W9-CPO-018

Encyclopedia
of
Bible Facts

Compiled and edited by

Mark Water

AMG
Publishers

AMG Publishers
6815 Shallowford Road
Chattanooga, Tennessee 37421

Copyright © 2004 John Hunt Publishing Ltd., UK

Text: © 2004 Mark Water

Designed by Jim Weaver Design, Basingstoke, UK

ISBN 0-89957-449-1

Printed by WS Bookwell, Finland

Introduction

The one thing needful

"'Now, what I want is, Facts. Teach these boys and girls nothing but Facts. Facts alone are wanted in life. Plant nothing else, and root out everything else. You can only form the minds of reasoning animals upon Facts: nothing else will ever be of any service to them. This is the principle on which I bring up my own children, and this is the principle on which I bring up these children. Stick to Facts, sir!'

"The scene was a plain, bare, monotonous vault of a school-room, and the speaker's square forefinger emphasized his observations by underscoring every sentence with a line on the schoolmaster's sleeve. The emphasis was helped by the speaker's square wall of a forehead, which had his eyebrows for its base, while his eyes found commodious cellarage in two dark caves, overshadowed by the wall. The emphasis was helped by the speaker's mouth, which was wide, thin, and hard set. The emphasis was helped by the speaker's voice, which was inflexible, dry, and dictatorial. The emphasis was helped by the speaker's hair, which bristled on the skirts of his bald head, a plantation of firs to keep the wind from its shining surface, all covered with knobs, like the crust of a plum pie, as if the head had scarcely warehouse-room for the hard facts stored inside. The speaker's obstinate carriage, square coat, square legs, square shoulders, – nay, his very neckcloth, trained to take him by the throat with an unaccommodating grasp, like a stubborn fact, as it was, – all helped the emphasis.

"'In this life, we want nothing but Facts, sir; nothing but Facts!'

"The speaker, and the schoolmaster, and the third grown person present, all backed a little, and swept with their eyes the inclined plane of little vessels then and there arranged in order, ready to have imperial gallons of facts poured into them until they were full to the brim."

In this, the opening scene of Charles Dickens' *Hard Times*, his most openly political novel, we discover the terrible human consequences of a ruthlessly materialistic philosophy in the lives of Thomas Gradgrind's family, brought up to believe that only "Facts! Facts! Facts!" have any meaning. Set in Coketown, a typical Lancashire milltown in northern England, the novel graphically exposes the truth about Victorian "progress."

The importance of facts

For the Christian, though facts are not everything, they are most important. Christianity is an historic religion based on countless verifiable facts. *Encyclopedia of Bible Facts* presents the facts recorded in the pages of the Bible, as well as facts about the Bible. Despite living in our age of information technology, with more information available on the Internet than any library, our general understanding about the contents of the Bible remains very poor.

For Christians, all facts are friends. We are certain that Christianity is true. All we desire is that the truth should be spread throughout the world. So there are no facts which should make Christians nervous. *Encyclopedia of Bible Facts* gives the example of the many manuscripts of the New Testament, more than for any other ancient text that still exist. The painstaking discoveries from the world of biblical archaeology are also detailed, as they always confirm the truth of the Bible.

The scandal of ignorance

It is nothing short of scandalous if we remain content about our own ignorance of the Bible and are unconcerned about the general lack of knowledge of the Bible among today's Christians. Leading Christians, from the past and present warn us of the dangers.

> Ignorance of the Scriptures is ignorance of Christ. Knowledge of Scripture is knowledge of Christ.
>
> *Jerome*

> Ignorance of God – ignorance both of his ways and of the practice of communion with him – lies at the root of much of the church's weakness today.
>
> *J.I. Packer*

> It is from ignorance of Scripture that all our evils arise; hence the plague of so many heresies, hence our careless lives, our fruitless labors.
>
> *John Chrysostom*

> All hindrance to prayer arises from ignorance of the teaching of God's Holy Word on the life of holiness He has planned for all His children, or from an unwillingness to consecrate ourselves fully to Him.
>
> *The Kneeling Christian*

As a result of the ignorance of Scripture, we have numberless ranters in our pulpits who do not deserve to be called preachers of the Word of God, as they seldom quote Scripture.

Bernard Lamy, 1699

Simple summaries and detailed descriptions

Encyclopedia of Bible Facts provides straightforward and basic summaries about hundreds of the most important topics found in the Bible. These are not only ideal for anyone who knows next to nothing about the Bible, but they are a useful springboard for the more detailed studies that are also given in this book. For example, in the overview of each Old Testament and New Testament book there are the most basic summaries of each book. However, more lengthy introductions are given to each Bible book in *Encouragements from Old Testament books* and in *Encouragements from New Testament books*.

Why are facts not enough?

To a group of people who were more knowledgeable about the Old Testament than we will ever be Jesus said, "'I have testimony weightier than that of John. For the very work that the Father has given me to finish, and which I am doing, testifies that the Father has sent me. And the Father who sent me has himself testified concerning me. You have never heard his voice nor seen his form, nor does his word dwell in you, for you do not believe the one he sent. You diligently study the Scriptures because you think that by them you possess eternal life. These are the Scriptures that testify about me, yet you refuse to come to me to have life.

"'I do not accept praise from men, but I know you. I know that you do not have the love of God in your hearts'" John 5:36–39 NIV.

From these words we see the importance of relating the Scriptures to the person of Jesus and of having "the love of God in our hearts." Many of the studies in *Encyclopedia of Bible Facts* show how particular topics and individuals direct us to the person of Jesus. Just as regurgitating endless reams of dry as dust facts should never be the criteria for passing any examination, so mere head knowledge about facts in the Bible will not ultimately help us. All the facts we learn need to be given a context and meaning.

It is the Holy Spirit who teaches us the meaning of the facts, and applies them to our lives. And this comes through prayer and faith on our part. It is not possible to be a faithful student of the Bible without being prayerful. You could define the best type of Bible study as "knowing the necessary facts and having the love of God active in our lives."

Encyclopedia of Bible Facts is concerned more about what the Bible says, than about what other people have said about the Bible. This does not mean to say that *Encyclopedia of Bible Facts* has not drawn heavily on the profound studies of the giant expositors of the Bible from today's and from previous generations. However, the main emphasis of this book is on the words of Scripture themselves. Many of the studies give direct quotations from the relevant Bible verses as well as tens of thousands of Bible references that will enhance and deepen our study of the Bible if they are looked up.

Jesus and the Bible

Christians aim to model their attitude toward the Bible on Jesus' attitude toward the Old Testament, which was his "Bible." For us it is the inspired Word of God. We especially treasure the words of Jesus, and these make up 30 studies in *Encyclopedia of Bible Facts*, for Jesus himself said, "Heaven and earth shall pass away: but my words shall not pass away" Luke 21:23.

Facts are like bricks that build up a house. It is the house that is important – but we cannot build without the bricks. *Encyclopedia of Bible Facts* will help us as we take on board the apostle Paul's advice to Timothy: "Study to shew thyself approved unto God, a workman that needeth not to be ashamed, rightly dividing the word of truth" 2 Timothy 2:15.

Mark Water

Acknowledgments

Unless otherwise stated Scripture quotations are taken from *King James Version/Authorized (KJV, AV)*: Oxford University Press.

All Scripture quotations marked *TAB*, are from *The Abbreviated Bible*, © Van Nostrand Reinhold (1971).

All Scripture quotations marked *AAT*, are from *An American Translation* 1963, 1976, © William F. Beck, Leader Publishing Company (1976).

All Scripture quotations marked *AB*, are from *The Amplified Bible* © Copyright 1954, 1958, 1962, 1964, 1965, 1987 The Lockman Foundation. All rights reserved.

All Scripture quotations marked *TBB*, are from *The Basic Bible*, 1950, C. K. Ogden of the Orthological Institute, E. P. Dutton (1950).

All Scripture quotations marked *TBR*, are from *The Bible Reader*, Abbott, Walter M.; Gilbert, Rabbi Arthur; Hunt, Rolfe Lanier; Swaim, J. Carter: New York: Bruce Books, 1968.

All Scripture quotations marked *TEB*, are from *The Emphasized Bible*, © Joseph Bryant Rotherham, Kregel Publications 1959.

All Scripture quotations marked *ESV* are from *The Holy Bible, English Standard Version*™ Copyright © 2001 by Crossway Bibles, a division of Good News Publishers. All rights reserved.

All Scripture quotations marked *EVD* are from *English Version for the Deaf*, Easy-to-Read Version, 1978, Baker Book House.

All Scripture quotations marked *GW* are from *God's Word, Today's Bible Translation That Says What It Means*, World Publishing, 1995.

All Scripture quotations marked *AIV* are from *An Inclusive Version*, Oxford University Press, 1995.

All Scripture quotations marked *IB* are from *The Interlinear Bible*, © Greene, Hendrickson Publishers (1976)

All Scripture quotations marked *JB* are from *The Jerusalem Bible*, Copyright © 1966, 1967 and 1968 by Darton, Longman and Todd Ltd. and Doubleday & Company Inc.

All Scripture quotations marked *KTC* are from *The Knox Translation*, © Ronald Knox, 1945, 1955, Sheed and Ward (1956).

All Scripture quotations marked *NLV* are from *The New Life Version*, © Gleason and Kathryn Ledyard 1969, Christian Literature International.

All Scripture quotations marked *NLT* are taken from the Holy Bible, *New Living Translation*, copyright © 1996. Used by permission of Tyndale House Publishers, Inc., Wheaton, Illinois 60189. All rights reserved.

The Scripture quotations contained herein (marked *NRSV*) are from the *New Revised Standard Version* of the Bible © 1989, 1995 by the Division of Christian Education of the National Council of Churches of Christ in the United States of America, and are used by permission. All rights reserved. Thomas Nelson, 1989.

All Scripture quotations marked *REB* are from *The Revised English Bible*, Oxford and Cambridge Universities Presses (1989).

All Scripture quotations marked *RSV* are from *The Revised Standard Version* 1946, © 1971. Division of Christian Education of the National Council of Churches of Christ in the United States of America, and are used by permission. All rights reserved.

All Scripture quotations marked *SSBE* are from *The Sacred Scriptures*, The Bethel Edition, Assemblies of Yahweh (1981).

All Scripture quotations marked *SISR* are from *The (ISR) Scriptures*, *The Institute for Scriptural Research* (ISR) © Institute for Scriptural Research (1998).

All Scripture quotations marked *TEV* are from *Today's English Version* (The Good News Bible) © American Bible Society 1966, 1971.

All Scripture quotations marked *SGAT* are from *Smith and Goodspeed – The Complete Bible: An American Translation* – © 1923, 1927, 1948 by the University of Chicago. Used by permission of the University of Chicago Press.

Scriptures marked as *CEV* are taken from the *Contemporary English Version* © 1995 by American Bible Society. Used by permission.

All Scripture quotations marked *KJ21* are from *The Holy Bible*, *21st Century King James Version*® (*KJ21*®) Copyright © 1994 by Deuel Enterprises, Inc., Gary, SD 57237. All rights reserved.

Complete Contents

Part One.. 1
Facts About The Bible's Background

Part Two...293
Facts From The Whole Bible

Part Three...691
Facts From The Old Testament

Part Four..915
Facts From The New Testament

Part Five...1125
Fascinating Bible Facts

Complete Contents in summary

Part One
Facts About The Bible's Background.................................... 1
The first Bible.. 10
The canon of Scripture.. 30
The history of Bible translation................................ 44
Descriptions of Bible translations 84
Archaeology...126
The land of the Bible 150
Nations and empires..166
Cities 186
Measurements, time and seasons.................................198
Plants..208
Metals and minerals..222
Animals...228
Homes and family life 260
Occupations...282
Music...288

Part Two
Facts From The Whole Bible..293
Bible statistics 302
Bible inspiration...318
Understanding the Bible..324
Bible reading...336
Bible study...366
Basic Bible teaching 376
Bible teaching in a catechism..................................510
Prayer 536
Key Bible words 542

Father, Son, and Holy Spirit 594

Persecution and martyrdom..630

Prophecy and prophets 642

Types of literature and typology 652

Supernatural events 672

Part Three
Facts From The Old Testament..**691**

Every Old Testament book: Overviews 698

Encouragement from Old Testament books.................................808

Old Testament people...846

Old Testament history and kings 868

Old Testament belief, worship and judges.................................892

Part Four
Facts From The New Testament...**915**

Every New Testament book: Overviews.....................................922

Studies in the New Testament 990

Encouragement from every New Testament book...................1004

Messianic prophecies..1062

Parables and miracles...1086

The resurrection of Jesus 1090

Conversions in Acts...1094

The early church 1100

Part Five
Fascinating Bible Facts.. **1125**

Bible symbols 1128

Dark Bible topics..1132

Bible contradictions...1140

Bible promises 1144

Complete Contents in detail

Part One
Facts About The Bible's Background

Part One Contents in summary 1

Part One Contents in detail 3

The first Bible

Glossary... 10

Writing the Bible... 12

Bible languages 14

Manuscript evidence of the New Testament 16

Early translations of the New Testament................................... 18

Quotations from the New Testament made by the early Church
Fathers.. 20

The number and early date of the New Testament manuscripts..... 22

Gap between originals and copies... 24

The first translations of the Bible (1).. 26

The first translations of the Bible (2) 28

The canon of Scripture

The canon of Scripture.. 30

The formation of the Old Testament... 32

The origin of the Bible... 34

Warfield on the New Testament canon (1) 36

Warfield on the New Testament canon (2).................................. 38

Jewish, Orthodox, Catholic, and Protestant Bibles (1) 40

Jewish, Orthodox, Catholic, and Protestant Bibles (2).................. 42

The history of Bible translation

The history of Bible translation... 44

Bible translations since the Middle Ages (1)................................. 46

Bible translations since the Middle Ages (2) 48

Bible translations since the Middle Ages (3) 50

Bible translations of Luther and Tyndale................................. 52

Coverdale's Bible, Matthew's Bible, the Great Bible 54

The first "authorized" Bible 56

The Geneva Bible, 1560.. 58

The Bishop's Bible, The Rheims/Douai Bible............................. 60

King James Version (1)... 62

King James Version (2) 64

King James Version (3)... 66

King James Version (4) 68

18th – 20th century Bible translations 70

20th century Bible translations (2)...................................... 72

A 21st century Bible translation (1)...................................... 74

A 21st century Bible translation (2) 76

An "internet" Bible (1).. 78

An "internet" Bible (2) 80

First American Bibles; Protestant and Catholic Bibles 82

Descriptions of Bible translations

Description of some of the major Bible translations (1)................. 84

Description of some of the major Bible translations (2) 86

Description of some of the major Bible translations (3) 88

Description of some of the major Bible translations (4) 90

Description of some of the major Bible translations (5) 92

Description of some of the major Bible translations (6)............... 94

Description of some of the major Bible translations (7) 96

Description of some of the major Bible translations (8) 98

Description of some of the major Bible translations (9)...............100

Description of some of the major Bible translations (10)..............102

Description of some of the major Bible translations (11)..............104

Description of some of the major Bible translations (12)..............106

Description of some of the major Bible translations (13) 108

Description of some of the major Bible translations (14)..............110

Description of some of the major Bible translations (15) 112

Description of some of the major Bible translations (16)..............114

Description of some of the major Bible translations (17) 116

Bibles printed with errors (1)..118

Bibles printed with errors (2) 120

Methodology used in Bible translations (1) 122

Methodology used in Bible translations (2)................................124

Archaeology

Bible facts confirmed by archaeologists 126

Archaeology and ancient languages...128

Archaeological discoveries explained...130

Archaeological discoveries about the Old Testament (1).............132

Archaeological discoveries about the Old Testament (2) 134

Archaeological discoveries about the Old Testament (3).............136

The Dead Sea Scrolls (1) 138

The Dead Sea Scrolls (2)..140

Historical evidence for the existence of Jesus 142

Archaeological discoveries about the New Testament (1).............144

Archaeological discoveries about the New Testament (2) 146

Archaeological discoveries about the New Testament (3).............148

The land of the Bible

Mountains..150

Valleys...152

Deserts..154

Seas (1) 156

Seas (2)...158

Seas (3)...160

Rivers and wells 162

Fountains and springs..164

Nations and empires

The Egyptians (1) 166

The Egyptians (2) 168

The Canaanites 170

The Assyrians (1) 172

The Assyrians (2) 174

The Assyrians (3) 176

Nineveh 178

The Babylonians 180

The Greeks 182

The Romans and Judah 184

Cities

Cities (1) 186

Cities (2) 188

Walls and towers 190

Jerusalem 192

Cities and towns of the New Testament (1) 194

Cities and towns of the New Testament (2) 196

Measurements, time and seasons

Bible measurements (1) 198

Bible measurements (2) 200

Time (1) 202

Time (2) 204

The Bible calendar 206

Plants

Trees (1) 208

Trees (2) 210

Trees (3) 212

Flowers, Grass, Gardens, Garden of Gethsemane 214

Fruit (1)...216

Fruit (2)...218

Herbs, spices, and incense...................................220

Metals and minerals

Metals and gold..222

Silver..224

Salt and precious stones.......................................226

Animals

Clean and unclean..228

Animals (1)...230

Animals (2)...232

Mythical animals..234

Animals (3)...236

Animals (4)...238

Animals (5)...240

Animals (6)...242

Animals (7)...244

Animals (8)...246

Animals (9)...248

Birds (1)..250

Birds (2)..252

Birds (3)..254

Insects and reptiles..256

Fish..258

Homes and family life

Homes...260

Houses..262

Food at home (1)...264

Food at home (2)...266

Illnesses 268

Death (1)..270

Death (2) 272

Families (1)..274

Families (2) 276

Clothes 278

Hair...280

Occupations

Farmers (1)..282

Farmers (2) 284

Shepherds 286

Music

Music (1)..288

Music (2) 290

Part Two
Facts From The Whole Bible

Part Two Contents in summary...293

Part Two Contents in detail..295

Bible statistics

Basic questions (Q) about the Bible answered (A) 302

Facts about the Bible...304

Bible statistics of the whole Bible (1).......................................306

Bible statistics of the whole Bible (2).......................................308

Links between the New Testament and the Old Testament (1) 310

Links between the New Testament and the Old Testament (2)......312

Links between the New Testament and the Old Testament (3)......314

Links between the New Testament and the Old Testament (4)......316

Bible inspiration

The importance of the Bible (1) 318

The importance of the Bible (2) 320

The inspiration of the Bible 322

Understanding the Bible

Understanding the Bible (1) 324

Understanding the Bible (2) 326

Understanding the Bible (3) 328

Quotations in the New Testament (1) 330

Quotations in the New Testament (2) 332

Interpreting the Bible 334

Bible reading

Bible reading (1) 336

Bible reading (2) 338

Bible reading (3) 340

Bible reading (4) 342

Bible readings in times of need (1) 344

Bible readings in times of need (2) 346

Bible readings in times of need (3) 348

Bible readings in times of need (4) 350

Bible readings in times of need (5) 352

Bible reading schedules (1) 354

Bible reading schedules (2) 356

Bible reading schedules (3) 358

Bible reading schedules (4) 360

Bible reading schedules (5) 362

Bible reading schedules (6) 364

Bible study

Bible study (1)..366

Bible study (2) 368

Memorizing the Bible...370

Meditating on the Bible (1)..372

Meditating on the Bible (2) 374

Basic Bible teaching

What the Bible says about (1)..376

What the Bible says about (2) 378

What the Bible says about (3)..380

What the Bible says about (4) 382

What the Bible says about (5)..384

What the Bible says about (6) 386

What the Bible says about (7)..388

What the Bible says about (8) 390

What the Bible says about (9) 392

What the Bible says about (10)...394

What the Bible says about (11)...396

What the Bible says about (12)...398

What the Bible says about (13)...400

What the Bible says about (14) 402

What the Bible says about (15) 404

What the Bible says about (16) 406

What the Bible says about (17) 408

What the Bible says about (18) 410

What the Bible says about (19) 412

What the Bible says about (20) 414

What the Bible says about (21) 416

What the Bible says about (22)...418

What the Bible says about (23)...420

What the Bible says about (24)...422

What the Bible says about (25)..424

What the Bible says about (26)..426

What the Bible says about (27)..428

What the Bible says about (28)..430

What the Bible says about (29)..432

What the Bible says about (30)..434

What the Bible says about (31)..436

What the Bible says about (32)..438

What the Bible says about (33)..440

What the Bible says about (34)..442

What the Bible says about (35)..444

What the Bible says about (36)..446

What the Bible says about (37)..448

What the Bible says about (38)..450

What the Bible says about (39)..452

What the Bible says about (40)..454

What the Bible says about (41)..456

What the Bible says about (42)..458

What the Bible says about (43)..460

What the Bible says about (44)..462

What the Bible says about (45)..464

What the Bible says about (46)..466

What the Bible says about (47)..468

What the Bible says about (48)..470

What the Bible says about (49)..472

What the Bible says about (50)..474

What the Bible says about (51)..476

What the Bible says about (52)..478

What the Bible says about (53)..480

What the Bible says about (54)..482

What the Bible says about (55)..484

What the Bible says about (56)..486

What the Bible says about (57) 488

What the Bible says about (58) 490

What the Bible says about (59) 492

What the Bible says about (60) 494

What the Bible says about (61) 496

What the Bible says about (62) 498

What the Bible says about (63) 500

What the Bible says about (64) 502

What the Bible says about (65) 504

What the Bible says about (66) 506

What the Bible says about (67) 508

Bible teaching in a catechism

The Heidelberg Catechism: Questions 1–8 510

The Heidelberg Catechism: Questions 9–20 512

The Heidelberg Catechism: Questions 21–27 514

The Heidelberg Catechism: Questions 28–35 516

The Heidelberg Catechism: Questions 36–45 518

The Heidelberg Catechism: Questions 46–53 520

The Heidelberg Catechism: Questions 54–61 522

The Heidelberg Catechism: Questions 62–71 524

The Heidelberg Catechism: Questions 72–78 526

The Heidelberg Catechism: Questions 79–84 528

The Heidelberg Catechism: Questions 85–92 530

The Heidelberg Catechism: Questions 93–100 532

The Heidelberg Catechism: Questions 101–110 534

Prayer

All the prayers in the Bible (1) 536

All the prayers in the Bible (2) 538

All the prayers in the Bible (3) 540

Key Bible words

Glossary of doctrinal words in the Bible (1) 542

Glossary of doctrinal words in the Bible (2) 544

Glossary of doctrinal words in the Bible (3)................................546

Glossary of doctrinal words in the Bible (4) 548

Glossary of doctrinal words in the Bible (5)................................550

Glossary of doctrinal words in the Bible (6) 552

Glossary of doctrinal words in the Bible (7)................................554

Glossary of doctrinal words in the Bible (8) 556

Glossary of doctrinal words in the Bible (9) 558

Glossary of doctrinal words in the Bible (10) 560

Glossary of doctrinal words in the Bible (11)..............................562

Glossary of doctrinal words in the Bible (12) 564

Glossary of doctrinal words in the Bible (13) 566

Glossary of doctrinal words in the Bible (14) 568

Glossary of doctrinal words in the Bible (15) 570

Glossary of doctrinal words in the Bible (16) 572

Glossary of doctrinal words in the Bible (17) 574

Glossary of doctrinal words in the Bible (18) 576

Glossary of doctrinal words in the Bible (19) 578

Glossary of doctrinal words in the Bible (20) 580

Glossary of doctrinal words in the Bible (21) 582

Glossary of doctrinal words in the Bible (22)..............................584

Glossary of doctrinal words in the Bible (23)..............................586

Glossary of doctrinal words in the Bible (24)..............................588

Glossary of doctrinal words in the Bible (25)..............................590

Glossary of doctrinal words in the Bible (26)..............................592

Father, Son, and Holy Spirit

The attributes of God the Father (1)..594

The attributes of God the Father (2) 596

The attributes of God the Father (3) 598

Titles, descriptions and names of Christ (1) 600

Titles, descriptions and names of Christ (2) 602

Titles, descriptions and names of Christ (3) 604

Titles, descriptions and names of Christ (4) 606

Titles, descriptions and names of Christ (5) 608

Titles, descriptions and names of Christ (6) 610

Titles, descriptions and names of Christ (7) 612

Titles, descriptions and names of Christ (8) 614

Titles, descriptions and names of Christ (9) 616

Titles, descriptions and names of Christ (10) 618

Titles, descriptions and names of Christ (11) 620

Titles, descriptions and names of Christ (12) 622

The attributes of God the Holy Spirit (1) 624

The attributes of God the Holy Spirit (2) 626

The Trinity 628

Persecution and martyrdom

Persecution (1) 630

Persecution (2) 632

Persecution (3) 634

Bible martyrs (1) 636

Bible martyrs (2) 638

Bible martyrs (3) 640

Prophecy and prophets

Prophecy 642

Prophets (1) 644

Prophets (2) 646

Prophets (3) 648

Prophets (4) 650

Types of literature and typology

Poetry 652

Idioms and figures of speech (1) 654

Idioms and figures of speech (2)..............................656

Idioms and figures of speech (3) 658

Idioms and figures of speech (4)..............................660

Idioms and figures of speech (5) 662

Old Testament parables...664

Typology (1)...666

Typology (2) 668

Types of Christ..670

Supernatural events

Miracles 672

Old Testament miracles..674

Miracles performed by God's followers (1) 676

Miracles performed by God's followers (2) 678

Miracles performed by God's followers (3).................680

Visions (1)..682

Visions (2) 684

Visions (3)..686

Dreams...688

Part Three
Facts From The Old Testament

Part Three Contents in summary 691

Part Three Contents in detail 693

Every Old Testament book: Overviews

Genesis (1) 698

Genesis (2)..700

Exodus (1)...702

Exodus (2) 704

Leviticus...706

Numbers (1) 708

Numbers (2) 710

Deuteronomy (1) 712

Deuteronomy (2) 714

Joshua (1) 716

Joshua (2) 718

Judges (1) 720

Judges (2) 722

Ruth 724

1 Samuel (1) 726

1 Samuel (2) 728

2 Samuel 730

1 Kings (1) 732

1 Kings (2) 734

2 Kings 736

1 Chronicles (1) 738

1 Chronicles (2) 740

2 Chronicles 742

Ezra 744

Nehemiah 746

Esther 748

Job (1) 750

Job (2) 752

Psalms (1) 754

Psalms (2) 756

Psalms (3) 758

Proverbs (1) 760

Proverbs (2) 762

Ecclesiastes 764

Song of Solomon 766

Isaiah (1) 768

Isaiah (2) 770

Jeremiah (1)..772

Jeremiah (2) 774

Lamentations...776

Ezekiel (1) 778

Ezekiel (2)..780

Daniel..782

Hosea 784

Joel...786

Amos 788

Obadiah...790

Jonah...792

Micah 794

Nahum 796

Habakkuk 798

Zephaniah...800

Haggai 802

Zechariah..804

Malachi..806

Encouragement from Old Testament books

Encouragement from Old Testament books (1) 808

Encouragement from Old Testament books (2)..........................810

Genesis 812

Exodus...814

Leviticus and Numbers....................................816

Deuteronomy 818

Joshua, Judges, Ruth, 1 and 2 Samuel 820

1 and 2 Samuel, 1 Kings 822

2 Kings, 1 Chronicles, 2 Chronicles 824

Ezra, Nehemiah, Esther....................................826

Esther and Job...828

Psalms and Proverbs 830

Proverbs and Ecclesiastes..832

Ecclesiastes, Song of Solomon, Isaiah 834

Isaiah and Jeremiah...836

Lamentations, Ezekiel, Daniel, Hosea 838

Hosea, Joel, Amos, Obadiah, Jonah 840

Jonah, Micah, Nahum, Habakkuk, Zephaniah....................842

Haggai, Zechariah, Malachi..844

Old Testament people

Noah 846

Abram, Abraham (1) 848

Abram, Abraham (2)...850

Abram, Abraham (3)...852

Esau and Jacob, and Joseph 854

Moses (1) 856

Moses (2)...858

Samuel...860

David, King of Israel (1)..862

David, King of Israel (2) 864

Solomon...866

Old Testament history and kings

Parallel passages in the historical books (1) 868

Parallel passages in the historical books (2)........................870

Kings of Israel (1)..872

Kings of Israel (2) 874

Kings of Israel (3) 876

Kings of Israel (4) 878

Kings of Judah (1)..880

Kings of Judah (2) 882

Kings of Judah (3)...884

Kings of Judah (4) 886

Kings of Judah (5)..888

The Apocrypha...890

Old Testament belief, worship and judges

The Law (1) 892

The Law (2)..894

The Tabernacle (1)...896

The Tabernacle (2) 898

The priesthood (1)...900

The priesthood (2) 902

Tabernacle worship 904

The judges..906

The beginning of the Hebrew monarchy...............................908

Feasts, festivals, and fasts (1)..910

Feasts, festivals, and fasts (2) 912

Part Four
Facts From The New Testament

Part Four Contents in summary..915

Part Four Contents in detail...917

Every New Testament book: Overviews

Matthew (1)..922

Matthew (2) 924

Mark (1)...926

Mark (2) 928

Luke (1) 930

Luke (2)...932

John 934

Acts (1)..936

Acts (2) 938

Romans (1)..940

Romans (2)...942

1 Corinthians (1)...944

1 Corinthians (2) 946

2 Corinthians...948

Galatians (1) 950

Galatians (2)..952

Ephesians (1) 954

Ephesians (2)...956

Philippians 958

Colossians..960

1 Thessalonians 962

2 Thessalonians..964

1 Timothy..966

2 Timothy 968

Titus..970

Philemon 972

Hebrews...974

James...976

1 Peter...978

2 Peter...980

1 John..982

2 John and 3 John 984

Jude...986

Revelation..988

Studies in the New Testament

Analysis of New Testament books (1).............................990

Analysis of New Testament books (2) 992

Authors of the New Testament....................................994

The synoptic Gospels...996

New Testament letters and Aramaic words 998

Harmony of the accounts of the resurrection, the resurrection appearances, and the ascension (1) 1000

Harmony of the accounts of the resurrection, the resurrection appearances, and the ascension (2).........................1002

Encouragement from every New Testament book

Matthew, Mark.........................1004

Mark, Luke 1006

Luke, John.........................1008

John 1010

Acts, Romans 1012

Romans, 1 Corinthians 1014

1 Corinthians 1016

1 Corinthians, 2 Corinthians.........................1018

2 Corinthians, Galatians 1020

Galatians, Ephesians 1022

Ephesians.........................1024

Ephesians, Philippians.........................1026

Philippians, Colossians.........................1028

1 Thessalonians 1030

2 Thessalonians, 1 Timothy 1032

1 Timothy, 2 Timothy.........................1034

2 Timothy, Titus.........................1036

Philemon, Hebrews 1038

Hebrews.........................1040

Hebrews, James.........................1042

James, 1 Peter 1044

1 Peter.........................1046

2 Peter, 1 John.........................1048

1 John, 2 John, 3 John.........................1050

Jude, Revelation (1).........................1052

Revelation (2).........................1054

Revelation (3) 1056

Symbols found in Revelation (1) 1058

Symbols found in Revelation (2) 1060

Messianic prophecies

Messianic prophecies in the Old Testament (1) 1062

Messianic prophecies in the Old Testament (2) 1064

Messianic prophecies in the Old Testament (3) 1066

Messianic prophecies in the Old Testament (4) 1068

Messianic prophecies in the Old Testament (5) 1070

Messianic prophecies in the Old Testament (6) 1072

Prophecies about the Messiah's birth and life 1074

Prophecies about the Messiah's ministry 1076

Prophecies about the Messiah's death (1) 1078

Prophecies about the Messiah's death (2) 1080

Prophecies about the Messiah's resurrection and ascension 1082

The Messiah's return 1084

Parables and miracles

All the miracles of Jesus 1086

All the parables of Jesus 1088

The resurrection of Jesus

The resurrection of Jesus (1) 1090

The resurrection of Jesus (2) 1092

Conversions in Acts

Conversions in Acts (1) 1094

Conversions in Acts (2) 1096

Conversions in Acts (3) 1098

The early church

Church (1)..1100

Church (2) 1102

The church of Christ (1) 1104

The church of Christ (2)................................1106

Worship...1108

Praise...1110

Baptism 1112

Lord's Supper..1114

Paul (1) 1116

Paul (2)..1118

The persecuted Paul 1120

The teachings of Paul 1122

Part Five
Fascinating Bible Facts

Part Five Contents in summary...............................1125

Part Five Contents in Detail....................................1127

Bible symbols

Bible symbols (1)...1128

Bible symbols (2) 1130

Dark Bible topics

Dark Bible topics (1) 1132

Dark Bible topics (2)......................................1134

Dark Bible topics (3)......................................1136

Dark Bible topics (4)......................................1138

Bible contradictions

Bible contradictions (1)...1140

Bible contradictions (2)...1142

Bible promises

Blessings promised to believers (1)..1144

Blessings promised to believers (2)..1146

Blessings promised to believers (3)..1148

Blessings promised to believers (4)..1150

Bible promises in times of need 1152

New Testament promises (1)..1154

New Testament promises (2)..1156

New Testament promises (3) 1158

New Testament promises (4)..1160

New Testament promises (5) 1162

Part One
Facts About
The Bible's Background

Part One Contents in summary

The first Bible..10

The canon of Scripture 30

The history of Bible translation.....................................44

Descriptions of Bible translations..................................84

Archaeology 126

The land of the Bible 150

Nations and empires..166

Cities..186

Measurements, time and seasons..................................198

Plants...208

Metals and minerals 222

Animals...228

Homes and family life 260

Occupations 282

Music..288

Part One Contents in detail

The first Bible

Glossary 10

Writing the Bible 12

Bible languages 14

Manuscript evidence of the New Testament 16

Early translations of the New Testament 18

Quotations from the New Testament made by the early Church Fathers 20

The number and early date of the New Testament manuscripts 22

Gap between originals and copies 24

The first translations of the Bible (1) 26

The first translations of the Bible (2) 28

The canon of Scripture

The canon of Scripture 30

The formation of the Old Testament 32

The origin of the Bible 34

Warfield on the New Testament canon (1) 36

Warfield on the New Testament canon (2) 38

Jewish, Orthodox, Catholic, and Protestant Bibles (1) 40

Jewish, Orthodox, Catholic, and Protestant Bibles (2) 42

The history of Bible translation

The history of Bible translation 44

Bible translations since the Middle Ages (1) 46

Bible translations since the Middle Ages (2) 48

Bible translations since the Middle Ages (3) 50

Bible translations of Luther and Tyndale 52

Coverdale's Bible, Matthew's Bible, the Great Bible 54

The first "authorized" Bible 56

The Geneva Bible, 1560 58

The Bishop's Bible, The Rheims/Douai Bible 60

King James Version (1) 62

King James Version (2) 64

King James Version (3) 66

King James Version (4) 68

18th – 20th century Bible translations 70

20th century Bible translations (2) 72

A 21st century Bible translation (1) 74

A 21st century Bible translation (2) 76

An "internet" Bible (1) 78

An "internet" Bible (2) 80

First American Bibles; Protestant and Catholic Bibles 82

Descriptions of Bible translations

Description of some of the major Bible translations (1) 84

Description of some of the major Bible translations (2) 86

Description of some of the major Bible translations (3) 88

Description of some of the major Bible translations (4) 90

Description of some of the major Bible translations (5) 92

Description of some of the major Bible translations (6) 94

Description of some of the major Bible translations (7) 96

Description of some of the major Bible translations (8) 98

Description of some of the major Bible translations (9) 100

Description of some of the major Bible translations (10) 102

Description of some of the major Bible translations (11) 104

Description of some of the major Bible translations (12) 106

Description of some of the major Bible translations (13) 108

Description of some of the major Bible translations (14) 110

Description of some of the major Bible translations (15) 112

Description of some of the major Bible translations (16) 114

Description of some of the major Bible translations (17) 116

Bibles printed with errors (1)..118

Bibles printed with errors (2) 120

Methodology used in Bible translations (1) 122

Methodology used in Bible translations (2)...............................124

Archaeology

Bible facts confirmed by archaeologists 126

Archaeology and ancient languages 128

Archaeological discoveries explained...130

Archaeological discoveries about the Old Testament (1)..............132

Archaeological discoveries about the Old Testament (2) 134

Archaeological discoveries about the Old Testament (3).............136

The Dead Sea Scrolls (1) 138

The Dead Sea Scrolls (2)...140

Historical evidence for the existence of Jesus 142

Archaeological discoveries about the New Testament (1).............144

Archaeological discoveries about the New Testament (2) 146

Archaeological discoveries about the New Testament (3).............148

The land of the Bible

Mountains..150

Valleys..152

Deserts..154

Seas (1) 156

Seas (2)..158

Seas (3)..160

Rivers and wells 162

Fountains and springs...164

Nations and empires

The Egyptians (1) 166

The Egyptians (2)..168

The Canaanites...170

The Assyrians (1)...172

The Assyrians (2)..174

The Assyrians (3)..176

Nineveh...178

The Babylonians...180

The Greeks...182

The Romans and Judah.....................................184

Cities

Cities (1)..186

Cities (2)..188

Walls and towers...190

Jerusalem..192

Cities and towns of the New Testament (1)................194

Cities and towns of the New Testament (2)...............196

Measurements, time and seasons

Bible measurements (1)......................................198

Bible measurements (2).....................................200

Time (1)...202

Time (2)...204

The Bible calendar..206

Plants

Trees (1)..208

Trees (2)..210

Trees (3)..212

Flowers, Grass, Gardens, Garden of Gethsemane.........214

Fruit (1)..216

Fruit (2)..218

Herbs, spices, and incense..................................220

Metals and minerals

Metals and gold..222

Silver 224

Salt and precious stones 226

Animals

Clean and unclean 228

Animals (1) 230

Animals (2)..232

Mythical animals..234

Animals (3) 236

Animals (4)..238

Animals (5) 240

Animals (6)..242

Animals (7) 244

Animals (8)..246

Animals (9)..248

Birds (1) 250

Birds (2)..252

Birds (3)..254

Insects and reptiles 256

Fish 258

Homes and family life

Homes..260

Houses...262

Food at home (1)..264

Food at home (2) 266

Illnesses 268

Death (1)..270

Death (2) 272

Families (1)..274

Families (2) 276

Clothes 278

Hair..280

Occupations

Farmers (1)..282

Farmers (2) 284

Shepherds 286

Music

Music (1)...288

Music (2) 290

Glossary

Words used of the Bible

The Bible

The word "Bible" comes from the Greek word *biblion* which simply means "book."

The Scriptures

This word is the word we use in our translation of the Greek word *graphai*, which can also be translated as "writings."

Testament

This word is derived from the Latin word *testamentum*, which was used in early Latin translations of both the Greek and Hebrew words for a "will" or "covenant."

Old Testament and New Testament

The words "Old Testament" and "New Testament" do not occur in the Bible.

TERTULLIAN
Tertullian was probably the first person to coin these words.

They come, in Latin, in his work *Against Marcion* Book 4 chapter 6, which he wrote in A.D. 207

Non-biblical words from ancient Jewish literature

Pseudepigrapha

Pseudepigrapha refers broadly to other ancient Jewish writings which are not part of the Hebrew Bible nor of the Septuagint, but are often attributed to a biblical figure

(e.g.
• Jubilees,
• 1 Enoch,
• the Testaments of the Twelve Patriarchs, etc.).

They were popular among ancient Jews, and thus are very valuable for historical purposes, even if they were never considered biblical.

Inter-Testamental literature

This literature is a collective term for a broader range of Jewish literature than the Pseudepigrapha which was written between the writing of the Old Testament and the writing of the New Testament.

Other words used in Bible study

Genre

MAJOR GENRES
Genre is the literary "form" or "category" of a text.

The major genres in the New Testament include:
• Gospels,
• Letters, and
• apocalyptic literature.

MINOR GENRES
Minor genres within the Gospels include:
• parables,
• sayings,
• controversy dialogues,
• healing miracles,
• exorcisms,
• nature miracles.

Pericope

A pericope is an individual passage within the Gospels, with a distinct beginning and ending. It forms an independent literary unit.

Pericopes include various genres such as parables, miracle stories, and evangelists' summaries.

Parable

A parable is a metaphorical story featuring common images and vivid comparisons, which usually has a twist at the end.

Exegesis

Exegesis is the careful investigation of the original meaning of a text in its various contexts, such as its historical context and its literary context.
The word "exegesis" comes from a Greek verb meaning "to lead out of" (Greek "*ex*" = "out"; "*ago*" = "to lead/go/draw").

Exegesis is the opposite is eisegesis, which means "reading into" the text.

Criticisms

Biblical criticism refers to the various methods of undertaking biblical exegesis. Each has a specific goal and a specific set of questions. So biblical criticism does not mean criticizing the text but asking critical questions based on criteria that are objective, such as the evidence from within a Bible book that points to when it was written.

TWO PEOPLE
Philo
Philo was an important Jewish writer who lived in Alexandria in the early 1st century A.D. He used Greek philosophical language to interpret Jewish biblical traditions.

Josephus
Josephus was the most important Jewish historian from the late 1st century A.D.

Glossary of archaeological terms

Archaeology

Archaeology is the science of studying the material remains of ancient cultures so that these people and their customs, habits, and history can be more fully understood.

Dating

Materials found in settlements can be dated through:
- samples of writing,
- everyday utensils such as pottery, and
- carbon-14 testing.

Dig

An archaeological dig is the site of an archaeological exploration in progress.

Stele

A stele is a stone slab.

Tell

A *tell* refers to an artificial hill that has been built up over hundreds, or even thousands of years, by layers of debris left at the place where people lived.

Writing the Bible

Writing materials

Papyrus

The use of papyrus as a writing material originated in Egypt and has been traced back to A.D. 2500.

In New Testament days it was still the most popular writing material.

Papyrus "paper" was made from the Egyptian papyrus plant. Thin strips from the stem of the papyrus plant were cut and laid side by side so that they just overlapped with each other. A second and similar layer was then put crossways over the first layer. Sheets of "paper" were made by pressing and gluing the Papyrus layers together.

Papyrus paper was cheaper, but not as durable as parchment.

Scrolls of papyrus were rolled out horizontally rather than vertically. They were about 10 inches high and up to about thirty-five feet in length.

On the scroll the text was written in columns about 2½ to 3 inches wide, and just over ½ an inch apart from one another.

The text was usually only on one side of the scroll, but an exception to this is alluded to in Revelation 5: 1: "And I saw in the right hand of him that sat on the throne a book written within and on the backside, sealed with seven seals."

Vellum and parchment

Animal skins used as writing material are known as vellum and parchment. Some such leather scrolls are still in existence and date back to 1500 B.C.

Animal skins were first of all soaked in limewater so they could be scraped of all their hair. After they had been dried they were rubbed clean with a pumice stone.

Vellum refers to the best quality animal skins and came from calves, while parchment refers to all other animal skin used in paper making, such as bulls and goats, and was inferior in quality to vellum.

Papyrus was displaced by vellum in the 4th century. Papyrus does not store well. If it becomes too dry it cracks and disintegrates; and if it becomes wet it rots. So it is not surprising that we have no complete or nearly complete copies of the Bible before the 4th century. But the oldest fragments of the New Testament are papyri.

Pens

Pens were simply made from dried reeds which had been cut to a point and then carefully slit at the end. Quills from bird feathers later replaced reed pens.

From scrolls to books

In Old Testament and New Testament times the papyrus paper was made into scrolls by joining the Papyrus sheets to each other. Later on papyrus sheets were used in book form, when books replaced scrolls.

SCROLLS

Scrolls, also known as "rolls," were long sheets of papyrus or vellum, written on one side only, before they were rolled up for storage.

CODEX

A codex was made up of written sheets of papyrus or vellum, written on both sides, which were then bound in book form.

Autographs

Autographs are original texts which were written either by the author or by a scribe under the author's personal direction.

The apostle Paul most often "dictated" his letters and sometimes added a few sentences in his own hand at the end of a letter.

Manuscripts

Manuscripts were not the original autographs. They could be copies, and more often, were copies of copies of copies.

Until Gutenberg first printed the Latin Bible in 1456, all Bible manuscripts were hand copied onto papyrus, parchment, and paper.

Ancient versions

Ancient versions of the Bible refer to translations of the Bible into other ancient languages, such as Latin, Coptic, Syriac, Armenian.

Translations

When the Bible is translated into a different language it is usually translated from the original Hebrew and Greek. However some translations in the past were made from an earlier translation. The first translation of the Bible into English, made by John Wycliffe in 1380, was prepared from the Latin Vulgate.

Print editions

Print editions of Bibles, as with any other books, refer to printed copies which will have been made after the invention of printing by Johannes Gutenberg in 1456.

Types of writing

Majuscule

Majuscules, or capital letters, are one type of case in a writing system. Capital letters are known as "upper case" and non-capitals are referred to as "lower case" letters today. Majuscules were capital letters.

Early manuscripts used majuscules. Their manuscripts had ALLCAPITALLETTERS, and usually there was NOPUNCTUATIONORSPAC ESBETWEEN WORDS.

Minuscule

Later manuscripts were written with small (lower case) letters, and had punctuation and spaces between words.

When cursive writing became common, the more difficult uncials were relied upon less.

Quote Unquote

"The essential truth and the will of God revealed in the Bible, have been preserved unchanged through all the vicissitudes in the transmission of the text."

Millard Burrows

Bible languages

Overview

Old Testament

Nearly all of the Old Testament was written in Hebrew.

There are a few Old Testament passages written in Aramaic which account for about 1% of the Old Testament.
- Genesis 31: 47 (two words only)
- Daniel 2: 4b–7: 28
- Ezra 4: 8–6: 18
- Ezra 7: 12–26
- Jeremiah 10: 11

New Testament

Nearly all the New Testament was written in Greek.

However, a relatively small number of words in the Gospels in the New Testament are in Aramaic.

EXAMPLES OF NEW TESTAMENT VERSES WITH ARAMAIC WORDS

Golgotha
"And when they were come unto a place called *Golgotha*, that is to say, a place of a skull" Matthew 27: 33. See also Mark 15: 22 and John 19: 17 for two other occurrences of the word *Golgotha*.

Eli, Eli, lama sabachthani?
And about the ninth hour Jesus cried with a loud voice, saying, Eli, Eli, lama sabachthani? that is to say, My God, my God, why hast thou forsaken me?" Matthew 27: 46. See also Mark 15: 34 for another occurrence of the phrase *Eli, Eli, lama sabachthani?*

Talitha cumi
"And he took the damsel by the hand, and said unto her, Talitha cumi; which is, being interpreted, Damsel, I say unto thee, arise" Mark 5: 41.

The Lord also addressed the Father as Abba (Aramaic for Father). "And he said, Abba, Father, all things are possible unto thee; take away this cup from me: nevertheless not what I will, but what thou wilt" Mark 14: 36.

The New Testament believers also addressed the Father as Abba in Romans 8: 15 and Galatians 4: 6.

They are also recorded as using the Aramaic phrase Marana tha, which means "The Lord comes" in 1 Corinthians 16: 22.

These phrases indicate that the spoken language of our Lord and the early believers was Aramaic.

Languages of New Testament times

Four languages played a significant role in the New Testament.

Two Semitic languages

1. ARAMAIC
(Aramaic should not be confused with the language spoken by the Arabs today, which is called Arabic.)
Aramaic was the everyday language of Palestine and would have most often been spoken by Jesus and His disciples. *Aramaic* comes from the former name

of Syria, Aram. The Arameans lived in the north-west of Palestine and are often mentioned in the Old Testament.

The Aramaic language is thought of as being a close cousin to the Hebrew language because of the similarities between them.

Aramaic is a Semitic language used by the neo-Babylonians of the time of Nebuchadnezzar II (cf. Book of Daniel). It became the major language of the ancient Near East and was spoken and written by most nations of the area until the rise of Islam subjugated it and replaced it with Arabic.

The language of Jesus

Aramaic was the language most commonly spoken in Israel in Jesus' day. Aramaic was the language that Jesus himself spoke. For this reason there are a few instances of Aramaic words being used in the New Testament. But nearly all of the New Testament translates all of Jesus' words into Greek, since the New Testament writers wrote in Greek. They used Greek because it was the language of the Roman Empire and they wanted to reach as wide an audience as possible with their writings.

2. HEBREW

Hebrew has been traced back to the old Phoenician alphabet from which Semitic and non-Semitic languages are drawn. Hebrew was the language spoken by the people of Israel in the Old Testament, and practically all of the Bible is written in Hebrew.

However, by the time of Jesus most Jews would not have spoken Hebrew,

although they would be familiar with some Old Testament passages written in Hebrew. The Pharisees and rabbis would still be thoroughly familiar with Hebrew, both as a spoken language and a written language.

Two Indo-European languages

1. LATIN

At the time of Jesus Latin was the official language of the Roman Empire. All well-educated people such as lawyers and poets knew Latin, and it was the language of the courtroom. Numerous Latin words are found in the New Testament. They are found in a number of proper names, such as:

- Agrippa, Augustus,
- Caesar, Claudius,
- Felix, Festus,
- Gallio, Julius.

Some Christians in New Testament times also had Latin names, such as:

- Aquila, Cornelius,
- Claudia, Clemens,
- Crescens, Crispus,
- Fortunatus, etc.

2. GREEK

Greek was the everyday language of the market place in Rome during the days of Jesus. The Greek of New Testament times was "koine" Greek, that is "common" Greek, which should be distinguished from the more refined classical Greek.

Manuscript evidence of the New Testament

Overview

There are three avenues to explore to determine whether the transmission of the text of the New Testament was accurate and kept to the original text.

1. There is the evidence of the copied Greek manuscripts of the New Testament.
2. There is the evidence of the copies of the early translations of the New Testament.
3. There is the evidence of the quotations from the New Testament made by the early church leaders, known as the Church Fathers.

1 Copied Greek manuscripts

A. AUTOGRAPHS

We do not have any of the original autographs of the New Testament. In their quest to reconstruct the text of the New Testament scholars do not have the assistance of any of the original writings of Paul or the Gospel writers.

Quote Unquote

"The books of the New Testament were written in the latter part of the first century; the earliest extant manuscripts (trifling scraps excepted) are of the fourth century — say from 250-300 years later."

Sir Frederick G. Kenyon, former director and principle librarian of the British Museum

B. BIBLICAL PAPYRUS

Archeologists and biblical scholars have collected more than seventy-five Greek manuscripts with part of the New Testament copied on to them. Many of the manuscripts are no more than quite small fragments with only a verse or two on them, although some are longer with a large section of the New Testament on them.

John Rylands Fragment

For example, the manuscript known as P52, called the "John Rylands Fragment" has just a short extract from John's Gospel on it. It has been dated to about A.D. 125.

C. UNCIAL MANUSCRIPTS

Uncial manuscripts are Greek manuscripts which take their name from the large box-like letters in which the Greek is written. The twenty-nine uncial letters are all in capitals, and as vellum was always so expensive these manuscripts are written with few spaces between words, very little punctuation and with word contractions.

The most important manuscripts are the oldest ones. The uncial manuscripts were copied from the 4th to the 9th centuries A.D. The uncial manuscripts are the most important of the Greek witnesses to the original text of the New Testament.

Important uncial manuscripts

Three of the most important of these uncial manuscripts are:

- Codex Vaticanus,
- Codex Sinaiticus, and
- Codex Alexandrinus.

Codex Vaticanus

Codex Vaticanus, represented by the letter B, is the oldest of the great uncial manuscripts, dating back to about A.D. 350.

It contains 759 vellum sheets out of its original 820 sheets, which are probably written on antelope skins.

It contains the entire Bible, both New Testament and Septuagint, except for Genesis 1-46, Psalms 105–137, and the New Testament after Hebrews 9:14.

Codex Sinaiticus

Except for 24 verses, Codex Sinaiticus, represented by the symbol for Aleph, is the second oldest of the uncial codices. It has the complete New Testament, except for 24 verses, but only 145 leaves of the Septuagint, that is, about half of the Old Testament. It is dated to early in the 4th century.

It is thought of as probably the most important witness to the New Testament because of its antiquity and accuracy.

Codex Alexandrinus

Codex Alexandrinus, represented by the letter A, is missing 34 chapters from the New Testament, mainly from Matthew's Gospel, but contains the whole of the Septuagint except for ten leaves.

It is dated to the beginning of the 5th century. Codex Alexandrinus is particularly important in the Greek studies of the New Testament because it contains the best extant text of the Revelation.

It also contains the oldest complete text of several Old Testament books.

Codex Vaticanus is housed in the Vatican Library while Sinaiticus and Alexandrinus are in the British Museum.

There are about three hundred New Testament uncial manuscripts still in existence.

D. MINUSCULE MANUSCRIPTS

Minuscule manuscripts are Greek manuscripts of the New Testament which derive their name from their style of lettering, which is a small cursive type of letter.

There are over 2,500 of these manuscripts which are all dated between the 9th to the 15th centuries.

E. LECTIONARIES

Lectionaries, lists of readings of passages from the Bible, testify to the existence of those parts of the original text of the New Testament which were used by the early church fellowships in their worship services.

More than 2000 lectionaries, from the 4th to the 12th centuries have been collected and preserved.

With the exception of the book of Revelation and of some chapters from Acts the New Testament can be assembled many times over from these lectionaries.

Early translations of the New Testament

A Latin versions of the New Testament

The first Latin translations of the original Greek manuscripts of the New Testament are the most important of the early versions of the New Testament. It was natural that the New Testament would be translated into Latin as Latin was the official language of the Roman Empire. As Latin became the dominant language of the West Latin versions of the New Testament became the only versions used by Christians in the West.

Two Latin versions of the New Testament existed, the "Old Latin" version, and the Vulgate, which included the Old Testament.

I. THE OLD LATIN TRANSLATION
Although these first Latin translations have been dated back to before A.D. 200 they contained a number of mistakes and variations.

These Latin translations are known as the "Old Latin" translation and about thirty of these manuscripts still exist.

II. THE LATIN VULGATE
Early church leaders saw the need to revise the "Old Latin" translation to ensure that they had a more accurate translation. This resulted in the Bible we know today as the Latin Vulgate.

In 382 Pope Damascus asked Jerome to make a revised Latin version of the whole Bible. The Vulgate was the first translation of the Bible based on Hebrew and Greek manuscripts.

Jerome, a Greek and Hebrew scholar, standardized the numerous Old Latin translations. Jerome's translation was called the Latin Vulgate as "Vulgate" means "common." This Bible came to be known as the *versio vulgata* (common translation).

The Latin Vulgate translation of the Bible meant that the Bible now existed in the ordinary language of the people

Jerome's new Latin version became the Bible of the Western church for the next one thousand years until the Reformation in the 16th century.

There are still about eight thousand copies of the Latin Vulgate in existence.

Psalm 117 in the Vulgate
laudate Dominum omnes gentes
conlaudate eum universi populi
quia confortata est super nos
misericordia eius et veritas Domini in
aeternum alleluia

1 Corinthians chapter 13 in the Vulgate
si linguis hominum loquar et
angelorum caritatem autem non
habeam factus sum velut aes sonans
aut cymbalum tinniens
    et si habuero prophetiam et noverim
mysteria omnia et omnem scientiam et
habuero omnem fidem ita ut montes
transferam caritatem autem non
habuero nihil sum
    et si distribuero in cibos pauperum
omnes facultates meas et si tradidero
corpus meum ut ardeam caritatem
autem non habuero nihil mihi prodest
    caritas patiens est benigna est caritas
non aemulatur non agit perperam non
inflatur

non est ambitiosa non quaerit quae
sua sunt non inritatur non cogitat
malum

non gaudet super iniquitatem
congaudet autem veritati

omnia suffert omnia credit omnia
sperat omnia sustinet

caritas numquam excidit sive
prophetiae evacuabuntur sive linguae
cessabunt sive scientia destruetur

ex parte enim cognoscimus et ex
parte prophetamus

cum autem venerit quod perfectum
est evacuabitur quod ex parte est

cum essem parvulus loquebar
ut parvulus sapiebam ut parvulus
cogitabam ut parvulus quando factus
sum vir evacuavi quae erant parvuli

videmus nunc per speculum in
enigmate tunc autem facie ad faciem
nunc cognosco ex parte tunc autem
cognoscam sicut et cognitus sum

nunc autem manet fides spes caritas
tria haec maior autem his est caritas

B Syrian Bible versions

The Syrian translation of the Bible
is another important early Bible
version. Syrian was the main language
of everyone who lived in Syria and
Mesopotamia. It was very similar to the
Aramaic language which was spoken
by Jesus and his disciples.

I. OLD SYRIAC
The first translation of the Bible into
Syrian is now known as the "Old
Syriac" version. It dates back to the end
of the 2nd century and only two of its
manuscripts still exist.

II. PESHITTA
The second Syriac version is now
known as the "Peshitta" or "simple"
Syrian version and dates back to the 5th
century.

Many languages

In addition to the Latin and Syrian
languages the Bible was also translated
into numerous other languages.

The following versions are some
examples of such translations.
- The Coptic version of Egypt
- The Ethiopic of Ethiopia
- The Gothic of the Germanic tribes
- The Armenian version of the Eastern
  church
- The Georgian of Georgia north of
  Armenia
- The Nestorian versions of central and
  east Asia
- The Arabic version
- The Slavonic version.

9000 copies

There are still more than 9000
copies of these early translations
of the Bible which are still quite
readable even after all these
centuries.

Quotations from the New Testament made by the early Church Fathers

Overview

"The church has always believed her Scriptures to be the book of God, of which God was in such a sense the author that every one of its affirmations of whatever kind is to be esteemed as the utterance of God, of infallible truth and authority."

B.B. Warfield

Treating the Bible as authoritative

The writings of the apostolic Fathers treat the Scriptures in the same way that the Scriptures treat themselves. The phrases that they use to introduce quotations from the Bible show how they treat the Bible as being authoritative.

In his first epistle to the Corinthians, Clement of Rome often introduces the Scriptures as God's words, and uses the following formulas:

"For He saith," "God said unto him," "And again He saith," "For the Holy Ghost saith," "For it is written," "For the Scripture saith," and "as it is written."

Why quotations by the early Church Fathers are important

- The earliest manuscripts we have of major portions of the New Testament are p45, p46, p66, and p75. These have been dated between A.D. 175 and A.D. 250 So this leaves a gap of about one hundred years between the autographs of the New Testament and the earliest existing fragments of the New Testament.
- The early Church Fathers (A.D. 97–180) through their quotations from the New Testament bear witness to even earlier New Testament manuscripts. They quoted from twenty-eight out of the twenty-nine New Testament books.
- They also bore witness to the authenticity of these New Testament books written by the apostles and those in the apostolic circle. They also rejected later books such as the Gospel of Thomas that claimed to have been written by the apostles, but were not.
- Every New Testament book was referred to prior to A.D. 150, with the possible exception of Philemon and 3 John.

Authentication of the New Testament

The apostolic fathers Ignatius (A.D. 30–107), Polycarp (A.D. 65–155), and Papias (A.D. 70–155) cite verses from every New Testament book except 2 and 3 John. So just these three early Church Fathers authenticated nearly all of the New Testament.

CLEMENT OF ROME
In his *Epistle of Clement to the Corinthians* in about A.D. 97 Clement cites verses from Luke, Acts, Romans, 1 Corinthians, Ephesians, Titus, 1 and 2 Peter, Hebrews, and James.

IGNATIUS

The letters of Ignatius (dated A.D. 115) were written to several churches in Asia Minor and cites verses from Matthew, John, Romans, 1 and 2 Corinthians, Galatians, Ephesians, Philippians, 1 and 2 Timothy, and Titus.

These letters indicate that the entire New Testament was written in the first century A.D.

JUSTIN MARTYR

Justin Martyr, (A.D. 110–165), cited verses from the following thirteen books of the New Testament: Matthew, Mark, Luke, John, Acts, Romans, 1 Corinthians, Galatians, 2 Thessalonians, Hebrews, 1 and 2 Peter, and Revelation.

IRENAEUS

In his book *Against Heresies* Irenaeus, (A.D. 130–20), quoted from every book of the New Testament except for 3 John. Irenaeus made over 1,200 quotations from the New Testament in his writings, and about 1,800 quotations and references from the New Testament

CLEMENT OF ALEXANDRIA

Clement of Alexandria, writing from A.D. 193 to 220, made about 2,400 quotations and references to every New Testament book except Philemon, James, 2 Peter, and possibly 3 John.

CYPRIAN

Cyprian, A.D. 200–258, made about 1,030 quotations and references from the New Testament. His quotes include every book except Philemon and 2 John, and possibly 3 John, which are the three shortest books in the New Testament.

There are enough quotations from the early Church Fathers that even if we did not have a single copy of the Bible, scholars could still reconstruct all but 11 verses of the entire New Testament from material written within 150 to 200 years from the time of Christ.

> **Quote Unquote**
>
> "The early church leaders wrote and quoted from the New Testament so that the New Testament could be re-written from their quotations with the exception of 11 verses."
>
> *Geisler and Nix*

Conclusion

Although there is a 250–300 year gap between the time of the original complete New Testament manuscript and the first complete copies that still exist, this gap is bridged by the quotations of the New Testament made by the early church leaders.

Over 86,000 quotations from the New Testament have been noted in the writings of the early Church Fathers. Christians believe that it is in God's providence that the text of the New Testament has been preserved in both quality and quantity, unlike any other document from antiquity.

The number and early date of the New Testament manuscripts

Writing the Bible

1,500–1,600 years

The whole Bible was written over a period of about 1,600 years dating from about 1,500 B.C. to about A.D. 100.

Date of writing

The first five books of the Old Testament were written by Moses in around 1,500 to 1,450 B.C.

The last book of the New Testament, the book of Revelation was written by John shortly before A.D. 100.

Over 400 years gap

The writing of the Old Testament was complete by about 400 B.C.

The New Testament was started within a few decades of the death of Jesus.

This leaves a gap of over 400 years between the end of the writing of the Old Testament and the starting of the writing of the New Testament.

Fragments of manuscripts

The existence of the unique manuscript evidence of the New Testament confirms its reliability.

The accurate transmission of the Bible is supported by more and better manuscripts than any other ancient piece of literature.

"The works of several ancient authors are preserved to us by the thinnest possible thread of transmission. In contrast the textual critic of the New Testament is embarrassed by the wealth of his material."

Bruce Metzger, Princeton professor, and leading biblical text critic

"To be skeptical of the resultant text of the New Testament Books is to allow all of classical antiquity to slip into obscurity, for no documents of the ancient period are as well attested bibliographically as the New Testament."

John Warwick Montgomery

"Jews preserved it as no other manuscript has ever been preserved. With their massora (parva, magna, and finalis) they kept tabs on every letter, syllable, word and paragraph. They had special classes of men within their culture whose sole duty was to preserve and transmit these documents with practically perfect fidelity – scribes, lawyers, massoretes. Who ever counted the letters and syllables and words of Plato or Aristotle? Cicero or Seneca?"

Bernard Ramm, speaking on the accuracy and number of biblical manuscripts

The integrity of the manuscript evidence

Like any other ancient book transmitted through a number of handwritten manuscripts, the question to ask about the biblical manuscripts is: How confident can we be that our present day Bibles resemble the original autographs?

Author	Book	Date written	Earliest copy	Time gap	No. of copies
Homer	Iliad	800 B.C.	c. 400 B.C.	c. 400 yrs.	643
Herodotus	History	480–425 B.C.	c. A.D. 900	c. 1,350 yrs.	8
Thucydides	History	460–400 B.C.	c. A.D. 900	c. 1,300 yrs.	8
Plato		400 B.C.	c. A.D. 900	c. 1,300 yrs.	7
Demosthenes		300 B.C.	c. A.D.1100	c. 1,400 yrs.	200
Caesar	Gallic wars	100–44 B.C.	c. A.D. 900	c. 1000 yrs.	10
Livy	History of Rome	59 B.C.–A.D. 17	4th cent. (partial) mostly 10th cent.	c. 400 yrs. c. 1000 yrs	1 partial 19 copies
Tacitus	Annals	A.D. 100	c. A.D. 1100	c. 1000 yrs.	20
Pliny Secundus	Natural History	A.D. 61–113	c. A.D. 850	c. 750 yrs.	7
New Testament		A.D. 50–100	c. 114 (fragment) c. 200 (books) c. 250 (most of N.T) c. 325 (complete N.T.)	+ 50 yrs. 100 yrs. 150 yrs. 225 yrs.	6000

"Although 250–300 years sounds like a long time from the writing of the original to the date of the first copy we have, the normal time for the Greek classical writers is 1000 years from the original to our first copy."

F.W. Hall, expert on ancient manuscripts

The reliability of the New Testament

"If we compare the present state of the text of the New Testament with that of no matter what other ancient work, we must. declare it marvelously exact."

Benjamin Warfield

"The records for the New Testament are vastly more abundant, clearly more ancient, and considerably more accurate in their text [than comparable ancient writings]."

Norman Geisler

Number of manuscripts

There are more copies of the New Testament than any other document in ancient history.

We have over 6000 manuscript copies of either the entire Greek New Testament, or parts of it.

By way of comparison, we have
- only about 650 manuscript copies of Homer's *Iliad*. However, they date from A.D. 200 to 300 which is over a thousand years after the *Iliad* was written,
- about 330 manuscript copies of Euripides' tragedies,
- only nine good copies of Caesar's Gallic Wars,
- and eight manuscripts of the *History* of Greek historian Herodotus.

Gap between originals and copies

Overview

The surviving manuscripts of the biblical texts are much closer in date to the publication of the originals than other ancient writings from the same era.

Classic writings

The date of the earliest manuscripts for most of the classical works of antiquity are 800 to 1000 years later than the date of original publication.

The average gap between the original composition and the earliest copy is over 1000 years for other books.

Josephus, a Jewish historian, wrote *The Jewish War* shortly after A.D. 70 There are nine manuscripts in Greek which date from A.D. 1000–1200 and one Latin translation from around A.D. 400.

Old Testament manuscripts

- The Old Testament autographs were written between about 1450 and 400 B.C.
- The fragments and manuscripts of the Old Testament among the Dead Sea Scrolls are the oldest collection of the Hebrew manuscripts and fragments.
- The Dead Sea Scrolls date between 200 B.C. to A.D. 70 and so are dated back to within 300 years from when the last book of the Old Testament was written. The Dead Sea Scrolls contain the entire book of Isaiah and parts of every other Old Testament book except for Esther.
- The Geniza Fragments are parts of the Old Testament in Hebrew and Aramaic which were discovered in 1947 in an old synagogue in Cairo, Egypt. They date back to about A.D. 400.
- The Ben Asher manuscripts are copies of the Old Testament from the Masoretic Hebrew text made by five or six generations of the Ben Asher family. They date back to about A.D. 700–950
- Two almost complete Greek LXX translations of the Old Testament date to about A.D. 350.
- The Aleppo Codex is the oldest complete Hebrew Old Testament and was copied in about A.D. 950.
- The Aleppo Codex, A.D. 900–950. Before a 1948 synagogue fire it was a complete copy of the Old Testament.
- The British Museum Codex has an incomplete copy of the Pentateuch, (A.D. 950).
- The St Petersburg (or Leningrad) Codex is the complete manuscript of the entire Old Testament and dates back to A.D. 1008. It is the basis of Kittel's *Biblia Hebraica* which is widely recognized as a standard Hebrew text.

New Testament manuscripts

- The New Testament autographs were written between A.D. 45 and 95.
- There are copies of part of the New Testament that were written within

about 40 or 50 years of the original.

- The New Testament has:
  - a fragment within one generation from its original composition,
  - whole books within about 100 years from the time of the autograph,
  - most of the New Testament dating back to within 200 years of its original writing, and
  - the entire New Testament within 250 years from the date of its completion.

NUMBER OF NEW TESTAMENT MANUSCRIPTS

- There are about 6000 Greek manuscripts of the New Testament, some of which date back to as early as A.D. 125, or even earlier. The earliest complete New Testament dates from A.D. 350.
- There are over 8000 manuscripts of Latin Vulgate or part of it.
- There are about 8000 manuscripts in Ethiopic, Coptic, Slavic, Syriac, and Armenian.

Important papyrus manuscripts

- P52 dates from c. A.D. 125. It is a fragment of a codex of the book of John (18: 31–33,37–38).
- P45, from the 3rd century, containing parts of all four Gospels on 30 leaves.
- P46, from c. 200, has 86 leaves on which are most of the letters of Paul and the letter to the Hebrews.
- P75, from between A.D. 175 and 225, contains 102 pages consisting of most of the Gospels of Luke and John.

Conclusion

There are no copies of Caesar's *Gallic Wars* or Herodotus' *History* that are within 900 years of the original composition.

Yet no classical scholar doubts the authenticity of Herodotus just because there is a gap of many hundreds of years between the earliest manuscripts of his works and his original manuscript.

The first translations of the Bible (1)

1 The Old Testament

The first translations of the Old Testament were made into Aramaic and Greek.

A Aramaic targums

From about 400 B.C. the Old Testament began to be translated into Aramaic. This translation is known as the Aramaic targums. This translation helped the Jewish people, who began to speak Aramaic from the time of their captivity in Babylon, to understand the Old Testament in their everyday language.

B The Greek Septuagint

In about 250 B.C., the Old Testament was translated into Greek. This translation is known as the Septuagint.

The Septuagint was the first translation of the Hebrew Old Testament into Greek.

The Jews who lived in Alexandria, Egypt, were no longer familiar with Hebrew, as they spoke Greek. These Jews could no longer read Hebrew but Greek had become their everyday language.

The Septuagint translation is thought to have been made near Alexandria.

The Septuagint, often abbreviated by the Roman numbers, LXX, is made up of the thirty-nine books of the Old Testament as well as the seven books of the Old Testament apocrypha, Tobit, Judith, 1 & 2 Maccabees, Wisdom, Ecclesiasticus, Baruch.

Traditionally it is supposed that the translation was made by 70 (or, 72) scholars and hence the translation is known as the "seventy." The word "Septuagint" is from the Latin "Septuaginta" or seventy. The Septuagint is often referred to by the Roman numerals for seventy, LXX.

There is a story recorded in the so-called Letter of Aristeas that says that seventy-two Jews from Jerusalem came to Alexandria and made their translation in seventy-two days.

It is probably more accurate to say that the Pentateuch was translated first during the reign of Philadelphius (285–247 B.C.) by 72 Jewish scholars. Eventually the name "Septuagint" was given to their translation of the entire Old Testament.

The Septuagint became the Bible for Greek-speaking synagogues all over the Roman Empire

New Testament writers most often used the Greek LXX in preference to the Hebrew text when they quoted from the Old Testament.

The LXX was the Old Testament translation used most of all by the early Church.

Jesus Christ would have used the Septuagint as his Bible.

In the Greek-speaking world the Septuagint became very important because it provided a version of the Old Testament in a language of the day.

C The Masoretic text

Before the discovery of the Dead Sea Scrolls, the earliest known surviving manuscripts of the Old Testament in the Hebrew language dated back to medieval times. For these manuscripts we are indebted to Tiberian Masoretes, the scholars who worked in Tiberias in Palestine. Over a period of about 500 years, from A.D. 500 to A.D. 1000, these scholars faithfully copied and standardized existing texts of the Old Testament.

"Masoretic" comes from a Hebrew word "masor" meaning "traditional." It means to hand down from person to person, and from one generation to the next generation. Hence the Masoretes have been called "transmitters."

The oldest dated Masoretic manuscript dates to A.D. 895.

A passion for accuracy

The Jews took great pride and care in copying the books of the Old Testament. Originally, the Old Testament was copied by men called Sopherim. These scribes preserved the ancient text by keeping various statistics about the books they copied. The Masoret copyists counted and knew exactly how many Hebrew letters were in each book of the Hebrew Bible. For example, there were 78,064 such letters in the book of Genesis. They even knew exactly how many letters of each letter of the alphabet were in the book of Genesis.

They also knew how many letters there were from the beginning of the text and from the end of the text to the middle of the text. They knew which letter should be the middle letter in the book of Genesis. When they had copied a Bible book they used the following checks to ensure the accuracy of their work. They counted the letters from the beginning of the book and from the end of the book to the middle of the book. If this was not accurate or if the letter in the middle was not correct, that manuscript was discarded and burned.

The first translations of the Bible (2)

Manuscripts of the LXX

The oldest Greek LXX translation of the Old Testament that still exists is the Chester Beatty Papyri. It contains nine Old Testament Books in the Greek Septuagint and used to be dated at the end of the 2nd century.

Codex Vaticanus and Codex Sinaiticus each contain almost the entire Old Testament of the Greek Septuagint and they both date around A.D. 350.

2 The New Testament

The autographs of the New Testament are dated to between about A.D. 45 and A.D. 95.

Oldest surviving New Testament manuscripts

Over 5,600 early Greek manuscripts of the New Testament have survived. The oldest manuscripts were written on papyrus and the later manuscripts were written on parchment. The letter "p" is used to identify these different manuscripts. "P" stands for papyrus. So "p52" refers to papyrus 52.

Suggested dates

The dates given below indicate the date when scholars believe the manuscript copies were made.

A.D. 125

The New Testament manuscript which dates most closely to the original autograph was copied around A.D. 125. The oldest New Testament manuscript is known as the John Rylands manuscript, and is called p52. It was discovered in Egypt.

This means it was copied within 35 years of the original autograph being written by the apostle John.

It contains a small part of John 18.

So the earliest copy of any of the New Testament is only one generation after its original writing.

A.D. 200

Bodmer II p66 was discovered in 1956. It has fourteen chapters of John's Gospel as well as parts of the last seven chapters of John's Gospel.

A.D. 225

Bodmer p75 contains the Gospels of Luke and John.

A.D. 250–300

The Chester Beatty papyri
The Chester Beatty p45, (A.D. 200–250) was discovered in 1931 and contains the Gospels, Acts, Paul's letters, except for 1 and 2 Timothy and Titus, and the book of Revelation.

Chester Beatty p46 contains Paul's letters and the letter to the Hebrews.

A.D. 350

Codex Sinaiticus contains the entire New Testament and almost the entire Old Testament in Greek. It was discovered by a German scholar Tisendorf in 1856 at an Orthodox monastery at Matt. Sinai.

A.D. 350
Codex Vaticanus B is an almost complete New Testament. It had been in the Vatican Library since 1475.

Changing dates

Over the past fifty years or so the dates given to the earliest New Testament manuscripts have changed. biblical scholars and archaeologists revise the probable dates of these manuscripts in the light of new dating techniques and as they reevaluate all the evidence. This has nearly always resulted in many of these papyri being given earlier dates than was previously thought.

If such early dating proves to be accurate then it is possible to place the following dates on this list of early manuscripts.

Revised dates

p46:A.D. 85	p66:A.D. 125
p32:A.D. 175	p45:A.D. 150
p87:A.D. 125	p90:A.D. 150
p64/67:A.D. 60	p4:A.D. 100
7Q4:<A.D. 68	7Q5:A.D. 50–68

Exceptionally early dates

The last two papyri in this list come from the Dead Sea Scrolls. They are identified with the letter "Q" instead of the letter "p." These exceptionally early dates are based on the identification of two new papyri of the New Testament found with the Dead Sea Scrolls in Cave 7 which some scholars believe to be the earliest New Testament papyri yet discovered.

Summary

Manuscripts containing most of the New Testament text have been dated back into the middle of the 3rd century, and some may be dated back into the 2nd century, or even 1st century.

Early New Testament translations

Early translations of the New Testament reveal important insights about the underlying Greek manuscripts they were translated from.

A.D. 180
Early translations of the New Testament from Greek into Latin, Syriac, and Coptic versions began about A.D. 180

A.D. 195
The first translations of the Old and New Testaments into Latin were called "Old Latin" translations. Parts of the Old Latin were found in quotes by Tertullian, 160–220.

A.D. 300
The Old Syriac version was a translation of the New Testament from the Greek into Syriac.

The Coptic versions were translated into the four Coptic dialects known in Egypt at that time.

A.D. 380
The Latin Vulgate was translated by St. Jerome. He translated into Latin the Old Testament from the Hebrew and the New Testament from Greek.

The canon of Scripture

What does the "canon" of Scripture mean?

The word "canon" is derived front the Greek word *kanon* which means a straight rod, a ruler, and a carpenter's measuring rod.

FIGURATIVE USE OF "CANON"

Figuratively "canon" came to mean the standard by which something could be measured. In 2 Corinthians 10: 13, "But we will not boast of things without *our* measure, but according to the measure of the rule which God hath distributed to us, a measure to reach even unto you"; and in Galatians 6: 16 "And as many as walk according to this rule, peace *be* on them, and mercy, and upon the Israel of God." The word *kanon* is translated as rule to denote the restriction and type of behavior that characterizes someone who is led by the Spirit.

APPLYING "CANON" TO SCRIPTURE

In time, the word *kanon* was applied to the books of Scripture themselves. The canon became the collection of books or writings accepted by the apostles and leadership of the early Christian church as a basis for Christian belief. It is the standard by which all Christians throughout the ages live and worship.

Athanasius

Athanasius is the first one known to have used "canon" in such a context.

Origen

Origen used the word "canon" to denote what we call the "rule of faith," the standard by which we are to measure and evaluate everything.

Canonicity

The process of recognizing the sixty-six books of the Bible as the word of God is known as canonicity.

The church did not create the canon. Rather, Christians came to recognize the books for what they were: God's inspired revelation. "All Scripture is God-breathed (inspired) and profitable for teaching, for conviction, for correction, for instruction in righteousness" 2 Timothy 3: 16.

The Old Testament canon

One way to answer the question: "How and when were the books of the Bible put together?" would be to say that ultimately it was God who decided which books would be included in the biblical canon and which books would be excluded from the biblical canon.

It was not a matter of some council or synod deciding which books they were going to have in the Old Testament. Rather it was a matter of God convincing the church which books should be included in the Bible.

Compared with the New Testament, there was very little controversy over the canon of the Old Testament.

The books of the Old Testament were recognized as being divinely inspired and authoritative almost as soon as they were written. The writers were accepted as being God's spokesmen.

Soon after the book of Malachi was written (in about 430 B.C.), the Jews officially recognized and closed the Old Testament canon.

The Council of Jamnia

The Council of Jamnia, held in about A.D. 90, established and closed the canon of the Old Testament for nearly all Jews. It has been their canon ever since and consists of the twenty-seven books of what we know as the Old Testament. However, the order of the books in the Hebrew Bible differs from the order of the books in what Christians call the Old Testament.

The canon of the whole Bible

All of the books of the New Testament as we know them today we officially recognized:
- In the Eastern Church in A.D. 367 in Athanasius' *Festal Letter;*
- In the Western Church in A.D. 397 at a conciliar decision at Carthage.

The sixty-six books which we are now used to seeing in our Bibles were recognized as being the canonical ones in the above 4th century letter and council.

Before the first church council formally ratified the question about which books made up the Christian Scriptures, the decisions had already been made. The council only went on record, approving what was already acknowledged.

Quote Unquote

"Some religious persons have had an incorrect view as to the basis of the determination of the true canon. They have said that the books were made canonical on the basis of the decision of church councils. In reality all that the church leaders could do would be to discover and recognize that list of books which were obviously inspired."

Roy D. Merritt

The formation of the Old Testament

A Early collections of writings

There are a number of instances recorded in the Old Testament which speak about early collections of formal writings being made.

The laws of Moses were stored by the Ark in the tabernacle. "And Moses wrote this law, and delivered it unto the priests the sons of Levi, which bare the ark of the covenant of the LORD, and unto all the elders of Israel" (Deuteronomy 31: 9–26); and later in the temple, "And Hilkiah the high priest said unto Shaphan the scribe, I have found the book of the law in the house of the LORD. And Hilkiah gave the book to Shaphan, and he read it" 2 Kings 22: 8.

The law was written down so that it could always be read by God's people (Joshua 24: 25–26). "Then Samuel told the people the manner of the kingdom, and wrote it in a book, and laid it up before the Lord" 1 Samuel 10: 25.

The rediscovery of part of the law written down in a book led to a revival in Josiah's reign (2 Kings 22 and 23). After the book of the law was read aloud the people repented (2 Kings 22: 11–12).

When Ezra had gathered all the people together in Jerusalem he read to them from the Law of Moses, (Nehemiah 8).

B Collecting together the collections of books

Some of the Old Testament books were immediately recognized as authoritative. Moses, after he wrote a book, put it in the Ark of the Covenant (Deut. 31: 24–26). After the temple was built, the sacred writings were kept there (2 Kings 22: 18). Early on, God commanded the kings to write for themselves a copy of the law. "And he shall read it all the days of his life, that he may learn to fear the Lord his God" (Deut. 17: 19). As the prophets spoke God's word, saying, "Thus saith the Lord," they also recognized that their message had to be recorded for future generations.

Criteria for accepting Old Testament books

A DOES THE BOOK AGREE WITH THE TORAH?

Any book that did not agree with the first five books of the OT could not be considered for inclusion in the OT canon.

B THE DIVINE AUTHORITY OF THE BOOK

Only books that were believed to be inspired by God were accepted.

It is not that the Jews gave these books their authority. Rather, they recognized the inherent authority contained in these books.

In the case of the Old Testament books the nation of Israel recognized a book as being authoritative because it is inspired of God. In the same way in the case of the New Testament books, the Christian church recognized a book as suitable for inclusion in the new book of Scriptures because it was already divinely inspired.

C The authors of the books

The author is the person to whom God revealed his word.

The words were either written down by him or by secretaries. For example, Jeremiah's scribe Baruch wrote down many of his prophecies. Jeremiah 51: 64 says, "...the words of Jeremiah end here."

Moses claimed to be the mouthpiece of God.

The Old Testament prophets repeatedly said, "And the word of the Lord came to me."

The New Testament canon

Criteria for accepting New Testament books

A APOSTOLIC AUTHORITY OR AUTHENTICATION
To be included in the NT books had to be written by the apostles themselves, or by those who were closely associated with the apostles.

B CHRIST-CENTERED CONTENT
The books had to agree with basic Christian teaching which included the known teaching of the other apostles and had to be Christ-honoring in its doctrinal teaching.

C ACCEPTED BY THE CHRISTIAN CHURCH
Books were only included which had been accepted and used by the Christian Church.

The Gospel of Thomas

The Gospel of Thomas is not found in our New Testament today. It was excluded from the canon of the New Testament because:

- the Gospel of Thomas fails the test of apostolic authority. It was not written by the apostle Thomas, (despite its name) and was probably not written until A.D. 140;

- none of the early church fathers from Clement to Irenaeus quoted from the Gospel of Thomas;

- the Gospel of Thomas fails to agree with accepted Christian teaching. It purports to contain 114 "secret sayings" of Jesus. But some of these sayings are wild in the extreme and one even says that women cannot receive salvation unless they become men.

The origin of the Bible

Overview

Christians have always believed, no matter how the Bible may have been transmitted to us over the centuries, that its origin is supernatural. Christians believe that the Bible exists because of divine revelation.

Revelation

In the pages of the Bible God has disclosed himself to men and women. We learn about God from reading the Bible.

General revelation

This does not exclude general revelation in which God has revealed himself: through nature and creation. In the beauty and wonder of creation we see God's signature (Psalm 19: 1, Romans 1: 20).

Special revelation

However, a more complete revelation of who God is, is only to be found in the Bible. What the biblical authors wrote were not their own ideas but God's revelation.

God's various methods of revelation to his chosen authors

VOICE
God spoke in an audible voice to some of them, telling them what to write down (Exodus 33: 1).

DREAMS
God used dreams as a channel through which he revealed some of his prophetic truths (Daniel 2: 1–49).

PEOPLE
The personal experiences and spiritual lives of individuals were used by God (Psalm 51).

HOLY SPIRIT
God's Spirit guided the biblical authors in all their writings (2 Peter 1: 21).

The formation of the New Testament

The process of recognizing and collecting the books for what we now call the New Testament started in the early days of the Christian church.

Some of the New Testament books were instantly regarded as being part of the Scriptures.

Paul considered Luke's writings to be as authoritative as the Old Testament (1 Tim. 5: 18, see Deut. 25: 4 and Luke 10: 7).

Peter recognized Paul's writings as Scripture (2 Pet. 3: 15–16).

Some of the books of the New Testament were being circulated among the churches (Col. 4: 1 6; 1 Thess. 5: 27).

Early church leaders

- Clement of Rome mentioned at least eight New Testament books (A.D. 95).
- Ignatius of Antioch acknowledged about seven books (A.D. 115).
- Polycarp, a disciple of John the Apostle, acknowledged 15 books (A.D. 108).
- Irenaeus mentioned 21 books (A.D. 185).
- Hippolytus recognized 22 books (A.D. 170–235).

The first "canon"

MURATORIAN CANON
The first "canon", the Muratorian Canon, compiled in A.D. 170, included all of the New Testament books except Hebrews, James, and 3 John.

COUNCIL OF LAODICEA
In A.D. 363, the Council of Laodicea stated that only the Old Testament and the 27 books of the New Testament were to be read in the churches.

COUNCIL OF HIPPO
The Council of Hippo (A.D. 393) declared that the twenty-seven books in our present day New Testament alone were authoritative.

COUNCIL OF CARTHAGE
The Council of Carthage (A.D. 397) affirmed that the same twenty-seven books were authoritative.

Summary

- The Christian church did not create the canon, but received the canon which God created.
- The Old Testament canon came from the hands of Christ and his apostles in the sense that the first Christians knew that the Jewish Scriptures were from God and were fulfilled by Jesus' coming.
- The New Testament canon came from the Holy Spirit. Only through the Holy Spirit were Jesus' apostles enabled to speak about and write down the truth about Jesus.

Key Bible passage

"For they that dwell at Jerusalem, and their rulers, because they knew him not, nor yet the voices of the prophets which are read every sabbath day, they have fulfilled *them* in condemning *him*. 28 And though they found no cause of death *in him*, yet desired they Pilate that he should be slain. 29 And when they had fulfilled all that was written of him, they took *him* down from the tree, and laid *him* in a sepulcher. 30 But God raised him from the dead: 31 And he was seen many days of them which came up with him from Galilee to Jerusalem, who are his witnesses unto the people. 32 And we declare unto you glad tidings, how that the promise which was made unto the fathers, 33 God hath fulfilled the same unto us their children, in that he hath raised up Jesus again; as it is also written in the second psalm, Thou art my Son, this day have I begotten thee"

Acts 13: 27–33.

See also:

Matthew 5: 17
Luke 4: 21; 18: 31
Romans 1: 2
1 Peter 1: 10–12
2 Peter 1: 19–21.

Warfield on the New Testament canon (1)

Overview

One of the classic statements about the New Testament canon was made by B.B. Warfield.

In 1892 he published the following article: *The Formation Of The Canon Of The New Testament*

An inherited idea

In order to obtain a correct understanding of what is called the formation of the Canon of the New Testament, it is necessary to begin by fixing very firmly in our minds one fact which is obvious enough when attention is once called to it. That is, that the Christian church did not require to form for itself the idea of a "canon," – or, as we should more commonly call it, of a "Bible," – that is, of a collection of books given of God to be the authoritative rule of faith and practice. It inherited this idea from the Jewish church, along with the thing itself, the Jewish Scriptures, or the "Canon of the Old Testament."

Something imposed on the church

The church did not grow up by natural law: it was founded. And the authoritative teachers sent forth by Christ to found His church, carried with them, as their most precious possession, a body of Divine Scriptures, which they imposed on the church that they founded as its code of law. No reader of the New Testament can need proof of this; on every page of that book is spread the evidence that from the very beginning the Old Testament was as cordially recognized as law by the Christian as by the Jew. The Christian church thus was never without a "Bible" or a "canon."

By divine authority

But the Old Testament books were not the only ones which the apostles (by Christ's own appointment the authoritative founders of the church) imposed upon the infant churches, as their authoritative rule of faith and practice. No more authority dwelt in the prophets of the old covenant than in themselves, the apostles, who had been "made sufficient ministers of a new covenant"; for (as one of themselves argued) "if that which passeth away was with glory, much more that which remaineth is in glory." Accordingly not only was the gospel they delivered, in their own estimation, itself a Divine revelation, but it was also preached "in the Holy Ghost" (1 Peter 1: 12); not merely the matter of it, but the very words in which it was clothed were "of the Holy Spirit" (1 Corinthians 2: 13). Their own commands were, therefore, of Divine authority (1 Thessalonians 4: 2), and their writings were the depository of these commands (2 Thessalonians 2: 15). "If any man obeyeth not our word by this epistle," says Paul to one church (2 Thessalonians 3: 14), "note that man, that ye have no company with him." To another he makes it the test of a Spirit-led man to recognize that what he was writing to them was "the commandments of the Lord" (1 Corinthians 14: 37).

Accepted like the Old Testament

Inevitably, such writings, making so awful a claim on their acceptance, were received by the infant churches as of a quality equal to that of the old "Bible"; placed alongside its older books as an additional part of the one law of God; and read as such in their meetings for worship – a practice which moreover was required by the apostles (1 Thessalonians 5: 27; Colossians 4: 16; Revelation 1: 3).

In the apprehension, therefore, of the earliest churches, the "Scriptures" were not a closed but an increasing "canon." Such they had been from the beginning, as they gradually grew in number from Moses to Malachi; and such they were to continue as long as there should remain among the churches "men of God who spake as they were moved by the Holy Ghost."

Spoken about from the start

We say that this immediate placing of new books – given the church under the seal of apostolic authority – among the Scriptures already established as such, was inevitable. It is also historically evinced from the very beginning. Thus the apostle Peter, writing in A.D. 68, speaks of Paul's numerous letters not in contrast with the Scriptures, but as among the Scriptures and in contrast with "the other Scriptures" (2 Peter 3: 16) – that is, of course, those of the Old Testament.

Uniting OT and NT quotes

Paul combines the book of Deuteronomy and the Gospel of Luke under the common head of "Scripture" (1 Timothy 5: 18): "For the Scripture saith, 'Thou shalt not muzzle the ox when he treadeth out the corn' [Deuteronomy 25: 4]; and, 'The laborer is worthy of his hire'" (Luke 10: 7).

New Testament books treated as additional Scriptures

What needs emphasis at present about these facts is that they obviously are not evidences of a gradually-heightening estimate of the New Testament books, originally received on a lower level and just beginning to be tentatively accounted Scripture; they are conclusive evidences rather of the estimation of the New Testament books from the very beginning as Scripture, and of their attachment as Scripture to the other Scriptures already in hand.

"New books," "old books"

The early Christians did not, then, first form a rival "canon" of "new books" which came gradually to be accounted as of equal divinity and authority with the "old books"; they received new book after new book from the apostolic circle, as equally "Scripture" with the old books, and added them one by one to the collection of old books as additional Scriptures, until at length the new books thus added were numerous enough to be looked upon as another section of the Scriptures.

Warfield on the New Testament canon (2)

New name modeled on Old Testament

The earliest name given to this new section of Scripture was framed on the model of the name by which what we know as the Old Testament was then known. Just as it was called "The Law and the Prophets and the Psalms" (or "the Hagiographa" – "Holy Writings"), or more briefly "The Law and the Prophets," or even more briefly still "The Law"; so the enlarged Bible was called "The Law and the Prophets, with the Gospels and the Apostles"; while the new books apart were called "The Gospel and the Apostles," or most briefly of all "The Gospel."

Ignatius

This earliest name for the new Bible, with all that it involves as to its relation to the old and briefer Bible, is traceable as far back as Ignatius (A.D. 115), who makes use of it repeatedly (e.g., "ad Philad." 5; "ad Smyrn." 7). In one passage he gives us a hint of the controversies which the enlarged Bible of the Christians aroused among the Judaizers ("ad Philad." 6). "When I heard some saying," he writes, "Unless I find it in the Old [Books]; his cross and death and resurrection, and the faith which is by him, the undefiled Old [Books] – by which I wish, by your prayers, to be justified. The priests indeed are good, but the High Priest better," etc.

The New Testament lies hidden in the Old

Here Ignatius appeals to the "Gospel" as Scripture, and the Judaizers object, receiving from him the answer in effect which Augustine afterward formulated in the well-known saying that the New Testament lies hidden in the Old and the Old Testament is first made clear in the New. What we need now to observe, however, is that to Ignatius the New Testament was not a different book from the Old testament, but part of the one body of Scripture with it; an accretion, so to speak, which had grown upon it.

Part of the oracles of God

From the evidence of the fragments which alone have been preserved to us of the Christian writings of that very early time, it appears that from the beginning of the second century (and that is from the end of the apostolic age) a collection (Ignatius, 2 Clement) of "New Books" (Ignatius), called the "Gospel and Apostles" (Ignatius, Marcion), was already part of the "Oracles" of God (Polycarp, Papias, 2 Clement), or "Scriptures (1 Timothy, 2 Peter, Barnabas, Polycarp, 2 Clement), or the "Holy Books" or "Bible" (Testt. XII. Patt.).

The "Gospel" and "The Apostles"

The number of books included in this added body of New Books, at the opening of the second century, cannot be satisfactorily determined by the evidence of these fragments alone. The section of it called the "Gospel" included Gospels written by the apostles and their companions" (Justin), which beyond legitimate question were our four Gospels now received. The section called "The Apostles" contained the book of Acts (The Testt. XII. Patt.) and epistles of Paul, John, Peter, and James. The evidence from various quarters is indeed enough to show that the collection in general use contained all the books which we at present receive, with the possible exceptions of Jude, 2 and 3 John and Philemon. And it is more natural to suppose that failure of very early evidence for these brief booklets is due to their insignificant size rather than to their non-acceptance. . . .

APOSTOLIC AUTHORSHIP

Let it be clearly understood that it was not exactly apostolic authorship which in the estimation of the earliest churches, constituted a book a portion of the "canon." Apostolic authorship was, indeed, early confounded with canonicity. It was doubt as to the apostolic authorship of Hebrews, in the West, and of James and Jude, apparently, which underlay the slowness of the inclusion of these books in the "canon" of certain churches. But from the beginning it was not so. The principle of canonicity was not apostolic authorship, but imposition by the apostles as "law." Hence Tertullian's name for the "canon" is "instrumentum"; and he speaks of

the Old and New Instrument as we would of the Old and New Testament. That the apostles so imposed the Old Testament on the churches which they founded – as their "Instrument," or "Law," or "Canon" – can be denied by none. And in imposing new books on the same churches, by the same apostolical authority, they did not confine themselves to books of their own composition. It is the Gospel according to Luke, a man who was not an apostle, which Paul parallels in 1 Timothy 5: 18 with Deuteronomy as equally "Scripture" with it, in the first extant quotation of a New Testament book as Scripture.

APOSTOLIC AUTHORITY

The Gospels which constituted the first division of the New Books, – of "The Gospel and the Apostles," – Justin tells us, were "written by the apostles and their companions." The authority of the apostles, as by Divine appointment founders of the church, was embodied in whatever books they imposed on the church as law, not merely in those they themselves had written.

B.B. Warfield

B.B. Warfield

B.B. Warfield (1851–1921) was the last great theologian of the conservative Presbyterians at Princeton Theological Seminary.

Warfield distinguished himself as a scholarly defender of Augustinian Calvinism, supernatural Christianity, and the inspiration of the Bible.

Jewish, Orthodox, Catholic, and Protestant Bibles (1)

Key Bible verse

"And a certain Jew named Apollos, born at Alexandria, an eloquent man, and mighty in the scriptures, came to Ephesus."
Acts 18: 24

Disagreement about the Old Testament

The New Testament used by almost all Christians contains the same twenty-seven books.

But when it comes to the Old Testament this is not the case.

Total number of biblical books

Jews, Orthodox, Catholic, and Protestant Christians differ in their view about the number of biblical books in the Old Testament.
• The Jews count twenty-four
• The Orthodox count forty-eight
• The Protestants count thirty-nine
• The Catholics count forty-six

Minor prophets

The Jews count "The Twelve" minor prophets as one book, but Christians count these as twelve separate books.

Order of Bible books

In the Hebrew Bible the group of books known as the "Latter Prophets" come before the "Writings."

So while the Protestant and Catholic Bibles end with the book of Malachi the Hebrew Bible ends with 2 Chronicles.

Catagorization of books

A few books are put into different categories in the different Bibles.

In the Hebrew Bible, Daniel and Ruth come in the "Writings" category, but the three Christian Bibles place Daniel among the prophets, and Ruth with the historical books.

Orthodox and Catholic Bibles

The following books are found in Orthodox and Catholic Bibles, but not in Jewish or Protestant Bibles.
The longer version of Esther
Judith
Tobit
1 Maccabees
2 Maccabees
Psalm 151
Wisdom of Solomon
Sirach, a.k.a. Ecclesiasticus
Baruch
Letter of Jeremiah
The longer version of Daniel

The Hebrew Bible

The following books are considered to be scriptural, or biblical, by both ancient and modern Hebrew-speaking Jews.

TORAH / LAW
Genesis
Exodus
Leviticus
Numbers
Deuteronomy

FORMER PROPHETS
Joshua
Judges
Samuel 1 and 2
Kings 1 and 2

LATTER PROPHETS
Isaiah
Jeremiah
Ezekiel

THE TWELVE:
Hosea
Joel
Amos
Obadiah
Jonah
Micah
Nahum
Habakkuk
Zephaniah
Haggai
Zechariah
Malachi

WRITINGS
Psalms (150)
Proverbs
Job
Song of Solomon
Ruth
Lamentations
Ecclesiastes
Esther
Daniel
Ezra-Nehemiah
Chronicles 1 and 2

Orthodox Bibles

Most Orthodox Bibles follow the
books which are found in the
Septuagint.

The Septuagint, abbreviated by the
initials LXX, was a larger version of the
Bible which had been translated into
Greek. It was used by ancient Greek-
speaking Jews and Christians outside of
Palestine.

Greek Orthodox Bibles

Greek Orthodox Bibles contain
the following 10 books from the
Apocrypha:

1 Esdras
Tobit
Judith
1, 2, and 3 Maccabees
Wisdom of Solomon
Ecclesiasticus
Baruch
The Letter of Jeremiah

COUNCIL OF JASSY
They were officially recognized at the
Council of Jassy in 1642, but even Greek
Orthodox scholars now see them as
being less inspired than the other Bible
books.

List of books in Orthodox Bible

LAW
Genesis
Exodus
Leviticus
Numbers
Deuteronomy

HISTORICAL BOOKS
Joshua
Judges
Ruth
1 Kingdoms 1 Samuel
2 Kingdoms 2 Samuel

Jewish, Orthodox, Catholic, and Protestant Bibles (2)

List of books in Orthodox Bible, continued

HISTORICAL BOOKS, CONTINUED

3 Kingdoms 1 Kings
4 Kingdoms 2 Kings
1 Chronicles
2 Chronicles
2 Esdras Ezra and Nehemiah
Esther longer version
Judith
Tobit
1 Maccabees
2 Maccabees
3 Maccabees

WISDOM BOOKS

Psalms 151
Prayer of Manasseh
Proverbs
Ecclesiastes
Song of Solomon
Job
Wisdom of Solomon
Sirach, a.k.a. Ecclesiasticus

PROPHETS

Hosea
Amos
Micah
Joel
Obadiah
Jonah
Nahum
Habakkuk
Zephaniah
Haggai
Zechariah
Malachi
Isaiah
Jeremiah

Baruch
Lamentations
Letter of Jeremiah
Ezekiel
Daniel longer version

Catholic Bibles

LIST OF BOOKS IN CATHOLIC BIBLES

LAW

Genesis
Exodus
Leviticus
Numbers
Deuteronomy

HISTORICAL BOOKS

Joshua
Judges
Ruth
1 Samuel
2 Samuel
1 Kings
2 Kings
1 Chronicles
2 Chronicles
Ezra
Nehemiah
Tobit
Judith
Esther longer
1 Maccabees
2 Maccabees

WISDOM BOOKS

Job
Psalms 150
Proverbs
Ecclesiastes

Song of Solomon
Wisdom of Solomon
Sirach, a.k.a. Ecclesiasticus

PROPHETS
Isaiah
Jeremiah
Lamentations
Baruch with Letter of Jeremiah
Ezekiel
Daniel longer
Hosea
Joel
Amos
Obadiah
Jonah
Micah
Nahum
Habakkuk
Zephaniah
Haggai
Zechariah
Malachi

Protestant Bibles

LIST OF BOOKS IN PROTESTANT BIBLES

LAW
Genesis
Exodus
Leviticus
Numbers
Deuteronomy

HISTORICAL BOOKS
Joshua
Judges
Ruth
1 Samuel
2 Samuel
1 Kings

2 Kings
1 Chronicles
2 Chronicles
Ezra
Nehemiah
Esther

WISDOM BOOKS
Job
Psalms 150
Proverbs
Ecclesiastes
Song of Solomon

PROPHETS
Isaiah
Jeremiah
Lamentations
Ezekiel
Daniel
Hosea
Joel
Amos
Obadiah
Jonah
Micah
Nahum
Habakkuk
Zephaniah
Haggai
Zechariah
Malachi

Quote Unquote

"The existence of the Bible as a book for the people is the greatest benefit which the human race has ever experienced."

Immanuel Kant, philosopher

The history of Bible translation

Overview

The first Anglo-Saxon translation of the Bible was initiated in the 7th century.

The first translation of the English Bible was initiated by John Wycliffe and completed by John Purvey in 1388.

The first American edition of the Bible was published in about 1752.

Today, the Bible has been translated in part or in whole into 1,200 different languages or dialects.

Some of the landmarks of the history of Bible translation now follow.

B.C.

430–420 B.C.

With the writing of the book of Malachi came the completion of the original writing of the Hebrew manuscripts of the Hebrew Bible.

200 B.C.

Completion of the Septuagint translation of the Old Testament Hebrew into Greek.

A.D.

1st century A.D.

Completion of all the original Greek manuscripts which make up the twenty-seven books of the New Testament.

390

Jerome's translation of the Bible into Latin, known as the Vulgate.

995

Anglo-Saxon translations of the New Testament made.

1384

Wycliffe is the first person to produce a manuscript copy, hand-written of course, of the complete Bible in English.

1455

Gutenberg's printing press enables books to be mass-produced instead of individually hand-written.

The first printed book was Gutenberg's Bible in Latin.

1516

Erasmus produces a Greek/Latin parallel New Testament.

1522

Martin Luther's German New Testament.

1524

First printed Hebrew Old Testament

In 1524, Jacob ben Hayyim used copies of the ben Asher manuscripts and had them printed and published. As this was the first text of the Hebrew Old Testament to be printed it soon became the standard for printed Bibles

The earliest complete copy of the Masoretic text of the Old Testament is housed in the St. Petersburg Public Library and dates back to about A.D. 1008.

1525

William Tyndale's New Testament is the first New Testament to be printed in the English language.

1535

Myles Coverdale's Bible is the first complete Bible to be printed in the English language.

1537

The Matthew's Bible was the second complete Bible to be printed in English.

1539

The "Great Bible" was the first English Language Bible to be authorized for public use.

1560

The Geneva Bible was the first English Language Bible to print chapter and verse numbers.

1568

The Bishop's Bible was printed. The *KJV* was a revision of this Bible.

1609

The Douai Old Testament is added to the Rheims New Testament of 1582 which make the first complete Roman Catholic translation of the Bible into English.

1611

The King James Bible is published.

1782

The Robert Aitken's Bible is printed and becomes the first English Language Bible (a King James Version without the Apocrypha) to be printed in America.

1791

Isaac Collins produces the first Family Bible printed in America, using the *KJV*. Isaiah Thomas produces the first illustrated Bible Printed in America, using the *KJV*.

1808

Jane Aitken's Bible becomes the first Bible to be printed by a woman.

1833

Noah Webster's Bible is published by the author of a famous dictionary. Webster printed his own revision of the *KJV*.

1841

The English Hexapla New Testament printed the Greek and 6 English translations in parallel columns.

1846

The Illuminated Bible was a lavishly illustrated Bible printed in America, using the *KJV*.

1885

The "Revised Version" Bible was the first major English revision of the *KJV*.

1901

The "American Standard Version" was the first major American revision of the *KJV*.

Bible translations since the Middle Ages (1)

Overview

The following is a list of some of the most important Bibles translated into Anglo-Saxon, German, and English since the Middle Ages, together with some of the people who did the translation work.

The Book of Armagh
Latin Bibles
Caedmon's paraphrase
Aldhelm
The Lindisfarne Gospels
Venerable Bede
Alcuin of York
King Alfred
Aelfric
The Ormulum Gospels and the Acts
Richard Rolle of Hampole
John Wycliffe
John Purvey
The Gutenberg Bible
Erasmus' *Greek New Testament*
Polyglot Bible
Martin Luther
William Tyndale
Miles Coverdale
Matthew's Bible
The Great Bible
Taverner's Bible
The Geneva Bible
The Bishop's Bible
Rheims/Douai

The Book of Armagh

In Ireland, the Book of Armagh, containing portions of the New Testament, was written in a tiny, compressed and abbreviated, pointed insular minuscule, designed to fit as much text into a page as possible.

It was written/copied in the early 9th century, partly in Irish and partly in Latin.

It contained parts of a non-Vulgate text of the New Testament.

The Book of Armagh is the only surviving complete copy of the New Testament produced by the Irish Church.

Latin Bibles

After Augustine of Canterbury arrived in England in Pope Gregory sent him a Gregorian Bible. The Greogorian Bible was not written in Hebrew in the Old Testament and Greek in the New Testament, but in Latin, since Latin had become the main spoken language throughout most of the Mediterranean world.

These two volumes consisted of two copies of the Gospels, two Psalters, and some expositions on the readings from the New Testament letters and Gospels.

First English Bibles

OLD ENGLISH AND MIDDLE ENGLISH BIBLES, A.D. 500–1100
No complete copy or translation of either the New Testament or Old Testament was made into the English language during this period.

Caedmon's paraphrase of the Scriptures in Anglo-Saxon, 650's

"The first attempt, of which we have certain knowledge, at any thing like a paraphrase of Scripture in the Anglo-Saxon tongue to which a date can be assigned, is the poet of Caedmon in the seventh century" (The English Hexapla; Preface: An Historical Account of the English Versions of the Scriptures).

FIRST SAXON POET
Caedmon, a lay monk from Whitby, and described as "the first Saxon poet," composed a metrical version of large portions of Old Testament history. "Now must we praise the author of the heavenly kingdom, the Creator's power and counsel, the deeds of the Father of glory: how He, the eternal God, was the author of all marvels – He, who first gave to the sons of men the heaven for a roof, and then, Almighty Guardian of mankind, created the earth."

Caedmon

ADDITIONAL CAEDMON WRITINGS
Caedmon also composed material that dealt with the main facts of Jesus' life and the preaching of the apostles.

Aldhelm, 640–709
Aldhelm, Abbot of Malmesbury and Bishop of Sherbome. He made a literal translation of the Psalms into Anglo-Saxon in about A.D. 706 to be used in the daily services of the church. No copy of this still exists. Aldhelm was the earliest translator of Scripture into Anglo-Saxon.

Chronology of the modern Bible

1611 Authorized King James Version	**1966** Jerusalem Bible	**1976** Good News Bible	**1989** Revised English Bible
1901 American Standard Version	**1970** New English Bible	**1982** New King James (Authorized) Version	**1995** Contemporary English Version
1952 Revised American Standard Version	**1971** Living Bible	**1985** New Jerusalem Bible	**1995** God's Word
1964 Amplified Bible	**1963/71** New American Standard Version	**1987** New Century Version	**1996** New Living Version
	1973 New International Version	**1989** New Revised Standard Version	**1998** New Light Bible (New International Reader's Version)

Bible translations since the Middle Ages (2)

First English translations, continued

The Lindisfarne Gospels

The beautiful Lindisfarne Gospels are a Latin translation of Matthew, Mark, Luke, and John, and was made around A.D. 700 in an uncial Irish script. In about A.D. 995 an interlinear translation written in Anglo-Saxon by Aldred was added.

Venerable Bede, 674–735

Bede, a monk who lived in Jarrow, translated John's Gospel. He completed this on the day of his death. No copy of this exists today.

"I gave all my attention to the study of the Scriptures. . . . From the time that I received the degree of Priest's Orders unto the fifty-ninth year of my age (A.D. 731)."

Venerable Bede

BEDE'S LAST HOURS
Bede's "English" was the Anglo-Saxon language, which resembled modern German.

This is the account of Bede's last hours during which he completed his translation work.

"The illness of Bede increased, but he only labored the more diligently (in the translation of St. John). On the Wednesday, his scribe told him that one chapter alone remained, but feared that it might be painful to him to dictate. 'It is easy,' Bede replied; 'take your pen and write quickly.' The work

continued for some time. Then Bede directed Cuthbert to fetch his little treasures from his casket (capsella) that he might distribute them among his friends. And so he passed the remainder of the day till evening in holy and cheerful conversation. His boy scribe at last found an opportunity to remind him, with pious importunity, of his unfinished work. 'One sentence, dear master, still remains unwritten.' He answered, 'Write quickly.' The boy soon said, 'It is completed now.' 'Well,' Bede replied, 'thou hast said the truth; all is ended. Support my head with thy hands; I would sit in the holy place in which I was wot to pray, that so sitting I may call upon my Father.' Thereupon, resting on the floor of his cell, he chanted the Gloria [Glory be to the Father, through the Son, in the Holy Spirit], and his soul immediately passed away, while the name of the Holy Spirit was on his lips."

A General View of the History of the English Bible by Brooke Foss Westcott; 1916 MacMillan

Alcuin of York, late 700's

Alcuin, the schoolmaster of York, translated the first five books of the Old Testament into Anglo-Saxon.

In one of his sermons, Alcuin wrote: "The reading of the Scriptures is the knowledge of everlasting blessedness. In them man may contemplate himself as in some mirror, what sort of person he is. The reading cleanseth the reader's soul, for, when we pray, we speak to God, and when we read the Holy Books, God speaks to us."

However, only the sons of nobility would have had the money and the ability to read Alcuin's translation.

King Alfred, 849–899

King Alfred prefaced his famous code of laws for his British subjects, with his own Anglo-Saxon translation of the Ten Commandments.

In the preface to Alfred's *Pope Gregory's "Pastoral Care"* the king states that he longs for:

"all the free-born youth of my people . . . may persevere in learning . . . until they can perfectly read the English Scriptures."

The king himself is generally thought to have been responsible for a translation of the first fifty psalms, complete with brief introductions explaining the origins and meaning of each psalm, as well as Augustine of Hippo's *The Soliloquies.*

Aelfric, 955–1020

Aelfric the Grammarian, a monk at Winchester, was later abbot of both Cerne and Eynsham.

From about A.D. 1000, Aelfric, Archbishop of Canterbury, preached in the West Saxon language, wrote commentaries on some Bible books.

HEPTATEUCH
He composed a condensed version of the first seven books of the Old Testament. This was known as *Aelfric's Heptateuch.*

The *Heptateuch* is partly translated literally and partly paraphrased. "He appears to have done this work with the express intention of enabling his countrymen to read the Scriptures for themselves."

In one of his sermons on the importance of reading the Bible he says:

"Happy is he, who reads the Scriptures, if he convert the words into action."

It was said of Aelfric: "He is among the first to stand out individually in the records of his contemporaries as one that labored to make the Scriptures available to English scholars in their native tongue."

The Ormulum Gospels and the Acts

At the beginning of the 14th century, or earlier, a poetical version of the Gospels and the Acts of the Apostles, accompanied by a commentary known as the Ormulum, the work of an Augustinian monk, Orm, was written. Fragments of this poetic work are preserved in the Bodleian Library in Oxford.

Later English Bibles

Richard Rolle of Hampole

Richard Rolle of Hampole translated a number of parts of the Scripture into early Middle English, which included a Psalter with a commentary, the Lord's Prayer, and parts of the Book of Job.

Bible translations since the Middle Ages (3)

Later English Bibles, continued

Richard Rolle of Hampole, continued

PSALM 23

Lord gouerns me and nathyng sall me want; in sted of pasture thare he me sett.

On the watere of rehetynge forth he me broght; my saule he turnyd.

He led me on the stretis of rightwisnes; for his name.

ffor whi, if i had gane in myddis of the shadow of ded; i. sall noght dred illes, for thou ert with me.

Thi wand and thi staf; thai haf confortyd me.

Thou has grayid (vr. ordand) in my syght the bord; agayns thaim that angirs me.

Thou fattid my heued in oyle; and my chalice drunkynand what it is bright.

And thi mercy sall folow me; all the dayes of my lif.

And that i. won in the hows of lord; in lenght of dayes.

Richard Rolle

John Wycliffe, 1320–84

The first English translation of the Bible was undertaken by John Wycliffe. He completed the translation of the New Testament in 1380 but did not complete his translation of the Old Testament before he died. This was completed by some of his friends, such as Nicholas of Hereford, and some of his former students after his death. His translation was not from the original Greek and Hebrew texts; instead he made use of the Latin Vulgate.

Wycliffe translated the Bible into English from the 4th century Latin Vulgate. Wycliffe, even though he was an Oxford educated theologian, did not know either Hebrew or Greek. Wycliffe's work has been called a "translation from a translation."

THE BIBLE IS FOR EVERYONE
Wycliffe longed to give the English-speaking people the Bible in their own language. He believed that the Bible should be studied by all Christians.

"HERETIC"
In 1414 the reading of the English Scriptures was outlawed. The Church Council of Constance declared Wycliffe a heretic. So in 1429 his bones were dug up, his remains were burned and his ashes were thrown into the River Severn.

QUOTATIONS FROM WYCLIFFE
"This Bible is for the government of the people, by the people, and for the people."

Preface to translation of the Bible by Hereford and Wycliffe

"Christian men and women, old and young, should study well in the New Testament, for it is of full authority, and open to understanding by simple men, as to the points that are most needful to salvation."

John Wycliffe, The Wicket

John Purvey

The Wycliffe Bible was improved by the work of John Purvey and his assistants as they managed to produce Wycliffe's translation in a smoother writing style. Purvey ensured that the idiom used in the translation was closer to the current language of the day than the earlier version.

Wycliffe's Bible translation was the only one in English which existed in Britain until Tyndale's arrived over a century later.

The Wycliffe Bible was the first complete Bible to appear in England.

The Gutenberg Bible

The first European printing press with moveable type changed the world.

"This was the single most important event of the second millennium" according to *Life* magazine.

It greatly helped in the transmission of the biblical texts.

42–LINE BIBLE
The first book to be printed in this revolutionary way was the Bible.

In 1454, Johannes Gutenberg invented the "type mold" print press and began to print the Bible.

Gutenberg's Bible was known as the *42–line Bible*, because most of its pages are 42 lines long. It was a Latin translation of the Bible and was printed in 3 volumes.

40 copies of the 42–line Bible survive.

Erasmus' *Greek New Testament*

In 1514 Erasmus printed his exceedingly influential *The Greek New Testament*.

TEXTUS RECEPTUS
He based his Greek translation of the New Testament on five Greek manuscripts, one of which dated back to the 12th century. With minor revisions, Erasmus' *Greek New Testament* came to be know as the *Textus Receptus* (the "received texts").

LATIN/GREEK NEW TESTAMENT
In 1516 Erasmus and printer and reformer John Froben published their *Latin/Greek New Testament*. This was the first non-Latin Vulgate text of the Bible in a millennium.

Polyglot Bible

In 1522 the Polyglot Bible was published.

It consisted of the Old Testament in four languages:
• Hebrew,
• Aramaic,
• Greek, and
• Latin;

and the New Testament in two languages:
• Latin and
• Greek.

Erasmus revised his *Greek New Testament* by making use of the Polyglot Bible.

Tyndale's translation of the Old Testament also made use of the Polyglot Bible.

Bible translations of Luther and Tyndale

Martin Luther

Luther translated the New Testament into German from Erasmus' Greek/Latin New Testament, and had it published it in 1522.

For non-Latin readers

In Luther's day most of the German people could not understand Latin, and so Jerome's Vulgate would be useless to them. Luther believed that the Bible should be the book of the people, and it should be used in church, in school, and in the home. So Luther made an accurate translation of the Bible into everyday German.

William Tyndale, 1494–1536

William Tyndale, an English reformer, was known as the "father of the English Bible."

Manuscripts used by Tyndale

Tyndale relied heavily on the Vulgate in his translation work. He did, however, make use of Hebrew and Greek manuscripts.

Since Tyndale was an accomplished Greek scholar he was able to make use of a number of manuscripts which Wycliffe did not use, including Erasmus' *Greek New Testament*. He also benefited from Martin Luther's German translation of the Bible.

Martyrdom

Tyndale completed his translation work on the New Testament in 1525 and the Pentateuch in 1530. However, he was martyred before he completed his translation of the Old Testament.

Plain English

Tyndale succeeded in translating the New Testament into "plain" English.

Two firsts

When his New Testament was published in the 1526 edition it became the first printed version in English.

He was the first to produce a translation of the New Testament from Greek to English.

Tyndale's influence

It has been calucalted that as many as 80% of the words from Tyndale's translation of the New Testament remained in the Authorized Version.

Quotations from Tyndale

"I had perceived by experience, how that it was impossible to stablish the lay people in any truth, except the Scripture were plainly laid before their eyes in their mother tongue, that they might see the process, order, and meaning of the text."

William Tyndale, Preface to the Pentateuch, 1530

"If God spare my life, ere many years pass, I will cause a boy that driveth the plough shall know more of the Scriptures than thou dost."

Tyndale speaking to a Roman Catholic priest

"Lord, open the King of England's eyes."

Tyndale's last reported words as he was martyred on October 6th, 1536

Tyndale's version of Romans chapter 8

Ther is then no damnacion to them which are in Christ Iesu, which walke not after the flesshe: but after the sprete. For the lawe of the sprete that bringeth life thorowe Iesus Christ, hath delivered me from the lawe of synne and deeth. For what the lawe coulde not doo in as moche it was weake because of the flesshe: that performed God, and sent his sonne in the similitude of synfull flesshe, and by synne damned synne in the flesshe: that the righteousnes requyred of the lawe myght be fulfilled in vs, which walke not after the flesshe, but after the sprete.

For they that are carnall, are carnally mynded. But they that are spirituall, are gostly mynded. To be carnally mynded, is deeth. But to be spiritually mynded is lyfe and peace. Because that the flesshly mynde is emnyte agaynst God: for it is not obedient to the lawe of God, nether can be. So then they that are geven to the flesshe, cannot please God.

But ye are not geven to the flesshe, but to the sprete: yf so be that the sprite of God dwell in you. If ther be eny man that hath not the sprite of Christ, ye same is none of his. Yf Christ be in you, the body is deed because of synne: but the sprite is lyfe for righteousnes sake. Wherfore if the sprite of him that raysed vppe Iesus from deeth, dwell in you: even he that raysed vp Christ from deeth, shall quycken youre mortall bodyes, because that this sprite dwelleth in you.

Coverdale's Bible, Matthew's Bible, the Great Bible

Miles Coverdale, 1488–1569

Miles Coverdale was responsible for having the first complete English Bible printed on October 4th, 1535.

It became known as the Coverdale Bible.

Coverdale and Tyndale

Coverdale, a friend of Tyndale, and his proof reader based his translation of the New Testament on Tyndale's version.

Manuscripts used

In addition to Tydale's translation, Coverdale based his translation on the Latin Vulgate and the German Bible of Martin Luther.

Influence of Coverdale Bible

Thomas Cromwell ordered all English clergymen to have Coverdale's Bible "set up in sum convenient place wythin the said church that ye have cure of, where as your parishioners may moste comodiously resorte to the same and reade it."

So his translation is notable for being the first one that was allowed to be circulated by the official church.

Coverdale was known as "a writers' writer" due to the beauty of the phrasing of the English language.

It has been well said of him that,

"Next to Tyndale, the man to whom lovers of the English Bible owe the greatest debt is Coverdale."

Apocrypha

Coverdale was the first Bible translator to separate the Apocrypha from the Old Testament. He relegated the Apocrypha to an appendix at the end of his Bible.

Chapter summaries

He was also the first Bible translator to introduce chapter summaries as distinct from brief chapter headings found in the Vulgate.

Coverdale's psalms

Coverdale's translation of the Psalms was revised by himself for the Great Bible of 1539.

The translation of the Psalms that is still printed in the *Book of Common Prayer* is Coverdale's translation.

PSALM 23
Dominus regit me.
THE Lord is my shepherd : therefore can I lack nothing.

2. He shall feed me in a green pasture: and lead me forth beside the waters of comfort.

3. He shall convert my soul : and bring me forth in the paths of righteousness, for his Name's sake.

4. Yea, thou I walk through the valley of the shadow of death, I will fear no evil : for thou art with me; thy rod and thy staff comfort me.

5. Thou shalt prepare a table before me against them that trouble me : thou hast anointed my head with oil, and my cup shall be full.

6. But thy loving-kindness and mercy shall follow me all the days of my life : and I will dwell in the house of the Lord for ever.

PSALM 24
Domini est terra
THE earth is the Lord's, and all that therein is : the compass of the world, and they that dwell therein.

2. For he hath founded it upon the seas : and prepared it upon the floods.

3. Who shall ascend into the hill of the Lord : or who shall rise up in his holy place?

4. Even he that hath clean hands, and a pure heart : and that hath not lift up his mind unto vanity, nor sworn to deceive his neighbor.

5. He shall receive the blessing from the Lord : and righteousness from the God of his salvation.

6. This is the generation of them that seek him : even of them that seek thy face, O Jacob.

7. Lift up your heads, O ye gates, and be ye lift up, ye everlasting doors : and the King of glory shall come in.

8. Who is the King of glory : it is the Lord strong and mighty, even the Lord mighty in battle.

9. Lift up your heads, O ye gates, and be ye lift up, ye everlasting doors : and the King of glory shall come in.

10. Who is the King of glory : even the Lord of hosts, he is the King of glory.

Matthew's Bible, 1537

Matthew's Bible was probably produced by John Rogers, a friend of Tyndale.

Second complete English Bible

John Rogers printed this second complete English Bible in 1537.

Pseudonym

He printed it under a pseudonym, Thomas Matthew, because Tyndale's translation of the Bible was still condemned by the English authorities.

Manuscripts used

Rogers relied on much of Tyndale's Pentateuch and New Testament, as well as the Coverdale Bible, and his own translation of the text. It is said that the Rogers Bible "was made up of two-thirds from Tyndale and one-third from Coverdale." This Bible became known as *Matthew's Bible*.

Quotation about *Matthew's Bible*

"It is Rogers' Bible which became the foundation of all later English authorized versions, and it is through Rogers' republication that Tyndale's 1535 version of the New Testament had its great influence upon subsequent versions."

L.A. Weigle

The Great Bible, 1539

The Great Bible, essentially a revision of Matthew's Bible largely carried out under Coverdale's judicious eye, derived its name *Great* from its size. The pages measured 9 x 15 inches and the printed text on the page covered an area of 8½ x 13 inches.

The first "authorized" Bible

Bibles in churches

In 1538 a copy of the English Bible was ordered to be set up in every parish church. The *Great Bible* was most often used to comply with this order.

This outsize volume was chained to the reading desk or pulpit in churches.

In 1546 King Henry VIII had ordered that, "no man or woman of whatever estate, condition, or degree was to receive, have, take, or keep Tyndale's or Coverdale's New Testament."

First authorized Bible

So the *Great Bible* has the distinction of being the first authorized Bible in English.

It was "authorized" in the sense that both the monarch and the church approved it for use in public worship. In this way it became the official church Bible.

Cranmer's Bible

Thomas Cranmer carried out the king's decree and ensured that a reader was provided so that the illiterate could hear the Scriptures in their own language.

Later editions of the *Great Bible*, those published in 1540 and 1541 included a preface by Archbishop Cranmer, and became known as Cranmer's Bible.

TITLE PAGE
On the title page of the later versions appeared for the first time the words,

"This is the Bible appointed to the use of churches."

EXTRACT FROM CRANMER'S PREFACE TO THE GREAT BIBLE

Light and food
"The word of God is light: *Lucerna pedibus meis, verbum tuum.* (See Psalm 119). Thy word is a lantern unto my feet.

It is food:

Non in solo pane viuit homo, sed in omni verbo dei. (See Matthew 4) Man shall not live by bread only, but by every word of God.

It is fire:

Ignem veni mittere in tertam, & quid volo nisi vt ardeat? (See Luke 12) I am come to send fire on the earth, and what is my desire but that it be kindled?

I would marvel (I say at this) save that I consider how much custom and usage may do.

So that if there were a people as some write, de Cymeriis, which never saw the sun, by reason that they be situated far toward the North pole, and be enclosed and overshadowed with high mountains, it is credible and like enough, that if by the power and will of God, the mountains should sink down and give place, that the light of the sun might have entrance to them, at the first some of them would be offended therewith.

Such is the nature of custom, that it causeth us to bear all things well and easily wherewith we have been accustomed, and to be offended with all things thereunto contrary.

But such as will persist still in their wilfulness, I must needs judge not only foolish, froward and obstinate, but also peevish, perverse, and indurate."

Chrysostom on reading the Bible at home
"Let us here discuss what it availeth Scripture to be had and read of the lay and vulgar people.

And to this question I intend here to say nothing but that was spoken and written by the noble doctor and most moral divine, saint John Chrysostom in his third sermon de Lazaro.

He exhorteth there his audience, that every man should read by himself at home in the mean days and time, between sermon and sermon, to the intent they might both more profoundly fix in their minds and memories that he had said before upon such texts whereupon he had already preached, and also that they might have their minds the more ready and better prepared to receive and perceive that which he should say from thenceforth in his sermons, upon such texts as he had not yet declared and preached upon.

Therefore saith he there,

My common usage is to give you warning before what matter I intend after to entreat upon, that you yourselves in the mean days may take the book in hand, read, weigh, and perceive the sum and effect of the matter, and mark what hath been declared and what remaineth yet to be declared."

Thomas Cranmer

Taverner's Bible, 1539

Matthew's Bible formed the basis for yet another Bible version. Richard Taverner improved the style of the translation of the Old Testament, but made more significant revisions of the New Testament as he was an able Greek scholar.

The Geneva Bible, 1560

Overview

The Geneva Bible of 1560 was produced by scholars who fled from England to Geneva, Switzerland, during the persecution instigated by Queen Mary. Mary had also banned the printing of Scriptures in English and no Bibles were printed in England in English in her reign.

- It was influenced by Calvinist thought.
- In turn, the Geneva Bible had marked influence over the King James Version.
- The Geneva Bible was said to be the first "Bible of the people."
- Between 1560 and 1644 140 editions of this Bible were published.

Manuscripts used

The translators of the Geneva Bible, headed by William Whittingham and Anthony Gilby, worked from the original Greek and Hebrew texts. In this way, the Geneva Bible became the first Bible to be translated into English from the original biblical languages.

1557, 1560

The New Testament was finished in 1557, and the complete Bible was published in 1560.

Verse divisions

In the Geneva Bible the verse divisions of Robert Estienne, originally used in his *Greek New Testament* of 1551, were printed. The Old Testament had been divided into verses by R. Nathan in A.D. 1448 and the New Testament by Robert Stephanus in A.D. 1551.

Chapter divisions

The Bible was divided into chapters by Stephen Langton in A.D. 1228. The whole of the Geneva Bible was divided into chapters and verses and it was the first Bible to print verse numbers in the text. The numbered verses were each set off as a separate paragraph.

Printing style

Instead of the heavy and clumsy-looking Gothic or black-letter type, which had always been used previously for Bibles, the 1560 version was printed with Roman type.

USE OF ITALICS

All added words which were not in the original Hebrew or Greek were italicized.

SIZE OF BIBLE

Previous English versions of the Bible were huge, unwieldy books, only suitable as lectern Bibles for reading in churches. Most printings of the Geneva Bible were small, conveniently-sized quarto editions, measuring 6½ x 9¾ inches.

They were much less expensive than previous Bibles.

Marginal notes

The outstanding feature of the Geneva Bible centered on its extensive marginal notes. It was the first Bible to be printed with such notes.

These notes were very extensive, and amounted to nearly 300,000 words.

Leading Reformers

Leading Reformation theologians such as John Calvin, John Knox, Miles Coverdale, William Whittingham, Anthony Gilby, William Keithe, Thomas Sampson, and Thomas Wood were responsible for writing these notes.

First study Bible

References to other parts of the Bible were included with these marginal notes and so the Geneva Bible became the first study Bible.

Purpose of marginal notes

These marginal notes are described as "brief annotations vpon all the hard places, aswel for the vnderstanding of suche wordes as are obscure, and for the declaration of the text, as for the application of the same as may moste apperteine to Gods glorie and the edification of his Churche."

OBSUCRE WORDS
An example of an explanation of an obscure word occurs at Matthew 9:16 where "newe cloth" is explained as "Or, rawe and vndressed."

UNDERSTANDING THE TEXT
An example of understanding the text comes in the marginal note on John 13:14. In the margin opposite Jesus' words, "Ye also oght to wash one anothers fete" (John 13:14), is added, "To serue one another."

Occasionally the same verse contains both kinds of the above comments. The word "vessels" in the statement, "Neither do they put newe wine into olde vessels" (Matt. 9:17), is described as, "Bottels or bagges of ledder or skinne, wherein wine was caried on asses or camels." The word "olde" is explained by the comment, "The minde which is infected with the dreggs of superstitious ceremonies, is not mete to receiue the pleasant wine of the Gospel."

Influence of Geneva Bible

- The Geneva Bible was the first Bible taken to America.
- The Geneva Bible was the Bible of the Pilgrim Fathers who came to America.
- The first Bible to be printed in Scotland was a Scottish edition of the Geneva Bible, in 1579.
- It became known as *The People's Bible* and was the most popular English Bible for 75 years.
- It was the Bible used by Shakespeare, John Bunyan, Oliver Cromwell, and the Puritans.

Breeches Bible

Although it was officially known as the Geneva Bible, due to a passage in Genesis describing the clothing that God made for Adam and Eve when they were expelled from the Garden of Eden as "breeches", this Bible also became known as the Breeches Bible.

The Bishop's Bible, The Rheims/Douai Bible

The Bishop's Bible

The Bishop's Bible was published in 1568 and was, in the main, a revision of the Great Bible.

It sought to replace the Geneva Bible and had the authority of Archbishop Parker and the Church of England and Queen Elizabeth I behind it. Despite becoming the second authorized Bible in English it never became as popular as the Geneva Bible.

Rheims/Douai

The Douai Bible was a Roman Catholic version translated from the Latin Vulgate. "The Nevv Testament of Iesvs Christ, translated faithfvlly into English, out of authentical Latin... 1582. " It was the first Roman Catholic version of the Bible published in English.

Rheims and Douai

NEW TESTAMENT
The New Testament was published at the English (Catholic) College which was then located in Rheims in 1582.

OLD TESTAMENT
The Old Testament translation, published in 1609, was mainly the work of Gregory Martin at the English College which returned to Douai by then.

The Bible became known as the Rheims-Douai Bible.

OFFICIAL CATHOLIC VERSION
It was generally accepted as the official English version of the Bible for the Catholic Church.

Controversial notes

It contained controversial notes written by Roman Catholic divines which Protestants did not approve of.
- There are a number of instances where the translation reveals its Roman Catholic bias.
- The word "repentance" is translated as "penance."
- "Elder" is translated as "priest."
- "The dispensation of the sacrament" is the translation of Ephesians 3: 9.

EXAMPLE OF THE WORD "PENANCE"
1 And in those days cometh John the Baptist preaching in the desert of Judea. 2 And saying: Do penance: for the kingdom of heaven is at hand. 3 For this is he that was spoken of by Isaias the prophet, saying: A voice of one crying in the desert, Prepare ye the way of the Lord, make straight his paths. 4 And the same John had his garment of camel's hair, and a leathern girdle about his loins: and his meat was locusts and wild honey. 5 Then went out to him Jerusalem and all Judea, and all the country about Jordan: 6 And were baptized by him in the Jordan, confessing their sins.

13 Then cometh Jesus from Galilee to the Jordan, unto John, to be baptized by him. 14 But John stayed him, saying: I ought to be baptized by thee,

and comest thou to me? 15 And Jesus answering, said to him: Suffer it to be so now. For so it becometh us to fulfill all justice. Then he suffered him. 16 And Jesus being baptized, forthwith came out of the water: and lo, the heavens were opened to him: and he saw the Spirit of God descending as a dove, and coming upon him. 17 And behold a voice from heaven saying: This is my beloved Son, in whom I am well pleased.

Matthew 3: 1–6,13–17, Douai Version

Onlyism

What many advocates of both King James-onlyism and Douai-Rheims-onlyism do not know is that neither Bible is the original issued in the 1600s.

Over the last three centuries, numerous minor changes (for example, of spelling and grammar) have been made in the King James, with the result that most versions of the *KJV* currently on the market are significantly different from the original. This has led one publisher to recently re-issue the 1611 King James Version Bible.

Richard Challoner

The Douai-Rheims currently on the market is also not the original, 1609 version. It is technically called the "Douai-Challoner" version because it is a revision of the Douai-Rheims carried out in the mid-eighteenth century by the English bishop Richard Challoner.

He also consulted early Greek and Hebrew manuscripts. So the Douai

Bible currently on the market is not simply a translation of the Vulgate.

Influence of the Douai Bible

The Douai-Reims Bible was commonly used by Roman Catholics in English-speaking countries until the 1900s. During the 19th and 20th centuries, the Douai and Challoner Bibles were replaced with other translations by Roman Catholics.

King James Version (1)

The King James (or Authorized) Version, 1611

The most famous English Bible ever printed takes its name from the English monarch, King James I, who wanted to produce another official, authorized Bible for use in churches of England. James longed for a Bible to circulate in England that had the popularity of the Geneva Bible but without the controversy linked with it.

James sought to have produced "the translation to end all translations."

Manuscripts used

Many sources were used in the translation work of the King James Bible. It was based on the Bishop's Bible.

TEXTUS RECEPTUS

Additionally, Greek and Hebrew texts were studied. For the New Testament the translators used the *Textus Receptus* as the basis for their work. Previous English translations were also freely consulted and used.

The story of the *KJV*

HAMPTON COURT CONFERENCE

At the Hampton Court Conference of 1604 Dr. John Reynolds, a leading Puritan and President of Corpus Christi College, Oxford, requested that a new translation of the Bible should be undertaken. He, "moved his Majesty, that there might be a new translation of the Bible, because those which were allowed in the reigns of Henry the eighth, and Edward the sixth, were corrupt and not answerable to the truth of the Original."

KING JAMES' SUPPORT

While most of the church leaders present at the conference were against this suggestion King James supported it.

The king responded by saying that he,

"Could never yet see a Bible well translated in English; but I think that, of all, that of Geneva is the worst. I wish some special pains were taken for an uniform translation, which should be done by the best learned men in both Universities, then reviewed by the Bishops, presented to the Privy Council, lastly ratified by the Royal authority, to be read in the whole Church, and none other."

TRANSLATION GUIDELINES

So it was resolved,

"That a translation be made of the whole Bible, as consonant as can be to the original Hebrew and Greek; and this to be set out and printed, without any marginal notes, and only to be used in all churches of England in time of divine service."

FORTY-SEVEN SCHOLARS

Fifty-four of the ablest biblical scholars in Great Britain were nominated to undertake this work, although it appears that only forty-seven of them took part in the translation work.

SIX GROUPS

The translators were organized into six groups, and met at Westminster, Cambridge, and Oxford.

Three groups worked on the Old Testament and three worked on the New Testament.

Two groups for the Old and New Testaments met at Oxford, two at Cambridge, and two at Westminster. Ten at Westminster were assigned Genesis through 2 Kings; seven had Romans through Jude.

At Cambridge, eight worked on 1 Chronicles through Ecclesiastes, and seven on the Apocrypha.

At Oxford seven translated Isaiah through Malachi and a further eight translated the Gospels, Acts, and Revelation.

The Oxford group

"The Oxford group was headed by Dr. John Hardinge, Regius Professor of Hebrew; and included Dr. John Reynolds, the originator of the project, 'his memory and reading were near to a miracle'; Dr. Miles Smith, who 'had Hebrew at his fingers' ends'; Dr. Richard Brett, 'skilled and versed to a criticism in the Latin, Greek, Chaldee, Arabic and Ethiopic tongues'; Sir Henry Saville, editor of the works of Chrysostom; and Dr. John Harmer, Professor of Greek, 'a most noted Latinist, Grecian and divine.'"

The Cambridge group

"The Cambridge committee was at first presided over by Edward Lively, Regius Professor of Hebrew, who died in 1605 before the work was really begun, and included Dr. Lawrence Chaderton,

'familiar with the Greek and Hebrew tongues, and the numerous writings of the Rabbis'; Thomas Harrison, 'noted for his exquisite skill in Hebrew and Greek idioms'; Dr. Robert Spalding, successor to Lively as Professor of Hebrew; Andrew Downes, 'one composed of Greek and industry,' and John Bois, 'a precious Greek and Hebrew scholar.'"

The Westminster group

"The Westminster group was headed by Lancelot Andrews, Dean of Westminster, afterwards Bishop of Chichester, of Ely, and finally of Winchester, 'who might have been interpreter general at Babel . . . the world wanted learning to know how learned be was'; and included the Hebraist Hadrian Saravia; and William Bedwell, the greatest living Arabic scholar."

H. Wheeler Robinson

Preface

In the Preface to the Reader which appeared in this version, the translators stated that they did not hesitate: "to consult the Translators or Commentators, Chaldee, Hebrew, Syrian, Gedi or Estienne no nor the Spanish, French, Italian, or Dutch."

Three years

The translation work started in 1607, was completed in 1610, and published in 1611.

King James Version (2)

Fifteen rules

The following fifteen rules guided the translators in their work.

1. The ordinary Bible read in the Church, commonly called the Bishop's Bible, to be followed, and as little altered as the Truth of the original will permit.

2. The names of the Prophets, and the Holy Writers, with the other Names of the Text, to be retained, as nigh as may be, accordingly as they were vulgarly used.

3. The Old Ecclesiastical Words to be kept, viz. the Word Church not to be translated Congregation, etc.

4. When a Word hath divers Significations, that to be kept which hath been most commonly used by the most of the Ancient Fathers, being agreeable to the Propriety of the Place, and the Analogy of the Faith.

5. The Division of the Chapters to be altered, either not at all, or as little as may be, if Necessity so require.

6. No Marginal Notes at all to be affixed, but only for the explanation of the Hebrew or Greek Words, which cannot without some circumlocution, so briefly and fitly be expressed in the Text.

7. Such Quotations of Places to be marginally set down as shall serve for the fit Reference of one Scripture to another.

8. Every particular Man of each Company, to take the same Chapter or Chapters, and having translated or amended them severally by himself, where he thinketh good, all to meet together, confer what they have done, and agree for their Parts what shall stand.

9. As any one Company hath dispatched any one Book in this Manner they shall send it to the rest, to be considered of seriously and judiciously, for His Majesty is very careful in this Point.

10. If any Company, upon the Review of the Book so sent, doubt or differ upon any Place, to send them Word thereof; note the Place, and withal send the Reasons, to which if they consent not, the Difference to be compounded at the general Meeting, which is to be of the chief Persons of each Company, at the end of the Work.

11. When any Place of special Obscurity is doubted of, Letters to be directed by Authority, to send to any Learned Man in the Land, for his Judgment of such a Place.

12. Letters to be sent from every Bishop to the rest of his Clergy, admonishing them of this Translation in hand; and to move and charge as many skillful in the Tongues; and having taken pains in that kind, to send his particular Observations to the Company, either at Westminster, Cambridge, or Oxford.

13. The Directors in each Company, to be the Deans of Westminster,

and Chester for that Place; and the King's Professors in the Hebrew or Greek in either University.

14. These translations to be used when they agree better with the Text than the Bishop's Bible: Tyndale's, Matthew's, Coverdale's, Whitchurch's, Geneva.

15. Besides the said Directors before mentioned, three or four of the most Ancient and Grave Divines, in either of the Universities, not employed in Translating, to be assigned by the vice-Chancellor, upon Conference with the rest of the Heads, to be Overseers of the Translations as well Hebrew as Greek, for the better observation of the 4th Rule above specified.

Title page

The King James Version (*KJV*), also known as The Authorized Version (*AV*), was printed with the following title:

"The Holy Bible, Containing the Old Testament and the New; Newly Translated out of the Originall tongues, with the former Translations diligently compared and revised, by His Majesties speciall commandement. Appointed to be read in Churches. Imprinted at London by Robert Barker, Printer to the Kings most Excellent Majestie. Anno Dom. 1611."

New Testament page

The *KJV* New Testament had a separate title page which read as follows:

"The New Testament of our Lord and Savior Jesus Christ, Newly translated out of the Originall Greeke; and with the former Translations diligently compared and revised, by His Majesties speciall Commandement. Imprinted at London by Robert Barker, Printer to the Kings most Excellent Majestie. Anno Dom. 1611. cum Privilegio."

Epistle Dedicatory

"The translators of the Bible wish Grace, Mercy, and Peace, through Jesus Christ our Lord."

"But among all our joys, there was no one that more filled our hearts, than the blessed continuance of the preaching of God's sacred Word among us; which is that inestimable treasure, which excelleth all the riches of the earth; because the fruit thereof extendeth itself, not only to the time spent in this transitory world, but directeth and disposeth men unto that eternal happiness which is above in heaven."

King James Version (3)

Preface to the *KJV*, 1611

The praise of the holy Scriptures

TRUTH

"But now what piety without truth? what truth (what saving truth) without the word of God? What word of God (whereof we may be sure) without the Scripture?

SEARCH AND STUDY

The Scriptures we are commanded to search. John 5: 39. Is. 8: 20. They are commended that searched and studied them. Acts 17: 11 and 8: 28,29. They are reproved that were unskillful in them, or slow to believe them. Matt. 22: 29; Luke 24: 25. They can make us wise unto salvation. 2 Tim. 3: 15.

TOLLE, LEGE

If we be ignorant, they will instruct us; if out of the way, they will bring us home; if out of order, they will reform us; if in heaviness, comfort us; if dull, quicken us; if cold, inflame us. Tolle, lege; Tolle, lege, Take up and read, take up and read the Scriptures [S. August. confess. lib 8 cap 12], (for unto them was the direction) it was said unto S. Augustine by a supernatural voice. "Whatsoever is in the Scriptures, believe me," saith the same S. Augustine, "is high and divine; there is verily truth, and a doctrine most fit for the refreshing of men's minds, and truly so tempered, that everyone may draw from thence that which is sufficient for him, if he come to draw with a devout and pious mind, as true Religion requireth." [S. August. de utilit. credendi cap. 6] Thus S. Augustine and S. Jerome: "Ama scripturas, et amabit te sapientia etc." [S. Jerome. ad Demetriad] Love the Scriptures, and wisdom will love thee.

CYRIL

And S. Cyril against Julian; "Even boys that are bred up in the Scriptures, become most religious, etc." [S. Cyril. 7 contra Iulianum] But what mention we three or four uses of the Scripture, whereas whatsoever is to be believed or practiced, or hoped for, is contained in them? or three or four sentences of the Fathers, since whosoever is worthy the name of a Father, from Christ's time downward, hath likewise written not only of the riches, but also of the perfection of the Scripture?

TERTULLIAN

"I adore the fullness of the Scripture," saith Tertullian against Hermogenes. [Tertul. advers. Hermo.] And again, to Apelles an heretic of the like stamp, he saith; "I do not admit that which thou bringest in (or concludest) of thine own (head or store, de tuo) without Scripture." [Tertul. de carne Christi.]

JUSTIN MARTYR

So Saint Justin Martyr before him; "We must know by all means," saith he, "that it is not lawful (or possible) to learn (anything) of God or of right piety, save only out of the Prophets, who teach us by divine inspiration."

Basil

So Saint Basil after Tertullian, "It is a manifest falling way from the Faith, and a fault of presumption, either to reject any of those things that are written, or to bring in (upon the head of them) any of those things that are not written.

Vocabulary

It is not always easy to say exactly where each word in the KJV came from, but the following calculations about the vocabulary of the KJV have been made.

- 39% is unique to the KJV
- 4% is possibly derived from Wycliffe
- 18% from Tyndale
- 13% from Coverdale
- 19% from the Geneva Bible
- 4% from the Bishop's Bible
- 3% from other preceding versions.

Notes excluded

In contrast with the Geneva Bible all controversial notes were excluded.

Marginal notes included

However, over four thousand marginal notes were included. In the Old Testament these gave the literal meaning of Hebrew words. The 765 New Testament marginal notes indicated variant or alternative renderings.

Chapter summaries

Chapter summaries and page headings were introduced.

Archbishop Ussher

In 1701 chronological dates based on the chronology of Archbishop Ussher were printed.

Continuous corrections

The 1611 edition was continually corrected.

Even by 1613 over 300 changes of some kind from the original of 1611 had been made.

By 1760 thirty thousand new marginal references had been added.

Versions of KJV

1611 – First Authorized Version. It included the Apocrypha.

1629 – First Authorized Version without the Apocrypha.

1632 – One of the earliest Bible concordances, entitled, A Concordance to the Bible of the Last Translation, by John Downham, was appended to the 1632 edition of the KJV Bible.

1701 – Insertion of dates of Archbishop Ussher in margins.

1769 – Today's Oxford Standard Authorized Version differs from the 1611 version in over 75,000 details

1777 – First KJV New Testament printed in US.

1782 – First KJV complete Bible printed in US.

King James Version (4)

The *KJV* and previous Bibles

The 1611 King James Version was a revision of earlier English Bibles.

The translators were quite open about their use of previous English translations.

"We are so far off from condemning any of their labors that travailed before us in this kind, either in this land or beyond sea, either in King Henry's time, or King Edward's … or Queen Elizabeth's of ever renowned memory, that we acknowledge them to have been raised up of God, for the building and furnishing of his Church, and that they deserve to be had of us and of posterity in everlasting remembrance."

Title page

This is backed by the title page of the 1611 Bible:

"THE HOLY BIBLE, Containing the Old Testament, and the New: Newly Translated out of the Original tongues: and with the former Translations diligently compared and revised …" It has been estimated that as much as 70% of the text of the *KJV* achieved its final literary form before 1611's translators began there work.

The *KJV* and William Tyndale

The *KJV* owes so much to Tyndale's work that the *KJV* has been called "the fifth revision of the work of William Tyndale."

It is possible to trace as much as one third of the wording of the New Testament of the *KJV* back to Tyndale's New Testament.

Tyndale's phrases

Hundreds of phrases and sentences which the King James translators took over from Tyndale have been retained in subsequent revisions.

A few examples of the above are:

"You cannot serve God and mammon" (Matt. 6: 24);

"Consider the lilies of the field, how they grow" (Matt. 6: 28);

"where two or three are gathered in my name, there am I in the midst of them" (Matt. 18: 20);

"It is more blessed to give than to receive" (Acts 20: 35);

"the unsearchable riches of Christ" (Eph.3: 8);

"out of darkness into his marvelous light" (1 Pet. 2: 9).

Coverdale and the Great Bible

The *KJV* translators adopted the following phrases from Coverdale and the Great Bible:

"till heaven and earth pass away" (Matt. 5: 18);

"none of us lives to himself, and none of us dies to himself" (Rom. 14: 7);

"death is swallowed up in victory" (1 Cor. 15: 54) ;

"the world has been crucified to me, and I to the world" (Gal. 6: 14).

Taverner's Bible

The *KJV* includes the following from Taverner's Bible:

"If any man will come after me, let him deny himself and take up his cross and follow me" (Matt. 16: 24);

"according to thy word" (Luke. 2: 29);

"a certain creditor" (Luke. 7: 41);

"Master, it is good for us to be here" (Luke. 9: 33);

"he would have given thee living water" (John.4: 10).

Geneva Bible

As much as 19% of the *KJV* text is derived from the Geneva Bible. Some such phrases are:

"He smote them hippe and thigh" (Judg. 15: 8);

"Remember now thy Creator in the daies of thy youth.... Vanitie of vanities, saith the Preacher" (Eccl. 12: 1 and 8);

"This is my beloued Sonne, in whome I am wel pleased" (Matt. 3: 17);

"his word was with authority" (Luke. 4: 32);

"Except a man be borne againe" (John 3: 3);

"in all these things we are more than conquerors through him that loved us" (Rom. 8: 37);

"we have the mind of Christ" (1 Cor. 2: 16);

"all the fullness of God" (Eph. 3: 19);

"the eyes of him with whom we have to do" (Heb. 4: 13);

"a cloude of witnesses" (Heb. 12: 1).

Bishop's Bible

The *KJV* took the following from the Bishop's Bible:

"persecuted for rigeousness' sake" (Matt. 5: 10);

"faithless and perverse generation" (Matt. 17: 17);

"overcome evil with good" (Rom. 12: 21);

"was made in the likeness of men" (Phil. 2: 7);

"the power of his resurrection" (Phil. 3: 10).

Rheims Version

The *KJV* took over the following expressions from the Rheims Version:

"Why, what evil has he done (Matt. 27: 23);

"owe no one anything" (Rom. 13: 8);

"the ministry of reconciliation" (2 Cor. 5: 18);

"to me to live is Christ, and to die gain" (Phil. 1: 21).

Contemporary expressions

Many of today's common expressions have their roots in the AV.

The fat of the land (Genesis 45: 18)

The skin of my teeth (Job 19: 20)

At their wit's end (Psalm 107: 27)

A soft answer (Proverbs 15: 1)

A thorn in the flesh (2 Corinthians 12: 7)

Labor of love (1 Thessalonians 1: 3; Hebrews 6: 10)

The root of all evil (1 Timothy 6: 10)

Clear as crystal (Revelation 21: 11; 22: 1)

Popularity of the *KJV*

Initially the Geneva Bible remained more popular that the King James Bible. But then the King James Bible gained great popularity and became the most popular translation in English for over 350 years.

For over 250 years, until the publication of the Revised Version in 1881, the *KJV* was unrivaled.

18th – 20th century Bible translations

Daniel Mace – The New Testament In Greek and English
1729

The Presbyterian minister, Daniel Mace aimed to produce a colloquial translation of the New Testament.

Richard Challoner

Richard Challoner produced a simplified and modernized version of the original Roman Catholic Rheims-Douai version in 1752. The Rheims-Douai-Challoner Bible became the version authorized for use by English-speaking Roman Catholics in America.

John Wesley – New Testament
1755

Wesley revised the King James Version of the New Testament for the benefit of "plain unlettered Men who understand only their Mother-Tongue."

Worsley believed that the Bible should be retranslated every century "according to the Present Idiom of the English Tongue."

The English Revised Version, 1885

This version replaced the archaic words and phrases in the KJV with the additional help of more recent manuscripts.

Fifty-four of the finest biblical scholars in Britain undertook this work.

GUIDELINES FOR TRANSLATORS
The following five statements guided the translators of the Revised Version.

1. That it is desirable that a revision of the Authorized Version of the Holy Scriptures be undertaken.

2. That the revision be so conducted as to comprise both marginal renderings and such emendations as it may be found necessary to insert in the text of the Authorized Version.

3. That in the above resolutions we do not contemplate any new translation of the Bible, or any alteration of the language, except when in the judgment of the most competent scholars such change is necessary.

4. That in such necessary changes, the style of the language employed in the existing version be closely followed.

5. That it is desirable that Convocation should nominate a body of its own members to undertake the work of revision, who shall be at liberty to invite the cooperation of any eminent for scholarship, to whatever nation or religious body they may belong.

> ## Quote Unquote
>
> "The Revised Version with these marginal references is still the most useful edition of the Bible for the careful student who knows no language but English."
>
> F. F. Bruce

20th century Bible translations

American Standard Version

The American Standard Version of 1900–1901 is the American version of the Revised Version.

Twentieth Century New Testament

The Twentieth Century New Testament, 1898–1901, was a careful retranslation based upon the Westcott and Hort text.

Weymouth's New Testament in Modern Speech

Dr. Weymouth's New Testament in Modern Speech, 1902

Edgar I. Goodspeed – Edgar I. Goodspeed, The New Testament: An American Translation, 1923

This was based on the Westcott and Hort text.

The Twentieth Century New Testament, 1904

This was a translation into modern English.

The Revised Standard Version

This translation was undertaken by thirty-two American scholars. The New Testament Revised Version was published in 1946 and the entire Bible in 1952.

A second edition of the Revised Standard Version was published in 1971, known as *RSV* II.

Berkeley Version – The Berkeley Version in Modern English, 1959

This version attempts to translate the whole Bible only using modern terms.

The New Testament was originally translated into modern English by Gerrit Verkuyl. Twenty translators assisted Verkuyl in his translation of the Old Testament.

J.B. Phillips – The New Testament in Modern Speech, J.B. Phillips, 1958

J.B. Phillips (1906–1982), an Anglican clergyman single-handedly translated the whole of the New Testament into contemporary English during the 1940s and 1950s.

His final version of the New Testament was published in 1972. He also translated a small part of the Old Testament. In writing about his earlier work on the New Testament, he speaks of the discovery he made as he worked on the Bible text that it was extraordinarily alive in a way he had never previously experienced with any other ancient text. Like the writer of Psalm 119 he also found that the Bible spoke to his condition in what he called an uncanny way.

The Amplified Bible, 1965

This version was commissioned by the Lockman Foundation. Its unusual feature is that it includes in brackets multiple expressions using associated words to convey the original thought. The New Testament uses the Greek text of Westcott and Hart plus 27 translations and revisions.

20th century Bible translations (2)

The Jerusalem Bible, 1966

This version was originally translated in French at the Dominican biblical School in Jerusalem in 1956. While the English version made use of the Hebrew Masoretic, Greek Septuagint, Dead Sea Scrolls, and accepted Greek and Aramaic New Testament texts, as well as the French version it usually follows the French version on matters of interpretation.

YAHWEH

It is the only major English translation that uses the divine name "Yahweh" in the Old Testament.

The translation includes the Apocrypha.

In 1989 a revised New Jerusalem Bible was published.

UBS – The United Bible Societies 4th Edition of the Greek New Testament, 1968

This Greek New Testament made use of the oldest Greek manuscripts which date from A.D. 175. This was the Greek New Testament text from which the NASV and the NIV were translated.

The New English Bible, 1970

This version, based on the original Greek and Hebrew texts, was produced by a committee of Bible scholars from leading denominations in England, Scotland, Wales, and Ireland. It includes the Apocrypha. A revised version of the New English Bible, the Revised English Bible was published in 1989.

This version,

"took pains to secure as best they could, the tone, and level of language appropriate to the different kinds of writing to be found in the Bible, whether narrative, familiar discourse, argument, law, rhetoric or poetry."

New American Bible, 1970

The New American Bible, a Catholic translation, took fifty scholars twenty-six years to complete. The translators were allowed to use manuscripts other than the Vulgate as the basis for translation.

The New American Standard Bible, 1971

The New American Standard Bible is a revision of the American Standard Version and was commissioned by the Lockman Foundation.

This version makes full use of many older Hebrew and Greek manuscripts than were available to the translators of the KJV. Its wording and sentence structure closely follow the Greek in a word for word style.

The fifty-four Greek and Hebrew scholars took over ten years to revise the American Standard Version of 1901 by incorporating recent discoveries of Hebrew and Greek textual sources and by updating the ASV into more current English.

The Living Bible, 1971

This is a paraphrase by one man, Kenneth N. Taylor who aimed to express what the writers of Scripture meant in the simplest modern English possible. It is not a translation from the original languages but rather a paraphrase of the American Standard Version.

THE LIVING BIBLE STORY

Ken Taylor began paraphrasing the New Testament Epistles on the train while commuting to Moody Press.

The project took seven years to complete.

Unable to interest publishers in his *Living Letters,* Taylor took out a loan for $2,000 and had his paraphrase printed privately.

It was not until Billy Graham recommended *Living Letters* from the pulpit that they became popular.

The success of this first publication resulted in

- the founding of Tyndale House Publishers,
- the completion of the Living Bible, and
- the establishment of the Tyndale Foundation.

Today's English Version (Good News Bible), 1976

A translation committee of Bible scholars aimed to produce a faithful translation of the Bible into natural, clear, and simple contemporary English.

The Translators' Preface states that: "every effort has been made to use language that is natural, clear, simple and unambiguous."

The New International Version, 1978

This version was sponsored by the New York International Bible Society (now the International Bible Society). It claims to be a completely new translation from the best original texts.

The Message

This version is a popular paraphrase by Dr. Eugene Peterson.

"When Paul of Tarsus wrote a letter, the people who received it understood it instantly," Peterson explains. "When the prophet Isaiah preached a sermon, I can't imagine that people went to the library to figure it out. That was the basic premise under which I worked."

The Red Letter Bible

Some Bible publishers print the words of Christ in red.

This idea originated with Louis Klopsch, the first editor for the Christian Herald.

German born Louis Klopsch was writing an editorial for the *Christian Herald* on June 19, 1899, when his attention was drawn to the words of Luke 22: 20: "This cup which is poured out for you is the new covenant in My blood."

Dr. Klopsch reasoned that all blood was red and thought to himself, "why not a red letter Bible with the red words to be those of our Lord?"

A 21st century Bible translation (1)

English Standard Version

The English Standard Version, (ESV) published by Crossway Books, is an example of a Bible translation published in the 21st century. The following quotation is the publisher's own description of this translation and illustrates many of the problems which all Bible translators have had to tackle.

Translation philosophy

"The ESV is an 'essentially literal' translation that seeks as far as possible to capture the precise wording of the original text and the personal style of each Bible writer. As such, its emphasis is on 'word-for-word' correspondence, at the same time taking into account differences of grammar, syntax, and idiom between current literary English and the original languages. Thus it seeks to be transparent to the original text, letting the reader see as directly as possible the structure and meaning of the original.

WORD-FOR-WORD
"In contrast to the ESV, some Bible versions have followed a 'thought-for-thought' rather than 'word-for-word' translation philosophy, emphasizing 'dynamic equivalence' rather than the 'essentially literal' meaning of the original. A 'thought-for-thought' translation is of necessity more inclined to reflect the interpretive opinions of the translator and the influences of contemporary culture.

TRADE-OFF
"Every translation is at many points a trade-off between literal precision and read-ability, between 'formal equivalence' in expression and 'functional equivalence' in communication, and the ESV is no exception. Within this framework we have sought to be 'as literal as possible' while maintaining clarity of expression and literary excellence.

Therefore, to the extent that plain English permits and the meaning in each case allows, we have sought to use the same English word for important recurring words in the original; and, as far as grammar and syntax allow, we have rendered Old Testament passages cited in the New in ways that show their correspondence.

Thus in each of these areas, as well as throughout the Bible as a whole, we have sought to capture the echoes and overtones of meaning that are so abundantly present in the original texts. As an essentially literal translation, then, the ESV seeks to carry over every possible nuance of meaning in the original words of Scripture into our own language. As such, it is ideally suited for in-depth study of the Bible.

LITERARY EXCELLENCE
"Indeed, with its emphasis on literary excellence, the ESV is equally suited for public reading and preaching, for private reading and reflection, for both academic and devotional study, and for Scripture memorization."

Translation style

RETAINS KEY THEOLOGICAL WORDS
"The *ESV* also carries forward classic translation principles in its literary style. Accordingly it retains theological terminology – words such as grace, faith, justification, sanctification, redemption, regeneration, reconciliation, propitiation – because of their central importance for Christian doctrine and also because the underlying Greek words were already becoming key words and technical terms in New Testament times.

STYLISTIC VARIETY
"The *ESV* lets the stylistic variety of the biblical writers fully express itself – from the exalted prose that opens Genesis, to the flowing narratives of the historical books, to the rich metaphors and dramatic imagery of the poetic books, to the ringing rhetorical indictments in the prophetic books, to the smooth elegance of Luke, to the profound simplicities of John, and the closely-reasoned logic of Paul.

CONNECTIVES
"In punctuating, paragraphing, dividing long sentences, and rendering connectives, the *ESV* follows the path that seems to make the ongoing flow of thought clearest in English. The biblical languages regularly connect sentences by frequent repetition of words such as 'and,' 'but,' and 'for,' in a way that goes beyond the conventions of literary English. Effective translation, however, requires that these links in the original be reproduced so that the flow of the argument will be transparent to the reader. We have therefore normally translated these connectives, though occasionally we have varied the rendering by using alternatives (such as 'also,' 'however,' 'now,' 'so,' 'then,' or 'thus') when they better capture the sense in specific instances.

GENDER LANGUAGE
"In the area of gender language, the goal of the *ESV* is to render literally what is in the original. For example, 'anyone' replaces 'any man' where there is no word corresponding to 'man' in the original languages, and 'people' rather than 'men' is regularly used where the original languages refer to both men and women. But the words 'man' and 'men' are retained where a male meaning component is part of the original Greek or Hebrew. Similarly, the English word 'brothers' (translating the Greek word *adelphoi*) is retained as an important familial form of address between fellow-Jews and fellow-Christians in the first century."

NOTE ON "BROTHERS"
A recurring note is included to indicate that the term "brothers" (*adelphoi*) was often used in Greek to refer to both men and women, and to indicate the specific instances in the text where this is the case.

A 21st century Bible translation (2)

English Standard Version, continued

Translation style, continued

NOTE ON "SONS"

In addition, the English word "sons" (translating the Greek word *huioi*) is retained in specific instances because of its meaning as a legal term in the adoption and inheritance laws of first-century Rome.

As used by the apostle Paul, this term refers to the status of all Christians, both men and women, who, having been adopted into God's family, now enjoy all the privileges, obligations, and inheritance rights of God's children.

APPRECIATING THE ORIGINAL

"The inclusive use of the generic 'he' has also regularly been retained, because this is consistent with similar usage in the original languages and because an essentially literal translation would be impossible without it.

Similarly, where God and man are compared or contrasted in the original, the *ESV* retains the generic use of 'man' as the clearest way to express the contrast within the framework of essentially literal translation.

In each case the objective has been transparency to the original text, allowing the reader to understand the original on its own terms rather than on the terms of our present-day culture."

Textual basis

MASORETIC TEXT

"The *ESV* is based on the Masoretic text of the Hebrew Bible as found in *Biblia Hebraica Stuttgartensia* (2nd ed., 1983).

The currently renewed respect among Old Testament scholars for the Masoretic text is reflected in the *ESV*'s attempt, wherever possible, to translate difficult Hebrew passages as they stand in the Masoretic text rather than resorting to emendations or to finding an alternative reading in the ancient versions."

GREEK TEXTS

The *ESV* is based on the Greek text in the 1993 editions of the *Greek New Testament* (4th corrected ed.), published by the United Bible Societies (UBS), and *Novum Testamentum Graece* (27th ed.), edited by Nestle and Aland.

OTHER SOURCES

"In exceptional, difficult cases,
• the Dead Sea Scrolls,
• the Septuagint,
• the Samaritan Pentateuch,
• the Syriac Peshitta,
• the Latin Vulgate, and
• other sources
were consulted to shed possible light on the text, or, if necessary, to support a divergence from the Masoretic text.

Similarly, in a few difficult cases in the New Testament, the *ESV* has followed a Greek text different from the text given preference in the UBS/Nestle-Aland 27th edition."

FOOTNOTES

In this regard the footnotes that accompany the *ESV* text are an integral part of the *ESV* translation, informing the reader of textual variations and difficulties and showing how these have been resolved by the *ESV* translation team.

SIGNIFICANT ALTERNATIVE READINGS

In addition to this, the footnotes indicate significant alternative readings and occasionally provide an explanation for technical terms or for a difficult reading in the text.

NEW TEXTUAL SOURCES

Throughout, the translation team has benefited greatly from the massive textual resources that have become readily available recently, from new insights into biblical laws and culture, and from current advances in Hebrew and Greek lexicography and grammatical understanding.

Sample extracts

PSALM 23

The Lord Is My Shepherd

A Psalm of David.

23: 1 The Lord is my shepherd; I shall not want.

2 He makes me lie down in green pastures.

He leads me beside still waters. [1]

3 He restores my soul.

He leads me in paths of righteousness [2]

for his name's sake.

4 Even though I walk through the valley of the shadow of death, [3]

I will fear no evil,

for you are with me;

your rod and your staff,

they comfort me.

5 You prepare a table before me

in the presence of my enemies;

you anoint my head with oil;

my cup overflows.

6 Surely [4] goodness and mercy [5] shall follow me

all the days of my life,

and I shall dwell [6] in the house of the Lord

forever. [7]

Footnotes

[1] 23: 2 Hebrew beside waters of rest
[2] 23: 3 Or in right paths
[3] 23: 4 Or the valley of deep darkness
[4] 23: 6 Or Only
[5] 23: 6 Or steadfast love
[6] 23: 6 Or shall return to dwell
[7] 23: 6 Hebrew for length of days

JOHN 3: 16

16 'For God so loved the world, [1] that he gave his only Son, that whoever believes in him should not perish but have eternal life.

Footnote

[1] 3: 16 Or For this is how God loved the world

An "internet" Bible (1)

The World English Bible (WEB) is a novel and unique translation of the Bible. It aims to make a modern version of the Bible freely available for all to use.

The following Frequently Asked Questions have been compiled by the compilers of the World English Bible.

Q: Why create yet another English translation of the Holy Bible?

That is a good question. There are many good English translations of the Holy Bible. Unfortunately, all of them are either: archaic (like the KJV and ASV of 1901), or covered by copyright restrictions that prevent unrestricted free posting on the internet or other media (like the NIV and NASB)

There is no other complete translation of the Holy Bible in normal Modern English that can be freely copied (except for some limited "fair use") without written permission from the publisher and (usually) payment of royalties.

This is the vacuum that the World English Bible is filling.

Why is the copyright such a big deal?

The copyright laws of most nations and the international treaties that support them grant authors and translators a legal monopoly (for a limited, but very long, time) on the right of copying and "first sale" of their works, the

law makers have made writing and translating very profitable for some people whose works are in great demand.

The problem with this system, with respect to the Holy Bible, is that it has had the effect of limiting distribution of God's Word in modern languages.

Liberation

What we are doing is liberating at least one modern English translation of the Holy Bible from all copyright restrictions – a translation that is trustworthy, accurate, and useful for evangelism and discipleship.

No copyright

Isn't it dangerous not to copyright the WEB?

No. Copyright protection is intended to protect the income of the copyright holder's sales of a work, but we are planning to give away the right to make copies of this version of the Holy Bible to anyone who wants it, so we have nothing to lose that way.

What is the WEB Revision?

The WEB Revision is an update of the American Standard Version of 1901, which is in the Public Domain.

The revision is also in the Public Domain, which sets it apart from other revisions of the American Standard Version, like the New American

Standard Bible and the Revised Standard Version.

FIRST PASS

The first pass of the translation, which has already been done, was to convert about 1000 archaic words and word forms to modern equivalents using a custom computer program.

SECOND TO SEVENTH PASSES

The second through seventh phases consist of manual editing and proofreading.

The initial manual pass is to add quotation marks (the ASV of 1901 had none), update other punctuation, update usage, and spot check the translation against the original languages in places where the meaning is unclear or significant textual variants exist.

The subsequent passes are to review the results of the previous pass.

Who is behind the WEB Revision work?

Rainbow Missions, Inc., a Colorado nonprofit corporation – and many volunteers. The Rainbow Missions gets its name from the rainbow that is a sign of the covenant between God and Noah, the rainbow around God's throne.

Is the WEB a one-man translation?

Many people have been involved in the production and editing of the World English Bible from a variety of backgrounds.

Because this is a revision of the American Standard Version of the Revised Bible, we start with the over 50 Evangelical scholars who worked on that project. They, in turn, relied on the work of those who had gone before them. We also rely on the work of many scholars who have found, compiled, combined, and published the excellent and highly accurate Hebrew and Greek texts from which we work.

We also rely on the excellent lexicons of Hebrew, Chaldee, and Greek that are available to us.

An "internet" Bible (2)

What is the WEB translation philosophy?

The WEB must

- be done with prayer – specifically prayer for inspiration by the Holy Spirit.
- be accurate and reliable (Revelation 22: 18–19).
- be understandable to the majority of the world's English-speaking population (and therefore should avoid locale-specific usage).
- be kept in the Public Domain (and therefore be done by volunteers).
- be made available in a short time, because we don't know the exact time of our Lord's return.
- preserve the essential character of the original 1901 publication.
- use language that is not faddish, but likely to retain its meaning for some time.
- render God's proper Name in the Old Testament as "Yahweh."
- resolve unclear passages by referring to the original Hebrew and Greek.
- be done with utmost respect for God and His Word.
- be done by Christians from a variety of denominations and backgrounds.
- retain (at least for now) the ASV 1901's pronoun capitalization rules (lower case "he" referring to God).
- retain (in most cases) the ASV 1901's use of "he" when that word might mean ("he and/or she").

- restrict footnotes to those which clarify the translation or provide significant alternate readings

BALANCING ACT

Bible translation (as with any natural language translation) is a balancing act, where the translators seek to preserve the following:

- The meaning of each thought or sentence.
- The meanings of individual words in their context.
- The shades of meaning implied by word forms, tense, etc.
- The impact and tone of each passage.
- The style of the original authors who were inspired by the Holy Spirit.
- Faithfulness to the target language (English, in this case).

Note that some of the above goals are at odds with one another, like preservation of the original style vs. faithfulness to the target language, and expressing the last bit of the shades of meaning vs. preserving the impact.

Still, it is possible to retain a good balance. For example,

- The Amplified Bible excels at getting the meaning across, but falls down hard on impact, style preservation, and faithfulness to the target language.
- The New Living Translation excels at preserving the meanings of entire thoughts, impact, and faithfulness to the target language, but loses some of the style and shades of meaning.

- The New International Version excels at most of the above, but loses some elements of style and some of the subtleties of wording.

The World English Bible attempts to balance all of the above with a fairly literal translation.

Some people like to use the terms "formal equivalent" and "dynamic equivalent." Neither of these exactly describe what we are doing, since we have borrowed ideas from both, but I suppose that we are closer to formal equivalence than dynamic equivalence.

What original language texts are you using?

Since this is primarily an update of the 1901 edition, the choices made by the original 50 or so Evangelical scholars that made this translation hold unless reference is made to the original languages to help with places where the Elizabethan English is not clear, or where major textual variants are known to exist. In this case, we are using the Biblia Hebraica Stuttgartensia, also called The Stuttgart Bible, in the Old Testament, and the Byzantine Majority Text. This choice of Greek text is very close to what the KJV translators used, but does take advantage of some more recently discovered manuscripts.

How does the WEB compare to other translations?

The WEB is different enough to avoid copyright infringement, but similar enough to avoid incurring the wrath of God. It is most similar to the ASV of 1901.

CAPITALS

The WEB doesn't capitalize pronouns pertaining to God's name in the Old Testament. The WEB, like the ASV of 1901, breaks the KJV tradition by printing God's proper Name in the Old Testament with a spelling closest to what we think it was pronounced like, instead of rendering that Name as "LORD" or "GOD" (with all caps or small caps). The current scholarly consensus has shifted from spelling this Name as "Jehovah" to spelling it as "Yahweh." There are a couple of other English translations that use "Yahweh," so this is not new, per se, but it does set it off a little from other translations.

First American Bibles; Protestant and Catholic Bibles

First American Bibles

The Eliot Indian Bible

The first complete Bible printed in America, published in the Algonquin language, was translated by John Eliot.

He fled England with the Puritans and arrived in Boston. Two miles from Boston he pastured the First Church of Roxbury from 1632 until his death in 1690.

THE APOSTLE TO THE INDIANS
As a result of his work among Native Americans Eliot became known as "The apostle to the Indians."

INDIAN TRACTS
Eliot issued a series of pamphlets known as "Eliot's Indian Tracts," to help the Native Americans grow in their Christian faith. It took Eliot eight years to translated the Bible into Algonquin.

The first New Testament printed in America was published in September of 1661. In 1663, the complete Eliot Indian Bible was printed.

The Aitken Bible

The Aitken Bible is also known as "The Bible of the American Revolution." It is also the only Bible that was printed with congressional approval.

It was the first English Bible printed in America.

When the American colonies declared their independence, Bibles became scarce as imports of Bible were curtailed.

CONGRESS RESOLUTION
The Scottish-born Quaker and American patriot Robert Aitken started to publish New Testaments in 1777. He then applied for congressional approval to print the complete Bible, and Congress resolved:

"That the United States in Congress assembled highly approve the pious and laudable undertaking of Mr. Aitken, as subservient to the interest of religion, as well as an instance of the progress of arts in this country, and being satisfied from the above report of his care and accuracy in the execution of the work, they recommend this edition of the Bible to the inhabitants of the United States, and hereby authorize him to publish this recommendation in the manner he shall think proper. CHA. THOMSON, Secy."

So the Aitken Bible received the approval of Congress. In 1782 the first Aitken Bible was printed.

GEORGE WASHINGTON
George Washington, one of the greatest supporters of the Aitken Bible, wrote to a friend:

"It would have pleased me well, if Congress had been pleased to make such an important present (a copy of the Aitken Bible) to the brave fellows, who have done so much for the security of their Country's rights and establishment."

Protestant and Catholic Bibles

Protestant printed Bibles

1525 Tyndale Bible
1535 Coverdale Bible
1537 Matthew's Bible
1539 The Great Bible
1560 Geneva Bible
1568 Bishop's Bible
1611 King James Version (Authorized Version)
1881–1885 Revised Version
1952 Revised Standard Version
1970 New English Bible
1973 New International Version
1980 New King James Version
1986 New Revised Standard Version

Catholic printed Bibles

1582–1609
Douai-Rheims

1749–1763
Challoner Revision
Bishop Challoner revised the Douai-Rheims and this remained in almost universal use among English-speaking Catholics for nearly 200 years..

1944–1950
Knox Bible
Ronald Knox was commissioned by the English bishops to make a new translation from the Vulgate.

1952–1970
New American
This translation, from the original languages, was commissioned by the American Catholic bishops. In 1964 it was adopted for use in the Roman Catholic Liturgy.

1966
Jerusalem Bible
The Jerusalem Dominicans edited this French translation. It was then translated into English.

1965
Revised Standard Version, Catholic edition
New Testament was prepared by a committee of the Catholic biblical Association of Great Britain. It included wording which reflects Catholic tradition.

1966
Revised Standard Version, Catholic edition

Ecumenical translations

New English Bible
Revised English Bible
Revised Standard Version
New Revised Standard Version

Description of some of the major Bible translations (1)

Information on each Bible

The following information about each of the Bible versions listed on the previous page is now given:
- The name of the Bible version
- The date of publication of the Bible version
- A description of the Bible version taken from the version itself
- Two sample extracts of the Bible version, from Genesis 1: 1,2 and John 1: 1–3.

Abbreviated Bible, The

Date of publication: 1971

A DESCRIPTION TAKEN FROM THE VERSION ITSELF

There were three goals in preparing this work. The first was to shorten the text sufficiently so that those lacking time or inclination for reading an unabridged version, yet wishing to obtain a workable knowledge of the Bible, might be able to do so. The second was to present the material in language easily understandable to the average layman. The third was to condense the content and simplify the language without omitting or changing any pertinent material.

Each chapter stands alone. It was felt that, although some people do not accept the Apocrypha, it should be included for several reasons. The compilers attempted not to allow any bias toward or against any particular code of religious beliefs. A dozen different translations were read by them in preparing this version, with the American Standard Version and the Revised Standard Version being followed more than any other one.

TWO SAMPLE EXTRACTS

Originally God created the cosmos. Then the earth was wasted, empty, and enveloped in darkness. God's Spirit hovered over the waters with Life-generating power.

Genesis 1: 1,2

The Word existed with God from the beginning, and all things were created through him.

John 1: 1–3

American Translation, An (Beck)

Date of publication: 1976

A DESCRIPTION TAKEN FROM THE VERSION ITSELF

This is the work of Dr. William F. Beck, whose cause was to simplify the English Bible for people of all ages. There are almost 5000 Greek manuscripts of the New Testament all over the earth, plus many thousands of the Latin, Syriac, and other translations. Dr. Beck felt that God wants us to have a passion for the truth; to use all the best evidences from the manuscripts, dictionaries, and grammars as light on the text; and to search with burning hearts for its exact meaning.

The translator did his utmost to make both the Old Testament and the New Testament the most accurate on the market, in regard to the best text, the most thorough lexiographical, grammatical, and archaeological evidence.

TWO SAMPLE EXTRACTS
In the beginning God created the heavens and the earth. The earth was desolate and uninhabitable, and it was dark on the deep sea, but God's Spirit hovered over the waters.

Genesis 1: 1,2

In the beginning was the Word, and the Word was with God, and the Word was God. He was in the beginning with God.

Everything was made by Him, and not one thing that was made was made without Him.

John 1: 1–3

American Translation, An (Smith-Goodspeed)

Date of publication: 1931

A DESCRIPTION TAKEN FROM THE VERSION ITSELF
The Old Testament was translated by Alexander R. Gordon (McGill University), Theopile J. Meek (University of Toronto), Leroy Waterman (University of Michigan), and J. M. Powis Smith (University of Chicago). The last person named was also the editor. The New Testament was translated by Edgar J. Goodspeed (University of Chicago).

There were basic reasons for the need of this translation of the Old Testament. The control of the Hebrew vocabulary and syntax available to the scholar at this time was vastly greater than that at the command of the translators of the Authorized Version or of its revisers. The science of textual criticism had made great progress in recent years, and no translation of the Old Testament could afford to ignore its results. There had developed a great interest in the stylistic qualities of Hebrew poetry. The English of King James's day was not wholly natural or clear to the average person at this time.

The New Testament was written in everyday Greek. It, thus, was translated into everyday English.

TWO SAMPLE EXTRACTS
When God began to create the heavens and the earth, the earth was a desolate waste, with darkness covering the abyss and a temptuous wind raging over the surface of the waters.

Genesis 1: 1,2

In the beginning the Word existed. The Word was with God, and the Word was divine.

It was he that was with God in the beginning. Everything came into existence through him, and apart from him nothing came to be.

John 1: 1–3

Description of some of the major Bible translations (2)

Amplified Bible

Date of publication: 1965

A DESCRIPTION TAKEN FROM THE
VERSION ITSELF
This translation is based on the
American Standard Version. It uses
a system of synonyms, punctuation,
typographical features, and clarifying
words or phrases to reveal shades
of meaning of the key words in the
original text.

The aim of the translation was that
it be true to the original languages, be
grammatically correct, be understandable to the masses, and give the Lord
Jesus Christ His proper place which the
Word gives Him. It is not an attempt
to duplicate what has already been
achieved but to progress beyond the
point where others have stopped.

TWO SAMPLE EXTRACTS
In the beginning God (prepared,
formed, fashioned,) and created the
heavens and the earth. [Heb. 11: 3.] The
earth was without form and an empty
waste, and darkness was upon the face
of the great deep. The Spirit of God was
moving, (hovering, brooding) over the
face of the waters.

Genesis 1: 1,2

In the beginning [before all time] was
the Word [Christ], and the Word was
with God, and the Word was God
Himself. [Is. 9: 6.] He was present
originally with God. All things were
made *and* came into existence through
Him; and without Him was not even
one thing made that has come into
being.

John 1: 1–3

Basic Bible, The

Date of publication: 1950

A DESCRIPTION TAKEN FROM THE
VERSION ITSELF
The language used is Basic English. This
version, produced by C. K. Ogden of
the Orthological Institute, is a simple
form of the English language which, in
850 words, is able to give the sense of
anything which may be said in English.
The version is designed to be used
wherever the English language has
taken root.

TWO SAMPLE EXTRACTS
At the first God made the heaven and
the earth. And the earth was waste and
without form; and it was dark on the
face of the deep: and the Spirit of God
was moving on the face of the waters.

Genesis 1: 1,2

From the first he was the Word, and
the Word was in relation with God
and was God. This Word was from the
first in relation with God. All things
came into existence through him, and
without him nothing was.

John 1: 1–3

Bible Designed to Be Read as Literature, The

Date of publication: 1930

A DESCRIPTION TAKEN FROM THE VERSION ITSELF
This volume is designed to present a selection of the greater part of the English Bible as literature. It is intended for all readers, of whatever belief, opinion, or bringing-up. It is not the first attempt, but the selection and arrangement of it are new. Ernest Sutherland Bates is the editor and arranger.

The following purposes are given:

- To afford a conservative narration from the creation to the exile, supplementing it with a selection from 1 Maccabees to complete the story down to the times of Jesus;
- To emphasize the greatest of the Prophets and minimize the others;
- To rearrange the drama, poetry, and fiction, adding parts of the Apocrypha;
- To give the basic biography of Jesus found in the Gospels;
- To restrict the utterances of Paul to those that have immortal value and to omit entirely the unimportant pseudonymous epistles;
- To print all the works in order of their composition, as far as possible.

TWO SAMPLE EXTRACTS
In the beginning God created the heaven and the earth. And the earth was without form, and void; and darkness was upon the face of the deep. And the Spirit of God moved upon the face of the waters.

Genesis 1: 1,2

In the beginning was the Word, and the Word was with God, and the Word was God. The same was in the beginning with God. All things were made by him; and without him was not any thing made that was made.

John 1: 1–3

Bible Reader, The

Date of publication: 1969

A DESCRIPTION TAKEN FROM THE VERSION ITSELF
This is an interfaith interpretation with notes from Catholic, Protestant and Jewish traditions, and references to art, literature, history and the social problems of modern man. It was prepared by Walter M. Abbott, S. J.; Rabbi Arthur Gilbert; Rolfe Lanier Hunt; and J. Carter Swaim.

The editors of this work came together in the early 1960's in a conviction that the preparation of citizens for life today requires an acquaintance with the Bible. Before starting their work, they asked themselves a number of questions regarding which passages to include. Then they selected the ones most associated with their respective religious observances and beliefs.

Attention was called to passages that have produced varied denominational emphases.

Description of some of the major Bible translations (3)

TWO SAMPLE EXTRACTS

When God began to create the heaven and the earth – the earth being unformed and void, with darkness over the surface of the deep and a wind from God sweeping over the water – .... (Torah)

Genesis 1: 1,2

In the beginning was the Word, and the Word was with God, and the Word was God. He was in the beginning with God; all things were made through him, and without him was not anything made that was made.

John 1: 1–3

Confraternity of Christian Doctrine Translation

Date of publication: 1953

A DESCRIPTION TAKEN FROM THE VERSION ITSELF

The editors have incorporated in this new edition of the Holy Bible the better translations which modern Bible scholarship has put at their disposal. The Old Testament, in prose paragraph format, is the venerable Douai Version, with the exception of the first eight books (Genesis to Ruth), translated by members of the Catholic biblical Association of America under the patronage of the Confraternity of Christian Doctrine. In addition, the Book of Psalms is a new English translation from the new Latin version approved by Pope Pius XII. The New Testament is the newly revised version of the Confraternity of Christian Doctrine.

TWO SAMPLE EXTRACTS
In the beginning God created the heavens and the earth; the earth was waste and void; darkness covered the abyss, and the spirit of God was stirring above the waters.

Genesis 1: 1,2

In the beginning was the Word, and the Word was with God; and the Word was God. He was in the beginning with God. All things were made through him, and without him nothing was made that has been made.

John 1: 1–3

Coverdale Bible, The

Date of publication: 1540

A DESCRIPTION OF THE VERSION
Miles Coverdale, ordained about 1514, became interested in the works of such men as Erasmus, Luther, and Tyndale. He helped Tyndale in Antwerp in 1529. He translated the Psalms and Ecclesiastes from the Latin works of Campensis and published them in 1534 and 1535, respectively. He may have started his own work on the Bible in 1534.

This Bible is divided into six parts, as was Luther's. The chapters are divided into paragraphs without systematic numbering. The notes, comparatively few, concern alternate readings. Marginal cross-references abound. There are over one hundred fifty illustrations.

It was not translated from Hebrew and Greek, but from German and Latin. Coverdale was competent in both of the latter two languages. He trusted five different interpreters, translating from them purely and faithfully, without favor to any sect and subject to correction. These were Jerome, Pagninus, Luther, the translators of the Zurich Bible, and Tyndale.

There is an extensive introduction. The spelling and type are Old English.

TWO SAMPLE EXTRACTS
In ye begynnynge God created heauen and earth: ye earth was voyde and emptie, and darcknes was vpon the depe, and ye sprete of God moued vpo the water.

Genesis 1: 1,2

In the begynnynge was the worde, and the worde was with God, and God was ye worde. The same was in the begynnynge wt God. All thinges were made by the same, and without the same was made nothinge that was made.

John 1: 1–3

Darby Holy Bible

Date of publication: 1923

A DESCRIPTION TAKEN FROM THE VERSION ITSELF
This translation of the Old Testament has been derived from a study of the common Hebrew text.

The purpose of this translation is not to offer to the man of letters a learned work, but rather to provide the simple and unlearned reader with as exact a translation as possible. To this end, all available helps have been used. The work is not a revision of the Bible in common use. The style of the Authorized Version [KJV] has been retained as far as possible within the purpose of the translation.

Poetical parts are distinguished from the rest by a metrical arrangement to which those are accustomed who use Paragraph Bibles.

TWO SAMPLE EXTRACTS
In the beginning God created the heavens and the earth. And the earth was waste and empty, and darkness was on the face of the deep, and the Spirit of God was hovering over the face of the waters.

Genesis 1: 1,2

Description of some of the major Bible translations (4)

TWO SAMPLE EXTRACTS, CONTINUED
In [the] beginning was the Word, and the Word was with God, and the Word was God. He was in the beginning with God. All things received being through him, and without him not one [thing] received being which has received being.

John 1: 1–3

Douai-Rheims Bible

Date of publication: 1899

A DESCRIPTION OF THE VERSION
This is a scrupulously faithful translation into English of the Latin Vulgate Bible which Jerome (342–420) translated into Latin from the original languages. The Latin Vulgate Bible had been declared by the Council of Trent to be the official Latin version of the canonical Scriptures. The *DRB* translators took great pains to translate exactly. When a passage seemed strange and unintelligible they left it alone, even if obscure.

The translators translated from a translation for ten reasons, ending by stating that the Latin Vulgate "is not onely better than al other Latin translations, but than the Greeke text itselfe, in those places where they disagree." They also state that the Vulgate is "more pure then the Hebrew or Greke now extant" and that "the same Latin hath bene farre better conserved from corruptions."

TWO SAMPLE EXTRACTS
In the beginning God created heaven, and earth. And the earth was void and empty, and darkness was upon the face of the deep; and the spirit of God moved over the waters.

Genesis 1: 1,2

In the beginning was the Word, and the Word was with God, and the Word was God.

The same was in the beginning with God.

All things were made by him; and without him was made nothing that was made.

John 1: 1–3

Emphasized Bible, The

Date of publication: 1959

A DESCRIPTION TAKEN FROM THE VERSION ITSELF
This is a translation designed to set forth the exact meaning, the proper terminology, and the graphic style of the sacred original. The translator was Joseph Bryant Rotherham.

Throughout are signs of emphasis for reading. (′) and (‖ ‖) call for slight stress. (‖ ‖) and (< >) call for more decided stress. The latter of these is confined to preplaced words and clauses, leading up to what follows.

"God" printed in upper case represents El. "God" printed in Gothic represents Eloah. "God" printed without peculiarity of type represents

Elohim. "Yahweh" is used instead of "Jehovah."

There is an extensive expository introduction dealing with special features of this translation, emphasis, the original texts, and the incommunicable name. For the Old Testament, the current Masoretic text was used.

For the New Testament, the text of Westcott and Hort was used.

TWO SAMPLE EXTRACTS

<In the beginning> God' created the heavens and the earth.
Now //the earth// had become waste and wild, and //darkness// was on the face of the roaring deep, – but //the Spirit of God// was brooding on the face of the waters.

Genesis 1: 1,2

//Originally// was /the Word,
And //the Word// was /with God;
And /the Word/ was //God//.
//The same// was originally /with God/.
//All things// through him' /came into existence/
And //without him// came into existence /not even one thing/:

John 1: 1–3

English Standard Version

Date of publication: 2002

A DESCRIPTION BY ITS PUBLISHERS
The English Standard Version (ESV) stands in the classic mainstream of English Bible translations of the past half-millennium.

The fountainhead of that stream was William Tyndale's New Testament of 1526; marking its course were the King James Version of 1611 (KJV), the Revised Version of 1885 (RV), the American Standard Version of 1901 (ASV), and the Revised Standard Version of 1952 and 1971 (RSV).

In that stream, faithfulness to the text and vigorous pursuit of accuracy were combined with simplicity, beauty, and dignity of expression. Our goal has been to carry forward this legacy for a new century.

To this end each word and phrase in the ESV has been carefully weighed against the original Hebrew, Aramaic, and Greek, to ensure the fullest accuracy and clarity and to avoid under-translating or overlooking any nuance of the original text. The words and phrases themselves grow out of this Tyndale–King James legacy. Archaic language has been brought to current usage and significant corrections have been made in the translation of key texts.

But throughout, our goal has been to retain the depth of meaning and enduring language that have made their indelible mark on the English-speaking world and have defined the life and doctrine of the church over the last four centuries.

Description of some of the major Bible translations (5)

TWO SAMPLE EXTRACTS

In the beginning, God created the heavens and the earth. The earth was without form and void, and darkness was over the face of the deep. And the Spirit of God was hovering over the face of the waters.

Genesis 1: 1,2

The Word of Life

1: 1 That which was from the beginning, which we have heard, which we have seen with our eyes, which we looked upon and have touched with our hands, concerning the word of life– 2 the life was made manifest, and we have seen it, and testify to it and proclaim to you the eternal life, which was with the Father and was made manifest to us– 3 that which we have seen and heard we proclaim also to you, so that you too may have fellowship with us; and indeed our fellowship is with the Father and with his Son Jesus Christ.

John 1: 1–3

English Version for the Deaf (Easy-to-Read Version)

Date of publication: 1989

A DESCRIPTION TAKEN FROM THE VERSION ITSELF

This version has been prepared to meet the special needs of the deaf. Whether it is published as the English Version for the Deaf or the Easy-to-Read Version, the text is the same.

Hearing persons learn English largely through oral conversation. However, for the deaf, this experience with language is severely limited. Children, people who learn English as a foreign language, and many others face similar difficulties in reading. This specialized English version is designed to help such people overcome or avoid the most common obstacles to reading with understanding.

One of the basic ideas that guided the work on this version was that good translation is good communication. The main concern of the translators was always to communicate to the reader the message of the biblical writers as effectively and as naturally as the original writings did to people in that time. The translators worked to convey to their special audience the meaning of the biblical text in a form that would be simple and natural.

TWO SAMPLE EXTRACTS

God made the sky and earth. At first, the sky was completely empty; nothing was on the earth. Darkness covered the ocean, and God's Spirit moved over the water.

Genesis 1: 1,2

Before the world began, the Word was there. The Word was there with God. The Word was God. He was there with God in the beginning. All things were made through him (the Word). Nothing was made without him.

John 1: 1–3

Geneva Bible, The

Date of publication: 1560

A DESCRIPTION TAKEN FROM THE
VERSION ITSELF
It was translated according to the Ebreu
and Greke, and conferred with the best
translations in diuers langages; with
the most profitable annotations vpon
all the hard places, and other things of
great importance as may appeare in the
Epistle to the Reader.

It contained original marginal notes.

The work was done in Geneva, Switzerland. The translators do not identify
themselves anywhere in the Bible. Several persons are considered to have been
involved with the work, namely, William
Whittingham (general editor), Miles Coverdale, John Knox, Christopher Goodman, Anthony Gilby, Thomas Sampson,
William Cole, and others. The translators
were motivated to prepare a new translation because it behooved Christians to
walk in the fear and love of God and this
could best be done when one had knowledge of the Word of God.

TWO SAMPLE EXTRACTS
In the beginning God created y
heauen and the earth. And the earth
was without forme and voyde, and
darkness was vpon the depe, and the
Spirit of God moued vpon the waters.

Genesis 1: 1,2

In the beginning was the Worde, and
the Worde was with God and that
Worde was God. The same was in
the beginning w God. All things were
made by it, and without it was made
nothing that was made.

John 1: 1–3

God's Word (Today's Bible Translation)

Date of publication: 1995

A DESCRIPTION TAKEN FROM THE
VERSION ITSELF
This translation, which is the work
of God's Word to the Nations Bible
Society, fills the need to communicate
clearly to contemporary Americans
without compromising the Bible's
message. It employed full-time Bible
scholars and full-time English editorial
reviewers. It uses natural grammar,
follows standard punctuation and
capitalization rules, and is printed in a
single column.

The theory followed by the Bible
Society's translators is closest natural
equivalent translation. The first
consideration was to find equivalent
English ways of expressing the
meaning of the original text. The
second consideration was readability.
The third consideration was to choose
the natural equivalent that most
clearly reflects the style of the Hebrew,
Aramaic, or Greek text.

In prose, this translation looks like
other works of literature. Poetry is
instantly recognized by its format.

Description of some of the major Bible translations (6)

A DESCRIPTION TAKEN FROM THE VERSION ITSELF, CONTINUED

It capitalizes the first letter in proper nouns and sentences and in all letters of the word Lord when it represents Yahweh. It does not capitalize any pronouns (except I and unless they begin sentences). In passages that apply to all people, it tries to use gender-neutral language so that all readers will apply these passages to themselves. If a passage focuses upon an individual, it does not use plural nouns and pronouns to avoid the gender-specific pronouns he, him, and his. It avoids using difficult theological terms, substituting words that carry the same meaning in common English. However, some traditional theological words are contained in footnotes the first time they occur in a chapter.

TWO SAMPLE EXTRACTS

In the beginning God created heaven and earth. The earth was formless and empty, and darkness covered the water. The Spirit of God was hovering over the water.

Genesis 1: 1,2

In the beginning the Word already existed. The Word was with God, and the Word was God. He was already with God in the beginning. Everything came into existence through him. Not one thing that exists was made without him.

John 1: 1–3

Holy Bible in Modern English, The

Date of publication: 1900

A DESCRIPTION TAKEN FROM THE VERSION ITSELF

The books of the Sacred Volume of our Faith, as they were arranged by the Editorial Committee appointed by the Great Sanhedrim, called at Jerusalem for the purpose, in the Third Century before Christ, were divided into Four Volumes, and put into the succession that this translator, Ferrar Fenton, has followed [Old Testament].

He used this order for the following reasons: It was the original one, and the accurate criticism, mental insight, and literary skill shown in it, and its grouping of both the Historical and the Divinely Inspired Writers, show a masterly comprehension of the work the Editors had before them, and the progressive nature of the Revelation from God to Man of the Everlasting Laws of Creation, Human Life, and Social and National health and duty, that has never been equalled, and which is itself, if studied, a commentary that cannot be excelled.

He first made, by his own hand and mental effort, the translation direct from the original, with no intermediary version between the Greek or Oriental Texts and his manuscript. He revised passages three to five times and submitted difficult ones to a few Orientalist and Grecianist friends. He tested their suggestions by various previous translators.

Then he collated his version with a Polyglot Bible. He was dismayed to find, in doing the latter, that translators to the various languages had repeated errors made by the Greek translators of the Hebrew or Chaldee text. He found the same with the Latin version of the Greek New Testament.

For many years he read the Old Testament in Hebrew and Chaldee and the New Testament in Greek, so as to arrive at their meaning from ancient writers themselves alone. He also had before him no theological or historic theories to assail or to support.

TWO SAMPLE EXTRACTS
By Periods GOD created that which produced the Solar Systems; then that which produced the Earth. But the Earth was unorganised and empty; and darkness covered its convulsed surface; while the breath of GOD rocked the surface of its waters.

Genesis 1: 1,2

The WORD existed in the beginning, and the WORD was with God, and the WORD was God. He was present with God at the beginning. All came into existence by means of Him; and nothing came into existence apart from Him.

John 1: 1–3

Holy Bible, Revised Version
Date of publication: 1885

A DESCRIPTION TAKEN FROM THE VERSION ITSELF
The Revised Version of the Bible was the first – and remains the only – officially authorized revision of the King James Version. The work was entrusted to some fifty scholars from various denominations in Britain; American scholars were invited to co-operate, by correspondence.

The revisers were charged with introducing alterations only if they were required in order to be faithful to the original text. In the New Testament alone more than 30,000 changes were made, over five thousand of them on the basis of a better Greek text.

The work was begun in 1879, and the Revised Version was published in 1885; the Apocrypha came out in 1895.

The American Standard Edition, based on the Revised Version, was published in 1901.

TWO SAMPLE EXTRACTS
In the beginning God created the heaven and the earth. And the earth was waste and void; and darkness was upon the face of the deep: and the spirit of God moved upon the face of the waters.

Genesis 1: 1,2

In the beginning was the Word, and the Word was with God, and the Word was God. The same was in the beginning with God. All things were made by him; and without him was not anything made that hath been made.

John 1: 1–3

Description of some of the major Bible translations (7)

Inclusive Version, An

Date of publication: 1995

A DESCRIPTION TAKEN FROM THE VERSION ITSELF
Only the Psalms and the New Testament were published.

This revolutionary new version, adapted from the New Revised Standard Version and edited by six scholars – three men and three women – pushes the English language to new levels of inclusive expression. This work addresses such issues as race, gender, and ethnicity more directly than ever before.

There are two reasons for this new version. The languages into which the Bible is rendered are changing. New manuscripts are discovered that are older and more reliable, and new investigations into the meanings of words reveal that more accurate renderings are possible.

People who have disabilities are not referred to as "the blind" or "the lame," but as "people who are blind" or "those who are lame." Because the church does not assume that God is a male being, in this version God is never referred to by a masculine pronoun, or by any pronoun at all. As the church does not believe that God is literally a father and understands "Father" to be a metaphor, "Father" is rendered in this version by a new metaphor, "Father-Mother." When Jesus is called "Son of God" or "Son of the Blessed One,"

and the maleness of the historical person Jesus is not relevant, but the "Son's" intimate relation to the "Father" is being spoken about, the formal equivalent "Child" is used for "Son," and gender-specific pronouns referring to the "Child" are avoided. This version uses "the Human One" as a formal equivalent to "the Son of Man." In the genealogy that begins the Gospel of Matthew, women's names, where they are known, have been added, e.g., David and Bathsheba, the wife of Uriah, were the parents of Solomon.

ONE SAMPLE EXTRACT
In the beginning was the Word, and the Word was with God, and the Word was God. The Word was in the beginning with God. All things came into being through the Word, and without the Word not one thing came into being.
John 1: 1–3

Interlinear Bible (Greene)

Date of publication: 1976

A DESCRIPTION TAKEN FROM THE VERSION ITSELF
It is the first such Bible available to students of Scriptures who speak English. With it, one can utilize lexicons, word books, and other recent aids.

The Hebrew text in the Old Testament is the Masoretic text. The Greek text in the New Testament is the Received Text (differing slightly from other printed editions).

There are two English translations: one located directly under each Hebrew or Greek word and "The Literal Translation of the Bible" in a narrow column to the left. The latter straight-forward translation makes it easy to see proper word order in English and to assimilate the message of the text. Both translations are word-for-word, but are not absolute, literal representations of the Hebrew and Greek words.

The personal name of God is rendered either Jehovah or Jah. The translators preferred JHWH to YHWH because of the established English usage for Bible names beginning with this letter (e.g., Jacob and Joseph). Greek names for Old Testament persons in the New Testament are spelled as in the Old Testament. "Mary" is rendered Miriam in consistency with the Greek form when translated under the Greek word.

TWO SAMPLE EXTRACTS

In the beginning God created the heavens and the earth; and the earth being without form and empty, and darkness on the face of the deep, and the Spirit of God moving gently on the face of the waters,

Genesis 1: 1,2

In the beginning was the Word, and the Word was with God, and the Word was God. He was in the beginning with God. All things came into being through Him, and without Him not even one thing came into being that has come into being.

John 1: 1–3

Jerusalem Bible, The

Date of publication: 1966

A DESCRIPTION TAKEN FROM THE VERSION ITSELF

The form and nature of this edition have been determined by two of the principal dangers facing the Christian religion today. The first is the reduction of Christianity to the state of a relic – affectionately regarded, but considered irrelevant to our times. The second is its rejection as a mythology, born and cherished in emotion with nothing at all to say to the mind.

Now for Christian thinking in the twentieth century two slogans have been wisely adopted: aggiornamento, or keeping abreast of the times, and approfondimento, or deepening of theological thought. Its first part can be carried out by translating into the language we use today, its second part by providing notes which are neither sectarian nor superficial.

In 1956, a one-volume edition, which came to be known popularly as La Bible de Jérusalem, appeared. This was prepared by the Dominican biblical School in Jerusalem. The edition being described here is the English equivalent of that.

Description of some of the major Bible translations (8)

A DESCRIPTION TAKEN FROM THE
VERSION ITSELF, CONTINUED
Parts of the English edition were
translated from the French, then
carefully compared with the Hebrew
or Aramaic texts. However, more
parts were translated from the Hebrew
or Greek and compared with the
French. The Psalms presented a special
problem because they are a collection
of verse not only to be read but also to
be sung or chanted.

TWO SAMPLE EXTRACTS
In the beginning God created the
heavens and the earth. Now the earth
was a formless void, there was darkness
over the deep, and God's spirit hovered
over the water.

Genesis 1: 1,2

In the beginning was the Word:
the Word was with God
and the Word was God.
He was with God in the beginning.
Through him all things came to be,
not one thing had its being but
through him.

John 1: 1–3

King James Version (Authorized Version)

Date of publication: 1611

A DESCRIPTION OF THE VERSION
It was translated out of the original
tongues and with previous translations,
including that of William Tyndale,
diligently compared and revised. In
the preface of the 1611 edition, the
translators stated that it was not their
purpose to make a new translation
but to make a good one better. It is a
revision of the Bishop's Bible of 1568.

It was the desire of the translators
to make God's holy Truth more and
more known unto the people, even
though they may be maligned by those
religious persons who would keep
the people in ignorance and darkness
concerning it. It was presented to King
James I when completed in 1611. It has
been the standard English translation
for almost four hundred years.

It is noted for the quality of
translation and the majesty of style.
The translators were committed
to producing an English Bible that
would be a precise translation and
by no means a paraphrase or broadly
approximate rendering. The scholars
were fully familiar with the original
languages of the Bible and especially
gifted in their use of their native
English. Because of their reverence for
God and His Word, only a principle of
utmost accuracy in their translation
could be accepted.

Appreciating the intrinsic beauty
of divine revelation, they disciplined
their talents to render well-chosen
English words of their time as well as a
graceful, often musical, arrangement of
language.

TWO SAMPLE EXTRACTS
In the beginning God created the
heaven and the earth.

And the earth was without form, and void; and darkness was upon the face of the deep. And the Spirit of God moved upon the face of the waters.

Genesis 1: 1,2

In the beginning was the Word, and the Word was with God, and the Word was God.

The same was in the beginning with God.

All things were made by him; and without him was not any thing made that was made.

John 1: 1–3

Knox Translation

Date of publication: 1956

A DESCRIPTION TAKEN FROM THE VERSION ITSELF

Ronald Knox was requested in 1936 by the hierarchy of England and Wales to undertake a completely new translation of the New Testament. This he produced single-handed in 1945. The Old Testament was completed in 1955. The translation is from the Vulgate "in light of" the originals and with many textual notes.

The purpose in preparing this translation was to give readers a greater knowledge and understanding of inspired Sacred Scripture. Prayer and the sacraments are a lay apostle's strength, the Bible, his armor. A knowledge of Holy Scripture is a valuable element in his participation in the Church's liturgy. The translation by Monsignor Knox was presented to meet the need of having in every home

a Bible that is easy to read and a joy to handle.

TWO SAMPLE EXTRACTS

God, at the beginning of time, created heaven and earth. Earth was still an empty waste, and darkness hung over the deep; but already, over its waters, stirred the breath of God.

Genesis 1: 1,2

At the beginning of time the Word already was; and God had the Word abiding with him, and the Word was God. He abode, at the beginning of time, with God. It was through him that all things came into being, and without him came nothing that has come to be.

John 1: 1–3

Lamsa Bible

Date of publication: 1957

A DESCRIPTION TAKEN FROM THE VERSION ITSELF

This translation of the Old and New Testaments is based on Peshitta manuscripts which have comprised the accepted Bible of all those Christians who have used Syriac as their language of prayer and worship for many centuries. From the Mediterranean east into India, the Peshitta is still the Bible of preference among Christians.

Description of some of the major Bible translations (9)

A DESCRIPTION TAKEN FROM THE
VERSION ITSELF, CONTINUED
George M. Lamsa, the translator,
devoted the major part of his life to this
work. He was an Assyrian and a native
of ancient Bible lands.

He and his people retained biblical
customs and Semitic culture, which
had perished elsewhere. With this
background and his knowledge of
the Aramaic (Syriac) language, he has
recovered much of the meaning that
has been lost in other translations of
the Scriptures.

Manuscripts used were the Codex
Ambrosianus for the Old Testament
and the Mortimer-McCawley
manuscript for the New Testament.
Comparisons have been made with
other Peshitta manuscripts, including
the oldest dated manuscript in
existence.

The term Peshitta means straight,
simple, sincere and true, that is, the
original.

TWO SAMPLE EXTRACTS
God created the heavens and the earth
in the very beginning.

And the earth was without form,
and void; and darkness was upon the
face of the deep. And the Spirit of God
moved upon the face of the water.

Genesis 1: 1,2

The Word was in the beginning, and
that very Word was with God, and God
was that Word.

The same was in the beginning with
God.

Everything came to be by his hand;
and without him not even one thing
that was created came to be.

John 1: 1–3

Living Bible

Date of publication: 1971

A DESCRIPTION TAKEN FROM THE
VERSION ITSELF
A paraphrase is the restatement of
an author's thoughts, using different
words. The purpose of this version is
for it to say as exactly as possible what
the writers of the Scriptures meant,
and to say it simply, expanding where
necessary for clear understanding by
the modern reader. There is a danger
in paraphrasing that the translator,
though honest, may give the English
reader something that the original
writer did not mean to say. When the
Greek or the Hebrew is not clear, the
theology of the translator and his sense
of logic are his guides. The theological
guide in this version has been a rigid
evangelical position.

This version has undergone several
manuscript revisions. It has also been
under the scrutiny of a team of Greek
and Hebrew experts to check the
content and of English critics to check
for style.

TWO SAMPLE EXTRACTS
When God began creating the heavens

and the earth, the earth was at first a shapeless, chaotic mass, with the Spirit of God brooding over the dark vapors.

Genesis 1: 1,2

Before anything else existed, there was Christ, with God. He has always been alive and is himself God. He created everything there is – nothing exists that he didn't make.

John 1: 1–3

Message, The

Date of publication: 2003

A DESCRIPTION TAKEN FROM THE VERSION ITSELF

This version is the work of Eugene H. Peterson. He was a pastor of a Presbyterian church in Maryland and is a professor of spiritual theology at a college in British Columbia and is a writer.

A feature of the original writings of the New Testament is that it was done in the street language of the day. At that time in the Greek-speaking world, there were two levels of language: formal and informal.

Formal language was used to write philosophy, history, government decrees, and epic poetry. Some people suppose that language dealing with a holy God and holy things should be elevated – stately and ceremonial. However, Jesus preferred down-to-earth stories and easy association with common people.

The followers of Jesus in their witness and preaching, translating and teaching, have always tried to get the Message – the "good news" – into the language of whatever street they happened to be living on.

In order to understand the Message right, the language must be a rough and earthy one that reveals God's presence and action where we least expect it.

This version is in a contemporary idiom that is current, fresh, and understandable in the same language that we use in all of our activities.

The goal was not to render a word-for-word conversion of Greek into English, but rather to convert the tone, the rhythm, the events, and the ideas into the way that we actually think and speak.

TWO SAMPLE EXTRACTS

First this: God created the Heavens and Earth – all you see, all you don't see. Earth was a soup of nothingness, a bottomless emptiness, an inky blackness. God's Spirit brooded like a bird above the watery abyss.

Genesis 1: 1,2

The Word was first,
   the Word present to God,
   God present to the Word.
The Word was God,
   in readiness for God from day one.
Everything was created through him;
nothing – not one thing! –
   came into being without him.

John 1: 1–3

Description of some of the major Bible translations (10)

MODERN READER'S BIBLE

Date of publication: 1923

A DESCRIPTION TAKEN FROM THE
VERSION ITSELF
This translation, presented in modern literary form, was edited by Richard G. Moulton, a professor of literary theory and interpretation at the University of Chicago. It is based on the English Revised Version.

When we look into our ordinary versions, we cannot see the lyrics, epics, dramas, essays, sonnets, and treatises as in other great literatures of the world. Instead, we see a monotonous uniformity of numbered sentences, more suggestive of an itemized legal instrument than literature.

The most ancient manuscripts could not distinguish verse and prose. In prose, they make no distinctions of sentences and paragraphs. In verse, they make no distinctions of meter. In drama, they do not discriminate speeches nor suggest the names of speakers. Many do not make divisions of words. The scribes, rabbis, and medieval doctors who have intervened between the authors and us can be described as commentators. These preserved the words of Scripture, but they did not consider the literary character. The purpose of this translation is to give assistance in meeting this difficulty. The spirit of this work is bounded by the idea of literature.

TWO SAMPLE EXTRACTS
In the beginning God created the heaven and the earth. And the earth was waste and void; and darkness was upon the face of the deep: and the spirit of God moved upon the face of the waters.

Genesis 1: 1,2

IN THE BEGINNING WAS THE WORD: AND THE WORD WAS WITH GOD: AND THE WORD WAS GOD. The same was in the beginning with God. All things were made through him, and without him was not anything made.

John 1: 1–3

Moffatt New Translation

Date of publication: 1922

A DESCRIPTION TAKEN FROM THE
VERSION ITSELF
The aim of the translator, James Moffatt, a doctor of divinity, was to present the Old and New Testaments in effective, intelligible English. No translation of an ancient classic can be quite intelligible unless the reader is sufficiently acquainted with its environment to understand some of its flying allusions and characteristic metaphors. The translator felt that ought to be done at the present day to offer the unlearned a transcript of the biblical literature as it lies in the light thrown upon it by modern research. A real translation is in the main an

interpretation. To the best of his ability he has tried to be exact and idiomatic.

Some Hebrew terms have no English equivalent which corresponds to the original meaning. Something is dropped if they pass from Hebrew to English. The Tetragrammaton is rendered "the Eternal," except in an enigmatic title like "the Lord of Hosts," although the translator would have preferred to use "Yahweh."

The text used for the New Testament was that of H. von Soden, whose critical edition of the Greek New Testament based upon unprecedented researches, appeared during the first decade of the twentieth century.

TWO SAMPLE EXTRACTS
When God began to form the universe, the world was void and vacant, darkness lay over the abyss; but the spirit of God was hovering over the waters, ...

Genesis 1: 1,2

The Logos existed in the very beginning,
   the Logos was with God,
   the Logos was divine.
He was with God in the very beginning:
   through him all existence came into being,
   no existence came into being apart from him.

John 1: 1–3

New American Bible
Date of publication: 1987

A DESCRIPTION TAKEN FROM THE VERSION ITSELF
In 1944, the Catholic Bible Association of America was requested to produce a completely new translation of the Bible from the original languages and to present the sense of biblical text as accurately as possible. The Old Testament was first published in a series of four volumes. The New Testament was completed in 1970, resulting in the New American Bible. It has widespread use by American Catholic people in public worship.

Further advances in biblical scholarship and identification of pastoral needs brought about a revision of the New Testament in 1986. This fulfilled the need for greater consistency of vocabulary, and provision of more abundant and upgraded explanatory material. Scholars from other Christian churches collaborated in preparing this version.

TWO SAMPLE EXTRACTS
In the beginning, when God created the heavens and the earth, the earth was a formless wasteland, and darkness covered the abyss, while a mighty wind swept over the waters.

Genesis 1: 1,2

In the beginning was the Word, and the Word was with God, and the Word was God. He was in the beginning with God. All things came to be through him, and without him nothing came to be.

John 1: 1–3

Description of some of the major Bible translations (11)

New American Standard Version

Date of publication: 1977

A DESCRIPTION TAKEN FROM THE VERSION ITSELF

The purposes were, first, to adhere as closely as possible to the original languages of the Holy Scripture and, secondly, to make the translation in a fluent and readable style according to current English usage.

The King James Version is the basis for the English Revised Version (New Testament, 1881; Old Testament, 1885). The American Standard Version (1901) is the American counterpart. The American Standard Version is the basis for the New American Standard Version, started in 1959. There was an attempt to preserve the qualities of scholarship and accuracy of the American Standard Version. Decisions about English renderings were made by a team of educators and pastors. A review and an evaluation were made by other Hebrew and Greek scholars.

The aids used were as follows: the latest edition of Biblia Hebraica; recent light from lexicography, cognate languages, and Dead Sea Scrolls; and the twenty-third edition of Novum Testamentum Graece. "Elohim" was translated to God; "Adonai" to Lord; and "YHWH" to Lord usually, but to God when it appears with "Adonai."

Footnotes are used only for clarification. Thou, thee, and thy are used only when addressing Deity. Personal pronouns for Deity are capitalized. In the New Testament, small capitals are used to indicate quotations from the Old Testament or allusions to Old Testament texts.

TWO SAMPLE EXTRACTS

In the beginning God created the heavens and the earth.
And the earth was formless and void, and darkness was over the surface of the deep; and the Spirit of God was moving over the surface of the waters.

Genesis 1: 1,2

In the beginning was the Word, and the Word was with God, and the Word was God.
He was in the beginning with God.
All things came into being by Him, and apart from Him nothing came into being that has come into being.

John 1: 1–3

New Berkeley Version

Date of publication: 1969

A DESCRIPTION TAKEN FROM THE VERSION ITSELF

This version of the New Testament (1945) has gained for Dr. Gerrit Verkuyl a place among the first rank of translators of the Bible into modern English. This version of the Old Testament (1959) under his editorship, exhibits the same characteristics of faithful rendering of the original texts into lively modern English that mark his New Testament.

The aim of this version was to achieve plain, up-to-date expression which reflects as directly as possible the meaning of the Hebrew, Aramaic, and Greek. It is not a paraphrase.

After twenty-five years, the need for revision became evident. This revision was very extensive, while not being a retranslation. Explanatory notes were revised as well as added. Topical headings were rephrased.

TWO SAMPLE EXTRACTS
In the beginning God created the heavens and the earth. The earth was formless and empty, and darkness lay upon the face of the deep, and the Spirit of God was moving over the surface of the waters.

Genesis 1: 1,2

In the beginning was the Word, and the Word was with God, and the Word was God. This is the One who was in the beginning with God. Through Him everything came into being and without Him nothing that exists came into being.

John 1: 1–3

New Century Version

Date of publication: 1987

A DESCRIPTION TAKEN FROM THE VERSION ITSELF
This translation of God's Word was made from the original Hebrew and Greek languages. The translation team was composed of the World Bible Translation Center and fifty additional, highly qualified and experienced Bible scholars and translators. Some had translation experience on the New International, the New American Standard, and the New King James Versions. The third edition of the United Bible Societies' Greek text, the latest edition of Biblia Hebraica and the Septuagint were among texts used.

Several guidelines were used to make the language clear for any reader.

- The Living Word Vocabulary, the standard used by World Book Encyclopedia, was the basis for vocabulary.

- Concepts were put into natural terms – modern measurements and geographical locations.

- Ancient customs were clarified in the text or footnotes.

- Rhetorical questions were stated according to the implied answers.

- Figures of speech and idiomatic expressions were translated according to their meanings.

- Obscure terms were clarified. An attempt was made to choose gender language that would convey the intent of the writers.

- The Tetragrammaton was indicated by putting LORD and GOD in capital letters.

- Hebrew parallelism in poetry and word plays were retained. Images of ancient languages were translated into equivalent English images, where possible.

Description of some of the major Bible translations (12)

TWO SAMPLE EXTRACTS
In the beginning God created the sky and the earth. The earth was empty and had no form. Darkness covered the ocean, and God's Spirit was moving over the water.

Genesis 1: 1,2

In the beginning there was the Word. The Word was with God, and the Word was God. He was with God in the beginning. All things were made by him, and nothing was made without him.

John 1: 1–3

New English Bible

Date of publication: 1970

A DESCRIPTION TAKEN FROM THE VERSION ITSELF
A presbytery in the Church of Scotland in 1946 recommended to the General Assembly that a translation of the Bible be made in the language of the present day because the language in the Authorized Version was archaic and less generally understood.

The General Assembly approached other churches. There was a desire for a completely new translation rather than a revision and that a contemporary idiom rather than a traditional biblical English be used.

It was planned and directed by representatives of the Baptist Union of Great Britain and Ireland, the Church of England, the Church of Scotland, the Congregational Church in England and Wales, the Council of Churches for Wales, the Irish Council of Churches, the London Yearly Meeting of the Society of Friends, the Methodist Church of Great Britain, the Presbyterian Church of England, the British and Foreign Bible Society, and the National Bible Society of Scotland. The Roman Catholic Church in England and Scotland sent representatives as observers. The translating was done by three panels drawn from scholars of British universities to deal, respectively, with the Old Testament, the Apocrypha, and the New Testament. A fourth panel of trusted literary advisers was to scrutinize the translation for English style.

TWO SAMPLE EXTRACTS
In the beginning of creation, when God made heaven and earth, the earth was without form and void, with darkness over the face of the abyss, and a mighty wind that swept over the surface of the waters.

Genesis 1: 1,2

When all things began, the Word already was. The Word dwelt with God, and what God was, the Word was. The Word, then, was with God at the beginning, and through him all things came to be; no single thing was created without him.

John 1: 1–3

New International Version

Date of publication: 1978

A DESCRIPTION TAKEN FROM THE
VERSION ITSELF
This is a completely new translation
of the Holy Bible done by over one
hundred scholars.

It followed several years of
exploratory study by committees from
the Christian Reformed Church and the
National Association of Evangelicals.
There were participants from the
United States, Canada, Australia, and
New Zealand in the translating process.

The denominations included:
Anglican, Assemblies of God, Baptist,
Brethren, Christian Reformed, Church
of Christ, Evangelical Free, Lutheran,
Mennonite, Methodist, Nazarene,
Presbyterian, Wesleyan, and others.

Each book was translated by a
team of scholars. An Intermediate
Editorial Committee revised their
work. A General Editorial Committee
checked it in detail and revised again.
The Committee on Bible Translation
reviewed, revised, then released the
translation for publication.

The goals were that the translation
would be accurate and have clarity
and literary quality so as to be suitable
for reading, teaching, preaching,
memorizing, and liturgical use. A
concern was that the English be
idiomatic but not idiosyncratic,
contemporary but not dated.

Texts used for the Old Testament
included the latest Biblia Hebraica,
Dead Sea Scrolls, Samaritan
Pentateuch, ancient scribal traditions,
Septuagint, Vulgate, Syriac Peshitta,
Targums, Juxta Hebraica, and others.
For the New Testament, the best
current Greek New Testament texts
were used.

The Tetragrammaton is rendered
as LORD, in capital letters. King
James pronouns and verb endings
were considered to be archaic. Poetic
passages are printed as poetry.

TWO SAMPLE EXTRACTS
In the beginning God created the
heavens and the earth. Now the earth
was formless and empty, darkness was
over the surface of the deep, and the
Spirit of God was hovering over the
waters.

Genesis 1: 1,2

In the beginning was the Word, and
the Word was with God, and the Word
was God. He was with God in the
beginning.

Through Him all things were made;
without Him nothing was made that
has been made.

John 1: 1–3

Description of some of the major Bible translations (13)

New Jerusalem Bible

Date of publication: 1985

A DESCRIPTION TAKEN FROM THE
VERSION ITSELF
This translation follows the original
Hebrew, Aramaic, and Greek texts.
For the Old Testament, the Masoretic
Text was used. Only when insuperable
difficulties occurred were the
Septuagint or other versions used.

In the Old Testament, italics indicate
passages found only in the Septuagint.
In the New Testament, italics indicate
quotations from other books of the
Bible. A gap indicates an unintelligible
word or an incomplete sentence in the
original. Brackets in the Old Testament
indicate an addition or an explanation
that is later than the original text.

Many devoted scholars who assisted
in Bible de Jérusalem (1956), the first
English Jerusalem Bible (1966), and
Bible de Jérusalem (revised 1973)
contributed to the New Jerusalem Bible
(1985).

TWO SAMPLE EXTRACTS
In the beginning God created heaven
and earth. Now the earth was a
formless void, there was darkness over
the deep, with a divine wind sweeping
over the waters.

Genesis 1: 1,2

In the beginning was the Word:
  and the Word was with God
  and the Word was God.
He was with God in the beginning.

Through him all things came into
being,
  not one thing came into being except
through him.

John 1: 1–3

New King James Version

Date of publication: 1990

A DESCRIPTION TAKEN FROM THE
VERSION ITSELF
The translators, the committees,
and the editors sought to maintain
the lyrical quality of the King James
Version while being sensitive to the
late twentieth century English idiom
and adhering faithfully to the Hebrew,
Aramaic, and Greek texts. Where
obsolescence and other reading
difficulties existed, present-day
vocabulary, punctuation, and grammar
were integrated. Words representing
ancient objects which have no
modern substitutes were retained.
A special feature is the conformity
to the thought flow of the 1611 Bible.
King James spelling of untranslated
words was retained, but made uniform
throughout. Standard doctrinal and
theological terms were retained.
Pronouns and verb endings no longer
in use were replaced by modern
words. Pronouns referring to God
were capitalized. Frequent use of "and"
was limited, and, where the original
language permitted, replaced by other
words. The format was designed to
enhance vividness and devotional

quality of the Scriptures.

The text used for the Old Testament was the 1967/1977 Stuttgart edition of Biblia Hebraica. There was supplementary use of the 1524/1525 Bomberg edition of Biblia Hebraica, Septuagint, Latin Vulgate, and Dead Sea Scrolls.

The New Testament was based on the traditional text of Greek-speaking churches, first published in 1516 and later referred to as the Received Text. It is the fifth revision of the New Testament translated from specific Greek texts.

TWO SAMPLE EXTRACTS
In the beginning God created the heavens and the earth. The earth was without form, and void; and darkness was on the face of the deep. And the Spirit of God was hovering over the face of the waters.

Genesis 1: 1,2

In the beginning was the Word, and the Word was with God, and the Word was God. He was in the beginning with God. All things were made through Him, and without Him nothing was made that was made.

John 1: 1–3

New Life Version

Date of publication: 1969

A DESCRIPTION TAKEN FROM THE VERSION ITSELF
The idea of a readable, but accurate, version of the Bible came to Gleason and Kathryn Ledyard as they worked in the Canadian Arctic with Eskimos who were starting to learn English. It was hoped that such a version would be useful wherever English is used as a second language.

For the most part, the words in this limited vocabulary edition have only one meaning. Difficult biblical words were broken down into simple, meaningful phrases. The use of today's street language and of paraphrasing were not considered. The wording and beauty of older versions were kept in many places.

The first copies of the Scriptures were considered to be perfect and without error. Because of language changes and the translation from one language to another, no version can claim the same perfection.

TWO SAMPLE EXTRACTS
In the beginning God made from nothing the heavens and the earth. The earth was an empty waste and darkness was over the deep waters. And the Spirit of God was moving over the top of the waters.

Genesis 1: 1,2

The Word (Christ) was in the beginning. The Word was with God. The Word was God. He was with God in the beginning. He made all things. Nothing was made without Him making it.

John 1: 1–3

Description of some of the major Bible translations (14)

New Living Translation

Date of publication: 1996

A DESCRIPTION TAKEN FROM THE
VERSION ITSELF

Ninety evangelical scholars from various theological backgrounds and denominations spent seven years in revising the New Living Bible. This version is based on the most recent scholarship in the theory of translation. Entire thoughts, rather than just words, were translated into natural, everyday English. Thus, this is a dynamic-equivalence translation. Three scholars were assigned to a portion of Scripture, usually one or two books. One general reviewer was assigned to each of the six groups of books.

The text used for the Old Testament was Biblia Hebraica Stuttgartensia (1977), along with such aids as The Dead Sea Scrolls, The Septuagint, other Greek manuscripts, The Samaritan Pentateuch, The Syriac Peshitta, The Latin Vulgate, and others. The texts for the New Testament were the Greek New Testament, published by the United Bible Societies (1977), and Novum Testamentum Graece, edited by Nestle and Aland (1993).

There was an attempt to use a gender-neutral rendering where the text applies generally to human beings or to the human condition. El, elohim, and eloah have been translated as "God." YHWH has been translated as "the LORD." Adonai has been translated "Lord."

TWO SAMPLE EXTRACTS

In the beginning God created the heavens and the earth. The earth was empty, a formless mass cloaked in darkness. And the Spirit of God was hovering over its surface.

Genesis 1: 1,2

In the beginning the Word already existed. He was with God, and he was God. He was in the beginning with God. He created everything there is. Nothing exists that he didn't make.

John 1: 1–3

New Revised Standard Version

Date of publication: 1989

A DESCRIPTION TAKEN FROM THE
VERSION ITSELF

This is the authorized revision of the Revised Standard Version (1952). A committee of about thirty members of various Protestant denominations and the Roman Catholic Church participated. Eastern Orthodox and Jewish representatives were members of the Old Testament section.

Since the publication of the Revised Standard Version, there have been advances made in the discovery and interpretation of documents in the Semitic languages. The Dead Sea Scrolls provided information on the Books of Isaiah and Habakkuk and fragments on the other books of the Old Testament. Greek manuscript copies of books of the New Testament also became available. Thus, authorization was given for revision of the entire Revised Standard Version of the Bible.

For the Old Testament, the 1977 edition of Biblia Hebraica Stuttgartensia was used. For the New Testament, the 1966 edition of The Greek New Testament was used.

Occasionally, it was necessary to make changes. Footnotes indicate how other ancient authorities read. The style of English used reflects current usage. Masculine-oriented language has been eliminated, where possible. The Tetragrammaton is rendered as LORD and GOD, in capital letters. Archaic English pronouns and verb endings are not used. Essentially, it is a literal translation, but it has a few paraphrastic renderings.

TWO SAMPLE EXTRACTS

In the beginning when God created the heavens and the earth, the earth was a formless void and darkness covered the face of the deep, while a wind from God swept over the face of the waters.

Genesis 1: 1,2

In the beginning was the Word, and the Word was with God, and the Word was God. He was in the beginning with God. All things came into being through him, and without him not one thing came into being.

John 1: 1–3

Revised English Bible

Date of publication: 1989

A DESCRIPTION TAKEN FROM THE VERSION ITSELF

In 1974, the Joint Committee of the Churches, which had produced the New English Bible, decided to begin a major revision of the text. By this time, there were changes in the composition of the Joint Committee. The Roman Catholic Church, with representatives from the hierarchies of England and Wales, of Scotland, and of Ireland, entered into full membership. The United Reformed Church, which was a recent union of the Presbyterian Church of England and the Congregational Church, was represented. Then representatives of the Salvation Army and the Moravian Church joined the committee.

The best available texts of both Testaments were used. Care was taken to ensure that the style of English used be fluent and of dignity for liturgical use, while maintaining intelligibility for all ages and backgrounds. Complex or technical terms were avoided, where possible. There was care that sentence structure and word order would facilitate congregational reading, without misrepresenting the meaning of the original text. "Thou" in addressing God has been replaced by you. A more inclusive gender reference than the male-oriented language was preferred. A more extensive use of textual sub-headings in italics has been used. These are not to be considered part of the text.

Description of some of the major Bible translations (15)

A DESCRIPTION TAKEN FROM THE
VERSION ITSELF, CONTINUED
The traditional verse numbering of the Authorized Version has been retained.

Passages that appear in the manuscripts used for the Authorized Version but left out of the Revised English Bible have been reproduced in footnotes. Some modern equivalents of ancient terms are used.

The publishers consider the Revised English Bible to be a radical revision of the New English Bible.

TWO SAMPLE EXTRACTS
In the beginning God created the heavens and the earth. The earth was a vast waste, darkness covered the deep, and the Spirit of God hovered over the surface of the water.

Genesis 1: 1,2

In the beginning the Word already was. The Word was in God's presence, and what God was, the Word was. He was with God at the beginning, and through him all things came to be; without him no created thing came into being.

John 1: 1–3

Revised Standard Version

Date of publication: 1952

A DESCRIPTION TAKEN FROM THE
VERSION ITSELF
This is the authorized revision of the American Standard Version (1901), a variant of the (British) Revised Version

(1881–1885), which was a revision of the King James Version (1611), which took into account several earlier versions. The King James Version has been termed "the noblest monument of English prose," yet it has grave defects. This was brought to light in the nineteenth century when more ancient manuscripts than those used for the King James Version were found.

The directive was that the revision should embody the best results of modern scholarship as to the meaning of the Scriptures and to express this meaning in English diction which is designed for use in private and public worship and preserves those qualities which have given to the King James Version a supreme place in English literature. Thirty-two scholars worked on the revision. Fifty representatives of cooperating denominations reviewed their work and counseled them. The aim was to make a good translation better.

Changes in the English language since 1611 were the main reason for revision. Except for the Dead Sea Scrolls, only late manuscripts of the Old Testament survive. This revision is based on Hebrew and Aramaic texts fixed early in the Christian era and revised by the Masoretes.

The Tetragrammaton was rendered as LORD or GOD, in capital letters.

TWO SAMPLE EXTRACTS
In the beginning God created the heavens and the earth. The earth was

without form and void, and darkness was upon the face of the deep; and the Spirit of God was moving over the face of the waters.

Genesis 1: 1,2

In the beginning was the Word, and the Word was with God, and the Word was God. He was in the beginning with God; all things were made through him, and without him was not anything made that was made.

John 1: 1–3

Sacred Scriptures, The, Bethel Edition

Date of publication: 1981

A DESCRIPTION TAKEN FROM THE VERSION ITSELF
This translation is based on the American Standard, 1901.

It is important to have the reader personally realize that the Tetragrammaton is of vital importance if one is to comprehend the distinctive flavor of the original text. The term "Lord" is not a name, but a title which cannot represent the unique word that stands for the Name of the Almighty. The form "Jehovah" originated as a corruption by the scribes who introduced foreign vowel points and attached them to the Tetragrammaton. The vowel points were those of the word "Adonai." The English hybrid "Jehovah" resulted when Peter Gallatin in 1520 published this form. He did not understand what the scribes had done in applying these vowel points so that the reader would pronounce "Adonai"

instead of "Yahweh." The Talmud explains that the Name of the Almighty is written "Yah," but pronounced "Adonai."

Although several Bible translations have retained the name "Yahweh" in the Old Testament, no Bible translation has restored all of the sacred titles to an accurate text. No translation has accurately restored the Name "Yahweh" to the New Testament.

Since the Assemblies of Yahweh have a singular desire to learn the truth of the Bible and to obey it, they have sought to go back to the source to find a proper transliteration of the Messiah's Name which He bore when He was on the earth. They have restored the Sacred Name and the sacred titles and the Name of Yahshua to the text.

TWO SAMPLE EXTRACTS
In the beginning Elohim created the heavens and the earth. And the earth had become waste and void; and darkness was upon the face of the deep; and the Spirit of Elohim moved upon the face of the waters.

Genesis 1: 1,2

In the beginning was the Word, and the Word was with Yahweh, and the Word was Elohim. The same was in the beginning with Yahweh. All things were made through him; and without him was not anything made that has been made.

John 1: 1–3

Description of some of the major Bible translations (16)

Scriptures, The (ISR)

Date of publication: 1998

A DESCRIPTION TAKEN FROM THE
VERSION ITSELF
There are four purposes for this
translation:

- To restore the Name of the Almighty
  to its rightful place in the text;
- To be recognizably Messianic in that
  it affirms the Hebraic roots of the
  Messianic belief;
- To restore the meaning to so many
  words which have become popular
  to use, but do not accurately reflect
  the meaning of the original, e.g.,
  church, glory, holy, sacrifice, soul;
- To be as far as possible a literal
  translation, wherever possible
  rendering key words uniformly.

The titles of the books are
transliterations of the names of the
books of the Old Covenant and, where
appropriate, likewise, of those of the
New covenant. The order of the Old
Covenant is the traditional Hebraic
order of the Tanakh.

The Old Covenant is based on the
Masoretic Hebrew and Aramaic text,
according to the 1937 edition of Kittel's
Biblia Hebraica. The New Covenant is
based on the Textus Receptus, being
modified with the use of such other
texts as the Nestle-Aland and Shem
Tob, as seemed appropriate.

TWO SAMPLE EXTRACTS
In the beginning Elohim created the
heavens and the earth.

And the earth came to be formless
and empty, and darkness was on the
face of the deep. And the Spirit of
Elohim was moving on the face of the
waters.

In the beginning Elohim created the
heavens and the earth.

Genesis 1: 1,2

In the beginning was the Word, and the
Word was with Elohim, and the Word
was Elohim.

He was in the beginning with Elohim.

All came to be through Him, and
without Him not even one came to be
that came to be.

John 1: 1–3

Standard American Edition, Revised Version

Date of publication: 1901

A DESCRIPTION TAKEN FROM THE
VERSION ITSELF
This is a revised version of the *KJV*
of 1611, completed in 1881–1885 and
newly edited by the American Revision
Committee in 1901.

In the course of the joint labors of
the English and American revisers, it
was agreed that the English should
have the decisive vote on points
of difference as they had initiated
the work. However, the American
preferences would be published as an
Appendix for the following fourteen
years. The Americans agreed not to
sanction any editions other than those
of the University Presses of England

during that period. After completing their work in 1885, the English revisers disbanded, but the American revisers decided to continue their organization.

In 1897, the American Revision Committee began work to issue an edition with the American preferences. This proved to be an elaborate task and could not be done until the Appendix was revised for fullness and accuracy. Then, they felt free to go beyond revising the Appendix and to introduce a text that included what had previously been suppressed. This edition contains a number of variations from the original Revised Version.

TWO SAMPLE EXTRACTS
In the beginning God created the heavens and the earth. And the earth was waste and void; and darkness was upon the face of the deep: and the Spirit of God moved upon the face of the waters.

Genesis 1: 1,2

In the beginning was the Word, and the Word was with God, and the Word was God. The same was in the beginning with God. All things were made through him; and without him was not anything made that hath been made.

John 1: 1–3

Today's English Version (The Good News Bible)

Date of publication: 1976

A DESCRIPTION TAKEN FROM THE VERSION ITSELF
It is a new translation which seeks to state clearly and accurately the meaning of the original texts in words and forms that are widely accepted by people who use English as a language. It attempts to set forth the biblical content and message in a standard, everyday, natural form of English.

The basic text used for the Old Testament was the Masoretic Text in the third edition of Biblica Hebraica. Other ancient versions (Greek, Syraic, Latin) were also used at times. The basic text used for the New Testament was The Greek New Testament, although other Greek manuscripts were also used.

The first task was to understand correctly the meaning of the original. The next task was to express that meaning in a manner and a form easily understood by readers.

The Tetragrammaton is translated as LORD, in capitals.

TWO SAMPLE EXTRACTS
In the beginning, when God created the universe, the earth was formless and desolate. The raging ocean that covered everything was engulfed in total darkness, and the power of God was moving over the water.

Genesis 1: 1,2

Before the world was created, the Word already existed; he was with God, and he was the same as God. From the very beginning the Word was with God. Through him God made all things; not one thing in all creation was made without him.

John 1: 1–3

Description of some of the major Bible translations (17)

World English Bible

Date of publication: 2004

A DESCRIPTION OF THE VERSION
The World English Bible is a Modern English update of the American Standard Version of 1901. The translation is in the Public Domain and is available to download freely from the Internet.

TWO SAMPLE EXTRACTS
In the beginning God created the heavens and the earth. Now the earth was formless and empty. Darkness was on the surface of the deep. God's Spirit was hovering over the surface of the waters.

Genesis 1: 1,2

That which was from the beginning, that which we have heard, that which we have seen with our eyes, that which we saw, and our hands touched, concerning the Word of life (and the life was revealed, and we have seen, and testify, and declare to you the life, the eternal life, which was with the Father, and was revealed to us); that which we have seen and heard we declare to you, that you also may have fellowship with us. Yes, and our fellowship is with the Father, and with his Son, Jesus Christ.

John 1: 1–3

William Tyndale Translation

Date of publication: 1530

TWO SAMPLE EXTRACTS
In the begynnynge God created heaven and erth. The erth was voyde and emptie, and darcknesse was vpon the depe, an the spirite of god moved vpon the water ... .

Genesis 1: 1,2

In the beginnynge was the worde, and the worde was with God: and the worde was God. The same was in the beginnynge with God. All thinges were made by it, and with out it, was made nothinge, that was made.

John 1: 1–3

Young's Literal Translation, Revised Edition

Date of publication: 1898

A DESCRIPTION TAKEN FROM THE VERSION ITSELF
The translation of the New Testament is based upon the belief that every word of the original is "God-breathed." (See 2 Timothy 3: 16 and 2 Peter 3: 15,16.) This inspiration extends only to the original text and not to any translation ever made by man.

A strictly literal rendering may not be as pleasant to the ear, yet truth is what ought to be sought. The translations available at the time that this one was published had frequent departures from the original. The meaning of what the writers did write was being replaced by what they ought to have written.

The Greek text used is the Received Text. A literal text was considered to be indispensable.

TWO SAMPLE EXTRACTS

In the beginning of God's preparing the heavens and the earth – the earth hath existed waste and void, and darkness is on the face of the deep, and the Spirit of God fluttering on the face of the waters.

Genesis 1: 1,2

In the beginning was the Word, and the Word was with God; and the Word was God; this one was in the beginning with God; all things through him did happen, and without him happened not even one thing that hath happened.

John 1: 1–3

List of some of the major Bible translations

TAB Abbreviated Bible, The
AAT American Translation, An (Beck)
SGAT American Translation, An (Smith-Goodspeed)
AB Amplified Bible
TBB Basic Bible, The
BDRL Bible Designed to Be Read as Literature, The
TBR Bible Reader, The
CCDT Confraternity of Christian Doctrine Translation
CEV Contemporary English Version
TCB Coverdale Bible, The
DHB Darby Holy Bible
DRB Douai-Rheims Bible
EBR Emphasized Bible, The
ESV English Standard Version
EVD English Version for the Deaf (Easy-to-Read Version)
TGB Geneva Bible, The

GW God's Word (Today's Bible Translation)
HBME Holy Bible in Modern English, The
HBRV Holy Bible, Revised Version
AIV Inclusive Version, An
IB Interlinear Bible (Greene)
TJB Jerusalem Bible, The
KJV King James Version (Authorized Version)
KTC Knox Translation
LBP Lamsa Bible
LB Living Bible
TM Message, The
MRB Modern Reader's Bible
MNT Moffatt New Translation
NAB New American Bible
NAS New American Standard Version
NBV New Berkeley Version
NCV New Century Version
NEB New English Bible
NIV New International Version
NJB New Jerusalem Bible
NKJ New King James Version
NLV New Life Version
NLT New Living Translation
NRS New Revised Standard Version
REB Revised English Bible
RSV Revised Standard Version
SSBE Sacred Scriptures, The, Bethel Edition
SISR Scriptures, The (ISR)
SBK Shorter Bible, The
SARV Standard American Edition, Revised Version
TEV Today's English Version (The Good News Bible)
WEB World English Bible
WTT William Tyndale Translation
YLR Young's Literal Translation, Revised Edition

Bibles printed with errors (1)

Bibles of the sects

The New World Translation is the Watch Tower (Jehovah's Witnesses) Bible.

The Inspired Version is the Bible of the Latter Day Saints Church, the Mormons.

Errors printed in Bibles

Some Bibles have been given special names because of a typographical error or peculiarity of vocabulary.

• The "Bug" Bible
• The "Placemakers" Bible
• The "Treacle" Bible
• The "He" Bible
• The "Repetitive" Bible
• The "Basketball" Bible
• The "Mistaken Identity" Bible
• Other misprints in the 1611 *KJV*
• The "Wicked" Bible
• The "More Sea" Bible
• The "Unrighteous" Bible
• The "Printer's" Bible
• The "Sin On" Bible

The "Bug" Bible

The Coverdale Bible of 1535 has been called the "Bug" Bible because of its translation of Psalm 91: 5: "Thou shalt not need to be afrayd for eny bugges by night."

The "Placemakers" Bible

The second edition of the Geneva Bible, published in 1562 has been given the name the "Placemakers" Bible because it printed: "Blessed are the placemakers" instead of "peacemakers" in Matthew 5: 9.

The "Treacle" Bile

The Bishop's Bible of 1568 was also known as the "Treacle" Bible on account of Jeremiah 8: 22 being printed: "Is there no tryacle in Gilead?" instead of "Is there no balm in Gilead?"

The "He" Bible

The first edition of the *KJV* is often called the "He" Bible because of the printing error that occurred at Ruth 3: 15. Here, it reads "he went into the city" instead of "she went into the city." The corrected edition is sometimes referred to as the "She" Bible.

The "Repetitive" Bible

The 1611 King James Version duplicates part of Exodus 14: 10 so that the following was printed: "And when Pharaoh drew nigh, the children of Israel lifted up their eyes, and, behold, the Egyptians marched after them; and they were sore afraid: the children of Israel lifted up their eyes, and, behold, the Egyptians marched after them; and they were sore afraid: and the children of Israel cried out unto the Lord." [Exodus 14: 10] Today's versions now correctly read: "And when Pharaoh drew nigh, the children of Israel lifted up their eyes, and, behold, the Egyptians marched after them; and they were sore afraid: and the children of Israel cried out unto the Lord." [Exodus 14: 10]

The "Basketball Bible"

The very first edition of the Authorized Version is the "Basketball" Bible because it speaks of "hoopes" instead of "hookes," Exodus 38: 11, which were used in the construction of the Tabernacle.

The "Mistaken Identity" Bible

More than one edition of the *KJV* was printed in 1611. The first printing of the 1611 edition of the King James Version, correctly prints Matthew 26: 36 as: "Then cometh Jesus with them unto a place called Gethsemane…" However, in the second printing of the 1611 edition Matthew 26: 36 now reads: "Then cometh Judas with them unto a place called Gethsemane…"

Other misprints in the 1611 *KJV*

Other misprints in the 1611 edition included:

Leviticus 13: 56, where "the plaine be" was printed instead of "the plague be."

In Ezra 3: 5 the printer repeated the word "offered."

The running head over the fourth chapter of Micah reads "Joel" instead of its correct name of Micah.

"He" is used instead of "ye" in Ezekiel 6: 8.

In Ezekiel 24: 7, the text should read, "She poured it not upon the ground." It was printed without the word "not."

The "Wicked" Bible

In a 1631 edition of the King James Bible, in Exodus 20 verse 14, the word "not" was left out. This changed the 7th commandment to read, "Thou shalt commit adultery." Most of the copies were recalled immediately and destroyed on the orders of Charles I. But there are 11 copies still remaining. They are known as the "Wicked" Bible. The Bible museum in Branson, Missouri, has one copy of the "Wicked Bible". The printer was fined heavily for his mistake. The "Wicked" Bible is also known as the "Adulterous" Bible.

The "More Sea" Bible

The 1641 edition of the *KJV* printed Revelation 21: 1 as: "the first heaven and the first earth were passed away and there was more sea," instead of "…there was no more sea."

The "Unrighteous" Bible

The word "not" was also left out in the 1653 edition of 1 Corinthians 6: 9 which was printed: "Know ye not that the unrighteous shall inherit the kingdom of God" instead of "Know ye not that the unrighteous shall not inherit the kingdom of God."

The "Printer's" Bible

In a 1702 edition of the Bible Psalm 119: 161 substituted the word "printers" for "princes" to give the phrase: "printers have persecuted me."

The "Sin On" Bible

In the 1716 King James Version John 8: 11 should read: "Go, and sin no more." However, the printer accidentally inverted the "n" and the "o" in the word "on," so it read, "Go and sin on more."

Bibles printed with errors (2)

- The "Vinegar" Bible
- The "Sting" Bible
- The "Fool" Bible
- The "Denial" Bible
- The "Murderer's" Bible
- The "Lions" Bible
- The "To Remain" Bible
- The "Discharge" Bible
- The "Standing Fishes" Bible
- The "Idle Shepherd" Bible
- The "Ears to Ear Bible"
- The "Wife-hater" Bible
- The "Large Family" Bible
- The "Camels" Bible

The "Vinegar" Bible

The heading in Luke 20 of the 1717 version of the Bible is printed "Parable of the Vinegar" instead of " Parable of the Vineyard."

The "Sting" Bible

At Mark 7: 35 a 1746 edition of the KJV printed: "And straightway his ears were opened, and the sting of his tongue was loosed, and he spake plain" instead of: "And straightway his ears were opened, and the string of his tongue was loosed, and he spake plain."

The "Fool" Bible

The printer of the 1763 KJV was ordered to pay £3,000 for his inadvertent printer's error which he made in Psalm 14: 1. There he printed: "the fool hath said in his heart there is a God," instead of: "the fool hath said in his heart there is no God." As soon as this error was spotted all copies of this Bible were suppressed.

The "Denial" Bible

In the so-called "Denial" Bible, an edition of the KJV printed in 1792, the name Philip is substituted for Peter as the apostle who would deny Jesus in Luke 22: 34.

The "Murderer's" Bible

In 1801, the following two errors crept into a printed Bible.

Jude 1: 16 should read, "These are murmurers, complainers." But the "Murderer's" Bible reads: "these are murderers."

Mark 7: 27 should read: "But Jesus said unto her, Let the children first be filled: for it is not meet to take the children's bread, and to cast it unto the dogs." Instead of "Let the children first be filled," the "Murderer's" Bible read, "let the children first be killed."

The "Lions" Bible

The 1804 KJV edition became known as the "Lions" Bible on account of one of its two memorable printer's errors. In 1 Kings 8: 19 it printed: "…but thy son that shall come forth out of thy lions…" instead of "but thy son that shall come forth out of thy loins."

The other error in this Bible occurs at Numbers 35: 18. This verse inadvertently read: "The murderer shall surely be put together" instead of "the murderer shall surely be put to death."

The "To Remain" Bible

The 1805 edition of the KJV has the words "to remain" inserted in the middle of Galatians 4: 29: "he that was born after the flesh persecuted him that was born after the Spirit to remain, even so it is now." A proofreader queried the comma after the words "the Spirit". The editor penciled in the words "to remain" and the printed version included those two words in the verse.

The "Discharge" Bible

In 1 Timothy 5: 2, the "Discharge" Bible, the KJV printed in 1806, reads: "I discharge thee... that thou observe these things," instead of "I charge thee."

The "Standing Fishes" Bible

The 1806 KJV is also known as the "Standing Fishes" Bible because at Ezekiel 47: 10 it printed: "And it shall come to pass, that the fishes shall stand upon it" instead of " And it shall come to pass, that the fishers shall stand upon it."

The "Idle Shepherd" Bible

The 1809 KJV edition replaces the sentence in Zechariah 11: 17: "Woe to the idol shepherd that leaveth the flock!" with the phrase: "Woe to the idle shepherd that leaveth the flock!"

The "Ears to Ear" Bible

The 1810 edition of the KJV prints Matthew 13: 43 as: "Who hath ears to ear, let him hear," instead of: "Who hath ears to hear, let him hear."

The "Wife-hater" Bible

The 1810 Bible is also known as the "Wife-hater" Bible because at Luke 14: 26 it reads: "If any man come to me, and hate not his father, and mother, and wife, and children, and brethren, and sisters, yea, and his own wife also, he cannot be my disciple," instead of "his own life."

The "Large Family" Bible

The 1820 edition of the KJV became known as the "Large Family" Bible because at Isaiah 66: 9 it printed: "Shall I bring to the birth, and not cease to bring forth?" instead of "Shall I bring to the birth, and not cause to bring forth?"

The "Camels" Bible

At Genesis 24: 61 the 1823 edition of the KJV printed, "Rebekah arose, and her camels," instead of "Rebekah arose, and her damsels."

Famous Bibles

The Gutenberg Bible

The first book that Johannes Gutenberg printed in 1454 was the Bible. It is thought that he printed about 180 copies, known as the 42–line Bible, of which significant parts of 48 copies still survive. Gutenberg did not make any printing errors.

The Thumb Bible

The Thumb Bible, printed in 1670, was one inch square and half an inch thick. It could be read only with a magnifying glass.

Methodology used in Bible translations (1)

Types of Bible translation

There are two basic philosophies or styles of translation which go under the names of "formal correspondence" and "dynamic equivalence." Some of the most popular versions of the Bible in English are, strictly speaking, not translations but are paraphrases.

1 Formal equivalence

Formal equivalence, also known as a literal translation, is where the translator tries to render the exact words of the original language.

These versions sometimes claim to be the most accurate translation because they are the most literal translation. While they are ideal for personal Bible study they sometimes fail to communicate very well when read aloud.

This is characterized as being a word-for-word translation.

An example of a word-for-word version is the *NASB*.

2 Dynamic equivalence

Dynamic (or functional) equivalence, is where the translator attempts to render the natural equivalent of the source language.

These translations do not always follow the exact wording or word-order of the Hebrew or Greek originals. While these translations are less literal than the formal correspondence translations they are not necessarily any less accurate.

This is characterized as being a thought-for-thought translation.

An example of a thought-for-thought version is the *NIV*.

Literal translations

It is true that a literal translation may be "closest" to the words of the original text. But that does not necessarily make it the "best" translation.

TWO EXAMPLES
Here are two examples of literal translations which are not the most helpful translations.

Chokwe

In Luke 18: 13, a man "beat his breast in remorse."

In Chokwe (a West Zambian language) this means to congratulate yourself which is the opposite of what Jesus meant.

Therefore, in the Chokwe Bible, the phrase "beat his breast" has been translated "beat his brow," which carries the idea of remorse.

This is not a literal translation, but a "thought-for-thought" translation.

Philippines

In the Philippines, repeating a word shows you are not sure.

So when Jesus said "Truly, truly . . . ", this would mean "I'm not sure of what I am about to say" instead of "I really mean this and want you to listen."

Again, a literal translation is not the best.

Paraphrase

Many Bible versions which are published are, strictly speaking, paraphrases and not Bible translations.

ADVANTAGES
Paraphrases have the great advantage that they are often much easier to understand than translations.

DISADVANTAGE
They are not, however, as accurate as Bible translations.

An example of a paraphrase version of the Bible is the LB.

Paraphrases often succeed in communicating the basic message of a sentence in a new and fresh way that more traditional translations do not.

Here are two versions of 1 Corinthians 16: 23.

"The grace of our Lord Jesus Christ be with you."

KJV

"Our Master Jesus has his arms wide open for you."

The Message

The KJV has the advantage of being an accurate translation, but The Message, while not being an accurate translation, conveys the sense of the verse in a fresh and invigorating way.

Psalm 23 in three contrasting versions

Comparing Psalm 23 in the
• NIV,
• NASB, and
• The Message
shows how the different Bible versions set about their work of translation.

PSALM 23 IN THE NIV
A psalm of David.

1 The Lord is my shepherd, I shall not be in want.

2 He makes me lie down in green pastures,
   he leads me beside quiet waters,

3 he restores my soul.
   He guides me in paths of righteousness
   for his name's sake.

4 Even though I walk
   through the valley of the shadow of death, [1]
   I will fear no evil,
   for you are with me;
   your rod and your staff,
   they comfort me.

5 You prepare a table before me
   in the presence of my enemies.
   You anoint my head with oil;
   my cup overflows.

6 Surely goodness and love will follow me
   all the days of my life,
   and I will dwell in the house of the Lord
   forever.

Footnote
[1] Or through the darkest valley

Methodology used in Bible translations (2)

Psalm 23 in three contrasting versions, continued

PSALM 23 IN THE *NASB*

A Psalm of David.

1 The Lord is my shepherd,
I shall not want.

2 He makes me lie down in green pastures;
He leads me beside quiet waters.

3 He restores my soul;
He guides me in the paths of righteousness
For His name's sake.

4 Even though I walk through the [1] valley of the shadow of death,
I fear no [2] evil, for You are with me;
Your rod and Your staff, they comfort me.

5 You prepare a table before me in the presence of my enemies;
You have anointed my head with oil;
My cup overflows.

6 Surely goodness and lovingkindness will follow me all the days of my life,
And I will [3] dwell in the house of the Lord forever.

Footnotes

[1] Or valley of deep darkness
[2] Or harm
[3] Another reading is return to

PSALM 23 IN *THE MESSAGE*

A David psalm

1 GOD, my shepherd! I don't need a thing.

2 You have bedded me down in lush meadows,
you find me quiet pools to drink from.

3 True to your word,
you let me catch my breath
and send me in the right direction.

4 Even when the way goes through Death Valley,
I'm not afraid
when you walk at my side.
Your trusty shepherd's crook
makes me feel secure.

5 You serve me a six-course dinner
right in front of my enemies.
You revive my drooping head;
my cup brims with blessing.

6 Your beauty and love chase after me
every day of my life.
I'm back home in the house of GOD
for the rest of my life.

Translations grouped by their translation philosophy

Many translations do not fit neatly into the two major methods of translation. For example, The Amplified Bible could be put into both or neither of such categories, as it amplifies the text by adding extra words and phrases.

Formal correspondence translations

- Douai-Rheims
- *KJV/NKJV*
- *RSV/NRSV*
- *NAB*
- *NIV*

Dynamic equivalence translations

- *NEB/REB*
- *TEV/CEV*
- *JB/NJB*

Bible manuscripts

In 1611 the translators of the *KJV* had fewer than twenty main Bible manuscripts to work from. We do not possess any original manuscripts written by the authors of the Bible books. All the manuscripts we now have are copies and copies of copies. This opens the door to inadvertent copying errors creeping in.

Textus Receptus

One of the earliest attempts to overcome this problem was the publication of the Received Text, (Textus Receptus.) The Textus Receptus is a printed Greek New Testament that provided the textual base for Bible translations in the time of the Reformation.

Erasmus edited this and it was printed in 1520. For this New Testament text Erasmus gathered together five Greek manuscripts he located in Basle,

the majority of which went back to the 12th century. Erasmus published two other revised editions, in 1527 and 1535. Erasmus' Greek text became the standard in the field. The *KJV* translators used the Textus Receptus.

However, since 1611 scores of Bible manuscripts have been discovered and so the Textus Receptus is no longer as up to date as it was when it was first compiled in 1520. The Textus Receptus became the dominant Greek text of the New Testament for the following two hundred and fifty years, until the publication of the Westcott and Hort Greek New Testament in 1881.

IMPROVED TRANSLATIONS

New Bible translations which use the most up to date and most accurate manuscripts have the opportunity of throwing new light on some obscure words or verses and should, in this sense, improve previous translations.

Bible facts confirmed by archaeologists

Overview

Christians who believe in the historical accuracy of the Old Testament and the New Testament have had this conviction confirmed again and again thanks to the archaeological finds over the past 200 years.

Modern archaeological discoveries have shed light on the background of and reinforced the accuracy of the biblical descriptions of people, places, and events.

Archaeology and the Bible

The science of archaeology has had a great impact on biblical studies:
• Archaeology has confirmed the historical accuracy of the Bible.
• Archaeology has increased our understanding of the world of the Bible.
• Archaeology has helped to explain certain Bible passages.

Limits of archaeology

Archaeology does not "prove" the Bible in the sense that the Bible is only to be believed as divinely inspired because archaeologists support its accuracy.

Secondly, like all other sciences archaeological finds are open to new evidence and in certain cases to reinterpretation. An archaeologist may review his understanding in the light of new finds.

Thirdly, we do not have a complete picture of all the Bible background we might want to know about as so much archaeological evidence has been lost, or waits to be discovered.

Leading theologians and archaeologists

Many scholars in the fields of theology and archaeology have witnessed to the impact archaeological finds have had on biblical studies.

RANDALL PRICE
"There are indeed instances where the information needed to resolve a historical or chronological question is lacking from both archaeology and the Bible, but it is unwarranted to assume the material evidence taken from the more limited content of archaeological excavations can be used to dispute the literary evidence from the more complete content of the canonical scriptures."

GEISLER AND NIX
"Historical confirmation of the Old Testament has come from all over the biblical world. Persons, places, and events have been substantiated: from the Patriarchs to Israel in Egypt, to the conquest of Canaan, to the kingdom under Solomon, to the deportations of Israel and Judah to Assyria and Babylonia respectively. In the field of New Testament studies, the evidence has also been abundant. Even a casual survey of any good book on New Testament archaeology will indicate that the accuracy of details in the events of Christ's life has been confirmed from the ruins of Palestine, as has been the

case with the details about the journeys of the Apostle Paul."

NELSON GLUECK

"It may be stated categorically that no archaeological discovery has ever controverted a biblical reference."

"Scores of archaeological findings have been made which confirm in clear outline or exact detail historical statements in the Bible."

Nelson Glueck, Jewish archaeologist

DONALD J. WISEMAN

"The geography of Bible lands and visible remains of antiquity were gradually recorded until today more than 25,000 sites within this region and dating to Old Testament times, in their broadest sense, have been located..."

Donald J. Wiseman, British Bible scholar

WILLIAM F. ALBRIGHT

"There can be no doubt that archaeology has confirmed the substantial historicity of the old Testament tradition."

"Discovery after discovery has established the accuracy of innumerable details, and has brought increased recognition of the value of the Bible as a source of history."

William F. Albright, 1891–1971

Albright was an evangelical Methodist archaeologist and director of the American School of Oriental Research at Johns Hopkins. Albright published over 800 books and articles and is famous for confirming the authenticity of the Dead Sea Scrolls. Albright used his combination of Christian interpretation and historical analysis of the Bible to demonstrate the historical reliability of the Old Testament.

MILLAR BURROWS

"Archaeology has in many cases refuted the views of modern critics. It has shown in a number of instances that these views rest on false assumptions and unreal, artificial schemes of historical development. This is a real contribution and not to be minimized."

Millar Burrows, Yale University

SIR WILLIAM RAMSAY

"Luke is a historian of the first rank; not merely are his statements of facts trustworthy; he is possessed of the true historic sense...In short this author should be placed along with the very greatest of historians."

William Ramsay, known as probably the world's greatest archaeologist

A.N. SHERWIN-WHITE

Referring to the book of Acts, Sherwin-White has written: "For Acts the confirmation of historicity is overwhelming...any attempt to reject its basic historicity even in matters of detail must now appear absurd."

A.N. Sherwin-White, a classical historian at Oxford University

Archaeology and ancient languages

Overview

Three archaeological finds have greatly helped us in our understanding of and deciphering of ancient languages.

Rosetta Stone

This was discovered in Egypt in 1801 by an engineer in Napoleon's army.

The slab of black basalt has three inscriptions on it. Two are forms of Egyptian writing and one of Greek. So while it has three kinds of script on it, it only has two languages.

SCRIPTS

The scripts are:
- Hieroglyphic (fourteen lines),
- Egyptian Demotic (thirty-two lines), and
- Koine Greek (fifty-four lines).

Hieroglyphic

Hieroglyphic means "sacred writing." This script is an old form of picture writing which dating back to 4000 B.C. It was used in making copies of funerary and religious texts.

Egyptian Demotic

The Egyptian Demotic (Greek for "people of the town") is the modified form of the Hieratic character. It allowed the writer to write hieroglyphics quickly and was used in literary circles.

Koine Greek

The Koine Greek was the language of the marketplace.

The languages used are technical at the top of the stone and straightforward at the bottom. The reason behind the diversity of the scripts could lie in the desire to communicate to everyone.

KEY TO DECIPHERING OTHER INSCRIPTIONS

The lasting significance of the Rosetta Stone cannot be estimated just by its content. Its descriptions of the Egyptian Pharaohs and priests are not in themselves unique.

Their significance lies in the method used to communicate the contents. The bilingual message found on the Rosetta Stone is the key to the ability to decipher all of the Egyptian hieroglyphics. Until 1822 Egyptian history with its inscriptions on the walls of tombs and tablets remained a mystery and looked just like a set of fascinating pictures.

Using this stone, the French scholar Jean F. Champollion was able to decipher Egyptian hieroglyphics for the first time. This opened the door to the entire written history of ancient Egypt, which covered 3000 years of history and civilization. It has become extremely valuable in the study of the background of the Bible.

Behistun Stone

This was carved on a mountainside during the reign of Darius I of Persia to record his achievements and contained some 1,200 lines of inscription.

It was written in three languages: Babylonian, Elamite, and Persian.

It was discovered in 1835, but no one managed to translate it until 1845 when an Englishman, Sir Henry Rawlinson succeeded in deciphering the cuneiform writing of the old Persian. Then the Elamite was translated, and finally the Babylonian was deciphered.

VALUE OF BEHISTUN STONE

Now, for the first time, the wealth of the literary remains of the Tigris-Euphrates Valley, including the historical documents from Assyria, Babylon, and Sumer, could be translated.

Reading these ancient languages greatly expanded our knowledge of the background and history of the Bible.

The Tablets of Ugarit

In the late 1920's a Syrian farmer who was plowing his field turned up some clay tablets.

Subsequently, French archaeologists excavated the site and found the city of Ugarit and many more clay tablets.

The discovery of the Ugaritic or Ras Shamra Tablets revealed a Semitic language closely related to Hebrew. It has a thirty letter alphabet and was used at the same time that Moses lived.

UNDERSTANDING *HAPAX LEGOMENA*

The meaning of words occurring only once in the Hebrew Bible (called *hapax legomena*), but fairly frequently in Ugaritic can now be determined with reasonable certainty.

THE GOD BAAL

The Ugaritic texts tell us about the god Baal who is often mentioned in the Old Testament. After the discovered of the Tablets of Ugarit it was possible to understand how the Canaanites thought of Baal.

BAAL TABLETS

Six large tablets were discovered in the ruins of the high priest's house at Ras Shamra.

From them we can see how the followers of Baal were a real danger to the ancient Israelites. These tablets are known as the "Baal tablets" and are like a Canaanite Bible.

BAAL'S INFLUENCE ON NATURE

It was seen that followers of Baal believed that their god had a great influence over nature. They worshiped him because he was supposed to bring rain for their crops and so sustain their cattle.

BAAL'S PREEMINENCE

Without Baal their life would quickly come to an end. So to the Canaanites the god Baal had to be given the highest possible preeminence, or else all human existence was threatened. They believed that their crops would fail and cattle die if they did not honor and worship Baal.

CONCLUSION

So from some of the religious texts discovered at Ugarit our knowledge of the Canaanite religion was greatly enhanced.

Archaeological discoveries explained

Overview

The following archaeological discoveries are now explained:
- Discovering the Hittites
- Mari Tablets
- Nuzi Tablets

Discovering the Hittites

THE PROBLEM

The "problem" with the Hittites is until just over a hundred years ago there was no extra-biblical evidence for their existence. So some commentators went as far as to say that they never existed and that they were a figment of the imagination of biblical authors.

The Hittites were quite prominent in Old Testament.

The lived in Canaan, 1 Kings 10: 29.

They bought chariots and horses from King Solomon.

Uriah, Bathsheba's husband, was the best known Hittite.

ARCHAEOLOGICAL FINDS

In 1876 the British scholar A.H. Sayce found inscriptions carved on rocks in Turkey which he believed belonged to the Hittites.

In 1887 more clay tablets were found in Turkey, at Boghaz-koy.

Hugo Winckler, a German cuneiform expert, studied these tablets and made his own investigation at Boghaz-koy in 1906.

Winckler was not disappointed by his excavations.

He discovered:
- five temples,
- a fortified citadel,
- a number of massive sculptures, and
- more than ten thousand clay tablets in just one storeroom.

He identified one document as the record of a treaty between Ramesses II and the Hittite king.

From these tablets it became clear that Boghaz-koy was the capital of the Hittite kingdom. Originally it had been called Hattusha and spread over 300 acres.

The existence of the Hittite nation could no longer be contested.

THE LAWS OF DEUTERONOMY AND LEVITICUS

Critics of the Bible had previously said that the instructions and detailed laws found in Leviticus and Deuteronomy were much too complicated for the time when they were supposed to have been given (about 1400 B.C.).

However, from the details gleaned from the numerous tablets discovered at the five Hittite temple sites it is clear that they described rites for purification from sin in lengthy and elaborate detail.

The Boghaz-koy texts along with others from Egyptian sites and a site along the Euphrates called Emar have proven that the ceremonies described in the Jewish Pentateuch are consistent with the ceremonies of the cultures of this time period.

Quote Unquote

"Now the Bible picture of this people fits in perfectly with what we know of the Hittite nation from the monuments. As an empire they never conquered the land of Canaan itself, although the Hittite local tribes did settle there at an early date. Nothing discovered by the excavators has in any way discredited the biblical account. Scripture accuracy has once more been proved by the archaeologist."

Dr Fred Wright

SUMMARY
The discovery of the Hittites, one of the all-time great archaeological finds, confirmed all the biblical narratives about them.

Mari Tablets

The Mari tablets were discovered in 1933 at Mari, the capital city of a Semitic state located in northern Mesopotamia.

Although the people of Mari lived before the patriarchs dwelt in Israel many of the customs discovered in Mari shed light on the lives of the Israelite patriarchs.

Among the twenty thousand tablets that were found are references to the Habiru (Akkadian form of *Hebrew*) people. They were described as warlike wanderers and "people from the other side." Such a term could be a reference to people of Israel after the crossing over of the River Jordan.

Nuzi Tablets

The Nuzi Tablets, discovered at the ancient city of Nuzi near the Tigris River, which have been dated to 5000–4000 B.C., shed light on the customs recorded in the book of Genesis and on the lives of Abraham, Isaac, and Jacob, such as legal customs like adoption and birthright sales.

An example of the Nuzi Tablets helping us to understand Genesis is illustrated by Genesis 16 where Sarah, Abraham's wife, because she was seemingly unable to have children, gave Hagar her servant to Abraham to have children through. Later Jacob's two wives, Rachel and Leah, did the same. Because of finds like the Nuzi Tablets, we now realize this was a common practice of that time and is mentioned in the laws and marriage contracts of that time.

Over 20,000 clay tablets, using cuneiform writing, have been discovered at Nuzi.

Writing and the Bible

A number of Bible critics used to claim that writing did not exist in the time of Moses and so his authorship of any of the first five books of the Bible was a fiction.

Archaeological discoveries about the Old Testament (1)

Overview

The following archaeological discoveries, all of which shed invaluable light on the Old Testament, are now explained.

- The Ebla tablets shed light on the patriarchal period
- The House of David Inscription: inscription about the "House of David"
- The Law Code of Hammurabi
- The Moabite Stone mentions Mesha, the Moabite king in 2 Kings 3
- The Black Obelisk: perhaps the only picture of a biblical figure
- The Taylor Prism: Sennacherib's boast about the siege of Hezekiah
- The Cyrus Cylinder describes the exile policies of the Persian monarch
- Hezekiah's Tunnel

The Ebla Tablets

OVERVIEW
The Ebla tablets shed light on the patriarchal period.

DETAILS
The Ebla tablets, discovered in Syria in the 1970s, are made up of 17,000 tablets. Several of them mention the "Five Cities of the Plain" which are mentioned in Genesis 14 (Sodom, Gomorrah, Admah, Zeboiim, and Zoar). These cities, which some critics had said were legendary, are listed on one tablet in the same order as occur in the Bible.

Some critics of the Bible once taught that the period described in Moses' time, 1400 B.C., was a time before the skill of writing had been acquired. However, the discovery of the Ebla tablets prove that a thousand years before Moses, laws, customs, and events were recorded in writing in the same region in which Moses and the patriarchs lived. The Ebla tablets also use the term "Canaan."

The House of David Inscription

OVERVIEW
This find reveals an inscription about the "House of David."

This is the first inscription that has been discovered that refers to the Davidic dynasty and to King David outside of the Bible.

DETAILS
Despite the major role King David played in the Bible it used to be thought that there was no evidence for his existence outside the Bible.

In 1993, the archaeologist Dr. Avraham Biran discovered a royal plaza as he excavated Tell Dan in northern Galilee at the foot of Matt. Hermon. Among the rubble he found the remains of a black basalt stele, which had parts of thirteen lines of Aramaic inscriptions. From these inscriptions the following two phrases are clearly visible: "The King of Israel" and "House of David." The stele had been erected to celebrate the defeat of the kings of Judah and Israel.

Additional inscriptions were discovered at this site in 1994. They refer to Jehoram, the son of Ahab, ruler over Israel, and Ahaziah, who was the ruler over the "House of David" (that is Judah.) See 2 Kings 8–9.

Quote Unquote

"The stele brings to life the biblical text in a very dramatic way. It also gives us more confidence in the historical reality of the biblical text."

Dr. Hershel Shanks of biblical Archaeological Review

The mention of the "House of David" implies that David and his heirs were rulers in Israel. King David's existence was now confirmed by this archaeological evidence. Skeptics could no longer assume that he was a heroic character invented by the Israelites.

Quote Unquote

"In our day, most scholars, archaeologist and biblical scholars would take a very critical view of the historical accuracy of many of the accounts in the Bible. ... Many scholars have said there never was a David or a Solomon, and now we have a stele that actually mentions David."

Dr. Bryant Wood

Law Code of Hammurabi

OVERVIEW
Laws similar to those found in the Pentateuch.

DETAILS
Archeologists have dated their discovery of a seven foot tall, black diorite carving (known as *The Black Stele*) containing about 300 laws of Babylon's King Hammurabi to about three centuries prior to Moses. Hammurabi's Law Code contains many civil laws that are similar to those found in the first five books of the Bible.

The Moabite Stone

OVERVIEW
On the Mesha or Moabite Stone, an ancient Palestinian slab, is the first definite inscribed evidence of an Old Testament event.

The Moabite Stone mentions Mesha, the Moabite king of 2 Kings 3.

DETAILS
This stone recounts the military achievements of one of the kings of Moab, Mesha.

It is an ancient monument discovered by the Rev. F. Klein in 1868 at Diban (the Dibon of the Old Testament) in Moab.

The inscription consists of thirty-four lines (the last two being undecipherable), and was written by Mesha king of Moab to commemorate his successful revolt from the yoke of Israel which is recorded in 2 Kings 1:1 and chapter 3.

Archaeological discoveries about the Old Testament (2)

The Moabite Stone, continued

"Then Moab rebelled against Israel after the death of Ahab" 2 Kings 1: 1.

The inscription also honors Moab's god, Chemosh, to whom he ascribed his successes. The inscription is in line with the passage in 2 Kings 3.

It reads as follows:

1. "I, Mesha son of Chemosh-Melech king of Moab, the Dibonite.

2. My father reigned over Moab thirty years and I reigned

3. after my father. I made this monument to Chemosh at Korkhah. A monument of salvation.

4. for he saved me from all invaders, and let me see my desire upon all my enemies. Omri

5. [was] king of Israel, and he oppressed Moab many days, for Chemosh was angry with his land.

6. His son followed him, and he also said : I will oppress Moab. In my days Che[mosh] said;

7. I will see my desire on him and his house. And Israel surely perished for ever. Omri took the land of

8. Medeba (1) and [Israel] dwelt in it during his days and half the days of his son (2), altogether forty years. But there dwelt in it

9. Chemosh in my days. I built Baal-Meon (3) and made therein the ditches; I built

10. Kirjathaim (4). The men of Gad dwelt in the land of Ataroth (5) from of old, and built there the king of

11. Israel Ataroth; and I made war against the town and seized it. And I slew all the [people of]

12. the town, for the pleasure of Chemosh and Moab : I captured from thence the Arel (6) of Dodah and tore

13. him before Chemosh in Kerioth (7) : And I placed therein the men of Sh(a)r(o)n, and the men

14. of M(e)kh(e)rth. And Chemosh said to me : Go, seize Nebo (8) upon Israel; and

15. I went in the night and fought against it from the break of dawn till noon : and I took

16. it, and slew all, 7,000 men, [boys?], women, [girls?]

17. and female slaves, for to Ashtar-Chemosh I devoted them. And I took from it the Arels (6) of Yahveh, and tore them before Chemosh. And the king of Israel built

18. Jahaz (9), and dwelt in it, while he waged war against me; Chemosh drove him out before me. And

19. I took from Moab 200 men, all chiefs, and transported them to Jahaz, which I took,

20. to add to it Dibon. I built Korkhah, the wall of the forests and the wall

21. of the citadel : I built its gates, and I built its towers. And

22. I built the house of Moloch, and I made sluices of the water-ditches in the middle

23. of the town. And there was no cistern in the middle of the town of Korkhah, and I said to all the people, Make for

24. yourselves every man a cistern in his house. And I dug the canals for Korkhah by means of the prisoners

25. of Israel. I built Aroer (10), and I made the road in [the province of] the Arnon. [And]

26. I built Beth-Bamoth (11), for it was destroyed. I built Bezer (12), for in ruins

27. [it was. And all the chiefs] of Dibon were 50, for all Dibon is subject; and I placed

28. one hundred [chiefs] in the towns which I added to the land : I built

29. Beth-Medeba and Beth-diblathaim (13), and Beth-Baal-Meon (14), and transported thereto the [shepherds]?...

30. and the pastors] of the flocks of the land. And at Horonaim (15) dwelt there

31. ...And Chemosh said to me, Go down, make war upon Horonaim. I went down [and made war]

32. ...And Chemosh dwelt in it during my days. I went up from thence..."

Footnotes

(1) Num. 21: 30; Is. 15: 2.

(2) "son" = successor.

(3) Now, Tell M'ain, Num. 32: 38. Josh. 13: 17.

(4) Num. 32: 37. Josh. 13: 19.

(5) Num. 32: 3. Josh. 16: 2.

(6) Arel, two lions, or, lion-like men cf 2 Sam. 23: 20.

(7) Now, Khan el Kureitin (?); Jer. 48: 24. Amos 2: 2.

(8) Num. 32: 3, 38. Is. 15: 2.

(9) Is. 15: 4.

(10) Now, 'Ar'air, Deut. 2: 36; 3: 12; 4: 48.

(11) Num. 21: 19. Is. 15: 2. (AV "high places"), cf. Josh. 13: 17.

(12) Deut. 4: 43.

(13) Jer. 48: 22.

(14) Josh. 13: 17. Jer. 48: 23.

(15) Is. 15: 5. Jer. 48: 3,5 34.

Translated by Dr. Neubauer

Archaeological discoveries about the Old Testament (3)

The Black Obelisk of Shalmaneser

OVERVIEW
The Black Obelisk may well have the only picture of a biblical figure that has yet been unearthed.

DETAILS
This monument, discovered in Nineveh in 1845, was erected by the Assyrian king Shalmaneser II. It mentions tribute being paid by Jehu, son of Ahab (2 Kings 10). Part of the relief depicts a figure bowing down to the Assyrian king. This could be King Jehu himself, or one of his representatives. If the figure is indeed King Jehu it is the only picture we have of a biblical figure.

The Taylor Prism, also known as Sennacherib's Cylinder

OVERVIEW
On this six-sided prism, King Sennacherib recorded eight military campaigns against those who refused to give in to the Assyrians.

The Taylor Prism contains Sennacherib's boast about the siege of Hezekiah.

DETAILS
The Taylor Prism, also known as Sennacherib's Cylinder, discovered in 1830, records the victories of the Assyrian king Sennacherib.

Part of this record describes Sennacherib's third victory, after the siege of Hezekiah, which is recorded in 2 Kings 18: "I (Sennacherib) … captured 46 towns and villages of Judah ... shut up Hezekiah the Jew like a bird in a cage in Jerusalem, his royal city."

The British Museum in London houses this hexagonal cylinder of Sennacherib, King of Assyria (607–583 B.C.).

Sennacherib's Cylinder is one of the finest and most perfect objects of its class ever discovered. Its importance as an historical document can hardly be overrated. It contains 487 lines of closely written but legible cuneiform text, inscribed in the Eponymy of Belimuranni, prefect of Karkemish.

Lines 11 to 24
In lines 11 to 24 of the central column of the cylinder Sennacherib says:

11. "I fixed upon him. And of Hezekiah [king of the]

12. Jews, who had not submitted to my yoke,

13. forty-six of his fenced cities, and the strongholds, and the smaller cities

14. which were round about them and which were without number,

15. by the battering of rams, and the attack of engines

16. and by the assaults of foot soldiers, and ....

17. I besieged, I captured, 200,150 people, small and great, male and female,

18. horses, and mules, and asses, and camels, and men,

19. and sheep innumerable from their

midst I brought out, and

20. I reckoned [them] as spoil. [Hezekiah] himself like a caged bird within Jerusalem,

21. his royal city, I shut in, andc.

The Cyrus Cylinder

OVERVIEW
The Cyrus Cylinder describes the exile policies of a Persian monarch.

DETAILS
The Cyrus Cylinder, discovered in 1879, contains inscriptions documenting the policy of Cyrus the Great. It records how Cyrus instigated the enlightened policy of allowing captured peoples, such as the Jews, to return home (see Ezra 1).

Hezekiah's Tunnel

OVERVIEW
Hezekiah's Tunnel explains how Jerusalem was able to obtain a secret supply of water and so survive sieges.

DETAILS
Sir Charles Warren discovered this rock-hewn tunnel connecting a spring of water with the Pool of Siloam in 1867.

Before the Assyrian invasion of 603 B.C. Hezekiah took precautions to help Jerusalem survive a siege. He constructed a tunnel and brought the water from Gihon to a pool that he had made for the purpose. "And the rest of the acts of Hezekiah, and all his might, and how he made a pool, and a conduit, and brought water into the city, *are* they not written in the book of the chronicles of the kings of Judah?" 2 Kings 20: 20.

This pool became known as "the King's Pool." "Then I went on to the gate of the fountain, and to the king's pool" Neh. 2: 14.

THE SILOAM INSCRIPTION
In 1880 the Siloam Inscription was discovered on a stone on the right wall of the tunnel about 20 feet after it left the Pool of Siloam.

TRANSLATION OF THE SILOAM INSCRIPTION
The inscription on the wall of Hezekiah's tunnel reads as follows:

Line 1. [Behold] the excavation. Now this is the history of the breaking through. While the workmen were still lifting up

Line 2. the pickax, each toward his neighbor, and while three cubits still remained to [cut through, each heard] the voice of the other calling

Line 3. to his neighbor, for there was an excess (or cleft) in the rock on the right ... And on the day of the

Line 4. breaking through, the excavators struck, each to meet the other, pickax against pickax; and there flowed

Line 5. the waters from the spring to the pool over [a space of] one thousand and two hundred cubits. And ...

Line 6. of a cubit was the height of the rock above the heads of the excavators.

The Dead Sea Scrolls (1)

Dead Sea Scroll facts

Discovery

The Dead Sea Scrolls were discovered in eleven caves on the upper northwest shore of the Dead Sea. The area is 13 miles east of Jerusalem, and is -1300 ft. below sea level (Jerusalem is +2400 ft. above sea level).

Isaiah scroll

The Isaiah Scroll is the oldest complete manuscript of a Hebrew Scripture yet discovered and was found in Cave 1 at Qumran in 1947 and purchased by the Syrian Orthodox archbishop of Jerusalem. The Isaiah scroll was acquired by Israel in 1954 and has been the central exhibit in Jerusalem's Shrine of the Book since 1965.

Number of scrolls

In all, scholars have identified the remains of over 800 separate scrolls.

Cave 4

Only Caves 1 and 11 have produced relatively intact manuscripts. Discovered in 1952, Cave 4 produced the largest find. About 15,000 fragments from more than 500 manuscripts were found.

All but Esther

Fragments of every book of the Hebrew canon (Old Testament) have been discovered except for the book of Esther.

Multiple copies

There are now identified among the scrolls, nineteen copies of the Book of Isaiah, twenty-five copies of Deuteronomy and thirty copies of the Psalms.

Non-biblical discoveries

Also found with the scrolls were nonbiblical writings. These are:
- commentaries on the OT,
- paraphrases that expand on the Law,
- rule books of the community,
- war conduct,
- thanksgiving psalms,
- hymnic compositions,
- benedictions,
- liturgical texts, and
- wisdom writings.

Before the Dead Sea Scrolls

1000 years older

Until 1947, scholars had only the clay tablets of Babylon and the Egyptian papyri to help them understand background information on the Bible, since no ancient Old Testament manuscripts were known to have survived. However, all this changed with the discovery of over 800 papyrus and parchment texts in caves along the northwest corner of the Dead Sea. These scrolls gave the world manuscripts of Old Testament books 1000 years older than any previously in existence.

Nash Papyrus

Before the discovery of the Dead Sea Scrolls the Nash Papyrus was the oldest known part of any of the Old Testament. It was dated to the 1st or 2nd century A.D. and contained the Ten Commandments.

CAIRO GENIZA

The second oldest part of the Old Testament were the Cairo Geniza fragments which date to the 5th century A.D.

Today the oldest known text of the OT was discovered in 1979 in tombs across the Hinnom valley from Jerusalem. The text is the benediction of Aaron (Numbers 6: 24–26) written on a silver amulet from the 7th century B.C. (Hoerth 1998, 386).

Accuracy of copying confirmed by the Dead Sea Scrolls

1,300 YEAR GAP

Before discovery of the Dead Sea Scrolls in 1947, the earliest known copy of the Old Testament was dated to about A.D. 900. Since the Old Testament was completed around 400 B.C., this meant that there was a 1,300 year gap between the writing of the last original book of the Old Testament and the first known copy. Some critics speculated that such a lengthy time-span must have allowed copying errors to creep into the text. This would then have meant that the Old Testament was unreliable.

In 1947, the discovery of many ancient manuscripts of the Old Testament in caves around the Dead Sea confirmed the accuracy of the Jewish copyists of the Old Testament books. Even though these new scrolls were nearly a thousand years older than those which were once thought to be the oldest, there was phenomenal agreement between the two sets of manuscripts.

ACCURATE TRANSMISSION

This suggests that careful preservation of the Hebrew manuscripts was an early priority in the transmission of the Old Testament writing.

Josephus

Concerning the faithful transcription of biblical manuscripts by the Jewish scribes, Jewish historian Flavius Josephus said the following:

"We have given practical proof of our reverence for our own Scriptures. For, although such long ages have now passed, no one has ventured either to add, or to remove, or to alter a syllable; and it is an instinct with every Jew from the day of his birth to regard them as the decrees of God, to abide by them, and, if need be, cheerfully to die for them."

Summary

The Dead Sea Scrolls confirm that from the 9th century A.D., the Jewish scribal copying of the Old Testament Scriptures contained remarkably few errors.

With the exception of minute copying errors here and there, the Dead Sea manuscripts exhibited virtually identical readings to their counterparts of the 9th century.

They proved that the many scholars who expressed doubts concerning the accuracy of the Masoretic text were unfounded.

The Dead Sea Scrolls (2)

John Allegro

John Allegro, who is not known for being a Christian sympathizer, said about the discovery of the Dead Sea Scrolls:

"Excitement had run high among scholars when it became known in 1948 that a cave near the Dead Sea had produced pre-Masoretic texts of the Bible.

Was it possible that we were at last going to see traditions differing seriously from the standard text, which would throw some important light on this hazy period of variant traditions?

In some quarters the question was raised with some apprehension, especially when news-hungry journalists began to talk about changing the whole Bible in view of the latest discoveries, but closer examination showed that, on the whole, the differences shown by the first Isaiah scroll were of little account, and could often be explained on the basis of scribal errors, or differing orthography, syntax, or grammatical form."

Conclusions to draw

Scholars have concluded that the remarkable similarity between the Masoretic texts and the Dead Sea Scrolls is compelling evidence that the original writings of the Old Testament, which were made well over 1000 years before the Dead Sea Scroll manuscripts, have also been faithfully preserved over the centuries.

RELIABLE RECORDS

They support this view with the words of Jesus himself who always treated the 1st century Old Testament manuscripts as if they were reliable records of the original, divine inspiration.

BACKGROUND INFORMATION

In addition to the Old Testament manuscripts the caves of Qumran had many other writings which provide interesting background to the times of the New Testament.

Finding the Dead Sea Scrolls

AN UNLIKELY STORY

The unlikely story of a Bedouin shepherd-boy searching for a lost goat and then discovering a cave near Qumran that contained jars with scrolls is perfectly true.

In 1947 the Bedouin boy, Muhammad Adh-Dhib was alerted to his find after he had thrown a stone into a cave which resulted in him hearing the crash of pottery. This led to the eventual discovery of a stored library of over 800 manuscripts from the time of Jesus.

Between 25% and 33% were manuscripts of Bible books.

The storage jars in which the scrolls were discovered had perfectly preserved the scrolls.

GREATEST MANUSCIPRT DISCOVERY

W.F. Albright of Johns Hopkins University, declared that these scrolls and fragments are "the greatest manuscript discovery of modern times."

The Qumran community

MONASTIC EVIDENCE

Out of the 1,200 graves unearthed in the cemetery, only six were of women and four of children. This is one of the pointers that indicate that the Qumran community, which numbered about 200 people, was similar to a monastery.

ENDED BY THE ROMANS

This community was in existence in Qumran from about 135 B.C. to A.D. 68, when the Romans captured Qumran and killed or enslaved all who did not escape.

Eleven caves

The treasure trove of wonderfully preserved manuscripts found in eleven caves at Qumran amounted to over 95,000 fragments.

Cave 1

In Cave 1 a well-preserved copy of the entire prophecy of Isaiah, the oldest copy of an Old Testament book ever to be discovered, was found.

Over 200 fragments from the Dead Sea Scrolls are now housed at the Shrine of the Book Museum in Jerusalem. The only fully intact scroll displayed at the Shrine of the Book is this Isaiah scroll, which is known as the "Great Isaiah Scroll" (1Qls-a).

"Despite the fact that the Isaiah scroll was about a thousand years older than the Masoretic version of Isaiah," says James VanderKam of the University of Notre Dame, "the two were nearly identical except for small details that rarely affected the meaning of the text."

Cave 4

Cave 4 alone housed 15,000 fragments of manuscripts and 574 complete manuscripts.

4Q17

One of the oldest scrolls, probably dating back to before 200 B.C., is 4Q17, which contains Exodus 38 to Leviticus 2. It is practically identical to the Masoretic text.

Summary

Among all of the archaeological discoveries,

"Probably the Dead Sea Scrolls have had the greatest biblical impact. They have provided Old Testament manuscripts approximately 1000 years older than our previous oldest manuscript.

The Dead Sea Scrolls have demonstrated that the Old Testament was accurately transmitted during this interval. In addition, they provide a wealth of information on the times leading up to, and during, the life of Christ."

Dr. Bryant Wood, archaeologist

Historical evidence for the existence of Jesus

Overview

There is relatively little recorded about Jesus in the secular history books of his day. But that might be expected as the Roman Empire had little interest in the life of a little known religious leader in one of its occupied territories.

However there is some evidence outside the pages of the Bible for the existence of Jesus.

1. It amounts to some 39 extra-biblical sources.
2. They witness to over one hundred facts concerning the life and teachings of Jesus.

Josephus

The Jewish historian, Flavius Josephus, (A.D. 37–A.D. 100) wrote a book called *Antiquites* which recorded the history of the Jewish people in Palestine from 70 A.D. to 100 A.D. In it he states:

"Now there was about this time, Jesus, a wise man, if it be lawful to call him a man, for he was a doer of wonderful works, a teacher of such men as receive the truth with pleasure. He drew over to him both many of the Jews and many of the gentiles.

He was the Christ and when Pilate, at the suggestion of the principal men amongst us, had condemned him to the cross, those that loved him at the first did not forsake him. For he appeared alive again the third day, as the divine prophets had foretold these and ten thousand other wonderful things concerning him; and the tribe of

Christians, so named from him, are not extinct to this day."

Pliny the Younger

While Pliny the Younger was Emperor of Bythynia in northwestern Turkey he wrote the following to Emperor Trajan in A.D. 112 in Epistles X.96, about the dedication of Christians whom he had been persecuting. He had:

"...made them curse Christ, which a genuine Christian cannot be induced to do."

In the same letter he describes the trials of Christians:

"They were in the habit of meeting on a certain fixed day before it was light, when they sang an anthem to Christ as God, and bound themselves by a solemn oath not to commit any wicked deed, but to abstain from all fraud, theft, and adultery, never to break their word, or deny a trust when called upon to honor it; after which it was their custom to separate, and then meet again to partake of food, but ordinary and innocent kind."

Cornelius Tacitus

Cornelius Tacitus, c A.D. 55–117, an important Roman historian, recorded Nero's persecution of the Christians, in A.D. 115.

Tacitus also wrote about "Christus" in his Annals Book XV, Chapter 44: a history of the Roman empire.

"Nero looked around for a scapegoat, and inflicted the most fiendish tortures on a group of persons already hated by the people for their crimes.

This was the sect known as Christians. Their founder, one Christus, had been put to death by the procurator Pontius Pilate in the reign of Tiberius.

This checked the abominable superstition for a while, but it broke out again and spread, not merely through Judea, where it originated, but even to Rome itself, the great reservoir and collecting ground for every kind of depravity and filth.

Those who confessed to being Christians were at once arrested, but on their testimony a great crowd of people were convicted, not so much on the charge of arson, but of hatred of the entire human race."

Thallus

Thallus, a Samaritan historian, c. A.D. 52, wrote (in a lost work, referred to by Julius Africanus in Chronography, XVIII from the 3rd century) attempting to give a natural explanation for the darkness which occurred at the crucifixion of Jesus.

"On the whole world there pressed a most fearful darkness; and the rocks were rent by an earthquake, and many places in Judea and other districts were thrown down. This darkness Thallus, in the third book of his History, calls, as appears to me without reason, an eclipse of the sun."

In this he did not deny the existence of Jesus, but only tried to explain away the strange circumstances which surrounded his death, as recorded in Mark 15: 33.

Mara-Serapion

In a letter written by Mara-Serapion to his son, c. A.D. 73 he recounts the deaths of Socrates, Pythagoras, and Jesus. Referring to Jesus he writes:

"What advantage did the Jews gain from executing their wise king? Nor did the wise king die for good; he lived on in the teaching which he had given."

Archaeological discoveries about the New Testament (1)

Overivew

Archaeology has played a major role in establishing the New Testament, as well as the Old Testament, as an accurate historical work divinely inspired by God.

There is a great deal of archaeological evidence which supports in general and in detail the account about Jesus as written in the Gospels and about his early followers as recorded in the remainder of the New Testament.

Accuracy of the Gospels

The discoveries of archaeology have supported the accuracy of the four Gospel writers, time and time again.

Herod the murderer

Matthew chapter 2 states that Jesus was born during the reign of wicked King Herod. Matthew records how evil Herod ordered the massacre of all boy toddlers who lived in and around Bethlehem.

Matthew's portrayal of Herod being a murderer is quite accurate. During his last years on his throne he had the following people killed:

- one of his ten wives,
- three of his own sons,
- a high priest,
- an ex-king, and
- two of his sister's husbands.

John's Gospel

It used to be fashionable in some scholarly circles to state that John's Gospel was not written until the 2nd century and that it contained many inaccurate if not imaginary tales. But archaeological finds have confirmed the accuracy of John's Gospel.

1   THE SHEEP POOL

In John 5: 1–15 it is recorded that Jesus heals a man at the Pool of Bethesda. John describes the pool as having five porticoes.

As such a site could not be found in Jerusalem some concluded that John must be making this up.

However, at a depth of 40 feet underground, archaeologists discovered a pool. It has five porticoes.

2   THE POOL OF SILOAM

In 9: 7 John mentions, in passing, the Pool of Siloam. The existence of this pool was often disputed until it was unearthed in 1897.

Pontius Pilate

Evidence confirming that Pontius Pilate was the Roman prefect (governor) in Palestine in Jesus' day was unearthed by Antonio Frova, an Italian archaeologist, in Caesarea Maritama in 1961. Fravo uncovered a fragment of a plaque in Jerusalem which bares a Latin inscription about Pilate.

It describes him as: "Pontius Pilatus, Prefect of Judea has dedicated to the people of Caesarea a temple in honor of Tiberius."

Emperor Tiberius reigned from A.D. 14–37, and Pilot ruled as procurator from A.D. 26–36.

Luke, the accurate historian

We often think of Luke as Paul's traveling companion and recall that he was called "Luke, the beloved physician" in Colossians 4: 14. He was also an accomplished and meticulously accurate historian.

Archaeological discoveries have rescued Luke from being accused of being a second-rate historian and have vindicated his Gospel and Acts as especially accurate accounts in all they describe.

Sir William Ramsay

Ramsay, the renowned archaeologist, had been schooled into thinking that the New Testament was not a historical document. So when he went to investigate the claims of the Bible in his work in Asia Minor he was greatly surprised by what he found. He records:

"I began with a mind unfavorable to it [Acts], for the ingenuity and apparent completeness of the Tubingen theory had at one time quite convinced me. It did not then in my line of life to investigate the subject minutely; but more recently I found myself often brought into contact with the Book of Acts as an authority for the topography, antiquities, and society

of Asia Minor. It was gradually borne in upon me that in various details the narrative showed marvelous truth."

Government officials

Luke's accuracy can be seen in various ways. He manages to name important historical figures with great attention to detail.

It is now agreed that he is accurate even in calling them by the correct titles. Different areas and different countries called their officials by different titles then, just as we do today.

- In Thessalonica Luke correctly refers to politarchs;
- In Ephesus Luke correctly refers to temple wardens;
- In Cyprus Luke correctly refers to a procouncil; and
- In Malta Luke correctly refers to the first man of the island.

THE *POLITARCHS* OF THESSALONICA

Luke stated in Acts 17: 5,6 that some of the Christian brethren were dragged before the "rulers of the city" *KJV* ("city authorities" – *NASV*). This phrase is a translation of the Greek word *politarchas*. In the whole of the New Testament it occurs only in Acts 17 verses 6 and 8.

Some Bible critics claimed that the title *politarchas* did not refer to the city officials of Thessalonica and that Luke should have been more careful and used the more common words, such as *strateegoi* (magistrates) and *exousiais* (authorities).

Archaeological discoveries about the New Testament (2)

Luke, the accurate historian, continued

The *politarchs* of Thessalonica, continued

Such critics believed that they had a cast iron case against the accuracy of Luke as the word *politarch* used as an official title is not found anywhere else in any Greek literature.

But all this changed when archaeologists dug up records which did refer to *politarchas* in some cities of Macedonia. Macedonia was the province in which Thessalonica was situated.

THIRTY-TWO INSCRIPTIONS
There are now 32 inscriptions dated between the 2nd and 3rd centuries in which the term *politarchas* have been found. Five of these inscriptions have been found in Thessalonica itself. One of these inscriptions was found on an ancient marble arch and it reads: "In the time of Politarchas...."

Gallio proconsul of Achaea

Luke states in Acts 18: 12–17 that Paul was brought before Gallio, the proconsul of Achaea.

This has been confirmed by an archaeological find at Delphi in a letter from Emperor Claudius. Claudius refers to:

"Lucius Junios Gallio, my friend, and the proconsul of Achaia ..."

The Erastus Inscription

One of the paved stones at Corinth bears an inscription concerning one of its city officials by the name of Erastus.

"Erastus the chamberlain of the city saluteth you" writes Paul in Romans 16: 23, thus naming Erastus as one of the city treasurers who belonged to the church at Corinth, from where Paul wrote his letter to the Romans.

From Acts 19: 22 it is clear that Erastus worked closely with Paul and, in Romans 16: 23, Erastus, a coworker of Paul, is named the Corinthian city treasurer.

In 1928 archaeologists were excavating a Corinthian theater when they came across the following inscription:

"Erastus in return for his aedilship laid the pavement at his own expense."

The pavement was laid in A.D. 50. The designation of treasurer describes the work of a Corinthian aedile.

Publius of Malta

In Acts 28: 7, Luke mentions a certain Publius, and speaks of him as the chief man on the island of Malta. Many scholars questioned this strange title and wrote it off as being part of Luke's inaccurate way of reporting. However, inscriptions have now been found on Malta giving Publius the title of "chief/first man."

"In all, Luke names thirty-two countries, fifty-four cities, and nine islands without error."

A.N. Sherwin-White

"For Acts the confirmation of historicity is overwhelming.... Any attempt to reject its basic historicity must now appear absurd. Roman historians have long taken it for granted."

A.N. Sherwin-White

Archaeology and the book of Acts

1 The cultural background in Acts

LYSTRA

Luke notes that the people of Lystra worshiped gods they called Zeus and Hermes in Acts 14: 12.

Inscriptions found near Lystra record a dedication to Zeus and Hermes which were made by men with Lycaonian names.

ATHENS

Luke states that in Athens Paul came across an inscription "to the unknown god." We now know that there were many such inscriptions on altars in Athens dedicated to "to an unknown god." 2nd century Pausanias, and 3rd century Diogenes Laertes both mentioned such altars to these anonymous deities.

EPHESUS

Luke mentions a number of significant features about the city of Ephesus, all of which have been confirmed by archaeological finds.

In Luke 19: 18–41 a host of significantly verifiable items are brought to our attention. According to Luke a number of people who practiced sorcery lived in Ephesus, Acts 19: 19.

It has been confirmed that in ancient times Ephesus was renowned for its sorcery and occultic practices. The phrase *Ephesia grammata* ("Ephesian scripts or writings") became a common term in the Greco-Roman world for magical texts.

The city of Ephesus made and sold silver idols dedicated to the goddess Artemis (Diana), Acts 19: 24,25
A number of such idols have been found in Ephesus.

Luke mentions that this goddess Artemis had a temple in Ephesus, Acts 19: 27
The remains of a temple, measuring 160 feet by 340 feet have been unearthed in Ephesus.

Luke also states that Ephesus had a theater in its city, Acts 19: 31
A theater almost 500 feet in diameter has been found in Ephesus. It is estimated that it could have seated up to 24,500 people. Inside the theater gold and silver images with inscriptions to Artemis have been found. Some of them weighed as much as 7 pounds.

Archaeological discoveries about the New Testament (3)

Archaeology and the book of Acts, continued

EPHESUS, CONTINUED

Luke also states that Ephesus had a theater in its city, Acts 19: 31, continued

Quote Unquote

"In Ephesus Paul taught 'in the school of Tyrannus'; in the city of Socrates he discussed moral questions in the market-place. But the narrative never makes a false step amid all the many details, as the scene changes from city to city; and that is the conclusive proof that it is a picture of real life."

Sir William Ramsay

2 Luke's knowledge of contemporary events

THE FAMINE

Luke refers to a severe famine taking place during the reign of Emperor Claudius, Acts 11: 27,28.

Suetonius, a Roman historian who lived at the beginning of the 2nd century, writes about austere conditions in Claudius' reign caused by, "a scarcity of provisions, occasioned by bad crops for several years."

3 Luke's nautical knowledge and Acts

Luke was a well-educated man and his account of Paul's journeys in Acts demonstrates that he was well-versed in nautical matters.

Luke's breath-taking account of a shipwreck in Acts 27 is not only a most exciting story to read but is full of information about boats and sailing that only an observant and informed eyewitness could have recorded.

Rackham says of Acts 27: "the story is told with such a wealth of detail that in all classical literature there is no passage which gives us so much information about the working of an ancient ship."

Luke uses precise terminology as he records some of the details of Paul's sea journey.

For example Luke says, "They sailed under [*hyperleusamen*] the lee of Cyprus, keeping northwards with a westerly wind on the beam" (Acts 27: 4); "here they ran before a wind under [*hypodramontes*] the lee of Clauda" (Acts 27: 14). In Acts 27: 14 Luke speaks of a wind of typhoon force, the "northeaster" (*euraquilo*), which swept down from an island (Crete). The island of Crete has mountains which rise to over 7000 feet. It is still true today that hurricane-like winds suddenly flow down the mountains and cause great difficulties for any passing ships.

Speaking of Luke's accuracy in describing his sea-voyages Robinson has written:

"it is to Luke that we owe the most vivid as well as the most accurate account of sea-voyaging that has come down to us from antiquity. Experts in navel science agree that it is without a parallel."

4 Historical framework

"In Acts or in that part of Acts which is concerned with the adventures of Paul in Asia Minor and Greece, one is aware all the time of the Hellenistic and Roman setting. The historical framework is exact. In terms of time and place the details are precise and correct. One walks the streets and market-places, the theatres and assemblies of first-century Ephesus or Thessalonica, Corinth or Philippi, with the author of Acts. ...The feel and tone of city life is the same as in the descriptions of Strabo and Dio of Prusa...In all these ways Acts takes us on a conducted tour of the Greco-Roman world. The detail is so interwoven with the narrative of the mission as to be inseparable."

A.N. Sherwin-White

SEUTONIUS
Suetonius, a court official and annalist under Hadrian, A.D. 120, wrote: "As the Jews were making constant disturbance at the instigation of Chrestus, he expelled them from Rome."

Luke makes reference to this same expulsion in Acts 18: 1–2.

Conclusion

It is hard to avoid the conclusion that Luke wrote his Acts in a reliable and trustworthy way, in every respect.

"The present writer takes the view that Luke's history is unsurpassed in respect of its trustworthiness. You may press the words of Luke in a degree beyond any other historian's and they will stand the keenest scrutiny and the hardest treatment, provided always that the critic knows the subject and does not go beyond the limits of science and of justice.

"Acts may be quoted as a trustworthy historical authority. Luke is a historian of the first rank; not merely are his statements of fact trustworthy; he is possessed of the true historic sense; he fixes his mind on the idea and plan that rules in the evolution of history."

Sir William Ramsay

Mountains

Overview

Mountains refer to the elevated parts of the earth. Gen. 7: 19,20.

God the Creator and mountains

God formed them.
   Amos 4: 13.
God founded them.
"Who by [Your] might have founded the mountains, being girded with power"
   Ps. 65: 6 AB.
Gives strength to.
   Ps. 95: 4.
Weighs, in a balance.
   Is. 40: 12.
Waters.
   Ps. 104: 13.
Bring draught on them.
   Hag. 1: 11.
Makes them smoke.
   Ps. 104: 32; 144: 5.
Sets them on fire.
   Deut. 32: 22.
Lays waste.
   Is. 42: 15.
Makes them tremble.
   Nah. 1: 5; Hab. 3: 10.
Makes them skip.
   Ps. 114: 4,6.
Makes them quake.
   Judg. 5: 5; Ps. 97: 5; Is. 64: 1,3.
Removes them.
   Job 9: 5.
Overturns them.
   Job 9: 5; 28: 9.
Crumbles them.
   Hab. 3: 6.

Purpose of

Made to glorify God.
   Ps. 148: 9.

Names given to mountains

God's mountains.
   Is. 49: 11.
The ancient mountains.
   Deut. 33: 15.
The everlasting mountains.
   Hab. 3: 6.
Perpetual hills.
   Heb. 3: 6.
Everlasting hills.
   Gen. 49: 26.
Pillars of heaven.
   Job 26: 11.

Features of mountains

Many very high
   Ps. 104: 18; Is. 2: 14.
Are the sources of springs and rivers
   Deut. 8: 7; Ps. 104: 8–10.
Canaan had many mountains
   Deut. 11: 11.
Allusions to volcanic fires
   Is. 64: 1,2; Jer. 51: 25; Nah. 1: 5,6.

Mountains mentioned in Scripture

- Ararat. Gen. 8: 4.
- Abarim. Num. 33: 47,48.
- Amalek. Judg. 12: 15.
- Bashan. Ps. 68: 15.
- Bethel. 1 Sam. 13: 2.
- Carmel. Josh. 15: 55; 19: 26;
   2 Kgs. 19: 23.
- Ebal. Deut. 11: 29; 27: 13.
- Ephraim. Josh. 17: 15; Judg. 2: 9.

- Gerizim. Deut. 11: 29; Judg. 9: 7.
- Gilboa. 1 Sam. 31: 1; 2 Sam. 1: 6,21.
- Gilead. Gen. 31: 21,25; Song 4: 1.
- Hachilah. 1 Sam. 23: 19.
- Hermon. Josh. 13: 11.
- Hor. Num. 20: 22; 34: 7,8.
- Horeb. Ex. 3: 1.
- Lebanon. Deut. 3: 25.
- Mizar. Ps. 42: 6.
- Moreh. Judg. 7: 1.
- Moriah. Gen. 22: 2; 2 Chr. 3: 1.
- Nebo. Num. 32: 3; Deut. 34: 1.
- Olives or mount of corruption.
  1 Kgs. 11: 7; 2 Kgs. 23: 13; Luke 21: 37.
- Pisgah. Num. 21: 20; Deut. 34: 1.
- Seir. Gen. 14: 6; 36: 8.
- Sinai. Ex. 19: 2; 18: 20,23; 31: 18.
- Sion. 2 Sam. 5: 7.
- Tabor. Judg. 4: 6,12,14.

Mount Sinai

This mountain is located in the peninsula east of the Red Sea, and is also sometimes called Sina-Hor.

Children of Israel arrive at it, during their wanderings in the desert: Ex. 16: 1; 19: 2; Deut. 1: 2.

THE LAW DELIVERED TO MOSES THERE
Ex. 19: 3–25

USED FIGURATIVELY
Galatians 4: 24–25 AB.

Usefulness of mountains

A defense to a country. Ps. 125: 2.
A refuge in time of danger.
  Gen. 14: 10; Judg. 6: 2; Matt. 24: 16.
Provided pasture
  Ex. 3: 1; 1 Sam. 25: 7; 1 Kgs. 22: 17;
  Ps. 147: 8; Amos 4: 1.
Mountains that had plenty of:
- Herbs. Prov. 27: 25.

- Minerals. Deut. 8: 9.
- Precious things. Deut. 33: 15.
- Stone for building. 1 Kgs. 5: 14,17;
  Dan. 2: 45.
- Forests. 2 Kgs. 19: 23; 2 Chr. 2: 2,8–10.
- Vineyards. 2 Chr. 26: 10; Jer. 31: 5.
- Spices. Song 4: 6; 8: 14.
- Deer. 1 Chr. 12: 8; Song 2: 8.
- Game. 1 Sam. 26: 20.
- Wild beasts. Song 4: 8; Hab. 2: 17.

Often inhabited

Gen. 36: 8; Josh. 11: 21.

Mountains and worship

Sometimes selected as places for divine worship. Gen. 22: 2,5; Ex. 3: 12.
Often selected for idolatrous worship.
  Deut. 12: 2; 2 Chr. 21: 11.

Proclamations and beacons

Proclamations often made from.
  Is. 40: 9.
Beacons often lifted up on them.
  Is. 13: 2; 30: 17.

Mountains in the Bible illustrate

Difficulties. Matt. 17: 20.
People in authority. Ps. 72: 3; Is. 44: 23.
God's church. Is. 2: 2; Dan. 2: 35,44,45.
God's righteousness. Ps. 36: 6.
Proud people. Is. 2: 14.
Burning: destructive enemies. Jer. 51: 25;
  Rev. 8: 8.
Breaking into song: expressing great
  joy. Is. 44: 23; 55: 12.
Lay waste: of desolation. Mal. 1: 3.
Dropping new wine: of abundance.
  Amos 9: 13.

Valleys

Overview

Referred to as tracts of land between mountains.
1 Sam. 17: 3.

Names for valleys

- Vales. Deut. 1: 7; Josh. 10: 40.
- Dales. Gen. 14: 17; 2 Sam. 18: 18.
- Fat valleys, when fruitful. Is. 28: 1,4.
- Rough valleys, when uncultivated and barren. Deut. 21: 4.

Watered by mountain streams

Ps. 104: 8,10.
"The mountains rose, the valleys sank down to the place which You appointed for them. . . .He sends forth springs into the valleys; their waters run among the mountains" Psalm 104: 8,10 AB.

Canaan abounded in

"But the land which you enter to possess is a land of hills and valleys which drinks water of the rain of the heavens" Deuteronomy 11: 11 AB.

Some valleys had plenty of:

Fountains and springs.
Deut. 8: 7; Is. 41: 18.

Rocks and caves.
Job 30: 6; Is. 57: 5.

Trees.
1 Kgs. 10: 27.

Lily of the valley.
Song 2: 1.

Ravens.
Prov. 30: 17.

Doves.
Ezek. 7: 16.

Valleys and humans

WELL TILLED AND FRUITFUL
Ps. 65: 13.
"Now the men of Beth-shemesh were reaping their wheat harvest in the valley, and they lifted up their eyes and saw the ark, and rejoiced to see it"
1 Samuel 6: 13 AB.

OFTEN THE SCENES OF IDOLATROUS RITES
Is. 57: 5.

THE HEATHEN BELIEVED THAT CERTAIN DEITIES PRESIDED OVER
1 Kgs. 20: 23,28.

THE CANAANITES HELD POSSESSION OF, AGAINST JUDAH
Judg. 1: 19.

OFTEN THE SCENES OF GREAT CONTESTS
Judg. 5: 15; 7: 8,22.
"Now Saul and the brothers and all the men of Israel were in the Valley of Elah, fighting with the Philistines" 1 Samuel 17: 19.

Valleys mentioned in scripture

- Achor. Josh. 7: 24; Is. 65: 10; Hos. 2: 5.

- Ajalon. Josh. 10: 12.
- Baca.
- "Passing through the Valley of Weeping (Baca), they make it a place of springs; the early rain also fills [the pools] with blessings" Psalm 84: 6 AB.
- Berachah. 2 Chr. 20: 26.
- Bochim. Judg. 2: 5.
- Charashim. 1 Chr. 4: 14.
- Elah. 1 Sam. 17: 2; 21: 9.
- Eshcol. Num. 32: 9; Deut. 1: 24.
- Gad. 2 Sam. 24: 5.
- Gerar. Gen. 26: 17.
- Gibeon. Is. 28: 21.
- Hebron. Gen. 37: 14.
- Hinnom or Tophet. Josh. 18: 16; 2 Kgs. 23: 10; 2 Chr. 28: 3; Jer. 7: 32.
- Jehoshaphat or decision. Joel 3: 2,14.
- Jericho. Deut. 34: 3.
- Jezreel. Hos. 1: 5.
- Jephthah-el. Josh. 19: 14,27.
- Keziz. Josh. 18: 21.
- Lebanon. Josh. 11: 17.
- Megiddo. 2 Chr. 35: 22; Zech. 12: 11.
- Moab where Moses was buried. Deut. 34: 6.
- Passengers or Hamongog. Ezek. 39: 11.
- Rephaim or giants. Josh. 15: 8; 18: 16; 2 Sam. 5: 18; Is. 17: 5.
- Salt. 2 Sam. 8: 13; 2 Kgs. 14: 17.
- Shaveh or king's dale. Gen. 14: 17; 2 Sam. 18: 18.
- Shittim. Joel 3: 18.
- Siddim. Gen. 14: 3,8.
- Sorek. Judg. 16: 4.
- Succoth. Ps. 60: 6.
- Zared. Num. 21: 12.
- Zeboim. 1 Sam. 13: 18.
- Zephathah. 2 Chr. 14: 10.

Unusual events linked to valleys

To be filled with hostile chariots, threatened as a punishment. Is. 22: 7.

Miracles connected with

THE MOON MADE TO STAND STILL OVER AJALON
"Then Joshua spoke to the Lord on the day when the Lord gave the Amorites over to the Israelites, and he said in the sight of Israel, Sun, be silent and stand still at Gibeon, and you, moon, in the Valley of Ajalon!
Joshua 10: 12 AB.

DITCHES IN, FILLED WITH WATER
2 Kgs. 3: 16,17.

WATER IN, MADE TO APPEAR TO THE MOABITES LIKE BLOOD
2 Kgs. 3: 22,23 AB.

Valleys are sometimes illustrative:

Of the church of Christ.
Song 6: 11.

(Fruitful and well watered,) of the tents of Israel.
Numbers 24: 6

(Dark,) of affliction and death.
Psalm 23: 4

(Filling up of,) of removing all obstructions to the gospel.
Isaiah 40: 4
Luke 3: 5

Deserts

Overview

Deserts are described as vast barren plains and as uninhabited places, Mark 6: 31.

"When evening came, the disciples came to Him and said, This is a remote and barren place, and the day is now over; send the throngs away into the villages to buy food for themselves" Matthew 14: 15 AB.

Characterized as

Lonely places.
Jer. 2: 6.

Uncultivated.
Num. 20: 5; Jer. 2: 2.

Desolate.
Ezek. 6: 14.

Dry and without water.
Ex. 17: 1; Deut. 8: 15.

Trackless.
Is. 43: 19.

Great and terrible.
Deut. 1: 19.

Howling void.
"He found him in a desert land, in the howling void of the wilderness; He kept circling around him, He scanned him [penetratingly], He kept him as the pupil of His eye" Deuteronomy 32: 10 AB.

Infested with wild beasts.
Is. 13: 21; Mark 1: 13.

Infested with snakes.
"He led you through the vast and dreadful desert, that thirsty and waterless land, with its venomous snakes and scorpions. He brought you water out of hard rock" Deuteronomy 8: 15 NIV.

Infested with robbers.
Jer. 3: 2; Lam. 4: 19.

Danger to travel through.
Ex. 14: 3; 2 Cor. 11: 26.

Guides required in.
Num. 10: 31; Deut. 32: 10.

Phenomena of, alluded to

Mirage or deceptive appearance of water.
Jer. 15: 18.

Hot wind.
2 Kgs. 19: 7
"At that time it will be said to this people and to Jerusalem, A hot wind from the bare heights in the wilderness [comes at My command] against the daughter of My people–not [a wind] to fan or cleanse [from chaff, as when threshing, but] A wind too strong and full for winnowing comes at My word. Now I will also speak in judgment against [My people]. Behold, [the enemy] comes up like clouds, his chariots like the whirlwind; his horses are swifter than eagles.
Woe to us, for we are ruined (destroyed)!" Jeremiah 4: 11–13 AB.

Tornadoes or whirlwinds.

Is. 21: 1.

CLOUDS OF DUST.

"The Lord shall make the rain of your land powdered soil and dust; from the heavens it shall come down upon you until you are destroyed" Deuteronomy 28: 24 AB.

Deserts mentioned in the Bible

- Arabian or great desert. Ex. 23: 31.
- Bethaven. Josh. 18: 12.
- Beersheba. Gen. 21: 14; 1 Kgs. 19: 3,4.

"Then he was afraid and arose and went for his life and came to Beersheba of Judah [over eighty miles, and out of Jezebel's realm] and left his servant there. But he himself went a day's journey into the wilderness and came and sat down under a lone broom or juniper tree and asked that he might die. He said, It is enough; now, O Lord, take away my life; for I am no better than my fathers" 1 Kings 19: 3,4 AB.

- Damascus. 1 Kgs. 19: 15.
- Edom. 2 Kgs. 3: 8.
- Engedi. 1 Sam. 24: 1.
- Gibeon. 2 Sam. 2: 24.
- Judea. Matt. 3: 1.
- Jeruel. 2 Chr. 20: 16.
- Kedemoth. Deut. 2: 26.
- Kadesh. Ps. 29: 8.
- Maon. 1 Sam. 23: 24,25.
- Paran. Gen. 21: 21; Num. 10: 12.
- Shur. Gen. 16: 7.
- Sin. Ex. 16: 1.
- Sinai. Ex. 19: 1,2; Num. 33: 16.
- Ziph. 1 Sam. 23: 14,15.
- Zin. Num. 20: 1; 27: 14.
- Of the Red Sea. Ex. 13: 18.

- Near Gaza. Acts 8: 26.

SHRUBS OFTEN FOUND IN
Jeremiah 17: 6

PARTS OF, GAVE PASTURE
Gen. 36: 24
Ex. 3: 1.

LIVED IN BY NOMADS
Gen. 21: 20,21; Ps. 72: 9; Jer. 25: 24.

THE PERSECUTED FLED TO
1 Sam. 23: 14; Heb. 11: 38.

THE DISAFFECTED FLED TO
1 Sam. 22: 2
Acts 21: 38.

DESERTS ARE OFTEN ILLUSTRATIVE OF:
Those deprived of blessings.

Hos. 2: 3.

The world.

Song 3: 6; 8: 5.

The Gentiles.

Is. 35: 1,6
Is. 41: 19.

What affords no support.

Jer. 2: 31.

Desolation by armies.

Jer. 50: 12.
Jer. 12: 10–13

Seas (1)

The gathering together of the waters originally called

"God called the dry land Earth, and the accumulated waters He called Seas. And God saw that this was good (fitting, admirable) and He approved it" Genesis 1: 10 AB.

Great rivers often called

Jer. 51: 36.
"And the Lord will utterly destroy (doom and dry up) the tongue of the Egyptian sea [the west fork of the Red Sea]; and with His [mighty] scorching wind He will wave His hand over the river [Nile] and will smite it into seven channels and will cause men to cross over dry-shod" Isaiah 11: 15 AB.

Lakes often called

Matt. 8: 24,27,32.
"The Arabah also, with the Jordan as its boundary, from Chinnereth as far as the Sea of the Arabah, the Salt [Dead] Sea, under the cliffs [of the headlands] of Pisgah on the east" Deuteronomy 3: 17 AB.

God

• Created. Ex. 20: 11; Ps. 95: 5; Acts 14: 15.
• Made the birds and fished out of. Gen. 1: 20–22.
• Founded the earth upon. Ps. 24: 2.
• Set bounds to, by a perpetual decree. Job 26: 10; 38: 8,10,11; Prov. 8: 27,29.
• Measures the waters of. Is. 40: 12.
• Does what he pleases in. Ps. 135: 6.
• Dries up, at his command. Is. 50: 2; Nah. 1: 4.

• Shakes, by his word. Hag. 2: 6.
• Stills, by his power. Ps. 65: 7; 89: 9; 107: 29.

Characteristics of seas

Of immense extent.
Job 11: 9; Ps. 104: 25.

Of great depth.
Ps. 68: 22.

Replenished by rivers.
Eccl. 1: 7; Ezek. 47: 8.

Called the

Deep.
Job 41: 31; Ps. 107: 24; 2 Cor. 11: 25.

Great waters.
Ps. 77: 19.

Great and wide sea.
Ps. 104: 25.

Inhabited by countless creatures

"Yonder is the sea, great and wide, in which are swarms of innumerable creeping things, creatures both small and great. There go the ships of the sea, and Leviathan (the sea monster), which You have formed to sport in it" Psalm 104: 25,26 AB.

The wonders of God seen in

Ps. 107: 24.

Made to glorify God

Ps. 69: 34; 148: 7.

Seas mentioned in the Bible

• The Adriatic or sea of Adria. Acts 27: 27.
• Mediterranean or great sea.

Num. 34: 6; Deut. 11: 24; 34: 2;
Zech. 14: 8.
- Red Sea. Ex. 10: 19; 13: 18; 23: 31.
- Sea of Joppa or sea of the Philistines.
  Ezra 3: 7; Ex. 23: 21.
- Salt or Dead Sea. Gen. 14: 3;
  Num. 34: 12.
- Sea of Galilee. Matt. 4: 18; 8: 32;
  John 6: 1.
- Sea of Jazer. Jer. 48: 32.

Raised by the wind

Ps. 107: 25,26; John. 1: 4.

Made to foam by Leviathan

"He makes the deep boil like a pot; he
makes the sea like a [foaming] pot of
ointment.

32 [His swift darting] makes a
shining track behind him; one would
think the deep to be hoary [with foam]"
Job 41: 31–32 AB.

The waves of

Raised up high.
  Ps. 93: 3; 107: 25.

Tossed to and fro.
  Jer. 5: 22.

Numerous.
  Jer. 51: 42.

Mighty.
  Ps. 93: 4; Acts 27: 41.

Tumultuous.
  Luke 21: 25; Jude 1: 13.

Sand the barrier of

Jer. 5: 22.

The shore of, covered with sand

Gen. 22: 17; 1 Kgs. 4: 29; Job 6: 3;
Ps. 78: 27.

Numerous islands in

Ezek. 26: 18.

Crossed over in ships

Ps. 104: 26; 107: 23.

Sailing on, dangerous

Acts 27: 9,20; 2 Cor. 11: 26.

Commercial nations

- Often built cities on the borders of.
  Gen. 49: 13; Ezek. 27: 3; Nah. 3: 8.
- Derived great wealth from.
  Deut. 33: 19.

Shall give up its dead at the last day

Rev. 20: 13.

The renewed earth shall be without

Rev. 21: 1.

Seas illustrative

- Of heavy afflictions. Is. 43: 2;
  Lam. 2: 13.
- (Trouble,) of the wicked. Is. 57: 20.
- (Roaring,) of hostile armies. Is. 5: 30;
  Jer. 6: 23.
- (Waves of,) of righteousness.
  Is. 48: 18.
- (Waves of,) of devastating armies.
  Ezek. 26: 3,4.
- (Waves of,) of the unsteady.
  James 1: 6.

"Only it must be in faith that he asks
with no wavering (no hesitating, no
doubting). For the one who wavers
(hesitates, doubts) is like the billowing
surge out at sea that is blown hither and
thither and tossed by the wind" James
1: 6 AB.

Seas (2)

Seas illustrative, continued

- (Covered with waters,) of the diffusion of spiritual knowledge over the earth in the latter days. Is. 11: 9; Hab. 2: 14.
- (Smooth as glass,) of the peace of heaven. Rev. 4: 6; 15: 2.
  "And in front of the throne there was also what looked like a transparent glassy sea, as if of crystal. And around the throne, in the center at each side of the throne, were four living creatures (beings) who were full of eyes in front and behind [with intelligence as to what is before and at the rear of them]" Revelation 4: 6 AB.

Sea of Galilee

Called:

SEA OF TIBERIAS
"AFTER THIS, Jesus let Himself be seen and revealed [Himself] again to the disciples, at the Sea of Tiberias. And He did it in this way" John 21: 1 AB.

LAKE GENNESARET
"NOW IT occurred that while the people pressed upon Jesus to hear the message of God, He was standing by the Lake of Gennesaret (Sea of Galilee)" Luke 5: 1 AB.

SEA OF CHINNERETH
Num. 34: 11; Deut. 3: 17; Josh. 13: 27.

SEA OF CHINNEROTH
Josh. 12: 3.

Jesus calls disciples on the shore of

Matt. 4: 18–22; Luke 5: 1–11.

Jesus teaches from a ship on

Matt. 13: 1–3.

Facts about Sea of Galilee

- This lake is 12½ miles long, and from 4 to 7½ miles wide.
- It surface is 682 feet below the level of the Mediterranean.
- Its varies in depth from 80 to 160 feet.
- The Jordan enters it 10½ miles below the southern extremity of the Huleh Lake.
- There is a fall in the river of 1,682 feet, or of more than 60 feet to the mile.
- It is 27 miles east of the Mediterranean, and about 60 miles north-east of Jerusalem.
- It is oval in shape.
- It is full of dozens of varieties of fish. This lake is linked with the public ministry of our Lord.
- Capernaum, "his own city" (Matt. 9: 1), stood on its shores.
- From among the fishermen who earned their living on Lake Galilee he chose Peter and his brother Andrew, and James and John, to be disciples, and sent them out to be "fishers of men" (Matt. 4: 18, 22; Mark 1: 16–20).

"And passing along the shore of the Sea of Galilee, He saw Simon [Peter] and Andrew the brother of Simon casting a net [to and fro] in the sea, for they were fishermen.

17 And Jesus said to them, Come after Me and be My disciples, and I will make you to become fishers of men.

18 And at once they left their nets and [yielding up all claim to them] followed [with] Him [joining Him as disciples and siding with His party].

19 He went on a little farther and saw James the son of Zebedee, and John his brother, who were in [their] boat putting their nets in order.

20 And immediately He called out to them, and [abandoning all mutual claims] they left their father Zebedee in the boat with the hired men and went off after Him [to be His disciples, side with His party, and follow Him]."

Mark 1: 16–20 AB

Miracles of Jesus on or beside Lake Galilee

Matt. 8: 24–32; Matt. 14: 22–33;
Matt. 17: 27; Mark 4: 37–39; Luke 5: 1–9;
Luke 8: 22–24; John 21: 1–11.

WALKING ON LAKE GALILEE
"22 Then He directed the disciples to get into the boat and go before Him to the other side, while He sent away the crowds.

23 And after He had dismissed the multitudes, He went up into the hills by Himself to pray. When it was evening, He was still there alone.

24 But the boat was by this time out on the sea, many furlongs [a furlong is one-eighth of a mile] distant from the land, beaten and tossed by the waves,

for the wind was against them.

25 And in the fourth watch [between 3: 00–6: 00 a.m.] of the night, Jesus came to them, walking on the sea.

26 And when the disciples saw Him walking on the sea, they were terrified and said, It is a ghost! And they screamed out with fright.

27 But instantly He spoke to them, saying, Take courage! I AM! Stop being afraid!

28 And Peter answered Him, Lord, if it is You, command me to come to You on the water.

29 He said, Come! So Peter got out of the boat and walked on the water, and he came toward Jesus.

30 But when he perceived and felt the strong wind, he was frightened, and as he began to sink, he cried out, Lord, save me [from death]!

31 Instantly Jesus reached out His hand and caught and held him, saying to him, O you of little faith, why did you doubt?

32 And when they got into the boat, the wind ceased.

33 And those in the boat knelt and worshiped Him, saying, Truly You are the Son of God!"

Matthew 14: 22–33 AB

A HEALING BESIDE LAKE GALILEE
"Soon after this, Jesus, coming back from the region of Tyre, passed through Sidon on to the Sea of Galilee, through the region of Decapolis [the ten cities].

Seas (3)

Sea of Galilee, continued

A HEALING BESIDE LAKE GALILEE,
CONTINUED

32 And they brought to Him a man
who was deaf and had difficulty in
speaking, and they begged Jesus to
place His hand upon him.

33 And taking him aside from
the crowd [privately], He thrust His
fingers into the man's ears and spat and
touched his tongue;

34 And looking up to heaven, He
sighed as He said, Ephphatha, which
means, Be opened!

35 And his ears were opened, his
tongue was loosed, and he began to
speak distinctly and as he should."

Mark 7: 31–35 AB

MIRACULOUS FISHING ON LAKE
GALILEE

"NOW IT occurred that while the
people pressed upon Jesus to hear the
message of God, He was standing by
the Lake of Gennesaret (Sea of Galilee).

2 And He saw two boats drawn up
by the lake, but the fishermen had gone
down from them and were washing
their nets.

3 And getting into one of the boats,
[the one] that belonged to Simon
(Peter), He requested him to draw
away a little from the shore. Then He
sat down and continued to teach the
crowd [of people] from the boat.

4 When He had stopped speaking,
He said to Simon (Peter), Put out into
the deep [water], and lower your nets
for a haul.

5 And Simon (Peter) answered,
Master, we toiled all night
[exhaustingly] and caught nothing [in
our nets]. But on the ground of Your
word, I will lower the nets [again].

6 And when they had done this,
they caught a great number of fish;
and as their nets were [at the point of]
breaking,

7 They signaled to their partners in
the other boat to come and take hold
with them. And they came and filled
both the boats, so that they began to
sink.

8 But when Simon Peter saw this, he
fell down at Jesus' knees, saying, Depart
from me, for I am a sinful man, O Lord.

9 For he was gripped with
bewildering amazement [allied to
terror], and all who were with him, at
the haul of fish which they had made;

10 And so also were James and
John, the sons of Zebedee, who were
partners with Simon (Peter). And Jesus
said to Simon, Have no fear; from now
on you will be catching men!

11 And after they had run their boats
on shore, they left everything and
joined Him as His disciples and sided
with His party and accompanied Him."

Luke 5: 1–11 AB

JESUS STILLED A STORM ON LAKE
GALILEE

"And after He got into the boat, His
disciples followed Him.

24 And suddenly, behold, there
arose a violent storm on the sea, so that
the boat was being covered up by the
waves; but He was sleeping.

25 And they went and awakened Him, saying, Lord, rescue and preserve us! We are perishing!

26 And He said to them, Why are you timid and afraid, O you of little faith? Then He got up and rebuked the winds and the sea, and there was a great and wonderful calm [a perfect peaceableness].

27 And the men were stunned with bewildered wonder and marveled, saying, What kind of Man is this, that even the winds and the sea obey Him!

Matthew 8: 23–27 AB

RESURRECTION APPEARANCE
Jesus showed himself to some of his disciples after his resurrection by Lake Galilee (John 21).

Dead Sea

Names given to the Dead Sea

GREEK WRITERS
The Dead Sea is the name given by Greek writers from the second century to the inland sea.

BIBLE NAMES
In Scripture it is called:
- the "salt sea" (Gen. 14: 3; Num. 34: 12),
- the "sea of the plain" (Deut. 3: 17),
- the "east sea" (Ezek. 47: 18; Joel 2: 20), and simply
- "the sea" (Ezek. 47: 8).

AN ARAB NAME
The Arabs call it Bahr Lut, i.e., the Sea of Lot.

Facts about the Dead Sea
- It lies about 16 miles east of Jerusalem.
- Its surface is 1,292 feet below the surface of the Mediterranean Sea.
- It covers an area of about 300 square miles.
- Its depth varies from 1,310 to 11 feet.
- It is about 53 miles long, and of an average width of 10 miles.
- It has no outlet.

Rapid evaporation

The very high temperatures of the area a cause such rapid evaporation that its average depth, notwithstanding the rivers that run into it, is maintained with little variation.

The River Jordan alone discharges six million gallons of water into it every twenty-four hours.

Saltiness

The waters of the Dead Sea contain 24.6%. of mineral salts, which is a concentration about seven times higher than ordinary sea-water.

If you swim in the Dead Sea you float as it is so buoyant.

It has huge quantities of magnesium chloride as well as sodium chloride (common salt).

Nothing living can exist in this sea. The fish carried down by the Jordan die at once.

Rivers and wells

Rivers

Source of
Job 28: 10; Ps. 104: 8,10.

Enclosed within banks
Dan. 12: 5.

Flow through valleys
Ps. 104: 8,10.

Some descriptions of
Great and mighty.
Gen. 15: 18; Ps. 74: 15.

Deep.
Ezek. 47: 5; Zech. 10: 11.

Broad.
Is. 33: 21.

Rapid.
Judg. 5: 21.

Parted into many streams.
Gen. 2: 10; Is. 11: 5.

Run into the sea.
Eccl. 1: 7; Ezek. 47: 8.

God's power over, unlimited.
Is. 50: 2; Nah. 1: 4.

Useful for
Supplying water for people.
Jer. 2: 18.

Commerce.
Is. 23: 3.

Promoting vegetation.
Gen. 2: 10.

Bathing.
Ex. 2: 5.

Baptism often performed in.
Matt. 3: 6.

Of Canaan full of fish.
Lev. 11: 9,10.

Banks of
Covered with bulrushes.
Ex. 2: 3,5.

Planted with trees.
Ezek. 47: 7.

Facts about rivers
Rivers and doves.
Song 5: 12.

Rivers and wild animals.
Jer. 49: 19.

Meeting places.
Ps. 137: 1.

Frequently overflowed.
Josh. 3: 15; 1 Chr. 12: 15.

Especially fruitful.
Ps. 1: 3; Is. 32: 20.

Gardens often made beside.
Num. 24: 6.

Cities often built beside.
Ps. 46: 4; 137: 1.

Often the boundaries of kingdoms.
Josh. 22: 25; 1 Kgs. 4: 24.

Rivers mentioned in the Bible
- Of Eden. Gen. 2: 10.
- Of Jotbath. Deut. 10: 7.
- Of Ethiopia. Is. 18: 1.
- Of Babylon. Ps. 137: 1.
- Of Egypt. Gen. 15: 18.
- Of Damascus. 2 Kgs. 5: 12.
- Of Ahava. Ezra 8: 15.
- Of Judah. Joel 3: 18.

- Of Philippi. Acts 16: 13.
- Abana. 2 Kgs. 5: 12.
- Arnon. Deut. 2: 36; Josh. 12: 1.
- Chebar. Ezek. 1: 1,3; 10: 15,20.
- Euphrates. Gen. 2: 14.
- Gihon. Gen. 2: 13.
- Gozan. 2 Kgs. 17: 6; 1 Chr. 5: 26.
- Hiddekel. Gen. 2: 14.
- Jabbok. Deut. 2: 37; Josh. 12: 2.
- Jordan. Josh. 3: 8; 2 Kgs. 5: 10.
- Kanah. Josh. 16: 8.
- Kishon. Judg. 5: 21.
- Pharpar. 2 Kgs. 5: 12.
- Pison. Gen. 2: 11.
- Ulai. Dan. 8: 16.

Rivers illustrative

- Of the abundance of grace in Christ. Is. 32: 2; John 1: 16.
- Of the gifts and graces of the Holy Spirit. Ps. 46: 4; Is. 41: 18; 43: 19,20; John 7: 38,39.
- Of heavy afflictions. Ps. 69: 2; Is. 43: 2.
- Of abundance. Job 20: 17; 29: 6.
- Of people flying from judgments. Is. 23: 10.
- (Steady course of,) of peace of saints. Is. 66: 12.
- (Fruitfulness of trees planted by,) of the permanent prosperity of saints. Ps. 1: 3; Jer. 17: 8.
- (Drying up of,) of God's judgments. Is. 19: 1–8; Jer. 51: 36; Nah. 1: 4; Zech. 10: 11.
- (Overflowing of,) of God's judgments. Is. 8: 7,8; 28: 2,18; Jer. 47: 2.

River Jordan

A river in Palestine:
Empties into the Dead Sea
  Josh. 15: 5

Fords of.
  Gen. 32: 10; Josh. 2: 7; Judg. 3: 28; Judg. 7: 24; Judg. 8: 4; Judg. 10: 9; Judg. 12: 5–6

Wells

First mention of

Gen. 16: 14.

Frequently made

Near encampments.
  Gen. 21: 30; 26: 18.

Outside cities.
  Gen. 24: 11; John 4: 6,8.

In the courts of houses.
  2 Sam. 17: 18.

In the desert.
  2 Chr. 26: 10.

Supplied by springs

Prov. 16: 22.

Supplied by the rain

Ps. 84: 6.

Surrounded by trees

Gen. 49: 22; Ex. 15: 27.

Names often given to

Gen. 16: 14; 21: 31.

Canaan had many
  Deut. 6: 11.

Many supplied from Lebanon.
  Song 4: 15.

Wells mentioned in the Bible

- Beerlahairoi. Gen. 16: 14.
- Bethlehem. 2 Sam. 23: 15; 1 Chr. 11: 17,18.
- Beer (east of Jordan). Num. 21: 16–18.
- Beer-sheba. Gen. 21: 30,31.
- Elim. Ex. 15: 27.

Fountains and springs

Overview

Created by God.
> Ps. 74: 15; 104: 10.

God to be praised for.
> Rev. 14: 7.

Come from the great deep.
> Gen. 7: 11; Job 38: 16.

Found in hills and valleys.
> Deut. 8: 7; Ps. 104: 10.

Only produce one kind of water.
> James 3: 11.

Purpose

For animals to drink.
> Ps. 104: 11.

Refresh birds.
> Ps. 104: 12.

Water the earth.
> 1 Kgs. 18: 5; Joel 3: 18.

Used by travelers.
> Gen. 16: 7.

Miscellaneous facts about

Abound in Canaan.
> Deut. 8: 7; 1 Kgs. 18: 5.

Sometimes dried up.
> Is. 58: 11.

Drying up of, a severe punishment.
> Ps. 107: 33,34; Hos. 13: 15.

Sometimes stopped to harm enemies.
> 2 Chr. 32: 3,4.

Mentioned in the Bible

In the way to Shur.
> Gen. 16: 7.

Of the waters of Nephtoah.
> Josh. 15: 9.

Of Jezreel.
> 1 Sam. 29: 1.

Of Pisgah.
> Deut. 4: 49.

Upper and nether springs.
> Josh. 15: 19; Judg. 1: 15.

Illustrative

Of God.
> Ps. 36: 9; Jer. 2: 13; 17: 13.

Of Christ.
> Zech. 13: 1.

Of the Holy Spirit.
> John 7: 38,39.
> "He who believes in Me [who cleaves to and trusts in and relies on Me] as the Scripture has said, From his innermost being shall flow [continuously] springs and rivers of living water.
> 39 But He was speaking here of the Spirit, Whom those who believed (trusted, had faith) in Him were afterward to receive. For the [Holy] Spirit had not yet been given, because Jesus was not yet glorified (raised to honor)"   *John 7: 38,29 AB.*

Of constant supplies of grace.
> Ps. 87: 7.

Of eternal life.
> But whoever takes a drink of the water that I will give him shall never, no never, be thirsty any more. But the water that I will give him shall become a spring of water welling up (flowing, bubbling) [continually] within him unto (into, for) eternal life"   *John 4: 14 AB.*
> And He [further] said to me, It is done! I am the Alpha and the Omega,

the Beginning and the End. To the thirsty I [Myself] will give water without price from the fountain (springs) of the water of Life"

Revelation 21: 6 AB

Of the means of grace.
I will open rivers on the bare heights, and fountains in the midst of the valleys; I will make the wilderness a pool of water, and the dry land springs of water" Isaiah 41: 18 AB.

"And in that day, the mountains shall drip with fresh juice [of the grape] and the hills shall flow with milk; and all the brooks and riverbeds of Judah shall flow with water, and a fountain shall come forth from the house of the Lord and shall water the Valley of Shittim"

Joel 3: 18 AB

Of a good wife.
Prov. 5: 18.

Of a numerous posterity.
Deut. 33: 28.

Of spiritual wisdom.
"Understanding is a wellspring of life to those who have it, but to give instruction to fools is folly"

Proverbs 16: 22 AB

"4 The words of a [discreet and wise] man's mouth are like deep waters [plenteous and difficult to fathom], and the fountain of skillful and godly Wisdom is like a gushing stream [sparkling, fresh, pure, and life-giving]"   *Proverbs 18: 4 AB*

Of the law of the wise.
Prov. 13: 14.

Of godly fear.
Prov. 14: 27.

(Sealed up,) of the church.
Song 4: 12.

(Not failing,) of the church.
Is. 58: 11.

(Always flowing,) of unceasing wickedness of the Jews.
Jer. 6: 7.

(Corrupt,) of the natural heart.
"Does a fountain send forth [simultaneously] from the same opening fresh water and bitter?"

James 3: 11 AB

Of the salvation of the gospel.
18 And in that day, the mountains shall drip with fresh juice [of the grape] and the hills shall flow with milk; and all the brooks and riverbeds of Judah shall flow with water, and a fountain shall come forth from the house of the Lord and shall water the Valley of Shittim"

Joel 3: 18 AB

"1 In that day there shall be a fountain opened for the house of David and for the inhabitants of Jerusalem [to cleanse them from] sin and uncleanness" *Zechariah 13: 1 AB*

"For the Lamb Who is in the midst of the throne will be their Shepherd, and He will guide them to the springs of the waters of life; and God will wipe away every tear from their eyes"

Revelation 7: 17 AB

Of being led astray.
Prov. 25: 26

The Egyptians (1)

Long history

The Nile River valley and delta has been home to the people of Egypt since 4000 B.C. Egypt is known as the land of the Nile and the pyramids (tombs of their monarchs). It is the oldest kingdom we have any record about and it has a significant place in Scripture.

When Cleopatra died in 30 B.C. the Roman Empire absorbed the country of Egypt.

Two halves

Egypt consists geographically of two halves, the northern being the Delta, and the southern Upper Egypt, between Cairo and the First Cataract. In the Old Testament, Northern or Lower Egypt is called Mazor, "the fortified land" (Is. 19: 6; 37: 25); while Southern or Upper Egypt is Pathros, the Egyptian Pa-to-Res, or "the land of the south" (Is. 11: 11). The whole country is known by the name of Mizraim, "the two Mazors."

The Egyptian religion was a strange mixture of pantheism and animal worship. They worshiped gods in the shape of animals.

General facts

Inhabited by Mizraim's descendants.
Gen. 10: 6,13,14.
Boundaries of.
Ezek. 29: 10.
Dry climate of.
Deut. 11: 10,11.
Watered by the Nile.
Gen. 41: 1–3; Ex. 1: 22.

Movement of the Nile
Amos 8: 8.
Subject to plague
Deut. 7: 15; 28: 27,60.
Sometimes experienced famine
Gen. 41: 30.

Names called in the Bible

• The land of Ham. Ps. 105: 23; 106: 22.
• The South. Jer. 13: 19; Dan. 11: 14,25.
• Sihor. Is. 23: 3.
• Rahab. Ps. 87: 4; 89: 10.
• House of Bondmen. Ex. 13: 3,14; Deut. 7: 8.

Celebrated for

• Fertility. Gen. 13: 10; 45: 18.
• Wealth. Heb. 11: 26.
• Literature. 1 Kgs. 4: 30; Acts 7: 22.
• Fine horses. 1 Kgs. 10: 28,29.
• Fine linen. Prov. 7: 16; Is. 19: 9.
• Commerce. Gen. 41: 57; Ezek. 27: 7.

Miscellaneous facts about

Religion of, idolatrous.
Ex. 12: 12; Num. 33: 4; Is. 19: 1; Ezek. 29: 7.
Idolatry of, followed by Israel
Ex. 32: 4; Ezek. 20: 8,19.
Magic practiced in
Ex. 7: 11,12,22; 8: 7.
Ruled by kings who assumed the name of Pharaoh
Gen. 12: 14,15; 40: 1,2; Ex. 1: 8,22.
Under a governor
Gen. 41: 41–44.
Had princes and counselors
Gen. 12: 15; Is. 19: 11.
Kind of hospitality.

Gen. 43: 32–34.

Diet used in
Num. 11: 5.

Kind of embalming in
Gen. 50: 3.

Often a refuge to strangers
Gen. 12: 10; 47: 4; 1 Kgs. 11: 17,40;
2 Kgs. 25: 26; Matt. 2: 12,13.

As a power was

Proud and arrogant.
Ezek. 29: 3; 30: 6.

Pompous.
Ezek. 32: 12.

Mighty.
Is. 30: 2,3.

Ambitious to conquer.
Jer. 46: 8.

Treacherous.
Is. 36: 6; 29: 6,7.

Characteristics of Egyptians

Superstitious.
Is. 19: 3.

Hospitable.
Gen. 47: 5,6; 1 Kgs. 11: 18.

Often intermarried with strangers.
Gen. 21: 21; 1 Kgs. 3: 1; 11: 19;
1 Chr. 2: 34,35.

Hated shepherds.
Gen. 46: 34.

Hated the sacrifice of oxen.
Ex. 8: 26.

Israelites and Egyptians

Israelites not to hate Egyptians.
"You shall not abhor an Egyptian,
because you were a stranger and
temporary resident in his land"
Deuteronomy 23: 7 AB

Might be received into the
congregation in the third generation.
Deut. 23: 8.

The armies of Egypt

Described.
Ex. 14: 7–9.

Destroyed in the Red Sea.
Ex. 14: 23–28.

Captured and burned Gezer.
1 Kgs. 9: 16.

Besieged and plundered Jerusalem in
Rehoboam's time.
1 Kgs. 14: 25,26.

Invaded Assyria and killed Josiah who
assisted it.
2 Kgs. 23: 29.

Deposed Jehoahaz and made Judea pay
tribute.
2 Kgs. 23: 31–35.

Assistance of, sought by Judah.
Ezek. 17: 15; Jer. 37: 5,7.

History of Israel in Egypt

• Their stay there, foretold. Gen. 15: 13.
• Joseph sold into. Gen. 37: 28; 39: 1.
• Potiphar blessed for Joseph's sake.
  Gen. 39: 2–6.
• Joseph unjustly thrown into prison.
  Gen. 39: 7–20.
• Joseph interprets the chief baker's
  and the chief butler's dreams.
  Gen. 40: 5–19.
• Joseph interprets Pharaoh's dreams.
  Gen. 41: 14–32.
• Joseph counsels Pharaoh.
  Gen. 41: 33–36.
• Joseph made governor. Gen. 41: 41–44.
• Joseph's successful provision for the
  years of famine. Gen. 41: 46–56.
• Joseph's ten brothers arrive.
  Gen. 42: 1–6.

The Egyptians (2)

History of Israel in Egypt, continued

- Joseph recognizes his brothers.
  Gen. 42: 7,8.
- Benjamin brought to Egypt.
  Gen. 43: 15.
- Joseph makes himself known to his brothers. Gen. 45: 1–8.
- Joseph sends for his father.
  Gen. 45: 9–11.
- Pharaoh invites Jacob into.
  Gen. 45: 16–20.
- Jacob's journey. Gen. 46: 5–7.
- Jacob presented to Pharaoh.
  Gen. 47: 1–10.
- Israel live in the land of Goshen.
  Gen. 46: 34; 47: 11,27.
- Joseph enriches the king. Gen. 47: 13–26.
- Jacob's death and burial. Gen. 49: 33; 50: 1–13.
- Israel increases and is oppressed.
  Ex. 1: 1–14.
- Male children killed. Ex. 1: 15–22.
- Moses born and hid for three months. Ex. 2: 2.
- Moses adopted and brought up by Pharaoh's daughter. Ex. 2: 5–10.
- Moses kills an Egyptian. Ex. 2: 11,12.
- Moses flees to Midian. Ex. 2: 15.
- Moses sent to Pharaoh. Ex. 3: 2–10.
- Pharaoh increases their affliction.
  Ex. 5: 1–23.
- Moses proves his divine mission by miracles. Ex. 4: 29–31; 7: 10.
- Egypt is plagued for Pharaoh's obstinacy. Ex. 7: 14–10: 29.
- The Passover instituted. Ex. 12: 1–28.

- Destruction of the first-born.
  Ex. 12: 29,30.
- Israel take jewelry from the Egyptians.
  "The Israelites did according to the word of Moses; and they [urgently] asked of the Egyptians jewels of silver and of gold, and clothing.

  36 The Lord gave the people favor in the sight of the Egyptians, so that they gave them what they asked. And they stripped the Egyptians [of those things]."   Ex. 12: 35,36. AB
- Israel driven out of. Ex. 12: 31–33.
- Date of the Exodus. Ex. 12: 41;
  Heb. 11: 27.
  "At the end of the 430 years, even that very day, all the hosts of the Lord went out of Egypt." *Exodus 12: 41 AB*
- Pharaoh pursues Israel and is miraculously destroyed.

  9 "The Egyptians pursued them, all the horses and chariots of Pharaoh and his horsemen and his army, and overtook them encamped at the [Red] Sea by Pi-hahiroth, in front of Baal-zephon.

  . . . 13 Moses told the people, Fear not; stand still [firm, confident, undismayed] and see the salvation of the Lord which He will work for you today. For the Egyptians you have seen today you shall never see again.

  14 The Lord will fight for you, and you shall hold your peace and remain at rest.

  15 The Lord said to Moses, Why do you cry to Me? Tell the people of Israel to go forward!

16 Lift up your rod and stretch out your hand over the sea and divide it, and the Israelites shall go on dry ground through the midst of the sea.

19 And the Angel of God Who went before the host of Israel moved and went behind them; and the pillar of the cloud went from before them and stood behind them,

20 Coming between the host of Egypt and the host of Israel. It was a cloud and darkness to the Egyptians, but it gave light by night to the Israelites; and the one host did not come near the other all night.

21 Then Moses stretched out his hand over the sea, and the Lord caused the sea to go back by a strong east wind all that night and made the sea dry land; and the waters were divided.

22 And the Israelites went into the midst of the sea on dry ground, the waters being a wall to them on their right hand and on their left.

23 The Egyptians pursued and went in after them into the midst of the sea, even all Pharaoh's horses, his chariots, and his horsemen.

24 And in the morning watch the Lord through the pillar of fire and cloud looked down on the host of the Egyptians and discomfited [them],

25 And bound [clogged, took off] their chariot wheels, making them drive heavily; and the Egyptians said, Let us flee from the face of Israel, for the Lord fights for them against the Egyptians!"

Exodus 14: 9,13–16,19–25, AB

Prophecies about

Dismay of its inhabitants.
Is. 19: 1,16,17.
Its princes.
Is. 19: 3,11–14.
Failure of internal resources.
Is. 19: 5–10.
Civil war and domestic strife.
Is. 19: 2.
Armies destroyed by Babylon.
Jer. 46: 2–12.
Invasion by Babylon.
Jer. 46: 13,24; Ezek. 32: 11.
Destruction of its power.
Ezek. 30: 24,25.
Destruction of its cities.
Ezek. 30: 14–18.
Destruction of its idols.
Jer. 43: 12,13; 46: 25; Ezek. 30: 13.
Capture of its people.
Is. 20: 4; Jer. 46: 19,24,26; Ezek. 30: 4.
Utter desolation of, for forty years.
Ezek. 29: 8–12; 30: 12; 32: 15.
Allies to share its misfortunes.
Ezek. 30: 4,6.
The Jews who practiced its idolatry to share its punishments.
Jer. 44: 7–28.
Terror brought about by its fall.
Ezek. 32: 9,10.
Christ to be called out of.
Hos. 11: 1; Matt. 2: 15.
Conversion of.
Is. 19: 18–20.
To be numbered and blessed along with Israel.
Is. 19: 23–25.
Prophetic illustration of its destruction.
Jer. 43: 9,10; Ezek. 30: 21,22; 32: 4–6.

The Canaanites

Overview

The Canaanites were the descendants of Canaan, the son of Ham.

The land of Canaan was situation on the east side of the Mediterranean Sea, from Sidon in the north, to Gaza in the south.

They were famous as merchants and seamen, as well as for their artistic skill.

They worshiped a sun-god, who was given the general name of Baal, "lord." Each locality had its special Baal, and the different local Baals were known by the name of Baalim, "lords."

Facts about

Descended from Ham.
Gen. 10: 6.
An accursed race.
Gen. 9: 25,26.
Different families of.
Gen. 10: 15–18.
Consisted of seven separate nations.
"WHEN THE Lord your God brings you into the land which you are entering to possess and has plucked away many nations before you, the Hittites, the Girgashites, the Amorites, the Canaanites, the Perizzites, the Hivites, and the Jebusites, seven nations greater and mightier than you"
Deuteronomy 7: 1 AB

Kind to the patriarchs.
Gen. 14: 13; 23: 6.
Possessions of, how bounded.
Gen. 10: 19.

Country of, fertile.
Ex. 3: 17; Num. 13: 27.
Had many strong cities.
Num. 13: 28; Deut. 1: 28.
Expelled for wickedness.
Deut. 9: 4; 18: 12.

Described as

Great and mighty.
Num. 13: 28; Deut. 7: 1.
Idolatrous.
Deut. 29: 17.
Superstitious.
"When you come into the land which the Lord your God gives you, you shall not learn to follow the abominable practices of these nations.

10 There shall not be found among you anyone who makes his son or daughter pass through the fire, or who uses divination, or is a soothsayer, or an augur, or a sorcerer,

11 Or a charmer, or a medium, or a wizard, or a necromancer"
Deuteronomy 18: 9–11 AB
Profane and wicked.
Lev. 18: 27.
Extremely numerous
Deut. 7: 17.

Abraham and the Canaanites

Called to live among.
Gen. 12: 1–5.
Was promised the country of, as inheritance.
Gen. 13: 14–17; 15: 18; 17: 8.

Had his faith tried will living among.
Gen. 12: 6; 13: 7.

Israel commanded

- To make no treaty with. Deut. 7: 2;
Judg. 2: 2.
- Not to intermarry with. Deut. 7: 3;
Josh. 23: 12.
- Not to follow their idols of. Ex. 23: 24;
Deut. 7: 25.
- Not to follow customs of.
Lev. 18: 26,27.
- To destroy, without mercy.
Deut. 7: 2,24.
- To destroy all their idols. Ex. 23: 24;
Deut. 7: 5,25.
- Not to fear. Deut. 7: 17,18; 31: 7.

The Canaanites and Israel

Terrified at the approach of Israel.
Ex. 15: 15,16; Josh. 2: 9–11; 5: 1.
Partially subdued by Israel.
Josh. 10: 1–11: 23; Judg. 1: 1–36.
Some of them were left to try Israel.
Judg. 2: 21,22; 3: 1–4.
Some of them were left to chastise
Israel.
Num. 33: 55; Judg. 2: 3; 4: 2.
Israel trapped by.
Judg. 2: 3,19; Ps. 106: 36–38.

The Assyrians (1)

Overview

Nineveh, chief city of.
Gen. 10: 11; 2 Kgs. 19: 36.
Governed by kings.
2 Kgs. 15: 19,29.

Assyria

Antiquity and origin of.
Gen. 10: 8–11.
Situated beyond the Euphrates.
Is. 7: 20.
Watered by the river Tigris.
Gen. 2: 14.

Called

The land of Nimrod.
Mic. 5: 6.
Shinar.
Gen. 11: 2; 14: 1.
Asshur.
Hos. 14: 3.

Celebrated for

• Fertility. 2 Kgs. 18: 32; Is. 36: 17.
• Extent of conquests. 2 Kgs. 18: 33–35;
19: 11–13; Is. 10: 9–14.
• Extensive commerce. Ezek. 27: 23,24.
• Idolatry, the religion of 2 Kgs. 19: 37.

As a power, was

Most formidable.
Is. 28: 2.
Intolerant and oppressive.
Nah. 3: 19.
Cruel and destructive.
Is. 10: 7.
Selfish and reserved.
Hos. 8: 9.

Unfaithful.
2 Chr. 28: 20,21.
Proud and haughty.
2 Kgs. 19: 22–24; Is. 10: 8.
An instrument of God's vengeance.
Is. 7: 18,19; 10: 5,6.

Leaders of, described

Ezek. 23: 6,12,23.

Armies of, described

Is. 5: 26–29.

Assyrian kings in the Bible

• (Pul) Tiglathpileser, 745–727 B.C.
• Shalmaneser, 727–721 B.C.
• Sennacherib, 705–681 B.C.

PUL, KING OF
Invaded Israel.
2 Kgs. 15: 19.
Bought off by Menahem.
2 Kgs. 15: 19,20.

TIGLATHPILESER KING OF
Ravaged Israel.
2 Kgs. 15: 29.
Asked to help Ahaz against Syria.
2 Kgs. 16: 7,8.
Took money from Ahaz, but did not
support him.
2 Chr. 28: 20,21.
Conquered Syria.
2 Kgs. 16: 9.

SHALMANESER KING OF
Reduced Israel to tribute.
2 Kgs. 17: 3.
Was conspired against by Hoshea.
2 Kgs. 17: 4.

Imprisoned Hoshea.

2 Kgs. 17: 4.

Took Israel captive.

2 Kgs. 17: 5,6.

Re-peopled Samaria from Assyria.

2 Kgs. 17: 24.

SENNACHERIB, KING OF

Invaded Judah.

2 Kgs. 18: 13.

Taken off by Hezekiah.

2 Kgs. 18: 14–16.

Insulted and threatened Judah.

2 Kgs. 18: 17–32; 19: 10–13.

Blasphemed the Lord.

2 Kgs. 18: 33–35.

Prayed against by Hezekiah.

2 Kgs. 19: 14–19.

Reproved for pride and blasphemy.

2 Kgs. 19: 12–34; Is. 37: 21–29.

His army destroyed by God.

2 Kgs. 19: 35.

Assassinated by his sons.

2 Kgs. 19: 36.

Condemned for oppressing God's people

Is. 52: 4.

Manasseh taken captive to

2 Chr. 33: 11.

The re-peopling of Samaria from, completed by Asnappar

Ezra 4: 10.

Idolatry of, brought into Samaria

2 Kgs. 17: 29.

Judah condemned for trusting to

Jer. 2: 18,36.

Israel condemned for trusting to

Hos. 5: 13; 7: 11; 8: 9.

The Jews condemned for following their idols

"You played the harlot also with the Assyrians because you were unsatiable; yes, you played the harlot with them, and yet you were not satisfied"   *Ezekiel 16: 28 AB*

"And Aholah played the harlot when she was Mine, and she was foolishly fond of her lovers and doted on the Assyrians her neighbors,

7 And she bestowed her harlotries upon them, the choicest men of Assyria all of them; and on whomever she doted, with all their idols she defiled herself.

8 Neither has she left her harlotries since the days of Egypt [from where she brought them], for in her youth men there lay with her and handled her girlish bosom, and they poured out their sinful desire upon her.

9 Wherefore I delivered her into the hand of her lovers, into the hand of the Assyrians upon whom she doted.

10 These uncovered her nakedness and shame; they took her sons and her daughters and they slew her with the sword, and her name became notorious and a byword among women when judgments were executed upon her.

11 And her sister Aholibah saw this; yet she was more corrupt in her foolish fondness than she, and in her harlotries she was more wanton than her sister in her harlotries.

12 She doted upon the Assyrians —governors and deputies, her neighbors, clothed most gorgeously, horsemen riding upon horses, all of them desirable young men."

Ezekiel 23: 5,7–19 AB

The Assyrians (2)

SENNACHERIB KING OF, CONTINUED

"And I saw that she was defiled, that both [of the sisters] took one way.

14 But [Aholibah] carried her harlotries further, for she saw men pictured upon the wall, the pictures of the Chaldeans sketched in bright red pigment,

15 Girded with girdles on their loins, with flowing turbans on their heads, all of them looking like officers, a picture of Babylonian men whose native land was Chaldea,

16 Then as soon as she saw [the sketches of] them, she doted on them and sent messengers to them in Chaldea.

17 And the Babylonians came to her into the bed of love, and they defiled her with their evil desire; and when she was polluted by them, she [Jerusalem] broke the relationship and pushed them away from her in disgust.

18 So she flaunted her harlotries and exposed her nakedness, and I was disgusted and turned from her, as I had turned in disgust from her sister.

19 Yet she multiplied her harlotries, remembering the days of her youth in which she had played the harlot in the land of Egypt."   *Ezekiel 23: 13–19 AB*

The greatness, extent, duration, and fall, illustrated

"Behold, [I will liken you to] Assyria, a cedar in Lebanon, with fair branches and with forestlike shade and of high stature, with its top among the thick boughs [even among the clouds].

4 The waters nourished it; the deep made it grow tall; its rivers ran round about its planting, sending out its streams to all the trees of the forest [the other nations].

5 Therefore it towered higher than all the trees of the forest; its boughs were multiplied and its branches became long, because there was much water when they were shot forth.

6 All the birds of the heavens made their nests in its boughs, and under its branches all the wild beasts of the field brought forth their young and under its shadow dwelt all of the great nations.

7 Thus was it beautiful in its greatness, in the length of its branches, for its root was by many and great waters.

8 The cedars in the garden of God could not hide or rival it; the cypress trees did not have boughs like it and the plane trees did not have branches like it, nor was any tree in the garden of God like it in its beauty.

9 I made it beautiful with the multitude of its branches, so that all the trees of Eden that were in the garden of God envied it [Assyria].

10 Therefore thus said the Lord God: Because it is exalted in stature and has set its top among the thick boughs and the clouds, and its heart is proud of its height,

11 I will even deliver it into the hand of a mighty one of the nations; he shall surely deal with it. I have driven it out for its wickedness and lawlessness.

12 And strangers, the most terrible of the nations, will cut it off and leave

it; upon the mountains and in all the valleys its branches will fall and its boughs will lie broken by all the watercourses of the land, and all the peoples of the earth will go down out of its shade and leave it.

13 Upon its ruins all the birds of the heavens will dwell, and all the wild beasts of the field will be upon [Assyria's fallen] branches.

14 All this is so that none of the trees by the waters may exalt themselves because of their height or shoot up their top among the thick boughs and the clouds, and that none of their mighty ones should stand upon [their own estimate of] themselves for their height, all that drink water. For they are all delivered over to death, to the lower world, in the midst of the children of men, with those who go down to the pit [the grave].

15 Thus says the Lord God: When [Assyria] goes down to Sheol [the place of the dead], I will cause a mourning; I will cover the deep for it and I will restrain its floods, and the many waters [that contributed to its prosperity] will be stayed; and I will cause Lebanon to be in black gloom and to mourn for it, and all the trees of the field, dismayed, will faint because of it.

16 I will make the nations quake at the sound of its fall when I cast it down to Sheol with those who descend into the pit, and all the trees of Eden, the choice and best of Lebanon, all [the trees] that drink water, will be comforted in the netherworld [at Assyria's downfall].

17 They also shall go down into Sheol with it to those who were slain by the sword – yes, those who were its arm, who dwelt under its shadow in the midst of the nations"

Ezekiel 3: 3–17 AB

Predictions about

Conquest of the Kenites by.
  Num. 24: 22.
Conquest of Syria by.
  Is. 8: 4.
Conquest and captivity of Israel by.
  Is. 8: 4; Hos. 9: 3; 10: 6; 11: 5.
Invasion of Judah by.
  Is. 5: 26; 7: 17–20; 8: 8; 10: 5,6,12.
Restoration of Israel from.
  Is. 27: 12,13; Hos. 11: 11; Zech. 10: 10.
Destruction of.
  Is. 10: 12–19; 14: 24,25; 30: 31–33;
  31: 8,9; Zech. 10: 11.
Participation in the blessings of the gospel.
  Is. 19: 23–25; Mic. 7: 12.

Assyria

The name "Assyria" is derived from the city of Asshur which was on the River Tigris.

It was a mountainous region to the north of Babylonia, extending along the Tigris as far as to the high mountain range of Armenia, the Gordiaean or Carduchian mountains.

The Assyrians (3)

The "Romans of the East"

The Assyrians were founded in 1700 B.C. under Bel-kap-kapu, and became an independent and a conquering power, and shook off the yoke of its Babylonian masters.

They subdued the whole of Northern Asia.

The Assyrians were Semites (Gen. 10: 22), but in process of time non-Semite tribes mingled with the inhabitants.

They were a military people, the "Romans of the East."

745 B.C.

In 745 B.C. the Assyrian crown was seized by a military adventurer called Pul, who assumed the name of Tiglath-pileser III. He fought against Syria, and took (740 B.C.) Arpad, near Aleppo, after a three year siege, and forced Hamath to submit to him. Azariah (Uzziah) was an ally of the king of Hamath, and thus was compelled by Tiglath-pileser to do him homage and pay him a yearly tribute.

738 B.C.

In 738 B.C., in the reign of Menahem, king of Israel, Pul invaded Israel, and imposed on it a heavy tribute (2 Kings 15: 19).

Ahaz, the king of Judah, when fighting against Israel and Syria, appealed for help from this Assyrian king and sent him gold and silver. "And Ahaz took the silver and gold in the house of the Lord and in the treasuries of the king's house and sent a present to the king of Assyria" 2 Kings 16: 8 AB.

He died 727 B.C., and was succeeded by Shalmanezer IV., who ruled till 721 B.C. He also invaded Syria. "Then the king of Assyria invaded all the land and went up to Samaria and besieged it for three years" 2 Kings 17: 5 AB.

722 B.C.

Assyia put an end to the kingdom of Israel, and deported the Israelites. carrying the people away into captivity, 722 B.C. (2 Kings 17: 1–6, 24; 18: 7, 9).

705 B.C.

Sennacherib (705 B.C.), the next king of Assyria, suffered one of the most amazing and mysterious military reversals while he was besieging Jerusalem. 185,000 of his men were killed by "an angel of the Lord."

185,000 killed by the angel of the Lord

"Then Isaiah son of Amoz sent to Hezekiah, saying, Thus says the Lord, the God of Israel: Your prayer to Me about Sennacherib king of Assyria I have heard.

21 This is the word that the Lord has spoken concerning him: The Virgin Daughter of Zion has despised you and laughed you to scorn; the Daughter of Jerusalem has wagged her head behind you.

22 Whom have you mocked and

reviled and insulted and blasphemed? Against Whom have you raised your voice and haughtily lifted your eyes? Against the Holy One of Israel!

23 By your messengers you have mocked, reproached, insulted, and defied the Lord, and have said, With my many chariots I have gone up to the heights of the mountains, to the far recesses of Lebanon. I cut down its tall cedar trees and its choicest cypress trees. I entered its most distant retreat, its densest forest.

24 I dug wells and drank foreign waters, and with the sole of my feet have I dried up all [the defense and] the streams of Egypt.

25 [But, says the God of Israel] Have you not heard how I ordained long ago what now I have brought to pass? I planned it in olden times, that you [king of Assyria] should [be My instrument to] lay waste fortified cities, making them ruinous heaps.

26 That is why their inhabitants had little power, they were dismayed and confounded; they were like plants of the field, the green herb, the grass on the housetops, blasted before it is grown up.

27 But [O Sennacherib] I [the Lord] know your sitting down, your going out, your coming in, and your raging against Me.

28 Because your raging against Me and your arrogance and careless ease have come to My ears, therefore I will put My hook in your nose and My bridle in your lips, and I will turn you back by the way you came, O king of Assyria.

29 And [Hezekiah, says the Lord] this shall be the sign [of these things] to you: you shall eat this year what grows of itself, also in the second year what springs up voluntarily. But in the third year sow and reap, plant vineyards and eat their fruit.

30 And the remnant that has survived of the house of Judah shall again take root downward and bear fruit upward.

31 For out of Jerusalem shall go forth a remnant, and a band of survivors out of Mount Zion. The zeal of the Lord of hosts shall perform this.

32 Therefore thus says the Lord concerning the king of Assyria: He shall not come into this city or shoot an arrow here or come before it with shield or cast up a siege mound against it.

33 By the way that he came, by that way shall he return, and he shall not come into this city, says the Lord.

34 For I will defend this city to save it, for My own sake and for My servant David's sake.

35 And it all came to pass, for that night the Angel of the Lord went forth and slew 185,000 in the camp of the Assyrians; and when [the living] arose early in the morning, behold, all these were dead bodies.

36 So Sennacherib king of Assyria departed and returned and dwelt at Nineveh.

37 And as he was worshiping in the house of Nisroch his god, Adrammelech and Sharezer his sons killed him with the sword, and they escaped to the land of Armenia or Ararat. Esarhaddon his son reigned in his stead."   *2 Kings 19: 14–37 AB*

Nineveh

Overview

Nineveh is first mentioned in the Bible in Gen. 10: 11, which is translated in the Revised Version, "He [i.e., Nimrod] went forth into Assyria and builded Nineveh."

It is not again mentioned until the days of Jonah, when it is described (Jonah 3: 3; 4: 11) as a great and well-populated city, the flourishing capital of the Assyrian empire (2 Kings 19: 36; Is. 37: 37).

The book of the prophet Nahum is almost exclusively taken up with prophetic denunciations against this city. Its ruin and utter desolation are foretold (Nah. 1: 14; 3: 19, etc.).

Zephaniah also (Zeph. 2: 13–15) predicts its destruction along with the fall of the empire of which it was the capital.

Nineveh is not mentioned again in the Bible until it is named in gospel history (Matt. 12: 41; Luke 11: 32).

Exceeding great city

This "exceeding great city" lay on the eastern or left bank of the river Tigris. It stretched along the riverbank for up to 30 miles, and extended up to 10 miles toward the eastern hills. This whole extensive space is now one immense area of ruins.

Occupying a central position on the great highway between the Mediterranean and the Indian Ocean, thus uniting the East and the West, wealth flowed into it from many sources, so that it became the greatest of all ancient cities.

Nineveh's end

About 633 B.C. the Assyrian empire began to show signs of weakness, and Nineveh was attacked by the Medes, who subsequently, about 625 B.C., being joined by the Babylonians, again attacked it, when it fell, and was razed to the ground.

The Assyrian empire then came to an end and the Medes and Babylonians divided its provinces between them.

"After having ruled for more than six hundred years with hideous tyranny and violence, from the Caucasus and the Caspian to the Persian Gulf, and from beyond the Tigris to Asia Minor and Egypt, it vanished like a dream" (Nah. 2: 6–11).

Its end was strange, sudden, tragic. It was God's doing, his judgment on Assyria's pride (Is. 10: 5–19).

Origin and antiquity of

Gen. 10: 11.

Situated on the river Tigris

Nah. 2: 6,8.

The ancient capital of Assyria

2 Kgs. 19: 36; Is. 37: 37.

Called the bloody city

Nah. 3: 1.

Described as

• Great.
  John 1: 2; 3: 2.

- Extensive.
  John 3: 3.
- Rich.
  Nah. 2: 9.
- Strong.
  Nah. 3: 12.
- Commercial.
  Nah. 3: 16.
- Populous.
  John 4: 11.
- Vile.
  Nah. 1: 14.
- Wicked.
  John. 1: 2.
- Idolatrous.
  Nah. 1: 14.
- Full of joy and carelessness.
  Zeph. 2: 15.
- Full of lies and robbery.
  Nah. 3: 1.
- Full of witchcraft.
  Nah. 3: 4.

Nineveh and Jonah

Jonah sent to proclaim the destruction of.
  John 1: 2; 3: 1,2,4.
Inhabitants of, repented at Jonah's preaching.
  John 3: 5–9; Matt. 12: 41; Luke 11: 32.
Destruction of, averted.
  John 3: 10; 4: 11.

Predictions about

Being faced with the Babylonian
  armies. Nah. 2: 1–4; 3: 2.
Destruction of its people. Nah. 1: 12;
  3: 3.
Spoiling of its treasures. Nah. 2: 9.
Destruction of its idols. Nah. 1: 14; 2: 7.

Utter destruction. Nah. 1: 8,9.
Degradation and contempt put on.
  Nah. 3: 5–7; Zeph. 2: 15.

"Behold, I am against you, says the Lord of hosts, and I will lift up your skirts over your face, and I will let the nations look on your nakedness [O Nineveh] and the kingdoms on your shame.

6 I will cast abominable things at you and make you filthy, treat you with contempt, and make you a gazingstock.

7 And all who look on you will shrink and flee from you and say, Nineveh is laid waste; who will pity and bemoan her? Where [then] shall I seek comforters for you?"
  Nahum 3: 5–7 AB.

Complete desolation.
"And [the Lord] will stretch out His hand against the north and destroy Assyria and will make Nineveh a desolation, dry as the desert.

14 Herds shall lie down in the midst of [Nineveh], all the [wild] beasts of the nations and of every kind; both the pelican and the hedgehog shall lodge on the upper part of her [fallen] pillars; the voice [of the nesting bird] shall sing in the windows; desolation and drought shall be on the thresholds, for her cedar paneling will He lay bare."
  Zephaniah 2: 13–14 AB

Feebleness of its people. Nah. 3: 13.
Being taken while people were drunk.
  Nah. 1: 10; 3: 11.
Captivity of its people. Nah. 3: 10.

The Babylonians

Babylon

"The Gate of God"

The Greek form of *Babel* and the Semitic form *Babilu*, both mean "The Gate of God."

In the Assyrian tablets it means "The city of the dispersion of the tribes."

Its long list of kings stretches back to 2300 B.C., and includes Khammu-rabi, or Amraphel.

Empire and city

In the Bible "Babylon" refers to both the city and the empire.

History of Babylon

The city of Babylon stood on the River Euphrates, about 200 miles above its junction with the River Tigris, which flowed through it and divided it into two almost equal parts.

On the fall of Nineveh (606 B.C.) it threw off the Assyrian yoke, and became the capital of the growing Babylonian empire. Under Nebuchadnezzar it became one of the most splendid cities of the ancient world.

The city was taken by Cyrus, "king of Elam," 539 B.C., who issued a decree allowing the Jews to return to their own land (Ezra 1). It then ceased to be the capital of an empire. It was repeatedly attacked by hostile armies until it was completely destroyed.

Was called

- Land of the Chaldeans.
  Ezek. 12: 13.
- Land of Shinar.
  Dan. 1: 2; Zech. 5: 11.
- Land of Merathaim.
  Jer. 50: 1,21.
- Desert of the sea.
  Is. 21: 1,9.
- Sheshach.
  Jer. 25: 12,26.
- Lady of kingdoms.
  Is. 47: 5.

Facts about Babylon

Origin of.
  Gen. 10: 8,10.
Origin of the name.
  Gen. 11: 8,9.
Situated beyond the Euphrates.
  Gen. 11: 31; Josh. 24: 2,3.
Formerly a part of Mesopotamia.
  Acts 7: 2.
Founded by the Assyrians, and a part of their empire.
  2 Kgs. 17: 24; Is. 23: 13.
Watered by the Rivers Euphrates and Tigris.
  Ps. 137: 1; Jer. 51: 13.
Composed of many nations.
  Dan. 3: 4; 3: 29.
Governed by kings.
  2 Kgs. 20: 12; Dan. 5: 1.
With Media and Persia divided by Darius into 120 provinces.
  Dan. 6: 1.
Babylon the chief province of.
  Dan. 3: 1.

Its antiquity.

Gen. 11: 4,9.

Enlarged by Nebuchadnezzar.

Dan. 4: 30.

Surrounded with a great wall and
fortified.

Jer. 51: 53,58.

Languages spoken in.

Dan. 1: 4; 2: 4.

Armies of, described.

Hab. 1: 7–9.

Ambassadors of, sent to Hezekiah

2 Kgs. 20: 12.

Known by different names

• The golden city. Is. 14: 4.
• The glory of kingdoms. Is. 13: 19.
• Beauty of Chaldee. Is. 13: 19.
• City of merchants. Ezek. 17: 4.
• Babylon the great. Dan. 4: 30.

Noted for

• Antiquity. Jer. 5: 15.
• Naval power. Is. 43: 14.
• Military power. Jer. 5: 16; 50: 23.
• National greatness. Is. 13: 19;
Jer. 51: 41.
• Wealth. Jer. 50: 37; 51: 13.
• Commerce. Ezek. 17: 4.
• Manufacture of garments. Josh. 7: 21.
• Wisdom of senators. Is. 47: 10;
Jer. 50: 35.

Inhabitants of

Idolatrous.

Jer. 50: 38; Dan. 3: 18.

Addicted to magic.

Is. 47: 9,12,13; Dan. 2: 1,2.

Profane and sacrilegious.

Dan. 5: 1–3.

Wicked.

Is. 47: 10.

As a power was

• Arrogant. Is. 14: 13,14; Jer. 50: 29,31,32.
• Secure and self-confident. Is. 47: 7,8.
• Grand and stately. Is. 47: 1,5.
• Covetous. Jer. 51: 13.
• Oppressive. Is. 14: 4.
• Cruel and destructive. Is. 14: 17; 47: 6;
Jer. 51: 25; Hab. 1: 6,7.
• An instrument of God's vengeance
on other nations. Jer. 51: 7; Is. 47: 6.

Represented by

• A great eagle. Ezek. 17: 3.
• A head of gold. Dan. 2: 32,37,38.
• A lion with eagle's wings. Dan. 7: 4.

Nebuchadnezzar king of

• Made Jehoiakim tributary.
2 Kgs. 24: 1.
• Besieged Jerusalem. 2 Kgs. 24: 10,11.
• Took Jehoiachin, and captives to
Babylon. 2 Kgs. 24: 12,14–16.
• Spoiled the temple. 2 Kgs. 24: 13.
• Made Zedekiah king. 2 Kgs. 24: 17.
• Rebelled against by Zedekiah.
2 Kgs. 24: 20.
• Besieged and took Jerusalem.
2 Kgs. 25: 1–4.
• Burned Jerusalem. 2 Kgs. 25: 9,10.
• Took Zedekiah, and captives to
Babylon. 2 Kgs. 25: 7,11,18–21.
• Spoiled and burned the temple.
2 Kgs. 25: 9,13–17; 2 Chr. 36: 18,19.

Predictions about destruction of

Is. 13: 1–22; 14: 4–22; 21: 1–10; 47: 1–15;
Jer. 25: 12; 50: 1–51: 64.

The Greeks

Greece

History of Greece

Originally consisted of the four provinces of Macedonia, Epirus, Achaia, and Peleponnesus.

Greece was conquered by the Romans 146 B.C.

Greece in the New Testament

In Acts 20: 2 it designates only the Roman province of Macedonia.

The cities of Greece were the special scenes of the labors of the apostle Paul.

Greek

In the New Testament the word "Greek" is used in a variety of ways.

"Greek" meaning "Greek by race"

See Acts 16: 1–3; 18: 17; Rom. 1: 14.

Paul states that Timothy's father was Greek.

"AND [Paul] went down to Derbe and also to Lystra. A disciple named Timothy was there, the son of a Jewish woman who was a believer [she had become convinced that Jesus is the Messiah and the Author of eternal salvation, and yielded obedience to Him]; but [Timothy's] father was a Greek.

2 He [Timothy] had a good reputation among the brethren at Lystra and Iconium.

3 Paul desired Timothy to go with him [as a missionary]; and he took him and circumcised him because of the Jews that were in those places, all of whom knew that his father was a Greek."   *Acts 16: 1–3 AB*

"Greek" meaning "Gentile as opposed to a Jew"

"[And] there will be tribulation and anguish and calamity and constraint for every soul of man who [habitually] does evil, the Jew first and also the Greek (Gentile).

10 But glory and honor and [heart] peace shall be awarded to everyone who [habitually] does good, the Jew first and also the Greek (Gentile)
                    Romans 2: 9,10 AB

"Grecians"

The word "Grecians" in Acts 11: 20 should be "Greeks," denoting the heathen Greeks of that city, as translated in the Revised Version.

Hellenists

Hellenists were Greek-Jews; Jews born in a foreign country, and thus did not speak Hebrew (Acts 6: 1; 9: 29), nor join in the Hebrew services of the Jews in Palestine, but had synagogues of their own in Jerusalem.

Athens

The capital of Attica, the most celebrated city of the ancient world, the seat of Greek literature and art during the golden period of Grecian history.

Its inhabitants were fond of novelty "For the Athenians, all of them, and the foreign residents and visitors among them spent all their leisure time in nothing except telling or hearing something newer than the last" Acts 17: 21 AB, and were remarkable for their zeal in the worship of the gods.

It was a sarcastic saying of the Roman satirist that it was "easier to find a god at Athens than a man."

Paul and Athens

On his second missionary journey Paul visited this city (Acts 17: 15; compare 1 Thess. 3: 1), and delivered in the Areopagus his famous speech (Acts 17: 22–31).

"So Paul, standing in the center of the Areopagus [Mars Hill meeting place], said: Men of Athens, I perceive in every way [on every hand and with every turn I make] that you are most religious or very reverent to demons.

23 For as I passed along and carefully observed your objects of worship, I came also upon an altar with this inscription, To the unknown god. Now what you are already worshiping as unknown, this I set forth to you.

24 The God Who produced and formed the world and all things in it, being Lord of heaven and earth, does not dwell in handmade shrines.

25 Neither is He served by human hands, as though He lacked anything, for it is He Himself Who gives life and breath and all things to all [people].

26 And He made from one [common origin, one source, one blood] all nations of men to settle on the face of the earth, having definitely determined [their] allotted periods of time and the fixed boundaries of their habitation (their settlements, lands, and abodes)..."

Acts 17: 22–26 AB

The Romans and Judah

Roman Empire

The Roman Empire was so widespread in Jesus' day that it was called "the world." See Luke 2: 1.

Represented by the

Legs of iron in Nebuchadnezzar's vision.
Dan. 2: 33,40.
Terrible beast in Daniel's vision.
Dan. 7: 7,19.

Rome and Judea

Rome the capitol of.
Acts 18: 2; 19: 21.
Judea a province of, under a procurator or a governor.
Luke 3: 2; Acts 23: 34,26; 25: 1.

Allusions to military affairs of

Strict obedience to superiors.
Matt. 8: 8,9.
Use of defensive armor.
Rom. 13: 12; 2 Cor. 6: 7; Eph. 6: 11–17.
Soldiers not allowed to entangle themselves with earthly cares.
2 Tim. 2: 4.
Hardship endured by soldiers.
2 Tim. 2: 3.
The soldier's special comrade who shared his toils and dangers.
Php 2: 25.
Danger of sleeping.
Matt. 28: 13,14.
Crowning of soldiers who distinguished themselves.
2 Tim. 4: 7,8.
Triumphs of victorious generals.
2 Cor. 2: 14–16; Col. 2: 15.

Different military officers.
Acts 21: 31; 23: 23,24.
Italian and Augustus' band.
Acts 10: 1; 27: 1.

Allusions to judicial affairs of

- Person accused, examined by scourging. Acts 22: 24,29.
- Criminals delivered over to the soldiers for execution. Matt. 27: 26,27.
- Accusation in writing placed over the head of those executed. John 19: 19.
- Garments of those executed given to the soldiers. Matt. 27: 35; John 19: 23.
- Prisoners chained to soldiers for safety. Acts 21: 33; 12: 6; 2 Tim. 1: 16; Acts 28: 16.
- Accusers and accused confronted together. Acts 23: 35; 25: 16–19.
- Accused person protected from popular violence. Acts 23: 20,24–27.
- Power of life and death vested in its authorities. John 18: 31,39,40; 19: 10.
- All appeals made to the emperor. Acts 25: 11,12.
- Those who appealed to Caesar, to be brought before him. Acts 26: 32.

Allusions to citizenship of

- Obtained by purchase. Acts 22: 28.
- Obtained by birth. Acts 22: 28.
- Exempted from the degradation scourging. Acts 16: 37,38; 22: 25.

Allusions to Grecian game adapted by

- Gladiatorial fights. 1 Cor. 4: 9; 15: 32.
- Foot races. 1 Cor. 9: 24; Php 2: 16; 3: 11–14; Heb. 12: 1,2.
- Wrestling. Eph. 6: 12.

- Training of combatants.
  1 Cor. 9: 25,27.
- Crowning of conquerors. 1 Cor. 9: 25;
  Php 3: 14; 2 Tim. 4: 8.
- Rules observed in conducting.
  2 Tim. 2: 5.

Emperors of, mentioned

- Tiberius. Luke 3: 1.
- Augustus. Luke 2: 1.
- Claudius. Acts 11: 28.
- Nero. Php 4: 22; 2 Tim. 4: 22.

Jews, Christians and the Roman Empire

Jews excluded from, by Claudius.
  Acts 18: 2
Paul visited by Onesiphorus.
  2 Tim. 1: 16–17
Paul desires to preach in.
  Rom. 1: 15
Abominations in.
  Rom. 1: 18–32
Christians in.
  Rom. 16: 5–17; Phil. 1: 12–18;
  Phil. 4: 22; 2 Tim. 4: 21

Judah

Overview

One of the divisions of the Holy Land
under the Romans .Luke 3: 1.
Made up the whole of the ancient
kingdom of Judah. 1 Kgs. 12: 21–24.

Names given to Judah

The land of Judah.
  Matt. 2: 6.
Jewry.
  Dan. 5: 13; John 7: 1.

Type of land

A mountainous district. Luke 1: 39,65.
Part desert. Matt. 3: 1; Acts 8: 26.

Capital

Jerusalem was the capital of Judah.
  Matt. 4: 25.

Towns of Judah

- Arimathea. Matt. 27: 57; John 19: 38.
- Azotus or Ashdod. Acts 8: 40.
- Bethany. John 11: 1,18.
- Bethlehem. Matt. 2: 1,6,16.
- Bethphage. Matt. 21: 1.
- Emmaus. Luke 24: 13.
- Ephraim. John 11: 54.
- Gaza. Acts 8: 26.
- Jericho. Luke 10: 30; 19: 1.
- Joppa. Acts 9: 36; 10: 5,8.
- Lydda. Acts 9: 32,35,38.

John the Baptist

John the Baptist preached in Judah
Matt. 3: 1.

Jesus and Judah

Born in. Matt. 2: 1,5,6.
Tempted in the wilderness of. Matt. 4: 1.
Frequently visited. John 11: 7.
Often left, to escape persecution.
  John 4: 1–3.

Several Christian churches in Judah

Acts 9: 31; 1 Thess. 2: 14.

Cities (1)

Overview

The earliest mention of a city-building is Enoch, which was built by Cain.

"Then Cain's wife became pregnant and gave birth to a son, and they named him Enoch. When Cain founded a city, he named it Enoch after his son" Genesis 4: 17 NLT.

After the confusion of tongues, the descendants of Nimrod founded several cities.

"He built the foundation for his empire in the land of Babylonia, with the cities of Babel, Erech, Akkad, and Calneh.

11 From there he extended his reign to Assyria, where he built Nineveh, Rehoboth-ir, Calah,

12 and Resen–the main city of the empire, located between Nineveh and Calah."   Genesis 10: 10–12 NLT

Early cities

The next cities mentioned are the cities of the Canaanites, Sidon, Gaza, Sodom, etc. (Gen. 10: 12,19; 11: 3, 9; 36: 31–39).

The earliest description of a city is that of Sodom (Gen. 19: 1–22).

Damascus is said to be the oldest existing city in the world.

Before the time of Abraham there were cities in Egypt (Num. 13: 22).

The Israelites in Egypt were used to build the "treasure cities" of Pithom and Raamses.

"So the Egyptians made the Israelites their slaves and put brutal slave drivers over them, hoping to wear them down under heavy burdens. They forced them to build the cities of Pithom and Rameses as supply centers for the king" Exodus 1: 11 NLT.

Pithom and Raamses were not places where royal treasures were kept, but were fortified towns where merchants stored their goods and conducted their business in safety, or cities in which weapons of war were stored.

Great cities with walls

In the kingdom of Og in Bashan there were sixty "great cities with walls," and twenty-three cities in Gilead partly rebuilt by the tribes on the east of Jordan (Num. 21: 21,32,33,35; 32: 1–3, 34–42; Deut. 3: 4,5,14; 1 Kings 4: 13).

Royal cities

On the west of Jordan were thirty-one "royal cities" (Josh. 12), besides many others spoken of in the history of Israel.

A fenced city

A fenced city was a city surrounded by fortifications and high walls, with watchtowers upon them (2 Chr. 11: 11; Deut. 3: 5).

A city with suburbs was a city surrounded with open pasture-grounds, such as the forty-eight cities which were given to the Levites (Num. 35: 2–7).

When David reduced the fortress of the Jebusites which stood on Mount Zion, he built on the site of it a palace and a city, which he called by his own name (1 Chr. 11: 5), the city of David. Bethlehem is also so called as being

David's native town (Luke 2: 4).

Jerusalem is called the Holy City, the holiness of the temple being regarded as extending in some measure over the whole city (Neh. 11: 1).

General facts about cities

- First mention of. Gen. 4: 17.
- Designed for habitations. Ps. 107: 7,36.
- Often built to perpetuate a name. Gen. 11: 4.
- Often founded and enlarged by blood and rapine. Mic. 3: 10; Hab. 2: 12.
- Inhabitants of, called citizens. Acts 21: 39.
- Prosperity of, increased by commerce. Gen. 49: 13; Deut. 33: 18,19; Ezek. 28: 5.
- Artificial mode of supplying water to. 2 Kgs. 18: 17; 20: 20.
- Infested by dogs. 1 Kgs. 14: 11; Ps. 59: 6,14.
- Under governors. 2 Chr. 33: 14; 2 Cor. 11: 32.

Built

- Of brick and slime. Gen. 11: 3.
- Of stone and wood. Ps. 102: 14; Ezek. 26: 12.
- Of brick and mortar. Ex. 1: 11,14.
- On solid foundations. Ezra 6: 3; Rev. 21: 14.
- With compactness. Ps. 122: 3.
- Often of a square form. Rev. 21: 16.
- Beside rivers. Ps. 46: 4; 137: 1.
- On hills. Matt. 5: 14; Luke 4: 29; Rev. 17: 9.
- In plains. Gen. 11: 2,4; 13: 12.
- In desert places. 2 Chr. 8: 4; Ps. 107: 35,36.
- In pleasant situations. 2 Kgs. 2: 19; Ps. 48: 2.

Details about cities

- Arranged in streets and lanes Num. 22: 39; Zech. 8: 5; Luke 14: 21.
- Entered through gates Gen. 34: 24; Neh. 13: 19,22.
- Surrounded with walls Deut. 1: 28; 3: 5.
- Often fortified by nature Ps. 125: 2.
- Often fortified by art 2 Chr. 11: 5–10,23; Ps. 48: 12,13; Jer. 4: 5; Dan. 11: 15.
- Sometimes had suburbs Num. 35: 2; Josh. 21: 3.
- Numerous Josh. 15: 21; 1 Chr. 2: 22; Jer. 2: 28.
- Densely inhabited John 4: 11; Nah. 3: 8.
- Often great and goodly Gen. 10: 12; Deut. 6: 10; Dan. 4: 30; John 3: 3.
- Often of great antiquity Gen. 10: 11,12.
- Often insignificant Gen. 19: 20; Eccl. 9: 14.

Were named after

- The family of the founder. Gen. 4: 17; Judg. 18: 29.
- The land owner. 1 Kgs. 16: 24.
- The country in which built. Dan. 4: 29,30.

Different kinds of

- Royal. Num. 21: 26; Josh. 10: 2; 2 Sam. 12: 26.
- Fenced. Josh. 10: 20; Is. 36: 1.
- Treasure. Ex. 1: 11.
- Commercial. Is. 23: 11; Ezek. 27: 3.
- Chariot. 2 Chr. 1: 14; 9: 25.
- Store. 2 Chr. 8: 4,6.

Levitical. Lev. 25: 32,33; Num. 35: 7,8.
Refuge. Num. 35: 6.

Cities (2)

More facts about cities

- Provided with judges. Deut. 16: 18; 2 Chr. 19: 5.
- Protected at night by watchmen. Ps. 127: 1; Song 5: 7; Is. 21: 11.
- Furnished with stores. 2 Chr. 11: 11,12.
- Garrisoned in war. 2 Chr. 17: 2,19.
- Often had citadels. Judg. 9: 51.
- A great defense to a country. 2 Chr. 11: 5.
- Afforded refuge in times of danger. Jer. 8: 14–16.
- Often deserted on the approach of an enemy. 1 Sam. 31: 7; Jer. 4: 20.

Were frequently

- Stormed. Josh. 8: 3–7; Judg. 9: 44.
- Besieged. Deut. 28: 52; 2 Kgs. 19: 24,25.
- Pillaged. Is. 13: 16; Jer. 20: 5.
- Wasted by pestilence. 1 Sam. 5: 11.
- Wasted by famine. Jer. 52: 6; Amos 4: 6.
- Depopulated. Is. 17: 9; Ezek. 26: 19.
- Burned. Judg. 20: 38,40; Is. 1: 7.
- Made heaps of ruins. Is. 25: 2.
- Razed and sown with salt. Judg. 9: 45.
- Difficulty of taking, alluded to Prov. 18: 19; Jer. 1: 18,19.
- Perishable nature of Heb. 13: 14.

Illustrative of

- Saints. Matt. 5: 14.

- Visible church. Song 3: 2,3; Rev. 11: 2.
- Church triumphant. Rev. 21: 2; 22: 19.
- Heavenly inheritance. Heb. 11: 16.
- The apostasy. Rev. 16: 10; 17: 18.
- Riches. Prov. 10: 15.

Walls of cities

- Often very high. Deut. 1: 28; 3: 5.
- Strongly fortified. Is. 2: 15; 25: 12.
- Had towers built on them. 2 Chr. 26: 9; 32: 5; Ps. 48: 12; Song 8: 10.
- Houses often built on. Josh. 2: 15.
- Were broad and places of public resort. 2 Kgs. 6: 26,30; Ps. 55: 10.
- Were strongly manned in war. 2 Kgs. 18: 26.
- Kept by watchmen night and day. Song 5: 7; Is. 62: 6.
- Houses sometimes broken down to repair, and fortify. Is. 22: 10.
- Danger of approaching too near to, in time of war. 2 Sam. 11: 20–1.
- Were battered by besieging armies. 2 Sam. 20: 15; Ezek. 4: 2,3.
- Adroitness of soldiers in scaling alluded to. Joel 2: 7–9.
- Sometimes burned. Jer. 49: 27; Amos 1: 7.
- Frequently laid in ruins. 2 Chr. 25: 23; 36: 19; Jer. 50: 15.
- Destruction of, a cause of grief. Deut. 28: 52; Neh. 1: 3; 2: 12–17.
- The falling of, sometimes with great

destruction. 1 Kgs. 20: 30.

- The bodies of enemies attached to, in disgrace. 1 Sam. 31: 10.
- Custom of dedicating. Neh. 12: 27.
- Idolatrous rites performed on. 2 Kgs. 3: 27.
- Instances of persons let down from. Josh. 2: 15; Acts 9: 24,25; 2 Cor. 11: 33.
- Small towns and villages were not surrounded by Lev. 25: 31.

Cities of refuge

Introduction

There were six cities of refuge, three on each side of Jordan, namely, Kadesh, Shechem, Hebron, on the west of Jordan; and on the east, Bezer, Ramoth-gilead, and Golan.

   The cities on each side of the river were nearly opposite each other. The regulations concerning these cities are given in Num. 35: 9–34; Deut. 19: 1–13; Ex. 21: 12–14.

Basic facts

- Design of Ex. 21: 13; Num. 35: 11; Josh. 20: 3.
- Names of Deut. 4: 41–43; Josh. 20: 7,8.
- Strangers might take advantage of Num. 35: 15.

Required to be

Easy of access. Deut. 19: 3; Is. 62: 10.
Open to all who committed manslaughter. Josh. 20: 4.

Those admitted to

Were put on their trial. Num. 35: 12,24.
Not protected outside of.
Num. 35: 26,27.
Obliged to remain in, until the high priest's death. Num. 35: 25,28.
Afforded no asylum to murderers
Ex. 21: 14; Num. 35: 16–21.

Illustrative

- Of Christ. Ps. 91: 2; Is. 25: 4.
- Of the hope of the gospel. Heb. 6: 18.
- (The way to,) of Christ. Is. 35: 8; John 14: 6.

Walls and towers

Walls

Overview

Designed for separation. Ezek. 43: 8;
Eph. 2: 14.
Designed for defense. 1 Sam. 25: 16.

Mentioned in the Bible

- Of cities. Num. 13: 28.
- Of temples. 1 Chr. 29: 4; Is. 56: 5.
- Of houses. 1 Sam. 18: 11.
- Of vineyards. Num. 22: 24;
  Prov. 24: 31.

Facts about walls

Frequently made of stone and wood
together. Ezra 5: 8; Hab. 2: 11.
Were probably often strengthened with
plates of iron or brass. Jer. 15: 20;
Ezek. 4: 3.
Hyssop frequently grew on. 1 Kgs. 4: 33.

Miracles connected with

Falling of the walls of Jericho. Josh. 6: 20.
Handwriting on the wall of
Belshazzar's palace. Dan. 5: 5,25–28.

Walls of houses

- Usually plastered. Ezek. 13: 10;
  Dan. 5: 5.
- Had nails or pegs fastened into them
  when built. Eccl. 12: 11; Is. 22: 23.
- Liable to leprosy. Lev. 14: 37.
- Often infested with serpents.
  Amos 5: 19.
- Could be easily dug through.
  Gen. 49: 6; Ezek. 8: 7,8; 12: 5.
- The seat next, was the place of
  distinction. 1 Sam. 20: 25.

Illustrative

- Of salvation. Is. 26: 1; 60: 18.
- Of the protection of God. Zech. 2: 5.
- Of those who afford protection.
  1 Sam. 25: 16; Is. 2: 15.
- Of the Church as a protection to the
  nation. Song 8: 9,10.
- Of ordinances as a protection to the
  Church. Song 2: 9; Is. 5: 5.
- Of the wealth of the rich in his own
  conceit. Prov. 18: 11.
- (Bronze,) of prophets in their
  testimony against the wicked.
  Jer. 22: 20.
- (Bowing or tottering,) of the wicked
  under judgments. Ps. 62: 3; Is. 30: 13.
- (Of partition,) of separation of Jews
  and Gentiles. Eph. 2: 14.
- (Daubed with untempered mortar,)
  of the teaching of false prophets.
  Ezek. 13: 10–15.
- (Whited,) of hypocrites. Acts 23: 3.

Towers

Introduction

Nearly all cities had a tower in which
citizens could take refuge in times of
danger.

"When the people who lived in the
tower of Shechem heard what had
happened, they took refuge within the
walls of the temple of Baal-berith.

47 Someone reported to Abimelech
that the people were gathered together
in the temple,

48 so he led his forces to Mount

Zalmon. He took an ax and chopped some branches from a tree, and he put them on his shoulder. "Quick, do as I have done!" he told his men.

49 So each of them cut down some branches, following Abimelech's example. They piled the branches against the walls of the temple and set them on fire. So all the people who had lived in the tower of Shechem died, about a thousand men and women.

50 Then Abimelech attacked the city of Thebez and captured it.

51 But there was a strong tower inside the city, and the entire population fled to it. They barricaded themselves in and climbed up to the roof of the tower.

52 Abimelech followed them to attack the tower"   *Judges 9: 46–52 NLT.*

Origin

Origin and antiquity of Gen. 11: 4.

Were built

- In cities. Judg. 9: 51.
- On the walls of cities. 2 Chr. 14: 7; 26: 9.
- In the forests. 2 Chr. 27: 4.
- In the deserts. 2 Chr. 26: 10.
- In vineyards. Is. 5: 2; Matt. 21: 33.

Facts about towers

- Frequently very high. Is. 2: 15.
- Frequently strong and well fortified. Judg. 9: 51; 2 Chr. 26: 9.
- Were used as armories. Song 4: 4.
- Were used as citadels in time of war. Judg. 9: 51; Ezek. 27: 11.
- Watchmen posted on, in times of danger. 2 Kgs. 9: 17; Hab. 2: 1.

Mentioned in the Bible

- Babel. Gen. 11: 9.
- Edar. Gen. 35: 21.
- Penuel. Judg. 8: 17.
- Shechem. Judg. 9: 46.
- Thebez. Judg. 9: 50,51.
- David. Song 4: 4.
- Lebanon. Song 7: 4.
- Of the furnaces. Neh. 3: 11.
- Meah. Neh. 12: 39.
- Jezreel. 2 Kgs. 9: 17.
- Hananeel. Jer. 31: 38; Zech. 14: 10.
- Syene. Ezek. 29: 10; 30: 6.
- Siloam. Luke 13: 4.

More facts about towers

- Of Jerusalem remarkable for number, strength, and beauty Ps. 48: 12.
- Frequently thrown down in war Judg. 8: 17; 9: 49; Ezek. 26: 4.
- Frequently left desolate Is. 32: 14; Zeph. 3: 6.

Illustrative

- Of God as the protector of his people. 2 Sam. 22: 3,51; Ps. 18: 2; 61: 3.
- Of the name of the Lord. Prov. 18: 10.
- Of ministers. Jer. 6: 27.
- Of Mount Sion. Mic. 4: 8.
- Of the grace and dignity of the church. Song 4: 4; 7: 4; 8: 10.
- Of the proud and haughty. Is. 2: 15; 30: 25.

Overview

Design of. Is. 62: 10.
Made of
- Brass. Ps. 107: 16; Is. 45: 2.
- Iron. Acts 12: 10.

Jerusalem

Introduction

Jerusalem, "city of peace," was the focal and most important city in ancient Israel, as it was in the New Testament, and as it remains today.

In Jesus' day King Herod's magnificent restoration of the Temple was taking place and the temple sacrifices flourished.

Devout Jewish pilgrims came from all over the world to Jerusalem, especially at festival time so that the 60,000 inhabitants of Jerusalem were increased to about 250,000.

Origin

• The ancient Salem. Gen. 14: 18; Ps. 76: 2.
• The ancient Jebusi or Jebus. Josh. 15: 8; 18: 28; Judg. 19: 10.
• The king of, defeated and slain by Joshua. Josh. 10: 5–23.
• Allotted to the tribe of Benjamin. Josh. 18: 28.
• Partly taken and burned by Judah. Judg. 1: 8.

The Jebusites

• Formerly dwelt in. Judg. 19: 10,11.
• Held possession of, with Judah and Benjamin. Josh. 15: 63; Judg. 1: 21.
• Finally dispossessed of, by David. 2 Sam. 5: 6–8.

Facts about Jerusalem

• Enlarged by David 2 Sam. 5: 9.
• Made the royal city 2 Sam. 5: 9; 20: 3.

• Specially chosen by God. 2 Chr. 6: 6; Ps. 135: 21.
• The seat of government under the Romans for a time. Matt. 27: 2,19.
• Roman government transferred from, to Caesarea. Acts 23: 23,24; 25: 1–13.
• Was the tomb of the prophets. Luke 13: 33,34.

Called

• City of God. Ps. 46: 4; 48: 1.
• City of the Lord. Is. 60: 14.
• City of Judah. 2 Chr. 25: 28.
• City of the great king. Ps. 48: 2; Matt. 5: 5.
• City of solemnities. Is. 33: 20.
• City of righteousness. Is. 1: 26.
• City of truth. Zech. 8: 3.
• A city not forsaken. Is. 62: 12.
• Faithful city. Is. 1: 21,26.
• Holy city. Neh. 11: 1; Is. 48: 2; Matt. 4: 5.
• Throne of the Lord. Jer. 3: 17.
• Zion. Ps. 48: 12; Is. 33: 20.
• Zion of the holy one of Israel. Is. 60: 14.

More facts about Jerusalem

• Surrounded by mountains. Ps. 125: 2.
• Surrounded by a wall. 1 Kgs. 3: 1.
• Protected by forts and bulwarks. Ps. 48: 12,13.
• Entered by gates. Ps. 122: 2; Jer. 17: 19–21.
• Hezekiah made an aqueduct for. 2 Kgs. 20: 20.

- Spoils of war placed in. 1 Sam. 17: 54; 2 Sam. 8: 7.
- The temple built in. 2 Chr. 3: 1; Ps. 68: 29.

God and Jerusalem

Protected by God. Is. 31: 5.
Instances of God's care and protection of. 2 Sam. 24: 16; 2 Kgs. 19: 32–34; 2 Chr. 12: 7.

The Jews

- Went up to celebrate the feasts. Luke 2: 42; Ps. 122: 4.
- Loved. Ps. 137: 5,6.
- Lamented the affliction of. Neh. 1: 2–4.
- Prayed for the prosperity of. Ps. 51: 18; 122: 6.
- Prayed towards. Dan. 6: 10; 1 Kgs. 8: 41.

Christ and Jerusalem

- Preached in. Luke 21: 37,38; John 18: 20.
- Did many miracles in. John 4: 45.
- Publicly entered, as king. Matt. 21: 9,10.
- Lamented over. Matt. 23: 37; Luke 19: 41.
- Put to death at. Luke 9: 31; Acts 13: 27,29.

Early church and Jerusalem

- Gospel first preached at. Luke 24: 47; Acts 2: 14.
- Miraculous gift of the Holy Spirit first given at. Acts 1: 4; 2: 1–5.
- Persecution of the Christian church commenced at. Acts 4: 1; 8: 1.
- First Christian council held at Acts 15: 4,6.

Rebuilding of

Rebuilt after the captivity by order of Cyrus. Ezra 1: 1–4.

Prophecies about

- To be taken by king of Babylon. Jer. 20: 5.
- To be made a heap of ruins. Jer. 9: 11; 26: 18.
- To be a wilderness. Is. 64: 10.
- To be rebuilt by Cyrus. Is. 44: 26–28.
- To be a quiet habitation. Is. 33: 20.
- To be a terror to her enemies. Zech. 12: 2,3.
- Christ to enter, as king. Zech. 9: 9.
- The gospel to go forth from. Is. 2: 3; 40: 9.
- To be destroyed by the Romans. Luke 19: 42–44.
- Its capture accompanied by severe calamities. Matt. 24: 21,29; Luke 21: 23,24.
- Signs preceding its destruction. Matt. 24: 6–15; Luke 21: 7–11,25,28.

Illustrative

- Of the church. Gal. 4: 25,26; Heb. 12: 22.
- Of the church glorified. Rev. 3: 12; 21: 2,10.
- (Its strong position,) of saints under God's protection. Ps. 125: 2.

Cities and towns of the New Testament (1)

In Judea

1. Azotus:
Near the Mediterranean; the ancient Ashod, visited by Philip (Acts 8: 40).

2. Bethlehem:
Six miles south of Jerusalem; the birthplace of Jesus (Matt. 2: 1).

3. Bethany:
Near Jerusalem, on a slope of the Mount of Olives; the home of Mary, Martha, and Lazarus (John 12: 1).

4. Gaza:
Near the Mediterranean, to which a road led from Jerusalem (Acts 8: 26).

5. Emmaus:
Four miles south of Jerusalem; the place to which the two disciples were walking when joined by Jesus (Luke 24: 13).

6. Joppa:
On the Mediterranean; the port of Jerusalem where Peter saw a vision (Acts 11: 5).

7. Jericho:
In the valley of the Jordan, where Jesus healed Bartimæus (Mark 10: 46).

8. Jerusalem:
The Holy City where all the great feasts were held (Luke 2: 41).

In Samaria

1. Antipatris:
East of Shechem; where the guard brought Paul by night (Acts 23: 31).

2. Cæsarea:
On the Mediterranean, where Paul made his defense before Agrippa (Acts 25).

3. Sychar:
In the valley between Ebal and Gerizim; the site of Jacob's well (John 4: 5,6).

In Galilee

1. Bethsaida:
A village on the Sea of Galilee; the native place of Peter, Andrew, and Philip (John 1: 44).

2. Cana:
A village four or five miles northeast of Nazareth, where Jesus performed his first miracle (John 2: 11).

3. Capernaum:
A city on the northwestern shore of the Sea of Galilee, where Jesus lived, and performed many miracles (Matt. 4: 13).

4. Chorazin:
A city on the northern shore of the Sea of Galilee, against which Jesus pronounced woes (Matt. 11: 21).

5. Magdala:
A village on the western shore of the Sea of Galilee, visited by Jesus (Matt. 15: 39).

6. Nazareth:
A town among the hills, about midway between the Sea of Galilee and the Mediterranean; the place where Jesus was brought up (Luke 4: 16).

7. Nain:
A village on a hill southeast of Nazareth, where Jesus raised to life the widow's son (Luke 7: 12).

8. Ptolemais:
On the Mediterranean, north of Mount Carmel, where Paul landed on his way to Jerusalem (Acts 21: 7).

9. Tiberias:
A city on the western shore of the Sea of Galilee, visited by Jesus (John 6: 1).

In Peræa

1. Bethabara:
A place east of the Jordan, nearly opposite Jericho, where John baptized (John 1: 28).

2. Machæus:
East of the Dead Sea; the place where John the Baptist was imprisoned and beheaded. Not named in the Bible.

Decapolis

1. Bethsaida:
On the northeastern shore of the Sea of Galilee; the place where Jesus fed the five thousand (Luke 9: 10–17).

2. Gadara:
A city south of the Sea of Galilee. This district was thus called: "the country of the Gadarenes" (Mark 5: 1).

3. Gergesa:
A little village east of the Sea of Galilee; near to where the demoniacs were cured, and the pigs drowned (Matt. 8: 28–34).

In Phoenicia

1. Tyre:
The commercial city of antiquity, on the Mediterranean; on "the coasts" of which Jesus cured the daughter of the Syro-Phoenician woman (Matt. 15: 21–28).

2. Sidon:
A city on the Mediterranean, about twenty miles north of Tyre, in a region once visited by Jesus (Mark 7: 24).

In Syria

1. Damascus: On a fertile plain, watered by the Abana and Pharpar, east of the Anti-Libanus mountains; the place of the Apostle Paul's conversion (Acts 9: 1–25).

2. Antioch: On the river Orontes, seventeen miles from the Mediterranean, the site of the first missionary church (Acts 11: 19–30).

Greece

1. Athens:
It was the seat of Grecian learning, where Paul delivered one of his most famous discourses (Acts 17: 15–34).

2. Corinth:
An important city forty miles west of Athens, where Paul preached, (Acts 18: 1–18).

Cities and towns of the New Testament (2)

In Asia Minor

1. Antioch:
A city in Pisidia, east of Ephesus, visited by Paul and Barnabas (Acts 13:14).

2. Ephesus:
A celebrated city one mile from the Ægean Sea, where Paul preached for a long time, (Acts 19) and one of the seven churches of Asia (Rev. 2:1).

3. Derbe:
A town in Lycaonia, visited by Paul and Barnabas (Acts 16:1).

4. Iconium:
Sixty miles east of Antioch, where Paul and Barnabas preached (Acts 14:1–5).

5. Lystra:
Not far from Derbe, also visited by Paul and Barnabas; the home of Timothy, (Acts 16:1) and where the two missionaries were thought to be gods (Acts 14:8–12).

6. Laodicea:
The capital of Phrygia, and the seat of one of the churches to which a message was sent by John (Rev. 3:14).

7. Miletus:
The port of Ephesus, where Paul delivered a farewell address (Acts 20:17–38).

8. Myra:
An important town of Lycia, where Paul changed ships on his journey to Rome (Acts 27:5).

9. Patara:
A sea-port of Lycia, where Paul took ship for Phoenicia (Rev. 2:12).

10. Pergamos:
A city of Mysia; the site of one of the seven churches of Asia (Rev. 2:12).

11. Perga:
A city of Pamphylia, visited by Paul and Barnabas, and where Mark left them (Acts 13:3).

12. Philadelphia:
A town on the borders of Lydia; the seat of one of the seven churches of Asia (Rev. 3:7).

13. Smyrna:
On the Ægean Sea, forty miles north of Ephesus; the seat of one of the seven churches in Asia (Rev. 2:8).

14. Sardis:
An important city of Lydia; the seat of one of the seven churches of Asia (Rev. 3:1).

15. Troas:
The ancient Troy, on the Ægean Sea, where Paul in a vision received the call to Macedonia (Acts 16:8–10).

16. Tarsus:
A city of Cilicia; the birthplace of the Apostle Paul (Acts 9:11).

17. Thyatira:
A city of Lydia, and the seat of one of the seven churches of Asia (Rev. 2:18).

In Macedonia

1. Amphipolis:
Thirty-three miles from Philippi, and three miles from the Ægean Sea, visited by Paul (Acts 17: 1).

2. Apollonia:
A city thirty miles from Amphipolis, where Paul remained one day (Acts 17: 1).

3. Berea:
A small city on the eastern side of Mount Olympus, where Paul preached, and where the people examined the Scriptures to see if his preaching was true (Acts 17: 10–13).

4. Philippi:
A flourishing city nine miles from the Ægean Sea, celebrated as the first foothold of the gospel in Europe (Acts 16: 12–40).

5. Thessalonica:
At the head of the Thermaic Gulf; an important commercial center, and the scene of Paul's labor (Acts 17: 1–9).

Islands

1. Fair Haven:
A harbor in the island of Crete; a place where the ship on which Paul was sailing anchored (Acts 27: 8).

2. Mitylene:
On the island of Lesbos, in the Ægean Sea, where Paul's ship anchored for a night (Acts 20: 14).

3. Paphos:
On the western shore of Cyprus; visited by Paul and Barnabas (Acts 13: 6).

4. Salamis:
On the eastern shore of Cyprus; visited by Paul and Barnabas (Acts 13: 5).

5. Syracuse:
A celebrated city on the eastern shore of Sicily, where Paul stopped on his journey to Rome (Acts 28: 12).

Italy

1. Puteoli: The leading port of Italy, where Paul disembarked (Acts 28: 13).

2. Appii Forum:
A village on the Appian Way, forty-three miles from Rome, where Christians met Paul (Acts 28: 15).

3. Three Taverns:
A place eleven miles from Rome, where Christians met Paul and accompanied him to Rome (Acts 28: 15).

4. Rome:
The great city of Italy, the capital of the Roman Empire, where Paul was taken for trial before Cæsar, (Acts 28: 16), and where it is believed that he was later executed.

Bible measurements (1)

Measurements of length

(American: mile=5280 feet or 1760 yards; yard=3 feet; foot=12 inches)

Handbreadth

A handbreadth was the width of the four fingers closely pressed together, thus, between 3 and 4 inches.

The table of showbread in Exodus 37: 12 mentions a handbreadth: "Also he made thereunto a border of an handbreadth round about; and made a crown of gold for the border thereof round about."

Cubit

A cubit was the length of the arm from the point of the elbow to the end of the middle finger, about 18 inches.

Goliath's height is recorded in 1 Samuel 17: 4: "And there went out a champion out of the camp of the Philistines, named Goliath, of Gath, whose height *was* six cubits and a span." Six cubits is 6x18=108 inches. Goliath was 6 cubits and one span (9 inches). That makes the giant 9 foot 9 inches tall.

Span

A span is the distance from the end of the thumb to that of the little finger, when these are extended. This is approximately 9 inches.

Aaron's breastplate was to measure: "Foursquare it shall be *being* doubled; a span *shall be* the length thereof, and a span *shall be* the breadth thereof." According to Exodus 28: 16.

Measuring Reed

This was an actual plant, the calamus or sweet cane which from its shape and length came to be used as a measure. See Ezekiel 40: 3,5. In verse 5 the length of this reed is said to be six cubits, each of which was of the length of a cubit and a handbreadth, thus 6 cubits and 6 handbreadths (nearly 11 feet).

Measurements of distance

Furlong

A furlong (Greek, *stadion*) measured about 600 feet, that is less than one eighth of a mile.

"So when they had rowed about five and twenty or thirty furlongs, they see Jesus walking on the sea, and drawing nigh unto the ship: and they were afraid."

John 6: 19

Sabbath day's journey

A sabbath day's journey was based on the instruction found in Exodus 16: 29 which did not allow excessive travel on the Sabbath day, which was meant to be a day of rest.

Jewish legislators ruled that a Sabbath day's journey should be no longer than 5 furlongs that, is about half a mile.

"Then returned they unto Jerusalem from the mount called Olivet, which is from Jerusalem a sabbath day's journey."

Acts 1: 12.

A day's journey

A day's journey was the distance a person could normally travel in one day, which usually amounted to about 20 to 30 miles. But traveling in a large group shortened a day's journey to about 10 miles.

"But they, supposing him to have been in the company, went a day's journey; and they sought him among *their* kinsfolk and acquaintance."

Luke 2: 44

Measurements of capacity

Dry measures

(American dry measurements: bushel=4 pecks; peck=8 quarts; quart=2 pints)

HANDFUL

A handful refers to the natural capacity of the human hand.

"And he shall bring it to Aaron's sons the priests: and he shall take thereout his handful of the flour thereof, and of the oil thereof, with all the frankincense thereof"

Leviticus 2: 2

OMER

An omer was about five pints. See Exodus 16: 16.

EPHAH

An ephah was equivalent to 10 omers.

"Now an omer *is* the tenth *part* of an ephah."

Exodus 16: 36

Liquid Measures

(American liquid measures: gallon=4 quarts; quart=2 pints)

LOG

A log is less than ½ pint.

"And on the eighth day he shall take two he lambs without blemish, and one ewe lamb of the first year without blemish, and three tenth deals of fine flour *for* a meat offering, mingled with oil, and one log of oil."

Leviticus 14: 10

HIN

An hin is nearly 6 pints/

"And with the one lamb a tenth deal of flour mingled with the fourth part of an hin of beaten oil; and the fourth part of an hin of wine *for* a drink offering."

Exodus 29: 40

BATH

A bath was the largest liquid measure used by the Jews in the Old Testament and amounted to about 7 gallons. The huge vessel or basin which Solomon built for the temple contained "two thousand baths" according to 1 Kings 7: 26.

FIRKIN

Firkin (Greek – Metretes) was equivalent to about 9 gallons.

"And there were set there six waterpots of stone, after the manner of the purifying of the Jews, containing two or three firkins apiece."

John 2: 6

Bible measurements (2)

Measures of weight

Shekel

The shekel was the most basic unit of weight among the Hebrew people. It was often used to weigh an amount of silver. Often when the Bible speaks of "pieces" of silver it is usually referring to "shekels" of silver.

Talent

A talent was the largest measure of weight used by the Hebrews. One talent was equivalent to about 3000 shekels.

A talent was about as much as anyone could carry.

"And Naaman said, Be content, take two talents. And he urged him, and bound two talents of silver in two bags, with two changes of garments, and laid *them* upon two of his servants; and they bare *them* before him."

2 Kings 5: 23

The talent weight was used for metals, such as

1. gold (1 Kings 9: 14),
2. silver (2 Kings 5: 22),
3. lead (Zechariah 5: 7),
4. bronze (Exodus 38: 29) or
5. iron (1 Chronicles 29: 7).

"And gave for the service of the house of God of gold five thousand talents and ten thousand drams, and of silver ten thousand talents, and of brass eighteen thousand talents, and one hundred thousand talents of iron."

1 Chronicles 29: 7

Measures of value/money

Dram

'Adarkon (Heb.)

"And gave for the service of the house of God of gold five thousand talents and ten thousand drams, and of silver ten thousand talents, and of brass eighteen thousand talents, and one hundred thousand talents of iron."

1 Chronicles 29: 7

See also Ezra 8: 27.

"They gave toward the work on the temple of God five thousand talents [1] and ten thousand darics [2] of gold, ten thousand talents [3] of silver, eighteen thousand talents [4] of bronze and a hundred thousand talents [5] of iron."

1 Chronicles 29: 7

Footnotes

[1] That is, about 190 tons (about 170 metric tons)

[2] That is, about 185 pounds (about 84 kilograms)

[3] That is, about 375 tons (about 345 metric tons)

[4] That is, about 675 tons (about 610 metric tons)

[5] That is, about 3,750 tons (about 3,450 metric tons)

The *Darkemon* was the Persian Daric gold coin.

"They gave after their ability unto the treasure of the work threescore and one thousand drams of gold, and five thousand pound of silver, and one hundred priests' garments."

Ezra 2: 69.

"According to their ability they gave to the treasury for this work 61,000 drachmas [1] of gold, 5,000 minas [2] of silver and 100 priestly garments."

Ezra 2: 69 NIV

Footnotes
[1] That is, about 1,100 pounds (about 500 kilograms)
[2] That is, about 3 tons (about 2.9 metric tons)
See also: Neh. 7: 70, 71,72.

Farthing

Kodrantes
A farthing, a bronze coin, was the smallest Roman coin in use.

Sixty-four farthings made one denarius.

One farthing was also equivalent to two mites.

"And there came a certain poor widow, and she threw in two mites, which make a farthing."

Mark 12: 42.

'Assarion
A second Greek word 'assarion was used to describe another coin which also had little value.

"Are not two sparrows sold for a farthing? and one of them shall not fall on the ground without your Father."

Matthew 10: 29

Mite

A mite (Greek: *lepta*) was the smallest Jewish coin in use.

"I tell thee, thou shalt not depart thence, till thou hast paid the very last mite."

Luke 21: 2

See also: Mark 12: 42. Luke 12: 59; 21: 2.

Penny

Penny is the translation of fourteen of the sixteen occurrences of the Greek word *denarion*.

This silver coin was equivalent to a day's wage of a working person: "And when he had agreed with the laborers for a penny a day, he sent them into his vineyard" Matthew 20: 2.

It is twice translated "pennyworth."

"He answered and said unto them, Give ye them to eat. And they say unto him, Shall we go and buy two hundred pennyworth of bread, and give them to eat?"

Mark 6: 37

Piece of Money/ four-drachma coin

"Take the first fish you catch; open its mouth and you will find a four-drachma coin" Matt. 17: 27 NIV.

It was tribute money, a temple tax, and in Matthew 17: 24 is referred to as "tribute money" which is a translation of the Greek word "didrachmon" which was the "double drachma" coin.

The Greek word used in Matthew 17: 27 for "four-drachma coin" NIV or, "piece of money" KJV is *Stater* and is the Jewish shekel which was equivalent to the necessary double drachma.

Time (1)

Measures of time

Year

Years were based on the changing of the seasons.

In Bible times, obviously before the use of B.C. and A.D. a year was often linked to a king's reign. "Now in the fifteenth year of the reign of Tiberius Caesar" Luke 3: 1.

Years were also reckoned from well-known historical events, such as:
1. The Exodus (see Numbers 33: 38; 1 Kings 6: 1).
2. The Babylonian captivity or exile.
"And it came to pass in the twelfth year of our captivity."

Ezekiel 33: 21

B.C. and A.D.

B.C. stands for Before Christ.
A.D. stands for *Anno Domini* (Latin words for, "in the year of the Lord").

Month

Months were based on the phases of the moon. The names of the months in Bible times were different than the names which we use today. Their first month, Nisan, was the month in which the Passover was always celebrated.

"In the fourteenth *day* of the first month at even *is* the Lord's Passover."

Leviticus 23: 5

Week

A week was the interval between two Sabbaths.

Sabbath

The Sabbath was the 7th day of the week, which was Saturday.

The first day of the week (Luke 24: 1) was Sunday, the day on which the early Christians meet together.

"And upon the first *day* of the week, when the disciples came together to break bread, Paul preached unto them, ready to depart on the morrow; and continued his speech until midnight."

Acts 20: 7

Day

A day was a 24 hour period based on the day-night cycle.

Jews calculated the day from sunset to sunset. So their new day started at sunset.

"... from even unto even, shall ye celebrate your Sabbath."

Leviticus 23: 32

Hour

For the Jews the hours of a day started at 6: 00 a.m.

Named hours

THIRD HOUR
The third hour was 9: 00 a.m.

"And it was the third hour, and they crucified him."

Mark 15: 25

See also: Matt. 20: 3; Acts 2: 15; 23: 23.

SIXTH HOUR
The sixth hour was about midday.

"Again he went out about the sixth

and ninth hour, and did likewise. And about the eleventh hour he went out, and found others standing idle, and saith unto them, Why stand ye here all the day idle?"

Matthew 20: 5,6

See also: Matt. 27: 45; Mark 15: 33. Luke 1: 26, 36; 23: 44; John 4: 6; 19: 14; Acts 10: 9.

SEVENTH HOUR

The seventh hour was about 1 p.m.

"Then inquired he of them the hour when he began to amend. And they said unto him, Yesterday at the seventh hour the fever left him."

John 4: 52

NINTH HOUR

The ninth hour was about 3 p.m. See Matt. 20: 5; 27: 45,46; Mark 15: 33,34; Luke 23: 44; Acts 3: 1; 10: 3,30.

TENTH HOUR

The tenth hour was about 4 p.m.

"He saith unto them, Come and see. They came and saw where he dwelt, and abode with him that day: for it was about the tenth hour."

John 1: 39

ELEVENTH HOUR

The eleventh hour was about 5 p.m. See Matt. 20: 6, 9.

Parts of the day

Different parts of the day were known by a variety of names in the Bible:

COCK-CROWING

This signified two times: one was after midnight, and one was before dawn.

Both are mentioned in Mark 14: 30:

"And Jesus saith unto him, Verily I say unto thee, That this day, *even* in this night, before the cock crow twice, thou shalt deny me thrice."

COOL OF THE DAY

The cool of the day was from about 2 p.m. to about 6 p.m.

"And they heard the voice of the Lord God walking in the garden in the cool of the day."

Genesis 3: 8

HEAT OF THE DAY

The heat of the day was from about 10 a.m. to 2 p.m.

"And the Lord appeared unto him in the plains of Mamre: and he sat in the tent door in the heat of the day"

Genesis 18: 1

The watches of the day and night

A "watch" lasted for about three hours.

Summary of Bible teaching on time

BEGINNING OF TIME

"In the beginning God created the heavens and the earth.

14 And God said, "Let bright lights appear in the sky to separate the day from the night. They will be signs to mark off the seasons, the days, and the years"

Genesis 1: 1,14 NLT

Time (2)

Summary of Bible teaching on time, continued

INDICATED BY A SUNDIAL

"Isaiah replied, 'This is the sign that the LORD will give you to prove he will do as he promised. Would you like the shadow on the sundial to go forward ten steps or backward ten steps?'

10 'The shadow always moves forward,' Hezekiah replied. 'Make it go backward instead.'

11 So Isaiah asked the LORD to do this, and he caused the shadow to move ten steps backward on the sundial of Ahaz!"

2 Kings 20: 9–11 NLT

"8 'I will cause the sun's shadow to move ten steps backward on the sundial of Ahaz!' ' So the shadow on the sundial moved backward ten steps."

Isaiah 38: 8 NJL

DIVISION OF, INTO WATCHES

Ex. 14: 24; Matt. 14: 25; Mark 6: 48

"And it was so on the morrow, that Saul put the people in three companies; and they came into the midst of the host in the morning watch, and slew the Ammonites until the heat of the day: and it came to pass, that they which remained were scattered, so that two of them were not left together."

1 Samuel 11: 11

ONE DAY AS A THOUSAND YEARS

"But you must not forget, dear friends, that a day is like a thousand years to the Lord, and a thousand years is like a day."

2 Peter 3: 8 NLT

FULLNESS OF

"But when the fullness of the time was come, God sent forth his Son, made of a woman, made under the law."

Galatians 4: 4

"That in the dispensation of the fullness of times he might gather together in one all things in Christ, both which are in heaven, and which are on earth; even in him."

Ephesians 1: 10

END OF

"He hath compassed the waters with bounds, until the day and night come to an end."

Job 26: 10

"And sware by him that liveth for ever and ever, who created heaven, and the things that therein are, and the earth, and the things that therein are, and the sea, and the things which are therein, that there should be time no longer."

Revelation 10: 6

Old Testament watches

FIRST WATCH

The first watch lasted from 9 p.m. to midnight.

BEGINNING OF THE WATCHES

This was about 9 p.m.

"Arise, cry out in the night: in the beginning of the watches pour out thine heart like water before the face of the Lord."

Lamentations 2: 19

MIDDLE WATCH

The middle watch lasted from midnight to 3 a.m.

"So Gideon, and the hundred men that *were* with him, came unto the outside of the camp in the beginning of the middle watch."

Judges 7: 19

MORNING WATCH

The morning watch lasted from 3 a.m. to 6 a.m.

"And it came to pass, that in the morning watch the LORD looked unto the host of the Egyptians through the pillar of fire and of the cloud, and troubled the host of the Egyptian."

Exodus 14: 24

New Testament watches

FIRST WATCH

The first watch lasted from 6 p.m. to 9 p.m.

SECOND WATCH

The second watch lasted from 9 p.m. to midnight.

"And if he shall come in the second watch, or come in the third watch, and find them so, blessed are those servants."

Luke 12: 38

THIRD WATCH

The third watch lasted from midnight to 3 a.m.

See Luke 12: 38.

FOURTH WATCH

The fourth watch lasted from 3 a.m. to 6 a.m.

"And in the fourth watch of the night Jesus went unto them, walking on the sea."

Matthew 14: 25

Chronos and *kairos*

The New Testament uses a number of words related to time. The two main words it uses are:

CHRONOS

This refers to a measurement of time.

KAIROS

This refers to a specific period of time in the way we say "it was the right time."

Jesus died at the "right time."

"You see, at just the right time, when we were still powerless, Christ died for the ungodly."

Romans 5: 6 NIV

"That in the dispensation of the fullness of times he might gather together in one all things in Christ, both which are in heaven, and which are on earth; even in him."

Ephesians 1: 10

"(For he saith, I have heard thee in a time accepted, and in the day of salvation have I succored thee: behold, now is the accepted time; behold, now is the day of salvation.)"

2 Corinthians 6: 2

The Bible calendar

Names of Months

The names of the months of the Hebrew Calendar are:

1. Abib or Nisan (Exodus 12: 2–37; Exodus 13: 4; Nehemiah 2: 1; Esther 3: 7);
2. Iyar or Zif (1 Kings 6: 1);
3. Sivan (Esther 8: 9);
4. Tammuz (Ezekiel 8: 14);
5. Ab;
6. Elul (Nehemiah 6: 15);
7. Ethanim or Tishri (1 Kings 8: 2);
8. Marchesvan or Bul (1 Kings 6: 38);
9. Chisleu (Zechariah 7: 1);
10. Tebeth (Esther 2: 16);
11. Sebat (Zechariah 1: 7);
12. Adar (Esther 3: 7).

The Jewish months

Certain important events are recorded as occurring in particular Jewish months.

1. Abib (April):

The Jewish calendar began with.
   Ex. 12: 2; Ex. 13: 4; Deut. 16: 1.
Passover instituted and celebrated in.
   Ex. 12: 1–28; Ex. 23: 15.
Israelites left Egypt in.
   Ex. 13: 4.
Tabernacle set up in.
   Ex. 40: 2; Ex. 40: 17.
Israelites arrive at Zin in.
   Num. 20: 1.
Cross Jordan in.
   Josh. 4: 19.
Jordan overflows in.
   1 Chr. 12: 15.
Decree to put the Jews to death in.
   Esth. 3: 12.
The death of Jesus in.
   Matt. 26–27.
After the captivity called Nisan.
   Neh. 2: 1; Esth. 3: 7.

Sacred month	Name of month	Corresponding english month	Festival of month
I	Abib, or Nisan	April	14th day. The Passover. 16th day. Firstfruits of Barley harvest presented.
II	Zif	May	14th day. Second Passover, for those who could not keep the first.
III	Sivan	June	6th day. Pentecost, or Feast of Weeks. Firstfruits of the Wheat harvest, and Firstfruits of all the ground.
IV	Thammuz	July	
V	Ab	August	
VI	Elul	September	
VII	Tisri, or Ethanim	October	1st day. Feast of Trumpets. 10th day. Day of Atonement. 15th day. Feast of Tabernacles. Firstfruits of Wine and Oil.
VIII	Bul	November	
IX	Chisleu	December	25th day. Feast of Dedication.
X	Tebeth	January	
XI	Shebat	February	
XII	Adar	March	14th and 15th days. Feast of Purim.

2. Zif (May):

General references.

1 Kgs. 6: 1; 1 Kgs. 6: 37.

Israel numbered in.

Num. 1: 1; Num. 1: 18.

Passover to be observed in, by the unclean and others who could not observe it in the first month.

Num. 9: 10–11.

Israel departed from the wilderness of Zin in.

Num. 10: 11.

Temple begun in.

1 Kgs. 6: 1; 2 Chr. 3: 2.

An irregular Passover celebrated in.

2 Chr. 30: 1–27.

Rebuilding of the temple begun in.

Ezra 3: 8.

3. Sivan (June):

General references.

Esth. 8: 9.

Asa renews the covenant of himself and people in.

2 Chr. 15: 10.

4. Tammuz (July): Mentioned by number, not by name

Jerusalem taken by Nebuchadnezzar in.

Jer. 39: 2; Jer. 52: 6–7.

5. Ab (August): mentioned by number, not by name

Aaron died on the first day of.

Num. 33: 38.

Temple destroyed in.

2 Kgs. 25: 8–10; Jer. 1: 3; Jer. 52: 12–30.

Ezra arrived at Jerusalem in.

Ezra 7: 8–9.

6. Elul (September):

Wall of Jerusalem finished in.

Neh. 6: 15.

Temple built in.

Hag. 1: 14–15.

7. Ethanim (October):

General references.

1 Kgs. 8: 2; Lev. 23: 24; Lev. 23: 27; Neh. 8: 13–15.

The feast of trumpets .

(Numbers 29: 1–6).

8. Bul (November):

The temple finished in.

1 Kgs. 6: 38.

Jeroboam's idolatrous feast in.

1 Kgs. 12: 32–33; 1 Chr. 27: 11.

9. Chisleu (December):

Ezra 10: 9; Jer. 36: 9; Jer. 36: 22; Zech. 7: 1.

10. Tebeth (January):

General references.

Esth. 2: 16.

Nebuchadnezzar besieges Jerusalem in.

2 Kgs. 25: 1; Jer. 52: 4.

11. Sebat (February):

General references.

Zech. 1: 7.

Moses probably died in.

Deut. 1: 3.

12. Adar (March):

General references.

Esth. 3: 7.

Second temple finished in.

"And this house was finished on the third day of the month of Adar, in the sixth year of the reign of King Darius"

Ezra 6: 15.

Feast of Purim in.

Esth. 9: 1–26.

Trees (1)

Overview

1. Originally created by God.
   Gen. 1: 11,12; 2: 9.
2. Made for the glory of God.
   Ps. 148: 9.
3. Of various sizes. Ezek. 17: 24.
4. Given as food. Gen. 1: 29,30;
   Deut. 20: 19.
5. Designed to beautify the earth.
   Gen. 2: 9.
6. Planted by man. Lev. 19: 23.
7. Each kind of, known by its fruit.
   Matt. 12: 33.

Different kinds of mentioned

Of the wood. Song 2: 3.
Of the forest. Is. 10: 19.
Bearing fruit. Neh. 9: 25; Eccl. 2: 5;
  Ezek. 47: 12.
Evergreen. Ps. 37: 35; Jer. 17: 2.
Deciduous. Is. 6: 13.

Parts of mentioned

- The roots. Jer. 17: 8.
- The stem or trunk. Is. 11: 1; 44: 19.
- The branches. Lev. 23: 40; Dan. 4: 14.
- The tender shoots. Luke 21: 29,30.
- The leaves. Is. 6: 13; Dan. 4: 12;
  Matt. 21: 19.
- The fruit or seeds. Lev. 27: 30;
  Ezek. 36: 30.

Propagation

Each kind has its own seed for
propagating its species. Gen. 1: 11,12.
Often propagated by birds who carry
the seeds along with them. Ezek. 17: 3,5.

Nourished

- By the earth. Gen. 1: 12; 2: 9.
- By the rain from heaven. Is. 44: 14.
- Through their own sap. Ps. 104: 16.

Growth of

- Specially flourished beside the rivers
  and streams of water. Ezek. 47: 12.
- When cut down often sprouted from
  their roots again. Job 14: 7.

Often suffered from

- Locusts. Ex. 10: 5,15; Deut. 28: 42.
- Hail and frost. Ex. 9: 25; Ps. 78: 47.
- Fire. Joel 1: 19.
- Desolating armies. 2 Kgs. 19: 23;
  Is. 10: 34.

Facts about

- Afford an agreeable shade in eastern
  countries during the heat of the day.
  Gen. 18: 4; Job 40: 21.
- Were sold with the land on which
  they grew. Gen. 23: 17.

Were cut down

- With axes. Deut. 19: 5; Ps. 74: 5;
  Matt. 3: 10.
- For building. 2 Kgs. 6: 2; 2 Chr. 2: 8,10.
- By besieging armies for erecting
  forts. Deut. 20: 20; Jer. 6: 6.
- For making idols. Is. 40: 20; 44: 14,17.
- For fuel. Is. 44: 14–16; Matt. 3: 10.

God and trees

- God increases and multiplies the fruit of, for his people. Lev. 26: 4; Ezek. 34: 27; Joel 2: 22.
- God often renders barren as a punishment. Lev. 26: 20.
- Early custom of planting, in consecrated grounds. Gen. 21: 33.

The Jews

- Prohibited from planting in consecrated places. Deut. 16: 21.
- Prohibited from cutting down fruit bearing, for sieges. Deut. 20: 19.
- Often pitched their tents under. Gen. 18: 1,4; Judg. 4: 5; 1 Sam. 22: 6.
- Often buried under. Gen. 35: 8; 1 Sam. 21: 13.
- Often executed criminals on. Deut. 21: 22,23; Josh. 10: 26; Gal. 3: 13; Gen. 40: 19.
- Considered trees on which criminals were executed abominable. Is. 14: 19.

Trees mentioned in the Bible

- Almond. Gen. 43: 11; Eccl. 12: 5; Jer. 1: 11.
- Almug or algum. 1 Kgs. 10: 11,12; 2 Chr. 9: 10,11.
- Apple. Song 2: 3; 8: 5; Joel 1: 12.
- Ash. Is. 44: 14.
- Bay. Ps. 37: 35.
- Box. Is. 41: 19.
- Cedar. 1 Kgs. 10: 27.
- Chestnut. Ezek. 31: 8.
- Cyprus. Is. 44: 14.
- Fig. Deut. 8: 8.
- Fir. 1 Kgs. 5: 10; 2 Kgs. 19: 23; Ps. 104: 17.
- Juniper. 1 Kgs. 19: 4,5.

- Lign-aloes. Num. 24: 6.
- Mulberry. 2 Sam. 5: 23,24.
- Myrtle. Is. 41: 19; 55: 13; Zech. 1: 8.
- Mustard. Matt. 13: 32.
- Oak. Is. 1: 30.
- Oil-tree. Is. 41: 19.
- Olive. Deut. 6: 11.

The olive tree

- Often grew wild. Rom. 11: 17.
- Canaan abounded in. Deut. 6: 11; 8: 8.
- Assyria abounded in. 2 Kgs. 18: 32.
- Kings of Israel largely cultivated. 1 Chr. 27: 28.
- Grafting of, alluded to. Rom. 11: 24.
- Pruning of, alluded to. Rom. 11: 18,19.
- Often cast its flowers. Job 15: 33.
- Often cast its fruit. Deut. 28: 40.
- Often attacked by caterpillars. Amos 4: 9.
- Good for the service of God and man Judg. 9: 9.
- Oil procured from. Ex. 27: 20; Deut. 8: 8.

Cultivated

- In olive yards. 1 Sam. 8: 14; Neh. 5: 11.
- Among rocks. Deut. 32: 13.
- On the sides of mountains. Matt. 21: 1.

Described as

- Green. Jer. 11: 16.
- Fair and beautiful. Jer. 11: 16.
- Fat and unctuous. Rom. 11: 17.
- Bearing goodly fruit. Jer. 11: 16; James 3: 12.

Trees (2)

Used for making

- The cherubim in the temple.
  1 Kgs. 6: 23.
- The doors and posts of the temple.
  1 Kgs. 6: 31–33.
- Booths at feast of tabernacles.
  Neh. 8: 15.

Trees and fruit

- Beaten to remove the fruit.
  Deut. 24: 20.
- Shaken when fully ripe. Is. 17: 6.
- Gleaning of, left for the poor.
  Deut. 24: 20.
- Fruit of, during sabbatical year left
  for the poor. Ex. 23: 11.
- The fruit of, trodden in presses to
  extract the oil. Mic. 6: 15; Hag. 2: 16.
- Failure of, a great calamity.
  Hab. 3: 17,18.

Illustrative

- Of Christ. Rom. 11: 17,24;
  Zech. 4: 3,12.
- Of the Jewish church. Jer. 11: 16.
- Of the righteous. Ps. 52: 8; Hos. 14: 6.
- Of children of pious parents.
  Ps. 128: 3.
- Of the two witnesses. Rev. 11: 3,4.
- (When wild,) of the Gentiles.
  Rom. 11: 17,24.
- (Gleaning of,) of the remnant of
  grace. Is. 17: 6; 24: 13.
- Probably origin of its being the
  emblem of peace. Gen. 8: 11.

The palm

Overview

1. First mention of, in Scripture.
   Ex. 15: 27.
2. Jericho celebrated for. Deut. 34: 3;
   Judg. 1: 16.

Described as

- Tall. Song 7: 7.
- Upright. Jer. 10: 5.
- Flourishing. Ps. 92: 12.
- Fruitful to a great age. Ps. 92: 14.

Facts about palms

- The fruit of, called dates. 2 Chr. 31: 5.
- Requires a moist and fertile soil.
  Ex. 15: 27.
- Tents often pitched under the shade
  of. Judg. 4: 5.
- Blasted as a punishment. Joel 1: 12.
- Represented in carved work on
  the walls and doors of the temple
  of Solomon. 1 Kgs. 6: 29,32,35;
  2 Chr. 3: 5.

The branches of, were

- The emblem of victory. Rev. 7: 9.
- Carried at feast of tabernacles.
  Lev. 23: 40.
- Used for constructing booths.
  Neh. 8: 15.
- Spread before Christ. John 12: 13.

Illustrative

- Of the church. Song 7: 7,8.
- Of the righteous. Ps. 92: 12.
- Of the upright appearance of idols.
  Jer. 10: 5.

Other trees

- Pine. Is. 41: 19.
- Pomegranate. Deut. 8: 8; Joel 1: 12.
- Shittah or shittim. Ex. 36: 20; Is. 41: 19.
- Sycamore. 1 Kgs. 10: 27; Ps. 78: 47; Amos 7: 14; Luke 19: 4.
- Teil. Is. 6: 13.
- Vine. Num. 6: 4; Ezek. 15: 2.
- Willow. Is. 44: 4; Ezek. 17: 5.

Book on

- Solomon wrote the history of 1 Kgs. 4: 33.

Illustrative

- Of Christ. Rom. 11: 24; Rev. 2: 7; 22: 2,14.
- Of wisdom. Prov. 3: 18.
- Of kings. Is. 10: 34; Ezek. 17: 24; 31: 7–10; Dan. 4: 10–14.
- Of the life and conversation of the righteous. Prov. 11: 30; 15: 4.
- (Green,) of the innocence of Christ. Luke 23: 31.
- (Good and fruitful,) of saints. Num. 24: 6; Ps. 1: 3; Is. 61: 3; Jer. 17: 8; Matt. 7: 17,18.
- (Evergreen,) of saints. Ps. 1: 1–3.
- (Duration of,) of continued prosperity of saints. Is. 65: 22.
- (Shedding their leaves yet retaining their substance,) of the elect remnant in the church. Is. 6: 13.
- (Barren,) of the wicked. Hos. 9: 16.
- (Shaking of the leaves off,) of the terror of the wicked. Is. 7: 2.
- (Producing evil fruit,) of the wicked. Matt. 7: 17–19.
- (Dry,) of useless persons. Is. 56: 3.
- (Dry,) of the wicked ripe for judgment. Luke 23: 31.

Forests

Overview

1. Tracts of land covered with trees Is. 44: 14.
2. Underbrush often in Is. 9: 18.
3. Infested by wild beasts Ps. 50: 10; 104: 20; Is. 56: 9; Jer. 5: 6; Mic. 5: 8.
4. Abounded with wild honey 1 Sam. 14: 25,26.
5. Often afforded pasture Mic. 7: 14.

Mentioned in scripture

- Bashan. Is. 2: 13; Ezek. 27: 6; Zech. 11: 2.
- Hareth. 1 Sam. 22: 5.
- Ephraim. 2 Sam. 18: 6,8.
- Lebanon. 1 Kgs. 7: 2; 10: 17.
- Carmel. 2 Kgs. 19: 23; Is. 37: 24.
- Arabian. Is. 21: 13.
- The south. Ezek. 20: 46,47.
- The king's. Neh. 2: 8.

Facts about forests

- Were places of refuge. 1 Sam. 22: 5; 23: 16.
- Jotham built towers, in. 2 Chr. 27: 4.
- The power of God extends over. Ps. 29: 9.
- Called on to rejoice at God's mercy. Is. 44: 23.
- Often destroyed by enemies. 2 Kgs. 19: 23; Is. 37: 24; Jer. 46: 23.

Trees (3)

Forests, continued

Illustrative

- Of the unfruitful world. Is. 32: 19.
- (A fruitful field turned into,) of the Jews rejected by God. Is. 29: 17; 32: 15.
- (Destroyed by fire,) of destruction of the wicked. Is. 9: 18; 10: 17,18; Jer. 21: 14.

The cedar

Overview

1. The cedar is (Heb. *e'rez*, Gr. *kedros*, Lat. *cedrus*) a tree often mentioned in Scripture.
2. It was stately (Ezek. 31: 3–5), long-branched (Ps. 80: 10; 92: 12; Ezek. 31: 6–9), durable, and therefore much used for boards, pillars, and ceilings (1 Kings 6: 9, 10; 7: 2; Jer. 22: 14), and for carved images (Is. 44: 14).
3. It grew very abundantly in Palestine, and particularly in Lebanon, of which it was "the glory" (Is. 35: 2; 60: 13).
4. Lebanon was celebrated for its cedar trees. Judg. 9: 15; Ps. 92: 12.
5. Hiram supplied Solomon with cedar trees from Lebanon for the construction of the temple and the king's palace (2 Sam. 5: 11; 7: 2,7; 1 Kings 5: 6,8,10; 6: 9,10,15,16,18,20; 7: 2,3,7,11,12; 9: 11, etc.).
6. Cedars were used also in the building of the second temple under Zerubbabel (Ezra 3: 7).

God and cedars

- Planted by God. Ps. 104: 16; Is. 41: 19.
- Made to glorify God. Ps. 148: 9.

Described as

- High. Is. 37: 24; Ezek. 17: 22; Amos 2: 9.
- Spreading. Ps. 80: 10,11.
- Fragrant. Song 4: 11; Hos. 14: 6.
- Graceful and beautiful. "The mountains were covered with the shadow of it, And the boughs thereof were like cedars of God" Psalm 80: 10 ASV.
- Strong and durable. Is. 9: 10.

Facts about

- Banks of rivers favorable to the growth of. Num. 24: 6.
- Destruction of, a punishment. Jer. 22: 7.
- Destruction of, exhibits God's power. Ps. 29: 5.
- Considered the first of trees. 1 Kgs. 4: 33.
- Extensive commerce in. 1 Kgs. 5: 10,11; Ezra 3: 7.

Used in

- Building temples. "And, behold, I purpose to build a house for the name of Jehovah my God, as Jehovah spake unto David my father, saying, Thy son, whom I will set upon thy throne in thy room, he shall build the house for my name.

6 Now therefore command thou that they cut me cedar-trees out of Lebanon; and my servants shall be with thy servants; and I will give thee hire for thy servants according to all that thou shalt say: for thou knowest that there is not among us any that knoweth how to cut timber like unto the Sidonians" 1 Kings 5: 5,6 ASV.

- Building palaces. 2 Sam. 5: 11; 1 Kgs. 7: 2,3.
- Making masts of ships. Ezek. 27: 5.
- Making wardrobes. Ezek. 27: 24.
- Making chariots. Song 3: 9.
- Purifying the leper. Lev. 14: 4–7,49–52.
- Preparing the water of separation. Num. 19: 6.
- Making idols. Is. 44: 14.

The eagle alluded to as

- Making its nest in. Jer. 22: 23.
- Perching on the high branches of. Ezek. 17: 3.
- Instrumental in propagating. Ezek. 17: 4,5.

Illustrative

- Of majesty, strength, and glory of Christ. Song 5: 15; Ezek. 17: 22,23.
- Of beauty and glory of Israel. Num. 24: 6.
- Of saints in their rapid growth. Ps. 92: 12.
- Of powerful nations. Ezek. 31: 3; Amos 2: 9.
- Of arrogant rulers. Is. 2: 13; 10: 33,34.

Tree of the Knowledge of Good and Evil

Stood in the middle of the garden of Eden, beside the tree of life (Gen. 2,3). Adam and Eve were forbidden to eat any of its fruit. But they disobeyed God, and so sin and death through sin entered the world.

Tree of Life

Stood in the middle of the garden of Eden (Gen. 2: 9; 3: 22).

"And out of the ground made Jehovah God to grow every tree that is pleasant to the sight, and good for food; the tree of life also in the midst of the garden, and the tree of the knowledge of good and evil" Genesis 2: 9 ASV.

It symbolized that life should be sought by humans, not from themselves or in their own power, but from outside themselves, from God who is life (John 1: 4; 14: 6).

Wisdom is compared to the tree of life (Prov. 3: 18).

The "tree of life" spoken of in the Book of Revelation is an emblem of the joys of the celestial paradise.

"He that hath an ear, let him hear what the Spirit saith to the churches. To him that overcometh, to him will I give to eat of the tree of life, which is in the Paradise of God" Revelation 2: 7 ASV.

"In the midst of the street thereof. And on this side of the river and on that was the tree of life, bearing twelve manner of fruits, yielding its fruit every month: and the leaves of the tree were for the healing of the nations."

Revelation 22: 2,14 ASV.

Flowers, Grass, Gardens, Garden of Gethsemane

Flowers

Overview

Very few species of flowers are mentioned in the Bible although they abounded in Palestine.

Flowers grew wild in fields, Ps. 103: 15, and were cultivated in gardens, Song 6: 2,3.

Described as

- Beautiful. Matt. 6: 29.
- Sweet. Song 5: 13.
- Temporary nature of. Is. 40: 8.
- Appear in spring. Song 2: 12.

Facts about

- Garlands of, used in worship of idols. Acts 14: 13.

Mentioned in the Bible

- The lily. Hos. 14: 5; Matt. 6: 28.
- The lily of the valley. Song 2: 1.
- The rose. Is. 35: 1.
- The rose of Sharon. Song 2: 1.
- Of the grass. 1 Pet. 1: 24.

Representations of, on the

- Golden candlestick. Ex. 25: 31,33; 2 Chr. 4: 21.
- Sea of brass. 1 Kgs. 7: 26; 2 Chr. 4: 5.
- Wood work of the temple. 1 Kgs. 6: 18,29,33,35.

Illustrative

- Of shortness of man's life. Job 14: 2; Ps. 103: 15.

- Of kingdom of Israel. Is. 28: 1.
- Of glory of man. 1 Pet. 1: 24.
- Of rich men. James 1: 10,11.

Grass

Overview

A green herb. Mark 6: 39.
Springs out of the earth. 2 Sam. 23: 4.

Called

- Grass of the earth. Rev. 9: 4.
- Grass of the field. Num. 22: 4.

God and grass

- Originally created. Gen. 1: 11,12.
- The giver of. Deut. 11: 15.
- Causes to grow. Ps. 104: 14.
- Adorns and clothes. Matt. 6: 30.

Facts about

- Often grew on the tops of houses. Ps. 129: 6.
- When young, soft and tender. Prov. 27: 25.
- Refreshed by rain and dew Deut. 32: 2; Prov. 19: 12.
- Cattle fed on. Job 6: 5; Jer. 50: 11.
- Ovens often heated with. Matt. 6: 30.
- Failure of, a great calamity. Is. 15: 5,6.
- Sufferings of cattle from failure of, described. Jer. 14: 5,6.

Destroyed by

- Locusts. Rev. 9: 4.
- Hail and lightning. Rev. 8: 7.

- Drought. 1 Kgs. 17: 1; 18: 5.

Illustrative

- Of shortness and uncertainty of life. Is. 40: 6,7; 1 Pet. 1: 24.
- Of prosperity of the wicked. Ps. 92: 7.
- (Refreshed by dew and showers,) of the saints refreshed by grace. Ps. 72: 6; Mic. 5: 7.
- (On tops of houses,) of the wicked. 2 Kgs. 19: 26; Is. 37: 27.

Gardens

Overview

Often made by the banks of rivers. Num. 24: 6.

Kinds of, mentioned in Scripture

- Herbs. Deut. 11: 10; 1 Kgs. 21: 2.
- Cucumbers. Is. 1: 8.
- Fruit trees. Eccl. 2: 5,6.
- Spices. Song 4: 16; 6: 2.

Facts about

- Often enclosed. Song 4: 12.
- Often refreshed by fountains. Song 4: 15.
- Taken care of by gardeners. John 20: 15.
- Lodges erected in. Is. 1: 8.
- Blasting of, a punishment. Amos 4: 9.
- Jews ordered to plant, in Babylon. Jer. 29: 5,28.

Often used for

- Entertainments. Song 5: 1.
- Rest. John 18: 1.

- Burial places. 2 Kgs. 21: 18,26; John 19: 41.
- Idolatrous worship. Is. 1: 29; 65: 3.

Of Eden

- Planted by the Lord. Gen. 2: 8.
- Called the garden of the Lord. Gen. 13: 10.
- Called the garden of God. Ezek. 28: 13.
- Had every tree good for food. Gen. 2: 9.
- Watered by a river. Gen. 2: 10–14.
- Man placed in, to tend. Gen. 2: 8,15.
- Man driven from, after the fall. Gen. 3: 23,24.

Comparisons with

- Fertility of Canaan like. Gen. 13: 10; Joel 2: 3.
- The future state of the Jews shall be like. Is. 51: 3; Ezek. 36: 35.

Illustrative

- (Well watered,) of spiritual prosperity of the church. Is. 58: 11; Jer. 31: 12.
- (When dried up,) of the wicked. Is. 1: 30.

Gethsemane

Gethsemane was a garden near Jerusalem.

"Gethsemane" means "oil -press," the name of an olive orchard at the foot of the Mount of Olives, to which Jesus often went (Luke 22: 39) with his disciples.

Jesus prayed there on the Thursday evening of his arrest (Mark 14: 32; John 18: 1; Luke 22: 44).

Fruit (1)

Overview

The word "fruit" in the Bible is used in a general sense and includes both vegetables and animals.

The Jews put the fruits of the land into three categories:

1. The fruit of the field, "corn-fruit" (Heb. *dagan*); all kinds of grain and pulse.
2. The fruit of the vine, "vintage-fruit" (Heb. *tirosh*); grapes, whether moist or dried.
3. "Orchard-fruits" (Heb. *yitshar*), as dates, figs, citrons, etc.

The word "fruit"

The word "fruit" is also used of:
- children (Gen. 30: 2; Deut. 7: 13; Luke 1: 42; Ps. 21: 10; 132: 11); and of
- the young of animals (Deut. 28: 51; Is. 14: 29).

Fruits

- The produce of corn. Deut. 22: 9; Ps. 107: 37.
- The produce of trees. Gen. 1: 29; Eccl. 2: 5.

Called the

- Fruit of the ground. Gen. 4: 3; Jer. 7: 20.
- Fruit of the earth. Is. 4: 2.
- Increase of the land. Ps. 85: 12.

Facts about fruits

- Given by God. Acts 14: 17.

- Preserved to us by God. Mal. 3: 11.
- Produced in their due seasons. Matt. 21: 41.
- First of, devoted to God. Deut. 26: 2.
- To be waited for with patience. James 5: 7.
- Often sent as presents. Gen. 43: 11.

Require

- A fruitful land. Ps. 107: 31.
- Rain from heaven. Ps. 104: 13; James 5: 18.
- Influence of the sun and moon. Deut. 33: 14.

Divided into

- Hasty or precocious. Is. 28: 4.
- Summer fruits. 2 Sam. 16: 1.
- New and old. Song 7: 13.
- Goodly. Jer. 11: 16.
- Pleasant. Song 4: 16.
- Precious. Deut. 33: 14.
- Evil or bad. Matt. 7: 17.

Often destroyed

- In God's anger. Jer. 7: 20.
- By blight. Joel 1: 12.
- By locusts. Deut. 28: 38,39; Joel 1: 4.
- By enemies. Ezek. 25: 4.
- By drought. Hag. 1: 10.

Illustrative

- Of effects of repentance. Matt. 3: 8.
- Of works of the Spirit. Gal. 5: 22,23; Eph. 5: 9.
- Of good works. Matt. 7: 17,18; Php 4: 17.

- Of godly conversation. Prov. 12: 14; 18: 20.
- Of praise. Heb. 13: 15.
- Of the example of the godly. Prov. 11: 30.
- Of effects of industry. Prov. 31: 16,31.
- Of the reward of saints. Is. 3: 10.
- Of the reward of the wicked. Jer. 17: 9,10.
- Of converts to the church. Ps. 72: 16; John 4: 36.
- (Bad,) of the conduct and conversation of evil men. Matt. 12: 33.

The fruit of the Spirit

The fruit of the Spirit (Gal. 5: 22,23; Eph. 5: 9; James 3: 17, 18) describe good characteristics of Christians which the Spirit produces in those in whom he lives and is allowed to flourish.

"(for the fruit of the light is in all goodness and righteousness and truth.)" Ephesians 5: 9 ASV.

"But the fruit of the Spirit is
- love,
- joy,
- peace,
- longsuffering,
- kindness,
- goodness,
- faithfulness,
- meekness,
- self-control;
against such there is no law"

Galatians 5: 22,23 ASV

"But the wisdom that is from above is first pure, then peaceable, gentle, easy to be entreated, full of mercy and good fruits, without variance, without hypocrisy. And the fruit of righteousness is sown in peace."

James 3: 17,18

Different spiritual fruits

The fruits of righteousness and the fruits of sin are contrasted many times in the Bible.

"The righteousness of the perfect shall direct his way; But the wicked shall fall by his own wickedness.

6 The righteousness of the upright shall deliver them; But the treacherous shall be taken in their own iniquity.

7 When a wicked man dieth, his expectation shall perish; And the hope of iniquity perisheth.

18 The wicked earneth deceitful wages; But he that soweth righteousness hath a sure reward.

19 He that is stedfast in righteousness shall attain unto life; And he that pursueth evil doeth it to his own death."

Proverbs 11: 5–7,18,19 ASV

Fruits of righteousness

OLD TESTAMENT
Deut. 6: 25; Josh. 22: 31; Ps. 1: 3; Ps. 15: 1–5; Ps. 24: 3–5; Ps. 101: 3–4; Ps. 106: 3; Ps. 112: 4–8; Prov. 2: 5–20; Prov. 10: 2; Prov. 11: 5–6; Prov. 11: 18–19; Prov. 11: 30; Prov. 12: 28; Prov. 10: 16; Prov. 13: 6; Prov. 14: 34; Prov. 21: 3; Prov. 29: 7; Is. 28: 17; Is. 32: 16–18; Is. 33: 15–17; Is. 55: 12–13; Is. 58: 6–14; Is. 62: 1; Ezek. 18: 5–9; Ezek. 33: 15; Dan. 12: 3; Hos. 10: 12; Mal. 3: 3; Mal. 4: 2.

Fruit (2)

Fruits of righteousness, continued

NEW TESTAMENT
Gospels
Matt. 5: 20; Matt. 12: 35; Mark 3: 33–35; Matt. 12: 50; Luke 3: 10–14; Luke 8: 15; John 3: 21; John 3: 33; John 8: 47; John 8: 49; John 13: 35; John 14: 21–24; John 15: 4–5; John 15: 8; John 15: 12;

Rest of the New Testament
Acts 9: 36; Acts 11: 29–30; Acts 19: 19; Rom. 5: 1–5; Rom. 6: 19–22; Rom. 7: 4–6; Rom. 8: 4–6; Rom. 14: 17–19; Rom. 15: 1–7; 1 Cor. 4: 19–20; 1 Cor. 12: 3; 1 Cor. 13: 1–13; 2 Cor. 5: 17; 2 Cor. 7: 10–11; 2 Cor. 9: 10; 2 Cor. 10: 5; 2 Cor. 13: 5; Gal. 4: 6; Gal. 5: 22–23; Gal. 6: 7–8; Eph. 1: 13–14; Eph. 5: 9; Phil. 1: 11; Phil. 1: 27–29; Phil. 2: 13; Phil. 3: 12–14; Phil. 4: 11–13; Col. 1: 12–13; Col. 3: 3; Col. 3: 5; Col. 3: 9–17. 1 Thess. 1: 3; 1 Thess. 1: 9–10; 2 Thess. 1: 3–5; 1 Tim. 2: 9–10; 1 Tim. 5: 9–10; 2 Tim. 2: 22; 2 Tim. 4: 6–8; Titus 2: 2; Titus 2: 11–12; Titus 3: 14; Phile. 1: 5–6; James 1: 27; James 2: 14–26; James 3: 11–18; 1 Pet. 3: 1–11; 1 Pet. 3: 14; 1 Pet. 4: 2; 2 Pet. 1: 5–9; 1 John 2: 3–6; 1 John 2: 10–11; 1 John 2: 24; 1 John 2: 29; 1 John 3: 3; 1 John 3: 6–7; 1 John 3: 9–11; 1 John 3: 14; 1 John 3: 17–24; 1 John 4: 4–21; 1 John 5: 1–5; 1 John 5: 10; 1 John 5: 13; 1 John 5: 18; 2 John 1: 9; 3 John 1: 11; Rev. 2: 2–3; Rev. 2: 19

Pictures of the fruit of righteousness in the psalms

STREAMS OF WATER
"And he shall be like a tree planted by the streams of water, That bringeth forth its fruit in its season, Whose leaf also doth not wither; And whatsoever he doeth shall prosper" Psalm 1: 3 ASV.

TRUTH
"Jehovah, who shall sojourn in thy tabernacle? Who shall dwell in thy holy hill?
2 He that walketh uprightly, and worketh righteousness, And speaketh truth in his heart;
3 He that slandereth not with his tongue, Nor doeth evil to his friend, Nor taketh up a reproach against his neighbor;
4 In whose eyes a reprobate is despised, But who honoreth them that fear Jehovah; He that sweareth to his own hurt, and changeth not;
5 He that putteth not out his money to interest, Nor taketh reward against the innocent. He that doeth these things shall never be moved"
Psalm 15: 1–5 ASV

A PURE HEART
"Who shall ascend into the hill of Jehovah? And who shall stand in his holy place?
4 He that hath clean hands, and a pure heart; Who hath not lifted up his soul unto falsehood, And hath not sworn deceitfully.
5 He shall receive a blessing from Jehovah, And righteousness from the God of his salvation"
Psalm 24: 3–5 ASV

ABSENCE OF EVIL
"I will set no base thing before mine eyes: I hate the work of them that turn

aside; It shall not cleave unto me.

4   A perverse heart shall depart from me: I will know no evil thing"

Psalm 101: 3,4 ASV

JUSTICE

"Blessed are they that keep justice, And he that doeth righteousness at all times"   *Psalm 106: 3 ASV*

MERCY

"Unto the upright there ariseth light in the darkness: He is gracious, and merciful, and righteous.

5   Well is it with the man that dealeth graciously and lendeth; He shall maintain his cause in judgment.

6   For he shall never be moved; The righteous shall be had in everlasting remembrance.

7   He shall not be afraid of evil tidings: His heart is fixed, trusting in Jehovah.

8   His heart is established, he shall not be afraid, Until he see his desire upon his adversaries"

Psalm 112: 4–8 ASV

Fruits of sin

Gen. 3: 7–24; Gen. 4: 9–14; Gen. 6: 5–7; Deut. 29: 18; 1 Kgs. 13: 33–34; Job 4: 8; Job 5: 2; Job 13: 26; Job 20: 11; Ps. 5: 10; Ps. 9: 15–16; Ps. 10: 2; Ps. 94: 23; Ps. 141: 10; Prov. 1: 31; Prov. 3: 35; Prov. 5: 22–23; Prov. 8: 36; Prov. 10: 24; Prov. 10: 29–31; Prov. 11: 5–7; Prov. 11: 18–19; Prov. 11: 27; Prov. 11: 29; Prov. 12: 13–14; Prov. 12: 21; Prov. 12: 26; Prov. 13: 5–6; Prov. 13: 15; Prov. 22: 8; Prov. 27: 8; Prov. 28: 1; Prov. 29: 6; Prov. 30: 20; Is. 3: 9; Is. 3: 11; Is. 9: 18; Is. 14: 21; Is. 50: 11; Is. 57: 20–21; Jer. 2: 17; Jer. 2: 19; Jer. 4: 18; Jer. 5: 25; Jer. 7: 19;

Jer. 14: 16; Jer. 21: 14; Ezek. 11: 21; Ezek. 22: 31; Ezek. 23: 31–35; Hos. 8: 7; Hos. 10: 13; Hos. 12: 14; Hos. 13: 9; Mic. 7: 13; Mark 7: 21–23; Acts 9: 5; Rom. 5: 12–21; Rom. 7: 5; 1 Cor. 3: 3; 1 Cor. 6: 9–11; Gal. 5: 19–21; Gal. 6: 7–8; 1 Pet. 4: 3

Pictures of the fruits of sin in Proverbs

ENGAGING IN EVIL

"The way of Jehovah is a stronghold to the upright; But it is a destruction to the workers of iniquity.

30   The righteous shall never be removed; But the wicked shall not dwell in the land.

31   The mouth of the righteous bringeth forth wisdom; But the perverse tongue shall be cut off"

Proverbs 10: 29–31 ASV

TREACHERY

"The righteousness of the perfect shall direct his way; But the wicked shall fall by his own wickedness.

6   The righteousness of the upright shall deliver them; But the treacherous shall be taken in their own iniquity.

7   When a wicked man dieth, his expectation shall perish; And the hope of iniquity perisheth"

Proverbs 11: 5–7 ASV

DECEIT

"The wicked earneth deceitful wages; But he that soweth righteousness hath a sure reward.

19   He that is stedfast in righteousness shall attain unto life; And he that pursueth evil doeth it to his own death"   *Proverbs 11: 18,19 ASV*

Herbs, spices, and incense

Herbs

Overview

1. Called the green herbs. 2 Kgs. 19: 26.
2. Each kind of, contains its own seed. Gen. 1: 11,12.

God

- Created. Gen. 1: 11,12; 2: 5.
- Causes to grow. Ps. 104: 14.
- Given as food to man. Gen. 1: 28,29.

Found in

- The fields. Jer. 12: 4.
- The mountains. Prov. 27: 25.
- The marshes. Job 8: 11.
- The deserts. Job 24: 5; Jer. 17: 6.

Cultivation of

- Cultivated in gardens. Deut. 11: 10; 1 Kgs. 21: 2.
- Cultivated for food. Prov. 15: 17; Heb. 6: 7.
- Require rain or dew. Deut. 32: 2.
- Mode of watering, alluded to. Deut. 11: 10.

Herbs, spices, and vegetables mentioned in the Bible

- Barley. Ex. 9: 31; 2 Sam. 14: 30.
- Beans. 2 Sam. 17: 28.
- Bulrushes. Ex. 2: 3; Is. 58: 5.
- Calamus. Song 4: 14.
- Cucumber. Num. 11: 5; Is. 1: 8.
- Cummin. Is. 28: 27; Matt. 23: 23.
- Dill. Matt. 23: 23.
- Flag. Ex. 2: 3; Job 8: 11.
- Flax. Ex. 9: 31.
- Garlic. Num. 11: 5.
- Gourds. 2 Kgs. 4: 39.
- Grass. Num. 22: 4.
- Heath. Jer. 17: 6; 48: 6.
- Hyssop. Ex. 12: 22; 1 Kgs. 4: 33.
- Leeks. Num. 11: 5.
- Lentils. Gen. 25: 34.
- Mandrakes. Gen. 30: 14; Song 7: 13.
- Mallows. Job 30: 4.
- Millet. Ezek. 4: 9.
- Melon. Num. 11: 5.
- Mint. Matt. 23: 23.
- Myrrh. Song 4: 14.
- Nard. Song 4: 14.
- Onions. Num. 11: 5.
- Reeds. Job 40: 21; Is. 19: 6.
- Rushes. Job 8: 11.
- Rye. Ex. 9: 32.
- Saffron. Song 4: 14.
- Spikenard. Song 4: 14.
- Tares or darnel. Matt. 13: 30.
- Wheat. Ex. 9: 32; Jer. 12: 13.

Facts about

- Bitter herbs, used at Passover. Ex. 12: 8; Num. 9: 11.
- Poisonous, not fit for man's use. 2 Kgs. 4: 39,40.
- Jews used to tithe. Luke 11: 42.
- Were sometimes used instead of animal food. Rom. 14: 2.

Destroyed by

- Hail and lightning. Ex. 9: 22–25.
- Locusts. Ex. 10: 12,15; Ps. 105: 34,35.
- Drought. Is. 42: 15.

Illustrative

Of the wicked. 2 Kgs. 19: 26; Ps. 37: 2. (Dew on,) of grace given to saints. Is. 18: 4.

Spices

Overview

Spices, aromatic substances, were used in oils for anointing and in embalming bodies, and were stored by Hezekiah in his treasure-house (2 Kings 20: 13; Is. 39: 2).

Facts about spices

In the formula for the sacred oil.
Ex. 25: 6; Ex. 35: 8.
Stores of.
2 Kgs. 20: 13.
Used in the temple.
1 Chr. 9: 29.
Exported from Gilead.
Gen. 37: 25.
Sent as a present by Jacob to Joseph.
Gen. 43: 11.
Presented by the queen of Sheba.
1 Kgs. 10: 2; 1 Kgs. 10: 10.
Sold in the markets of Tyre.
Ezek. 27: 22.
Used in the embalming of Asa.
2 Chr. 16: 14.
Prepared for embalming the body of Jesus.
Mark 16: 1; Luke 23: 56; Luke 24: 1; John 19: 39–40.

Incense

Formula for making.
Ex. 30: 34–35.

Strange incense

Incorrectly prepared incense (Ex. 30: 9).

Uses of

Ex. 30: 36–38; Lev. 16: 12; Num. 16: 17; Num. 16: 40; Num. 16: 46; Deut. 33: 10.

Made by

Bezaleel. Ex. 37: 29.
Priests. 1 Chr. 9: 30.

Offered

Incense was offered along with every meat-offering; and daily on the golden altar in the holy place, and on the day of atonement was burnt by the high priest in the holy of holies.
Morning and evening.
Ex. 30: 7–8; 2 Chr. 13: 11.
On the golden altar.
Ex. 30: 1–7; Ex. 40: 5; Ex. 40: 27; 2 Chr. 2: 4; 2 Chr. 32: 12.
In making atonement.
Lev. 16: 12–13; Num. 16: 46–47; Luke 1: 10.

UNLAWFULLY OFFERED BY:
Nadab and Abihu. Lev. 10: 1–2.
Korah, Dathan, and Abiram.
Num. 16: 16–35.
Uzziah. 2 Chr. 26: 16–21.

Offered in idolatrous worship

1 Kgs. 12: 33; Jer. 41: 5; Ezek. 8: 11

Presented by the wise men to Jesus

Matt. 2: 11.

Figurative

Of prayer. Ps. 141: 2.
Of praise. Mal. 1: 11.
Of an acceptable sacrifice. Eph. 5: 2.
Symbolic of the prayers of saints.
Rev. 5: 8; Rev. 8: 3–4.

Metals and gold

Metals

Dug out of the earth. Job 28: 1,2,6.

Mentioned in the Bible

- Gold. Gen. 2: 11,12.
- Silver. Gen. 44: 2.
- Brass. Ex. 27: 2,4; 2 Chr. 12: 10.
- Copper. Ezra 8: 27; 2 Tim. 4: 14.
- Iron. Num. 35: 16; Prov. 27: 17.
- Lead. Ex. 15: 10; Jer. 6: 29.
- Tin. Num. 31: 22.

Facts about metals

- Comparative value of. Is. 60: 17; Dan. 2: 32–45.
- Often mixed with dross. Is. 1: 25.
- The holy land abounded in. Deut. 8: 9.
- Antiquity of the art of working in. Gen. 4: 21.
- Freed from dross by fire. Ezek. 22: 18,20.
- Ceremonially cleansed by fire. Num. 31: 21–23.
- Cast in mold. Judg. 17: 4; Jer. 6: 29.
- Clay of Jordan used for molding. 1 Kgs. 7: 46.
- An extensive commerce in. Ezek. 27: 12.

Gold

Meaning of words for gold

1. Heb. *zahab*, so called from its yellow color (Ex. 25: 11; 1 Chr. 28: 18; 2 Chr. 3: 5).
2. Heb. *segor*, from its compactness, or as being enclosed or treasured up; thus precious or "fine gold" (1 Kings 6: 20; 7: 49).
3. Heb. *paz*, native or pure gold (Job 28: 17; Ps. 19: 10; 21: 3, etc.).
4. Heb. *betzer*, "ore of gold or silver" as dug out of the mine (Job 36: 19, where it means simply riches).
5. Heb. *kethem*, i.e., something concealed or separated (Job 28: 16, 19; Ps. 45: 9; Prov. 25: 12). Rendered "golden wedge" in Is. 13: 12.
6. Heb. *haruts*, i.e., dug out; poetic for gold (Prov. 8: 10; 16: 16; Zech. 9: 3).

Introduction

- Gold was known from the earliest times. Gen. 2: 11.
- It was principally used for ornaments. Gen. 24: 22.
- It was very abundant. 1 Chr. 22: 14; Nah. 2: 9; Dan. 3: 1.
- Many tons used on the temple 2 Chr. 1: 15.
- It was found in Arabia, Sheba, and Ophir 1 Kings 9: 28; 10: 1; Job 28: 16, but not in Palestine.
- In Dan. 2: 38, the Babylonian Empire is spoken of as a "head of gold" because of its great riches.

Facts about

- Found in the earth. Job 28: 1,6.
- Abounded in:
  Havilah. Gen. 2: 11.
  Ophir. 1 Kgs. 9: 28; Ps. 45: 9.
  Sheba. Ps. 72: 15; Is. 60: 6.

Parvaim. 2 Chr. 3: 6.
- Belongs to God. Joel 3: 5; Hag. 2: 8.
- Most valuable when pure and fine.
  Job 28: 19; Ps. 19: 10; 21: 3; Prov. 3: 14.
- Refined and tried by fire. Zech. 13: 9;
  1 Pet. 1: 7.
- Working in, a trade. Neh. 3: 8;
  Is. 40: 19.
- An article of commerce. Ezek. 27: 22.
- The patriarchs were rich in.
  Gen. 13: 2.
- Imported by Solomon. 1 Kgs. 9: 11,28;
  10: 11.
- Abundance of, in Solomon's reign.
  2 Chr. 1: 15.
- Offerings of, for tabernacle. Ex. 35: 22.
- Offerings of, for temple. 1 Chr. 22: 14;
  29: 4,7.
- Used as money. Matt. 10: 9; Acts 3: 6.
- Priestly and royal garments adorned
  with. Ex. 28: 4–6.

Described as

- Yellow. Ps. 68: 13.
- Malleable. Ex. 39: 3.
- Fusible. Ex. 32: 3,4; Prov. 17: 3.
- Precious. Ezra 8: 27; Is. 13: 12.
- Valuable. Job 28: 15,16.

Was used for

- Overlaying the tabernacle.
  Ex. 36: 34,38.
- Overlaying the temple. 1 Kgs. 6: 21,22.
- Overlaying cherubims in temple.
  2 Chr. 3: 10.
- Overlaying the Ark. Ex. 25: 11–13.
- Overlaying floor of temple.
  1 Kgs. 6: 30.
- Overlaying throne of Solomon.
  1 Kgs. 10: 18.

- Mercy seat and cherubims.
  Ex. 25: 17,18.
- Sacred candlesticks. Ex. 25: 31.
- Sacred utensils. 2 Chr. 4: 19–22.
- Crowns. 2 Sam. 12: 30; Ps. 21: 3.
- Scepters. Esth. 4: 11.
- Chains. Gen. 41: 42; Dan. 5: 29.
- Rings. Song 5: 14; James 2: 2.
- Earrings. Judg. 8: 24,26.
- Ornaments. Jer. 4: 30.
- Shields. 2 Sam. 8: 7; 1 Kgs. 10: 16,17.
- Vessels. 1 Kgs. 10: 21; Esth. 1: 7.
- Idols. Ex. 20: 23; Ps. 115: 4.
- Couches. Esth. 1: 6.
- Footstools. 2 Chr. 9: 18.

More facts about gold

- Estimated by weight. 1 Chr. 28: 14.
- Given as presents. Matt. 2: 11.
- Exacted as tribute. 1 Kgs. 20: 3,5;
  2 Kgs. 23: 33,35.
- Taken in war, dedicated to God.
  Josh. 6: 19; 2 Sam. 8: 11; 1 Kgs. 15: 15.
- Kings of Israel not to multiply.
  Deut. 17: 17.
- Jews condemned for multiplying.
  Is. 2: 7.
- Vanity of heaping up. Eccl. 2: 8,11.

Liable to

- Grow dim. Lam. 4: 1.
- Canker and rust. James 5: 3.

Illustrative

- Of saints after affliction. Job 23: 10.
- Of tried faith. 1 Pet. 1: 7.
- Of the doctrines of grace. Rev. 3: 18.
- Of true converts. 1 Cor. 3: 12.
- Of Babylonian Empire. Dan. 2: 38.

Silver

Overview

Veins of, found in the earth. Job 28: 1.
Generally found in an impure state.
Prov. 25: 4.
Comparative value of. Is. 60: 17.

Described as

- White and shining. Ps. 68: 13,14.
- Fusible. Ezek. 22: 20,22.
- Malleable. Jer. 10: 9.

Facts about silver

- Purified by fire. Prov. 17: 3; Zech. 13: 9.
- Purified, called:
  Refined silver. 1 Chr. 29: 4.
  Choice silver. Prov. 8: 19.
- Tarshish carried on extensive
  commerce in. Jer. 10: 9; Ezek. 27: 12.
- The patriarchs rich in. Gen. 13: 2;
  24: 35.
- Used as money from the earliest
  times. Gen. 23: 15,16; 37: 28.
- Very abundant in the reign of.
  Solomon 1 Kgs. 10: 21,22,27.
- The working in, a trade. Acts 19: 24.

Made into

- Cups. Gen. 44: 2.
- Dishes. Num. 7: 13,84,85.
- Bowls. Num. 7: 13,84.
- Thin plates. Jer. 10: 9.
- Chains. Is. 40: 19.
- Wires (alluded to). Eccl. 12: 6.

- Sockets for the boards of the
  tabernacle. Ex. 26: 19,25,32.
- Ornaments and hooks for the pillars
  of the tabernacle. Ex. 27: 17.
- Candlesticks. 1 Chr. 28: 15.
- Tables. 1 Chr. 28: 16.
- Beds or couches. Esth. 1: 6.
- Vessels. 2 Sam. 8: 10; Ezra 6: 5.
- Idols. Ps. 115: 4; Is. 2: 20; 30: 22.
- Ornaments for the person. Ex. 3: 22.

More facts about silver

- Given by the Israelite for making the
  tabernacle. Ex. 25: 3; 35: 24.
- Given by David and his subjects for
  making the temple. 1 Chr. 28: 14;
  29: 2,6–9.
- Taken in war often consecrated
  to God. Josh. 6: 19; 2 Sam. 8: 11;
  1 Kgs. 15: 15.
- Taken in war purified by fire.
  Num. 31: 22,23.
- Often given as presents. 1 Kgs. 10: 25;
  2 Kgs. 5: 5,23.
- Tribute often paid in. 2 Chr. 17: 11;
  Neh. 5: 15.
- From Tarshish Ezek. 27: 12

Illustrative

- Of the words of the Lord. Ps. 12: 6.
- Of the tongue of the just. Prov. 10: 20.
- Of good rulers. Is. 1: 22,23.
- Of the Medo-Persian kingdom.
  Dan. 2: 32,39.

- Of saints purified by affliction.
  Ps. 66: 10; Zech. 13: 9.
- (Labor of seeking for,) of diligence
  required for attaining knowledge.
  Prov. 2: 4.
- (Reprobate,) of the wicked. Jer. 6: 30.
- (Dross of,) of the wicked. Is. 1: 22;
  Ezek. 22: 18.

Silver and wisdom

- Wisdom to be esteemed more than.
  Job 28: 15; Prov. 3: 14; 8: 10,19.

Refining of

Prov. 17: 3; Prov. 25: 4; Prov. 26: 23;
Ezek. 22: 18–22; Jer. 6: 29–30;
Zech. 13: 9; Mal. 3: 3.

Used for money

Gen. 13: 2; Gen. 17: 12; Gen. 20: 16;
Gen. 23: 13–16; Amos 8: 6; Matt. 10: 9;
Matt. 26: 15; Mark 14: 11; Acts 19: 19.

For ornamentation

For the tabernacle. Ex. 26; 27; 35; 36;
Num. 7.

Of the temple. 1 Chr. 28: 14;
1 Chr. 29: 2–5; Ezra 5: 14; Ezra 6: 5;
Ezra 8: 26; Dan. 5: 2.

Cups made of. Gen. 44: 2.

Trumpets made of. Num. 10: 2.

Cords made of. Eccl. 12: 6.

Chains made of. Is. 40: 19.

Shrines made of. Acts 19: 24.

Idols made of. Ex. 20: 23; Is. 30: 22;
Hos. 13: 2.

Baskets or filigree made of. Prov. 25: 11.

Symbolic

Dan. 2: 32; Dan. 2: 3.

Salt and precious stones

Salt

Characteristics of
- Good and useful. Mark 9: 50.
- Lost its savor when exposed to the air. Matt. 5: 13; Mark 9: 50.

Used For
- Seasoning food. Job 6: 6.
- Seasoning sacrifices. Lev. 2: 13; Ezek. 43: 24.
- Ratifying covenants. Num. 18: 19; 2 Chr. 13: 5.
- Strengthening new-born infants. Ezek. 16: 4.

Often found
- In pits. Josh. 11: 8; Zeph. 2: 9.
- In springs. James 3: 12.
- Near the Dead Sea. Num. 34: 12; Deut. 3: 17.

Miracles connected with
- Lot's wife turned into a pillar of. Gen. 19: 26.
- Elisha healed the bad water with. 1 Kgs. 2: 21.

Facts about salt
- Places sown with, to denote perpetual desolation. Judg. 9: 45.
- Liberally afforded to the Jews after the captivity. Ezra 6: 9; 7: 22.
- Places where it abounded barren and unfruitful. Jer. 17: 6; Ezek. 47: 11.
- The valley of, celebrated for victories. 2 Sam. 8: 13; 2 Kgs. 14: 7; 1 Chr. 18: 12.

Illustrative
- Of saints. Matt. 5: 13.
- Of grace in the heart. Mark 9: 50.
- Of wisdom in speech. Col. 4: 6.
- (Without savor,) of graceless professors. Matt. 5: 13; Mark 9: 50.
- (Pits of,) of desolation. Zeph. 2: 9.
- (Salted with fire,) of preparation of the wicked for destruction. Mark 9: 49.
- Partaking of another's a bond of friendship. Ezra 4: 14.

Precious stones

Overview
1. Frequently referred to (1 Kings 10: 2; 2 Chr. 3: 6; 9: 10; Rev. 18: 16; 21: 19).
2. About twenty different precious stones are mentioned in the Bible.
3. Used figuratively Song of Songs 5: 14; Is. 54: 11,12; Lam. 4: 7.

Facts about precious stones
- Dug out of the earth. Job 28: 5,6.
- Brought from Ophir. 1 Kgs. 10: 11; 2 Chr. 9: 10.
- Brought from Sheba. 1 Kgs. 10: 1,2; Ezek. 27: 22.
- Of great variety. 1 Chr. 29: 2.
- Of many colors. 1 Chr. 29: 2.
- Brilliant and glittering. 1 Chr. 29: 2; Rev. 21: 11.

Called
- Stones of fire. Ezek. 28: 14,16.
- Stones to be set. 1 Chr. 29: 2.
- Jewels. Is. 61: 10; Ezek. 16: 12.

- Precious jewels. 2 Chr. 20: 25;
  Prov. 20: 15.

Mentioned in the Bible

- Agate. Ex. 28: 19; Is. 54: 12.
- Amethyst. Ex. 28: 19; Rev. 21: 20.
- Beryl. Dan. 10: 6; Rev. 21: 20.
- Carbuncle. Ex. 28: 17; Is. 54: 12.
- Coral. Job 28: 18.
- Chalcedony. Rev. 21: 19.
- Chrysolite. Rev. 21: 20.
- Chrysoprasus. Rev. 21: 20.
- Diamond. Ex. 28: 18; Jer. 17: 1;
  Ezek. 28: 13.
- Emerald. Ezek. 27: 16; Rev. 4: 3.
- Jacinth. Rev. 9: 17; 21: 20.
- Jasper. Rev. 4: 3; 21: 11,19.
- Onyx. Ex. 28: 20; Job 28: 16.
- Pearl. Job 28: 18; Matt. 13: 45,46;
  Rev. 21: 21.
- Ruby. Job 28: 18; Lam. 4: 7.
- Sapphire. Ex. 24: 10; Ezek. 1: 26.
- Sardine or Sardius. Ex. 28: 17;
  Rev. 4: 3.
- Sardonyx. Rev. 21: 20.
- Topaz. Job 28: 19; Rev. 21: 20.

More facts about precious stones

- Highly prized by the ancients.
  Prov. 17: 8.
- Extensive commerce in. Ezek. 27: 22;
  Rev. 18: 12.
- Often given as presents.
  1 Kgs. 10: 2,10.
- Art of engraving on. Ex. 28: 9,11,21.
- Art of setting Ex. 28: 20.
- A part of the treasure of kings
  2 Chr. 32: 27.
- Given by the Jews for the tabernacle.
  Ex. 25: 7.

- Prepared by David for the temple.
  1 Chr. 29: 2.
- Given by chief men for the temple.
  1 Chr. 29: 8.

Used for

- Adorning the high priest's ephod.
  Ex. 28: 12.
- Adorning the breastplate of
  judgment.
  Ex. 28: 17–20; 39: 10–14.
- Decorating the person. Ezek. 28: 13.
- Ornamenting royal crowns.
  2 Sam. 12: 30.
- Setting in seals and rings. Song 5: 12.
- Adorning the temple.
  2 Chr. 3: 6.
- Honoring idols.
  Dan. 11: 38.

Illustrative

- Of preciousness of Christ. Is. 28: 16;
  1 Pet. 2: 6.
- Of beauty and stability of the church.
  Is. 54: 11,12.
- Of saints.
  Mal. 3: 17; 1 Cor. 3: 12.
- Of seductive splendor and false glory
  of the apostasy.
  Rev. 17: 4; 18: 16.
- Of worldly glory of nations.
  Ezek. 28: 13–16.
- Of glory of heavenly Jerusalem.
  Rev. 21: 11.
- Of stability of heavenly Jerusalem.
  Rev. 21: 19.

Clean and unclean

Overview

1. The concept of "clean" and "unclean" refers to Old Testament ritual in which some things had or did not have a place in worshiping God.
2. There were clean and unclean animals, fish, birds and insects.
3. The concept of clean and unclean extended beyond sacrificial animals to places and priests.
4. Everything used in the worship of God had to be holy and set apart for that purpose.
5. By coming into contact with anything that was unclean made a person unclean.
6. Only a "clean" person was fit to worship God.
7. God's followers in the Old Testament were not allowed to come into contact with anything unclean.

"Do not render yourselves detestable through any of the swarming things that swarm; and you shall not make yourselves unclean with them so that you become unclean.

"For I am the LORD your God. Consecrate yourselves therefore, and be holy, for I am holy. And you shall not make yourselves unclean with any of the swarming things that swarm on the earth." *Leviticus 11: 43,44 NASV*

Clean and unclean animals

For animals the principle of classification rested on the animal having a split hoof and that it also chewed the cud. Such animals were clean. Unclean animals, those that had paws or that did not travel by means of a split hoof, were deemed to be unclean.

Clean and unclean fish

Fish and any water creatures that had fins and scales were clean.

Clean and unclean birds

Certain birds were categorized as being unclean.

Clean and unclean insects

All flying insects that walked, unless they had jointed legs, were said to be unclean.

Moral cleanness and uncleanness

Ceremonial uncleanness in the Old Testament paved the way for the Israelites to understand about moral cleanness. Sins made a person unclean in God's sight. So on the Day of Atonement the people of Israel were made clean.

"For it is on this day that atonement shall be made for you to cleanse you; you will be clean from all your sins before the LORD" Leviticus 16: 30 *NASB.*

Jesus and cleanness and uncleanness

Jesus emphasized the importance of inner cleanliness.

"The Pharisees and some of the

scribes gathered around Him when they had come from Jerusalem,

2 and had seen that some of His disciples were eating their bread with impure hands, that is, unwashed.

5 The Pharisees and the scribes asked Him, "Why do Your disciples not walk according to the tradition of the elders, but eat their bread with impure hands?"

6 And He said to them, 'Rightly did Isaiah prophesy of you hypocrites, as it is written:

"THIS PEOPLE HONORS ME WITH THEIR LIPS,
BUT THEIR HEART IS FAR AWAY FROM ME.

7 'BUT IN VAIN DO THEY
WORSHIP ME,
TEACHING AS DOCTRINES THE
PRECEPTS OF MEN."

8 Neglecting the commandment of God, you hold to the tradition of men.

The Heart of Man

15 there is nothing outside the man which can defile him if it goes into him; but the things which proceed out of the man are what defile the man.'

18 And He said to them, 'Are you so lacking in understanding also? Do you not understand that whatever goes into the man from outside cannot defile him,

19 because it does not go into his heart, but into his stomach, and is eliminated?' (Thus He declared all foods clean.)

20 And He was saying, 'That which proceeds out of the man, that is what defiles the man.

21 For from within, out of the heart of men, proceed the evil thoughts,

fornications, thefts, murders, adulteries,

22 deeds of coveting and wickedness, as well as deceit, sensuality, envy, slander, pride and foolishness.

23 All these evil things proceed from within and defile the man.'"

Mark 7: 1–2, 5–8, 15, 18–23, NASV

Animals (1)

Overview

1. Created by God. Gen. 1: 24,25; 2: 19.
2. Creation of, exhibits God's power. Jer. 27: 5.
3. Made for the praise and glory of God. Ps. 148: 10.
4. Differ from birds and fishes. 1 Cor. 15: 39.
5. Feed on grass. Gen. 1: 30.
6. Humans to rule over. Gen. 1: 26,28; Ps. 8: 7.
7. Adam named them. Gen. 2: 19,20.
8. Given to humans for food after the flood. Gen. 9: 3.
9. Not to be eaten alive or with blood. Gen. 9: 4; Deut. 12: 16,23.
10. Not to be eaten that died naturally or were injured. Ex. 22: 31; Lev. 17: 15; 22: 8.
11. Supply clothing to man. Gen. 3: 21; Job 31: 20.
12. Belong to God. Ps. 50: 10.
13. Subjects of God's care. Ps. 36: 6; 104: 10,11.

Described as

- Devoid of speech. 2 Pet. 2: 16.
- Devoid of understanding. Ps. 32: 9; 73: 22.
- Devoid of immortality. Ps. 49: 12–15.
- Possess an instinct. Is. 1: 3.
- Capable of being tamed. James 3: 7.

Facts about animals

- Many kinds of destructive animals. Lev. 26: 6; Ezek. 5: 17.
- Many kinds of domestic animals. Gen. 36: 6; 45: 17.

- Often suffered on account of the sins of men. Joel 1: 18,20; Hag. 1: 11.
- Liable to diseases. Ex. 9: 3.

Learning wisdom from

- Job 12: 7.

Found in

- Deserts. Is. 13: 21.
- Fields. Deut. 7: 22; Joel 2: 22.
- Mountains. Song 4: 8.
- Forests. Is. 56: 9; Mic. 5: 8.

Make their homes in

- Caves. Job 37: 8; 38: 40.
- Under spreading trees. Dan. 4: 12.
- Deserted cities. Is. 13: 21,22; Zeph. 2: 15.

Clean animals

- Ox. Ex. 21: 28; Deut. 14: 4.
- Wild ox. Deut. 14: 5.
- Sheep. Deut. 7: 13; 14: 4.
- Goat. Deut. 14: 4.
- Deer. Deut. 14: 5; Job 39: 1. "the deer, the gazelle, the roebuck, the wild goat, the ibex, the antelope and the mountain sheep" Deuteronomy 14: 5 NASV.
- Roebuck. Deut. 14: 5; 2 Sam. 2: 18.
- Wild goat. Deut. 14: 5.
- Ibex. Deut. 14: 5.
- Antelope. Deut. 14: 5.
- Mountain sheep. Deut. 14: 5.
- Used for food. Lev. 11: 2; Deut. 12: 15. "You shall not eat any detestable thing.

4 These are the animals which you may eat: the ox, the sheep, the goat,

5 the deer, the gazelle, the roebuck, the wild goat, the ibex, the antelope and the mountain sheep.

6 Any animal that divides the hoof and has the hoof split in two and chews the cud, among the animals, that you may eat.

7 Nevertheless, you are not to eat of these among those which chew the cud, or among those that divide the hoof in two: the camel and the rabbit and the shaphan, for though they chew the cud, they do not divide the hoof; they are unclean for you.

8 The pig, because it divides the hoof but does not chew the cud, it is unclean for you. You shall not eat any of their flesh nor touch their carcasses.

9 These you may eat of all that are in water: anything that has fins and scales you may eat,

10 but anything that does not have fins and scales you shall not eat; it is unclean for you.

11 You may eat any clean bird.

12 But these are the ones which you shall not eat: the eagle and the vulture and the buzzard,

13 and the red kite, the falcon, and the kite in their kinds,

14 and every raven in its kind,

15 and the ostrich, the owl, the sea gull, and the hawk in their kinds,

16 the little owl, the great owl, the white owl,

17 the pelican, the carrion vulture, the cormorant,

18 the stork, and the heron in their kinds, and the hoopoe and the bat.

19 And all the teeming life with wings are unclean to you; they shall not be eaten.

20 You may eat any clean bird.

21 You shall not eat anything which dies of itself. You may give it to the alien who is in your town, so that he may eat it, or you may sell it to a foreigner, for you are a holy people to the LORD your God. You shall not boil a young goat in its mother's milk."

Deuteronomy 14: 3–21 NASB

• Used for sacrifice. Gen. 8: 20.

Clean and unclean

• First distinction between clean and unclean. Gen. 7: 2.
• Distinguishing between clean and unclean. Lev. 11: 3; Deut. 14: 6.

Unclean animals

• Camel. Gen. 24: 64; Lev. 11: 4.
• Horse. Job 39: 19–25.
• Donkey. Gen. 22: 3; Matt. 21: 2.

JESUS AND A DONKEY
Jesus rode into Jerusalem on a donkey.

"Go into the village opposite you, and immediately you will find a donkey tied there and a colt with her; untie them and bring them to Me."

Matthew 21: 2 NASV

Animals (2)

Unclean animals, continued

- Wild donkey. Job 6: 5; 39: 5–8.

    "Does the wild donkey bray over
    his grass,
    Or does the ox low over his fodder?"
    Job 6: 5 NASV.

- Mule. 2 Sam. 13: 29; 1 Kgs. 10: 25.

    "They brought every man his gift,
    articles of silver and gold, garments,
    weapons, spices, horses, and mules,
    so much year by year" 1 Kings 10: 25
    NASV.

- Lion. Judg. 14: 5,6.
- Leopard. Song 4: 8.
- Bear. 2 Sam. 17: 8.
- Wolf. Gen. 49: 27; John 10: 12.
- Wild ox. Num. 23: 22.

    "God brings them out of Egypt,
    He is for them like the horns of the
    wild ox" Numbers 23: 22 NASV.

- Behemoth. Job 40: 15.

    "Behold now, Behemoth, which I
    made as well as you;
    He eats grass like an ox" Job 40: 15
    NASV.

- Ape. 1 Kgs. 10: 22.
- Fox. Ps. 63: 10; Song 2: 5.
- Dog. Ex. 22: 31; Luke 16: 2.
- Pigs. Lev. 11: 7; Is. 66: 17.

    "Some of you get yourselves ready
    and go to a garden to worship a
    foreign goddess. You eat the meat
    of pigs, lizards, and mice. But I, the
    LORD, will destroy you for this"
    Isaiah 66: 17 CEV.

- Hare. Lev. 11: 6; Deut. 14: 7.
- Rock badger. Lev. 11: 5; Ps. 104: 18.

    "High in the mountains are
    pastures for the wild goats,
    and the rocks form a refuge for rock
    badgers" Psalm 194: 18 NLT.

- Mouse. Lev. 11: 29; Is. 66: 17.
- Mole. Lev. 11: 30; Is. 2: 20.
- Weasel. Lev. 11: 29.
- Ferret. Lev. 11: 30.
- Badger. Ex. 25: 5; Ezek. 16: 10.

Distinguishing between clean and unclean animals

Lev. 11: 26.

"Any animal that has divided but
unsplit hooves or that does not chew
the cud is unclean for you. If you touch
the dead body of such an animal, you
will be defiled until evening."

Leviticus 11: 26, NLT

ANIMALS NOT TO BE EATEN. LEV. 11: 4–
8; DEUT. 1: 7,8.

"You may not, however, eat the
animals named here because they
either have split hooves or chew the
cud, but not both. The camel may not
be eaten, for though it chews the cud,
it does not have split hooves. 5 The
same is true of the rock badger 6 and
the hare, so they also may never be
eaten. 7 And the pig may not be eaten,
for though it has split hooves, it does
not chew the cud. 8You may not eat the
meat of these animals or touch their
dead bodies. They are ceremonially
unclean for you."

Leviticus 11: 4–8 NLT

First born to be redeemed. Num. 18: 15.

"The firstborn of every mother,
whether human or animal, that is
offered to the LORD will be yours. But

you must always redeem your firstborn sons and the firstborn males of ritually unclean animals"

Numbers 18: 15 NLT.

Caused uncleanness when dead. Lev. 5: 2.

"Or if they touch something that is ceremonially unclean, such as the dead body of an animal that is ceremonially unclean–whether a wild animal, a domesticated animal, or an animal that scurries along the ground–they will be considered ceremonially unclean and guilty, even if they are unaware of their defilement."

Leviticus 5: 2 NLT

Domestic animals

- To enjoy the sabbath. Ex. 20: 10; Deut. 5: 14.
- To be taken care of. Lev. 25: 7; Deut. 25: 4.
  "Even your cattle and the animals that are in your land shall have all its crops to eat" Leviticus 25: 7 *NASB.*
  "You shall not muzzle the ox while he is threshing" Deuteronomy 25: 4 *NASB.*
- Not to be cruelly used. Num. 22: 27–32; Prov. 12: 10.

Facts about animals

- No likeness of, to be worshiped. Deut. 4: 17.
- Idols of, worshiped by the heathen. Rom. 1: 23.
- Often used as instruments of punishment. Lev. 26: 22; Deut. 32: 24; Jer. 15: 3; Ezek. 5: 17.
- Humans by nature no better than.

"I said in mine heart concerning the estate of the sons of men, that God might manifest them, and that they might see that they themselves are beasts.
19 For that which befalleth the sons of men befalleth beasts; even one thing befalleth them: as the one dieth, so dieth the other; yea, they have all one breath; so that a man hath no preeminence above a beast: for all is vanity"

Ecclesiastes 3: 18,19

Illustrative

- Of the wicked. Ps. 49: 20; Titus 1: 12.
- Of the ungodly. 2 Pet. 2: 12; Jude 1: 10.
- Of persecutors. 1 Cor. 15: 32; 2 Tim. 4: 17.
- Of kingdoms. Dan. 7: 11,17; 8: 4.
- Of people of different nations. Dan. 4: 12,21,22.
- Of antichrist. Rev. 13: 2; 20: 4.
  "This beast looked like a leopard, but it had bear's feet and a lion's mouth! And the dragon gave him his own power and throne and great authority."

Revelation 13: 2 NLT

Mythical animals

Overview

There are several animals mentioned in the *KJV* that are mythical:

Unicorns

* Generally had a single horn.
  "But my horn shalt thou exalt like the horn of an unicorn: I shall be anointed with fresh oil" Psalm 92: 10.

DESCRIBED AS

* Intractable in disposition. Job 39: 9,10,12.
* Of vast strength. Job 39: 11.
* The young of, remarkable for agility. Ps. 29: 6.

LLUSTRATIVE

* Of God as the strength of Israel. Num. 23: 22; 24: 8.

"God brought them out of Egypt; he hath as it were the strength of an unicorn" Numbers 23: 22.

* Of the wicked. Is. 34: 7.
* (Horns of,) of the strength of the descendants of Joseph. Deut. 33: 17.
* (Horns of,) of the strength of powerful enemies. Ps. 22: 21.
* (The position of its horns,) of the exaltation of saints. Ps. 92: 10.

The "Unicorn" is mentioned nine times in the *KJV* (Numbers 23: 22; 24: 8; Deuteronomy 33: 17; Job 39: 9,10; Psalm 22: 21; 29: 6; 92: 10; Isaiah 34: 7). In Deuteronomy 33: 17 it says the unicorn has "horns" plural, so the *KJV* solved this problem by translating "unicorn" as plural "unicorns." It is an unfortunate translation of the Hebrew

"reem" which means "wild ox." "You have exalted my horn like that of a wild ox; fine oils have been poured upon me" Psalm 92: 10 *NIV*. It seems that the LXX translation made the error which was carried over into the Latin *unicornis*. The idea of a unicorn probably came from seeing a rhinoceros.

Dragons

* Often of a red color. Rev. 12: 3.

DESCRIBED AS

* Powerful. Rev. 12: 4.
* Poisonous. Deut. 32: 33.
* Of solitary habits. Job 30: 29.
* Its mournful voice alluded to. Mic. 1: 8.
* Its wailing alluded to. Mic. 1: 8.
* Its snuffing up the air alluded to. Jer. 14: 6.
* Its swallowing of its prey alluded to. Jer. 51: 34.

FOUND IN

* The wilderness. Mal. 1: 3.
* Deserted cities. Is. 13: 22; Jer. 9: 11.
* Dry places. Is. 34: 13; 43: 20.
* A species of, in rivers. Ps. 74: 13; Is. 27: 1.

LLUSTRATIVE

* Of cruel and persecuting kings. Is. 27: 1; 51: 9; Ezek. 29: 3.
  "In that day the LORD with his sore and great and strong sword shall punish leviathan the piercing serpent, even leviathan that crooked serpent; and he shall slay the dragon that is in the sea" Isaiah 27: 1.

"Awake, awake, put on strength,
O arm of the LORD; awake, as in
the ancient days, in the generations
of old. Art thou not it that hath cut
Rahab, and wounded the dragon?"
Isaiah 51: 9.

- Of wicked people. Ps. 44: 19.
- Of the devil. Rev. 13: 2; 20: 2,7.

"And he laid hold on the dragon,
that old serpent, which is the
Devil, and Satan, and bound him a
thousand years,

7 And when the thousand years
are expired, Satan shall be loosed out
of his prison" Revelation 20: 2,7.

- (Poison of,) of wine. Deut. 32: 33.

Mistranslation

In the Old Testament the *KJV* uses the
term "dragon" for the Hebrew words
tannim meaning "jackals" and *tannin*
meaning "serpent, or sea monster." It
seems the *KJV* mistranslated these two
separate words.

Tannim is from the root tan meaning
"to howl" and tannin is from the root
tanan "to smoke." Jackals are known for
their howling, and are associated with
desolate areas.

Tannin or "smokers" probably came
from seeing the spouts of whales or
the snorting of animals which looked
like smoke coming from a fire inside.
Our warm breath in winter looks
like smoke. This is probably how the
idea of fire-breathing dragons started.
The Hebrew is not referring to any
dinosaurs.

The *KJV* uses the term "dragon"
which comes from the Greek word
drakon which means "serpent." It refers

to a monster with a scaly snake-like
body. The Greek New Testament uses
drakon 12 times only in the book of
Revelation which the *KJV* translates as
"dragon" (Rev. 12–13; 16: 13; 20: 2). The
dragon in Revelation has seven heads
similar to the leviathan in Ugaritic and
Psalm 74: 14. Satan is called a "dragon"
in Revelation 20: 2.

Satyr

The Satyr is a mythical creature that
was half-man and half-goat. Isaiah 13: 21
and 34: 14 mentions this creature in the
KJV.

"But wild beasts of the desert shall lie
there; and their houses shall be full of
doleful creatures; and owls shall dwell
there, and satyrs shall dance there"
Isaiah 13: 21.

The *NIV* uses the word "wild goat" in
place of the word Satyr.

"But desert creatures will lie there,
jackals will fill her houses;
there the owls will dwell,
and there the wild goats will leap
about" Isaiah 13: 21 NIV.

In the Hebrew there are two more
occurrences in Leviticus 17: 7 and
2 Chronicles 11: 15; also possibly 2 Kings
23: 8.

Animals (3)

Tamed donkey

Overview

1. Unclean. Lev. 11: 2,3,26; Ex. 13: 13.
2. Often fed on vine-leaves. Gen. 49: 11.
3. Formed a part of patriarchal wealth.
   Gen. 12: 16; 30: 43; Job 1: 3;
   42: 12.

Described as

- Not devoid of instinct. Is. 1: 3.
- Strong. Gen. 49: 14.
- Fond of ease. Gen. 49: 14,15.

Was used

- In agriculture. Is. 30: 6,24.
- For bearing burdens. Gen. 42: 26;
  1 Sam. 25: 18.
- For riding. Gen. 22: 3; Num. 22: 21.
- In harness. Is. 21: 7.
- In war. 2 Kgs. 7: 7,10.

Facts about donkeys

- Governed by a bridle. Prov. 26: 3.
- Urged on with a staff. Num. 22: 23,27.
- Women often rode on. Josh. 15: 18;
  1 Sam. 25: 20.
- People of rank rode on. Judg. 10: 3,4;
  2 Sam. 16: 2.
- Judges of Israel rode on white
  donkeys. Judg. 5: 10.
- Young, most valued for labor.
  Is. 30: 6,24.
- Trustworthy people appointed to
  take care of. Gen. 36: 24; 1 Sam. 9: 3;
  1 Chr. 27: 30.

- Often taken unlawfully by corrupt
  rulers. Num. 16: 15; 1 Sam. 8: 16; 12: 3.
- Later thought of as an ignoble
  creature. Jer. 22: 19.

Laws about

- Not to be coveted. Ex. 20: 17.
- Fallen under a burden, to be assisted.
  Ex. 23: 5.
- Astray, to be brought back to its
  owners. Ex. 23: 4; Deut. 22: 1.
- Astray, to be taken care of till its
  owner appeared. Deut. 22: 2,3.
- Not to be yoked with an ox.
  Deut. 22: 10.
- To enjoy the rest of the Sabbath.
  Deut. 5: 14.

SYMBOLIC USE OF DONKEY
- Jesus entered Jerusalem on.
  Zech. 9: 9; John 12: 14.

Miracles connected with

- Mouth of Balaam's opened to speak.
  2 Pet. 2: 16.
  "But God was angry because
  he was going, and the angel of the
  LORD took his stand in the way as
  an adversary against him. Now he
  was riding on his donkey and his two
  servants were with him.
  23 When the donkey saw the angel
  of the LORD standing in the way
  with his drawn sword in his hand,
  the donkey turned off from the way
  and went into the field; but Balaam
  struck the donkey to turn her back
  into the way.
  24 Then the angel of the LORD
  stood in a narrow path of the

vineyards, with a wall on this side and a wall on that side.

25 When the donkey saw the angel of the LORD, she pressed herself to the wall and pressed Balaam's foot against the wall, so he struck her again.

26 The angel of the LORD went further, and stood in a narrow place where there was no way to turn to the right hand or the left.

27 When the donkey saw the angel of the LORD, she lay down under Balaam; so Balaam was angry and struck the donkey with his stick.

28 And the LORD opened the mouth of the donkey, and she said to Balaam, 'What have I done to you, that you have struck me these three times?'

29 Then Balaam said to the donkey, "'Because you have made a mockery of me! If there had been a sword in my hand, I would have killed you by now.'

30 The donkey said to Balaam, 'Am I not your donkey on which you have ridden all your life to this day? Have I ever been accustomed to do so to you?' And he said, 'No.'

31 Then the LORD opened the eyes of Balaam, and he saw the angel of the LORD standing in the way with his drawn sword in his hand; and he bowed all the way to the ground.

32 The angel of the LORD said to him, 'Why have you struck your donkey these three times? Behold, I have come out as an adversary, because your way was contrary to me.

33 'But the donkey saw me and turned aside from me these three times. If she had not turned aside from me, I would surely have killed you just now, and let her live.'"

Numbers 22: 18–33 NASV

- A thousand men killed by Samson with a jaw-bone of. Judg. 15: 19.
- Water brought from the jaw-bone of. Judg. 15: 19.
- Not torn by a lion. 1 Kgs. 13: 28.
- Eaten during famine in Samaria. 2 Kgs. 6: 25.

Untamed donkey

Overview

1. Inhabits wild and solitary places. Job 39: 6; Is. 32: 14; Dan. 5: 21.
2. Ranges the mountains for food. Job 39: 8.
3. Brays when hungry. Job 6: 5.
4. Suffers in time of scarcity. Jer. 14: 6.
5. Despises his pursuers. Job 39: 7.
6. Supported by God. Ps. 104: 10,11.

Described as

- Fond of freedom. Job 39: 5.
- Intractable. Job 11: 12.
- Unsocial. Hos. 8: 9.

Illustrative

- Of intractableness of natural man. Job 11: 12.
- Of the wicked in their pursuit of sin. Job 24: 5.
- Of Israel in their love of idols. Jer. 2: 23,24.
- Of the Assyrian power. Hos. 8: 9.
- Of the Ishmaelites. Gen. 16: 12.

Animals (4)

Bear

Overview

1. Inhabits woods. 2 Kgs. 2: 24.
2. Often attacks men. 2 Kgs. 2: 24; Amos 5: 19.
3. Attacks the flock in the presence of the shepherd. 1 Sam. 17: 34.
4. Particularly fierce when deprived of its young. 2 Sam. 17: 8; Prov. 17: 12.
5. Growls when annoyed. Is. 59: 11.
6. Killed by David. 1 Sam. 17: 36,37.

Described as

- Voracious. Dan. 7: 5.
- Cunning. Lam. 3: 10.
- Cruel. Amos 5: 19.

Illustrative

- Of God in his judgments. Lam. 3: 10; Hos. 13: 8.

  "He is to me like a bear lying in wait, Like a lion in secret places" Lamentations 3: 10 NASB.

  "I will encounter them like a bear robbed of her cubs,

  And I will tear open their chests;

  There I will also devour them like a lioness,

  As a wild beast would tear them" Hosea 13: 8 NASB.
- Of the natural man. Is. 11: 7.
- Of wicked rulers. Prov. 28: 15.
- Of the kingdom of the Medes. Dan. 7: 5.
- Of the kingdom of Antichrist. Rev. 13: 2.

Calf

Overview

1. The young of the herd. Job 21: 10; Jer. 31: 12.
2. Playfulness of, alluded to. Ps. 29: 6.

Fed on

- Milk. 1 Sam. 6: 10.
- Branches of trees. Is. 27: 10.

Facts about calves

- Fattened in stalls. 1 Sam. 28: 24; Amos 6: 4.
- Offered in sacrifice. Lev. 9: 2,3; Heb. 9: 12,19.
- Of a year old best for sacrifice. Mic. 6: 6.
- Eaten in the patriarchal age. Gen. 18: 7,8.
- When fattened considered a delicacy. 1 Sam. 28: 24,25; Amos 6: 4; Luke 15: 23,27.

Illustrative

- Of the godly nourished by grace. Mal. 4: 2.
- Of sacrifices of praise. Hos. 14: 2; Heb. 13: 5.
- Of patient endurance. Ezek. 1: 7; Rev. 4: 7.

Golden calf

Overview

Made while Moses was on Mount Sinai Ex. 32: 1.

"Now when the people saw that

Moses delayed to come down from the mountain, the people assembled about Aaron and said to him, 'Come, make us a god who will go before us; as for this Moses, the man who brought us up from the land of Egypt, we do not know what has become of him.'

2 Aaron said to them, 'Tear off the gold rings which are in the ears of your wives, your sons, and your daughters, and bring them to me.'

3 Then all the people tore off the gold rings which were in their ears and brought them to Aaron.

4 He took this from their hand, and fashioned it with a graving tool and made it into a molten calf; and they said, 'This is your god, O Israel, who brought you up from the land of Egypt.'

5 Now when Aaron saw this, he built an altar before it; and Aaron made a proclamation and said, 'Tomorrow shall be a feast to the LORD.'

6 So the next day they rose early and offered burnt offerings, and brought peace offerings; and the people sat down to eat and to drink, and rose up to play.

7 Then the LORD spoke to Moses, 'Go down at once, for your people, whom you brought up from the land of Egypt, have corrupted themselves.

8 'They have quickly turned aside from the way which I commanded them. They have made for themselves a molten calf, and have worshiped it and have sacrificed to it and said, "This is your god, O Israel, who brought you up from the land of Egypt!"'

Exodus 32: 1–8 NASB

Was made

- Of the ornaments. Ex. 32: 2,3.
- To represent God. Ex. 32: 4,5.
- After an Egyptian model. Acts 7: 39,41.
- To go before the congregation. Ex. 32: 1.
- Sacrifices offered to. Ex. 32: 6.
- Worshiped with profane revelry. Ex. 32: 6,18,19,25; 1 Cor. 10: 7.

Resulted in

- A very great sin. Ex. 32: 21,30,31.
- Forgetting of God. Ps. 106: 21.
- A turning aside from the divine command. Ex. 32: 8; Deut. 9: 12,16.
- Brought anger against Aaron. Deut. 9: 20.
- Brought anger against Israel. Ex. 32: 10; Deut. 9: 14,19.
- Caused Moses to break the tables of the testimony. Ex. 32: 19; Deut. 9: 17.
- Israel punished for. Ex. 32: 26–29,35.
- Moses interceded for those who worshiped Ex. 32: 11–14,30–34; Deut. 9: 18–20.
- Destroyed by Moses Ex. 32: 20; Deut. 9: 21.
- Punishment of those who worshiped a warning to others.

"Do not be idolaters, as some of them were; as it is written, "THE PEOPLE SAT DOWN TO EAT AND DRINK, AND STOOD UP TO PLAY."

1 Corinthians 10: 7 NASB

Animals (5)

Calves of Jeroboam

Overview

1. Reason for making. 1 Kgs. 12: 26–28
2. Made of gold. 1 Kgs. 12: 28.
3. Made to prevent the Israelites going to Jerusalem. 1 Kgs. 12: 26,27.

Called the

- Golden calves. 2 Kgs. 10: 29;
  2 Chr. 13: 8.
- Calves of Bethaven. Hos. 10: 5.
- Calves of Samaria. Hos. 8: 5.

Facts about the calves of Jeroboam

- Placed in Dan and Bethel.
  1 Kgs. 12: 29.
- Probably from an Egyptian model.
  1 Kgs. 11: 40.
- Designed to represent God.
  1 Kgs. 12: 28.
- Priests appointed for. 1 Kgs. 12: 31;
  2 Chr. 11: 15.
- Sacrifices offered to. 1 Kgs. 12: 32; 13: 1.
- Feasts appointed for. 1 Kgs. 12: 32,33.
- Were kissed in adoration. Hos. 13: 2.

Worship of

- Denounced by a prophet. 1 Kgs. 13: 1–3.
- Adopted by succeeding kings.
  1 Kgs. 15: 34; 16: 26; 2 Kgs. 10: 29,31;
  14: 24.
- Became the sin of Israel. 1 Kgs. 12: 30;
  2 Kgs. 10: 31; 2 Chr. 13: 8.

Predictions respecting

- Captivity. Hos. 10: 6.
- Destruction. Hos. 8: 6; 10: 8.
- Punishment of the worshipers.
  Hos. 8: 13,14.

Camel

Overview

1. Unclean. Lev. 11: 4; Deut. 14: 7.
2. Found in deserted places. Ezek. 25: 5.

Characterized by

- Humps its back. Is. 30: 6.
- Its docility. Gen. 24: 11.
- The dromedary, noted for its
  swiftness. Jer. 2: 23.
- Abounded in the east. 1 Chr. 5: 21;
  Is. 60: 6.
- Part of patriarchal wealth. Gen. 12: 16;
  30: 43; Job 1: 3.

Used for

- Riding. Gen. 24: 61.
- Drawing chariots. Is. 21: 7.
- Carrying burdens. Gen. 37: 25;
  1 Kgs. 10: 2; 2 Kgs. 8: 9.
- War. Judg. 7: 12; 1 Sam. 30: 17.
- The rich. Judg. 8: 21,26.

Facts about camels

- Treated with great care.
  Gen. 24: 31,32.
- A valuable booty. 1 Chr. 5: 20,21;
  2 Chr. 14: 15; Job 1: 17; Jer. 49: 29,32.
- Coarse cloth made from its hair.
  Matt. 3: 4.
- Referred to in illustrations by Christ.
  Matt. 19: 24; 23: 24.

Deer

Overview

1. Clean and used as food. Deut. 12: 15;
   14: 5.
2. Often hunted. Lam. 1: 6.

Illustrative

- Of Christ. Song 2: 9,17; 8: 14.
- Of converted sinners. Is. 35: 6.
- (Sure-footedness of,) of experienced saints. Ps. 18: 33; Hab. 3: 19.
- (Panting for water,) of afflicted saints longing for God. Ps. 42: 1,2.
- (Without pasture,) of the persecuted. Lam. 1: 6.

Dog

Overview

Despised by the Jews. 2 Sam. 3: 8.

Facts about dogs

- Nothing holy to be given to. Matt. 7: 6; 15: 26.
- Things torn by beasts given to. Ex. 22: 31.

When domesticated

- Used to guard flocks. Job 30: 1.
- Fed with the crumbs. Matt. 15: 27.

Illustrative

- Of Gentiles. Matt. 15: 22,26.
- Of covetous ministers. Is. 56: 11.
- Of fools. Prov. 26: 11.
- Of apostates. 2 Pet. 2: 22.
- Of persecutors. Ps. 22: 16,20.
- Of obstinate sinners. Matt. 7: 6; Rev. 22: 15.
- Of false teachers. Php 3: 2.
- (Dumb,) of unfaithful ministers. Is. 56: 10.
- (Dead,) of the mean. 1 Sam. 24: 14; 2 Sam. 9: 8.

Fox

Overview

1. Found in deserts. Ezek. 13: 4.
2. Abounded in Palestine. Judg. 15: 4; Lam. 5: 18.

Described as

- Active. Neh. 4: 3.
- Crafty. Luke 13: 32.
- Carnivorous. Ps. 63: 10.

Facts about foxes

- Destructive to vines. Song 2: 15.
- Lived in holes. Matt. 8: 20; Luke 9: 58.

Illustrative of

- False prophets. Ezek. 13: 4.
- Cunning and deceitful people. Luke 13: 32.
- Enemies of the church. Song 2: 15.

Gazelle

Facts about

- Wild. 2 Sam. 2: 18.
- Swift. 1 Chr. 12: 8.
- Inhabits the mountains. 1 Chr. 12: 8.
- Often hunted by men. Prov. 6: 5.

Illustrative

- Of a good wife. Prov. 5: 19.
- Of the swift of foot. 2 Sam. 2: 18.

Animals (6)

Goat

Overview

1. Clean and fit for food. Deut. 14: 4,5.
2. Offered in sacrifice. Gen. 15: 9;
   Lev. 16: 5,7.
3. The male, best for sacrifice.
   Lev. 22: 19; Ps. 50: 9.
4. Jews had large flocks of. Gen. 32: 14;
   1 Sam. 25: 2.
5. Most profitable to the owner.
   Prov. 27: 26.
6. Milk of, used as food. Prov. 27: 27.

The young of

- Called kids. Gen. 37: 31.
- Kept in small flocks. 1 Kgs. 20: 27.
- Fed near the shepherds' tents.
  Song 1: 8.
- Not to be boiled in own mother's
  milk. Ex. 23: 19.
- Offered in sacrifice. Lev. 4: 23; 5: 6.
- Offered at the Passover. Ex. 12: 5;
  2 Chr. 35: 7.
- Considered a delicacy. Gen. 27: 9;
  Judg. 6: 19.
- Given as a present. Gen. 38: 17;
  Judg. 15: 1.

The hair of

- Offered for tabernacle. Ex. 25: 4;
  35: 23.
- Made into curtains, for covering the
  tabernacle. Ex. 35: 26; 36: 14–18.
- Made into pillows. 1 Sam. 19: 13.

Facts about goats

- Skin of, often used as clothing.
  Heb. 11: 37.
- Bashan celebrated for. Deut. 32: 14.
- The Arabians traded in. Ezek. 27: 21.
- Flocks of, always led by a male.
  Jer. 50: 8.
- When wild lived in the hills and
  rocks. 1 Sam. 24: 2; Job 39: 1;
  Ps. 104: 18.

Illustrative

- Of Macedonian Empire. Dan. 8: 5,21.
- Of the wicked. Zech. 10: 3;
  Matt. 25: 32,33.

Horse

Overview

Endued with strength by God.
Job 39: 19.

Colors of, mentioned

- White. Zech. 1: 8; 6: 3; Rev. 6: 2.
- Black. Zech. 6: 2,6; Rev. 6: 5.
- Red. Zech. 1: 8; 6: 2; Rev. 6: 4.
- Brown. Zech. 1: 8.
- Bay. Zech. 6: 3,7.
- Dappled. Zech. 6: 3,6.
- Pale or ash color. Rev. 6: 8.

Used for

- Mounting cavalry. Ex. 14: 9;
  1 Sam. 13: 5.

- Drawing chariots. Mic. 1: 13;
  Zech. 6: 2.
- Bearing burdens. Ezra 2: 66;
  Neh. 7: 68.
- Hunting. Job 39: 18.

Horses and war

- Numbers of, kept for war. Jer. 51: 27;
  Ezek. 26: 10.
- Prepared and trained for war.
  Prov. 21: 31.
- In battle protected by armour.
  Jer. 46: 4.

The Jews

- Not to trust in. Hos. 14: 3.
- Condemned for trusting to.
  Is. 30: 16; 31: 3.
- Brought back many, from Babylon.
  Ezra 2: 66.

Illustrative

- Of beauty of the church. Song 1: 9;
  Zech. 10: 3.
- Of deliverance of the church.
  Is. 63: 13.
- Of a dull headstrong disposition.
  Ps. 32: 9.
- Of impetuosity of the wicked in sin.
  Jer. 8: 6.

Lamb

Overview

The young of the flock. Ex. 12: 5;
Ezek. 45: 15.

Described as

- Patient. Is. 53: 7.
- Playful. Ps. 114: 4,6.

Facts about lambs

- Exposed to danger from wild beasts.
  1 Sam. 17: 34.
- The shepherd's care for. Is. 40: 11.
- Considered a great delicacy.
  Amos 6: 4.
- An extensive commerce in. Ezra 7: 17;
  Ezek. 27: 21.
- Tribute often paid in. 2 Kgs. 3: 4;
  Is. 16: 1.
- Covenants confirmed by gift of.
  Gen. 21: 28–30.
- Image on coins. Gen. 33: 19;
  Josh. 24: 32.

Used for

- Food. Deut. 32: 14; 2 Sam. 12: 4.
- Clothing. Prov. 27: 26.
- Sacrifice. 1 Chr. 29: 21; 2 Chr. 29: 32.

Offered in sacrifice

- Every morning and evening.
  Ex. 29: 38,39; Num. 28: 3,4.
- At the Passover. Ex. 12: 3,6,7.

Illustrative

- Of purity of Christ. 1 Pet. 1: 19.
- Of Christ as a sacrifice. John 1: 29;
  Rev. 5: 6.
- Of any thing dear or cherished.
  2 Sam. 12: 3,9.
- Of the Lord's people. Is. 5: 17; 11: 6.
- Of weak believers. Is. 40: 11;
  John 21: 15.
- (Patience of,) of the patience of
  Christ. Is. 53: 7; Acts 8: 32.
- (Among wolves,) of ministers among
  the ungodly. Luke 10: 3.
- (Deserted and exposed,) of Israel
  deprived of God's protection.
  Hos. 4: 16.

Animals (7)

Leopard

Overview

Lies in wait for its prey Jer. 5: 6;
Hos. 13: 7.

Described as

- Spotted. Jer. 13: 23.
- Fierce and cruel. Jer. 5: 6.
- Swift. Hab. 1: 8.

Illustrative

- Of God in his judgments. Hos. 13: 7.
- Of the Macedonian Empire. Dan. 7: 6.
- Of antichrist. Rev. 13: 2.
- (Tamed,) of the wicked subdued by the gospel. Is. 11: 6.

Lion

Described as

- Superior in strength. Judg. 14: 18; Prov. 30: 30.
- Active. Deut. 33: 22.
- Courageous. 2 Sam. 17: 10.
- Fearless even of man. Is. 31: 4; Nah. 2: 11.
- Fierce. Job 10: 16; 28: 8.
- Voracious. Ps. 17: 12.
- Majestic in movement. Prov. 30: 29,30.

Facts about lions

- Canaan full of. 2 Kgs. 17: 25,26.
- Greatness of its teeth alluded to. Ps. 58: 6; Joel 1: 6.
- God's power exhibited in restraining. 1 Kgs. 13: 28; Dan. 6: 22,27.

- God provides for. Job 38: 39; Ps. 104: 21,28.
- Lurks for its prey. Ps. 10: 9.
- Roars when seeking prey. Ps. 104: 21; Is. 31: 4.
- Tears its prey. Deut. 33: 20; Ps. 7: 2.
- Often carries its prey to its den. Nah. 2: 12.
- Conceals itself by day. Ps. 104: 22.
- Often dies through lack of food. Job 4: 11.
- A swarm of bees found in the carcass of, by Samson. Judg. 14: 8.
- Disobedient prophet killed by. 1 Kgs. 13: 24,26.

Inhabits

- Forests. Jer. 5: 6.
- Thickets. Jer. 4: 7.
- Mountains. Song 4: 8.
- Deserts. Is. 30: 6.

Human fear of lions

- Attacks the sheepfolds. 1 Sam. 17: 34; Amos 3: 12; Mic. 5: 8.
- Attacks and kills men. 1 Kgs. 13: 24; 20: 36.
- Roar frightens. Jer. 2: 15; Amos 3: 8.
- Criminals often thrown to. Dan. 6: 7,16,24.
- Hunting of, alluded to. Job 10: 16.

Killed by

- Samson. Judg. 14: 5,6.
- David. 1 Sam. 17: 35,36.
- Benaiah. 2 Sam. 23: 20.

Illustrative

- Of Israel. Num. 24: 9.
- Of the tribe of Judah. Gen. 49: 9.
- Of the tribe of Gad. Deut. 33: 20.
- Of Christ. Rev. 5: 5.
- Of God in protecting his church. Is. 31: 4.
- Of God in executing judgments. Is. 38: 13; Lam. 3: 10; Hos. 5: 14; 13: 8.
- Of boldness of saints. Prov. 28: 1.
- Of brave men. 2 Sam. 1: 23; 23: 20.
- Of cruel and powerful enemies. Is. 5: 29; Jer. 49: 19; 51: 38.
- Of persecutors. Ps. 22: 13; 2 Tim. 4: 17.
- Of the devil.
  "Be on your guard and stay awake. Your enemy, the devil, is like a roaring lion, sneaking around to find someone to attack" 1 Peter 5: 8 CEV.
- Of imaginary fears of the slothful. Prov. 22: 13; 26: 13.
- (Tamed,) of the natural man subdued by grace. Is. 11: 7; 65: 25.
- (Roaring of,) of a king's wrath. Prov. 19: 12; 20: 2.

Ox

Overview

Often found wild. Deut. 14: 5.

Includes the

- Bull. Gen. 32: 15; Job 21: 10.
- Bullock. Ps. 50: 9; Jer. 46: 21.
- Cow. Num. 18: 17; Job 21: 10.
- Heifer. Gen. 15: 9; Num. 19: 2.

Clean

- Was clean and fit for food. Deut. 14: 4.

Described as

- Strong. Ps. 144: 14; Prov. 14: 4.
- Beautiful. Jer. 46: 20; Hos. 10: 11.
- Not without sagacity. Is. 1: 3.

Characteristics of

- Horns and hoofs of, alluded to. Ps. 69: 31.
- Lowing of, alluded to. 1 Sam. 15: 14; Job 6: 5.

Was fed

- With grass. Job 40: 15; Ps. 106: 20; Dan. 4: 25.
- With corn. Is. 30: 24.
- With straw. Is. 11: 7.
- On the hills. Is. 7: 25.
- In the valleys. 1 Chr. 27: 29; Is. 65: 10.
- In stalls. Hab. 3: 17.

Facts about oxen

- Rapid manner of collecting its food alluded to. Num. 22: 4.
- Formed a part of the patriarchal wealth. Gen. 13: 2,5; 26: 14; Job 1: 3.
- Formed a part of the wealth of Israel in Egypt. Gen. 50: 8; Ex. 10: 9; 12: 32.
- Formed a part of the wealth of the Jews. Num. 32: 4; Ps. 144: 14.
- Required great care and attention. Prov. 27: 23.
- Herdsmen appointed over. Gen. 13: 7; 1 Sam. 21: 7.
- Urged on by the goad. Judg. 3: 31.

Animals (8)

Ox, continued

Used for

- Drawing wagons. Num. 7: 3; 1 Sam. 6: 7.
- Carrying burdens. 1 Chr. 12: 40.
- Plowing. 1 Kgs. 19: 19; Job 1: 14; Amos 6: 12.
- Treading out the corn. Hos. 10: 11.
- Sacrifice. Ex. 20: 24; 2 Sam. 24: 22.
- Food. 1 Kgs. 1: 9; 19: 21; 2 Chr. 18: 2.

Laws about

- To rest on the Sabbath. Ex. 23: 12; Deut. 5: 14.
- Not to be yoked with an ass in the same plow. Deut. 22: 10.
- Not to be muzzled when treading out the corn. Deut. 25: 4; 1 Cor. 9: 9.
- If stolen to be restored double. Ex. 22: 4.
- Not to be coveted. Ex. 20: 17; Deut. 5: 21.
- If lost or hurt through neglect, to be made good. Ex. 22: 9–13.
- Killing a man, to be stoned. Ex. 21: 28–32.
- Method of reparation for one, killing another. Ex. 21: 35,36.
- Straying to be brought back to its owner. Ex. 23: 4; Deut. 22: 1,2.
- Fallen under its burden to be raised up again. Deut. 22: 4.
- Fat of, not to be eaten. Lev. 7: 23.

Illustrative

- (Engaged in husbandry,) of ministers. Is. 30: 24; 32: 20.
- (Not muzzled in treading corn,) of

Minister's right to support.

"I am not saying this on my own authority. The Law of Moses tells us not to muzzle an ox when it is grinding grain. But was God concerned only about an ox? 10 No, he wasn't! He was talking about us. This was written in the Scriptures so that all who plow and all who grind the grain will look forward to sharing in the harvest! 1 Corinthians 9: 8–10 CEV.

- (Prepared for a feast,) of the provision of the gospel. Prov. 9: 2; Matt. 22: 4.
- (Led to slaughter,) of a rash youth. Prov. 7: 22.
- (Led to slaughter,) of saints under persecution. Jer. 11: 19.
- (Stall fed,) of sumptuous living. Prov. 15: 17.

Bull or bullock illustrative

- Of fierce enemies. Ps. 22: 12; 68: 30.
- (Firstling of,) of the glory of Joseph. Deut. 33: 17.
- (In a net,) of the impatient under judgment. Is. 51: 20.
- (Fatted,) of greedy mercenaries. Jer. 46: 21.
- (Unaccustomed to the yoke,) of intractable sinners. Jer. 31: 18.

Cows illustrative

- Of proud and wealthy rulers. Amos 4: 1.

  " You women of Samaria are fat cows! You mistreat and abuse the poor and needy, then you say to your husbands, 'Bring us more drinks!'" Amos 4: 1 *CEV*

- (well favored,) of years of plenty. Gen. 41: 2,26,29.
- (Lean,) of years of scarcity. Gen. 41: 3; 27: 30.

Heifer illustrative

- Of a beloved wife. Judg. 14: 18.
- Of backsliding Israel.
  " You people of Israel are charmed by idols. Leave them alone!" Hosea 4: 17 *CEV*.
- (Taught) of Israel's fondness for ease in preference to obedience. Hos. 10: 11.
- (Of three years old,) of Moab in affliction. Is. 15: 5; Jer. 48: 34.
- (Fair,) of the beauty and wealth of Egypt. Jer. 46: 20.
- (At grass,) of the luxurious Chaldees. Jer. 50: 11.

Pigs

Overview

1. When wild inhabited the woods. Ps. 80: 13.
2. Unclean and not to be eaten. Lev. 11: 7,8.

Described

- Fierce and ungenerous. Matt. 7: 6.
- Filthy. 2 Pet. 2: 22.
- Destructive to agriculture. Ps. 80: 13.

Facts about

- Fed on husks. Luke 15: 16.
- Sacrificing of, and abomination. Is. 66: 3.
- Kept in large herds. Matt. 8: 30.
- Herding of, considered as the greatest degradation to a Jew. Luke 15: 15.
- The Gergesenes punished for having. Matt. 8: 31,32; Mark 5: 11,14.
- The ungodly Jews condemned for eating. Is. 65: 4; 66: 17.
  "Some of you get yourselves ready and go to a garden to worship a foreign goddess. You eat the meat of pigs, lizards, and mice. But I, the LORD, will destroy you for this" Isaiah 66: 17 *CEV*.

Illustrative

- Of the ungodly. Matt. 7: 6.
  "Don't give to dogs what belongs to God. They will only turn and attack you. Don't throw pearls down in front of pigs. They will trample all over them" Matthew 7: 6 *CEV*.
- Of hypocrites.
  "What happened to them is just like the true saying,
  "A dog will come back
  to lick up its own vomit.
  A pig that has been washed
  will roll in the mud" 2 Peter 2: 22 *CEV*.

Animals (9)

Sheep

Overview
Clean and used as food. Deut. 14: 4.

Described as
- Innocent. 2 Sam. 24: 17.
- Sagacious. John 10: 4,5.
- Agile. Ps. 114: 4,6.
- Being covered with a fleece. Job 31: 20.
- Remarkably prolific. Ps. 107: 41; 144: 13; Song 4: 2; Ezek. 36: 37.

Facts about sheep
- Bleating of, alluded to. Judg. 5: 16; 1 Sam. 15: 14.
- Under man's care from the earliest age. Gen. 4: 4.
- A great part of patriarchal wealth. Gen. 13: 5; 24: 25; 26: 14.
- Males of called rams. 1 Sam. 15: 22; Jer. 51: 40.
- Females of, called ewes. Ps. 78: 71.
- Young of, called lambs. Ex. 12: 3; Is. 11: 6.

Places celebrated for
- Kedar. Ezek. 27: 21.
- Bashan. Deut. 32: 14.
- Nebaioth. Is. 60: 7.
- Bozrah. Mic. 2: 12.

Uses of
- Flesh of, extensively used as food 1 Sam. 25: 18; 1 Kgs. 1: 19; 4: 23; Neh. 5: 18; Is. 22: 13.
- Milk of, used as food. Deut. 32: 14; Is. 7: 21,22; 1 Cor. 9: 7.
- Skins of, worn as clothing by the poor. Heb. 11: 37.
- Skins of, made into a covering for the tabernacle. Ex. 25: 5; 36: 10; 39: 34.
- Wool of, made into clothing. Job 31: 20; Prov. 31: 13; Ezek. 34: 3.
- Offered in sacrifice from the earliest age. Gen. 4: 4; 8: 20; 15: 9,10.
- Offered in sacrifice under the law. Ex. 20: 24; Lev. 1: 10; 1 Kgs. 8: 5,63.

Flocks of
- Cared for by members of the family. Gen. 29: 9; Ex. 2: 16; 1 Sam. 16: 11.
- Cared for by servants. 1 Sam. 17: 20; Is. 61: 5.
- Guarded by dogs. Job 30: 1.
- Kept in folds. 1 Sam. 24: 3; 2 Sam. 7: 8; John 10: 1.
- Taken to the richest pastures. Ps. 23: 2.
- Fed on the mountains. Ex. 3: 1; Ezek. 34: 6,13.
- Fed in the valleys. Is. 65: 10.
- Frequently covered the pastures. Ps. 65: 13.
- Watered every day. Gen. 29: 8–10; Ex. 2: 16,17.
- Made to rest at noon. Ps. 23: 2; Song 1: 7.
- Followed the shepherd. John 10: 4,27.
- Fled from strangers. John 10: 5.

Tithes and wool
- Tithe of, given to the Levites. 2 Chr. 31: 4–6.

- First wool of, given to the priests. Deut. 18: 4.
- Time of shearing, a time of rejoicing. 1 Sam. 25: 2,11,36; 2 Sam. 13: 23.

Were frequently

- Given as presents. 2 Sam. 17: 29; 1 Chr. 12: 40.
- Given as tribute. 2 Kgs. 3: 4; 2 Chr. 17: 11.
- Destroyed by wild beasts. Jer. 50: 17; Mic. 5: 8; John 10: 12.
- Taken in great numbers in war. Judg. 6: 4; 1 Sam. 14: 32; 1 Chr. 5: 21; 2 Chr. 14: 15.
- Cut off by disease. Ex. 9: 3.

Illustrative

- Of the Jews. Ps. 74: 1; 78: 52; 79: 13.
- Of the people of Christ. John 10: 7–26; 21: 16,17; Heb. 13: 20; 1 Pet. 5: 2.
- Of the wicked in their death. Ps. 49: 14.
- Of those under God's judgment. Ps. 44: 1.
- (In patience and simplicity,) of patience, of Christ. Is. 53: 7.
- (In proneness to wander,) of those who depart from God. Ps. 119: 176; Is. 53: 6; Ezek. 34: 16.
- (Lost,) of the unregenerate. Matt. 10: 6.
- (When found,) of restored sinners. Luke 15: 5,7.
- (Separation from the goats,) of the separation of saints from the wicked. Matt. 25: 32,33.
- False prophets assume the simple appearance Matt. 7: 15.

Wolf

Overview

1. Rapacious nature of. Gen. 49: 27.
2. Particularly fierce in the evening when it seeks its prey. Jer. 5: 6; Hab. 1: 8.
3. Kills flocks of sheep. John 10: 12.

Illustrative

- Of the wicked. Matt. 10: 16; Luke 10: 3.
- Of wicked rulers. Ezek. 22: 27; Zeph. 3: 3.
- Of false teachers. Matt. 7: 15; Acts 20: 29.
- Of the devil. John 10: 12.
- Of the tribe of Benjamin. Gen. 49: 27.
- Of fierce enemies. Jer. 5: 6; Hab. 1: 8.
- (Taming of,) of new order.

    "The wolf will romp with the lamb, the leopard sleep with the kid.
    Calf and lion will eat from the same trough,
    and a little child will tend them."

    Isaiah 11: 6 The Message

    "Wolf and lamb will graze the same meadow, lion and ox eat straw from the same trough, but snakes – they'll get a diet of dirt! Neither animal nor human will hurt or kill anywhere on my Holy Mountain," says GOD.

    Isaiah 65: 25 The Message

Birds (1)

Overview

1. Created by God. Genesis 1: 20,21; 2: 19.
2. Created for the glory of God. Psalms 148: 10.
3. Given as food. Genesis 1: 30; 9: 2,3.
4. Differ from animals and fishes. 1 Corinthians 15: 39.
5. Under the control of humans. Genesis 1: 26; Psalms 8: 8.
6. Given names by Adam. Genesis 2: 19,20.
7. Instinctively fear humans. Genesis 9: 2.
8. Provide lessons in wisdom. Job 12: 7.
9. Can be tamed James 3: 7.
10. Belong to God. Psalms 50: 11.
11. Are provided for by God. Psalms 104: 1–12; Matthew 6: 26; Luke 12: 23,24.

Names given to birds

- Fowls of the air. Genesis 7: 3.
- Fowls of heaven. Job 35: 11.
- Feathered fowl. Ezekiel 39: 17.
- Winged fowl. Deuteronomy 4: 17.
- Birds of the air. Matthew 8: 20.

Varieties of birds

- Graniverous. Matthew 13: 4.
- Carnivorous. Genesis 15: 11; 40: 19; Deuteronomy 28: 26.

Birds and their nests

- In trees. Psalms 104: 17; Ezekiel 31: 6.
- On the ground. Deuteronomy 22: 6.
- In cracks in rocks. Numbers 24: 21; Jeremiah 48: 28.
- In deserted cities. Isaiah 34: 15.
- Under the roofs of houses. Psalms 84: 3.

Clean and unclean birds

Birds are divided into these two categories Genesis 8: 20

List of clean birds

Birds that were designated as "clean" birds could be eaten (Deuteronomy 14: 11,20) and offered in sacrifice (Genesis 8: 20; Leviticus 1: 14).

- Dove. Genesis 8: 8.
- Turtle. Leviticus 14: 22; Song of Solomon 2: 12.
- Pigeon. Leviticus 1: 14; 12: 6.
- Quail. Exodus 16: 12,13; Numbers 11: 31,32.
- Sparrow. Leviticus 14: 4; Matthew 10: 29–31.
- Swallow. Psalms 84: 3; Isaiah 38: 14.
- Cock and hen. Matthew 23: 37; 26: 34,74.
- Partridge. 1 Samuel 26: 20; Jeremiah 17: 11.
- Crane. Isaiah 38: 14; Jeremiah 8: 7.

List of unclean birds

Unclean birds were not allowed to be eaten (Leviticus 11: 13,17; Deuteronomy 14: 12), or sacrificed.

- Eagle. Leviticus 11: 13; Job 39: 27.
- Black vulture. Leviticus 11: 13.
- Vulture. Leviticus 11: 14; Job 28: 7; Isaiah 34: 15.
- Falcon. Deuteronomy 14: 13.
- Kite. Leviticus 11: 14.

- Raven. Leviticus 11: 15; Job 38: 41.
- Owl. Leviticus 11: 16; Job 30: 29.
- Nighthawk. Leviticus 11: 16.
- Cuckoo Leviticus 11: 16.
- Hawk. Leviticus 11: 17; Job 39: 26.
- Little owl. Leviticus 11: 17.
- Cormorant. Leviticus 11: 17; Isaiah 34: 11.
- Great owl. Leviticus 11: 17.
- Swan. Leviticus 11: 18.
- Pelican. Leviticus 11: 18; Psalms 102: 6.
- Gier eagle. Leviticus 11: 18.
- Stork. Leviticus 11: 19; Psalms 104: 17.
- Heron. Leviticus 11: 19.
- Lapwing. Leviticus 11: 19.
- Bat. Leviticus 11: 19; Isaiah 2: 20.
- Ostrich. Job 39: 13,18.
- Bittern. Isaiah 14: 23; 34: 11.
- Peacock. 1 Kings 10: 22; Job 39: 13.

Protection for birds

Birds were not allowed:
- to be eaten with their young. Deuteronomy 22: 6,7.
- to be captured in snares or nets. Proverbs 1: 17.

Birds and idolatry

Birds were often worshiped by idolaters (Romans 1: 23) even though no images of them were allowed to be made for worship (Deuteronomy 4: 17).

Birds used as illustrations

The Bible compares birds to a variety of things:
- To cruel kings. Isaiah 46: 11.
- To hostile nations. Jeremiah 12: 9.
- To people from different countries. Ezekiel 31: 6; Matthew 13: 32.
- To the devil and his spirits. Matthew 13: 4,19.

Capturing birds are used to picture death. Ecclesiastes 9: 12.

Hen

The "hen" is only alluded to once in the Bible, in Luke 13: 34.

Quails

Quail are ground-dwelling birds that were known to migrate in vast numbers.

Israelites and quails

The Israelites were twice saved from hunger by a miraculous supply of quails,
1. in the wilderness of Sin (Ex. 16: 13), and
2. again at Kibroth-hattaavah (q.v.), Num. 11: 31.

God "rained flesh upon them as dust, and feathered fowls like as the sand of the sea" (Ps. 78: 27).

The quails flew at "about two cubits above the face of the earth," and so could be caught by hand.

The Israelites "spread them all abroad" (Num. 11: 32) in order to salt and dry them.

These birds (the *Coturnix vulgaris* of naturalists) are found in great numbers on the coastal regions of the Mediterranean, and their annual migration is a spectacular event.

Birds (2)

Quails, continued

"And there went forth a wind from The Lord, and it brought quails from the sea, and let them fall beside the camp, about a day's journey on this side and a day's journey on the other side, round about the camp, and about two cubits above the face of the earth. And the people rose all that day, and all night, and all the next day, and gathered the quails; he who gathered least gathered ten homers; and they spread them out for themselves all around the camp."

(Numbers 11: 31–32 RSV)

Vulture

Heb. *nesher*; properly the griffon vulture or great vulture, so called from its tearing its prey with its beak), referred to for
- its swiftness of flight. Deut. 28: 49; 2 Sam. 1: 23.
- its mounting high in the air. Job 39: 27.
- its strength. Ps. 103: 5.
- its setting its nest in high places. Jer. 49: 16.
- its power of vision Job 39: 27–30.

This "ravenous bird" is a symbol of those nations whom God uses in acts of destruction, sweeping away whatever is decaying (Matt. 24: 28; Is. 46: 11; Ezek. 39: 4; Deut. 28: 49; Jer. 4: 13; 48: 40).

It is said that the eagle sheds his feathers in the beginning of spring, and with fresh plumage assumes the appearance of youth. To this, allusion is made in Ps. 103: 5 and Is. 40: 31.

"Yet those who wait for the LORD
Will gain new strength;
They will mount up with wings like eagles,
They will run and not get tired,
They will walk and not become weary" Isaiah 40: 31 *NASB*.

God's care over his people is likened to that of the eagle in training its young to fly (Ex. 19: 4; Deut. 32: 11,12).

"As an eagle stirs up its nest,
Hovers over its young,
Spreading out its wings, taking them up,
Carrying them on its wings,
12 So the LORD alone led him,
And there was no foreign god with him" Deuteronomy 32: 11,12 *NKJV*.

Eagles observed in Palestine
- the golden eagle (Aquila chrysaetos).
- the spotted eagle (Aquila naevia).
- the common species, the imperial eagle (Aquila heliaca).
- the Circaetos gallicus, which preys on reptiles.

The eagle was unclean by the Levitical law (Lev. 11: 13; Deut. 14: 12).

Learning from the birds

"Therefore I say to you, do not worry about your life, what you will eat or what you will drink; nor about your body, what you will put on. Is not life more than food and the body more than clothing?

26 Look at the birds of the air, for they neither sow nor reap nor gather into barns; yet your heavenly Father feeds them. Are you not of more value than they?

27 Which of you by worrying can add one cubit to his stature?"

Matthew 6: 25–27 NKJV

Conservation

Caring for the environment and caring for animals should be based on God's care for his created world and the creatures in it.

10 He sends the springs into the valleys;

They flow among the hills.

11 They give drink to every beast of the field;

The wild donkeys quench their thirst.

12 By them the birds of the heavens have their home;

They sing among the branches.

13 He waters the hills from His upper chambers;

The earth is satisfied with the fruit of Your works.

14 He causes the grass to grow for the cattle,

And vegetation for the service of man,

That he may bring forth food from the earth,

15 And wine that makes glad the heart of man,

Oil to make his face shine,

And bread which strengthens man's heart.

16 The trees of the LORD are full of sap,

The cedars of Lebanon which He planted,

17 Where the birds make their nests;

The stork has her home in the fir trees.

18 The high hills are for the wild goats;

The cliffs are a refuge for the rock badgers.

Psalm 104: 10-18

Birds (3)

Eagle

Overview

1. A bird of prey. Job 9: 26; Matt. 24: 28.
   "They pass by like swift ships,
   Like an eagle swooping on its prey"
   Job 9: 26 *NKJV*.
   "For wherever the carcass is, there
   the eagles will be gathered together"
   Matthew 24: 28 *NKJV*.
2. Unclean. Lev. 11: 13; Deut. 14: 12.
3. Different kinds of. Lev. 11: 13,18;
   Ezek. 17: 3.
4. Called the eagle of the heavens.
   Lam. 4: 19.

Described as

- Long-sighted. Job 39: 29.
- Swift. 2 Sam. 1: 23.
- Soaring to heaven. Prov. 23: 5.
- Strength of its feathers alluded to.
  Dan. 4: 33.
- Greatness of its wings alluded to.
  Ezek. 17: 3,7.
- Peculiarity of its flight alluded to.
  Prov. 30: 19.
- Delights in the lofty cedars.
  Ezek. 17: 3,4.
- Lives in the high rocks. Job 39: 27,28.

Illustrative

- Of wisdom and zeal of God's
  ministers. Ezek. 1: 10; Rev. 4: 7.
- Of great and powerful kings.
  Ezek. 17: 3; Hos. 8: 1.
- Renewed strength and beauty of, of
  the renewal of saints. Ps. 103: 5.
  "Who satisfies your mouth with
  good things,

So that your youth is renewed like
the eagle's" Psalm 103: 5 *NKJV*.
- Method of teaching her young to fly,
  of God's care of his church. Ex. 19: 4;
  Deut. 32: 11.
- Wings of, of protection afforded to
  the church. Rev. 12: 14.
- Upward flight of, of the saint's rapid
  progress toward heaven.
  "But those who wait on the LORD
  Shall renew their strength;
  They shall mount up with wings like
  eagles,
  They shall run and not be weary,
  They shall walk and not faint" Isaiah
  40: 31 *NKJV*.
- Swiftness of, of the melting away of
  riches. Prov. 23: 5.
- Swiftness of, of the swiftness of
  hostile armies. Deut. 28: 49; Jer. 4: 13;
  48: 40; Lam. 4: 19.
- Height and security of its dwelling, of
  the fatal security of the wicked.
  "Your fierceness has deceived you,
  The pride of your heart,
  O you who dwell in the clefts of the
  rock,
  Who hold the height of the hill!
  Though you make your nest as high
  as the eagle,
  I will bring you down from there,"
  says the LORD"
  Jeremiah 49: 16 NKJV
- Was the standard of the Roman
  armies. Matt. 24: 15,28.

Ostrich

- Unclean and unfit for food. Lev. 11: 13.
- Furnished with wings and feathers. Job 39: 13.
- Lays her eggs in the sand. Job 39: 14.

Described as

- Void of wisdom. Job 39: 17.
- Imprudent. Job 39: 15.
- Cruel to her young. Job 39: 16.
- Rapid in movement. Job 39: 18.

Illustrative

- Of the unnatural cruelty of the Jews in their calamities. Lam. 4: 3.
- Companionship with, of extreme desolation. Job 30: 29.

Owls

- Owls are a metaphor for loneliness. "I am like a vulture of the wilderness, like an owl of the waste places; I lie awake, I am like a lonely bird on the housetop" Psalm 102: 6–7 RSV.
- Varieties of. Lev. 11: 16,17; Deut. 14: 15,16.
- Unclean and not to be eaten. Lev. 11: 13,16.

Described as

- Mournful in voice. Mic. 1: 8.
- Solitary in disposition. Ps. 102: 6.
- Careful of its young. Is. 34: 15.

Illustrative

- Of mourners. "I am like an owl in the desert,
like a lonely owl in a far-off wilderness" Psalm 102: 6 NL.

Raven

- Unclean and not to be eaten. Lev. 11: 15; Deut. 14: 14.
- Called the raven of the valley. Prov. 30: 17.

Described as

- Black. Song 5: 11.
- Solitary in disposition. Is. 34: 11.
- Improvident. Luke 12: 24.
- Carnivorous. Prov. 30: 17.
- God provides food for Job 38: 41; Ps. 147: 9; Luke 12: 24.

  "Who provides food for the raven, When its young ones cry to God, And wander about for lack of food? Job 38: 41 NKJV

  He gives to the beast its food, And to the young ravens that cry" Psalm 147: 9 NKJV.

  24 Consider the ravens, for they neither sow nor reap, which have neither storehouse nor barn; and God feeds them. Of how much more value are you than the birds?"

  Luke 12: 24 NKJV

- Sent by Noah from the ark Gen. 8: 7. Elijah fed by

  "And it will be that you shall drink from the brook, and I have commanded the ravens to feed you there."

  5 So he went and did according to the word of the LORD, for he went and stayed by the Brook Cherith, which flows into the Jordan. 6The ravens brought him bread and meat in the morning, and bread and meat in the evening; and he drank from the brook."

  1 Kings 17: 4–6 NKJV

Insects and reptiles

Insects

Overview

1. Created by God.

   "Then God said, "Let the earth bring forth the living creature according to its kind: cattle and creeping thing and beast of the earth, each according to its kind"; and it was so. 25And God made the beast of the earth according to its kind, cattle according to its kind, and everything that creeps on the earth according to its kind. And God saw that it was good."

   Genesis 1: 24,25 NKJV

2. Fed by God Ps. 104: 25,27; 145: 9,15.

Divided into

• Clean and fit for food. Lev. 11: 21,22.
• Unclean and abominable. Lev. 11: 23,24.

   "Yet these you may eat of every flying insect that creeps on all fours: those which have jointed legs above their feet with which to leap on the earth. 22 These you may eat: the locust after its kind, the destroying locust after its kind, the cricket after its kind, and the grasshopper after its kind. 23 But all other flying insects which have four feet shall be an abomination to you."

   Leviticus 11: 21–25 NKJV

Insects Mentioned in the Bible

• Ant. Prov. 6: 6; 30: 25.

   Lessons to learn from the ant:
   "Go to the ant, you sluggard! Consider her ways and be wise" Proverbs 6: 6 *NKJV*.

   "The ants are a people not strong, Yet they prepare their food in the summer" Proverbs 30: 25 *NKJV*.

• Bee. Judg. 14: 8; Ps. 118: 12; Is. 7: 18.
• Beetle. Lev. 11: 22.
• Caterpillar. Ps. 78: 46; Is. 33: 4.
• Earthworm. Job 25: 6; Mic. 7: 17.
• Flea. 1 Sam. 24: 14.
• Fly. Ex. 8: 22; Eccl. 10: 1; Is. 7: 18.
• Gnat. Matt. 23: 24.
• Grasshopper. Lev. 11: 22; Judg. 6: 5; Job 39: 20.
• Hornet. Deut. 7: 20.
• Locust. Ex. 10: 12,13.
• Lice. Ex. 8: 16; Ps. 105: 31.
• Maggot. Ex. 16: 20.
• Moth. Job 4: 19; 27: 18; Is. 50: 9.
• Spider. Job 8: 14; Prov. 30: 28.

Locust

Overview

1. A small insect. Prov. 30: 24,27.
2. Clean and fit for food. Lev. 11: 21,22.

Described as

• Wise. Prov. 30: 24,27.
• Voracious. Ex. 10: 15.
• Rapid in movement. Is. 33: 4.
• Like to horses prepared for battle. Joel 2: 4; Rev. 9: 7.

Facts about locusts

• Carried by the wind. Ex. 10: 13,19.
• Immensely numerous. Ps. 105: 34; Nah. 3: 15.

- Flies in bands and with order.
  Prov. 30: 27.
- One of the plagues of Egypt.
  Ex. 10: 4–15.

The Jews and locusts

- Used as food. Matt. 3: 4.
- Threatened with, as a punishment for
  sin. Deut. 28: 38,42.
- Deprecated the plague of.
  1 Kgs. 8: 37,38.
- Often plagued by. Joel 1: 4; 2: 25.
- Promised deliverance from the
  plague of. 2 Chr. 7: 13,14.

Illustrative

- Of destructive enemies. Joel 1: 6,7;
  2: 2–9.
- Of false teachers of the apostasy.
  Rev. 9: 3.
- Of ungodly rulers. Nah. 3: 17.
- (Destruction of,) of destruction of
  God's enemies. Nah. 3: 15.

Reptiles

Overview

1. Created by God. Gen. 1: 24,25.
2. Made for praise and glory of God.
   Ps. 148: 10.
3. Placed under the dominion of man.
   Gen. 1: 26.
4. Unclean and not eaten.
   Lev. 11: 31,40–43.

Mentioned in the Bible

- Chameleon. Lev. 11: 30.
- Lizard. Lev. 11: 30.

- Tortoise. Lev. 11: 29.
- Snail. Lev. 11: 30; Ps. 58: 8.
- Frog. Ex. 8: 2; Rev. 16: 13.
- Leech. Prov. 30: 15.
- Scorpion. Deut. 8: 15.
- Snake. Job 26: 13; Matt. 7: 10.
- Flying fiery serpent. Deut. 8: 15;
  Is. 30: 6.
- Dragon. Deut. 32: 33; Job 30: 29;
  Jer. 9: 11.
- Viper. Acts 28: 3.
- Adder. Ps. 58: 4; 91: 13; Prov. 23: 32.
- Cobra. Is. 11: 8.

Snakes and worship

- Worshiped by Gentiles. Rom. 1: 23.
- No image of similitude of, to be made
  for worshiping. Deut. 4: 16,18.
- Jews condemned for worshiping.
  Ezek. 8: 10.

Scorpion

- Armed with a sharp sting in its tail.
  Rev. 9: 10.
- Sting of, venomous and caused
  torment. Rev. 9: 5.
- Abounded in the great desert.
  Deut. 8: 15.
- Unfit for food. Luke 11: 12.

ILLUSTRATIVE
- Of wicked men. Ezek. 2: 6.
- Of ministers of antichrist.
  Rev. 9: 3,5,10.
- Of severe scourges. 1 Kgs. 12: 11.

CHRIST AND SCORPIONS
Christ gave his disciples power over
Luke 10: 19.

Fish

Key Bible verse

"The fowl of the air, and the fish of the sea, *and whatsoever* passeth through the paths of the seas." Psalm 8: 8

Had you ever noticed before?

The word "fish" comes sixty times in the Bible.

Neither the Old Testament nor the New Testament gives the name of any of them.

FIGURATIVE USES OF FISH
God's judgment on the people of Egypt is likened to fish: Ezekiel 29: 4,5.

The visible church are likened to fish: Matthew 13: 48.

Defenseless people captured by the Babylonians: Habakkuk 1: 14.

FISHING USED BY JESUS IN A SYMBOLIC WAY

"Come, follow me," Jesus said, "and I will make you fishers of men." At once they left their nets and followed him. Matthew 4: 19.

Fishermen like Peter and Andrew realized that Jesus was inviting them to change professions: from being fishermen to become evangelists.

Fish in the Bible	Bible reference	Significance
GENESIS – DEUTERONOMY "Rule over the fish of the sea."	Genesis 1: 28; see Psalm 8: 8	It is God's wish that humans are in control of fish.
"The fear and dread of you will fall upon . . . all the fish of the sea; they are given into your hands. Everything that lives and moves will be food for you."	Genesis 9: 2,3	Fish were given for us to eat.
"The fish in the Nile will die. . . . The fish in the Nile died, and the river smelled so bad that the Egyptians could not drink its water."	Exodus 7: 18, 21; see Psalm 105: 29	One of the ten plagues in Egypt involved the death of the fish in the River Nile.
"We remember the fish we ate in Egypt."	Numbers 11: 5.	The Israelites must have enjoyed eating the fresh-water fish from the River Nile, before the plagues.
"Would they have enough if all the fish in the sea were caught for them?"	Numbers 11: 22	As the Israelites grumble, the Lord asks this sarcastic question.
". . . like any creature that moves along the ground or any fish in the waters below."	Deuteronomy 4: 18	No idols in the shape of fish are to be made.

SOLOMON He also taught about animals and birds, reptiles and fish.	1 Kings 4: 33	Solomon's knowledge extended to the animal kingdom.
The Fish Gate	2 Chronicles 33: 14	The different gates in the walls of Jerusalem were given different names. Gates were often named after the items traded there. It is assumed that this gate was originally given this name due to all the dried and salted fish brought into Jerusalem through it.
"On that day," declares the Lord, "a cry will go up from the Fish Gate . . ."	Zephaniah 1: 10	The Fish Gate was one of the main entrances into Jerusalem in the days of the first temple.
The Fish Gate was rebuilt by the sons of Hassenaah.	Nehemiah 3: 3	Under Nehemiah's instruction the Fish Gate was repaired by the tribe of Hassenaah when the exiles returned to Jerusalem.
"Men from Tyre who lived in Jerusalem were bringing in fish and all kinds of merchandise and selling them in Jerusalem on the Sabbath to the people of Judah."	Nehemiah 13: 16	Fish was sold in Jerusalem on the Sabbath, thus breaking the law. But this also shows that the Phoenicians of Tyre. traded in Jerusalem as fish dealers.
	Matthew 13: 47	One of Jesus' parables focuses on fish and teaches that there will be a final separation between the righteous and the wicked.
	Matthew 14: 19 Matthew 15: 34	Two fish, and a few fish are mentioned in Jesus' feeding of the 5000 and the 4000.
"Take the first fish you catch; open its mouth and you will find a four-drachma coin. Take it and give it to them for my tax and yours."	Matthew 17: 27	This is a remarkable miracle involving a *tilapia,* one of the most common fish in the Sea of Galilee to this day. It is still known as *St Peter's fish.* One of its characteristics is that it carries its young fish in its mouth. When the mother fish thinks it is time for the baby fish to leave her mouth she puts a bright object in her mouth to prevent them from entering. The four-drachma coin found in the *tilapiais* mouth was the exact amount of money needed by two adults for the annual temple tax.
Or if he asks for a fish, will give him a snake?	Matthew 7: 10	In Galilee, together with bread, fish made the normal diet of ordinary people.

Homes

Caves

Overview

Caves were frequently used as dwelling-places (Num. 24: 21; Jer. 49:16; Obad. 3).

"Then he looked on the Kenites, and
he took up his oracle and said:
'Firm is your dwelling place,
And your nest is set in the rock'"

Numbers 24: 21 NKJV

"Your fierceness has deceived you,
The pride of your heart,
O you who dwell in the clefts of the
rock,
Who hold the height of the hill!
Though you make your nest as high as
the eagle,
I will bring you down from there," says
the LORD"   *Jeremiah 49: 16 NKJV*

"The pride of your heart has deceived
you,
You who dwell in the clefts of the rock,
Whose habitation is high;
You who say in your heart, 'Who will
bring me down to the ground?'"

Obadiah 3 NKJV

Pits or cavities in rocks were also
sometimes used as prisons (Is. 24: 22;
51: 14; Zech. 9: 11).

Were lived in:

- By Lot Gen. 19: 30.
- By Elijah 1 Kgs. 19: 9.
- By Israelites Ezek. 33: 27.
- By God's followers Heb. 11: 38.

Used as a place of refuge

Josh. 10: 16–27; Judg. 6: 2; 1 Sam. 13: 6;
1 Kin 18: 4; 1 Kgs. 18: 13; 1 Kgs. 19: 9;
1 Kgs. 19: 13.

Tents

Overview

Origin and antiquity of. Gen. 4: 20.

Called

- Tabernacles. Num. 24: 5; Job 12: 6;
  Heb 11: 9.
- Curtains. Is. 54: 2; Heb. 3: 7.

Facts about tents

- Were spread out. Is. 40: 22.
- Fastened by cords to stakes or nails.
  Is. 54: 2; Jer. 10: 20; Judg. 4: 21.
- Separate, for females of the family.
  Gen. 24: 67.
- Separate, for the servants. Gen. 31: 33.
- Of the Jews contrasted with those of
  the Arabs. Num. 24: 5; Song 1: 5.
- Custom of sitting and standing at the
  door of. Gen. 18: 1; Judg. 4: 20.

Were used by

Patriarchs. Gen. 13: 5; 25: 27; Heb. 11: 9.
- Israel in the desert. Ex. 33: 8;
  Num. 24: 2.
- Noah. Gen. 9: 21.
- Abraham. Gen. 12: 8; Gen. 13: 18;
  Gen. 18: 1.
- Lot. Gen. 13: 5.
- Moses. Ex. 18: 7.
- Children of Israel. Num. 24: 5–6;
  2 Sam. 20: 1; 1 Kgs. 12: 16.

• "Now when all Israel saw that the king did not listen to them, the people answered the king, saying: 'What share have we in David? We have no inheritance in the son of Jesse.
To your tents, O Israel!
Now, see to your own house, O David!'
So Israel departed to their tents"
1 Kings 12: 16 NKJV.
• The Midianites. Judg. 6: 5
• Cushites. Hab. 3: 7
• Arabians. Is. 13: 20
• shepherds. Is. 38: 12; Jer. 6: 3
• The people of Israel in all their wars. 1 Sam. 4: 3,10; 29: 1; 1 Kgs. 16: 16.
• The Rechabites. Jer. 35: 7,10.
• The Arabs. Is. 13: 20.
• Shepherds while tending their flocks. Song 1: 8; Is. 38: 12.
• All eastern nations. Judg. 6: 5; 1 Sam. 17: 4; 2 Kgs. 7: 7; 1 Chr. 5: 10.
• Used for cattle. 2 Chr. 14: 15.

Manufacture of

Paul was a tent-maker by trade.
"and because he was a tentmaker as they were, he stayed and worked with them" Acts 18: 3 NIV.

Were pitched

• With order and regularity. Num. 1: 52.
• In the neighborhood of wells. Gen. 13: 10,12; 26: 17,18; 1 Sam. 29: 1.
• Under trees. Gen. 18: 1,4; Judg. 4: 5.
• On the tops of houses. 2 Sam. 16: 22.

Illustrative

(Spread out,) of the heavens. Is. 40: 22.
(Enlarging of,) of the great extension of the Church. Is. 54: 2.

Palaces

Introduction

Today we think of palaces as applying only to royal buildings. But originally the Latin word *palatium*, from which "palace" is derived, meant any building surrounded by a fence.

In the Authorized Version palaces include citadels, lofty fortresses, and royal residences (Neh. 1: 1; Dan. 8: 2).

Solomon's palace

It appears that Solomon was distracted from wholly serving the Lord and building the temple by his foreign wives, and their gods, and his own building projects.

Solomon's palace is described in 1 Kings 7: 1–12 as a series of buildings rather than a single great structure. It took thirteen years to build.

For kings

• 1 Kgs. 21: 1; 2 Kgs. 15: 25; Jer. 49: 27; Amos 1: 12; Nah. 2: 6.
• Of David 2 Sam. 7: 2.
• Of Solomon 1 Kgs. 7: 1–12.
• At Babylon Dan. 4: 29; Dan. 5: 5.
• At Shushan Neh. 1: 1; Esth. 1: 2; Esth. 7: 7; Dan. 8: 2.

Facts about palaces

Archives kept in. Ezra 6: 2.
Proclamations issued from. Amos 3: 9.

Figurative, of a government

Amos 1: 12; Amos 2: 2; Nah. 2: 6.

Houses

Introduction

Before their stay in Egypt the Jews lived in tents. Then, for the first time, they lived in cities (Gen. 47: 3; Ex. 12: 7; Heb. 11: 9).

Overview

1. Antiquity of. Gen. 12: 1; 19: 3.
2. Deep and solid foundations required for. Matt. 7: 24; Luke 6: 48.
3. Sometimes built without foundation. Matt. 7: 26; Luke 6: 49.

Built of

- Clay. Job 4: 19.
- Bricks. Ex. 1: 11–14; Is. 9: 10.
- Stone and wood. Lev. 14: 40,42; Hab. 2: 11.
- Hewn or cut stone. Is. 3: 10; Amos 5: 11.
- Plastered. Ezek. 13: 10,11.
- Easily broken through. Job 24: 16; Ezek. 12: 5.
- Often swept away by torrents. Ezek. 13: 13,14.

The flat roofs of

- Surrounded with battlements. Deut. 22: 8.
- Had booths on them. 2 Sam. 16: 22; Neh. 8: 16; Prov. 2: 19.
- Used for worship Acts 1: 13–14; Acts 12: 12; Rom. 16: 5; 1 Cor. 16: 19; Col. 4: 15; Phile. 1: 2
- Had idolatrous altars on them. 2 Kgs. 23: 12; Jer. 19: 13; Zeph. 1: 5.

- Used for drying flax. Josh. 2: 6.
- Used for exercise. 2 Sam. 11: 2; Dan. 4: 29.
- Used as place to sleep. Josh. 2: 8; Acts 10: 9
- Used for devotion. Acts 10: 9.
- Used for making proclamations. Luke 12: 3.
- Used for secret conference. 1 Sam. 9: 25,26.
- Resorted to in grief. Is. 15: 3; Jer. 48: 38.
- Often covered with grass. Ps. 129: 6,7.

Facts about houses

- Accessible from the outside. Matt. 24: 17.
- The courts of, large and used as apartments. Esth. 1: 5; Luke 5: 19.
- Entered by a gate or door. Gen. 43: 19; Ex. 12: 22; Luke 16: 20; Acts 10: 17.
- Doors of, low and small for safety. Prov. 17: 19.
- Doors of, how fastened. 2 Sam. 13: 18; Song 5: 5; Luke 11: 7.
- Admission to, gained by knocking at the door. Acts 12: 13; Rev. 3: 20.
- Walls of, plastered. Lev. 14: 42,43.
- Snakes often lived in their walls. Amos 5: 19.
- Several stories high. Ezek. 41: 16; Acts 20: 9.
- Divided into apartments. Gen. 43: 30; Is. 26: 20.
- Texts of Scripture on doorposts of.
- Deut. 6: 9
- Laws regarding sale of.
- Lev. 25: 29–33; Neh. 5: 3

Apartments were often

- Large and airy. Jer. 22: 14.
- Paneled. Jer. 22: 14; Hag. 1: 4.
- Inlaid with ivory. 1 Kgs. 22: 39; Amos 3: 15.
- Hung with rich tapestries. Esth. 1: 6.
- Heated with fires. Jer. 36: 22; John 18: 18.
- Top of apartments were the best, and used for entertainment. Mark 14: 15.
- Had detached apartments for secrecy and for strangers. Judg. 3: 20–23; 2 Kgs. 4: 10,11; 9: 2,3.
- Windows for light. 1 Kgs. 7: 4.
- Street windows of, high and dangerous. 2 Kgs. 1: 2; 9: 30,33; Acts 20: 9.

House of the rich

- Great. Is. 5: 9; Amos 6: 11; 2 Tim. 2: 20.
- Pleasant. Ezek. 26: 12; Mic. 2: 9.

More facts about houses

- When finished were usually dedicated. Deut. 20: 5; Ps. 30: 1.
- For summer residence. Amos 3: 15.
- Liable to leprosy. Lev. 14: 34–53.
- Not to be coveted. Ex. 20: 17; Mic. 2: 2.
- Were hired Acts 28: 30.
- Were mortgaged. Neh. 5: 3.
- Were sold Acts 4: 34.
- Law about the sale of. Lev. 25: 29–33.
- Of criminals, desolated. Dan. 2: 5; 3: 29.
- Desolation of, threatened as a punishment. Is. 5: 9; 13: 16,21,22; Ezek. 16: 41; 26: 12.
- Often broken down to repair city walls before sieges. Is. 22: 10.

Illustrative

- Of the body. Job 4: 19; 2 Cor. 5: 1.
- Of the grave. Job 30: 23.
- Of the church. Heb. 3: 6; 1 Pet. 2: 5.
- Heaven. John 14: 2; 2 Cor. 5: 1.
- (On sand,) of the delusive hope of hypocrites. Matt. 7: 24,25.
- (On a rock,) of the hope of God's followers. Matt. 7: 24,25.
- (Insecurity of,) of earthly trust. Matt. 6: 19,20.
- (Building of,) of great prosperity. Is. 65: 21; Ezek. 28: 26.
- (Built and not inhabited,) of calamity. Deut. 28: 30; Amos 5: 11; Zeph. 1: 13.
- (To inhabit those, built by others,) of abundant feelings. Deut. 6: 10,11.

Kings' houses

- Called the king's house. 2 Kgs. 25: 9; 2 Chr. 7: 11.
- Called the house of the kingdom. 2 Chr. 2: 1,12.
- Called the king's palace. Esth. 1: 5.
- Called the royal house. Esth. 1: 9.
- Splendidly furnished. Esth. 1: 6.
- Surrounded with gardens. Esth. 1: 5.
- Surrounded with terraces. 2 Chr. 9: 11.
- Royal decrees issued from. Esth. 3: 15; 8: 14.
- Contained treasures of the king. 1 Kgs. 15: 18; 2 Chr. 12: 9; 25: 24.

Food at home (1)

Types of

- Milk. Gen. 49: 12; Prov. 27: 27.
- Butter. Deut. 32: 14; 2 Sam. 17: 29.
- Cheese. 1 Sam. 17: 18; Job 10: 10.
- Bread. Gen. 18: 5; 1 Sam. 17: 17.
- Parched corn. Ruth 2: 14; 1 Sam. 17: 17.
- Flesh. 2 Sam. 6: 19; Prov. 9: 2.
- Fish. Matt. 7: 10; Luke 24: 42.
- Herbs. Prov. 15: 17; Rom. 14: 2; Heb. 6: 7.
- Fruit. 2 Sam. 16: 2.
- Dried fruit. 1 Sam. 25: 18; 1 Sam. 30: 12.
- Honey. Song 5: 1; Is. 7: 15.
- Oil. Deut. 12: 17; Prov. 21: 17; Ezek. 16: 13.
- Vinegar. Num. 6: 3; Ruth 2: 14.
- Wine. 2 Sam. 6: 19; John 2: 3; John 2: 10.

Facts about food

- Prepared by females. Gen. 27: 9; 1 Sam. 8: 13; Prov. 31: 15.
- Thanks given before Mark 8: 6; Acts 27: 35.
- A hymn sung after Matt. 26: 30.
- Men and women ate together Gen. 18: 8–9; Esth. 1: 3; Esth. 1: 9.

Food comes from God

- Gen. 1: 29–30; Gen. 9: 3; Gen. 48: 15; Ps. 23: 5; Ps. 103: 5; Ps. 104: 14–15; Ps. 111: 5; Ps. 136: 25; Ps. 145: 15; Ps. 147: 9; Prov. 30: 8; Is. 3: 1; Matt. 6: 11; Rom. 14: 14; Rom. 14: 21; 1 Tim. 4: 3–5.

Things prohibited as food

- Ex. 22: 31; Lev. 11: 1–47; Deut. 14; Lev. 17: 13–15

Bread

- Given by God. Ruth 1: 6; Matt. 6: 11.
- Yielded by the earth. Job 28: 5; Is. 55: 10.

Made of

- Wheat. Ex. 29: 2; Ps. 81: 16.
- Barley. Judg. 7: 13; John 6: 9.
- Beans, millet, etc. Ezek. 4: 9.
- Manna (in the wilderness). Num. 11: 8.

Bread making

- Corn ground for making. Is. 28: 28.
- Was kneaded. Gen. 18: 6; Jer. 7: 18; Hos. 7: 4.
- Troughs used for kneading. Ex. 12: 34.
- Usually leavened. Lev. 23: 17; Matt. 13: 33.
- Sometimes unleavened. Ex. 12: 18; 1 Cor. 5: 8.

Was formed into

- Loaves. 1 Sam. 10: 3,4; Matt. 14: 17.
- Cakes. 2 Sam. 6: 19; 1 Kgs. 17: 13.
- Wafers. Ex. 16: 31; 29: 23.

Was baked

- On hearths. Gen. 18: 6.
- On coals of fire. Is. 44: 19; John 21: 9.
- In ovens. Lev. 26: 26; Hos. 7: 4–7.

Facts about bread

- Making of, a trade. Gen. 40: 2; Jer. 37: 21.
- Ordinary, called common bread. 1 Sam. 21: 4.
- Sacred, called hallowed bread. 1 Sam. 21: 4,6.
- Often put for the whole substance of man. Gen. 3: 19; 39: 6; Matt. 6: 11.
- The principal food used by the ancients. Gen. 18: 5; 21: 14; 27: 17.
- Broken when used. Lam. 4: 4; Matt. 14: 19.
- Kept in baskets. Gen. 40: 16; Ex. 29: 32.
- With water, the food of prisons. 1 Kgs. 22: 27.
- First fruit of, offered to God. Num. 15: 19,20.
- Offered with sacrifices. Ex. 29: 2,23; Num. 28: 2.

Illustrative

- Of Christ. John 6: 33–35.
- (When broken,) of the death of Christ. Matt. 26: 26; 1 Cor. 11: 23,24.
- (Partaking of,) of communion of saints. Acts 2: 46; 1 Cor. 10: 17.
- (Lack of,) of extreme poverty. Prov. 12: 9; Is. 3: 7.
- (Seeking or begging,) of extreme poverty. 1 Sam. 2: 36; Ps. 37: 25.
- (Fullness of,) of abundance. Ezek. 16: 49.
- (Eating without scarceness,) of plenty. Deut. 8: 9.
- (Of adversity,) of heavy affliction. Is. 30: 20.
- (Of tears,) of sorrow. Ps. 80: 5.
- (Of deceit,) of unlawful gain. Prov. 20: 17.
- (Of wickedness,) of oppression. Prov. 4: 17.
- (Of idleness,) of sloth. Prov. 31: 27.

Manna

Overview

Miraculously given to Israel for food in the wilderness Ex. 16: 4,15; Neh. 9: 15.

Called

- God's manna. Neh. 9: 20.
- Bread of heaven. Ps. 105: 40.
- Bread from heaven. Ex. 16: 4; John 6: 31.
- Corn of heaven. Ps. 78: 24.
- Angel's food. Ps. 78: 25.
- Spiritual meat. 1 Cor. 10: 3.

Described as

- Like coriander seed. Ex. 16: 31; Num. 11: 7.
- White. Ex. 16: 31.
- Like in color to bdellium. Num. 11: 7.
- Like in taste to wafers made with honey. Ex. 16: 31.
- Like in taste to oil. Num. 11: 18.
- Like hoar frost. Ex. 16: 14.

Facts about manna

- Previously unknown. Deut. 8: 3,16.
- Fell after the evening dew. Num. 11: 9.
- None fell on the Sabbath day. Ex. 16: 26,27.
- Gathered every morning. Ex. 16: 21.
- Ceased when Israel entered Canaan. Ex. 16: 35; Josh. 5: 12.

Food at home (2)

Given

- When Israel murmured for bread. Ex. 16: 2,3.
- In answer to prayer. Ps. 105: 40.
- Through Moses. John 6: 31,32.
- To exhibit God's glory. Ex. 16: 7.
- As a sign of Moses' divine mission. John 6: 30,31.
- For forty years. Neh. 9: 21.
- As a test of obedience. Ex. 16: 4.
- To teach that man does not live by bread only. Deut. 8: 3; Matt. 4: 4.
- To humble and prove Israel. Deut. 8: 16.

The Israelites

- At first covetous of. Ex. 16: 17.
- Ground, made into cakes and baked in pans. Num. 11: 8.
- Counted inferior to food of Egypt. Num. 11: 4–6.
- Loathed. Num. 21: 5.
- Punished for despising. Num. 11: 10–20.
- Punished for loathing. Num. 21: 6.

Illustrative

- Of Christ.

   "Jesus said, 'I assure you, Moses didn't give them bread from heaven. My Father did. And now he offers you the true bread from heaven.

   33 The true bread of God is the one who comes down from heaven and gives life to the world.'

   34 'Sir,' they said, 'give us that bread every day of our lives.'

   35 Jesus replied, 'I am the bread of life. No one who comes to me will ever be hungry again. Those who believe in me will never thirst.'"

   John 6: 32–35 NLT

- Of blessedness given to God's followers. Rev. 2: 17.
- A golden pot of, put in the ark of the covenant:

   "Then Moses gave them this command from the Lord: 'Take two quarts of manna and keep it forever as a treasured memorial of the Lord's provision. By doing this, later generations will be able to see the bread that the Lord provided in the wilderness when he brought you out of Egypt.'

   33 Moses said to Aaron, 'Get a container and put two quarts of manna into it. Then store it in a sacred place as a reminder for all future generations.'

   34 Aaron did this, just as the Lord had commanded Moses. He eventually placed it for safekeeping in the Ark of the Covenant."

   Exodus 16: 32–34 NLT

   "In that room were a gold incense altar and a wooden chest called the Ark of the Covenant, which was covered with gold on all sides. Inside the Ark were a gold jar containing some manna, Aaron's staff that sprouted leaves, and the stone tablets of the covenant with the Ten Commandments written on them."

   Hebrews 9: 4 NJT

Gluttony

General references

OLD TESTAMENT

Ex. 16: 20–21; Ex. 16: 27; Num. 11: 32–33; Deut. 21: 20–21; Prov. 23: 21; Prov. 30: 21–22; Eccl. 10: 17; Is. 22: 13; Amos 6: 4–7

NEW TESTAMENT

Luke 12: 19–20; Luke 12: 45–46; Luke 21: 34; Rom. 13: 13–14; 1 Cor. 15: 32; Phil. 3: 19; 1 Pet. 4: 3; Jude 1: 12.

Instances of:

- Esau. Gen. 25: 30–34; Heb. 12: 16–17.
- Israel. Num. 11: 4; Ps. 78: 18.
- Sons of Eli. 1 Sam. 2: 12–17.
- Belshazzar. While Belshazzar was feasting and drinking from the golden goblets taken from the temple God announced his imminent death.

    "A number of years later, King Belshazzar gave a great feast for a thousand of his nobles and drank wine with them.

    2 While Belshazzar was drinking, he gave orders to bring in the gold and silver cups that his predecessor, Nebuchadnezzar, had taken from the Temple in Jerusalem, so that he and his nobles, his wives, and his concubines might drink from them.

    3 So they brought these gold cups taken from the Temple of God in Jerusalem, and the king and his nobles, his wives, and his concubines drank from them.

    4 They drank toasts from them to honor their idols made of gold, silver, bronze, iron, wood, and stone.

    5 At that very moment they saw the fingers of a human hand writing on the plaster wall of the king's palace, near the lamp stand. The king himself saw the hand as it wrote,

    6 and his face turned pale with fear. Such terror gripped him that his knees knocked together and his legs gave way beneath him . . .

    13 So Daniel was brought in before the king . . .

    'O Belshazzar, . . . you have not humbled yourself.

    24 So God has sent this hand to write a message.

    25 This is the message that was written: MENE, MENE, TEKEL, PARSIN.

    26 This is what these words mean: Mene means "numbered" – God has numbered the days of your reign and has brought it to an end.

    27 Tekel means "weighed" – you have been weighed on the balances and have failed the test.

    28 Parsin means "divided" – your kingdom has been divided and given to the Medes and Persians.'

    29 Then at Belshazzar's command, Daniel was dressed in purple robes, a gold chain was hung around his neck, and he was proclaimed the third highest ruler in the kingdom.

    30 That very night Belshazzar, the Babylonian king, was killed.

    31 And Darius the Mede took over the kingdom at the age of sixty-two."
    Daniel 5: 1–6,13,22,24–31 NLT

Illnesses

Overview

1. Often sent as punishment.
   Lev. 14: 34; Deut. 28: 21; Ps. 107: 17;
   Is. 3: 17; John 5: 14.
2. Often brought from other countries.
   Deut. 7: 15.
3. Often through Satan. 1 Sam. 16: 14–
   16; Job 2: 7.
4. Regarded as visitations. Job 2: 7–10;
   Ps. 38: 2,7.
5. Intemperance a cause of. Hos. 7: 5.
6. Sins of youth a cause of. Job 20: 11.
7. Over-excitement a cause of.
   Dan. 8: 27.
8. Were many and divers. Matt. 4: 24.

Instances of:

- Upon Nabal. 1 Sam. 25: 38.
- Upon David's child. 2 Sam. 12: 15.
- Upon Gehazi. 2 Kgs. 5: 27.
- Upon Jeroboam. 2 Chr. 13: 20.
- Upon Jehoram. 2 Chr. 21: 12–19.
- Upon Uzziah. 2 Chr. 26: 17–20.
- Threatened as judgments. Lev. 26: 16;
  Deut. 7: 15; Deut. 28: 22; Deut. 28: 27–
  28; Deut. 29: 22.

Illnesses mentioned in the Bible

- Abscess. 2 Kgs. 20: 7.
- Atrophy. Job 16: 8; 19: 20.
- Bleeding. Matt. 9: 20.
- Blindness. Job 29: 15; Matt. 9: 27.
- Boils. Ex. 9: 10.
- Demoniacal possession. Matt. 15: 22;
  Mark 5: 15.
- Deafness. Ps. 38: 13; Mark 7: 32.
- Dropsy. Luke 14: 2.
- Dumbness. Prov. 31: 8; Matt. 9: 32.
- Dysentery. 2 Chr. 21: 12–19;
  Acts 28: 8.
- Fever. Deut. 28: 22; Matt. 8: 14.
- Impediment of speech. Mark 7: 32.
- Itch. Deut. 28: 27.
- Inflammation. Deut. 28: 22.
- Lameness. 2 Sam. 4: 4; 2 Chr. 16: 12.
- Leprosy. Lev. 13: 2; 2 Kgs. 5: 1.
- Loss of appetite. Job 33: 20; Ps. 107: 18.
- Melancholy. 1 Sam. 16: 14.
- Mental illness. Matt. 4: 24; 17: 15.
- Paralysis
  "Lord, my young servant lies in
  bed, paralyzed and racked with pain"
  Matthew 8: 6.
- Plague. Num. 11: 33;
  2 Sam. 24: 15,21,25.
- Sunstroke. 2 Kgs. 4: 18–20; Is. 49: 10.
- Tumors. Deut. 28: 27; 1 Sam. 5: 6,12.
- Ulcers. Is. 1: 6; Luke 16: 20.
- Wasting disease. Lev. 26: 16.
- Worms. Acts 12: 23.
  "Instantly, an angel of the Lord
  struck Herod with a sickness,
  because he accepted the people's
  worship instead of giving the glory
  to God. So he was consumed with
  worms and died" Acts 12: 23 NLT.

Frequently

- Loathsome. Ps. 38: 7; 41: 8.
- Painful. 2 Chr. 21: 15; Job 33: 19.
- Tedious. Deut. 28: 59; John 5: 5;
  Luke 13: 16.
- Complicated. Deut. 28: 60,61;
  Acts 28: 8.
- Incurable. 2 Chr. 21: 18; Jer. 14: 19.

Facts and illnesses

- Children subject to. 2 Sam. 12: 15; 1 Kgs. 17: 17.
- Doctors tried to cure. 2 Chr. 16: 12; Jer. 8: 22; Matt. 9: 12; Mark 5: 26; Luke 4: 23
- Medicine used for curing. Prov. 17: 22; Is. 1: 6.
- God often called on to cure. 2 Sam. 12: 16; 2 Kgs. 20: 1–3; Ps. 6: 2; James 5: 14.
- Not calling on God when ill, condemned. 2 Chr. 16: 12.
- Treatment of fractures. Ezek. 30: 21.

Healing of:

- From God. Ex. 15: 26; Ex. 23: 25; Deut. 7: 15; 2 Chr. 16: 12; Ps. 103: 3; Ps. 107: 20.
- In answer to prayer: Of Hezekiah.
- 2 Kgs. 20: 1–11; Is. 38: 1–8. Of David. Ps. 21: 4; Ps. 116: 3–8.

Miraculous healing of:

- A sign to accompany the preaching of the word. Mark 16: 18.

Those afflicted with

- Anointed. Mark 6: 13; James 5: 14.
- Often laid in the streets to receive advice from passers by. Mark 6: 56; Acts 5: 15.
- Often divinely supported. Ps. 41: 3.
- Often divinely cured. 2 Kgs. 20: 5; James 5: 15.

Illustrative

- Of sin. Is. 1: 5.
- Figurative. Ps. 38: 7; Is. 1: 6; Jer. 30: 12.

Remedies used:

General references:
Prov. 17: 22; Prov. 20: 30; Is. 38: 21; Jer. 30: 13; Jer. 46: 11.

- Poultices 2 Kgs. 20: 7.
- Ointments Is. 1: 6; Jer. 8: 22.
- Emulsions Luke 10: 34.

Paul and illness

Paul performed many miraculous healings. However, he himself suffered some kind of illness. The precise nature of his illness has never been diagnosed. Although he asked the Lord to heal him he was not healed, as far as we know.

"... even though I have received wonderful revelations from God. But to keep me from getting puffed up, I was given a thorn in my flesh, a messenger from Satan to torment me and keep me from getting proud.

8 Three different times I begged the Lord to take it away.

9 Each time he said, 'My gracious favor is all you need. My power works best in your weakness.' So now I am glad to boast about my weaknesses, so that the power of Christ may work through me"

2 Corinthians 12: 7–9 NLT

Paul did not heal everyone he met and some fellow-Christians he never managed to cure. "Erastus stayed at Corinth, and I left Trophimus sick at Miletus" 2 Timothy 4: 20 *NLT*.

Death (1)

Overview

May be simply defined as the termination of life.

It is described in a variety of ways in Scripture:

Dust

"The dust shall return to the earth as it was" (Eccl. 12: 7).

Breath

"Thou takest away their breath, they die" (Ps. 104: 29).

House

It is the dissolution of "our earthly house of this tabernacle" (2 Cor. 5: 1); the "putting off this tabernacle" (2 Pet. 1: 13, 14).

Nakedness

Being "unclothed" (2 Cor. 5: 3, 4).

Being asleep

"Falling on sleep" (Ps. 76: 5; Jer. 51: 39; Acts 13: 36; 2 Pet. 3: 9).

A departure

"... to depart .. " (Phil. 1: 23).

Shadow of death

The grave is represented as "the gates of death" (Job 38: 17; Ps. 9: 13; 107: 18).

The gloomy silence of the grave is spoken of under the figure of the "shadow of death" (Jer. 2: 6).

Death is the effect of sin (Heb. 2: 14), and not a "debt of nature." It is but once (Heb. 9: 27), universal (Gen. 3: 19), necessary (Luke 2: 28–30). Jesus has by his own death taken away its sting for all his followers (1 Cor. 15: 55–57).

Spiritual death

There is a spiritual death in trespasses and sins, i.e., the death of the soul under the power of sin (Rom. 8: 6; Eph. 2: 1,3; Col. 2: 13).

Second death

The "second death" (Rev. 2: 11) is the everlasting perdition of the wicked (Rev. 21: 8), and "second" in respect to natural or temporal death.

Physical death

- Came into the world through Adam. Gen. 3: 19; 1 Cor. 15: 21,22.
- Consequence of sin. Gen. 2: 17; Rom. 5: 12.
- Comes to everyone. Eccl. 8: 8; Heb. 9: 27.
- Ordered by God. Deut. 32: 39; Job 14: 5.
- Puts an end to earthly projects. Eccl. 9: 10.
- Strips of earthly possessions. Job 1: 21; 1 Tim. 6: 7.
- Levels all ranks. Job 3: 17–19.
  "For in death the wicked cease from troubling, and the weary are at rest.
  18 Even prisoners are at ease in death, with no guards to curse them.

19 Rich and poor are there alike,
and the slave is free from his master"
Job 3: 17–19 NLT.

- Take note, as at hand. Job 14: 1,2;
Ps. 39: 4,5; 90: 9; 1 Pet. 1: 24.
- Prepare for. 2 Kgs. 20: 1.
- Pray to be prepared for. Ps. 39: 4,13;
90: 12.
- Consideration of, a motive to
diligence. Eccl. 9: 10; John 9: 4.
- When averted for a season, is a
motive to increased devotedness
Ps. 56: 12,13; 118: 17; Is. 38: 18,20.

Jesus and death

- Conquered by Christ. Rom. 6: 9;
Rev. 1: 18.
- Abolished by Christ. 2 Tim. 1: 10.
- Will finally be destroyed by Christ.
Hos. 13: 14; 1 Cor. 15: 26.
- Christ delivers from the fear of.
Heb. 2: 15.

Exemption from:

- Enoch. Gen. 5: 24; Heb. 11: 5.
- Elijah. 2 Kgs. 2: 11.

Facts about death

- All shall be raised from. Acts 24: 15.
- No death in heaven. Luke 20: 36;
Rev. 21: 4.
- Promised to God's followers at the
second coming of Christ. 1 Cor. 15: 51;
1 Thess. 4: 15; 1 Thess. 4: 17.

Is described as

- The earthly house of this tabernacle
being dissolved. 2 Cor. 5: 1.
- Putting off this tabernacle. 2 Pet. 1: 14.
- God requiring the soul. Luke 12: 20.

- Going where there is no return.
Job 16: 22.
- Gathering to your people.
Gen. 49: 33.
- Going to your fathers. Gen. 15: 15;
Gen. 25: 8; Gen. 35: 29.
- Going down into silence. Ps. 115: 17.
- Yielding up the spirit. Acts 5: 10.
- Returning to dust. Gen. 3: 19;
Ps. 104: 29.
- Being cut down. Job 14: 2.
- Fleeing as a shadow. Job 14: 2.
- Departing. Php 1: 23.
- Illustrates the change produced in
conversion. Rom. 6: 2; Col. 2: 20.
- Giving up the Ghost. Gen. 25: 8;
Gen. 35: 29; Lam. 1: 19; Acts 5: 10.
- King of terrors. Job 18: 14.
- A change. Job 14: 14.
- Putting off this tabernacle. 2 Pet. 1: 14.
- Requiring the soul. Luke 12: 20.
- Sleep Deut. 31: 16; Job 7: 21;
Job 14: 12; Jer. 51: 39; Dan. 12: 2;
John 11: 11; Acts 7: 60; Acts 13: 36;
1 Cor. 15: 6; 1 Cor. 15: 18; 1 Cor. 15: 51;
1 Thess. 4: 14–15.

Symbolized

- By the pale horse. Rev. 6: 8.
- Referred to in poety. Hos. 13: 14;
1 Cor. 15: 55.
- Figurative of regeneration.
Rom. 6: 2–11; 7: 1–11; 8: 10–11;
Col. 2: 20.

Desired:

- General references. Jer. 8: 3; Rev. 9: 6.
- By Moses. Num. 11: 15.
- By Elijah. 1 Kgs. 19: 4.
- By Job. Job 3; Job 6: 8–11; Job 7: 1–3;
Job 7: 15–16; Job 10: 1; Job 14: 13.

Death (2)

Desired, continued:

- By Jonah Jonah 4: 8
- By Simeon Luke 2: 29
- By Paul

"We grow weary in our present bodies, and we long for the day when we will put on our heavenly bodies like new clothing" 2 Corinthians 5: 2 NLT.

"Yes, we are fully confident, and we would rather be away from these bodies, for then we will be at home with the Lord" 2 Corinthians 5: 8 NLT.

"20   For I live in eager expectation and hope that I will never do anything that causes me shame, but that I will always be bold for Christ, as I have been in the past, and that my life will always honor Christ, whether I live or I die.

21   For to me, living is for Christ, and dying is even better.

22   Yet if I live, that means fruitful service for Christ. I really don't know which is better.

23   I'm torn between two desires: Sometimes I want to live, and sometimes I long to go and be with Christ. That would be far better for me" *Philippians 1: 20–23 NLT*

As a judgment

- On those who lived before the flood. Gen. 6: 7; Gen. 6: 11–13.
- Upon Sodomites. Gen. 19: 12–13; Gen. 19: 24–25.
- Upon Saul. 1 Chr. 10: 13–14

Preparation for

Deut. 32: 29; 2 Kgs. 20: 1; Ps. 39: 4; Ps. 39: 13; Ps. 90: 12; Eccl. 9: 4; Eccl. 9: 10; Eccl. 11: 7–8; Is. 38: 18–19; Luke 12: 35–37; John 9: 4; Rom. 14: 8; Phil. 1: 21; Heb. 13: 14; James 4: 15; 1 Pet. 1: 17.

Of the righteous

Num. 23: 10; 2 Sam. 12: 23; 2 Kgs. 22: 19–20; Ps. 23: 4; Ps. 31: 5; Ps. 37: 37; Ps. 49: 15; Ps. 73: 24; Ps. 116: 15; Prov. 14: 32; Eccl. 7: 1; Is. 57: 1–2; Dan. 12: 13; Luke 2: 29; Luke 16: 22; Luke 23: 43; John 11: 11; Acts 7: 59; Rom. 14: 7–8; 1 Cor. 3: 21–23; 1 Cor. 15: 51–57; 2 Cor. 1: 9–10; 2 Cor. 5: 1; 2 Cor. 5: 4; 2 Cor. 5: 8; Phil. 1: 20–21; Phil. 1: 23–24; 1 Thess. 4: 13–14; 1 Thess. 5: 9–10; 2 Tim. 4: 6–8; Heb. 2: 14–15; Heb. 11: 13; 2 Pet. 1: 11; 2 Pet. 1: 14; Rev. 14: 13.

Scenes of

- Isaac. Gen. 27: 1–4; Gen. 27: 22–40.
- Jacob. Gen. 49: 1–33; Heb. 11: 21.
- Moses. Deut. 31: 14–30; Deut. 32: 1–52; Deut. 33: 1–29; Deut. 34: 1–7.

"So Moses, the servant of the LORD, died there in the land of Moab, just as the LORD had said.

6   He was buried in a valley near Beth-peor in Moab, but to this day no one knows the exact place.

7   Moses was 120 years old when he died, yet his eyesight was clear, and he was as strong as ever."
Deuteronomy 34: 5–7 NLT.

- David. 1 Kgs. 2: 1–10.
- Zechariah. 2 Chr. 24: 22.
- Jesus. Matt. 27: 34–53; Mark 15: 23–38; Luke 23: 27–49; John 19: 16–30.
- Stephen. Acts 7: 59–60.
- Paul. 2 Tim. 4: 6–8.

Of the wicked

OLD TESTAMENT

Num. 16: 30; 1 Sam. 25: 38; 2 Chr. 21: 6; 2 Chr. 21: 20; Job 4: 21; Job 18: 14; Job 18: 18; Job 20: 4–5; Job 20: 8; Job 20: 11; Job 21: 13; Job 21: 17–18; Job 21: 23–26; Job 24: 20; Job 24: 24; Job 27: 8; Job 27: 19–23; Job 34: 20; Job 36: 12; Job 36: 14; Job 36: 18; Job 36: 20; Ps. 37: 1–2; Ps. 37: 9–10; Ps. 37: 35–36; Ps. 49: 7; Ps. 49: 9–10; Ps. 49: 14; Ps. 49: 17; Ps. 49: 19–20; Ps. 55: 15; Ps. 55: 23; Ps. 58: 9; Ps. 73: 3–4; Ps. 73: 17–20; Ps. 78: 50; Ps. 92: 7; Prov. 2: 22; Prov. 5: 22–23; Prov. 10: 25; Prov. 10: 27; Prov. 11: 7; Prov. 11: 10; Prov. 13: 9; Prov. 14: 32; Prov. 21: 16; Prov. 24: 20; Prov. 29: 1; Prov. 29: 16; Eccl. 8: 10; Is. 14: 11; Is. 14: 15; Is. 17: 14; Is. 26: 14; Jer. 16: 3–4; Ezek. 28: 8; Ezek. 28: 10; Amos 9: 10.

NEW TESTAMENT

Luke 12: 20; Luke 16: 22–28; Acts 5: 3–10; 1 Thess. 5: 3.

SPIRITUAL

Luke 1: 79; John 5: 24–26; John 6: 50–51; John 6: 53; John 11: 26; Rom. 5: 12; Rom. 5: 15; Rom. 7: 11; Rom. 8: 5–6; Rom. 8: 12–13; 2 Cor. 5: 14; Eph. 2: 1; Eph. 2: 5–6; Eph. 4: 18; Eph. 5: 14; Col. 2: 13; 1 Tim. 5: 6; 1 Pet. 2: 24; 1 John 5: 12.

SECOND DEATH

Prov. 14: 12; Ezek. 18: 4; Ezek. 18: 10–13; Ezek. 18: 21; Ezek. 18: 23–24; Ezek. 33: 8–9; Ezek. 33: 11; Ezek. 33: 14–16; Matt. 7: 13; Matt. 10: 28; Matt. 25: 30; Matt. 25: 41; Matt. 25: 46; Mark 9: 43–44; Rom. 1: 32; Rom. 6: 16; Rom. 6: 21; Rom. 6: 23; Rom. 8: 13; Rom. 9: 22; 2 Thess. 1: 9; James 1: 15; James 4: 12; 2 Pet. 2: 12; Rev. 2: 11; Rev. 19: 20; Rev. 20: 14; Rev. 21: 8.

Families (1)

Family

Overview

1. Instituted. Gen. 2: 23–24
2. Government of. Gen. 3: 16;
   Gen. 18: 19; Esth. 1: 20; Esth. 1: 22;
   1 Cor. 7: 10; 1 Cor 11: 3; 1 Cor. 11: 7–9
3. Of God's followers blessed.
   Ps. 128: 3–6.
4. Are a gift from. God Gen. 33: 5;
   Ps. 127: 3.
5. Are capable of glorifying God.
   Ps. 8: 2; 148: 12,13; Matt. 21: 15,16.
6. An heritage from the Lord. Ps. 113: 9;
   127: 3.

Godly families should

- Be taught the Scriptures.
  Deut. 4: 9,10.
- Worship God together. 1 Cor. 16: 19.
- Be duly regulated. Prov. 31: 27;
  1 Tim. 3: 4,5,12.
- Live in unity. Gen. 45: 24; Ps. 133: 1.
- Live in mutual forbearance.
  Gen. 50: 17–21; Matt. 18: 21,22.
- Rejoice together before God.
  Deut. 14: 26.
- Deceivers and liars should be
  removed from. Ps. 101: 7.
- Warning against departing from
  God. Deut. 29: 18.
- Punishment of irreligious. Jer. 10: 25.

Good exemplified

- Abraham. Gen. 18: 19.
- Jacob. Gen. 35: 2.
- Joshua. Josh. 24: 15.
- David. 2 Sam. 6: 20.
- Job. Job 1: 5.
- Lazarus of Bethany. John 11: 1–5.
- Cornelius. Acts 10: 2,33.
- Lydia. Acts 16: 15.
- Jailor of Philippi. Acts 16: 31–34.
- Crispus. Acts 18: 8.
- Lois. 2 Tim. 1: 5.

Jesus and the family

- Jesus was an example to. Luke 2: 51;
  John 19: 26,27.

Families should be

- Brought to Christ. Mark 10: 13–16.
- Brought early to the house of God.
  1 Sam. 1: 24.
- Instructed in the ways of God.
  Deut. 31: 12,13; Prov. 22: 6.
- Judiciously trained. Prov. 22: 15;
  29: 17; Eph. 6: 4.

Families should

- Obey God. Deut. 30: 2.
- Fear God. Prov. 24: 21.
- Remember God. Eccl. 12: 1.
- Obey parental teaching. Prov. 1: 8,9.
- Honor parents. Ex. 20: 12; Heb. 12: 9.
- Fear parents. Lev. 19: 3.
- Obey parents. Prov. 6: 20; Eph. 6: 1.
- Take care of parents. 1 Tim. 5: 4.
- Honor the aged. Lev. 19: 32; 1 Pet. 5: 5.
- Not imitate bad parents. Ezek. 20: 18.

Not to have a family

- Considered an affliction. Gen. 15: 2,3; Jer. 22: 30.
- A reproach in Israel. 1 Sam. 1: 6,7; Luke 1: 25.

Babies

- Often prayed for. 1 Sam. 1: 10,11; Luke 1: 13.
- Often given in answer to prayer. Gen. 25: 21; 1 Sam. 1: 27; Luke 1: 13.

Were named

- After relatives. Luke 1: 59,61.
- From remarkable events. Gen. 21: 3,6; 18: 13; Ex. 2: 10; 18: 3,4.
- From circumstances connected with their birth. Gen. 25: 25,26; 35: 18; 1 Chr. 4: 9.
- Often by God. Is. 8: 3; Hos. 1: 4,6,9.
- Numerous, considered an especial blessing. Ps. 115: 14; 127: 4,5.
- Sometimes born when parents were old. Gen. 15: 3,6; 17: 17; Luke 1: 18.

Male

- If first born, belonged to God and were redeemed. Ex. 13: 12,13,15.
- Birth of, announced to the father by a messenger. Jer. 20: 15.
- Under the care of tutors, till they came of age. 2 Kgs. 10: 1; Gal. 4: 1,2.
- Usefully employed. 1 Sam. 9: 3; 17: 15.
- Inherited the possessions of their father. Deut. 21: 16,17; Luke 12: 13,14.
- Received the blessing of their father before his death. Gen. 27: 1–4; 48: 15; 49: 1–33.

Female

- Taken care of by nurses. Gen. 35: 8.
- Usefully employed. Gen. 24: 13; Ex. 2: 16.
- Inherited property in default of sons. Num. 27: 1–8; Josh. 17: 1–6.

Loss of babies

- Grief occasioned by loss of. Gen. 37: 35; 44: 27–29; 2 Sam. 13: 37; Jer. 6: 26; 31: 15.
- Resignation manifested at loss of. Lev. 10: 19,20; 2 Sam. 12: 18–23; Job 1: 19–21.

Husbands

Overview

Should have but one wife. Gen. 2: 24; Mark 10: 6–8; 1 Cor. 7: 2–4.

Duty of, to wives

- To respect them. 1 Pet. 3: 7.
- To love them. Eph. 5: 25–33; Col. 3: 19.
- To regard them as themselves. Gen. 2: 23; Matt. 19: 5.
- To be faithful to them. Prov. 5: 19; Mal. 2: 14,15.
- To dwell with them for life. Gen. 2: 24; Matt. 19: 3–9.
- To comfort them. 1 Sam. 1: 8.
- To consult with them. Gen. 31: 4–7.
- Not to leave them, though unbelieving. 1 Cor. 7: 11,12,14,16.

Families (2)

Husbands, continued

Duty of, to wives, continued

Duties of, not to interfere with
their duties to Christ. Luke 14: 26;
Matt. 19: 29.

Good examples

- Isaac. Gen. 24: 67.
- Elkanah. 1 Sam. 1: 4,5.

Bad examples

- Solomon. 1 Kgs. 11: 1.
- Ahasuerus. Esth. 1: 10,11.

Wives

Overview

- Not to be selected from among the
  ungodly. Gen. 24: 3; 26: 34,35; 28: 1.

Duties of, to their husbands

- To love them. Titus 2: 4.
- To reverence them. Eph. 5: 33.
- To be faithful to them. 1 Cor. 7: 3–5,10.
- To be subject to them. Gen. 3: 16;
  Eph. 5: 22,24; 1 Pet. 3: 1.
- To obey them. 1 Cor. 14: 34; Titus 2: 5.
- To remain with them for life.
  Rom. 7: 2,3.

Should be adorned

- Not with ornaments. 1 Tim. 2: 9;
  1 Pet. 3: 3.
- With modesty and sobriety.
  1 Tim. 2: 9.

- With a meek and quiet spirit.
  1 Pet. 3: 4,5.
- With good works. 1 Tim. 2: 10; 5: 10.

Good

- Are from the Lord. Prov. 19: 14.
- Are a token of the favor of God.
  Prov. 18: 22.
- Are a blessing to husbands.
  Prov. 12: 4; 31: 10,12.
- Bring honor on husbands.
  Prov. 31: 23.
- Secure confidence of husbands.
  Prov. 31: 11.
- Are praised by husbands. Prov. 31: 28.
- Are diligent and prudent. Prov. 31: 13–
  27.
- Are benevolent to the poor.
  Prov. 31: 20.
- Duty of, to unbelieving husbands.
  1 Cor. 7: 13,14,16; 1 Pet. 3: 1,2.
- Should be silent in the Churches.
  1 Cor. 14: 34.
- Should seek religious instruction
  from their husbands. 1 Cor. 14: 35.
- Of ministers should be exemplary.
  1 Tim. 3: 11.

Good examples

- Wife of Manoah. Judg. 13: 10.
- Orpah and Ruth. Ruth 1: 4,8.
- Abigail. 1 Sam. 25: 3.
- Esther. Esth. 2: 15–17.
- Elizabeth. Luke 1: 6.
- Priscilla. Acts 18: 2,26.
- Sarah. 1 Pet. 3: 6.

Bad Exemplified

- Samson's wife. Judg. 14: 15–17.
- Michal. 2 Sam. 6: 16.
- Jezebel. 1 Kgs. 21: 25.
- Zeresh. Esth. 5: 14.
- Job's wife. Job 2: 9.
- Herodias. Mark 6: 17.
- Sapphira. Acts 5: 1,2.

Widows

Overview

1. Character of true. Luke 2: 37;
   1 Tim. 5: 5,10.
2. Exhorted to trust in God. Jer. 49: 11.
3. Though poor, may be liberal.
   Mark 12: 42,43.
4. When young, exposed to many
   temptations. 1 Tim. 5: 11–14.

God

- Surely hears the cry of. Ex. 22: 23.
- Judges for. Deut. 10: 18; Ps. 68: 5.
- Relieves. Ps. 146: 9.
- Establishes the border of. Prov. 15: 25.
- Will witness against oppressors of.
  Mal. 3: 5.

Should not be

- Afflicted. Ex. 22: 22.
- Oppressed. Jer. 7: 6; Zech. 7: 10.
- Treated with violence. Jer. 22: 3.
- Deprived of raiment in pledge.
  Deut. 24: 17.

Should be

- Pleaded for. Is. 1: 17.
- Honored, if widows indeed.
  1 Tim. 5: 3.
- Relieved by their friends.
  1 Tim. 5: 4,16.
- Relieved by the Church. Acts 6: 1; 1
  Ti 5: 9.
- Visited in affliction. James 1: 27.
- Allowed to share in our blessings.
  Deut. 14: 29; 16: 11,14; 24: 19–21.

God's followers should

- Relieve. Acts 9: 39.
- Bring joy to. Job 29: 13.
- Disappoint not. Job 31: 16.

The wicked

- Do no good to. Job 24: 21.
- Send away empty. Job 22: 9.
- Take pledges from. Job 24: 3.
- Reject the cause of. Is. 1: 23.
- Vex. Ezek. 22: 7.
- Make a prey of. Is. 10: 2; Matt. 23: 14.
- Slay. Ps. 94: 6.

Facts about widows

- Woe to those who oppress. Is. 10: 1,2.
- Blessings on those who relieve.
  Deut. 14: 29.
- A type of Zion in affliction. Lam. 5: 3.
- Were released from all obligation to
  former husbands. Rom. 7: 3.
- Allowed to marry again. Rom. 7: 3.
- Were under the special protection of
  God. Deut. 10: 18; Ps. 68: 5.
- Specially taken care of by the Church
  Acts 6: 1; 1 Tim. 5: 9.

Clothes

Materials used

The earliest and simplest clothes mentioned in the Bible are an apron of fig-leaves sewed together (Genesis 3: 7).

After this skins of animals (3: 21) are mentioned.

Elijah's dress was probably the skin of a sheep (2 Kings 1: 8).

Animals' hair

The Jews learned the art of weaving hair into cloth (Exodus 26: 7; 35: 6), which formed the sackcloth of mourners. This was the material of John the Baptist's robe (Matthew 3: 4).

Wool

Wool was also woven into garments (Leviticus 13: 47; Deuteronomy 22: 11; Ezekiel 34: 3; Job 31: 20; Proverbs 27: 26).

Linen

The Israelites probably learned the art of weaving linen when they were in Egypt (1 Chronicles 4: 21). Fine linen was used in the vestments of the high priest (Exodus 28: 5), as well as by the rich (Genesis 41: 42; Proverbs 31: 22; Luke 16: 19).

The use of mixed material, as wool and flax, was forbidden (Leviticus 19: 19; Deuteronomy 22: 11).

Color

The prevailing color was the natural white of the material used.

Dyeing

The Jews knew about the art of dyeing (Genesis 37: 3,23).

Ornaments

Different types of ornamentation were used in weaving (Exodus 28: 6; 26: 1,31; 35: 25), and needle-work (Judges 5: 30; Psalms 45: 13). Dyed robes were imported from foreign countries, particularly from Phoenicia (Zephaniah 1: 8). Purple and scarlet robes were the marks of the wealthy (Luke 16: 19; 2 Sam. 1: 24).

Types of clothes

The robes of men and women were not very different from each other.

COAT

The "coat" (*kethoneth*), made of wool, cotton, or linen, was worn by both sexes. It was a closely-fitting garment, similar to our shirt (John 19: 23). It was kept close to the body by a belt (John 21: 7). A person wearing this "coat" alone was described as naked (1 Samuel 19: 24; Isaiah 20: 2; 2 Kings 6: 30; John 21: 7); deprived of it he would be absolutely naked.

LINEN CLOTH

A linen cloth or wrapper (*sadin*) of fine linen, used like a night-shirt (Mark 14: 51). It is mentioned in Judg. 14: 12,13, and rendered there "sheets."

UPPER TUNIC

An upper tunic (*meil*), longer than the

"coat" (1 Samuel 2: 19; 24: 4; 28: 14). In 1 Samuel 28: 14 it is the garment which Samuel wore; in 1 Samuel 24: 4 it is the "robe" under which Saul slept. The disciples were forbidden to take two "coats" with them on their work of preaching and healing (Matthew 10: 10; Luke 9: 3).

OUTER GARMENT

The usual outer garment consisted of a piece of woolen cloth like a Scottish plaid, either wrapped round the body or thrown over the shoulders like a shawl, with the ends hanging down in front, or it might be thrown over the head so as to conceal the face (2 Samuel 15: 30; Esther 6: 12). It was fastened to the waist by a belt, and the fold formed by the overlapping of the robe served as a pocket (2 Kings 4: 39; Psalms 79: 12; Haggai 2: 12; Proverbs 17: 23; 21: 14).

Female dress

The "coat" was common to both sexes (Song of Songs 5: 3). But peculiar to females were:

VEIL

The "veil" or "wimple," a kind of shawl (Ruth 3: 15; translated "mantle," RSV, Isaiah 3: 22);

MANTLE

The "mantle," also a kind of shawl (Isaiah 3: 22).

VEIL

A "veil" was probably a light summer dress (Genesis 24: 65).

The outer garment ended in an ample fringe or border, which concealed the feet (Isaiah 47: 2; Jeremiah 13: 22).

Facts about clothes

The clothing worn by the Persians is described in Daniel 3: 21.

References to sewing are few, as the clothes came ready-to-wear from the loom. Making clothes was regarded as women's work, (Proverbs 31: 22; Acts 9: 39).

Extravagance in dress is referred to in Jeremiah 4: 30; Ezek. 16: 10; 1 Peter 3: 3 NLT.

Tearing robes expressed

- grief. Genesis 37: 29,34,
- fear. 1 Kings 21: 27,
- indignation. 2 Kings 5: 7, or
- despair. Judges 11: 35; Esther 4: 1.

Other symbolic actions associated with clothing

- Shaking the garments, or shaking the dust from them, was a sign of renunciation. Acts 18: 6;
- wrapping them round the head, of awe 1 Kings 19: 13 or grief 2 Samuel 15: 30.
- throwing them off, of excitement. Acts 22: 23.
- they were set aside also when they would impede action. Mark 10: 50; John 13: 4; Acts 7: 58.
- laying hold of them, of supplication. 1 Samuel 15: 27.
- When traveling, the outer garments were drawn up. 1 Kings 18: 46.

Hair

Cosmetics

When Jezebel, the queen mother, heard that Jehu had come to Jezreel, she painted her eyelids and fixed her hair and sat at a window" 2 Kings 9: 30.

Perfume

The Jews anointed the hair profusely with fragrant ointments (Ruth 3: 3; 2 Sam. 14: 2; Ps. 23: 5; 45: 7), especially in times of rejoicing (Matt. 6: 17; Luke 7: 46).

"Wash and perfume yourself, and put on your best clothes. Then go down to the threshing floor, but don't let him know you are there until he has finished eating and drinking."

Ruth 3: 3 NIV

"So Joab sent someone to Tekoa and had a wise woman brought from there. He said to her, 'Pretend you are in mourning. Dress in mourning clothes, and don't use any cosmetic lotions. Act like a woman who has spent many days grieving for the dead.'"

2 Samuel 14: 2 NIV

"You prepare a table before me in the presence of my enemies.
You anoint my head with oil;
my cup overflows."

Psalm 23: 5 NIV

"You love righteousness and hate wickedness; therefore God, your God, has set you above your companions by anointing you with the oil of joy."

Psalm 45: 7 NIV

Hair

Introduction
EGYPTIANS
The Egyptians let the hair of their head and beard grow only when they were in mourning, shaving it off at other times. Joseph shaved himself before going in to Pharaoh (Gen. 41: 14). The women of Egypt wore their hair long and plaited. Wigs were worn by priests and laymen to cover the shaven skull, and false beards were common.

GREEKS
In the time of the apostle Paul, Greeks men wore short hair, while women wore long hair (1 Cor. 11: 14, 15).

JEWS
Among the Jews the natural distinction between the sexes was preserved by the women wearing long hair (Luke 7: 38; John 11: 2; 1 Cor. 11: 6), while men kept theirs as a rule at a moderate length by frequent clipping.

Baldness
Baldness disqualified any one for the priest's office (Lev. 21).

Long hair
Long hair is especially noticed in the description of Absalom's person (2 Sam. 14: 26); but the wearing of long hair was unusual, and was only practiced as an act of religious observance by Nazarites (Num. 6: 5; Judg. 13: 5) and others in token of special mercies (Acts 18: 18).

Facts about hair

- The natural covering of the head. Ps. 68: 21.
- Innumerable. Ps. 40: 12; 69: 4.
- Numbered. Matt. 10: 30; Luke 12: 7
- Growth of. Judg. 16: 22.

God

- Takes care of. Dan. 3: 27; Luke 21: 18.

Color of

- Color of, changed by leprosy. Lev. 13: 3,10.
- Black, particularly esteemed. Song 5: 11.

WHITE OR GRAY

- A token of age. 1 Sam. 12: 2; Ps. 71: 18.
- A token of weakness and decay. Hos. 7: 9.
- An emblem of wisdom. Dan. 7: 9; Job 12: 12.
- With righteousness, a crown of glory. Prov. 16: 31.
- To be reverenced. Lev. 19: 32.
- People cannot even change the color of Matt. 5: 36.

"And do not swear by your head, for you cannot make even one hair white or black" Matthew 5: 36 NIV.

Hair of women

- Worn long by women. Is. 3: 24; Luke 7: 38; 1 Cor. 11: 5–6; 1 Tim. 2: 9; 1 Pet. 3: 3; Rev. 9: 8.
- Worn long for a covering. 1 Cor. 11: 15.
- Plaited and broidered. 1 Tim. 2: 9; 1 Pet. 3: 3.
- Well set and ornamented. Is. 3: 24.
- Neglected in grief. Luke 7: 38; John 12: 3.

Hair of men

- Men condemned for wearing long. 1 Cor. 11: 14.
- Worn long by Absalom. 2 Sam. 14: 26
- Worn short by men. 1 Cor. 11: 14

Anointing hair

- Often expensively anointed. Eccl. 9: 8.

Hair of Nazarites

- Not to be cut during their vow. Num. 6: 5; Judg. 16: 17,19,20.
- Shorn after completion of vow. Num. 6: 18.

Symbolic acts linked to hair

- Plucked out in extreme grief. Ezra 9: 3.
- Plucking out of, a reproach. Neh. 13: 25; Is. 50: 6.
- Judgments expressed by sending baldness for. Is. 3: 24; Jer. 47: 5.
- Symbolic, dividing of. Ezek. 5: 1–2
- In times of affliction the hair was cut off. Is. 3: 17, 24; 15: 2; 22: 12; Jer. 7: 29; Amos 8: 10
- Shaving symbolizes the destruction of a people. Is. 7: 20.

Farmers (1)

Overview

1. The cultivation of the earth.
   Gen. 3: 23.
2. Man's occupation before the Fall.
   Gen. 2: 15.
3. Made laborious by the curse on the
   earth. Gen. 3: 17–19.
4. Contributes to supporting everyone.
   Eccl. 5: 9.
- God's providence should be
  acknowledged in fruits of farming.
  Jer. 5: 24; Hos. 2: 8.
- The promises of God's blessings on.
  Lev. 26: 4; Deut. 7: 13; 11: 14,15.

Farming requires

- Wisdom. Is. 28: 26.
- Diligence. Prov. 27: 23–27; Eccl. 11: 6.

General illustrations

Paul mentions the idea of the hard
working farming.
  "The husbandman who laboreth
must be the first partaker of the fruits"
2 Timothy 2: 6 KJ21.

James counsels his readers to be patient
and points to the patience of the farmer
to reinforce his point.
  "Be patient therefore, brethren, unto
the coming of the Lord. Behold, the
husbandman waiteth for the precious
fruit of the earth, and hath long
patience for it, until he receive the early
and latter rain" James 5: 7 KJ21.

A farming metaphor is used to
illustrate the truth that diligence is
rewarded.

"Much food is in the tillage of
the poor, but there is that which is
destroyed for want of judgment"
Proverbs 13: 23 KJ21.

"He that tilleth his land shall have
plenty of bread, but he that followeth
after vain persons shall have poverty
enough" Proverbs 28: 19 KJ21.

"For the earth which drinketh in
the rain that cometh oft upon it, and
bringeth forth herbs meet for those by
whom it is dressed, receiveth blessing
from God" Hebrews 6: 7 KJ21.

Farmers were given a variety of names.
- Tillers of the ground. Gen. 4: 2.
- Husbandmen. 2 Chr. 26: 10.
- Laborers. Matt. 9: 37; 20: 1.

Rules about farming

- Charging interest on loans forbidden
  "If you lend money to a fellow
  Hebrew in need, do not be like a
  money lender, charging interest"
  Exodus 22: 25 NLT.
- Not to covet the fields of another.
  Deut. 5: 21.
- Not to move landmarks. Deut. 19: 14;
  Prov. 22: 28.
- Not to cut down crops of another.
  Deut. 23: 25.
- Against the trespass of cattle.
  Ex. 22: 5.
- Against injuring the produce of.
  Ex. 22: 5.

Types of work engaged in by farmers

- Hedging. Is. 5: 2,5; Hos. 2: 6.
- Ploughing. Job 1: 14.
- Digging. Is. 5: 6; Luke 13: 8; 16: 3.
- Manuring. Is. 25: 10
- Harrowing. Job 39: 10; Is. 28: 24.
- Gathering out the stones. Is. 5: 2.
- Sowing. Eccl. 11: 4; Is. 32: 20.
- Planting. Prov. 31: 16; Is. 44: 14.
- Watering. Deut. 11: 10; 1 Cor. 3: 6–8.
- Weeding. Matt. 13: 28.
- Grafting. Rom. 11: 17–19,24.
- Pruning. Is. 5: 6; John 15: 2.
- Mowing. Ps. 129: 7; Amos 7: 1.
- Reaping. Is. 17: 5.
- Binding. Gen. 37: 7; Matt. 13: 30.
- Gleaning. Lev. 19: 9; Ruth 2: 3.
- Stacking. Ex. 22: 6.
- Threshing. Deut. 25: 4; Judg. 6: 11.
- Winnowing. Ruth 3: 2; Matt. 3: 12.
- Storing in barns. Matt. 6: 26; 13: 30.

Animals used in farming

- The ox. Deut. 25: 4.
- The ass. Deut. 22: 10.
- The horse. Is. 28: 28.

Implements used in farming

- The plow. 1 Sam. 13: 20.
- The harrow. 2 Sam. 12: 31.
- The mattock. 1 Sam. 13: 20; Is. 7: 25.
- The sickle. Deut. 16: 9; 23: 25.
- The pruning-hook. Is. 18: 5; Joel 3: 10.
- The fork. 1 Sam. 13: 21.
- The axe. 1 Sam. 13: 20.
- The teethed threshing instrument. Is. 41: 15.
- The flail. Is. 28: 27.
- The cart. 1 Sam. 6: 7; Is. 28: 27,28.

- The shovel. Is. 30: 24.
- The sieve. Amos 9: 9.
- The fan. Is. 30: 24; Matt. 3: 12.

Illustrations taken from farming

PLOWING

The breaking up or tilling of the earth Jer. 4: 3; Hos. 10: 12.

Performed:

- By a plow. Luke 9: 62.
- With oxen. 1 Sam. 14: 14; Job 1: 14.
- During the cold winter season. Prov. 20: 4.
- In long and straight furrows. Ps. 129: 3.
- Generally by servants. Is. 61: 5; Luke 17: 7.
- Sometimes by the owner of the land himself. 1 Kgs. 19: 19.

Plowing was followed by harrowing and sowing Is. 28: 24,25.

GLEANING

- Laws concerning. Lev. 23: 22; Deut. 24: 19–20.

  "And when ye reap the harvest of your land, thou shalt not wholly reap the corners of thy field, neither shalt thou gather the gleanings of thy harvest.

  10 And thou shalt not glean thy vineyard, neither shalt thou gather every grape of thy vineyard. Thou shalt leave them for the poor and stranger: I am the Lord your God." Leviticus 19: 9,10 KJ21.

- Instances of, Ruth in the field of Boaz. Ruth 2: 2–3.

Farmers (2)

Farming activities used as illustrations: Fallow ground and repentance

"For thus saith the Lord to the men of Judah and Jerusalem: 'Break up your fallow ground, and sow not among thorns'" Jeremiah 4: 3 KJ21.

SOWING WHEAT, BUT REAPING THORNS

"They have sown wheat, but shall reap thorns; they have put themselves to pain, but shall not profit; and they shall be ashamed of your produce because of the fierce anger of the Lord" Jeremiah 12: 13 KJ21.

PEACE AND PROSPERITY

"And He shall judge among the nations, and shall rebuke many people; and they shall beat their swords into plowshares, and their spears into pruning hooks; nation shall not lift up sword against nation, neither shall they learn war anymore" Isaiah 2: 4 KJ21.

"And He shall judge among many people, and rebuke strong nations afar off. And they shall beat their swords into plowshares, and their spears into pruning hooks; nation shall not lift up a sword against nation, neither shall they learn war any more" Micah 4: 3 KJ21.

SIN

"Even as I have seen, they that plow iniquity and sow wickedness reap the same" Job 4: 8 KJ21.

"Ye have plowed wickedness, ye have reaped iniquity, ye have eaten the fruit of lies, because thou didst trust in thy way, in the multitude of thy mighty men" Hosea 10: 13 KJ21.

PARABLE OF THE SOWER

Matt. 13: 3–8; Matt. 13: 19–23; Luke 8: 5–15.

PARABLE OF THE WEEDS

Matt. 13: 24–30; Matt. 13: 36–43.

A PICTURE OF THE CHURCH

"For we are fellow workmen (joint promoters, laborers together) with and for God; you are God's [1] garden and vineyard and field under cultivation, [you are] God's building" 1 Corinthians 3: 9 AB.

A PICTURE OF THE HEART

Jer. 4: 3; Hos. 10: 12.

Gleaning used in a figurative way

"And he said unto them, 'What have I done now in comparison with you? Is not the gleaning of the grapes of Ephraim better than the vintage of Abiezer?'" Judges 8: 2 KJ21

"'Yet gleaning grapes shall be left in it, as the shaking of an olive tree, two or three berries in the top of the uppermost bough, four or five in the outmost fruitful branches thereof,' saith the Lord God of Israel" Isaiah 17: 6 KJ21.

"If grape-gatherers come to thee, would they not leave some gleaning grapes? If thieves by night, they will destroy till they have enough" Jeremiah 49: 9 KJ21.

Threshing

The removing or separating corn, from the straw. 1 Chr. 21: 20.
Was achieved:

- By a rod or staff. Is. 28: 27.
- By cart wheels. Is. 28: 27,28.
- By implements which had teeth. Is. 41: 15; Amos 1: 3.
- By the hooves of horses and oxen. Is. 28: 28; Hos. 10: 11; 2 Sam. 24: 22.

Facts about threshing

While cattle were threshing they were not to be muzzled.

"Thou shalt not muzzle the ox when he treadeth out the corn" Deuteronomy 25: 4 KJ21.

PAUL APPLIES THIS PRINCIPLE IN TWO OF HIS LETTERS

"For it is written in the Law of Moses: 'Thou shalt not muzzle the mouth of the ox that treadeth out the corn.' Doth God take care for oxen or doth He say it altogether for our sakes? For our sakes, no doubt, this is written: that he that ploweth should plow in hope, and that he that thresheth in hope should be partaker of his hope" 1 Corinthians 9: 9,10 KJ21.

"For the Scripture saith, 'Thou shalt not muzzle the ox that treadeth out the corn,' and, 'The laborer is worthy of his reward'" 1 Timothy 5: 18 KJ21.

Winnowing

Threshing was followed by winnowing which was performed by a shovel.

"The oxen and donkeys that till the ground will eat good grain, its chaff having been blown away by the wind" Isaiah 30: 24 NLT.

"You will toss them in the air, and the wind will blow them all away; a whirlwind will scatter them. And the joy of the Lord will fill you to overflowing. You will glory in the Holy One of Israel" Isaiah 41: 16 NLT.

WINNOWING USED TO ILLUSTRATE
Jesus used the idea of winnowing to illustrate how we will be judged.

"He is ready to separate the chaff from the grain with his winnowing fork. Then he will clean up the threshing area, storing the grain in his barn but burning the chaff with never-ending fire" Matthew 3: 12 NLT.

God's judgments

Is. 21: 10; Jer. 51: 33; Hab. 3: 12.

- Of the church in her conquests. Is. 41: 15,16; Mic. 4: 13.

- Gathering the sheaves for. Of preparing the enemies of the Church for judgment. Mic. 4: 12.

- Dust made by. Of complete destruction. 2 Kgs. 13: 7; Is. 41: 15.

- An instrument for, with teeth. Of the Church overcoming opposition. Is. 41: 15.

Shepherds

Overview

The work of the eastern shepherd, as described in the Bible, was a tough and dangerous one.

He was exposed to the extremes of heat and cold (Genesis 31: 40).

Prowling wild beasts were a danger to his flock and to himself. He was constantly on his guard against lions, leopards, and bears (1 Samuel 17: 34; Isaiah 31: 4; Jeremiah 5: 6; Amos 5: 12).

Shepherds' equipment

A SHEPHERD'S BAG
A shepherd's bag, containing a small amount of food.

"Then he took his staff in his hand and chose five smooth stones out of the brook and put them in his shepherd's [lunch] bag [a whole kid's skin slung from his shoulder], in his pouch, and his sling was in his hand, and he drew near the Philistine" 1 Samuel 17: 40 AB

A SLING
A sling, which is still the favorite weapon of the Bedouin shepherd.

A STAFF
A staff, which was used as weapon against enemies and a crook to look after his flock with.

"Yes, though I walk through the [deep, sunless] valley of the shadow of death, I will fear or dread no evil, for You are with me; Your rod [to protect] and Your staff [to guide], they comfort me" Psalm 23: 4 AB

"So I [Zechariah] shepherded the flock of slaughter, truly [as the name implies] the most miserable of sheep. And I took two [shepherd's] staffs, the one I called Beauty or Grace and the other I called Bands or Union; and I fed and shepherded the flock" Zechariah 11: 7 AB.

The shepherd's routine

THE MORNING
In the morning he led his flock from the fold (John 10: 4) which he did by going in front of them and calling to them, as is still usual in the East.

"I ASSURE you, most solemnly I tell you, he who does not enter by the door into the sheepfold, but climbs up some other way (elsewhere, from some other quarter) is a thief and a robber.

2 But he who enters by the door is the shepherd of the sheep.

3 The watchman opens the door for this man, and the sheep listen to his voice and heed it; and he calls his own sheep by name and brings (leads) them out."

John 10: 1–3 AB

If any sheep stray, he went and searched for them until he found them (Ezekiel 34: 12; Luke 15: 4).

The shepherd found water for his sheep, either from a stream or troughs attached to wells (Genesis 29: 7; 30: 38; Exodus 2: 16; Psalms 23: 2).

THE EVENING
In the evening he brought them back to the fold, and checked that none

were missing, by passing them "under the rod" as they entered the door of the enclosure (Leviticus 27: 32; Ezekiel 20: 37) checking each sheep, as it passed, by a motion of the hand, (Jeremiah 33: 13). He guarded the entrance of the fold through the night by sleeping across its opening.

Caring shepherds

Shepherds were gentle toward the young and sick sheep (Isaiah 40: 11).

"He will feed His flock like a shepherd: He will gather the lambs in His arm, He will carry them in His bosom and will gently lead those that have their young" Isaiah 40: 11 AB

Shepherds demonstrated their care for their sheep by:

- Knowing them individually. John 10: 14.
- Going before and leading them. Ps. 77: 20; 78: 52; 80: 1.
- Seeking out good pasture for them. 1 Chr. 4: 39–41; Ps. 23: 2.
- Numbering them when they return from pasture. Jer. 33: 13.
- Watching over them by night. Luke 2: 8.
- Tenderness to the ewes, and to the young. Gen. 33: 13,14; Ps. 78: 71.
- Defending them when attacked by wild beasts. 1 Sam. 17: 34–36; Amos 3: 12.

"And David said to Saul, Your servant kept his father's sheep. And when there came a lion or again a bear and took a lamb out of the flock,

35 I went out after it and smote it and delivered the lamb out of its mouth; and when it arose against me, I caught it by its beard and smote it and killed it.

36 Your servant killed both the lion and the bear; and this uncircumcised Philistine shall be like one of them, for he has defied the armies of the living God!"

1 Samuel 17: 34–36 AB

- Searching for them out when lost. Ezek. 34: 12; Luke 15: 4,5.
- Attending to them when sick. Ezek. 34: 16.

Illustrative

- Of God as leader of Israel. Ps. 77: 20; 80: 1.
- Of Christ as the good shepherd. Ezek. 34: 23; Zech. 13: 7; John 10: 14; Heb. 13: 20.
- Of kings as the leaders of the people. Is. 44: 28; Jer. 6: 3; 49: 19.
- Of ministers of the gospel. Jer. 23: 4.
- (Searching for stray sheep,) of Christ seeking the lost. Ezek. 34: 12; Luke 15: 2–7.
- (Their care and tenderness,) of tenderness of Christ. Is. 40: 11; Ezek. 34: 13–16.
- (Ignorant and foolish,) of bad ministers. Is. 56: 11; Jer. 50: 6; Ezek. 34: 2,10; Zech. 11: 7,8,15–17.

"Yes, the dogs are greedy; they never have enough. And such are the shepherds who cannot understand; they have all turned to their own way, each one to his own gain, from every quarter [one and all]" Isaiah 56: 11 AB.

"My people have been lost sheep; their shepherds have led them astray" Zechariah 11: 6 AB.

Music (1)

Overview

FIRST MENTION OF MUSIC
"His brother's name was Jubal; he was the father of all those who play the lyre and pipe" Genesis 4: 21 NASB.

Musical instruments

CYMBALS
1 Chr. 16: 5; Ps. 150: 5.

TRUMPET

HORN
Ps. 98: 6; Hos. 5: 8.
"With trumpets and the sound of the horn
Shout joyfully before the King, the Lord" Psalm 98: 6 NASB.

FLUTE

HARP

LYRE

PIPES

ZITHER
"As soon as you hear the sound of the horn, flute, zither, lyre, harp, pipes and all kinds of music, you must fall down and worship the image of gold that King Nebuchadnezzar has set up" Daniel 3: 5 NIV.

TEN-STRINGED HARP
"Give thanks to the Lord with the lyre; sing praises to Him with the harp of ten strings" Psalm 33: 2 AB.

TAMBOURINE
"Praise Him with tambourine and

[single or group] dance; praise Him with stringed and wind instruments or flutes!" Psalm 150: 4 AB.

TIMBREL
"The mirth of the timbrels is stilled, the noise of those who rejoice ends, the joy of the lyre is stopped" Isaiah 24: 8 AB.

CASTANETS
"And David and all the house of Israel played before the Lord with all their might, with songs, lyres, harps, tambourines, castanets, and cymbals" 2 Samuel 6: 5 AB.

Musical instruments were made from

ALMUG WOOD
"Of the almug wood the king made pillars for the house of the Lord and for the king's house, and lyres also and harps for the singers. No such almug wood came again or has been seen to this day" 1 Kings 10: 12 AB.

SILVER
"Make two trumpets of silver; of hammered or turned work you shall make them, that you may use them to call the congregation and for breaking camp" Numbers 10: 2 AB.

HORNS OF ANIMALS
"When Joshua had spoken to the people, the seven priests bearing the seven trumpets of rams' horns passed on before the Lord and blew the trumpets, and the ark of the covenant of the Lord followed them" Joshua 6: 8 AB.

Various uses of musical instruments

TO THANK GOD FOR DELIVERANCE
"THEN MOSES and the Israelites sang this song to the Lord, saying, I will sing to the Lord, for He has triumphed gloriously; the horse and his rider or its chariot has He thrown into the sea.

2 The Lord is my Strength and my Song, and He has become my Salvation; this is my God, and I will praise Him, my father's God, and I will exalt Him.

3 The Lord is a Man of War; the Lord is His name."

Exodus 15: 1–3 AB

FOR WORSHIP IN THE TEMPLE
"He appointed Levites to minister before the ark of the Lord and to celebrate [by calling to mind], thanking and praising the Lord, the God of Israel:

5 Asaph was the chief, next to him Zechariah, Jeiel (Jaaziel), Shemiramoth, Jehiel, Mattithiah, Eliab, and Benaiah, Obed-edom and Jeiel, who were to play harps and lyres; Asaph was to sound the cymbals;

6 Benaiah and Jahaziel the priests were to blow trumpets continually before the ark of the covenant of God."

1 Chronicles 16: 4–6 AB

"And, said David, 4,000 shall be gatekeepers and 4,000 are to praise the Lord with the instruments which I made for praise.

6 And David organized them in sections according to the sons of Levi: Gershon, Kohath, and Merari."

1 Chronicles 23: 5,6 AB

"ALSO DAVID and the chiefs of the host [of the Lord] separated to the [temple] service some of the sons of Asaph, Heman, and Jeduthun, who should prophesy [being inspired] with lyres, harps, and cymbals. The list of the musicians according to their service was."

1 Chronicles 25: 1 AB

"Hezekiah stationed the Levites in the Lord's house with cymbals, harps, and lyres, as David [his forefather] and Gad the king's seer and Nathan the prophet had commanded; for the commandment was from the Lord through His prophets"

2 Chronicles 29: 25 AB

WHEN FRIENDS LEFT
"Why did you flee secretly and cheat me and did not tell me, so that I might have sent you away with joy and gladness and with singing, with tambourine and lyre?"

Genesis 31: 27 AB

IN SACRED PROCESSIONS
2 Sam. 6: 4,5,15; 1 Chr. 13: 6–8; 15: 27,28.

AT THE LAYING OF THE FOUNDATION OF THE TEMPLE.
Ezra 3: 9,10.

Quote Unquote

"The aim and final end of all music should be none other than the glory of God and the refreshment of the soul. If heed is not paid to this, it is not true music but a diabolical bawling and twanging."

J.S. Bach

Music (2)

Various uses of musical instruments, continued

AT THE CONSECRATION OF THE TEMPLE

"And all the Levites who were singers–all of those of Asaph, Heman, and Jeduthun, with their sons and kinsmen, arrayed in fine linen, having cymbals, harps, and lyres – stood at the east end of the altar, and with them 120 priests blowing trumpets;

13 And when the trumpeters and singers were joined in unison, making one sound to be heard in praising and thanking the Lord, and when they lifted up their voice with the trumpets and cymbals and other instruments for song and praised the Lord, saying, For He is good, for His mercy and loving-kindness endure forever, then the house of the Lord was filled with a cloud,

14 So that the priests could not stand to minister because of the cloud, for the glory of the Lord filled the house of God."

2 Chronicles 5: 12–14 AB

AT CORONATION OF KINGS
2 Chr. 23: 11,13.

AT DEDICATION OF CITY WALLS
Neh. 12: 27,28.

TO CELEBRATE VICTORIES
Ex. 15: 20; 1 Sam. 18: 6,7.

IN RELIGIOUS FEASTS
2 Chr. 30: 21.

IN PRIVATE, FOR PERSONAL PLEASURE
Is. 5: 12; Amos 6: 5.

IN DANCES
Matt. 11: 17; Luke 15: 25.

IN FUNERAL CEREMONIES
Matt. 9: 23.

IN COMMEMORATING GREAT MEN
2 Chr. 35: 25.

IN IDOL WORSHIP
Dan. 3: 5.

TO DIRECT THE MOVEMENT OF ARMIES

"And if the war bugle gives an uncertain (indistinct) call, who will prepare for battle?" 1 Corinthians 14: 8 AB.

No music

In times of affliction music was not played.

"On the willow trees in the midst of [Babylon] we hung our harps.

3 For there they who led us captive required of us a song with words, and our tormentors and they who wasted us required of us mirth, saying, Sing us one of the songs of Zion.

4 How shall we sing the Lord's song in a strange land?"

Psalm 137: 2–4 AB

THE CESSATION OF MUSIC MARKED A CALAMITY
"The mirth of the timbrels is stilled, the noise of those who rejoice ends, the joy of the lyre is stopped" Isaiah 24: 8 AB.

"And the sound of harpists and minstrels and flute players and trumpeters shall never again be heard in you" Revelation 18: 22 AB.

Music illustrated

- Joy and gladness
  Zeph. 3: 17; Eph. 5: 19.

- Heavenly happiness
  "And when He had taken the scroll, the four living creatures and the twenty-four elders [of the heavenly Sanhedrin] prostrated themselves before the Lamb. Each was holding a harp (lute or guitar), and they had golden bowls full of incense (fragrant spices and gums for burning), which are the prayers of God's people (the saints).

  9 And [now] they sing a new song, saying, You are worthy to take the scroll and to break the seals that are on it, for You were slain (sacrificed), and with Your blood You purchased men unto God from every tribe and language and people and nation."
  Revelation 5: 8,9 AB

The golden age of Hebrew music

The period of Samuel, David, and Solomon was the golden age of Hebrew music, as it was of Hebrew poetry.

Music was an essential part of training in the schools of the prophets (1 Sam. 10: 5; 19: 19–24; 2 Kings 3: 15; 1 Chr. 25: 6).

A class of professional singers arose (2 Sam. 19: 35; Eccl. 2: 8).

The temple was the great school of music. During temple services large choirs of trained singers and instrumentalists were constantly used (2 Sam. 6: 5; 1 Chr. 15; 16; 23: 5; 25: 1–6).

In private life music was greatly appreciated by the Jews (Eccl. 2: 8; Amos 6: 4–6; Is. 5: 11,12; 24: 8, 9; Ps. 137; Jer. 48: 33; Luke 15: 25).

Music and worship

Some of the psalms greatly encourage the use of musical instruments in our praise of God.

"PRAISE THE Lord! Praise God in His sanctuary; praise Him in the heavens of His power!

2 Praise Him for His mighty acts; praise Him according to the abundance of His greatness!

3 Praise Him with trumpet sound; praise Him with lute and harp!

4 Praise Him with tambourine and [single or group] dance; praise Him with stringed and wind instruments or flutes!

5 Praise Him with resounding cymbals; praise Him with loud clashing cymbals!

6 Let everything that has breath and every breath of life praise the Lord! Praise the Lord! (Hallelujah!)"
Psalm 150: 1–6 AB

Quote Unquote

"Next to the Word of God, the noble art of music is the greatest treasure in the world."
Martin Luther

Part Two
Facts From The Whole Bible

Part Two Contents in summary

Bible statistics 302

Bible inspiration 318

Understanding the Bible 324

Bible reading 336

Bible study 366

Basic Bible teaching 376

Bible teaching in a catechism 510

Prayer 536

Key Bible words 542

Father, Son, and Holy Spirit 594

Persecution and martyrdom 630

Prophecy and prophets 642

Types of literature and typology 652

Supernatural events 672

Part Two
Facts From The Whole Bible

Part Two Contents in Summary

Part Two Contents in detail

Bible statistics

Basic questions (Q) about the Bible answered (A) 302

Facts about the Bible 304

Bible statistics of the whole Bible (1) 306

Bible statistics of the whole Bible (2) 308

Links between the New Testament and the Old Testament (1) 310

Links between the New Testament and the Old Testament (2) 312

Links between the New Testament and the Old Testament (3) 314

Links between the New Testament and the Old Testament (4) 316

Bible inspiration

The importance of the Bible (1) 318

The importance of the Bible (2) 320

The inspiration of the Bible 322

Understanding the Bible

Understanding the Bible (1) 324

Understanding the Bible (2) 326

Understanding the Bible (3) 328

Quotations in the New Testament (1) 330

Quotations in the New Testament (2) 332

Interpreting the Bible 334

Bible reading

Bible reading (1) 336

Bible reading (2) 338

Bible reading (3) 340

Bible reading (4) 342

Bible readings in times of need (1) 344

Bible readings in times of need (2) 346

Bible readings in times of need (3) 348

Bible readings in times of need (4) 350

Bible readings in times of need (5) 352

Bible reading schedules (1)..354

Bible reading schedules (2) 356

Bible reading schedules (3) 358

Bible reading schedules (4)...360

Bible reading schedules (5) 362

Bible reading schedules (6)...364

Bible study

Bible study (1)..366

Bible study (2) 368

Memorizing the Bible..370

Meditating on the Bible (1)..372

Meditating on the Bible (2) 374

Basic Bible teaching

What the Bible says about (1)..376

What the Bible says about (2) 378

What the Bible says about (3)..380

What the Bible says about (4) 382

What the Bible says about (5)..384

What the Bible says about (6) 386

What the Bible says about (7)..388

What the Bible says about (8) 390

What the Bible says about (9) 392

What the Bible says about (10) 394

What the Bible says about (11)..396

What the Bible says about (12) 398

What the Bible says about (13)...400

What the Bible says about (14) 402

What the Bible says about (15) 404

What the Bible says about (16) 406

What the Bible says about (17) 408

What the Bible says about (18) 410

What the Bible says about (19) 412

What the Bible says about (20) 414

What the Bible says about (21) 416

What the Bible says about (22)...418

What the Bible says about (23)...420

What the Bible says about (24)...422

What the Bible says about (25)...424

What the Bible says about (26)...426

What the Bible says about (27)...428

What the Bible says about (28)...430

What the Bible says about (29)...432

What the Bible says about (30)...434

What the Bible says about (31)...436

What the Bible says about (32)...438

What the Bible says about (33) 440

What the Bible says about (34)...442

What the Bible says about (35) 444

What the Bible says about (36)...446

What the Bible says about (37) 448

What the Bible says about (38)...450

What the Bible says about (39)...452

What the Bible says about (40) 454

What the Bible says about (41) 456

What the Bible says about (42)...458

What the Bible says about (43)...460

What the Bible says about (44)...462

What the Bible says about (45)...464

What the Bible says about (46)..466

What the Bible says about (47)..468

What the Bible says about (48)..470

What the Bible says about (49)..472

What the Bible says about (50)..474

What the Bible says about (51) 476

What the Bible says about (52)..478

What the Bible says about (53) 480

What the Bible says about (54)..482

What the Bible says about (55)..484

What the Bible says about (56)..486

What the Bible says about (57)..488

What the Bible says about (58)..490

What the Bible says about (59)..492

What the Bible says about (60) 494

What the Bible says about (61) 496

What the Bible says about (62)..498

What the Bible says about (63)..500

What the Bible says about (64)..502

What the Bible says about (65)..504

What the Bible says about (66)..506

What the Bible says about (67)..508

Bible teaching in a catechism

The Heidelberg Catechism: Questions 1–8................................510

The Heidelberg Catechism: Questions 9–20 512

The Heidelberg Catechism: Questions 21–27.............................514

The Heidelberg Catechism: Questions 28–35 516

The Heidelberg Catechism: Questions 36–45 518

The Heidelberg Catechism: Questions 46–53 520

The Heidelberg Catechism: Questions 54–61..............................522

The Heidelberg Catechism: Questions 62–71.............................524

The Heidelberg Catechism: Questions 72–78 526

The Heidelberg Catechism: Questions 79–84 528

The Heidelberg Catechism: Questions 85–92 530

The Heidelberg Catechism: Questions 93–100 532

The Heidelberg Catechism: Questions 101–110 534

Prayer

All the prayers in the Bible (1) 536

All the prayers in the Bible (2)...538

All the prayers in the Bible (3)...540

Key Bible words

Glossary of doctrinal words in the Bible (1)...............................542

Glossary of doctrinal words in the Bible (2) 544

Glossary of doctrinal words in the Bible (3)...............................546

Glossary of doctrinal words in the Bible (4) 548

Glossary of doctrinal words in the Bible (5)...............................550

Glossary of doctrinal words in the Bible (6) 552

Glossary of doctrinal words in the Bible (7)...............................554

Glossary of doctrinal words in the Bible (8) 556

Glossary of doctrinal words in the Bible (9) 558

Glossary of doctrinal words in the Bible (10) 560

Glossary of doctrinal words in the Bible (11)..............................562

Glossary of doctrinal words in the Bible (12) 564

Glossary of doctrinal words in the Bible (13) 566

Glossary of doctrinal words in the Bible (14) 568

Glossary of doctrinal words in the Bible (15) 570

Glossary of doctrinal words in the Bible (16) 572

Glossary of doctrinal words in the Bible (17) 574

Glossary of doctrinal words in the Bible (18) 576

Glossary of doctrinal words in the Bible (19) 578

Glossary of doctrinal words in the Bible (20) 580

Glossary of doctrinal words in the Bible (21) 582

Glossary of doctrinal words in the Bible (22)..............................584

Glossary of doctrinal words in the Bible (23)..............................586

Glossary of doctrinal words in the Bible (24)..............................588

Glossary of doctrinal words in the Bible (25)..............................590

Glossary of doctrinal words in the Bible (26)..............................592

Father, Son, and Holy Spirit

The attributes of God the Father (1)..............................594

The attributes of God the Father (2) 596

The attributes of God the Father (3) 598

Titles, descriptions and names of Christ (1) 600

Titles, descriptions and names of Christ (2)..............................602

Titles, descriptions and names of Christ (3)..............................604

Titles, descriptions and names of Christ (4)..............................606

Titles, descriptions and names of Christ (5)..............................608

Titles, descriptions and names of Christ (6)..............................610

Titles, descriptions and names of Christ (7)..............................612

Titles, descriptions and names of Christ (8)..............................614

Titles, descriptions and names of Christ (9)..............................616

Titles, descriptions and names of Christ (10) 618

Titles, descriptions and names of Christ (11) 620

Titles, descriptions and names of Christ (12)..............................622

The attributes of God the Holy Spirit (1) 624

The attributes of God the Holy Spirit (2)..............................626

The Trinity 628

Persecution and martyrdom

Persecution (1)..............................630

Persecution (2) 632

Persecution (3)..............................634

Bible martyrs (1) 636

Bible martyrs (2) 638

Bible martyrs (3) 640

Prophecy and prophets

Prophecy...642

Prophets (1)...644

Prophets (2)...646

Prophets (3)...648

Prophets (4)...650

Types of literature and typology

Poetry...652

Idioms and figures of speech (1)......................654

Idioms and figures of speech (2)......................656

Idioms and figures of speech (3)......................658

Idioms and figures of speech (4)......................660

Idioms and figures of speech (5)......................662

Old Testament parables................................664

Typology (1)..666

Typology (2)..668

Types of Christ.......................................670

Supernatural events

Miracles..672

Old Testament miracles................................674

Miracles performed by God's followers (1).............676

Miracles performed by God's followers (2).............678

Miracles performed by God's followers (3).............680

Visions (1)...682

Visions (2)...684

Visions (3)...686

Dreams..688

Basic questions (Q) about the Bible answered (A)

Q: *How many books are in the Bible?*
A: There are sixty-six books in the Bible.

Q: *How many books are there in the Old Testament?*
A: There are thirty-nine books in the Old Testament.

Q: *How many books are there in the New Testament?*
A: There are twenty-seven books in the New Testament.

Q: *What does "testament" mean?*
A: Testament means "covenant" or "contract."

Q: *Who wrote the Bible?*
A1: The Bible was written under the inspiration of the Holy Spirit.
A2: The Bible was written by over 40 authors.

Q: *What kinds of people wrote the Bible?*
A: People from all walks of life:
• doctors
• farmers
• fishermen
• kings
• military leaders
• philosophers
• priests
• shepherds
• tent-makers
• theologians

Q: *Who wrote the most in the Old Testament?*
A: Moses. He wrote the first five books of the Bible.

Q: *Who wrote the most number of books in the New Testament?*
A: Paul. He wrote thirteen books of the New Testament.

Q: *Who wrote the most number of verses in the New Testament?*
A: Luke. Luke wrote the Gospel bearing his name and the book of Acts. These amount to 28% of the New Testament.
  Paul's thirteen letters add up to 2,033 verses, but Luke's Gospel and Acts add up to 2,138 verses.

Q: *When was the Bible written?*
A: The Bible was written over a period of about 1,550 years.
  The first Old Testament books were probably written around 1450 B.C.
  The last New Testament book was probably written before A.D. 100.

Q: *Which is the oldest book in the Old Testament?*
A1: Job. The book of Job is anonymous and although scholars disagree about the exact date of its writing many of them believe that it was the first book of the Bible to be written.
A2: Genesis, Exodus, Leviticus, Numbers, and Deuteronomy. Those

who do not think that Job is the oldest book usually say that the first five books of the Bible are the oldest books.

Q: *Which is the last Old Testament book to have been written?*

A: The book of Malachi. It was written around 400 B.C.

Q: *Which languages were the books of the Bible originally written in?*

A: Nearly all of the Old Testament was written in Hebrew. There are a handful of verses in Aramaic.

All of the New Testament was written in Greek.

Q: *When was the first translation of the Bible made into English?*

A: In 1382, by John Wycliffe.

Q: *When was the Bible first printed?*

A: The first printed Bible was produced in 1454 by Johannes Gutenberg.

Q: *What is the oldest copy (or nearly complete copy) of the Old Testament?*

A: The *Codex Vaticanus*, A.D. 350. It is now housed in the library of the Vatican in Rome.

Q: *What is the oldest copy of any part of the Old Testament?*

A: Fragments of the Bible from the Dead Sea Scrolls which have been dated back to the 2nd century B.C.

Q: *What is the oldest fragment of the New Testament?*

A: A scrap of John's Gospel, found in Egypt, has been dated back to around A.D. 125. It is now housed in the Rayland's Library in Manchester, England.

Q: *Which is the longest book in the Bible?*

A: The book of Psalms.

Q: *Which is the shortest book in the Bible?*

A: 2 John.

Q: *Which is the longest chapter in the Bible?*

A: Psalm 119.

Q: *Which is the shortest chapter in the Bible?*

Psalm 117.
"Praise God, everybody!
Applaud God, all people!
His love has taken over our lives;
God's faithful ways are eternal.
Hallelujah!"

The Message

Q: *Which is the longest verse in the Bible?*

A: Esther 8: 9.

Q: *Which is the shortest verse in the Bible?*

A: John 11: 35.

Q: *Which books in the Bible do not mention the word "God?"*

A: The book of Esther and Song of Solomon.

Facts about the Bible

Number of Old Testament chapters

The average number of chapters in the books of Old Testament is just under twenty-four chapters, 23.8 chapters, to be precise.

Jeremiah

There are seven different Jeremiahs in the Bible! (1 Chronicles 5: 24; 12: 4, 10, 13; 2 Kings 23: 30; Jeremiah 1: 1; 35: 3).

Jeremiah's 15 recorded prayers make him the "praying prophet" as well as the "weeping prophet."

No mention of God

Esther and Song of Solomon are the only two books in the Old Testament (and the whole bible) that do not mention God.

Hebrews

Hebrews has approximately 102 references to the Old Testament. Hebrews uses over 20 different names and titles for Jesus Christ.

2 Timothy

2 Timothy is the most personal of the pastoral epistles. It mentions twenty-three people, and twelve of those people are not mentioned anywhere else in the New Testament.

Colossians

The book of Colossians has some interesting words.

There are fifty-five words used in Colossians that Paul uses nowhere else!

Revelation

Revelation has more references to the Old Testament, a total of 278, than any other New Testament book!

Galatians

Galatians has no praise or prayer of thanksgiving.

Romans

More Old Testament quotations are used by Paul in Romans than in all his other letters put together. Romans is the longest New Testament letter with 7,100 words.

Paul

Paul was a man of four cultures: a Roman citizen, a Jew who spoke Greek as well as Hebrew and a Christian.

People and places

There are nearly 3000 different people and more than 1,500 places cited in the Bible.

Breakdown of Bible

These statistics are based on the King James Version of the Bible.

Bible books

The Bible contains 66 books:
   39 in the Old Testament
   27 in the New Testament

From chapters to letters

In the whole Bible there are:
   1,189 chapters
   31,173 verses
   774,746 words
   3,566,480 letters

Breakdown of the Old Testament

39 Books
929 Chapters
23,214 Verses

593,493 Words
2,278,100 Letters

Type of books
17 historical books
5 poetic books
17 prophetic books

Middles
The middle book of the Old Testament
is Proverbs.
Middle chapter: Job 20.
Middle verses: 2 Chronicles 20: 17,18.

Shortest and longest
Shortest book: Obadiah.
Longest book: Psalms.
The shortest verse in the Old Testament
is 1 Chr. 1: 25.
The longest verse in the Old Testament
is Esther 8: 9, (89 words, 425 letters).

*Old Testament writers often mentioned each
other*

- The five books of the Law are
  mentioned in Joshua 1: 7; 8: 31; 23: 6;
  1 Kings 2: 3; 2 Kings 14: 6; 17: 37; 18: 6;
  1 Chronicles 16: 40; 2 Chronicles 17: 9;
  23: 18; 30: 5,16,18; 31: 3; 35: 26; Ezra
  3: 2,4; 6: 18; 7: 6; Daniel 9: 11,13; Hosea
  8: 12.
- Ezra is mentioned in Nehemiah 8: 1;
  Nehemiah 12: 32.
- Nehemiah is mentioned in Ezra 2: 2.
- Isaiah is mentioned in 2 Kings 19: 2;
  2 Chronicles 32: 20.
- Jeremiah is mentioned in Daniel 9: 2;
  2 Chronicles 36: 22.
- Jonah is mentioned in 2 Kings 14: 25.
- Micah: is mentioned in Jeremiah
  26: 18.
- Haggai is mentioned in Ezra 5: 1; Ezra
  6: 14.
- Zechariah is mentioned in Nehemiah
  12: 1,4,16, Ezra 5: 1; 6: 14.

Breakdown of the New Testament

27 Books
260 Chapters
7,959 Verses
181,253 Words
838,380 Letters

Type of books
4 Gospels
1 historical book
22 letters
1 apocalyptic book

Middles
The middle book of New Testament is
2 Thessalonians.
The middle chapters of the New
Testament are Romans 8 and 9.
Middle verse: Acts 27: 17

Shortest and longest

Longest chapter: Luke 1.

Shortest and longest books
Shortest book: 3 John, counting words.
Shortest book: 2 John, counting verses.
Longest book: Luke.

Shortest and longest verses
The shortest verse is John 11: 35.
The longest verse is Revelation 20: 4,
with 68 words.

NUMBERS
43: The four Gospels make up 43% of
the New Testament
12: Acts makes up 12% of the New
Testament.
38: The 21 letters make up 38% of the
New Testament.
7: The book of Revelation makes up 7%
of the New Testament.

Bible statistics of the whole Bible (1)

> **Key Bible verse**
> "I will delight myself in thy statutes: I will not forget thy word." Psalm 119: 16

Middles

MIDDLE BOOKS
The middle books of the whole Bible are Micah and Nahum.

MIDDLE CHAPTER
Psalm 118 is the middle chapter of the entire bible.

MIDDLE VERSE
The middle verse of the entire Bible is Psalm 118: 8.

The Bible has 594 chapters before Psalm 118 and 594 chapters after Psalm 118.

All the chapters of the Bible, except Psalm 118, add up to a total of 1188 chapters.

11:88, or Psalm 118 verse 8 is the middle verse of the entire Bible.

The contents of Psalm 118: 8 could be said to be the central message of the Bible:

"It is better to take refuge in the Lord than to trust in man." Psalm 118: 8

Shortest and longest

SHORTEST AND LONGEST BOOKS
The little New Testament letter, 3 John, counting words, is the shortest book in the Bible.

The psalms are the longest book.

SHORTEST AND LONGEST CHAPTERS
Psalm 117 is the shortest chapter in the Bible.

Psalm 119 is the longest chapter in the Bible.

SHORTEST AND LONGEST VERSES
The longest verse in the entire Bible is Esth. 8: 9.

The shortest verse in the Bible is John 11: 35, "Jesus wept."

The shortest verse in the New International Version is Job 3: 2: "Job said,".

Ten longest books in the Bible

The number of chapters in a book does not necessarily indicate the length of the book. For example, Isaiah has 66 chapters, amounting to 37,044 words, but the 50 chapters of Genesis amount to 38,267 words.

In the same way the Acts of the Apostles is often said to be the longest book in the New Testament, as its twenty-eight chapters are more than any other New Testament book. However, it has 1,007 verses, which amount to 24,250 words, whereas although Luke only has twenty-four chapters, Luke has 1,151 verses which amount to 25,944 words. So, in this sense, it is correct to say that Luke is the longest New Testament book.

1. PSALMS
150 chapters, 2,461 verses, 43,743 words.

2. JEREMIAH
52 chapters, 1,364 verses, 42,659 words.

3. EZEKIEL
48 chapters, 1,273 verses, 39,407 words.

4. GENESIS
50 chapters, 1,533 verses, 38,267 words.

5. ISAIAH
66 chapters, 1,292 verses, 37,044 words.

6. NUMBERS
36 chapters, 1,288 verses, 32,902 words.

7. EXODUS
40 chapters, 1,213 verses, 32.602 words.

8. DEUTERONOMY
34 chapters, 959 verses, 28,461 words.

9. 2 CHRONICLES
36 chapters, 822 verses, 26,074 words.

10. LUKE
24 chapters, 1,151 verses, 25,944 words.

Ten shortest books in the Bible

1. 3 John
1 chapter, 14 verses, 299 words.

2. 2 JOHN
1 chapter, 13 verses, 303 words.

3. PHILEMON
1 chapter, 25 verses, 445 words.

4. JUDE
1 chapter, 25 verses, 613 words.

5. OBADIAH
1 chapter, 21 verses, 670 words.

6. TITUS
3 chapters, 46 verses, 921 words.

7. 2 THESSALONIANS
3 chapters, 47 verses, 1,042 words.

8. HAGGAI
2 chapters, 38 verses, 1,131 words.

9. NAHUM
3 chapters, 47 verses, 1,285 words.

10. JONAH
4 chapters, 48 verses, 1,321 words.

Only one appearance

Words that appear only once in Bible:
- Reverend Psalms 111: 9
- Eternity Isaiah 57: 15
- Grandmother 2 Timothy 1: 5

Twenty-three letters of the alphabet

A number of verses in the Bible contain all but one letter of the alphabet:

ALL BUT J

Ezra 7: 21 contains all the letters of the alphabet except the letter j.

"And I, even I Artaxerxes the king, do make a decree to all the treasurers which are beyond the river, that whatsoever Ezra the priest, the scribe of the law of the God of heaven, shall require of you, it be done speedily."

ALL BUT Q

Joshua 7: 24, 1 Kings 1: 9, 1 Chronicles 12: 40, 2 Chronicles 36: 10, Ezekiel 28: 13, Daniel 4: 37, and Haggai 1: 1 contain all the letters of the alphabet except the letter q.

ALL BUT Z

2 Kings 16: 15 and 1 Chronicles 4: 10 contain all the letters of the alphabet except the letter z.

ALL BUT K

Galatians 1: 14. "And profited in the Jews' religion above many my equals in mine own nation, being more exceedingly zealous of the traditions of my fathers."

Bible statistics of the whole Bible (2)

Most mentioned humans in the Bible

- David is mentioned 1118 times.
- Moses is mentioned 740 times.
- Aaron is mentioned 339 times.
- Saul is mentioned 338 times.
- Abraham is mentioned 306 times.
- Solomon is mentioned 295 times.
- Jacob is mentioned 270 times.
- Joseph is mentioned 208 times.
- Joshua is mentioned 197 times.
- Paul is mentioned 185 times.
- Peter is mentioned 166 times.
- Joab is mentioned 137 times.
- Jeremiah is mentioned 136 times.
- Samuel is mentioned 135 times.
- Isaac is mentioned 127 times.

The second most commonly occurring name in the Bible is "Jesus," which occurs 973 times.

The ten most frequently mentioned women in the Bible

- Sarah, Abraham's wife, 57 times.
- Rachel, Jacob's second wife, 47 times.
- Leah, Jacob's first wife, 34 times.
- Rebekah, Isaac's wife, 31 times.
- Jezebel, wicked queen, 23 times.
- Mary, Jesus' mother, 19 times.
- Abigail, 15 times.
- Miriam, 15 times.
- Mary Magdalene, 14 times.
- Hagar, Abraham's concubine 14 times.
- Eve, is mentioned only 4 times.

Longest names found in the Bible

Words which are not names are excluded from this list.

18 LETTERS

JONATH-ELEM-RECHO-KIM in the title of Psalm 56. This is the name of a song and means "the silent dove of far-off places."

MAHER-SHALAL-HASH-BAZ Isaiah 8: 1. This is the name given to Isaiah's son, meaning "swift is booty, speedy is prey."

17 LETTERS

CHU-SHAN-RISH-A-THA-IM Judges 3: 8.

Top ten occurring names, by Bible book

The percentages given relate to the number of Bible books. As there are 66 Bible books and the word "God" appears in 64 of them, all except Song of Solomon and Esther, the word God is said to appear in 97% of the Bible books.

GOD appears in 64 Books of the Bible 97.0%

LORD appears in 61 Books of the Bible 92.4%

ISRAEL appears in 47 Books of the Bible 71.2%

JERUSALEM appears in 36 Books of the Bible 54.5%

MOSES appears in 31 Books of the Bible 47.0%

JACOB appears in 29 Books of the Bible 43.9%

DAVID appears in 28 Books of the Bible 42.4%

ABRAHAM appears in 27 Books of the Bible 40.9%

CHRIST appears in 26 Books of the Bible 39.4%

JESUS appears in 26 Books of the Bible 39.4%

The shortest names in the Bible

AI Joshua 7: 2

AR Numbers 21: 15

ED Joshua 22: 34

ER Genesis 38: 3

IR 1 Chronicles 7: 12

NO Jeremiah 46: 25

OG Numbers 21: 33

ON Numbers 16: 11

PE Psalm 119: 129

SO 2 Kings 17: 4

UR Genesis 11: 28

UZ Genesis 10: 23

Longest words found in the Bible

Names are excluded from this list.

16 LETTERS

COVENANTBREAKERS Rom. 1: 31

EVILFAVOUREDNESS Deut. 17: 1

LOVINGKINDNESSES Psalm 25: 6

UNPROFITABLENESS Hebrews 7: 18

15 LETTERS

ADMINISTRATIONS 1 Cor. 12: 5

BLOODGUILTINESS Psalm 51: 14

CONFECTIONARIES 1 Samuel 8: 13

FELLOWDISCIPLES John 11: 16

FELLOWLABOURERS Phil. 4: 3

FELLOWPRISONERS Romans 16: 7

INTERPRETATIONS Genesis 40: 8

KNEADINGTROUGHS Exodus 8: 3

NOTWITHSTANDING Exodus 16: 20

PROGNOSTICATORS Isaiah 47: 13

RIGHTEOUSNESSES Isaiah 64: 6

STUMBLINGBLOCKS Jeremiah 6: 21

THRESHINGFLOORS 1 Samuel 23: 1

UNRIGHTEOUSNESS Lev. 19: 15

Identical verses

In Ps. 107, vv 8,15,21,31 are identical.

Unusual things recorded in the Bible

Methuselah who lived to be 969 years old, Gen. 5: 27.

Man was spoken to by a donkey, Num. 22: 28–30.

A bed measuring 13½ feet in length and 6 feet in width, Deut. 3: 11.

Women who shaved their heads before they married, Deut. 21: 11–13.

The sun standing still for a whole day, Josh. 10: 13.

An army with 700 left-handed men, Judges 20: 16.

A man whose hair weighed about 6 pounds when it was cut annually, 2 Sam. 14: 26.

A man who had 12 fingers and 12 toes, 2 Sam. 21: 20.

Man had seven hundred wives and three hundred concubines 1 Kgs.. 11: 3

A father who had eighty-eight children, 2 Chr. 11: 21.

Army of 185,000 destroyed in one night, Is. 37: 36.

A man whose life was increased by fifteen years in answer to prayer, Is. 38: 1–5.

A day the sun went backward, Is 38: 8.

A prostitute who was an ancestor of Christ, Matt. 1: 5.

Links between the New Testament and the Old Testament (1)

Key Bible verse

"Search the scriptures; for in them ye think ye have eternal life: and they are they which testify of me."

John 5: 39

The ten Old Testament books most referred to in the New Testament

1. Isaiah
The book of Isaiah is referred to 419 times in twenty-three New Testament books.

2. Psalms
The psalms are referred to 414 times in twenty-three New Testament books.

3. Genesis
The book of Genesis is referred to 260 times in twenty-one New Testament books.

4. Exodus
The book of Exodus is referred to 250 times in nineteen New Testament books.

5. Deuteronomy
The book of Deuteronomy is referred to 208 times in twenty-one New Testament books.

6. Ezekiel
The book of Ezekiel is referred to 141 times in fifteen New Testament books.

7. Daniel
The book of Daniel is referred to 133 times in seventeen New Testament books.

8. Jeremiah
The book of Jeremiah is referred to 125 times in seventeen New Testament books.

9. Leviticus
The book of Leviticus is referred to 107 times in fifteen New Testament books.

10. Numbers
The book of Numbers is referred to 73 times in four New Testament books.

Link between different Bible books

GENESIS AND REVELATION
Many similarities and contrasts between the first book of the Old Testament and the last book of the New Testament have been noted.

1. Genesis, the book of the beginning.
1. Apocalypse, the book of the end.
2. The Earth created (1: 1).
2. The Earth passed away (21: 1).
3. Satan's first rebellion.
3. Satan's final rebellion (20: 3, 7–10).
4. Sun, moon, and stars for Earth's government (1: 14–16).
4. Sun, moon, and stars, connected with Earth's judgment (6: 13; 8: 12; 16: 8).
5. Sun to govern the day (1: 16).
5. No need of the sun (21: 23).
6. Darkness called night (1: 5).
6. "No night there" (22: 5).
7. Waters called seas (1: 10).
7. "No more sea" (21: 1).

8. A river for Earth's blessing (2: 10–14).

8. A river for the New Earth (22: 1,2).

9. Man in God's image (1: 26).

9. Man headed by one in Satan's image (13).

10. Entrance of sin (3).

10. Development and end of sin (21,22).

11. Curse pronounced (3: 14, 17).

11. "No more curse" (22: 3).

12. Death entered (3: 19).

12. "No more death" (21: 4).

13. Cherubim, first mentioned in connection with man (3: 24).

13. Cherubim, finally mentioned in connection with man (4: 6).

14. Man driven out from Eden (3: 24).

14. Man restored (22).

15. Tree of life guarded (3: 24).

15. "Right to the Tree of Life" (22: 14).

16. Sorrow and suffering enter (3: 17).

16. No more sorrow (21: 4).

17. Man's religion, art, and science, resorted to for enjoyment, apart from God (4).

17. Man's religion, luxury, art, and science, in their full glory, judged and destroyed by God (18).

18. Nimrod, a great rebel and king, and hidden anti-God, the founder of Babylon (10: 8, 9).

18. The Beast, the great rebel, a king and manifested anti-God, the reviver of Babylon (13–18).

19. A flood from God to destroy an evil generation (6–9).

19. A flood from Satan to destroy an elect generation (12).

20. The Bow, the token of God's covenant with the Earth (9: 13).

20. The Bow, betokening God's

remembrance of His covenant with the Earth (4: 3; 10: 1).

21. Sodom and Egypt, the place of corruption and temptation (13, 19).

21. Sodom and Egypt again: (spiritually representing Jerusalem) (11: 8).

22. A confederacy against Abraham's people overthrown (14).

22. A confederacy against Abraham's seed overthrown (12).

23. Marriage of first Adam (2: 18–23).

23. Marriage of last Adam (19).

24. A bride sought for Abraham's son (Isaac) and found (24).

24. A Bride made ready and brought to Abraham's Son (19: 9). See Matt. 1: 1.

25. Two angels acting for God on behalf of His people (19).

25. Two witnesses acting for God on behalf of His People (11).

26. A promised seed to possess the gate of his enemies (22: 17).

26. The promised seed coming into possession (11: 18).

27. Man's dominion ceased and Satan's begun (3: 24).

27. Satan's dominion ended, and man's restored (22).

28. The old serpent causing sin, suffering, and death (3: 1).

28. The old serpent bound for 1000 years (20: 1–3).

29. The doom of the old serpent pronounced (3: 15).

29. The doom on the old serpent executed (20: 10).

30. Sun, moon, and stars, associated with Israel (37: 9).

30. Sun, moon, and stars, associated again with Israel (12).

Links between the New Testament and the Old Testament (2)

10 New Testament books containing material from the greatest number of Old Testament books

1

Revelation has material from thirty-two Old Testament books.

2

Luke has material from thirty-one Old Testament books.

3

John has material from twenty-six Old Testament books.

4

Acts has material from twenty-five Old Testament books.

5

Mark has material from twenty-four Old Testament books.

6

Romans has material from twenty-three Old Testament books.

7

Hebrews has material from twenty-one Old Testament books.

8

1 Corinthians has material from eighteen Old Testament books.

9

James has material from seventeen Old Testament books.

10

1 Peter has material from fifteen Old Testament books.

New Testament quotations of the Old Testament

Jesus quoted from twenty-two Old Testament books.

The book of Hebrews quotes the Old Testament eight-five times.

Revelation quotes the Old Testament 245 times.

Ten Old Testament passages most frequently quoted or referred to in the New Testament

1. Psalm 110: 1

"The Lord said unto my Lord, Sit thou at my right hand, until I make thine enemies thy footstool."

This verse is quoted or referred to eighteen times in the New Testament:
Matt. 22: 44, 26: 64, Mark 12: 36, 14: 62, 16: 19, Luke 20: 42–43, 22: 69, Acts 2: 34–35, Rom. 8: 34, 1 Cor. 15: 25, Eph. 1: 20, Col. 3: 1, Heb.1: 3,13, 8: 1, 10: 12–13, 12: 2.

2. Ezekiel 1: 26–28

These verses are quoted or referred to twelve times in the New Testament:
Rev. 4: 2–3, 9–10; 5: 1,7, 13; 6: 16, 7: 10, 15, 19: 14, 21: 5.

3. Daniel 12: 1

This verse is quoted or referred to eleven times in the New Testament.
Matt. 24: 21, Mark 13: 19, Phil. 4: 3, Jude 9, Rev. 3: 5, 7: 14, 12: 7, 13: 8, 16: 18, 17: 18, 20: 12.

4. Isaiah 6: 1

This verse is quoted or referred to eleven times in the New Testament:

Rev. 4: 2, 9–10, 5: 1,7, 13, 6: 16, 7: 10, 15, 19: 4, 21: 5.

5. 2 Chronicles 18: 18; Psalms 47: 8; 1 Kings 22: 19

The above three verses are quoted or referred to eleven times in the New Testament:

Rev. 4: 2, 9–10, 5: 1,7, 13, 6: 16, 7: 10, 15, 19: 4, 21: 5.

6. Psalms 2: 7

"I will declare the decree: the Lord hath said unto me, Thou art my Son; this day have I begotten thee."

This verse is quoted or referred to ten times in the New Testament:

Matt. 3: 17, 17: 5, Mark 1: 11, 9: 7, Luke 1: 49, Acts 13: 33, Heb.1: 5, 5: 5.

7. Isaiah 53: 7

"He was oppressed, and he was afflicted, yet he opened not his mouth: he is brought as a lamb to the slaughter, and as a sheep before her shearers is dumb, so he openeth not his mouth."

This verse is quoted or referred to 10 times in the New Testament:

Matt. 26: 63, Mark 27: 12,14, Mark 14: 60–61, 15: 4–5, 1 Cor. 5: 7, 1 Peter 2: 23, Rev. 5: 6, 12, 13: 8.

8. Amos 3: 13

"Hear ye, and testify in the house of Jacob, saith the Lord GOD, the God of hosts."

This verse is quoted or referred to 10 times in the New Testament:

Rev. 1: 8, 4: 8, 13, 11: 17, 15: 3, 16: 7, 14, 19: 6, 15, 21: 22.

9. Amos 4: 13

"For, lo, he that formeth the mountains, and createth the wind, and declareth unto man what is his thought, that maketh the morning darkness, and treadeth upon the high places of the earth, The Lord, The God of hosts, is his name."

This verse is quoted or referred to 10 times in the New Testament:

2 Cor. 6: 18, Rev. 1: 8, 4: 8, 11: 17, 15: 3, 16: 7, 14, 19: 6, 15, 21: 22.

10. Leviticus 19: 18

"Thou shalt not avenge, nor bear any grudge against the children of thy people, but thou shalt love thy neighbor as thyself: I am the Lord."

This verse is quoted or referred to 10 times in the New Testament:

Matt. 5: 43, 19: 19, 22: 39, Mark 12.31,33, Luke 10: 27, Rom. 12: 19, 13: 19, Gal. 5: 14, James 2: 8.

> **Quote Unquote**
>
> "In the Old Testament the New is concealed.
> In the New Testament the Old is revealed."
>
> *Augustine of Hippo*

Links between the New Testament and the Old Testament (3)

Quotations from the Old Testament in the New Testament

The following list gives the number of direct Old Testament quotations in the New Testament. They are arranged in Bible book order of New Testament.

In addition to this list there are hundreds of allusions, verbal echoes, and non-direct quotations from the Old Testament in the New Testament

Matthew 54

Mark 28

Luke 25

John 14

Acts 40

Romans 60

1 Corinthians 17

2 Corinthians 10

Galatians 10

Ephesians 5

Philippians 0

Colossians 0

1 Thessalonians 0

2 Thessalonians 0

1 Timothy 1

2 Timothy 1

Titus 0

Philemon 0

Hebrews 37

James 4

1 Peter 12

2 Peter 1

1 John 0

2 John 0

3 John 0

Jude 0

Revelation 0

List of Old Testament Quotations and allusions in the New Testament

These quotations are arranged in Bible book order of the Old Testament.

Gen. 1: 27	Matt. 19: 4
Gen. 5: 2	Mark 10: 6
Gen. . 2: 2	Heb. 4: 4
Gen. 2: 7	1 Cor. 15: 45
Gen. 2: 24	Matt. 19: 5, Mark 10: 7–8; 1 Cor. 6: 17; Eph. 5: 31
Gen. 5: 24	Heb. 11: 5
Gen. 12: 1	Acts. 7: 3
Gen. 12: 3	Gal. 3: 8
Gen. 12: 7	Acts 7: 5
Gen. 13: 15	Gal. 3: 16
Gen. 14: 17–20	Heb. 7: 1–2
Gen. 15: 5	Rom. 4: 18
Gen. 15: 6	Rom. 4: 3,9,22; Gal. 3: 6, James 2: 23
Gen. 15: 13–14	Acts 7: 6–7
Gen. 17: 5	Rom. 4: 17
Gen. 17: 7	Gal. 3: 16
Gen. 17: 8	Acts 7: 5
Gen. 18: 10	Rom. 9: 9
Gen. 18: 14	Rom. 9: 9
Gen. 21: 10	Gal. 4: 30
Gen. 21: 22	Rom. 9: 7; Heb. 11: 18
Gen. 22: 16–17	Heb. 6: 13–14
Gen. 22: 18	Acts 3: 15
Gen. 25: 23	Rom. 9: 12
Gen. 25: 23	Rom. 9: 12
Gen. 38: 8	Luke 20: 28
Gen. 47: 31	Heb. 11: 21
Ex. 1: 8	Acts 7: 18
Ex. 2: 14	Acts 7: 27–28,38
Ex. 3: 5–10	Acts 7: 33–34

Ex. 3: 6	Matt. 22: 32	Deut. 5: 16–20	Mark 10: 1; Luke 18: 20
Ex. 3: 15	Mark 12: 26; Acts 3: 13	Deut. 5: 17	James 2: 11
Ex. 4: 16	Rom. 9: 17	Deut. 6: 4–5	Mark 12: 29–30
Ex. 5: 2	Acts 7: 30	Deut. 6: 5	Matt. 22: 37
Ex. 5: 18	James 2: 11	Deut. 6: 5	Luke 10: 27
Ex. 12: 46	John 19: 36	Deut. 6: 13	Matt. 4: 10; Luke 4: 8
Ex. 13: 2	Luke 2: 23	Deut. 6: 16	Matt. 4: 7; Luke 4: 12
Ex. 16: 18	2 Cor. 8: 15	Deut. 8: 3	Matt. 4: 4; Luke 4: 4
Ex. 19: 6	1 Pet. 2: 9	Deut. 9: 4	Rom. 10: 6
Ex. 19: 12–13	Heb. 12: 20	Deut. 9: 19	Heb. 12: 21
Ex. 20: 12	Matt. 15: 4	Deut. 17: 7	1 Cor. 5: 13
Ex. 20: 12–16	Matt. 19: 18–19	Deut. 18: 15–16	Acts 7: 37; 3: 12
Ex. 20: 13	Matt. 5: 21	Deut. 19: 15	Matt. 18: 16; 2 Cor. 13: 1
Ex. 20: 13–17	Rom. 13: 2 9	Deut. 21: 23	Gal. 3: 13
Ex. 20: 14	Matt. 5: 27	Deut. 24: 1,3	Matt. 5: 31; Matt. 19: 7;
Ex. 20: 17	Rom. 7: 7		Mark 10: 4
Ex. 21: 17	Matt. 15: 4; Mark 7: 10	Deut. 24: 14	Mark 10: 19
Ex. 21: 24	Matt. 5: 38	Deut. 25: 4	1 Cor. 9: 9; 1 Tim. 5: 18
Ex. 22: 27	Acts 23: 5	Deut. 25: 5,7	Matt. 22: 24;
Ex. 23: 20	Mark 1: 2; Luke 7: 27		Mark 12: 19
Ex. 24: 8	Heb. 9: 20	Deut. 27: 26	Gal. 3: 10
Ex. 25: 40	Heb. 8: 5	Deut. 29: 3	Rom. 11: 8
Ex. 32: 1	Acts 7: 40	Deut. 30: 12–14	Rom. 10: 6–8
Ex. 32: 6	1 Cor. 10: 17	Deut. 31: 6	Heb. 13: 5
Ex. 33: 19	Rom. 9: 15	Deut. 32: 21	Rom. 10: 19
Lev. 10: 9	Luke 1: 15	Deut. 32: 35–36	Rom. 12: 19
Lev. 12: 8	Luke 2: 24	Deut. 32: 43	Rom. 15: 10
Lev. 18: 5	Rom. 10: 5; Gal. 3: 12	1 Sam. 12: 22	Rom. 11: 2
Lev. 19: 2	1 Pet. 1: 16	1 Sam. 13: 14	Acts 13: 22
Lev. 19: 12, 30: 2	Matt. 5: 33	2 Sam. 7: 8	2 Cor. 6: 18
Lev. 19: 18	Mark 12: 33	2 Sam. 7: 14	Heb. 1: 5
Lev. 19: 18	Matt. 5: 43,19: 19; 22: 39	2 Sam. 22: 50	Rom. 15: 9
Lev. 19: 18	Mark 12: 31; Gal. 5: 14;	1 Kgs. 19: 10,12	Rom. 11: 3
	James 2: 8	1 Kgs. 19: '8	Rom. 11: 4
Lev. 23: 29	Acts 3: 23	2 Kgs. 1: 10,11	Luke 9: 54; Rev. 20: 9
Lev. 24: 20	Matt. 5: 38	1 Chr. 17: 13	Rev. 21: 7
Lev. 26: 12	2 Cor. 6: 16	2 Ch. 18: 16; 30: 2	Mark 6: 34
Num. 16	2 Tim. 2: 19	Job 5: 13	1 Cor. 3: 19
Num. 27: 17	Matt. 9: 36	Job 16: 19	Mark 11: 10
Deut. 4: 3	Mark 12: 32	Job 41: 3	Rom. 11: 35
Deut. 4: 24	Heb. 12: 29		
Deut. 5: 16	Mark 7: 10; Phil. 6: 2–3		

Links between the New Testament and the Old Testament (4)

List of Old Testament Quotations and allusions in the New Testament

Ps. 2: 1–2	Acts 4: 25–26
Ps. 2: 7	Acts 13: 33, Heb. 1: 5; 5: 5
Ps. 2: 9	Rev. 2: 26–27
Ps. 4: 5	Eph. 4: 26
Ps. 5: 10	Rom. 3: 13
Ps. 6: 9	Matt. 7: 23
Ps. 8: 3	Matt. 21: 16
Ps. 8: 5–7	Heb. 2: 6–8; 1 Cor. 15: 27
Ps. 10: 7	Rom. 3: 14
Ps. 14: 1–3	Rom. 3: 10–12
Ps. 16: 8–11	Acts 2: 25–28; 2: 31; 13: 35
Ps. 19: 5	Rom. 10: 18
Ps. 22: 2	Matt. 27: 46; Mark 15: 34
Ps. 22: 19	John 19: 24; Matt. 27: 35; Mark 15: 24; Luke 23: 24
Ps. 22: 23	Heb. 2: 12
Ps. 24: 1	1 Cor. 10: 26
Ps. 31: 6	Luke 23: 46
Ps. 32: 1–2	Rom. 4: 7–8
Ps. 34: 9	1 Pet. 2: 3
Ps. 34: 13–17	1 Pet. 3: 10–12
Ps. 34: 21	John 15: 25
Ps. 36: 2	Rom. 3: 18
Ps. 40: 10	Heb. 10: 5–7
Ps. 41: 10	John 13: 18
Ps. 42: 6, 12	Matt. 26: 38
Ps. 43: 5	Mark 14: 34
Ps. 44: 23	Rom. 8: 36
Ps. 45: 7–8	Heb. 1: 8–9
Ps. 51: 6	Rom. 3: 4
Ps. 62: 13	Matt. 16: 27
Ps. 68: 19	Eph. 4: 8
Ps. 69: 10	John 2: 17
Ps. 69: 23–24	Rom. 11: 9–10
Ps. 69: 26	Acts 1: 20
Ps. 78: 2	Matt. 13: 35
Ps. 78: 24	John 6: 31
Ps. 82: 6	John 10: 34
Ps. 86: 9	Rev. 15: 4
Ps. 91: 11–12	Matt. 4: 6; Luke 4: 10–11
Ps. 94: 11	1 Cor. 3: 20
Ps. 95: 7	Heb. 1: 6
Ps. 95: 7–11	Heb. 3: 7–11; 3: 15; 4: 3,5,7
Ps. 102: 26–28	Heb. 1: 10–12
Ps. 104: 4	Heb. 1: 7
Ps. 104: 12	Matt. 13: 32, Mark 4: 32; Luke 13: 19
Ps. 110: 1	Matt. 22: 44; Mark 12: 36; Luke 20: 42–43; Acts 2: 34–35; Heb. 1: 13
Ps. 110: 4	Heb. 5: 6,-10; Heb. 7: 17,21
Ps. 111: 2	Rev. 15: 3–4
Ps. 112: 9	2 Cor. 9: 9
Ps. 116: 10	2 Cor. 4: 13
Ps. 117: 2	Rom. 15: 11
Ps. 118: 6	Heb. 13: 6
Ps. 118: 22–23	Matt. 21: 42; Mark 12: 10–11; Luke 20: 17
Ps. 118: 22	Acts 4: 11, 1 Pet. 2: 7
Ps. 118: 25–26	Matt. 21: 9, Mark 11: 9–10; John 12: 13; Matt. 23: 39
Ps. 118: 26	Luke 13: 35; Luke 19: 38
Ps. 132: 11	Acts 2: 30
Ps. 135: 14	Heb. 10: 30
Prov. 3: 11–12	Heb. 12: 5–6
Prov. 3: 34	James 4: 6; 1 Pet. 5: 5
Prov. 11: 31	1 Pet. 4: 18

Pro 24: 12	Rom. 2: 6	Is. 59: 20–21	Rom.11: 26–27
Prov. 25: 21–22	Rom. 12: 20	Is. 61: 1–2	Luke 4: 18–19
Prov. 26: 11	2 Pet. 2: 22	Is. 62: 11	Matt. 21: 5
Is. 1: 9	Rom. 9: 29	Is. 64: 3	1 Cor. 2: 9
Is. 6: 9–10	Matt. 13: 14–15;	Is. 65: 1–2	Rom. 10: 10–21
	Mark 4: 12;	Is. 65: 17	2 Pet. 3: 13
	Acts 28: 26–27	Is. 66: 1–2	Acts 7: 49–50
Is. 6: 9	Luke 8: 10	Jer. 5: 21	Mark 8: 18
Is. 6: 10	John 12: 40	Jer. 7: 11	Mark 11: 17; Luke 19: 46
Is. 7: 14	Matt. 1: 23	Jer. 9: 23	1 Cor. 1: 31; 2 Cor. 10: 17
Is. 8: 12–13	1 Pet. 3: 14–15	Jer.31: 15	Matt. 2: 18
Is. 8: 17–18	Heb. 2: 13	Jer. 31: 31–34	Heb. 8: 8–12
Is. 8: 23–9: 1	Matt. 4: 15–16	Ezk. 11: 20	Rev. 21: 7
Is. 11: 10	Rom. 15: 12	Ezk. 37: 5, 10	Rev. 11: 11
Is. 13: 10	Matt. 24: 29;	Dan. 3: 6	Matt.13: 42,50
	Mark 13: 24–25	Dan. 7: 13	Matt. 24: 30, 26: 64;
Is. 22: 13	1 Cor. 15: 32		Mark 13: 26; 14: 62,
Is. 25: 8	1 Cor. 15: 54; Rev. 7: 17		Luke 21: 27; 22: 69
Is. 26: 19	Matt. 11: 5	Dan. 9: 27	Matt. 24: 15
Is. 26: 20	Heb. 10: 37–38	Dan. 11: 31	Mark 13: 14
Is. 28: 11–12	1 Cor. 14: 21	Hos. 2: 1,3	Rom. 9: 25–28
Is. 29: 13	Matt. 15: 8–9; Mark 1: 3,	Hos. 6: 6	Matt. 9: 13; Matt. 12: 7
	John 1: 23	Hos. 10: 8	Luke 23: 30; Rev. 6: 16
Is. 34: 4	Luke 21: 26	Hos. 11: 1	Matt. 2: 15
Is. 35: 5–6	Luke 7: 22	Hos. 13: 14	1 Cor. 15: 55
Is. 40: 6–8	1 Pet. 1: 24–25	Joel 3: 1–5	Acts 2: 17–21;
Is. 40: 13	Rom. 11: 34; 1 Cor. 2: 16		Rom. 10: 13
Is. 42: 1–4	Matt. 12: 18–21	Amos 5: 25–27	Acts 7: 42–43
Is. 45: 23	Rom. 14: 11	Amos 9: 11–12	Acts 15: 16–17
Is. 49: 6	Acts 13: 47	Jonah 2: 1	Matt. 12: 40
Is. 49: 8	2 Cor. 6: 2	Mic. 5: 1	Matt. 2: 6
Is. 52: 5	Rom. 2: 24	Mic. 7: 6	Matt. 10: 35–36
Is. 52: 7	Rom. 10: 15	Hab. 1: 5	Acts 13: 41
Is. 52: 11	2 Cor. 6: 17	Hab.2: 3–4	Rom. 1: 17; Gal. 3: 11
Is. 52: 15	Rom. 15: 21	Hag. 2: 6, 21	Heb. 12: 26
Is. 53: 1	John 12: 38; Rom. 8: 17	Zech. 8: 16	Eph. 4: 25
Is. 53: 7–8	Acts 8: 32–33	Zech. 9: 9	John 12: 15
Is. 53: 9	1 Pet. 2: 23	Zech. 11: 12–13	Matt. 27: 9–10
Is. 53: 12	Luke 22: 37	Zech. 12: 10	John 19: 37
Is. 54: 1	Gal. 4: 27	Zech. 13: 7	Matt. 26: 31;
Is. 54: 13	John 6: 45		Mark 14: 27
Is. 55: 3	Acts 13: 34	Mal. 1: 2–3	Rom. 9: 13
Is. 55: 10	2 Cor. 9: 10	Mal. 3: 1	Matt. 11: 10
Is. 56: 7	Matt. 21: 13	Mal. 3: 23–24	Matt. 17: 10–11
Is. 59: 7–8	Rom. 3: 15–17		

The importance of the Bible (1)

Overview

Christians take the Bible seriously because Jesus did.

Our view of the Bible should be molded by:
1. What Jesus said about the Scriptures.
2. What the Scriptures say about themselves.

1. What Jesus said about the Scriptures

A. SEARCH THE SCRIPTURES
"Search the scriptures; for in them ye think ye have eternal life: and they are they which testify of me."

John 5: 39

B. THE SCRIPTURES POINT TO JESUS
"And beginning at Moses and all the prophets, he expounded unto them in all the scriptures the things concerning himself."

Luke 24: 27

C. IGNORANCE OF THE SCRIPTURES BRINGS ERROR
"Jesus answered and said unto them, Ye do err, not knowing the scriptures, nor the power of God."

Matthew 22: 29

D. JESUS CAME TO FULFILL THE SCRIPTURES
"Think not that I am come to destroy the law, or the prophets: I am not come to destroy, but to fulfill. For verily I say unto you, Till heaven and earth pass, one jot or one title shall in no wise pass from the law, till all be fulfilled."

Matthew 5: 17

E. THEY WILL NEVER PASS AWAY
"And it is easier for heaven and earth to pass, than one title of the law to fail."

Luke 16: 17

"Heaven and earth will pass away, but my words will not pass away."

Matthew 24: 35

F. THE SCRIPTURES CANNOT BE BROKEN
"The Scripture cannot be broken."

John 10: 35

G. THE SCRIPTURES ARE THE FINAL AUTHORITY
"But he answered and said, It is written, Man shall not live by bread alone, but by every word that proceedeth out of the mouth of God.

Jesus said unto him, It is written again, Thou shalt not tempt the Lord thy God.

Then saith Jesus unto him, Get thee hence, Satan: for it is written, Thou shalt worship the Lord thy God, and him only shalt thou serve."

Matthew 4: 4,7,10

H. THE SCRIPTURES ARE HISTORICALLY TRUE
"For as Jonas was three days and three nights in the whale's belly; so shall the Son of man be three days and three nights in the heart of the earth"

Matthew 12: 40."

I. THE SCRIPTURES ARE TRUE
"Sanctify them through thy truth: thy word is truth."

John 17: 17

2. What the Bible says about itself

A. THE BIBLE IS GOD-INSPIRED

"All Scripture is given by inspiration of God, and is profitable for doctrine, for reproof, for correction, for instruction in righteousness: That the man of God may be perfect, thoroughly furnished unto all good works."

2 Timothy 3: 16

B. THE BIBLE WAS ORIGINALLY WRITTEN BY MEANS OF THE HOLY SPIRIT

"Knowing this first, that no prophecy of the Scripture is of any private interpretation. For the prophecy came not in old time by the will of man: but holy men of God spake as they were moved by the Holy Spirit."

2 Peter 1: 20

C. THE BIBLE MAKES PEOPLE WISE

"The law of the Lord is perfect, converting the soul: the testimony of the Lord is sure, making wise the simple."

Psalms 19: 7

D. THE BIBLE DELIVERS HAMMER BLOWS

"Is not my word like fire, says the Lord, and like a hammer which breaks the rock in pieces?"

Jeremiah 23: 29

E. THE BIBLE BRINGS HEALING

"Then they cried to the Lord in their trouble, and he delivered them from their distress; he sent forth his word and healed them, and delivered them from destruction."

Psalm 107: 19,20

F. THE BIBLE BRINGS ABOUT SPIRITUAL LIFE

"You have been born anew, not of perishable seed but of imperishable, through the living and abiding word of God; for, 'All flesh is like grass and all its glory like the flower of the grass. The grass withers, and the flower falls, but the word of the Lord abides forever.'

That word is the good news which was preached to you."

1 Peter 1: 23–25

G. THE BIBLE CAN BE AN OFFENSIVE WEAPON, LIKE A SWORD

"And take...the sword of the Spirit which is the word of God."

Ephesians 6: 17

H. NOBODY CAN THWART GOD'S WORD

"For as the rain and snow come down from heaven and return not thither but water the earth, making it bring forth and sprout, giving seed to the sower and bread to the eater, so shall my word be that goes forth from my mouth; it shall not return to me empty, but it shall accomplish that which I purpose, and prosper in the thing for which I sent it."

Isaiah 55: 9–11

The importance of the Bible (2)

What the Bible says about itself, continued

I. THE BIBLE PIERCES THROUGH TO THE HEART OF THE MATTER

"For the word of God is living and active, sharper than any two-edged sword, piercing to the division of soul and spirit, of joints and marrow, and discerning the thoughts and intentions of the heart."

Hebrews 4: 12

J. THE WORD OF THE LORD BROUGHT ABOUT CREATION

"For the word of the Lord is upright, and all his work is done in faithfulness. He loves righteousness and justice; the earth is full of the steadfast love of the Lord.

By the word of the Lord the heavens were made, and all their host by the breath of his mouth. He gathered the waters of the sea as in a bottle; he put the deeps in storehouses. Let all the earth fear the Lord, let all the inhabitants of the world stand in awe of him!

For he spoke, and it came to be; he commanded, and it stood forth."

Psalm 33: 4–9

Christians and the Bible

The following nine points about the Bible indicate how important the Bible is to the Christian.

1. STUDY THE BIBLE

"Study to show thyself approved unto God, a workman that needeth not to be ashamed, rightly dividing the word of truth."

2 Timothy 2: 15

2. USE THE BIBLE TO WITNESS WITH

"But sanctify the Lord God in your hearts: and be ready always to give an answer to every man that asketh you a reason of the hope that is in you with meekness and fear."

1 Peter 3: 15

3. DEFEAT SIN WITH THE HELP OF THE BIBLE

"Thy word have I hid in mine heart, that I might not sin against thee."

Psalms 119: 11

4. MEDITATE ON THE BIBLE

"This book of the law shall not depart out of thy mouth; but thou shalt meditate therein day and night, that thou mayest observe to do according to all that is written therein: for then thou shalt make thy way prosperous, and then thou shalt have good success."

Joshua 1: 8

5. THE BIBLE EQUIPS US FOR CHRISTIAN LIVING

"All Scripture is inspired by God and profitable for teaching, for reproof, for correction, and for training in righteousness, that the man of God may be complete, equipped for every good work."

2 Timothy 3: 16

6. THE BIBLE HELPS TO KEEP US HOLY

"How can a young man keep his way pure? By guarding it according to thy word. With my whole heart I seek thee; let me not wander from your commandments! I have laid up thy word in my heart, that I might not sin against thee."

Psalm 119: 9–11

"7. Seek God's guidance from the Bible"

"When thou goest, it shall lead thee; when thou sleepest, it shall keep thee; and when thou awakest, it shall talk with thee. For the commandment is a lamp; and the law is light; and reproofs of instruction are the way of life."

Proverbs 6: 22

8. THE BIBLE SHIELDS US

"Every word of God proves true. He is a shield to all those who take refuge in him."

Proverbs 30: 5

9. THE MESSAGE OF THE BIBLE IS TO BE SPREAD

"And we also thank God constantly for this, that when you received the word of God which you heard from us, you accepted it not as the word of men but as what it really is, the word of God, which is at work in you believers."

1 Thessalonians 2: 13

The authority of the Bible

Christians claim that God's authority is behind the Bible.

The authority of the Bible is derived from it being inspired. It is authoritative for believe and

behavior for all time because it is God's revelation. The Bible is no mere collection of human wisdom.

Quote Unquote

"When the questions of revelation and inspiration with regard to the Bible have been answered, the issue of authority will have been settled. In other words, how one views revelation and inspiration will determine how he views the Bible's authority.... Since the written revelation from God has been recorded under the Spirit's superintendence and is "the very breath of God," it is therefore authoritative – just as authoritative as the One who gave it.

"The authority of Scripture cannot be separated from the authority of God. Whatever the Bible affirms, God affirms. And what the Bible affirms (or denies), it affirms (or denies) with the very authority of God."

Robert Lightner

"If God entirely inspired Scripture (as we have seen that he did), then Scripture is vested with his authority."

Rene Pache

The inspiration of the Bible

Overview

We talk of Shakespeare's writings as being inspired. But Christians believe that the Bible is divinely inspired in a way that is unique to the Bible.

This inspiration came about when the Holy Spirit used human writers to produce the Scripture so that what they wrote was precisely what God wanted written.

Doctrine of inspiration

The doctrine of the inspiration of the Bible contains at least the following seven elements:

1. DIVINE ORIGIN
The origin of the Bible is divine.

2. HUMAN AGENCY
The Bible was indeed written under the power of the Holy Spirit, but also through the agency of human writers.

3. THE BIBLE IS VERBALLY INSPIRED
The Bible is a book consisting of words and so can be said to be verbally inspired.

4. CHRISTIANS BELIEVE IN THE PLENARY INSPIRATION OF THE BIBLE
The whole of the Bible, and not just parts of it are divinely inspired.

5. ONLY AUTOGRAPHS ARE INSPIRED
Only the autographs, that is the original documents penned by the biblical authors, are inspired. If the King James Version, or any other Bible version, should contain a tiny mistake that does not undermine the inspiration of the whole Bible. For Christians only believe that the Bible as originally given was inspired by God.

6. THE BIBLE IS INERRANT
Christians are happy to say that because Scripture is divinely inspired, it is inerrant and has no errors in it.

7. THE BIBLE IS THE FINAL AUTHORITY
Since Scripture is inspired and inerrant, it follows that it, and it alone, has final authority in all matters of Christian teaching and Christian practice.

A question of logic

The following syllogism has been proposed:
Major Premise:
    God is true (Romans 3: 4).
Minor Premise:
    God breathed out the Scriptures (2 Timothy 3: 16).
Conclusion:
    Therefore, the Scriptures are true (John 17: 17).

Truth and the Word of God

Truth is one of God's attributes: (Jeremiah 10: 10; John 1: 14; 14: 6; 17: 3).

So when he speaks he speaks truthfully. God never lies. Numbers 23: 19; 1 Samuel 15: 29; Titus 1: 2; Romans 3: 3–4.

Paul states that Scripture is "breathed out" by God (2 Timothy 3: 16).

So all that God "breathes out" is true. So the Word of God is true. John 17: 14,17; cf. Psalm 119: 142; 151; 160; Revelation 21: 5; 22: 6.

The Holy Spirit is the Agent of inspiration

2 Peter 1: 21 says that "prophecy came not in old time by the will of man: but holy men of God spake as they were moved by the Holy Spirit."

The word moved in this verse literally means to be "borne along" or "carried along."

So while human beings were used in the process of writing down God's Word, they were all literally "borne along" by the Holy Spirit.

Because they were carried along by God's Spirit they did not record their own fallible and faulty ideas but God's perfect revelation.

The Old Testament states that the Holy Spirit speaks through its writers.

"The Spirit of the Lord spake by me, and his word was in my tongue.

3 The God of Israel said, the Rock of Israel spake to me, He that ruleth over men must be just, ruling in the fear of God." *2 Samuel 23: 2–3*

Divine inspiration and the New Testament

Jesus promised His followers that it would be the work of the Holy Spirit to provide an accurate recounting of the events of His life.

"But the Comforter, which is the Holy Spirit, whom the Father will send in my name, he shall teach you all things, and bring all things to your remembrance, whatsoever I have said unto you."

John 14: 26

Divine authority claimed by biblical writers

Some of the writers of the New Testament are on record as claiming to have divine authority for their writings.

In 1 Corinthians 2: 13 the apostle Paul said he spoke "not in the words which man's wisdom teacheth, but which the Holy Spirit teacheth; comparing spiritual things with spiritual."

Paul claims that what he wrote was given to him by the Holy Spirit.

In 1 Corinthians 14: 37 Paul says, "If any man think himself to be a prophet, or spiritual, let him acknowledge that the things that I write unto you are the commandments of the Lord."

Paul claims that the words he wrote were God's commands, not human wisdom.

1 Thessalonians 2: 13. To his Christian friends at Thessalonica Paul says, "For this cause also thank we God without ceasing, because, when ye received the word of God which ye heard of us, ye received it not as the word of men, but as it is in truth, the word of God."

From this verse it is clear that God used Paul to convey his words to his readers.

Understanding the Bible (1)

The Westminster Confession

The Confession was commissioned from an assembly of 121 Puritan ministers in Westminster Abbey, called the Westminster Assembly, which was convened in 1643 for the purpose of drafting official documents for the reformation of the Church of England. It has been prized as a trustworthy yardstick for explaining biblical doctrine ever since it was written in 1646.

1:1 The writing of Scripture

Although the light of nature and the wonder of creation and providence itself all bear witness to God's goodness, wisdom, and power, so that men and women have no excuse (Ps. 19: 1–3; Rom. 1: 19, 20, 32; Rom. 2: 1, 14,15); these things in themselves are not enough to give that knowledge of God and of His will, which is necessary unto salvation (1 Cor. 1: 21; 2: 13, 14).

Therefore it pleased the Lord, at sundry times, and in diverse manners, to reveal Himself, and to declare that His will unto His Church (Heb. 1: 1); and afterwards, for the better preserving and propagating of the truth, and for the more sure establishment and comfort of the Church against the corruption of the flesh, and the malice of Satan and of the world, to commit the same wholly unto writing (Prov. 22: 19–21; Is. 8: 19, 20; Matt. 4: 4, 7, 10; Luke 1: 3, 4; Rom. 15: 4); which maketh the Holy Scripture to be most necessary (2 Tim. 3: 15; 2 Pet. 1: 19); those former ways of God's revealing His will unto His people being now ceased (Heb. 1: 1,2).

"God, who at sundry times and in divers manners spake in time past unto the fathers by the prophets, Hath in these last days spoken unto us by his Son, whom he hath appointed heir of all things, by whom also he made the world" Hebrews 1: 1,2.

Books of the Old Testament			
Genesis	1 Kings	Ecclesiastes	Obadiah
Exodus	2 Kings	The Song of Solomon	Jonah
Leviticus	1 Chronicles	Isaiah	Micah
Numbers	2 Chronicles	Jeremiah	Nahum
Deuteronomy	Ezra	Lamentations	Habakkuk
Joshua	Nehemiah	Ezekiel	Zephaniah
Judges	Esther	Daniel	Haggai
Ruth	Job	Hosea	Zechariah
1 Samuel	Psalms	Joel	Malachi
2 Samuel	Proverbs	Amos	

1:2 The books of the Bible

Under the name of Holy Scripture, or the Word of God written, are now contained all the books of the Old and New Testament, which are these: All which are given by inspiration of God to be the rule of faith and life (Luke 16: 29, 31; Eph. 2: 20; 2 Tim. 3: 16; Rev. 22: 18, 19).

"For I testify unto every man that heareth the words of the prophecy of this book, If any man shall add unto these things, God shall add unto him the plagues that are written in this book: And if any man shall take away from the words of the book of this prophecy, God shall take away his part out of the book of life, and out of the holy city, and from the things which are written in this book" Revelation 22: 18,19.

1:3 The Apocrypha

The books commonly called Apocrypha, not being of divine inspiration, are no part of the canon of the Scripture; and therefore are of no authority in the Church of God, nor to be any otherwise approved, or made use of, than other human writings (Luke 24: 27, 44; Rom. 3: 2; 2 Pet. 1: 21).

1:4 The authority of Scripture

The authority of the Holy Scripture, for which it ought to be believed and obeyed, dependeth not upon the testimony of any man, or Church; but wholly upon God (who is truth itself) the author thereof: and therefore it is to be received because it is the Word of God (1 Thes 2: 13; 2 Tim. 3: 16; 2 Pet. 1: 19, 21; 1 John 5: 9).

"We have also a more sure word of prophecy; whereunto ye do well that ye take heed, as unto a light that shineth in a dark place, until the day dawn, and the day star arise in your hearts : Knowing this first, that no prophecy of the Scripture is of any private interpretation. For the prophecy came not in old time by the will of man: but holy men of God spake as they were moved by the Holy Spirit" 2 Peter 1: 19–21.

Books of the New Testament			
Matthew	2 Corinthians	1 Timothy	2 Peter
Mark	Galatians	2 Timothy	1 John
Luke	Ephesians	Titus	2 John
John	Philippians	Philemon	3 John
Acts	Colossians	The Epistle to the Hebrews	Jude
Romans	1 Thessalonians	James	Revelation
1 Corinthians	2 Thessalonians	1 Peter	

Understanding the Bible (2)

The Westminster Confession, continued

1:5 The inward work of the Holy Spirit

We may be moved and induced by the testimony of the Church to a high and reverent esteem of the Holy Scripture (1 Tim. 3:15).

And the heavenliness of the matter, the efficacy of the doctrine, the majesty of the style, the consent of all the parts, the scope of the whole (which is, to give all glory to God), the full discovery it makes of the only way of man's salvation, the many other incomparable excellencies, and the entire perfection thereof, are arguments whereby it doth abundantly evidence itself to be the Word of God: yet notwithstanding, our full persuasion and assurance of the infallible truth and divine authority thereof, is from the inward work of the Holy Spirit bearing witness by and with the Word in our hearts.

(See Isaiah 59: 21; John 16: 13, 14; 1 Corinthians 2: 10–12; 1 John 2: 20, 27).

1:6 The whole counsel of God

The whole counsel of God, concerning all things necessary for
• His own glory,
• man's salvation,
• faith, and
• life,
is either expressly set down in Scripture, or by good and necessary

consequence may be deduced from Scripture: unto which nothing at any time is to be added, whether by new revelations of the Spirit, or traditions of men (Gal. 1: 8, 9; 2 Thes 2: 2; 2 Tim. 3: 15–17).

Nevertheless we acknowledge the inward illumination of the Spirit of God to be necessary for the saving understanding of such things as are revealed in the Word (John 6: 45; 1 Cor. 2: 9, 10, 12): and that there are some circumstances concerning the worship of God, and government of the Church, common to human actions and societies, which are to be ordered by the light of nature and Christian prudence, according to the general rules of the Word, which are always to be observed.

(See 1 Cor. 11: 13, 14; 14: 26, 40).

1:7 Things necessary for salvation

All things in Scripture are not alike in plain themselves, nor alike clear unto all (2 Pet. 3: 16): yet those things which are necessary to be known, believed, and observed for salvation, are so clearly propounded and opened in some place of Scripture or other, that not only the learned, but the unlearned, in a due use of the ordinary means, may attain unto a sufficient understanding of them.

"Thy word is a lamp unto my feet, and a light unto my path" Psalm 119: 105.

"The entrance of thy words giveth light; it giveth understanding unto the simple" Psalm 119: 130.

1:8 The final court of appeal

The Old Testament in Hebrew (which was the native language of the people of God of old), and the New Testament in Greek (which at the time of writing of it was most generally known to the nations), being immediately inspired by God, and by His singular care and providence kept pure in all ages, are therefore authentic (Matt. 5: 18); so as, in all controversies of religion, the Church is finally to appeal unto them.

(See Is. 8: 20; John 5: 39, 46; Acts 15: 15).

But, because these original tongues are not known to all the people of God, who have right unto, and interest in the Scriptures, and are commanded, in the fear of God, to read and search them (John 5: 39), therefore they are to be translated into the vulgar language of every nation unto which they come (1 Cor. 14: 6,9,11,12,24,27,28), that the Word of God dwelling plentifully in all, they may worship Him in an acceptable manner (Col. 3: 16); and, through patience and comfort of the Scriptures, may have hope (Rom. 15: 4).

1:9 Interpret Scripture with Scripture

The infallible rule of interpretation of Scripture is the Scripture itself: and therefore, when there is a question about the true and full sense of any Scripture (which is not manifold, but

one), it must be searched and known by other places that speak more clearly.

(See Acts 15: 15; 2 Pet. 1: 20, 21).

1:10 The Holy Spirit speaking in Scripture

The supreme judge by which all controversies of religion are to be determined, and all decrees of councils, opinions of ancient writers, doctrines of men, and private spirits, are to be examined; and in whose sentence we are to rest; can be no other but the Holy Spirit speaking in the Scripture.

(See Matt. 22: 29, 31; Acts 28: 25; Eph. 2: 20).

The Westminster Confession, 1646

Understanding the Bible (3)

The Belgic Confession

Introduction

The first of the doctrinal standards of the Christian Reformed Churches is the Confession of Faith. It is usually called the Belgic Confession because it originated in the Southern Netherlands, now known as Belgium.

GUIDO DE BRÈS

Its chief author was Guido de Brès, a preacher of the Reformed Churches of The Netherlands, who died a martyr to the faith in the year 1567.

FIRES OF PERSECUTION

During the 16th century the Churches in this country were exposed to the most terrible persecution by the Roman Catholic government. To protest against this cruel oppression, and to prove to the persecutors that the adherents of the Reformed faith were no rebels, as was laid to their charge, but law-abiding citizens who professed the true Christian doctrine according to the Holy Scriptures, de Brès prepared this Confession in the year 1561.

OBEY GOD FIRST

In the following year a copy was sent to King Philip II, together with an address in which the petitioners declared that they were ready to obey the government in all lawful things, but that they would "offer their backs to stripes, their tongues to knives, their mouths to gags, and their whole bodies to fire," rather than deny the truth expressed in this Confession. Its excellence as one of the best statements of Reformed doctrine continues to be acclaimed.

Article 2

HOW GOD MAKES HIMSELF KNOWN TO US

We know Him by two means: First, by the creation, preservation, and government of the universe; which is before our eyes as a most beautiful book, wherein all creatures, great and small, are as so many letters leading us to perceive clearly the invisible qualities of God namely His eternal power and deity, as the apostle Paul says in Rom. 1: 20. All these things are sufficient to convict men and leave them without excuse. Second, He makes Himself more clearly and fully known to us by His holy and divine Word as far as is necessary for us in this life, to His glory and our salvation.

Article 3

THE WORD OF GOD

We confess that this Word of God did not come by the impulse of man, but that men moved by the Holy Spirit spoke from God, as the apostle Peter says. Thereafter, in His special care for us and our salvation, God commanded His servants, the prophets and apostles, to commit His revealed word to writing and He Himself wrote with His own finger the two tables of the law. Therefore we call such writings holy and divine Scriptures.

Article 5

THE AUTHORITY OF HOLY SCRIPTURE

We receive all these books, and these only, as holy and canonical, for the regulation, foundation, and confirmation of our faith. We believe without any doubt all things contained in them, not so much because the Church receives and approves them as such, but especially because the Holy Spirit witnesses in our hearts that they are from God, and also because they contain the evidence thereof in themselves; for, even the blind are able to perceive that the things foretold in them are being fulfilled.

Article 7

THE SUFFICIENCY OF HOLY SCRIPTURE

We believe that this Holy Scripture fully contains the will of God and that all that man must believe in order to be saved is sufficiently taught therein. The whole manner of worship which God requires of us is written in it at length. It is therefore unlawful for any one, even for an apostle, to teach otherwise than we are now taught in Holy Scripture: yes, even if it be an angel from heaven, as the apostle Paul says. Since it is forbidden to add to or take away anything from the Word of God, it is evident that the doctrine thereof is most perfect and complete in all respects.

We may not consider any writings of men, however holy these men may have been, of equal value with the divine Scriptures; nor ought we to consider custom, or the great multitude, or antiquity, or succession of times and people, or councils, decrees, or statutes, as of equal value with the truth of God, since the truth is above all; for all men are of themselves liars, and lighter than a breath. We therefore reject with all our heart whatever does not agree with this infallible rule, as the apostles have taught us: Test the spirits to see whether they are of God. Likewise: If any one comes to you and does not bring this doctrine, do not receive him into your house or give him any greeting.

Quotations in the New Testament (1)

Introduction

Most of the quotations from the Old Testament made in the New Testament are not made according to any uniform method.

When the New Testament was written there were no chapter and verse divisions in the Old Testament. In order to identify the passage in Exodus 3: 6 Luke could not say, "this quotation comes from Exodus 3: 6." So he identifies the passage in Luke 20: 37 by referring to "Moses at the bush." "Now that the dead are raised, even Moses showed at the bush, when he calleth the Lord the God of Abraham, and the God of Isaac, and the God of Jacob."

Most of the time, the New Testament writers quote from the Septuagint version of the Old Testament. This was the version of the Old Testament most often used by the Jews at that time.

New Testament quotes of the Old Testament

Some Old Testament passages that are quoted in the New Testament are said to have the Holy Spirit as their author, even though the Old Testament records that a human prophet actually spoke the words.

For example, Mark 12: 36 says, "For David himself said by the Holy Spirit, The LORD said to my Lord, Sit thou on my right hand, till I make thine enemies thy footstool."

This is a quotation from Psalm 110: 1 which does not actually state that David is speaking by the Holy Spirit, although, clearly, he was: "The LORD said unto my Lord, Sit thou at my right hand, until I make thine enemies thy footstool."

The Holy Spirit designated by New Testament quotations

On a number of occasions, where the Old Testament states that some words were said by the psalmist or by one of the prophets, the New Testament specifically attributes to the Lord, to God and to the Holy Spirit.

OLD TESTAMENT DESIGNATION	NEW TESTAMENT DESIGNATION
The psalmist said (Psalm 95: 7)	The Holy Spirit said (Heb. 3: 7)
The psalmist said (Psalm 45: 6)	God said (Hebrews 1: 8)
The psalmist said (Ps. 102: 25,27)	God said (Hebrews 1: 10–12)
Isaiah said (Isaiah 7: 14)	The Lord spoke by the prophet (Matthew 1: 22–23)
Hosea said (Hosea 11: 1)	The Lord spoke by the prophet (Matthew 2: 15).

"When Israel was a child, I loved him,
And out of Egypt I called My son."

Hosea 11: 1 NKJV

"... and was there until the death of Herod, that it might be fulfilled which was spoken by the Lord through the prophet, saying, 'Out of Egypt I called My Son.'"

Matthew 2: 15 NKJV

God's words and the mouths of the prophets

In the Old Testament we often find that God's words are said to be in the mouths of the prophets.

This picture indicates that God was in control of the process of communicating his word to humankind.

DAVID

In 2 Samuel 23: 2, David is speaking, and he says: "The Spirit of the lord spake by me, and his word was in my tongue."

There could hardly be a clearer reference to a human being used as a mouthpiece for God's Spirit.

ISAIAH

Similarly, we read in Isaiah 59: 21, "As for me, this is my covenant with them, saith the lord; My spirit that is upon thee, and my words which I have put in thy mouth."

JEREMIAH

Jeremiah was all too conscious of the Lord's hand on him and his words. In Jeremiah 1: 9 he says:

"Then the lord put forth his hand, and touched my mouth. And the lord said unto me, Behold, I have put my words in thy mouth."

Non-literal quotations

For a quotation to be a valid quotation in the days of the New Testament the quotation did not have to be a literal quotation.

There are about one hundred instances of quotations in the New Testament which do not exactly match either the Septuagint or the Hebrew text of the Old Testament.

There are about ninety instances of the Septuagint being literally quoted in the New Testament.

There are about eighty instances of the Septuagint being quoted in a slightly corrected or altered way in the New Testament.

Less often there are quotations made directly from the Hebrew text (Matt. 4: 15, 16; John 19: 37; 1 Cor. 15: 54).

Quotations in the New Testament (2)

283 direct quotations

There are direct quotations from the Old Testament in the New Testament.

There is not one clear cut quotation from the Apocrypha in the New Testament.

Greek poets

Paul was an exceptionally well educated person. On three occasions he quotes from Greek poets:

- Acts 17: 28
- 1 Cor. 15: 33
- Titus 1: 12

The principles underlying the quotations from the Old Testament in the New Testament

Quotations from the Old Testament Greek text sometimes differ from the Hebrew.

This only creates difficulties when we think of the Bible only as a book written by human authors. Difficulties about differences between Old Testament verses as they are found in the Old Testament and then quoted in the New Testament vanish when we recall that the Bible is the Word of God. It is the record of the words which he himself used, "at sundry times and in divers manners" (Heb. 1: 1). We need to constantly recall that the Bible is the result of godly authors writing under the Holy Spirit's direction: "holy men of God spake as they were moved by the Holy Spirit" (2 Pet. 1: 27).

The Holy Spirit, in referring to words which he previously caused to be written in connection with one particular set of circumstances, frequently refers to them again in connection with different circumstances.

All this is for our benefit, even if the words are sometimes changed, in order to highlight some new truth.

1. SOMETIMES THE MEANING ORIGINALLY INTENDED BY THE HOLY SPIRIT IS KEPT IN THE QUOTATION, EVEN THOUGH THE WORDS MAY VARY. Such instances are:

Gospels

Matt. 1: 23 (Is. 7: 13,14); Matt. 2: 6 (Mic. 5: 2); Matt. 3: 3 (Is. 40: 3); 11: 10 (Mal. 3: 1); Matt. 12: 17 (Is. 42: 1–4); Matt. 26: 31 (Zech. 13: 7)
Mark 15: 28 (Is. 53: 12).
Luke 4: 18–21 (Is. 61: 1,2).
John 19: 37 (Zech. 12: 10)

Rest of the New Testament

Acts 15: 16,17 (Amos 9: 11,12)
Rom. 14: 11 (Is. 45: 23)
Eph. 4: 8 (Ps. 68: 18)
Heb. 5: 6 and 7: 17,21 (Ps. 110: 4)

2. SOMETIMES THE ORIGINAL SENSE IS MODIFIED, AND USED WITH A NEW AND DIFFERENT APPLICATION Such instances are:
Matt. 12: 40 (Jonah 1: 17)
John 3: 14,15 (Num. 21: 8,9)
John 19: 36 (Ex. 12: 46)
Eph. 5: 31,32 (Gen. 2: 23,24)

3. SOMETIMES THE ORIGINAL SENSE IS ADAPTED TO SUIT A VERY DIFFERENT EVENT OR SITUATION

Such instances are:

Gospels

Matt. 2: 15 (Hos. 11: 1); Matt. 2: 17,18
(Jer. 31: 15); Matt. 8: 17 (Is. 53: 4);
Matt. 13: 35, "spoken" (Ps. 78: 2);
Matt. 15: 8,9 (Is. 29: 13); Matt. 27: 9,10
(Zech. 11: 12,13)

Rest of the New Testament

Acts 13: 40,41 (Hab. 1: 5). Rom. 9: 27,28
(Is. 10: 22,23); 9: 29 (Is. 1: 9); 10: 6,7,8
(Deut. 30: 12–14). 1 Cor. 1: 19,20
(Is. 29: 14; 33: 18); 1 Cor. 10: 6 (Ex. 32: 6–
25). Rev. 1: 7 (Zech. 12: 10); Rev. 1: 17
(Is. 41: 4); Rev. 11: 4 (Zech. 4: 3,11,14).

4. COMPOSITE QUOTATIONS.
Sometimes the quotations in the New
Testament combine two or more
quotations from the Old Testament.
This is a common practice in all
literature. Humans may make mistakes
as they do this, but there are no such
mistakes in the Bible because of the
ministry of the Holy Spirit.

Such instances are:

- In Matt. 21: 5, Is. 62: 11 is combined
  with Zech. 9: 9.

"Tell the daughter of Zion,
'Behold, your King is coming to you,
Lowly, and sitting on a donkey,
A colt, the foal of a donkey.'"

Matthew 21: 5 NKJV

"Indeed the Lord has proclaimed
To the end of the world:
'Say to the daughter of Zion,
"Surely your salvation is coming;
Behold, His reward is with Him,
And His work before Him."'"

Isaiah 62: 11 NKJV

"Rejoice greatly, O daughter of Zion!
Shout, O daughter of Jerusalem!

Behold, your King is coming to you;
He is just and having salation,
Lowly and riding on a donkey,
A colt, the foal of a donkey."

Zechariah 9: 9 NKJV

- In Matt. 21: 13, Is. 56: 7 is combined
  with Jer. 7: 11.

- In Mark 1: 2,3, Mal. 3: 1 is combined
  with Is. 40: 3.

- In Luke 1: 16,17, Mal. 4: 5,6 is
  combined with 3: 1.

- In Luke 3: 4,5, Mal. 3: 1 is combined
  with Is. 40: 3.

- In Acts 1: 20, Ps. 69: 25 is combined
  with 109: 8.

- In Rom. 3: 10–12, Eccles. 7: 20 is
  combined with Ps. 14: 2,3 and 53: 2,3.

- In Rom. 3: 13–18, Ps. 5: 9 is combined
  with Is. 59: 7,8 and Ps. 36: 1.

- In Rom. 9: 33, Is. 28: 16 is combined
  with 8: 14.

- In Rom. 11: 26,27 Is. 59: 20,21 is
  combined with 27: 9.

- In 1 Cor. 15: 54–56, Is. 25: 8 is
  combined with Hos. 13: 14.

- In 2 Cor. 6: 16, Lev. 26: 11 is combined
  with Ezek. 37: 27.

- In Gal. 3: 8, Gen. 12: 3 is combined
  with 18: 18.

- In 1 Pet. 2: 7,8, Ps. 118: 22 is combined
  with Is. 8: 14.

Interpreting the Bible

Methods of interpreting the Bible

The aim of all biblical interpretation should be to travel down the correct path in order to arrive at scriptural truth.

"Improper" paths

Interpreting the Bible by means of improper methodology is nothing new. Peter warns against this in 2 Peter 3: 16, where he refers to Paul's inspired writings, "which they that are unlearned and unstable wrest [that is distort], as they do also the other scriptures, unto their own destruction."

The need for revelation

The Bible teaches us that we need revelation from God if we are to know about him and know him for ourselves. The Bible as a body of literature exists because human beings need to know certain spiritual truths to which they cannot attain by themselves.

Our need for revelation is indicated in Deuteronomy 29: 29; "The secret things belong unto the LORD our God: but those things which are revealed belong unto us and to our children for ever, that we may do all the words of this law."

Guidelines for interpreting Scripture

1. LOOK FOR THE AUTHOR'S INTENDED MEANING

As we read we should never ignore the ordinary, plain, literal sense of each passage.

We should try never to superimpose a meaning on the Bible that is really not there.

The idea is to discover the meaning the author had in mind.

2. LOOK AT THE CONTEXT

A text taken out of context can all too easily become a pretext for almost anything.

The context is discovered by looking at the whole verse in question, the surrounding verses, the preceding chapter and the following chapter and the whole drift of the topic under discussion in the Bible passage.

"If we would understand the parts, our wisest course is to get to know the whole." *J.I. Packer*

3. LOOK AT THE TYPE OF LITERATURE YOU ARE READING

The Bible contains many different types of literature and each type should be read for what it is. If one reads a parable as if it is history or poetry as if it is straightforward narrative one is likely to misinterpret the passage.

4. LOOK AT THE OLD TESTAMENT IN LIGHT OF THE NEW TESTAMENT

The Old Testament should always be interpreted in the light of the New

Testament. And the New Testament should always be interpreted against the background of the Old Testament.

"In the Old Testament the New is concealed. In the New Testament the Old is revealed." *Augustine of Hippo*

5. COMPARE SCRIPTURE WITH SCRIPTURE

The best commentary on the Bible is the Bible itself. Compare relevant parts of Scripture with each other.

Any part of the human body can only be properly explained in reference to the whole body. And any part of the Bible can only be properly explained in reference to the whole Bible.

6. RELY ON THE HOLY SPIRIT

The Bible itself says that we are to rely on the Holy Spirit's illumination as we seek its meaning.

See John 16: 12–15; 1 Corinthians 2: 9–11.

He who inspired the Word, the Holy Spirit, (2 Peter 1: 21) is also its supreme interpreter. "For the prophecy came not in old time by the will of man: but holy men of God spake *as they were* moved by the Holy Spirit" 2 Peter 1: 21.

7. READING THE GOSPELS

"We must not fall into the error of thinking that when we have come to a conclusion about the sources of a literary work we have learned all that needs to be known about it. Source criticism is merely a preliminary piece of spade-work. Whatever their sources were, the Gospels are there before our eyes, each an individual literary work with its own characteristic viewpoint, which has in large measure

controlled the choice and presentation of the subject matter. In attempting to discover how they were composed, we must beware of regarding them as scissors-and-paste compilations." *F.F. Bruce*

> **Quote Unquote**
>
> "If in these books I meet anything which seems contrary to truth, I shall not hesitate to conclude either that the text is faulty, or that the translator has not expressed the meaning of the passage, or that I myself do not understand."
>
> *Augustine of Hippo*

Bible reading (1)

Short list of famous Bible passages

While the Bible remains the world's best-selling book it is in danger of being the world's best-selling unread book.

Its thousand pages are usually printed in two columns of small type. For someone who is not at all familiar with the Bible it may appear to be a daunting book to read. One way to start is to turn to and become familiar with some of the most inspiriting chapters of the Bible.

1. Old Testament

The creation account
"In the beginning, God created the heavens and the earth..."
Genesis 1: 1–2: 3

The Ten Commandments
Exodus 20: 1–17

The Lord is my shepherd
Psalm 23

2. New Testament

A. WORDS OF JESUS
Beatitudes. Matthew 5: 1–12.

The Greatest Commandment
"Love the Lord thy God." Mark 12: 28–34.

The Golden Rule
"And as ye would that men should do to you, do ye also to them likewise." Luke 6: 31.

THE LORD'S PRAYER
Matthew 6: 9–13.

God's great love (John 3: 16)

The last words of Jesus
"Go ye therefore and teach all nations" Matthew 28: 18.

THREE FAMOUS PARABLES
The Sower and the Seed
"Behold, a sower went forth to sow seed." Matthew 13: 3.

The Good Samaritan (Luke 10: 33)

The Prodigal Son (Luke 15: 11–32)

THE APOSTLE PAUL
Paul on love
"If I have not love I am nothing."
1 Corinthians 13.

Finding famous Bible passages

This list answers the question: "where does that famous Bible passage come?"

Titles of and references of over two hundred and fifty of some of the most-loved Bible passages are set out.

1. THE OLD TESTAMENT

A. *Readings from the first five books of the Bible*
Creation and Sin: Genesis 1: 1–3: 24
The First Murder: Genesis 4: 1–16
Noah and The Flood: Genesis 6: 1–9: 17
Tower of Babel: Genesis 11: 1–9
Call of Abraham (Abram):
    Genesis 12: 1–9
Destruction of Sodom and Gomorrah:
    Genesis 19: 1–29
Hagar and Ishmael: Genesis 16: 1–15;
    21: 9–21
Birth of Isaac: Genesis 21: 1–8
Abraham offers Isaac as a sacrifice:
    Genesis 22: 1–19
The Jacob and Esau stories:

Genesis 25: 19–35: 29
The Joseph story: Genesis 37 – 50
Moses in Egypt: Exodus 1 – 14
Moses wanders in the desert:
  Exodus 15: 22–20: 26; Numbers 20–21: 25
The Ten Commandments:
  Exodus 20: 1–17; Deuteronomy 5: 1–21
Balak, Balaam and his talking donkey: Numbers 22–24
The death of Moses: Deuteronomy 34

B. People of faith in the rest of the Old Testament
Rahab helps the Israelite spies: Joshua 2
Joshua and his military strategy: Joshua 3; 6
Deborah and her power: Judges 4 – 5
Gideon and his conquests: Judges 6: 1 – 8: 32
Samson and his strength: Judges 13 – 16
Ruth and her loyalty: Ruth 1 – 4
Samuel: the prophet who listened to God: 1 Samuel 1–3; 7–10; 12; 15; 16; 25: 1
Saul: Israel's first king: 1 Samuel 8–11; 13; 15; 28; 31
David, the shepherd king: 1 Samuel 16–27; 29–30; 2 Samuel 1–24; 1 Kings 1: 1–31; 2: 1–11
Solomon and his wisdom: 1 Kings 2: 12–11: 43
Elijah and his prophetic actions: 1 Kings 17–19; 21; 2 Kings 1
Elisha succeeds Elijah: Nehemiah 1; 2; 4; 5
Esther and her bravery: Esther 1 – 10
Daniel and his faithfulness: Daniel 1 – 6
Jonah, the reluctant missionary: Jonah 1 – 4

2. The New Testament

A. The Life of Jesus
The birth of Jesus: Matthew 1: 18–2: 15; Luke 2: 1–20
Jesus is given his name and presented in the Temple: Luke 2: 21–40
The 12 year old Jesus in the Temple: Luke 2: 41–52
The baptism of Jesus: Matthew 3: 13–17; Mark 1: 9–11
The temptation of Jesus: Matthew 4: 1–11; Mark 1: 12–13; Luke 4: 1–13
Jesus calls his first disciples: Matthew 4: 18–22; Mark 1: 16–20
Jesus chooses the twelve apostles: Matthew 10: 1–4; Mark 3: 13–19; Luke 6: 12–16
The transfiguration of Jesus: Matthew 17: 1–13; Mark 9: 2–13; Luke 9: 28–36

Jesus' death, resurrection and ascension
Jesus' enters Jerusalem: Matthew 21: 1–11; Mark 11: 1–11; Luke 19: 28–40; John 12: 12–19
The Last Supper: Matthew 26: 17–35; Mark 14: 12–26; Luke 22: 1–38
Jesus prays in Gethsemane: Matthew 26: 36–46; Mark 14: 32–42; Luke 22: 39–46
Jesus' trial and crucifixion: Matthew 26: 47–27: 66; Mark 14: 43–15: 47; Luke 22: 47–23: 56; John 18; 19
The resurrection of Jesus: Matthew 28: 1–10; Mark 16; Luke 24: 1–12; John 20
The great commission: Matthew 28: 16–20
The ascension of Jesus: Luke 24: 50–53; Acts 1: 1–11

Bible reading (2)

B. The miracles and healings of Jesus

Jesus changes water into wine:
John 2: 1–11

Jesus feeds thousands of people:
Matt. 14: 13–21; Mark 6: 30–40;
Luke 9: 10–17; John 6: 1–15;
Matt. 15: 32–39; Mark 8: 1–10

Jesus calms a storm: Matt. 8: 23–27;
Mark 4: 35–41; Luke 8: 22–25

The miraculous catch of fish: Luke 5: 1–11

Jesus walks on water: Matt. 14: 22–33;
Mark 6: 45–52; John 6: 16–21

Jesus heals people who had skin
diseases: Matt. 8: 1–4; Mark 1: 40–45;
Luke 5: 12–16; Luke 17: 11–19

Jesus expels demons: Matt. 8: 28–34;
Mark 5: 1–20; Luke 8: 26–39;
Matt. 12: 22–32; Mark 3: 20–30;
Luke 11: 14–23; Matt. 17: 14–20;
Mark 9: 14–29; Luke 9: 37–43;
Mark 1: 21–28; Luke 4: 31–37

Jesus heals blind people: Matt. 9: 27–31;
Matt. 20: 29–34; Mark 10: 46–52;
Luke 18: 35–43

Jesus heals a deaf man: Mark 7: 31–37

Jesus paralyzed and crippled people:
Matt. 9: 1–8; Mark 2: 1–12; Luke 5: 17–26; Matt. 12: 9–14; Mark 3: 1–6; Luke
6: 6–11; Luke 14: 1–6; John 5: 1–18

Jesus heals many women: Matt. 9: 18–26; Mark 5: 25–43; Luke 8: 1–3;
Luke 8: 42–48; Luke 13: 10–17;
Matt. 15: 21–28; Mark 7: 24–30

Jesus heals a centurion's servant:
Matt. 8: 5–13; Luke 7: 1–10

Jesus heals Peter's mother-in-law: Matt.
8: 14; Mark 1: 29–31; Luke 4: 38–39

Jesus heals an official's son: John 4: 46–54

Jesus bring Lazarus back to life:
John 11: 1–44

C. The teachings and parables of Jesus

The Sermon on the Mount: Matt. 5 – 7

The Beatitudes: Matt. 5: 3–11;
Luke 6: 20–26

The great commandment: Matt. 22: 37–39; Mark 12: 29–31; Luke 10: 27

The golden rule: Matt. 7: 12; Luke 6: 31

The parable of the Mustard Seed:
Matt. 13: 31–32; Mark 4: 30–32;
Luke 13: 18–19

The parable of the Sower: Matt. 13: 1–23;
Mark 4: 1–20; Luke 8: 4–15

The parable of the Growing Seed:
Mark 4: 26–29

Parables About the Kingdom of
Heaven: Matt. 13: 24–52

The parable of the Unforgiving Servant:
Matt. 18: 21–35

The parable of the Workers in the
Vineyard: Matt. 20: 1–16

The parable of the Tenants in the
Vineyard: Matt. 21: 33–46; Mark 12: 1–11; Luke 20: 9–18

The parable of the Wedding Feast:
Matt. 22: 1–14; Luke 14: 15–24

The parable of the Ten Virgins:
Matt. 25: 1–13

The parable of the Servants and their
Coins: Matt. 25: 14–30; Luke 19: 11–27

The parable of the Sheep and the Goats:
Matt. 25: 31–46

The parable of the Good Samaritan:
Luke 10: 25–37

The parable of the Good Shepherd:
John 10: 1–21

The parable of the Rich Fool:
Luke 12: 16–21

The parable of the Watchful Servants:
Luke 12: 35–48
The parable of the Barren Fig Tree:
Luke 13: 6–9
The parable of the Lost Sheep:
Matt. 18: 12–14; Luke 15: 3–7
The parable of the Lost Coin:
Luke 15: 8–10
The parable of the Lost Son: Luke 15: 11–
32
The parable of the Shrewd Steward:
Luke 16: 1–13
The parable of the Rich Man and
Lazarus: Luke 16: 19–31
The parable of the Widow and the
Judge: Luke 18: 1–8
The parable of the Pharisee and the Tax
Collector: Luke 18: 9–14

D. Other New Testament events
Birth of John the Baptist: Luke 1: 57–66
Preaching of John the Baptist:
Matt. 3: 1–12; Mark 1: 1–8; Luke 3: 1–
20; John 1: 19–28
Execution of John the Baptist:
Matt. 14: 1–12; Mark 6: 14–29
The Holy Spirit at Pentecost: Acts 2
Stephen becomes the first Christian
martyr: Acts 6: 5–15; 7: 54–60
Saul is converted: Acts 9: 1–31
Peter and Cornelius: Acts 10
Peter in prison: Acts 12: 1–19
Baptism of Lydia: Acts 16: 11–15
Paul and Silas in prison: Acts 16: 16–40
Riot at Ephesus: Acts 19: 23–41
Paul's sea voyage to Rome: Acts 27; 28

3. SONGS OF THE BIBLE
Moses' song of deliverance: Ex. 15: 1–18
Miriam's song of victory: Ex. 15: 19–21
Deborah and Barak's song of victory:
Judges 5: 1–31
Hannah's song of praise: 1 Samuel
2: 1–10
David's lament: 2 Samuel 1: 17–27
David's song of victory: 2 Samuel 22;
Psalm 18
Hezekiah's song of praise: Isaiah
38: 10–20
Mary's song of praise: Luke 1: 46–55
Zechariah's song of praise: Luke 1: 68–79
The angels' song of praise: Luke 2: 14
Simeon's song of thanksgiving:
Luke 2: 29–32
A hymn about Jesus: Philippians 2: 6–11
Songs of praise to the Lamb of God:
Revelation 5: 9–13; 15: 3–4

4. BIBLE PRAYERS
David's prayer of thanksgiving:
2 Samuel 7: 18–29; 1 Chron 17: 16–27
Solomon's personal prayer: 1 Kings
3: 1–15; 2 Chr. 1: 1–12
Solomon's public prayer: 1 Kings
8: 22–61; 2 Chr. 6: 12–42
Jabez's prayer: 1 Chron 4: 10
Hezekiah's prayer: 2 Kings 19: 14–19;
Isaiah 37: 14–20
Job's prayer: Job 42: 1–6
Jeremiah's prayer: Jeremiah 32: 16–25
Daniel's prayer: Daniel 9: 1–19
Jonah's prayer: Jonah 2: 1–9
The Lord's Prayer: Matt. 6: 9–13
Jesus' prayer in Gethsemane:
Matt. 26: 36–46
Jesus' prayer for his disciples: John 17
Paul's prayer for believers: Ephesians
3: 14–21

BIBLE BLESSINGS AND INVOCATIONS
Psalm 19: 14; Numbers 6: 24–26; 1 Kings
8: 57–58; Romans 15: 5,6,13; Romans
16: 25–27; 1 Cor. 1: 3; 2 Cor. 13: 13;
Ephesians 6: 23–24; Philippians 4: 7;
1 Timothy 1: 2; Hebrews 13: 20–21;
2 John 3; Jude 24–25; Revelation 1: 4–6

Bible reading (3)

Bible history

The following Bible passages give a bird's eye view of the history of the Bible.

1. Old Testament

Genesis 1–4, 6–9, 11: Beginnings

Genesis 12–24: Abraham

Genesis 25–35: Jacob's Deceptions

Genesis 37–50: Joseph

Exodus 1–10: Call of Moses

Exodus 11–20, 32–34: From Egypt to Matt. Sinai

Numbers 9–17, 19–32: Rebellions in the Wilderness

Joshua 1–11: Conquering Canaan

Judges 2–4, 6–12: Early Judges

Judges 13–21: Samson, and Civil War

1 Samuel 1–12: Last Judge, First King

1 Samuel 13–31: Reign of Saul

2 Samuel 1–12: Early Reign of David

2 Samuel 13–21,24: End of David's Reign

1 Kings 1–11: Reign of Solomon

1 Kings 12–22: Divided Kingdom, Elijah

2 Kings 1–11: Elisha and end of Ahab and Jezebel Family

2 Kings 12–25: Israel and Judah Taken Captive

Jeremiah 34–45, Daniel 1–3: Captivity

Ezra 1–10: Return from Captivity

2. New Testament

Mark 1–10: Ministry of Jesus

Mark 11–16: Crucifixion and Resurrection of Jesus

Acts 1–12: Ministry of Peter

Acts 13–28: Ministry of Paul

Where can I find this verse?

Here is a list of some of the most well known Bible phrases together with their Bible references.

"Do unto others as you would have them do unto you." – Matthew 7: 12 and Luke 6: 31

"For God so loved the world that he gave his one and only Son..." – John 3: 16

"For where two or three have gathered together in My name, there I am in their midst." – Matthew 18: 20

"I am the Alpha and Omega..." – Revelation 1: 8

"Love is patient, love is kind.." – 1 Corinthians 13: 4–13

"Love of money is the root of all evil..." – 1 Timothy 6: 10

"Love your neighbor as yourself." – Leviticus 19: 18; Matthew 19: 19; 22: 39, Mark 12: 31,33, Luke 10: 27; Romans 13: 9; Galatians 5: 14; James 2: 8

"Man shall not live by bread alone..." – Matthew 4: 4

"Many are called, but few are chosen." – Matthew 22: 14

"Seek and you will find; knock and the door will be opened" – Matthew 7: 7, Luke 11: 9

"Seek ye first the kingdom of God." – Matthew 6: 33

The Golden Rule – Matthew 7: 12 and Luke 6: 31

"The Lord is my shepherd.." – Psalms 23: 1–6

"To every thing there is a season, and a time to every purpose under the heaven" – Ecclesiastes 3: 1–8

"You cannot serve both God and money (mammon)" – Matthew 6: 24; Luke 16: 13

Golden chapters

Certain chapters in the Bible have been called "golden" chapters because of their great importance.

A-Z LIST

Ascension: Acts 1
Backsliders: Hos. 14
Beatitudes: Matt. 5
Bread of Life: John 6
Brotherhood: Rom. 14
Builders: Neh. 4
Burden-bearers: Gal. 6
Call, Universal Is. 55
Call, Workers: Is. 6
Chastening: 2 Cor. 4
Confession: Ps. 51
Consecration: Phil. 3
Constancy: Ruth 1
Contrast: Deut. 28
Converts: Ps. 32
Deliverance: Acts 12
Divinity: John 1
Duty: Rom. 12
Faith: Heb. 11
Flood: Gen. 7
Friendship: 1 Sam. 20
Fruit: John 15
Gifts: 1 Cor. 12
Gideon's Band: Judg. 7
Good Shepherd: John 10
Heaven: John 14; Rev. 7–22
Holy Spirit: John 14–15
Humility: John 13
Instruction: Prov. 1
Intercession: John 17

Joy: Is. 12
Jubilee: Lev. 25
Judgment: Matt. 25
Law: Ex. 20
Life, Frailty of: Ps. 90
Love: 1 Cor. 13
Messianic: Is. 53
Missions: Ps. 72; Rom. 10
New Covenant: Heb. 8
Old Age: Eccl. 12
Omniscience: Ps. 139
Overcomers: Rev. 2–3
Passover: Ex. 12
Praise: Ps. 103
Prayer: Dan. 6; Luke 11–18
Prosperity: Ps. 73
Providence: Ps. 121
Refuge: Num. 35
Regeneration: John 3
Rest: Heb. 4
Resurrection: 1 Cor. 15
Revival: 2 Chr. 30; Luke 3
Safety: Ps. 91
Service: Luke 10
Shepherd: John 10
Soldier's: Eph. 6
Teacher's: 1 Cor. 2
Temperance: Prov. 23
Tither's: Mal. 3
Tongue: James 3
Transfiguration: Matt. 17
Unity: Eph.4
Vanity: Eccl. 2
Watchman's: Ezek. 33
Water of Life: John 4
Wisdom: Prov. 3
Word of God: Deut. 6
Worship: Ps. 84

Bible reading (4)

Key chapters of the Bible

1. Old Testament

Genesis 1–3: Creation, Fall, first promise
of a Redeemer
"In the beginning"
Genesis 12: Abraham's call
"Through you all peoples will be
blessed"
Exodus 20: Giving of the Ten
Commandments
"I am the Lord your God"
Joshua 24: Joshua's call to decide for
God
"Choose you this day"
Isaiah 53: The "suffering servant"
passage that looks forward to the
coming Messiah
"The Lord has laid on him the
iniquity of us all"
Psalm 23: The Shepherd's Psalm
"The Lord is my shepherd"
Psalm 51: David's prayer for forgiveness
"Create in me a clean heart, O God"
Proverbs 31: The virtuous and godly
woman
"Far more precious than jewels"

2. New Testament

Matthew 5–7: Sermon on the Mount
"Blessed are you . . ."
John 17: Jesus' high priestly prayer
"Sanctify them"
Acts 2: The Holy Spirit's coming on
Day of Pentecost
"All of them were filled with the Holy
Spirit"
Acts 15: The Jerusalem Council

"He has made no distinction between
them and us"
1 Cor. 13: Love chapter
"The greatest of these is love"
Hebrews 11: Hall of fame: heroes of the
faith
"By faith . . ."
Revelation 7: A glimpse of heaven
"A great multitude that no man could
count"

Verses and chapters and their names

Certain chapters and verses have been
given the following titles.

VERSES
Most precious verse: John 3: 16
"For God so loved the world that
He gave His only begotten Son, that
whoever believes in Him should
not perish but have everlasting life"
John 3: 16 NKJV.

Saddest verse: Mark 15: 34
"And at the ninth hour Jesus cried
out with a loud voice, saying, 'Eloi, Eloi,
lama sabachthani?' which is translated,
'My God, My God, why have You forsaken
Me?'" Mark 15: 34 NKJV

Grandest verse: Romans 8: 11
"But if the Spirit of Him who raised
Jesus from the dead dwells in you, He
who raised Christ from the dead will
also give life to your mortal bodies
through His Spirit who dwells in you"
Romans 8: 11 NKJV.

CHAPTERS

The Ten Commandments
chapter: Exodus 20

God's promised presence
chapter: Joshua 1

The Lord is my Shepherd
chapter: Psalms 23

Confession of sin chapter: Psalms 51

The praise of God chapter: Psalms 103

The Word of God chapter: Psalms 119

The wisdom chapter: Proverbs 8

The virtuous woman chapter: Prov. 31

The majesty of God chapter: Isaiah 40

The great invitation chapter: Isaiah 55

The Beatitudes chapter: Matthew 5

The Lord's Prayer chapter: Matthew 6

The sower and seed chapter: Matt. 13

The protection of the sheep chapter:
John 10

The comfort chapter: John 14

The abiding chapter: John 15

The justification chapter: Romans 5

The sanctification chapter: Romans 6

The glorification chapter: Romans 8

The marriage chapter: 1 Cor. 7

The gifts chapter: 1 Cor. 12

The love chapter: 1 Cor. 13

The Resurrection chapter: 1 Cor. 15

The fruit of the Spirit chapter: Gal. 5

The faith chapter: Hebrews 11

The chastisement chapter: Hebrews 12

The tongue chapter: James 3
"If anyone does not stumble in word,
he is a perfect man, able also to bridle
the whole body. Indeed, we put bits
in horses' mouths that they may
obey us, and we turn their whole
body. Look also at ships: although
they are so large and are driven by
fierce winds, they are turned by a
very small rudder wherever the pilot
desires. Even so the tongue is a little
member and boasts great things.

See how great a forest a little fire
kindles! And the tongue is a fire, a
world of iniquity. The tongue is so set
among our members that it defiles
the whole body, and sets on fire the
course of nature; and it is set on fire
by hell. For every kind of beast and
bird, of reptile and creature of the
sea, is tamed and has been tamed
by mankind. But no man can tame
the tongue. It is an unruly evil, full of
deadly poison. With it we bless our
God and Father, and with it we curse
men, who have been made in the
similitude of God. Out of the same
mouth proceed blessing and cursing.
My brethren, these things ought not
to be so. Does a spring send forth
fresh water and bitter from the same
opening? Can a fig tree, my brethren,
bear olives, or a grapevine bear figs?
Thus no spring yields both salt water
and fresh."

James 3: 2–12 NKJV

The reason for suffering chapter:
1 Peter 4

The fellowship chapter: 1 John 1

Bible readings in times of need (1)

Bible reading

It takes about seventy hours to read the entire Bible, reading at the speed the Bible is read aloud.

So by spending twelve minutes a day the whole Bible could be read aloud in one year.

Emergency numbers

Just as we may have a list of telephone numbers to call in an emergency it is useful to have a list of Bible passages which are particularly appropriate for challenging situations.

When in sorrow: call John 14.

When people let you down: call Psalm 27.

When longing to be spiritually fruitful: call John 15.

When you have sinned: call Psalm 51.

When you worry: call Matthew 6: 19–34.

When you are in danger: call Psalm 91.

When God seems far away: call Psalm 139.

When your faith needs stirring: call Hebrews 11.

When you are lonely and fearful: call Psalm 23.

When you grow bitter and critical: call 1 Cor. 13.

For Paul's secret to happiness: call Col. 3: 12–17.

For understanding of Christianity: call 2 Cor. 5: 15–19.

When you feel down and out: call Romans 8: 31.

When you want rest: call Matthew 11: 25–30.

When seeking God's assurance: call Romans 8: 1–30.

When away from home: call Psalm 121.

When you need courage: call Joshua 1.

When you are depressed: call Psalm 27.

Finding the right verse

The Bible is full of advice, comfort, and compassion. It has appropriate counsel for every situation.

The topics which now follow are:

WHERE TO TURN IN TIMES OF:

• spiritual aridity
• serious upset

WHERE TO TURN WHEN IN NEED OF:

• courage
• patience
• peace

WHERE TO TURN:

• in times of fear
• in times of doubt
• in times of grief
• when you need confidence
• when troubles hit you
• in times of illness
• when you have marriage problems
• if you are deserted by loved ones
• in times of perplexity

WHERE TO TURN IN TIMES OF
SPIRITUAL ARIDITY

Revelation 3: 2,15,16

"Be watchful, and strengthen the
things which remain, that are ready
to die: for I have not found thy works
perfect before God. I know thy works,
that thou are neither cold nor hot: I
would thou wert cold or hot. So then
because thou are lukewarm, and
neither cold nor hot, I will spue thee
out of my mouth."

Revelation 2: 4

"Nevertheless I have somewhat
against thee, because thou hast left thy
first love."

Hosea 6: 4

"O Ephraim, what shall I do unto
thee? O Judah, what shall I do unto
thee? for your goodness is as a morning
cloud, and as the early dew it goeth
away."

Deuteronomy 4: 9

"Only take heed to thyself, and keep
thy soul diligently, lest thou forget the
things which thine eyes have seen, and
lest they depart from thy heart all the
days of thy life: but teach them thy
sons, and thy sons' sons."

Deuteronomy 8: 11–14

"Beware that thou forget not the
Lord thy God, in not keeping his
commandments, and his judgments,
and his statutes, which I command thee
this day. Lest when thou hast eaten and
art full, and hast build goodly houses,
and dwelt therein; And when thy herds
and thy flocks multiply, and thy silver
and thy gold is multiplied, and all that

thou hast is multiplied; Then thine
heart be lifted up, and thou forget the
Lord thy God, which brought thee
house of bondage."

Psalm 44: 20,21

"If we have forgotten the name of our
God, or stretched out our hands to a
strange god; Shall not God search this
our? for he knoweth the secrets of the
heart."

Hebrews 3: 12,13

"Take heed, brethren, lest there be
in any of you an evil heart of unbelief,
in departing from the living God.
But exhort one another daily, while
it is called Today; lest any of you be
hardened through the deceitfulness of
sin."

Jeremiah 6: 16

WHERE TO TURN IN TIMES OF SERIOUS
UPSET

2 Timothy 1: 7

1 Corinthians 14: 33a

"For God is not the author of
confusion, but of peace."

Bible readings in times of need (2)

Finding the right verse, continued

Isaiah 41: 10

"Fear thou not; for I am with thee: be not dismayed; for I am thy God: I will strength thee; yea, I will help thee; yea, I will uphold thee with the right hand of my righteousness."

James 3: 16–18

"For where envying and strife is, there is confusion and every evil work: But the wisdom that is from above is first pure, then peaceable, gentle, and easy to be intreated, full of mercy and good fruits, without partiality, and without hypocrisy. And the fruit of righteousness is sown in peace of them that make peace."

1 Peter 2: 6

"Wherefore also it is contained in the scripture. Behold, I lay in Sion a chief cornerstone, elect, precious: and he that believeth on him shall not be confounded."

Isaiah 50: 7

"For the Lord God will help me; therefore shall I not be confounded: therefore have I set my face like a flint, and I know that I shall not be ashamed."

Psalm 55: 22

"Cast thy burden upon the Lord, and he shall sustain thee; he shall never suffer the righteous to be moved. "

Philippians 4: 6,7

"Be careful for nothing, but in every thing by prayer and supplication with thanksgiving let your requests be made known unto God. And the peace of God, which passeth all understanding, shall keep your hearts and minds through Jesus Christ."

Psalm 110: 165

"Great peace have they which love thy law: and nothing shall offend them."

Psalm 30: 5

"For this anger endureth but a moment; in his favor is life: weeping may endure for a night, but joy cometh in the morning. "

Isaiah 43: 2

"When thou passest through the waters, I will be with thee; and through the rivers, they shall not overflow thee: when thou walkest through the fire, thou shalt not be burned; neither shall the flame kindle upon thee."

Psalm 147: 3

"He healeth the broken in heart, and bindeth up their wounds."

Philippians 4: 8

"Finally brethren, whatsoever things are true, whatsoever things are honest, whatsoever things are just, whatsoever things are pure, whatsoever things are lovely, whatsoever things are of good report; if there be any virtue, and if there be any praise, think on these things."

Where to turn when in need of courage

Psalm 27: 14

"Wait on the Lord: be of good courage, and he shall strengthen thine heart: wait, I say, on the Lord."

Psalm 30: 5

"For his anger endureth but a moment; in his favor is life: weeping may endure for a night, but joy cometh in the morning."

1 Peter 4: 12,13

"Beloved, think it not strange concerning the fiery trial which is to try you, as through some strange thing happened unto you:

But rejoice, in as much as ye are partakers of Christ's suffering; that when his glory shall be revealed, ye may be glad also with exceeding joy."

Deuteronomy 33: 27

"The eternal God is thy refuge, and underneath are the everlasting arms: and he shall thrust out the enemy from before thee; and shall say, Destroy them. "

Psalm 118: 17

"I shall not die, but live, and declare the works of the Lord."

Philippians 4: 13

"I can do all things through Christ which strengtheneth me."

Psalm 31: 24

"Be of good courage, and he shall strengthen your heart, all ye that hope in the Lord."

Isaiah 40: 31

"But they that wait upon the Lord shall renew their strength; they shall mount up with wings of eagles; they shall run and not be weary; and they shall walk and not faint."

Isaiah 51: 11

"Therefore the redeemed of the Lord shall return, and come with singing unto Zion; and everlasting joy shall be upon their head; they shall obtain gladness and joy; and sorrow and mourning shall flee away."

Where to turn when in need of patience

Galatians 5: 22

"But the fruit of the Spirit is love, joy, peace, longsuffering, gentleness, goodness faith."

Isaiah 40: 31

"But they that wait upon the Lord shall renew their strength; they shall mount up with wings of eagles; they shall run and not be weary; and they shall walk and not faint."

Psalm 27: 14

"Wait on the Lord, be of good courage, and he shall strengthen thine heart: wait, I say, on the Lord."

Lamentations 3: 26

"It is good that a man should both hope and quietly wait for the salvation of the Lord."

Bible readings in times of need (3)

Finding the right verse, continued

WHERE TO TURN WHEN IN NEED OF PATIENCE, CONTINUED

Romans 8: 25

"But if we hope for that we see not, then do we with patience wait for it."

Hebrews 6: 12

"Rest in the Lord, and wait patiently for him: fret not thyself because of him who prospereth in his way, because of the man who bringeth wicked devices to pass. That ye be not slothful, but followers of them who through faith in patience inherit the promises."

Hebrews 10: 35–37

"Cast not away therefore your confidence, which hath great recompense of reward. For ye have need of patience, that, after ye have done the will of God, ye might receive the promise. For yet a little while, and he that shall come will come, and will not tarry."

WHERE TO TURN WHEN IN NEED OF PEACE

Isaiah 26: 3

"Thou wilt keep him in perfect Peace, whose mind is stayed on thee: because he trusteth in thee."

John 14: 27

"Peace, I leave with you, my peace I give unto you; not as the world giveth, give I unto you. Let not your heart be troubled, neither let it be afraid."

Philippians 4: 7

"And the peace of God, which passeth all understanding, shall keep your hearts and minds through Jesus Christ."

Romans 5: 1

"Therefore being justified by faith, we have peace with God through our Lord Jesus Christ."

Isaiah 26: 12

"Lord thou wilt ordain peace for us: for thou also hast wrought all our works in us."

Isaiah 55: 12

"For ye shall go out with joy, and shall be lead forth with peace: the mountains and the hills shall break forth before you into singing, and all the trees of the field shall clap their hands."

Psalm 37: 37

"Mark the perfect man, and behold the upright, for the end of that man is peace."

Romans 8: 6

"For to be carnally minded is death: but to be spiritually minded is life and peace."

Psalm 119: 165

"Great peace have they which love thy law: and nothing shall offend them."

Isaiah 57: 2

"He shall enter into peace: they shall rest in their beds, each one walking in his uprightness."

Romans 14: 17

"For the kingdom of God is not meat and drink; but righteousness, and peace and joy in the Holy Spirit."

Psalm 37: 11

"But the meek shall inherit the earth; and shall delight themselves in the abundance of peace."

Roman 15: 13

"Now the God of hope fill you with all joy and peace in believing, that ye may abound in hope, through the power of the Holy Spirit."

WHERE TO TURN IN TIMES OF FEAR

2 Timothy 1: 7

"For God hath not given us the spirit of fear; but of power, and of love, and of a sound mind. "

Romans 8: 15

"For ye have not received the spirit of bondage again to fear, but ye have received the Spirit of adoption, whereby we cry, Abba, Father."

1 John 4: 18

"There is no fear in love; but perfect love casteth out fear: because fear hath torment. He that feareth is not made perfect in love."

Psalm 91: 1

"He that dwelleth in the secret place of the most High shall abide under the shadow of the Almighty."

Psalm 91: 4 – 7

"He shall cover thee with his feathers, and under his wings shalt thou trust: his trust shall be thy shield and buckler. Thou shalt not be afraid for the terror by night; nor for the arrow that flieth by day; Nor for the pestilence that walketh in darkness: nor for the destruction that wasteth at noonday."

Proverbs 3: 25, 26

"Be not afraid of sudden fear, neither of the desolation of the wicked, when it cometh. For the Lord shall be thy confidence, and shall keep thy foot from being taken."

Isaiah 54: 14

"In righteousness shalt thou be established: thou shalt be far from oppression: for thou shalt not fear: and from terror; for it shall not come near thee."

Psalm 56: 11

"In God have I put my trust: I will not be afraid what man can do unto me."

Psalm 23: 4, 5

"Yea, though I walk through the valley of the shadow of death, I will fear no evil: for thou art with me; thy rod and thy staff they comfort me. Thou preparest a table before me in the presence of mine enemies: thou anointest my head with oil; my cup runneth over."

Bible readings in times of need (4)

Finding the right verse, continued

WHERE TO TURN IN TIMES OF DOUBT
Mark 11: 22–24

"And Jesus answering saith unto them, Have faith in God. For verily I say unto you, That whosoever shall say unto this mountain, Be thou removed, and be thou cast into the sea; and shall not doubt in his heart, but shall believe that those things which he saith shall come to pass: he shall have whatsoever he saith. Therefore I say unto you, What things soever ye desire, when you pray, believe that ye received them, and ye shall have them."

Luke 12: 29–31

"And seek not ye what ye shall eat, or what ye shall drink, neither be ye of doubtful mind. For all these things do the nations of the world seek after: and your Father knoweth that ye have need of these things. But rather seek ye the kingdom of God; and all these things shall be added unto you."

2 Peter 3: 9

"The Lord is not slack concerning his promise, as some men count slackness; but is longsuffering to us-ward, not willing that any should perish, but that all should come to repentance."

Isaiah 59: 1

"Behold, the Lord's hand is not shortened, that it cannot save; neither his ear heavy, that it cannot hear."

Isaiah 55: 10, 11

"For as the rain cometh down, and the snow from heaven, and returneth not thither, but watereth the earth, and maketh it bring fourth and bud, that it may give seed to the sower, and bread to the eater; So shall my word be that goeth forth out of my mouth: it shall not return unto me void, but it shall accomplish that which I please, and it shall prosper in the thing whereto I sent it."

WHERE TO TURN IN TIMES OF GRIEF
1 Thessalonians 4: 13,14

"But I would not have you be ignorant, brethren, concerning them which are asleep, that ye sorrow not, even as others which have no hope. If we believe that Jesus died and rose again, even so them also which sleep in Jesus will God bring with him."

Isaiah 49: 13b

"For the Lord hath comforted his people, and will have mercy upon the afflicted."

Isaiah 43: 2

"When thou passest through the waters, I will be with thee; and through the rivers, they shall not overflow thee; when thou walkest through the fire, thou shalt not be burned; neither shall the flame kindle upon thee."

Matthew 5: 4

"Blessed are they that mourn: for they shall be comforted."

Psalm 119: 50

"This is my comfort in my affliction: for thy word hath quickened me."

1 Peter 5: 7

"Casting all your care upon him; for he careth for you."

1 Corinthians 15: 55–57

"O death, where is thy sting? O grave, where is thy victory? The sting of death is sin; and the strength of sin is the law. But thanks be to God, which giveth us the victory through our Lord Jesus Christ."

WHERE TO TURN WHEN YOU NEED CONFIDENCE

Hebrews 10: 35,36

"Cast not away therefore your confidence, which hath great recompense of reward. for ye have need of patience, that, after ye have done the will of God, ye might receive the promise."

Philippians 1: 6

"Being confident of this very thing, that he which hath begun a good work in you will perform it until the day of Jesus Christ."

1 John 5: 14, 15

"And this is the confidence that we have in him, that, if we ask any thing according to his will, he heareth us: And if we know that he hear us, whatsoever we ask, we know that we have the petitions that we desired of him."

WHERE TO TURN WHEN TROUBLES HIT YOU

Isaiah 33: 16

"He shall dwell on high: his place of defense shall be the munitions of rocks: bread shall be given him; his waters shall be sure."

Nahum 1: 7

"The Lord is good, a strong hold in the day of trouble; and he knoweth them that trust in him."

2 Corinthians 4: 8,9

"We are troubled on every side, yet not distressed; we are perplexed, but not in despair; Persecuted, but no forsaken; cast down, but not destroyed."

Psalm 138: 7

"Through I walk in the midst of trouble, thou wilt revive me: thou shalt stretch forth thine hand against the wrath of mine enemies, and thy right hand shall save me."

Isaiah 43: 2

"When thou passes through the waters, I will be with thee: and through the rivers, they shall not overflow thee: when thou walkest through the fire, thou shalt not be burned; neither shall the flame kindle upon thee."

Bible readings in times of need (5)

Finding the right verse, continued

WHERE TO TURN WHEN TROUBLES
HIT YOU, CONTINUED
Romans 8: 28
"And we know that all things work together for good to them that love God, to them who are the called according to his purpose."

Psalm 31: 7
"I will be glad and rejoice in thy mercy: for thou hast considered my trouble; thou hast known my soul in adversities."

Psalm 121: 1,2
"I will lift up mine eyes unto the hills, from whence cometh my help. My help cometh from the Lord, which made heaven and earth."

Hebrews 4: 15,16
"For we have no and high priest which cannot be touched with the feeling of our infirmities; but was in all poinst tempted like as we are, yet without sin. Let us therefore come boldly unto the throne of grace, that we may obtain mercy, and find grace to help in time of need."

1 Peter 5: 7
"Casting all your care upon him; for he careth for you."

WHERE TO TURN IN TIMES OF ILLNESS
2 John 2
"Beloved, I wish above all things that thou mayest prosper and be in health, even as they soul prospereth."

Psalm 102: 3
"Who forgiveth all thine iniquities; who healeth all thy diseases."

Isaiah 53: 5
"But he was wounded for our transgressions, he was bruised for our iniquities: the chastisement of our peace was upon him; and with his stripes we are healed."

Jeremiah 30: 17a
"For I will restore health unto thee, and I will heal thee of thy wounds, saith the Lord."

Matthew 10: 8
"Heal the sick, cleanse the lepers, raise the dead, cast out devils: freely ye have received, freely give."

WHERE TO TURN WHEN YOU HAVE
MARRIAGE PROBLEMS
Genesis 2: 24
"Therefore shall a man leave his father and mother, and shall cleave unto his wife: and they shall be one flesh."

Ephesians 5: 21–33
"Submitting yourselves one to another in the fear of God.
Wives, submit yourselves unto your own husbands, as unto the Lord.
For the husband is the head of the wife, even as Christ is the head of the church: and he is the savior of the body.
Therefore as the church is subject

unto Christ, so let the wives be to their own husband in every thing.

Husbands, love your wives, even as Christ also loved the church, and gave himself for it;

That he might sanctify and cleanse it with the washing of water by the word.

That he might present it to himself a glorious church, not having spot, or wrinkle, or any such things; but that it should be holy and without blemish.

So ought men to love their wives as their own bodies. He that loveth his wife loveth himself.

For no man ever yet hated his own flesh; but nourished and cherisheth it, even as the Lord the church:

For we are member of his body, of his flesh, and of his bones.

For this cause shall a man leave his father and mother, and shall be joined unto his wife, and they two shall be one flesh.

This is a great mystery: but I speak concerning Christ and the church.

Nevertheless let everyone of you in particular so love his wife even as himself; and the wife see that she reverence her husband."

WHERE TO TURN IF YOU ARE
DESERTED BY LOVED ONES
Psalm 94: 14

"For the Lord will not cast off his people, neither will he forsake his inheritance."

Psalm 27: 10

"When my father and my mother forsake me, then the Lord will take me up."

Matthew 28: 20

"Teaching them to observe all thing whatsoever I have commanded you: and, lo, I am with you always, even unto the end of the world. Amen."

2 Corinthians 4: 9

"Persecuted, but not forsaken; cast down, but not destroyed;"

1 Peter 5: 7

"Casting all your care upon him; for he careth for you."

WHERE TO TURN IN TIMES OF
PERPLEXITY
Isaiah 55: 8,9

"For my thoughts are not your thoughts, neither are your ways my ways, saith the Lord.

For as the heavens are higher than the earth, so are my ways higher than your ways, and my thoughts than your thoughts."

Jeremiah 33: 3

"Call unto me, and I will answer thee, and shew thee great and mighty things, which thou knowest not."

Romans 8: 31

"What shall we then say to these things? If God be for us, who can be against us?"

Bible reading schedules (1)

Reading all the Psalms and Proverbs in a month

Some people read two psalms every day and one chapter from the book of Proverbs every day.

One simple way to read through all the Psalms and Proverbs each month is as follows.

Read the Psalm which corresponds to today's date, "plus 30." So if today is the 15th of the month you read Psalm 15. The "plus 30" means that you add 30 to today's date and read that psalm as well. You keep on adding 30 to the last psalm you read until you reach the end of the psalms. So for the 15th of the month you will read the following psalms: Psalm 15, Psalm 45, Psalm 75, Psalm 105, and Psalm 135.

Then read Proverbs 15 also.

Daily Bible reading schedule

Some people find it helpful to read the Bible every day in a systematic way. The following readings are designed to take you through the Bible in one year.

The day of the month is followed by the reference for the Bible reading for each day.

THE BIBLE IN ONE YEAR

JANUARY

Genesis thru Exodus

1 – Genesis 1–2
2 – Genesis 3–5
3 – Genesis 6–9
4 – Genesis 10–11
5 – Genesis 12–14
6 – Genesis 15–17
7 – Genesis 18–20

8 – Genesis 21–24
9 – Genesis 25–26
10 – Genesis 27–30
11 – Genesis 31–33
12 – Genesis 34–36
13 – Genesis 37–38
14 – Genesis 39–41
15 – Genesis 42–43
16 – Genesis 44–45
17 – Genesis 46–47
18 – Genesis 48–50
19 – Exodus 1–2
20 – Exodus 3–6
21 – Exodus 7–10
22 – Exodus 11–12
23 – Exodus 13–15
24 – Exodus 16–18
25 – Exodus 19–20
26 – Exodus 21–24
27 – Exodus 25–27
28 – Exodus 28–29
29 – Exodus 30–31
30 – Exodus 32–34
31 – Exodus 35–40

FEBRUARY

Leviticus thru Deuteronomy

1 – Leviticus 1–3
2 – Leviticus 4–7
3 – Leviticus 8–10
4 – Leviticus 11–13
5 – Leviticus 14–15
6 – Leviticus 16–17
7 – Leviticus 18–20
8 – Leviticus 21–23
9 – Leviticus 24–27
10 – Numbers 1–2
11 – Numbers 3–4
12 – Numbers 5–8
13 – Numbers 9–12

14 – Numbers 13–16
15 – Numbers 17–20
16 – Numbers 21–25
17 – Numbers 26–27
18 – Numbers 28–30
19 – Numbers 31–33
20 – Numbers 34–36
21 – Deuteronomy 1–4
22 – Deuteronomy 5–7
23 – Deuteronomy 8–11
24 – Deuteronomy 12–16
25 – Deuteronomy 17–20
26 – Deuteronomy 21–26
27 – Deuteronomy 27–30
28 – Deuteronomy 31–34

MARCH
Joshua thru Samuel
1 – Joshua 1–5
2 – Joshua 6–8
3 – Joshua 9–12
4 – Joshua 13–17
5 – Joshua 18–21
6 – Joshua 22–24
7 – Judges 1–2
8 – Judges 3–5
9 – Judges 6–8
10 – Judges 9–12
11 – Judges 13–16
12 – Judges 17–19
13 – Judges 20–21
14 – Ruth
15 – 1 Samuel 1–3
16 – 1 Samuel 4–8
17 – 1 Samuel 9–12
18 – 1 Samuel 13–15
19 – 1 Samuel 16–17
20 – 1 Samuel 18–19
21 – 1 Samuel 20–23
22 – 1 Samuel 24–26
23 – 1 Samuel 27–31
24 – 2 Samuel 1–4

25 – 2 Samuel 5–7
26 – 2 Samuel 8–10
27 – 2 Samuel 11–12
28 – 2 Samuel 13–14
29 – 2 Samuel 15–18
30 – 2 Samuel 19–20
31 – 2 Samuel 21–24

APRIL
1 Kings thru 2 Chronicles
1 – 1 Kings 1–4
2 – 1 Kings 5–6
3 – 1 Kings 7–8
4 – 1 Kings 9–11
5 – 1 Kings 12–14
6 – 1 Kings 15–16
7 – 1 Kings 17–19
8 – 1 Kings 20–22
9 – 2 Kings 1–3
10 – 2 Kings 4–8
11 – 2 Kings 9–12
12 – 2 Kings 13–17
13 – 2 Kings 18–21
14 – 2 Kings 22–25
15 – 1 Chronicles 1–4
16 – 1 Chronicles 5–9
17 – 1 Chronicles 10–13
18 – 1 Chronicles 14–16
19 – 1 Chronicles 17–21
20 – 1 Chronicles 22–27
21 – 1 Chronicles 28–29
22 – 2 Chronicles 1–5
23 – 2 Chronicles 6–9
24 – 2 Chronicles 10–12
25 – 2 Chronicles 13–16
26 – 2 Chronicles 17–20
27 – 2 Chronicles 21–25
28 – 2 Chronicles 26–28
29 – 2 Chronicles 29–32
30 – 2 Chronicles 33–36

Bible reading schedules (2)

The Bible in one year, continued

MAY

Ezra thru Job

1 – Ezra 1–2
2 – Ezra 3–4
3 – Ezra 5–6
4 – Ezra 7–8
5 – Ezra 9–10
6 – Nehemiah 1–2
7 – Nehemiah 3–4
8 – Nehemiah 5–6
9 – Nehemiah 7
10 – Nehemiah 8
11 – Nehemiah 9–10
12 – Nehemiah 11–12
13 – Nehemiah 13
14 – Esther 1–2
15 – Esther 3–4
16 – Esther 5–7
17 – Esther 8–10
18 – Job 1–3
19 – Job 4–7
20 – Job 8–10
21 – Job 11–14
22 – Job 15–17
23 – Job 18–19
24 – Job 20–21
25 – Job 22–24
26 – Job 25–28
27 – Job 29–31
28 – Job 32–34
29 – Job 35–37
30 – Job 38–39
31 – Job 40–42

JUNE

Psalms

1 – Psalms 1–6
2 – Psalms 7–12
3 – Psalms 13–18
4 – Psalms 19–24
5 – Psalms 25–30
6 – Psalms 31–33
7 – Psalms 34–36
8 – Psalms 37–41
9 – Psalms 42–45
10 – Psalms 46–49
11 – Psalms 50–54
12 – Psalms 55–59
13 – Psalms 60–66
14 – Psalms 67–69
15 – Psalms 70–72
16 – Psalms 73–77
17 – Psalms 78–79
18 – Psalms 80–83
19 – Psalms 84–89
20 – Psalms 90–97
21 – Psalms 98–103
22 – Psalms 104–106
23 – Psalms 107–110
24 – Psalms 111–118
25 – Psalms 119: 1–112
26 – Psalms 119: 113–176;
and Psalms 120–127
27 – Psalms 128–134
28 – Psalms 135–139
29 – Psalms 140–145
30 – Psalms 146–150

JULY

Proverbs thru Isaiah

1 – Proverbs 1–4
2 – Proverbs 5–9
3 – Proverbs 10–13
4 – Proverbs 14–17
5 – Proverbs 18–21
6 – Proverbs 22–24
7 – Proverbs 25–27
8 – Proverbs 28–29

9 – Proverbs 30–31
10 – Eccles. 1–6
11 – Eccles. 7–12
12 – Song of Solomon 1–4
13 – Song of Solomon 5–8
14 – Isaiah 1–4
15 – Isaiah 5–8
16 – Isaiah 9–12
17 – Isaiah 13–16
18 – Isaiah 17–20
19 – Isaiah 21–23
20 – Isaiah 24–27
21 – Isaiah 28–30
22 – Isaiah 31–35
23 – Isaiah 36–39
24 – Isaiah 40–41
25 – Isaiah 42–43
26 – Isaiah 44–45
27 – Isaiah 46–48
28 – Isaiah 49–51
29 – Isaiah 52–57
30 – Isaiah 58–62
31 – Isaiah 63–66

AUGUST
Jeremiah thru Daniel
1 – Jeremiah 1–3
2 – Jeremiah 4–6
3 – Jeremiah 7–10
4 – Jeremiah 11–15
5 – Jeremiah 16–20
6 – Jeremiah 21–25
7 – Jeremiah 26–29
8 – Jeremiah 30–31
9 – Jeremiah 32–33
10 – Jeremiah 34–36
11 – Jeremiah 37–39
12 – Jeremiah 40–45
13 – Jeremiah 46–49
14 – Jeremiah 50–52
15 – Lamentations
16 – Ezekiel 1–6

17 – Ezekiel 7–11
18 – Ezekiel 12–15
19 – Ezekiel 16–19
20 – Ezekiel 20–21
21 – Ezekiel 22–23
22 – Ezekiel 24–28
23 – Ezekiel 29–32
24 – Ezekiel 33–36
25 – Ezekiel 37–39
26 – Ezekiel 40–43
27 – Ezekiel 44–48
28 – Daniel 1–3
29 – Daniel 4–6
30 – Daniel 7–9
31 – Daniel 10–12

SEPTEMBER
Hosea thru Malachi
1 – Hosea 1–3
2 – Hosea 4–6
3 – Hosea 7–8
4 – Hosea 9–11
5 – Hosea 12–14
6 – Joel 1
7 – Joel 2–3
8 – Amos 1–2
9 – Amos 3–5
10 – Amos 6–7
11 – Amos 8–9
12 – Obadiah
13 – Jonah 1–2
14 – Jonah 3–4
15 – Micah 1–2
16 – Micah 3–5
17 – Micah 6–7
18 – Nahum
19 – Habakkuk
20 – Zephaniah 1–2
21 – Zephaniah 3
22 – Haggai
23 – Zechariah 1–2

Bible reading schedules (3)

The Bible in one year, continued

SEPTEMBER, CONTINUED
Hosea thru Malachi, continued

24 – Zechariah 3–4

25 – Zechariah 5–6

26 – Zechariah 7–8

27 – Zechariah 9–11

28 – Zechariah 12–14

29 – Malachi 1–2

30 – Malachi 3–4

OCTOBER
Matthew thru John

1 – Matthew 1–4

2 – Matthew 5–7

3 – Matthew 8–11

4 – Matthew 12–13

5 – Matthew 14–15

6 – Matthew 16–19

7 – Matthew 20–23

8 – Matthew 24–25

9 – Matthew 26–28

10 – Mark 1–3

11 – Mark 4–5

12 – Mark 6–7

13 – Mark 8–10

14 – Mark 11–13

15 – Mark 14–16

16 – Luke 1–2

17 – Luke 3–4

18 – Luke 5–6

19 – Luke 7–9

20 – Luke 10–12

21 – Luke 13–15

22 – Luke 16–18

23 – Luke 19–21

24 – Luke 22–24

25 – John 1–2

26 – John 3–5

27 – John 6–8

28 – John 9–12

29 – John 13–14

30 – John 15–17

31 – John 18–21

NOVEMBER
Acts thru Colossians

1 – Acts 1–2

2 – Acts 3–4

3 – Acts 5–7

4 – Acts 8–9

5 – Acts 10–12

6 – Acts 13–15

7 – Acts 16–18

8 – Acts 19–20

9 – Acts 21–23

10 – Acts 24–26

11 – Acts 27–28

12 – Romans 1–3

13 – Romans 4–5

14 – Romans 6–8

15 – Romans 9–11

16 – Romans 12–16

17 – 1 Corinthians 1–3

18 – 1 Corinthians 4–6

19 – 1 Corinthians 7–10

20 – 1 Corinthians 11–14

21 – 1 Corinthians 15–16

22 – 2 Corinthians 1–5

23 – 2 Corinthians 6–9

24 – 2 Corinthians 10–13

25 – Galatians 1–2

26 – Galatians 3–6

27 – Ephesians 1–3

28 – Ephesians 4–6

29 – Philippians

30 – Colossians

DECEMBTER
1 *Thessalonians thru Revelation*

1 – 1 Thessalonians 1–3

2 – 1 Thessalonians 4–5

3 – 2 Thessalonians

4 – 1 Timothy 1–3

5 – 1 Timothy 4–6

6 – 2 Timothy 1–2

7 – 2 Timothy 3–4

8 – Titus

9 – Philemon

10 – Hebrews 1–2

11 – Hebrews 3–4

12 – Hebrews 5–7

13 – Hebrews 8–10

14 – Hebrews 11–13

15 – James 1–2

16 – James 3–5

17 – 1 Peter 1–2

18 – 1 Peter 3–5

19 – 2 Peter

20 – 1 John 1–2

21 – 1 John 3–5

22 – 2 John

23 – 3 John

24 – Jude

25 – Revelation 1–3

26 – Revelation 4–6

27 – Revelation 7–9

28 – Revelation 10–13

29 – Revelation 14–16

30 – Revelation 17–19

31 – Revelation 20–22

Bible reading schedules (4)

Robert Murray McCheyne's Bible reading schedule

The following Bible reading schedule was compiled by the godly Scottish minister, Robert Murray McCheyne, in 1842.

It gives four portions of Scripture for each day, two for the morning and two for the evening.

By following this plan you will read through the whole of the Old Testament once in a year and the whole of the New Testament and the Psalms twice in a year.

JANUARY				
Date	**Morning**		**Evening**	
1	Gen. 1	Matt. 1	Ezra 1	Acts 1
2	Gen. 2	Matt. 2	Ezra 2	Acts 2
3	Gen. 3	Matt. 3	Ezra 3	Acts 3
4	Gen. 4	Matt. 4	Ezra 4	Acts 4
5	Gen. 5	Matt. 5	Ezra 5	Acts 5
6	Gen. 6	Matt. 6	Ezra 6	Acts 6
7	Gen. 7	Matt. 7	Ezra 7	Acts 7
8	Gen. 8	Matt. 8	Ezra 8	Acts 8
9	Gen. 9,10	Matt. 9	Ezra 9	Acts 9
10	Gen. 11	Matt. 10	Ezra 10	Acts 10
11	Gen. 12	Matt. 11	Neh. 1	Acts 11
12	Gen. 13	Matt. 12	Neh. 2	Acts 12
13	Gen. 14	Matt. 13	Neh. 3	Acts 13
14	Gen. 15	Matt. 14	Neh. 4	Acts 14
15	Gen. 16	Matt. 15	Neh. 5	Acts 15
16	Gen. 17	Matt. 16	Neh. 6	Acts 16
17	Gen. 18	Matt. 17	Neh. 7	Acts 17
18	Gen. 19	Matt. 18	Neh. 8	Acts 18
19	Gen. 20	Matt. 19	Neh. 9	Acts 19
20	Gen. 21	Matt. 20	Neh. 10	Acts 20
21	Gen. 22	Matt. 21	Neh. 11	Acts 21
22	Gen. 23	Matt. 22	Neh. 12	Acts 22
23	Gen. 24	Matt. 23	Neh. 13	Acts 23
24	Gen. 25	Matt. 24	Esther 1	Acts 24
25	Gen. 26	Matt. 25	Esther 2	Acts 25
26	Gen. 27	Matt. 26	Esther 3	Acts 26
27	Gen. 28	Matt. 27	Esther 4	Acts 27
28	Gen. 29	Matt. 28	Esther 5	Acts 28
29	Gen. 30	Mark 1	Esther 6	Rom. 1
30	Gen. 31	Mark 2	Esther 7	Rom. 2
31	Gen. 32	Mark 3	Esther 8	Rom. 3

FEBRUARY				
Date	**Morning**		**Evening**	
1	Gen. 33	Mark 4	Esther 9,10	Rom. 4
2	Gen. 34	Mark 5	Job 1	Rom. 5
3	Gen. 35,36	Mark 6	Job 2	Rom. 6
4	Gen. 37	Mark 7	Job 3	Rom. 7
5	Gen. 38	Mark 8	Job 4	Rom. 8
6	Gen. 39	Mark 9	Job 5	Rom. 9
7	Gen. 40	Mark 10	Job 6	Rom. 10
8	Gen. 41	Mark 11	Job 7	Rom. 11
9	Gen. 42	Mark 12	Job 8	Rom. 12
10	Gen. 43	Mark 13	Job 9	Rom. 13
11	Gen. 44	Mark 14	Job 10	Rom. 14
12	Gen. 45	Mark 15	Job 11	Rom. 15
13	Gen. 46	Mark 16	Job 12	Rom. 16
14	Gen. 47	Luke 1:1-38	Job 13	1 Cor. 1
15	Gen. 48	Luke 1:39-80	Job 14	1 Cor. 2
16	Gen. 49	Luke 2	Job 15	1 Cor. 3
17	Gen. 50	Luke 3	Job 16,17	1 Cor. 4
18	Ex. 1	Luke 4	Job 18	1 Cor. 5
19	Ex. 2	Luke 5	Job 19	1 Cor. 6
20	Ex. 3	Luke 6	Job 20	1 Cor. 7
21	Ex. 4	Luke 7	Job 21	1 Cor. 8
22	Ex. 5	Luke 8	Job 22	1 Cor. 9
23	Ex. 6	Luke 9	Job 23	1 Cor. 10
24	Ex. 7	Luke 10	Job 24	1 Cor. 11
25	Ex. 8	Luke 11	Job 25,26	1 Cor. 12
26	Ex. 9	Luke 12	Job 27	1 Cor. 13
27	Ex. 10	Luke 13	Job 28	1 Cor. 14
28	Ex. 11,12:21	Luke 14	Job 29	1 Cor. 15

Date	Morning		Evening	
MARCH				
1	Ex.12:22-51	Luke 15	Job 30	1 Cor. 16
2	Ex. 13	Luke 16	Job 31	2 Cor. 1
3	Ex. 14	Luke 17	Job 32	2 Cor. 2
4	Ex. 15	Luke 18	Job 33	2 Cor. 3
5	Ex. 16	Luke 19	Job 34	2 Cor. 4
6	Ex. 17	Luke 20	Job 35	2 Cor. 5
7	Ex. 18	Luke 21	Job 36	2 Cor. 6
8	Ex. 19	Luke 22	Job 37	2 Cor. 7
9	Ex. 20	Luke 23	Job 38	2 Cor. 8
10	Ex. 21	Luke 24	Job 39	2 Cor. 9
11	Ex. 22	John 1	Job 40	2 Cor. 10
12	Ex. 23	John 2	Job 41	2 Cor. 11
13	Ex. 24	John 3	Job 42	2 Cor. 12
14	Ex. 25	John 4	Prov. 1	2 Cor. 13
15	Ex. 26	John 5	Prov. 2	Gal. 1
16	Ex. 27	John 6	Prov. 3	Gal. 2
17	Ex. 28	John 7	Prov. 4	Gal. 3
18	Ex. 29	John 8	Prov. 5	Gal. 4
19	Ex. 30	John 9	Prov. 6	Gal. 5
20	Ex. 31	John 10	Prov. 7	Gal. 6
21	Ex. 32	John 11	Prov. 8	Eph. 1
22	Ex. 33	John 12	Prov. 9	Eph. 2
23	Ex. 34	John 13	Prov. 10	Eph. 3
24	Ex. 35	John 14	Prov. 11	Eph. 4
25	Ex. 36	John 15	Prov. 12	Eph. 5
26	Ex. 37	John 16	Prov. 13	Eph. 6
27	Ex. 38	John 17	Prov. 14	Phil. 1
28	Ex. 39	John 18	Prov. 15	Phil. 2
29	Ex. 40	John 19	Prov. 16	Phil. 3
30	Lev. 1	John 20	Prov. 17	Phil. 4
31	Lev. 2,3	John 21	Prov. 18	Col. 1

Date	Morning		Evening	
APRIL				
1	Lev. 4	Ps. 1,2	Prov. 19	Col. 2
2	Lev. 5	Ps. 3,4	Prov. 20	Col. 3
3	Lev. 6	Ps. 5,6	Prov. 21	Col. 4
4	Lev. 7	Ps. 7,8	Prov. 22	1 Thess.1
5	Lev. 8	Ps. 9	Prov. 23	1 Thess.2
6	Lev. 9	Ps. 10	Prov. 24	1 Thess.3
7	Lev. 10	Ps. 11,12	Prov. 25	1 Thess.4
8	Lev. 11,12	Ps. 13,14	Prov. 26	1 Thess.5
9	Lev. 13	Ps. 15,16	Prov. 27	2 Thess.1
10	Lev. 14	Ps. 17	Prov. 28	2 Thess.2
11	Lev. 15	Ps. 18	Prov. 29	2 Thess.3
12	Lev. 16	Ps. 19	Prov. 30	1 Tim. 1
13	Lev. 17	Ps. 20,21	Prov. 31	1 Tim. 2
14	Lev. 18	Ps. 22	Eccles. 1	1 Tim. 3
15	Lev. 19	Ps. 23,24	Eccles. 2	1 Tim. 4
16	Lev. 20	Ps. 25	Eccles. 3	1 Tim. 5
17	Lev. 21	Ps. 26,27	Eccles. 4	1 Tim. 6
18	Lev. 22	Ps. 28,29	Eccles. 5	2 Tim. 1
19	Lev. 23	Ps. 30	Eccles. 6	2 Tim. 2
20	Lev. 24	Ps. 31	Eccles. 7	2 Tim. 3
21	Lev. 25	Ps. 32	Eccles. 8	2 Tim. 4
22	Lev. 26	Ps. 33	Eccles. 9	Titus 1
23	Lev. 27	Ps. 34	Eccles. 10	Titus 2
24	Num. 1	Ps. 35	Eccles. 11	Titus 3
25	Num. 2	Ps. 36	Eccles. 12	Philemon 1
26	Num. 3	Ps. 37	Song 1	Heb. 1
27	Num. 4	Ps. 38	Song 2	Heb. 2
28	Num. 5	Ps. 39	Song 3	Heb. 3
29	Num. 6	Ps. 40,41	Song 4	Heb. 4
30	Num. 7	Ps. 42,43	Song 5	Heb. 5

Bible reading schedules (5)

MAY				
Date	Morning		Evening	
1	Num. 8	Ps. 44	Song 6	Heb. 6
2	Num. 9	Ps. 45	Song 7	Heb. 7
3	Num.10	Ps. 46,47	Song 8	Heb. 8
4	Num.11	Ps. 48	Is. 1	Heb. 9
5	Num. 12,13	Ps. 49	Is. 2	Heb. 10
6	Num.14	Ps. 50	Is. 3,4	Heb. 11
7	Num.15	Ps. 51	Is. 5	Heb. 12
8	Num.16	Ps. 52-54	Is. 6	Heb. 13
9	Num. 17,18	Ps. 55	Is. 7	James 1
10	Num. 19	Ps. 56,57	Is. 8-9:7	James 2
11	Num. 20	Ps. 58,59	Isa. 9:8-10:4	James 3
12	Num. 21	Ps. 60,61	Isa.10:5-34	James 4
13	Num. 22	Ps. 62,63	Is. 11,12	James 5
14	Num. 23	Ps. 64,65	Is. 13	1 Pet. 1
15	Num. 24	Ps. 66,67	Is. 14	1 Pet. 2
16	Num. 25	Ps. 68	Is. 15	1 Pet. 3
17	Num. 26	Ps. 69	Is. 16	1 Pet. 4
18	Num. 27	Ps. 70,71	Is. 17,18	1 Pet. 5
19	Num. 28	Ps. 72	Is. 19,20	2 Pet. 1
20	Num. 29	Ps. 73	Is. 21	2 Pet. 2
21	Num. 30	Ps. 74	Is. 22	2 Pet. 3
22	Num. 31	Ps. 75,76	Is. 23	1 John 1
23	Num. 32	Ps. 77	Is. 24	1 John 2
24	Num. 33	Ps. 78:1-37	Is. 25	1 John 3
25	Num. 34	Ps. 78:38-72	Is. 26	1 John 4
26	Num. 35	Ps. 79	Is. 27	1 John 5
27	Num. 36	Ps. 80	Is. 28	2 John 1
28	Deut. 1	Ps. 81,82	Is. 29	3 John 1
29	Deut. 2	Ps. 83,84	Is. 30	Jude 1
30	Deut. 3	Ps. 85	Is. 31	Rev. 1
31	Deut. 4	Ps. 86,87	Is. 32	Rev. 2

JUNE				
Date	Morning		Evening	
1	Deut. 5	Ps. 88	Is. 33	Rev. 3
2	Deut. 6	Ps. 89	Is. 34	Rev. 4
3	Deut. 7	Ps. 90	Is. 35	Rev. 5
4	Deut. 8	Ps. 91	Is. 36	Rev. 6
5	Deut. 9	Ps. 92,93	Is. 37	Rev. 7
6	Deut. 10	Ps. 94	Is. 38	Rev. 8
7	Deut. 11	Ps. 95,96	Is. 39	Rev. 9
8	Deut. 12	Ps. 97,98	Is. 40	Rev. 10
9	Deut. 13,14	Ps. 99-101	Is. 41	Rev. 11
10	Deut. 15	Ps.102	Is. 42	Rev. 12
11	Deut. 16	Ps.103	Is. 43	Rev. 13
12	Deut. 17	Ps.104	Is. 44	Rev. 14
13	Deut. 18	Ps.105	Is. 45	Rev. 15
14	Deut. 19	Ps.106	Is. 46	Rev. 16
15	Deut. 20	Ps.107	Is. 47	Rev. 17
16	Deut. 21	Ps.108,109	Is. 48	Rev. 18
17	Deut. 22	Ps.110,111	Is. 49	Rev. 19
18	Deut. 23	Ps.112,113	Is. 50	Rev. 20
19	Deut. 24	Ps.114,115	Is. 51	Rev. 21
20	Deut. 25	Ps.116	Is. 52	Rev. 22
21	Deut. 26	Ps.117,118	Is. 53	Matt. 1
22	Deut. 27-28:19	Ps.119:1-24	Is. 54	Matt. 2
23	Deut. 28:20-68	Ps.119:25-48	Is. 55	Matt. 3
24	Deut. 29	Ps.119:49-72	Is. 56	Matt. 4
25	Deut. 30	Ps.119:73-96	Is. 57	Matt. 5
26	Deut. 31	Ps.119:97-120	Is. 58	Matt. 6
27	Deut. 32	Ps.119:121-144	Is. 59	Matt. 7
28	Deut. 33,34	Ps.119:145-176	Is. 60	Matt. 8
29	Josh. 1	Ps.120-122	Is. 61	Matt. 9
30	Josh. 2	Ps.123-125	Is. 62	Matt.10

JULY			
Date	Morning		Evening
1	Josh. 3	Ps.126-128	Is. 63	Matt. 11
2	Josh. 4	Ps.129-131	Is. 64	Matt. 12
3	Josh. 5-6:5	Ps.132-134	Is. 65	Matt. 13
4	Josh. 6:6-27	Ps.135-136	Is. 66	Matt. 14
5	Josh. 7	Ps.137,138	Jer. 1	Matt. 15
6	Josh. 8	Ps.139	Jer. 2	Matt. 16
7	Josh. 9	Ps.140,141	Jer. 3	Matt. 17
8	Josh. 10	Ps.142,143	Jer. 4	Matt. 18
9	Josh. 11	Ps.144	Jer. 5	Matt. 19
10	Josh. 12,13	Ps.145	Jer. 6	Matt. 20
11	Josh. 14,15	Ps.146,147	Jer. 7	Matt. 21
12	Josh. 16,17	Ps.148	Jer. 8	Matt. 22
13	Josh. 18,19	Ps.149,150	Jer. 9	Matt. 23
14	Josh. 20,21	Acts 1	Jer. 10	Matt. 24
15	Josh. 22	Acts 2	Jer. 11	Matt. 25
16	Josh. 23	Acts 3	Jer. 12	Matt. 26
17	Josh. 24	Acts 4	Jer. 13	Matt. 27
18	Judg. 1	Acts 5	Jer. 14	Matt. 28
19	Judg. 2	Acts 6	Jer. 15	Mark 1
20	Judg. 3	Acts 7	Jer. 16	Mark 2
21	Judg. 4	Acts 8	Jer. 17	Mark 3
22	Judg. 5	Acts 9	Jer. 18	Mark 4
23	Judg. 6	Acts 10	Jer. 19	Mark 5
24	Judg. 7	Acts 11	Jer. 20	Mark 6
25	Judg. 8	Acts 12	Jer. 21	Mark 7
26	Judg. 9	Acts 13	Jer. 22	Mark 8
27	Judg.10-11:11	Acts 14	Jer. 23	Mark 9
28	Judg. 11:12-40	Acts 15	Jer. 24	Mark 10
29	Judg. 12	Acts 16	Jer. 25	Mark 11
30	Judg. 13	Acts 17	Jer. 26	Mark 12
31	Judg. 14	Acts 18	Jer. 27	Mark 13

AUGUST			
Date	Morning		Evening
1	Judg. 15	Acts 19	Jer. 28	Mark 14
2	Judg. 16	Acts 20	Jer. 29	Mark 15
3	Judg. 17	Acts 21	Jer. 30,31	Mark 16
4	Judg. 18	Acts 22	Jer. 32	Ps. 1,2
5	Judg. 19	Acts 23	Jer. 33	Ps. 3,4
6	Judg. 20	Acts 24	Jer. 34	Ps. 5,6
7	Judg. 21	Acts 25	Jer. 35	Ps. 7,8
8	Ruth 1	Acts 26	Jer. 36,45	Ps. 9
9	Ruth 2	Acts 27	Jer. 37	Ps. 10
10	Ruth 3,4	Acts 28	Jer. 38	Ps. 11,12
11	1 Sam. 1	Rom. 1	Jer. 39	Ps. 13,14
12	1 Sam. 2	Rom. 2	Jer. 40	Ps. 15,16
13	1 Sam. 3	Rom. 3	Jer. 41	Ps. 17
14	1 Sam. 4	Rom. 4	Jer. 42	Ps. 18
15	1 Sam. 5,6	Rom. 5	Jer. 43	Ps. 19
16	1 Sam. 7,8	Rom. 6	Jer. 44	Ps. 20,21
17	1 Sam. 9	Rom. 7	Jer. 46	Ps. 22
18	1 Sam. 10	Rom. 8	Jer. 47	Ps. 23,24
19	1 Sam. 11	Rom. 9	Jer. 48	Ps. 25
20	1 Sam. 12	Rom. 10	Jer. 49	Ps. 26,27
21	1 Sam. 13	Rom. 11	Jer. 50	Ps. 28,29
22	1 Sam. 14	Rom. 12	Jer. 51	Ps. 30
23	1 Sam. 15	Rom. 13	Jer. 52	Ps. 31
24	1 Sam. 16	Rom. 14	Lam. 1	Ps. 32
25	1 Sam. 17	Rom. 15	Lam. 2	Ps. 33
26	1 Sam. 18	Rom. 16	Lam. 3	Ps. 34
27	1 Sam. 19	1 Cor. 1	Lam. 4	Ps. 35
28	1 Sam. 20	1 Cor. 2	Lam. 5	Ps. 36
29	1 Sam. 21,22	1 Cor. 3	Ezek. 1	Ps. 37
30	1 Sam. 23	1 Cor. 4	Ezek. 2	Ps. 38
31	1 Sam. 24	1 Cor. 5	Ezek. 3	Ps. 39

Bible reading schedules (6)

SEPTEMBER			
Date	**Morning**	**Evening**	
1	1 Sam. 25	1 Cor. 6	Ezek. 4	Ps.40,41
2	1 Sam. 26	1 Cor. 7	Ezek. 5	Ps.42,43
3	1 Sam. 27	1 Cor. 8	Ezek. 6	Ps.44
4	1 Sam. 28	1 Cor. 9	Ezek. 7	Ps.45
5	1 Sam. 29,30	1 Cor.10	Ezek. 8	Ps.46,47
6	1 Sam. 31	1 Cor.11	Ezek. 9	Ps.48
7	2 Sam. 1	1 Cor.12	Ezek.10	Ps.49
8	2 Sam. 2	1 Cor.13	Ezek.11	Ps.50
9	2 Sam. 3	1 Cor.14	Ezek.12	Ps.51
10	2 Sam.4,5	1 Cor.15	Ezek.13	Ps.52-54
11	2 Sam. 6	1 Cor.16	Ezek.14	Ps.55
12	2 Sam. 7	2 Cor. 1	Ezek.15	Ps.56,57
13	2 Sam.8,9	2 Cor. 2	Ezek.16	Ps.58,59
14	2 Sam. 10	2 Cor. 3	Ezek.17	Ps.60,61
15	2 Sam. 11	2 Cor. 4	Ezek.18	Ps.62,63
16	2 Sam. 12	2 Cor. 5	Ezek.19	Ps.64,65
17	2 Sam. 13	2 Cor. 6	Ezek.20	Ps.66,67
18	2 Sam. 14	2 Cor. 7	Ezek.21	Ps.68
19	2 Sam. 15	2 Cor. 8	Ezek.22	Ps.69
20	2 Sam. 16	2 Cor. 9	Ezek.23	Ps.70,71
21	2 Sam. 17	2 Cor.10	Ezek.24	Ps.72
22	2 Sam. 18	2 Cor.11	Ezek.25	Ps.73
23	2 Sam. 19	2 Cor.12	Ezek.26	Ps.74
24	2 Sam. 20	2 Cor.13	Ezek.27	Ps.75,76
25	2 Sam. 21	Gal. 1	Ezek.28	Ps.77
26	2 Sam. 22	Gal. 2	Ezek.29	Ps.78:1-37
27	2 Sam. 23	Gal. 3	Ezek.30	Ps.78:38-72
28	2 Sam. 24	Gal. 4	Ezek.31	Ps.79
29	1 Kings 1	Gal. 5	Ezek.32	Ps.80
30	1 Kings 2	Gal. 6	Ezek.33	Ps.81,82

OCTOBER			
Date	**Morning**	**Evening**	
1	1 Kings 3	Eph. 1	Ezek.34	Ps.83,84
2	1 Kings 4,5	Eph. 2	Ezek.35	Ps.85
3	1 Kings 6	Eph. 3	Ezek.36	Ps.86
4	1 Kings 7	Eph. 4	Ezek.37	Ps.87,88
5	1 Kings 8	Eph. 5	Ezek.38	Ps.89
6	1 Kings 9	Eph. 6	Ezek.39	Ps.90
7	1 Kings 10	Phil. 1	Ezek.40	Ps.91
8	1 Kings 11	Phil. 2	Ezek.41	Ps.92,93
9	1 Kings 12	Phil. 3	Ezek.42	Ps.94
10	1 Kings 13	Phil. 4	Ezek.43	Ps.95,96
11	1 Kings 14	Col. 1	Ezek.44	Ps.97,98
12	1 Kings 15	Col. 2	Ezek.45	Ps.99-101
13	1 Kings 16	Col. 3	Ezek.46	Ps.102
14	1 Kings 17	Col. 4	Ezek.47	Ps.103
15	1 Kings 18	1 Thess. 1	Ezek.48	Ps.104
16	1 Kings 19	1 Thess. 2	Dan. 1	Ps.105
17	1 Kings 20	1 Thess. 3	Dan. 2	Ps.106
18	1 Kings 21	1 Thess. 4	Dan. 3	Ps.107
19	1 Kings 22	1 Thess. 5	Dan. 4	Ps.108,109
20	2 Kings 1	2 Thess. 1	Dan. 5	Ps.110,111
21	2 Kings 2	2 Thess. 2	Dan. 6	Ps.112,113
22	2 Kings 3	2 Thess. 3	Dan. 7	Ps.114-115
23	2 Kings 4	1 Tim. 1	Dan. 8	Ps.116
24	2 Kings 5	1 Tim. 2	Dan. 9	Ps.117,118
25	2 Kings 6	1 Tim. 3	Dan. 10	Ps.119:1-24
26	2 Kings 7	1 Tim. 4	Dan. 11	Ps.119:25-48
27	2 Kings 8	1 Tim. 5	Dan. 12	Ps.119:49-72
28	2 Kings 9	1 Tim. 6	Hos. 1	Ps.119:73-96
29	2 Kings 10,11	2 Tim. 1	Hos. 2	Ps.119:97-120
30	2 Kings 12	2 Tim. 2	Hos. 3,4	Ps.119:121-144
31	2 Kings 13	2 Tim. 3	Hos. 5,6	Ps.119:145-176

NOVEMBER			
Date	Morning		Evening
1	2 Kings 14	2 Tim. 4	Hos. 7	Ps.120-122
2	2 Kings 15	Titus 1	Hos. 8	Ps.123-125
3	2 Kings 16	Titus 2	Hos. 9	Ps.126-128
4	2 Kings 17	Titus 3	Hos. 10	Ps.129-131
5	2 Kings 18	Philem.	Hos. 11	Ps.132-134
6	2 Kings 19	Heb. 1	Hos. 12	Ps.135-136
7	2 Kings 20	Heb. 2	Hos. 13	Ps.137,138
8	2 Kings 21	Heb. 3	Hos. 14	Ps.139
9	2 Kings 22	Heb. 4	Joel 1	Ps.140,141
10	2 Kings 23	Heb. 5	Joel 2	Ps.142
11	2 Kings 24	Heb. 6	Joel 3	Ps.143
12	2 Kings 25	Heb. 7	Amos 1	Ps.144
13	1 Chron. 1,2	Heb. 8	Amos 2	Ps.145
14	1 Chron. 3,4	Heb. 9	Amos 3	Ps.146,147
15	1 Chron. 5,6	Heb. 10	Amos 4	Ps.148-150
16	1 Chron. 7,8	Heb. 11	Amos 5	Lk.1:1-38
17	1 Chron. 9,10	Heb. 12	Amos 6	Lk.1:39-80
18	1 Chron. 11,12	Heb. 13	Amos 7	Luke 2
19	1 Chron. 13,14	James 1	Amos 8	Luke 3
20	1 Chron. 15	James 2	Amos 9	Luke 4
21	1 Chron. 16	James 3	Obad. 1	Luke 5
22	1 Chron. 17	James 4	Jonah 1	Luke 6
23	1 Chron. 18	James 5	Jonah 2	Luke 7
24	1 Chron. 19,20	1 Pet. 1	Jonah 3	Luke 8
25	1 Chron. 21	1 Pet. 2	Jonah 4	Luke 9
26	1 Chron. 22	1 Pet. 3	Micah 1	Luke 10
27	1 Chron. 23	1 Pet. 4	Micah 2	Luke 11
28	1 Chron. 24,25	1 Pet. 5	Micah 3	Luke 12
29	1 Chron. 26,27	2 Pet. 1	Micah 4	Luke 13
30	1 Chron. 28	2 Pet. 2	Micah 5	Luke 14

DECEMBER			
Date	Morning		Evening
1	1 Chron. 29	2 Pet. 3	Micah 6	Luke 15
2	2 Chron. 1	1 John 1	Micah 7	Luke 16
3	2 Chron. 2	1 John 2	Nahum 1	Luke 17
4	2 Chron. 3,4	1 John 3	Nahum 2	Luke 18
5	2 Chron. 5-6:11	1 John 4	Nahum 3	Luke 19
6	2 Chron. 6:12-42	1 John 5	Hab. 1	Luke 20
7	2 Chron. 7	2 John 1	Hab. 2	Luke 21
8	2 Chron. 8	3 John 1	Hab. 3	Luke 22
9	2 Chron. 9	Jude 1	Zeph. 1	Luke 23
10	2 Chron. 10	Rev. 1	Zeph. 2	Luke 24
11	2 Chron. 11,12	Rev. 2	Zeph. 3	John 1
12	2 Chron. 13	Rev. 3	Haggai 1	John 2
13	2 Chron. 14,15	Rev. 4	Haggai 2	John 3
14	2 Chron. 16	Rev. 5	Zech. 1	John 4
15	2 Chron. 17	Rev. 6	Zech. 2	John 5
16	2 Chron. 18	Rev. 7	Zech. 3	John 6
17	2 Chron. 19,20	Rev. 8	Zech. 4	John 7
18	2 Chron. 21	Rev. 9	Zech. 5	John 8
19	2 Chron. 22,23	Rev. 10	Zech. 6	John 9
20	2 Chron. 24	Rev. 11	Zech. 7	John 10
21	2 Chron. 25	Rev. 12	Zech. 8	John 11
22	2 Chron. 26	Rev. 13	Zech. 9	John 12
23	2 Chron. 27,28	Rev. 14	Zech. 10	John 13
24	2 Chron. 29	Rev. 15	Zech. 11	John 14
25	2 Chron. 30	Rev. 16	Zech. 12-13:1	John 15
26	2 Chron. 31	Rev. 17	Zech. 13:2-9	John 16
27	2 Chron. 32	Rev. 18	Zech.14	John 17
28	2 Chron. 33	Rev. 19	Malachi 1	John 18
29	2 Chron. 34	Rev. 20	Malachi 2	John 19
30	2 Chron. 35	Rev. 21	Malachi 3	John 20
31	2 Chron. 36	Rev. 22	Malachi 4	John 21

Bible study (1)

Two purposes of Bible study

Every one ought to study the Bible with two ends in view:
- his own growth in knowledge and grace, and
- passing it on to others.

We ought to have four ears, – two for ourselves, and two for other people.

> ### Quote Unquote
>
> "My Bible is worth a good deal to me because I have so many passages marked that, if I am called upon to speak at any time, I am ready. We ought to be prepared to pass around heavenly thoughts and truths, just as we do the coin of the realm." *John Wesley*

A servant of memory

"Bible-marking should be made the servant of memory; a few words will recall a whole sermon. It sharpens the memory, instead of blunting it, if properly done, because it gives prominence to certain things that catch the eye, which by constant reading you get to learn by heart. It helps you to locate texts. It saves preachers and class-leaders the trouble of writing out notes of their addresses. Once in the margin, always ready." *John Wesley*

Don't overdo it

There is a danger, however, of overdoing a system of marking, and of making your marks more prominent than the Scripture itself. If the system is complicated it becomes a burden, and you are liable to get confused. It is easier to remember the texts than the meaning of your marks.

Methods of marking

The simplest way to mark is to underline the words, or to make a stroke alongside the verse. Another good way is to go over the printed letters with your pen, and make them thicker. The word will standout like heavier type.

For example, mark "only" in Psalm 62 in this way.

Numbering

When any word or phrase is often repeated in a book or chapter, put consecutive numbers in the margin over against each text.

Thus, "the fear of the Lord" in Prov. 1: 7, 29, and so on.

Number the ten plagues in this way. In the second chapter of Habakkuk are five "woes" against five common sins.

NUMBERING PROMISES
When there is a succession of promises or charges in a verse, it is better to write the numbers small at the beginning of each promise.

Thus, there is a sevenfold promise to Abraham in Gen. 12: 2,3:

1
I will make of thee a great nation,

2
and I will bless thee,

3
and make thy name great,

4

and thou shalt be a blessing,

5

and I will bless them that bless thee,

6

and curse him that curseth thee,

7

and in thee shall all families of the earth be blessed."

In Prov. 1: 22, we have:

1

simple ones,

2

scorners,

3

fools.

The use of a cross

Put a cross in the margin against things not generally observed. For example, the law regarding women's wearing men's clothes, and regarding bird's-nesting, in Deut. 22: 5, 6; the sleep of the poor man and of the rich man compared, Eccl. 5: 12.

Using blank spaces

On blank pages at the beginning and end of your Bible, jot down texts to answer the various kinds of difficulties that you meet in talking to people. Also on these blank pages write short Bible readings and outlines of sermons.

Things to mark

1. SCRIPTURE REFERENCES

Opposite Gen. 1: 1 write, "Through faith. Heb. 11: 3," because there we read, "Through faith we understand that the worlds were framed by the word of God."

Opposite Gen. 28: 2 write, "An answer to prayer, Gen. 35: 3."

Opposite Matt. 6: 33 write, "1 Kings 17: 3" and "Luke 10: 42," which give illustrations of seeking the kingdom of God first.

Opposite Gen. 37: 7 write, "Gen. 50: 18," which gives the fulfillment of the dream.

You can link up the prophets with the historical books, and Paul's letters with the book of Acts, in this way.

2. NOTES TO RECALL A SERMON, STORY, OR HYMN

Against Ps. 119: 59,60, I have written, "The prodigal son's epitaph."

3. RAILWAY CONNECTIONS

"Railway connections" are links that can be made by fine lines running across the page.

In Dan. 6, link "will deliver" (v.16), "able to deliver" (v.20), and "hath delivered" (v.27).

In Ps. 66, link "Come and see" (v.5) with "come and hear" (v.16).

4. BOOK SUMMARIES

At the beginning of every Bible book, write a short summary of its contents.

5. WRITE IN KEY-WORDS FOR BOOKS AND CHAPTERS

Genesis is the book of beginnings; Exodus, of redemption.

The key-word of the first chapter of John is "receiving"; second chapter, "obedience"; and so on.

An interleaved Bible gives the most room for notes and suggestions.

Bible study (2)

Overview

Among the wealth of printed material now readily available for studying the Bible the following books are some of the basic ones which have been published to help one's appreciation of the Scriptures.

Study Bible

Study Bibles not only print the biblical text itself but also include extensive editorial material which includes such material as footnotes, cross-references, and appendices with maps, charts, and time-lines.

Bible atlas

A Bible atlas contains maps, diagrams, and pictures to assist one's appreciation of biblical geography.

Bible commentary

Bible commentaries give explanations of biblical texts as they have been understood by scholars and preachers. A Bible commentary may be on just one Bible book, a one volume Bible commentary may cover all the Bible books from Genesis to Revelation. They go through the Bible, book-by-book, chapter-by-chapter, and, to a certain extent, verse-by-verse.

Bible Dictionary

Bible dictionaries contains articles on such things as biblical names, places, and themes. They often have much helpful background information on the Bible which increases our understanding of the Bible.

Lexicon

A Bible lexicon is a dictionary which explains the meaning of ancient Hebrew or Greek words.

Concordance

A Bible concordance lists some or all of the passages in the Bible in which a particular word is used.

Parallel Bible

A parallel Bible prints several English translations of the Bible, or just the New Testament, often 4, or 8 different ones, in parallel columns on the same pages. This allows one to compare different translations with each other at a glance.

Interlinear Bible

An interlinear Bible prints the original biblical text, Hebrew in the case of the Old Testament and Greek in the case of the New Testament, with the literal English equivalent printed underneath each Hebrew or Greek word. Additionally, a standard translation of the verses are printed in the margin.

Types of Bible study

Topical

Select a subject/word, and by using a concordance trace its use from Genesis to Revelation.

Such topical studies could be:
1. About people: God, Jesus, Holy Spirit, etc.

2. About places: Jerusalem, Bethlehem, etc.

3. About important objects: The Ark, the Temple, etc.

4. About themes: Prophecy: etc.

5. About words: Choose one Hebrew/ Greek word

6. About doctrines: Salvation, sanctification, etc.

Biographical

Select a person and study everything the Bible says about him.

Character studies on some of the most important people in the Bible may take many hours.

Such biographical studies could be on:

Adam
Abraham
David
Jesus
Paul

Book survey

Select a Bible book and discover everything you can about it.

The book of Proverbs has a wide variety of topics in it. One way to study its different topics is to list them under different headings.

WISDOM FROM THE BOOK OF PROVERBS

Here are ten selected quotes from the book of Proverbs about ten different topics.

1. Wisdom
"The fear of the Lord is the beginning of wisdom, and the knowledge of the Holy One is understanding."
Proverbs 9: 10

2. Prayer
"The Lord is far from the wicked, but He hears the prayer of the righteous."
Proverbs 15: 29

3. A good word
"Anxiety in the heart of a man weighs it down, but a good word makes it glad."
Proverbs 12: 25

4. Keeping silent
"'He who despises his neighbor lacks sense, but a man of understanding keeps silent."
Proverbs 11: 12

5. Gossip
"A perverse man spreads strife, and a slanderer separates intimate friends."
Proverbs 16: 28

6. Anger
"A fool always loses his temper, but a wise man holds it back."
Proverbs 29: 11

7. Correction
"Whoever loves discipline loves knowledge, but he who hates reproof is stupid."
Proverbs 12: 1

8. Adultery
"The one who commits adultery with a woman is lacking sense; he who would destroy himself does it."
Proverbs 6: 32

9. Learning from ants
"Go to the ant, O sluggard, observe her ways and be wise; which, having no chief, officer or ruler, prepares her food in the summer, and gathers her provisions in the harvest."
Proverbs 6: 6–8

10. Things God hates
Proverbs 6: 16–19.

Memorizing the Bible

Benefits of memorizing the Bible

1. It helps one to follow God's will

"This book of the law shall not depart from your mouth, but you shall meditate on it day and night, so that you may be careful to do according to all that is written in it; for then you will make your way prosperous, and then you will have success" Joshua 1: 8.

2. It helps one to live a holy life

Frances Ridley Havergal, 1836–1879, commenting on Ps119: 11 said:

"In proportion as the word of the King is present in the heart there is power against sin. Let us use this means of absolute power more, and more life and more holiness will be ours."

"Thy word have I hid in mine heart, that I might not sin against thee" Psalm 119: 11.

3. It helps to keep one on the straight and narrow

"The law of his God is in his heart. His steps do not slip" Psalm 37: 31.

"I know of no other single practice in the Christian life more rewarding, practically speaking, than memorizing Scripture...No other single exercise pays greater spiritual dividends! Your prayer life will be strengthened. Your witnessing will be sharper and much more effective. Your attitudes and outlook will begin to change. Your mind will become alert and observant.

Your confidence and assurance will be enhanced. Your faith will be solidified."

Dr. Chuck Swindle, Bible teacher

Study and memorization is commanded by God

Study

The first question in the Westminster Shorter Catechism of 1674 asks is: "What is the chief end of man?" The answer is: "Man's chief end is to glorify God, and to enjoy Him for ever."

We cannot do this unless we obey his word.

We need to
1. read the Bible over and over again,
2. study it as much as possible,
3. pray about it,
4. meditate on it, and
5. memorize portions of it.

Then we will be able to obey it.

Memorize verses

We are, in fact, commanded to memorize parts of the Bible.

"And these words which I command you today shall be in your heart. You shall teach them diligently to your children, and shall talk of them when you sit in your house, when you walk by the way, when you lie down, and when you rise up. You shall bind them as a sign on your hand, and they shall be as frontlets between your eyes. You shall write them on the doorposts of your house and on your gates."

Deuteronomy 6: 6–9 NKJV

Scripture memorization

Memorizing the Bible verses helps you
1. pray,
2. meditate on God's Word, and
3. understand God's Word.

Simple steps

Some people find it much easier to
learn a passage of Scripture than single
verses from different Bible books.
Here are some simple steps to take for
learning a passage from the Bible.

Step one

Select an interesting short passage to
memorize.
Beatitudes: Matthew 5: 3–10
Lord's Prayer: Matthew 6: 9–13
Psalm 23
John 15: 1–9
1 Corinthians 13

Step two

Aim to learn one verse a day.

Don't worry when you don't manage
to do this.

Just go over what you have already
memorized and then carry on with one
extra verse a day.

In the long run, you will find that
you learn more verses if you keep on
revising those you have already learned
until you are word perfect with them,
before you continue with new verses.

Step three

Add a verse a day until you have
learned a whole paragraph. Then give
yourself a day off from learning a new
verse and just revise what you have
already memorized.

Step four

Learn the second paragraph of your
Bible passage, following the above
steps.

Step five

Test yourself on what you have learned
each month.

REVISION

There are hundreds of helpful tips
about memorizing the Bible. One
of the most important things to
remember is to revise. If you want to
make real progress you need to make
revision a life-time habit.

Simple steps for revision

Step one

Add verse two to verse 1.
Once you have learned your first Bible
verse so that you can say it perfectly
without having to look at it all, learn
your second verse in the same way. But
before you move on to your third verse,
revise.

Do this by putting verses 1 and 2
together until you can say both of them
perfectly.

Step two

When you have successfully learned
verse 3, add it to your first two verses.

Say verses one, two, and three until
they are word perfect.

Step three

Keep doing the above each time you
learn a new verse.

Meditating on the Bible (1)

Overview

"O how I love Thy law: it is my meditation all the day" Ps. 119: 97.

"My eyes stay open through the watches of the night, that I may meditate on your promises" Ps. 119: 148.

Watch, watch, watch

Watch your thoughts; they become words.

Watch your words; they become actions.

Watch your actions; they become habits.

Watch your habits; they become character.

Watch your character; it becomes your destiny.

Author unknown

Thinking

If there is any truth in the saying: "you are what you eat," there is more truth in the saying "you are (and are becoming) what you think."

Our hearts judge us

"The good man brings good things out of the good stored up in his heart, and the evil man brings evil things out of the evil stored up in his heart. For out of the overflow of his heart his mouth speaks" Luke 6: 45.

"But the things that come out of the mouth come from the heart, and these make a man 'unclean'" Matt. 15: 18.

"What comes out of a man is what makes him 'unclean.' For from within, out of men's hearts, come evil thoughts, sexual immorality, theft, murder, adultery, greed, malice, deceit, lewdness, envy, slander, arrogance and folly. All these evils come from inside and make a man 'unclean'" Matt. 7: 20–23.

"As water reflects a face, so a man's heart reflects the man" Prov. 27: 19.

"Above all else, guard your heart, for it is the wellspring of life" Prov. 4: 23.

The inner life

Jesus publicly rebuked the church leaders of his day for being outright hypocrites. They came top of the class when it came to doing good deeds, but Jesus always looked into people hearts and motives.

"Woe to you, teachers of the law and Pharisees, you hypocrites! You clean the outside of the cup and dish, but inside they are full of greed and self-indulgence. Blind Pharisee! First clean the inside of the cup and dish, and then the outside also will be clean. "Woe to you, teachers of the law and Pharisees, you hypocrites! You are like whitewashed tombs, which look beautiful on the outside but on the inside are full of dead men's bones and everything unclean. In the same way, on the outside you appear to people as righteous but on the inside you are full of hypocrisy and wickedness."

Matthew 23: 25–28

Webster's definition of meditation

Meditate:
to engage in contemplation or reflection, to focus one's thoughts on: reflect or ponder over. to plan or project in the mind.

Think:
to form or have in the mind, to have as an opinion, to regard as or consider, to reflect on or ponder, to determine by reflecting, to call to mind or remember, to center one's thoughts on or form a mental picture of, to have in the mind engaged in reflection, to consider.

Reflect:
to think quietly and calmly

ponder:
to weigh in the mind, to think about, reflect on, to think about – especially quietly, soberly and deeply.

The words Ponder, Meditate, Muse, and Ruminate are synonyms and mean to consider or examine attentively or deliberately.

PONDER
implies a careful weighing of a problem or, often, prolonged inconclusive thinking about a matter;

MEDITATE
implies a definite focusing of one's thoughts on something so as to understand it deeply;

MUSE
suggests a more or less focused daydreaming as in remembrance;

RUMINATE
implies going over the same matter in one's thoughts again and again but suggests little of either purposive thinking or rapt absorption.

MIND AND HEART
Meditation is a function of the mind and the heart.

It is what we think about in our hearts and it is something we each do every day.

Whether we realize it or not, we all spend a large portion of our time in some form of meditation.

The thing is, what we meditate on may or may not be worthwhile.

In fact, what we habitually think about is frequently unhealthy for our growth as Christians. Often it is simply sinful.

This is why it is such a good idea to make notes about what we meditate about.

This can be the first step in the process of training ourselves to think correctly.

Defining Bible meditation

"Meditation is simply thought prolonged and directed to a single object. Your mystic chambers where thoughts abide are the secret workshop of an unseen Sculptor chiseling living forms for a deathless future. Personality and influence are modeled here. Hence, the biblical injunction: 'Keep thy heart with all diligence, for out of it are the issues of life', Proverbs 4: 23."

A.T. Pierson

Meditating on the Bible (2)

The Bible and meditation

There are scores of Bible verses which encourage the practice of Bible meditations

The Old Testament

"Do not let this Book of the Law depart from your mouth; meditate on it day and night, so that you may be careful to do everything written in it. Then you will be prosperous and successful. (Josh. 1: 8)

The Psalms

"May the words of my mouth and the meditation of my heart be pleasing in your sight, O LORD, my Rock and my Redeemer." Ps. 19: 14

"Within your temple, O God, we meditate on your unfailing love." Ps. 48: 9

"I will meditate on all your works and consider all your mighty deeds." Ps. 77: 12

"I meditate on your precepts and consider your ways." Ps. 119: 15

"Though rulers sit together and slander me, your servant will meditate on your decrees." Ps. 119: 23

"Let me understand the teaching of your precepts; then I will meditate on your wonders." Ps. 119: 27

"I lift up my hands to your commands, which I love, and I meditate on your decrees." Ps. 119: 48

"May the arrogant be put to shame for wronging me without cause; but I will meditate on your precepts." Ps. 119: 78

"Oh, how I love your law! I meditate on it all day long." Ps. 119: 97

"I have more insight than all my teachers, for I meditate on your statutes." Ps. 119: 99

"My eyes stay open through the watches of the night, that I may meditate on your promises." Ps. 119: 148

"I remember the days of long ago; I meditate on all your works and consider what your hands have done." Ps. 143: 5

"They will speak of the glorious splendor of your majesty, and I will meditate on your wonderful works." Ps. 145: 5

"May my meditation be pleasing to him, as I rejoice in the LORD." Ps. 104: 34

"Blessed is the man who does not walk in the counsel of the wicked or stand in the way of sinners or sit in the seat of mockers. But his delight is in the law of the LORD, and on his law he meditates day and night. He is like a tree planted by streams of water, which yields its fruit in season and whose leaf does not wither. Whatever he does prospers. Not so the wicked! They are like chaff that the wind blows away. Therefore the wicked will not stand in the judgment, nor sinners in the assembly of the righteous. For the

LORD watches over the way of the righteous, but the way of the wicked will perish." Psalm 1

Paul

WE MEDITATE ON WHAT OUR HEARTS ARE FULL OF

In the place of our own thoughts that can so easily fill our minds Paul tells us what we should do.

"Since, then, you have been raised with Christ, set your hearts on things above, where Christ is seated at the right hand of God. Set your minds on things above, not on earthly things. For you died, and your life is now hidden with Christ in God." Col. 3: 1–3

"Reflect on what I am saying, for the Lord will give you insight into all this." 2 Tim 2: 7

"Finally, brothers, whatever is true, whatever is noble, whatever is right, whatever is pure, whatever is lovely, whatever is admirable – if anything is excellent or praiseworthy – think about such things." Phil. 4: 8

"Therefore, I urge you, brothers, in view of God's mercy, to offer your bodies as living sacrifices, holy and pleasing to God – his is your spiritual act of worship. Do not conform any longer to the pattern of this world, but be transformed by the renewing of your mind. Then you will be able to test and approve what God's will is – his good, pleasing and perfect will. For by the grace given me I say to every one of you: Do not think of yourself more highly than you ought, but rather think of yourself with sober judgment, in accordance with the measure of faith God has given you." Romans 12: 1–3

Quote Unquote

"You see, much of this is reflection on the relationship we have with God, it is thinking about His love and influence in your life, it is wondering about His awesome power and mighty deeds. It is joyfully giving thanks to Him for all he has done. It is sitting in awe and appreciation of his works. It is using all your energy to understand and obey his word. Just as your digestive system processes the food you eat so it can be of use to your body, so also meditation digests all things concerning God and makes them a power which can renew your heart."

The Saints' Everlasting Rest, Richard Baxter

What the Bible says about (1)

The Bible in 50 words

God made
Adam bit
Noah arked
Abraham split
Joseph ruled
Jacob fooled
Bush talked
Moses balked
Pharaoh plagued
People walked
Sea divided
Tablets guided
Promise landed
Saul freaked
David peeked
Prophets warned
Jesus born
God walked
Love talked
Anger crucified
Hope died
Love rose
Spirit flamed
Word spread
God remained

Words and themes

One way to study the Bible in a topical way is to look up a particular word in a Bible concordance and read all the Bible references. Another way is to group together some of the Bible verses which illustrate the topic or word under investigation, even if the actual word itself does not appear in the Bible. The following topical list of words, arranged in alphabetical order, list some of the most well known and important verses on each subject.

A

Abandonment

He will not forsake thee, neither destroy thee, nor forget the covenant of thy fathers which He sware unto them. (Deut. 4: 31)

The Lord will not forsake His people for His great name's sake. (1 Sam. 12: 22)

God will not cast away a perfect man, neither will He help the evil doers. (Job 8: 20)

When my father and my mother forsake me, then the Lord will take me up. (Ps. 27: 10)

Forsake me not, O Lord: O my God, be not far from me. (Ps. 38: 21)

I will not leave you comfortless: I will come to you. (John 14: 18)

I will never leave thee, nor forsake thee. (Heb. 13: 5)

Absence

The Lord watch between me and thee, when we are absent one from another. (Gen. 31: 49)

Though I be absent in the flesh, yet am I with you in the spirit. (Col. 2: 5)

Abundance

And ye shall eat the fat of the land. (Gen. 45: 18)

My cup runneth over. (Ps. 23: 5)

Acceptance

The Lord gave, and the Lord hath taken away; blessed be the name of the Lord. (Job 1: 21)

Let the righteous smite me; it shall be a kindness. (Ps. 141: 5)

Whether it be good, or whether it be evil, we will obey the voice of the Lord. (Jer. 42: 6)

Not what I will, but what Thou wilt. (Mark 14: 36)

Father, into Thy hands I commend my spirit. (Luke 23: 46)

The will of the Lord be done. (Acts 21: 14)

If a spirit or an angel hath spoken to him, let us not fight against God. (Acts 23: 9)

Being reviled, we bless; being persecuted, we suffer it. (1 Cor. 4: 12)

Do all things without murmurings and disputings. (Phil. 2: 14)

Despise not thou the chastening of the Lord. (Heb. 12: 5)

If, when ye do well, and suffer for it, ye take it patiently, this is acceptable with God. (1 Pet. 2: 20)

It is better, if the will of God be so, that ye suffer for well doing, than for evil doing. (1 Pet. 3: 17)

Accusations

Wherefore have ye rewarded evil for good? (Gen. 44: 4)

How long wilt thou be drunken? put away thy wine from thee. (1 Sam. 1: 14)

And Nathan said to David, Thou art the man. (2 Sam. 12: 7)

He that is without sin among you, let him first cast a stone. (John 8: 7)

Acknowledgment

In all thy ways acknowledge Him. (Prov. 3: 6)

Hear, ye that are far off, what I have done: and, ye that are near, acknowledge My might. (Is. 33: 13)

I will say, It is My people: and they shall say, The Lord is my God. (Zech. 13: 9)

Truly this was the Son of God. (Matt. 27: 54)

Whosoever shall confess me before men, him shall the Son of man also confess before the angels of God. (Luke 12: 8)

Every tongue should confess that Jesus Christ is Lord. (Phil. 2: 11)

Adaptability

Unto the Jews I became as a Jew, that I might gain the Jews. (1 Cor. 9: 20)

To the weak became I as weak, that I might gain the weak. (1 Cor. 9: 22)

I am made all things to all men, that I might by all means save some. (1 Cor. 9: 22)

Adultery

Thou shalt not commit adultery. (Ex. 20: 14)

Thou shalt not covet thy neighbor's wife. (Ex. 20: 17)

Lust not after her beauty in thine heart; neither let her take thee with her eyelids. (Prov. 6: 25)

What the Bible says about (2)

A continued

Adultery

Whoso committeth adultery with a woman lacketh understanding: he that doeth it destroyeth his own soul. (Prov. 6: 32)

Whosoever looketh on a woman to lust after her hath committed adultery with her already in his heart. (Matt. 5: 28)

Whosoever shall put away his wife, saving for the cause of fornication, causeth her to commit adultery. (Matt. 5: 32)

Whosoever shall marry her that is divorced committeth adultery. (Matt. 5: 32)

It is not lawful for thee to have thy brother's wife. (Mark 6: 18)

Adversity

The more they afflicted them, the more they multiplied and grew. (Ex. 1: 12)

Princes have persecuted me without a cause: but my heart standeth in awe of Thy word. (Ps. 119: 161)

We are perplexed, but not in despair; Persecuted, but not forsaken; cast down, but not destroyed. (2 Cor. 4: 8–9)

Advice

Consider of it, take advice, and speak your minds. (Judg. 19: 30)

But he forsook the counsel which the old men gave him. (2 Chr. 10: 8)

Receive my sayings; and the years of thy life shall be many. (Prov. 4: 10)

Hear instruction, and be wise, and refuse it not. (Prov. 8: 33)

Give instruction to a wise man, and he will yet be wiser: teach a just man, and he will increase in learning. (Prov. 9: 9)

In the multitude of counselors there is safety. (Prov. 11: 14)

The thoughts of the righteous are right: but the counsels of the wicked are deceit. (Prov. 12: 5)

The way of a fool is right in his own eyes: but he that hearkeneth unto counsel is wise. (Prov. 12: 15)

A word spoken in due season, how good is it! (Prov. 15: 23)

Hear counsel, and receive instruction, that thou mayest be wise in thy latter end. (Prov. 19: 20)

Age

Honor the face of the old man. (Lev. 19: 32)

Ambition

Should I forsake my sweetness, and my good fruit, and go to be promoted over the trees? (Judg. 9: 11)

Anger

Wrath killeth the foolish man, and envy slayeth the silly one. (Job 5: 2)

Cease from anger, and forsake wrath. (Ps. 37: 8)

Antichrist

Antichrist shall come. (1 John 2: 18)

Even now are there many antichrists. (1 John 2: 18)

He is antichrist, that denieth the Father and the Son. (1 John 2: 22)

Appearance

The Lord seeth not as man seeth, for man looketh on the outward appearance, but the Lord looketh on the heart. (1 Sam. 16: 7)

Ye are like unto whited sepulchers, which indeed appear beautiful outward. (Matt. 23: 27)

Ye also outwardly appear righteous unto men, but within ye are full of hypocrisy and iniquity. (Matt. 23: 28)

Judge not according to the appearance, but judge righteous judgment. (John 7: 24)

Ye judge after the flesh; I judge no man. (John 8: 15)

Appreciation

And they shall know that I am the Lord their God, that brought them forth out of the land of Egypt. (Ex. 29: 46)

Thou art good in my sight, as an angel of God. (1 Sam. 29: 9)

He was in the world, and the world was made by Him, and the world knew Him not. (John 1: 10)

He came unto His own, and His own received Him not. (John 1: 11)

Arguments

Strive not with a man without cause, if he have done thee no harm. (Prov. 3: 30)

Hatred stirreth up strifes: but love covereth all sins. (Prov. 10: 12)

It is an honor for a man to cease from strife. (Prov. 20: 3)

A soft tongue breaketh the bone. (Prov. 25: 15)

An angry man stirreth up strife. (Prov. 29: 22)

Arrogance

Who is the Lord, that I should obey His voice to let Israel go? (Ex. 5: 2)

How long wilt thou refuse to humble thyself before Me? let My people go. (Ex. 10: 3)

Let not arrogancy come out of your mouth: for the Lord is a God of knowledge, and by Him actions are weighed. (1 Sam. 2: 3)

Thine eyes are upon the haughty, that Thou mayest bring them down. (2 Sam. 22: 28)

Atheism

The fool hath said in his heart, There is no God. (Ps. 14: 1)

Attitude

Thy heart is not right in the sight of God. (Acts 8: 21)

We should serve in newness of spirit, and not in the oldness of the letter. (Rom. 7: 6)

To be carnally minded is death; but to be spiritually minded is life and peace. (Rom. 8: 6)

Awe

Who is like unto Thee, O Lord, among the gods? who is like Thee, glorious in holiness, fearful in praises, doing wonders? (Ex. 15: 11)

What the Bible says about (3)

B

Backsliding

And the children of Israel remembered not the Lord their God. (Judg. 8: 34)

Baptism

He that believeth and is baptized shall be saved; but he that believeth not shall be damned. (Mark 16: 16)

Repent, and be baptized every one of you in the name of Jesus Christ. (Acts 2: 38)

The baptism of repentance. (Acts 13: 24)

Arise, and be baptized, and wash away thy sins. (Acts 22: 16)

One Lord, one faith, one baptism. (Eph. 4: 5)

Behavior

Ye shall walk in all the ways which the Lord your God hath commanded you, that ye may live, and that it may be well with you. (Deut. 5: 33)

Do that which is right and good in the sight of the Lord. (Deut. 6: 18)

Walk in all His ways. (Deut. 10: 12)

I have set before thee this day life and good, and death and evil. (Deut. 30: 15)

Take good heed therefore unto yourselves, that ye love the Lord your God. (Josh. 23: 11)

Turn ye from your evil ways, and keep My commandments and My statutes. (2 Kings 17: 13)

Belief

If ye will not believe, surely ye shall not be established. (Is. 7: 9)

He that believeth shall not make haste. (Is. 28: 16)

With God all things are possible. (Matt. 19: 26, Mark 10: 27)

He that believeth and is baptized shall be saved; but he that believeth not shall be damned. (Mark 16: 16)

As many as received Him, to them gave He power to become the sons of God. (John 1: 12)

He that believeth not is condemned already, because he hath not believed in the name of the only begotten Son of God. (John 3: 18)

He that believeth not the Son shall not see life; but the wrath of God abideth on him. (John 3: 36)

He that heareth my word, and believeth on Him that sent me, hath everlasting life. (John 5: 24)

Had ye believed Moses, ye would have believed me: for he wrote of me. (John 5: 46)

Lord, I believe. (John 9: 38)

Though ye believe not me, believe the works. (John 10: 38)

He that believeth in me, though he were dead, yet shall he live. (John 11: 25)

Blessed are they that have not seen, and yet have believed. (John 20: 29)

I believe that Jesus Christ is the Son of God. (Acts 8: 37)

By Him all that believe are justified. (Acts 13: 39)

Blasphemy

Thou shalt not take the name of the Lord thy God in vain. (Ex. 20: 7)

Whosoever curseth his God shall bear his sin. (Lev. 24: 15)

Blood

It is the blood that maketh an atonement for the soul. (Lev. 17: 11)

The life of all flesh is the blood thereof. (Lev. 17: 14)

This is my blood of the new testament, which is shed for many for the remission of sins. (Matt. 26: 28)

Without shedding of blood is no remission. (Heb. 9: 22)

The blood of Jesus Christ His Son cleanseth us from all sin. (1 John 1: 7)

Boasting

A prudent man concealeth knowledge: but the heart of fools proclaimeth foolishness. (Prov. 12: 23)

Boast not thyself of tomorrow; for thou knowest not what a day may bring forth. (Prov. 27: 1)

He that glorieth, let him glory in the Lord. (1 Cor. 1: 31)

God forbid that I should glory, save in the cross of our Lord Jesus Christ. (Gal. 6: 14)

Born again

Except a man be born again, he cannot see the kingdom of God. (John 3: 3)

Except a man be born of water and of the Spirit, he cannot enter into the kingdom of God. (John 3: 5)

Ye must be born again. (John 3: 7)

If any man be in Christ, he is a new creature. (2 Cor. 5: 17)

Borrowing

The wicked borroweth, and payeth not again: but the righteous showeth mercy, and giveth. (Ps. 37: 21)

The borrower is servant to the lender. (Prov. 22: 7)

Better is it that thou shouldest not vow, than that thou shouldest vow and not pay. (Eccl. 5: 5)

Give to him that asketh thee, and from him that would borrow of thee turn not thou away. (Matt. 5: 42)

Bribery

A gift doth blind the eyes of the wise, and pervert the words of the righteous. (Deut. 16: 19)

Burdens

Come unto me, all ye that labor and are heavy laden, and I will give you rest. (Matt. 11: 28)

Bear ye one another's burdens. (Gal. 6: 2)

What the Bible says about (4)

C

Candor

Open rebuke is better than secret love.
(Prov. 27: 5)

A time to keep silence, and a time to speak. (Eccl. 3: 7)

Celebration

To every one a loaf of bread, and a good piece of flesh, and a flagon of wine.
(1 Chr. 16: 3)

Go your way, eat the fat, and drink the sweet. (Neh. 8: 10)

The joy of Jerusalem was heard even afar off. (Neh. 12: 43)

Let the heavens rejoice, and let the earth be glad; let the sea roar, and the fullness thereof. (Ps. 96: 11)

Challenges

Give me a man, that we may fight together. (1 Sam. 17: 10)

Call ye on the name of your gods, and I will call on the name of the Lord. (1 Kings 18: 24)

Touch all that he hath, and he will curse Thee to Thy face. (Job 1: 11)

Chance

The lot is cast into the lap; but the whole disposing thereof is of the Lord.
(Prov. 16: 33)

Change

Can the Ethiopian change his skin, or the leopard his spots? then may ye also do good, that are accustomed to do evil. (Jer. 13: 23)

Old things are passed away; behold, all things are become new. (2 Cor. 5: 17)

Jesus Christ the same yesterday, and today, and for ever. (Heb. 13: 8)

Charity

Thou shalt not harden thine heart, nor shut thine hand from thy poor brother. (Deut. 15: 7)

Thou shalt open thine hand wide unto thy brother, to thy poor, and to thy needy, in thy land. (Deut. 15: 11)

Every man shall give as he is able, according to the blessing of the Lord thy God which He hath given thee. (Deut. 16: 17)

Childlessness

Give me children, or else I die.
(Gen. 30: 1)

Sing, O barren, thou that didst not bear; break forth into singing, and cry aloud, thou that didst not travail with child: for more are the children of the desolate than the children of the married wife, saith the Lord. (Is. 54: 1)

Children

Be fruitful, and multiply. (Gen. 1: 28)

Thy seed shall be as the dust of the earth. (Gen. 28: 14)

Choice

If thou wilt take the left hand, then I will go to the right; or if thou depart to the right hand, then I will go to the left. (Gen. 13: 9)

Behold, I set before you this day a blessing and a curse; A blessing, if ye obey the commandments of the Lord your God, which I command you this day: And a curse, if ye will not obey. (Deut. 11: 26–28)

I have set before thee this day life and good, and death and evil. (Deut. 30: 15)

Choose you this day whom ye will serve. (Josh. 24: 15)

Christians

By this shall all men know that ye are my disciples, if ye have love one to another. (John 13: 35)

The disciples were called Christians first in Antioch. (Acts 11: 26)

Circumcision

Ye shall circumcise the flesh of your foreskin; and it shall be a token of the covenant betwixt Me and you. (Gen. 17: 11)

Circumcise therefore the foreskin of your heart, and be no more stiffnecked. (Deut. 10: 16)

Circumcise yourself to the Lord. (Jer. 4: 4)

Comfort

Fear not, for I am with thee, and will bless thee, and multiply thy seed. (Gen. 26: 24)

Miserable comforters are ye all. (Job 16: 2)

Commandments

If a soul sin, and commit any of these things which are forbidden to be done by the commandments of the Lord; though he wist it not, yet is he guilty. (Lev. 5: 17)

Do them, that ye may live. (Deut. 4: 1)

Commitment

With all thy heart and with all thy soul. (Deut. 10: 12)

I am my beloved's, and my beloved is mine. (Song 6: 3)

Complaints

I will speak in the anguish of my spirit; I will complain in the bitterness of my soul. (Job 7: 11)

Neither murmur ye. (1 Cor. 10: 10)

Do all things without murmurings and disputings. (Phil. 2: 14)

Murmurers, complainers, walking after their own lusts. (Jude 16)

Confession

I have sinned against the Lord. (2 Sam. 12: 13)

We have sinned, and have done perversely, we have committed wickedness. (1 Kings 8: 47)

We have sinned, we have done amiss, and have dealt wickedly. (2 Chr. 6: 37)

What the Bible says about (5)

C continued

Conformity

Be not conformed to this world.
(Rom. 12: 2)
   Love not the world, neither the things
that are in the world. (1 John 2: 15)

Conscience

Thou knowest all the wickedness
which thine heart is privy to. (1 Kings
2: 44)
   My righteousness I hold fast, and
will not let it go: my heart shall not
reproach me so long as I live. (Job 27: 6)
   The wicked flee when no man
pursueth. (Prov. 28: 1)

Consequences

His wife looked back from behind
him, and she became a pillar of salt.
(Gen. 19: 26)
   Because ye are turned away from
the Lord, therefore the Lord will not be
with you. (Num. 14: 43)
   Because thou hast rejected the word
of the Lord, He hath also rejected thee
from being king. (1 Sam. 15: 23)

Consistency

Of thorns men do not gather figs, nor
of a bramble bush gather they grapes.
(Luke 6: 44)
   He that is faithful in that which is
least is faithful also in much. (Luke
16: 10)

Can the fig tree, my brethren, bear
olive berries? (James 3: 12)

Contamination

A little leaven leaveneth the whole
lump. (1 Cor. 5: 6, Gal. 5: 9)
   Be not partakers of her sins.
(Rev. 18: 4)

Contemplation

Whatsoever things are true, whatsoever
things are honest, whatsoever things
are just, whatsoever things are
pure, whatsoever things are lovely,
whatsoever things are of good report; if
there be any virtue, and if there be any
praise, think on these things. (Phil. 4: 8)

Controversy

Him that is weak in the faith receive
ye, but not to doubtful disputations.
(Rom. 14: 1)
   Foolish and unlearned questions
avoid, knowing that they do gender
strifes. (2 Tim. 2: 23)
   The servant of the Lord must not
strive. (2 Tim. 2: 24)
   Avoid foolish questions. (Titus 3: 9)

Conversion

Thy people shall be my people, and thy
God my God. (Ruth 1: 16)
   Except ye be converted, and become
as little children, ye shall not enter into
the kingdom of heaven. (Matt. 18: 3)

Cooperation

I am as thou art, and my people as thy people. (2 Chr. 18: 3)

Courtesy

The poor useth intreaties; but the rich answereth roughly. (Prov. 18: 23)

Give none offence. (1 Cor. 10: 32)

Let your speech be alway with grace, seasoned with salt, that ye may know how ye ought to answer every man. (Col. 4: 6)

Love as brethren, be pitiful, be courteous. (1 Pet. 3: 8)

Covenant

I do set My bow in the cloud, and it shall be for a token of a covenant between Me and the earth. (Gen. 9: 13)

I will make of thee a great nation. (Gen. 12: 2)

In thee shall all families of the earth be blessed. (Gen. 12: 3)

My covenant is with thee, and thou shalt be a father of many nations. (Gen. 17: 4)

Cowardice

The sound of a shaken leaf shall chase them. (Lev. 26: 36)

The hearts of the people melted, and became as water. (Josh. 7: 5)

Creation

In the beginning God created the heaven and the earth. (Gen. 1: 1)

And God said, Let there be light: and there was light. (Gen. 1: 3)

God created man in His own image, in the image of God created He him; male and female created He them. (Gen. 1: 27)

Crime

Thou shalt not steal. (Ex. 20: 15)

Criticism

Ye are forgers of lies, ye are all physicians of no value. (Job 13: 4)

Reprove not a scorner, lest he hate thee: rebuke a wise man, and he will love thee. (Prov. 9: 8)

He that refuseth reproof erreth. (Prov. 10: 17)

Crucifixion

They shall mock Him, and shall scourge Him, and shall spit upon Him, and shall kill Him: and the third day He shall rise again. (Mark 10: 34)

Father, into Thy hands I commend my spirit. (Luke 23: 46)

Ye shall weep and lament, but the world shall rejoice. (John 16: 20)

Cruelty

The merciful man doeth good to his own soul: but he that is cruel troubleth his own flesh. (Prov. 11: 17)

The tender mercies of the wicked are cruel. (Prov. 12: 10)

What the Bible says about (6)

D

Dance

Let them praise His name in the dance: let them sing praises unto Him with the timbrel and harp. (Ps. 149: 3)

A time to mourn, and a time to dance. (Eccl. 3: 4)

We have piped unto you, and ye have not danced; we have mourned unto you, and ye have not lamented. (Matt. 11: 17)

Danger

Thou shalt fear day and night, and shalt have none assurance of thy life. (Deut. 28: 66)

There is but a step between me and death. (1 Sam. 20: 3)

He that seeketh my life seeketh thy life. (1 Sam. 22: 23)

The wicked watcheth the righteous, and seeketh to slay him. (Ps. 37: 32)

We are counted as sheep for the slaughter. (Ps. 44: 22)

We went through fire and through water. (Ps. 66: 12)

Though I walk in the midst of trouble, Thou wilt revive me. (Ps. 138: 7)

Sharp as a two-edged sword. (Prov. 5: 4)

Our God whom we serve is able to deliver us from the burning fiery furnace. (Dan. 3: 17)

I send you forth as sheep in the midst of wolves: be ye therefore wise as serpents, and harmless as doves. (Matt. 10: 16)

Death

Dust thou art, and unto dust shalt thou return. (Gen. 3: 19)

Now let me die, since I have seen thy face, because thou art yet alive. (Gen. 46: 30)

Let me die the death of the righteous, and let my last end be like his! (Num. 23: 10)

There be some standing here, which shall not taste death, till they see the Son of man coming in His kingdom. (Matt. 16: 28)

Wheresoever the carcass is, there will the eagles be gathered together. (Matt. 24: 28)

Except ye repent, ye shall all likewise perish. (Luke 13: 13)

Whosoever believeth in Him should not perish, but have eternal life. (John 3: 15)

If a man keep my saying, he shall never see death. (John 8: 51)

Yet a little while, and the world seeth me no more. (John 14: 19)

I come to Thee. (John 17: 11)

It is finished. (John 19: 30)

Decadence

Ye are like unto whited sepulchers, which indeed appear beautiful outward. (Matt. 23: 27)

Wasted his substance with riotous living. (Luke 15: 13)

Be not partakers of her sins. (Rev. 18: 4)

Deception

Why didst thou not tell me that she was thy wife? (Gen. 12: 18)

Wherefore have ye beguiled us? (Josh. 9: 22)

I have a secret errand unto thee, O king. (Judg. 3: 19)

Thou dost but hate me, and lovest me not. (Judg. 14: 16)

As one man mocketh another, do ye so mock Him? (Job 13: 9)

Saying, Peace, peace; when there is no peace. (Jer. 6: 14; Jer. 8: 11)

Cursed be the deceiver. (Mal. 1: 14)

Beware of false prophets, which come to you in sheep's clothing, but inwardly they are ravening wolves. (Matt.7: 15)

Take heed that ye be not deceived. (Luke 21: 8)

Let no man deceive himself. (1 Cor. 3: 18)

Let no man deceive you with vain words. (Eph. 5: 6)

Beware lest any man spoil you through philosophy and vain deceit. (Col. 2: 8)

By thy sorceries were all nations deceived. (Rev. 18: 23)

Decisions

Do what seemeth good unto thee. (1 Sam. 14: 40)

Let us choose to us judgment: let us know among ourselves what is good. (Job 34: 4)

A time to keep, and a time to cast away. (Eccl. 3: 6)

A time to keep silence, and a time to speak. (Eccl. 3: 7)

Not as I will, but as Thou wilt. (Matt. 26: 39)

Deeds

The Lord is a God of knowledge, and by Him actions are weighed. (1 Sam. 2: 3)

Even a child is known by his doings. (Prov. 20: 11)

God shall bring every work into judgment. (Eccl. 12: 14)

Let your light so shine before men, that they may see your good works. (Matt. 5: 16)

By their fruits ye shall know them. (Matt. 7: 20)

Whosoever heareth these sayings of mine, and doeth them, I will liken him unto a wise man, which built his house upon a rock. (Matt. 7: 24)

He shall reward every man according to his works. (Matt. 16: 27)

Every tree is known by his own fruit. (Luke 6: 44)

Why call ye me, Lord, Lord, and do not the things which I say? (Luke 6: 46)

With such sacrifices God is well pleased. (Heb. 13: 16)

Be ye doers of the word, and not hearers only. (James 1: 22)

I have not found thy works perfect before God. (Rev. 3: 2)

What the Bible says about (7)

D continued

Defeat

Knowest thou not yet that Egypt is destroyed? (Ex. 10: 7)

How should one chase a thousand, and two put ten thousand to flight, except their Rock had sold them, and the Lord had shut them up? (Deut. 32: 30)

Thus shall the Lord do to all your enemies against whom ye fight. (Josh. 10: 25)

Whithersoever they went out, the hand of the Lord was against them for evil. (Judg. 2: 15)

How are the mighty fallen, and the weapons of war perished! (2 Sam. 1: 27)

Deliverance

I am the Lord thy God, which have brought thee out of the land of Egypt, out of the house of bondage. (Ex. 20: 2)

The Lord brought us forth out of Egypt with a mighty hand, and with an out-stretched arm. (Deut. 26: 8)

Slack not thy hand from thy servants; come up to us quickly, and save us. (Josh. 10: 6)

Ye cried to Me, and I delivered you out of their hand. (Judg. 10: 12)

He hath sent me to heal the brokenhearted, to preach deliverance to the captives. (Luke 4: 18)

I was delivered out of the mouth of the lion. (2 Tim. 4: 17)

Denial

Shall the work say of him that made it, He made me not? (Is. 29: 16)

Whosoever shall deny me before men, him will I also deny before my Father which is in heaven. (Matt. 10: 33)

Before the cock crow, thou shalt deny me thrice. (Matt. 26: 34,75)

Though I should die with Thee, yet will I not deny Thee. (Matt. 26: 35)

And immediately the cock crew. (Matt. 26: 74; John 18: 27)

I know not this man of whom ye speak. (Mark 14: 71)

If I should say, I know Him not, I shall be a liar like unto you: but I know Him, and keep His saying. (John 8: 55)

If we deny Him, He also will deny us. (2 Tim. 2: 12)

If we believe not, yet He abideth faithful: He cannot deny Himself. (2 Tim. 2: 13)

Whosoever denieth the Son, the same hath not the Father. (1 John 2: 23)

Depravity

Do you with them what seemeth good unto you: but unto this man do not so vile a thing. (Judg. 19: 24)

There was no such deed done nor seen from the day that the children of Israel came up out of the land of Egypt unto this day. (Judg. 19: 30)

He that is of a perverse heart shall be despised. (Prov. 12: 8)

Babylon the great, the mother of harlots and abominations of the earth. (Rev. 17: 5)

Depression

Why is thy countenance sad, seeing thou art not sick? (Neh. 2: 2)

My soul is weary of my life. (Job 10: 1)

Save me, O God; for the waters are come in unto my soul. (Ps. 69: 1)

A merry heart doeth good like a medicine: but a broken spirit drieth the bones. (Prov. 17: 22)

Desire

Get her for me; for she pleaseth me well. (Judg. 14: 3)

The desire accomplished is sweet to the soul. (Prov. 13: 19)

Better is the sight of the eyes than the wandering of the desire. (Eccl. 6: 9)

In the broad ways I will seek him whom my soul loveth. (Song 3: 2)

I am my beloved's, and his desire is toward me. (Song 7: 10)

We should not lust after evil things. (1 Cor. 10: 6)

When lust hath conceived, it bringeth forth sin. (James 1: 15)

Ye lust, and have not. (James 4: 2)

The world passeth away, and the lust thereof: but he that doeth the will of God abideth for ever. (1 John 2: 17)

Desolation

Jerusalem is ruined, and Judah is fallen: because their tongue and their doings are against the Lord. (Is. 3: 8)

The land shall be utterly emptied, and utterly spoiled: for the Lord hath spoken this word. (Is. 24: 3)

All they that look upon thee shall flee from thee. (Nah. 3: 7)

Despair

Give me children, or else I die. (Gen. 30: 1)

What shall I do unto this people? they be almost ready to stone me. (Ex. 17: 4)

If I wait, the grave is mine house: I have made my bed in the darkness. (Job 17: 13)

Where is now my hope? (Job 17: 15)

Eli, Eli, lama sabachthani? (Matt. 27: 46)

He that cometh to me shall never hunger; and he that believeth on me shall never thirst. (John 6: 35)

What the Bible says about (8)

D continued

Destiny

It was not you that sent me hither, but God. (Gen. 45: 8)

Such as are for death, to death; and such as are for the sword, to the sword; and such as are for the famine, to the famine; and such as are for the captivity, to the captivity. (Jer. 15: 2)

As the clay is in the potter's hand, so are ye in Mine hand, O house of Israel. (Jer. 18: 6)

Determination

Intreat me not to leave thee. (Ruth 1: 16)

He turned not to the right hand nor to the left. (2 Sam. 2: 19)

If thou seek Him, He will be found of thee. (1 Chr. 28: 9)

I shall not die, but live, and declare the works of the Lord. (Ps. 118: 17)

Stand fast in the faith. (1 Cor. 16: 13)

Devotion

Set your heart and your soul to seek the Lord your God. (1 Chr. 22: 19)

With a perfect heart and with a willing mind. (1 Chr. 28: 9)

With all thy heart, and with all thy soul, and with all thy mind. (Matt. 22: 37; Mark 12: 29)

Whosoever he be of you that forsaketh not all that he hath, he cannot be my disciple. (Luke 14: 33)

The good shepherd giveth his life for the sheep. (John 10: 11)

The hireling fleeth, because he is an hireling, and careth not for the sheep. (John 10: 13)

Diligence

Seek, and ye shall find. (Matt. 7: 7; Luke 11: 9)

No man, having put his hand to the plow, and looking back, is fit for the kingdom of God. (Luke 9: 62)

Be ye stedfast, unmoveable, always abounding in the work of the Lord. (1 Cor. 15: 58)

Discernment

Give therefore Thy servant an understanding heart to judge Thy people, that I may discern between good and bad. (1 Kings 3: 9)

A wise man's heart discerneth both time and judgment. (Eccl. 8: 5)

O ye hypocrites, ye can discern the face of the sky; but can ye not discern the signs of the times? (Matt. 16: 3)

Disciples

Follow me, and I will make you fishers of men. (Matt. 4: 19)

I send you forth as sheep in the midst of wolves: be ye therefore wise as serpents, and harmless as doves. (Matt. 10: 16)

The disciple is not above his master, nor the servant above his lord. (Matt. 10: 24)

He that taketh not his cross, and

followeth after me, is not worthy of me. (Matt. 10: 38)

Whosoever will come after me, let him deny himself, and take up his cross, and follow me. (Mark 8: 34)

Go ye into all the world, and preach the gospel to every creature. (Mark 16: 15)

He that despiseth you despiseth me; and he that despiseth me despiseth Him that sent me. (Luke 10: 16)

Whosoever he be of you that forsaketh not all that he hath, he cannot be my disciple. (Luke 14: 33)

Have not I chosen you twelve, and one of you is a devil? (John 6: 70)

If ye continue in my word, then are ye my disciples indeed. (John 8: 31)

If any man serve me, him will my Father honor. (John 12: 26)

By this shall all men know that ye are my disciples, if ye have love one to another. (John 13: 35)

I am the vine, ye are the branches. (John 15: 5)

Ye have not chosen me, but I have chosen you. (John 15: 16)

Follow me. (John 21: 19)

Discipline

As a man chasteneth his son, so the Lord thy God chasteneth thee. (Deut. 8: 5)

Correction is grievous unto him that forsaketh the way. (Prov. 15: 10)

He that refuseth instruction despiseth his own soul. (Prov. 15: 32)

As many as I love, I rebuke and chasten. (Rev. 3: 19)

Dishonesty

Put not thine hand with the wicked to be an unrighteous witness. (Ex. 23: 1)

With flattering lips and with a double heart do they speak. (Ps. 12: 2)

He that worketh deceit shall not dwell within my house. (Ps. 101: 7)

He that telleth lies shall not tarry in my sight. (Ps. 101: 7)

Deceit is in the heart of them that imagine evil. (Prov. 12: 20)

He that hath a perverse tongue falleth into mischief. (Prov. 17: 20)

He that speaketh lies shall perish. (Prov. 19: 9)

A poor man is better than a liar. (Prov. 19: 22)

He that is unjust in the least is unjust also in much. (Luke 16: 10)

Disobedience

She took of the fruit thereof, and did eat. (Gen. 3: 6)

His wife looked back from behind him, and she became a pillar of salt. (Gen. 19: 26)

How long wilt thou refuse to humble thyself before Me? let My people go. (Ex. 10: 3)

What the Bible says about (9)

Disobedience, continued

They hear thy words, but they do them not. (Ezek. 33: 32)

Every one that heareth these sayings of mine, and doeth them not, shall be likened unto a foolish man, which built his house upon the sand. (Matt. 7: 26)

Laying aside the commandment of God, ye hold the tradition of men. (Mark 7: 8)

Remember Lot's wife. (Luke 17: 32)

He that loveth me not keepeth not my sayings. (John 14: 24)

He that saith, I know Him, and keepeth not His commandments, is a liar. (1 John 2: 4)

Distance

From Dan even to Beersheba. (Judg. 20: 1)

Diversity

All the people, both small and great. (2 Kings 23: 2)

There are diversities of gifts, but the same Spirit. (1 Cor. 12: 4)

There are differences of administrations, but the same Lord. (1 Cor. 12: 5)

In a great house there are not only vessels of gold and of silver, but also of wood and of earth. (2 Tim. 2: 20)

Divorce

Whosoever shall put away his wife, saving for the cause of fornication, causeth her to commit adultery. (Matt. 5: 32)

Whosoever shall marry her that is divorced committeth adultery. (Matt. 5: 32)

What therefore God hath joined together, let not man put asunder. (Matt. 19: 6; Mark 10: 9)

Whosoever shall put away his wife, except it be for fornication, and shall marry another, committeth adultery. (Matt. 19: 9)

If a woman shall put away her husband, and be married to another, she committeth adultery. (Mark 10: 12)

Whosoever putteth away his wife, and marrieth another, committeth adultery. (Luke 16: 18)

Let not the husband put away his wife. (1 Cor. 7: 11)

Art thou bound unto a wife? seek not to be loosed. (1 Cor. 7: 27)

Doubt

Is the Lord among us, or not? (Ex. 17: 7)

We have here but five loaves, and two fishes. (Matt. 14: 17)

O thou of little faith, wherefore didst thou doubt? (Matt. 14: 31)

O ye of little faith. (Matt. 16: 8)

O faithless and perverse generation, how long shall I be with you? how long shall I suffer you? (Matt. 17: 17)

Reach hither thy hand, and thrust it into my side: and be not faithless, but believing. (John 20: 27)

Dreams

Thou scarest me with dreams, and terrifiest me through visions. (Job 7: 14)

Show me the dream, and the interpretation thereof. (Dan. 2: 6)

There is a God in heaven that revealeth secrets. (Dan. 2: 28)

Your old men shall dream dreams, your young men shall see visions. (Joel 2: 28)

Drunkenness

I have drunk neither wine nor strong drink, but have poured out my soul before the Lord. (1 Sam. 1: 15)

The drunkard and the glutton shall come to poverty. (Prov. 23: 21)

As a drunken man staggereth in his vomit. (Is. 19: 14)

Woe unto him that giveth his neighbor drink. (Hab. 2: 15)

Be not drunk with wine, wherein is excess; but be filled with the Spirit. (Eph. 5: 18)

Duty

What doth the Lord thy God require of thee, but to fear the Lord thy God, to walk in all His ways, and to love Him, and to serve the Lord thy God with all thy heart and with all thy soul. (Deut. 10: 12)

Fear God, and keep His commandments: for this is the whole duty of man. (Eccl. 12: 13)

Say not, I am a child: for thou shalt go to all that I shall send thee, and whatsoever I command thee thou shalt speak. (Jer. 1: 7)

It becometh us to fulfill all righteousness. (Matt. 3: 15)

Wist ye not that I must be about my Father's business? (Luke 2: 49)

Go thou and preach the kingdom of God. (Luke 9: 60)

This is the work of God, that ye believe on Him whom He hath sent. (John 6: 29)

I must work the works of Him that sent me, while it is day. (John 9: 4)

The cup which my Father hath given me, shall I not drink it? (John 18: 11)

It shall be told thee what thou must do. (Acts 9: 6)

Duty, Neglect of

Curse ye bitterly the inhabitants thereof; because they came not to the help of the Lord. (Judg. 5: 23)

This thing is not good that thou hast done. (1 Sam. 26: 16)

As the Lord liveth, ye are worthy to die. (1 Sam. 26: 16)

What doest thou here, Elijah? (1 Kings 19: 9)

The stork in the heaven knoweth her appointed times; and the turtle and the crane and the swallow observe the time of their coming; but my people know not the judgment of the Lord. (Jer. 8: 7)

Cursed be he that doeth the work of the Lord deceitfully. (Jer. 48: 10)

What the Bible says about (10)

E

Earth

And God called the dry land Earth; and the gathering together of the waters called He Seas. (Gen. 1: 10)

All the earth is Mine. (Ex. 19: 5)

The pillars of the earth are the Lord's, and He hath set the world upon them. (1 Sam. 2: 8)

Who laid the corner stone thereof? (Job 38: 6)

Education

And thou shalt teach them diligently unto thy children, and shalt talk of them when thou sittest in thine house, and when thou walkest by the way, and when thou liest down, and when thou risest up. (Deut. 6: 7)

Teach them the good way wherein they should walk. (1 Kings 8: 36)

Fools despise wisdom and instruction. (Prov. 1: 7)

Effort

Let not your hands be weak: for your work shall be rewarded. (2 Chr. 15: 7)

Whosoever shall compel thee to go a mile, go with him twain. (Matt. 5: 41)

He that seeketh findeth. (Matt. 7: 8; Luke 11: 10)

To him that knocketh it shall be opened. (Matt. 7: 8; Luke 11: 10)

With what measure ye mete, it shall be measured to you. (Mark 4: 24)

Eloquence

I am slow of speech, and of a slow tongue. (Ex. 4: 10)

Go, and I will be with thy mouth, and teach thee what thou shalt say. (Ex. 4: 12)

My speech shall distil as the dew, as the small rain upon the tender herb, and as the showers upon the grass. (Deut. 32: 2)

Empathy

As thou livest, and as thy soul liveth, I will not do this thing. (2 Sam. 11: 11)

Rejoice with them that do rejoice, and weep with them that weep. (Rom. 12: 15)

Absent in body, but present in spirit. (1 Cor. 5: 3)

Who is weak, and I am not weak? who is offended, and I burn not? (2 Cor. 11: 29)

Though I be absent in the flesh, yet am I with you in the spirit. (Col. 2: 5)

Employees

Thou shalt not oppress an hired servant that is poor and needy. (Deut. 24: 14)

Thou shalt not muzzle the ox when he treadeth out the corn. (Deut. 25: 4)

A wicked messenger falleth into mischief: but a faithful ambassador is health. (Prov. 13: 17)

Encouragement

Fear ye not, stand still, and see the salvation of the Lord, which He will show to you today. (Ex. 14: 13)

The Lord shall fight for you, and ye shall hold your peace. (Ex. 14: 14)

Rebel not ye against the Lord, neither fear ye the people of the land. (Num. 14: 9)

Fear not, neither be discouraged. (Deut. 1: 21)

Get thee up; wherefore liest thou thus upon thy face? (Josh. 7: 10)

Go up; for to morrow I will deliver them into thine hand. (Judg. 20: 28)

Be of good cheer; thy sins be forgiven thee. (Matt. 9: 2)

When thou art converted, strengthen thy brethren. (Luke 22: 32)

Be not afraid, but speak, and hold not thy peace: For I am with thee. (Acts 18: 9–10)

Enemies

Dread not, neither be afraid of them. The Lord your God which goeth before you, He shall fight for you. (Deut. 1: 29–30)

Ye shall not fear them: for the Lord your God He shall fight for you. (Deut. 3: 22)

The souls of thine enemies, them shall He sling out. (1 Sam. 25: 29)

Let me see Thy vengeance on them: for unto Thee have I opened my cause. (Jer. 20: 12)

Love your enemies. (Matt. 5: 44; Luke 6: 27)

Bless them that curse you, do good to them that hate you. (Matt. 5: 44)

If ye love them which love you,
what reward have ye? do not even the publicans the same? (Matt. 5: 46)

If ye do good to them which do good to you, what thank ye have ye? for sinners also do even the same. (Luke 6: 33)

He that hateth me hateth my Father also. (John 15: 23)

Enlightenment

Your eyes shall be opened, and ye shall be as gods, knowing good and evil. (Gen. 3: 5)

The Lord will lighten my darkness. (Ii Sam. 22: 29)

I will bring the blind by a way that they knew not; I will lead them in paths that they have not known. (Is. 42: 16)

To give light to them that sit in darkness. (Luke 1: 79)

He hath anointed me to preach the gospel to the poor. (Luke 4: 18)

I am come a light into the world, that whosoever believeth on me should not abide in darkness. (John 12: 46)

Open their eyes. (Acts 26: 18)

What the Bible says about (11)

E continued

Enthusiasm

With all thy heart and with all thy soul. (Deut. 10: 12)

What ye shall say, that will I do for you. (2 Sam. 21: 4)

Thou shouldest have smitten five or six times. (2 Kings 13: 19)

Whatsoever ye do, do it heartily, as to the Lord, and not unto men. (Col. 3: 23)

I know thy works, that thou art neither cold nor hot: I would thou wert cold or hot. (Rev. 3: 16)

I heard as it were the voice of a great multitude, and as the voice of many waters, and as the voice of mighty thunderings. (Rev. 19: 6)

Envy

Thou shalt not covet. (Ex. 20: 17; Rom. 13: 9)

Wrath killeth the foolish man, and envy slayeth the silly one. (Job 5: 2)

A little that a righteous man hath is better than the riches of many wicked. (Ps. 37: 16)

Is thine eye evil, because I am good? (Matt. 20: 15)

Ephemera

Riches certainly make themselves wings; they fly away as an eagle toward heaven. (Prov. 23: 5)

They shall be as the morning cloud, and as the early dew that passeth away,

as the chaff that is driven with the whirlwind out of the floor, and as the smoke out of the chimney. (Hos. 13: 3)

Equality

One law shall be to him that is homeborn, and unto the stranger that sojourneth among you. (Ex. 12: 49)

They all are the work of His hands. (Job 34: 19)

All are of the dust, and all turn to dust again. (Eccl. 3: 20)

The last shall be first, and the first shall be last. (Matt. 20: 16)

The servant is not greater than his lord; neither he that is sent greater than he that sent him. (John 13: 16)

Ye are all the children of God by faith in Christ Jesus. (Gal. 3: 26)

Escape

Arise, and let us flee. (2 Sam. 15: 14)

I am escaped with the skin of my teeth. (Job 19: 20)

Oh that I had wings like a dove! for then would I fly away, and be at rest. (Ps. 55: 6)

The darkness hideth not from Thee; but the night shineth as the day. (Ps. 139: 12)

There is no peace, saith the Lord, unto the wicked. (Is. 48: 22)

Eternal life

Thou wilt not leave my soul in hell; neither wilt Thou suffer Thine Holy One to see corruption. (Ps. 16: 10)

He that loseth his life for my sake shall find it. (Matt. 10: 39)

There be some standing here, which shall not taste of death, till they see the Son of man coming in His kingdom. (Matt. 16: 28)

If thou wilt enter into life, keep the commandments. (Matt. 19: 17)

Go and sell that thou hast, and give to the poor, and thou shalt have treasure in heaven. (Matt. 19: 21)

Thou knowest the commandments, Do not commit adultery, Do not kill, Do not steal, Do not bear false witness, Defraud not, Honor thy father and mother. (Mark 10: 19)

Come, take up the cross, and follow me. (Mark 10: 21)

Eternity

The Lord shall reign for ever and ever. (Ex. 15: 18)

This God is our God for ever and ever: He will be our guide even unto death. (Ps. 48: 14)

But Thou, O Lord, shalt endure for ever. (Ps. 102: 12)

Thou art the same, and Thy years shall have no end. (Ps. 102: 27)

Thou, O Lord, remainest for ever; Thy throne from generation to generation. (Lam. 5: 19)

For Thine is the kingdom, and the power, and the glory, for ever. (Matt. 6: 13)

Holy, holy, holy, Lord God Almighty, which was, and is, and is to come. (Rev. 4: 8)

Evangelism

Follow me, and I will make you fishers of men. (Matt. 4: 19)

The harvest is truly plenteous, but the laborers are few. (Matt. 9: 37)

I send you forth as sheep in the midst of wolves: be ye therefore wise as serpents, and harmless as doves. (Matt. 10: 16)

I am not sent but unto the lost sheep of the house of Israel. (Matt. 15: 24)

Go ye therefore, and teach all nations, baptizing them in the name of the Father, and of the Son, and of the Holy Spirit. (Matt. 28: 19)

The sower soweth the word. (Mark 4: 14)

The gospel must first be published among all nations. (Mark 13: 10)

Go ye into all the world, and preach the gospel to every creature. (Mark 16: 15)

Go thou and preach the kingdom of God. (Luke 9: 60)

Repentance and remission of sins should be preached in His name among all nations. (Luke 24: 47)

What the Bible says about (12)

Evangelism, continued

He that reapeth receiveth wages,
and gathereth fruit unto life eternal.
(John 4: 36)

Other sheep I have, which are not of
this fold. (John 10: 16)

He that receiveth whomsoever I send
receiveth me. (John 13: 20)

Go and bring forth fruit. (John 15: 16)

Ye also shall bear witness, because ye
have been with me from the beginning.
(John 15: 27)

He is a chosen vessel unto me, to bear
my name. (Acts 9: 15)

The hand of the Lord was with
them: and a great number believed.
(Acts 11: 21)

The word of God grew and
multiplied. (Acts 12: 24)

Open their eyes. (Acts 26: 18)

Turn them from darkness to light,
and from the power of Satan unto God.
(Acts 26: 18)

Evil

The imagination of man's heart is evil
from his youth. (Gen. 8: 21)

Sodom and Gomorrah. (Gen. 18: 20;
Gen. 19: 28)

I will not justify the wicked. (Ex. 23: 7)

Thou knowest the people, that they
are set on mischief. (Ex. 32: 22)

Put the evil away from the midst of
thee. (Deut. 13: 5)

Sons of Belial. (Judg. 19: 22)

The thing that David had done
displeased the Lord. (2 Sam. 11: 27)

Thou knowest all the wickedness

which thine heart is privy to. (1 Kings
2: 44)

There was none like unto Ahab,
which did sell himself to work
wickedness in the sight of the Lord.
(1 Kings 21: 25)

Keep me from evil, that it may not
grieve me! (1 Chr. 4: 10)

Exaltation

Thou, Lord, art high above all the
earth: Thou art exalted far above all
gods. (Ps. 97: 9)

Hereafter shall the Son of man sit on
the right hand of the power of God.
(Luke 22: 69)

Sit thou on my right hand, Until
I make thy foes thy footstool.
(Acts 2: 34–35)

Exasperation

How long refuse ye to keep My
commandments and My laws?
(Ex. 16: 28)

How long will this people provoke
Me? (Num. 14: 11)

Ye have forsaken Me, and served
other gods: wherefore I will deliver you
no more. (Judg. 10: 13)

Excess

Thou wilt surely wear away, both
thou, and this people that is with thee.
(Ex. 18: 18)

After whom dost thou pursue? after
a dead dog, after a flea. (1 Sam. 24: 14)

The king of Israel is come out

to seek a flea, as when one doth hunt a partridge in the mountains. (1 Sam. 26: 20)

Be not righteous over much; neither make thyself over wise. (Eccl. 7: 16)

Much study is a weariness of the flesh. (Eccl. 12: 12)

Be not drunk with wine, wherein is excess; but be filled with the Spirit. (Eph. 5: 18)

Excuses

I was afraid, because I was naked. (Gen. 3: 10)

The serpent beguiled me, and I did eat. (Gen. 3: 13)

I did but taste a little honey with the end of the rod. (1 Sam. 14: 43)

I feared the people, and obeyed their voice. (1 Sam. 15: 24)

Exile

He made them wander in the wilderness forty years, until all the generation, that had done evil in the sight of the Lord, was consumed. (Num. 32: 13)

The Lord shall scatter you among the nations, and ye shall be left few in number among the heathen. (Deut. 4: 27)

Ye have sinned against the Lord, and have not obeyed His voice, therefore this thing is come upon you. (Jer. 40: 3)

Exorcism

How can Satan cast out Satan? (Mark 3: 23)

Come out of the man, thou unclean spirit. (Mark 5: 8)

In my name shall they cast out devils. (Mark 16: 17)

I command thee in the name of Jesus Christ to come out of her. (Acts 16: 18)

Expectation

The desire of the righteous is only good: but the expectation of the wicked is wrath. (Prov. 11: 23)

We looked for peace, but no good came; and for a time of health, and behold trouble! (Jer. 8: 15)

The harvest is past, the summer is ended, and we are not saved. (Jer. 8: 20)

Ye looked for much, and, lo, it came to little. (Hag. 1: 9)

To whom men have committed much, of him they will ask the more. (Luke 12: 48)

Experience

Thou mayest be to us instead of eyes. (Num. 10: 31)

Remember the days of old, consider the years of many generations: ask thy father, and he will show thee; thy elders, and they will tell thee. (Deut. 32: 7)

Let not him that girdeth on his harness boast himself as he that putteth it off. (1 Kings 20: 11)

With the ancient is wisdom; and in length of days understanding. (Job 12: 12)

Days should speak, and multitude of years should teach wisdom. (Job 32: 7)

What the Bible says about (13)

F

Failure

If thou doest not well, sin lieth at the door. (Gen. 4: 7)

By the way that he came, by the same shall he return. (2 Kings 19: 33, Is. 37: 34)

He that trusteth in his riches shall fall. (Prov. 11: 28)

Pride goeth before destruction, and an haughty spirit before a fall. (Prov. 16: 18)

Fairness

Wilt Thou also destroy the righteous with the wicked? (Gen. 18: 23)

He that gathered much had nothing over, and he that gathered little had no lack. (Ex. 16: 18)

God do so and more also: for thou shalt surely die, Jonathan. (1 Sam. 14: 44)

He shall not judge after the sight of his eyes, neither reprove after the hearing of his ears. (Is. 11: 3)

Faith

Is any thing too hard for the Lord? (Gen. 18: 14)

If the Lord delight in us, then He will bring us into this land. (Num. 14: 8)

How long will it be ere they believe Me, for all the signs which I have showed among them? (Num. 14: 11)

Speak ye unto the rock before their eyes; and it shall give forth his water. (Num. 20: 8)

He will not fail thee, neither forsake thee: fear not, neither be dismayed. (Deut. 31: 8)

Faithfulness

Hath He said, and shall He not do it? or hath He spoken, and shall He not make it good? (Num. 23: 19)

Beware lest thou forget the Lord. (Deut. 6: 12)

Him shalt thou serve, and to Him shalt thou cleave, and swear by His name. (Deut. 10: 20)

Cleave unto the Lord your God, as ye have done unto this day. (Josh. 23: 8)

But as for me and my house, we will serve the Lord. (Josh. 24: 15)

Faithlessness

We be not able to go up against the people; for they are stronger than we. (Num. 13: 31)

He will not be slack to him that hateth Him, He will repay him to his face. (Deut. 7: 10)

They would not hearken unto their judges, but they went a whoring after other gods. (Judg. 2: 17)

False gods

Take heed to yourselves, that your heart be not deceived. (Deut. 11: 16)

If he be a god, let him plead for himself, because one hath cast down his altar. (Judg. 6: 31)

Go and cry unto the gods which ye have chosen; let them deliver you. (Judg. 10: 14)

False prophets

Thou shalt not hearken unto the words of that prophet, or that dreamer of dreams: for the Lord your God proveth you, to know whether ye love the Lord your God with all your heart and with all your soul. (Deut. 13: 3)

When a prophet speaketh in the name of the Lord, if the thing follow not, nor come to pass, that is the thing which the Lord hath not spoken. (Deut. 18: 22)

I am a prophet also as thou art; and an angel spake unto me by the word of the Lord. (1 Kings 13: 18)

Fame

His fame was noised throughout all the country. (Josh. 6: 27)

Saul hath slain his thousands, and David his ten thousands. (1 Sam. 18: 7)

Riches and honor come of Thee. (1 Chr. 29: 12)

Family

Be fruitful, and multiply. (Gen. 1: 28)

In thee and in thy seed shall all the families of the earth be blessed. (Gen. 28: 14)

He that troubleth his own house shall inherit the wind. (Prov. 11: 29)

He that loveth father or mother more than me is not worthy of me: and he that loveth son or daughter more than me is not worthy of me. (Matt. 10: 37)

Whosoever shall do the will of my Father which is in heaven, the same is my brother, and sister, and mother. (Matt. 12: 50)

My mother and my brethren are these which hear the word of God, and do it. (Luke 8: 21)

The father shall be divided against the son, and the son against the father; the mother against the daughter, and the daughter against the mother. (Luke 12: 53)

What the Bible says about (14)

F continued

Fasting

I humbled my soul with fasting.
(Ps. 35: 13)

In the day of your fast ye find
pleasure. (Is. 58: 3)

Is not this the fast that I have chosen?
to loose the bands of wickedness, to
undo the heavy burdens, and to let the
oppressed go free. (Isa. 58: 6)

When they fast, I will not hear thy
cry. (Jer. 14: 12)

When thou fastest, anoint thine head,
and wash thy face. (Matt. 6: 17)

Appear not unto men to fast, but
unto thy Father. (Matt. 6: 18)

Favoritism

He was the son of his old age.
(Gen. 37: 3)

He made him a coat of many colors.
(Gen. 37: 3)

Thou shalt not respect the person of
the poor, nor honor the person of the
mighty. (Lev. 19: 15)

Though he was not the firstborn,
yet his father made him the chief.
(1 Chr. 26: 10)

There is no respect of persons with
God. (Rom. 2: 11)

Fear

Fear not, for I am with thee, and will
bless thee, and multiply thy seed.
(Gen. 26: 24)

Deliver me, I pray Thee, from the
hand of my brother. (Gen. 32: 11)

It had been better for us to serve the
Egyptians, than that we should die in
the wilderness. (Ex. 14: 12)

Ye shall flee when none pursueth
you. (Lev. 26: 17)

We were in our own sight as
grasshoppers. (Num. 13: 33)

Ye shall not fear them: for the Lord
your God He shall fight for you.
(Deut. 3: 22)

Be not afraid, neither be thou
dismayed: for the Lord thy God is with
thee whithersoever thou goest.
(Josh. 1: 9)

Fear of God

O that there were such an heart in
them, that they would fear Me, and
keep all My commandments always.
(Deut. 5: 29)

Fear the Lord thy God. (Deut. 10: 12)

Fear before Him, all the earth.
(1 Chr. 16: 30)

The fear of the Lord, that is wisdom.
(Job 28: 28)

The secret of the Lord is with them
that fear Him. (Ps. 25: 14)

When He slew them, then they
sought Him. (Ps. 78: 34)

God is greatly to be feared in the
assembly of the saints. (Ps. 89: 7)

Fellowship

Behold, how good and how pleasant
it is for brethren to dwell together in
unity! (Ps. 133: 1)

Have we not all one father? hath not

one God created us? (Mal. 2: 10)

Whosoever shall do the will of my Father which is in heaven, the same is my brother, and sister, and mother. (Matt. 12: 50)

Where two or three are gathered together in my name, there am I in the midst of them. (Matt. 18: 20)

Have salt in yourselves, and have peace one with another. (Mark 9: 50)

He that loveth me shall be loved of my Father. (John 14: 21)

I am the vine, ye are the branches. (John 15: 5)

Woman, behold thy son! (John 19: 26)

Fertility

Be fruitful, and multiply. (Gen. 1: 28)

I will make thy seed as the dust of the earth: so that if a man can number the dust of the earth, then shall thy seed also be numbered. (Gen. 13: 16)

Shall a child be born unto him that is an hundred years old? and shall Sarah, that is ninety years old, bear? (Gen. 17: 17)

Flattery

As thou art, so were they; each one resembled the children of a king. (Judg. 8: 18)

The half was not told me. (1 Kings 10: 7)

With flattering lips and with a double heart do they speak. (Ps. 12: 2)

He that hideth hatred with lying lips, and he that uttereth a slander, is a fool. (Prov. 10: 18)

Folly

But he forsook the counsel which the old men gave him. (2 Chr. 10: 8)

In his disease he sought not to the Lord, but to the physicians. (2 Chr. 16: 12)

Forsake the foolish, and live. (Prov. 9: 6)

The foolishness of fools is folly. (Prov. 14: 24)

He that is hasty of spirit exalteth folly. (Prov. 14: 29)

Food

Every moving thing that liveth shall be meat for you. (Gen. 9: 3)

Eat, that thou mayest have strength, when thou goest on thy way. (1 Sam. 28: 22)

He hath given meat unto them that fear Him. (Ps. 111: 5)

Fools

The fool hath said in his heart, There is no God. (Ps. 14: 1; Ps. 53: 1)

The foolish man reproacheth Thee daily. (Ps. 74: 22)

Fools despise wisdom and instruction. (Prov. 1: 7)

Scorners delight in their scorning, and fools hate knowledge. (Prov. 1: 22)

What the Bible says about (15)

F continued

Foreigners

I have been a stranger in a strange land. (Ex. 2: 22)

One law shall be to him that is homeborn, and unto the stranger that sojourneth among you. (Ex. 12: 49)

Thou shalt neither vex a stranger, nor oppress him: for ye were strangers in the land of Egypt. (Ex. 22: 21)

Thou shalt love him as thy self. (Lev. 19: 34)

Love ye therefore the stranger: for ye were strangers in the land of Egypt. (Deut. 10: 19)

Unto a stranger thou mayest lend upon usury; but unto thy brother thou shalt not lend upon usury. (Deut. 23: 20)

Learn not the way of the heathen. (Jer. 10: 2)

Forgiveness

Hear Thou in heaven Thy dwelling place: and when Thou hearest, forgive. (1 Kings 8: 30)

Render unto every man according unto all his ways, whose heart Thou knowest. (2 Chr. 6: 30)

They have humbled themselves; therefore I will not destroy them. (2 Chr. 12: 7)

Nevertheless there are good things found in thee. (2 Chr. 19: 3)

Serve the Lord your God, that the fierceness of His wrath may turn away from you. (2 Chr. 30: 8)

The good Lord pardon every one that prepareth his heart to seek God. (2 Chr. 30: 18–19)

Remember not the sins of my youth. (Ps. 25: 7)

Fornication

The body is not for fornication, but for the Lord. (1 Cor. 6: 13)

Flee fornication. (1 Cor. 6: 18)

He that committeth fornication sinneth against his own body. (1 Cor. 6: 18)

To avoid fornication, let every man have his own wife, and let every woman have her own husband. (1 Cor. 7: 2)

Frailty

Remember, I beseech Thee, that Thou hast made me as the clay. (Job 10: 9)

Have mercy upon me, O Lord; for I am weak. (Ps. 6: 2)

Every man at his best state is altogether vanity. (Ps. 39: 5)

If thou faint in the day of adversity, thy strength is small. (Prov. 24: 10)

We all do fade as a leaf. (Is. 64: 6)

The law maketh men high priests which have infirmity. (Heb. 7: 28)

Freedom

When ye go, ye shall not go empty. (Ex. 3: 21)

Thus saith the Lord God of Israel, Let My people go. (Ex. 5: 1)

It is a night to be much observed unto the Lord. (Ex. 12: 42)

Friendship

The Lord do so to me, and more also, if ought but death part thee and me. (Ruth 1: 17)

The soul of Jonathan was knit with the soul of David, and Jonathan loved him as his on soul. (1 Sam. 18: 1)

Whatsoever thy soul desireth, I will even do it for thee. (1 Sam. 20: 4)

He loved him as he loved his own soul. (1 Sam. 20: 17)

Fulfillment

He satisfieth the longing soul, and filleth the hungry soul with goodness. (Ps. 107: 9)

Surely as I have thought, so shall it come to pass; and as I have purposed, so shall it stand. (Is. 14: 24)

Every one that thirsteth, come ye to the waters, and he that hath no money; come ye, buy, and eat. (Is. 55: 1)

I am not come to destroy, but to fulfill. (Matt. 5: 17)

Ye are complete in Him, which is the head of all principality and power. (Col. 2: 10)

Futility

Ye shall sow your seed in vain, for your enemies shall eat it. (Lev. 26: 16)

Wherefore then dost thou ask of me, seeing the Lord is departed from thee, and is become thine enemy? (1 Sam. 28: 16)

Knowest thou not that it will be bitterness in the latter end? (2 Sam. 2: 26)

The Lord hath said unto him, Curse David. Who shall then say, Wherefore hast thou done so? (2 Sam. 16: 10)

Fight ye not against the Lord God of your fathers; for ye shall not prosper. (2 Chr. 13: 12)

Future

What God is about to do He showeth unto Pharaoh. (Gen. 41: 28)

Hast thou not heard long ago how I have done it, and of ancient times that I have formed it? (2 Kings 19: 25, Is. 37: 26)

Boast not thyself of tomorrow; for thou knowest not what a day may bring forth. (Prov. 27: 1)

Shut thou up the vision; for it shall be for many days. (Dan. 8: 26)

Take therefore no thought for the morrow: for the morrow shall take thought for the things of itself. (Matt. 6: 34)

Sufficient unto the day is the evil thereof. (Matt. 6: 34)

It is not for you to know the times or the seasons. (Acts 1: 7)

Known unto God are all His works from the beginning of the world. (Acts 15: 18)

Ye know not what shall be on the morrow. (James 4: 14)

Ye ought to say, If the Lord will, we shall live, and do this, or that. (James 4: 15)

What the Bible says about (16)

G

Generosity

Every man shall give as he is able, according to the blessing of the Lord thy God which He hath given thee. (Deut. 16: 17)

Let her glean even among the sheaves, and reproach her not. (Ruth 2: 15)

Ask what I shall give thee. (1 Kings 3: 5; 2 Chr. 1: 7)

Gifts

He made him a coat of many colors. (Gen. 37: 3)

A gift in secret pacifieth anger. (Prov. 21: 14)

They presented unto Him gifts; gold, and frankincense, and myrrh. (Matt. 2: 11)

Gloating

Let not them that are mine enemies wrongfully rejoice over me. (Ps. 35: 19)

Rejoice not when thine enemy falleth, and let not thine heart be glad when he stumbleth. (Prov. 24: 17)

All mine enemies have heard of my trouble; they are glad that Thou hast done it. (Lam. 1: 21)

Glory

The journey that thou takest shall not be for thine honor. (Judg. 4: 9)

Let them that love Him be as the sun when he goeth forth in his might. (Judg. 5: 31)

A chariot of fire. (2 Kings 2: 11)

Gluttony

Put a knife to thy throat, if thou be a man given to appetite. (Prov. 23: 2)

The drunkard and the glutton shall come to poverty. (Prov. 23: 21)

Let us eat and drink; for tomorrow we shall die. (Is. 22: 13; 1 Cor. 15: 32)

God

I Am That I Am. (Ex. 3: 14)

I am the Lord. (Ex. 6: 2)

The Lord shall reign for ever and ever. (Ex. 15: 18)

Thou shalt find Him, if thou seek Him with all thy heart and with all thy soul. (Deut. 4: 29)

He is thy praise. (Deut. 10: 21)

He is thy life, and the length of thy days. (Deut. 30: 20)

He is the Rock, His work is perfect. (Deut. 32: 4)

The Lord liveth. (2 Sam. 22: 47, Ps. 18: 46)

The Lord is God. (1 Kings 8: 60)

Him shall ye fear, and Him shall ye worship, and to Him shall ye do sacrifice. (2 Kings 17: 36)

Lord, Thou art God. (1 Chr. 17: 26)

As for God, His way is perfect. (Ps. 18: 30, 2 Sam. 22: 31)

Blessed be the Lord. (Ps. 31: 21)

Blessed be God. (Ps. 68: 35)

Thou art my father, my God, and the rock of my salvation. (Ps. 89: 26)

Remember now thy Creator in the days of thy youth. (Eccl. 12: 1)

The Lord is our judge, the Lord is our lawgiver, the Lord is our king; He will save us. (Is. 33: 22)

I am the Lord thy God, that divided the sea, whose waves roared: The Lord of hosts is His name. (Is. 51: 15)

I the Lord am thy Savior and thy redeemer. (Is. 60: 16)

O Lord, Thou art our Father. (Is. 64: 8)

The Lord is the true God, He is the living God, and an everlasting king. (Jer. 10: 10)

All that forsake Thee shall be ashamed. (Jer. 17: 13)

Behold, all souls are Mine. (Ezek. 18: 4)

The Lord our God is righteous in all His works which He doeth. (Dan. 9: 14)

The ways of the Lord are right, and the just shall walk in them: but the transgressors shall fall therein. (Hos. 14: 9)

I am the Lord, I change not. (Mal. 3: 6)

Our Father which art in heaven, Hallowed be Thy name. Thy kingdom com. Thy will be done in earth, as it is in heaven. (Matt. 6: 9–10)

God is not the God of the dead, but of the living. (Matt. 22: 32)

Call no man your father upon the earth: for one is your Father, which is in heaven. (Matt. 23: 9)

God is true. (John 3: 33)

He that sent me is true, whom ye know not. (John 7: 28)

God is light, and in Him is no darkness at all. (1 John 1: 5)

God is love. (1 John 4: 8, 16)

We love Him, because He first loved us. (1 John 4: 19)

Holy, holy, holy, Lord God Almighty, which was, and is, and is to come. (Rev. 4: 8)

God, Characteristics of

I the Lord thy God am a jealous God. (Ex. 20: 5)

The Lord, The Lord God, merciful and gracious, longsuffering, and abundant in goodness and truth. (Ex. 34: 6)

The Lord, whose name is Jealous, is a jealous God. (Ex. 34: 14)

What the Bible says about (17)

God, Characteristics of, continued

The Lord thy God is a consuming fire, even a jealous God. (Deut. 4: 24)

The Lord thy God is a merciful God. (Deut. 4: 31)

A God of truth and without iniquity, just and right is He. (Deut. 32: 4)

He is an holy God; He is a jealous God; He will not forgive your transgressions nor your sins. (Josh. 24: 19)

With the merciful Thou wilt show Thyself merciful, and with the upright man Thou wilt show Thyself upright. (2 Sam. 22: 26)

The Lord is righteous. (2 Chr. 12: 6)

God will not do wickedly, neither will the Almighty pervert judgment. (Job 34: 12)

All the paths of the Lord are mercy and truth unto such as keep His covenant. (Ps. 25: 10)

Thy mercy is great unto the heavens, and Thy truth unto the clouds. (Ps. 57: 10)

The Lord is good; His mercy is everlasting; and His truth endureth to all generations. (Ps. 100: 5)

The Lord is merciful and gracious, slow to anger, and plenteous in mercy. (Ps. 103: 8)

The Lord is righteous in all His ways, and holy in all His works. (Ps. 145: 17)

The Lord is a God of judgment: blessed are all they that wait for Him. (Is. 30: 18)

He is gracious and merciful, slow to anger, and of great kindness. (Joel 2: 13)

God is faithful. (1 Cor. 1: 9)

The Father of mercies, and the God of all comfort. (2 Cor. 1: 3)

God's anger

They provoked Him to jealousy with their sins. (1 Kings 14: 22)

Great is the wrath of the Lord that is kindled against us, because our fathers have not hearkened unto the words of this book. (2 Kings 22: 13)

His power and His wrath is against all them that forsake Him. (Ezra 8: 22)

Lest My fury come forth like fire, and burn that none can quench it. (Jer. 4: 4)

Ye provoke Me unto wrath with the works of your hands. (Jer. 44: 8)

In the day of the Lord's anger none escaped nor remained. (Lam. 2: 22)

Thus saith the Lord God; Behold, I, even I, am against thee. (Ezek. 5: 8)

I will cause My fury to rest upon them, and I will be comforted. (Ezek. 5: 13)

He reserveth wrath for His enemies. (Nah. 1: 2)

His fury is poured out like fire. (Nah. 1: 6)

All the earth shall be devoured with the fire of My jealousy. (Zeph. 3: 8)

The wrath of God cometh on the children of disobedience. (Col. 3: 6)

It is a fearful thing to fall into the hands of the living God. (Heb. 10: 31)

Our God is a consuming fire. (Heb. 12: 29)

The great winepress of the wrath of God. (Rev. 14: 19)

Pour out the vials of the wrath of God upon the earth. (Rev. 16: 1)

God's glory

As truly as I live, all the earth shall be filled with the glory of the Lord. (Num. 14: 21)

Declare His glory among the heathen; His marvelous works among all nations. (1 Chr. 16: 24)

He saved them for His name's sake, that He might make His mighty power to be known. (Ps. 106: 8)

Great is the glory of the Lord. (Ps. 138: 5)

The whole earth is full of His glory. (Is. 6: 3)

Peace in heaven, and glory in the highest. (Luke 19: 38)

Ye shall see heaven open, and the angels of God ascending and descending upon the Son of man. (John 1: 51)

This sickness is not unto death, but for the glory of God. (John 11: 4)

The hour is come, that the Son of man should be glorified. (John 12: 23)

Father, glorify Thy name. (John 12: 28)

Now is the Son of man glorified, and God is glorified in Him. (John 13: 31)

Whatsoever ye shall ask in my name, that will I do, that the Father may be glorified in the Son. (John 14: 13)

Glorify Thy Son, that Thy Son also may glorify Thee. (John 17: 1)

The city had no need of the sun, neither of the moon, to shine in it: for the glory of God did lighten it, and the Lamb is the light thereof. (Rev. 21: 23)

God's greatness

I know that the Lord is greater than all gods. (Ex. 18: 11)

God is great. (Job 36: 26)

Great is the Lord, and greatly to be praised. (Ps. 48: 1)

For Thine is the kingdom, and the power, and the glory, for ever. (Matt. 6: 13)

My Father is greater than I. (John 14: 28)

Every house is builded by some man; but He that built all things is God. (Heb. 3: 4)

Great and marvelous are Thy works, Lord God Almighty. (Rev. 15: 3)

What the Bible says about (18)

G continued

God's knowledge

Your Father knoweth what things ye have need of, before ye ask Him. (Matt. 6: 8)

Are not five sparrows sold for two farthings, and not one of them is forgotten before God? (Luke 12: 6)

Even the very hairs of your head are all numbered. (Luke 12: 7)

God knoweth your hearts. (Luke 16: 15)

The Lord knoweth the thoughts of the wise, that they are vain. (1 Cor. 3: 20)

God is greater than our heart, and knoweth all things. (1 John 3: 20)

God's love

Thy loving kindness is better than life. (Ps. 63: 3)

The Lord loveth the righteous. (Ps. 146: 8)

Whom the Lord loveth He correcteth. (Prov. 3: 12)

For God so loved the world, that He gave His only begotten Son, that whosoever believeth in Him should not perish, but have everlasting life. (John 3: 16)

Whom the Lord loveth He chasteneth. (Heb. 12: 6)

Draw nigh to God, and He will draw nigh to you. (James 4: 8)

God's mercy

I have looked upon My people, because their cry is come unto Me. (1 Sam. 9: 16)

My mercy shall not depart away from him. (2 Sam. 7: 15)

Thou art a God ready to pardon. (Neh. 9: 17)

Spare me according to the greatness of Thy mercy. (Neh. 13: 22)

Thou, O Lord, art a God full of compassion, and gracious, longsuffering, and plenteous in mercy and truth. (Ps. 86: 15)

His mercy is everlasting. (Ps. 100: 5)

His mercy endureth for ever. (Ps. 118: 1)

With the Lord there is mercy. (Ps. 130: 7)

His mercy is on them that fear Him from generation to generation. (Luke 1: 50)

God's people

In thee shall all families of the earth be blessed. (Gen. 12: 3)

Ye are the children of the Lord your God. (Deut. 14: 1)

The Lord will not forsake His people for His great name's sake. (1 Sam. 12: 22)

Blessed is the nation whose God is the Lord. (Ps. 33: 12)

He that is of God heareth God's words. (John 8: 47)

Other sheep I have, which are not of this fold. (John 10: 16)

Ye are all the children of God by faith in Christ Jesus. (Gal. 3: 26)

I will be to them a God, and they shall be to Me a people. (Heb. 8: 10)

God's power

And God said, Let there be light: and there was light. (Gen. 1: 3)

Fear ye not, stand still, and see the salvation of the Lord, which He will show to you today. (Ex. 14: 13)

Speak ye unto the rock before their eyes; and it shall give forth his water. (Num. 20: 8)

Surely as I have thought, so shall it come to pass; and as I have purposed, so shall it stand. (Is. 14: 24)

The Lord is His name. (Amos 9: 6)

For Thine is the kingdom, and the power, and the glory, for ever. (Matt. 6: 13)

Father, all things are possible unto Thee. (Mark 14: 36)

With God nothing shall be impossible. (Luke 1: 37)

All things are delivered to me of my Father. (Luke 10: 22)

The Son can do nothing of Himself, but what He seeth the Father do. (John 5: 19)

All things are of God. (2 Cor. 5: 18)

Alleluia: for the Lord God omnipotent reigneth. (Rev. 19: 6)

God's presence

The eye of the Lord run to and fro throughout the whole earth. (2 Chr. 16: 9)

The eyes of the Lord are in every place, beholding the evil and the good. (Prov. 15: 3)

Thy Father which seeth in secret shall reward thee openly. (Matt. 6: 6; Matt. 6: 18)

Where two or three are gathered together in my name, there am I in the midst of them. (Matt. 18: 20)

He be not far from every one of us. (Acts 17: 27)

Ye are the temple of the living God. (2 Cor. 6: 16)

The Lord is at hand. (Phil. 4: 5)

God's protection

I will bless them that bless thee, and curse him that curseth thee. (Gen. 12: 3)

I am thy shield, and thy exceeding great reward. (Gen. 15: 1)

As I was with Moses, so I will be with thee. (Josh. 1: 5; Josh. 3: 7)

He shall deliver you out of the hand of all your enemies. (2 Kings 17: 39)

Thou, O Lord, art a shield for me; my glory, and the lifter up of mine head. (Ps. 3: 3)

O God, lift up Thine hand: forget not the humble. (Ps. 10: 12)

In the Lord put I my trust. (Ps. 11: 1)

The Lord is my shepherd, I shall not want. (Ps. 23: 1)

Thy rod and Thy staff they comfort me. (Ps. 23: 4)

What the Bible says about (19)

God's protection, continued

The Lord is my strength and my shield. (Ps. 28: 7)

Deliver me from the deceitful and unjust man. (Ps. 43: 1)

God is my defense. (Ps. 59: 17)

The Lord is thy keeper. (Ps. 121: 5)

I will surely deliver thee. (Jer. 39: 18)

The Lord is faithful, who shall stablish you, and keep you from evil. (2 Thess. 3: 3)

The face of the Lord is against them that do evil. (1 Pet. 3: 12)

God's support

The Lord bless thee, and keep thee. (Num. 6: 24)

He will not fail thee, nor forsake thee. (Deut. 31: 6)

The living God is among you. (Josh. 3: 10)

I will deliver thine enemy into thine hand, that thou mayest do to him as it shall seem good unto thee. (1 Sam. 24: 4)

I will be his father, and he shall be My son. (2 Sam. 7: 14; 1 Chr. 17: 13)

Seek His face continually. (1 Chr. 16: 11)

O Lord, Thou art our God; let not man prevail against Thee. (2 Chr. 14: 11)

Our God shall fight for us. (Neh. 4: 20)

The Lord is far from the wicked: but He heareth the prayer of the righteous. (Prov. 15: 29)

I will help thee, saith the Lord. (Is. 41: 14)

I am with you, saith the Lord. (Hag. 1: 13; Hag. 2: 4)

God's uniqueness

There is none like Me in all the earth. (Ex. 9: 14)

I am He; I am the first, I also am the last. (Is. 48: 12)

To us there is but one God, the Father, of whom are all things, and we in Him. (1 Cor. 8: 6)

God is one. (Gal. 3: 20)

There is one God, and one mediator between God and men, the man Christ Jesus. (1 Tim. 2: 5)

God's will

It is the Lord: let Him do what seemeth Him good. (1 Sam. 3: 18)

Our Father which art in heaven, Hallowed be Thy name. Thy kingdom come. Thy will be done in earth, as it is in heaven. (Matt. 6: 9–10)

Not my will, but Thine, be done. (Luke 22: 42)

The will of the Lord be done. (Acts 21: 14)

God's word

Thus saith the Lord. (1 Kings 12: 24)

In His word do I hope. (Ps. 130: 5)

I the Lord have spoken it. (Ezek. 5: 13, 17)

My doctrine is not mine, but His that sent me. (John 7: 16)

Thy word is truth. (John 17: 17)

Let the word of Christ dwell in you. (Col. 3: 16)

The word of God is quick, and powerful, and sharper than any two-edged sword. (Heb. 4: 12)

God, Names of

I am God Almighty. (Gen. 35: 11)

I Am That I Am. (Ex. 3: 14)

The Lord your God is God of gods, and Lord of lords. (Deut. 10: 17)

The Most High. (Deut. 32: 8)

Lord God of Israel. (1 Chr. 29: 10)

The Lord of hosts, He is the King of glory. (Ps. 24: 10)

Thou, whose name alone is JEHOVAH. (Ps. 83: 18)

Know ye that the Lord He is God. (Ps. 100: 3)

The Lord of hosts is His name. (Jer. 31: 35)

Their Redeemer is strong; the Lord of hosts is His name. (Jer. 50: 34)

The Lord is His name. (Amos 9: 6)

Our Father. (Matt. 6: 9)

Godlessness

The way of the ungodly shall perish. (Ps. 1: 6)

The wicked shall be turned into hell, and all the nations that forget God. (Ps. 9: 17)

My people is foolish, they have not known Me. (Jer. 4: 22)

Learn not the way of the heathen. (Jer. 10: 2)

O faithless and perverse generation. (Matt. 17: 17)

Gomorrha in the day of judgment than for that city. (Mark 6: 11)

He that denieth me before men shall be denied before that angels of God. (Luke 12: 9)

Ye are of your father the devil, and the lusts of your father ye will do. (John 8: 44)

The enemies of the cross of Christ: Whose end is destruction, whose God is their belly, and whose glory is in their shame. (Phil. 3: 18–19)

Murmurers, complainers, walking after their own lusts. (Jude 16)

Godliness

Happy is that people, whose God is the Lord. (Ps. 144: 15)

Ye cannot serve God and mammon. (Matt. 6: 24;Luke 16: 13)

Great is the mystery of godliness. (1 Tim. 3: 16)

Godliness with contentment is great gain. (1 Tim. 6: 6)

All that will live godly in Christ Jesus shall suffer persecution. (2 Tim. 3: 12)

Whomsoever is born of God doth not commit sin. (1 John 3: 9)

Whomsoever shall confess that Jesus is the Son of God, God dwelleth in him, and he in God. (1 John 4: 15)

Whatsoever is born of God overcometh the world. (1 John 5: 4)

What the Bible says about (20)

Godliness, continued

He that doeth good is of God: but he that doeth evil hath not seen God. (3 John 11)

Keep yourselves in the love of God, looking for the mercy of our Lord Jesus Christ. (Jude 21)

Good and evil

Of every tree of the garden thou mayest freely eat: But of the tree of the knowledge of good and evil, thou shalt not eat. (Gen. 2: 16–17)

Ane the Lord God said, Behold, the man is become as one of us, to know good and evil. (Gen. 3: 22)

I have set before thee this day life and good, and death and evil. (Deut. 30: 15)

Seek good, and not evil, that ye may live. (Amos 5: 14)

He maketh His sun to rise on the evil and on the good, and sendeth rain on the just and on the unjust. (Matt. 5: 45)

Every good tree bringeth forth good fruit; but a corrupt tree bringeth forth evil fruit. (Matt. 7: 17)

How can ye, being evil, speak good things? (Matt. 12: 34)

A good man out of the good treasure of the heart bringeth forth good things: and an evil man out of the evil treasure bringeth forth evil things. (Matt. 12: 35)

They that have done good, unto the resurrection of life; and they that have done evil, unto the resurrection of damnation. (John 5: 29)

Ye are from beneath; I am from above: ye are of this world; I am not of this world. (John 8: 23)

We know that we are of God, and the whole world lieth in wickedness. (1 John 5: 19)

Follow not that which is evil, but that which is good. (3 John 11)

He that doeth good is of God: but he that doeth evil hath not seen God. (3 John 11)

Goodness

Thou art not a God that hath pleasure in wickedness. (Ps. 5: 4)

The earth is full of the goodness of the Lord. (Ps. 33: 5)

The Lord is good. (Ps. 100: 5)

He maketh His sun to rise on the evil and on the good, and sendeth rain on the just and on the unjust. (Matt. 5: 45)

Why callest thou me good? there is none good but one, that is, God. (Matt. 19: 17; Mark 10: 18)

Is thine eye evil, because I am good? (Matt. 20: 15)

If ye do good to them which do good to you, what thank have ye? for sinners also do even the same. (Luke 6: 33)

Go, and do thou likewise. (Luke 10: 37)

Hold fast to that which is good. (1 Thess. 5: 21)

Do good. (1 Tim. 6: 18)

Every good gift and every perfect gift is from above. (James 1: 17)

Gossip

Thou shalt not go up and down
as a talebearer among thy people.
(Lev. 19: 16)

A talebearer revealeth secrets.
(Prov. 11: 13)

A whisperer separateth chief friends.
(Prov. 16: 28)

The words of a talebearer are as
wounds. (Prov. 18: 8; Prov. 26: 22)

Meddle not with him that flattereth
with his lips. (Prov. 20: 19)

Where no wood is, there the fire
goeth out: so where there is no
talebearer, the strife ceaseth. (Prov.
26: 20)

Grace

The law was given by Moses, but
grace and truth came by Jesus Christ.
(John 1: 17)

No man can come unto me, except
it were given unto him of my Father.
(John 6: 65)

The gift of God is eternal life through
Jesus Christ our Lord. (Rom. 6: 23)

By grace are ye saved through faith.
(Eph. 2: 8)

It is the gift of God. (Eph. 2: 8)

Grace be with all them that love our
Lord Jesus Christ in sincerity. (Eph.
6: 24)

Grandchildren

He shall be unto thee a restorer of thy
life, and a nourisher of thine old age.
(Ruth 4: 15)

A good man leaveth an inheritance
to his children's children. (Prov. 13: 22)

Children's children are the crown of
old men. (Prov. 17: 6)

Gratitude

My cup runneth over. (Ps. 23: 5)

Give unto the Lord the glory due
unto His name. (Ps. 29: 2)

O Lord my God, I will give thanks
unto Thee for ever. (Ps. 30: 12)

Blessed be the Lord. (Ps. 31: 21)

It is a good thing to give thanks unto
the Lord. (Ps. 92: 1)

To whom little is forgiven, the same
loveth little. (Luke 7: 47)

All things are delivered to me of my
Father. (Luke 10: 22)

In every thing give thanks: for this is
the will of God in Christ Jesus. (1 Thess.
5: 18)

What the Bible says about (21)

G continued

Greatness

Great men are not always wise: neither do the aged understand judgment. (Job 32: 9)

God is greater than man. (Job 33: 12)

Whosoever shall do and teach them, the same shall be called great in the kingdom of heaven. (Matt. 5: 19)

He that is least among you all, the same shall be great. (Luke 9: 48)

The servant is not greater than his lord; neither he that is sent greater than he that sent him. (John 13: 16)

Greed

Better is a little with righteousness than great revenues without right. (Prov. 16: 8)

Hell and destruction are never full; so the eyes of man are never satisfied. (Prov. 27: 20)

He that maketh haste to be rich shall not be innocent. (Prov. 28: 20)

Beware of covetousness. (Luke 12: 15)

The love of money is the root of all evil. (1 Tim. 6: 10)

Be content with such things as ye have. (Heb. 13: 5)

Grief

If I be bereaved of my children, I am bereaved. (Gen. 43: 14)

How long wilt thou mourn for Saul, seeing I have rejected him? (1 Sam. 16: 1)

They had no more power to weep. (1 Sam. 30: 4)

My friends scorn me: but mine eye poureth out tears unto God. (Job 16: 20)

Pour out your heart before Him: God is a refuge for us. (Ps. 62: 8)

Thou feedest them with the bread of tears. (Ps. 80: 5)

Weep not for me, but weep for yourselves, and for your children. (Luke 23: 28)

Ye shall weep and lament, but the world shall rejoice. (John 16: 20)

Growth

Spreading himself like a green bay tree. (Ps. 37: 35)

A little one shall become a thousand, and a small one a strong nation. (Is. 60: 22)

First the blade, then the ear, after that the full corn in the ear. (Mark 4: 28)

It is like a grain of mustard seed, which a man took, and cast into his garden; and it grew, and waxed a great tree. (Luke 13: 19)

Grudges

He that repeateth a matter separateth very friends. (Prov. 17: 9)

Agree with thine adversary quickly, whiles thou art in the way with him. (Matt. 5: 25)

When ye stand praying, forgive, if ye have ought against any: that your Father also which is in heaven may forgive you your trespasses. (Mark 11: 25)

If ye do not forgive, neither will your Father which is in heaven forgive your trespasses. (Mark 11: 26)

Let not the sun go down upon your wrath. (Eph. 4: 26)

Guidance

The Lord went before them by day in a pillar of a cloud, to lead them the way; and by night in a pillar of fire, to give them light. (Ex. 13: 21)

Thou art my lamp, O Lord. (2 Sam. 22: 29)

He maketh me lie down in green pastures: He leadeth me beside the still waters. He restoreth my soul. (Ps. 23: 2–3)

Show me Thy ways, O Lord; teach me Thy paths. (Ps. 25: 4)

The meek will He guide in judgment: and the meek will He teach His way. (Ps. 25: 9)

The steps of a good man are ordered by the Lord: and he delighteth in his way. (Ps. 37: 23)

Attend to my words; incline thine ear unto my sayings. (Prov. 4: 20)

The commandment is a lamp; and the law is light. (Prov. 6: 23)

Where no counsel is, the people fall. (Prov. 11: 14)

The Lord shall be unto thee an everlasting light. (Is. 60: 19)

O Lord, correct me, but with judgment. (Jer. 10: 24)

When I sit in darkness, the Lord shall be a light unto me. (Mic. 7: 8)

I am the light of the world. (John 8: 12)

I am the way, the truth, and the life: no man cometh unto the Father, but by me. (John 14: 6)

It shall be told thee what thou must do. (Acts 9: 6)

Remember the words of the Lord Jesus. (Acts 20: 35)

Let the word of the Lord dwell in you. (Col. 3: 16)

Guilt

Thy blood be upon thy head. (2 Sam. 1: 16)

Every man shall be put to death for his own sin. (2 Kings 14: 6)

If I be wicked, woe unto me. (Job 10: 15)

Thy mouth uttereth thine iniquity. (Job 15: 5)

Thine own lips testify against thee. (Job 15: 6)

Your hands are full of blood. (Is. 1: 15)

Our sins testify against us. (Is. 59: 12)

His blood shall be upon him. (Ezek. 18: 13)

He that is without sin among you, let him first cast a stone. (John 8: 7)

Woman, where are those thine accusers? (John 8: 10)

Ye are not all clean. (John 13: 11)

What the Bible says about (22)

H

Habit

As a dog returneth to his vomit, so a fool returneth to his folly. (Prov. 26: 11)

Can the Ethiopian change his skin, or the leopard his spots? then may ye also do good, that are accustomed to do evil. (Jer. 13: 23)

Handicapped

Who hath made man's mouth? or who maketh the dumb, or deaf, or the seeing, or the blind? have not I the Lord? (Ex. 4: 11)

Thou shalt not curse the deaf, nor put a stumblingblock before the blind. (Lev. 19: 14)

He maketh both the deaf to hear, and the dumb to speak. (Mark 7: 37)

The blind see, the lame walk, the lepers are cleansed, the deaf hear, the dead are raised, to the poor the gospel is preached. (Luke 7: 22)

When thou makest a feast, call the poor, the maimed, the lame, the blind: And thou shalt be blessed; for they cannot recompense thee. (Luke 14: 13–14)

Happiness

My heart rejoiceth in the Lord. (1 Sam. 2: 1)

Happy is the man whom God correcteth. (Job 5: 17)

Weeping may endure for a night, but joy cometh in the morning. (Ps. 30: 5)

Be glad in the Lord. (Ps. 32: 11)

Light is sown for the righteous, and gladness for the upright in heart. (Ps. 97: 11)

Glory ye in His holy name. (Ps. 105: 3; 1 Chr. 16: 10)

Let the heart of them rejoice that seek the Lord. (Ps. 105: 3)

Whoso trusteth in the Lord, happy is he. (Prov. 16: 20)

Rejoice not, that the spirits are subject unto you; but rather rejoice, because your names are written in heaven. (Luke 10: 20)

Rejoice with me; for I have found my sheep which was lost. (Luke 15: 6)

If ye know these things, happy are ye if ye do them. (John 13: 17)

Ask, and ye shall receive, that your joy may be full. (John 16: 24)

Let us be glad and rejoice, and give honor to Him. (Rev. 19: 7)

Hatred

My soul shall abhor you. (Lev. 26: 30)

Let them that hate Thee flee before Thee. (Num. 10: 35)

He that hideth hatred with lying lips, and he that uttereth a slander, is a fool. (Prov. 10: 18)

He that despiseth his neighbor sinneth. (Prov. 14: 21)

A time to love, and a time to hate. (Eccl. 3: 8)

Do good to them that hate you. (Matt. 5: 44)

If the world hate you, ye know that it hated me before it hated you. (John 15: 18)

Whosoever hateth his brother is a murderer. (1 John 3: 15)

If a man say, I love God, and hateth his brother, he is a liar. (1 John 4: 20)

Healing

Heal me, O Lord, and I shall be healed; save me, and I shall be saved. (Jer. 17: 14)

They that be whole need not a physician, but they that are sick. (Matt. 9: 12)

If I may but touch His garment, I shall be whole. (Matt. 9: 21)

Thy faith hath made thee whole. (Matt. 9: 22; Mark 5: 34; Mark 10: 52; Luke 8: 48)

Heal the sick, cleanse the lepers, raise the dead, cast out devils. (Matt. 10: 8)

Ephphatha, that is, Be opened. (Mark 7: 34)

They shall lay hands on the sick, and they shall recover. (Mark 16: 18)

He hath sent me to heal the brokenhearted, to preach deliverance to the captives. (Luke 4: 18)

He laid His hands on every one of them, and healed them. (Luke 4: 18)

Go thy way; thy son liveth. (John 4: 50)

Rise, take up thy bed, and walk. (John 5: 8)

Go, wash in the pool of Siloam. (John 9: 7)

By Him doth this man stand here before you whole. (Acts 4: 10)

Heaven

If I ascend up into heaven, Thou art there: if I make my bed in hell, behold, Thou art there. (Ps. 139: 8)

It is better for thee to enter into the kingdom of God with one eye, than having two eyes to be cast into hell fire. (Mark 9: 47)

In my Father's house are many mansions. (John 14: 2)

I go to prepare a place for you. (John 14: 2)

Whither I go ye know, and the way ye know. (John 14: 4)

Heaven is My throne, and earth is My footstool: what house will ye build Me? saith the Lord. (Acts 7: 49)

The gates of it shall not be shut at all by day: for there shall be no night there. (Rev. 21: 25)

What the Bible says about (23)

H continued

Heaven and earth

And God called the firmament Heaven. (Gen. 1: 8)

In six days the Lord made heaven and earth, the sea, and all that in them is. (Ex. 20: 11)

All that is in the heaven and in the earth is Thine. (1 Chr. 29: 11)

The heavens declare the glory of God; and the firmament showeth His handywork. (Ps. 19: 1)

The world is Mine, and the fullness thereof. (Ps. 50: 12)

The heaven, even the heavens, are the Lord's: but the earth hath He given to the children of men. (Ps. 115: 16)

Hell

Hell and destruction are never full. (Prov. 27: 20)

Hell hath enlarged herself, and opened her mouth without measure. (Is. 5: 14)

The fire that never shall be quenched. (Mark 9: 43,45)

Where their worm dieth not, and the fire is not quenched. (Mark 9: 44,46,48)

I am tormented in this flame. (Luke 16: 24)

I looked, and behold a pale horse: and his name that sat on him was Death, and Hell followed with him. (Rev. 6: 8)

The bottomless pit. (Rev. 9: 1)

Death and hell were cast into the lake of fire. This is the second death. (Rev. 20: 14)

Heresy

Thou shalt not hearken unto the words of that prophet, or that dreamer of dreams: for the Lord your God proveth you, to know whether ye love the Lord your God with all your heart and with all your soul. (Deut. 13: 3)

Put the evil away from the midst of thee. (Deut. 13: 5)

Thou shalt die, because thou hast taught rebellion against the Lord. (Jer. 28: 16)

In vain they do worship me, teaching for doctrines the commandments of men. (Matt. 15: 9; Mark 7: 7)

False Christs and false prophets shall rise, and shall show signs and wonders, to seduce, if it were possible, even the elect. (Mark 13: 22)

There shall be false teachers among you. (2 Pet. 2: 1)

He that biddeth him God speed is partaker of his evil deeds. (2 John 11)

Heritage

My covenant is with thee, and thou shalt be a father of many nations. (Gen. 17: 4)

In thee and in thy seed shall all the families of the earth be blessed. (Gen. 28: 14)

He is my God, and I will prepare Him an habitation; my father's God, and I will exalt Him. (Ex. 15: 2)

As is the mother, so is her daughter. (Ezek. 16: 44)

If the root be holy, so are the branches. (Rom. 11: 16)

History

Remember the days of old, consider the years of many generations: ask thy father, and he will show thee; thy elders, and they will tell thee. (Deut. 32: 7)

Write it before them in a table, and note it in a book, that it may be for the time to come for ever and ever. (Is. 30: 8)

Have ye forgotten the wickedness of your fathers? (Jer. 44: 9)

He that saw it bare record, and his record is true. (John 19: 35)

If they should be written every one, I suppose that even the world itself could not contain the books that should be written. (John 21: 25)

That which we have seen and heard declare we unto you. (1 John 1: 3)

Holidays

It is a night to be much observed unto the Lord. (Ex. 12: 42)

This day is holy unto the Lord your God; mourn not, nor weep. (Neh. 8: 9)

Holiness

I will be sanctified in them that come nigh Me. (Lev. 10: 3)

Ye shall be holy: for I the Lord your God am holy. (Lev. 19: 2)

Every devoted thing is most holy unto the Lord. (Lev. 27: 28)

There is none holy as the Lord. (1 Sam. 2: 2)

Holy, holy, holy, is the Lord of hosts: the whole earth is full of His glory. (Is. 6: 3)

Before thou camest forth out of the womb I sanctified thee. (Jer. 1: 5)

Now ye are clean through the word which I have spoken unto you. (John 15: 3)

Sanctify them through Thy truth. (John 17: 17)

Holy, holy, holy, Lord God Almighty, which was, and is, and is to come. (Rev. 4: 8)

Thou only art holy. (Rev. 15: 4)

Holy Spirit

And the Spirit of God moved upon the face of the waters. (Gen. 1: 2)

The Spirit of the Lord God is upon me. (Is. 61: 1)

The Spirit of God descending like a dove. (Matt. 3: 16)

Whosoever speaketh against the Holy Spirit, it shall not be forgiven him, neither in this world, neither in the world to come. (Matt. 12: 32)

What the Bible says about (24)

Holy Spirit, continued

Except a man be born of water and of the Spirit, he cannot enter into the kingdom of God. (John 3: 5)

It is the Spirit that quickeneth; the flesh profiteth nothing. (John 6: 63)

He shall give you another Comforter, that He may abide with you for ever. (John 14: 16)

The Comforter, which is the Holy Spirit. (John 14: 26)

If I go not away, the Comforter will not come unto you. (John 16: 7)

Receive ye the Holy Spirit. (John 20: 22)

Wait for the promise of the Father. (Acts 1: 4)

It is the Spirit that beareth witness, because the Spirit is the truth. (1 John 5: 6)

Homage

We have seen His star in the east, and are come to worship Him. (Matt. 2: 2)

Whosoever shall receive me, receiveth not me, but Him that sent me. (Mark 9: 37)

He that honoreth not the Son honoreth not the Father which hath sent Him. (John 5: 23)

I receive not honor from men. (John 5: 41)

He that receiveth whomsoever I send receiveth me. (John 13: 20)

At the name of Jesus every knee should bow. (Phil. 2: 10)

Home

Bury me not, I pray thee, in Egypt. (Gen. 47: 29)

How goodly are thy tents, O Jacob, and thy tabernacles, O Israel! (Num. 24: 5)

By the rivers of Babylon, there we sat down, yea, we wept, when we remembered Zion. (Ps. 137: 1)

Every wise woman buildeth her house: but the foolish plucketh it down with her hands. (Prov. 14: 1)

Foxes have holes, and birds of the air have nests; but the Son of man hath not where to lay His head. (Luke 9: 58)

Honesty

Keep thee far from a false matter. (Ex. 23: 7)

He that hath clean hands, and a pure heart. (Ps. 24: 4)

Keep thy tongue from evil, and thy lips from speaking guile. (Ps. 34: 13)

The wicked borroweth, and payeth not again: but the righteous showeth mercy and giveth. (Ps. 37: 21)

A true witness delivereth souls. (Prov. 14: 25)

The just man walketh in his integrity. (Prov. 20: 7)

Deceive not with thy lips. (Prov. 24: 28)

Ye shall have just balances. (Ezek. 45: 10)

He that is faithful in that which is least is faithful also in much. (Luke 16: 10)

God is my witness. (Rom. 1: 9)

Lie not to one another. (Col. 3: 9)

Ye know that our record is true. (3 John 12)

Hope

The poor hath hope. (Job 5: 16)

I wait for the Lord, my soul doth wait. (Ps. 130: 5)

In His word do I hope. (Ps. 130: 5)

In Thee is my trust; leave not my soul destitute. (Ps. 141: 8)

The eyes of all wait upon Thee. (Ps. 145: 15)

The last shall be first. (Matt. 19: 30)

Ye shall be sorrowful, but your sorrow shall be turned into joy. (John 16: 20)

Hope maketh not ashamed. (Rom. 5: 5)

We are saved by hope. (Rom. 8: 24)

Hope that is seen is not hope. (Rom. 8: 24)

And now abideth faith, hope, charity, these three; but the greatest of these is charity. (1 Cor. 13: 13)

I will give unto him that is athirst of the fountain of the water of life freely. (Rev. 21: 6)

Hospitality

If the house be worthy, let your peace come upon it: but if it be not worthy, let your peace return to you. (Matt. 10: 13)

He that receiveth a prophet in the name of a prophet shall receive a prophet's reward. (Matt. 10: 41)

He that receiveth a righteous man in the name of a righteous man shall receive a righteous man's reward. (Matt. 10: 41)

For I was an hungered, and ye gave me meat: I was thirsty, and ye gave me drink: I was a stranger, and ye took me in: Naked, and ye clothed me: I was sick, and ye visited me: I was in prison, and ye came unto me. (Matt. 25: 35,36)

Inasmuch as ye have done it unto one of the least of these my brethren, ye have done it unto me. (Matt. 25: 40)

Whosoever shall give you a cup of water to drink in my name, because ye belong to Christ, verily I say unto you, he shall not lose his reward. (Mark 9: 41)

He that receiveth whomsoever I send receiveth me. (John 13: 20)

Use hospitality one to another without grudging. (1 Pet. 4: 9)

What the Bible says about (25)

Human nature

The imagination of man's heart is evil from his youth. (Gen. 8: 21)

The heart of the sons of men is full of evil, and madness is in their heart while they live. (Eccl. 9: 3)

Destruction and misery are in their ways: And the way of peace have they not known. (Rom. 3: 16–17)

The law is spiritual: but I am carnal. (Rom. 7: 14)

In me (that is, in my flesh,) dwelleth no good thing. (Rom. 7: 18)

The flesh lusteth against the Spirit, and the Spirit against the flesh. (Gal. 5: 17)

Humiliation

Upon thy belly shalt thou go, and dust shalt thou eat all the days of thy life. (Gen. 3: 14)

I will show the nations thy nakedness, and the kingdoms thy shame. (Nah. 3: 5)

I will corrupt your seed, and spread dung upon your faces. (Mal. 2: 3)

God hath chosen the foolish things of the world to confound the wise. (1 Cor. 1: 27)

Humility

I am slow of speech, and of a slow tongue. (Ex. 4: 10)

He shall save the humble person. (Job 22: 29)

Serve the Lord with fear, and rejoice with trembling. (Ps. 2: 11)

Walk humbly with thy God. (Mic. 6: 8)

Blessed are the poor in spirit: for theirs is the kingdom of heaven. (Matt. 5: 3)

Blessed are the meek: for they shall inherit the earth. (Matt. 5: 5)

I am meek and lowly in heart: and ye shall find rest unto your souls. (Matt. 11: 29)

Except ye be converted, and become as little children, ye shall not enter into the kingdom of heaven. (Matt. 18: 3)

Whosoever will be great among you, let him be your minister. (Matt. 20: 26)

Whosoever will be chief among you, let him be your servant. (Matt. 20: 27)

Whosoever shall exalt himself shall be abased; and he that shall humble himself shall be exalted. (Matt. 23: 12)

If any man desire to be first, the same shall be last of all, and servant of all. (Mark 9: 35)

He that is least among you all, the same shall be great. (Luke 9: 48)

I am among you as He that serveth. (Luke 22: 27)

I can of mine own self do nothing. (John 5: 30)

The servant is not greater than his lord; neither he that is sent greater than he that sent him. (John 13: 16)

Remember therefore from whence thou art fallen, and repent. (Rev. 2: 5)

Hunger

Men do not despise a thief, if he steal to satisfy his soul when he is hungry. (Prov. 6: 30)

Thou shalt eat, but not be satisfied. (Mic. 6: 14)

He that cometh to me shall never hunger; and he that believeth on me shall never thirst. (John 6: 35)

If any would not work, neither should he eat. (2 Thess. 3: 10)

Hypocrisy

They love to pray standing in the synagogues and in the corners of the streets, that they may be seen of men. (Matt. 6: 5)

They have their reward. (Matt. 6: 5)

They disfigure their faces, that they may appear unto men to fast. (Matt. 6: 16)

Why beholdest thou the mote that is in thy brother's eye, but considerest not the beam that is in thine own eye? (Matt. 7: 3)

In vain they do worship me, teaching for doctrines the commandments of men. (Matt. 15: 9, Mark 7: 7)

O ye hypocrites, ye can discern the face of the sky; but can ye not discern the signs of the times? (Matt. 16: 3)

Do not ye after their works: for they say, and do not. (Matt. 23: 3)

They bind heavy burdens and grievous to be borne, and lay them on men's shoulders; but they themselves will not move them with one of their fingers. (Matt. 23: 4)

All their works they do for to be seen of men. (Matt. 23: 5)

Woe unto you, scribes and Pharisees, hypocrites! (Matt. 23: 14)

Ye blind guides, which strain at a gnat, and swallow a camel. (Matt. 23: 24)

Ye also outwardly appear righteous unto men, but within ye are full of hypocrisy and iniquity. (Matt. 23: 28)

This people honoreth me with their lips, but their heart is far from me. (Mark 7: 6)

Ye reject the commandment of God, that ye may keep your own tradition. (Mark 7: 9)

Beware of the scribes, which love to go in long clothing, and love salutations in the marketplaces, And the chief seats in the synagogues, and the uppermost rooms at feasts. (Mark 12: 38–40)

Woe unto you also, ye lawyers! (Luke 11: 46)

Beware ye of the leaven of the Pharisees, which is hypocrisy. (Luke 12: 1)

What the Bible says about (26)

I

Idolatry

Thou shalt have no other gods before Me. (Ex. 20: 3)

Thou shalt not make unto thee any graven images. (Ex. 20: 4)

The Lord, whose name is Jealous, is a jealous God. (Ex. 34: 14)

God forbid that we should forsake the Lord, to serve other gods. (Josh. 24: 16)

Flee from idolatry. (1 Cor. 10: 14)

Little children, keep yourselves from idols. (1 John 5: 21)

They have no rest day nor night, who worship the beast and his image. (Rev. 14: 11)

Idols

Against all the gods of Egypt I will execute judgment: I am the Lord. (Ex. 12: 12)

Thou shalt not make thee any graven image. (Deut. 4: 28)

It is an abomination to the Lord. (Deut. 7: 25)

Ye shall not fear other gods. (2 Kings 17: 37)

Let them arise, if they can save thee in the time of thy trouble. (Jer. 2: 28)

Ignorance

He multiplieth words without knowledge. (Job 35: 16)

They seeing see not; and hearing they hear not, neither do they understand. (Matt. 13: 13)

If the blind lead the blind, both shall fall into the ditch. (Matt. 15: 14)

O ye hypocrites, ye can discern the face of the sky; but can ye not discern the signs of the times? (Matt. 16: 3)

Father, forgive them; for they not know what they do. (Luke 23: 34)

He was in the world, and the world was made by Him, and the world knew Him not. (John 1: 10)

Art thou a master of Israel, and knoweth not these things? (John 3: 10)

Ye worship ye know not what. (John 4: 22)

He that followeth me shall not walk in darkness. (John 8: 12)

He that walketh in darkness knoweth not whither he goeth. (John 12: 35)

Imminence

The time is come, the day draweth near. (Ezek. 7: 12)

The day of the Lord is near. (Ezek. 30: 3)

My time is at hand. (Matt. 26: 18)

Behold, the hour is at hand, and the Son of man is betrayed into the hands of sinners. (Matt. 26: 45)

The hour is coming, in the which all that are in the graves shall hear His voice. (John 5: 28)

The hour is come, that the Son of man should be glorified. (John 12: 23)

Yet a little while, and the world seeth me no more. (John 14: 19)

Behold, the hour cometh. (John 16: 32)

The Lord is at hand. (Phil. 4: 5)

The coming of the Lord draweth nigh. (James 5: 8)

Behold, the judge standeth before the door. (James 5: 9)

The end of all things is at hand: be ye therefore sober, an watch unto prayer. (1 Pet. 4: 7)

The time is at hand. (Rev. 1: 3)

Immorality

Do not prostitute thy daughter, to cause her to be a whore; lest the land fall to whoredom, and the land become full of wickedness. (Lev. 19: 29)

How is the faithful city become an harlot! (Is. 1: 21)

Thy silver is become dross, thy wine mixed with water. (Is. 1: 22)

Thou hast polluted the land with thy whoredoms and with thy wickedness. (Jer. 3: 2)

As is the mother, so is her daughter. (Ezek. 16: 44)

Flee fornication. (1 Cor. 6: 18)

She that liveth in pleasure is dead while she liveth. (1 Tim. 5: 6)

Whoremongers and adulterers God will judge. (Heb. 13: 4)

Woe unto them! for they have gone in the way of Cain. (Jude 11)

Impartiality

Ye shall not respect persons in judgment. (Deut. 1: 17)

Ye shall hear the small as well as the great. (Deut. 1: 17)

He maketh His sun to rise on the evil and on the good, and sendeth rain on the just and on the unjust. (Matt. 5: 45)

God is no respecter of persons. (Acts 10: 34)

God accepteth no man's person. (Gal. 2: 6)

If ye have respect to persons, ye commit sin. (James 2: 9)

Impatience

He that maketh haste to be rich shall not be innocent. (Prov. 28: 20)

O thou sword of the Lord, how long will it be ere thou be quiet? (Jer. 47: 6)

O Lord, how long shall I cry, and Thou wilt not hear! (Hab. 1: 2)

Impenitence

This is a rebellious people, lying children, children that will not hear the law of the Lord. (Is. 30: 9)

They have made they faces harder than a rock. (Jer. 5: 3)

They hearkened not, nor inclined their ear to turn from their wickedness. (Jer. 44: 5)

Harden not your hearts. (Heb. 3: 8)

What the Bible says about (27)

I continued

Imprisonment

Let the sighing of the prisoner come before Thee. (Ps. 79: 11)

The Lord looseth the prisoners. (Ps. 146: 7)

They have cut off my life in the dungeon, and cast a stone upon me. (Lam. 3: 53)

The earth with her bars was about me for ever: yet hast Thou brought up my life from corruption. (Jonah 2: 6)

Remember my bonds. (Col. 4: 18)

Incest

The nakedness of thy father, or the nakedness of thy mother, shalt thou not uncover. (Lev. 18: 7)

For theirs is thine own nakedness. (Lev. 18: 10)

Cursed be he that lieth with his father's wife. (Deut. 27: 20)

Do not thou this folly. (2 Sam. 13: 12)

Whither shall I cause my shame to go? (2 Sam. 13: 13)

Indecision

Choose you this day whom ye will serve. (Josh. 24: 15)

How long halt ye between two opinions? (1 Kings 18: 21)

As a drunken man staggereth in his vomit. (Is. 19: 14)

No man, having put his hand to the plow, and looking back, is fit for the kingdom of God. (Luke 9: 62)

We henceforth be no more children, tossed to and fro, and carried about with every wind of doctrine, by the sleight of men, and cunning craftiness, whereby they lie in wait to deceive. (Eph. 4: 14)

He that wavereth is like a wave of the sea driven with the wind. (James 1: 6)

A double minded man is unstable in all his ways. (James 1: 8)

Independence

Thou shalt lend unto many nations, but thou shalt not borrow. (Deut. 15: 6)

Thou shalt reign over many nations, but they shall not reign over thee. (Deut. 15: 6)

Every one turned to his course, as the horse rusheth into the battle. (Jer. 8: 6)

Individual, Importance Of

Ye are of more value than many sparrows. (Matt. 10: 31; Luke 12: 7)

Are not five sparrows sold for two farthings, and not one of them is forgotten before God? (Luke 12: 6)

Rejoice with me; for I have found my sheep which was lost. (Luke 15: 6)

Joy shall be in heaven over one sinner that repenteth, more than over ninety and nine just persons, which need no repentance. (Luke 15: 7)

There is joy in the presence of the angels of God over one sinner that repenteth. (Luke 15: 10)

By one man sin entered into the world. (Rom. 5: 12)

Every man hath his proper gift of God. (1 Cor. 7: 7)

I seek not yours, but you. (2 Cor. 12: 14)

Infinity

I will multiply thy seed as the stars of the heaven, and as the sand which is upon the sea shore. (Gen. 22: 17)

He telleth the number of the stars; He calleth them all by their names. (Ps. 147: 4)

Even the very hairs of your head are all numbered. (Luke 12: 7)

Ingratitude

Ye have wept in the ears of the Lord. (Num. 11: 18)

They have rewarded me evil for good, and hatred for my love. (Ps. 109: 5)

Give not that which is holy unto the dogs, neither cast ye your pearls before swine, lest they trample them under their feet, and turn again and rend you. (Matt. 7: 6)

When they knew God, they glorified Him not as God. (Rom. 1: 21)

Inheritance

If a man die, and have no son, then ye shall cause his inheritance to pass unto his daughter. (Num. 27: 8)

The Lord is the portion of mine inheritance. (Ps. 16: 5)

A good man leaveth an inheritance of fathers: and a prudent wife is from the Lord. (Prov. 19: 14)

Injustice

Keep thee far from a false matter. (Ex. 23: 7)

He destroyeth the perfect and the wicked. (Job 9: 22)

The earth is given into the hand of the wicked: He covereth the faces of the judges thereof. (Job 9: 24)

If, when ye do well, and suffer for it, ye take it patiently, this is acceptable with God. (1 Pet. 2: 20)

Innocence

Wickedness proceedeth from the wicked: but mine hand shall not be upon thee. (1 Sam. 24: 13)

As a man falleth before wicked men, so fellest thou. (2 Sam. 3: 34)

God will not cast away a perfect man, neither will He help the evil doers. (Job 8: 20)

If ye were blind, ye should have no sin. (John 9: 41)

What the Bible says about (28)

Innocence, continued

Unto the pure all things are pure. (Titus 1: 15)

If we say that we have no sin, we deceive ourselves. (1 John 1: 8)

If we say that we have not sinned, we make Him a liar. (1 John 1: 10)

In their mouth was found no guile: for they are without fault before the throne of God. (Rev. 14: 5)

Innovation

There is no new thing under the sun. (Eccl. 1: 9)

That which hath been is now; and that which is to be hath already been. (Eccl. 3: 15)

That which hath been is named already. (Eccl. 6: 10)

No man also having drunk old wine straightway desireth new. (Luke 5: 39)

Inspiration

Go, and I will be with thy mouth, and teach thee what thou shalt say. (Ex. 4: 12)

The word that God putteth in my mouth, that shall I speak. (Num. 22: 38)

The Spirit of the Lord will come upon thee. (1 Sam. 10: 6)

The Spirit of the Lord spake by me, and His word was in my tongue. (2 Sam. 23: 2)

The hand of the Lord was upon me.

(Ezek. 37: 1)

Your old men shall dream dreams, your young men shall see visions. (Joel 2: 28)

It is not ye that speak, but the Spirit of your Father which speaketh in you. (Matt. 10: 20)

A man can receive nothing, except it be given him from heaven. (John 3: 27)

He was a burning and a shining light: and ye were willing for a season to rejoice in his light. (John 5: 35)

Write the things which thou hast seen, and the things which are, and the things which shall be hereafter. (Rev. 1: 19)

Instability

Unstable as water, thou shalt not excel. (Gen. 49: 4)

Your goodness is as a morning cloud, and as the early dew it goeth away. (Hos. 6: 4)

Instinct

The stork in the heaven knoweth her appointed times; and the turtle and the crane and the swallow observe the time of their coming; but My people know not the judgment of the Lord. (Jer. 8: 7)

Instruction

God exalteth by His power: who teacheth like Him? (Job 36: 22)

Make me to understand the way of Thy precepts: so shall I talk of Thy wondrous works. (Ps. 119: 27)

How sweet are Thy words unto my taste! yea, sweeter than honey to my mouth! (Ps. 119: 103)

He will teach us of His ways, and we walk in His paths. (Is. 2: 3; Mic. 4: 2)

He that hath ears to hear, let him hear. (Luke 14: 35)

Though ye have ten thousand instructors in Christ, yet have ye not many fathers. (1 Cor. 4: 15)

Insults

Am I a dog, that thou comest to me with staves? (1 Sam. 17: 43)

Am I a dog's head? (2 Sam. 3: 8)

A fool's wrath is presently known: but a prudent man covereth shame. (Prov. 12: 16)

A brother offended is harder to be won than a strong city. (Prov. 18: 19)

Take no heed unto all words that are spoken; lest thou hear thy servant curse thee. (Eccl. 7: 21)

Integrity

Till I die I will not remove mine integrity from me. (Job 27: 5)

As for me, I will walk in mine integrity. (Ps. 26: 11)

What shall a man give in exchange for his soul? (Matt. 16: 26; Mark 8: 37)

What shall it profit a man, if he shall gain the whole world, and lose his own soul? (Mark 8: 36)

Walk as children of light. (Eph. 5: 8)

Swear not, neither by heaven, neither by the earth, neither by any other oath: but let your yea be yea: and your nay, nay. (James 5: 12)

Intentions

They shall not deliver the slayer up into his hand; because he smote his neighbor unwittingly, and hated him not beforetime. (Josh. 20: 5)

Man looketh on the outward appearance, but the Lord looketh on the heart. (1 Sam. 16: 7)

Thou didst well in that it was in thine heart. (2 Chr. 6: 8)

Whosoever looketh on a woman to lust after her hath committed adultery with her already in his heart. (Matt. 5: 28)

Wherefore think ye evil in your hearts? (Matt. 9: 4)

The good that I would I do not: but the evil which I would not, that I do. (Rom. 7: 19)

What the Bible says about (29)

J

Jealousy

Give me children, or else I die. (Gen. 30: 1)

They hated him yet the more for his dreams, and for his words. (Gen. 37: 8)

They have ascribed unto David ten thousands, and to me they have ascribed but thousands. (1 Sam. 18: 8)

What can he have more but the kingdom? (1 Sam. 18: 8)

Saul eyed David from that day and forward. (1 Sam. 18: 9)

Fret not thyself because of him that prospereth. (Ps. 37: 7)

Jealousy is the rage of a man. (Prov. 6: 34)

Let not thine heart envy sinners. (Prov. 23: 17)

Wrath is cruel, and anger is outrageous; but who is able to stand before envy? (Prov. 27: 4)

Better is the sight of the eyes than the wandering of the desire. (Eccl. 6: 9)

Jealousy is cruel as the grave: the coals thereof are coals of fire, which hath a most vehement flame. (Song 8: 6)

Charity envieth not. (1 Cor. 13: 4)

Jerusalem

The city of David, which is Zion. (1 Kings 8: 1)

Jerusalem, the city where I have chosen Me to put My name. (1 Kings 11: 36)

Jerusalem, the city which the Lord did choose out of all the tribes of Israel, to put His name there. (1 Kings 14: 21)

Jesus

He shall save His people from their sins. (Matt. 1: 21)

We have seen His star in the east, and are come to worship Him. (Matt. 2: 2)

He that cometh after me is mightier than I, whose shoes I am not worthy to bear. (Matt. 3: 11)

This is My beloved Son, in whom I am well pleased. (Matt. 3: 17)

What manner of man is this, that even the winds and the sea obey Him! (Matt. 8: 27)

The Son of man hath power on earth to forgive sins. (Matt. 9: 6; Mark 2: 10)

Whosoever therefore shall confess me before men, him will I confess also before my Father which is in heaven. But whosoever shall deny me before men, him will I also shall I deny before my Father which is in heaven. (Matt. 10: 32–33)

He that taketh not his cross, and followeth after me, is not worthy of me. (Matt. 10: 38)

In His name shall the Gentiles trust. (Matt. 12: 21)

He that is not with me is against me. (Matt. 12: 30; Luke 11: 23)

Behold, a greater than Solomon is here. (Matt. 12: 42; Luke 11: 31)

Jesus, Acceptance of

Take my yoke upon you, and learn of me; for I am meek and lowly in heart: and ye shall find rest unto your souls. (Matt. 11: 29)

Flesh and blood hath not revealed it unto thee, but my Father which is in heaven. (Matt. 16: 17)

Whosoever will come after me, let him deny himself, and take up his cross, and follow me. (Mark 8: 34)

Whosoever shall confess me before men, him shall the Son of man also confess before the angels of God. (Luke 12: 8)

Whosoever he be of you that forsaketh not all that he hath, he cannot be my disciple. (Luke 14: 33)

As many as received Him, to them gave He power to become the sons of God. (John 1: 12)

Ye must be born again. (John 3: 7)

This is the work of God, that ye believe on Him whom He hath sent. (John 6: 29)

He that cometh to me shall never hunger; and he that believeth on me shall never thirst. (John 6: 35)

No man can come to me, except the Father which hath sent me draw him. (John 6: 44)

Lord, I believe. (John 9: 38)

I believe that Thou art the Christ, the Son of God. (John 11: 27)

He that believeth on me, believeth not on me, but on Him that sent me. (John 12: 44)

He that receiveth me receiveth Him that sent me. (John 13: 20)

Ye believe in God, believe also in me. (John 14: 1)

He that loveth me shall be loved of my Father. (John 14: 21)

If a man love me, he will keep my words. (John 14: 23)

If thou shalt confess with thy mouth the Lord Jesus, and shalt believe in thine heart that God hath raised Him from the dead, thou shalt be saved. (Rom. 10: 9)

What the Bible says about (30)

Jesus, Acceptance of, continued

To whom He was not spoken of, they shall see: and they that have not heard shall understand. (Rom. 15: 21)

Ye were sometimes darkness, but now are ye light in the Lord. (Eph. 5: 8)

Every tongue should confess that Jesus Christ is Lord. (Phil. 2: 11)

What things were gain to me, those I counted loss for Christ. (Phil. 3: 7)

Ye are dead, and your life is hid with Christ in God. (Col. 3: 3)

He that acknowledgeth the Son hath the Father also. (1 John 2: 23)

Whosoever shall confess that Jesus is the Son of God, God dwelleth in him, and he in God. (1 John 4: 15)

He that hath the Son hath life. (1 John 5: 12)

If any man hear my voice, and open the door, I will come in to him. (Rev. 3: 20)

Jesus, Birth of

She shall bring forth a son, and thou shalt call His name JESUS. (Matt. 1: 21)

Behold, a virgin shall be with child, and shall bring forth a son. (Matt. 1: 23)

They presented unto Him gifts, gold, and frankincense, and myrrh. (Matt. 2: 11)

The Lord is with thee: blessed art thou among women. (Luke 1: 28)

Behold, thou shalt conceive in thy womb, and bring forth a son, and shalt call His name JESUS. (Luke 1: 31)

How shall this be, seeing I know not a man? (Luke 1: 34)

With God nothing shall be impossible. (Luke 1: 37)

He that is mighty hath done to me great things; and holy is His name. (Luke 1: 49)

There was no room for them in the inn. (Luke 2: 7)

Unto you is born this day in the city of David a Savior, which is Christ the Lord. (Luke 2: 11)

His name was called JESUS. (Luke 2: 21)

To this end was I born, and for this cause came I into the world, that I should bear witness unto the truth. (John 18: 37)

Jesus, Last words on the Cross

Eli, Eli, lama sabachthani? (Matt. 27: 46)

My God, my God, why hast Thou forsaken me? (Matt. 27: 46; Mark 15: 34)

Father, forgive them; for they know not what they do. (Luke 23: 34)

Verily I say unto thee, Today shalt thou be with me in paradise. (Luke 23: 43)

Father, into Thy hands I commend my spirit. (Luke 23: 46)

Woman, behold thy son! (John 19: 26)

Behold thy mother! (John 19: 27)

I thirst. (John 19: 28)

It is finished. (John 19: 30)

Jesus, Titles of

His name shall be called Wonderful, Counselor, The mighty God, The everlasting Father, The Prince of Peace. (Is. 9: 6)

They shall call His name Emmanuel. (Matt. 1: 23)

Thou art the Christ, the Son of the living God. (Matt. 16: 16)

A Savior, which is Christ the Lord. (Luke 2: 11)

His name was called JESUS. (Luke 2: 21)

The Lamb of God. (John 1: 29)

The Son of God. (John 1: 34)

The Messiah. (John 1: 41; Dan. 9: 25)

The Son of man. (John 1: 51)

The bread of life. (John 6: 35)

I am the light of the world. (John 8: 12)

I am the door. (John 10: 9)

The good shepherd. (John 10: 11)

I am the way, the truth, and the life. (John 14: 6)

I am the true vine. (John 15: 1)

Jesus of Nazareth the King of the Jews. (John 19: 19)

The Holy One and the Just. (Acts 3: 14)

The Deliverer. (Rom. 11: 26)

That great shepherd of the sheep. (Heb. 13: 20)

The judge. (James 5: 9)

The chief Shepherd. (1 Pet. 5: 4)

The true light. (1 John 2: 8)

The faithful witness. (Rev. 1: 5)

The prince of the kings of the earth. (Rev. 1: 5)

The morning star. (Rev. 2: 28)

The Word of God. (Rev. 19: 13)

KING OF KINGS, AND LORD OF LORDS. (Rev. 19: 16)

I am Alpha and Omega, the beginning and the end, the first and the last. (Rev. 22: 13)

Jews

The lost sheep of the house of Israel. (Matt. 15: 24)

He came unto His own, and His own received Him not. (John 1: 11)

Forty years suffered He their manners in the wilderness. (Acts 13: 18)

I am a Pharisee, the son of a Pharisee. (Acts 23: 6)

He is not a Jew, which is one outwardly. (Rom. 2: 28)

What advantage then hath the Jew? or what profit is there of circumcision? (Rom. 3: 1)

Unto them were committed the oracles of God. (Rom. 3: 2)

They have a zeal of God, but not according to knowledge. (Rom. 10: 2)

What the Bible says about (31)

Jews, continued

Hath God cast away His people? God forbid. (Rom. 11: 1)

I also am an Israelite, of the seed of Abraham. (Rom. 11: 1)

Through their fall salvation is come unto the Gentiles. (Rom. 11: 11)

Unto the Jews I became as a Jew, that I might gain the Jews. (1 Cor. 9: 20)

Are they Hebrews? so am I. Are they Israelites? so am I. Are they the seed of Abraham? so am I. (2 Cor. 11: 22)

John The Baptist

Elias is come already, and they knew him not. (Matt. 17: 12)

One mightier than I cometh, the latchet of whose shoes I am not worthy to unloose. (Luke 3: 16)

He was not that Light , but was sent to bear witness of that Light. (John 1: 8)

I am the voice of one crying in the wilderness, Make straight the way of the Lord. (John 1: 23)

He was a burning and a shining light: and ye were willing for a season to rejoice in his light. (John 5: 35)

Judas

None of them is lost, but the son of perdition. (John 17: 12)

Judging

Thou shalt not respect the person of the poor, nor honor the person of the mighty. (Lev. 19: 15)

In righteousness shalt thou judge thy neighbor. (Lev. 19: 15)

Judge righteously between every man and his brother, and the stranger that is with him. (Deut. 1: 16)

Ye shall not be afraid of the face of man; for the judgment is God's. (Deut. 1: 17)

Thou shalt not respect persons, neither take a gift. (Deut. 16: 19)

A gift doth blind the eyes of the wise, and pervert the words of the righteous. (Deut. 16: 19)

Take heed what ye do: for ye judge not for man, but for the Lord. (2 Chr. 19: 6)

Let the fear of the Lord be upon you. (2 Chr. 19: 7)

Judgment

Shall not the Judge of all the earth do right? (Gen. 18: 25)

The Lord shall judge His people. (Deut. 32: 36)

I will render vengeance to Mine enemies, and will reward them that hate Me. (Deut. 32: 41)

The Lord shall judge the ends of the earth. (1 Sam. 2: 10)

Judgment day

Alas for the day! for the day of the Lord is at hand. (Joel 1: 15)

The day of the Lord cometh. (Joel 2: 1)

The day of the Lord is great and very terrible; and who can abide it? (Joel 2: 11)

Woe unto you that desire the day of the Lord! (Amos 5: 18)

Behold, the day cometh, that shall burn as an oven; and all the proud, yea, and all that do wickedly, shall be stubble. (Mal. 4: 1)

He shall separate them from one another, as a shepherd divideth his sheep from the goats. (Matt. 25: 32)

These be the days of vengeance, that all things which are written may be fulfilled. (Luke 21: 22)

He hath appointed a day, in the which He will judge the world in righteousness. (Acts 17: 31)

We must all appear before the judgment seat of Christ. (2 Cor. 5: 10)

The great day of His wrath is come; and who shall be able to stand? (Rev. 6: 17)

Fear God, and give glory to Him; for the hour of His judgment is come. (Rev. 14: 7)

I saw the dead, small and great, stand before God. (Rev. 20: 12)

Death and hell delivered up the dead which were in them: and they were judged every man according to their works. (Rev. 20: 13)

Whosoever was not found written in the book of life was cast into the lake of fire. (Rev. 20: 15)

Justice

Whoso sheddeth man's blood, by man shall his blood be shed. (Gen. 9: 6)

One law shall be to him that is homeborn, and unto the stranger that sojourneth among you. (Ex. 12: 49)

Thou shalt give life for life, Eye for eye, tooth for tooth, hand for hand, foot for foot, Burning for burning, wound for wound, stripe for stripe. (Ex. 21: 23–25)

Thou shalt not wrest the judgment of thy poor in his cause. (Ex. 23: 6)

I will not justify the wicked. (Ex. 23: 7)

Justification

By Him all that believe are justified. (Acts 13: 39)

A man is justified by faith without the deeds of the law. (Rom. 3: 28)

It is God that justifieth. (Rom. 8: 33)

Ye are justified in the name of the Lord Jesus, and by the Spirit of our God. (1 Cor. 6: 11)

No man is justified by the law in the sight of God. (Gal. 3: 11)

What the Bible says about (32)

K

Kindness

The Lord deal kindly with you, as ye have dealt with the dead, and with me. (Ruth 1: 8)

Let her glean even among the sheaves, and reproach her not. (Ruth 2: 15)

Thou hast showed more kindness in the latter end than at the beginning. (Ruth 3: 10)

Let them be of those that eat at thy table. (1 Kings 2: 7)

The merciful man doeth good to his own soul: but he that is cruel troubleth his own flesh. (Prov. 11: 17)

The tender mercies of the wicked are cruel. (Prov. 12: 10)

If thine enemy be hungry, give him bread to eat, and if he be thirsty, give him water to drink. (Prov. 25: 21)

Let none of you imagine evil against his brother in your heart. (Zech. 7: 10)

What man is there of you, whom if his son ask bread, will he give him a stone? (Matt. 7: 9)

Be ye kind to one another. (Eph. 4: 32)

Be gentle unto all men, apt to teach, patient. (2 Tim. 2: 24)

Kingdom of God

It is easier for a camel to go through the eye of a needle, than it is for a rich man to enter into the Kingdom of God. (Matt. 19: 24)

Whosoever shall not receive the Kingdom of God as a little child, he shall not enter therein. (Mark 10: 15)

No man, having put his hand to the plow, and looking back, is fit for the Kingdom of God. (Luke 9: 62)

The Kingdom of God is come nigh unto you. (Luke 10: 9)

Seek ye the Kingdom of God; and all things shall be added unto you. (Luke 12: 31)

Fear not, little flock; for it is your Father's good pleasure to give you the Kingdom. (Luke 12: 32)

It is like a grain of mustard seed, which a man took, and cast into his garden; and it grew, and waxed a great tree. (Luke 13: 19)

The law and the prophets were until John: since that time the Kingdom of God is preached. (Luke 16: 16)

The Kingdom of God cometh not with observation. (Luke 17: 20)

The Kingdom of God is within you. (Luke 17: 21)

Except a man be born of water and of the Spirit, he cannot enter into the Kingdom of God. (John 3: 5)

We must through much tribulation enter into the Kingdom of God. (Acts 14: 22)

The Kingdom of God is not meat and drink; but righteousness, and peace, and joy in the Holy Spirit. (Rom. 14: 17)

The Kingdom of God is not in word, but in power. (1 Cor. 4: 20)

The unrighteous shall not inherit the Kingdom of God. (1 Cor. 6: 9)

Flesh and blood cannot inherit the Kingdom of God. (1 Cor. 15: 50)

Kingdom of Heaven

Repent, for the kingdom of heaven is at hand. (Matt. 4: 17)

Blessed are the poor in spirit: for theirs is the kingdom of heaven. (Matt. 5: 3)

Blessed are they which are persecuted for righteousness' sake: for theirs is the kingdom of heaven. (Matt. 5: 10)

Not every one that saith unto me, Lord, Lord, shall enter into the kingdom of heaven. (Matt. 7: 21)

The kingdom of heaven is like unto treasure hid in a field. (Matt. 13: 44)

I will give unto thee the keys of the kingdom of heaven. (Matt. 16: 19)

Except ye be converted, and become as little children, ye shall not enter into the kingdom of heaven. (Matt. 18: 3)

A rich man shall hardly enter into the kingdom of heaven. (Matt. 19: 23)

Knowledge

Of every tree of the garden thou mayest freely eat: But of the tree of the knowledge of good and evil, thou shalt not eat. (Gen. 2: 16–17)

Your eyes shall be opened, and ye shall be as gods, knowing good and evil. (Gen. 3: 5)

The Lord God said, Behold, the man is become as one of us, to know good and evil. (Gen. 3: 22)

The secret things belong unto the Lord our God: but those things which are revealed belong unto us and to our children for ever. (Deut. 29: 29)

The Lord is a God of knowledge, and by Him actions are weighed. (1 Sam. 2: 3)

Canst thou by searching find out God? (Job 11: 7)

Shall any teach God knowledge? (Job 21: 22)

What the Bible says about (33)

Knowledge, continued

Let us choose to us judgment: let us know among ourselves what is good. (Job 34: 4)

Have the gates of death been opened unto thee? or hast thou seen the doors of the shadow of death? (Job 38: 17)

I understand more than the ancients, because I keep Thy precepts. (Ps. 119: 100)

A wise man will hear, and will increase learning. (Prov. 1: 5)

The fear of the Lord is the beginning of knowledge. (Prov. 1: 7)

Get wisdom, get understanding: forget it not. (Prov. 4: 5)

Wise men lay up knowledge. (Prov. 10: 14)

Through knowledge shall the just be delivered. (Prov. 11: 9)

Knowledge is easy unto him that understandeth. (Prov. 14: 6)

The heart of him that hath understanding seeketh knowledge. (Prov. 15: 14)

The ear of the wise seeketh knowledge. (Prov. 18: 15)

He that increaseth knowledge increaseth sorrow. (Eccl. 1: 18)

Have ye not known? have ye not heard? hath it not been told you from the beginning? (Is. 40: 21)

The stork in the heaven knoweth her appointed times; and the turtle and the crane and the swallow observe the time of their coming; but My people know not the judgment of the Lord. (Jer. 8: 7)

Because thou hast rejected knowledge, I will also reject thee. (Hos. 4: 6)

Hear, and understand. (Matt. 15: 10)

Flesh and blood hath not revealed it unto thee, but my Father which is in heaven. (Matt. 16: 17)

If ye were blind, ye should have no sin. (John 9: 41)

Walk while ye have the light, lest darkness come upon you. (John 12: 35)

It is not for you to know the times or the seasons. (Acts 1: 7)

I had not known lust, except the law had said, Thou shalt not covet. (Rom. 7: 7)

I would have you wise unto that which is good, and simple concerning evil. (Rom. 16: 19)

I know nothing by myself. (1 Cor. 4: 4)

If any man think that he knoweth any thing, he knoweth nothing yet as he ought to know. (1 Cor. 8: 2)

Though I be rude in speech, yet not in knowledge. (2 Cor. 11: 6)

Ye know not what shall be on the morrow. (James 4: 14)

To him that knoweth to do good, and doeth it not, to him it is sin. (James 4: 17)

As newborn babes, desireth the sincere milk of the word, that ye may grow thereby. (1 Pet. 2: 2)

Add to your faith virtue; and to virtue knowledge. (2 Pet. 1: 5)

Knowledge of God

And they shall know that I am the Lord their God, that brought them forth out of the land of Egypt. (Ex. 29: 46)

And ye shall know that I am the Lord. (1 Kings 20: 28)

Know thou the God of thy father. (1 Chr. 28: 9)

We know Him not, neither can the number of His years be searched out. (Job 36: 26)

The secret of the Lord is with them that fear Him. (Ps. 25: 14)

Be still, and know that I am God. (Ps. 46: 10)

The earth shall be full of the knowledge of the Lord, as the waters cover the sea. (Is. 11: 9)

They shall all know Me, from the least of them unto the greatest. (Jer. 31: 34)

Ye shall know that I am the Lord, when I set My face against them. (Ezek. 15: 7)

I will be known in the eyes of many nations, and they shall know that I am the Lord. (Ezek. 38: 23)

No man knoweth the Son, but the Father; neither knoweth any man the Father, save the Son, and he to whomsoever the Son will reveal Him. (Matt. 11: 27)

I know Him: for I am from Him, and He hath sent me. (John 7: 29)

If ye had known me, ye should have known my Father also. (John 8: 19)

If I should say, I know Him not, I shall be a liar like unto you: but I know Him, and keep His saying. (John 8: 55)

As the Father knoweth me, even so know I the Father. (John 10: 15)

They know not Him that sent me. (John 15: 21)

They profess that they know God; but in the works they deny Him. (Titus 1: 16)

Grace and peace be multiplied unto you through the knowledge of God, and of Jesus our Lord. (2 Pet. 1: 2)

Grow in grace, and in the knowledge of our Lord. (2 Pet. 3: 18)

What the Bible says about (34)

L

Lament

How are the mighty fallen! (2 Sam. 1: 19)

I have no son to keep my name in remembrance. (2 Sam. 18: 18)

How doth the city sit solitary, that was full of people! how is she become as a widow! (Lam. 1: 1)

Alas for the day! for the day of the Lord is at hand. (Joel 1: 15)

Woe is me! (Mic. 7: 1)

O faithless and perverse generation. (Matt. 17: 17)

Laughter

Even in laughter the heart is sorrowful. (Prov. 14: 13)

I said of laughter, It is mad: and of mirth, What doeth it? (Eccl. 2: 2)

A time to weep, and a time to laugh. (Eccl. 3: 4)

Sorrow is better than laughter: for by the sadness of the countenance the heart is made better. (Eccl. 7: 3)

As the crackling of thorns under a pot, so is the laughter of the fool. (Eccl. 7: 6)

Blessed are ye that weep now: for ye shall laugh. (Luke 6: 21)

Woe unto you that laugh now! for ye shall mourn and weep. (Luke 6: 25)

Let your laughter be turned to mourning, and your joy to heaviness. (James 4: 9)

Law

Ye shall have one manner of law, as well for the stranger, as for one of your own country. (Lev. 24: 22)

If any man will sue thee at the law, and take away thy coat, let him have thy cloak also. (Matt. 5: 40)

Woe unto you also, ye lawyers! (Luke 11: 46)

Lawlessness

The earth is given into the hand of the wicked: He that covereth the faces of the judges thereof. (Job 9: 24)

If the foundations be destroyed, what can the righteous do? (Ps. 11: 3)

The wicked watcheth the righteous, and seeketh to slay him. (Ps. 37: 32)

Deliver me from the workers of iniquity, and save me from bloody men. (Ps. 59: 2)

When the wicked spring as the grass, and when all the workers of iniquity do flourish; it is that they shall be destroyed for ever. (Ps. 92: 7)

Laziness

He becometh poor that dealeth with a slack hand: but the hand of the diligent maketh rich. (Prov. 10: 4)

He that sleepeth in harvest is a son that causeth shame. (Prov. 10: 5)

As vinegar to the teeth, and as smoke to the eyes, so is the sluggard to them that send him. (Prov. 10: 26)

Leadership

Can we find such a one as this is, a man in whom the Spirit of God is? (Gen. 41: 38)

The scepter shall not depart from Judah, nor a lawgiver from between his feet, until Shiloh come. (Gen. 49: 10)

Who made thee a prince and a judge over us? (Ex. 2: 14)

Lies

The Strength of Israel will not lie. (1 Sam. 15: 29)

Should thy lies make men hold their peace? (Job 11: 3)

Ye are forgers of lies, ye are all physicians of no value. (Job 13: 4)

I said in my haste, All men are liars. (Ps. 116: 11)

These six things doth the Lord hate: yea, seven are an abomination unto Him: A proud look, a lying tongue, and hands that shed innocent blood, An heart that deviseth wicked imaginations, feet that be swift in running to mischief, A false witness that speaketh lies, and he that soweth discord among brethren. (Prov. 6: 16–19)

The wicked is snared by the transgression of his lips. (Prov. 12: 13)

A lying tongue is but for a moment. (Prov. 12: 19)

Lying lips are abomination to the Lord. (Prov. 12: 22)

A righteous man hateth lying. (Prov. 13: 5)

Excellent speech becometh not a fool: much less do lying lips a prince. (Prov. 17: 7)

Woe unto them that call evil good, and good evil; that put darkness for light, and light for darkness; that put bitter for sweet, and sweet for bitter! (Is. 5: 20)

Their tongue is deceitful in their mouth. (Mic. 6: 12)

Thou speakest lies in the name of the Lord. (Zech. 13: 3)

He is a liar, and the father of it. (John 8: 44)

Thou hast not lied unto men, but unto God. (Acts 5: 4)

The poison of asps is under their lips. (Rom. 3: 13)

No lie is of the truth. (1 John 2: 21)

Who is a liar but he that denieth that Jesus is the Christ. (1 John 2: 22)

What the Bible says about (35)

L continued

Life

The Lord God formed man of the dust of the ground, and breathed into his nostrils the breath of life. (Gen. 2: 7)

The life of all flesh is the blood thereof. (Lev. 17: 14)

Wherefore is light given to him that is in misery, and life unto the bitter in soul? (Job 3: 20)

What is mine end, that I should prolong my life? (Job 6: 11)

Wherefore then hast Thou brought me forth out of the womb? Oh that I had given up the Spirit, and no eye had seen me! (Job 10: 18)

Man that is born of a woman is of few days, and full of trouble. (Job 14: 1)

The spirit of God hath made me, and the breath of the Almighty hath given me life. (Job 33: 4)

We spend our years as a tale that is told. (Ps. 90: 9)

Life and death

I have set before you life and death, blessing and cursing: therefore choose life, that both thou and thy seed may live. (Deut. 30: 19)

There is no god with Me: I kill, and I make alive; I wound, and I heal: neither is there any that can deliver out of My hand. (Deut. 32: 39)

The Lord killeth, and maketh alive: He bringeth down to the grave, and bringeth up. (1 Sam. 2: 6)

Naked came I out of my mother's womb, and naked shall I return hither. (Job 1: 21)

Unto God the Lord belong the issues from death. (Ps. 68: 20)

According to the greatness of Thy power preserve Thou those that are appointed to die. (Ps. 79: 11)

Shall Thy lovingkindness be declared in the grave? or Thy faithfulness in destruction? (Ps. 88: 11)

Take me not away in the midst of my days. (Ps. 102: 24)

I shall not die, but live, and declare the works of the Lord. (Ps. 118: 17)

Man is like to vanity: his days are as a shadow that passeth away. (Ps. 144: 4)

He that keepeth the commandment keepeth his own soul; but he that despiseth His ways shall die. (Prov. 19: 16)

A time to be born, and a time to die. (Eccl. 3: 2)

Light and darkness

And God said, Let there be light: and there was light. (Gen. 1: 3)

Darkness which may be felt. (Ex. 10: 21)

The people that walked in darkness have seen a great light. (Is. 9: 2)

Ye are the light of the world. A city that is set on an hill cannot be hid. (Matt. 5: 14)

Take heed therefore that the light which is in thee be not darkness. (Luke 11: 35)

The light shineth in darkness; and the darkness comprehended it not. (John 1: 5)

Men loved darkness rather than light, because their deeds were evil. (John 3: 19)

Every one that doeth evil hateth the light. (John 3: 20)

As long as I am in the world, I am the light of the world. (John 9: 5)

Turn them from darkness to light, and from the power of Satan unto God. (Acts 26: 18)

All things that are reproved are made manifest by the light. (Eph. 5: 13)

God is light, and in Him is no darkness at all. (1 John 1: 5)

The city had no need of the sun, neither of the moon, to shine in it: for the glory of God did lighten it, and the Lamb is the light thereof. (Rev. 21: 23)

Liquor

Wine that maketh glad the heart of man. (Ps. 104: 15)

Wine is a mocker, strong drink is raging. (Prov. 20: 1)

Look not thou upon the wine when it is red. (Prov. 23: 31)

It biteth like a serpent, and stingeth like an adder. (Prov. 23: 32)

Give strong drink unto him that is ready to persih, and wine unto those that be of heavy hearts. (Prov. 31: 6)

Whoredom and wine and new wine take away the heart. (Hos. 4: 11)

No man also having drunk old wine straightway desireth new. (Luke 5: 39)

Loneliness

It is not good that the man should be alone; I will make him an help meet for him. (Gen. 2: 18)

My kinsfolk have failed, and my familiar friends have forgotten me. (Job 19: 14)

I am a brother to dragons, and a companion to owls. (Job 30: 29)

How long wilt Thou forget me, O Lord? for ever? how long wilt Thou hide Thy face from me? (Ps. 13: 1)

When my father and my mother forsake me, then the Lord will take me up. (Ps. 27: 10)

What the Bible says about (36)

L continued

Loss

The Lord gave, and the Lord hath taken away; blessed be the name of the Lord. (Job 1: 21)

A time to get, and a time to lose. (Eccl. 3: 6)

I will restore to you the years that the locust hath eaten. (Joel 2: 25)

If the salt have lost his savor, wherewith shall it be salted? it is thenceforth good for nothing. (Matt. 5: 13)

The last shall be first. (Matt. 19: 30)

Many are called, but few are chosen. (Matt. 22: 14)

From him that hath not shall be taken away even that which he hath. (Matt. 25: 29)

He that hath, to him shall be given: and he that hath not, from him shall be taken even that which he hath. (Mark 4: 25)

What shall it profit a man, if he shall gain the whole world, and lose his own soul? (Mark 8: 36)

The fruits that thy soul lusted after are departed from thee. (Rev. 18: 14)

Love

Thou shalt love thy neighbor as thyself. (Lev. 19: 18; Matt. 19: 19)

The apple of His eye. (Deut. 32: 10)

How canst thou say, I love thee, when thine heart is not with me? (Judg. 16: 15)

In their death they were not divided. (2 Sam. 1: 23)

Hatred stirreth up strifes: but love covereth all sins. (Prov. 10: 12)

Better is a dinner of herbs where love is, than a stalled ox and hatred therewith. (Prov. 15: 17)

A time to love, and a time to hate. (Eccl. 3: 8)

Let him kiss me with the kisses of his mouth: for thy love is better than wine. (Song 1: 2)

Love your enemies. (Matt. 5: 44; Luke 6: 27)

Bless them that curse you, do good to them that hate you. (Matt. 5: 44)

If ye love them which love you, what reward have ye? do not even the publicans the same? (Matt. 5: 46)

He that loveth father or mother more than me is not worthy of me: and he that loveth son or daughter more than me is not worthy of me. (Matt. 10: 37)

This do, and thou shalt live. (Luke 10: 28)

A new commandment I give unto you, That ye love one another. (John 13: 34)

By this shall all men know that ye are my disciples, if ye have love one to another. (John 13: 35)

He that loveth me shall be loved of my Father. (John 14: 21)

This is my commandment, That ye love one another, as I have loved you. (John 15: 12)

Greater love hath no man than this, that a man lay down his life for his friends. (John 15: 13)

Love of God

Thou shalt Love the Lord thy God with all thine heart, and with all thy soul, and with all thy might. (Deut. 6: 5)

Love Him. (Deut. 10: 12)

Love the Lord thy God. (Deut. 19: 9)

Take good heed therefore unto yourselves, that ye love the Lord your God. (Josh. 23: 11)

Let them that love Him be as the sun when he goeth forth in his might. (Judg. 5: 31)

As the hart panteth after the water brooks, so panteth my soul after Thee, O God. (Ps. 42: 1)

My soul thirsteth after Thee, as a thirsty land. (Ps. 143: 6)

Thou shalt love the Lord thy God with all thine heart, and with all thy soul, and with all thy mind. This is the first and great commandment. (Matt. 22: 37–38)

Loyalty

Where your treasure is, there will your heart be also. (Matt. 6: 21; Luke 12: 34)

Ye cannot serve God and mammon. (Matt. 6: 24; Luke 16: 13)

No man can serve two masters: for either he will hate the one, and love the other; or else he will hold to the one, and despise the other. (Matt. 6: 24; Luke 16: 13)

He that is not with me is against me. (Matt. 12: 30; Luke 11: 23)

Render therefore unto Caesar the things which are Caesar's; and unto God the things that are God's. (Matt. 22: 21)

Though I should die with Thee, yet will I not deny Thee. (Matt. 26: 35)

Lust

Keep thee from the evil woman, from the flattery of the tongue of a strange woman. (Prov. 6: 24)

Lust not after her beauty in thine heart; neither let her take thee with her eyelids. (Prov. 6: 25)

Can a man take fire in his bosom, and his clothes not be burned? (Prov. 6: 27)

Whosoever looketh on a woman to lust after her hath committed adultery with her already in his heart. (Matt. 5: 28)

What the Bible says about (37)

M

Marriage

And they shall be one flesh. (Gen. 2: 24)

Thy desire shall be to thy husband, and he shall rule over thee. (Gen. 3: 16)

A virtuous woman is a crown to her husband. (Prov. 12: 4)

Whoso findeth a wife findeth a good thing, and obtaineth favor of the Lord. (Prov. 18: 22)

What therefore God hath joined together, let not man put asunder. (Matt. 19: 6; Mark 10: 9)

They twain shall be one flesh. (Mark 10: 8)

Husbands, love your wives, even as Christ also loved the church. (Eph. 5: 25)

He that loveth his wife, loveth himself. (Eph. 5: 28)

Martyrdom

Precious in the sight of the Lord is the death of His saints. (Ps. 116: 15)

Blessed are they which are persecuted for righteousness' sake: for theirs is the kingdom of heaven. (Matt. 5: 10)

Great is your reward in heaven. (Matt. 5: 12)

Whosoever shall lose his life for my sake and the gospel's, the same shall save it. (Mark 8: 35)

Lord Jesus, receive my spirit. (Acts 7: 59)

Materialism

Lay not up for yourselves treasures upon earth, where moth and rust doth corrupt, and where thieves break through and steal. (Matt. 6: 19)

What shall it profit a man, if he shall gain the whole world, and lose his own soul? (Mark 8: 36)

Man shall not live by bread alone, but by every word of God. (Luke 4: 4)

A man's life consisteth not in the abundance of the things which he possesseth. (Luke 12: 15)

That which is highly esteemed among men is abomination in the sight of God. (Luke 16: 15)

Labor not for the meat which perisheth, but for that meat which endureth unto everlasting life. (John 6: 27)

Thou sayest I am rich, and increased with goods, and have need of nothing; and knowest not that thou art wretched, and miserable, and poor, and blind, and naked. (Rev. 3: 17)

Maturity

He is of age; ask him. (John 9: 21,23)

Be not children in understanding. (1 Cor. 14: 20)

Grow in grace, and in the knowledge of our Lord. (2 Pet. 3: 18)

Mediation

A mediator is not a mediator of one. (Gal. 3: 20)

Jesus the mediator of the new covenant. (Heb. 12: 24)

Meekness

The meek shall eat and be satisfied: they shall praise the Lord that seek Him. (Ps. 22: 26)

The meek will He guide in judgment: and the meek will He teach His way. (Ps. 25: 9)

The meek shall inherit the earth. (Ps. 37: 11)

The Lord lifteth up the meek: He casteth the wicked down to the ground. (Ps. 147: 6)

He is brought as a lamb to the slaughter. (Is. 53: 7)

Seek righteousness, seek meekness: it may be ye shall be hid in the day of the Lord's anger. (Zeph. 2: 3)

Behold, I send you forth as lambs among wolves. (Luke 10: 3)

Like a lamb dumb before His shearer, so opened He not His mouth. (Acts 8: 32)

Mercy

And God Almighty give you mercy before the man. (Gen. 43: 14)

The Lord thy God is a merciful God. (Deut. 4: 31)

It is enough: stay now thine hand. (2 Sam. 24: 16; 1 Chr. 21: 15)

In thy days I will not do it for David thy father's sake: but I will rend it out of the hand of thy son. (1 Kings 11: 12)

I am merciful, saith the Lord, and I will not keep anger for ever. (Jer. 3: 12)

I will spare them, as a man spareth his own son that serveth him. (Mal. 3: 17)

Blessed are the merciful: for they shall obtain mercy. (Matt. 5: 7)

Be ye therefore merciful, as your Father also is merciful. (Luke 6: 36)

Messiah

But whom say ye that I am? (Matt. 16: 15; Mark 8: 29, Luke 9: 20)

Take heed that no man deceive you. For many shall come in my name, saying, I am Christ. (Matt. 24: 4,5)

False Christs and false prophets shall rise, and shall show signs and wonders, to seduce, if it were possible, even the elect. (Mark 13: 22)

The Son of man is not come to destroy men's lives, but to save them. (Luke 9: 56)

He whom God hath sent speaketh the words of God. (John 3: 34)

I that speak unto thee am He. (John 4: 26)

Whom He hath sent, Him ye believe not. (John 5: 38)

The bread of God is He which cometh down from heaven, and giveth life unto the world. (John 6: 33)

What the Bible says about (38)

M continued

Messianic hopes and prophecies

I am not come to destroy, but to fulfill. (Matt. 5: 17)

This is he, of whom it is written, Behold, I send my messenger before Thy face, which shall prepare Thy way before Thee. (Matt. 11: 10; Luke 7: 27)

All this was done, that the scriptures of the prophets might be fulfilled. (Matt. 26: 56)

This day is this Scripture fulfilled in your ears. (Luke 4: 21)

Search the scriptures. (John 5: 39)

Had ye believed Moses, ye would have believed me: for he wrote of me. (John 5: 46)

Ministry

Serve Him in sincerity and in truth. (Josh. 24: 14)

Cursed be he that doeth the work of the Lord deceitfully. (Jer. 48: 10)

The harvest truly is plenteous, but the laborers are few. (Matt. 9: 37)

Freely ye have received, freely give. (Matt. 10: 8)

Feed my lambs. (John 21: 15)

Feed my sheep. (John 21: 16,17)

We are ambassadors for Christ. (2 Cor. 5: 20)

Miracles

Speak ye unto the rock before their eyes; and it shall give forth his water. (Num. 20: 8)

An evil and adulterous generation seeketh after a sign; and there shall no sign be given to it, but the sign of the prophet Jonas. (Matt. 12: 39)

In my name shall they cast out devils. (Mark 16: 17)

The blind see, the lame walk, the lepers are cleansed, the deaf hear, the dead are raised, to the poor the gospel is preached. (Luke 7: 22)

Go thy way; thy son liveth. (John 4: 50)

Misjudgment

Thou art but a youth, and he a man of war. (1 Sam. 17: 33)

Behold, I have played the fool, and have erred exceedingly. (1 Sam. 26: 21)

He hath borne our griefs, and carried our sorrows: yet we did esteem him stricken, smitten of God, and afflicted. (Is. 53: 4)

Mission

Whom shall I send, and who will go for us? Then said I, Here am I; send me. (Is. 6: 8)

And ye shall know that the Lord of hosts hath sent me. (Zech. 2: 9)

Heal the sick, cleanse the lepers, raise the dead, cast out devils. (Matt. 10: 8)

He hath sent me to heal the

brokenhearted, to preach deliverance to the captives. (Luke 4: 18)

Behold, I send you forth as lambs among wolves. (Luke 10: 3)

My meat is to do the will of Him that sent me, and to finish His work. (John 4: 34)

I came down from heaven, not to do mine own will, but the will of Him that sent me. (John 6: 38)

I know Him: for I am from Him, and He hath sent me. (John 7: 29)

But for this cause came I unto this hour. (John 12: 27)

To this end was I born, and for this cause came I unto the world, that I should bear witness unto the truth. (John 18: 37)

As my Father hath sent me, even so send I you. (John 20: 21)

Arise, and go into Damascus. (Acts 22: 10)

I have appeared unto thee for this purpose, to make thee a minister and a witness. (Acts 26: 16)

Mockery

Go and cry unto the gods which ye have chosen; let them deliver you. (Judg. 10: 14)

Be ye not mockers. (Is. 28: 22)

God is not mocked. (Gal. 6: 7)

Models

Ye are the light of the world. A city that is set on an hill cannot be hid. (Matt. 5: 14)

Let your light so shine before men, that they may see your good works. (Matt. 5: 16)

It is enough for the disciple that he be as his master, and the servant as his lord. (Matt. 10: 25)

Do not ye after their works: for they say, and do not. (Matt. 23: 3)

Go and do thou likewise. (Luke 10: 37)

He was a burning and a shining light: and ye were willing for a season to rejoice in his light. (John 5: 35)

Do as I have done to you. (John 13: 15)

Modesty

Few and evil have the days of the years of my life been. (Gen. 47: 9)

Seemeth it to you a light thing to be a king's son in law? (1 Sam. 18: 23)

Let another man praise thee, and not thine own mouth. (Prov. 27: 2)

When thou doest thine alms, do not sound a trumpet before thee, as the hypocrites do. (Matt. 6: 2)

Appear not unto men to fast, but unto thy Father. (Matt. 6: 18)

What the Bible says about (39)

Modesty, continued

See that no man know it. (Matt. 9: 30)

Thou sayest it. (Mark 15: 2; Luke 23: 3)

He must increase, but I must decrease. (John 3: 30)

Money

Money answereth all things. (Eccl. 10: 19)

Ye cannot serve God and mammon. (Matt. 6: 24; Luke 16: 13)

Thy money perish with thee, because thou hast thought that the gift of God may be purchased with money. (Acts 8: 20)

Filthy lucre. (1 Tim. 3: 3)

The love of money is the root of all evil. (1 Tim. 6: 10)

Monotheism

Hear, O Israel: The Lord our God is one Lord. (Deut. 6: 4)

There is none beside Thee. (1 Sam. 2: 2)

There is none else. (1 Kings 8: 60)

Thou art the God, even Thou alone. (2 Kings 19: 15)

Be still, and know that I am God. (Ps. 46: 10)

Know ye that the Lord He is God. (Ps. 100: 3)

And ye shall know that I am the Lord. (Ezek. 25: 5)

Thou shalt worship the Lord thy God, and Him only shalt thou serve. (Matt. 4: 10)

The devils also believe, and tremble. (James 2: 19)

Motivation

Every way of a man is right in his own eyes: but the Lord pondereth the hearts. (Prov. 21: 2)

I do not this for your sakes, O house of Israel, but for Mine holy name's sake, which ye have profaned. (Ezek. 36: 22)

Will a lion roar in the forest, when he hath no prey? (Amos 3: 4)

Out of the heart proceed evil thoughts, murders, adulteries, fornications, thefts, false witness, blasphemies. (Matt. 15: 19)

Ye ask, and receive not, because ye ask amiss. (James 4: 3)

Not for filthy lucre. (1 Pet. 5: 2)

Mourning

A time to weep, and a time to laugh; a time to mourn, and a time to dance. (Eccl. 3: 4)

Blessed are they that mourn: for they shall be comforted. (Matt. 5: 4)

We have piped unto you, and ye have not danced; we have mourned unto you, and ye have not lamented. (Matt. 11: 17)

Murder

Whoso sheddeth man's blood, by man shall his blood be shed. (Gen. 9: 6)

Let not our hand be upon him; for he is our brother and our flesh. (Gen. 37: 27)

Thou shalt not kill. (Ex. 20: 13)

The murderer shall surely be put to death. (Num. 35: 16)

Ye shall take no satisfaction for the life of a murderer, which is guilty of death: but he shall be surely put to death. (Num. 35: 31)

Thine eye shall not pity him. (Deut. 19: 13)

Cursed be he that taketh reward to slay an innocent person. (Deut. 27: 25)

As a man falleth before wicked men, so fellest thou. (2 Sam. 3: 34)

These six things doth the Lord hate: yea, seven are an abomination unto Him: A proud look, a lying tongue, and hands that shed innocent blood, An heart that deviseth wicked imaginations, feet that be swift in running to mischief, A false witness that speaketh lies, and he that soweth discord among brethren. (Prov. 6: 16–19)

No murderer hath eternal life abiding in him. (1 John 3: 15)

Music

Praise the Lord with harp: sing unto Him with the psaltery and an instrument of ten strings. (Ps. 33: 2)

Praise Him with the sound of the trumpet: praise Him with the psaltery and harp. (Ps. 150: 3)

Praise Him with the timbrel and dance: praise Him with stringed instruments and organs. (Ps. 150: 4)

Praise Him upon the loud cymbals: praise Him upon the high sounding cymbals. (Ps. 150: 5)

Mystery

The way of an eagle in the air; the way of a serpent upon a rock; the way of a ship in the midst of the sea; and the way of a man with a maid. (Prov. 30: 19)

Watchman, what of the night? (Is. 21: 11)

There is a God in heaven that revealeth secrets. (Dan. 2: 28)

Mene, Mene, Tekel, Upharsin. (Dan. 5: 25)

The wind bloweth where it listeth, and thou hearest the sound thereof, but canst not tell whence it cometh, and whither it goeth. (John 3: 8)

He that was healed wist not who it was. John 5: 13)

Who is worthy to open the book, and to loose the seals thereof? (Rev. 5: 2)

When He had opened the seventh seal, there was silence in heaven about the space of half an hour. (Rev. 8: 1)

Myth

Refuse profane and old wives' fables. (1 Tim. 4: 7)

What the Bible says about (40)

N

Nature

And God made two great lights; the greater light to rule the day, and the lesser light to rule the night: He made the stars also. (Gen. 1: 16)

Ye shall not pollute the land wherein ye are. (Num. 35: 33)

Defile not therefore the land which ye shall inhabit. (Num. 35: 34)

The tree of the field is man's life. (Deut. 20: 19)

Speak to the earth, and it shall teach thee: and the fishes of the sea shall declare unto thee. (Job 12: 8)

Stand still, and consider the wondrous works of God. (Job 37: 14)

The trees of the Lord are full of sap. (Ps. 104: 16)

How manifold are Thy works! in wisdom hast Thou made them all. (Ps. 104: 24)

The earth is full of Thy riches. (Ps. 104: 24)

He commandeth, and raiseth the stormy wind, which lifteth up the waves thereof. (Ps. 107: 25)

The works of the Lord are great. (Ps. 111: 2)

The mountains skipped like rams, and the little hills like lambs. (Ps. 114: 4)

All are Thy servants. (Ps. 119: 91)

Let them praise the name of the Lord: for He commanded, and they were created. (Ps. 148: 5)

The sun also ariseth. (Eccl. 1: 5)

To every thing there is a season, and a time to every purpose under the heaven. (Eccl. 3: 1)

A time to be born, and a time to die; a time to plant, and a time to pluck up that which is planted. (Eccl. 3: 2)

A pleasant thing it is for the eyes to behold the sun. (Eccl. 11: 7)

For the mountains will I take up a weeping and wailing, and for the habitations of the wilderness a lamentation. (Jer. 9: 10)

The Lord hath His way in the whirlwind and in the storm, and the clouds are the dust of His feet. (Nah. 1: 3)

Consider the lilies of the field, how they grow; they toil not, neither do they spin: And yet I say unto you, that even Solomon in all his glory was not arrayed like one of these. (Matt. 6: 28–29)

The wind bloweth where it listeth, and thou hearest the sound thereof, but canst not tell whence it cometh, and whither it goeth. (John 3: 8)

Hath not My hand made all these things? (Acts 7: 50)

The earth is the Lord's, and the fullness thereof. (1 Cor. 10: 26, 28)

The grass withereth, and the flower thereof falleth away: But the word of the Lord endureth forever. (1 Pet. 1: 24,25)

Need

Your Father knoweth what things ye have need of, before ye ask Him. (Matt. 6: 8)

They that be whole need not a physician, but they that are sick. (Matt. 9: 12)

Let him that is athirst come. And whosoever will, let him take the water of life freely. (Rev. 22: 17)

Neighbors

Thou shalt not covet thy neighbor's house, thou shalt not covet thy neighbor's wife, nor his manservant, nor his maidservant, nor his ox, nor his ass, nor any thing that is thy neighbor's. (Ex. 20: 17)

Thou shalt love thy neighbor as thyself. (Lev. 19: 18)

He that is void of wisdom despiseth his neighbor: but a man of understanding holdeth his peace. (Prov. 11: 12)

Let none of you imagine evil in your hearts against his neighbor. (Zech. 8: 17)

Love worketh no ill to his neighbor. (Rom. 13: 10)

Neutrality

Curse ye bitterly the inhabitants thereof; because they came not to the help of the Lord. (Judg. 5: 23)

He that is not with me is against me. (Matt. 12: 30)

He that is not against us is for us. (Luke 9: 50)

I know thy works, that thou art neither cold nor hot: I would thou wert cold or hot. (Rev. 3: 15)

Because thou art lukewarm, and neither cold nor hot, I will spue thee out of my mouth. (Rev. 3: 16)

News

It is no good report that I hear. (1 Sam. 2: 24)

Tell it not in Gath, publish it not in the streets of Askelon. (2 Sam. 1: 20)

I am sent to thee with heavy tidings. (1 Kings 14: 6)

He shall hear a rumor, and shall return to his own land. (2 Kings 19: 7)

As cold waters to a thirsty soul, so is good news from a far country. (Prov. 25: 25)

He that sendeth a message by the hand of a fool cutteth off the feet. (Prov. 26: 6)

How beautiful upon the mountains are the feet of him that bringeth good tidings, that publisheth peace. (Is. 52: 7)

Publish, and set up a standard; publish, and conceal not. (Jer. 50: 2)

I bring you good tidings of great joy. (Luke 2: 10)

What the Bible says about (41)

O

Oaths

Swear unto me by the Lord.(Josh. 2: 12)
As the Lord thy God liveth. (1 Kings
18: 10)

So let the gods do to me, and more.
(1 Kings 19: 2)

Thus saith the Lord God; As I live.
(Ezek. 33: 27)

Swear not at all; neither by heaven;
for it is God's throne: Nor by the
earth; for it is His footstool: neither by
Jerusalem; for it is the city of the great
King. (Matt. 5: 34,35)

Neither shalt thou swear by thy head,
because thou canst not make one hair
white or black. (Matt. 5: 36)

He that shall swear by heaven,
sweareth by the throne of God, and by
Him that sitteth thereon. (Matt.23: 22)

Swear not, neither by heaven, neither
by earth, neither by any other oath: but
let your yea be yea; and your nay be
nay. (James 5: 12)

Obedience

Of every tree of the garden thou
mayest freely eat: But of the tree of the
knowledge of good and evil, thou shalt
not eat. (Gen. 2: 16,17)

Walk before Me, and be thou perfect.
(Gen. 17: 1)

In thy seed shall all the nations of
the earth be blessed; because thou hast
obeyed My voice. (Gen. 22: 18)

Upon me be thy curse, my son: only
obey my voice. (Gen. 27: 13)

Obligation

Unto whomsoever much is given, of
him shall be much required. (Luke
12: 48)

To whom men have committed
much, of him they will ask the more.
(Luke 12: 48)

Owe no man any thing, but to love
one another. (Rom. 13: 8)

Though I be free from all men, yet
have I made myself servant unto all.
(1 Cor. 9: 19)

Obstacles

The way of the wicked is as
darkness: they know not at what they
stumble. (Prov. 4: 19)

I will break in pieces the gates of
brass, and cut in sunder the bars of
iron. (Is. 45: 2)

Prepare the way, take up the
stumblingblock out of the way of My
people. (Is. 57: 14)

I will lay stumbling blocks before this
people, and the fathers and the sons
together shall fall upon them. (Jer. 6: 21)

I will hedge up thy way with thorns,
and make a wall, that she shall not find
her paths. (Hos. 2: 6)

Every valley shall be filled, and every
mountain and hill shall be brought low.
(Luke 3: 5)

The crooked shall be made straight,
and rough ways shall be made smooth.
(Luke 3: 5)

Make straight paths for your feet, lest
that which is lame be turned out of the
way. (Heb. 12: 13)

Omens

Shall the shadow go forward ten degrees, or go back? (2 Kings 20: 9)

Let the shadow return backward ten degrees. (2 Kings 20: 10)

He delivereth and rescueth, and He worketh signs and wonders in heaven and in earth. (Dan. 6: 27)

An evil and adulterous generation seeketh after a sign; and there shall no sign be given to it, but the sign of the prophet Jonas. (Matt. 12: 39)

O ye hypocrites, ye can discern the face of the sky; but can ye not discern the signs of the times? (Matt. 16: 3)

Opportunism

Why are ye come unto me now when ye are in distress? (Judg. 11: 7)

Let us build with you: for we seek your God, as ye do. (Ezra 4: 2)

Wealth maketh many friends; but the poor is separated from his neighbor. (Prov. 19: 4)

Every man is a friend to him that giveth gifts. (Prov. 19: 6)

O generation of vipers, who hath warned you to flee from the wrath to come? (Matt. 3: 7; Luke 3: 7)

Wheresoever the carcass is, there will the eagles be gathered together. (Matt. 24: 28)

Opportunity

The Lord thy God hath set the land before thee: go up and possess it. (Deut. 1: 21)

Seek ye the Lord while He may be found, call ye upon Him while He is near. (Is. 55: 6)

I called you, but ye answered not. (Jer. 7: 13)

Seek, and ye shall find. (Matt. 7: 7; Luke 11: 9)

Knock, and it shall be opened unto you. (Matt. 7: 7; Luke 11: 9)

Many are called, but few are chosen. (Matt. 22: 14)

Oppression

Ye shall no more give the people straw to make brick. (Ex. 5: 7)

Fulfill your works, your daily tasks, as when there was straw. (Ex. 5: 13)

My father chastised you with whips, but I will chastise you with scorpions. (2 Chr. 10: 11,14)

Let not the proud oppress me. (Ps. 119: 122)

Deliver me from the oppression of man. (Ps. 119: 134)

The Lord looseth the prisoners. (Ps. 146: 7)

What the Bible says about (42)

P

Parents

Shall a child be born unto him that is an hundred years old? and shall Sarah, that is ninety years old bear? (Gen. 17: 17)

I am Joseph; doth my father yet live? (Gen. 45: 3)

Honor thy father and thy mother. (Ex. 20: 12)

He that smiteth his father, or his mother, shall be surely put to death. (Ex. 21: 15)

He that curseth his father, or his mother, shall surely be put to death. (Ex. 21: 17)

Ye shall fear every man his mother, and his father. (Lev. 19: 3)

Honor thy father and thy mother, as the Lord thy God hath commanded thee; that thy days may be prolonged. (Deut. 5: 16)

Password

Say now Shibboleth. (Judg. 12: 6)

Patience

How long shall I bear with this evil congregation, which murmur against Me? (Num. 14: 27)

Their foot shall slide in due time. (Deut. 32: 35)

Let not Thine anger be hot against me, and I will speak but this once. (Judg. 6: 39)

Would ye tarry for them till they were grown? (Ruth 1: 13)

His day shall come to die. (1 Sam. 26: 10)

After that I have spoken, mock on. (Job 21: 3)

I gave ear to your reasons, whilst ye searched out what to say. (Job 32: 11)

Wait on the Lord. (Ps. 27: 14)

Peace

If thou wilt take the left hand, then I will go to the right; or if thou depart to the right hand, then I will go to the left. (Gen. 13: 9)

Go in peace. (Ex. 4: 18)

And the land rested from war. (Josh. 11: 23)

How long shall it be then, ere thou bid the people return from following their brethren? (2 Sam. 2: 26)

Is it not good, if peace and truth be in my days? (2 Kings 20: 19)

Ye shall not go up, nor fight against your brethren. (2 Chr. 11: 4; 1 Kings 12: 24)

He maketh peace in His high places. (Job 25: 2)

Seek peace, and pursue it. (Ps. 34: 14)

Perfection

He is the Rock, His work is perfect. (Deut. 32: 4)

And the Lord said unto Satan, Hast thou considered my servant Job? (Job 1: 8)

There is none like him in the earth, a perfect and an upright man, one

that feareth God, and escheweth evil.
(Job 1: 8; Job 2: 3)

As for God, His way is perfect.
(Ps. 18: 30; 2 Sam. 22: 31)

Perjury

Thou shalt not bear false witness.
(Ex. 20: 16)

Do unto him, as he had thought to
have done unto his brother. (Deut. 19: 19)

A false witness will utter lies.
(Prov. 14: 5)

Every one that sweareth shall be cut
off. (Zech. 5: 3)

Love no false oath. (Zech. 8: 17)

Permanence

It is a covenant of salt for ever before
the Lord. (Num. 18: 19)

Oh that my words were now written!
oh that they were printed in a book!
(Job 19: 23)

The counsel of the Lord standeth for
ever. (Ps. 33: 11)

Riches are not for ever. (Prov. 27: 24)

One generation passeth away, and
another generation cometh: but the
earth abideth for ever. (Eccl. 1: 4)

That which now is in the days to
come shall all be forgotten. (Eccl. 2: 16)

Whatsoever God doeth, it shall be for
ever. (Eccl. 3: 14)

Persecution

I have not sinned against thee; yet thou
huntest my soul to take it. (1 Sam. 24: 11)

I, even I only, am left; and they
seek my life, to take it away. (1 Kings
19: 10,14)

Think not with thyself that thou shalt
escape in the king's house, more than
all the Jews. (Esther 4: 13)

How can I endure to see the evil that
shall come unto my people? (Esther 8: 6)

Behold, He findeth occasions against
me, He counteth me for His enemy.
(Job 33: 10)

The wicked in his pride doth
persecute the poor. (Ps. 10: 2)

The assembly of the wicked have
inclosed me: they pierced my hands
and my feet. (Ps. 22: 16)

Deliver me not over unto the will of
mine enemies: for false witnesses are
risen up against me. (Ps. 27: 12)

The wicked watcheth the righteous,
and seeketh to slay him. (Ps. 37: 32)

Perseverance

O God, strengthen my hands. (Neh. 6: 9)

The Lord gave Job twice as much as
he had before. (Job 42: 10)

We went through fire and through
water. (Ps. 66: 12)

Harder than flint have I made thy
forehead. (Ezek. 3: 9)

Blessed is he that waiteth. (Dan. 12: 12)

What the Bible says about (43)

P continued

Perspective

Behold, I am at the point to die: and
what profit shall this birthright do to
me? (Gen. 25: 32)

O that they were wise, that they
understood this, that they would
consider their latter end! (Deut. 32: 29)

Is not the gleaning of the grapes of
Ephraim better than the vintage of
Abiezer? (Judg. 8: 2)

After whom dost thou pursue? after
a dead dog, after a flea. (1 Sam. 24: 14)

How long have I to live, that I should
go up with the king unto Jerusalem?
(2 Sam. 19: 34)

Shall we receive good at the hand
of God, and shall we not receive evil?
(Job 2: 10)

Our days upon earth are a shadow.
(Job 8: 9)

Mine age is as nothing before Thee.
(Ps. 39: 5)

Persuasion

Stand still, that I may reason with you
before the Lord. (1 Sam. 12: 7)

How forcible are right words!
(Job 6: 25)

Produce your cause, saith the Lord;
bring forth your strong reasons.
(Is. 41: 21)

If they hear not Moses and the
prophets, neither will they be
persuaded, though one rose from the
dead. (Luke 16: 31)

Paul, Almost thou persuadest me to
be a Christian. (Acts 26: 28)

Some believed the things which
were spoken, and some believed not.
(Acts 28: 24)

Let no man deceive you with vain
words. (Eph. 5: 6)

For love's sake I rather beseech thee.
(Philem. 9)

Physical fitness

Bodily exercise profiteth little: but
godliness is profitable unto all things.
(1 Tim. 4: 8)

Planning

Consider of it, take advice, and speak
your minds. (Judg. 19: 30)

The Lord bringeth the counsel of the
heathen to nought. (Ps. 33: 10)

The counsel of the Lord standeth for
ever. (Ps. 33: 11)

Ponder the path of thy feet.
(Prov. 4: 26)

Pleasure

Can that which is unsavory be eaten
without salt? (Job 6: 6)

Is there any taste in the white of an
egg? (Job 6: 6)

Stolen waters are sweet, and bread
eaten in secret is pleasant. (Prov. 9: 17)

He that loveth pleasure shall be a
poor man. (Prov. 21: 17)

He that loveth wine and oil shall not
be rich. (Prov. 21: 17)

Possibility

Is any thing too hard for the Lord?
(Gen. 18: 14)

If Balak would give me his house full
of silver and gold, I cannot go beyond
the word of the Lord my God, to do less
or more. (Num. 22: 18)

Shall the shadow go forward ten
degrees, or go back? (2 Kings 20: 9)

Who can make that straight, which
He hath made crooked? (Eccl. 7: 13)

I am the Lord, the God of all flesh: is
there any thing too hard for Me?
(Jer. 32: 27)

It is a rare thing that the king
requireth. (Dan. 2: 11)

If ye have faith as a grain of mustard
seed, ye shall say unto this mountain,
Remove hence to yonder place; and it
shall remove. (Matt. 17: 20)

It is easier for a camel to go through
the eye of a needle, than for a rich man
to enter into the kingdom of God.
(Matt. 19: 24; Mark 10: 25)

With God all things are possible.
(Matt. 19: 26; Mark 10: 27)

Ye know not what ye ask.
(Matt. 20: 22; Mark 10: 38)

If ye shall say unto this mountain, Be
thou removed, and be thou cast into
the sea; it shall be done. (Matt. 21: 21)

All things are possible to him that
believeth. (Mark 9: 23)

With men it is impossible, but not
with God. (Mark 10: 27)

With God nothing shall be
impossible. (Luke 1: 37)

Posterity

I will make thy seed as the dust of the
earth: so that if a man can number the
dust of the earth, then shall thy seed
also be numbered. (Gen. 13: 16)

A nation and a company of nations
shall be of thee, and kings shall come
out of thy loins. (Gen. 35: 11)

Who shall declare his generation?
(Is. 53: 8)

The promise is unto you, and to your
children, and to all that are afar off.
(Acts 2: 39)

Poverty

The poor shall never cease out of the
land. (Deut. 15: 11)

He raiseth up the poor out of the
dust, and lifteth up the beggar from the
dunghill. (1 Sam. 2: 8)

Naked came I out of my mother's
womb, and naked shall I return hither.
(Job 1: 21)

He saveth the poor from the sword,
from their mouth, and from the hand
of the mighty. (Job 5: 15)

The poor hath hope. (Job 5: 16)

What the Bible says about (44)

P continued

Power

How shall I curse, whom God hath not cursed? or how shall I defy, whom the Lord hath not defied? (Num. 23: 8)

He will take your fields, and your vineyards, and your oliveyards, even the best of them, and give them to his servants. (1 Sam. 8: 14)

Am I God, to kill and to make alive? (2 Kings 5: 7)

Praise

Saul hath slain his thousands, and David his ten thousands. (1 Sam. 18: 7)

Because the Lord loved Israel for ever, therefore made He thee king. (1 Kings 10: 9)

A man shall be commended according to his wisdom. (Prov. 12: 8)

Out of the mouths of babes and sucklings Thou hast perfected praise. (Matt. 21: 16)

If I honor myself, my honor is nothing: it is my Father that honoreth me. (John 8: 54)

Prayer

Remember me, I pray Thee, and strengthen me, I pray Thee, only this once, O God. (Judg. 16: 28)

For this child I prayed; and the Lord hath given me my petition. (1 Sam. 1: 27)

God forbid that I should sin against the Lord in ceasing to pray for you. (1 Sam. 12: 23)

In my distress I called upon the Lord. (2 Sam. 22: 7; Ps. 18: 6)

Preaching

Hear, O Israel: The Lord our God is one Lord. (Deut. 6: 4)

The Lord gave the word: great was the company of those that published it. (Ps. 68: 11)

Give ye ear, and hear my voice; hearken, and hear my speech. (Is. 28: 23)

Blessed are ye that sow beside all waters. (Is. 32: 20)

Pride

How are the mighty fallen! (2 Sam. 1: 19)

Pride compasseth them about as a chain; violence covereth them as a garment. (Ps. 73: 6)

When pride cometh, then cometh shame. (Prov. 11: 2)

Pride goeth before destruction, and an haughty spirit before a fall. (Prov. 16: 18)

A man's pride shall bring him low. (Prov. 29: 23)

Priesthood

All the firstborn are Mine. (Num. 3: 13)

The priesthood of the Lord is their inheritance. (Josh. 18: 7)

I have lent him to the Lord. (1 Sam. 1: 28)

As long as he liveth he shall be lent to the Lord. (1 Sam. 1: 28)

They shall go in, for they are holy. (2 Chr. 23: 6)

I am their inheritance. (Ezek. 44: 28)

He is the messenger of the Lord of hosts. (Mal. 2: 7)

Procrastination

If we tarry till the morning light, some mischief will come upon us. (2 Kings 7: 9)

He that observeth the wind shall not sow; and he that regardeth the clouds shall not reap. (Eccl. 11: 4)

Seek ye the Lord while He may be found, call ye upon Him while He is near. (Is. 55: 6)

Exhort one another daily, while it is called To day. (Heb. 3: 13)

Profanity

Put off all these; anger, wrath, malice, blasphemy, filthy communication out of your mouth. (Col. 3: 8)

Profit

Shall I drink the blood of these men that have put their lives in jeopardy? (1 Chr. 11: 19)

Treasures of wickedness profit nothing. (Prov. 10: 2)

In all labor there is a profit. (Prov. 14: 23)

Promises

Is the Lord's hand waxed short? (Num. 11: 23)

Hath He said, and shall He not do it? or hath He spoken, and shall He not make it good? (Num. 23: 19)

When thou shalt vow a vow unto the Lord thy God, thou shalt not slack to pay it. (Deut. 23: 21)

If thou shalt forbear to vow, it shall be no sin in thee. (Deut. 23: 22)

Proof

The God that answereth by fire, let Him be God. (1 Kings 18: 24)

Hear me, O Lord, hear me, that this people may know that Thou art the Lord God, and that Thou hast turned their heart back again. (1 Kings 18: 37)

And ye shall know that I am the Lord. (1 Kings 20: 28)

Property

The land shall not be sold for ever: for the land is Mine; for ye are strangers and sojourners with Me. (Lev. 25: 23)

Cursed be he that removeth his neighbor's landmark. (Deut. 19: 14)

The world is Mine, and the fullness thereof. (Ps. 50: 12)

Remove not the ancient landmark, which thy fathers have set. (Prov. 22: 28)

Prophecy

Would God that all the Lord's people were prophets, and that the Lord would put His spirit upon them! (Num. 11: 29)

What the Bible says about (45)

Prophecy, continued

When a prophet speaketh in the name of the Lord, if the thing follow not, nor come to pass, that is the thing which the Lord hath not spoken. (Deut. 18: 22)

I hate him; for he doth not prophesy good concerning me, but evil. (1 Kings 22: 8)

Speak that which is good. (1 Kings 22: 13)

Hear ye the word of the Lord. (II Kings 7: 1)

Prosperity

If ye walk in My statutes, and keep My commandments, and do them; Then I will give you rain in due season, and the land shall yield her increase, and the trees of the field shall yield their fruit. (Lev. 26: 3,4)

The Lord make His face shine upon thee, and be gracious unto thee. (Num. 6: 25)

The Lord maketh poor, and maketh rich: He bringeth low, and lifteth up. (1 Sam. 2: 7)

Give rain upon Thy land, which Thou hast given to Thy people. (1 Kings 8: 36)

Prostitution

Do not prostitute thy daughter, to cause her to be a whore; lest the land fall to whoredom, and the land become full of wickedness. (Lev. 19: 29)

Thou shalt not bring the hire of a whore, or the price of a dog, into the house of the Lord. (Deut. 23: 18)

The lips of a strange woman drop as an honeycomb, and her mouth is smoother than oil. (Prov. 5: 3)

Keep thee from the evil woman, from the flattery of the tongue of a strange woman. (Prov. 6: 24)

Provocation

Now shall I be more blameless than the Philistines, though I do them a displeasure. (Judg. 15: 3)

They provoked Him to jealousy with their sins. (1 Kings 14: 22)

Provoke Me not to anger with the works of your hands; and I will do you no hurt. (Jer. 25: 6)

Prudence

He that is surety for a stranger shall smart for it. (Prov. 11: 15)

He that keepeth his mouth keepeth his life: but he that openeth wide his lips shall have destruction. (Prov. 13: 3)

The wisdom of the prudent is to understand his ways. (Prov. 14: 8)

Whoso keepeth his mouth and his tongue keepeth his soul from troubles. (Prov. 21: 23)

Public opinion

Ye shall not be afraid of the face of man; for the judgment is God's. (Deut. 1: 17)

Hearken unto their voice, and make them a king. (1 Sam. 8: 22)

I feared the people, and obeyed their voice. (1 Sam. 15: 24)

No doubt but ye are the people, and

wisdom shall die with you. (Job 12: 2)

Hath he not sent me to the men that sit upon the wall? (Is. 36: 12)

They feared the people, lest they should have been stoned. (Acts 5: 26)

Publicity

His fame was noised throughout all the country. (Josh. 6: 27)

For men to search their own glory is not glory. (Prov. 25: 27)

A city that is set on an hill cannot be hid. (Matt. 5: 14)

Neither do men light a candle, and put it under a bushel, but on a candlestick. (Matt. 5: 15)

Let your light so shine before men, that they may see your good works. (Matt. 5: 16)

He that doeth truth cometh to the light, that his deeds may be made manifest. (John 3: 21)

Punishment

Upon thy belly shalt thou go, and dust shalt thou eat all the days of thy life. (Gen. 3: 14)

In sorrow thou shalt bring forth children. (Gen. 3: 16)

In the sweat of thy face shalt thou eat bread, till thou return unto the ground. (Gen. 3: 19)

A fugitive and a vagabond shalt thou be in the earth. (Gen. 4: 12)

My punishment is greater than I can bear. (Gen. 4: 13)

Purity

Neither will I be with you any more, except ye destroy the accursed from among you. (Josh. 7: 12)

Sanctify yourselves against to morrow. (Josh. 7: 13)

Thou canst not stand before thine enemies, until ye take away the accursed thing from among you. (Josh. 7: 13)

Purpose

God did send me before you to preserve life. (Gen. 45: 5)

The Lord hath made all things for Himself: yea, even the wicked for the day of evil. (Prov. 16: 4)

I will give them one heart, and one way, that they may fear Me for ever. (Jer. 32: 39)

The thief cometh not, but for to steal, and to kill, and to destroy. (John 10: 10)

Do all to the glory of God. (1 Cor. 10: 31)

What the Bible says about (46)

R

Rain

A little cloud out of the sea, like a man's hand. (1 Kings 18: 44)

Hath the rain a father? or who hath begotten the drops of dew? (Job 38: 28)

He watereth the hills from His chambers. (Ps. 104: 13)

Rainbow

I do set My bow in the cloud, and it shall be for a token of a covenant between Me and the earth. (Gen. 9: 13)

Rashness

I have opened my mouth unto the Lord, and I cannot go back. (Judg. 11: 35)

Set a watch, O Lord, before the door of my lips. (Ps. 141: 3)

He that is hasty of spirit exalteth folly. (Prov. 14: 29)

He that hasteth with his feet sinneth. (Prov. 19: 2)

Let not thine heart be hasty to utter any thing before God. (Eccl. 5: 2)

Readiness

Sanctify yourselves against to morrow. (Josh. 7: 13)

Speak, Lord; for Thy servant heareth. (1 Sam. 3: 9)

Be thou prepared. (Ezek. 38: 7)

I will send My messenger, and he shall prepare the way before Me. (Mal. 3: 1)

Prepare ye the way of the Lord, make His paths straight. (Matt. 3: 3; Mark 1: 3; Luke 3: 4)

This is he, of whom it is written, Behold, I send my messenger before Thy face, which shall prepare Thy way before Thee. (Matt. 11: 10; Luke 7: 27)

Elias is come already, and they knew him not. (Matt. 17: 12)

Be ye therefore ready also: for the Son of man cometh at an hour when ye think not. (Luke 12: 40)

Lift up your eyes, and look on the fields; for they are white already to harvest. (John 4: 35)

Reciprocity

Thou shalt give life for life, Eye for eye, tooth for tooth, hand for hand, foot for foot, Burning for burning, wound for wound, stripe for stripe. (Ex. 21: 23–25)

Blessed is he that blesseth thee, and cursed is he that curseth thee. (Num. 24: 9)

Do unto him, as he had thought to have done unto his brother. (Deut. 19: 19)

As they did unto me, so have I done unto them. (Judg. 15: 11)

The Lord is with you, while ye be with Him. (2 Chr. 15: 2)

They shall be My people, and I will be their God. (Jer. 24: 7)

Turn ye unto Me, saith the Lord of hosts, and I will turn unto you. (Zech. 1: 3)

All things whatsoever ye would that men should do to you, do ye even so to them. (Matt. 7: 12)

Redemption

Redeem us for Thy mercies' sake. (Ps. 44: 26)

Fear not: for I have redeemed thee, I have called thee by thy name; thou art Mine. (Is. 43: 1)

With his stripes we are healed. (Is. 53: 5)

Behold the Lamb of God, which taketh away the sin of the world. (John 1: 29)

The bread that I will give is my flesh, which I will give for the life of the world. (John 6: 51)

Christ hath redeemed us from the curse for the law. (Gal. 3: 13)

We have redemption through His blood, even the forgiveness of sins. (Col. 1: 14)

The blood of Jesus Christ His Son cleanseth us from all sin. (1 John 1: 7)

Regret

It repented the Lord that He had made man on earth. (Gen. 6: 6)

Ye shall lothe yourselves in your own sight for all your evils that ye have committed. (Ezek. 20: 43)

There shall be weeping and gnashing of teeth. (Matt. 24: 51)

He found no place of repentance, though he sought it carefully with tears. (Heb. 12: 17)

Rejection

Thus saith the Lord God; Behold, I, even I, am against thee. (Ezek. 5: 8)

Ye are not My people, and I will not be your God. (Hos. 1: 9)

He that despiseth you despiseth me; and he that despiseth me despiseth Him that sent me. (Luke 10: 16)

He that denieth me before men shall be denied before the angels of God. (Luke 12: 9)

Depart from me, all ye workers of iniquity. (Luke 13: 27)

Whom He hath sent, Him ye believe not. (John 5: 38)

Reliability

It is better to trust in the Lord than to put confidence in man. (Ps. 118: 8)

A wicked messenger falleth into mischief: but a faithful ambassador is health. (Prov. 13: 17)

He that sendeth a message by the hand of a fool cutteth off the feet. (Prov. 26: 6)

The mountains shall depart, and the hills be removed; but My kindness shall not depart from thee. (Is. 54: 10)

What the Bible says about (47)

R continued

Remembrance

Forget not the Lord thy God.
(Deut. 8: 11)

They may forget, yet will I not forget thee. (Is. 49: 15)

They consider not in their hearts that I remember all their wickedness. (Hos. 7: 2)

This is my body, which is broken for you: this do in remembrance of me. (1 Cor. 11: 24)

This cup is the new testament in my blood: this do ye, as oft as ye drink it, in remembrance of me. (1 Cor. 11: 25)

Renewal

Be fruitful, and multiply, and replenish the earth. (Gen. 9: 1)

He restoreth my soul. (Ps. 23: 3)

A time to break down, and a time to build up. (Eccl. 3: 3)

Come, and let us join ourselves to the Lord. (Jer. 50: 5)

Turn Thou us into Thee, O Lord, and we shall be turned; renew our days as of old. (Lam. 5: 21)

Be renewed in the spirit of your mind. (Eph. 4: 23)

Behold, I make all things new. (Rev. 21: 5)

Repentance

I have sinned this time: the Lord is righteous, and I and my people are wicked. (Ex. 9: 27)

It is the blood that maketh an atonement for the soul. (Lev. 17: 11)

Make confession unto Him. (Josh. 7: 19)

Turn again unto the Lord. (2 Chr. 30: 9)

Fear the Lord, and depart from evil. (Prov. 3: 7)

By the fear of the Lord men depart from evil. (Prov. 16: 6)

Put away the evil of your doings from before Mine eyes. (Is. 1: 16)

Cease to do evil. (Is. 1: 16)

Turn thou unto Me. (Jer. 3: 7)

Come, and let us return unto the Lord. (Hos. 6: 1)

It is time to seek the Lord. (Hos. 10: 12)

Seek the Lord, and ye shall live. (Amos 5: 6)

Repent, for the kingdom of heaven is at hand. (Matt. 4: 17)

I am not come to call the righteous, but sinners to repentance. (Matt. 9: 13)

Except ye repent, ye shall all likewise perish. (Luke 13: 3)

Rejoice with me; for I have found my sheep which was lost. (Luke 15: 6)

Joy shall be in heaven over one sinner that repenteth, more than over ninety and nine just persons, which need no repentance. (Luke 15: 7)

There is joy in the presence of the angels of God over one sinner that repenteth. (Luke 15: 10)

When thou art converted, strengthen

thy brethren. (Luke 22: 32)

Repentance and remission of sins should be preached in His name among all nations. (Luke 24: 47)

Repent, and be baptized every one of you in the name of Jesus Christ. (Acts 2: 38)

The goodness of God leadeth thee to repentance. (Rom. 2: 4)

Remember therefore from whence thou art fallen, and repent. (Rev. 2: 5)

Repent; or else I will come unto thee quickly. (Rev. 2: 16)

Reputation

How are the mighty fallen! (2 Sam. 1: 19)

A good name is better than precious ointment. (Eccl. 7: 1)

A prophet is not without honor, save in his own country, and in his own house. (Matt. 13: 57)

Woe unto you, when all men shall speak well of you! (Luke 6: 26)

Ye know that our record is true. (3 John 12)

Respect

The excellency of dignity. (Gen. 49: 3)

Honor the face of the old man. (Lev. 19: 32)

My people shall know My name. (Is. 52: 6)

A prophet is not without honor, save in his own country, and in his own house. (Matt. 13: 57)

If I honor myself, my honor is nothing: it is my Father that honoreth me. (John 8: 54)

Walk honestly toward them that are without. (1 Thess. 4: 12)

Fear God. Honor the king. (1 Pet. 2: 17)

Submit yourselves unto the elder. (1 Pet. 5: 5)

Responsibility

Hast thou not procured this unto thyself, in that thou hast forsaken the Lord thy God? (Jer. 2: 17)

The soul that sinneth, it shall die. (Ezek. 18: 4,20)

Let the dead bury their dead. (Matt. 8: 22; Luke 9: 60)

Every idle word that men shall speak, they shall give account thereof in the day of judgment. (Matt. 12: 36)

Unto whomsoever much is given, of him shall be much required. (Luke 12: 48)

He that is faithful in that which is least is faithful also in much. (Luke 16: 10)

Father, forgive them; for they know not what they do. (Luke 23: 34)

The hireling fleeth, because he is an hireling, and careth not for the sheep. (John 10: 13)

Feed my lambs. (John 21: 15)

Feed my sheep. (John 21: 16,17)

Bear ye one another's burdens. (Gal. 6: 2)

Every man shall bear his own burdens. (Gal. 6: 5)

What the Bible says about (48)

R continued

Restitution

When ye go, ye shall not go empty. (Ex. 3: 21)

If the thief be found, let him pay double. (Ex. 22: 7)

Whom the judges shall condemn, he shall pay double unto his neighbor. (Ex. 22: 9)

He shall make amends for the harm that he hath done. (Lev. 5: 16)

He shall restore that which he took violently away. (Lev. 6: 4)

He that killeth a beast shall make it good; beast for beast. (Lev. 24: 18)

Restoration

The desert shall rejoice, and blossom as the rose. (Is. 35: 1)

The eyes of the blind shall be opened, and the ears of the deaf shall be unstopped. (Is. 35: 5)

Then shall the lame man leap as an hart, and the tongue of the dumb sing. (Is. 35: 6)

Restraint

Return every man to his house; for this thing is from Me. (1 Kings 12: 24)

Ye shall not go up, nor fight against your brethren. (2 Chr. 11: 4; 1 Kings 12: 24)

He that is slow to anger appeaseth strife. (Prov. 15: 18)

It is an honor for a man to cease from strife. (Prov. 20: 3)

Whoso keepeth his mouth and his tongue keepeth his soul from troubles. (Prov. 21: 23)

I will not ask, neither will I tempt the Lord. (Is. 7: 12)

Unto him that smiteth thee on the one cheek offer also the other. (Luke 6: 29)

Resurrection

He will swallow up death in victory. (Is. 25: 8)

Awake and sing, ye that dwell in dust. (Is. 26: 19)

The third day He shall rise again. (Matt. 20: 19; Mark 10: 34; Luke 18: 33)

God is not the God of the dead, but of the living. (Matt. 22: 32)

He is risen. (Matt. 28: 6; Mark 16: 6)

After that He is killed, He shall rise the third day. (Mark 9: 31)

They shall mock Him, and shall scourge Him, and shall spit upon Him, and shall kill Him: and the third day He shall rise again. (Mark 10: 34)

They are equal unto the angels; and are the children of God. (Luke 20: 36)

Destroy this temple, and in three days I will raise it up. (John 2: 19)

The hour is coming, in the which all that are in the graves shall hear His voice. (John 5: 28)

They that have done good, unto the resurrection of life; and they that have done evil, unto the resurrection of damnation. (John 5: 29)

Thy brother shall rise again.
(John 11: 23)
I am the resurrection, and the life.
(John 11: 25)
Lazarus, come forth. (John 11: 43)
I am He that liveth, and was dead.
(Rev. 1: 18)
I am alive for evermore. (Rev. 1: 18)

Revelation

No man knoweth the Son, but the
Father; neither knoweth any man
the Father, save the Son, and he to
whomsoever the Son reveal Him.
(Matt. 11: 27)
Flesh and blood hath not revealed
it unto thee, but my Father which is in
heaven. (Matt. 16: 17)
I that speak unto thee am He.
(John 4: 26)
I speak to the world those things
which I have heard of Him. (John 8: 26)
I have not spoken of myself; but the
Father which sent me. (John 12: 49)
He that hath seen me hath seen the
Father. (John 14: 9)
All things that I have heard of my
Father I have made known unto you.
(John 15: 15)
I have appeared unto thee for this
purpose, to make thee a minister and a
witness. (Acts 26: 16)

Revenge

Thou shalt give life for life, Eye for eye,
tooth for tooth, hand for hand, foot for
foot, Burning for burning, wound for
wound, stripe for stripe. (Ex. 21: 23–25)

Turn their reproach upon their own
head. (Neh. 4: 4)
Destroy Thou them, O God; let them
fall by their own counsels. (Ps. 5: 10)
Keep not Thou silence, O God: hold
not Thy peace. (Ps. 83: 1)
God, to whom vengeance belongeth.
(Ps. 94: 1)
Take vengeance upon her; as she
hath done, do unto her. (Jer. 50: 15)
Do unto them, as Thou hast done
unto me. (Lam. 1: 22)
As thou hast done, it shall be done
unto thee. (Obad. 15)
God is jealous, and the Lord
revengeth. (Nah. 1: 2)
Whosoever shall smite thee on thy
right cheek, turn to him the other also.
(Matt. 5: 39)
Unto him that smiteth thee on the
one cheek offer also the other.
(Luke 6: 29)
The Son of man is not come to
destroy men's lives, but to save them.
(Luke 9: 56)
Vengeance belongeth unto Me, I will
recompense, saith the Lord.
(Heb. 10: 30)
The great winepress of the wrath of
God. (Rev. 14: 19)

What the Bible says about (49)

R continued

Reverence

Thou shalt fear the Lord thy God; Him shalt thou serve, and to Him shalt thou cleave, and swear by His name. (Deut. 10: 20)

Fear the Lord, and serve Him, and obey His voice. (1 Sam. 12: 14)

As the heaven is high above the earth, so great is His mercy toward them that fear Him. (Ps. 103: 11)

Every tongue should confess that Jesus Christ is Lord. (Phil. 2: 11)

Fear God, and give glory to him; for the hour of His judgment is come. (Rev. 14: 7)

Reward

If thou doest well, shalt thou not be accepted? (Gen. 4: 7)

In thy seed shall all the nations of the earth be blessed; because thou hast obeyed My voice. (Gen. 22: 18)

If ye will obey My voice indeed, and keep My covenant, then ye shall be a peculiar treasure unto Me above all people: for all the earth is Mine. (Ex. 19: 5)

I will walk among you, and will be your God, and ye shall be My people. (Lev. 26: 12)

The Lord render to every man his righteousness and his faithfulness. (1 Sam. 26: 23)

Ask what I shall give thee. (1 Kings 3: 5; 2 Chr. 1: 7)

I have also given thee that which thou hast not asked, both riches, and honor. (1 Kings 3: 13)

Blessed are the meek: for they shall inherit the earth. (Matt. 5: 5)

Great is your reward in heaven. (Matt. 5: 12)

Thy Father which seeth in secret shall reward thee openly. (Matt. 6: 6; Matt. 6: 18)

Every one that asketh receiveth. (Matt. 7: 8; Luke 11: 10)

According to your faith be it unto you. (Matt. 9: 29)

Freely ye have received, freely give. (Matt. 10: 8)

He shall reward every man according to his works. (Matt. 16: 27)

To sit on my right hand, and on my left, is not mine to give, but it shall be given to them for whom it is prepared of my Father. (Matt. 20: 23)

He that hath, to him shall be given: and he that hath not, from him shall be taken even that which he hath. (Mark 4: 25)

Seek ye the kingdom of God; and all these things shall be added unto you. (Luke 12: 31)

When thou makest a feast, call the poor, the maimed, the lame, the blind: And thou shalt be blessed; for they cannot recompense thee. (Luke 14: 13,14)

Thou shalt be recompensed at the resurrection of the just. (Luke 14: 14)

He that reapeth receiveth wages, and gathereth fruit unto life eternal. (John 4: 36)

If any man serve me, him will my Father honor. (John 12: 26)

To him that overcometh will I give to eat of the hidden manna. (Rev. 2: 17)

And I will give him the morning star. (Rev. 2: 28)

They shall walk with me in white: for they are worthy. (Rev. 3: 4)

Him that overcometh will I make a pillar in the temple of my God. (Rev. 3: 12)

Rich

And again I say unto you, It is easier for a camel to go through the eye of a needle, than for a rich man to enter into the kingdom of God. (Matt. 19: 24)

Riddles

Out of the eater came forth meat, and out of the strong came forth sweetness. (Judg. 14: 14)

What is sweeter than honey? and what is stronger than a lion? (Judg. 14: 18)

Righteousness

O Lord, righteousness belongeth unto Thee. (Dan. 9: 7)

Sow to yourselves in righteousness, reap in mercy. (Hos. 10: 12)

Do justly. (Mic. 6: 8)

It becometh us to fulfill all righteousness. (Matt. 3: 15)

Blessed are they which do hunger and thirst after righteousness: for they shall be filled. (Matt. 5: 6)

Blessed are they which are persecuted for righteousness' sake: for theirs is the kingdom of heaven. (Matt. 5: 10)

He that receiveth a righteous man in the name of a righteous man shall receive a righteous man's reward. (Matt. 10: 41)

If ye were Abraham's children, ye would do the works of Abraham. (John 8: 39)

The just shall live by faith. (Rom. 1: 17)

All unrighteousness is sin. (1 John 5: 17)

They shall walk with me in white: for they are worthy. (Rev. 3: 4)

Just and true are Thy ways, Thou King of saints. (Rev. 15: 3)

Behold a white horse; and he that sat upon him was called Faithful and True. (Rev. 19: 11)

Robbery

Thou shalt not steal. (Ex. 20: 15)

If the thief be found, let him pay double. (Ex. 22: 7)

Rob not the poor, because he is poor: neither oppress the afflicted in the gate. (Prov. 22: 22)

What the Bible says about (50)

S

Sabbath

And God blessed the seventh day, and sanctified it: because that in it He had rested from all His work which God created and made. (Gen. 2: 3)

Remember the sabbath day, to keep it holy. (Ex. 20: 8)

Six days thou shalt do thy work, and on the seventh day thou shalt rest. (Ex. 23: 12)

My sabbaths ye shall keep: for it is a sign between Me and you throughout your generations. (Ex. 31: 13)

Sacrifice

He that loseth his life for my sake shall find it. (Matt. 10: 39)

Whosoever will save his life shall lose it: and whosoever will lose his life for my sake shall find it. (Matt. 16: 25)

The Son of man came not to be ministered unto, but to minister, and to give His life a ransom for many. (Matt. 20: 28; Mark 10: 45)

For God so loved the world, that He gave His only begotten Son, that whosoever believeth in Him should not perish, but have everlasting life. (John 3: 16)

The bread that I will give is my flesh, which I will give for the life of the world. (John 6: 51)

The good shepherd giveth his life for the sheep. (John 10: 11)

Greater love hath no man than this, that a man lay down his life for his friends. (John 15: 13)

Glorify Thy Son, that Thy Son also may glorify Thee. (John 17: 1)

This is my body, which is broken for you: this do in remembrance of me. (1 Cor. 11: 24)

Christ died for our sins. (1 Cor. 15: 3)

He died for all. (2 Cor. 5: 15)

Sacrifices

Behold the fire and the wood: but where is the lamb for the burnt offering? (Gen. 22: 7)

He that sacrificeth unto any god, save unto the Lord only, he shall be utterly destroyed. (Ex. 22: 20)

If thou wilt offer a burnt offering, thou must offer it unto the Lord. (Judg. 13: 16)

To obey is better than sacrifice, and to hearken than the fat of rams. (1 Sam. 15: 22)

I desired mercy, and not sacrifice; and the knowledge of God more than burnt offerings. (Hos. 6: 6)

Sacrilege

I will curse your blessings. (Mal. 2: 2)

My house is the house of prayer: but ye have made it a den of thieves. (Luke 19: 46)

Make not my Father's house an house of merchandise. (John 2:16)

If any man defile the temple of God, him shall God destroy. (1 Cor. 3:17)

Safety

Deliver me not over unto the will of mine enemies: for false witnesses are risen up against me. (Ps. 27:12)

God is our refuge and strength, a very present help in trouble. (Ps. 46:1)

Hold Thou me up, and I shall be safe. (Ps. 119:117)

He that followeth me shall not walk in darkness. (John 8:12)

I am with thee, and no man shall set on thee to hurt thee. (Acts 18:10)

Salvation

Salvation belongeth unto the Lord. (Ps. 3:8)

My soul waiteth upon God: from Him cometh my salvation. (Ps. 62:1)

Strait is the gate, and narrow is the way, which leadeth unto life, and few there be that find it. (Matt. 7:14)

The kingdom of heaven is at hand. (Matt. 10:7)

The keys of the kingdom of heaven. (Matt. 16:19)

Whosoever will save his life shall lose it: and whosoever will lose his life for my sake shall find it. (Matt. 16:25)

The Son of man is come to save that which was lost. (Matt. 18:11)

Who then can be saved? (Matt. 19:25, Mark 10:26)

He that shall endure unto the end, the same shall be saved. (Matt. 24:13; Mark 13:13)

The kingdom of God is at hand: repent ye, and believe the gospel. (Mark 1:15)

The Son of man is not come to destroy men's lives, but to save them. (Luke 9:56)

Sanctuary

And they shall be your refuge from the avenger of blood. (Josh. 20:3)

They shall not deliver the slayer up into his hand; because he smote his neighbor unwittingly, and hated him not beforetime. (Josh. 20:5)

Let her not be slain in the house of the Lord. (2 Kings 11:15)

What the Bible says about (51)

S continued

Satan

If Satan cast out Satan, he is divided against himself; how shall then his kingdom stand? (Matt. 12: 26)

Get thee behind me, Satan: thou art an offence unto me. (Matt. 16: 23)

I beheld Satan as lightning fall from heaven. (Luke 10: 18)

Ye are of your father the devil, and the lusts of your father ye will do. (John 8: 44)

There is no truth in him. (John 8: 44)

He is a liar, and the father of it. (John 8: 44)

Now is the judgment of this world: now shall the prince of this world be cast out. (John 12: 31)

Satisfaction

And God saw the light, that it was good. (Gen. 1: 4)

And God saw every thing that He had made, and, behold, it was very good. (Gen. 1: 31)

Glory of this, and tarry at home. (2 Kings 14: 10)

A good man shall be satisfied from himself. (Prov. 14: 14)

Hell and destruction are never full; so the eyes of man are never satisfied. (Prov. 27: 20)

Thou sayest, I am rich, and increased with goods, and have need of nothing; and knowest not that thou art wretched, and miserable, and poor, and blind, and naked. (Rev. 3: 17)

Scapegoat

One lot for the Lord, and the other lot for the scapegoat. (Lev. 16: 8)

Let him go for a scapegoat into the wilderness. (Lev. 16: 10)

The goat shall bear upon him all their iniquities. (Lev. 16: 22)

Scheming

Let the wicked fall into their own nets. (Ps. 141: 10)

The way of the wicked He turneth upside down. (Ps. 146: 9)

The wicked shall fall by his own wickedness. (Prov. 11: 5)

Whoso diggeth a pit shall fall therein. (Prov. 26: 27)

Let none of you imagine evil in your hearts against his neighbor. (Zech. 8: 17)

Scorn

Hear, O our God; for we are despised. (Neh. 4: 4)

When thou mockest, shall no man make thee ashamed? (Job 11: 3)

He addeth rebellion unto his sin. (Job 34: 37)

Ye have wearied the Lord with your words. (Mal. 2: 17)

A crown of thorns. (Matt. 27: 29, Mark 15: 17; John 19: 2)

So is the will of God, that with well doing ye may put to silence the ignorance of foolish men. (1 Pet. 2: 15)

Scripture

Thy word is a lamp unto my feet, and a light unto my path. (Ps. 119: 105)

Thy word is true from the beginning. (Ps. 119: 160)

Seek ye out of the book of the Lord, and read. (Is. 34: 16)

I am not come to destroy, but to fulfill. (Matt. 5: 17)

This day is this Scripture fulfilled in your ears. (Luke 4: 21)

The law and the prophets were until John: since that time the kingdom of God is preached. (Luke 16: 16)

If ye believe not his writings, how shall ye believe my words? (John 5: 47)

Blessed is he that readeth, and they that hear the words of this prophecy. (Rev. 1: 3)

Searching

Ye shall seek Me, and find Me, when ye shall search for Me with all your heart. (Jer. 29: 13)

It is time to seek the Lord. (Hos. 10: 12)

Seek good, and not evil, that ye may live. (Amos 5: 14)

Seek ye first the kingdom of God, and His righteousness. (Matt. 6: 33)

Seek, and ye shall find. (Matt. 7: 7; Luke 11: 9)

Ye shall seek me, and shall not find me: and where I am, thither ye cannot come. (John 7: 34)

The Spirit searcheth all things. (1 Cor. 2: 10)

I am He which searcheth the reins and hearts. (Rev. 2: 23)

Seasons

While the earth remaineth, seedtime and harvest, and cold and heat, and summer and winter, and day and night shall not cease. (Gen. 8: 22)

By the breath of God frost is given. (Job 37: 10)

Who can stand before His cold? (Ps. 147: 17)

To every thing there is a season, and a time to every purpose under the heaven. (Eccl. 3: 1)

Lo, the winter is past, the rain is over and gone. (Song 2: 11)

The flowers appear on the earth; the time of the singing of birds is come, and the voice of the turtle is heard in our land. (Song 2: 12)

The harvest is past, the summer is ended, and we are not saved. (Jer. 8: 20)

Second coming

The end is not yet. (Matt. 24: 6)

As the lightning cometh out of the east, and shineth even unto the west; so shall also the coming of the Son of man be. (Matt. 24: 27)

Of that day and hour knoweth no man, no, not the angels of heaven, but my Father only. (Matt. 24: 36)

What the Bible says about (52)

Second coming, continued

Watch therefore: for ye know not what hour your Lord doth come. (Matt. 24: 42)

Be ye also ready. (Matt. 24: 44)

Take ye heed, watch and pray: for ye know not when the time is. (Mark 13: 33)

If the goodman of the house had known what hour the thief would come, he would have watched. (Luke 12: 39)

Be ye therefore ready also: for the Son of man cometh at an hour when ye think not. (Luke 12: 40)

I will come again. (John 14: 3)

If I will that he tarry till I come, what is that to thee? (John 21: 22)

I will come on thee as a thief. (Rev. 3: 3)

Thou shalt not know what hour I will come upon thee. (Rev. 3: 3)

Behold, I come quickly. (Rev. 22: 7,12)

Secrecy

Be sure your sin will find you out. (Num. 32: 23)

The secret things belong unto the Lord our God: but those things which are revealed belong unto us and to our children for ever. (Deut. 29: 29)

See that no man know it. (Matt. 9: 30)

Nothing is secret, that shall not be made manifest; neither any thing hid, that shall not be known. (Luke 8: 17)

There is nothing covered, that shall not be revealed; neither hid, that shall not be known. (Luke 12: 2)

That which ye have spoken in the ear in closets shall be proclaimed upon the housetops. (Luke 12: 3)

God knoweth your hearts. (Luke 16: 15)

Every one that doeth evil hateth the light. (John 3: 20)

I have called you friends; for all things that I have heard of my Father I have made known unto you. (John 15: 15)

The Spirit searcheth all things. (1 Cor. 2: 10)

I am He which searcheth the reins and hearts. (Rev. 2: 23)

Security

As thy days, so shall thy strength be. (Deut. 33: 25)

The Lord is our defense. (Ps. 89: 18)

Foxes have holes, and birds of the air have nests; but the Son of man hath not where to lay His head. (Luke 9: 58)

Self-awareness

let us search and try our ways, and turn again to the Lord. (Lam. 3: 40)

Why beholdest thou the mote that is in thy brother's eye, but considerest not the beam that is in thine own eye. (Matt. 7: 3)

Examine yourselves, whether ye be in the faith. (2 Cor. 13: 5)

Self-control

Take ye therefore good heed unto yourselves. (Deut. 4: 15)

Set a watch, O Lord, before my mouth; keep the door of my lips. (Ps. 141: 3)

He that hath no rule over his own spirit is like a city that is broken down. (Prov. 25: 28)

What I hate, that do I. (Rom. 7: 15)

The good that I would I do not: but the evil which I would not, that I do. (Rom. 7: 19)

Be sober, be vigilant; because your adversary the devil, as a roaring lion, walketh about, seeking whom he may devour. (1 Pet. 5: 8)

Self-deception

Deceive not yourselves. (Jer. 37: 9)

Thy terribleness hath deceived thee, and the pride of thine heart. (Jer. 49: 16)

Professing themselves to be wise, they became fools. (Rom. 1: 22)

If any man think that he knoweth any thing, he knoweth nothing yet as he ought to know. (1 Cor. 8: 2)

Thou sayest, I am rich, and increased with goods, and have need of nothing; and knowest not that thou art wretched, and miserable, and poor, and blind, and naked. (Rev. 3: 17)

Self-denial

As thou livest, and as thy soul liveth, I will not do this thing. (2 Sam. 11: 11)

Be it as far from me, O Lord, that I should do this. (2 Sam. 23: 17)

Whosoever will come after me, let him deny himself, and take up his cross, and follow me. (Mark 8: 34)

Whosoever he be of you that forsaketh not all that he hath, he cannot be my disciple. (Luke 14: 33)

Make not provision for the flesh, to fulfill the lusts thereof. (Rom. 13: 14)

Self-hatred

I abhor myself, and repent in dust and ashes. (Job 42: 6)

Whoso is partner with a thief hateth his own soul. (Prov. 29: 24)

Ye shall lothe yourselves in your own sight for all your evils that ye have committed. (Ezek. 20: 43)

O wretched man that I am! who shall deliver me from the body of this death? (Rom. 7: 24)

Self-incrimination

The man that hath done this thing shall surely die. (2 Sam. 12: 5)

Thine own lips testify against thee. (Job 15: 6)

Wherein thou judgest another, thou condemnest thyself. (Rom. 2: 1)

What the Bible says about (53)

S continued

Self-Interest

If ye do good to them which do good to you, what thank have ye? for sinners also do even the same. (Luke 6: 33)

Sinners also lend to sinners, to receive as much again. (Luke 6: 34)

When thou makest a feast, call the poor, and maimed, the lame, the blind: And thou shalt be blessed; for they cannot recompense thee. (Luke 14: 13–14)

We preach not ourselves, but Christ Jesus the Lord. (2 Cor. 4: 5)

Self-Pity

Kill me, I pray thee, out of hand, if I have found favor in Thy sight; and let me not see my wretchedness. (Num. 11: 15)

Mark me, and be astonished. (Job 21: 5)

Woe is me now! for the Lord hath added grief to my sorrow. (Jer. 45: 3)

Self-Righteousness

He was righteous in his own eyes. (Job 32: 1)

Be not righteous over much; neither make thyself over wise. (Eccl. 7: 16)

I am holier than thou. (Is. 65: 5)

The time cometh, that whosoever killeth you will think that he doeth God service. (John 16: 2)

Selfishness

I was an hungered, and ye gave me no meat: I was thirsty, and ye gave me no drink. (Matt. 25: 42)

Whosoever shall seek to save his life shall lose it; and whosoever shall lose his life shall preserve it. (Luke 17: 33)

He that loveth his life shall lose it; and he that hateth his life in this world shall keep it unto life eternal. (John 12: 25)

Selflessness

Would God that all the Lord's people were prophets, and that the Lord would put His spirit upon them! (Num. 11: 29)

Thou shalt be king over Israel, and I shall be next unto thee. (1 Sam. 23: 17)

Shall I drink the blood of these men that have put their lives in jeopardy? (1 Chr. 11: 19)

If I go not away, the Comforter will not come unto you. (John 16: 7)

I have coveted no man's silver, or gold, or apparel. (Acts 20: 33)

Even Christ pleased not Himself. (Rom. 15: 3)

Separation

The Lord do so to me, and more also, if ought but death part thee and me. (Ruth 1: 17)

In their death they were not divided. (2 Sam. 1: 23)

Whither I go, ye cannot come. (John 8: 21; John 13: 33)

Who shall separate us from the love of Christ? shall tribulation, or distress, or persecution, or famine, or nakedness, or peril, or sword? (Rom. 8: 35)

Serenity

The Lord is my shepherd; I shall not want. (Ps. 23: 1)

Great peace have they which love Thy law. (Ps. 119: 165)

There is no peace, saith the Lord, unto the wicked. (Is. 48: 22)

Peace be with you all that are in Christ Jesus. (1 Pet. 5: 14)

Service to God

Serve the Lord thy God with all thy heart and with all thy soul. (Deut. 10: 12)

Serve ye the Lord. (Josh. 24: 14)

Deliver us out of the hand of our enemies, and we will serve Thee. (1 Sam. 12: 10)

Let it be known this day that Thou art God in Israel, and that I am Thy servant. (1 Kings 18: 36)

Serve Him with a perfect heart and with a willing mind. (1 Chr. 28: 9)

Minister unto Him. (2 Chr. 29: 11)

Serve the Lord your God, that the fierceness of His wrath may turn away from you. (2 Chr. 30: 8)

Serve the Lord with gladness: come before His presence with singing. (Ps. 100: 2)

If any man serve me, him will my Father honor. (John 12: 26)

We should serve in newness of spirit, and not in the oldness of the letter. (Rom. 7: 6)

He that is called, being free, is Christ's servant. (1 Cor. 7: 22)

There are differences of administrations, but the same Lord. (1 Cor. 12: 5)

Severity

My punishment is greater than I can bear. (Gen. 4: 13)

My little finger shall be thicker than my father's loins. (1 Kings 12: 10; 2 Chr. 10: 10)

Thou hast broken the yokes of wood; but thou shalt make for them yokes of iron. (Jer. 28: 13)

It shall be more tolerable for the land of Sodom in the day of judgment, than for thee. (Matt. 11: 24)

Shame

Let me not be ashamed, let not mine enemies triumph over me. (Ps. 25: 2)

When pride cometh, then cometh shame. (Prov. 11: 2)

All that forsake Thee shall be shamed. (Jer. 17: 13)

Whosoever shall be ashamed of me and of my words, of him shall the son of man be ashamed. (Luke 9: 26)

What the Bible says about (54)

S continued

Sharing

It is not meet to take the children's bread, and to cast it to dogs. (Matt. 15: 26)

Him they compelled to bear His cross. (Matt. 27: 32)

I have called you friends; for all things that I have heard of my Father I have made known unto you. (John 15: 15)

Bear ye one another's burdens. (Gal. 6: 2)

Sight

The light of the body is the eye. (Matt. 6: 22; Luke 11: 34)

If thine eye offend thee, pluck it out, and cast it from thee. (Matt. 18: 9)

It is better for thee to enter into the kingdom of God with one eye, than having two eyes to be cast into hell fire. (Mark 9: 47)

We walk by faith, not by sight. (2 Cor. 5: 7)

Anoint thine eyes with eyesalve, that thou mayest see. (Rev. 3: 18)

Silence

As people being ashamed steal away when they flee in battle. (2 Sam. 19: 3)

If I hold my tongue, I shall give up the Spirit. (Job 13: 19)

Hold thy peace, and I shall teach thee wisdom. (Job 33: 33)

He that refraineth his lips is wise. (Prov. 10: 19)

Even a fool, when he holdeth his peace, is counted wise. (Prov. 17: 28)

A time to keep silence, and a time to speak. (Eccl. 3: 7)

Sin

She took of the fruit thereof, and did eat. (Gen. 3: 6)

If thou doest not well, sin lieth at the door. (Gen. 4: 7)

Be sure your sin will find you out. (Num. 32: 23)

We have sinned, because we have forsaken the Lord. (1 Sam. 12: 10)

There is no man that sinneth not. (1 Kings 8: 46; 2 Chr. 6: 36)

Every man shall be put to death for his own sin. (2 Kings 14: 6)

All manner of sin and blasphemy shall be forgiven unto men: but the blasphemy against the Holy Spirit shall not be forgiven unto men. (Matt. 12: 31)

Not that which goeth into the mouth defileth a man; but that which cometh out of the mouth, this defileth a man. (Matt. 15: 11)

Out of the heart proceed evil thoughts, murders, adulteries, fornications, thefts, false witness, blasphemies. (Matt. 15: 19)

The spirit indeed is willing, but the flesh is weak. (Matt. 26: 41)

All these evil things come from within, and defile the man. (Mark 7: 23)

It is better for thee to enter into the kingdom of God with one eye, than

having two eyes to be cast into hell fire.
(Mark 9: 47)

Forgive us our sins. (Luke 11: 4)

There is nothing covered, that shall
not be revealed; neither hid, that shall
not be known. (Luke 12: 2)

Sin no more, lest a worse thing come
unto thee. (John 5: 14)

He that is without sin among you, let
him first cast a stone. (John 8: 7)

Woman, where are those thine
accusers? (John 8: 10)

Go, and sin no more. (John 8: 11)

Whosoever committeth sin is the
servant of sin. (John 8: 34)

If ye were blind, ye should have no
sin. (John 9: 41)

Now they have no cloak for their sin.
(John 15: 22)

In Him is no sin. (1 John 3: 5)

Whosoever abideth in Him sinneth
not. (1 John 3: 6)

All unrighteousness is sin. (1 John 5: 17)

Be not partakers of her sins. (Rev. 18: 4)

Her sins have reached unto heaven,
and God hath remembered her
iniquities. (Rev. 18: 5)

Sincerity

Not every one that saith unto me, Lord,
Lord, shall enter into the kingdom of
heaven. (Matt. 7: 21)

Why call ye me, Lord, Lord, and do
not the things which I say? (Luke 6: 46)

They that worship Him must
worship Him in spirit and in truth.
(John 4: 24)

If God were your Father, ye would
love me: for I proceeded forth and
came from God. (John 8: 42)

The kingdom of God is not in word,
but in power. (1 Cor. 4: 20)

Be ye doers of the word, and not
hearers only. (James 1: 22)

Sanctify the Lord God in your hearts.
(1 Pet. 3: 15)

Sinners

The light of the wicked shall be put out,
and the spark of his fire shall not shine.
(Job 18: 5)

The Lord knoweth the way of the
righteous: but the way of the ungodly
shall perish. (Ps. 1: 6)

Let the sinners be consumed out
of the earth, and let the wicked be no
more. (Ps. 104: 35)

Evil pursueth sinners. (Prov. 13: 21)

Let not thine heart envy sinners.
(Prov. 23: 17)

They that be whole need not a
physician, but they that are sick.
(Matt. 9: 12)

Sinners also lend to sinners, to
receive as much again. (Luke 6: 34)

Christ died for the ungodly.
(Rom. 5: 6)

What the Bible says about (55)

S continued

Size

There were giants in the earth in those days. (Gen. 6: 4)

We were in our own sight as grasshoppers. (Num. 13: 33)

The ants are a people not strong, yet they prepare their meat in the summer. (Prov. 30: 25)

Which of you by taking thought can add one cubit unto his stature? (Matt. 6: 27)

A little leaven leaveneth the whole lump. (1 Cor. 5: 6, Gal. 5: 9)

Skepticism

An evil and adulterous generation seeketh after a sign; and there shall no sign be given to it, but the sign of the prophet Jonas. (Matt. 12: 39)

But whom say ye that I am? (Matt. 16: 15; Mark 8: 29)

If they hear not Moses and the prophets, neither will they be persuaded, though one rose from the dead. (Luke 16: 31)

O fools, and slow of heart to believe all that the prophets have spoken. (Luke 24: 25)

If I have told you earthly things, and ye believe not, how shall ye believe, if I tell you of heavenly things? (John 3: 12)

Except ye see signs and wonders, ye will not believe. (John 4: 48)

Had ye believed Moses, ye would have believed me: for he wrote of me. (John 5: 46)

Because I tell you the truth, ye believe me not. (John 8: 45)

Though ye believe not me, believe the works. (John 10: 38)

Blessed are they that have not seen, and yet have believed. (John 20: 29)

Believe not every spirit. (1 John 4: 1)

Slander

Thy tongue deviseth mischiefs; like a sharp razor, working deceitfully. (Ps. 52: 2)

Swords are in their lips. (Ps. 59: 7)

Deliver my soul, O Lord, from lying lips, and from a deceitful tongue. (Ps. 120: 2)

Do violence to no man, neither accuse any falsely. (Luke 3: 14)

Speak evil of no man. (Titus 3: 2)

Slavery

I am the Lord thy God, which have brought thee out of the land of Egypt, out of the house of bondage. (Ex. 20: 2)

Thou shalt not deliver unto his master the servant which is escaped from his master unto thee. (Deut. 23: 15)

He that leadeth into captivity shall go into captivity. (Rev. 13: 10)

Sleep

I will not give sleep to mine eyes, or slumber to mine eyelids, Until I find out a place for the Lord. (Ps. 132: 4–5)

Love not sleep, lest thou come to poverty. (Prov. 20: 13)

Drowsiness shall clothe a man with rags. (Prov. 23: 21)

The sleep of a laboring man is sweet. (Eccl. 5: 12)

Snakes

Now the serpent was more subtle than any beast of the field. (Gen. 3: 1)

Thou art cursed above all cattle, and above every beast of the field. (Gen. 3: 14)

Upon thy belly shalt thou go, and dust shalt thou eat all the days of thy life. (Gen. 3: 14)

Be ye therefore wise as serpents, and harmless as doves. (Matt. 10: 16)

Sodomy

Sodom and Gomorrah. (Gen. 18: 20, Gen. 19: 28)

Whosoever lieth with a beast shall surely be put to death. (Ex. 22: 19)

Cursed be he that lieth with any manner of beast. (Deut. 27: 21)

Song

With my song will I praise Him. (Ps. 28: 7)

Sing unto God, ye kingdoms of the earth; O sing praises unto the Lord. (Ps. 68: 32)

Sing unto the Lord, all the earth. (Ps. 96: 1; 1 Chr. 16: 23)

Sing unto Him, sing psalms unto Him: talk ye of all His wondrous works. (Ps. 105: 2; 1 Chr. 16: 9)

Sing unto the Lord; for He hath done excellent things. (Is. 12: 5)

Sorrow

Mine eye affecteth mine heart. (Lam. 3: 51)

Ye shall be sorrowful, but your sorrow shall be turned into joy. (John 16: 20)

Be of good cheer; I have overcome the world. (John 16: 33)

There shall be no more death, neither sorrow, nor crying, neither shall there be any more pain: for the former things are passed away. (Rev. 21: 4)

Soul

None can keep alive his own soul. (Ps. 22: 29)

He restoreth my soul. (Ps. 23: 3)

He that winneth souls is wise. (Prov. 11: 30)

A true witness delivereth souls. (Prov. 14: 25)

He that keepeth the commandment keepeth his own soul; but he that despiseth His ways shall die. (Prov. 19: 16)

Behold, all souls are Mine. (Ezek. 18: 4)

Fear not them which kill the body, but are not able to kill the soul. (Matt. 10: 28)

What shall a man give in exchange for his soul? (Matt. 16: 26; Mark 8: 37)

What shall it profit a man, if he shall gain the whole world, and lose his own soul? (Mark 8: 36)

What the Bible says about (56)

S continued

Sovereignty

The Lord shall reign for ever and ever. (Ex. 15: 18)

The kingdom is the Lord's. (Ps. 22: 28)

God is the King of all the earth: sing ye praises with understanding. (Ps. 47: 7)

The Lord reigneth; let the earth rejoice. (Ps. 97: 1)

The kingdom shall be the Lord's. (Obad. 21)

Of His kingdom there shall be no end. (Luke 1: 33)

Thy throne, O God, is for ever and ever. (Heb. 1: 8)

Speech

How can ye, being evil, speak good things? (Matt. 12: 34)

Out of the abundance of the heart the mouth speaketh. (Matt. 12: 34)

A good man out of the good treasure of the heart bringeth forth good things: and an evil man out of the evil treasure bringeth forth evil things. (Matt. 12: 35)

Every idle word that men shall speak, they shall give account thereof in the day of judgment. (Matt. 12: 36)

By thy words thou shalt be justified, and by thy words thou shalt be condemned. (Matt. 12: 37)

Not that which goeth into the mouth defileth a man; but that which cometh out of the mouth, this defileth a man. (Matt. 15: 11)

Speed

They were swifter than eagles, they were stronger than lions. (2 Sam. 1: 23)

He did fly upon the wings of the wind. (Ps. 18: 10)

That thou doest, do quickly. (John 13: 27)

In the twinkling of an eye. (1 Cor. 15: 52)

Spies

Ye are spies; to see the nakedness of the land ye are come. (Gen. 42: 9)

Spiritualism

Regard not them that have familiar spirits, neither seek after wizards, to be defiled by them. (Lev. 19: 31)

All that do these things are an abomination unto the Lord. (Deut. 18: 12)

Bring me up Samuel. (1 Sam. 28: 11)

Why hast thou disquieted me, to bring me up? (1 Sam. 28: 15)

Spirituality

In Thy light shall we see light. (Ps. 36: 9)

Create in me a clean heart, O God; and renew a right spirit within me. (Ps. 51: 10)

Lay up for yourselves treasures in heaven, where neither moth nor rust doth corrupt, and where thieves do not break through nor steal. (Matt. 6: 20)

The light of the body is the eye. (Matt. 6: 22; Luke 11: 34)

Seek ye first the kingdom of God, and His righteousness. (Matt. 6: 33)

To give light to them that sit in darkness. (Luke 1: 79)

Take heed therefore that the light which is in thee be not darkness. (Luke 11: 35)

Except a man be born again, he cannot see the kingdom of God. (John 3: 3)

That which is born of the flesh is flesh; and that which is born of the Spirit is spirit. (John 3: 6)

I have meat to eat that ye know not of. (John 4: 32)

If any man thirst, let him come unto me, and drink. (John 7: 37)

The darkness is past, and the true light now shineth. (1 John 2: 8)

Spoils of war

There shall cleave nought of the cursed thing to thine hand. (Deut. 13: 17)

Keep yourselves from the accursed thing, lest ye make yourselves accursed. (Josh. 6: 18)

Divide the spoil of your enemies with your brethren. (Josh. 22: 8)

Whomsoever the Lord our God shall drive out from before us, them will we possess. (Judg. 11: 24)

Spokesmen

He shall be to thee instead of a mouth, and thou shalt be to him instead of God. (Ex. 4: 16)

I am come in my Father's name, and ye receive me not. (John 5: 43)

He that receiveth whomsoever I send

receiveth me. (John 13: 20)

He is a chosen vessel unto me, to bear my name. (Acts 9: 15)

I am an ambassador in bonds. (Eph. 6: 20)

Status

The Lord maketh poor, and maketh rich: He bringeth low, and lifteth up. (1 Sam. 2: 7)

The disciple is not above his master, nor the servant above his lord. (Matt. 10: 24)

The servant is not greater than his lord; neither he that is sent greater than he that sent him. (John 13: 16)

Steadfastness

Be not moved away from the hope of the gospel. (Col. 1: 23)

Hold fast to that which is good. (1 Thess. 5: 21)

We are not of them who draw back unto perdition; but of them that believe to the saving of the soul. (Heb. 10: 39)

What the Bible says about (57)

S continued

Strategy

Take an heifer with thee, and say, I am come to sacrifice to the Lord. (1 Sam. 16: 2)

I will be a lying spirit in the mouth of all his prophets. (1 Kings 22: 22)

Be ye therefore wise as serpents, and harmless as doves. (Matt. 10: 16)

Strength

The Lord is my strength and song, and He is become my salvation. (Ex. 15: 2)

Hast thou an arm like God? (Job 40: 9)

The Lord is my strength and my shield. (Ps. 28: 7)

A wise man is strong. (Prov. 24: 5)

Wisdom is better than strength. (Eccl. 9: 16)

Wisdom and might are His. (Dan. 2: 20)

The Lord God is my strength. (Hab. 3: 19)

Upon this rock I will build my church; and the gates of hell shall not prevail against it. (Matt. 16: 18)

My strength is made perfect in weakness. (2 Cor. 12: 9)

Strife

A man's foes shall be they of his own household. (Matt. 10: 36)

If a house be divided against itself, that house cannot stand. (Mark 3: 25)

Suppose ye that I am come to give peace on earth? I tell you, Nay; but rather division. (Luke 12: 51)

The father shall be divided against the son, and the son against the father; the mother against the daughter, and the daughter against the mother. (Luke 12: 53)

Be at peace among yourselves. (1 Thess. 5: 13)

Stubbornness

Thou art a stiffnecked people. (Ex. 33: 3)

Stubbornness is as iniquity and idolatry. (1 Sam. 15: 23)

If ye will hear His voice, Harden not your heart. (Ps. 95: 7–8)

They are brass and iron; they are all corrupters. (Jer. 6: 28)

Having eyes, see ye not? and having ears, hear ye not? (Mark 8: 18)

Success

The righteous shall inherit the land. (Ps. 37: 29)

They go from strength to strength. (Ps. 84: 7)

This is the Lord's doing; it is marvelous in our eyes. (Ps. 118: 23)

Many that are first shall be last; and the last shall be first. (Mark 10: 31)

The stone which the builders rejected is become the head of the corner. (Mark 12: 10)

A man's life consisteth not in the abundance of the things which he possesseth. (Luke 12: 15)

Unto whomsoever much is given, of him shall be much required. (Luke 12: 48)

The word of God grew and multiplied. (Acts 12: 24)

Suddenness

As the lightning cometh out of the east, and shineth even unto the west; so shall also the coming of the Son of man be. (Matt. 24: 27)

Suffering

The wicked man travaileth with pain all his days. (Job 15: 20)

My sighs are many, and my heart is faint. (Lam. 1: 22)

Though He cause grief, yet will He have compassion. (Lam. 3: 32)

Let this cup pass from me. (Matt. 26: 39)

We count them that endure. (James 5: 11)

If ye suffer for righteousness' sake, happy are ye. (1 Pet. 3: 14)

He that hath suffered in the flesh hath ceased from sin. (1 Pet. 4: 1)

Superstition

Be not dismayed at the signs of heaven; for the heathen are dismayed at them. (Jer. 10: 2)

The gods are come down to us in the likeness of men. (Acts 14: 11)

Survival

Of every living thing of all flesh, two of every sort shalt thou bring into the ark, to keep them alive with thee. (Gen. 6: 19)

The more they afflicted them, the more they multiplied and grew. (Ex. 1: 12)

I am escaped with the skin of my teeth. (Job 19: 20)

We are left but a few of many. (Jer. 42: 2)

I send you forth as sheep in the midst of wolves: be ye therefore wise as serpents, and harmless as doves. (Matt. 10: 16)

Swearing

Swear not at all; neither by heaven; for it is God's throne: Nor by the earth; for it is His footstool: neither by Jerusalem; for it is the city of the great King. (Matt. 5: 34,35)

Sympathy

Miserable comforters are ye all. (Job 16: 2)

Though all shall cry unto Me, I will not hearken unto them. (Jer. 11: 11)

Is it nothing to you, all ye that pass by? (Lam. 1: 12)

He that despiseth you despiseth me; and he that despiseth me despiseth Him that sent me. (Luke 10: 16)

Jesus wept. (John 11: 35)

Remember them that are in bonds, as bound with them; and them which suffer adversity, as being yourselves also in the body. (Heb. 13: 3)

What the Bible says about (58)

T

Tact

A soft answer turneth away wrath. (Prov. 15: 1)

Pleasant words are as an honeycomb, sweet to the soul, and health to the bones. (Prov. 16: 24)

A soft tongue breaketh the bone. (Prov. 25: 15)

Taxation

If ye love them which love you, what reward have ye? do not even the publicans the same? (Matt. 5: 46)

Of whom do the kings of the earth take custom or tribute? of their own children, or of strangers? (Matt. 17: 25)

Take, and give unto them for me and thee. (Matt. 17: 27)

Render therefore unto Caesar the things which are Caesar's; and unto God the things that are God's. (Matt. 22: 21)

Exact no more than that which is appointed you. (Luke 3: 13)

Pay ye tribute also: for they are God's ministers. (Rom. 13: 6)

Tribute to whom tribute is due. (Rom. 13: 7)

Teaching

Show them the way wherein they must walk, and the work that they must do. (Ex. 18: 20)

Whosoever shall do and teach them, the same shall be called great in the kingdom of heaven. (Matt. 5: 19)

My doctrine is not mine, but His that sent me. (John 7: 16)

Tears

All the night make I my bed to swim; I water my couch with my tears. (Ps. 6: 6)

Weeping may endure for a night, but joy cometh in the morning. (Ps. 30: 5)

Rivers of waters run down mine eyes, because they keep not Thy law. (Ps. 119: 136)

They that sow in tears shall reap in joy. (Ps. 126: 5)

Temper

Let not the anger of my lord wax hot. (Ex. 32: 22)

Cease from anger, and forsake wrath. (Ps. 37: 8)

A fool's wrath is presently known: but a prudent man covereth shame. (Prov. 12: 16)

He that is soon angry dealeth foolishly. (Prov. 14: 17)

For a small moment have I forsaken thee; but with great mercies will I gather thee. (Is. 54: 7)

Temptation

And the serpent said unto the woman, Ye shall not surely die. (Gen. 3: 4)

She took of the fruit thereof, and did eat. (Gen. 3: 6)

If thou doest not well, sin lieth at the door. (Gen. 4: 7)

Ye shall not tempt the Lord your God. (Deut. 6: 16)

If sinners entice thee, consent thou not. (Prov. 1: 10)

Enter not into the path of the wicked, and go not in the way of evil men. (Prov. 4: 14)

Keep thee from the evil woman, from the flattery of the tongue of a strange woman. (Prov. 6: 24)

Thou shalt not tempt the Lord thy God. (Matt. 4: 7; Luke 4: 12)

Lead us not into temptation, but deliver us from evil. (Matt. 6: 13; Luke 11: 4)

Wide is the gate, and broad is the way, that leadeth to destruction. (Matt. 7: 13)

Get thee behind me, Satan: thou art an offence unto me. (Matt. 16: 23)

Woe to that man by whom the offence cometh! (Matt. 18: 7)

Why tempt ye me, ye hypocrites? (Matt. 22: 18)

Watch and pray, that ye not enter into temptation. (Matt. 26: 41)

The spirit indeed is willing, but the flesh is weak. (Matt. 26: 41)

Blessed is the man that endureth temptation. (James 1: 12)

God cannot be tempted with evil, neither tempteth He any man. (James 1: 13)

Resist the devil, and he will flee from you. (James 4: 7)

Ten Commandments

And he was there with the Lord forty days and forty nights. (Ex. 34: 28)

Two tables of stone written with the finger of God. (Deut. 9: 10)

The Ten Commandments:

I am the Lord thy God, which have brought thee out of the land of Egypt, out of the house of bondage.

Thou shalt have no others gods before Me.

Thou shalt not make unto thee any graven image, or any likeness of any thing that is in heaven above, or that is in the earth beneath, or that is in the water under the earth:

Thou shalt not bow down thyself to them, nor serve them: for I the Lord thy God am a jealous God, visiting the iniquity of the fathers upon the children unto the third and fourth generation of them that hate Me;

And showing mercy unto thousands of them that love Me, and keep My commandments.

Thou shalt not take the name of the Lord thy God in vain; for the Lord will not hold him guiltless that taketh His name in vain.

What the Bible says about (59)

Ten Commandments, continued

Remember the sabbath day, to keep it holy.

Six days shalt thou labor, and do all thy work:

But the seventh day is the sabbath of the Lord thy God: in it thou shalt not do any work, thou, nor thy son, nor thy daughter, thy manservant, nor thy maidservant, nor thy cattle, nor thy stranger that is within thy gates:

For in six days the Lord made heaven and earth, the sea, and all that in them is, and rested the seventh day: wherefore the Lord blessed the sabbath day, and hallowed it.

Honor thy father and thy mother: that thy days may be long upon the land which the Lord thy God giveth thee.

Thou shalt not kill.

Thou shalt not commit adultery.

Thou shalt not steal.

Thou shalt not bear false witness against thy neighbor.

Thou shalt not covet thy neighbor's house, thou shalt not covet thy neighbor's wife, nor his manservant, nor his maidservant, nor his ox, nor his ass, nor any thing that is thy neighbor's. (Ex. 20: 2–17)

Terror

The sword without, and terror within, shall destroy both the young man and the virgin, the suckling also with the man of gray hairs. (Deut. 32: 25)

Let not Thy dread make me afraid. (Job 13: 21)

The terrors of the shadow of death. (Job 24: 17)

I have caused My terror in the land of the living. (Ezek. 32: 32)

The abomination of desolation. (Matt. 24: 15; Mark 13: 14)

Every island fled away, and the mountains were not found. (Rev. 16: 20)

Testimony

Speak ye unto the rock before their eyes; and it shall give forth his water. (Num. 20: 8)

Ye are My witness, saith the Lord. (Is. 43: 10,12)

Whosoever therefore shall confess me before men, him will I confess also before my Father which is in heaven. But whosoever shall deny me before men, him will I also deny before my Father which is in heaven. (Matt. 10: 32,33)

The blind see, the lame walk, the lepers are cleansed, the deaf hear, the dead are raised, to the poor the gospel is preached. (Luke 7: 22)

Whosoever shall confess me before men, him shall the Son of man also confess before the angels of God. (Luke 12: 8)

I saw, and bare record that this is the Son of God. (John 1: 34)

If I bear witness of myself, my witness is not true. (John 5: 31)

The works that I do in my Father's

name, they bear witness of me.
(John 10: 25)

Ye also shall bear witness, because ye have been with me from the beginning. (John 15: 27)

To this end was I born, and for this cause came I into the world, that I should bear witness unto the truth. (John 18: 37)

Ye shall be witnesses unto me. (Acts 1: 8)

What thou seest, write in a book, and send it unto the seven churches. (Rev. 1: 11)

Write the things which thou hast seen, and the things which are, and the things which shall be hereafter. (Rev. 1: 19)

Testing

Through them I may prove Israel, whether they will keep the way of the Lord to walk therein. (Judg. 2: 22)

Thou art weighed in the balances, and art found wanting. (Dan. 5: 27)

Thirst

Oh that one would give me drink of the water of the well of Bethlehem. (2 Sam. 23: 15; 1 Chr. 11: 17)

In my thirst they gave me vinegar to drink. (Ps. 69: 21)

The tongue of the sucking child cleaveth to the roof of his mouth for thirst. (Lam. 4: 4)

Whosoever drinketh of this water shall thirst again: But whosoever drinketh of the water that I shall give him shall never thirst. (John 4: 13–14)

I thirst. (John 19: 28)

Thoughts

Thou, even Thou only, knowest the hearts of all the children of men. (1 Kings 8: 39)

The Lord knoweth the thoughts of man, that they are vanity. (Ps. 94: 11)

There is not a word in my tongue, but, lo, O Lord, Thou knowest it altogether. (Ps. 139: 4)

The thoughts of the wicked are an abomination to the Lord. (Prov. 15: 26)

My thoughts are not your thoughts, neither are your ways My ways, saith the Lord. (Is. 55: 8)

How long shall thy vain thoughts lodge within thee? (Jer. 4: 14)

I know the things that come into your mind, every one of them. (Ezek. 11: 5)

Think soberly. (Rom. 12: 3)

The Lord knoweth the thoughts of the wise, that they are vain. (1 Cor. 3: 20)

Gird up the loins of your mind. (1 Pet. 1: 13)

I am He which searcheth the reins and hearts. (Rev. 2: 23)

What the Bible says about (60)

T continued

Threat

Neither will I be with you any more, except ye destroy the accursed from among you. (Josh. 7: 12)

Show us, we pray thee, the entrance into the city, and we will show thee mercy. (Judg. 1: 24)

So let the gods do to me, and more. (1 Kings 19: 2)

My father chastised you with whips, but I will chastise you with scorpions. (2 Chr. 10: 11, 14)

I have not said in vain that I would do this evil unto them. (Ezek. 6: 10)

Time

And God called the light Day, and the darkness He called Night. And the evening and the morning were the first day. (Gen. 1: 5)

Our days upon the earth are a shadow. (Job 8: 9)

Waters wear the stones. (Job 14: 19)

A thousand years in Thy sight are but as yesterday when it is past. (Ps. 90: 4)

That which now is in the days to come shall all be forgotten. (Eccl. 2: 16)

To every thing there is a season, and a time to every purpose under the heaven. (Eccl. 3: 1)

A time to be born, and a time to die; a time to plant, and a time to pluck up that which is planted. (Eccl. 3: 2)

A time to kill, and a time to heal; a time to break down, and a time to build up. (Eccl. 3: 3)

That which hath been is now; and that which is to be hath already been. (Eccl. 3: 15)

Mine hour is not yet come. (John 2: 4)

Lift up your eyes, and look on the fields; for they are white already to harvest. (John 4: 35)

The night cometh, when no man can work. (John 9: 4)

Timidity

The children of Israel have not hearkened unto me; how then shall Pharaoh hear me? (Ex. 6: 12)

If thou wilt go with me, then I will go. (Judg. 4: 8)

When I have a convenient season, I will call for thee. (Acts 24: 25)

God hath not given us the spirit of fear; but of power, and of love, and of a sound mind. (2 Tim. 1: 7)

Tithe

Of all that Thou shalt give me I will surely give the tenth unto Thee. (Gen. 28: 22)

The tithe of the land, whether of the seed of the land, or of the fruit of the tree, is the Lord's. (Lev. 27: 30)

Honor the Lord with thy substance, and with the firstfruits of all thine increase. (Prov. 3: 9)

Tolerance

For all this His anger is not turned away, but His hand is stretched out still. (Is. 5: 25; Is. 9: 17)

Thou art of purer eyes than to behold evil. (Hab. 1: 13)

O faithless and perverse generation, how long shall I be with you? how long shall I suffer you? (Matt. 17: 17)

Judge not, and ye shall not be judged: condemn not, and ye shall not be condemned. (Luke 6: 37)

Forgive, and ye shall be forgiven. (Luke 6: 37)

Tradition

He did evil in the sight of the Lord, and walked in the way of his father. (1 Kings 15: 26)

As did their fathers, so do they unto this day. (2 Kings 17: 41)

Laying aside the commandment of God, ye hold the tradition of men. (Mark 7: 8)

Ye reject the commandment of God, that ye may keep your own tradition. (Mark 7: 9)

As your fathers did, so do ye. (Acts 7: 51)

Traps

Say now Shibboleth. (Judg. 12: 6)

As a bird hasteth to the snare, and knoweth not that it is for his life. (Prov. 7: 23)

I will spread My net upon him, and he shall be taken in My snare. (Ezek. 17: 20)

Treachery

Let not mine hand be upon him, but let the hand of the Philistines be upon him. (1 Sam. 18: 17)

The words of his mouth were smoother than butter, but war was in his heart. (Ps. 55: 21)

His words were softer than oil, yet were they drawn swords. (Ps. 55: 21)

One speaketh peaceably to his neighbor with his mouth, but in heart he layeth his wait. (Jer. 9: 8)

By thy sorceries were all nations deceived. (Rev. 18: 23)

Trinity

Go ye therefore, and teach all nations, baptizing them in the name of the Father, and of the Son, and of the Holy Spirit. (Matt. 28: 19)

The grace of the Lord Jesus Christ, and the love of God, and the communion of the Holy Spirit, be with you all. (2 Cor. 13: 14)

What the Bible says about (61)

Trinity, continued

There are three that bear record in heaven, the Father, the Word, and the Holy Spirit: and these three are one. (1 John 5: 7)

Trouble

Evil will befall you in the latter days. (Deut. 31: 29)

Let Him deliver me out of all tribulation. (1 Sam. 26: 24)

Man is born unto trouble. (Job 5: 7)

I was brought low, and He helped me. (Ps. 116: 6)

He that seeketh mischief, it shall come unto him. (Prov. 11: 27)

The Lord is good, a strong hold in the day of trouble. (Nah. 1: 7)

Sufficient unto the day is the evil thereof. (Matt. 6: 34)

This sickness is not unto death, but for the glory of God. (John 11: 4)

Give no offence. (1 Cor. 10: 32)

Trust

Let Him do to me as seemeth good unto Him. (2 Sam. 15: 26)

Our eyes upon Thee. (2 Chr. 20: 12)

Blessed are all they that put their trust in Him. (Ps. 2: 12)

Let all those that put their trust in thee rejoice: let them ever shout for joy. (Ps. 5: 11)

The Lord is my rock, and my fortress, and my deliverer; my God, my strength, in whom I will trust. (Ps. 18: 2)

Into Thine hand I commit my spirit. (Ps. 31: 5)

Commit thy way unto the Lord; trust also in Him. (Ps. 37: 5)

Blessed is that man that maketh the Lord his trust. (Ps. 40: 4)

As for me, I will call upon God; and the Lord shall save me. (Ps. 55: 16)

In God I have put my trust; I will not fear what flesh can do unto me. (Ps. 56: 4)

In Thee, O Lord, do I put my trust. (Ps. 71: 1)

Trust thou in the Lord. (Ps. 115: 9)

Hold Thou me up, and I shall be safe. (Ps. 119: 117)

Trust in the Lord with all thine heart. (Prov. 3: 5)

Blessed is the man that trusteth in the Lord, and whose hope the Lord is. (Jer. 17: 7)

I will look unto the Lord; I will wait for the God of my salvation. (Mic. 7: 7)

He knoweth them that trust in Him. (Nah. 1: 7)

We trust in the living God, who is the Savior of all men. (1 Tim. 4: 10)

Truth

What the Lord saith unto me, that will I speak. (1 Kings 22: 14)

The truth of the Lord endureth for ever. (Ps. 117: 2)

Thy law is the truth. (Ps. 119: 142)

Thy word is true from the beginning. (Ps. 119: 160)

Love the truth and peace. (Zech. 8: 19)

Heaven and earth shall pass away, but my words shall not pass away. (Matt. 24: 35, Mark 13: 31)

The law was given by Moses, but grace and truth came by Jesus Christ. (John 1: 17)

He that doeth truth cometh to the light, that his deeds may be made manifest. (John 3: 21)

God is true. (John 3: 33)

He that sent me is true, whom ye know not. (John 7: 28)

Ye shall know the truth, and the truth shall make you free. (John 8: 32)

Because I tell you the truth, ye believe me not. (John 8: 45)

These are not the words of him that hath a devil. (John 10: 21)

I am the way, the truth, and the life: no man cometh unto the Father, but by me. (John 14: 6)

Sanctify them through Thy truth. (John 17: 17)

Thy word is truth. (John 17: 17)

To this end was I born, and for this cause came I unto the world, that I should bear witness unto the truth. (John 18: 37)

Every one that is of the truth heareth my voice. (John 18: 37)

Let God be true, but every man a liar. (Rom. 3: 4)

We can do nothing against the truth, but for the truth. (2 Cor. 13: 8)

Behold, before God, I lie not. (Gal. 1: 20)

The truth is in Jesus. (Eph. 4: 21)

Tyrants

Princes have persecuted me without a cause: but my heart standeth in awe of Thy word. (Ps. 119: 161)

Envy thou not the oppressor, and choose none of his ways. (Prov. 3: 31)

Woe unto them that decree unrighteous decrees. (Is. 10: 1)

How art thou fallen from heaven, O Lucifer, son of the morning! (Is. 14: 12)

He shall come to his end, and none shall help him. (Dan. 11: 45)

As thou hast done, it shall be done unto thee. (Obad. 15)

What the Bible says about (62)

U

Underprivileged

Thou shalt open thine hand wide unto thy brother, to thy poor, and to thy needy, in thy land. (Deut. 15: 11)

He heareth the cry of the afflicted. (Job 26: 14)

He forgetteth not the cry of the humble. (Ps. 9: 12)

O God, lift up Thine hand: forget not the humble. (Ps. 10: 12)

He shall deliver the needy when he crieth; the poor also, and him that hath no helper. (Ps. 72: 12)

Precious shall their blood be in His sight. (Ps. 72: 14)

Defend the poor and fatherless: do justice to the afflicted and needy. (Ps. 82: 3)

Though the Lord be high, yet hath He respect unto the lowly. (Ps. 138: 6)

The Lord upholdeth all that fall, and raiseth up all those that be bowed down. (Ps. 145: 14)

Rob not the poor, because he is poor: neither oppress the afflicted in the gate. (Prov. 22: 22)

Open thy mouth, judge righteously, and plead the cause of the poor and needy. (Prov. 31: 9)

Relieve the oppressed, judge the fatherless, plead for the widow. (Is. 1: 17)

I the God of Israel will not forsake them. (Is. 41: 17)

Ye have the poor with you always. (Mark 14: 7)

He hath filled the hungry with good things; and the rich He hath sent empty away. (Luke 1: 53)

Support the weak. (1 Thess. 5: 14)

Understanding

The thunder of His power who can understand? (Job 26: 14)

Man knoweth not the price thereof. (Job 28: 13)

To depart from evil is understanding. (Job 28: 28)

The ear trieth words, as the mouth tasteth meat. (Job 34: 3)

Great things doeth He, which we cannot comprehend. (Job 37: 5)

Be ye not as the horse, or as the mule, which have no understanding. (Ps. 32: 9)

Teach me, O Lord, the way of Thy statutes; and I shall keep it unto the end. (Ps. 119: 33)

Give me understanding, and I shall keep the law. (Ps. 119: 34)

Give me understanding, and I shall live. (Ps. 119: 144)

Wisdom is the principal thing; therefore get wisdom: and with all thy getting get understanding. (Prov. 4: 7)

O ye simple, understand wisdom: and, ye fools, be ye of an understanding heart. (Prov. 8: 5)

In the lips of him that hath understanding wisdom is found. (Prov. 10: 13)

A man of understanding hath wisdom. (Prov. 10: 23)

The wisdom of the prudent is to understand his way. (Prov. 14: 8)

He that is slow to wrath is of great understanding. (Prov. 14: 29)

Understanding is a wellspring of life unto him that hath it: but the instruction of fools is folly. (Prov. 16: 22)

Hear ye indeed, but understand not; and see ye indeed, but perceive not. (Is. 6: 9)

In the latter days ye shall consider it. (Jer. 30: 24)

Who hath ears to hear, let him hear. (Matt. 13: 9)

They seeing see not; and hearing they hear not, neither do they understand. (Matt. 13: 13)

Having eyes, see ye not? and having ears, hear ye not? (Mark 8: 18)

We do hear them speak in our tongues the wonderful works of God. (Acts 2: 11)

When I was a child, I spake as a child, I understood as a child, I thought as a child: but when I became a man, I put away childish things. (1 Cor. 13: 11)

Now we see through a glass, darkly; but then face to face. (1 Cor. 13: 12)

Be not children in understanding. (1 Cor. 14: 20)

The peace of God, which passeth all understanding. (Phil. 4: 7)

Anoint thine eyes with eyesalve, that thou mayest see. (Rev. 3: 18)

Let him that hath understanding count the number of the beast. (Rev. 13: 18)

Unity

The whole earth was of one language, and of one speech. (Gen. 11: 1)

Now nothing will be restrained from them, which they have imagined to do. (Gen. 11: 6)

Behold, how good and how pleasant it is for brethren to dwell together in unity! (Ps. 133: 1)

A threefold cord is not quickly broken. (Eccl. 4: 12)

If a kingdom be divided against itself, that kingdom cannot stand. (Mark 3: 24)

If a house be divided against itself, that house cannot stand. (Mark 3: 25)

I and my Father are one. (John 10: 30)

All that believed were together, and had all things in common. (Acts 2: 44)

We, being many, are one body in Christ, and every one members one of another. (Rom. 12: 5)

We being many are one bread, and one body: for we are all partakers of that one bread. (1 Cor. 10: 17)

One Lord, one faith, one baptism. (Eph. 4: 5)

Both He that sanctifieth and they who are sanctified are all of one. (Heb. 2: 11)

What the Bible says about (63)

V

Values

He that killeth a beast, he shall restore it: and he that killeth a man, he shall be put to death. (Lev. 24: 21)

Man looketh on the outward appearance, but the Lord looketh on the heart. (1 Sam. 16: 7)

I dwell in an house of cedar, but the ark of God dwelleth within curtains. (2 Sam. 7: 2)

Thou lovest thine enemies, and hatest thy friends. (2 Sam. 19: 6)

If the foundations be destroyed, what can the righteous do? (Ps. 11: 3)

Teach us to number our days, that we may apply our hearts unto wisdom. (Ps. 90: 12)

The law of Thy mouth is better unto me than thousands of gold and silver. (Ps. 119: 72)

Wisdom is the principal thing; therefore get wisdom: and with all thy getting get understanding. (Prov. 4: 7)

In the house of the righteous is much treasure: but in the revenues of the wicked is trouble. (Prov. 15: 6)

Labor not to be rich. (Prov. 23: 4)

Wherefore do ye spend money for that which is not bread? (Is. 55: 2)

Eat ye that which is good, and let your soul delight itself in fatness. (Is. 55: 2)

Let him that glorieth glory in this, that he understandeth and knoweth Me, that I am the Lord. (Jer. 9: 24)

Lay up yourselves treasures in heaven, where neither moth nor rust doth corrupt, and where thieves do not break through nor steal. (Matt. 6: 20)

Is not the life more than meat, and the body than raiment? (Matt. 6: 25)

He that loveth father or mother more than me is not worthy of me: and he that loveth son or daughter more than me is not worthy of me. (Matt. 10: 37)

Thou savorest not the things that be of God, but those that be of men. (Matt. 16: 23)

What shall a man give in exchange for his soul? (Matt. 16: 26)

What shall it profit a man, if he shall gain the whole world, and lose his own soul? (Mark 8: 36)

If thy foot offend thee, cut it off: it is better for thee to enter halt into life, than having two feet to be cast into hell. (Mark 9: 45)

It is better for thee to enter into the kingdom of God with one eye, than having two eyes to be cast into hell fire. (Mark 9: 47)

Take no thought for your life, what ye shall eat; neither for the body, what ye shall put on. (Luke 12: 22)

That which is highly esteemed among men is abomination in the sight of God. (Luke 16: 15)

Labor not for the meat which perisheth, but for that meat which endureth unto everlasting life. (John 6: 27)

They loved the praise of men more than the praise of God. (John 12: 43)

The things which are seen are temporal; but the things which are not seen are eternal. (2 Cor. 4: 18)

What things were gain to me, those I counted loss for Christ. (Phil. 3: 7)

Above all these things put on charity, which is the bond of perfectness. (Col. 3: 14)

Hold fast to that which is good. (1 Thess. 5: 21)

He that said, Do not commit adultery, said also, Do not kill. (James 2: 11)

Know ye not that the friendship of the world is enmity with God? (James 4: 4)

Buy of me gold tried in the fire, that thou mayest be rich; and white raiment, that thou mayest be clothed. (Rev. 3: 18)

Verbosity

Should a wise man utter vain knowledge, and fill his belly with the east wind? (Job 15: 2)

How long will it be ere ye make an end of words? (Job 18: 2)

He multiplieth words without knowledge. (Job 35: 16)

He that hath knowledge spareth his words. (Prov. 17: 27)

A fool uttereth all his mind: but a wise man keepeth it in till afterwards. (Prov. 29: 1)

A fool's voice is known by multitude of words. (Eccl. 5: 3)

They think that they shall be heard for their much speaking. (Matt. 6: 7)

Victory

Let us flee from the face of Israel; for the Lord fighteth for them. (Ex. 14: 25)

I will sing unto the Lord, for He hath triumphed gloriously: the horse and his rider hath He thrown into the sea. (Ex. 15: 1)

Thy right hand, O Lord, is become glorious in power: Thy right hand, O Lord, hath dashed in pieces the enemy. (Ex. 15: 6)

Thou hast overthrown them that rose up against Thee: Thou sentest forth Thy wrath, which consumed them as stubble. (Ex. 15: 7)

Ye shall chase your enemies, and they shall fall before you by the sword. (Lev. 26: 7)

Ye shall be saved from your enemies. (Num. 10: 9)

Not for thy righteousness, or for the uprightness of thine heart, dost thou go to possess their land: but for the wickedness of these nations the Lord thy God doth drive them out. (Deut. 9: 5)

What the Bible says about (64)

Victory, continued

Every place whereon the soles of your feet shall tread shall be yours. (Deut. 11: 24)

Shout; for the Lord hath given you the city. (Josh. 6: 16)

Fear them not: for I delivered them into thine hand. (Josh. 10: 8)

The Lord fought for Israel. (Josh. 10: 14)

No man hath been able to stand before you unto this day. (Josh. 23: 9)

The Lord your God, He it is that fighteth for you. (Josh. 23: 10)

Go up; for to morrow I will deliver them into thine hand. (Judg. 20: 28)

My mouth is enlarged over mine enemies; because I rejoice in Thy salvation. (1 Sam. 2: 1)

David prevailed over the Philistine with a sling and with a stone. (1 Sam. 17: 50)

The victory that day was turned into mourning. (2 Sam. 19: 2)

I beat them as small as the dust of the earth, I did stamp them as the mire of the street. (2 Sam. 22: 43)

The God that answereth by fire, let Him be God. (1 Kings 18: 24)

Have the gods of the nations delivered them which my fathers have destroyed? (2 Kings 19: 12)

I know that Thou favorest me, because mine enemy doth not triumph over me. (Ps. 41: 11)

His enemies shall lick the dust. (Ps. 72: 9)

Sit thou at My right hand, until I make thine enemies thy footstool. (Ps. 110: 1)

This is the day which the Lord hath made; we will rejoice and be glad in it. (Ps. 118: 24)

It is He that giveth salvation unto kings. (Ps. 144: 10)

The horse is prepared against the day of battle: but safety is of the Lord. (Prov. 21: 31)

He shall cry, yea, roar; He shall prevail against His enemies. (Is. 42: 13)

A little one shall become a thousand, and a small one a strong nation. (Is. 60: 22)

He shall array himself with the land of Egypt, as a shepherd putteth on his garment. (Jer. 43: 12)

Their mighty ones are beaten down, and are fled apace, and look not back. (Jer. 46: 5)

Let not the swift flee away, nor the mighty man escape. (Jer. 46: 6)

The kingdom shall be the Lord's. (Obad. 21)

Thine hand shall be lifted up upon thine adversaries, and all thine enemies shall be cut off. (Mic. 5: 9)

Be of good cheer; I have overcome the world. (John 16: 33)

Sit Thou on my right hand, Until I make Thy foes Thy footstool. (Acts 2: 34,35)

They which run in a race run all, but one receiveth the prize. (1 Cor. 9: 24)

Thanks be to God, which giveth us the victory through our Lord Jesus Christ. (1 Cor. 15: 57)

Whatsoever is born of God overcometh the world. (1 John 5: 4)

To him that overcometh will I give to eat of the hidden manna. (Rev. 2: 17)

They overcame him by the blood of the Lamb. (Rev. 12: 11)

The Lamb shall overcome them: for He is Lord of lords, and King of kings. (Rev. 17: 14)

Alleluia: for the Lord God omnipotent reigneth. (Rev. 19: 6)

He that overcometh shall inherit all things. (Rev. 21: 7)

Vigilance

He that keepeth Israel shall neither slumber nor sleep. (Ps. 121: 4)

Except the Lord keep the city, the watchman waketh but in vain. (Ps. 127: 1)

Go, set a watchman, let him declare what he seeth. (Is. 21: 6)

Awake, awake, stand up, O Jerusalem. (Is. 51: 17)

Take heed that no man deceive you. For many shall come in my name, saying, I am Christ. (Matt. 24: 4,5)

Watch therefore: for ye know not what hour your Lord doth come. (Matt. 24: 42)

What, could ye not watch with me one hour? (Matt. 26: 41)

Watch and pray, that ye enter not into temptation. (Matt. 26: 41)

Take heed to yourselves. (Mark 13: 9)

Take ye heed, watch and pray: for ye know not when the time is. (Mark 13: 33)

Watch ye therefore: for ye know not when the master of the house cometh. (Mark 13: 35)

If the goodman of the house had known what hour the thief would come, he would have watched. (Luke 12: 39)

Watch ye therefore, and pray always. (Luke 21: 36)

Take heed therefore unto yourselves, and to all the flock. (Acts 20: 28)

Now it is high time to awake out of sleep. (Rom. 13: 11)

What the Bible says about (65)

Vigilance, continued

Let us not sleep, as do others; but let us watch and be sober. (1 Thess. 5: 6)

They that sleep sleep in the night; and they that be drunken are drunken in the night. (1 Thess. 5: 7)

Be sober, be vigilant; because your adversary the devil, as a roaring lion, walketh about, seeking whom he may devour. (1 Peter 5: 8)

Look to yourselves, that we lose not those things which we have wrought. (2 John 8)

Blessed is he that watcheth, and keepeth his garments, lest he walk naked, and they see his shame. (Rev. 16: 15)

Vindication

Why are ye come unto me now when ye are in distress? (Judg. 11: 7)

The stone which the builders refused is become the head stone of the corner. (Ps. 118: 22)

Where are now your prophets which prophesied unto you, saying, The king of Babylon shall not come? (Jer. 37: 19)

They shall lick the dust like a serpent, they shall move out of their holes like worms of the earth: they shall be afraid of the Lord our God. (Mic. 7: 17)

Many that are first shall be last; and the last shall be first. (Mark 10: 31)

Sit Thou on my right hand, Until I make Thy foes Thy footstool. (Acts 2: 34,35)

Violence

He that smiteth his father, or his mother, shall be surely put to death. (Ex. 21: 15)

He smote them hip and thigh. (Judg. 15: 8)

The sword shall never depart from thine house. (2 Sam. 12: 10)

Thou shalt not build an house unto My name, because thou hast shed much blood upon the earth. (1 Chr. 22: 8)

The Lord trieth the righteous: but the wicked and him that loveth violence His soul hateth. (Ps. 11: 5)

Evil shall hunt the violent man to overthrow him. (Ps. 140: 11)

Envy thou not the oppressor, and choose none of his ways. (Prov. 3: 31)

The land is full of bloody crimes, and the city is full of violence. (Ezek. 7: 23)

Woe to the bloody city! it is all full of lies and robbery. (Nah. 3: 1)

Woe to him that buildeth a town with blood. (Hab. 2: 12)

All they that take the sword shall perish with the sword. (Matt. 26: 52)

Do violence to no man, neither accuse any falsely. (Luke 3: 14)

Be ye come out, as against a thief, with swords and staves? (Luke 22: 52)

Their feet are swift to shed blood. (Rom. 3: 15)

Destruction and misery are in their ways: And the way of peace have they not known. (Rom. 3: 16,17)

With violence shall that great city Babylon be thrown down. (Rev. 18: 21)

Virtue

A virtuous woman is a crown to her husband. (Prov. 12: 4)

Who can find a virtuous woman? for her price is far above rubies. (Prov. 31: 10)

Many daughters have done virtuously, but thou excellest them all. (Prov. 31: 29)

Whatsoever things are true, whatsoever things are honest, whatsoever things are just, whatsoever things are pure, whatsoever things are of good report; if there be any virtue, and if there be any praise, think on these things. (Phil. 4: 8)

Add to your faith virtue; and to virtue knowledge. (2 Pet. 1: 5)

Visions

The word of the Lord was precious in those days. (1 Sam. 3: 1)

O ye dry bones, hear the word of the Lord. (Ezek. 37: 4)

Your old men shall dream dreams, your young men shall see visions. (Joel 2: 28)

Behold, I see the heavens opened, and the Son of man standing on the right hand of God. (Acts 7: 56)

They heard not the voice of Him that spake to me. (Acts 22: 9)

If a spirit or an angel hath spoken to him, let us not fight against God. (Acts 23: 9)

Who is worthy to open the book, and to loose the seals thereof? (Rev. 5: 2)

Vitality

The life of all flesh is the blood thereof. (Lev. 17: 14)

The trees of the Lord are full of sap. (Ps. 104: 16)

Whatsoever thy hand findeth to do, do it with thy might. (Eccl. 9: 10)

Lift up the hands which hang down, and the feeble knees. (Heb. 12: 12)

Volunteers

Let no man's heart fail because of him; thy servant will go and fight with this Philistine. (1 Sam. 17: 32)

Who is there among you of all His people? The Lord his God be with him, and let him go up. (2 Chr. 36: 23; Ezra 1: 3)

Whom shall I send, and who will go for us? Then said I, Here am I; send me. (Is. 6: 8)

What the Bible says about (66)

W

Wages

Because thou art my brother, shouldest thou therefore serve me for nought? tell me, what shall thy wages be? (Gen. 29:15)

Did not I serve with thee for Rachel? (Gen. 29:25)

Let them deliver it into the hand of the doers of the work. (2 Kings 22:5)

The recompense of a man's hands shall be rendered unto him. (Prov. 12:14)

Whatsoever is right, that shall ye receive. (Matt. 20:7)

Be content with your wages. (Luke 3:14)

The laboreth is worthy of his reward. (1 Tim. 5:18)

War

Ye shall be saved from your enemies. (Num. 10:9)

Go not up, for the Lord is not among you. (Num. 14:42)

Because ye are turned away from the Lord, therefore the Lord will not be with you. (Num. 14:43)

War and peace

Go not up, neither fight, for I am not among you. (Deut. 1:42)

When thou comest nigh unto a city to fight against it, then proclaim peace unto it. (Deut. 20:10)

Thou doest me wrong to war against me. (Judg. 11:27)

What hast thou to do with peace? turn thee behind me. (2 Kings 9:18,19)

Warning

The Lord set a mark upon Cain. (Gen. 4:15)

Look not behind thee. (Gen. 19:17)

Go not up, for the Lord is not among you. (Num. 14:42)

Beware lest thou forget the Lord. (Deut. 6:12)

Ye shall not tempt the Lord thy God. (Deut. 6:16)

Evil will befall you in the latter days. (Deut. 31:29)

The Lord will not hear you in that day. (1 Sam. 8:18)

If ye shall still do wickedly, ye shall be consumed. (1 Sam. 12:25)

Waste

Give not that which is holy unto the dogs, neither cast ye your pearls before swine. (Matt. 7:6)

It is not meet to take the children's bread, and to cast it to dogs. (Matt. 15:26)

Gather up the fragments that remain, that nothing be lost. (John 6:12)

Water

Unstable as water, thou shalt not excel. (Gen. 49:4)

Can the rush grow up without mire?
can the flag grow without water?
(Job 8: 11)

Waters wear the stones. (Job 14: 19)

Wealth

Thou shalt remember the Lord thy
God: for it is He that giveth thee power
to get wealth. (Deut. 8: 18)

The Lord maketh poor, and maketh
rich: He bringeth low, and lifteth up.
(1 Sam. 2: 7)

I have also given thee that which
thou hast not asked, both riches, and
honor. (1 Kings 3: 13)

None were of silver. (1 Kings 10: 21)

All that is in the heaven and in the
earth is Thine. (1 Chr. 29: 11)

Riches and honor come of Thee.
(1 Chr. 29: 12)

All things come of Thee.
(1 Chr. 29: 14)

Wickedness

Thou shalt not follow a multitude to do
evil. (Ex. 23: 2)

Not for thy righteousness, or for the
uprightness of thine heart, dost thou
go to possess their land: but for the
wickedness of these nations the Lord
thy God doth drive them out.
(Deut. 9: 5)

Count not thine handmaid for a
daughter of Belial. (1 Sam. 1: 16)

The children of Belial. (1 Sam. 10: 27)

If ye shall still do wickedly, ye shall be
consumed. (1 Sam. 12: 25)

He walked in all the sins of his father.
(1 Kings 15: 3)

Widows and orphans

If thou afflict them in any wise, and
they cry at all unto Me, I will surely
hear their cry. (Ex. 22: 23)

A father of the fatherless, and a judge
of the widows, is God in His holy
habitation. (Ps. 68: 5)

Defend the poor and fatherless: do
justice to the afflicted and needy.
(Ps. 82: 3)

Plead for the widow. (Is. 1: 17)

Leave thy fatherless children, I will
preserve them alive; and let thy widows
trust in Me. (Jer. 49: 11)

In Thee the fatherless findeth mercy.
(Hos. 14: 3)

Oppress not the widow, nor the
fatherless, the stranger, nor the poor.
(Zech. 7: 10)

Honor widows that are widows
indeed. (1 Tim. 5: 3)

Visit the fatherless and widows in
their affliction. (James 1: 27)

Wisdom

In the hearts of all that are wise hearted
I have put wisdom. (Ex. 31: 6)

Give therefore Thy servant an
understanding heart to judge Thy
people, that I may discern between
good and bad. (1 Kings 3: 9)

Divide the living child in two, and
give half to the one, and half to the
other. (1 Kings 3: 25)

What the Bible says about (67)

Wisdom, continued

Give her the living child, and in no wise slay it: she is the mother thereof.
(1 Kings 3: 27)

The wisdom of God was in him.
(1 Kings 3: 28)

Give me now wisdom and knowledge. (2 Chr. 1: 10)

Witchcraft

Thou shalt not suffer a witch to live.
(Ex. 22: 18)

Regard not them that have familiar spirits, neither seek after wizards, to be defiled by them. (Lev. 19: 31)

All that do these things are an abomination unto the Lord.
(Deut. 18: 12)

I will be a swift witness against the sorcerers. (Mal. 3: 5)

Thou child of the devil, thou enemy of all righteousness. (Acts 13: 10)

Women

It is not good that the man should be alone; I will make him an help meet for him. (Gen. 2: 18)

The rib, which the Lord God had taken from man, made He a woman.
(Gen. 2: 22)

This is now bone of my bones, and flesh of my flesh. (Gen. 2: 23)

Work

In the sweat of thy face shalt thou eat bread, till thou return unto the ground.
(Gen. 3: 19)

The Lord God sent him forth from the garden of Eden, to till the ground from whence he was taken. So He drove out the man. (Gen. 3: 23,24)

Because thou art my brother, shouldest thou therefore serve me for nought? tell me, what shall thy wages be? (Gen. 29: 15)

Worldliness

Thou savorest not the things that be of God, but those that be of men.
(Matt. 16: 23)

The children of this world are in their generation wiser than the children of light. (Luke 16: 8)

Ye are from beneath; I am from above: ye are of this world; I am not of this world. (John 8: 23)

Be not conformed to this world.
(Rom. 12: 2)

Worry

Why tarry the wheels of his chariots?
(Judg. 5: 28)

Cast thy burden upon the Lord, and He shall sustain thee. (Ps. 55: 22)

Pour out your heart before Him: God is a refuge for us. (Ps. 62: 8)

Worship

He is my God, and I will prepare Him an habitation; my father's God, and I will exalt Him. (Ex. 15: 2)

Ye shall serve the Lord your God.
(Ex. 23: 25)

Let them make Me a sanctuary; that I may dwell among them. (Ex. 25: 8)

Thou shalt love the Lord thy God with all thine heart, and with all thy soul, and with all thy might. (Deut. 6: 5)

Serve Him with all your heart and with all your soul. (Deut. 11: 13)

Y

Youth

The flower of their age. (1 Sam. 2: 33)

His bones are full of the sins of his youth. (Job 20: 11)

Remember not the sins of my youth. (Ps. 25: 7)

The young lions roar after their prey, and seek their meat from God. (Ps. 104: 21)

The glory of young men is their strength: and the beauty of old men is the gray head. (Prov. 20: 29)

Rejoice, O young man, in thy youth. (Eccl. 11: 9)

Let thy heart cheer thee in the days of thy youth. (Eccl. 11: 9)

Remember now thy Creator in the days of thy youth. (Eccl. 12: 1)

Say not, I am a child: for thou shalt go to all that I shall send thee, and whatsoever I command thee thou shalt speak. (Jer. 1: 7)

It is good for a man that he bear the yoke in his youth. (Lam. 3: 27)

Your young men shall see visions, and your old men shall dream dreams. (Acts 2: 17)

Let no man despise thy youth. (1 Tim. 4: 12)

For every one that useth milk is unskillful in the word of righteousness: for he is a babe. (Heb. 5: 13)

Z

Zeal

I the Lord thy God am a jealous God. (Ex. 20: 5)

Come with me, and see my zeal for the Lord. (2 Kings 10: 16)

Preach ye upon the housetops. (Matt. 10: 27)

I persecuted them even unto strange cities. (Acts 26: 11)

I continue unto this day, witnessing both to small and great. (Acts 26: 22)

They have a zeal of God, but not according to knowledge. (Rom. 10: 2)

I seek not yours, but you. (2 Cor. 12: 14)

He which persecuted us in times past now preacheth the faith which once he destroyed. (Gal. 1: 23)

It is good to be zealously affected always in a good thing. (Gal. 4: 18)

Earnestly contend for the faith which was once delivered unto the saints. (Jude 3)

As many as I love, I rebuke and chasten: be zealous therefore, and repent. (Rev. 3: 19)

The Heidelberg Catechism: Questions 1–8

Introduction

The Heidelberg Catechism derives its name because it originated in Heidelberg, the capital of the German Electorate of the Palatinate. It was asked for by its godly Elector, Frederick III. In order that the Calvinistic Reformation might spread throughout his country, Frederick III commissioned Zacharias Ursinus, professor at the Heidelberg University, and Caspar Olevianus, the court preacher, to prepare a manual which could be used to teach the Christian faith. This resulted in the Heidelberg Catechism, which was published in 1563. The Heidelberg Catechism remains one of the most influential and the most generally accepted of the catechisms of Reformation times.

QUESTION 1

Q.
What is your only comfort in life and death?

A.
That I, with body and soul, both in life and death (Rom. 14: 8), am not my own (1 Cor. 6: 19), but belong unto my faithful Savior Jesus Christ (1 Cor. 3: 23; Tit. 2: 14), who with His precious blood has fully satisfied for all my sins (1 Pet. 1: 18, 19; 1 John 1: 7; 2: 2,12), and delivered me (Heb. 2: 14; 1 John 3: 8; John 8: 34–36) from all the power of the devil (John 6: 39; 10: 28,29; 2 Thess. 3: 3; 1 Pet. 1: 5), and so preserves me that without the will of my heavenly Father not a hair can fall from my head (Matt. 10: 30; Luke 21: 18); indeed, that everything must fit His purpose for my salvation, (Rom. 8: 28) therefore by His Holy Spirit He also assures me of eternal life (2 Cor. 1: 22; 5: 5; Eph. 1: 14; Rom. 8: 16) and makes me heartily willing and ready, always, to live for him. (Rom. 8: 14; 1 John 3: 3)

QUESTION 2

Q.
How many things are necessary for you to know that you may live and die happily, enjoying this comfort?

A.
Three (Matt. 11: 28–30; Eph. 5: 8).
First, how great my sins and misery are, (John 9: 41; Matt. 9: 12; Rom. 3: 10; 1 John 1: 9,10)
    second, how I am delivered from all my sins and misery (John 17: 3; Acts 4: 12; 10: 43),
    third, how I am to express my thankfulness to God for such deliverance (Eph. 5: 10; Ps. 50: 14; Matt. 5: 16; 1 Pet. 2: 12; Rom. 6: 13; 2 Tim. 2: 15).

QUESTION 3

Q.
Where do you learn of your sin and its miserable consequences?
A.
Out of the law of God (Rom. 3: 20).

QUESTION 4

Q.
What does God require of you in His law?

A.
Jesus Christ teaches this in summary in Matthew 22: 37–40: You shall love the Lord your God with all your heart, and with all your soul, and with all your mind. This is the great and first commandment. And the second is like unto it. You shall love your neighbor as yourself. On these two commandments hang all the law and the prophets (Deut. 6: 5; Lev. 19: 18; Mark 12: 30; Luke 10: 27).

QUESTION 5

Q.
Are you able to keep God's law?

A.
In no way (Rom. 3: 10,20,23; 1 John 1: 8,10), for by nature I am inclined to hate God and my neighbor, and to break God's commandments in thought, word, and deed (Rom. 8: 7; Eph. 2: 3; Tit. 3: 3; Gen. 6: 5; 8: 21; Jer. 17: 9; Rom. 7: 23).

QUESTION 6

Q.
Did God create man so wicked and perverse like this?

A.
By no means. On the contrary, God created man good (Gen. 1: 31) and in His own image (Gen. 1: 26,27); that is, in true righteousness and holiness, so that

he might rightly know God his Creator, love Him with his whole heart, and live with Him in eternal blessedness, praising and glorifying Him always. (Eph. 4: 24; Col. 3: 10; 2 Cor. 3: 18)

QUESTION 7

Q.
Where, then, does this depraved nature of man come from?

A.
From the fall and disobedience of our first parents, Adam and Eve, in the Garden of Eden (Gen. 3; Rom. 5: 12,18,19); by which our nature became so corrupt that we are all conceived and born in sin. (Ps. 51: 5; Gen. 5: 3)

QUESTION 8

Q.
But are we so corrupt that we are wholly unable to do any good, and inclined to all evil?

A.
Yes, indeed, (Gen. 8: 21; 6: 5; Job 14: 4; 15: 14,16,35; John 3: 6; Is. 53: 6) unless we are born again by the Spirit of God. (John 3: 3,5; 1 Cor. 12: 3; 2 Cor. 3: 5)

The Heidelberg Catechism: Questions 9–20

QUESTION 9

Q. Does not God, then, wrong man by requiring of him in His law that which he cannot do?

A. Not at all; for God created man capable of doing it (Eph. 4: 24). But man, following the urging of the devil (Gen. 3: 13; 1 Tim. 2: 13,14), by deliberate disobedience, deprived himself and all his descendants of these gifts (Gen. 36; Rom. 5: 12)

QUESTION 10

Q. Will God allow such disobedience and rebellion to go unpunished?

A. Certainly not, for the wrath of God is revealed from heaven, (Gen. 2: 17; Rom. 5: 12) both against our inborn sinfulness as well as our actual sins, and He will punish them according to His righteous judgment both in time and eternity (Ps. 50: 20; 5: 5; Nah. 1: 2; Ex. 20: 5; 34: 7; Rom. 1: 18; Eph. 5: 6). Just as He has declared: Cursed is every one who does not continue in all things that are written in the book of the law, and do them (Deut. 27: 26; Gal. 3: 10).

QUESTION 11

Q. But is not God also merciful?

A. God is indeed merciful and gracious (Ex. 34: 6,7; 20: 6), but He is also true and righteous (Ps. 7: 9; Ex. 20: 5; 23: 7; 34: 7; Ps. 5: 4,5; Nah. 1: 2,3). And His truth and righteousness require that

He punish sin committed against His supreme majesty with extreme, that is, with eternal punishment of body and soul.

QUESTION 12

Q. Since, then by the righteous judgment of God we deserve punishment both in this life and forever, is there no way by which we may escape that punishment and again be received into favor?

A. God will have His righteousness satisfied (Gen. 2: 17; Ex. 23: 7; Ezek. 18: 4; Matt. 5: 26; 2 Thes. 1: 6; Luke 16: 2); therefore, full payment must be made to His righteousness, either by ourselves or by another (Rom. 8: 4).

QUESTION 13

Q. Can we make this payment ourselves?

A. By no means. On the contrary, we increase our debt each day (Job 9: 2; 15: 15,16; 4: 18,19; Ps. 130: 3; Matt. 6: 12; 18: 25; 16: 26).

QUESTION 14

Q. Can any mere creature make the payment for us?

A. None. First of all, God does not want to punish any other creature for the sin which man has committed (Ezek. 18: 4; Gen. 3: 17). And, further, no mere creature can bear the burden of God's eternal wrath against sin and redeem others from it (Nah. 1: 6; Ps. 130: 3).

QUESTION 15

Q. Then, what kind of mediator and redeemer must we seek?

A. One who is a true (1 Cor. 15: 21) and righteous (Heb. 7: 26) man and yet more powerful than all creatures, that is, one who is at the same time true God (Is. 7: 14; 9: 6; Jer. 23: 6; Luke 11: 22)

QUESTION 16

Q. Why must he be a true and righteous man?

A. Because God's righteousness requires that the same human nature which has sinned should make satisfaction for sin (Ezek. 18: 4,20; Rom. 5: 18; 1 Cor. 15: 21; Heb. 2: 14–16), but one who himself is a sinner cannot pay for others (Heb. 7: 26,27; Ps. 49: 8; 1 Pet. 3: 18).

QUESTION 17

Q. Why must he at the same time be true God?

A. So that by the power of His deity (Is. 9: 6; 63: 3) He might bear in His human nature (Deut. 4: 24; Nah. 1: 6; Ps. 130: 3) the burden of God's wrath (Is. 53: 4,11), and recover for us and restore to us righteousness and life. (Is. 53: 5,11)

QUESTION 18

Q. But who is this Mediator who is at the same time true God (1 John 5: 20; Rom. 9: 5; 8: 3; Gal. 4: 4; Is. 9: 6; Jer. 23: 6; Mal. 3: 1) and a true (Luke 1: 42; 2: 6,7; Rom. 1: 3; 9: 5; Phil. 2: 7; Heb. 2: 14–17; 4: 15) and perfectly righteous man (Is. 53: 9,11; Jer. 23: 5; Luke 1: 35; John 8: 46; Heb. 4: 15; 7: 26; 1 Pet. 1: 19; 2: 22; 3: 18)?

A. Our Lord Jesus Christ (1 Tim. 2: 5; Matt. 1: 23; 1 Tim. 3: 16; Luke 2: 11; Heb. 2: 9), who was made to us wisdom of God, and righteousness and sanctification and redemption (1 Cor. 1: 30).

QUESTION 19

Q. From where do you know this?

A. From the Holy Bible which is God's inspired revelation of Himself (Ps. 19: 1–3; 2 Tim. 3: 15,16).

QUESTION 20

Q. What do you mean by inspired revelation?

A. That the Holy Spirit moved men to write the scriptures and guided them in their work so they wrote the Word of God without any kind of error. (2 Pet. 1: 19)

The Heidelberg Catechism: Questions 21–27

QUESTION 21

Q:
Why did God give us this true and complete revelation?

A:
To tell us about Himself. Especially of His holy gospel which He first revealed in the Garden of Eden (Gen. 3: 15), afterward proclaimed by the holy patriarchs (Gen. 22: 18; 12: 3; 49: 10) and prophets (Is. 53; 42: 1–4; 43: 25; 49: 5,6,22,23; Jer. 23: 5,6; 31: 32,33; 32: 39–41; Mic. 7: 18–20; Acts 10: 43; 3: 22–24; Rom. 1: 2; Heb. 1: 1) an foreshadowed through the sacrifices and other rites of the Old Testament (Heb. 10: 1,7; Col. 2: 7; John 5: 46), and finally fulfilled by His only begotten Son (Rom. 10: 4; Gal. 4: 4; 3: 24; Col. 2: 17).

QUESTION 22

Q:
Will everyone, then, be saved through this gospel as they became lost through Adam?

A:
No (Matt. 7: 14; 22: 14).
But only those who are made to share in Christ and all His benefits by a true and living faith (Mark 16: 16; John 1: 12; 3: 16,18,36; Is. 53: 11; Ps. 2: 12; Rom. 11: 20; 3: 22; Heb. 4: 3; 5: 9; 10: 39; 11: 6).

QUESTION 23

Q:
What is true faith?

A:
It is not only a certain knowledge by which I accept as true all that God has revealed to us in His Word (James 2: 19), but also a firm confidence (Heb. 11: 1,7; Rom. 4: 18–21; 10: 10; Eph. 3: 12; Heb. 4: 16; Jms. 1: 6) which the Holy Spirit (Gal. 5: 22; Matt. 16: 17; 2 Cor. 4: 13; John 6: 29; Eph. 2: 8; Phil. 1: 19; Acts 16: 14) creates in me through the gospel (Rom. 1: 16; 10: 17; 1 Cor. 1: 21; Acts 10: 44; 16: 14), that, not only to others but to me also God has given the forgiveness of sins, everlasting righteousness and salvation (Rom. 1: 17; Gal. 3: 11; Heb. 10: 10, 38; Gal. 2: 16), out of sheer grace solely for the sake of Christ's saving work (Eph. 2: 8; Rom. 3: 24; 5: 19; Luke 1: 77, 78).

QUESTION 24

Q:
What, then, must a Christian believe?

A:
All that God has revealed to us about Himself as Father, Son, and Holy Spirit (Matt. 28: 19); and about how He has created us, and redeemed us when fallen (Gen. 1: 1; Mark 1: 15; John 20: 31); as well as the reason, result, and goal of His great and marvelous work of salvation (2 Tim. 1: 13; Heb. 11: 6; 1 John 5: 7; Luke 1: 1).

QUESTION 25

Q:
Since there is but one Divine Being
(Dt. 6: 4; Eph. 4: 6; Is. 44: 6; 45: 5;
1 Cor. 8: 4,6), why do you speak of
three: Father, Son, and Holy Spirit?

A:
Because God has thus revealed
Himself in His Word (Is. 61: 1; Luke
4: 18; Gen. 1: 2,3; Ps. 33: 6; Is. 48: 16;
Matt. 3: 16,17; 28: 19; 1 John 5: 7), that
these three distinct persons are the one,
true, eternal God (Is. 6: 1,3; John 14: 26;
15: 26; 2 Cor. 13: 14; Gal. 4: 6; Eph. 2: 18;
Tit. 3: 5,6)

QUESTION 26

Q:
What do you believe concerning God
the Father Almighty, Creator of all
things?

A:
That the eternal Father of our Lord
Jesus Christ, who out of nothing
created heaven and earth with all that
is in them (Gen. 1,2; Ex. 20: 11; Job 38,39;
Acts 4: 24; 14: 15; Ps. 33: 6; Is. 45: 7) is
for the sake of Christ, His Son, my God
and my Father (John 1: 12; Rom. 8: 15;
Gal. 4: 5–7; Eph. 1: 5).

I trust in Him so completely that I
have no doubt that He will provide me
with all things necessary for body and
soul (Ps. 55: 22; Matt. 6: 25,26; Luke
12: 22).

Moreover, whatever evil He sends
upon me in this troubled and tearful
life He will turn to my good (Rom.
8: 28); for He is able to do it, being

almighty God (Is. 46: 4; Rom. 10: 12),
and is willingly determined to do it,
being a faithful Father (Matt. 6: 32, 33;
7: 9, 10, 11).

QUESTION 27

Q:
What do you mean by the providence
of God?

A:
The almighty and everywhere
present power of God (Acts 17: 25–28;
Jer. 23: 23,24; Is. 29: 15, 16; Ezek. 8: 12)
whereby He still upholds, as it were
by His own hand, heaven and earth
together with all creatures, and rules
in such a way (Heb. 1: 3) that plants and
animals, rain and drought (John 9: 3),
fruitful and unfruitful years, food and
drink, health and sickness (Jer. 5: 24;
Acts 14: 17), riches and poverty
(Prov. 22: 2), and everything else, come
to us not by chance but by His fatherly
hand (Matt. 10: 29; Prov. 16: 33).

The Heidelberg Catechism: Questions 28–35

QUESTION 28

Q:
What advantage comes from acknowledging God's creation and providence?

A:
We learn that we are to be patient in adversity (Rom. 5: 3; Jms. 1: 3; Ps. 39: 9; Job 1: 21,22), thankful in prosperity (1 Thes. 5: 18; Dt. 8: 10), and to trust our faithful God and Father (Ps. 55: 22; Rom. 5: 4) for the future, assured that no creature shall separate us from His love (Rom. 8: 38,39), since all creatures are so completely in His hand that without His will they cannot so much as move (Job 1: 12; 2: 6; Prov. 21: 1; Acts 17: 25).

QUESTION 29

Q:
Why is Jesus Christ called God's only begotten Son, since we also are God's children?

A:
Because Christ alone is God and He is God's own eternal, natural Son (John 1: 14; Heb. 1: 1,2; John 3: 16; 1 John 4: 9; Rom. 8: 32), but we are children of God by adoption, through grace, for Christ's sake (Rom. 8: 16; John 1: 12; Gal. 4: 6; Eph. 1: 5,6).

QUESTION 30

Q:
How did the eternal Son of God become our Savior?

A:
The Son of God, who always remained (1 John 5: 20; John 1: 1; 17: 3; Rom. 1: 3) and always (Col. 1: 15; Rom. 9: 5) is true and eternal God, took upon Himself our human nature from the flesh and blood of a virgin woman (Gal. 4: 4; Luke 1: 31,42,43) by the working of the Holy Spirit (Matt. 1: 20; Luke 1: 35), so that He might also be the true seed of David (Rom. 1: 3; Ps. 132: 11; 2 Sam. 7: 12; Luke 1: 32; Acts 2: 30), just like those He was to save (Phil. 2: 7; Heb. 2: 14,17), except for sin (Heb. 4: 15).

QUESTION 31

Q:
What benefit is it to you that Jesus was miraculously conceived and born?

A:
That He is our Mediator (Heb. 7: 26, 27), and that, He covers over with His innocence and perfect holiness the sinfulness in which I have been conceived and born (1 Pet. 1: 18,19; 3: 18; 1 Cor. 1: 30,31; Rom. 8: 3,4; Is. 53: 11; Ps. 32: 1).

QUESTION 32

Q:
Why do you call Him Jesus, which means Savior?

A:
Because He saves us from our sins
(Matt. 1: 21; Heb. 7: 25), and because
salvation is not to be sought or found in
any other (Acts 4: 12; John 15: 4,5; 1 Tim.
2: 5; Is. 43: 11; 1 John 5: 11).

QUESTION 33

Q:
Do those who seek their salvation and
well-being by their own efforts, from
saints, or by other means really believe
in the only Savior Jesus?

A:
They do not. Rather, by such actions
they deny Jesus, the only Savior and
Mediator (1 Cor. 1: 13,31; Gal. 5: 4), even
though they boast of Him in words.
Therefore, one or the other must be
true: Either Jesus is not a perfect Savior,
or those who have truly received
Him possess ALL that is necessary
for their salvation (Heb. 12: 2; Is. 9: 6;
Col. 1: 19,20; 2: 10; 1 John 1: 7).

QUESTION 34

Q:
Why is Jesus called Christ, that is, the
Anointed One?

A:
Because He is ordained by God the
Father and anointed with the Holy
Spirit (Ps. 45: 7; Heb. 1: 9; Is. 61: 1; Luke
4: 18) to be our Prophet-Teacher (Dt.
18: 15; Acts 3: 22; 7: 32; Is. 55: 4) fully
revealing to us the secret purpose
and will of God concerning our

redemption (John 1: 18; 15: 15), to be
our only High Priest (Ps. 110: 4), having
redeemed us by the one sacrifice of
His body (Heb. 10: 12,14; 9: 12,14,28)
and continually interceding for us
with the Father (Rom. 8: 34; Heb. 9: 24;
1 John 2: 1; Rom. 5: 9,10), and to be
our eternal King, governing us by His
Word and Spirit, and defending and
preserving us in the redemption He
has won for us (Ps. 2: 6; Zech. 9: 9;
Matt. 21: 5; Luke 1: 33; Matt. 28: 18;
John 10: 28; Rev. 12: 10,11).

QUESTION 35

Q:
But why are you called a Christian
(Acts 11: 26)?

A:
Because He has made me a prophet,
priest, and king (1 John 2: 27; Acts 2: 17)
by sharing in Him and His anointing
(Acts 11: 26); so that I may confess His
name (Matt. 10: 32; Rom. 10: 10), offer
myself a living sacrifice of gratitude to
Him (Rom. 12: 1; 1 Pet. 2: 5,9; Rev. 1: 6;
5: 8,10), and fight against sin and the
devil with a free and good conscience
throughout this life (1 Pet. 2: 11; Rom.
6: 12,13; Gal. 5: 16,17; Eph. 6: 11; 1 Tim.
1: 18,20) and hereafter rule with Him in
eternity over all creatures (2 Tim. 2: 12;
Matt. 25: 34).

The Heidelberg Catechism: Questions 36–45

QUESTION 36

Q:
Why do you call Him, Our Lord?

A:
Because He has redeemed us, body and soul, from all our sins, not with gold or silver, but with His precious blood, and has delivered us from all the power of the devil, and has made us His own possession (1 Pet. 1: 18,19; 2: 9; 1 Cor. 6: 20; 1 Tim. 2: 6; John 20: 28).

QUESTION 37

Q:
What is the meaning of our Lord's suffering?

A:
That all the time He lived on earth, but especially at the end of His life, He bore in body and soul the wrath of God against the sins of a multitude of all kinds of sinners (even the worst) from all over the world and out of every race and every age of human history (Is. 53: 4; 1 Pet. 2: 24; 3: 18; 1 Tim. 2: 6), so that by His suffering, as the only atoning sacrifice (Is. 53: 10; Eph. 5: 2; 1 Cor. 5: 7; 1 John 2: 2; Rom. 3: 25; Heb. 9: 28; 10: 14), He might redeem our body and soul from everlasting damnation (Gal. 3: 13; Col. 1: 13; Heb. 9: 12; 1 Pet. 1: 18,19), and might obtain for us God's blessing, righteousness and eternal life (Rom. 3: 25; 2 Cor. 5: 21; John 3: 16; 6: 51; Heb. 9: 15; 10: 19).

QUESTION 38

Q:
Why was He judged of men like Pontius Pilate and the Jewish leaders?

A:
They were God's instruments to prove Christ's innocence, to execute God's judgment, and to show the wickedness of mankind even in its highest attainments of human justice and religion (John 18: 38; 19: 4–6; Acts 2: 33).

QUESTION 39

Q:
Is there something more in His having been crucified than if He had died some other death?

A:
Yes, for by this I am assured that He took upon Himself the curse which lay upon me (Gal. 3: 13), because the death of the cross was cursed of God (Dt. 21: 23).

QUESTION 40

Q:
Why was it necessary for Christ to suffer death?

A:
Because the justice and truth of God (Gen. 2: 17) are such that nothing else could satisfy for our sins except the death of the Son of God (Rom. 8: 3,4; Heb. 2: 14,15).

QUESTION 41

Q:
What is the deepest meaning of death?

A:
To be separated from God which is the greatest agony of hell (Ps. 16: 10,11; 89: 46).

QUESTION 42

Q:
Did Christ then go into hell in my place?

A:
Even though He did not go into the place of the damned, yet while He was on the cross at Calvary He bore all the inexpressible horrors, pains, and agonies in His body and soul which that place ever had or could have (Ps. 18: 4,5; 116: 3; Matt. 26: 38; 27: 46; Heb. 5: 7), and so He has delivered me from all its torments (Is. 53: 5).

QUESTION 43

Q:
Since then Christ suffered and died for us, why do we also suffer and die?

A:
Our suffering and death is not a satisfaction for our sins (Mk. 8: 37; Ps. 49: 7), but a subduing of the evil passions of our mortal bodies and a dying to sins, and an entering into eternal life, leaving behind the corruption which cleaves to our flesh

as it is in this present world (Phil. 1: 23; John 5: 24; Rom. 7: 24).

QUESTION 44

Q:
For whom did Christ endure all His sufferings and His terrible death?

A:
In His suffering and death Christ had His heart set upon a particular people (Matt. 1: 21), His body, His church (Acts 20: 28), His sheep (John 10: 11), those chosen from eternity to be His own (Eph. 1: 3–12) and given to Him before the world began (John 17: 1–11,20,24–26).

QUESTION 45

Q:
What comfort is it to you that the purpose of Christ's death was definite and particular?

A:
Much, in that it means that Christ does not fail in His purposes (John 6: 35–40) nor lose any who were given to Him by the Father (John 10: 14–18); and that His love toward me is everlasting (Eph. 5: 25–27) and unchangeable (Is. 46: 9–11) rather than general; that the salvation He wrought is certain and not a mere possibility (Is. 55: 11); and that His purchase was full and complete, leaving no part undone in my free salvation (Eph. 1: 3,4; Rom. 5: 8,9).

The Heidelberg Catechism: Questions 46–53

QUESTION 46

Q:
Why was He buried?

A:
Since the grave is the place of corruption, the finality of death, the return unto dust, Christ was buried to set the seal upon His death. His burial accomplished all of death and thereby fulfilled all righteousness (Acts 13: 29; Matt. 27: 59,60; Luke 23: 53; John 19: 38).

QUESTION 47

Q:
What benefit do we receive from the resurrection of Christ?

A:
First, by His resurrection He has overcome death that He might make us share in the righteousness which He has obtained for us through His death (Rom. 4: 25; 1 Pet. 1: 3; 1 Cor. 15: 16). Second, we too are now raised by His power to a new life while in this world (Rom. 6: 4; Col. 3: 1,3; Eph. 2: 5,6). Third, the resurrection of Christ is a sure pledge to us of our blessed resurrection (1 Cor. 15: 20,21).

QUESTION 48

Q:
Where is Christ's human nature at this time?

A:
Christ was taken up from the earth into heaven (Acts 1: 9; Mk. 16: 19; Luke 24: 51) before the eyes of His disciples and remains there on our behalf (Heb. 9: 24; 4: 14; Rom. 8: 34; Col. 3: 1) until He comes again to judge the living and the dead. (Acts 1: 11; Matt. 24: 30)

QUESTION 49

Q:
Is not Christ with us until the end of the world, as He has promised us (Matt. 28: 20)?

A:
Christ is true man and true God. As a man He is no longer on earth, (Heb. 8: 4; Matt. 26: 11; John 16: 28; 17: 11; Acts 3: 21) but in His divinity, majesty, grace, and Spirit, He is always present with us (John 14: 18; Matt. 28: 20).

QUESTION 50

Q:
But are not the two natures in Christ separated from each other in this way, if His humanity is not present wherever His divinity is?

A:
Not at all; for since the divine nature has no limits and is present everywhere (Jer. 23: 24; Acts 7: 49), that nature is certainly beyond the limits of the humanity it has assumed

(Col. 2: 9; John 3: 13; 11: 15; Matt. 28: 6). Nevertheless, it is ever in that humanity as well and remains personally united to it, so that the sympathies of His human nature can be with us in this world, even though His body is not.

QUESTION 51

Q:
What benefit do we receive from Christ's ascension into heaven?

A:
First, that He is our Advocate in the presence of His Father in heaven (1 John 2: 1; Rom. 8: 34).

Second, that we have our flesh in heaven as a sure pledge that He, as the Head, will also take us, His members, up to Himself (John 14: 2; 17: 24; 20: 17; Eph. 2: 6).

Third, that He sends us His Spirit as a security pledge, (John 14: 16; 16: 7; Acts 2: 33; 2 Cor. 1: 22; 5: 5) by whose power we seek what is above, where Christ is seated at the right hand of God, and not things that are on earth (Col. 3: 1)

QUESTION 52

Q:
What do you mean that Christ sits at the right hand of God; and what benefit do we receive from this glory of Christ, our Head?

A:
That He is seated means that He is the acknowledged Head (Eph. 1: 20–23;

Col. 1: 18) over all things for the sake of His Church, (Matt. 28: 18; John 5: 22) and through Him the Father pours out upon His members all the heavenly gifts of the Holy Spirit (Acts 2: 33; Eph. 4: 8), that by His irresistible power and absolute authority He may defend and support us against all His and our enemies (Ps. 2: 9; 110: 1,2; John 10: 28; Eph. 4: 8).

QUESTION 53

Q:
What comfort does the return of Christ to judge the living and the dead give you?

A:
That in all my sorrows and persecutions, with uplifted head I look for the very same Person who before has offered Himself for my sake to the judgment of God, and has removed all curse from me, to come as judge from heaven (Phil. 3: 20; Luke 21: 28; Rom. 8: 23; Tit. 2: 13), who shall cast all His and my enemies into everlasting condemnation (Matt. 25: 41; 2 Th. 1: 6), but shall take me with all His chosen ones to Himself into heavenly joy and glory.
(Matt. 25: 34; 2 Th. 1: 7)

The Heidelberg Catechism: Questions 54–61

QUESTION 54

Q:
What comfort does the resurrection of the body give you?

A:
That after this life my soul shall immediately be taken up to Christ, its Head (Luke 16: 22; 23: 43; Phil. 1: 21,23); and rest there awaiting the great day when it shall be reunited with my body, which shall be raised by the power of Christ and be made like unto His glorious body (Job 19: 25,26; 1 John 3: 2; Phil. 3: 21).

QUESTION 55

Q:
What comfort does the teaching concerning the life everlasting give you?

A:
That, since I now feel in my heart the beginning of eternal joy (2 Cor. 5: 2,3,6), I shall possess, after this life, perfect blessedness, which no eye has seen, nor ear heard, nor has the heart of man conceived, and I shall forever praise and rejoice in God (1 Cor. 2: 9).

QUESTION 56

Q:
What do you believe concerning the Holy Spirit?

A:
First, that with the Father and the Son (1 John 5: 7; Gen. 1: 2; Is. 48: 16; 1 Cor. 3: 16; 6: 19; Acts 5: 3,4), He is equally eternal God; second, that He is also given to me (Gal. 4: 6; Matt. 28: 19,20; 2 Cor. 1: 22; Eph. 1: 13) to make me by true faith share in Christ and all His benefits (Gal. 3: 14; 1 Pet. 1: 2; 1 Cor. 6: 17); third, that He comforts and guides me (John 15: 26; Acts 9: 31) in the way of truth and obedience and will abide with me forever (John 14: 16; 1 Pet. 4: 14).

QUESTION 57

Q:
What do you believe concerning the holy universal church?

A:
I believe that, from the beginning to the end of the world (Gen. 26: 4; Rev. 5: 9), and out of the whole human race (Ps. 71: 17,18; Is. 59: 21; 1 Cor. 11: 26), the Son of God (Eph. 5: 26; John 10: 11; Acts 20: 28; Eph. 4: 11–13), by His Spirit and Word (Is. 59: 21; Rom. 1: 16; 10: 14–17; Eph. 5: 26), gathers, protects, and preserves for Himself (Matt. 16: 18; John 10: 28–30; Ps. 129: 1–5), in the unity of the faith (Acts 2: 42; Eph. 4: 3–5), a congregation chosen for eternal life. (Rom. 8: 29; Eph. 1: 10–13).

Also, I believe that I am and forever will remain a living member of this great assembly (Ps. 23: 6; 1 Cor. 1: 8,9; John 10: 28; 1 John 2: 19; 1 Pet. 1: 5).

QUESTION 58

Q:
When was this church chosen for eternal life?

A:
God chose each of its members in Christ before the creation of the world according to the purpose of His eternal and unchangeable will, having predestinated us unto the adoption of children by Jesus Christ unto Himself so that we might be built into a holy temple which is pleasing, beautiful, and glorious unto Him (Eph. 1: 4–23).

QUESTION 59

Q:
How is this elect church of the Lord Jesus Christ manifest in the world?

A:
The Son of God, by His Word and Spirit, calls the elect to a saving faith in Himself and these are gathered and united in local congregations for worship, instruction in righteousness, and the proclamation and defense of the gospel (2 Th. 2: 13,14; 2 Tim. 1: 8,9; Acts 2: 41,42; Matt. 28: 20; Phil. 1: 27).

QUESTION 60

Q:
What do you understand of the communion of saints?

A:
That believers one and all, as members of Christ, share Christ and all His treasures and gifts (1 John 1: 3; Rom. 8: 32; 1 Cor. 12: 12,13; 1 Cor. 6: 17) together; and, because of this togetherness, every one ought to know that he is obligated to use his gifts freely and cheerfully for the benefit and welfare of other members (1 Cor. 12: 21; 13: 1,5; Phil. 2: 4–8).

QUESTION 61

Q:
What do you believe concerning the forgiveness of sins?

A:
That, for the sake of Christ's reconciling work, God will no more remember my sins or the sinfulness with which I have to struggle all my life long (1 John 2: 2; 1: 7; 2 Cor. 5: 19); but that He graciously grants to me the righteousness of Christ (Rom. 7: 23–25; Jer. 31: 34; Mic. 7: 19; Ps. 103: 3,10,12) so that I may never come into condemnation (John 3: 18; 5: 24).

The Heidelberg Catechism: Questions 62–71

QUESTION 62

Q:
How are you righteous before God?

A:
Though in myself I am guilty of grievously sinning against all the commandments of God and have not kept any one of them (Rom. 3: 9); and though I still have inclinations and desires toward all sorts of evils (Rom. 7: 23), yet, God out of pure grace freely gives me all the benefits of Christ's perfect satisfaction (Tit. 3: 5; Dt. 9: 6; Ezek. 36: 22), placing all His righteousness and holiness to my account (Rom. 3: 24; Eph. 2: 8); God looks upon me in Christ and sees perfection as if I had never committed a single sin or had ever been sinful (1 John 2: 2; 2 Cor. 5: 21), as if I myself had fulfilled all the obedience which Christ has carried out for me. All of this is given to me through faith alone (Rom. 3: 22; John 3: 18).

QUESTION 63

Q:
Why do you say that you are righteous by faith alone?

A:
It is not that faith has any worth or merit to God, for it is not a work or meriting condition, but it is God's instrument through which He gives me the satisfaction, righteousness, and holiness of Christ (1 Cor. 1: 30; 2: 2), and it is the only way that He does this (1 John 5: 10).

QUESTION 64

Q:
Since, then, faith alone makes us share in Christ and all His benefits, where does such faith originate?

A:
It is the gracious gift of God created in our hearts by the Holy Spirit (Eph. 2: 8; 6: 23; John 3: 5; Phil. 1: 29) along with the preaching of the Word (Matt. 28: 19; 1 Pet. 1: 22,23).

QUESTION 65

Q:
But why cannot our good works or own efforts be our righteousness before God, or at least part of it?

A:
Because the righteousness which can stand before the judgment of God must be absolutely perfect and wholly identical to every line and dot of God's law (Gal. 3: 10; Dt. 27: 26). But even our best efforts in this life are all imperfect and defiled with sin. (Is. 64: 6)

QUESTION 66

Q:
Since God rewards good works both in this and the future life, does not this mean there is some merit in them?

A:
In no way, for it is a reward of grace (Lk. 17: 10), because even my good

works are but fruits which Christ bears in and through me (Eph. 2: 8,9).

QUESTION 67

Q:
But does not this teaching make people careless and sinful?

A:
No, for it is utterly impossible for one who is in union with Christ by true faith, and renewed by the Holy Spirit, not to bring forth the fruits of gratitude (Matt. 7: 18; John 15: 5).

QUESTION 68

Q:
What two fruits of gratitude should one who has been renewed unto true faith soon exhibit by public rite?

A:
Baptism (Matt. 28: 19) and the Lord's Supper (Acts 2: 42).

QUESTION 69

Q:
What are baptism and the Lord's Supper?

A:
They are holy ordinances which declare by symbols the saving truth of the gospel, which were appointed by the Lord Jesus to be observed until the end of the world (Matt. 28: 19).

QUESTION 70

Q:
Are these only then mere symbols and not sacraments?

A:
They are the Word of God in symbol and must always be understood in connection with that Word. When they are received by faith they draw our attention to Christ's crucifixion and resurrection and thereby strengthen our souls. Unbelievers and hypocrites profess by their act of partaking to believe something they do not possess, therefore receive nothing but guilt for taking God's Word in vain (1 Cor. 11: 28,29).

QUESTION 71

Q:
What is baptism?

A:
It is the immersing of a believer in water (Rom. 6: 3,4,5; Col. 2: 11; Gal. 3: 27) as a sign unto him (1 Pet. 3: 21) that he has union with Christ in His atoning death and powerful resurrection (Rom. 6: 2, 4), thus having the remission of sins and the washing of regeneration (Mk. 1: 4; Acts 26: 16), and so is to walk and live as a new creature (Col. 3: 1–5).

The Heidelberg Catechism: Questions 72–78

QUESTION 72

Q:
How does holy baptism remind you that Christ's sacrificial death and mighty resurrection avail for you?

A:
In this way:

Christ has instituted this immersing and washing in water to signify His promise that, as certainly as I go down beneath the water and come up again, I am one with Him (Rom. 6: 4) as He was overwhelmed by sufferings and death (Luke 12: 50), then rose victoriously to life (Rom. 6: 8–11); and that by this union, just as my whole body is washed externally with water, so have I been wholly cleansed from the uncleanness of my soul and all my sins by the blood and Spirit of Christ, and made a victor over death.

QUESTION 73

Q:
What does it mean to be one with Christ as He was baptized in sufferings and death, and as He arose victoriously over the grave?

A:
That God places to my account the death of Christ just as if I myself had borne this overwhelming penalty for sin (Rom. 4: 24,25), and I share also in His resurrection by being granted His victory over sin and death and all spiritual foes (Eph. 1: 3,4), for Christ

my risen Lord dwells in me by His Spirit with the same energizing power which raised Him from the dead (Eph. 1: 19,20), giving me strength to live a new life and finally raising my body on the last day (Rom. 6: 8,9).

QUESTION 74

Q:
What does it mean to be washed in the blood and Spirit of Christ?

A:
It means to have the forgiveness of sins from God, through grace for the sake of Christ's blood which He shed for us in His sacrifice on the cross (Heb. 12: 24; 1 Pet. 1: 2; Rev. 1: 5; 7: 14; Zech. 13: 1; Ezek. 36: 25), and because of this to be renewed by the Holy Spirit and separated unto God as members of Christ so that we may more and more die unto sin and live in a consecrated and blameless way (John 1: 33; 3: 5; 1 Cor. 6: 11; 12: 13; Rom. 6: 4; Col. 2: 12).

QUESTION 75

Q:
Who, then, should be baptized?

A:
Only those who possess the things signified (Mk. 16: 16) Otherwise, we declare another gospel which says one may be forgiven in, by, through, or because of baptism, or by inheritance

from parents (John 1: 13), rather than by Christ's work alone applied to us by God's Spirit (John 3: 6).

QUESTION 76

Q:
What is the Lord's Supper?

A:
It is an eating of bread and drinking of wine by believers as a memorial to relive symbolically the deliverance from sin Christ made for them on Calvary (Matt. 26: 26–28; Mk. 14: 22–24; Luke 22: 19,20).

It is a joyous confession and thanksgiving proclamation that the work which Christ did on the cross is the continuing source of their spiritual life (1 Cor. 10: 16,17; 11: 23–25; 12: 13), and that they are sharers together in it.

QUESTION 77

Q:
What does it mean to eat the crucified body of Christ and to drink His shed blood?

A:
It means that we embrace with a trusting heart the whole suffering and death of Christ upon the cross and by it receive the forgiveness of sins and spiritual life (John 6: 35,40,47,48,50,5 1,53,54), and thus become more and more united to Him by the Holy Spirit who dwells both in Christ and in us (John 6: 55,56), that, as bread and wine provide for our physical needs, Christ's

work upon the cross provides for our spiritual needs (Col. 3: 1; Eph. 5: 29; 1 John 3: 24).

QUESTION 78

Q:
Do the bread and wine become the very body and blood of Christ?

A:
No (Matt. 26: 26–28).

For these elements refer to the historical event of Calvary done by our Lord Jesus (1 Cor. 11: 23–26) and our incorporation into what He did there (1 Cor. 10: 16).

Just as baptism is not the actual burial and resurrection of Christ, nor does the water change into the blood or Spirit of Christ, but is a divine memorial, even so, Christ is not offered, nor any real sacrifice made in the Lord's Supper, but we are made by the Spirit to relive by faith the Calvary event which is the source of our life.

The Heidelberg Catechism: Questions 79–84

QUESTION 79

Q:
Then why does Christ call the bread His body, and the cup His blood, or the new covenant in His blood, and why does the apostle Paul call the Supper a sharing in the body and blood of Christ?

A:
Not without strong reason, for the Supper is a special time set apart to take us back to Calvary in memory by faith to relive that event, and to remind ourselves that we receive the reality of spiritual life, from the work of Christ there, with our spiritual mouth, which is faith, in just as real a way as the mouth of the body receives these physical elements; for the flesh and blood of Christ sacrificed once for all on the cross is indeed the true spiritual food and drink of our souls (Jn. 6: 55; 1 Cor. 10: 16).

QUESTION 80

Q:
Does the Scripture use any other such symbolic language?

A:
Yes, of the old Passover it is written: This is the bread of affliction which our fathers ate in the land of Egypt (Dt. 16: 3); Jesus says: The field is the world, I am the door (Matt. 13: 3,8; John 10: 9); and the apostle Paul says the veil on Moses' face is the same that remains on Israel's heart (2 Cor. 3: 15);

also, the book of Hebrews calls the temple veil Christ's flesh (Heb. 10: 20).

QUESTION 81

Q:
What difference is there between the Lord's Supper and the Roman Catholic Mass?

A:
The Lord's Supper testifies to us that we have complete forgiveness of all our sins through the one sacrifice of Jesus Christ which He Himself has accomplished on the cross once for all (Heb. 10: 10,12; 7: 26,27; 9: 12,25; John 19: 30; Matt. 26: 28; Luke 22: 19); and that through the Holy Spirit we are incorporated into Christ (1 Cor. 10: 16, 17; 6: 17), who according to His human nature is not now on earth but in heaven, at the right hand of the Father (John 20: 17; Col. 3: 1; Heb. 1: 3; 8: 1), and is there to be worshiped (Matt. 6: 20,21; Acts 7: 55; Phil. 3: 20; 1 Th. 1: 10).

But the Mass teaches that the living and the dead do not have forgiveness of sins through the sufferings of Christ unless He is again offered for them daily by the priest, and that Christ is bodily under the form of bread and wine and is therefore to be worshiped in them. Therefore, the Mass is fundamentally a complete denial of the once for all sacrifice and suffering of Christ and as such an idolatry to be condemned (Heb. 9: 26; 10: 12,14).

QUESTION 82

Q:
Who ought to come to the table of the Lord?

A:
Only Christians, that is, those who have inwardly mourned over their sinfulness, but nevertheless trust that their sins are forgiven for Christ's sake, and who have heart-felt desire to live the new life of Christian gratitude. But those with hypocritical hearts who have not turned to God with sincerity eat and drink judgment to themselves (1 Cor. 11: 28, 29; 10: 19–22).

QUESTION 83

Q:
Should those who show themselves to be unbelievers and enemies of God by their confession and life be admitted to this Supper?

A:
No, these should not be received by the church, nor welcomed to the Supper, but rather excluded from the fellowship and warned that all who do not sincerely repent stand exposed to the wrath of God and eternal condemnation as long as they remain unconverted (1 Cor. 11: 20,34; Is. 1: 11; 66: 3; Jer. 7: 21).

QUESTION 84

Q:
Does Christ require that His church withhold full fellowship from any other than unbelievers?

A:
Yes, any who persist to act in a disorderly manner or have settled in errors which tend to destroy the unity of the faith, though they are not damnable in themselves, should be barred from full communion as a warning against such disorderly ways. However, such an offender should be counted as a brother and not an enemy (2 Th. 3: 14,15).

The Heidelberg Catechism: Questions 85–92

QUESTION 85

Q:
Since we are redeemed from our sin and God's wrath wholly by grace through Christ without any merit of our own, why must we do good works?

A:
Because just as certain as Christ has redeemed us with His blood, He has also certainly renewed us by His Holy Spirit after His own image, and this inward renewal will always bear fruit (Eph. 2: 10; John 15: 5; Matt. 7: 16–20), because true faith is the life of God implanted in the soul and this life will work itself out in humble gratitude to God its source and seek to glorify Him before all men (Jms. 2: 26; 3: 12).

QUESTION 86

Q:
Can those who profess Christ with their mouths, but continue to walk in sin and live being ruled by fleshly desire be saved?

A:
Certainly not! Scripture says, Surely you know that the unjust will never come into possession of the kingdom of God. Make no mistake; no fornicator, or idolater, none who are guilty of either adultery or of homosexual perversion, no thieves or greedy or drunkards or slanderers or swindlers, will possess the kingdom of God (1 Cor. 6: 9,10; Eph. 5: 5,6;

1 John 3: 14); and, without sanctification (holiness) no one shall see the Lord (Heb. 12: 14).

QUESTION 87

Q:
What is this practical sanctification?

A:
Practical sanctification is the continuing work of God, which He began at regeneration, by His Holy Spirit applying His Word to the heart of each of His children (Phil. 1: 6; 2: 12,13), thereby separating them from the control of sinful thoughts and actions (Rom. 6: 12–14), and setting them apart to become more like Himself in thought and act, in order that they may glorify Him by good works (Eph. 2: 10; 1 Tim. 2: 10; Tit. 2: 7, 14; 3: 14; 1 Pet. 2: 12).

QUESTION 88

Q:
What are good works?

A:
The only works which are good in God's sight are those which flow out of gratitude to Him, from a believing heart (Rom. 14: 23; 1 Cor. 10: 31), for what He has done for us through His Son, Jesus Christ; and those which reflect His image (John 17: 23; 2 Cor. 3: 18; Col. 3: 10; Rom. 8: 29).

QUESTION 89

Q:
How do I reflect the image of God?

A:
I reflect the image of God as my character and conduct are, in loving fear by the Spirit, conformed to His will and commandments (Col. 3: 5–10).

QUESTION 90

Q:
How do I know the character and commandments of God?

A:
God has revealed His law and His character in various ways: In the lives of His saints, such as, Abraham, Moses, David, Peter, John, and Paul; (2 Th. 3: 9; 1 Cor. 10: 11) in His acts and words to and through O.T. Israel and the N.T. churches (Rom. 15: 4); in the ten commandments given to Israel by Moses (Rom. 14: 9); in the message of the holy prophets (Jer. 31: 10; Ezek. 20: 47); but especially in Jesus Christ, who was the fullness of God come in our flesh, (so He was the perfect image of God incarnate (Col. 3: 9; Heb. 1: 1–3)), and whose Spirit was the source of all those other revelations (1 Pet. 1: 11).

QUESTION 91

Q:
Where do I find the permanent, final, and inerrant record of these revelations?

A:
In the Holy Bible, which is God's Word, and the only sufficient, certain, infallible, and complete rule of truth that we have (Matt. 4: 4,7,10; 2 Tim. 3: 16,17).

QUESTION 92

Q:
Are not the ten commandments a special rule summing up how we might be holy?

A:
We should not ignore Moses or any of the O.T. (1 Tim. 5: 18; Eph. 6: 2), for they are the Word of Christ too. However, the divine standard of holiness became incarnate in Jesus Christ, and the fullness of God's law is embodied and set forth in His perfect humanity (Gal. 4: 4; Col. 2: 9); so our use of the O.T. must always be subordinate to and in light of the full and complete revelation of God's eternal law given to us in His Son (Luke 9: 35; Heb. 3: 3–7; 12: 25; John 1: 17,18)

The Heidelberg Catechism: Questions 93–100

QUESTION 93

Q:
Then, do you mean the O.T. saints were not fully God's children like we are?

A:
Indeed they were God's children, but they lived in a time of shadow and infancy (Gal. 4: 1–5; Rom. 3: 25; Heb. 8: 8–13; 10: 1; 11: 40) and looked forward to the coming of the great Light (Luke 2: 32; John 1: 9,14), the gospel of Jesus Christ, which contains the sum and substance and glory of all the laws which God ever gave from His throne (Col. 1: 19).

QUESTION 94

Q:
Is Christ's example or the gospel, then, just a new or a fuller set of rules we must follow in order to be saved?

A:
Certainly not! For all things pertaining to our salvation were won and are treasured up for us in the Lord Jesus Christ (1 Cor. 1: 30; Col. 2: 3), including our sanctification; and we follow Christ's example and commandments because He dwells in us (Col. 1: 27; John 14: 16,20) and works in us and gives us His mind and power as His Holy Spirit applies His Word to our hearts (Rom. 12: 2; 1 Cor. 2: 16; Phil. 2: 5); all this is part of the one great salvation He merited for us on the cross (Rom. 8: 32–34).

QUESTION 95

Q:
Do you, then, walk in Christ as you received Him, that is, by faith alone?

A:
Having begun in the Spirit by faith (Gal. 3: 2–5) I put no confidence in the flesh to continue, but look to the cross of Christ, not only for my pardon, but for my purification as well (Gal. 3: 13,14; 6: 14; Heb. 12: 2), for there is but one great principle of grace, through faith that covers the whole Christian life (Gal. 3: 11; 1 John 4: 9).

QUESTION 96

Q:
Does this mean you have no struggle and warfare?

A:
Quite the contrary! For the loving fear of God, which His Spirit worked in my heart at my conversion (2 Cor. 7: 1; Eph. 5: 21; Phil. 2: 12; 1 Pet. 1: 17), by revealing His love to me in Christ and the cross, continues to motivate me to obey His Word and struggle against sin and long for perfection (1 John 3: 9; 5: 4; Rom. 8: 16); and so, I fight to put off the old life of sin and put on the new life of holiness (Eph. 4: 22; Col. 3: 8–14).

QUESTION 97

Q:
As you become more holy do you need Christ's work on the cross and His Spirit's work within any less?

A:
Just the opposite. For my sanctification always remains in Christ (John 15: 2–4), and, the more I grow in grace, the more I learn of my own sinfulness (Rom. 7: 18–20) and my need of His Spirit to apply the benefits of His crucifixion and resurrection. In myself there ever remains no good thing, and it is only in fellowship with Him that I conform to God's standard of holiness.

QUESTION 98

Q:
Will you ever in this life attain perfect conformity to God's standard of holiness?

A:
No, for even the holiest of God's children make only a small beginning in obedience (1 John 1: 8; Rom. 7: 14,15; Eccl. 7: 20; 1 Cor. 13: 9) in this life. Nevertheless, they begin with serious purpose to live not only according to some, but according to all the commandments of God in Christ Jesus (Rom. 7: 22; Ps. 1: 2).

QUESTION 99

Q:
If weakness and imperfection is mixed with all our good works, how are they acceptable to God at all?

A:
As my whole being is accepted through Christ, so also are my good works (2 Cor. 8: 12; Eph. 1: 6); not as though they were in this life wholly unblamable and perfect in God's sight, but that He, looking upon them in His Son, is pleased to accept and reward that which is sincere, although accompanied with many weaknesses and imperfections.

QUESTION 100

Q:
Why, then, does God set before us such a standard of perfection, since none can attain it in this life?

A:
First, that all our life long we may become increasingly aware of our sinfulness (Rom. 3: 20; 1 John 1: 9; Ps. 32: 5), and therefore more eagerly seek forgiveness of sins and righteousness in Christ (Matt. 5: 6; Rom. 7: 24,25). Second, that we may constantly and diligently pray to God for the grace of the Holy Spirit, so that we may be renewed in the image of God, until we attain the goal of full perfection after this life (1 Cor. 9: 24; Phil. 3: 12–14). Third, that we may never forget God's wonderful grace toward us, but continually praise and thank Him (Ps. 103: 1–3).

The Heidelberg Catechism: Questions 101–110

QUESTION 101

Q:
Why is prayer and thanksgiving necessary for Christians?

A:
Because it is the chief part of the gratitude which God works in and requires of us (Ps. 50: 14; Rom. 14: 6; Eph. 5: 4,20; Col. 3: 17; Heb. 13: 5), and because God will give His grace and Holy Spirit only to those who sincerely beseech Him in prayer without ceasing, and who thank Him for all these gifts He gives us in His Son (Matt. 7: 7; Luke 11: 9,13; 1 Th. 5: 17).

QUESTION 102

Q:
What is contained in a prayer which pleases God and is heard by Him?

A:
First, that we sincerely (John 4: 24; Ps. 145: 18) call upon the one true God, who has revealed Himself to us in His Word (Rev. 19: 10; John 4: 22–24) for all that He has commanded us to ask of Him (Rom. 8: 26; 1 John 5: 14; Jms. 1: 5). Then, that we thoroughly acknowledge our need and evil condition (2 Chr. 20: 12) so that we may humble ourselves in the presence of His majesty (Ps. 2: 11; 34: 18; Is. 66: 2). Third, that we rest assured (Rom. 10: 13; Jms. 1: 6), that, in spite of our unworthiness, He will certainly hear our prayer (John 14: 13; 16: 23; Dan. 9: 18) for the

sake of Christ our Lord, as He has promised us in His Word (Matt. 7: 8; Ps. 27: 8).

QUESTION 103

Q:
What guide has God given to direct us in our prayers?

A:
The whole Word of God is of use to direct us in prayer; but we have a special guide in that pattern of prayer which Christ taught His disciples, commonly called, THE LORD'S PRAYER.

QUESTION 104

Q:
Where is this found?
A:
In Matthew 6: 9–13, or Luke 11: 1–4.

QUESTION 105

Q:
Why has Christ commanded us to address God: Father?

A:
That at the very beginning of our prayer He may awaken in us the inner knowledge that we are God's dearly beloved children through Christ (Matt. 7: 9–11; Luke 11: 11–13), and that with a heart of tenderness, compassion,

loving kindness, and mercy He who so freely gave His Son for us will certainly provide all our needs (Rom. 8: 16–21; Gal. 3: 26; Eph. 5: 1; Gal. 4: 5–7).

QUESTION 106

Q:
How should you, God's child, approach Him then?

A:
I should come to Him with the reverence, expectation, and wonder of a little child (Ps. 131: 2) which acknowledges Him the only true God and Source of all my good (Ps. 73: 25; 37: 7; Matt. 11: 28,29); finds my trust and comfort and rest in Him alone; loves, honors, and obeys Him with my whole heart (Matt. 5: 29; 10: 37; Acts 5: 29); and rather than do the least thing against the will of Him who loves me so, I should rather turn my back on all creatures.

QUESTION 107

Q:
Who denies the Fatherhood of God?

A:
All those who deny that Jesus Christ is the only way to the Father have denied the Father and set up an idol (John 14: 6; Eph. 5: 5), which is to imagine or possess something in which one puts one's trust in place of or beside the true God who has revealed Himself in His Word (Phil. 3: 19; Gal. 4: 8; Eph. 2: 12; 1 John 2: 23; John 5: 23).

QUESTION 108

Q:
Why does Christ say: OUR Father?

A:
So that we may remember to pray not only for ourselves, but with and for our brothers and sisters in Christ also (2 Cor. 1: 11; 9: 14; Phil. 1: 4,19; Col. 3: 4).

QUESTION 109

Q:
Why is there added: Who is in heaven?

A:
That we may have no earthly conception of the heavenly majesty of God (Jer. 23: 23,24; Acts 17: 24,25,27), but that we may expect from His almighty power all things that are needed for body and soul (Rom. 10: 12).

QUESTION 110

Q:
Should we, then, not make any images of God at all?

A:
God cannot and should not be pictured in any way. (Is. 40: 25) As for creatures, although they may indeed be portrayed, God forbids making or having any likeness of them in order to worship them or use them to serve Him (Ex. 34: 17; 23: 24; 34: 13; Num. 33: 52).

All the prayers in the Bible (1)

Overview

In the New American Standard Bible [NASB]
- the word "prayer" occurs 112 times ("prayers" = 27 times);
- the verb "pray" occurs 109 ("prays" = 5; "prayed" = 46; "praying" = 35);

in total: prayer is used 334 times.

The 221 prayers of the Bible

176 prayers from the Old Testament and 45 from the New Testament are now listed.

They only include actual prayers, and not references to prayer, such as statements like "he prayed."

Old Testament

Genesis: Six prayers

Other references to prayer: Gen. 12: 7–8; 13: 4; 16: 11; 20: 17–18; 25: 21–23.

1. Abraham for an heir (Gen. 15: 2–3). Answered [A'd] (Gen. 21: 1–8). This is the first prayer in the Bible.

2. Abraham for Ishmael to be his heir (Gen. 17: 18). Not Answered [Not A'd].

3. Abraham for God to spare Sodom (Gen. 18: 23–32). Not A'd (Gen. 19: 24).

4. Eliezer, Abraham's servant, for a bride for Isaac (Gen. 24: 12–14). A'd (Gen. 24: 15ff)

5. Jacob for a blessing (Gen. 28: 20–22). A'd (Gen. 32: 1–33: 17).

6. Jacob for deliverance from Esau (Gen. 32: 9–12). A'd (Gen. 33).

Exodus: Four prayers

Other references to prayer: Ex. 2: 11,23–25; 3: 7,9; 10: 16.

7. Moses for Aaron to go with him (Ex. 4: 13). A'd (Ex. 4: 14–17).

8. Moses for not delivering Israel (Ex. 5: 22–23). A'd (Ex. 3: 8,12,17–22).

9. Moses for forgiveness for Israel (Ex. 32: 11–13; 31–32). A'd (Ex. 32: 14, 33–35).

10. Moses for God's presence to go with Israel to Canaan (Ex. 33: 12–13,15–16,18). A'd (Ex. 33: 14,17,19–23).

Numbers: Nine prayers

Other references to prayer: Num. 11: 2; 21: 7.

11. Aaron for the blessing of God on the people (Num. 6: 24–26). A'd (Num. 6: 27).

12. Moses for God to bless on the journey (Num. 10: 35–36). A'd (Ex. 32: 32–33).

13. Moses complaining over his burden (Num. 11: 10–15). A'd (Num. 11: 16–20, 25–30).

14. Moses for the people to have meat (Num. 11: 21–22). A'd (Num. 11: 21,23,31–33).

15. Moses for the healing of Miriam (Num. 12: 13). A'd (Num. 12: 14–16).

16. Moses for God to spare Israel (Num. 14: 13–19). A'd (Num. 14: 20).

17. Moses for judgment on sin (Num. 16: 15). A'd (Num. 16: 23–34)

18. Israel for forgiveness of sin (Num. 21: 7). A'd (Num. 21: 7–9)

19. Moses for a new leader of Israel (Num. 27: 16–17). A'd (Num. 27: 18–23).

Deuteronomy: Two prayers

Other references to prayer: Dt. 9: 20,26; 21: 6–9; 26: 5–15.

20. Moses asking to go over into Canaan (Dt. 3: 24–25). Not A'd (Dt. 3: 26; Num. 20: 12).

21. Moses for Israel to be spared (Dt. 9: 26–29). A'd (Ex. 32: 11–14).

Joshua: Two prayers

22. Joshua because God had not given victory (Josh. 7: 7–9). A'd (Josh. 7: 10–15).

23. Joshua for the sun and moon to stand still (Josh. 10: 12). A'd (Josh. 10: 13).

Judges: Nine prayers

24. Israel for guidance (Judg. 1: 1). A'd (Judg. 1: 2).

25. Gideon for guidance (Judg. 6: 13,15,17–18,22). A'd (Judg. 6: 12,14,16,20–21,23).

26. Israel for deliverance and forgiveness of sins (Judg. 10: 10,15). A'd (Judg. 11: 1–33).

27. Jephthah for victory (Judg. 11: 30–31). A'd (Judg. 11: 32).

28. Manoah for an angel to appear and direct him (Judg. 13: 8,11–12,15,17). A'd (Judg. 13: 9,11,13,16,18).

29. Samson for one last victory (Judg. 16: 28). A'd (Judg. 13: 4–5; 16: 22).

30. Israel for guidance (Judg. 20: 23). A'd (Judg. 20: 23)

31. Israel for guidance (Judg. 20: 28). A'd (Judg. 20: 28)

32. Israel for revelation (Judg. 21: 3). Not A'd.

1 Samuel: Six prayers

Other references to prayer: 1 Sam. 7: 9; 8: 6; 12: 18; 15: 11; 28: 6.

33. Hannah for a son (1 Sam. 1: 11). A'd (1 Sam. 1: 20–23).

34. Hannah to express gratitude for A'd prayer (1 Sam. 2: 1–10).

35. Saul for guidance (1 Sam. 14: 37). Not A'd (1 Sam. 14: 37).

36. David for guidance (1 Sam. 23: 2). A'd (1 Sam. 23: 2).

37. David for revelation (1 Sam. 23: 10–12).

38. David for revelation (1 Sam. 30: 8).

2 Samuel: Four prayers

Other references to prayer: 2 Sam. 5: 23; 12: 16; 15: 7–8; 21: 1.

39. David for revelation (2 Sam. 2: 1).

40. David for revelation (2 Sam. 5: 19). A'd (2 Sam. 5: 19).

41. David for fulfillment of Davidic covenant (2 Sam. 7: 18–29) A'd in Christ (Is. 9: 6–7; Luke 1: 32–33; Acts 15: 13–18; Rev. 11: 15; 20: 1–10).

42. David for forgiveness of sin (2 Sam. 24: 10). A'd, but the consequences of David's sin were not removed (2 Sam. 24: 11–25).

1 Kings: Five prayers

Other references to prayer: 1 Kgs. 13: 6; 18: 42–43.

43. Solomon for wisdom (1 Kgs. 3: 6–9). A'd (1 Kgs. 3: 10–14).

44. Solomon, prayer of dedication (1 Kgs. 8: 23–53).

45. Elijah for resurrection of boy (1 Kgs. 17: 20–21). A'd (1 Kgs. 17: 22–24; Heb. 11: 35).

All the prayers in the Bible (2)

1 Kings: Five prayers, continued

46. Elijah for fire from heaven
(1 Kgs. 18: 36–37). A'd (1 Kgs. 18: 38).

47. Elijah for death (1 Kgs. 19: 4). Not
A'd because God later took him to
heaven without dying (2 Kgs. 2: 9).

2 Kings: Three prayers

48. Elisha for his servant's eyes to be
opened (2 Kgs. 6: 17). A'd (2 Kgs. 6: 17).

49. Hezekiah for deliverance (2 Kgs.
19: 15–19). A'd (2 Kgs. 19: 35).

50. Hezekiah for a longer life
(2 Kgs. 20: 3). A'd: he lived fifteen more
yrs (2 Kgs. 20: 3,5–6).

1 Chronicles: Two prayers

Other references to prayer: 1 Chr. 5: 20;
21: 26; 23: 30.

51. Jabez for enlarged coast (1 Chr.
4: 10). A'd (1 Chr. 4: 10).

52. David for Solomon and Israel
(1 Chr. 29: 10–19). A'd.

2 Chronicles: Two prayers

Other references to prayer: 2 Chr. 15: 13;
33: 13.

53. Asa for victory (2 Chr. 14: 11). A'd
(2 Chr. 14: 12–14).

54. Jehoshaphat for victory (2 Chr.
20: 6–12). A'd (2 Chr. 20: 20–25).

Ezra: Two prayers

Other references to prayer: Ezra
8: 21–23.

55. Ezra – prayer of thanksgiving
(Ezra 7: 27–28).

56. Ezra for forgiveness and help
(Ezra 9: 5–15). A'd (Ezra 10: 1–19).

Nehemiah: Nine prayers

Other references to prayer: Neh. 2: 4;
4: 9; 8: 6.

57. Nehemiah for confession of sins
and help (Neh. 1: 5–11).

58. Nehemiah for judgment
(Neh. 4: 1–6).

59. Nehemiah for help (Neh. 6: 9).

60. Nehemiah for help (Neh. 6: 14).

61. Israel's confession of sins
(Neh. 9: 5–38). This is the Bible's longest
prayer.

62. Nehemiah for blessing
(Neh. 13: 14).

63. Nehemiah for blessing
(Neh. 13: 22).

64. Nehemiah for judgment
(Neh. 13: 29).

65. Nehemiah for blessing
(Neh. 13: 31).

Job: Seven prayers

66. Job's thanksgiving and
resignation (Job 1: 20–22).

67. Job in complaint and for relief
and forgiveness (Job 7: 17–21). A'd
(Job 42: 10).

68. Job in complaint and for relief
(Job 9: 25–10: 22). A'd (Job 42: 10).

69. Job in complaint and for life
and forgiveness (Job 14: 13–22). A'd
(Job 42: 10).

70. Job for a fair trial (Job 23: 3–5). A'd
(Job 38–42).

71. Job's confession (Job 40: 3–5). A'd
Job 42: 10)

72. Job, prayer of repentance
(Job 42: 1–6). A'd (Job 42: 10).

Psalms: Seventy-two out of 150 Psalms are prayers

73–123. David. In fifty psalms, he requested various blessings, most of them A'd (Pss. 3–7; 9; 12–13; 16–17; 19–20; 22; 25–31; 35–36; 38–41; 51; 54–61; 64; 69–70; 86; 108–109; 124; 132; 139–144).

124–138. An unknown psalmist prayed for blessings (Pss 10; 33; 43–44; 71; 85; 88; 102; 106; 118; 119; 120; 123; 125; 129; 137).

139–143. Asaph asked God for various blessings (Pss. 74; 79–80; 82–83).

144. Moses makes requests to God (Ps. 90).

145. Ethan made requests for God to remember the reproach of His servants (Ps. 89).

Twenty prayers of distress (Pss. 3; 4; 6; 12; 13; 17; 25; 27; 31; 38; 43; 56; 57; 70; 80; 109; 120; 123; 130; 143)

Isaiah: Three prayers

Other references to prayer: Is. 1: 15; 7: 11; 16: 12; 26: 16; 55: 6,7).

146. Isaiah for cleansing (Is. 6: 5). A'd (Is. 6: 6,7).

147. Hezekiah for deliverance (Is. 37: 16–20). A'd (Is. 37: 36).

148. Hezekiah for healing and length of days (Is. 38: 3). A'd (Is. 38: 5).

Jeremiah: Eleven prayers

Other references to prayer: Jer.7: 16; 11: 14; 14: 11; 21: 2; 29: 7,12; 37: 3; 42: 2,4,20.

149. Jeremiah, confession of inability to obey God (Jer. 1: 6).

150. Jeremiah, accusing God (Jer. 4: 10).

151. Jeremiah for judgment (Jer. 10: 23–25). A'd (Dan. 5).

152. Jeremiah, questioning God (Jer. 12: 1–4).

153. Jeremiah for help for Judah (Jer. 14: 7–9).

154. Jeremiah for help for Judah (Jer. 14: 20–22).

155. Jeremiah, judgment (Jer. 15: 15–18).

156. Jeremiah for judgment (Jer. 17: 13–18).

157. Jeremiah for judgment (Jer. 18: 19–23).

158. Jeremiah for judgment (Jer. 20: 7–12).

159. Jeremiah, concerning captivity of Judah (Jer. 32: 17–25).

Lamentations: Four prayers

160. Jeremiah for judgment (Lam. 1: 20–22).

161. Jeremiah for consideration (Lam. 2: 20–22).

162. Jeremiah for judgment (Lam. 3: 55–66).

163. Jeremiah for the oppressed people of Judah (Lam. 5: 1–22).

Ezekiel: Three prayers

164. Ezekiel protesting what God wanted him to do (Ezek. 4: 14).

165. Ezekiel for the remnant (Ezek. 9: 8).

166. Ezekiel for the remnant (Ezek. 11: 13).

All the prayers in the Bible (3)

Daniel: Two prayers

Other references to prayer: Dan. 2: 17–18; 6: 10.

167. Daniel for forgiveness of sins and fulfillment of prophecy (Dan. 9: 1–19).

168. Daniel for revelation (Dan. 12: 8).

Amos: Two prayers

169. Amos for forgiveness (Amos 7: 2).

170. Amos for help (Amos 7: 5).

Jonah: Three prayers

171. Sailors for mercy (Jonah 1: 14).

172. Jonah for deliverance from the fish (Jonah 2: 1–9).

173. Jonah for death (Jonah 4: 2,3).

Habakkuk: Three prayers

174. Habakkuk for God to act (Hab. 1: 1–5).

175. Habakkuk for judgment (Hab. 1: 12–17).

176. Habakkuk for revival (Hab. 3: 2–19).

New Testament

Matthew: Seventeen prayers

Other references to prayer: Matt. 6: 5–13; 7: 7–11; 9: 37–39; 14: 23; 18: 19–20; 21: 22; 23: 14.

177. Jesus' Lord's Prayer (Matt. 6: 9–13).

178. Leper for healing (Matt. 8: 2). A'd (Matt. 8: 3).

179. Centurion for healing of his servant (Matt. 8: 6–9). A'd (Matt. 8: 13).

180. Disciples for help from drowning (Mt.8: 25). A'd (Matt. 8: 26).

181. Demons for temporary liberty (Matt. 8: 29–31). A'd (Matt. 8: 32).

182. A ruler for healing (Matt. 9: 18). A'd (Matt. 9: 25).

183. A woman for healing (Matt. 9: 21). A'd (Matt. 9: 22).

184. Two blind men for healing (Matt. 9: 27). A'd (Matt. 9: 29,30).

185. Jesus giving thanks to God (Matt. 11: 25)

186. Peter to walk on water (Matt. 14: 28). A'd (Matt. 14: 29).

187. Peter for help from drowning (Matt. 14: 30). A'd (Matt. 14: 31).

188. A woman for healing of her daughter (Matt. 15: 22–27). A'd (Matt. 15: 28).

189. A man for healing of his son (Matt. 17: 15,16). A'd (Matt. 17: 18).

190. James and John's mother (Matt. 20: 21). Not A'd (Matt. 20: 23).

191. Two blind men for healing (Matt. 20: 30–33). A'd (Matt. 20: 34).

192. Jesus in the garden of Gethsemane (Matt. 26: 39–44).

193. Jesus on the cross (Matt. 27: 46).

Mark: Two prayers

Other references to prayer: Mk. 1: 35; 6: 41,46; 9: 23; 11: 22–24.

194. A demon for temporary freedom (Mk. 1: 23–24).

195. Jesus in healing a deaf mute (Mk. 7: 34). A'd (v 35). The Bible's shortest prayer: one 6–letter Greek word.

Luke: Seven prayers

Other references to prayer: Luke

3: 21,22; 5: 16; 6: 12; 9: 28,29; 11: 1–13; 18: 1–18; 22: 31,32.

196. Simeon in blessing Jesus (Luke 2: 29–32).

197. Rich man in hell (Luke 16: 24–31).

198. Ten lepers for healing (Luke 17: 13). A'd (Luke 17: 14,19).

199. A Pharisee in boasting of his righteousness (Luke 18: 11,12). Not A'd.

200. A tax collector for mercy (Luke 18: 13). A'd (Luke 18: 14).

201. Jesus on the cross for the forgiveness of his murderers (Luke 23: 34).

202. Jesus dying on the cross, commending His Spirit to God (Luke 23: 46).

John: Five prayers

Other references to prayer: Jn.7: 37–39; 14: 12–15; 15: 7,16; 16: 23–26.

203. Nobleman for healing of child (John 4: 49). A'd (John 4: 50).

204. People for living bread (John 6: 34).

205. Jesus for resurrection of Lazarus (John 11: 41–43). A'd (John 11: 44).

206. Jesus for glorification (John 12: 27,28). A'd (John 12: 28).

207. Jesus for disciples (Jn.17: 1–26)

Acts: Six prayers

Other references to prayer: Acts 1: 14; 3: 1; 6: 4; 8: 22,24,34; 10: 9,31; 12: 5; 16: 13–16.

208. Disciples for successor to Judas (Acts 1: 24,25). A'd (Acts 1: 26).

209. Peter for healing of lame man (Acts 3: 6). (Acts 3: 7,8).

210. Disciples for boldness and power (Acts 4: 24–30). A'd (Acts 4: 31–33).

211. Stephen for enemies (Acts 7: 59,60).

212. Paul for instruction (Acts 9: 5,6). A'd (Acts 9: 5,6).

213. Peter for resurrection of Tabitha/ Dorcas (Acts 9: 40). A'd (Acts 9: 40,41).

New Testament letters

(Rom. 1: 8–10; 16: 20; Eph. 1: 15–20; 3: 13–21; Phil. 1: 2–7; 4: 6,7; Col. 1: 3–14; 1 Thess. 1: 2,3; 3: 9–13; 1 Tim. 1: 3–7; 2 Tim. 4: 14–18; James 5: 13–18). Paul was the only NT writer who asked for the prayers of those he wrote to (Rom. 15: 30; 2 Cor. 1: 11; Eph. 6: 18–20; Phil. 1: 19; Col. 4: 3; Philm. 1: 22) other than the author to Hebrews (Heb.13: 18). Paul's written prayers in his letters: Eph. 1: 15–23; 3: 14–21; Phil. 1: 9–11; Col. 1: 9–12.

Revelation: Eight prayers

214. Elders in worship (Rev. 4: 11).

215. Angels in worship (Rev. 5: 12).

216. All creatures in worship (Rev. 5: 13).

217. Martyrs for vengeance (Rev. 6: 10).

218. Great multitude in worship (Rev. 7: 10).

219. Angels in worship (Rev. 7: 12).

220. Glorified saints in worship (Rev. 19: 1–6).

221. John for Jesus Christ's second coming (Rev. 22: 20).

Books with no prayers

Many books in the Bible have no actual, worded prayers said by Bible characters: Lev, Ru, Est, Prov, Ecc, SS, Ho, Jo, Ob, Mi, Na, Zeph, Hag, Zec, Mal, Ro, 1 Co, Gal, Eph, Phi, Col, 1 The, 2 The, 1 Ti, 2 Ti, Tit, Phile, Heb, Ja, 1 Pe, 2 Pe, 1 Jn, 2 Jn, 3 Jn, Ju.

Glossary of doctrinal words in the Bible (1)

Overview

The following entries are based on an edited and shortened version of some of the entries from one of the most helpful classic Bible dictionaries, *Easton's Bible Dictionary*. Easton was a past-master at explaining the meaning of key Bible words.

A

Alpha

Alpha is the first letter of the Greek alphabet, just as Omega is the last. These letters occur in the text of Rev. 1: 8,11; 21: 6; 22: 13, and are represented by "Alpha" and "Omega". They mean "the first and last." (Cf. Heb. 12: 2; Is. 41: 4; 44: 6; Rev. 1: 11,17; 2: 8.)

In the symbols of the early Christian Church these two letters are frequently combined with the cross or with Christ's monogram to denote his divinity.

Abaddon

Abaddon means destruction. It is the Hebrew name (equivalent to the Greek Apollyon, i.e., destroyer) of "the angel of the bottomless pit" (Rev. 9: 11). It is rendered "destruction" in Job 28: 22; 31: 12; 26: 6; Prov. 15: 11; 27: 20. In the last three of these passages the Revised Version retains the word "Abaddon."

Abaddon is a personification of the idea of destruction, or as Sheol, the realm of the dead.

Adoption

Adoption is the giving to any one the name and place and privileges of a son who is not a son by birth.

(1) NATURAL ADOPTION
Pharaoh's daughter adopted Moses (Ex. 2: 10), and Mordecai adopted Esther (Esther 2: 7).

(2) NATIONAL ADOPTION
God adopted Israel (Ex. 4: 22; Deut. 7: 6; Hos. 11: 1; Rom. 9: 4).

(3) SPIRITUAL ADOPTION
Spiritual adoption is an act of God's grace by which he brings people into his redeemed family, and enables them to take part in his blessings, such as: God's love (John 17: 23; Rom. 5: 5–8), a spiritual nature (2 Pet. 1: 4; John 1: 13), possessing God's Spirit and so becoming children of God (1 Pet. 1: 14; 2 John 4; Rom. 8: 15–21; Gal. 5: 1; Heb. 2: 15), and a future inheritance (Rom. 8: 17,23; James 2: 5; Phil. 3: 21).

Adore

The word itself does not occur in the Bible, although the concept does. Adore means to worship and to express reverence and homage. As a sign of adoration godly Jews took off their shoes (Ex. 3: 5; Josh. 5: 15), and prostrated themselves (Gen. 17: 3; Ps. 95: 6; Is. 44: 15,17,19; 46: 6).

Adultery

Adultery refers to unfaithfulness in marriage. An adulterer was a man who had sexual intercourse with a married woman, and such a woman was an adulteress. Sexual intercourse between a married man and an unmarried woman was fornication. Adultery was regarded as a great social wrong, as well as a sin.

Afflictions

Afflictions are common to all (Job 5: 7; 14: 1; Ps. 34: 19); are for the good of people (James 1: 2,3,12; 2 Cor. 12: 7) and are for the glory of God (2 Cor. 12: 7–10; 1 Pet. 4: 14).

They are to be borne with patience by the Lord's people (Ps. 94: 12; Prov. 3: 12).

They are all directed by God (Lam. 3: 33), and will benefit his people (2 Cor. 4: 16–18) as they are in Christ Jesus (Rom. 8: 35–39).

Alien

An alien is a foreigner, or person born in another country, and therefore not entitled to the rights and privileges of the country where he lives. Aliens could become members of the congregation of the Lord's people by submitting to circumcision and abandoning idolatry (Deut. 23: 3–8). This term is used (Eph. 2: 12) to denote people who have no interest in Christ.

Allegory

The word "allegory" is used only in Gal. 4: 24, where the apostle refers to the history of Isaac the free-born, and Ishmael the slave-born, and makes use of it allegorically.

Every parable is an allegory. Nathan (2 Sam. 12: 1–4) addresses David in an allegorical narrative. In the eightieth Psalm there is a beautiful allegory: "Thou broughtest a vine out of Egypt," etc. In Eccl. 12: 2–6, there is a striking allegorical description of old age.

Alleluia

Alleluia is the Greek form (Revelation 19: 1,3,4,6) of the Hebrew word *Hallelujah* meaning, "Praise ye Jehovah," which begins or ends several of the psalms (106, 111, 112, 113).

Alms

The word "alms" is not found in the Old Testament, but it is often used in the New Testament. The Mosaic legislation (Lev. 25: 35; Deut. 15: 7) encouraged a spirit of charity, and discouraged destitution among the people. Such passages as Ps. 41: 1; 112: 9; Prov. 14: 31; Is. 10: 2; Amos 2: 7; Jer. 5: 28; Ezek. 22: 29, would also naturally foster the same spirit of caring and generosity.

In our Lord's day begging was common (Mark 10: 46; Acts 3: 2). The Pharisees were very ostentatious in their almsgivings (Matt. 6: 2).

The Christian attitude to giving comes in 1 John 3: 17. Christians were expected to help the poor and needy, (Luke 3: 11; 6: 30; Matt. 6: 1; Acts 9: 36; 10: 2,4).

Glossary of doctrinal words in the Bible (2)

A continued

Amen

This Hebrew word means firm, and hence also faithful (Revelation 3: 14). In Isaiah 65: 16, the Authorized Version has "the God of truth," which in Hebrew is "the God of Amen." It was often used by Jesus to give emphasis to his words. It such cases it is translated "verily" or, "I tell you the truth." Sometimes, only however in John's Gospel, it is repeated, "Verily, verily." It is used as an epithet of the Lord Jesus Christ (Revelation 3: 14).

It is found singly and sometimes doubly at the end of prayers (Psalms 41: 13; 72: 19; 89: 52), to confirm the words and invoke the fulfillment of them. It is used when taking an oath (Numbers 5: 22; Deuteronomy 27: 15–26; Nehemiah 5: 13; 8: 6; 1 Chronicles 16: 36). In the early churches it was common for the general audience to say "Amen" at the close of the prayer (1 Corinthians 14: 16).

The promises of God are said to be Amen; that is, they are all true and sure (2 Corinthians 1: 20).

Ancient of Days

This phrase is made three times of Jehovah in the vision of Daniel (7: 9,13,22). Each time it conveys the sense of eternal.

Angel

The word "angel" in both the Hebrew and Greek means a "messenger," and so is used of anyone sent by Go to carry out his will.
It is used:
- of an ordinary messenger (Job 1: 14: 1 Sam. 11: 3; Luke 7: 24; 9: 52),
- of prophets (Is. 42: 19; Hag. 1: 13),
- of priests (Mal. 2: 7)
- of ministers in the New Testament (Rev. 1: 20).

The word is also applied to impersonal agents such as the pestilence (2 Sam. 24: 16,17; 2 Kings 19: 35), the wind (Ps. 104: 4).

Its distinctive use is of heavenly beings whom God uses as he rules the world. The appearances to Abraham at Mamre (Gen. 18: 2,22. Cf. 19: 1), to Jacob at Peniel (Gen. 32: 24,30), to Joshua at Gilgal (Josh. 5: 13,15), of the Angel of the Lord, were doubtless manifestations of God's presence.

THE NUMBER AND DIFFERENT TYPES OF ANGELS
The personal existence of angels is taught in Gen. 16: 7,10,11; Judg. 13: 1–21; Matt. 28: 2–5; Heb. 1: 4, etc.

Angels are very numerous, there being "Thousand thousands," of them, (Dan. 7: 10; Matt. 26: 53; Luke 2: 13; Heb. 12: 22,23). They had different ranks and a variety of power (Zech. 1: 9,11; Dan. 10: 13; 12: 1; 1 Thess. 4: 16; Jude 1: 9; Eph. 1: 21; Col. 1: 16).

THE NATURE OF ANGELS

Angels are spirits (Heb. 1: 14). They do not have bodies like humans. They are called "holy" (Luke 9: 26), "elect" (1 Tim. 5: 21). The redeemed in glory are "like unto the angels" (Luke 20: 36). They are not to be worshiped (Col. 2: 18; Rev. 19: 10).

THE PURPOSE OF ANGELS

(a) Angels are agents of God's providence (Ex. 12: 23; Ps. 104: 4; Heb. 11: 28; 1 Cor. 10: 10; 2 Sam. 24: 16; 1 Chr. 21: 16; 2 Kings 19: 35; Acts 12: 23).

(b) Angels assist in carrying out God's work of redemption. There are no recorded angelic appearances to man until after the call of Abraham. From then on there are frequent references to their ministry on earth (Gen. 18; 19; 24: 7,40; 28: 12; 32: 1). They appear to rebuke idolatry (Judg. 2: 1–4), to call Gideon (Judg. 6: 11,12), and to consecrate Samson (13: 3).

ANGELS AND JESUS

During and after Jesus' birth angels are very active. They serve their Lord while he is on earth.

They predicted his coming (Matt. 1: 20; Luke 1: 26–38), ministered to him after his temptations (Matt. 4: 11), ministered to him after his agony in the garden of Gethsemane (Luke 22: 43), and declare his resurrection and ascension (Matt. 28: 2–8; John 20: 12,13; Acts 1: 10,11).

Anoint

The practice of anointing with perfumed oil was common among the Hebrews.

(1) The act of anointing signified consecration to a holy or sacred purpose. So the high priest was anointed (Ex. 29: 29; Lev. 4: 3). The high priest and the king are thus called "the anointed" (Lev. 4: 3,5,16; 6: 20; Ps. 132: 10). Anointing a king was equivalent to crowning him (1 Sam. 16: 13; 2 Sam. 2: 4, etc.). Prophets were also anointed (1 Kings 19: 16; 1 Chr. 16: 22; Ps. 105: 15).

(2) Anointing was also an act of hospitality (Luke 7: 38,46). Jews also anointed themselves with oil to refresh and invigorate their bodies (Deut. 28: 40; Ruth 3: 3; 2 Sam. 14: 2; Ps. 104: 15).

(3) Oil was used also for medicinal purposes. It was given to the sick, and helped to dress wounds (Ps. 109: 18; Is. 1: 6; Mark 6: 13; James 5: 14).

(4) The bodies of the dead were sometimes anointed (Mark 14: 8; Luke 23: 56).

(5) The promised Deliverer is twice called the "Anointed" or Messiah (Ps. 2: 2; Dan. 9: 25,26), because he was anointed with the Holy Spirit (Is. 61: 1), figuratively styled the "oil of gladness" (Ps. 45: 7; Heb. 1: 9). Jesus of Nazareth is this anointed One.

Glossary of doctrinal words in the Bible (3)

A continued

Antichrist

Antichrist is against Christ, or an opposing Christ in the sense of being a rival Christ. The word is used only by the apostle John. Referring to false teachers, he says (1 John 2: 18, 22; 4: 3; 2 John 1: 7), "Even now are there many antichrists."

Antichrists have been identified as follows:

(1) This name has been applied to the "little horn" of the "king of fierce countenance" (Dan. 7: 24,25; 8: 23–25).

(2) It has been applied also to the "false Christs" spoken of by our Lord (Matt. 24: 5, 23,24).

(3) To the "man of sin" described by Paul (2 Thess. 2: 3,4,8–10).

(4) And to the "beast from the sea" (Rev. 13: 1; 17: 1–18).

Apocalypse

The Apocalypse is the Greek name of the Book of Revelation.

Apollyon

Apollyon, the destroyer, is the name given to the king of the hosts represented by the locusts (Rev. 9: 11). It is the Greek translation of the Hebrew word "Abaddon."

Apostle

An apostle is a person sent by another, a messenger or an envoy.

"Apostle" is once used as a title of Jesus Christ, the Sent of the Father (Heb. 3: 1; John 20: 21).

The apostles is the name given to the twelve disciples Jesus chose. They are referred to as "the twelve" There are four lists of the apostles, (Matt. 10: 2–4; Mark 3: 16; Luke 6: 14, 1: 13).

Our Lord gave them the "keys of the kingdom," and through the gift of his Spirit equipped them to be the founders and the first leaders of his church (John 14: 16,17,26; 15: 26,27; 16: 7–15; Acts 2: 4; 1 Cor. 2: 16; 2: 7,10,13; 2 Cor. 5: 20; 1 Cor. 11: 2).

Judas Iscariot, one of "the twelve," was replaced by Matthias (Acts 1: 21). Saul of Tarsus was later added to their number (Acts 9: 3–20; 20: 4; 26: 15–18; 1 Tim. 1: 12; 2: 7; 2 Tim. 1: 11).

Luke provides some information about Peter, John, and the two Jameses (Acts 12: 2,17; 15: 13; 21: 18), but beyond this nothing more is recorded in the Bible about the original twelve.

QUALIFICATIONS OF AN APOSTLE

(1) The twelve apostles saw the Lord, and were able to witness about him and his resurrection from personal knowledge (John 15: 27; Acts 1: 21,22; 1 Cor. 9: 1; Acts 22: 14,15).

(2) They were called to be apostles by Christ himself (Luke 6: 13; Gal. 1: 1).

(3) Their teaching was divinely inspired (John 14: 26; 16: 13; 1 Thess. 2: 13).

(4) They were given the power to perform miracles (Mark 16: 20; Acts 2: 43; 1 Cor. 12: 8–11).

Archangel

An archangel (1 Thess. 4: 16; Jude 1: 9), was the prince of the angels.

Arm

The word "arm" is used to denote power (Ps. 10: 15; Ezek. 30: 21; Jer. 48: 25).

It is also used of the omnipotence of God (Ex. 15: 16; Ps. 89: 13; 98: 1; 77: 15; Is. 53: 1; John 12: 38; Acts 13: 17).

Armageddon

Armageddon occurs only in Rev. 16: 16, as symbolically designating the place where the "battle of that great day of God Almighty" (ver. 14) will be fought. The word means the "mount of Megiddo." It is the scene of the final conflict between Christ and antichrist.

Ashes

The ashes of a red heifer (Num. 19: 5) when sprinkled on the unclean made them ceremonially clean (Heb. 9: 13).

To cover the head with ashes indicated self-abhorrence and humiliation (2 Sam. 13: 19; Esther 4: 3; Jer. 6: 26).

Ashtoreth

Ashtoreth was the moon goddess of the Phoenicians, representing the passive principle in nature, their principal female deity; frequently associated with the name of Baal, the sun-god, their main male deity (Judg. 10: 6; 1 Sam. 7: 4; 12: 10). These names often occur in the plural as Ashtaroth and Baalim. This deity is spoken of as Ashtoreth of the Zidonians. She was the Ishtar of the Accadians and the Astarte of the Greeks (Jer. 44: 17; 1 Kings 11: 5,33; 2 Kings 23: 13). In Saul's day the Philistines had a temple dedicated to her. Solomon introduced the worship of this idol (1 Kings 11: 33). Jezebel's 400 priests were probably in her service (1 Kings 18: 19). She was called the "queen of heaven" (Jer. 44: 25).

Assurance

The resurrection of Jesus (Acts 17: 31) is the "assurance" (Gr. *pistis,* generally rendered "faith") or pledge God has given that his revelation is true and so should be accepted.

The "full assurance (Gr. *plerophoria,* 'full bearing') of faith" (Heb. 10: 22) is a fullness of faith in God which leaves no room for doubt.

The "full assurance of understanding" (Col. 2: 2) is an entire unwavering conviction of the truth of the declarations of Scripture.

The "full assurance of hope" (Heb. 6: 11) is a sure and well-grounded expectation of eternal glory (2 Tim. 4: 7,8).

Glossary of doctrinal words in the Bible (4)

Assurance, continued

This assurance, which each believer may experience, is founded on the truth of the promises (Heb. 6: 18), on the inner evidence of Christian graces, and on the testimony of the Spirit of adoption (Rom. 8: 16).

That such a certainty should be normal for a Christ is seen: from the testimony of Scripture (Rom. 8: 16; 1 John 2: 3; 3: 14), from the command to seek after it (Heb. 6: 11; 2 Pet. 1: 10), and from the fact that it has been attained (2 Tim. 1: 12; 4: 7,8; 1 John 2: 3; 4: 16).

Atonement

The word "atonement" does not occur in the Authorized Version of the New Testament except in Rom. 5: 11, where in the Revised Version the word "reconciliation" is used. In the Old Testament it often occurs.

Simply stated the word means "at-one-ment," that is, being at one or being reconciled. So atonement is reconciliation. Atonement describes the result of Jesus' death.

Atonement also describes how this reconciliation is brought about, that is, it describes the death of Jesus itself. So when it is said that Jesus made an atonement for someone it means that he dealt with their offenses against God, thus reconciling that person to God.

B

Baal

Baal, meaning, "lord," was the name of the principal male god of the Phoenicians, and is often used in the plural, "Baalim" (Judg. 2: 11; 10: 10; 1 Kings 18: 18; Jer. 2: 23; Hos. 2: 17). Baal is identified with Molech (Jer. 19: 5).

He was known to the Israelites as Baal-peor (Num. 25: 3; Deut. 4: 3), was worshiped till the time of Samuel (1 Sam. 7: 4), and later became the religion of the ten tribes in the time of Ahab (1 Kings 16: 31–33; 18: 19,22). The sun-god, under the general title of Baal, or "lord," was worshiped by the Canaanites. Each locality had its special Baal.

Baptism, Christian

Christian baptism, with the original meaning of "to dip, plunge, or to dye," is an ordinance instituted by Christ (Matthew 28: 19,20), and, like that of the Lord's Supper meant to be observed in the church, "till he come." The words "baptize" and "baptism" are simply Greek words transferred into English.

THE BAPTISM OF JOHN AND THE BAPTISM OF JESUS
There is one important similarity, and one important difference between the baptisms John undertook and the baptism Jesus preached about.

Both baptisms stressed the need for the person being baptized to repent. John's baptism is described as "a baptism of repentance for the forgiveness of sins" Mark 1: 4 NIV.

But the baptism Jesus spoke of added one crucial modification to the baptisms John performed in the River Jordan. As John himself said, referring to the baptism Jesus ushered in: "He will baptize you with the Holy Spirit and with fire" Matthew 3: 11 NIV.

Jesus would baptize with "fire" and the "Spirit" and not just with water, as John did. So the baptism of Jesus could never be thought of as a mere mechanical act. Water-baptism and Spirit-baptism were intended to go hand in hand.

JESUS' COMMISSION TO HIS DISCIPLES TO BAPTIZE

Jesus' final command in Matthew's Gospel is that his followers are to teach and to baptize. Those who are baptized are called "disciples." From this it seems reasonable to conclude that such people should be both repentant and have faith in Jesus.

Such baptism was to be in the name of Jesus or in the name of the Trinity. This Christian baptism was totally different from pagan baptism, or Jewish baptism, and also qualitatively different from John's baptism.

PAUL AND BAPTISM

Paul carried out Jesus' teaching about baptism in his own ministry. It is clear that his converts were baptized. "Is Christ divided? Was Paul crucified for you? Were you baptized into the name of Paul? I am thankful that I did not baptize any of you except Crispus and Gaius" 1 Corinthians 1: 13,14, NIV.

Paul could never be accused of using

or thinking of baptism as some magical rite. Paul thought of Christian baptism as the means for entering into the Christian community and fellowship and doing so in a spiritual way. "For we were all baptized by one Spirit into one body-whether Jews or Greeks, slave or free-and we were all given the one Spirit to drink" 1 Corinthians 12: 13, NIV.

Paul emphasizes the spiritual meaning of this baptism and teaches that it is only by the Spirit that any true baptism takes place.

Christian baptism should therefore never be restricted to one type of person: "for all of you who were baptized into Christ have clothed yourselves with Christ. There is neither Jew nor Greek, slave nor free, male nor female, for you are all one in Christ Jesus" Galatians 3: 27,28, NIV. For the Christian Church was never meant to have distinctions between race (Jews and Greeks), or between the sexes (male and female), or between social status (slave or free). For those who had been "baptized into Christ" had "put on Christ." See Romans 13: 14; Ephesians 4: 24; Colossians 3: 10.

Bible, Meaning of, and covenant

TESTAMENT

The word *Testament* means covenant or agreement. God made an agreement with humankind about our salvation which was based on law (Deut. 4: 5).

The law of the Old Testament sets out how humankind could be saved before the coming of Christ.

Glossary of doctrinal words in the Bible (5)

B continued

Bible, Meaning of, and covenant, continued

God's new agreement, the New Testament, is a covenant of grace (Gal. 3: 17–25). This new covenant describes our salvation after the coming of Christ.

The word "Bible" never appears in the Bible.

Bible, the English form of the Greek name *Biblia*, meaning "books," was the name which in the fifth century began to be given to the entire collection of sacred books, the "Library of Divine Revelation." The name Bible was adopted by Wickliffe, and came gradually into use in our English language.

Birthright

This word denotes the special privileges held by the first-born son among the Jews.

The first-born son received a double share of his father's inheritance (Deuteronomy 21: 15–17). Reuben was deprived of his birthright (Genesis 49: 4; 1 Chronicles 5: 1) and Esau transferred his birthright to Jacob (Genesis 25: 33).

The first-born inherited the judicial authority of his father, whatever it might be (2 Chronicles 21: 3). By divine appointment, however, David excluded Adonijah in favor of Solomon.

The Jews attached a sacred importance to the rank of "first-born" and "first-begotten" as applied to the Messiah (Romans 8: 29; Colossians 1: 18; Hebrews 1: 4–6). As first-born he had an inheritance superior to his brethren, and is alone the true priest.

Bishop

A "bishop" means an overseer. In apostolic times, it appears that there was little difference between bishops and elders or presbyters (Acts 20: 17–28; 1 Peter 5: 1,2; Phil. 1: 1; 1 Timothy 3).

The term bishop is never once used to denote a different office from that of elder or presbyter. These different names are simply titles of the same office, "bishop" designating the function, namely, that of oversight, and "presbyter" the dignity appertaining to the office.

Christ is figuratively called "the bishop [*episcopos*] of souls" (1 Peter 2: 25).

Blasphemy

In the sense of speaking evil of God this word is found in Psalms 74: 18; Isaiah 52: 5; Romans 2: 24; Revelation 13: 1,6; 16: 9,11,21. It denotes also any kind of calumny, or evil-speaking, or abuse (1 Kings 21: 10; Acts 13: 45; 18: 6, etc.). Our Lord was accused of blasphemy when he claimed to be the Son of God (Matthew 26: 65; cf. Matthew 9: 3; Mark 2: 7). They who deny his Messiahship blaspheme Jesus (Luke 22: 65; John 10: 36).

Blasphemy against the Holy Spirit

Blasphemy against the Holy Spirit (Matthew 12: 31,32; Mark 3: 28,29; Luke 12: 10) is regarded by some as a continued and obstinate rejection of the gospel, and hence is an unpardonable sin, simply because as long as a sinner remains in unbelief he voluntarily excludes himself from pardon. Others regard the expression as designating the sin of attributing to the power of Satan those miracles which Christ performed, or generally those works which are the result of the Spirit's agency.

Bless

God blesses his people when he bestows on them some gift temporal or spiritual (Genesis 1: 22; 24: 35; Job 42: 12; Psalms 45: 2; 104: 24,35).

We bless God when we thank him for his mercies (Psalms 103: 1,2; 145: 1,2). A man blesses himself when he invokes God's blessing (Isaiah 65: 16), or rejoices in God's goodness to him (Deuteronomy 29: 19; Psalms 49: 18). One blesses another when he expresses good wishes or offers prayer to God for his welfare (Genesis 24: 60; 31: 55; 1 Samuel 2: 20). Sometimes blessings were uttered under divine inspiration, as in the case of Noah, Isaac, Jacob, and Moses (Genesis 9: 26,27; 27: 28,29,40; 48: 15–20; 49: 1–28; Deuteronomy 33). The priests were divinely authorized to bless the people (Deuteronomy 10: 8; Numbers 6: 22–27). We have many examples of apostolic benediction (2 Corinthians 13: 14; Ephesians 6: 23,24; 3: 16,18; Hebrews 13: 20,21; 1 Peter 5: 10,11).

Among the Jews in their thank-offerings the master of the feast took a cup of wine in his hand, and after having blessed God for it and for other mercies then enjoyed, handed it to his guests, who all partook of it. Psalms 116: 13 refers to this custom. It is also alluded to in 1 Corinthians 10: 16, where the apostle speaks of the "cup of blessing."

Blood

As food, prohibited in Genesis 9: 4, where the use of animal food is first allowed. Cf. Deuteronomy 12: 23; Leviticus 3: 17; 7: 26; 17: 10–14. The injunction to abstain from blood is renewed in the decree of the council of Jerusalem (Acts 15: 29). It has been held by some, and we think correctly, that this law of prohibition was only ceremonial and temporary; while others regard it as still binding on all. Blood was eaten by the Israelites after the battle of Gilboa (1 Samuel 14: 32–34).

The blood of sacrifices was caught by the priest in a basin, and then sprinkled seven times on the altar; that of the Passover on the doorposts and lintels of the houses (Exodus 12; Leviticus 4: 5–7; 16: 14–19). At the giving of the law (Exodus 24: 8) the blood of the sacrifices was sprinkled on the people as well as on the altar, and thus the people were consecrated to God, or entered into covenant with him, hence the blood of the covenant (Matthew 26: 28; Hebrews 9: 19,20; 10: 29; 13: 20).

Glossary of doctrinal words in the Bible (6)

B continued

Human blood

The murderer was to be punished (Genesis 9: 5). The blood of the murdered "crieth for vengeance" (Genesis 4: 10). The "avenger of blood" was the nearest relative of the murdered, and he was required to avenge his death (Numbers 35: 24,27). No satisfaction could be made for the guilt of murder (Numbers 35: 31).

Blood used metaphorically to denote race (Acts 17: 26), and as a symbol of slaughter (Isaiah 34: 3). To "wash the feet in blood" means to gain a great victory (Psalms 58: 10). Wine, from its red color, is called "the blood of the grape" (Genesis 49: 11). Blood and water issued from our Savior's side when it was pierced by the Roman soldier (John 19: 34). This has led pathologists to the conclusion that the proper cause of Christ's death was rupture of the heart. (Compare Psalms 69: 20.)

Bloody sweat

The sign and token of our Lord's great agony (Luke 22: 44).

Book

This word has a comprehensive meaning in Scripture. In the Old Testament it is the rendering of the Hebrew word *sepher*, which properly means a "writing," and then a "volume" (Exodus 17: 14; Deuteronomy 28: 58; 29: 20; Job 19: 23) or "roll of a book"

(Jeremiah 36: 2,4).

Books were originally written on skins, on linen or cotton cloth, and on Egyptian papyrus, whence our word "paper." The leaves of the book were generally written in columns, designated by a Hebrew word properly meaning "doors" and "valves."

Among the Hebrews books were generally rolled up like our maps, or if very long they were rolled from both ends, forming two rolls (Luke 4: 17–20). Thus they were arranged when the writing was on flexible materials; but if the writing was on tablets of wood or brass or lead, then the several tablets were bound together by rings through which a rod was passed.

A SEALED BOOK
A sealed book is one whose contents are secret (Isaiah 29: 11; Revelation 5: 1–3). To "eat" a book (Jeremiah 15: 16; Ezekiel 2: 8–10; 3: 1–3; Revelation 10: 9) is to study its contents carefully.

THE BOOK OF JUDGMENT
The book of judgment (Daniel 7: 10) refers to the method of human courts of justice as illustrating the proceedings which will take place at the day of God's final judgment.

The book of the wars of the Lord (Numbers 21: 14), the book of Jasher (Joshua 10: 13), and the book of the chronicles of the kings of Judah and Israel (2 Chronicles 25: 26), were probably ancient documents known to the Hebrews, but not forming a part of the canon.

THE BOOK OF LIFE

The book of life (Psalms 69: 28) suggests the idea that as the redeemed form a community or citizenship (Phil. 3: 20; 4: 3), a catalogue of the citizens' names is preserved (Luke 10: 20; Revelation 20: 15). Their names are registered in heaven (Luke 10: 20; Revelation 3: 5).

THE BOOK OF THE COVENANT

The book of the covenant (Exodus 24: 7), containing Exodus 20: 22–23: 33, is the first book actually mentioned as a part of the written word. It contains a series of laws, civil, social, and religious, given to Moses at Sinai immediately after the delivery of the Decalogue. These were written in this "book."

Branch

A symbol of kings descended from royal ancestors (Ezekiel 17: 3,10; Daniel 11: 7); of prosperity (Job 8: 16); of the Messiah, a branch out of the root of the stem of Jesse (Isaiah 11: 1), the "beautiful branch" (4: 2), a "righteous branch" (Jeremiah 23: 5), "the Branch" (Zechariah 3: 8; 6: 12).

Disciples are branches of the true vine (John 15: 5,6).

The "abominable branch" is a tree on which a malefactor has been hanged (Isaiah 14: 19).

The "highest branch" in Ezekiel 17: 3 represents Jehoiakim the king.

Bread

Among the Jews was generally made of wheat (Exodus 29: 2; Judg. 6: 19), though also sometimes of other grains (Genesis 14: 18; Judg. 7: 13). Parched grain was sometimes used for food without any other preparation (Ruth 2: 14).

Bread was prepared by kneading in wooden bowls or "kneading troughs" (Genesis 18: 6; Exodus 12: 34; Jeremiah 7: 18). The dough was mixed with leaven and made into thin cakes, round or oval, and then baked. The bread eaten at the Passover was always unleavened (Exodus 12: 15–20; Deuteronomy 16: 3). In the towns there were public ovens, which were much made use of for baking bread; there were also bakers by trade (Hosea 7: 4; Jeremiah 37: 21). Their ovens were not unlike those of modern times. But sometimes the bread was baked by being placed on the ground that had been heated by a fire, and by covering it with the embers (1 Kings 19: 6). This was probably the mode in which Sarah prepared bread on the occasion referred to in Genesis 18: 6.

In Leviticus 2 there is an account of the different kinds of bread and cakes used by the Jews.

SHEW-BREAD

The shew-bread consisted of twelve loaves of unleavened bread prepared and presented hot on the golden table every Sabbath. They were square or oblong, and represented the twelve tribes of Israel. The old loaves were removed every Sabbath, and were to be eaten only by the priests in the court of the sanctuary (Exodus 25: 30; Leviticus 24: 8; 1 Samuel 21: 1–6; Matthew 12: 4).

Glossary of doctrinal words in the Bible (7)

Bread, continued

BREAD USED FIGURATIVELY
The word bread is used figuratively in such expressions as "bread of sorrows" (Psalms 127: 2), "bread of tears" (80: 5), i.e., sorrow and tears are like one's daily bread, they form so great a part in life. The bread of "wickedness" (Proverbs 4: 17) and "of deceit" (20: 17) denote in like manner that wickedness and deceit are a part of the daily life.

Breastplate

That piece of ancient armor that protected the breast. This word is used figuratively in Ephesians 6: 14 and Isaiah 59: 17.

An ornament covering the breast of the high priest, first mentioned in Exodus 25: 7. It was made of embroidered cloth, set with four rows of precious stones, three in each row. On each stone was engraved the name of one of the twelve tribes (Exodus 28: 15–29; 39: 8–21). It was in size about ten inches square. The two upper corners were fastened to the ephod by blue ribbons. It was not to be "loosed from the ephod" (Exodus 28: 28). The lower corners were fastened to the girdle of the priest. As it reminded the priest of his representative character, it was called the memorial (28: 29). It was also called the breastplate of judgment (28: 15).

Bride

Frequently used in the ordinary sense (Isaiah 49: 18; 61: 10, etc.).

The relationship between Christ and his church is likened to that between a bridegroom and bride (John 3: 29). The church is called "the bride" (Revelation 21: 9; 22: 17).

Brother

In the natural and common usage (Matthew 1: 2; Luke 3: 1,19).

A near relation, a cousin (Genesis 13: 8; 14: 16; Matthew 12: 46; John 7: 3; Acts 1: 14; Galatians 1: 19).

Simply a fellow-countryman (Matthew 5: 47; Acts 3: 22; Hebrews 7: 5).

A disciple or follower (Matthew 25: 40; Hebrews 2: 11,12).

One of the same faith (Amos 1: 9; Acts 9: 30; 11: 29; 1 Corinthians 5: 11). From this the early disciples of our Lord were known to each other as brethren.

A colleague in office (Ezra 3: 2; 1 Corinthians 1: 1; 2 Corinthians 1: 1).

A fellow-man (Genesis 9: 5; 19: 7; Matthew 5: 22,23,24; 7: 5; Hebrews 2: 17).

One closely united with another in affection (2 Samuel 1: 26; Acts 6: 3; 1 Thessalonians 5: 1).

C

Calling

A profession, or as we usually say, a vocation (1 Corinthians 7: 20). The "hope of your calling" in Ephesians 4: 4 is the hope resulting from your being called into the kingdom of God.

Calvary

Only found in Luke 23: 33, the Latin name Calvaria, which was used as a translation of the Greek word Kranion, by which the Hebrew word Gulgoleth was interpreted, "the place of a skull." It probably took this name from its shape, being a hillock or low, rounded, bare elevation somewhat in the form of a human skull. It is nowhere in Scripture called a "hill." The crucifixion of our Lord took place outside the city walls (Hebrews 13: 11–13) and near the public thoroughfare. "This thing was not done in a corner."

Chosen

spoken of warriors (Exodus 15: 4; Judges 20: 16), of the Hebrew nation (Psalms 105: 43; Deuteronomy 7: 7), of Jerusalem as the seat of the temple (1 Kings 11: 13). Christ is the "chosen" of God (Isaiah 42: 1); and the apostles are "chosen" for their work (Acts 10: 41). It is said with regard to those who do not profit by their opportunities that "many are called, but few are chosen" (Matthew 20: 16).

Christian

the name given by the Greeks or Romans, probably in reproach, to the followers of Jesus. It was first used at Antioch. The names by which the disciples were known among themselves were "brethren," "the faithful," "elect," "saints," "believers." But as distinguishing them from the multitude without, the name "Christian" came into use, and was universally accepted. This name occurs but three times in the New Testament (Acts 11: 26; 26: 28; 1 Peter 4: 16).

Church

Derived probably from the Greek kuriakon (i.e., "the Lord's house"), which was used by ancient authors for the place of worship.

In the New Testament it is the translation of the Greek word *ecclesia*, which is synonymous with the Hebrew *kahal* of the Old Testament, both words meaning simply an assembly, the character of which can only be known from the connection in which the word is found. There is no clear instance of its being used for a place of meeting or of worship, although in post-apostolic times it early received this meaning. Nor is this word ever used to denote the inhabitants of a country united in the same profession, as when we say the "Church of England," the "Church of Scotland," etc.

We find the word *ecclesia* used in the following senses in the New Testament:

- It is translated "assembly" in the ordinary classical sense (Acts 19: 32,39,41).

Glossary of doctrinal words in the Bible (8)

Church, continued

- It denotes the whole body of the redeemed, all those whom the Father has given to Christ, the invisible catholic church (Ephesians 5: 23,25,27,29; Hebrews 12: 23).
- A few Christians associated together in observing the ordinances of the gospel are an *ecclesia* (Romans 16: 5; Colossians 4: 15).
- All the Christians in a particular city, whether they assembled together in one place or in several places for religious worship, were an *ecclesia*. Thus all the disciples in Antioch, forming several congregations, were one church (Acts 13: 1); so also we read of the "church of God at Corinth" (1 Corinthians 1: 2), "the church at Jerusalem" (Acts 8: 1), "the church of Ephesus" (Revelation 2: 1), etc.
- The whole body of professing Christians throughout the world (1 Corinthians 15: 9; Galatians 1: 13; Matthew 16: 18) are the church of Christ.

Visible church

The church visible "consists of all those throughout the world that profess the true religion, together with their children." It is called "visible" because its members are known and its assemblies are public. Here there is a mixture of "wheat and chaff," of saints and sinners. "God has commanded his people to organize themselves into distinct visible ecclesiastical communities, with constitutions, laws, and officers, badges, ordinances, and discipline, for the great purpose of giving visibility to his kingdom, of making known the gospel of that kingdom, and of gathering in all its elect subjects. Each one of these distinct organized communities which is faithful to the great King is an integral part of the visible church, and all together constitute the catholic or universal visible church." A credible profession of the true religion constitutes a person a member of this church. This is "the kingdom of heaven," whose character and progress are set forth in the parables recorded in Matthew 13.

Church and children

The children of all who thus profess the true religion are members of the visible church along with their parents.

Church and children, continued

Children are included in every covenant God ever made with man. They go along with their parents (Genesis 9: 9–17; 12: 1–3; 17: 7; Exodus 20: 5; Deuteronomy 29: 10–13). Peter, on the day of Pentecost, at the beginning of the New Testament dispensation, announces the same great principle. "The promise [just as to Abraham and his seed the promises were made] is unto you, and to your children" (Acts 2: 38,39). The children of believing parents are "holy", i.e., are "saints", a title which designates the members of the Christian church (1 Corinthians 7: 14).

INVISIBLE CHURCH

The church invisible "consists of the whole number of the elect that have been, are, or shall be gathered into one under Christ, the head thereof." This is a pure society, the church in which Christ dwells. It is the body of Christ. It is called "invisible" because the greater part of those who constitute it are already in heaven or are yet unborn, and also because its members still on earth cannot certainly be distinguished. The qualifications of membership in it are internal and are hidden. It is unseen except by Him who "searches the heart." "The Lord knoweth them that are his" (2 Timothy 2: 19).

The church to which the attributes, prerogatives, and promises appertaining to Christ's kingdom belong, is a spiritual body consisting of all true believers, i.e., the church invisible.

UNITY OF CHURCH

• Its unity.
God has ever had only one church on earth. We sometimes speak of the Old Testament church and of the New Testament church, but they are one and the same.

The Old Testament church was not to be changed but enlarged (Isaiah 49: 13–23; 60: 1–14). When the Jews are at length restored, they will not enter a new church, but will be grafted again into "their own olive tree" (Romans 11: 18–24; Compare Ephesians 2: 11–22). The apostles did not set up a new organization. Under their ministry disciples were "added" to the "church" already existing (Acts 2: 47).

• Its universality.
It is the "catholic" church; not confined to any particular country or outward organization, but comprehending all believers throughout the whole world.

• Its perpetuity.
It will continue through all ages to the end of the world. It can never be destroyed. It is an "everlasting kingdom."

Circumcision

The word means "cutting around." This rite, previously practiced by difference races, was appointed by God to be the special sign to his chosen people of their consecration to him. It was established as a national ordinance (Genesis 17: 10,11). Following God's command Abraham, though ninety-nine years old, was circumcised on the same day with Ishmael, who was thirteen years old (17: 24–27). Slaves were circumcised (17: 12,13); and all foreigners had to have their males circumcised before they could enjoy the privileges of Jewish citizenship (Exodus 12: 48). During the journey through the wilderness, the practice of circumcision fell into disuse, but was resumed on the orders of Joshua before they entered the Promised Land (Joshua 5: 2–9). It was observed always afterwards among the tribes of Israel, although it is not mentioned from the time of the settlement in Canaan until the time of Christ, about 1,450 years.

Glossary of doctrinal words in the Bible (9)

Circumcision, continued

The Jews prided themselves on the possession of this covenant distinction (Judg. 14: 3; 15: 18; 1 Samuel 14: 6; 17: 26; 2 Sam. 1: 20; Ezekiel 31: 18).

CIRCUMCISION AND THE NEW TESTAMENT

As a rite of the church it ceased when the New Testament times began (Galatians 6: 15; Colossians 3: 11). Some Jewish Christians sought to impose it, however, on the Gentile converts; but this the apostles resolutely resisted (Acts 15: 1; Galatians 6: 12). Our Lord was circumcised, for it "became him to fulfill all righteousness," as of the descendant of Abraham; and Paul "took and circumcised" Timothy (Acts 16: 3), to avoid giving offense to the Jews. It would make Timothy more acceptable to the Jews. But Paul would not consent to the demand that Titus should be circumcised (Galatians 2: 3–5). The great point for which he fought was the free admission of uncircumcised Gentiles into the church.

CIRCUMCISION'S SPIRITUAL DIMENSION

In the Old Testament a spiritual idea is attached to circumcision. It was the symbol of purity (Isaiah 52: 1). We read of:
• uncircumcised lips (Exodus 6: 12,30)
• ears (Jeremiah 6: 10)
• hearts (Leviticus 26: 41).
The fruit of a tree that is unclean is spoken of as uncircumcised (Leviticus 19: 23).

Comforter

The name for the Holy Spirit, (John 14: 16,26; 15: 26; 16: 7; or Advocate, or Helper; Gr. *paracletos*).

The same Greek word thus translated is translated "Advocate" in 1 John 2: 1 and is applied to Christ. It means "one who is summoned to the side of another" to help him in a court of justice by defending him, "one who is summoned to plead a cause."

"Advocate" is the correct translation of the word in every case where it occurs.

Although Paul nowhere uses the word *paracletos*, he uses the idea when he speaks of the "intercession" both of Christ and the Spirit (Romans 8: 27,34).

Coming of Christ

(1) with reference to his first advent "in the fullness of the time" (1 John 5: 20; 2John 1: 7), or

(2) with reference to his coming again the second time at the last day (Acts 1: 11; 3: 20,21; 1 Thessalonians 4: 15; 2 Tim 4: 1; Hebrews 9: 28).

The expression is used metaphorically of:
• the introduction of the gospel into any place (John 15: 22; Ephesians 2: 17),
• the visible establishment of his kingdom in the world (Matthew 16: 28),
• the conferring on his people of the peculiar tokens of his love (John 14: 18,23,28), and
• his executing judgment on the wicked (2 Thessalonians 2: 8).

Communion

Fellowship with God (Genesis 18: 17–33; Exodus 33: 9–11; Numbers 12: 7,8), between Christ and his people (John 14: 23), by the Spirit (2 Corinthians 13: 14; Phil. 2: 1), of believers with one another (Ephesians 4: 1–6).

The Lord's Supper is so called (1 Corinthians 10: 16,17), because in it there is fellowship between Christ and his disciples, and of the disciples with one another.

Conscience

That faculty of the mind, or inborn sense of right and wrong, by which we judge of the moral character of human conduct. Everyone has a conscience. Like all our other faculties, it has been perverted by the Fall (John 16: 2; Acts 26: 9; Romans 2: 15). It is spoken of as "defiled" (Titus 1: 15), and "seared" (1 Timothy 4: 2). A "conscience void of offense" is to be cultivated (Acts 24: 16; Romans 9: 1; 2 Cor. 1: 12; 1 Timothy 1: 5,19; 1 Peter 3: 21).

Consecration

The devoting or setting apart of anything to the worship or service of God. The race of Abraham and the tribe of Levi were thus consecrated (Exodus 13: 2,12,15; Numbers 3: 12). The Hebrews devoted their fields and cattle, and sometimes the spoils of war, to the Lord (Leviticus 27: 28,29). According to the Mosaic law the first-born both of man and beast were consecrated to God.

In the New Testament, Christians are regarded as consecrated to the Lord (1 Peter 2: 9).

Contentment

A state of mind in which one's desires are confined to his lot whatever it may be (1 Timothy 6: 6; 2 Cor. 9: 8). It is contrasted with envy (James 3: 16), greed (Hebrews 13: 5), ambition (Proverbs 13: 10), anxiety (Matthew 6: 25,34), and complaining (1 Corinthians 10: 10). It comes from the inner disposition, and is the fruit of humility, and an awareness of divine providence (Psalms 96: 1,2; 145), of the divine promises (2 Peter 1: 4), and our own unworthiness (Genesis 32: 10).

Conversion

The turning of a sinner to God (Acts 15: 3). In a general sense pagans are said to be "converted" when they abandon heathenism and embrace the Christian faith; and in a more special sense men are converted when, by the influence of divine grace in their souls, their whole life is changed, old things pass away, and all things become new (Acts 26: 18). Thus we speak of the conversion of the Philippian jailer (16: 19–34), of Paul (9: 1–22), of the Ethiopian treasurer (8: 26–40), of Cornelius (10), of Lydia (16: 13–15), and others.

Glossary of doctrinal words in the Bible (10)

C continued

Covenant

A contract or agreement between two parties. In the Old Testament the Hebrew word *berith* is always thus translated. *Berith* is derived from a root which means "to cut," and hence a covenant is a "cutting," with reference to the cutting or dividing of animals into two parts, and the contracting parties passing between them, in making a covenant (Genesis 15; Jeremiah 34: 18,19).

The corresponding word in the New Testament Greek is *diatheke* , which is, however, translated "testament" generally in the Authorized Version. It ought to be translated, just as the word *berith* of the Old Testament, "covenant."

This word is used of a covenant or compact between man and man (Genesis 21: 32), or between tribes or nations (1 Samuel 11: 1; Joshua 9: 6,15). In entering into a covenant, Jehovah was solemnly called on to witness the transaction (Genesis 31: 50), and hence it was called a "covenant of the Lord" (1 Samuel 20: 8). The marriage compact is called "the covenant of God" (Proverbs 2: 17), because the marriage was made in God's name. Wicked men are spoken of as acting as if they had made a "covenant with death" not to destroy them, or with hell not to devour them (Isaiah 28: 15,18).

The word also refers to God's revelation of himself to men and women.

Thus God's promise to Noah after the Flood is called a covenant (Genesis 9; Jeremiah 33: 20, "my covenant"). We have an account of God's covenant with Abraham (Genesis 17, cf. Leviticus 26: 42), of the covenant of the priesthood (Numbers 25: 12,13; Deuteronomy 33: 9; Nehemiah 13: 29), and of the covenant of Sinai (Exodus 34: 27,28; Leviticus 26: 15).

Later, this was renewed at different times in the history of Israel (Deuteronomy 29; Joshua 1: 24; 2 Chronicles 15; 23; 29; 34; Ezra 10; Nehemiah 9). God's covenant is said to be confirmed with an oath (Deuteronomy 4: 31; Psalms 89: 3), and to be accompanied by a sign (Genesis 9; 17). Hence the covenant is called God's "counsel," "oath," "promise" (Psalms 89: 3,4; 105: 8–11; Hebrews 6: 13–20; Luke 1: 68–75). God's covenant consists wholly in him bestowing his blessing (Isaiah 59: 21; Jeremiah 31: 33,34).

The term covenant is also used to designate the regular succession of day and night (Jeremiah 33: 20), the Sabbath (Exodus 31: 16), circumcision (Genesis 17: 9,10), and in general any ordinance of God (Jeremiah 34: 13,14).

COVENANT OF SALT

A "covenant of salt" signifies an everlasting covenant, in the sealing or ratifying of which salt, as an emblem of perpetuity, is used (Numbers 18: 19; Leviticus 2: 13; 2 Chronicles 13: 5).

Covetousness

A strong desire for the possession of worldly things (Colossians 3: 5; Ephesians 5: 5; Hebrews 13: 5; 1 Timothy 6: 9,10; Matthew 6: 20). It assumes sometimes the more aggravated form of avarice, which is the mark of cold-hearted worldliness.

Creation

"In the beginning" God created, i.e., called into being, all things out of nothing. This creative act on the part of God was absolutely free, and for infinitely wise reasons. The cause of all things exists only in the will of God. The work of creation is attributed:

- to the Godhead (Genesis 1: 1,26)
- to the Father (1 Corinthians 8: 6)
- to the Son (John 1: 3; Colossians 1: 16,17)
- to the Holy Spirit (Genesis 1: 2; Job 26: 13; Psalms 104: 30).

The fact that he is the Creator distinguishes Jehovah as the true God (Isaiah 37: 16; 40: 12,13; 54: 5; Psalms 96: 5; Jeremiah 10: 11,12). The one great goal in the work of creation is the manifestation of the glory of the Creator (Colossians 1: 16; Revelation 4: 11; Romans 11: 36). God's works, equally with God's word, are a revelation from him; and between the teachings of the one and those of the other, when rightly understood, there is no contradiction.

Glossary of doctrinal words in the Bible (11)

D

Death

Death may be simply defined as the termination of life. It is spoken of in a variety of ways in Scripture:

"The dust shall return to the earth as it was" (Eccl. 12: 7).

"Thou takest away their breath, they die" (Psalms 104: 29).

It is the dissolution of "our earthly house of this tabernacle" (2 Corinthians 5: 1); the "putting off this tabernacle" (2 Peter 1: 13,14).

Being "unclothed" (2 Corinthians 5: 3,4).

"Falling on sleep" (Psalms 76: 5; Jeremiah 51: 39; Acts 13: 36; 2 Pet. 3: 9).

"I go whence I shall not return" (Job 10: 21); "Make me to know mine end" (Psalms 39: 4); "to depart" (Phil. 1: 23).

The grave is represented as "the gates of death" (Job 38: 17; Psalms 9: 13; 107: 18). The gloomy silence of the grave is spoken as the "shadow of death" (Jeremiah 2: 6).

Death is the result of sin (Hebrews 2: 14), and not a "debt of nature." It is but once (9: 27), universal (Genesis 3: 19), necessary (Luke 2: 28–30). Jesus has by his own death taken away the sting of death for all his followers (1 Corinthians 15: 55–57).

There is a spiritual death in trespasses and sins, i.e., the death of the soul under the power of sin (Romans 8: 6; Ephesians 2: 1,3; Colossians 2: 13).

THE DEATH OF CHRIST

The death of Christ gives rise to all the blessings people enjoy on earth. It especially brings about the actual salvation of all his people. It does not make their salvation merely possible, but certain (Matthew 18: 11; Romans 5: 10; 2 Corinthians 5: 21; Galatians 1: 4; 3: 13; Ephesians 1: 7; 2: 16; Romans 8: 32–35).

Devil

(Gr. *diabolos*), a slanderer, the arch-enemy of man's spiritual interest (Job 1: 6; Revelation 2: 10; Zechariah 3: 1). He is called also "the accuser of the brethren" (Revelation 12: 10).

In Leviticus 17: 7 the word "devil" is the translation of the Hebrew *sair*, meaning a "goat" or "satyr" (Isaiah 13: 21; 34: 14), alluding to the wood-demons, the objects of idolatrous worship among the heathen.

In Deuteronomy 32: 17 and Psalms 106: 37 it is the translation of Hebrew *shed*, meaning lord, and idol, regarded by the Jews as a "demon," as the word is translated in the Revised Version.

In the narratives of the Gospels in connection with the "casting out of devils" a different Greek word (*daimon*) is used. In our Lord's time demon possession was frequent (Matthew 12: 25–30; Mark 5: 1–20; Luke 4: 35; 10: 18, etc.).

Disciple

A scholar, sometimes applied to the followers of John the Baptist (Matthew 9: 14), and of the Pharisees (22: 16), but principally to the followers of Christ.

A disciple of Christ is one who:
• believes his doctrine
• trusts in his sacrifice
• imbibes his spirit
• imitates his example
(Matthew 10: 24; Luke 14: 26,27,33; John 6: 69).

Dream

God has frequently used dreams to communicate his will to men and women. The most remarkable instances of this are recorded in the history of Jacob (Genesis 28: 12; 31: 10), Laban (31: 24), Joseph (37: 9–11), Gideon (Judg. 7), and Solomon (1 Kings 3: 5). Other significant dreams are also recorded, such as those of Abimelech (Genesis 20: 3–7), Pharaoh's chief butler and baker (40: 5), Pharaoh (41: 1–8), the Midianites (Judges 7: 13), Nebuchadnezzar (Daniel 2: 1; 4: 10,18), the wise men from the east (Matthew 2: 12), and Pilate's wife (27: 19).

To Joseph "the Lord appeared in a dream," and gave him instructions regarding the infant Jesus (Matthew 1: 20; 2: 12,13,19). In a vision of the night a "man of Macedonia" stood before Paul and said, "Come over into Macedonia and help us" (Acts 16: 9; see also 18: 9; 27: 23).

E

Easter

Originally a Saxon word (*Eostre*), denoting a goddess of the Saxons, in honor of whom sacrifices were offered about the time of the Passover. Hence the name came to be given to the festival of the Resurrection of Christ, which occurred at the time of the Passover. In the early English versions this word was frequently used as the translation of the Greek *pascha* (the Passover). When the Authorized Version (1611) was made, the word "Passover" was used in all passages in which this word *pascha* occurred, except in Act 12: 4. In the Revised Version the proper word, "Passover," is always used.

Eternal death

The miserable fate of the wicked in hell (Matthew 25: 46; Mark 3: 29; Hebrews 6: 2; 2 Thess. 1: 9; Matthew 18: 8; 25: 41; Jude 1: 7). The same Greek words in the New Testament (*aion, aionios, aidios*) are used to express

(1) the eternal existence of God (1 Timothy 1: 17; Romans 1: 20; 16: 26);

(2) of Christ (Revelation 1: 18);

(3) of the Holy Spirit (Hebrews 9: 14); and

(4) the eternal duration of the sufferings of the lost (Matthew 25: 46; Jude 1: 6).

Their condition is spoken of as:
"Fire that shall not be quenched" (Mark 9: 45,46),
"fire unquenchable" (Luke 3: 17),
"the worm that never dies,"
the "bottomless pit" (Revelation 9: 1),

Glossary of doctrinal words in the Bible (12)

Eternal death, continued

"the smoke of their torment ascending up for ever and ever" (Revelation 14: 10,11).

The supposition that God will ultimately secure the repentance and restoration of all sinners is unscriptural. There is not the slightest trace in all the Scriptures of any such restoration. The atoning death of Christ and the sanctifying power of the Holy Spirit are the only means of bringing people to repentance. In the case of those who perish these means have been rejected, and "there remaineth no more sacrifice for sins" (Hebrews 10: 26,27).

Eternal life

This expression occurs in the Old Testament only in Daniel 12: 2 (RSV, "everlasting life").

It occurs frequently in the New Testament (Matthew 7: 14; 18: 8,9; Luke 10: 28; 18: 18). It comprises the whole future of the redeemed (Luke 16: 9), and is contrasted with "eternal punishment" (Matthew 19: 29; 25: 46). It is the final reward and glory into which the children of God enter (1 Timothy 6: 12,19; Romans 6: 22; Galatians 6: 8; 1 Timothy 1: 16; Romans 5: 21); their Sabbath of rest (Hebrews 4: 9; 12: 22).

The newness of life which the believer derives from Christ (Romans 6: 4) is the very essence of salvation, and hence the life of glory or the eternal life must also be theirs (Romans

6: 8; 2 Tim 2: 11,12; Romans 5: 17,21; 8: 30; Ephesians 2: 5,6).

It is the "gift of God in Jesus Christ our Lord" (Romans 6: 23). The life the faithful have here on earth (John 3: 36; 5: 24; 6: 47,53–58) is inseparably connected with the eternal life beyond, the endless life of the future, the happy future of the saints in heaven (Matthew 19: 16,29; 25: 46).

Evangelist

A "publisher of glad tidings"; a missionary preacher of the gospel (Ephesians 4: 11). This title is applied to Philip (Acts 21: 8), who appears to have gone from city to city preaching the word (8: 4,40). Judging from the case of Philip, evangelists had neither the authority of an apostle, nor the gift of prophecy, nor the responsibility of pastoral supervision over a portion of the flock. They were itinerant preachers, having it as their special function to carry the gospel to places where it was previously unknown. The writers of the four Gospels are known as the Evangelists.

Everlasting

Eternal, applied to God (Genesis 21: 33; Deuteronomy 33: 27; Psalms 41: 13; 90: 2). We also read of the "everlasting hills" (Genesis 49: 26); an "everlasting priesthood" (Exodus 40: 15; Numbers 25: 13).

F

Faith

Faith is in general the persuasion of the mind that a certain statement is true (Phil. 1: 27; 2 Thessalonians 2: 13). Its primary idea is trust. A thing is true, and therefore worthy of trust.

Faith is the result of teaching (Romans 10: 14–17). Knowledge is an essential element in all faith, and is sometimes spoken of as an equivalent to faith (John 10: 38; 1 John 2: 3). Yet the two are distinguished in this respect, that faith includes in it assent, which is an act of the will in addition to the act of the understanding. Assent to the truth is of the essence of faith, and the ultimate ground on which our assent to any revealed truth rests is the veracity of God.

TEMPORARY FAITH

Temporary faith is that state of mind which is awakened in men and women (e.g., Felix) by the sight of the truth and by the influence of religious sympathy, or by what is sometimes styled the common operation of the Holy Spirit.

SAVING FAITH

Saving faith is so called because it has eternal life inseparably connected with it. It cannot be better defined than in the words of the Assembly's Shorter Catechism: "Faith in Jesus Christ is a saving grace, whereby we receive and rest upon him alone for salvation, as he is offered to us in the gospel."

The object of saving faith is the whole revealed Word of God. Faith accepts and believes it as the very truth. But the special act of faith which unites to Christ has as its object the person and the work of the Lord Jesus Christ (John 7: 38; Acts 16: 31). This is the specific act of faith by which a sinner is justified before God (Romans 3: 22,25; Galatians 2: 16; Philippians 3: 9; John 3: 16–36; Acts 10: 43; 16: 31). In this act of faith the believer appropriates and rests on Christ alone as Mediator.

This assent to or believe in the truth has always associated with it:

- a deep sense of sin,
- a distinct view of Christ,
- a consenting will, and
- a loving heart, together with
- a reliance on, a trusting in, or resting in Christ.

It is that state of mind in which a poor sinner, conscious of his sin, flees from his guilty self to Christ his Savior, and rolls over the burden of all his sins on him. It consists chiefly, not in the assent given to the testimony of God in his Word, but in embracing with trust the one and only Savior whom God reveals.

This trust and reliance is of the essence of faith.

By faith the believer directly and immediately appropriates Christ as his or her own.

Glossary of doctrinal words in the Bible (13)

Faith, continued

SAVING FAITH, CONTINUED
Faith makes Christ ours. It is not a work which God graciously accepts instead of perfect obedience, but is only the hand by which we take hold of the person and work of our Redeemer as the only ground of our salvation.

Saving faith is a moral act, as it proceeds from a renewed will, and a renewed will is necessary to believing assent to the truth of God (1 Corinthians 2: 14; 2 Cor. 4: 4). Faith, therefore, has its origin in the moral part of our nature as much as in the intellectual. The mind must first be enlightened by divine teaching (John 6: 44; Acts 13: 48; 2 Cor. 4: 6; Ephesians 1: 17,18) before it can discern the things of the Spirit.

Faith is necessary to our salvation (Mark 16: 16), not because there is any merit in it, but simply because it is the sinner's taking the place assigned to him or her by God, his or her falling in with what God is doing.

The basis or ground of faith is the divine testimony, not the reasonableness of what God says, but the simple fact that he says it. Faith rests immediately on, "Thus saith the Lord." But in order to appropriate this faith the veracity, sincerity, and truth of God must be owned and appreciated, together with his unchangeableness. God's word encourages the sinner personally to accept Christ as God's gift, to embrace him, to take Christ as his or hers.

Faith in Christ secures for the believer:
• freedom from condemnation, or
• justification before God;
• a participation in the life that is in Christ,
• the divine life (John 14: 19; Romans 6: 4–10; Ephesians 4: 15,16, etc.);
• "peace with God" (Romans 5: 1); and
• sanctification (Acts 26: 18; Galatians 5: 6; Acts 15: 9).

All who thus believe in Christ will certainly be saved (John 6: 37,40; 10: 27,28; Romans 8: 1). The faith=the gospel (Acts 6: 7; Romans 1: 5; Galatians 1: 23; 1 Timothy 3: 9; Jude 1: 3).

Faithful

As a name given to Christians, it means full of faith, full of trust, and not simply trustworthy (Acts 10: 45; 16: 1; 2 Cor. 6: 15; Colossians 1: 2; 1 Timothy 4: 3,12; 5: 16; 6: 2; Titus 1: 6; Ephesians 1: 1; 1 Corinthians 4: 17, etc.).

It is used also of God's word or covenant as true and to be trusted (Psalms 119: 86,138; Isaiah 25: 1; 1 Timothy 1: 15; Revelation 21: 5; 22: 6, etc.).

Father

A name applied
• to any ancestor (Deuteronomy 1: 11; 1 Kings 15: 11; Matthew 3: 9; 23: 30, etc.);
• as a title of respect to a chief, ruler, or elder, etc. (Judges 17: 10; 18: 19; 1 Samuel 10: 12; 2 Kings 2: 12; Matthew 23: 9, etc.).

The author or beginner of anything is also so called; e.g., Jabal and Jubal (Genesis 4: 20,21; cf. Job 38: 28).

Applied to God (Exodus 4: 22; Deuteronomy 32: 6; 2 Sam. 7: 14; Psalms 89: 27,28, etc.).

It denoting his covenant relation to the Jews (Jeremiah 31: 9; Isaiah 63: 16; 64: 8; John 8: 41, etc.).

Believers are called God's "sons" (John 1: 12; Romans 8: 16; Matthew 6: 4,8,15,18; 10: 20,29). They also call him "Father" (Romans 1: 7; 1 Corinthians 1: 3; 2 Cor. 1: 2; Galatians 1: 4)

Fear of the Lord

The fear of the Lord is used in the Old Testament of true piety (Proverbs 1: 7; Job 28: 28; Psalms 19: 9). It is a fear linked with love and hope, and is therefore not a slavish dread, but rather loving reverence. (Cf. Deuteronomy 32: 6; Hosea 11: 1; Isaiah 1: 2; 63: 16; 64: 8.) God is called "the Fear of Isaac" (Genesis 31: 42,53), i.e., the God whom Isaac feared.

A holy fear is ordered also in the New Testament to prevent carelessness in religion, and as an incentive to penitence (Matthew 10: 28; 2 Cor. 5: 11; 7: 1; Phil. 2: 12; Ephesians 5: 21; Hebrews 12: 28,29).

Fellowship

With God, consisting in:
- the knowledge of his will (Job 22: 21; John 17: 3)
- agreement with his designs (Amos 3: 2)
- enjoyment of his presence (Psalms 4: 6)
- conformity to his image (1 John 2: 6; 1: 6); and
- participation of his love (1 John 1: 3,4; Ephesians 3: 14–21).

Of saints with one another, in duties (Romans 12: 5; 1 Corinthians 12: 1; 1 Thessalonians 5: 17,18); in ordinances (Hebrews 10: 25; Acts 2: 46); in grace, love, joy, etc. (Malachi 3: 16; 2 Cor. 8: 4); mutual interest, spiritual and temporal (Romans 12: 4,13; Hebrews 13: 16); in sufferings (Romans 15: 1,2; Galatians 6: 1,2; Romans 12: 15; and in glory (Revelation 7: 9).

Foreknowledge of God

God's foreknowledge, (Acts 2: 23; Rom. 8: 29; 11: 2; 1 Pet. 1: 2), is one of God's attributes which we cannot fully understand. In the most absolute sense his knowledge is infinite (1 Sam. 23: 9–13; Jer. 38: 17–23; 42: 9–22, Matt. 11: 21, 23; Acts 15: 18).

Forgiveness of sins

One of the parts of justification. In pardoning sin, God absolves the sinner from the condemnation of the law, and on account of the work of Christ, i.e., he removes the guilt of sin.

All sins are forgiven freely (Acts 5: 31; 13: 38; 1 John 1: 6–9). The sinner is by this act of grace for ever freed from the guilt and penalty of his sins. This is God's special prerogative (Ps. 130: 4; Mark 2: 5). It is offered to all in the gospel.

Glossary of doctrinal words in the Bible (14)

F continued

Fornication

In every form it was sternly condemned by the Mosaic law (Lev. 21: 9; 19: 29; Deut. 22: 20,21,23–29; 23: 18; Ex. 22: 16). But this word is more frequently used in a symbolical than in its ordinary sense. It frequently means forsaking God or following idols (Is. 1: 2; Jer. 2: 20; Ezek. 16; Hos. 1: 2; 2: 1–5; Jer. 3: 8,9).

G

Glory

(Heb. *kabhod*; Gr. *doxa*).

(1) Abundance, wealth, treasure, and hence honor (Ps. 49: 12); glory (Gen. 31: 1; Matt. 4: 8; Rev. 21: 24,26).

(2) Honor, dignity (1 Kings 3: 13; Heb. 2: 7 1 Pet. 1: 24); of God (Ps. 19: 1; 29: 1); of the mind or heart (Gen. 49: 6; Ps. 7: 5; Acts 2: 46).

(3) Splendor, brightness, majesty (Gen. 45: 13; Is. 4: 5; Acts 22: 11; 2 Cor. 3: 7); of Jehovah (Is. 59: 19; 60: 1; 2 Thess. 1: 9).

(4) The glorious moral attributes, the infinite perfections of God (Is. 40: 5; Acts 7: 2; Rom. 1: 23; 9: 23; Eph. 1: 12). Jesus is the "brightness of the Father's glory" (Heb. 1: 3; John 1: 14; 2: 11).

(5) The happiness of heaven (Rom. 2: 7, 10; 5: 2; 8: 18; Heb. 2: 10; 1 Pet. 5: 1,10).

(6) The phrase "Give glory to God" (Josh. 7: 19; Jer. 13: 16) is a Hebrew idiom meaning, "Confess your sins." The words of the Jews to the blind man, "Give God the praise" (John 9: 24), are a command to confess sin. They are equivalent to, "Confess that you are an impostor," "Give God the glory by speaking the truth"; for they denied that a miracle had been performed.

God

God is the name of the Divine Being. It is the translation

(1) of the Hebrew *'El*, from a word meaning to be strong;

(2) of *'Eloah*, plural *'Elohim*. The singular form, *Eloah*, is used only in poetry. The plural form is more commonly used in all parts of the Bible, The Hebrew word Jehovah, the only other word generally used to denote the Supreme Being, is uniformly translated in the Authorized Version by "Lord," printed in small capitals. The existence of God is taken for granted in the Bible. There is nowhere any argument to prove it. He who disbelieves this truth is spoken of as one devoid of understanding (Ps. 14: 1).

ARGUMENTS FOR THE EXISTENCE OF GOD
The arguments generally adduced by theologians in proof of the being of God are:

(1) The *a priori* argument, which is the testimony suggested by reason.

(2) The *a posteriori* argument, by

which we proceed logically from the facts of experience to causes. These arguments are,

(a) The cosmological, by which it is proved that there must be a First Cause of all things, for every effect must have a cause.

(b) The teleological, or the argument from design. We see everywhere the results of the work of an intelligent Cause in nature.

(c) The moral argument, also called the anthropological argument, based on the moral consciousness and the history of humankind, which shows a moral order and purpose which can only be explained on the supposition of the existence of God. Conscience and human history testify that "verily there is a God that judgeth in the earth."

The attributes of God are set forth in order by Moses in Ex. 34: 6,7. (See also Deut. 6: 4; 10: 17; Num. 16: 22; Ex. 15: 11; 33: 19; Is. 44: 6; Hab. 3: 6; Ps. 102: 26; Job 34: 12.) They are also systematically classified in Rev. 5: 12 and Rev. 7: 12.

God's attributes are spoken of by some as absolute, i.e., such as belong to his essence as Jehovah, Jah, etc.; and relative, i.e., such as are ascribed to him with relation to his creatures. Others distinguish them into communicable, i.e., those which can be imparted in degree to his creatures: goodness, holiness, wisdom, etc.; and incommunicable, which cannot be so imparted: independence, immutability, immensity, and eternity. Some have divided them into natural attributes, eternity, immensity, etc.; and moral, holiness, goodness, etc.

Godhead

The godhead, (Acts 17: 29; Rom. 1: 20; Col. 2: 9), is the essential being or the nature of God.

Godliness

The whole of practical piety (1 Tim. 4: 8; 2 Pet. 1: 6). "It supposes knowledge, veneration, affection, dependence, submission, gratitude, and obedience." In 1 Tim. 3: 16 it denotes the substance of revealed religion.

Goodness of God

A perfection of his character which he brings to his creatures (Ps. 145: 8,9; 103: 8; 1 John 4: 8). It is seen in connection with the miseries of his creatures in its mercy, pity, compassion, and in the case of impenitent sinners, in long-suffering patience. "Goodness and justice are the different aspects of one unchangeable, infinitely wise, and sovereign moral perfection.

God is not sometimes merciful and sometimes just, but he is eternally infinitely just and merciful." God is infinitely and unchangeably good (Zeph. 3: 17), and his goodness is incomprehensible by the finite mind (Rom. 11: 35,36). "God's goodness appears in two things, giving and forgiving."

Glossary of doctrinal words in the Bible (15)

G

Gospel

A word of Anglo-Saxon origin, and meaning "God's spell," i.e., word of God, or rather, according to others, "good spell," i.e., good news. It is the translation of the Greek *evangelion*, i.e., "good message." It denotes:

(1) the message of salvation as preached by our Lord and his followers.

(2) It was later applied to each of the four histories of our Lord's life, written by those who are therefore called "Evangelists," writers of the history of the gospel (the *evangelion*).

(3) The term is often used to express collectively the gospel doctrines; and "preaching the gospel" is often used to include not only the proclaiming of the good tidings, but teaching men and women how to accept the offer of salvation. It is spoken of as:

- "the gospel of the grace of God" (Acts 20: 24),
- "the gospel of the kingdom" (Matt. 4: 23),
- "the gospel of Christ" (Rom. 1: 16),
- "the gospel of peace (Eph. 6: 15),
- "the glorious gospel,"
- "the everlasting gospel,"
- "the gospel of salvation" (Eph. 1: 13).

Grace

(1) Of form or person (Prov. 1: 9; 3: 22; Ps. 45: 2).

(2) Favor, kindness, friendship (Gen. 6: 8; 18: 3; 19: 19; 2 Tim. 1: 9).

(3) God's forgiving mercy (Rom. 11: 6; Eph. 2: 5).

(4) The gospel as distinguished from the law (John 1: 17; Rom. 6: 14; 1 Pet. 5: 12).

(5) Gifts freely bestowed by God; as miracles, prophecy, tongues (Rom. 15: 15; 1 Cor. 15: 10; Eph. 3: 8).

(6) Christian virtues (2 Cor. 8: 7; 2 Pet. 3: 18).

(7) The glory hereafter to be revealed (1 Pet. 1: 13).

Grace, Means of

An expression not used in Scripture, but used:

(1) to denote those institutions ordained by God to be the normal channels of grace to men and women. These are the Word, Sacraments, and Prayer.

(2) But in popular language the expression is used in a wider sense to denote those exercises in which we engage for the purpose of obtaining spiritual blessing; as hearing the gospel, reading the Word, meditation, self-examination, Christian fellowship, etc.

H

Hatred

Hatred is listed as one of the deeds of sinful human nature (Gal. 5: 20). Totally different from the meaning of the word in Deut. 21: 15; Matt. 6: 24; Luke 14: 26; Rom. 9: 13, where it denotes only a lesser degree of love.

Heart

According to the Bible, the heart is the center not only of spiritual activity, but of all human life. "Heart" and "soul" are often used interchangeably (Deut. 6: 5; 26: 16; cf. Matt. 22: 37; Mark 12: 30,33), but this is not generally the case.

The heart is the "home of the personal life," and hence a man or woman is designated, according to his or her heart, wise (1 Kings 3: 12, etc.), pure (Ps. 24: 4; Matt. 5: 8, etc.), upright and righteous (Gen. 20: 5,6; Ps. 11: 2; 78: 72), pious and good (Luke 8: 15), etc. In these and such passages the word "soul" could not be substituted for "heart."

The heart is also the seat of the conscience (Rom. 2: 15). It is naturally wicked (Gen. 8: 21), and hence it contaminates the whole life and character (Matt. 12: 34; 15: 18; cf. Eccl. 8: 11; Ps. 73: 7). Hence the heart must be changed, regenerated (Ezek. 36: 26; 11: 19; Ps. 51: 10–14), before a person can willingly obey God.

The process of salvation begins in the heart by the believing reception of the testimony of God, while the rejection of that testimony hardens the heart (Ps. 95: 8; Prov. 28: 14; 2 Chr. 36: 13). "Hardness of heart evidences itself by light views of sin; partial acknowledgment and confession of it; pride and conceit; ingratitude; unconcern about the word and ordinances of God; inattention to divine providences; stifling convictions of conscience; shunning reproof; presumption, and general ignorance of divine things."

Heaven

DEFINITIONS
The phrase "heaven and earth" is used to indicate the whole universe (Gen. 1: 1; Jer. 23: 24; Acts 17: 24). According to the Jewish ideas there were three heavens,

(a) The firmament, as "fowls of the heaven" (Gen. 2: 19; 7: 3,23; Ps. 8: 8, etc.), "the eagles of heaven" (Lam. 4: 19), etc.

(b) The starry heavens (Deut. 17: 3; Jer. 8: 2; Matt. 24: 29).

(c) "The heaven of heavens," or "the third heaven" (Deut. 10: 14; 1 Kings 8: 27; Ps. 115: 16; 148: 4; 2 Cor. 12: 2).

Glossary of doctrinal words in the Bible (16)

Heaven, continued

MEANING OF WORDS IN THE ORIGINAL

(a) The usual Hebrew word for "heavens" is *shamayim*, a plural form meaning "heights," "elevations" (Gen. 1: 1; 2: 1).

(b) The Hebrew word *marom* is also used (Ps. 68: 18; 93: 4; 102: 19, etc.) as equivalent to *shamayim*, "high places," "heights."

(c) Heb. *galgal*, literally a "wheel," is translated "heaven" in Ps. 77: 18 (RV, "whirlwind").

(d) Heb. *shahak*, translated "sky" (Deut. 33: 26; Job 37: 18; Ps. 18: 11), plural "clouds" (Job 35: 5; 36: 28; Ps. 68: 34, marg. "heavens"), means probably the firmament.

(e) Heb. *rakia* is closely connected with (d), and is translated *firmamentum* in the Vulgate, from which is derived our "firmament" (Gen. 1: 6; Deut. 33: 26, etc.), regarded as a solid expanse.

METAPHORICAL MEANING OF TERM

Is. 14: 13,14; "doors of heaven" (Ps. 78: 23); heaven "shut" (1 Kings 8: 35); "opened" (Ezek. 1: 1). (See 1 Chr. 21: 16.)

SPIRITUAL MEANING

The place of the everlasting blessedness of the righteous; the abode of departed spirits.

(a) Christ calls it his "Father's house" (John 14: 2).

(b) It is called "paradise" (Luke 23: 43; 2 Cor. 12: 4; Rev. 2: 7).

(c) "The heavenly Jerusalem" (Gal. 4: 26; Heb. 12: 22; Rev. 3: 12).

(d) The "kingdom of heaven" (Matt. 25: 1; James 2: 5).

(e) The "eternal kingdom" (2 Pet. 1: 11).

(f) The "eternal inheritance" (1 Pet. 1: 4; Heb. 9: 15).

(g) The "better country" (Heb. 11: 14,16).

(h) The blessed are said to "sit down with Abraham, Isaac, and Jacob," and to be "in Abraham's bosom" (Luke 16: 22; Matt. 8: 11); to "reign with Christ" (2 Tim. 2: 12); and to enjoy "rest" (Heb. 4: 10, 11).

In heaven the blessedness of the righteous consists in the possession of "life everlasting," "an eternal weight of glory" (2 Cor. 4: 17), freedom from all sufferings forever, freedom from all evils (2 Cor. 5: 1, 2) freedom from the wicked (2 Tim. 4: 18), bliss without termination, the "fullness of joy" for ever (Luke 20: 36; 2 Cor. 4: 16,18; 1 Pet. 1: 4; 5: 10; 1 John 3: 2). The believer's heaven is not only a state of everlasting blessedness, but also a "place", a place "prepared" for them (John 14: 2).

Heresy

From a Greek word signifying
(1) a choice
(2) the opinion chosen
(3) the sect holding the opinion.
In the Acts of the Apostles (Acts 5: 17; 15: 5; 24: 5,14; 26: 5) it denotes a sect, without reference to its character. Elsewhere, however, in the New Testament it has a different meaning attached to it. Paul ranks "heresies" with crimes and seditions (Gal. 5: 20).

This word also denotes divisions or schisms in the church (1 Cor. 11: 19). In Titus 3: 10 a "heretical person" is one who follows his own self-willed "questions," and who is to be avoided. Heresies thus came to signify self-chosen doctrines not emanating from God (2 Pet. 2: 1).

Holiness

In the highest sense belongs to God (Is. 6: 3; Rev. 15: 4), and to Christians as consecrated to God's service, and in so far as they conform in all things to the will of God (Rom. 6: 19,22; Eph. 1: 4; Titus 1: 8; 1 Pet. 1: 15). Personal holiness is a work of gradual development. It is often hindered and hence the frequent commands to watchfulness, prayer, and perseverance (1 Cor. 1: 30; 2 Cor. 7: 1; Eph. 4: 23,24).

Holy Spirit

The third Person of the Trinity.

HIS PERSONALITY IS PROVED:

(1) from the fact that the attributes of personality, as intelligence and volition, are ascribed to him (John 14: 17, 26; 15: 26; 1 Cor. 2: 10,11; 12: 11). He reproves, helps, glorifies, intercedes (John 16: 7–13; Rom. 8: 26).

(2) He does things only a person does (Luke 12: 12; Acts 5: 32; 15: 28; 16: 6; 28: 25; 1 Cor. 2: 13; Heb. 2: 4; 3: 7; 2 Pet. 1: 21).

HIS DIVINITY IS ESTABLISHED:

(1) from the fact that the names of God are ascribed to him (Ex. 17: 7; Ps. 95: 7; compare Heb. 3: 7–11); and

(2) that divine attributes are also ascribed to him, omnipresence (Ps. 139: 7; Eph. 2: 17,18; 1 Cor. 12: 13); omniscience (1 Cor. 2: 10, 11); omnipotence (Luke 1: 35; Rom. 8: 11); eternity (Heb. 9: 4).

(3) Creation is ascribed to him (Gen. 1: 2; Job 26: 13; Ps. 104: 30), as are miracles (Matt. 12: 28; 1 Cor. 12: 9–11).

(4) Worship is required and ascribed to him (Is. 6: 3; Acts 28: 25; Rom. 9: 1; Rev. 1: 4; Matt. 28: 19).

Hope

One of the three main elements of Christian character (1 Cor. 13: 13). It is linked to faith and love, and is opposed to seeing or possessing (Rom. 8: 24; 1 John 3: 2). "Hope is an essential and fundamental element of Christian life, so essential indeed, that, like faith and love, it can itself designate the essence of Christianity (1 Pet. 3: 15; Heb. 10: 23). In it the whole glory of the Christian vocation is centered (Eph. 1: 18; 4: 4)."

Glossary of doctrinal words in the Bible (17)

Hope, continued

Unbelievers are without this hope (Eph. 2: 12; 1 Thess. 4: 13). Christ is the actual object of the believer's hope, because it is in his second coming that the hope of glory will be fulfilled (1 Tim. 1: 1; Col. 1: 27; Titus 2: 13). It is spoken of as "lively," i.e., a living, hope, a hope not frail and perishable, but having a perennial life (1 Pet. 1: 3). In Rom. 5: 2 the "hope" spoken of is probably objective, i.e., "the hope set before us," namely, eternal life (cf. Rom. 12: 12). In 1 John 3: 3 the expression "hope in him" ought rather to be, as in the Revised Version, "hope on him," i.e., a hope based on God.

Humiliation of Christ

(Phil. 2: 8), seen in:

(1) his birth (Gal. 4: 4; Luke 2: 7; John 1: 46; Heb. 2: 9),

(2) his circumstances,

(3) his reputation (Is. 53; Matt. 26: 59,67; Ps. 22: 6; Matt. 26: 68),

(4) his soul (Ps. 22: 1; Matt. 4: 1–11; Luke 22: 44; Heb. 2: 17, 18; 4: 15),

(5) his death (Luke 23; John 19; Mark 15: 24,25),

(6) and his burial (Is. 53: 9; Matt. 27: 57,58, 60).

His humiliation was necessary:

(1) to execute the purpose of God (Acts 2: 23,24; Ps. 40: 6–8),

(2) fulfill the Old Testament types and prophecies,

(3) satisfy the law in the room of the guilty (Is. 53; Heb. 9: 12,15), procure for them eternal redemption,

(4) and to show us an example.

Humility

A prominent Christian grace (Rom. 12: 3; 15: 17,18; 1 Cor. 3: 5–7; 2 Cor. 3: 5; Phil. 4: 11–13). It is a state of mind well pleasing to God (1 Pet. 3: 4); it preserves the soul in tranquility (Ps. 69: 32, 33), and makes us patient under trials (Job 1: 22).

Christ has set us an example of humility (Phil. 2: 6–8). We should become humble as we recall our sins (Lam. 3: 39), and by the thought that it is the way to honor (Prov. 16: 18), and that the greatest promises are made to the humble (Ps. 147: 6; Is. 57: 15; 66: 2; 1 Pet. 5: 5). It is a "great paradox in Christianity that it makes humility the avenue to glory."

Hypocrite

One who puts on a mask and pretends to be what he is not. Our Lord severely rebuked the scribes and Pharisees for their hypocrisy (Matt. 6: 2,5,16). "The hypocrite's hope shall perish" (Job 8: 13). The Hebrew word here translated "hypocrite" rather means the "godless" or "profane," as it is translated in Jer. 23: 11, i.e., polluted with crimes.

I

Idolatry

Image-worship or divine honor paid to any created object. Paul describes the origin of idolatry in Rom. 1: 21–25: humankind forsook God, and sank into ignorance and moral corruption (Rom. 1: 28).

The forms of idolatry are:

(1) Fetishism, or the worship of trees, rivers, hills, stones, etc.

(2) Nature worship, the worship of the sun, moon, and stars, as the supposed powers of nature.

(3) Hero worship, the worship of dead ancestors, or of heroes.

In Scripture, idolatry is regarded as of heathen origin, and as being introduced to the Hebrews through contact with heathen nations. The first allusion to idolatry is in the account of Rachel stealing her father's teraphim (Gen. 31: 19), which were the relics of the worship of other gods by Laban's progenitors "on the other side of the river in old time" (Josh. 24: 2). During their long stay in Egypt the Hebrews fell into idolatry (Josh. 24: 14; Ezek. 20: 7).

The first and second commandments are directed against idolatry of every form.

In the New Testament the term idolatry is used of covetousness (Matt. 6: 24; Luke 16: 13; Col. 3: 5; Eph. 5: 5).

Immortality

Perpetuity of existence. The doctrine of immortality is taught in the Old Testament. It is plainly implied in the writings of Moses (Gen. 5: 22,24; 25: 8; 37: 35; 47: 9; 49: 29, compare Heb. 11: 13–16; Ex. 3: 6, compare Matt. 22: 23). It is more clearly and fully taught in the later books (Is. 14: 9; Ps. 17: 15; 49: 15; 73: 24). It was thus a doctrine obviously well known to the Jews.

With the full revelation of the gospel this doctrine was "brought to light" (2 Tim. 1: 10; 1 Cor. 15; 2 Cor. 5: 1–6; 1 Thess. 4: 13–18).

Incarnation

The incarnation took place when Christ took our human nature on himself and became a human being. Christ is both God and man. A Divine Person was united to a human nature (Acts 20: 28; Rom. 8: 32; 1 Cor. 2: 8; Heb. 2: 11–14; 1 Tim. 3: 16; Gal. 4: 4, etc.). The union is hypostatical, i.e., is personal; the two natures are not mixed, and it is perpetual.

J

Jew

The name derived from the patriarch Judah, at first given to a member of the tribe of Judah or to the separate kingdom of Judah (2 Kings 16: 6; 25: 25; Jer. 32: 12; 38: 19; 40: 11; 41: 3), in contrast to those belonging to the kingdom of the ten tribes, who were called Israelites.

Glossary of doctrinal words in the Bible (18)

Jew, continued

During the Captivity, and after the Restoration, the name, however, was extended to the whole Jewish nation (Esther 3: 6,10; Dan. 3: 8, 12; Ezra 4: 12; 5: 1,5).

Originally this people were called Hebrews (Gen. 39: 14; 40: 15; Ex. 2: 7; 3: 18; 5: 3; 1 Sam. 4: 6,9, etc.), but after the Exile this name fell into disuse. But Paul was called a Hebrew (2 Cor. 11: 22; Phil. 3: 5).

There are three names used in the New Testament to designate this people,

(1) Jews, referring to their nationality, to distinguish them from Gentiles.

(2) Hebrews, referring to their language and education, to distinguish them from Hellenists, i.e., Jews who spoke the Greek language.

(3) Israelites, referring to their sacred privileges as the chosen people of God. "To other races we owe the splendid inheritance of modern civilization and secular culture; but the religious education of mankind has been the gift of the Jew alone."

Jewess

A woman of Hebrew birth, such as Eunice, the mother of Timothy (Acts 16: 1; 2 Tim. 1: 5), and Drusilla (Acts 24: 24), wife of Felix, and daughter of Herod Agrippa I.

Judgment, The final

The sentence that will be passed on our actions at the last day (Matt. 25; Rom. 14: 10, 1; 2 Cor. 5: 10; 2 Thess. 1: 7–10).

The judge is Jesus Christ, as mediator. All judgment is committed to him (Acts 17: 31; John 5: 22,27; Rev. 1: 7). The people to be judged are:

(1) the whole race of Adam without a single exception (Matt. 25: 31–46; 1 Cor. 15: 51,52; Rev. 20: 11–15); and

(2) the fallen angels (2 Pet. 2: 4; Jude 6).

The yardstick of judgment is the standard of God's law as revealed to men and women,

• the heathen by the law as written on their hearts (Luke 12: 47, 48; Rom. 2: 12–16);

• the Jew who "sinned in the law shall be judged by the law" (Rom. 2: 12);

• the Christian enjoying the light of revelation, by the will of God as made known to him (Matt. 11: 20–24; John 3: 19).

Then the secrets of all hearts will be brought to light (1 Cor. 4: 5; Luke 8: 17; 12: 2,3) to vindicate the justice of the sentence pronounced.

The time of the judgment will be after the resurrection (Heb. 9: 27; Acts 17: 31).

Judgments of God

(1) The secret decisions of God's will (Ps. 110: 5; 36: 6).

(2) The revelations of his will

(Ex. 21: 1; Deut. 6: 20; Ps. 119: 7–175).

(3) The infliction of punishment on the wicked (Ex. 6: 6; 12: 12; Ezek. 25: 11; Rev. 16: 7), such as is mentioned in Gen. 7; 19: 24,25; Judg. 1: 6,7; Acts 5: 1–10, etc.

Justice of God

That perfection of his nature in which he is infinitely righteous in himself and in all he does, the righteousness of the divine nature exercised in his moral rule. At first God imposes righteous laws on his creatures and executes them righteously. Justice is not an optional product of his will, but an unchangeable principle of his very nature. He cannot, as he is infinitely righteous, do other than hate sin as it must be punishment.

"He cannot deny himself" (2 Tim. 2: 13). His essential and eternal righteousness immutably determines him to visit every sin as such with deserved punishment.

Justification

A forensic term, in contrast with condemnation.

In its nature, it is God's judicial act, by which he pardons all the sins of those who believe in Christ, and accounts, accepts, and treats them as righteous in the eye of the law, i.e., as conformed to all its demands. In addition to the pardon of sin, justification declares that all the claims of the law are satisfied in the justified. It is the act of a judge and not of a sovereign.

The law is not relaxed or set aside, but is declared to be fulfilled in the strictest sense; and so the person justified is declared to be entitled to all the advantages and rewards arising from perfect obedience to the law (Rom. 5: 1–10).

It comes about through the imputing or crediting to the believer by God himself of the perfect righteousness, of his Representative Jesus Christ (Rom. 10: 3–9). Justification is not the forgiveness of a man without righteousness, but a declaration that he possesses a righteousness which perfectly and for ever satisfies the law, namely, Christ's righteousness (2 Cor. 5: 21; Rom. 4: 6–8).

The sole condition on which this righteousness is imputed or credited to the believer is faith in or on the Lord Jesus Christ. Faith is called a "condition," not because it possesses any merit, but only because it is the instrument, the only instrument by which the soul appropriates or apprehends Christ and his righteousness (Rom. 1: 17; 3: 25,26; 4: 20,22; Phil. 3: 8–11; Gal. 2: 16).

The act of faith which thus secures our justification secures also at the same time our sanctification; and thus the doctrine of justification by faith does not lead to licentiousness (Rom. 6: 2–7).

Good works, while not the ground, are the certain consequence of justification (Rom. 6: 14; 7: 6).

Glossary of doctrinal words in the Bible (19)

K

Key

Frequently mentioned in Scripture. It is called in Hebrew *maphteah*, i.e., the opener (Judg. 3: 25); and in the Greek New Testament *kleis*, from its use in shutting (Matt. 16: 19; Luke 11: 52; Rev. 1: 18, etc.). Figures of ancient Egyptian keys are frequently found on monuments, also of Assyrian locks and keys of wood, and of a large size (Cf. Is. 22: 22).

The word is used figuratively of power or authority or office (Is. 22: 22; Rev. 3: 7; Rev. 1: 8; cf. Rev. 9: 1; 20: 1; cf. also Matt. 16: 19; 18: 18). The "key of knowledge" (Luke 11: 52; cf. Matt. 23: 13) is the means of attaining the knowledge regarding the kingdom of God. The "power of the keys" is a phrase in general use to denote the extent of ecclesiastical authority.

Kingdom of God

(Matt. 6: 33; Mark 1: 14,15; Luke 4: 43) = "kingdom of Christ" (Matt. 13: 41; 20: 21) = "kingdom of Christ and of God" (Eph. 5: 5) = "kingdom of David" (Mark 11: 10) = "the kingdom" (Matt. 8: 12; 13: 19) = "kingdom of heaven" (Matt. 3: 2; 4: 17; 13: 41), all denote facets of the same thing:

(1) Christ's mediatorial authority, or his rule on the earth;

(2) the blessings and advantages of all kinds that flow from this rule;

(3) the subjects of this kingdom taken collectively, or the Church.

L

Lord

There are various Hebrew and Greek words translated by this phase.

(1) Heb. *Jehovah*, has been translated in the English Bible Lord, printed in small capitals. This is the proper name of the God of the Hebrews. The form "Jehovah" is retained only in Ex. 6: 3; Ps. 83: 18; Is. 12: 2; 26: 4, both in the Authorized and the Revised Version.

(2) Heb. *'adon*, means one possessed of absolute control. It denotes a master, as of slaves (Gen. 24: 14,27), or a ruler of his subjects (Gen. 45: 8), or a husband, as lord of his wife (Gen. 18: 12).The old plural form of this Hebrew word is *'adonai*. From a superstitious reverence for the name "Jehovah," the Jews, in reading their Scriptures, whenever that name occurred, always pronounced it *'Adonai*.

(3) Greek *kurios*, a supreme master, etc. In the LXX this is invariably used for "Jehovah" and "'Adonai."

(4) Heb. *ba'al*, a master, as having domination. This word is applied to human relationships, as that of husband, to people skilled in some art or profession, and to heathen deities. "The men of Shechem," literally "the baals of Shechem" (Judg. 9: 2, 3). These

were the Israelite inhabitants who had reduced the Canaanites to slavery (Josh. 16: 10; 17: 13).

(5) Heb. *seren*, applied exclsively to the "lords of the Philistines" (Judg. 3: 3). The LXX Translates it by *satrapies*. At this period the Philistines were not, as at a later period (1 Sam. 21: 10), under a kingly government. (See Josh. 13: 3; 1 Sam. 6: 18.) There were five such lordships, i.e., Gath, Ashdod, Gaza, Ashkelon, and Ekron.

Lord's Day

Only once, in Rev. 1: 10, was this in the early Christian times used of the first day of the week, which commemorated the Lord's resurrection. There is every reason to conclude that John thus used the name.

Lust

Sinful longing; the inward sin which leads to the falling away from God (Rom. 1: 21). "Lust, the origin of sin, has its place in the heart, not of necessity, but because it is the center of all moral forces and impulses and of spiritual activity." In Mark 4: 19 "lusts" are objects of desire.

M

Man and woman

(1) Heb. *'Adam*, used as the name of the first man. The name is derived from a word meaning "to be red," and thus the first man was called Adam because he was formed from the red earth. It is also the generic name of the human race (Gen. 1: 26,27; 5: 2; 8: 21; Deut. 8: 3). Its equivalents are the Latin *homo* and the Greek *anthropos* (Matt. 5: 13,16). It denotes also man as opposed to woman (Gen. 3: 12; Matt. 19: 10).

(2) Heb. *'ish*, like the Latin *vir* and Greek *aner*, means a man in contrast with a woman (1 Sam. 17: 33; Matt. 14: 21); a husband (Gen. 3: 16; Hos. 2: 16).

(3) Heb. *'enosh*, man as mortal, transient, perishable (2 Chr. 14: 11; Is. 8: 1; Job 15: 14; Ps. 8: 4; 9: 19,20; 103: 15). It is used of women (Josh. 8: 25).

(4) Heb. *geber*, man with reference to his strength, in contrast with women (Deut. 22: 5) and children (Ex. 12: 37); a husband (Prov. 6: 34).

(5) Heb. *methim*, men as mortal (Is. 41: 14).

Man was created by the hand of God, and is generically different from all other creatures (Gen. 1: 26,27; 2: 7). His complex nature is composed of two elements, two distinct substances, body and soul (Gen. 2: 7; Eccl. 12: 7; 2 Cor. 5: 1–8).

The words translated "spirit" and "soul," in 1 Thess. 5: 23, Heb. 4: 12, are used interchangeably (Matt. 10: 28; 16: 26; 1 Pet. 1: 22). The "spirit" (Gr. *pneuma*) is the soul as rational; the "soul" (Gr. *psuche*) is the same, considered as the animating and vital principle of the body.

Glossary of doctrinal words in the Bible (20)

Man and woman, continued

Man was created in the likeness of God in the perfection of his nature, in knowledge (Col. 3: 10), righteousness, and holiness (Eph. 4: 24), and in having dominion over all the inferior creatures (Gen. 1: 28). He had in his original state God's law written on his heart, and had power to obey it, and yet was capable of disobeying, being left to the freedom of his own will. He was created with holy inclinations, prompting him to holy actions; but he was fallible, and did fall (Gen. 3: 1–6).

Martyr

One who bears witness of the truth, and suffers death in the cause of Christ (Acts 22: 20; Rev. 2: 13; 17: 6). In this sense Stephen was the first martyr. The Greek word so translated in all other cases is translated "witness."

(1) In a court of justice (Matt. 18: 16; 26: 65; Acts 6: 13; 7: 58; Heb. 10: 28; 1 Tim. 5: 19).

(2) As bearing testimony to the truth of what is seen or known (Luke 24: 48; Acts 1: 8,22; Rom. 1: 9; 1 Thess. 2: 5,10; 1 John 1: 2).

Mediator

One who intervenes between two people who are in dispute, with the aim to reconcile them. This word is not found in the Old Testament; but the idea it expresses is found in Job 9: 33, in the word "daysman," marg., "umpire."

This word is used in the New Testament to denote an *internuncius*, an ambassador, one who acts as a medium of communication between two contracting parties. In this sense Moses is called a mediator in Gal. 3: 19.

Christ is the one and only mediator between God and humankind (1 Tim. 2: 5; Heb. 8: 6; 9: 15; 12: 24). He makes reconciliation between God and men and women by his all-perfect atoning sacrifice. Such a mediator must be at one and the same time both divine and human; divine, that his obedience and his sufferings might possess infinite worth, and that he might possess infinite wisdom and knowledge and power to direct all things in the kingdoms of providence and grace which are committed to his hands (Matt. 28: 18; John 5: 22, 25, 26, 27); and human, that in his work he might represent men and women, and be capable of obedience to the law and satisfying the claims of justice (Heb. 2: 17,18; 4: 15,16), and that in his glorified humanity he might be the head of a glorified Church (Rom. 8: 29).

This office involves the three functions of prophet, priest, and king, all of which are discharged by Christ both in his estate of humiliation and exaltation. These functions are so inherent in the one office that the quality of each gives character to every mediatorial act. They are never separated in the exercise of the office of mediator.

Mercy

Compassion for the miserable. Its object is misery. By the atoning sacrifice of Christ a way is open for the exercise of mercy toward men and women, in harmony with the demands of truth and righteousness (Gen. 19: 19; Ex. 20: 6; 34: 6,7; Ps. 85: 10; 86: 15, 16). In Christ mercy and truth meet together. Mercy is also a Christian grace (Matt. 5: 7; 18: 33–35).

Minister

One who serves, as distinguished from the master.

(1) Heb. *meshereth*, applied to an attendant on one of superior rank, as to Joshua, the servant of Moses (Ex. 33: 11), and to the servant of Elisha (2 Kings 4: 43). This name is also given to attendants at court (2 Chr. 22: 8), and to the priests and Levites (Jer. 33: 21; Ezek. 44: 11).

(2) Heb. *pelah* (Ezra 7: 24), a "minister" of religion. It is here used of sanctuary servants called "Solomon's servants" in Ezra 2: 55–58 and Neh. 7: 57–60.

(3) Greek *leitourgos*, a subordinate public administrator, and in this sense applied to magistrates (Rom. 13: 6). It is applied also to our Lord (Heb. 8: 2), and to Paul in his relationship to Christ (Rom. 15: 16).

(4) Greek *hyperetes* (literally, "under-rower"), a personal attendant on a superior, thus of the person who waited on the officiating priest in the synagogue (Luke 4: 20). It is applied also to John Mark, the attendant on Paul and Barnabas (Acts 13: 5).

(5) Greek *diaconos*, usually a subordinate officer or assistant employed in the ministry of the gospel, as to Paul and Apollos (1 Cor. 3: 5), Tychicus (Eph. 6: 21), Epaphras (Col. 1: 7), Timothy (1 Thess. 3: 2), and also to Christ (Rom. 15: 8).

Mystery

The calling of the Gentiles into the Christian Church, so designated (Eph. 1: 9,10; 3: 8–11; Col. 1: 25–27); a truth undiscoverable except by revelation, long hidden, now made known.

- The resurrection of the dead (1 Cor. 15: 51), and other doctrines which need to be explained but which cannot be fully understood by finite intelligence (Matt. 13: 11; Rom. 11: 25; 1 Cor. 13: 2);
- the union between Christ and his people symbolized by the marriage union (Eph. 5: 31,32; cf. Eph. 6: 19);
- the seven stars and the seven candlesticks (Rev. 1: 20); and
- the woman clothed in scarlet (Rev. 17: 7), are also in this sense mysteries.

The anti-Christian power working in his day is called by the apostle (2 Thess. 2: 7) the "mystery of iniquity."

Glossary of doctrinal words in the Bible (21)

P

Passion

Only once found, in Acts 1: 3, meaning suffering, referring to the sufferings of our Lord.

Predestination

This word is used only with reference to God's plan or purpose of salvation. The Greek word translated "predestinate" is found only in these six passages, Acts 4: 28; Rom. 8: 29, 30; 1 Cor. 2: 7; Eph. 1: 5,11; and in all of them it has the same meaning.

It teaches that the eternal, sovereign, immutable, and unconditional decree or "determinate purpose" of God governs all events.

This doctrine of predestination or election is beset with many difficulties. It belongs to the "secret things" of God. But if we take the revealed word of God as our guide, we must accept this doctrine with all its mysteriousness, and settle all our questionings in the humble, devout acknowledgment, "Even so, Father: for so it seemed good in thy sight."

For the teaching of Scripture on this subject see: Gen. 21: 12; Ex. 9: 16; 33: 19; Deut. 10: 15; 32: 8; Josh. 11: 20; 1 Sam. 12: 22; 2 Chr. 6: 6; Ps. 33: 12; 65: 4; 78: 68; 135: 4; Is. 41: 1–10; Jer. 1: 5; Mark 13: 20; Luke 22: 22; John 6: 37; 15: 16; 17: 2,6,9; Acts 2: 28; 3: 18; 4: 28; 13: 48; 17: 26; Rom. 9: 11,18,21; 11: 5; Eph. 3: 11; 1 Thess. 1: 4; 2 Thess. 2: 13; 2 Tim. 1: 9; Titus 1: 2; 1 Pet. 1: 2.

Pride

Pride is sometimes viewed in a positive way in the Bible, as in 2 Corinthians 7:4 where delight is taken in someone's achievements: "I have great confidence in you; I take great pride in you. I am greatly encouraged; in all our troubles my joy knows no bounds."

However, the term pride is most often used in a negative way in the Scriptures. It is a rebellious attitude towards God, which, at times, can even be present in God's followers: "But after Uzziah became powerful, his pride led to his downfall. He was unfaithful to the Lord his God, and entered the temple of the Lord to burn incense on the altar of incense" 2 Chronicles 26: 16.

Providence

Literally means foresight, but is generally used to denote God's preserving and governing all things by means of secondary causes (Ps. 18: 35; 63: 8; Acts 17: 28; Col. 1: 17; Heb. 1: 3). God's providence extends to the natural world (Ps. 104: 14; 135: 5–7; Acts 14: 17), the brute creation (Ps. 104: 21–29; Matt. 6: 26; 10: 29), and the affairs of men and women (1 Chr. 16: 31; Ps. 47: 7; Prov. 21: 1; Job 12: 23; Dan. 2: 21; 4: 25), and of individuals (1 Sam. 2: 6; Ps. 18: 30; Luke 1: 53; James 4: 13–15). It extends also to the free actions of men and women (Ex. 12: 36; 1 Sam. 24: 9–15; Ps. 33: 14,15; Prov. 16: 1; 19: 21; 20: 24; 21: 1), and things sinful (2 Sam. 16: 10; 24: 1; Rom. 11: 32;

Acts 4: 27,28), as well as to their good actions (Phil. 2: 13; 4: 13; 2 Cor. 12: 9,10; Eph. 2: 10; Gal. 5: 22–25).

With regard to sinful actions of men and women, they are represented as occurring by God's permission (Gen. 45: 5; 50: 20. Cf. 1 Sam. 6: 6; Ex. 7: 13; 14: 17; Acts 2: 3; 3: 18; 4: 27,28), and as controlled (Ps. 76: 10) and overruled for good (Gen. 50: 20; Acts 3: 13). God does not cause or approve of sin, but only limits, restrains, overrules it for good.

The method of God's providential rule is unexplained. We only know that it is a fact that God does govern all his creatures and all their actions; that this rule is universal (Ps. 103: 17–19), particular (Matt. 10: 29–31), effective (Ps. 33: 11; Job 23: 13), embraces events apparently contingent (Prov. 16: 9,33; 19: 21; 21: 1), is consistent with his own perfection (2 Tim. 2: 13), and to his own glory (Rom. 9: 17; 11: 36).

R

Rabbi

My master, a title of dignity given by the Jews to their doctors of the law and their distinguished teachers. It is sometimes applied to Christ (Matt. 23: 7,8; Mark 9: 5 (RV); John 1: 38,49; 3: 2; 6: 25, etc.); also to John (John 3: 26).

Rabboni

Occurs only twice in the New Testament (Mark 10: 51, AV, "Lord," RV, "Rabboni"; John 20: 16). It was the most honorable of all the titles.

Raca

Vain, empty, worthless, only found in Matt. 5: 22. The Jews used it as a word of contempt. It is derived from a root meaning "to spit."

Ransom

The price or payment made for our redemption, as when it is said that the Son of man "gave his life a ransom for many" (Matt. 20: 28; cf. Acts 20: 28; Rom. 3: 23,24; 1 Cor. 6: 19,20; Gal. 3: 13; 4: 4,5; Eph. 1: 7; Col. 1: 14; 1 Tim. 2: 6; Titus 2: 14; 1 Pet. 1: 18,19. In all these passages the same idea is expressed). This word is derived from the Fr. *rancon*; Lat. *redemptio*. The debt is represented not as canceled but as fully paid.

The slave or captive is not liberated by a mere gratuitous favor, but a ransom price has been paid, in consideration of which he is set free. The original owner receives back his alienated and lost possession because he has bought it back "with a price." This price or ransom (Gr. *lutron*) is always said to be Christ, his blood, his death. He secures our redemption by the payment of a ransom.

Glossary of doctrinal words in the Bible (22)

R continued

Reconciliation

A change from enmity to friendship. It is mutual, i.e., it is a change in both parties who have enemies.

(1) In Col. 1: 21,22, the word there used refers to a change brought about in the personal character of the sinner who ceases to be an enemy to God by wicked deeds, and gives him his full confidence and love. In 2 Cor. 5: 20 the apostle pleads with the Corinthians to be "reconciled to God," i.e., to lay aside their enmity.

(2) Rom. 5: 10 refers not to any change in our disposition toward God, but to God himself, as the party reconciled. Romans 5: 11 teaches the same truth. From God we have received "the reconciliation" (RV), i.e., he has conferred on us the token of his friendship. So also 2 Cor. 5: 18,19 speaks of a reconciliation originating with God, and consisting in the removal of his merited wrath. In Eph. 2: 16 it is clear that the apostle does not refer to the winning back of the sinner in love and loyalty to God, but to the restoration of God's forfeited favor. This is effected by his justice being satisfied, so that he can, in consistency with his own nature, be favorable toward sinners. Justice demands the punishment of sinners. The death of Christ satisfies justice, and so reconciles God to us. This reconciliation makes God our friend, and enables him to pardon and save us.

Redeemer

Heb. *goel*; i.e., one charged with the duty of restoring the rights of another and avenging his wrongs (Lev. 25: 48,49; Num. 5: 8; Ruth 4: 1; Job 19: 25; Ps. 19: 14; 78: 35, etc.). This title is peculiarly applied to Christ. He redeems us from all evil by the payment of a ransom.

Redemption

The purchase back of something that had been lost, by the payment of a ransom. The Greek word is *apolutrosis*, a word occurring nine times in Scripture, and always with the idea of a ransom or price paid, i.e., redemption by a *lutron* (see Matt. 20: 28; Mark 10: 45). There are instances in the LXX version of the Old Testament of the use of *lutron* in man's relation to man (Lev. 19: 20; 25: 51; Ex. 21: 30; Num. 35: 31,32; Is. 45: 13; Prov. 6: 35), and in the same sense of man's relation to God (Num. 3: 49; 18: 15).

There are many passages in the New Testament which present Christ's sufferings using the idea of a ransom or price, resulting in a purchase or redemption (Compare Acts 20: 28; 1 Cor. 6: 19,20; Gal. 3: 13; 4: 4,5; Eph. 1: 7; Col. 1: 14; 1 Tim. 2: 5,6; Titus 2: 14; Heb. 9: 12; 1 Pet. 1: 18,19; Rev. 5: 9). The idea running through all these texts is that of payment made for our redemption. The debt against us is not viewed as simply canceled, but is fully paid. Christ's blood or life, which he translated for them, is the "ransom" by which the deliverance of his people from the servitude of sin and from its penal consequences is secured. Scripture teaches that "Christ saves us neither by the mere exercise of power, nor by his doctrine, nor by his example, nor by the moral influence which he exerted, nor by any subjective influence on his people, whether natural or mystical, but as a satisfaction to divine justice, as an expiation for sin, and as a ransom from the curse and authority of the law, thus reconciling us to God by making it consistent with his perfection to exercise mercy toward sinners" (Hodge).

Repentance

There are three Greek words used in the New Testament to denote repentance.

(1) The verb *metamelomai* is used of a change of mind, such as to produce regret or even remorse on account of sin, but not necessarily a change of heart. This word is used of the repentance of Judas (Matt. 27: 3).

(2) *Metanoeo*, meaning to change one's mind and purpose, in the light of knowledge.

(3) This verb, with the cognate noun *metanoia*, is used of true repentance, a change of mind and purpose and life, to which remission of sin is promised. Evangelical repentance consists of

• a true sense of one's own guilt and sinfulness;
• an apprehension of God's mercy in Christ;
• an actual hatred of sin (Ps. 119: 128; Job 42: 5, 6; 2 Cor. 7: 10) and turning

from it to God; and
• a persistent endeavor after a holy life in a walking with God in the way of his commandments.

The true penitent is conscious of guilt (Ps. 51: 4,9), of pollution (Ps. 51: 5,7,10), and of helplessness (Ps. 51: 11; 109: 21,22). Thus he understands himself to be just what God has always seen him to be and declares him to be. But repentance acknowledges not only such a sense of sin, but also an appreciation of mercy, without which there can be no true repentance (Ps. 51: 1; 130: 4).

Reprobate

That which is rejected on account of its own worthlessness (Jer. 6: 30; Heb. 6: 8; Gr. *adokimos*, "rejected"). This word is also used of people who have failed to make use of opportunities offered them (1 Cor. 9: 27; 2 Cor. 13: 5–7).

Rest

(1) Gr. *katapausis*, equivalent to the Hebrew word noah (Heb. 4: 1).

(2) Gr. *anapausis*, "rest from weariness" (Matt. 11: 28).

(3) Gr. *anesis*, "relaxation" (2 Thess. 1: 7).

(4) Gr. *sabbatismos*, a Sabbath rest, a rest from all work (Heb. 4: 9; RV, "sabbath"), a rest like that of God when he had finished the work of creation.

Glossary of doctrinal words in the Bible (23)

R continued

Righteousness

See JUSTIFICATION.

S

Sabachthani

Thou hast forsaken me, one of the Aramaic words uttered by our Lord on the cross (Matt. 27: 46; Mark 15: 34).

Sabaoth

The transliteration of the Hebrew word *sebha'oth*, meaning "hosts," "armies" (Rom. 9: 29; James 5: 4). In the LXX the Hebrew word is translated by "Almighty." (See Rev. 4: 8; cf. Is. 6: 3.) It may designate Jehovah as either

(1) God of the armies of earth, or

(2) God of the armies of the stars, or

(3) God of the unseen armies of angels; or perhaps it may include all these ideas.

Sabbath

(Heb. verb *shabbath*, meaning "to rest from labor"), the day of rest. It is first mentioned as having been instituted in Paradise, when man was in innocence (Gen. 2: 2). "The sabbath was made for man," as a day of rest and refreshment for the body and of blessing to the soul.

It is next referred to in connection with the gift of manna to the children of Israel in the wilderness (Ex. 16: 23); and later, when the law was given from Sinai (Ex. 20: 11), the people were solemnly charged to "remember the sabbath day, to keep it holy." Thus it is spoken of as an institution already existing.

In the Mosaic law strict regulations were laid down regarding its observance (Ex. 35: 2, 3; Lev. 23: 3; 26: 34). These were peculiar to that dispensation.

In the subsequent history of the Jews frequent references are made to the sanctity of the Sabbath (Is. 56: 2,4,6,7; 58: 13,14; Jer. 17: 20–22; Neh. 13: 19). In later times they perverted the Sabbath by their traditions. Our Lord rescued it from their perversions, and recalled to them its true nature and intent (Matt. 12: 10–13; Mark 2: 27; Luke 13: 10–17).

The Sabbath, originally instituted for man at his creation, is of permanent and universal obligation. The physical necessities of humanity require a Sabbath of rest. Humanity is so constituted that his bodily welfare needs at least one day in seven for rest from ordinary labor. Experience also proves that the moral and spiritual necessities of men also demand a Sabbath of rest.

"I am more and more sure by experience that the reason for the observance of the Sabbath lies deep in the everlasting necessities of human nature, and that as long as man is man the blessedness of keeping it, not as a day of rest only, but as a day of spiritual rest, will never be annulled. I certainly do feel by experience the eternal obligation, because of the eternal necessity, of the Sabbath. The soul withers without it. It thrives in proportion to its observance."

"The Sabbath was made for man. God made it for men in a certain spiritual state because they needed it. The need, therefore, is deeply hidden in human nature. He who can dispense with it must be holy and spiritual indeed. And he who, still unholy and unspiritual, would yet dispense with it is a man that would fain be wiser than his Maker" (F. W. Robertson).

THE CHANGE OF THE DAY

Originally at creation the seventh day of the week was set apart and consecrated as the Sabbath. The first day of the week is now observed as the Sabbath. Has God authorized this change? There is an obvious distinction between the Sabbath as an institution and the particular day set apart for its observance. The question, therefore, as to the change of the day in no way affects the perpetual obligation of the Sabbath as an institution. Change of the day or no change, the Sabbath remains as a sacred institution the same. It cannot be abrogated.

If any change of the day has been made, it must have been by Christ or by his authority. Christ has a right to make such a change (Mark 2: 23–28). As Creator, Christ was the original Lord of the Sabbath (John 1: 3; Heb. 1: 10). It was originally a memorial of creation. A work vastly greater than that of creation has now been accomplished by him, the work of redemption. We would naturally expect just such a change as would make the Sabbath a memorial of that greater work.

True, we can give no text authorizing the change in so many words. We have no express law declaring the change. But we know for a fact that the first day of the week has been observed from apostolic times, and the necessary conclusion is, that it was observed by the apostles and their immediate disciples. This, we may be sure, they never would have done without the permission or the authority of their Lord.

After his resurrection, which took place on the first day of the week (Matt. 28: 1; Mark 16: 2; Luke 24: 1; John 20: 1), we never find Christ meeting with his disciples on the seventh day. But he specially honored the first day by showing himself to them on four separate occasions (Matt. 28: 9; Luke 24: 18–33,34; John 20: 19–23). Again, on the next first day of the week, Jesus appeared to his disciples (John 20: 26).

The observance of this "Lord's day" as the Sabbath was the general custom of the primitive churches.

Glossary of doctrinal words in the Bible (24)

Sabbath, continued

So it must have had apostolic sanction (compare Acts 20: 3–7; 1 Cor. 16: 1,2) and authority, and so the sanction and authority of Jesus Christ.

The words "at her sabbaths" (Lam. 1: 7, AV) ought probably to be, as in the Revised Version, "at her desolations."

Sabbath Day's Journey

Supposed to be a distance of 2,000 cubits, or less than half-a-mile, the distance which, according to Jewish tradition, one was allowed to travel on the Sabbath day without violating the law (Acts 1: 12; cf. Ex. 16: 29; Num. 35: 5; Josh. 3: 4).

Saint

One separated from the world and consecrated to God; one holy by profession and by covenant; a believer in Christ (Ps. 16: 3; Rom. 1: 7; 8: 27; Phil. 1: 1; Heb. 6: 10).

The "saints" spoken of in Jude 14 are probably not the disciples of Christ, but the "innumerable company of angels" (Heb. 12: 22; Ps. 68: 17), with reference to Deut. 33: 2.

This word is also used of the holy dead (Matt. 27: 52; Rev. 18: 24). It was not used as a distinctive title of the apostles and evangelists and of a "spiritual nobility" till the fourth century. In that sense it is not a scriptural title.

Salvation

This word is used of the deliverance of the Israelites from the Egyptians (Ex. 14: 13), and of deliverance generally from evil or danger. In the New Testament it is specially used with reference to the great deliverance from the guilt and the pollution of sin wrought out by Jesus Christ, "the great salvation" (Heb. 2: 3).

Sanctification

Involves more than a mere moral reformation of character, brought about by the power of the truth: it is the work of the Holy Spirit bringing the whole nature more and more under the influences of the new gracious principles implanted in the soul in regeneration.

In other words, sanctification is the carrying on to perfection the work begun in regeneration, and it extends to the whole person (Rom. 6: 13; 2 Cor. 4: 6; Col. 3: 10; 1 John 4: 7; 1 Cor. 6: 19). It is the special work of the Holy Spirit in the plan of redemption (1 Cor. 6: 11; 2 Thess. 2: 13).

Faith is instrumental in securing sanctification, inasmuch as it:

(1) secures union to Christ (Gal. 2: 20), and

(2) brings the believer into living contact with the truth, whereby he is led to yield obedience "to the commands, trembling at the threatenings, and embracing the promises of God for this life and that which is to come."

Perfect sanctification is not attainable in this life (1 Kings 8: 46; Prov. 20: 9; Eccl. 7: 20; James 3: 2; 1 John 1: 8). See Paul's account of himself in Rom. 7: 14–25; Phil. 3: 12–14; and 1 Tim. 1: 15; also the confessions of David (Ps. 19: 12,13; 51), of Moses (Ps. 90: 8), of Job (Job 42: 5,6), and of Daniel (Dan. 9: 3–20).

"The more holy a man is, the more humble, self-renouncing, self-abhorring, and the more sensitive to every sin he becomes, and the more closely he clings to Christ. The moral imperfections which cling to him he feels to be sins, which he laments and strives to overcome. Believers find that their life is a constant warfare, and they need to take the kingdom of heaven by storm, and watch while they pray. They are always subject to the constant chastisement of their Father's loving hand, which can only be designed to correct their imperfections and to confirm their graces. And it has been notoriously the fact that the best Christians have been those who have been the least prone to claim the attainment of perfection for themselves." Hodge

Satan

Adversary; accuser. When used as a proper name, the Hebrew word so translated has the article "the adversary" (Job 1: 6–12; 2: 1–7). In the New Testament it is used as interchangeable with Diabolos, or the devil, and is so used more than thirty times.

He is also called

- "the dragon"
- "the old serpent" (Rev. 12: 9; 20: 2)
- "the prince of this world" (John 12: 31; 14: 30)
- "the prince of the power of the air" (Eph. 2: 2)
- "the god of this world" (2 Cor. 4: 4)
- "the spirit that now worketh in the children of disobedience" (Eph. 2: 2).

The distinct personality of Satan and his activity among men and women are easy to see.

He tempted our Lord in the wilderness (Matt. 4: 1–11).

He is "Beelzebub, the prince of the devils" (Matt. 12: 24).

He is "the constant enemy of God, of Christ, of the divine kingdom, of the followers of Christ, and of all truth; full of falsehood and all malice, and exciting and seducing to evil in every possible way."

His power is very great in the world.

He is a "roaring lion, seeking whom he may devour" (1 Pet. 5: 8).

Men and women are said to be "taken captive by him" (2 Tim. 2: 26).

Christians are warned against his "devices" (2 Cor. 2: 11), and called on to "resist" him (James 4: 7).

Christ redeems his people from "him that had the power of death, that is, the devil" (Heb. 2: 14). Satan has the "power of death," not as lord, but simply as executioner.

Glossary of doctrinal words in the Bible (25)

S continued

Scripture

Invariably in the New Testament denotes that definite collection of sacred books, regarded as given by inspiration of God, which we usually call the Old Testament (2 Tim. 3: 15,16; John 20: 9; Gal. 3: 22; 2 Pet. 1: 20). It was God's purpose to give this permanent record of his revealed will. From time to time he raised up men to commit to writing in an infallible record the revelation he gave. The "Scripture," or collection of sacred writings, was thus enlarged from time to time as God saw necessary. We have now a completed "Scripture," consisting of the Old and New Testaments.

The Old Testament canon in the time of our Lord was precisely the same as that which we now possess under that name. He placed the seal of his own authority on this collection of writings, as all equally given by inspiration (Matt. 5: 17; 7: 12; 22: 40; Luke 16: 29,31).

Seek

In the Bible the word "seek", meaning "to choose to follow" refers to giving the top priority to God and to seeking the good of other people.

Jesus told his followers: "But seek first his kingdom and his righteousness, and all these things will be given to you as well" Matthew 6:33, NIV.

Paul told Christians: "Nobody should seek his own good, but the good of others" 1 Corinthians 10: 24, NIV.

Jesus' mission can be summed up by saying that he gave top priority to seeking out the lost: "For the Son of Man came to seek and to save what was lost." Luke 19: 10, NIV.

The letter to the Hebrews teaches that, "without faith it is impossible to please God, because anyone who comes to him must believe that he exists and that he rewards those who earnestly seek him." Hebrews 11: 6, NIV.

Selah

This strange word occurs at the beginning of a number of psalms and Bible scholars are still uncertain about its precise meaning.

It is probably some kind of liturgical direction or musical notation. It comes in 71 psalms and three times in the book of Habakkuk.

"To the LORD I cry aloud, and he answers me from his holy hill. Selah" Psalm 3:4, NIV.

The word "selah" many have been a direction for the worshippers to meditate quietly, or to sing loudly.

Shaddai

The Omnipotent, the name of God in frequent use in the Hebrew Scriptures, generally translated "the Almighty."

Sheol

(Heb., "the all-demanding world" = Gr. *Hades*, "the unknown region"), the invisible world of departed souls.

Shekinah

This is a Hebrew word meaning, "that which dwells." It refers to God's presence appearing in a visible or special way.

An example of God's Shekinah is seen in the pillar of cloud that went ahead of the Israelites: "Then the angel of God, who had been traveling in front of Israel's army, withdrew and went behind them. The pillar of cloud also moved from in front and stood behind them, coming between the armies of Egypt and Israel. Throughout the night the cloud brought darkness to the one side and light to the other side; so neither went near the other all night long." Exodus 14: 19,20, NIV

The cloud that filled Solomon's temple was God's shekinah presence, 2 Chronicles 7: 1.

Sin

Is "any want of conformity unto or transgression of the law of God" (1 John 3: 4; Rom. 4: 15), in the inward state and habit of the soul, as well as in the outward conduct of the life, whether by omission or commission (Rom. 6: 12–17; 7: 5–24). It is "not a mere violation of the law of our constitution, nor of the system of things, but an offense against a personal lawgiver and moral governor who vindicates his law with penalties.

The soul that sins is always conscious that his sin is

(1) intrinsically vile and polluting, and
(2) that it justly deserves punishment, and calls down the righteous wrath of God.

Hence sin carries with it two inalienable characters,

(1) ill-desert, guilt (*reatus*); and
(2) pollution (*macula*)." Hodge

The moral character of a man's actions is determined by the moral state of his heart. The disposition to sin, or the habit of the soul that leads to the sinful act, is itself also sin (Rom. 6: 12–17; Gal. 5: 17; James 1: 14,15).

The origin of sin is a mystery, and will always remain a mystery to us. It is plain that for some reason God has permitted sin to enter this world, and that is all we know. His permitting it, however, in no way makes God the author of sin.

Adam's sin (Gen. 3: 1–6) consisted in his yielding to the assaults of temptation and eating the forbidden fruit. It involved in it,

• the sin of unbelief, virtually making God a liar; and
• the guilt of disobedience to a positive command.

By this sin he became an apostate from God, a rebel against his Creator. He lost the favor of God and communion with him; his whole nature became depraved, and he incurred the penalty involved in the covenant of works.

Glossary of doctrinal words in the Bible (26)

Sin, continued
ORIGINAL SIN, CONTINUED
- From its early manifestation
(Ps. 58: 3; Prov. 22: 15).

  It is proved also from the necessity, absolutely and universally, of regeneration (John 3: 3; 2 Cor. 5: 17).
- From the universality of death
(Rom. 5: 12–20).

Various kinds of sin are mentioned:
- "Presumptuous sins," or as literally translated, "sins with an uplifted hand," i.e., defiant acts of sin, in contrast with "errors" or "inadvertencies" (Ps. 19: 13).
- "Secret," i.e., hidden sins (Ps. 19: 12); sins which escape the notice of the soul.
- "Sin against the Holy Spirit," or a "sin unto death" (Matt. 12: 31,32; 1 John 5: 16), which amounts to a willful rejection of grace.

Son of God

The plural, "sons of God," is used (Gen. 6: 2,4) to denote the pious descendants of Seth. In Job 1: 6; 38: 7 this name is applied to the angels. Hosea uses the phrase (Hos. 1: 10) to designate the gracious relation in which men stand to God.

In the New Testament this phrase is often used of God's adoption of us (Rom. 8: 14,19; 2 Cor. 6: 18; Gal. 4: 5,6; Phil. 2: 15; 1 John 3: 1,2).

It occurs thirty-seven times in the New Testament as the distinctive title of our Savior. He does not bear this title because of his miraculous birth, or because of his incarnation, his resurrection, and exaltation to the Father's right hand. This is a title of nature and not of office. The sonship of Christ denotes his equality with the Father. To call Christ the Son of God is to assert his true and proper divinity. The second Person of the Trinity, because of his eternal relation to the first Person, is the Son of God. He is the Son of God as to his divine nature, while as to his human nature he is the Son of David (Rom. 1: 3,4. Cf. Gal. 4: 4; John 1: 1–14; 5: 18–25; 10: 30–38, which prove that Christ was the Son of God before his incarnation, and that his claim to this title is a claim of equality with God.)

When used with reference to creatures, whether men or angels, this word is always in the plural. In the singular it is always used of the second Person of the Trinity, with the single exception of Luke 3: 38, where it is used of Adam.

Son of man

(1) Denotes humankind generally, with special reference to their weakness and frailty (Job 25: 6; Ps. 8: 4; 144: 3; 146: 3; Is. 51: 12, etc.).

(2) It is a title frequently given to the prophet Ezekiel, probably to remind him of his human weakness.

(3) In the New Testament it is used forty-three times as a distinctive title of the Savior. In the Old Testament it is used only in Ps. 80: 17 and Dan. 7: 13 with this application. It denotes the

true humanity of our Lord. He had a true body (Heb. 2: 14; Luke 24: 39) and a rational soul. He was perfect man.

Sovereignty

Of God, his absolute right to do all things according to his own good pleasure (Dan. 4: 25,35; Rom. 9: 15–23; 1 Tim. 6: 15; Rev. 4: 11).

Spirit

(Heb. *ruah*; Gr. *pneuma*), refers to wind or breath. In 2 Thess. 2: 8 it means "breath," and in Eccl. 8: 8 the vital principle in man. It also denotes the rational, immortal soul by which man is distinguished (Acts 7: 59; 1 Cor. 5: 5; 6: 20; 7: 34), and the soul in its separate state (Heb. 12: 23), and hence also an apparition (Job 4: 15; Luke 24: 37,39), an angel (Heb. 1: 14), and a demon (Luke 4: 36; 10: 20). This word is used also metaphorically as denoting a tendency (Zech. 12: 10; Luke 13: 11).

In Rom. 1: 4, 1 Tim. 3: 16, 2 Cor. 3: 17, 1 Pet. 3: 18, it designates the divine nature.

T

Tradition

Any kind of teaching, written or spoken, handed down from generation to generation. In Mark 7: 3,9,13, Col. 2: 8, this word refers to the arbitrary interpretations of the Jews. In 2 Thess. 2: 15; 3: 6, it is used in a good sense. Peter (1 Pet. 1: 18) uses this word

of degenerate Judaism (cf. Acts 15: 10; Matt. 15: 2–6; Gal. 1: 14).

Truth

Used in various senses in Scripture. In Prov. 12: 17,19, it denotes opposition to falsehood. In Is. 59: 14,15; Jer. 7: 28, it means fidelity or truthfulness. The teaching of Christ is called "the truth of the gospel" (Gal. 2: 5), "the truth" (2 Tim. 3: 7; 4: 4).

W

Word of God

(Heb. 4: 12, etc.). The Bible so called because its writers were used by God to communicate. It is his "word," because he speaks to us in its sacred pages. Whatever the inspired writers here declare to be true and binding upon us, God declares to be true and binding. This word is infallible, because written under the guidance of the Holy Spirit, and therefore free from all error of fact or doctrine or precept. All saving knowledge is obtained from the word of God. It is an indispensable means of salvation, and is effective because of the work of the Holy Spirit (John 17: 17; 2 Tim. 3: 15,16; 1 Pet. 1: 23).

The attributes of God the Father (1)

Overview

Some of the most important characteristics of God found in the Bible are listed below.

- God and his goodness
- God and his grace
- God and his holiness
- God and his immanence
- God and his immutability
- God and his eternal nature
- God and his love
- God and his mercy
- God and his omnipotence
- God and his justice
- God and his omnipresence
- God and his omniscience
- God and his self-existence
- God and his sovereignty
- God and his transcendence

God and his goodness

Psalm 25: 8 – Good and upright is the Lord.

James 1: 17 – Every good gift and every perfect gift is from above, and comes down from the Father of lights with whom there is no variation or shadow of turning.

God is the source of goodness. In the lives of Christians God works for good.

Romans 8: 28 states that "God causes all things to work together for good to those who love God, to those who are called according to His purpose."

God and his grace

Psalm 145: 17 – The Lord is righteous in all His ways, gracious in all His works.

Romans 1: 5 – Through Him we have received grace and apostleship for obedience to the faith among all nations for His name.

Romans 3: 24 – [We] being justified freely by His grace through the redemption that is in Christ Jesus.

Romans 5: 15,20 – But the free gift is not like the offense. For if by the one man's offense many died, much more the grace of God and the gift by the grace of the one Man Jesus Christ, abounded to many. Moreover the law entered that the offense might abound. But where sin abounded, grace abounded much more.

Ephesians 4: 7 – But to each one of us grace was given according to the measure of Christ's gift.

Hebrews 4: 16 – Let us therefore come boldly to the throne of grace, that we may obtain mercy and find grace to help in time of need.

APPRECIATING ONE FACET OF GOD'S NATURE
Grace is the bestowal of blessing unearned or unmerited. When we speak of God's grace, we speak of those wonderful gifts (e.g., salvation) that no one deserves but God grants anyway. There are several ways in which God demonstrates His grace to us.

God and his holiness

1 Samuel 2: 2 – "No one is holy like the Lord."

Psalm 99: 2–3 – The Lord is great in Zion, and He is high above all the peoples. Let them praise Your great and awesome name – He is holy.

Revelation 4: 8 – "Holy, holy, holy, Lord God Almighty, who was and is and is to come!"

APPRECIATING ONE FACET OF GOD'S NATURE

Holiness is synonymous with God's total purity and separation from the rest of creation. God's holiness sets him apart from sinful humans. God's holiness is closely linked to Jesus' first coming. It is only as a result of our salvation that we, as forgiven people, are able to approach God in his perfect holiness.

God and his immanence

Jeremiah 23: 23–24 – "Am I a God near at hand?" says the Lord, "And not a God afar off? Can anyone hide himself in secret places, so I shall not see him?" says the Lord; "Do I not fill heaven and earth?" says the Lord.

Acts 17: 27–28 – He is not far from each one of us; for in Him we live and move and have our being.

Haggai 2: 5 – "According to the word that I covenanted with you when you came out of Egypt, so My Spirit remains among you; do not fear!"

APPRECIATING ONE FACET OF GOD'S NATURE

Immanence describes a God who is close at hand. God is at work through the countless details of his creation. The Christian God is no absentee landlord. He is present and actively participates in his world. For this reason Christians know that there is no place or situation that is not under God's protecting hand.

God and his immutability

Malachi 3: 6 – "For I am the Lord, I do not change."

James 1: 17 – Every good gift and every perfect gift is from above, and comes down from the Father of lights with whom there is no variation or shadow of turning.

APPRECIATING ONE FACET OF GOD'S NATURE

God's immutability is a great source of comfort for the believer. God's immutability means that God does not change his mind, his characteristics, his plan, or anything else about himself. God's character never changes and nor do his covenants, his prophecies, or his promises. God is therefore utterly dependable.

God and his eternal nature

Exodus 3: 14 – And God said to Moses, "I AM WHO I AM."

Psalm 102: 12 – But You, O Lord, shall endure forever, and the remembrance of Your name to all generations.

God and his love

Deuteronomy 7: 7–8 – "The Lord did not set His love on you nor choose you because you were more in number than any other people, for you were the least of all peoples; but because the Lord loves you, and because He would keep the oath which He swore to your fathers, the Lord has brought you out with a might hand, and redeemed you from the house of bondage, from the hand of Pharaoh king of Egypt."

The attributes of God the Father (2)

God and his love, continued

John 14: 31 – "But that the world may know that I love the Father, and as the Father gave Me commandment, so I do."

Romans 5: 5,8 – Now hope does not disappoint, because the love of God has been poured out in our hearts by the Holy Spirit who was given to us.

Romans 8: 35,39 – Who shall separate us from the love of God? Shall tribulation, or distress, or persecution, or famine, or nakedness, or peril, or sword? [Neither] height nor depth, nor any other created thing, shall be able to separate us from the love of God which is in Christ Jesus our Lord.

1 John 4: 8,16 – He who does not love does not know God, for God is love. And we have known and believed the love that God has for us. God abides in him, and who abides in love abides in God, and God in him.

APPRECIATING ONE FACET OF GOD'S NATURE
We all have a basic understanding of what love is, but we are unable to comprehend the depths of true love. This is the love that God embodies. God is the source of love and it is through him that we experience love. God loves us. In spite of who we are God still loves us.

God and his mercy

Psalm 6: 4 – Return, O Lord, deliver! Oh, save me for Your mercies' sake!

Hebrews 4: 16 – Let us therefore come boldly to the throne of grace, that we may obtain mercy and find grace to help in time of need.

Romans 9: 23,24 – And that he might make known the riches of His glory on the vessels of mercy, which He had prepared beforehand for glory, even us whom He called, not of the Hews only, but also of the Gentiles?

Ephesians 2: 4 – God, who is rich in mercy.

Titus 3: 5 – Not by works of righteousness which we have done, but according to His mercy He saved us, through the washing of regeneration and renewing of the Holy Spirit.

1 Peter 1: 3 – Blessed be the God and Father of our Lord Jesus Christ, who according to His abundant mercy has begotten us again to a loving hope through the resurrection of Jesus Christ from the dead.

APPRECIATING ONE FACET OF GOD'S NATURE
Mercy is when what is deserved is withheld so that this benefits the person in question. We deserved to receive punishment for our sins, but because of God's mercy, we have received forgiveness instead.

God and his omnipotence

Romans 11: 36 – For of Him and through Him and to Him are all things, to whom be glory forever. Amen.

Ephesians 1: 11 – In Him also we have obtained an inheritance, being predestined according to the purpose of Him who works all things according to the counsel of His will.

Hebrews 1: 3 – [God's Son upholds] all things by the word of His power.

Mark 14: 36 – And He said, "Abba, Father, all things are possible for You. Take this cup away from me; nevertheless, not what I will, but what You will."

Jeremiah 32: 17 – "Ah, Lord GOD! Behold, You have made the heavens and the earth by Your great power and outstretched arm. There is nothing too hard for you."

Matthew 19: 26 – "With God all things are possible."

Psalm 115: 3 – "But our God is in heaven; He does what He pleases."

APPRECIATING ONE FACET OF GOD'S NATURE

God has the unlimited power to accomplish anything that can be accomplished – this is known as omnipotence. The things God does are neither difficult nor easy for God; they are only either done or not done. God has the power to accomplish everything he desires to do.

God and his justice

Genesis 18: 25 – Far be it from You to do such a thing as this, to slay the righteous with the wicked, so that the righteous should be as the wicked; far be it from You! Shall not the Judge of all the earth do right?

Nehemiah 9: 32–33 – However You are just in all that has befallen us.

Romans 9: 14–33 – What shall we say then? Is there unrighteousness with God?

Psalm 99: 4 – The King's strength also loves justice; You have established equity; You have executed justice and righteousness in Jacob.

Romans 1: 32 – Who, knowing the righteous judgment of God, that those who practice such things are deserving of death, not only do the same but also approve of those who practice them.

1 Peter 1: 17 – The Father... without partiality judges according to each one's work, conduct yourselves throughout the time of your stay here in fear.

APPRECIATING ONE FACET OF GOD'S NATURE

Since God is the God of justice, God is the ultimate judge over the lives and actions of men. There seems to be so much injustice in the world. People lie, cheat, steal, and kill all the time and, so often it seems they do this with total impunity. That is how it is on this earth. But on the day of judgment everyone will receive his just deserts at the hands of an immutable God. Unlike a corrupt human judge, God's justice will be fair and perfect in every respect. God is not open to persuasion or bribes. In God's justice, we can find a comfort for all the wrongs perpetrated against us and against mankind. It is only because of the Christian's faith in Jesus that we need not fear God's justice as we know that we are eternally safe.

God and his omnipresence

Job 11: 7–9 – Can you search out the deep things of God? Can you find out the limits of the Almighty? They are higher than heaven – what can you do?

The attributes of God the Father (3)

God and his omnipresence, continued

Deeper than Sheol – what can you know? Their measure is longer than the earth and broader than the sea.

Jeremiah 23: 23–24 – "Am I a God near at hand?" says the Lord, "And not a God afar off? Can anyone hide himself in secret places, so I shall not see him?" says the Lord; "Do I not fill heaven and earth?" says the Lord.

Psalm 139: 7–10 – "Where can I go from Your Spirit? Or where can I flee from your Spirit? If I ascend into heaven, You are there; If I make my bed in hell, behold, you are there. If I take the wings of the morning, and dwell in the utter most parts of the sea, even there your hand shall lead me, and Your right hand shall hold me."

Psalm 90: 1–2 – Lord, You have been our dwelling place in all generations. Before the mountains were brought forth, or ever You had formed the earth and the world, even from everlasting to everlasting, You are God.

APPRECIATING ONE FACET OF GOD'S NATURE
Because of God's omnipresence he is present everywhere. There is nowhere we can go to and not be in his presence.

God and his omniscience

Psalm 147: 5 – [God's] understanding is infinite.

Ezekiel 11: 5 – Then the Spirit of the Lord fell upon me, and said to me, "Speak! Thus says the Lord: "Thus you

have said, O house of Israel; for I know the things that come into your mind"'."

1 John 3: 20 – For if our heart condemns us, God is greater than our heart, and knows all things.

Hebrews 4: 13 – And there is no creature hidden from His sight, but all things are naked and open to the eyes of Him to whom we must give account.

Romans 2: 16 – God will judge the secret things of men by Jesus Christ, according to [Paul's] gospel.

APPRECIATING ONE FACET OF GOD'S NATURE
When we say God is omniscient, we mean that he knows all that there is to know. There is nothing that is outside the scope of his conception, or understanding.

God and his self-existence

Exodus 3: 14 – And God said to Moses, "I AM WHO I AM."

Psalm 90: 2 – Before the mountains were brought forth, or ever You had formed the earth and the world, even from everlasting to everlasting, You are God.

John 5: 26 – "For as the Father has life in Himself, so He has granted the Son to have life in Himself."

Colossians 1: 15–17 – He is the image of the invisible God, the firstborn over all creation. For by Him all things were created that are in heaven and that are on earth, visible and invisible, whether thrones or dominions or principalities or powers. All things were created through Him and for Him. And He is before all things, and in Him all things consist.

APPRECIATING ONE FACET OF GOD'S NATURE

By God's self-existence we mean God's unique attribute through which he has existed eternally and will always exist. Unlike all other things that relate to our existence, God does not owe his being to any other thing. I owe my existence to my mother and father and all my ancestors. All events have causes. All creatures have been created. Except for God. God is the uncaused cause and the uncreated Creator.

God and his sovereignty

Genesis 14: 19 – "Blessed be Abram of God Most High, possessor of heaven and earth; and blessed be God Most High, who has delivered your enemies into your hand."

Exodus 18: 11 – Now I know that the Lord is greater than all the gods.

Psalm 115: 3 – But our God is in heaven; he does whatever he pleases.

Matthew 10: 29 – "Are not two sparrows sold for a copper coin? And not one of them falls to the ground apart from your Father's will."

Romans 9: 15 – For He says to Moses, "I will have mercy on whomever I will have mercy, and I will have compassion on whomever I will have compassion."

APPRECIATING ONE FACET OF GOD'S NATURE

Sovereignty speaks of God's divine control over everything that happens. There is nothing outside the control of his loving hand. Romans 8: 28 tells us that all things work together for the good of God's children and verses 38–39 implies that there is nothing beyond the control of God's sovereign hand. God's sovereignty reminds Christians to fear nothing as God is always in charge, no matter how dreadful the situation.

God and his transcendence

Isaiah 55: 8–9 – "For my thoughts are not your thoughts, nor are your ways My ways," says the Lord. "For as the heavens are higher than the earth, so are My ways higher than your ways, and My thoughts than your thoughts."

Isaiah 57: 15 – For thus says the High and Lofty One who inhabits eternity, whose name is Holy: "I dwell in the high and holy place, with him who has a contrite and humble spirit, to revive the spirit of the humble, and to revive the heart of the contrite ones."

Psalm 113: 5,6 – Who is like the Lord our God, who dwells on high, who humbles Himself to behold the things that are in the heavens and in the earth?

APPRECIATING ONE FACET OF GOD'S NATURE

Transcendence refers to the fact that God is unlike any other being in our experience and so no analogy or comparison can come close to perfectly describing him. His ways are so other than our ways that we cannot predict Him, categorize Him, or comprehend Him with any sort of accuracy.

Titles, descriptions and names of Christ (1)

Introduction

In the Bible a person's title or name was reckoned as an extension of the person himself or herself. To speak in somebody's name was to speak with the authority of that person, as if he or she was actually speaking.

Adam, Second

1 Corinthians 15: 45.

Advocate

"My little children, these things write I unto you, that ye sin not. And if any man sin, we have an advocate with the Father, Jesus Christ the righteous" 1 John 2: 1.

Alive for Evermore

"I am he that liveth, and was dead; and, behold, I am alive for evermore, Amen; and have the keys of hell and of death" Revelation 1: 18.

All, and in All

"Where there is neither Greek nor Jew, circumcision nor uncircumcision, Barbarian, Scythian, bond nor free: but Christ is all, and in all" Colossians 3: 11.

Almighty

Revelation 1: 18.

Alpha and Omega

Revelation 1: 8; 22: 13.

Amen

Revelation 3: 14.

Angel

"And unto the angel of the church of the Laodiceans write; These things saith the Amen, the faithful and true witness, the beginning of the creation of God" Revelation 3: 14.

Angel

Genesis 48: 16; Exodus 23: 20,21.

Angel of the Lord

Exodus 3: 2; Judges 13: 15–18.

Angel of God's presence

Isaiah 63: 9.

Apostle

Hebrews 3: 1.

Arm of the Lord

Isaiah 51: 9; 53: 1.

Author and Finisher of our faith

"Looking unto Jesus the author and finisher of our faith; who for the joy that was set before him endured the cross, despising the shame, and is set down at the right hand of the throne of God" Hebrews 12: 2.

Babe

"And they came with haste, and found Mary, and Joseph, and the babe lying in a manger" Luke 2: 16.

Before All Things

"And he is before all things, and by him all things consist" Colossians 1: 17.

Beginning

"And he is the head of the body, the church: who is the beginning, the firstborn from the dead; that in all things he might have the preeminence" Colossians 1: 18.

Beginning and the Ending

"I am Alpha and Omega, the beginning and the ending, saith the Lord, which is, and which was, and which is to come, the Almighty" Revelation 1: 8.

Beginning of the Creation of God

!And unto the angel of the church of the Laodiceans write; These things saith the Amen, the faithful and true witness, the beginning of the creation of God" Revelation 3: 14.

Beloved

"Behold my servant, whom I have chosen; my beloved, in whom my soul is well pleased: I will put my spirit upon him, and he shall shew judgment to the Gentiles" Matthew 12: 18.

Beloved Son

"And lo a voice from heaven, saying, This is my beloved Son, in whom I am well pleased" Matthew 3: 17.

Bishop of Your Souls

"For ye were as sheep going astray; but are now returned unto the Shepherd and Bishop of your souls" 1 Peter 2: 25.

Blessed and only Potentate

1 Timothy 6: 15.

Blessed for Evermore

"The God and Father of our Lord Jesus Christ, which is blessed for evermore, knoweth that I lie not" 2 Corinthians 11: 31.

Blessed Hope

"Looking for that blessed hope, and the glorious appearing of the great God and our Savior Jesus Christ" Titus 2: 13.

Branch

Jeremiah 23: 5; Zechariah 3: 8; 6: 12.

Branch of Righteousness

Jeremiah 33: 15.

Branch of the Lord

"In that day shall the branch of the Lord be beautiful and glorious, and the fruit of the earth shall be excellent and comely for them that are escaped of Israel" Isaiah 4: 2.

Bread

"The Jews then murmured at him, because he said, I am the bread which came down from heaven" John 6: 41.

Bread of God

"For the bread of God is he which cometh down from heaven, and giveth life unto the world" John 6: 33.

Bread of Life

John 6: 35,48.

Bridegroom

John 3: 29.

Bright and Morning Star

Revelation 22:16.

Titles, descriptions and names of Christ (2)

Brightness of His [the Father's] Glory

"Who being the brightness of his glory, and the express image of his person, and upholding all things by the word of his power, when he had by himself purged our sins, sat down on the right hand of the Majesty on high" Hebrews 1: 3.

Captain of the Lord's hosts

Joshua 5: 14,15.

Captain of salvation

Hebrews 2: 10.

Carpenter

"Is not this the carpenter, the son of Mary, the brother of James, and Joses, and of Juda, and Simon? and are not his sisters here with us? And they were offended at him" Mark 6: 3.

Carpenter's Son

"Is not this the carpenter's son? is not his mother called Mary? and his brethren, James, and Joses, and Simon, and Judas?" Matthew 13: 55.

Chief Corner Stone

"And are built upon the foundation of the apostles and prophets, Jesus Christ himself being the chief corner stone" Ephesians 2: 20.

"Wherefore also it is contained in the scripture, Behold, I lay in Sion a chief corner stone, elect, precious: and he that believeth on him shall not be confounded" 1 Peter 2: 6.

Chief Shepherd

"And when the chief Shepherd shall appear, ye shall receive a crown of glory that fadeth not away" 1 Peter 5: 4.

Child

"For unto us a child is born, unto us a son is given: and the government shall be upon his shoulder: and his name shall be called Wonderful, Counselor, The mighty God, The everlasting Father, The Prince of Peace" Isaiah 9: 6.

Child Jesus

"And he came by the Spirit into the temple: and when the parents brought in the child Jesus, to do for him after the custom of the law" Luke 2: 27.

Chosen of God

"To whom coming, as unto a living stone, disallowed indeed of men, but chosen of God, and precious" 1 Peter 2: 4.

"And the people stood beholding. And the rulers also with them derided him, saying, He saved others; let him save himself, if he be Christ, the chosen of God" Luke 23: 35.

Christ

"And Jacob begat Joseph the husband of Mary, of whom was born Jesus, who is called Christ" Matthew 1: 16.
"And when he had gathered all the chief priests and scribes of the people together, he demanded of them where Christ should be born" Matthew 2: 4.
"And Simon Peter answered and said,

Thou art the Christ, the Son of the living God" Matthew 16: 16. "Whosoever believeth that Jesus is the Christ is born of God: and every one that loveth him that begat loveth him also that is begotten of him" 1 John 5: 1.

Christ a King

"And they began to accuse him, saying, We found this fellow perverting the nation, and forbidding to give tribute to Caesar, saying that he himself is Christ a King" Luke 23: 2.

Christ Crucified

"But we preach Christ crucified, unto the Jews a stumblingblock, and unto the Greeks foolishness" 1 Corinthians 1: 23.

Christ Jesus

"Then said Paul, John verily baptized with the baptism of repentance, saying unto the people, that they should believe on him which should come after him, that is, on Christ Jesus" Acts 19: 4.

Christ Jesus our Lord

"Nor height, nor depth, nor any other creature, shall be able to separate us from the love of God, which is in Christ Jesus our Lord" Romans 8: 39.

Christ Jesus the Lord

"For we preach not ourselves, but Christ Jesus the Lord; and ourselves your servants for Jesus' sake" 2 Corinthians 4: 5.

Christ of God

Luke 9: 20.

The word "Christ"

Anointed, the Greek translation of the Hebrew word rendered Messiah, the official title of our Lord, occurs five hundred and fourteen times in the New Testament.

It denotes that he was anointed or consecrated to his great redemptive work as

- Prophet,
- Priest, and
- King of his people.

He is Jesus the Christ (Acts 17: 3; 18: 5; Matthew 22: 42), the Anointed One. He is thus spoken of by Isaiah (Isaiah 61: 1), and by Daniel (Daniel 9: 24–26), who styles him Messiah the Prince. The Messiah is the same person as

- the seed of the woman (Genesis 3: 15),
- the seed of Abraham (Genesis 22: 18),
- the Prophet like unto Moses (Deuteronomy 18: 15),
- the priest after the order of Melchizedek (Psalm 110: 4),
- the rod out of the stem of Jesse (Isaiah 11: 1,10),
- the Immanuel, the virgin's son (Isaiah 7: 14),
- the branch of Jehovah (Isaiah 4: 2), and
- the messenger of the covenant (Malachi 3: 1).

Titles, descriptions and names of Christ (3)

The word "Christ", continued

The Old Testament Scripture is full of prophetic declarations regarding the Great Deliverer and the work he was to accomplish. Jesus the Christ is Jesus:
- the Great Deliverer,
- the Anointed One,
- the Savior of men.

This name denotes that Jesus was divinely appointed, commissioned, and accredited as the Savior of men (Hebrews 5: 4; Isaiah 11: 2–4; 49: 6; John 5: 37; Acts 2: 22).

To believe that Jesus is the Christ is to believe that he is:
- the Anointed,
- the Messiah of the prophets,
- the Savior sent of God.

It is to believe that he was what he claimed to be. This is to believe the gospel, by the faith of which alone men and women can be brought to God. That Jesus is the Christ is the belief of Christians (1 Corinthians 12: 3; 1 John 5: 1).

Characteristics of Jesus Christ

The four Gospel writers and the writers of the New Testament letters give us a great deal of information about the person and work of Jesus.

The example of Christ is perfect, Hebrews 7: 26.

Christians should be like Christ in:
- Holiness. 1 Peter 1: 15,16; Romans 1: 6.
- Righteousness. 1 John 2: 6.
- Purity. 1 John 3: 3.

- Love. John 13: 34; Ephesians 5: 2; 1 John 3: 16.
- Humility. Luke 22: 27; Philippians 2: 5,7.
- Meekness. Matthew 11: 29.
- Obedience. John 15: 10.
- Self-denial. Matthew 16: 24; Romans 15: 3.
- Ministering to others. Matthew 20: 28; John 13: 14,15.
- Forgiving. Colossians 3: 13.
- Overcoming the world. John 16: 33; 1 John 5: 4.
- Being not of the world. John 17: 16.
- Being guileless. 1 Peter 2: 21,22.
- Suffering wrongfully. 1 Peter 2: 21–23.
- Suffering for righteousness. Hebrews 12: 3,4.

Consolation of Israel

Luke 2: 25.

Commander

Isaiah 55: 4.

Counselor

"For unto us a child is born, unto us a son is given: and the government shall be upon his shoulder: and his name shall be called Wonderful, Counselor, The mighty God, The everlasting Father, The Prince of Peace" Isaiah 9: 6.

David

Jeremiah 30: 9; Ezekiel 34: 23.

Day Star

"We have also a more sure word of prophecy; whereunto ye do well that ye take heed, as unto a light that shineth in a dark place, until the day dawn, and the day star arise in your hearts" 2 Peter 1: 19.

Day-spring

Luke 1: 78.

Deliverer

Romans 11: 26.

Desire of all nations

Haggai 2: 7.

Diadem of Beauty

"In that day shall the Lord of hosts be for a crown of glory, and for a diadem of beauty, unto the residue of his people" Isaiah 28: 5.

Door

John 10: 7.

Door of the Sheep

"Then said Jesus unto them again, Verily, verily, I say unto you, I am the door of the sheep" John 10: 7.

Elect of God

Isaiah 42: 1.

Emmanuel

See Immanuel.

End of the Law

"For Christ is the end of the law for righteousness to every one that believeth" Romans 10: 4.

Ensign of the People

"And in that day there shall be a root of Jesse, which shall stand for an ensign of the people; to it shall the Gentiles seek: and his rest shall be glorious" Isaiah 11: 10.

Eternal life

1 John 1: 2; 5: 20.

Everlasting Father

Isaiah 9: 6.

Everlasting Light

"The sun shall be no more thy light by day; neither for brightness shall the moon give light unto thee: but the Lord shall be unto thee an everlasting light, and thy God thy glory. Thy sun shall no more go down; neither shall thy moon withdraw itself: for the Lord shall be thine everlasting light, and the days of thy mourning shall be ended" Isaiah 60: 19,20.

Express Image of His Person

"Who being the brightness of his glory, and the express image of his person, and upholding all things by the word of his power, when he had by himself purged our sins, sat down on the right hand of the Majesty on high" Hebrews 1: 3.

Faithful

"Faithful is he that calleth you, who also will do it" 1 Thessalonians 5: 24/

Faithful and True

Revelation 19: 11.

Titles, descriptions and names of Christ (4)

Faithful and True Witness

"And unto the angel of the church of the Laodiceans write; These things saith the Amen, the faithful and true witness, the beginning of the creation of God" Revelation 3: 14.

Faithful Creator

"Wherefore let them that suffer according to the will of God commit the keeping of their souls to him in well doing, as unto a faithful Creator" 1 Peter 4: 19.

Faithful High Priest

"Wherefore in all things it behoved him to be made like unto his brethren, that he might be a merciful and faithful high priest in things pertaining to God, to make reconciliation for the sins of the people" Hebrews 2: 17.

Faithful witness

Revelation 1: 5; 3: 14.

First and Last

Revelation 1: 17; 2: 8.

First-begotten of the dead

Revelation 1: 5.

First-born of every creature

Colossians 1:15.

Firstborn among Many Brethren

"For whom he did foreknow, he also did predestinate to be conformed to the image of his Son, that he might be the firstborn among many brethren" Romans 8: 29.

Firstborn from the Dead

"And he is the head of the body, the church: who is the beginning, the firstborn from the dead; that in all things he might have the preeminence" Colossians 1: 18.

First-Fruits

"But every man in his own order: Christ the firstfruits; afterward they that are Christ's at his coming" 1 Corinthians 15: 23.

Firstfruits of Them That Slept

"But now is Christ risen from the dead, and become the firstfruits of them that slept" 1 Corinthians 15: 20.

Flesh

"And the Word was made flesh, and dwelt among us, (and we beheld his glory, the glory as of the only begotten of the Father,) full of grace and truth" John 1: 14.

Foreordained before the Foundation of the World

"Who verily was foreordained before the foundation of the world, but was manifest in these last times for you" 1 Peter 1: 20.

Forerunner

Hebrews 6: 20.

Foundation

"For other foundation can no man lay than that is laid, which is Jesus Christ" 1 Corinthians 3: 11.

Fountain

"In that day there shall be a fountain opened to the house of David and to the inhabitants of Jerusalem for sin and for uncleanness" Zechariah 13: 1.

Fountain of Living Waters

"O Lord, the hope of Israel, all that forsake thee shall be ashamed, and they that depart from me shall be written in the earth, because they have forsaken the Lord, the fountain of living waters" Jeremiah 17: 13.

Friend

"A man that hath friends must shew himself friendly: and there is a friend that sticketh closer than a brother" Proverbs 18: 24.

Friend of Publicans and Sinners

"The Son of man is come eating and drinking; and ye say, Behold a gluttonous man, and a winebibber, a friend of publicans and sinners!" Luke 7: 34.

Fuller's Soap

"But who may abide the day of his coming? and who shall stand when he appeareth? for he is like a refiner's fire, and like fullers' soap" Malachi 3: 2.

Gift of God

"Jesus answered and said unto her, If thou knewest the gift of God, and who

it is that saith to thee, Give me to drink; thou wouldest have asked of him, and he would have given thee living water" John 4: 10.

Glory of the Lord

"And the glory of the Lord shall be revealed, and all flesh shall see it together: for the mouth of the Lord hath spoken it" Isaiah 40: 5.

Glory of Thy People Israel

"A light to lighten the Gentiles, and the glory of thy people Israel" Luke 2: 32.

God

Isaiah 40: 9; John 20: 28.

God blessed for ever

Romans 9: 5.

God our Savior

"For this is good and acceptable in the sight of God our Savior" 1 Timothy 2: 3.

God with Us

"Behold, a virgin shall be with child, and shall bring forth a son, and they shall call his name Emmanuel, which being interpreted is, God with us" Matthew 1: 23.

God's fellow

Zechariah 13: 7.

Glory of the Lord

Isaiah 40: 5.

Titles, descriptions and names of Christ (5)

The glory of Christ

The glory of Jesus Christ is spelled out in the following titles which have been given to him. This glory was also revealed in his miracles and in his life and in many of his other deeds.

- As God: John 1: 1–5; Philippians 2: 6,9,10.
- As the Son of God: Matthew 3: 17; Hebrews 1: 6,8.
- As one with the Father: John 10: 30,38.
- As the First-born: Colossians 1: 15,18.
- As the First-begotten: Hebrews 1: 6.
- As Lord of lords: Revelation 17: 14.
- As the image of God: Colossians 1: 15; Hebrews 1: 3.
- As creator: John 1: 3; Colossians 1: 16; Hebrews 1: 2.
- As the Blessed of God: Psalm 45: 2.
- As Mediator: 1 Timothy 2: 5; Hebrews 8: 6.
- As Prophet: Deuteronomy 18: 15,16; Acts 3: 22.
- As Priest: Psalm 110: 4; Hebrews 4: 15.
- As King: Isaiah 6: 1–5; John 12: 41.
- As Judge: Matthew 16: 27; 25: 31,33.
- As Shepherd: Isaiah 40: 10,11; John 10: 11,14.
- As Head of the Church: Ephesians 1: 22.
- As the true Light: Luke 1: 78,79; John 1: 4,9.
- As the foundation of the Church: Isaiah 28: 16.
- As the way: John 14: 6; Hebrews 10: 19,20.
- As the truth: 1 John 5: 20; Revelation 3: 7.
- As the life: John 11: 25; Colossians 3: 4; 1 John 5: 11.
- As incarnate: John 1: 14.
- In his words: Luke 4: 22; John 7: 46.
- In his deeds: Matthew 13: 54; John 2: 11.
- In his sinless perfection: Hebrews 7: 26–28.
- In the fullness of his grace and truth: Psalm 45: 2; John 1: 14.
- In his transfiguration: Matthew 17: 2.

"For we have not followed cunningly devised fables, when we made known unto you the power and coming of our Lord Jesus Christ, but were eyewitnesses of his majesty. For he received from God the Father honor and glory, when there came such a voice to him from the excellent glory, This is my beloved Son, in whom I am well pleased. And this voice which came from heaven we heard, when we were with him in the holy mount."
2 Peter 1: 16–18

- In his exaltation: Acts 7: 55,56; Ephesians 1: 21.
- In his triumph: Isaiah 63:1–3; Revelation 19:11,16.
- It followed his sufferings: 1 Peter 1: 10,11.

God's followers will see Christ's glory in heaven John 17: 24.

Good Master

"And, behold, one came and said unto him, Good Master, what good thing shall I do, that I may have eternal life?" Matthew 19: 16.

Good Shepherd

John 10: 14.

Great High Priest

Hebrews 4: 14.

Governor

Matthew 2: 6.

Gracious

"If so be ye have tasted that the Lord is gracious" 1 Peter 2: 3.

Great God

"Looking for that blessed hope, and the glorious appearing of the great God and our Savior Jesus Christ" Titus 2: 13.

Great High Priest

"Seeing then that we have a great high priest, that is passed into the heavens, Jesus the Son of God, let us hold fast our profession" Hebrews 4: 14.

Great King

"Nor by the earth; for it is his footstool: neither by Jerusalem; for it is the city of the great King" Matthew 5: 35.

Great Prophet

"And there came a fear on all: and they glorified God, saying, That a great prophet is risen up among us; and, That God hath visited his people" Luke 7: 16.

Great Shepherd of the Sheep

"Now the God of peace, that brought again from the dead our Lord Jesus, that great shepherd of the sheep, through the blood of the everlasting covenant" Hebrews 13: 20.

Greater than Jonas

"The men of Nineveh shall rise in judgment with this generation, and shall condemn it: because they repented at the preaching of Jonas; and, behold, a greater than Jonas is here" Matthew 12: 41.

Greater than Solomon

"The queen of the south shall rise up in the judgment with this generation, and shall condemn it: for she came from the uttermost parts of the earth to hear the wisdom of Solomon; and, behold, a greater than Solomon is here" Matthew 12: 42.

Guide

"For this God is our God for ever and ever: he will be our guide even unto death" Psalm 48: 14.

Harmless

"For such an high priest became us, who is holy, harmless, undefiled, separate from sinners, and made higher than the heavens" Hebrews 7: 26.

Head

Ephesians 4: 15.

Titles, descriptions and names of Christ (6)

Head of All Principality and Power

"And ye are complete in him, which is the head of all principality and power" Colossians 2: 10.

Head of Every Man

"But I would have you know, that the head of every man is Christ; and the head of the woman is the man; and the head of Christ is God". 1 Corinthians 11: 3.

Head of the Church

Ephesians 5: 23; Colossians 1: 18.

Head of the Corner

"Unto you therefore which believe he is precious: but unto them which be disobedient, the stone which the builders disallowed, the same is made the head of the corner" 1 Peter 2: 7.

Head over All Things

"And hath put all things under his feet, and gave him to be the head over all things to the church" Ephesians 1: 22.

Heir of all things

Hebrews 1: 2.

High Priest

"Wherefore, holy brethren, partakers of the heavenly calling, consider the Apostle and High Priest of our profession, Christ Jesus" Hebrew 3: 1.

"Whither the forerunner is for us entered, even Jesus, made an high priest for ever after the order of Melchisedec" Hebrews 6: 20.

High Priest after the Order of Melchisedec

"Called of God an high priest after the order of Melchisedec" Hebrews 5: 10.

High Priest For Ever

"Whither the forerunner is for us entered, even Jesus, made an high priest for ever after the order of Melchisedec" Hebrews 6: 20.

His Dear Son

"Who hath delivered us from the power of darkness, and hath translated us into the kingdom of his dear Son" Colossians 1: 13.

His Son from Heaven

"And to wait for his Son from heaven, whom he raised from the dead, even Jesus, which delivered us from the wrath to come" 1 Thessalonians 1: 10.

Holy Child Jesus

"For of a truth against thy holy child Jesus, whom thou hast anointed, both Herod, and Pontius Pilate, with the Gentiles, and the people of Israel, were gathered together" Acts 4: 27.

Holy One

Psalm 16: 10; Acts 2: 27,31.

Holy One of God

Mark 1: 24.

Holy One and the Just

"But ye denied the Holy One and the Just, and desired a murderer to be granted unto you" Acts 3: 14.

Holy One of Israel

Isaiah 41: 14.

Holy Thing

"And the angel answered and said unto her, The Holy Ghost shall come upon thee, and the power of the Highest shall overshadow thee: therefore also that holy thing which shall be born of thee shall be called the Son of God" Luke 1: 35.

Horn of salvation

Luke 1: 69.

Hope of Gory

"To whom God would make known what is the riches of the glory of this mystery among the Gentiles; which is Christ in you, the hope of glory" Colossians 1: 27.

Hope of Israel

"For this cause therefore have I called for you, to see you, and to speak with you: because that for the hope of Israel I am bound with this chain" Acts 28: 20.

I Am

"Jesus said unto them, Verily, verily, I say unto you, Before Abraham was, I am" John 8: 58.

Immortal

"Now unto the King eternal, immortal, invisible, the only wise God, be honor and glory for ever and ever. Amen" 1 Timothy 1: 17.

Image of the Invisible God.

"Who is the image of the invisible God, the firstborn of every creature" Colossians 1: 15.

Immanuel

"Therefore the Lord himself shall give you a sign; Behold, a virgin shall conceive, and bear a son, and shall call his name Immanuel" Isaiah 7: 14.

"Behold, a virgin shall be with child, and shall bring forth a son, and they shall call his name Emmanuel, which being interpreted is, God with us" Matthew 1: 23.

Jehovah

Isaiah 26: 4.

Jesus

Matthew 1: 21; 1Thess. 1: 10.

Jesus Christ

Hebrews 13: 8.

Jesus Christ Our Lord

"I thank God through Jesus Christ our Lord. So then with the mind I myself serve the law of God; but with the flesh the law of sin" Romans 7: 25.

Jesus Christ Our Savior

"Which he shed on us abundantly through Jesus Christ our Savior" Titus 3: 6.

Jesus Christ the Righteous

1 John 2: 1.

Titles, descriptions and names of Christ (7)

Jesus of Galilee

""Now Peter sat without in the palace: and a damsel came unto him, saying, Thou also wast with Jesus of Galilee" Matthew 26: 69.

Jesus of Nazareth

"Philip findeth Nathanael, and saith unto him, We have found him, of whom Moses in the law, and the prophets, did write, Jesus of Nazareth, the son of Joseph" John 1: 45.

Jesus of Nazareth the King of the Jews

"And Pilate wrote a title, and put it on the cross. And the writing was, JESUS OF NAZARETH THE KING OF THE JEWS" John 19: 19.

Jesus the Son of God

"Seeing then that we have a great high priest, that is passed into the heavens, Jesus the Son of God, let us hold fast our profession". Hebrews 4: 14.

Jesus, the Son of Joseph

"And they said, Is not this Jesus, the son of Joseph, whose father and mother we know? how is it then that he saith, I came down from heaven?" John 6: 42.

A Jew

"Then saith the woman of Samaria unto him, How is it that thou, being a Jew, askest drink of me, which am a woman of Samaria? for the Jews have no dealings with the Samaritans" John 4: 9.

Joseph's Son

"And all bare him witness, and wondered at the gracious words which proceeded out of his mouth. And they said, Is not this Joseph's son?" Luke 4: 22.

Judge

"And he commanded us to preach unto the people, and to testify that it is he which was ordained of God to be the Judge of quick and dead" Acts 10: 42.

Judge of All the Earth

"That be far from thee to do after this manner, to slay the righteous with the wicked: and that the righteous should be as the wicked, that be far from thee: Shall not the Judge of all the earth do right?" Genesis 18: 25.

Judge of Israel

Micah 5: 1.

Judge of Quick and Dead

"And he commanded us to preach unto the people, and to testify that it is he which was ordained of God to be the Judge of quick and dead" Acts 10: 42.

Just Man

"When he was set down on the judgment seat, his wife sent unto him, saying, Have thou nothing to do with that just man: for I have suffered many things this day in a dream because of him" Matthew 27: 19.

Just One

Acts 7: 52.

Just Person

"When Pilate saw that he could prevail nothing, but that rather a tumult was made, he took water, and washed his hands before the multitude, saying, I am innocent of the blood of this just person: see ye to it" Matthew 27: 24.

King

Zechariah 9: 9; Matthew 21: 5.

King Eternal

"Now unto the King eternal, immortal, invisible, the only wise God, be honor and glory for ever and ever. Amen" 1 Timothy 1: 17.

King in His Beauty

"Thine eyes shall see the king in his beauty: they shall behold the land that is very far off" Isaiah 33: 17.

King of Glory

"Lift up your heads, O ye gates; and be ye lift up, ye everlasting doors; and the King of glory shall come in. Who is this King of glory? The Lord strong and mighty, the Lord mighty in battle" Psalms 24: 7,8.

King of Israel

John 1: 49.

King of Kings

1 Timothy 6: 15; Revelation 17: 14.

King of Saints

"And they sing the song of Moses the servant of God, and the song of the Lamb, saying, Great and marvelous are thy works, Lord God Almighty; just and true are thy ways, thou King of saints" Revelation 15: 3.

King of the Jews

Matthew 2: 2.

King over All the Earth

"And the Lord shall be king over all the earth: in that day shall there be one Lord, and his name one" Zechariah 14: 9.

King That Cometh in the Name of the Lord

"Saying, Blessed be the King that cometh in the name of the Lord: peace in heaven, and glory in the highest" Luke 19: 38.

Law giver

Isaiah 33: 22.

Lamb

Revelation 5: 6,12; 13: 8; 21: 22; 22: 3.

Lamb of God

John 1:2 9,36.

Lamb Slain from the Foundation of the World

"And all that dwell upon the earth shall worship him, whose names are not written in the book of life of the Lamb slain from the foundation of the world" Revelation 13: 8.

Titles, descriptions and names of Christ (8)

Lamb That was Slain

"Saying with a loud voice, Worthy is the Lamb that was slain to receive power, and riches, and wisdom, and strength, and honor, and glory, and blessing" Revelation 5: 12.

Lamb Who Is in the Midst of the Throne

"For the Lamb which is in the midst of the throne shall feed them, and shall lead them unto living fountains of waters: and God shall wipe away all tears from their eyes" Revelation 7: 17.

Last Adam

"And so it is written, The first man Adam was made a living soul; the last Adam was made a quickening spirit" 1 Corinthians 15: 45.

Leader

Isaiah 55: 4.

Life

John 14: 6; Colossians 3: 4; 1 John 1: 2.

Light

"The same came for a witness, to bear witness of the Light, that all men through him might believe" John 1: 7.

Light of the world

John 8: 12.

Light to Lighten the Gentiles

"A light to lighten the Gentiles, and the glory of thy people Israel" Luke 2: 32 (also Isaiah 42: 6; 49: 6; 60: 3).

Lion of the tribe of Judah

Revelation 5: 5.

Living Bread

"I am the living bread which came down from heaven: if any man eat of this bread, he shall live for ever: and the bread that I will give is my flesh, which I will give for the life of the world" John 6: 51.

Living Stone

"To whom coming, as unto a living stone, disallowed indeed of men, but chosen of God, and precious" 1 Peter 2: 4.

Lord

"Ye call me Master and Lord: and ye say well; for so I am" John 13: 13.

Lord Also of the Sabbath

"Therefore the Son of man is Lord also of the Sabbath" Mark 2: 28 (also Matthew 12: 8).

Lord and Savior Jesus Christ

"For so an entrance shall be ministered unto you abundantly into the everlasting kingdom of our Lord and Savior Jesus Christ" 2 Peter 1: 11 (see also 2 Peter 3: 18).

Lord Both of the Dead and the Living

"For to this end Christ both died, and rose, and revived, that he might be Lord both of the dead and living" Romans 14: 9.

Lord Christ

"Knowing that of the Lord ye shall receive the reward of the inheritance: for ye serve the Lord Christ" Colossians 3: 24.

Lord from Heaven

"The first man is of the earth, earthy: the second man is the Lord from heaven" 1 Corinthians 15: 47.

Lord God Almighty

Revelation 15: 3.

Lord God of the holy prophets

Revelation 22: 6.

Lord God Omnipotent

"And I heard as it were the voice of a great multitude, and as the voice of many waters, and as the voice of mighty thunderings, saying, Alleluia: for the Lord God omnipotent reigneth" Revelation 19: 6.

Lord Jesus

"That if thou shalt confess with thy mouth the Lord Jesus, and shalt believe in thine heart that God hath raised him from the dead, thou shalt be saved" Romans 10: 9 (see also Acts 7: 59; Colossians 3: 17).

Lord Jesus Christ

"My brethren, have not the faith of our Lord Jesus Christ, the Lord of glory, with respect of persons" James 2: 1 (see also Acts 16: 31; Romans 5: 1).

Lord Jesus Christ our Savior

"To Titus, mine own son after the common faith: Grace, mercy, and peace, from God the Father and the Lord Jesus Christ our Savior" Titus 1: 4.

Lord of all

Acts 10: 36.

Lord of glory

1 Corinthians 2: 8.

Lord of Hosts

"Thus saith the Lord the King of Israel, and his redeemer the Lord of hosts; I am the first, and I am the last; and beside me there is no God" Isaiah 44: 6.

Lord of Lords

"Which in his times he shall shew, who is the blessed and only Potentate, the King of kings, and Lord of lords" 1 Timothy 6: 15.

"And he hath on his vesture and on his thigh a name written, KING OF KINGS, AND LORD OF LORDS" Revelation 19: 16.

Lord of Peace

"Now the Lord of peace himself give you peace always by all means. The Lord be with you all" 2 Thessalonians 3: 16.

Lord of the Harvest

Matthew 9: 38.

Titles, descriptions and names of Christ (9)

Lord our righteousness

Jeremiah 23: 6.

Lord's Christ

"And it was revealed unto him by the Holy Ghost, that he should not see death, before he had seen the Lord's Christ" Luke 2: 26.

Man, The

"Then came Jesus forth, wearing the crown of thorns, and the purple robe. And Pilate saith unto them, Behold the man!" John 19: 5.

Man Approved of God

"Ye men of Israel, hear these words; Jesus of Nazareth, a man approved of God among you by miracles and wonders and signs, which God did by him in the midst of you, as ye yourselves also know" Acts 2: 22.

Man Christ Jesus

"For there is one God, and one mediator between God and men, the man Christ Jesus" 1 Timothy 2: 5.

Man of sorrows

"He is despised and rejected of men; a man of sorrows, and acquainted with grief: and we hid as it were our faces from him; he was despised, and we esteemed him not" Isaiah 53: 3.

Man Whom He Hath Ordained

"Because he hath appointed a day, in the which he will judge the world in righteousness by that man whom he hath ordained; whereof he hath given assurance unto all men, in that he hath raised him from the dead" Acts 17: 31.

Master

"But be not ye called Rabbi: for one is your Master, even Christ; and all ye are brethren" Matthew 23: 8.

Mediator

1 Timothy 2: 5.

Mediator of a Better Covenant

"But now hath he obtained a more excellent ministry, by how much also he is the mediator of a better covenant, which was established upon better promises" Hebrews 8: 6.

Mediator of the New Covenant

"And to Jesus the mediator of the new covenant, and to the blood of sprinkling, that speaketh better things than that of Abel" Hebrews 12: 24.

Mediator of the New Testament

"And for this cause he is the mediator of the new testament, that by means of death, for the redemption of the transgressions that were under the first testament, they which are called might receive the promise of eternal inheritance" Hebrews 9: 15.

Meek

Matthew 11: 29.

Merciful and Faithful High Priest

"Wherefore in all things it behoved him to be made like unto his brethren, that he might be a merciful and faithful high priest in things pertaining to God, to make reconciliation for the sins of the people" Hebrews 2: 17.

Messenger of the covenant

Malachi 3: 1.

Messiah

Daniel 9: 25; John 1: 41.

Mighty God

"For unto us a child is born, unto us a son is given: and the government shall be upon his shoulder: and his name shall be called Wonderful, Counselor, The mighty God, The everlasting Father, The Prince of Peace" Isaiah 9: 6.

Mighty One of Jacob

Isaiah 60: 16.

More Excellent Name

"Being made so much better than the angels, as he hath by inheritance obtained a more excellent name than they" Hebrews 1: 4.

Morning-star

Revelation 22: 16.

Most High

"When he saw Jesus, he cried out, and fell down before him, and with a loud voice said, What have I to do with thee, Jesus, thou Son of God most high? I beseech thee, torment me not" Luke 8: 28.

My Lord and My God

"And Thomas answered and said unto him, My Lord and my God" John 20: 28.

Nazarene

Matthew 2: 23.

Offering and a Sacrifice to God

"And walk in love, as Christ also hath loved us, and hath given himself for us an offering and a sacrifice to God for a sweetsmelling savor". Ephesians 5: 2.

Offspring of David

Revelation 22: 16.

Omega

See Alpha and Omega.

One of the Prophets

"And they said, Some say that thou art John the Baptist: some, Elias; and others, Jeremias, or one of the prophets" Matthew 16: 14.

Only Begotten of the Father

"And the Word was made flesh, and dwelt among us, (and we beheld his glory, the glory as of the only begotten of the Father,) full of grace and truth" John 1: 14.

Only Begotten Son

"For God so loved the world, that he gave his only begotten Son, that whosoever believeth in him should not perish, but have everlasting life" John 3: 16.

Only Potentate

1 Timothy 6: 15.

Titles, descriptions and names of Christ (10)

Only Wise God

"Now unto the King eternal, immortal, invisible, the only wise God, be honor and glory for ever and ever. Amen" 1 Timothy 1: 17.

Only Wise God Our Savior

"To the only wise God our Savior, be glory and majesty, dominion and power, both now and ever. Amen" Jude 25.

Our Passover

1 Corinthians 5: 7.

Our Peace

"For he is our peace, who hath made both one, and hath broken down the middle wall of partition between us" Ephesians 2: 14.

Plant of renown

Ezekiel 34: 29.

Potentate

See Blessed and Only Potentate.

Power of God

"But unto them which are called, both Jews and Greeks, Christ the power of God, and the wisdom of God" 1 Corinthians 1: 24.

Precious

"Unto you therefore which believe he is precious: but unto them which be disobedient, the stone which the builders disallowed, the same is made the head of the corner" 1 Peter 2: 7.

Precious Corner Stone

"Therefore thus saith the Lord God, Behold, I lay in Zion for a foundation a stone, a tried stone, a precious corner stone, a sure foundation: he that believeth shall not make haste" Isaiah 28: 16.

Priest

"For he testifiedth, Thou art a priest for ever after the order of Melchisedec" Hebrews 7: 17.

Prince

"Him hath God exalted with his right hand to be a Prince and a Savior, for to give repentance to Israel, and forgiveness of sins" Acts 5: 31.

Prince of life

Acts 3: 15.

Prince of peace

Isaiah 9: 6.

Prince of Princes

"And through his policy also he shall cause craft to prosper in his hand; and he shall magnify himself in his heart, and by peace shall destroy many: he shall also stand up against the Prince of princes; but he shall be broken without hand" Daniel 8: 25.

Prince of the kings of the earth
Revelation 1: 5.

Prophet

Luke 24: 19; John 7: 40.

Prophet Mighty in Deed and Word

Luke 24: 19.

Prophet of Nazareth of Galilee

"And the multitude said, This is Jesus the prophet of Nazareth of Galilee" Matthew 21: 11.

Propitiation for Our Sins

"And he is the propitiation for our sins: and not for ours only, but also for the sins of the whole world" 1 John 2: 2.

Quickening Spirit

"And so it is written, The first man Adam was made a living soul; the last Adam was made a quickening spirit" 1 Corinthians 15: 45.

Rabbi

"The same came to Jesus by night, and said unto him, Rabbi, we know that thou art a teacher come from God: for no man can do these miracles that thou doest, except God be with him" John 3: 2.

Rabboni

"Jesus saith unto her, Mary. She turned herself, and saith unto him, Rabboni; which is to say, Master" John 20: 16.

Ransom

1 Timothy 2: 6.

Redeemer

Job 19: 25; Isaiah 59: 20; 60: 16.

Refiner's Fire

Malachi 3: 2.

Resurrection and life

John 11:.25.

Righteous

"My little children, these things write I unto you, that ye sin not. And if any man sin, we have an advocate with the Father, Jesus Christ the righteous" 1 John 2: 1.

Righteous Branch

Jeremiah 23: 5.

Righteous Judge

"Henceforth there is laid up for me a crown of righteousness, which the Lord, the righteous judge, shall give me at that day: and not to me only, but unto all them also that love his appearing" 2 Timothy 4: 8.

Righteous Man

"Now when the centurion saw what was done, he glorified God, saying, Certainly this was a righteous man" Luke 23: 47.

Righteous Servant

"He shall see of the travail of his soul, and shall be satisfied: by his knowledge shall my righteous servant justify many; for he shall bear their iniquities" Isaiah 53: 11.

Rock

1 Corinthians 10: 4.

Rock of Offense

Romans 9: 33.

Titles, descriptions and names of Christ (11)

Rod out of the Stem of Jesse

"And there shall come forth a rod out of the stem of Jesse, and a Branch shall grow out of his roots" Isaiah 11: 1.

Root and Offspring of David

"I Jesus have sent mine angel to testify unto you these things in the churches. I am the root and the offspring of David, and the bright and morning star" Revelation 22: 16.

Root of David

Revelation 22: 16.

Root of Jesse

Isaiah 11: 10.

Royal Diadem

"Thou shalt also be a crown of glory in the hand of the Lord, and a royal diadem in the hand of thy God" Isaiah 62: 3.

Ruler of Israel

Micah 5: 2.

Salvation

"For mine eyes have seen thy salvation" Luke 2: 30.

Salvation of God

"And all flesh shall see the salvation of God" Luke 3: 6.

Same Yesterday, To day, and For ever

"Jesus Christ the same yesterday, and to day, and for ever" Hebrews 13 :8.

Savior

2 Peter 2: 20; 3: 18.

Savior of All Men

"For therefore we both labor and suffer reproach, because we trust in the living God, who is the Savior of all men, specially of those that believe" 1 Timothy 4: 10.

Savior of the World

"And said unto the woman, Now we believe, not because of thy saying: for we have heard him ourselves, and know that this is indeed the Christ, the Savior of the world" John 4: 42.

Second Man

"The first man is of the earth, earthy: the second man is the Lord from heaven" 1 Corinthians 15: 47.

Separate from Sinners

"For such an high priest became us, who is holy, harmless, undefiled, separate from sinners, and made higher than the heavens" Hebrews 7: 26.

Servant

Isaiah 42: 1; 52: 13.

Shepherd

"And Jesus saith unto them, All ye shall be offended because of me this night: for it is written, I will smite the shepherd, and the sheep shall be scattered" Mark 14: 27.

Shepherd and Bishop of souls

1 Peter 2: 25.

Shiloh

Genesis 49: 10.

Son

"All things are delivered unto me of my Father: and no man knoweth the Son, but the Father; neither knoweth any man the Father, save the Son, and he to whomsoever the Son will reveal him" Matthew 11: 27 (see also Colossians 1: 13).

Son of Abraham

"The book of the generation of Jesus Christ, the son of David, the son of Abraham" Matthew 1: 1.

Son of David

Matthew 9: 27.

Son of God

Luke 1: 35; John 1: 49.

Son of Joseph

John 1: 45.

Son of man

John 5: 27; 6: 37.

Son of Mary

"Is not this the carpenter, the son of Mary, the brother of James, and Joses, and of Juda, and Simon? and are not his sisters here with us? And they were offended at him" Mark 6: 3.

Son of the blessed

Mark 14: 61.

Son of the Father

"Grace be with you, mercy, and peace, from God the Father, and from the Lord Jesus Christ, the Son of the Father, in truth and love" 2 John 3.

Son of the Highest

Luke 1: 32.

Son of the Living God

"And Simon Peter answered and said, Thou art the Christ, the Son of the living God" Matthew 16: 16.

Son of the Most High God

Mark 5: 7.

Son over His Own House

"But Christ as a son over his own house; whose house are we, if we hold fast the confidence and the rejoicing of the hope firm unto the end" Hebrews 3: 6.

Star

Numbers 24: 17.

Stone

"Therefore thus saith the Lord God, Behold, I lay in Zion for a foundation a stone, a tried stone, a precious corner stone, a sure foundation: he that believeth shall not make haste" Isaiah 28: 16.

Stone of Stumbling

"And a stone of stumbling, and a rock of offence, even to them which stumble at the word, being disobedient: whereunto also they were appointed" 1 Peter 2: 8.

Titles, descriptions and names of Christ (12)

Stone which the Builders Rejected

"Jesus saith unto them, Did ye never read in the scriptures, The stone which the builders rejected, the same is become the head of the corner: this is the Lord's doing, and it is marvelous in our eyes?" Matthew 21: 42.

Sun of righteousness

Malachi 4: 2.

Surety

Hebrews 7: 22.

Sure Foundation

"Therefore thus saith the Lord God, Behold, I lay in Zion for a foundation a stone, a tried stone, a precious corner stone, a sure foundation: he that believeth shall not make haste" Isaiah 28: 16.

Surety of a Better Testament

Hebrews 7: 22.

Sweet Smelling Savor

"And walk in love, as Christ also hath loved us, and hath given himself for us an offering and a sacrifice to God for a sweetsmelling savor" Ephesians 5: 2.

Teacher Come from God

"The same came to Jesus by night, and said unto him, Rabbi, we know that thou art a teacher come from God: for no man can do these miracles that thou doest, except God be with him" John 3: 2.

Tried Stone

"Therefore thus saith the Lord God, Behold, I lay in Zion for a foundation a stone, a tried stone, a precious corner stone, a sure foundation: he that believeth shall not make haste" Isaiah 28: 16.

True

"And I saw heaven opened, and behold a white horse; and he that sat upon him was called Faithful and True, and in righteousness he doth judge and make war" Revelation 19: 11.

True Bread from Heaven

"Then Jesus said unto them, Verily, verily, I say unto you, Moses gave you not that bread from heaven; but my Father giveth you the true bread from heaven2 John 6: 32.

True God

"And we know that the Son of God is come, and hath given us an understanding, that we may know him that is true, and we are in him that is true, even in his Son Jesus Christ. This is the true God, and eternal life" 1 John 5: 20.

True Witness

"And unto the angel of the church of the Laodiceans write; These things saith the Amen, the faithful and true witness, the beginning of the creation of God" Revelation 3 14.

True Light

John 1: 9.

True Vine

John 15: 1.

Truth

John 14: 6.

Undefiled

"For such an high priest became us, who is holy, harmless, undefiled, separate from sinners, and made higher than the heavens" Hebrews 7: 26.

Unspeakable Gift

"Thanks be unto God for his unspeakable gift" 2 Corinthians 9: 15.

Very Christ

"But Saul increased the more in strength, and confounded the Jews which dwelt at Damascus, proving that this is very Christ" Acts 9: 22.

Vine

"I am the vine, ye are the branches: He that abideth in me, and I in him, the same bringeth forth much fruit: for without me ye can do nothing" John 15: 5.

Way

John 14: 6.

Wisdom

Proverbs 8: 12.

Wisdom of God

"But unto them which are called, both Jews and Greeks, Christ the power of God, and the wisdom of God" 1 Corinthians 1: 24.

Witness

Isaiah 55: 4.

Wonderful

Isaiah 9: 6.

Word

"In the beginning was the Word, and the Word was with God, and the Word was God" John 1: 1.

Word of God

"And he was clothed with a vesture dipped in blood: and his name is called The Word of God" Revelation 19: 13.

Word of Life

"That which was from the beginning, which we have heard, which we have seen with our eyes, which we have looked upon, and our hands have handled, of the Word of life" 1 John 1: 1.

Young Child

"And when they were come into the house, they saw the young child with Mary his mother, and fell down, and worshipped him: and when they had opened their treasures, they presented unto him gifts; gold, and frankincense, and myrrh" Matthew 2: 11.

Quote Unquote

"The name Jesus is not only light but food. It is oil without which food for the soul is dry and salt without which it is insipid. It is honey in the mouth, music in the ear and joy in the heart."

Bernard of Clairvaux

The attributes of God the Holy Spirit (1)

Wealth of teaching

The Holy Spirit has been called the "forgotten" person of the Trinity. This is no longer the case. The amount of teaching about the Holy Spirit in the Bible is quite amazing.

General references to the Holy Spirit

OLD TESTAMENT

Gen. 1: 2; Gen. 6: 3; Gen. 41: 38; Ex. 31: 3; Ex. 35: 31; Num. 27: 18; Neh. 9: 20; Job 16: 19; Job 32: 8; Job 33: 4; Ps. 51: 11,12; Ps. 103: 9; Ps. 139: 7; Is. 4: 4; Is. 6: 8; Is. 11: 2; Is. 28: 6; Is. 30: 1; Is. 32: 15; Is. 40: 13; Is. 42: 1; Is. 44: 3–4; Is. 48: 16; Is. 51: 12; Is. 54: 13; Is. 59: 19; Is. 59: 21; Is. 61: 1; Luke 4: 18; Is. 63: 10–11; Is. 63: 14; Ezek. 36: 27; Ezek. 37: 9; Ezek. 37: 14; Ezek. 39: 29; Joel 2: 28–29; Mic. 2: 7; Mic. 3: 8; Hag. 2: 5; Zech. 4: 1–7; Zech. 12: 10.

NEW TESTAMENT

Gospels

Matt. 1: 18; Matt. 1: 20; Matt. 3: 11; Matt. 3: 16,17; John 1: 33; Mark 1: 10; Luke 3: 22; John 1: 32; Matt. 4: 1; Matt. 10: 20; Matt. 12: 28; Matt. 28: 19; Mark 12: 36; Mark 13: 11; Luke 1: 15; Luke 1: 35; Luke 1: 67; Luke 2: 25–27; Luke 11: 13; Luke 12: 12; Luke 24: 49; John 1: 9; John 3: 5,6; John 3: 34; John 4: 14; John 6: 45; John 6: 63; John 7: 38,39; John 14: 16,17; John 14: 26; John 15: 26; John 16: 7–14; John 20: 22.

ACTS

The books of Acts has been accurately named "the acts of the Holy Spirit." Acts 1: 2; Acts 1: 5; Acts 1: 8; Acts 1: 16; Acts 2: 2–4; Acts 2: 33; Acts 2: 38; Acts 4: 8; Acts 4: 31; Acts 5: 3,4; Acts 5: 9; Acts 5: 32; Acts 6: 5; Acts 7: 51; Acts 8: 15–19; Acts 9: 31; Acts 10: 19,20; Acts 10: 44–47; Acts 11: 15–17; Acts 11: 24; Acts 13: 2; Acts 13: 4; Acts 13: 9; Acts 13: 52; Acts 15: 8; Acts 15: 28; Acts 16: 6,7; Acts 19: 2–6; Acts 20: 28.

PAUL'S LETTERS

Rom. 1: 4; Rom. 5: 3–5; Rom. 8: 1–27; Rom. 9: 1; Rom. 14: 17; Rom. 15: 13; Rom. 15: 16; Rom. 15: 18,19; Rom. 15: 30; 1 Cor. 2: 4; 1 Cor. 2: 10–14; Rom. 11: 33,34; 1 Cor. 3: 16; 1 Cor. 6: 19; 1 Cor. 6: 11; 1 Cor. 12: 3–11; 2 Cor. 1: 22; 2 Cor. 5: 5; 2 Cor. 3: 3; 2 Cor. 3: 6; 2 Cor. 3: 8; 2 Cor. 3: 17,18; 2 Cor. 6: 4–6; 2 Cor. 13: 14; Gal. 3: 2,3; Gal. 3: 14; Gal. 4: 6; Gal. 5: 5; Gal. 5: 16–18; Gal. 5: 22,23; Gal. 5: 25; Gal. 6: 8; Eph. 1: 12–14; Eph. 1: 17; Eph. 2: 18; Eph. 2: 22; Eph. 3: 5; Eph. 3: 16; Eph. 4: 3,4; Eph. 4: 30; Eph. 5: 9; Eph. 5: 18; Eph. 6: 17,18; Phil. 1: 19; Phil. 2: 1; Col. 1: 8; 1 Thess. 1: 5,6; 1 Thess. 4: 8,9; 1 Thess. 5: 19; 2 Thess. 2: 13; 1 Tim. 4: 1; 2 Tim. 1: 7; 2 Tim. 1: 14; Titus 3: 5,6.

NON-PAULINE LETTERS

Heb. 2: 4; Heb. 3: 7; Heb. 6: 4; Heb. 9: 14; Heb. 10: 15; Heb. 10: 29; 1 Pet. 1: 2; 1 Pet. 1: 11,12; 1 Pet. 1: 22; 1 Pet. 3: 18; 1 Pet. 4: 14; 2 Pet. 1: 21; 1 John 2: 20; 1 John 3: 24; 1 John 4: 2; 1 John 4: 13; 1 John 5: 6–8; Jude 1: 19,20.

The book of Revelation
Rev. 2: 7; Rev. 2: 11; Rev. 2: 29; Rev. 11: 11;
Rev. 14: 13; Rev. 19: 10; Rev. 22: 17.

Introduction

The third Person of the adorable
Trinity.

His personality is proved

(1) from the fact that the attributes
of personality are ascribed to him
(John 14: 17,26; 15: 26; 1 Cor. 2: 10,11;
12: 11). He reproves, helps, glorifies,
intercedes (John 16: 7–13; Rom. 8: 26).

(2) He performs work that can only
be attributed to a person. (Luke 12: 12;
Acts 5: 32; 15: 28; 16: 6; 28: 25; 1 Cor.
2: 13; Heb. 2: 4; 3: 7; 2 Pet. 1: 21).

His divinity is demonstrated

(1) from the fact that God's names are
ascribed to him (Ex. 17: 7; Ps. 95: 7; cf.
Heb. 3: 7–11); and

(2) that divine attributes are also
ascribed to him,

• omnipresence (Ps. 139: 7; Eph. 2: 17,
18; 1 Cor. 12: 13);
• omniscience (1 Cor. 2: 10, 11);
• omnipotence (Luke 1: 35; Rom. 8: 11);
• eternity (Heb. 9: 14).

"How much more will the blood of
Christ, who through the eternal Spirit
offered himself without blemish to
God, purify our conscience from dead
works to serve the living God" Hebrews
9: 14 *ESV*.

(3) Creation is ascribed to him
(Gen. 1: 2; Job 26: 13; Ps. 104: 30), and
the working of miracles (Matt. 12: 28;

1 Cor. 12: 9–11).

(4) Worship is required and ascribed
to him (Is. 6: 3; Acts 28: 25; Rom. 9: 1;
Rev. 1: 4; Matt. 28: 19).

The Holy Spirit is God

As Jehovah. Ex. 17: 7; Heb. 3: 7–9;
    Num. 12: 6; 2 Pet. 1: 21.
As Jehovah of hosts. Is. 6: 3,8–10;
    Acts 28: 25.
As Jehovah, Most High. Ps. 78: 17,21;
    Acts 7: 51.
Being invoked as Jehovah. Luke
    2: 26–29; Acts 4: 23–25; 1: 16,20;
    2 Thess. 3: 5.
As called God. Acts 5: 3,4.
As the Spirit of glory and of God.
    1 Pet. 4: 14.
As Creator. Gen. 1: 26,27; Job 33: 4.
As equal to, and one with the Father.
    Matt. 28: 19; 2 Cor. 13: 14.
As Sovereign. Dan. 4: 35; 1 Cor. 12: 6,11.
As Author of the new birth. John 3: 5,6;
    1 John 5: 4.
As raising Christ from the dead.
    Acts 2: 24; 1 Pet. 3: 18; Heb. 13: 20;
    Rom. 1: 4.
As inspiring Scripture. 2 Tim. 3: 16;
    2 Pet. 1: 21.
As the source of wisdom. 1 Cor. 12: 8;
    Is. 11: 2; John 16: 13; 14: 26.
Linked with the Father and the Son in
    the baptismal formula. Matt. 28: 19.

Quote Unquote

"Without the Holy Spirit true
Christian discipleship would
be inconceivable, indeed
impossible."

John R.W. Stott

The attributes of God the Holy Spirit (2)

The Holy Spirit is God, continued

As the source of miraculous power.
Matt. 12: 28; Luke 11: 20; Acts 19: 11; Rom. 15: 19.
As appointing ministers. Acts 13: 2,4; 9: 38; 20: 28.
As directing evangelism. Acts 16: 6,7,10.
As indwelling saints. John 14: 17; 1 Cor. 14: 25; 3: 16; 6: 19.
As Comforter of the Church. Acts 9: 31; 2 Cor. 1: 3.
As sanctifying the Church. Ezek. 37: 28; Rom. 15: 16.
As the Witness. Heb. 10: 15; 1 John 5: 9.
As convincing of sin, of righteousness, and of judgment. John 16: 8–11.

The personality of Holy Spirit

He creates and gives life. Job 33: 4.
He commissions ministers. Is. 48: 16.
He instructs ministers what to preach. 1 Cor. 2: 13.
He spoke in, and by, the prophets Acts 1: 16; 1 Pet. 1: 11,12; 2 Pet. 1: 21.
He strives with sinners. Gen. 6: 3.
He reproves. John 16: 8.
He comforts. Acts 9: 31.
He helps our infirmities. Rom. 8: 26.
He teaches. John 14: 26; 1 Cor. 12: 3.
He guides. John 16: 13.
He sanctifies. Rom. 15: 16; 1 Cor. 6: 11.
He testifies of Christ. John 15: 26.
He glorifies Christ. John 16: 14.
He has a power of his own. Rom. 15: 13.
He searches all things. Rom. 11: 33,34; 1 Cor. 2: 10,11.
He works according to his own will. 1 Cor. 12: 11.

He can be grieved. Eph. 4: 30.
He can be resisted. Acts 7: 51.
He can be tempted. Acts 5: 9.

The Holy Spirit as Teacher

Promised. Prov. 1: 23.
As the Spirit of wisdom. Is. 11: 2; 40: 13,14.

GIVEN
In answer to prayer. Eph. 1: 16,17.
To saints. Neh. 9: 20; 1 Cor. 2: 12,13.
Necessity for. 1 Cor. 2: 9,10.

AS SUCH HE
Reveals the things of God. 1 Cor. 2: 10,13.
Reveals the things of Christ. John 16: 14.
Reveals the future. Luke 2: 26; Acts 21: 11.
Brings the words of Christ to remembrance. John 14: 26.
Directs in the way of godliness. Is. 30: 21; Ezek. 36: 27.
Teaches saints to answer persecutors. Mark 13: 11; Luke 12: 12.
Enables ministers to teach. 1 Cor. 12: 8.
Guides into all truth. John 14: 26; 16: 13.
Directs the decisions of the Church. Acts 15: 28.
Attend to instruction. Rev. 2: 7,11,29.
The natural man will not receive the things of. 1 Cor. 2: 14.

Holy Spirit as the Comforter

Proceeds from the Father. John 15: 26.

GIVEN
By the Father. John 14: 16.
By Christ. Is. 61: 3.
Through Christ's intercession.

John 14: 16.
Sent in the name of Christ. John 14: 26.
Sent by Christ from the Father.
John 15: 26; 16: 7.

AS SUCH HE
Communicates joy to saints.
Rom. 14: 17; Gal. 5: 22; 1 Thess. 1: 6.
Builds the Church. Acts 9: 31.
Testifies of Christ. John 15: 26.
Imparts the love of God. Rom. 5: 3–5.
Imparts hope. Rom. 15: 13; Gal. 5: 5.
Teaches saints. John 14: 26.
Abides for ever with saints. John 14: 16.
Is known by saints. John 14: 17.
The world cannot receive. John 14: 17.

Examples of the Holy Spirit's inspiration

OLD TESTAMENT
Joseph. Gen. 41: 38.
Bezalee. Ex. 31: 3; Ex. 35: 31.
The seventy elders. Num. 11: 17.
Balaam. Num. 24: 2.
Joshua. Num. 27: 18.

The Judges:
Othniel. Judg. 3: 10.
Gideon. Judg. 6: 34.
Jephthah. Judg. 11: 29.
Samson. Judg. 13: 25; Judg. 14: 6;
Judg. 14: 19.
King David. 1 Chr. 28: 11–12.

The prophets:
Azariah. 2 Chr. 15: 1.
Zechariah. 2 Chr. 24: 20; Zech. 1: 1.
Ezekiel. Ezek. 8: 3; Ezek. 11: 1; Ezek. 11: 5;
Ezek. 11: 24.
Daniel. Dan. 4: 8.

NEW TESTAMENT
Zacharias. Luke 1: 67.
Elizabeth. Luke 1: 41.

Simeon. Luke 2: 25–26.
The disciples. Acts 6: 3; Acts 7: 55;
Acts 8: 29; Acts 9: 17; Acts 10: 45.

Blasphemy/sin against the Holy Spirit

Is. 63: 10; Matt. 12: 31–32; Luke 12: 10;
Mark 3: 29; Luke 2: 10; 1 John 5: 16;
Acts 5: 3; Acts 5: 9; Acts 7: 51; Acts 8: 18–
22; Eph. 4: 30; Heb. 10: 29.

Withdrawn from incorrigible sinners

GENERAL REFERENCES
Gen. 6: 3; Deut. 32: 30; Ps. 51: 11;
Prov. 1: 24–28; Jer. 7: 29; Hos. 4: 17–18;
Hos. 5: 6; Hos. 9: 12; Matt. 15: 14; Luke
13: 7; Rom. 1: 24; Rom. 1: 26; Rom. 1: 28.

INSTANCES OF:
Those who lived before the flood.
Gen. 6: 3–7.
People of Sodom. Gen. 19: 13;
Gen. 19: 24–25.
Israelites. Num. 14: 26–45; Deut. 1: 42;
Deut. 28: 15–68; Deut. 31: 17–18.
Samson. Judg. 16: 20.
Saul. 1 Sam. 16: 14; 1 Sam. 18: 10–12;
1 Sam. 19: 9–11; 1 Sam. 20: 30–33;
1 Sam. 22: 7–19; 1 Sam. 28: 15–16;
2 Sam. 7: 15.

Quote Unquote

"Only where the Spirit is sighed, cried, and prayed for does he become present and newly active."

Karl Barth

The Trinity

Introduction

The word "Trinity" is not found in the Bible.

Summary

This word "Trinity" is used to express the doctrine of the unity of God as subsisting in three distinct Persons.

This word is derived from the Gr. *trias*, or from the Lat. *trinitas*.

First uses of the word

FIRST USE OF THE WORD "TRINITY"
The first person to use the term Trinity was bishop Theophilus of Antioch, in the late 2nd century, about 178. He does so in his *Letter to Autolycus 2: 15*.

SECOND USE OF THE WORD "TRINITY"
Tertullian, in the early 3rd century was the second to make use of the term "Trinity." He does so in his letter *Against Praxeus*.

Three other theologians from the 3rd century who used this word are Novatian, Clement of Alexandria, and Origen.

Propositions of the early theologians

The propositions put forward by the Christians teachers who first coined and used the word "trinity" were:

(1) That God is one, and that there is but one God (Deut. 6: 4; 1 Kings 8: 60; Is. 44: 6; Mark 12: 29,32; John 10: 30).

(2) That the Father is a distinct divine Person (*hypostasis, subsistentia, persona,*

suppositum intellectuale), distinct from the Son and the Holy Spirit.

(3) That Jesus Christ was truly God, and yet was a Person distinct from the Father and the Holy Spirit.

(4) That the Holy Spirit is also a distinct divine Person.

Proved from the Bible

The key Bible verses which verify the doctrine of the Trinity are:

Matt. 3: 16,17; 28: 19; Rom. 8: 9; 1 Cor. 12: 3–6; 2 Cor. 13: 14; Eph. 4: 4–6; 1 Pet. 1: 2; Jude 1: 20,21; Rev. 1: 4,5.

Divine titles applied to the three persons in Ex. 20: 2; John 20: 28; Acts 5: 3,4.

EACH PERSON IN, DESCRIBED AS

Eternal. Rom. 16: 26; Rev. 22: 13; Heb. 9: 14.

Holy. Rev. 4: 8; 15: 4; Acts 3: 14; 1 John 2: 20.

True. John 7: 28; Rev. 3: 7.

Omnipresent. Jer. 23: 24; Eph. 1: 23; Ps. 139: 7.

Omnipotent. Gen. 17: 1; Rev. 1: 8; Rom. 15: 19; Jer. 32: 17; Heb. 1: 3; Luke 1: 35.

Omniscient. Acts 15: 18; John 21: 17; 1 Cor. 2: 10,11.

Creator. Gen. 1: 1; Col. 1: 16; Job 33: 4; Ps. 148: 5; John 1: 3; Job 26: 13.

Source of all spiritual work. Heb. 13: 21; Col. 1: 29; 1 Cor. 12: 11.

"make you perfect in every good thing to do his will, working in us that which is well-pleasing in his sight, through Jesus Christ; to whom

be the glory for ever and ever. Amen"
Hebrews 13: 21 *ASV*.

"whereunto I labor also, striving
according to his working, which
worketh in me mightily" Colossians
1: 29 *ASV*.

"but all these worketh the one
and the same Spirit, dividing to
each one severally even as he will"
1 Corinthians 12: 11 *ASV*.

Source of eternal life. Rom. 6: 23;
John 10: 28; Gal. 6: 8.

Teacher. Is. 54: 13; Luke 21: 15;
John 14: 26; Is. 48: 17; Gal. 1: 12;
1 John 2: 20.

The Trinity and the inspiring of the prophets

Heb. 1: 1; 2 Cor. 13: 3; Mark 13: 11.

The Trinity and God's ministers in his Church

Jer. 3: 15; Eph. 4: 11; Acts 20: 28; Jer. 26: 5;
Matt. 10: 5; Acts 13: 2.

Salvation is the work of the Trinity

"But we are bound to give thanks to
God always for you, brethren beloved
of the Lord, for that God chose you
from the beginning unto salvation in
sanctification of the Spirit and belief of
the truth:

14 whereunto he called you through
our gospel, to the obtaining of the
glory of our Lord Jesus Christ."
2 Thessalonians 2: 13,14 ASV

"But when the kindness of God
our Savior, and his love toward man,
appeared,

5 not by works done in
righteousness, which we did ourselves,
but according to his mercy he saved us,
through the washing of regeneration
and renewing of the Holy Spirit,

6 which he poured out upon us
richly, through Jesus Christ our Savior."
Titus 3: 4–6 ASV

"According to the foreknowledge of
God the Father, in sanctification of the
Spirit, unto obedience and sprinkling
of the blood of Jesus Christ: Grace to
you and peace be multiplied."
1 Peter 1: 2 ASV

Baptism was to be administered in name of the Trinity

"Go ye therefore, and make disciples of
all the nations, baptizing them into the
name of the Father and of the Son and
of the Holy Spirit." Matthew 28: 19 *ASV*.

Blessings were given in name of the Trinity

"The grace of the Lord Jesus Christ, and
the love of God, and the communion
of the Holy Spirit, be with you all."
2 Corinthians 13: 14 ASV

Quote Unquote

"Every divine action begins from
the Father, proceeds through the
Son and is completed in the Holy
Spirit."

Basil

Persecution (1)

General references

The volume of references to the persecution of God's followers found in the Bible bears eloquent testimony to the evil intentions and actions of persecutors and the faithfulness of many of those who were persecuted.

Old Testament

Gen. 49: 23; Job 1: 9; Job 2: 4,5; Job 12: 4,5; Prov. 29: 10; Prov. 29: 27; Is. 26: 20; Is. 29: 20,21; Is. 51: 12,13; Is. 59: 15; Jer. 2: 30; Jer. 11: 19; Jer. 15: 10; Jer. 18: 18; Jer. 20: 7,8; Jer. 26: 11–14; Jer. 50: 7; Amos 5: 10; Hab. 1: 13.

PERSECUTION IN THE PSALMS
Ps. 11: 2; Ps. 37: 32; Ps. 38: 20; Ps. 42: 3; Ps. 42: 10; Ps. 44: 15–18; Ps. 44: 22; Ps. 56: 5; Ps. 69: 10–12; Ps. 74: 7,8; Ps. 94: 5; Ps. 119: 51; Ps. 119: 61; Ps. 119: 69; Ps. 119: 78; Ps. 119: 85–87; Ps. 119: 95; Ps. 119: 110; Ps. 119: 157; Ps. 119: 161.

New Testament

THE GOSPELS
Matt. 5: 10–12; Matt. 5: 44; Luke 6: 26–27; Matt. 10: 16–18; Matt. 10: 21–23; M,tt. 10: 28; Matt. 20: 22,23; Matt. 23: 34,35; Matt. 24: 8–10; Mark 8: 35; Luke 17: 33; Mark 9: 42; Mark 13: 9; Mark 13: 11–13; Luke 6: 22,23; Luke 21: 12–19; John 12: 42; John 15: 18,19; John 16: 1,2; John 17: 14

Jesus and persecution

Jesus made it abundantly clear, on numerous occasions, that his followers would face severe persecution.

"But when you are arrested and stand trial, don't worry about what to say in your defense. Just say what God tells you to. Then it is not you who will be speaking, but the Holy Spirit.

12 "Brother will betray brother to death, fathers will betray their own children, and children will rise against their parents and cause them to be killed. 13And everyone will hate you because of your allegiance to me. But those who endure to the end will be saved."

Mark 13: 11–13 NLT

ACTS THR REVELATION
Acts 4: 16–20; Acts 5: 29; Acts 5: 40–42; Acts 7: 52; Acts 8: 4; Acts 28: 22; Rom. 8: 17; Rom. 8: 35–37; 1 Cor. 4: 9–13; 1 Cor. 13: 3; 2 Cor. 4: 8–12; 2 Cor. 6: 4,5; 2 Cor. 6: 8–10; 2 Cor. 11: 23–27; 2 Cor. 12: 10; Gal. 4: 29; Gal. 6: 12; Gal. 6: 17; Phil. 1: 12–14; Phil. 1: 28,29; Col. 1: 24; 1 Thess. 1: 6; 1 Thess. 2: 2; 1 Thess. 2: 14,15; 2 Thess. 1: 4; 2 Tim. 1: 8; 2 Tim. 1: 12; 2 Tim. 2: 9,10; 2 Tim. 2: 12; 2 Tim. 3: 2,3; 2 Tim. 3: 12; 2 Tim. 4: 16,17; Heb. 10: 32–34; Heb. 11: 25–27; Heb. 11: 33–38; Heb. 12: 3,4; Heb. 13: 13; James 2: 6; James 5: 6; James 5: 10; 1 Pet. 3: 14; 1 Pet. 3: 16–17; 1 Pet. 4: 3,4; 1 Pet. 4: 12–14; 1 Pet. 4: 16; 1 Pet. 4: 19; 1 John 3: 1; 1 John 3: 13; Rev. 2: 3; Rev. 2: 10; Rev. 2: 13; Rev. 6: 9–11; Rev. 7: 13–17; Rev. 12: 11; Rev. 17: 6; Rev. 20: 4.

Paul

The apostle Paul never left the first Christians in any doubt that they would experience all kinds of persecution.

"So you must never be ashamed to tell others about our Lord. And don't be ashamed of me, either, even though I'm in prison for Christ. With the strength God gives you, be ready to suffer with me for the proclamation of the Good News."

2 Timothy 1: 8 NLT.

PERSECUTION PREDICTED
The Old Testament frequently predicted that the coming Messiah would suffer greatly.

Gen. 3: 15; Ps. 2: 1–5; Ps. 22: 1,2; Ps. 22: 6–8; Ps. 22: 11–21; Ps. 69: 1–21; Ps. 69: 26; Ps. 109: 25; Is. 49: 7; Is. 50: 6; Is. 52: 14; Is. 53: 2–5; Is. 53: 7–10; Mic. 5: 1.

PERSECUTION FROM ALL SIDES
Jesus himself suffered all kinds of opposition, which ranged from verbal insults to the most severe physical persecution. This came not just from hypocritical religious leaders, but also at the hands of his friends and even his family.

Reading through the Gospels

Reading through the Gospels it is clear that Jesus endured endless personal attacks.

Matthew
Matt. 2: 13; Matt. 11: 19; Matt. 12: 14; Matt. 12: 24; Matt. 16: 1; Matt. 26: 3,4; Matt. 26: 14–16; Matt. 26: 59; Matt. 27: 25–30; Matt. 27: 39–44;

Mark
Mark 3: 6; Mark 3: 21; Mark 3: 22; Mark 14: 1; Mark 14: 48; Mark 15.

Luke
Luke 4: 28,29; Luke 6: 11; Luke 7: 34; Luke 11: 15; Luke 11: 53,54; Luke 12: 50Luke 13: 31; Luke 19: 14; Luke 19: 47; Luke 20: 20; Luke 22: 2–5; Luke 22: 52,53; Luke 22: 63–65; Luke 23: 11; Luke 23: 23.

John
John 5: 16; John 7: 1; John 7: 7; John 7: 19,20; John 7: 30; John 7: 32; John 8: 37; John 8: 40; John 8: 48; John 8: 52; John 8: 59; John 10: 31; John 10: 20; John 10: 39; John 11: 57; John 14: 30; John 15: 18; John 15: 20,21; John 15: 24,25; John 18: 22,23; John 18: 29,30.

Acts
Acts 2: 23; Acts 3: 13–15; Acts 4: 27; Acts 7: 52; Acts 13: 27–29.

New Testament letters
Heb. 12: 2,3; 1 Pet. 4: 1.

Spreading the Gospel

One positive result from the persecution of the early Christians is that the Gospel spread from Jerusalem into every corner of the known world and to the capital of the Roman Empire itself, Rome.

Acts 8: 1; Acts 8: 4; Acts 11: 19–21; Phil. 1: 12–14.

Persecution (2)

Spreading the Gospel, continued

"Meanwhile, the believers who had fled from Jerusalem during the persecution after Stephen's death traveled as far as Phoenicia, Cyprus, and Antioch of Syria. They preached the Good News, but only to Jews.

20 However, some of the believers who went to Antioch from Cyprus and Cyrene began preaching to Gentiles about the Lord Jesus.

21 The power of the Lord was upon them, and large numbers of these Gentiles believed and turned to the Lord."

Acts 11: 19–21 NLT

Persecution greatly influenced Paul

But for witnessing Stephen's martyrdom Saul may never have become Paul.

"Saul was one of the official witnesses at the killing of Stephen"
Acts 8: 1 *NLT*.

Prayer for deliverance from persecution

Ps. 70: 1–4; Ps. 83; Ps. 140: 1; Ps. 140: 4; Ps. 142: 6.

Deliverance from persecution

Ps. 124; Ps. 129: 1,2.

Examples of persecution in the Old Testament

Of Abel.
Gen. 4: 8; Matt. 23: 35; 1 John 3: 12.

Of Lot.
Gen. 19: 9.

Of Moses.
Ex. 2: 15; Ex. 17: 4.

Of David.
Ps. 31: 13; Ps. 59: 1,2.

Of prophets martyred by Jezebel.
1 Kgs. 18: 4.

Of Gideon.
Judg. 6: 28–32.

Of Elijah.
1 Kgs. 18: 10; 1 Kgs. 19; 2 Kgs. 1: 9; 2 Kgs. 2: 23.

Of Micaiah.
1 Kgs. 22: 26; 2 Chr. 18: 26.

Of Elisha.
2 Kgs. 6: 31.

Of Hanani.
2 Chr. 16: 10.

Of Zachariah.
2 Chr. 24: 21; Matt. 23: 35.

Of Job.
Job 13: 4–13; Job 16: 1–4; Job 17: 2; Job 19: 1–5; Job 30: 1–10.

Of Jeremiah.
Jer. 15: 10; Jer. 15: 15; Jer. 17: 15–18; Jer. 18: 18–23; Jer. 26; Jer. 32: 2; Jer. 33: 1; Jer. 36: 26; Jer. 37; Jer. 38: 1–6.

JEREMIAH AND PERSECUTION

There are more details about the persecution of Jeremiah the prophet than any other Old Testament prophet.

"Then I said, 'What sadness is mine, my mother. Oh, that I had died at birth! I am hated everywhere I go. I am neither a lender who has threatened to foreclose nor a borrower who refuses to pay – yet they all curse me.'" Jeremiah 15: 10 NLT.

"Then I said, 'Lord, you know I am suffering for your sake. Punish my persecutors! Don't let them kill me! Be merciful to me and give them what they deserve!'" Jeremiah 15: 15 NLT.

JEREMIAH'S COMPLAINT

"People scoff at me and say, 'What is this "message from the Lord" you keep talking about? Why don't your predictions come true?'

16 Lord, I have not abandoned my job as a shepherd for your people. I have not urged you to send disaster. It is your message I have given them, not my own.

17 Lord, do not desert me now! You alone are my hope in the day of disaster.

18 Bring shame and terror on all who persecute me, but give me peace. Yes, bring double destruction upon them!"   *Jeremiah 17: 15–17 NLT*

A PLOT AGAINST JEREMIAH

"Then the people said, 'Come on, let's find a way to stop Jeremiah. We have our own priests and wise men and prophets. We don't need him to teach the law and give us advice and prophecies. Let's spread rumors about him and ignore what he says.'

19 Lord, help me! Listen to what they are planning to do to me!

20 Should they repay evil for good? They have set a trap to kill me, though I pleaded for them and tried to protect them from your anger.

21 So let their children starve! Let the sword pour out their blood! Let their wives become widows without any children! Let their old men die in a plague, and let their young men be killed in battle!

22 Let screaming be heard from their homes as warriors come suddenly upon them. For they have dug a pit for me, and they have hidden traps along my path.

23 Lord, you know all about their murderous plots against me. Don't forgive their crimes and blot out their sins. Let them die before you. Deal with them in your anger."

Jeremiah 18: 18–23 NLT

Persecution (3)

Examples of persecution in the Old Testament, continued

Of Urijah.

Jer. 26: 23.

Of prophets.

Matt. 21: 35–36.

Of the three Jews in captivity.

Dan. 3: 8–23.

Of Daniel.

Dan. 6.

Of the Jews.

Ezra 4; Neh. 4.

Examples of persecution in the New Testament

Of John the Baptist.

Matt. 14: 3–12.

Of James.

Acts 12: 2.

Of Simon.

Mark 15: 21.

Of the disciples.

John 9: 22; John 9: 34; John 20: 19.

Of Lazarus.

John 12: 10.

Of the apostles.

Acts 4: 3–18; Acts 5: 18–42; Acts 12: 1–19; Rev. 1: 9.

"Saul was one of the official witnesses at the killing of Stephen" Acts 8: 1 NLT.

"They arrested the apostles and put them in the jail.

19 But an angel of the Lord came at night, opened the gates of the jail, and brought them out. Then he told them,

20 'Go to the Temple and give the people this message of life!'

21 So the apostles entered the Temple about daybreak and immediately began teaching. When the high priest and his officials arrived, they convened the high council, along with all the elders of Israel. Then they sent for the apostles to be brought for trial.

22 But when the Temple guards went to the jail, the men were gone. So they returned to the council and reported,

23 'The jail was locked, with the guards standing outside, but when we opened the gates, no one was there!'

24 When the captain of the Temple guard and the leading priests heard this, they were perplexed, wondering where it would all end.

25 Then someone arrived with the news that the men they had jailed were out in the Temple, teaching the people.

26 The captain went with his Temple guards and arrested them, but without violence, for they were afraid the people would kill them if they treated the apostles roughly.

27 Then they brought the apostles in before the council.

28 'Didn't we tell you never again to teach in this man's name?' the high priest demanded. 'Instead, you have filled all Jerusalem with your teaching about Jesus, and you intend to blame us for his death!'

29 But Peter and the apostles replied, 'We must obey God rather than human authority.

30 The God of our ancestors raised

Jesus from the dead after you killed him by crucifying him.

31 Then God put him in the place of honor at his right hand as Prince and Savior. He did this to give the people of Israel an opportunity to turn from their sins and turn to God so their sins would be forgiven.

32 We are witnesses of these things and so is the Holy Spirit, who is given by God to those who obey him.'

33 At this, the high council was furious and decided to kill them.

34 But one member had a different perspective. He was a Pharisee named Gamaliel, who was an expert on religious law and was very popular with the people. He stood up and ordered that the apostles be sent outside the council chamber for a while.

35 Then he addressed his colleagues as follows: 'Men of Israel, take care what you are planning to do to these men!

36 Some time ago there was that fellow Theudas, who pretended to be someone great. About four hundred others joined him, but he was killed, and his followers went their various ways. The whole movement came to nothing.

37 After him, at the time of the census, there was Judas of Galilee. He got some people to follow him, but he was killed, too, and all his followers were scattered.

38 So my advice is, leave these men alone. If they are teaching and doing these things merely on their own, it will soon be overthrown.

39 But if it is of God, you will not be able to stop them. You may even find yourselves fighting against God.'

40 The council accepted his advice. They called in the apostles and had them flogged. Then they ordered them never again to speak in the name of Jesus, and they let them go.

41 The apostles left the high council rejoicing that God had counted them worthy to suffer dishonor for the name of Jesus. 42And every day, in the Temple and in their homes, they continued to teach and preach this message: "The Messiah you are looking for is Jesus.""

Acts 5: 18–42 NLT

Of Stephen.
    Acts 6: 9–15; Acts 7.

Of the church.
    Acts 8: 1; Acts 9: 1–14; Gal. 1: 13.

Of Timothy.
    Heb. 13: 23.

Of John.
    Rev. 1: 9.

Of Antipas.
    Rev. 2: 13.

Of the church of Smyrna.
    Rev. 2: 8–10.

Bible martyrs (1)

Definition

A martyr is a witness. A Christian martyr may be defined as someone who bears witness of the truth, and suffers death in the cause of Christ (Acts 22: 20; Rev. 2: 13; 17: 6). In this sense Stephen was the first martyr.

The Greek word from which we derive the word "martyr" means "witness."

Christians as witnesses

In the New Testament Christians are called on to be witnesses to Jesus:

(1) In a court of justice (Matt. 18: 16; 26: 65; Acts 6: 13; 7: 58; Heb. 10: 28; 1 Tim. 5: 19).

(2) In bearing testimony to the truth about what has been seen or known (Luke 24: 48; Acts 1: 8, 22; Rom. 1: 9; 1 Thess. 2: 5, 10; 1 John 1: 2).

Overview

Ps. 44: 22; Rom. 8: 36; Matt. 10: 21,22; Mark 13: 12; Luke 21: 16,17; Matt. 10: 39; Matt. 16: 25; Matt. 23: 34,35; Luke 11: 50; Matt. 24: 9; Luke 9: 24; John 12: 25; 1 Cor. 13: 3; Rev. 6: 9–11; Rev. 11: 7–12; Rev. 12: 11; Rev. 16: 6; Rev. 17: 6.

"And the brother shall deliver up the brother to death, and the father the child; and the children shall rise up against their parents and cause them to be put to death.

22 And ye shall be hated by all men for My name's sake, but he that endureth to the end shall be saved"

Matthew 10: 21,22 ASV

"As it is written: "For Thy sake we are killed all the day long; we are accounted as sheep for the slaughter." Romans 8: 36 ASV.

Examples of martyrdom:

ABEL
Gen. 4: 3–8

PROPHETS KILLED BY JEZEBEL
1 Kgs. 18: 4; 1 Kgs. 18: 13.

ZECHARIAH
2 Chr. 24: 21–22.

JOHN THE BAPTIST
Mark 6: 18–28.

STEPHEN
Acts 7: 58–60.

JAMES THE APOSTLE
Acts 12: 2.

THE PROPHETS
Matt. 22: 6; Matt. 23: 35; Rom. 11: 3; 1 Thess. 2: 15; Heb. 11: 32–37.

Jesus' followers and martyrdom

Forewarned of. Matt. 10: 21; 24: 9; John 16: 2.

Should not fear. Matt. 10: 28; Rev. 2: 10.

Should be prepared for. Matt. 16: 24,25; Acts 21: 13.

Facts about Christian martyrdom

IT WILL BE REWARDED
Rev. 2: 10; 6: 11.

IT IS INFLICTED BY THE DEVIL
Rev. 2: 10,13.

THOSE COMMITTING APOSTASY ARE
GUILTY OF INFLICTING IT
Rev. 17: 6; 18: 24.

Jesus and Old Testament martyrdoms

Jesus once summarized the martyr-
doms recorded in the Old Testament.

"God in his wisdom said, 'I will send
them prophets and apostles, some of
whom they will kill and others they will
persecute.' Therefore this generation
will be held responsible for the blood
of all the prophets that has been shed
since the beginning of the world,
from the blood of Abel to the blood of
Zechariah, who was killed between the
altar and the sanctuary. Yes, I tell you,
this generation will be held responsible
for it all"   Acts 11: 49–51 NIV.

Martyrs and the book of Revelation

Christian martyrs are graphically
portrayed in the book of revelation.
"I saw under the altar the souls of them
that were slain for the word of God,
and for the testimony which they held"
Revelation 6: 9 ASV.

Hebrews and martyrs

The author of the letter to the Hebrews
summarizes how God's faithful
followers in Old Testament times were
persecuted and martyred.

"These all died in faith, not having
received the promises, but having seen
them afar off, and were persuaded
of them, and embraced them, and
confessed that they were strangers and
pilgrims on the earth.... Others were
tortured, not accepting deliverance;

that they might obtain a better
resurrection: and others had trial
of cruel mockings and scourgings,
yea, moreover of bonds and
imprisonment: they were stoned, they
were sawn asunder, were tempted, were
slain with the sword: they wandered
about in sheepskins and goatskins;
being destitute, afflicted, tormented; (of
whom the world was not worthy): they
wandered in deserts, and in mountains,
and in dens and caves of the earth."
                Hebrews 11: 13, 35–38 NKJV

Old Testament martyrs

1 Obadiah explains to Elijah

"And it came to pass after many days
that the word of the Lord came to Elijah
in the third year, saying, 'Go, show
thyself unto Ahab, and I will send rain
upon the earth.'

2 And Elijah went to show himself
unto Ahab. And there was a sore
famine in Samaria.

3 And Ahab called Obadiah, who
was the governor of his house. (Now
Obadiah feared the Lord greatly.

4 For it was so, when Jezebel cut off
the prophets of the Lord, that Obadiah
took a hundred prophets and hid them
by fifty in a cave, and fed them with
bread and water.)

5 And Ahab said unto Obadiah, 'Go
into the land unto all fountains of water
and unto all brooks. Perhaps we may
find grass to save the horses and mules
alive, that we lose not all the beasts.'

6 So they divided the land between
them to pass throughout it; Ahab

Bible martyrs (2)

Old Testament martyrs, continued

1 Obadiah explains to Elijah, continued

went one way by himself, and Obadiah went another way by himself.

7 And as Obadiah was on the way, behold, Elijah met him; and he knew him, and fell on his face and said, 'Art thou my lord Elijah?'

8 And he answered him, 'I am. Go, tell thy lord: "Behold, Elijah is here."'

9 And he said, 'What have I sinned, that thou wouldest deliver thy servant into the hand of Ahab to slay me?

10 As the Lord thy God liveth, there is no nation or kingdom whither my lord hath not sent to seek thee; and when they said, "He is not there," he took an oath from the kingdom and nation that they found thee not.

11 And now thou sayest, "Go, tell thy lord: 'Behold, Elijah is here.'"

12 And it shall come to pass, as soon as I am gone from thee, that the Spirit of the Lord shall carry thee whither I know not; and so when I come and tell Ahab, and he cannot find thee, he shall slay me. But I thy servant fear the Lord from my youth.

13 Was it not told my lord what I did when Jezebel slew the prophets of the Lord, how I hid a hundred men of the Lord's prophets by fifty in a cave, and fed them with bread and water?'"

1 Kings 18: 1–13 ASV

2 Uriah the prophet

"And there was also a man that prophesied in the name of Jehovah, Uriah the son of Shemaiah of Kiriath-jearim; and he prophesied against this city and against this land according to all the words of Jeremiah:

21 and when Jehoiakim the king, with all his mighty-men, and all the princes, heard his words, the king sought to put him to death; but when Uriah heard it, he was afraid, and fled, and went into Egypt:

22 and Jehoiakim the king sent men into Egypt, namely, Elnathan the son of Achbor, and certain men with him, into Egypt;

23 and they fetched forth Uriah out of Egypt, and brought him unto Jehoiakim the king, who slew him with the sword, and cast his dead body into the graves of the common people.

24 But the hand of Ahikam the son of Shaphan was with Jeremiah, that … should not give him into the hand of the people to put him to death."

Jeremiah 26: 20–24 ASV

3 Zechariah the priest

"Now after the death of Jehoiada came the princes of Judah, and made obeisance to the king. Then the king hearkened unto them.

18 And they forsook the house of Jehovah, the God of their fathers, and served the Asherim and the idols: and wrath came upon Judah and Jerusalem for this their guiltiness.

19 Yet he sent prophets to them, to

bring them again unto Jehovah; and they testified against them: but they would not give ear.

20 And the Spirit of God came upon Zechariah the son of Jehoiada the priest; and he stood above the people, and said unto them, Thus saith God, Why transgress ye the commandments of Jehovah, so that ye cannot prosper? because ye have forsaken Jehovah, he hath also forsaken you.

21 And they conspired against him, and stoned him with stones at the commandment of the king in the court of the house of Jehovah.

22 Thus Joash the king remembered not the kindness which Jehoiada his father had done to him, but slew his son. And when he died, he said, Jehovah look upon it, and require it"

2 Chronicles 24: 17–22 ASV

New Testament martyrs

1 Holy innocents

The horrific massacre of male toddlers who lived around Bethlehem, ordered by King Herod, is often considered as an example of "martyrdom."

"Then Herod, when he saw that he was mocked of the Wise-men, was exceeding wroth, and sent forth, and slew all the male children that were in Bethlehem, and in all the borders thereof, from two years old and under, according to the time which he had exactly learned of the Wise-men.

17 Then was fulfilled that which was spoken through Jeremiah the prophet, saying,

18 A voice was heard in Ramah, Weeping and great mourning, Rachel weeping for her children; And she would not be comforted, because they are not."   *Matthew 2: 16–18 ASV*

2 John the Baptist

John the Baptist fearlessly preached the gospel and spoke out against sin wherever he saw it.

"This is John the Baptist; he is risen from the dead; and therefore do these powers work in him.

3 For Herod had laid hold on John, and bound him, and put him in prison for the sake of Herodias, his brother Philip's wife.

4 For John said unto him, It is not lawful for thee to have her.

5 And when he would have put him to death, he feared the multitude, because they counted him as a prophet.

6 But when Herod's birthday came, the daughter of Herodias danced in the midst, and pleased Herod.

7 Whereupon he promised with an oath to give her whatsoever she should ask.

8 And she, being put forward by her mother, saith, Give me here on a platter the head of John the Baptist.

9 And the king was grieved; but for the sake of his oaths, and of them that sat at meat with him, he commanded it to be given;

10 and he sent and beheaded John in the prison.

11 And his head was brought on a platter, and given to the damsel: and she brought it to her mother.

12 And his disciples came, and took up the corpse, and buried him; and they went and told Jesus"

Matthew 14: 1–12 ASV.

Bible martyrs (3)

3 Stephen

The deacon Stephen is usually thought of as being the first Christian martyr because his stoning to death is the first death of a Christian for the cause of Christ recorded after the death of Jesus.

"And all that sat in the council, fastening their eyes on him, saw his face as it had been the face of an angel.

1 And the high priest said, Are these things so?

2 And he said, Brethren and fathers, hearken: The God of glory appeared unto our father Abraham, when he was in Mesopotamia, before he dwelt in Haran...

51 Ye stiffnecked and uncircumcised in heart and ears, ye do always resist the Holy Spirit: as your fathers did, so do ye.

52 Which of the prophets did not your fathers persecute? and they killed them that showed before of the coming of the Righteous One; of whom ye have now become betrayers and murderers;

53 ye who received the law as it was ordained by angels, and kept it not.

54 Now when they heard these things, they were cut to the heart, and they gnashed on him with their teeth.

55 But he, being full of the Holy Spirit, looked up steadfastly into heaven, and saw the glory of God, and Jesus standing on the right hand of God,

56 and said, Behold, I see the heavens opened, and the Son of Man standing on the right hand of God.

57 But they cried out with a loud voice, and stopped their ears, and rushed upon him with one accord;

58 and they cast him out of the city, and stoned him: and the witnesses laid down their garments at the feet of a young man named Saul.

59 And they stoned Stephen, calling upon the Lord, and saying, Lord Jesus, receive my spirit.

60 And he kneeled down, and cried with a loud voice, Lord, lay not this sin to their charge. And when he had said this, he fell asleep."

Acts 6: 15–7: 2, 51–60 ASV

Death of the twelve apostles and the Gospel writers

CHURCH TRADITION

The Bible does not record many details about the ministry of the apostles, apart from Peter and Paul, and gives no details of any of their deaths except for James being beheaded.

Some of the traditions that have grown up about the deaths of the apostles and Gospel writers are not at all trustworthy, while some of the traditions are supported by historical records. One things is certain: the early church suffered great persecution and most of Jesus' twelve apostles became martyrs.

GOSPEL WRITERS

Matthew

Matthew is said to have been martyred in Ethopia, killed by a sword wound.

Mark

Mark, it is believed, died in Alexandria, Egypt, dragged by horses through the streets until he was dead.

Luke

Luke, tradition maintains, was hanged in Greece as a result of his preaching.

THE APOSTLES

John

Tradition states that John, who was the only apostle to write a Gospel, was boiled in a huge basin of boiling oil during a wave of persecution in Rome. However, he was miraculously delivered from death. John was then sentenced to the mines on the prison island of Patmos where he wrote the book of Revelation. The Apostle John was later freed and returned to serve as a bishop in modern Turkey. He died an old man, the only apostle to die peacefully.

Peter

Peter was crucified upside down on an x-shaped cross, according to Church tradition, because he told his tormentors that he felt unworthy to die the same way that Jesus Christ had died.

James the Just

James the Just, the leader of the Church in Jerusalem and brother of Jesus, is said to have been thrown down more than a hundred feet from the southeast pinnacle of the Temple when he refused to deny his faith in Christ. He survived the fall and so was clubbed to death.

James the Greater

James, a son of Zebedee, was beheaded at Jerusalem, according to the Bible record.

"Now about that time Herod the king put forth his hands to afflict certain of the church.

2 And he killed James the brother of John with the sword" Acts 12: 1–2 ASV.

Tradition says that the Roman soldier who guarded James watched amazed as James defended his faith at his trial. Later, the officer walked beside James to the place of execution. Overcome by conviction, he declared his new faith to the judge and knelt beside James to accept beheading as a Christian.

Bartholomew

Bartholomew, also known as Nathanael, became a missionary in present day Turkey. He was whipped to death for his preaching in Armenia.

Thomas

Thomas was speared to death on one of his missionary trips to India.

Jude

Jude was killed with arrows after refusing to deny his faith in Christ.

Matthias

Matthias, the apostle chosen to replace the traitor Judas Iscariot, was stoned and beheaded.

Barnabas

Barnabas, one of the group of seventy disciples, was stoned to death at Salonica.

Paul

Paul was tortured and then beheaded by Emperor Nero at Rome in A.D. 67.

Prophecy

Overview

God is the author of prophecy.
Is. 44: 7; 45: 21.
"21 Declare and present your case;
let them take counsel together! Who
told this long ago? Who declared it
of old? Was it not I, the Lord? And
there is no other god besides me, a
righteous God and a Savior; there is
none besides me" Isaiah 45: 21 ESV.

Foretelling and forth-telling

Biblical prophecy is not confined to
foretelling future events, Gen. 49: 1;
Num. 24: 14, as it includes a divine
message to the contemporary
situation.

Jacob tells his sons, in an example
of predictive prophecy, what is going
to happen to each of them and to
their whole family: "Then Jacob called
his sons and said, 'Gather yourselves
together, that I may tell you what
shall happen to you in days to come'"
Genesis 49: 1 ESV.

PROPHETS AND DISHONESTY
But the prophet was being no less
prophetic when he spoke out against
the dishonest business practices and
immoral ways of his present day
hearers:
"'So I will send a fire upon Judah,
and it shall devour the strongholds of
Jerusalem.'
6 Thus says the Lord:
'For three transgressions of Israel,
and for four, I will not revoke the
punishment, because they sell the
righteous for silver, and the needy for a
pair of sandals –
7 those who trample the head of the
poor into the dust of the earth and turn
aside the way of the afflicted; a man
and his father go in to the same girl, so
that my holy name is profane'"
Amos 2: 5–7 ESV

Features of true prophecy

GOD GIVES PROPHECY, THROUGH
CHRIST
Rev. 1: 1.

PROPHECY IS A GIFT FROM CHRIST
Eph. 4: 11; Rev. 11: 3.

A GIFT OF THE HOLY SPIRIT
1 Cor. 12: 10.

Prophecy never came by the will of
man. 2 Pet. 1: 21.

PROPHECY WAS GIVEN FROM THE
BEGINNING
Luke 1: 70.

PROPHECY CAN BE RELIED ON
2 Pet. 1: 19.

PEOPLE WHO SPOKE PROPHECIES WERE:
Raised up by God. Amos 2: 11.
Ordained by God. 1 Sam. 3: 20; Jer. 1: 5.
Sent by God. 2 Chr. 36: 15; Jer. 7: 25.
Sent by Christ. Matt. 23: 34.
Filled with the Holy Spirit. Luke 1: 67.
Moved by the Holy Spirit. 2 Pet. 1: 21.
Spoke by the Holy Spirit. Acts 1: 16;
    11: 28; 28: 25.
Spoke in the name of the Lord.
    2 Chr. 33: 18; James 5: 10.
Spoke with authority. 1 Kgs. 17: 1.

Facts about prophecy

GOD FULFILS PROPHECIES
Is. 44: 26; Acts 3: 18.

CHRIST THE GREAT SUBJECT OF
Acts 3: 22–24; 10: 43; 1 Pet. 1: 10,11.

FULFILLED RESPECTING CHRIST
Luke 24: 44.

Gift of prophecy was promised.
Joel 2: 28; Acts 2: 16,17.

IS FOR THE BENEFIT FUTURE
GENERATIONS
1 Pet. 1: 12.

IS A LIGHT IN DARK PLACE
2 Pet. 1: 19.

SHOULD NOT BE INTERPRETED
ACCORDING TO ONE'S OWN PERSONAL
INTERPRETATION
"knowing this first of all, that no
prophecy of Scripture comes from
someone's own interpretation" 2 Peter
1: 20 ESV.

Correct attitudes toward prophecy

Despise not. 1 Thess. 5: 20.
Pay attention to. 2 Pet. 1: 19.
Receive in faith. 2 Chr. 20: 20.
    "And they rose early in the morning
and went out into the wilderness
of Tekoa. And when they went out,
Jehoshaphat stood and said, "Hear me,
Judah and inhabitants of Jerusalem!
Believe in the Lord your God, and
you will be established; believe his
prophets, and you will succeed.'"
                    2 Chronicles 20: 20 ESV

Benefits of prophecy

BLESSEDNESS OF READING, HEARING,
AND KEEPING
Rev. 1: 3; 22: 7.

PEOPLE HAVE PRETENDED TO HAVE
THE GIFT OF PROPHECY
Jer. 14: 14; 23: 13,14; Ezek. 13: 2,3.

Prophecy and punishments

PUNISHMENT FOR:
Not following prophecies. Neh. 9: 30.
Adding to, or taking from.
    Rev. 22: 18,19.
Pretending to the gift of. Deut. 18: 20;
    Jer. 14: 15; 23: 15.

True and false prophecy

The gift of prophecy was sometimes
given to ungodly people:
Num. 24: 2–9; 1 Sam. 19: 20,23;
Matt. 7: 22; John 11: 49–51; 1 Cor. 13: 2.

How to test the genuineness of prophecy

"If a prophet or a dreamer of dreams
arises among you and gives you a sign
or a wonder, and the sign or wonder
that he tells you comes to pass, and
if he says, 'Let us go after other gods,'
which you have not known, 'and let us
serve them,' you shall not listen to the
words of that prophet or that dreamer
of dreams. For the Lord your God is
testing you, to know whether you
love the Lord your God with all your
heart and with all your soul . . . when
a prophet speaks in the name of the
Lord, if the word does not come to pass
or come true, that is a word that the
Lord has not spoken;"
                    Deuteronomy 13: 1–3, 22 ESV

Prophets (1)

Divine origin of prophetic messages

God spoke through the Old Testament prophets

"I spoke to the prophets – often I spoke in visions. And so, I will send my prophets with messages of doom" Hosea 12: 10 CEV.

"Long ago in many ways and at many times God's prophets spoke his message to our ancestors" Hebrews 1: 1 CEV.

Names given to prophets

THE MESSENGERS OF GOD
2 Chr. 36: 15; Is. 44: 26.

THE SERVANTS OF GOD
Jer. 35: 15.

THE WATCHMEN OF ISRAEL
Ezek. 3: 17.

MEN OF GOD
1 Sam. 9: 6.

PROPHETS OF GOD
Ezra 5: 2.

HOLY PROPHETS
Luke 1: 70; Rev. 18: 20; 22: 6.

HOLY MEN OF GOD
2 Pet. 1: 21.

SEERS
1 Sam. 9: 9.

God communicated to the prophets:

His secret things. Amos 3: 7.

At different times and in different ways. Heb. 1: 1.

By an audible voice. Num. 12: 8; 1 Sam. 3: 4–14.

By angels. Dan. 8: 15–26; Rev. 22: 8,9.

By dreams and visions. Num. 12: 6; Joel 2: 28.

How the prophets spoke

The prophets were under the direct influence of the Holy Spirit when they prophesied. Luke 1: 67; 2 Pet. 1: 21.

The prophets spoke in the name of the Lord. 2 Chr. 33: 18; Ezek. 3: 11; James 5: 10.

Often in parables and riddles. 2 Sam. 12: 1–6; Is. 5: 1–7; Ezek. 17: 2–10.

Often they acted out parables or made signs to the people. Is. 20: 2–4; Jer. 19: 1,10,11; 27: 2,3; 43: 9; 51: 63; Hos. 1: 2–9; Acts 21: 11.

Ezekiel and his "signs"

Ezekiel used more signs than any other Old Testament prophet. Some of them seem quite strange, but they were effective in arresting people's attention to some divine message the prophet was passing on to them. Ezek. 4: 1–13; 5: 1–4; 7: 23; 12: 3–7; 21: 6,7; 24: 1–24.

Infrequent prophecies

The prophets explained why God's people were frequently left without any divine communication from the prophets. It was because of sins of the people. 1 Sam. 28: 6; Lam. 2: 9; Ezek. 7: 26.

"Samuel served the Lord by helping Eli the priest, who was by that time almost blind. In those days, the Lord hardly ever spoke directly to people, and he did not appear to them in dreams very often" 1 Samuel 3: 1–2 CEV.

"I, the Lord, also promise you a terrible shortage, but not of food and water. You will hunger and thirst to hear my message.

12 You will search everywhere – from north to south, from east to west. You will go all over the earth, seeking a message from me, the Lord. But you won't find one."

Amos 8: 11,12 CEV

Different prophets were given different tasks, but all were required

- To be bold and undaunted. Ezek. 2: 6; 3: 8,9.
- To be vigilant and faithful. Ezek. 3: 17–21.
- To receive with attention all God's communications. Ezek. 3: 10.
- Not to speak anything but what they received from God. Deut. 18: 20.
- To declare everything that the Lord commanded. Jer. 26: 2.

Ways in which the prophecies were communicated

- Sometimes the prophets were physically greatly upset as they received their divine messages and passed on their God-given predictions. Jer. 23: 9; Ezek. 3: 14,15; Dan. 7: 28; 10: 8; Hab. 3: 2,16.
- Sometimes the prophets spoke their predictions in verse Deut. 32: 44; Is. 5: 1.

"Moses spoke the words of the song so that all the Israelites could hear, and Joshua helped him" Deuteronomy 32: 44 CEV.

"I will sing a song about my friend's vineyard that was on the side of a fertile hill.

2 My friend dug the ground, removed the stones, and planted the best vines. He built a watchtower and dug a pit in rocky ground for pressing the grapes. He hoped they would be sweet, but bitter grapes were all it produced.

3 Listen, people of Jerusalem and of Judah! You be the judge of me and my vineyard.

4 What more could I have done for my vineyard? I hoped for sweet grapes, but bitter grapes were all that grew.

5 Now I will let you know what I am going to do. I will cut down the hedge and tear down the wall. My vineyard will be trampled and left in ruins.

6 It will turn into a desert, neither pruned nor hoed; it will be covered with thorns and briars. I will command the clouds not to send rain.

7 I am the Lord All-Powerful! Israel is the vineyard, and Judah is the garden I tended with care. I had hoped for honesty and for justice, but dishonesty and cries for mercy were all I found."

Isaiah 5: 1–7 CEV

Prophets (2)

Ways in which the prophecies were communicated, continued

• Prophecies often had a musical accompaniment

"Next, go to Gibeah, where the Philistines have an army camp. As you're going into the town, you'll meet a group of prophets coming down from the place of worship. They'll be going along prophesying while others are walking in front of them, playing small harps, small drums, and flutes"
1 Samuel 10: 5 CEV.

"Then Elisha said, 'Send for someone who can play the harp.'

The harpist began playing, and the Lord gave Elisha this message for Joram. The Lord says that this dry riverbed will be filled with water. You won't feel any wind or see any rain, but there will be plenty of water for you and your animals. That simple thing isn't all the Lord is going to do. He will also help you defeat Moab's army. You will capture all their walled cities and important towns. You will chop down every good tree and stop up every spring of water, then ruin their fertile fields by covering them with rocks."
2 Kings 3: 15–19 CEV

Prophecies supplied evidence about God's foreknowledge

Is. 43: 9.

Prophecies were certain of fulfillment

Ezek. 12: 22–25; Ezek. 12: 28; Hab. 2: 3; Matt. 5: 18; Matt. 24: 35; Acts 13: 27; Acts 13: 29.

Warnings of the prophets

OF APOSTASY
1 John 2: 18; Jude 1: 17–18.

OF FALSE TEACHERS
2 Pet. 2: 3.

OF TRIBULATIONS OF THE RIGHTEOUS
Rev. 2: 10.

Ordinary and extraordinary prophets

ORDINARY
Numerous in Israel. 1 Sam. 10: 5;
    1 Kgs. 18: 4.
Trained up and instructed in schools.
    2 Kgs. 2: 3,5; 1 Sam. 19: 20.
The sacred bards of the Jews.
    Ex. 15: 20,21; 1 Sam. 10: 5,10;
    1 Chr. 25: 1.
Great patience of, under suffering
    James 5: 10.

EXTRAORDINARY
Specially raised up in times of
    emergency. 1 Sam. 3: 19–21; Is. 6: 8,9;
    Jer. 1: 5.
Often given some miraculous power.
    Ex. 4: 1–4; 1 Kgs. 17: 23; 2 Kgs. 5: 3–8.

Facts about prophets

Often the prophets were married men.
    2 Kgs. 4: 1; Ezek. 24: 18.
Wore coarse hair-cloth garments.
    2 Kgs. 1: 8; Zech. 13: 4; Matt. 3: 4;
    Rev. 11: 3.
Often led a nomadic life. 1 Kgs. 18: 10–
    12; 19: 3,8,15; 2 Kgs. 4: 10.
Often had a simple lifestyle. Matt. 3: 4.
They were often the historians of
    the Jewish nation. 1 Chr. 29: 29;
    2 Chr. 9: 29.

They often had the gift of being
interpreters of dreams. Dan. 1: 17.
Were consulted in all difficulties.
1 Sam. 9: 6; 28: 15; 1 Kgs. 14: 2–4; 22: 7.
Presented with gifts by those who
consulted them. 1 Sam. 9: 7,8;
1 Kgs. 14: 3.
Sometimes thought it right to reject
presents. 2 Kgs. 5: 15,16.

Varied ministry of the prophets

PROPHETS WERE SENT TO:
*Reprove the wicked and exhort them to
repent*
2 Kgs. 17: 13; 2 Chr. 24: 19; Jer. 25: 4,5.

Denounce the wickedness of kings
1 Sam. 15: 10,16–19; 2 Sam. 12: 7–12;
1 Kgs. 18: 18; 21: 17–22.

*Exhort people to be faithful in God's
service*
2 Chr. 15: 1,2,7.

Predict the coming of Christ
Luke 24: 44; John 1: 45; Acts 3: 24;
10: 43.

Predict the downfall of nations
Is. 15: 1; 17: 1; Jer. 47: 1–51: 64.

*Help the Jews in their great national
enterprises*
Ezra 5: 2.

Emotions of the prophets

The prophets themselves were often
deeply moved by the theme of their
own prophecies. Is. 16: 9–11; Jer. 9: 1–7.

Facts about prophetic predictions

Frequently proclaimed at the gate of
the Lord's house. Jer. 7: 2.

Proclaimed in public in the cities and
streets. Jer. 11: 6.
Written on tablets and hung up in a
public place. Hab. 2: 2.
Written on scrolls and read to the
people. Is. 8: 1; Jer. 36: 2.
Were all fulfilled. 2 Kgs. 10: 10;
Is. 44: 26; Acts 3: 18; Rev. 10: 7.
One generally attached to the
king's household. 2 Sam. 24: 11;
2 Chr. 29: 25; 35: 15.
Many prophecies were written down.
2 Chr. 21: 12; Jer. 36: 2.
Written in books. Jer. 45: 1; Jer. 51: 60
Writings of the prophets were read
in the synagogues every Sabbath
Luke 4: 17; Acts 13: 15.
Sometimes prophecies were written
down by an amanuensis. Jer. 45: 1

Bible prophets

We tend to restrict our thinking about
the prophets of the Bible to the writers
of the Old Testament prophetic books.
However, the term "prophet" includes
many other people. Some people, such
as Noah and Aaron, we may not have
thought of as being prophets at all.
Other prophets, such as Zadok, Iddo,
and Oded, we may never have heard of.
Enoch. Gen. 5: 21–24; Jude 1: 14.
Noah. Gen. 9: 25–27.
Jacob. Gen. 49: 1.
Aaron. Ex. 7: 1.
Moses. Deut. 18: 18.
Miriam. Ex. 15: 20.
Deborah. Judg. 4: 4.
Prophet set to Israel. Judg. 6: 8.
Prophet sent to Eli. 1 Sam. 2: 27.
Samuel. 1 Sam. 3: 20.
David. Ps. 16: 8–11; Acts 2: 25,30.
Nathan. 2 Sam. 7: 2; 12: 1; 1 Kgs. 1: 10.

Prophets (3)

Bible prophets, continued

Zadok. 2 Sam. 15: 27.

Gad. 2 Sam. 24: 11; 1 Chr. 29: 29.

Ahijah. 1 Kgs. 11: 29; 12: 15; 2 Chr. 9: 29.

Prophet of Judah. 1 Kgs. 13: 1.

Iddo. 2 Chr. 9: 29; 12: 15.

Shemaiah. 1 Kgs. 12: 22; 2 Chr. 12: 7,15.

Azariah the son of Oded. 2 Chr. 15: 2,8.

Hanani. 2 Chr. 16: 7.

Jehu the son of Hanani. 1 Kgs. 16: 1,7,12.

Elijah. 1 Kgs. 17: 1.

Elisha. 1 Kgs. 19: 16.

Micaiah the son of Imlah. 1 Kgs. 22: 7,8.

Jonah. 2 Kgs. 14: 25; John 1: 1;
Matt. 12: 39.

Isaiah. 2 Kgs. 19: 2; 2 Chr. 26: 22; Is. 1: 1.

Hosea. Hos. 1: 1.

Amos. Amos 1: 1; 7: 14,15.

Micah. Mic. 1: 1.

Oded. 2 Chr. 28: 9.

Nahum. Nah. 1: 1.

Joel. Joel 1: 1; Acts 2: 16.

Zephaniah. Zeph. 1: 1.

Huldah. 2 Kgs. 22: 14.

Jeduthun. 2 Chr. 35: 15.

Jeremiah. 2 Chr. 36: 12,21; Jer. 1: 1,2.

Habakkuk. Hab. 1: 1.

Obadiah. Obad. 1: 1.

Ezekiel. Ezek. 1: 3.

Daniel. Dan. 12: 11; Matt. 24: 15.

Haggai. Ezra 5: 1; 6: 14; Hag. 1: 1.

Zechariah son of Iddo. Ezra 5: 1;
Zech. 1: 1.

Malachi. Mal. 1: 1.

Zacharias the father of John. Luke 1: 67.

Anna. Luke 2: 36.

Agabus. Acts 11: 28; 21: 10.

Daughters of Philip. Acts 21: 9.

Paul. 1 Tim. 4: 1.

Peter. 2 Pet. 2: 1,2.

John. Rev. 1: 1.

The Jews and the prophets

Required to hear and believe them.
De 18: 15; 2 Chr. 20: 20.

Often tried to make them give the
message they wanted to hear
1 Kgs. 22: 13; Is. 30: 10; Amos 2: 12.

Persecuted them. 2 Chr. 36: 16;
Matt. 5: 12.

Often imprisoned them. 1 Kgs. 22: 27;
Jer. 32: 2; 37: 15,16.

Sometimes killed them. 1 Kgs. 18: 13;
19: 10; Matt. 23: 34–37.

More facts about the prophets

Perhaps the most typical characteristic
of the faithful prophets was their
dynamic faith in God. Because of this
they were full of physical courage and
moral integrity.

"What else can I say? There isn't
enough time to tell about Gideon,
Barak, Samson, Jephthah, David,
Samuel, and the prophets. Their faith
helped them conquer kingdoms, and
because they did right, God made
promises to them. They closed the
jaws of lions and put out raging fires
and escaped from the swords of their
enemies. Although they were weak,
they were given the strength and power
to chase foreign armies away.

Some women received their loved
ones back from death. Many of these
people were tortured, but they refused
to be released. They were sure that
they would get a better reward when
the dead are raised to life. Others were

made fun of and beaten with whips, and some were chained in jail. Still others were stoned to death or sawed in two or killed with swords. Some had nothing but sheep skins or goat skins to wear. They were poor, mistreated, and tortured. The world did not deserve these good people, who had to wander in deserts and on mountains and had to live in caves and holes in the ground. All of them pleased God because of their faith! But still they died without being given what had been promised. This was because God had something better in store for us. And he did not want them to reach the goal of their faith without us.

Hebrews 11: 32–40 CEV

Prophets

SCHOOLS OF
1 Kgs. 20: 35; 2 Kgs. 2: 3–15; 2 Kgs. 4: 1; 2 Kgs. 4: 38; 2 Kgs. 9: 1.

KEPT THE CHRONICLES
1 Chr. 29: 29; 2 Chr. 9: 29; 2 Chr. 12: 15.

COUNSELORS TO KINGS
Is. 37: 2,3.

NOT HONORED IN THEIR OWN COUNTRY
Matt. 13: 57; Luke 4: 24–27; John 4: 44.

PERSECUTIONS OF
2 Chr. 36: 16; Amos 2: 12

MARTYRS
Jer. 2: 30; Matt. 23: 37; Mark 12: 5; Luke 13: 34; 1 Thess. 2: 15; Heb. 11: 37; Rev. 16: 6.

Warnings

The New Testament is full of warnings against being taken in by false prophets.

General references to false Old Testament prophets

1 Kgs. 13: 18; Neh. 6: 12; Jer. 23: 25–27; Jer. 23: 30–32; Lam. 2: 14.

ADMONITIONS TO FALSE PROPHETS
Deut. 13: 1–3.

DENUNCIATIONS AGAINST
Deut. 18: 20; Jer. 14: 15.

PUNISHMENT OF
Jer. 14: 13–16; Jer. 20: 6; Jer. 28: 16,17; Jer. 29: 32; Zech. 13: 3

INSTANCES OF:
Noadiah
Neh. 6: 14.

Four hundred in Samaria
1 Kgs. 22: 6–12; 2 Chr. 18: 5.

Inspiration of the prophets

The prophets were messengers. Their visions and prophecies did not originate in their own fertile imaginations. They just passed on the divine communication they had received. They were inspired by God. They said, "Thus saith the Lord." The divine inspiration is the basic fact that underpins everything else about the prophets in the Bible.

> **Quote Unquote**
>
> "The false and the genuine prophet will be known by their ways. If a prophet teaches the truth but does not practice what he teaches, he is a false prophet."
> *Didache*

Prophets (4)

Inspired prophets

Elijah

1 Kgs. 17: 8; 1 Kgs. 21: 17; 1 Kgs. 21: 28.

Isaiah

Is. 2: 1; Is. 8: 5; Is. 13: 1; Is. 14: 28; Is. 38: 4

Jeremiah

Jer. 1: 4; Jer. 7: 1; Jer. 11: 1; Jer. 13: 8;
Jer. 16: 1; Jer. 18: 1; Jer. 25: 1–2; Jer. 26: 1;
Jer. 27: 1; Jer. 29: 30; Jer. 30: 1; Jer. 30: 4;
Jer. 32: 1; Jer. 32: 6; Jer. 32: 26; Jer. 33: 1;
Jer. 33: 19; Jer. 33: 23; Jer. 34: 12; Jer. 35: 12;
Jer. 36: 1; Jer. 37: 6; Jer. 40: 1; Jer. 43: 8;
Jer. 44: 1; Jer. 46: 1; Jer. 49: 34; Jer. 50: 1.

Ezekiel

Ezek. 3: 16; Ezek. 6: 1; Ezek. 7: 1;
Ezek. 11: 14; Ezek. 12: 1; Ezek. 12: 8;
Ezek. 12: 17; Ezek. 12: 21; Ezek. 13: 1;
Ezek. 14: 12; Ezek. 15: 1; Ezek. 16: 1;
Ezek. 17: 1; Ezek. 17: 11; Ezek. 18: 1;
Ezek. 20: 45; Ezek. 21: 1; Ezek. 21: 8;
Ezek. 21: 18; Ezek. 22: 1; Ezek. 22: 17;
Ezek. 22: 23; Ezek. 23: 1; Ezek. 24: 1;
Ezek. 24: 15; Ezek. 24: 20; Ezek. 25: 1;
Ezek. 26: 1; Ezek. 27: 1; Ezek. 28: 1;
Ezek. 28: 11; Ezek. 28: 20; Ezek. 29: 1;
Ezek. 29: 17; Ezek. 30: 1; Ezek. 30: 20;
Ezek. 31: 1; Ezek. 32: 1; Ezek. 32: 17;
Ezek. 33: 1; Ezek. 33: 23; Ezek. 34: 1;
Ezek. 35: 1; Ezek. 36: 16; Ezek. 37: 15;
Ezek. 38: 1.

Amos

Amos 7: 14,15.

Jonah

Jonah 3: 1.

Haggai

Hag. 2: 1; Hag. 2: 10; Hag. 2: 20.

Zechariah

Zech. 1: 7; Zech. 4: 8; Zech. 6: 9;
Zech. 7: 1; Zech. 7: 4; Zech. 7: 8;
Zech. 8: 1; Zech. 8: 18.

Inspired by angels

Zech. 1: 9; Zech. 1: 13–14; Zech. 1: 19;
Acts 7: 53; Gal. 3: 19; Heb. 2: 2.

The most important biblical prophecies concerned Jesus. But there were many other types of prophecy in addition to the messianic prophecies

Predictive prophecies that were fulfilled:

The birth and zeal of Josiah. 1 Kgs. 13: 2;
   2 Kgs. 23: 1–20.
Death of the prophet of Judah.
   1 Kgs. 13: 21,22; 1 Kgs. 13: 24–30.
Extinction of Jeroboam's house.
   1 Kgs. 14: 5–17.
Extinction of Baasha's house.
   1 Kgs. 16: 2,3; 1 Kgs. 16: 9–13.
Concerning the rebuilding of Jericho
   Josh. 6: 26; 1 Kgs. 16: 34.
The drought, foretold by Elijah.
   1 Kgs. 17: 14.
Destruction of Benhadad's army.
   1 Kgs. 20: 13–30.
The death of a man who refused to
   smite a prophet. 1 Kgs. 20: 35,36.
The death of Ahab. 1 Kgs. 20: 42;
   1 Kgs. 21: 18–24; 1 Kgs. 22: 31–38.
The death of Ahaziah. 2 Kgs. 1: 3–17.
Elijah's translation. 2 Kgs. 2: 3–11.
Cannibalism among the children

of Israel. Lev. 26: 29; Deut. 28: 53;
2 Kgs. 6: 28,29; Jer. 19: 9; Lam. 4: 10.
The death of the Samaritan lord.
2 Kgs. 7: 2; 2 Kgs. 7: 19,20.
The end of the famine in Samaria.
2 Kgs. 7: 1–18.
Jezebel's tragic death. 1 Kgs. 21: 23;
2 Kgs. 9: 10; 2 Kgs. 9: 33–37.
The smiting of Syria by Joash.
2 Kgs. 13: 16–25.
Conquests of Jeroboam. 2 Kgs. 14: 25–28.
Four generations of Jehu to sit upon
the throne of Israel. 2 Kgs. 10: 30;
2 Kgs. 15: 12.
Destruction of Sennacherib's army, and
his death. 2 Kgs. 19: 6,7; 2 Kgs. 19: 20–37.
The captivity of Judah. 2 Kgs. 20: 17,18;
2 Kgs. 24: 10–16.
About John the Baptist. Matt. 3: 3.
Rachel weeping for her children.
Jer. 31: 15; Matt. 2: 17,18.
Deliverance of Jeremiah. Jer. 39: 15–18.
Invasion of Judah by the Chaldeans.
Hab. 1: 6–11.
(Fulfilled) 2 Kgs. 25; 2 Chr. 36: 17–21.
The coming of the Holy Spirit. Joel
2: 28,29.
(Fulfilled) Acts 2: 16–21.

PROPHECY ABOUT THE CAPTIVITY OF
THE JEWS

Jer. 25: 11–12; Jer. 29: 10; Jer. 29: 14;
Jer. 32: 3–5; Dan. 9: 2; 2 Kgs. 25: 1–8;
Ezra 1.

"Zedekiah had ordered me to be
held there because I told everyone that
the Lord had said: I am the Lord, and I
am about to let the king of Babylonia
conquer Jerusalem. King Zedekiah
will be captured and taken to King

Nebuchadnezzar, who will speak with
him face to face. Then Zedekiah will be
led away to Babylonia, where he will
stay until I am finished with him. So,
if you people of Judah fight against the
Babylonians, you will lose. I, the Lord,
have spoken."

Jer. 32: 3–5 CEV

Prophecy about the destruction of the
ship in which Paul sailed. Acts 27: 10;
Acts 27: 18–44.

Prophetesses

There are prophetesses to be found in
both the Old Testament and the New
Testament.

GENERAL REFERENCES
Ezek. 13: 17; Joel 2: 28,29.

LIST OF PROPHETESSES
Miriam. Ex. 15: 20.
Deborah. Judg. 4: 4.
Huldah. 2 Kgs. 22: 14.
Noadiah. Neh. 6: 14.
Isaiah's wife. Is. 8: 3.
Elizabeth. Luke 1: 41–45.
Anna. Luke 2: 36–38.
The four daughters of Philip. Acts 21: 9.
The symbol of evil, Jezebel. Rev. 2: 20.

Quote Unquote

"God gave the prophecies, not
to gratify men's curiosity by
enabling them to foreknow
things, but that after they were
fulfilled they might be interpreted
by the event, and His own
providence, not the interpreter's,
be thereby manifested to the
world."

Isaac Newton

Poetry

The poetical books

The Bible books classed as poetical are
• Job,
• Psalms,
• Proverbs,
• Ecclesiastes,
• Song of Solomon, and
• Lamentations.

Meaning of "poetical"

The term "poetical" does not imply anything fanciful or unreal. When applied to Bible books the term "poetical" relates to the construction and form of that particular type of writing.

Three categories of poetry

Three kinds of poetry are found in the Hebrew Bible:

1 DRAMATIC POETRY

The Book of Job and the Song of Solomon have dramatic poetry.

2 LYRICAL POETRY

The Psalms have lyrical poetry.

3 DIDACTIC POETRY

The book of Ecclesiastes has didactic poetry.

Hebrew poetry

Hebrew poetry is quite different from much of the traditional poetry we are familiar with.

It has neither meter nor rhyme.

Hebrew rhythm is not achieved by matching similar sounding words with each other, as in rhymed verse; nor by rhythmic accent as in blank verse, but by repetition of ideas. This is called parallelism.

Parallelism is characterized by the links between sentences or clauses and so is sometimes called "thought-rhyme."

Parallelism

There are various kinds of parallelism in the poetry of the Bible.
1 Synonymous parallelism
2 Antithetic parallelism
3 Compound parallelism
4 Emblemic parallelism

1 SYNONYMOUS PARALLELISM

This is where:
The same idea is repeated in the same words.
"The Lord also will be a refuge for the oppressed,
A refuge in times of trouble" Psalms 9: 9.
"The floods have lifted up, O Lord, the floods have lifted up their voice; the floods lift up their waves" Psalm 93: 3.
"Thou art snared with the words of thy mouth, thou art taken with the words of thy mouth" Proverbs 6: 2.
The same idea is repeated in different words.
"The sea saw it, and fled: Jordan was driven back. The mountains skipped like rams, and the little hills like lambs" Psalm 114: 3,4. The same

idea is sometimes expressed in three successive clauses.

"Let them be desolate for a reward of their shame that say unto me, Aha, aha.

Let all those that seek thee rejoice and be glad in thee:

let such as love thy salvation say continually, The Lord be magnified" Psalm 40: 15,16.

2 ANTITHETIC PARALLELISM

This is where the poet expresses an idea in one line and in the next line the opposite idea.

"A wise son maketh a glad father: but a foolish man despiseth his mother" Proverbs 15: 20.

The next example of antithetic poetry is achieved as the primary and secondary thoughts are in contrast:

"For the Lord knoweth the way of the righteous:

But the way of the ungodly shall perish" Psalms 1: 6.

3 COMPOUND PARALLELISM

This parallelism is also called synthetic parallelism as the thought in the sentence is developed or enriched by the parallel thought.

This is where each clause or sentence contains an extra idea which emphasizes the main idea.

"And thou shalt be secure, because there is hope;

Yea, thou shalt dig about thee, and thou shalt take thy rest in safety" Job 11: 18.

See also Job 3: 3–9.

4 EMBLEMIC PARALLELISM

This is where an idea is repeated in a figurative or symbolic way.

"As coals are to burning coals, and wood to fire; so is a contentious man to kindle strife" Proverbs 26: 21.

Other types of Hebrew poetry

1 ACROSTIC POETRY

This alphabetical arrangement of the first words in each line of poetry links the sentences to each other.

The following are so arranged that in Hebrew the initial words of each verse begin with succeeding letters of the alphabet.

Prov. 31: 10–31; Lam. 1,2,3,4; Ps. 25,34,37,145.

Every eighth verse of Psalm 119 has a successive letter of the alphabet.

2 REFRAINS

This is where a verse is repeated at intervals.

In Psalm 42 most of verse 5 is repeated at verse 11.,

In Psalm 107 verse 8, "Oh that men would praise the Lord for his goodness, and for his wonderful works to the children of men!" is repeated in 15, 21, and 31.

3 SONGS

There are a number of very beautiful songs found in the Old Testament:
- the song of Moses (Ex. 15),
- the song of Deborah (Judg. 5),
- the song of Hannah (1 Sam. 2),
- the song of Hezekiah (Is. 38: 9–20),
- the song of Habakkuk (Hab. 3), and
- David's "song of the bow" (2 Sam. 1: 19–27).

Idioms and figures of speech (1)

Definition

An idiom is a saying or figure of speech which often cannot be understood by the individual words that make it up.

Avoiding false interpretations

It is useful to know that the pages of the Bible are crammed full of different figures of speech. If one is ignorant about them it is all too easy to make a false interpretation of a particular verse.

A figure of speech relates to the form in which the words are used. It refers to words or phrases in which words are not used in the normal way, or sense. Such figures of speech are a device which is used to attract our attention to what is being said.

Figures of speech deliberately depart from the normal laws of language, in order to emphasize what is said.

The danger of taking everything in a literal way

Figures of speech should not be taken in a literal way, any more than what is literal should be taken as a figure of speech.

DR. BULLINGER
The greatest classical work on figures of speech in the Bible was published at the end of the 19th century by Dr. Bullinger. He identified two hundred and seventeen figures of speech used in the Bible. The following list draws on his work.

Each example of a figure of speech is given a descriptive name. This is followed by a Bible reference illustrating the figure of speech. The entry closes with a few words of explanation about the figure of speech.

Apparent refusal (Matt. 15: 22–26). So named because it is an apparent or assumed refusal. Initially, Jesus did not reply to the cries of the woman of Canaan. The reason for this apparent refusal to help becomes clear by the end of the incident.

Acrostic (Ps. 119)
Repetition of the same successive letters at the beginnings of words or clauses.

Dark Saying (Gen. 49: 10)
A truth expressed in obscure language.

Riddle (Judges 14: 14)

Explaining a reason (Rom. 1: 16). This states the reason for what is said or done.

Affirmation (Phil. 1: 18)
Emphasizing words to affirm what no one has disputed.

Indignation (Gen. 3: 13; Acts 13: 10)
An expression of feeling by way of indignation.

Allegory; or, continuous comparison

This may be achieved by use of a metaphor (Gen. 49: 9; Gal. 4: 22, 24), or by implication (Matt. 7: 3–5). This figure of speech teaches a truth about one thing by substituting another for it, even though it is not like it.

Refrain (Ps. 136)
The repetition of the same phrase at the end of successive paragraphs.

Double meaning (Ezek. 12: 13)
A word or phrase open to two interpretations, both of which are true.

Am'-phi-di-or-tho'-sis; or, Double Correction (1 Cor. 11: 22)
A correction setting right both hearer and speaker.

Gradual ascent (Ps. 18: 37,38)
An increase of emphasis or sense in successive sentences.

Regression (Eph. 3: 14)
A return to the original subject after a digression.

Common cause (1 Cor. 4: 21)
An appeal to others as having interests in common.

Non-sequence (Gen. 35: 3. Mark 11: 32)
A breaking off the sequence of thought.

Similar sentence endings and beginnings (Gen. 1: 1,2. Ps. 121: 1,2)
The word or words concluding one sentence are repeated at the beginning of another.

Recalling (Rom. 9: 3)
An expression which calls something to mind.

Similar sentence beginnings (Deut. 28: 3–6)
The repetition of the same word at the beginning of successive sentences.

Abating (2 Kings 5: 1)
The addition of a concluding sentence which diminishes the effect of what has been said.

Counter question (Matt. 21: 23–25)
The answering of one question by asking another.

Anthropomorphism (Gen. 1: 2; 8: 21; Ps. 74: 11; Jer. 2: 13; Hos. 11: 10)
Ascribing human characteristics to God.

Dialogue (1 Cor. 7: 16)
Addressing the reader as if he/she were actually present.

Anti-personification (2 Sam. 16: 9)
People represented as inanimate things.

Retort (Matt. 15: 26,27)
Turning the words of the speaker against himself.

Contrast (Prov. 15: 17)
Setting one phrase in contrast with another.

Name change (Gen. 31: 21)
Changing a name.

Idioms and figures of speech (2)

A-po'-ria; or, Doubt (Luke 16: 3).
Expressing doubt.

Sudden Silence
It may be associated with:
1. Some great promise (Ex. 32: 32).
2. Anger (Gen. 3: 22).
3. Grief (Gen. 25: 22; Ps. 6: 3).
4. Inquiry (John 6: 62).

Apostrophe
When the speaker changes the person
he is addressing. This person may be:
1. God (Neh. 6: 9).
2. Men (2 Sam. 1: 24,25).
3. Animals (Joel 2: 22).
4. Inanimate things (Jer. 47: 6).

Association (Acts 17: 27)
When the speaker associates himself
with those whom he addresses, or of
whom he speaks.

Not using "ands" (Mark 7: 21–23.
Luke 14: 13).
Leaving out the usual conjunction is
omitted in order to arrive at the point
which is being emphasized.

Vain Repetition (1 Kings 18: 26)

Blessing (Gen. 1: 22, 28; Matt. 5: 3–11).

Gradual descent (Phil. 2: 6–8)
Used to emphasize humiliation or
sorrow.

Sudden exclamation (Ezek. 16: 23)
A parenthesis in the form of a sudden
exclamation.

Mocking (Ps. 2: 4)

Description of time (John 10: 22)
The teaching of something important
by mentioning the time when it
happened.

Gradation (2 Pet. 1: 5–7)
Repetition in successive sentences

Combined repetition (Ps. 118: 8,9)
The repetition of two different phrases,
one at the beginning, and the other at
the end of successive paragraphs.

Circular repetition (Ps. 80: 3,7,19)
The repetition of the same phrase at
regular intervals.

Encircling (Gen. 9: 3; Ps. 27: 14)
The repetition of the same word or
words at the beginning and end of a
sentence.

Adjuration (Deut. 4: 26)
An expression of deep feeling by means
of an oath.

Exclamation (Rom. 7: 24)

Irony
The expression of thought in a form
that naturally conveys its opposite.

1. Divine irony
Where the speaker is Divine (Gen.
3: 22). "Go and cry unto the gods which
ye have chosen; let them deliver you
in the time of your tribulation" Judges
10: 14.

2. Human irony
Where the speaker is a human being.
   "And Job answered and said, No
doubt but ye *are* the people, and
wisdom shall die with you" Job 12: 2.

Arrow prayer (Hos. 9: 14)
A short wish or prayer.

Candor (Luke 13: 32)
The speaker, without intending offense, speaks with total freedom and boldness.

Resumption (1 Cor. 10: 29; Phil. 1: 24)
The repetition of the same word after a break or parenthesis.

Litotes
A phrase that lessens one thing in order to exalt another.
  "Once you were not a people, but now you are the people of God; once you had not received mercy, but now you have received mercy" 1 Peter 2: 10 *NIV.*

Inversion (Gen. 10: 1–31; Is. 6: 10)
The repetition of the same word or words in an inverse order, without changing the sense.

Overlaid repetition
(Ps. 29: 3,4,7,8,9)
The repetition of the same phrase at irregular intervals.

Euphemism
Substituting a harsh or offensive term with a less offensive one.
  "After he had said this, he went on to tell him, 'Our friend Lazarus has fallen asleep; but I am going there to wake him up.' (Jesus was speaking of the death of Lazarus)" John 11: 11 *NIV.*

Judgment (John 12: 33)
A short sentence added at the end by way of an additional conclusion.

Lingering (John 21: 15–17)
Repetition added for the sake of emphasis.

Exclamation (Ps. 135: 21)
An exclamation at the conclusion of a sentence.

Epistrophe in argument (2 Cor. 11: 22)
The repetition of the same word or words at the end of successive sentences used in argument.

Like sentence-endings (Gen. 13: 6. Ps. 24: 10)
The repetition of the same word or words at the end of successive sentences.

Amplification (Ex. 3: 19)
Adding a concluding sentence for the sake of emphasis.

Qualification (Phil. 4: 10
A sentence added at the end to heal, soften, mitigate, or modify what has been before said.

Epithet (Gen. 21: 16; Luke 22: 41)
To name something by describing it.

Reprimand (Luke 24: 25)

Idioms and figures of speech (3)

Summarizing (Heb. 11: 32)

A running lightly over by way of summary.

Admission (Ecc. 11: 9)

Admission of wrong, in order to gain what is right.

Duplication (Gen. 22: 11; Ps. 77: 16)

The repetition of the same word in the same sense.

Interrogating (Gen. 13: 9; Ps. 35: 10)

To ask questions, but not for information, or for an answer.

Euphemism (Gen. 15: 15)

Where a pleasing expression is used for one that is unpleasant.

Example (Luke 17: 32)

Concluding a sentence by using an example.

Contempt (2 Sam. 6: 20).

Quotation

The citation of a well-known saying without quoting the author's name.

1. Where the sense originally intended is preserved, though the words may vary (Matt. 26: 31).

2. Where the original sense is modified in the quotation or reference (Matt. 12: 40).

3. Where the sense is quite different from that which was first intended (Matt. 2: 15).

4. Where the words are from the Hebrew of from the Septuagint (Luke 4: 18).

5. Where the words are varied by omission, addition, or transposition (1 Cor. 2: 9).

6. Where the words are changed by a reading, or an inference, or in number, person, mood, or tense (Matt. 4: 7).

7. Where two or more citations are amalgamated (Matt. 21: 13).

8. Where quotations are from books other than the Bible (Acts 17: 28).

Two for one (Gen. 2: 9; Eph. 6: 18)

Where two words are used, but only one thing is meant.

Three for one (Dan. 3: 7)

Where three words used, but only one thing is meant.

Interpretation (John 7: 39)

An explanation immediately following a statement.

Hyperbole

When more is said than is literally meant. Hyperbole is an idiom of overstatement. It is an exaggeration made to reinforce a point (Gen. 41: 47; Deut. 1: 28).

"And if thy right eye offend thee, pluck it out, and cast it from thee: for it is profitable for thee that one of thy members should perish, and not that thy whole body should be cast into hell" Matthew 5: 29.

Hendiadys

The combination of two or three things to express the same meaning.

"May the God of peace sanctify you through and through. May your whole spirit, soul and body be kept blameless at the coming of the Lord Jesus Christ" 1 Thessalonians 5: 23 NIV

Implication (Matt. 15: 13; 16: 6)

Word picture (Is. 5: 26–30)

Objects or actions represented by words.

Interjection (Ps. 42: 2)

Belittling (Gen. 18: 27. Num. 13: 33)

Belittling one thing in order to magnify another.

Transition (1 Cor. 12: 31)

Passing from one subject to another.

Double metonymy (Gen. 19: 8; Ecc. 12: 6; Hos. 14: 2)

Two metonymies, one contained in the other, but only one is expressed.

Changing over (Hos. 4: 18)

A different subject is substituted for the original subject.

Metaphor (Matt. 26: 26)

A declaration that one thing is (or represents) another. A metaphor, like a simile, is a comparison between two things without using words such as "like" or "as."

"Ye are the salt of the earth" Matthew 5: 13.

Counter-blame (1 Kings 18: 17,18)

Transferring of the blame from one's self to another.

Metonymy, or, change of noun

Here one name or noun is used instead of another.

"He is the one who will build a house for me, and I will establish his throne forever" 1 Chronicles 17: 12 NIV.

1. Of the Cause.
When the cause is substituted for the effect (Gen. 23: 8. Luke 16: 29).

2. Of the Effect.
When the effect is substituted for the cause producing it (Gen. 25: 23; Acts 1: 18).

3. Of the Subject.
When the subject is substituted for something linked to it (Gen. 41: 13; Deut. 28: 5).

4. Of the Adjunct.
When something linked to the subject is put for the subject itself (Gen. 28: 22; Job 32: 7).

Negation (Gal. 2: 5)

A denial of something that has not been affirmed.

Wishing (Ps. 55: 6)

Oxymoron; or, wise folly (1 Tim. 5: 6)

A wise saying that seems foolish.

Exultation (Zeph. 3: 14)

Calling others to rejoice over something.

Parable, extended simile (Luke 14: 16–24)

Idioms and figures of speech (4)

Neithers and nors (Ex. 20: 10; Rom. 8: 35,38,39)

The repetition of the disjunctives neither and nor, or, either and or.

Parallelism

The repetition of similar, synonymous, or opposite thoughts or words in parallel or successive lines.

1. Simple synonymous, or gradational. When the lines are parallel in thought, and in the use of synonymous words (Gen. 4: 23,24; Ps. 1: 1).

2. Simple antithetic, or opposite. When the words are contrasted in two or more lines, being opposed in sense one to the other (Prov. 10: 1).

3. Simple synthetic, or constructive. When the parallelism consists only in the similar form of construction (Ps. 19: 7–9).

4. Complex alternate. When the lines are placed alternately (Gen. 19: 25; Prov. 24: 19,20).

5. Complex repeated alternation. The repetition of the two parallel subjects in several lines (Is. 65: 21,22).

6. Complex extended alternation. Alternation extended so as to consist of three or more lines (Judg. 10: 17).

7. Complex introversion. When the parallel lines are so placed that the first corresponds with the last, the second with the last but one, etc. (Gen. 3: 19; 2 Chron, 32: 7,8).

Antithesis

A direct contrast.

"For the sinful nature desires what is contrary to the Spirit, and the Spirit what is contrary to the sinful nature" Galatians 5: 17 NIV.

Digression (Gen. 2: 8–15)

Insertion (Phil. 3: 18,19)

Insertion of a sentence between others which is independent and complete in itself.

Parenthesis (2 Pet. 1: 19)

Insertion of a word or sentence, parenthetically, which is necessary to explain the context.

Proverb (Gen. 10: 9; 1 Sam, 10: 12)

A well known saying.

Pathos (Luke 19: 41, 42)

Circumlocution (Gen. 20: 16; Judg. 5: 10)

When a description is used instead of the name.

Description of circumstances (John 4: 6)

Word-folding (Jer. 34: 17)

The repetition of the same word in a different sense, implying more that the first use of it.

Many names (Gen. 26: 34,35; 2 Kings 23: 13)

People or places mentioned under different names

Justification (Matt. 12: 12)

A sentence added at the end by way of justification.

Anticipation (Heb. 2: 8).

Anticipating what is going to be, and speaking of future things as present. Answering an argument by anticipating it before it is used.

1. Open.
When the anticipated objection is both answered and stated (Matt. 3: 9).

2. Closed.
When the anticipated objection is either not plainly stated or not answered (Rom. 10: 18).

Merismus

A combination of parts of the whole to express totality.
  "At midnight the Lord struck down all the firstborn in Egypt, from the firstborn of Pharaoh, who sat upon the throne, to the firstborn of the prisoner, who was in the dungeon, and the firstborn of all the livestock as well" Exodus 12: 29 NIV.

Personification

Things or concepts represented as persons.

1. Parts of the human body (Gen. 48: 14; Ps. 35: 10).

2. Animals (Gen. 9: 5; Job 12: 7).

3. The products of the earth (Nah. 1: 4).

4. Inanimate things (Gen. 4: 10).
5. Kingdoms, countries, and states (Ps. 45: 12).

6. Human actions attributed to things (Gen. 18: 20; Ps. 85: 10).

7. Wisdom (Proverbs 1: 20,21).

Idioms and figures of speech (5)

Apostrophe

A personification in which the writer addresses the object or concept that he has personified.
"Where, O death, is your victory? Where, O death, is your sting?"
1 Corinthians 15: 55 *NIV*.

Repeated negation (John 10: 28)

The repetition of negatives

Simile

In a simile one thing is compared with another thing. The words "as" or "like" are often used. Gen. 25: 25; Matt. 7: 24–27.
"His head and *his* hairs *were* white like wool, as white as snow; and his eyes *were* as a flame of fire" Revelation 1: 14.

Omission of the conclusion
(1 Sam. 17: 4–7)

The conclusion, though implied, is unexpressed, in order to add emphasis to it.

Symbol (Is. 22: 22)

A material object substituted for a moral or spiritual truth.

Concluding summary (Matt. 1: 17)

When what has been said is briefly summed up.

Intertwining (1 Cor. 15: 42–44)

The repetition of different words in successive sentences in the same order and having the same sense.

Ellipsis

A passage that is grammatically incomplete which requires the reader to complete it.
"Do all have gifts of healing? Do all speak in tongues? Do all interpret?"
1 Corinthians 12: 30 *NIV*.

Enumeration (1 Tim. 4: 1–3)

The enumeration of the parts of a whole which has not been mentioned.

Concession (Hab. 1: 13)

Making a concession of one point in order to gain another.

Repeated Simile (Is. 32: 2)

Synecdoche, or, transfer

The exchange of one idea for another associated idea. A figure of speech in which the part represents the whole or the whole represents the part.

1. Of the genus.
When the genus is put for the species, or universals for particulars (Gen. 6: 12; Matt. 3: 5).

2. Of the species.
When the species is put for the genus, or particulars for universals (Gen. 3: 19. Matt. 6: 11).

3. Of the whole.
When the whole is put for a part
(Gen. 6: 12).

4. Of the part.
When a part is put for the whole
(Gen. 3: 19; Matt. 27: 4).
    "Let me know that it is your hand,
that you, O Lord, have done it"
Psalm 109: 27 NIV.

Expanding a narrative

Not uncommonly in the Old
Testament, a story is presented in a way
that is similar to a modern newspaper
article. There is a line or paragraph that
summarizes the rest of the story.

Four examples

1. Genesis 1: 1–3: 25.

2. Jonah 3: 5–9: The result of Jonah
preaching to the evil city of Nineveh
comes in Jonah 3: 5. Jonah 3: 6–9 goes
on to spell out this out in much greater
detail.

3. Proverbs 1: 10–19: The summary of
Proverbs 1: 10–19 comes in verse 10,
with the advice: "My son, if sinners
entice you do not go."
    The rest of the passage unpacks this
summary in two sections:
1: 11–14 – How sinners entice.
1: 15–19 – Do not go with them.

4. Ecclesiastes 2: 1–26: In Ecclesiastes
2: 1 the scene is set for the whole of 2: 1–
26: "I spoke in my heart, 'Come now, I
will test pleasure and examine good.'
Behold: all of it is also meaningless."
    The remaining verses fall into two
parts:
2: 2–10 – Testing with pleasure to
discover what's good.
2: 11–26 – Everything is meaningless.

Old Testament parables

Overview

A parable, from the Greek word *parabole*, means a placing beside; a comparison. It is equivalent to the Hebrew word *mashal*, which means a similitude.

Old Testament

The word "parable" in the Old Testament

(1) a proverb (1 Sam. 10: 12; 24: 13; 2 Chr. 7: 20),

(2) a prophetic utterance (Num. 23: 7; Ezek. 20: 49),

(3) an enigmatic saying (Ps. 78: 2; Prov. 1: 6).

New Testament

The word "parable" in the New Testament:

(1) a proverb (Mark 7: 17; Luke 4: 23),

(2) a typical emblem (Heb. 9: 9; 11: 19),

(3) a similitude or allegory (Matt. 15: 15; 24: 32; Mark 3: 23; Luke 5: 36; 14: 7);

(4) most often it refers to a comparison between an earthly thing with heavenly things. Jesus' parables were earthly stories with heavenly meanings.

All the Old Testament parables

NATHAN'S PARABLE

After David's adultery with Bathsheba and after David had arranged for Bathsheba's husband, Uriah, to be killed in battle, the Lord sent Nathan to David. David was convicted of his evil deeds by the parable Nathan told him.

"And the Lord sent Nathan unto David. And he came unto him, and said unto him, There were two men in one city; the one rich, and the other poor. The rich *man* had exceeding many flocks and herds: But the poor *man* had nothing, save one little ewe lamb, which he had bought and nourished up: and it grew up together with him, and with his children; it did eat of his own meat, and drank of his own cup, and lay in his bosom, and was unto him as a daughter. And there came a traveler unto the rich man, and he spared to take of his own flock and of his own herd, to dress for the wayfaring man that was come unto him; but took the poor man's lamb, and dressed it for the man that was come to him. And David's anger was greatly kindled against the man; and he said to Nathan, As the Lord liveth, the man that hath done this *thing* shall surely die: And he shall restore the lamb fourfold, because he did this thing, and because he had no pity. And Nathan said to David, Thou *art* the man. Thus saith the Lord God of Israel, I anointed thee king over Israel, and I delivered thee out of the hand of Saul; And I gave thee thy master's house, and thy master's wives into thy bosom, and gave thee the house of Israel and of Judah; and if *that* had been too little, I would moreover have given unto thee such and such things. Wherefore hast thou despised the commandment of the Lord, to do evil in his sight? thou hast killed Uriah the Hittite with the sword, and hast taken his wife *to be* thy wife, and

Old Testament parables, proverbs, and sayings			
Spoken by	Concerning	Spoken at	Recorded
Balaam	The Moabites and Israelites	Mount Pisgah	Num. 23: 24
Jotham	Trees making a king	Mount Gerizim	Judg. 9: 7–15
Samson	Sweetness coming forth from the strong	Timnath	Judg. 14: 14
Nathan	The poor man's ewe lamb	Jerusalem	2 Sam. 12: 1–4
Woman of Tekoah	Two brothers striving	Jerusalem	2 Sam. 14: 1
One of the sons of the prophets	The escaped prisoner	Near Samaria	1 Kings 20: 35–49
Jehoash, king of Israel	The thistle and the cedar	Jerusalem	2 Kings 14: 9
Isaiah	The vineyard yielding wild grapes	Jerusalem	Is. 5: 1–6
Ezekiel	Lion's whelps	Babylon	Ezek. 19: 2–9
Ezekiel	The great eagles and the vine	Babylon	Ezek. 17: 3–10
Ezekiel	The boiling pot	Babylon	Ezek. 24: 3–5

hast slain him with the sword of the children of Ammon."

2 Samuel 12: 1–9 NKJV

THE VINE

When Jesus called himself "the true vine" in John 15: 1 his listeners would have been familiar with Isaiah's parable about an unfruitful vineyard.

"Now will I sing to my wellbeloved a song of my beloved touching his vineyard. My wellbeloved hath a vineyard in a very fruitful hill: And he fenced it, and gathered out the stones thereof, and planted it with the choicest vine, and built a tower in the midst of it, and also made a winepress therein: and he looked that it should bring forth grapes, and it brought forth wild grapes. And now, O inhabitants of Jerusalem, and men of Judah, judge, I pray you, betwixt me and my vineyard. What could have been done more to my vineyard, that I have not done in it? wherefore, when I looked that it should bring forth grapes, brought it forth wild grapes?"

Isaiah 5: 1–4 NKJV

Typology (1)

Defining the term

A "type" has been defined as: "A pre-ordained representative relationship which certain persons, events and institutions of the Old Testament bear to corresponding persons, events, and institutions in the New Testament."

Bernard Ramm

A type may be defined as "a figure or ensample of something future and more or less prophetic, called the 'Antitype.'"

E. W. Bullinger

A type is "the preordained representative relation which certain persons, events, and institutions of the Old Testament bear to corresponding persons, events, and institutions in the New."

Muenscher

"A type is a shadow cast on the pages of Old Testament history by a truth whose full embodiment or antitype is found in the New Testament revelation."

Wick Broomall

"A type is a real, exalted happening in history which was divinely ordained by the omniscient God to be a prophetic picture of the good things which He purposed to bring to fruition in Christ Jesus."

Wayne Jackson

Typology in the Old Testament

A person as a type:

MELCHIZEDEK
The New Testament gives ample justification for the use of typology. Melchizedek, in Hebrews 7, is an example of a person being used as a type.

Melchizedek corresponds to Jesus in many ways.

He is both a king and a priest like Christ.

An event as a type:

THE EXODUS
The Exodus from Egypt is an example of an event serving as a type.

Just as Israel was redeemed from slavery by God's power, the New Testament teaches that God's followers today are redeemed from sin.

The Exodus event bears an obvious correspondence with our salvation.

A God-given institution as a type:

THE OLD TESTAMENT SACRIFICES
The sacrifices of Leviticus 1–5 are an example of an institution which constitutes a type.

For example, Hebrews 9 draws the parallel between the shedding of the blood of the animal and the shedding of the blood of Christ.

New Testament words for "type"

1 tupos

Tupos is the basis of our English word "type". In Romans 5: 14 Paul declares that Adam "is a figure (tupos) of him that was to come," that is, Christ.

2 skia

The word *skia*, is translated as "shadow" in Colossians 2: 17. Some parts of the Mosaic system are said to be "a shadow of the things to come."

See also: Heb. 8: 5; 10: 1.

3 hupodeigma

The term *hupodeigma* is translated "copy," and used in conjunction with "shadow" in Hebrews 8: 5.

"They serve at a sanctuary that is a copy and shadow of what is in heaven. This is why Moses was warned when he was about to build the tabernacle: 'See to it that you make everything according to the pattern shown you on the mountain'" Hebrews 8: 5.

See also Heb. 9: 23.

4 parabole

The Greek word *parabole* (hence the English word, "parable") in Hebrews 9: 9, states that parts of the tabernacle are "a figure for the present time."

See also Heb. 11: 19.

5 antitupon

Antitupon is translated "figure" (*KJV*) or "pattern" (*ASV*) in Hebrews 9: 24, and "like figure" (*KJV*) or "true likeness" (*ASV*) in 1 Peter 3: 21.

People as types

A number of Old Testament people are rightly thought of as "types" because of the link they have with some aspect of God's salvation.

ADAM

Adam is a type of Christ. Adam introduced sin into the world, Christ brought the remedy for sin.

"For as by one man's disobedience many were made sinners, so also by one Man's obedience many will be made righteous" Romans 5: 19 *NKJV*.

MELCHIZEDEK IS A TYPE OF CHRIST

Melchizedek was king of Salem and a priest of God, Gen. 14: 18–20. Christ at his ascension, began to reign on David's throne and to be our high priest. See. Ps. 110: 4; Zech. 6: 12,13; Heb. 5: 5–10; 6: 20; 7: 1–17.

"So also Christ did not glorify Himself to become High Priest, but it was He who said to Him:
'You are My Son,
Today I have begotten You.'

As He also says in another place:
'You are a priest forever
According to the order of Melchizedek';
who, in the days of His flesh, when He had offered up prayers and supplications, with vehement cries and tears to Him who was able to save Him from death, and was heard because of His godly fear, though He was a Son, yet He learned obedience by the things which He suffered.

And having been perfected, He became the author of eternal salvation to all who obey Him, called by God as High Priest 'according to the order of Melchizedek.'"   *Hebrews 5: 5–10 NKJV*

Typology (2)

Places as types

JERUSALEM

Jerusalem is a type of the church and also of believers in heaven.

"But you have come to Mount Zion and to the city of the living God, the heavenly Jerusalem, to an innumerable company of angels, to the general assembly and church of the firstborn *who are* registered in heaven."

Hebrews 12: 22 NKJV

BABYLON

Babylon attacked and captured God's people in the Old Testament. In the New Testament Babylon stands for apostate members of the Christian church.

"Babylon is fallen, is fallen, that great city, because she has made all nations drink of the wine of the wrath of her fornication."

Revelation 14: 8 NKJV

Objects as types

THE BRONZE SNAKE

The bronze snake mentioned in Numbers 21: 8 is referred to by John as a type of Christ, who brings spiritual healing.

"And as Moses lifted up the serpent in the wilderness, even so must the Son of Man be lifted up, 15that whoever believes in Him should not perish but have eternal life."

John 3: 14,15 NKJV

Events as types

A number of Old Testament events are earmarked as "types" by New Testament writers.

THE FLOOD

The flood of Noah's day, recorded in Genesis 6–8 is seen as a type of the destruction that will take place at the end of the world.

"But as the days of Noah were, so also will the coming of the Son of Man be. For as in the days before the flood, they were eating and drinking, marrying and giving in marriage, until the day that Noah entered the ark, and did not know until the flood came and took them all away, so also will the coming of the Son of Man be."

Matthew 24: 37–39 NKJV

WATER FROM THE ROCK

When the Israelites were wandering in the desert God provided them, miraculously, with water from a rock, Exodus 17: 6.

This is taken up in the New Testament to be a type of the spiritual life given by Jesus.

"and all drank the same spiritual drink. For they drank of that spiritual Rock that followed them, and that Rock was Christ."

1 Corinthians 10: 4 NKJV

MANNA IN THE DESERT

In answer to Moses' request the Lord miraculously provided manna for the Israelites in the desert, Exodus 16: 14–16. This is pointed to as a type of spiritual bread, who is Jesus, through whom Christians are spiritually nourished.

"Then Jesus said to them, 'Most assuredly, I say to you, Moses did not give you the bread from heaven, but My Father gives you the true bread from heaven. For the bread of God is He who comes down from heaven and gives life to the world.'"

John 6: 32,33 NKJV

THE DESERT EXPERIENCES

Paul points to the time the Israelites spent in the desert so that spiritual lessons can be drawn from it.

Note Paul's statement after discussing the experiences of Israel in the wilderness of Sinai. "Now these things were our examples (tupoi), to the intent we should not lust after evil things, as they also lusted" (1 Cor. 10: 6; cf. 10: 11).

"Now these things were our examples, to the intent we should not lust after evil things, as they also lusted"

1 Corinthians 19: 6 NKJV

The deliverance of Noah's family from a corrupted world, by means of "water," prefigured our salvation, through baptism, from the power of darkness into the kingdom of Christ (cf. 1 Pet. 3: 20–21; Col. 1: 13).

Offices as types

Three offices in the Old Testament were entered into through an anointing: prophets (1 Kings 19: 16), priests (Ex. 28: 41), and kings (1 Sam. 10: 1).

Each of these offices are seen as types of Jesus who was to be the Anointed One.

Jesus is a prophet, "For Moses truly said unto the fathers, A prophet shall the Lord your God raise up unto you of your brethren, like unto me; him shall ye hear in all things whatsoever he shall say unto you" Acts 3: 22 *NKJV*.

Jesus is a priest, "Wherefore, holy brethren, partakers of the heavenly calling, consider the Apostle and High Priest of our profession, Christ Jesus; Who was faithful to him that appointed him, as also Moses *was faithful* in all his house" Hebrews 3: 1,2 *NKJV*.

Jesus is a king, "These shall make war with the Lamb, and the Lamb shall overcome them: for he is Lord of lords, and King of kings" Revelation 17: 14 *NKJV*.

Types of Christ

Overview

This alphabetical list of some of the leading types of Christ found in the Bible give two of the most important Bible references about each type.

In each instance at least one Old Testament reference is matched with at least one relevant New Testament verse.

Adam. Rom. 5: 14; 1 Cor. 15: 45.

Abel. Gen. 4: 8,10; Heb. 12: 24.

Abraham. Gen. 17: 5; Eph. 3: 15.

Aaron. Ex. 28: 1; Heb. 5: 4,5; Lev. 16: 15; Heb. 9: 7,24.

Ark. Gen. 7: 16; 1 Pet. 3: 20,21.

Ark of the Covenant. Ex. 25: 16; Ps. 40: 8; Is. 42: 6.

"And you shall put inside the ark the Testimony [the Ten Commandments] which I will give you" Exodus 25: 16 AB.

"I delight to do Your will, O my God; yes, Your law is within my heart" Psalm 40: 8 AB.

"Hence, when He [Christ] entered into the world, He said, Sacrifices and offerings You have not desired, but instead You have made ready a body for Me [to offer]" Hebrews 10: 5 AB.

Atonement, sacrifices offered on the day of. Lev. 16: 15,16; Heb. 9: 12,24.

Bronze snake. Num. 21: 9; John 3: 14,15.

Bronze altar. Ex. 27: 1,2; Heb. 13: 10.

Burnt offering. Lev. 1: 2,4; Heb. 10: 10.

Cities of refuge. Num. 35: 6; Heb. 6: 18.

David. 2 Sam. 8: 15; Ezek. 37: 24;

Ps. 89: 19,20; Php 2: 9.

Eliakim. Is. 22: 20–22; Rev. 3: 7.

First-fruits. Ex. 22: 29; 1 Cor. 15: 20.

Golden candlestick. Ex. 25: 31; John 8: 12.

Golden altar. Ex. 40: 5,26,27; Rev. 8: 3; Heb. 13: 15.

Isaac. Gen. 22: 1,2; Heb. 11: 17–19.

Jacob. Gen. 32: 28; John 11: 42; Heb. 7: 25.

Jacob's ladder. Gen. 28: 12; John 1: 51.

Joshua. Josh. 1: 5,6; Heb. 4: 8,9; Josh. 11: 23; Acts 20: 32.

Jonah. John 1: 17; Matt. 12: 40.

Laver of brass. Ex. 30: 18–20; Zech. 13: 1; Eph. 5: 26,27.

"Thou shalt also make a laver of brass, and the base thereof of brass, whereat to wash. And thou shalt put it between the tent of meeting and the altar, and thou shalt put water therein.

19   And Aaron and his sons shall wash their hands and their feet thereat:

20   when they go into the tent of meeting, they shall wash with water, that they die not; or when they come near to the altar to minister, to burn an offering made by fire unto Jehovah."   *Exodus 30: 18–20 ASV*

"In that day there shall be a fountain opened to the house of David and to the inhabitants of Jerusalem, for sin and for uncleanness" Zechariah 13: 1 ASV.

"that he might sanctify it, having

cleansed it by the washing of water with the word,

27 that he might present the church to himself a glorious church, not having spot or wrinkle or any such thing; but that it should be holy and without blemish"

Ephesians 5: 26,27 ASV

Leper's offering. Lev. 14: 4–7; Rom. 4: 25.

Manna. Ex. 16: 11–15; John 6: 32–35.

Melchizedek. Gen. 14: 18–20; Heb. 7: 1–17.

Mercy-seat. Ex. 25: 17–22; Rom. 3: 25; Heb. 4: 16.

Morning and evening sacrifices. Ex. 29: 38–41; John 1: 29,36.

Moses. Num. 12: 7; Heb. 3: 2; Deut. 18: 15; Acts 3: 20–22.

Noah. Gen. 5: 29; 2 Cor. 1: 5.

Paschal lamb. Ex. 12: 3–6,46; John 19: 36; 1 Cor. 5: 7.

Peace offerings. Lev. 3: 1; Eph. 2: 14,16.

Red heifer. Num. 19: 2–6; Heb. 9: 13,14.

Rock of Horeb. Ex. 17: 6; 1 Cor. 10: 4.

Samson. Judg. 16: 30; Col. 2: 14,15.

Scapegoat. Lev. 16: 20–22; Is. 53: 6,12.

Sin offering. Lev. 4: 2,3,12; Heb. 13: 11,12.

Solomon. 2 Sam. 7: 12,13; Luke 1: 32,33; 1 Pet. 2: 5.

Tabernacle. Ex. 40: 2,34; Col. 2: 9; Heb. 9: 11.

"On the first day of the first month shalt thou rear up the tabernacle of the tent of meeting.

34 Then the cloud covered the tent of meeting, and the glory of Jehovah filled the tabernacle."

Exodus 40: 2 ASV

"for in him dwelleth all the fullness of the Godhead bodily" Colossians 2: 9 ASV.

"But Christ having come a high priest of the good things to come, through the greater and more perfect tabernacle, not made with hands, that is to say, not of this creation" Hebrews 9: 11 ASV.

Table and show bread. Ex. 25: 23–30; John 1: 16; 6: 48.

Temple. 1 Kgs. 6: 1,38; John 2: 19,21.

Tree of life. Gen. 2: 9; John 1: 4; Rev. 22: 2.

Trespass offering. Lev. 6: 1–7; Is. 53: 10.

Veil of the tabernacle and temple. Ex. 40: 21; 2 Chr. 3: 14; Heb. 10: 20.

"and he brought the ark into the tabernacle, and set up the veil of the screen, and screened the ark of the testimony; as Jehovah commanded Moses" Exodus 40: 21 ASV.

"And he made the veil of blue, and purple, and crimson, and fine linen, and wrought cherubim thereon" 2 Chronicles 3: 14 ASV.

"by the way which he dedicated for us, a new and living way, through the veil, that is to say, his flesh" Hebrews 10: 20 ASV.

Zerubbabel. Zech. 4: 7–9; Heb. 12: 2,3.

Miracles

1 General Bible teaching on

Overview

Power of God necessary for miracles.
John 3: 2.

Described as

Marvelous things. Ps. 78: 12.
Marvelous works. Is. 29: 14; Ps. 105: 5.
Signs and wonders. Jer. 32: 21;
John 4: 48; 2 Cor. 12: 12.

Miracles demonstrate

The glory of God. John 11: 4.
The glory of Christ. John 2: 11; 11: 4.
The works of God. John 9: 3.

FACTS ABOUT BIBLE MIRACLES
Were evidences of a divine
commission. Ex. 4: 1–5; Mark 16: 20.
The Messiah was expected to perform.
Matt. 11: 2,3; John 7: 31.
Jesus was proved to be the Messiah
by. Matt. 11: 4–6; Luke 7: 20–22;
John 5: 36; Acts 2: 22.
Jesus was followed on account of
Matt. 4: 23–25; 14: 35,36; John 6: 2,26;
12: 18.
A gift of the Holy Spirit. 1 Cor. 12: 10.

Were performed

By the power of God. Ex. 8: 19;
Acts 14: 3; 15: 12; 19: 11.
By the power of Christ. Matt. 10: 1.
By the power of the Holy Spirit.
Matt. 12: 28; Rom. 15: 19.
In the name of Christ. Matt. 16: 17;
Acts 3: 16; 4: 30.

Miracles and the gospel

First preaching of the gospel confirmed
by. Mark 16: 20; Heb. 2: 4.
The who wrought, disclaimed all power
of their own. Acts 3: 12.
Should produce faith. John 2: 23;
20: 30,31.
Should produce obedience. Deut. 11: 1–
3; 29: 2,3,9.
Instrumental to the early propagation
of the gospel. Acts 8: 6;
Rom. 15: 18,19.

Faith required in

Those who performed. Matt. 17: 20;
21: 21; John 14: 12; Acts 3: 16; 6: 8.
Those for whom they were performed.
Matt. 9: 28; 13: 58; Mark 9: 22–24;
Acts 14: 9.

Recount miracles

Should be remembered. 1 Chr. 16: 12;
Ps. 105: 5.
Should be told to future generations
Ex. 10: 2; Judg. 6: 13.

2 The wicked and miracles

The wicked:

Desire to see. Matt. 27: 42; Luke 11: 29;
23: 8.
Often acknowledge. John 11: 47;
Acts 4: 16.
Do not understand. Ps. 106: 7.
Do not consider. Mark 6: 52.
Forget. Neh. 9: 17; Ps. 78: 1,11.
Proof against. Num. 14: 22; John 12: 37.

Rejection of miracles

Guilt of rejecting the evidence of miracles Matt. 11: 20–24; John 15: 24. "Then he began to denounce the cities where most of his mighty works had been done, because they did not repent. 'Woe to you, Chorazin! Woe to you, Bethsaida! For if the mighty works done in you had been done in Tyre and Sidon, they would have repented long ago in sackcloth and ashes. But I tell you, it will be more bearable on the day of judgment for Tyre and Sidon than for you. And you, Capernaum, will you be exalted to heaven? You will be brought down to Hades. For if the mighty works done in you had been done in Sodom, it would have remained until this day. But I tell you that it will be more tolerable on the day of judgment for the land of Sodom than for you.'" *Matthew 11: 20–24 ESV*

"If I had not done among them the works that no one else did, they would not be guilty of sin, but now they have seen and hated both me and my Father" John 15: 24 *ESV*.

Miracles need faith

Miracles in themselves may or may not produce faith in God. Jesus warned that miracles are insufficient in themselves to produce conversion. "31 He said to him, If they do not hear and listen to Moses and the Prophets, neither will they be persuaded and convinced and believe [even] if someone should rise from the dead" Luke 16: 31 *AB*.

Faith needs to accompany miracles.

Godless miracles

Some godless people have been able to perform counterfeit miracles. These are recorded and warned against in many places in the Bible.

Some miracles are performed through the power of the devil.
2 Thess. 2: 9; Rev. 16: 14.

Some miracles are performed to support of false religions. Deut. 13: 1–2.

Some miracles are performed:
• By false christs. Matt. 24: 24.
• By false prophets. Matt. 24: 24; Rev. 19: 20.

Some miracles are a mark of the lawless one.

"Let no one deceive you in any way. For that day will not come, unless the rebellion comes first, and the man of lawlessness is revealed, the son of destruction … The coming of the lawless one is by the activity of Satan with all power and false signs and wonders" 2 Thessalonians 2: 3,9 *ESV*.

"It performs great signs, even making fire come down from heaven to earth in front of people" Revelation 13: 13 *ESV*.

Some miracles should be disregarded. Deut. 13: 3.

Some miracles deceive the ungodly. 2 Thess. 2: 10–12; Rev. 13: 14; 19: 20.

Examples of godless miracles

Magicians of Egypt. Ex. 7: 11,22; 8: 7.
Witch of Endor. 1 Sam. 28: 7–14.
Simon Magus. Acts 8: 9–11.

> ### Quote Unquote
> "We must remember that Satan has his miracles, too."
> *John Calvin*

Old Testament miracles

A chronological list of Old Testament miracles	
1. The flood	Gen. 7, 8
2. Destruction of Sodom and Gomorrah	Gen. 19: 24
3. Lot's wife turned into a pillar of salt	Gen. 19: 26
4. Birth of Isaac at Gerar	Gen. 21: 1
5. The burning bush not consumed	Ex. 3: 3
6. Aaron's rod changed into a snake	Ex. 7: 10–12
7. The ten plagues of Egypt – (1) waters become blood, (2) frogs, (3) lice, (4) flies, (5) murrain, (6) boils, (7) thunder and hail, (8) locusts, (9) darkness, (10) death of the first-born	Ex. 7: 20–12: 30
8. The Red Sea divided; Israel passes through	Ex. 14: 21–31
9. The waters of Marah purified	Ex. 15: 23–25
10. Manna sent daily, except on Sabbath	Ex. 16: 14–35
11. Water from the rock at Rephidim	Ex. 17: 5–7
12. Nadab and Abihu killed	Lev. 10: 1, 2
13. Some of the people killed by fire at Taberah	Num. 11: 1–3
14. The earth opens and swallows up Korah and his men; fire and plague follow at Kadesh	Num. 16: 32
15. Aaron's rod budding at Kadesh	Num. 17: 8
16. Water from the rock, Desert of Zin	Num. 20: 7–11
17. The bronze snake, the Desert of Zin	Num. 21: 8,9
18. Balaam's ass speaks	Num. 22: 21–35
19. The Jordan divided, so that Israel passed over on dry ground	Josh. 3: 14–17
20. The walls of Jericho fall down	Josh. 6: 6–20
21. The sun and moon stand still. Hailstorm	Josh. 10: 12–14
22. The strength of Samson	Judg. 14–16
23. Water from a hollow place	Judg. 15: 19
24. Dagon falls twice before the Ark. Tumors on the Philistines	1 Sam. 5: 1–12
25. Men of Beth-shemesh killed for looking into the Ark	1 Sam. 6: 19
26. Thunderstorm causes a panic among the Philistines at Eben-ezer	1 Sam. 7: 10–12
27. Thunder and rain in harvest at Gilgal	1 Sam. 12: 18
28. Sound in the mulberry trees at Rephaim	2 Sam. 5: 23–25
29. Uzzah punished for touching the Ark at Perez-uzzah	2 Sam. 6: 6,7
30. Jeroboam's hand withered. His new altar destroyed at Bethel	1 Kings 13: 4–6

31.	Widow of Zarephath's flour and oil do not run out	1 Kings 17: 14–16
32.	Widow's son raised from the dead	1 Kings 17: 17–24
33.	Drought, fire, and rain after Elijah's prayers, and Elijah fed by ravens	1 Kings 17, 18
34.	Ahaziah's captains consumed by fire near Samaria	2 Kings 1: 10–12
35.	Jordan divided by Elijah and Elisha near Jericho	2 Kings 2: 7,8,14
36.	Elijah taken up into heaven	2 Kings 2: 11
37.	Waters of Jericho purified by Elisha	2 Kings 2: 21,22
38.	Bears out of the wood destroy forty-two young men	2 Kings 2: 24
39.	Water provided for Jehoshaphat and the allied army	2 Kings 3: 16–20
40.	The widow's oil multiplied	2 Kings 4: 2–7
41.	The Shunammite's son given, and raised from the dead at Shunem	2 Kings 4: 32–37
42.	The deadly soup made wholesome at Gilgal	2 Kings 4: 38–41
43.	An hundred men fed with twenty loaves at Gilgal	2 Kings 4: 42–44
44.	Naaman cured of leprosy, Gehazi becomes leprous	2 Kings 5: 10–27
45.	The iron axe-head floats, river Jordan	2 Kings 6: 5–7
46.	Ben-hadad's plans discovered	2 Kings 6: 12
47.	The Syrian army blinded at Dothan	2 Kings 6: 18
48.	The Syrian army cured of blindness at Samaria	2 Kings 6: 20
49.	Elisha's bones revive the dead	2 Kings 13: 21
50.	Sennacherib's army destroyed, Jerusalem	2 Kings 19: 35
51.	Shadow of sun goes back ten degrees on the sun-dial of Ahaz, Jerusalem	2 Kings 20: 9–11
52.	Uzziah and his leprosy, Jerusalem	2 Chr. 26: 16–21
53.	Shadrach, Meshach, and Abed-nego delivered from the furnace, Babylon	Dan. 3: 10–27
54.	Daniel saved in the lions' den	Dan. 6: 16–23
55.	Jonah inside the large fish	Jonah 2: 1–10

The sun and moon stand still

"Then spake Joshua to Jehovah in the day when Jehovah delivered up the Amorites before the children of Israel; and he said in the sight of Israel, Sun, stand thou still upon Gibeon; And thou, Moon, in the valley of Aijalon.

13 And the sun stood still, and the moon stayed, Until the nation had avenged themselves of their enemies. Is not this written in the book of Jashar? And the sun stayed in the midst of heaven, and hasted not to go down about a whole day.

14 And there was no day like that before it or after it, that Jehovah hearkened unto the voice of a man: for Jehovah fought for Israel."

Joshua 10: 12–14 ASV

Miracles performed by God's followers (1)

Old Testament miracles (1)

Moses and Aaron

Staff turned into a snake. Ex. 4: 3; 7: 10.
Staff restored. Ex. 4: 4.
Hand made leprous. Ex. 4: 6.
Hand healed. Ex. 4: 7.
Ten plagues of Egypt. Exodus 7–12.
The red-sea divided. Ex. 14: 21,22.

"The Egyptians pursued them, all
Pharaoh's horses and chariots and
his horsemen and his army, and
overtook them encamped at the
sea, by Pi-hahiroth, in front of Baal-
zephon.

When Pharaoh drew near, the
people of Israel lifted up their eyes,
and behold, the Egyptians were
marching after them, and they feared
greatly. And the people of Israel cried
out to the Lord. They said to Moses,
"Is it because there are no graves in
Egypt that you have taken us away
to die in the wilderness? What have
you done to us in bringing us out
of Egypt? Is not this what we said to
you in Egypt, 'Leave us alone that
we may serve the Egyptians'? For
it would have been better for us to
serve the Egyptians than to die in the
wilderness." And Moses said to the
people, "Fear not, stand firm, and
see the salvation of the Lord, which
he will work for you today. For the
Egyptians whom you see today, you
shall never see again. The Lord will
fight for you, and you have only to be
silent....

Then Moses stretched out his hand
over the sea, and the Lord drove the
sea back by a strong east wind all
night and made the sea dry land, and
the waters were divided. And the
people of Israel went into the midst
of the sea on dry ground, the waters
being a wall to them on their right
hand and on their left.

Exodus 14: 9–13, 21,22 CEV

Egyptians overwhelmed. Ex. 14: 26–28.
Water made pure. Ex. 15: 25.
Water from rock in Horeb. Ex. 17: 6.
Amalek defeated. Ex. 17: 11–13.
Destruction of Korah. Num. 16: 28–32.
Water from rock in Kadesh.
Num. 20: 11.
Healing by bronze snake. Num. 21: 8,9.

Joshua

Waters of Jordan divided. Josh. 3: 10–17.
Jordan restored. Josh. 4: 18.
Jericho taken. Josh. 6: 6–20.
The sun and moon stand still.
Josh. 10: 12–14.

Gideon

Midianites destroyed. Judg. 7: 16–22.

Samson

A lion killed. Judg. 14: 6.
Philistines killed. Judg. 14: 19; 15: 15.
The gates of Gaza carried away.
Judg. 16: 3.
Dagon's house pulled down.
Judg. 16: 30.

Samuel

Thunder and rain in harvest.
1 Sam. 12: 18.

The prophet of Judah

Jeroboam's hand withered. 1 Kgs. 13: 4.
The altar broken. 1 Kgs. 13: 5.
The withered hand restored. 1 Kgs. 13: 6.
"And when the king heard the saying of the man of God, which he cried against the altar at Bethel, Jeroboam stretched out his hand from the altar, saying, 'Seize him.' And his hand, which he stretched out against him, dried up, so that he could not draw it back to himself. The altar also was torn down, and the ashes poured out from the altar, according to the sign that the man of God had given by the word of the Lord. And the king said to the man of God, 'Entreat now the favor of the Lord your God, and pray for me, that my hand may be restored to me.' And the man of God entreated the Lord, and the king's hand was restored to him and became as it was before."
                    1 Kings 13: 4–6 ESV

Elijah

Drought caused. 1 Kgs. 17: 1; James 5: 17.
Flour and oil increased. 1 Kgs. 17: 14–16.
A child restored to life. 1 Kgs. 17: 22,23.
"For thus says the Lord the God of Israel, 'The jar of flour shall not be spent, and the jug of oil shall not be empty, until the day that the Lord sends rain upon the earth.' And she went and did as Elijah said. And she and he and her household ate for many days. The jar of flour was not spent, neither did the jug of oil become empty, according to the word of the Lord that he spoke by Elijah"   *1 Kings 17: 14–16 ESV*
Sacrifice consumed by fire.
1 Kgs. 18: 36,38.
Men destroyed by fire. 2 Kgs. 1: 10–12.
Rain brought. 1 Kgs. 18: 41–45;
James 5: 18.
Waters of Jordan divided. 2 Kgs. 2: 8.
Taken to heaven. 2 Kgs. 2: 11.

Elisha

Waters of Jordan divided. 2 Kgs. 2: 14.
Waters healed. 2 Kgs. 2: 21,22.
Children torn by bears. 2 Kgs. 2: 24.
Oil provided. 2 Kgs. 4: 1–7.
Child restored to life. 2 Kgs. 4: 32–35.

Quote Unquote

"God creates the vine and teaches it to draw up water by its roots and, with the aid of the sun, to turn that water into a juice which will ferment and take on certain qualities. Thus every year, from Noah's time till ours, God turns water into wine."

                    C.S. Lewis

Miracles performed by God's followers (2)

Old Testament miracles (2)

Naaman healed

2 Kgs. 5:10,14.

"Naaman, commander of the army of the king of Syria, was a great man with his master and in high favor, because by him the LORD had given victory to Syria. He was a mighty man of valor, but he was a leper. Now the Syrians on one of their raids had carried off a little girl from the land of Israel, and she worked in the service of Naaman's wife.

3 She said to her mistress, 'Would that my lord were with the prophet who is in Samaria! He would cure him of his leprosy.'

4 So Naaman went in and told his lord, 'Thus and so spoke the girl from the land of Israel.'

5 And the king of Syria said, 'Go now, and I will send a letter to the king of Israel.' So he went, taking with him ten talents of silver, six thousand shekels of gold, and ten changes of clothes.

6 And he brought the letter to the king of Israel, which read, 'When this letter reaches you, know that I have sent to you Naaman my servant, that you may cure him of his leprosy.'

7 And when the king of Israel read the letter, he tore his clothes and said, 'Am I God, to kill and to make alive, that this man sends word to me to cure a man of his leprosy? Only consider, and see how he is seeking a quarrel with me.'

8 But when Elisha the man of God heard that the king of Israel had torn his clothes, he sent to the king, saying, 'Why have you torn your clothes? Let him come now to me, that he may know that there is a prophet in Israel.'

9 So Naaman came with his horses and chariots and stood at the door of Elisha's house.

10 And Elisha sent a messenger to him, saying, 'Go and wash in the Jordan seven times, and your flesh shall be restored, and you shall be clean.'

11 But Naaman was angry and went away, saying, 'Behold, I thought that he would surely come out to me and stand and call upon the name of the LORD his God, and wave his hand over the place and cure the leper.

12 Are not Abana and Pharpar, the rivers of Damascus, better than all the waters of Israel? Could I not wash in them and be clean?' So he turned and went away in a rage.

13 But his servants came near and said to him, 'My father, it is a great word the prophet has spoken to you; will you not do it? Has he actually said to you, "Wash, and be clean"?'

14 So he went down and dipped himself seven times in the Jordan, according to the word of the man of God, and his flesh was restored like the flesh of a little child, and he was clean."

2 Kings 5:1-14 ESV

Gehazi struck with leprosy

2 Kgs. 5: 27.

Iron floats

2 Kgs. 6: 6.

Syrians blinded

2 Kgs. 6: 20.

Sight restored to Syrians

2 Kgs. 6: 20.

A man restored to life

2 Kgs. 13: 21.

Hezekiah healed

2 Kgs. 20: 7.

"And before Isaiah had gone out of the middle court, the word of the LORD came to him:

5 'Turn back, and say to Hezekiah the leader of my people, Thus says the LORD, the God of David your father: I have heard your prayer; I have seen your tears. Behold, I will heal you. On the third day you shall go up to the house of the LORD,

6 and I will add fifteen years to your life. I will deliver you and this city out of the hand of the king of Assyria, and I will defend this city for my own sake and for my servant David's sake.'

7 And Isaiah said, 'Bring a cake of figs. And let them take and lay it on the boil, that he may recover.'"

2 Kings 20: 4-7 ESV.

Shadow goes back on sun-dial

2 Kgs. 20: 11.

Quote Unquote

"Why, they ask, do not those miracles, which you preach as of past events, happen nowadays? I might reply that they were necessary before the world believed, to bring the world to believe; but whoever is still looking for prodigies to make him believe is himself a great prodigy for refusing to believe where the world believes."

Augustine of Hippo

Miracles performed by God's followers (3)

New Testament miracles

The seventy disciples

Various miracles. Luke 10: 9,17.

The apostles

Many miracles. Acts 2: 43; 5: 12.

"Now many signs and wonders were regularly done among the people by the hands of the apostles. And they were all together in Solomon's Portico.

13 None of the rest dared join them, but the people held them in high esteem.

14 And more than ever believers were added to the Lord, multitudes of both men and women,

15 so that they even carried out the sick into the streets and laid them on cots and mats, that as Peter came by at least his shadow might fall on some of them.

16 The people also gathered from the towns around Jerusalem, bringing the sick and those afflicted with unclean spirits, and they were all healed."

Acts 5: 12–16 ESV

Peter

Lame man cured. Acts 3: 7.
Death of Ananias. Acts 5: 5.
Death of Sapphira. Acts 5: 10.
The sick healed. Acts 5: 15,16.
Aeneas made whole. Acts 9: 34.

"Now as Peter went here and there among them all, he came down also to the saints who lived at Lydda.

33 There he found a man named Aeneas, bedridden for eight years, who was paralyzed.

34 And Peter said to him, 'Aeneas, Jesus Christ heals you; rise and make your bed.' And immediately he rose.

35 And all the residents of Lydda and Sharon saw him, and they turned to the Lord"

Acts 9: 32–35 ESV

Dorcas restored to life. Acts 9: 40.

"Now there was in Joppa a disciple named Tabitha, which, translated, means Dorcas. She was full of good works and acts of charity.

37 In those days she became ill and died, and when they had washed her, they laid her in an upper room.

38 Since Lydda was near Joppa, the disciples, hearing that Peter was there, sent two men to him, urging him, "Please come to us without delay."

39 So Peter rose and went with them. And when he arrived, they took him to the upper room. All the widows stood beside him weeping and showing tunics and other garments that Dorcas made while she was with them.

40 But Peter put them all outside, and knelt down and prayed; and turning to the body he said, "Tabitha, arise." And she opened her eyes, and when she saw Peter she sat up.

41 And he gave her his hand and raised her up. Then calling the saints and widows, he presented her alive.

42 And it became known throughout all Joppa, and many believed in the Lord.

43 And he stayed in Joppa for many days with one Simon, a tanner"

Acts 9: 26–42 ESV

Stephen

Great miracles. Acts 6: 8.

Philip

Various miracles. Acts 8: 6,7,13.

Paul

Elymas made blind. Acts 13: 11.
Lame man cured. Acts 14: 10.

"Now at Lystra there was a man sitting who could not use his feet. He was crippled from birth and had never walked.

9 He listened to Paul speaking. And Paul, looking intently at him and seeing that he had faith to be made well,

10 said in a loud voice, 'Stand upright on your feet.' And he sprang up and began walking."   *Acts 14: 8–10 ESV.*
An unclean spirit expelled. Acts 16: 18.
Special miracles. Acts 19: 11,12.
Eutychus restored to life. Acts 20: 10–12.

"But Paul went down and bent over him, and taking him in his arms, said, 'Do not be alarmed, for his life is in him.'

11 And when Paul had gone up and had broken bread and eaten, he conversed with them a long while, until daybreak, and so departed.

12 And they took the youth away alive, and were not a little comforted."
Acts 20: 10–12 ESV
Viper's bite made harmless. Acts 28: 5.
Father of Publius healed. Acts 28: 8.

"Now in the neighborhood of that place were lands belonging to the chief man of the island, named Publius, who received us and entertained us hospitably for three days.

8 It happened that the father of Publius lay sick with fever and dysentery. And Paul visited him and prayed, and putting his hands on him healed him.

9 And when this had taken place, the rest of the people on the island who had diseases also came and were cured."
Acts 28: 7–9 ESV

Paul and Barnabas

Various miracles. Acts 14: 3.

> ### Quote Unquote
>
> "However skillfully the modern ingenuity of semi-belief may have tampered with supernatural interpositions, it is clear to every honest and unsophisticated mind that, if miracles be incredible, Christianity is false."
> *Frederic William Farrar*

Visions (1)

Introduction

Visions are one of God's methods of revelation.

Num. 12: 6; 1 Sam. 3: 1; 2 Chr. 26: 5; Ps. 89: 19; Prov. 29: 18; Jer. 14: 14; Jer. 23: 16; Dan. 1: 17; Hos. 12: 10; Joel 2: 28; Obad. 1: 1; Hab. 2: 2; Acts 2: 17.

"And the child Samuel ministered unto the Lord before Eli. And the word of the Lord was precious in those days; there was no open vision" 1 Samuel 3: 1 KJ21.

"And he sought God in the days of Zechariah, who had understanding in the visions of God; and as long as he sought the Lord, God made him to prosper" 2 Chronicles 26: 5 KJ21.

Visions and dreams

Visions are (Luke 1: 22) vivid apparitions and are to be differentiated from dreams (cf. Luke 24: 23; Acts 26: 19; 2 Cor. 12: 1).

"And when he came out, he could not speak unto them, and they perceived that he had seen a vision in the temple; for he beckoned unto them and remained speechless" Luke 1: 22 KJ21.

"And when they found not His body, they came saying that they had also seen a vision of angels, who said that He was alive" Luke 24: 23 KJ21.

Overview

God often made known his will by visions

"Then Thou didst speak in a vision to Thy holy one and said, 'I have laid help upon one that is mighty; I have exalted one chosen out of the people'" Psalm 89: 19 KJ21.

God especially made himself known to prophets by visions

"And He said, 'Hear now My words: If there be a prophet among you, I, the Lord, will make Myself known unto him in a vision, and will speak unto him in a dream." Numbers 12: 6 KJ21.

Visions often accompanied

A representative of the divine person and glory. Is. 6: 1.

An audible voice from heaven.
Gen. 15: 1; 1 Sam. 3: 4,5.

An appearance of angels. Luke 1: 22,11; 24: 23; Acts 10: 3.

An appearance of human beings.
Acts 9: 12; 16: 9.

Visions were often perplexing to those who received them. Dan. 7: 15; 8: 15; Acts 10: 17.

When communicated

In the night season. Gen. 46: 2; Dan. 2: 19.

In a trance. Num. 24: 16; Acts 11: 5.

Purpose of visions

Often recorded for the benefit of the people. Hab. 2: 2.

Numerous visions for the benefit of the people.

"I have also spoken by the prophets, and I have multiplied visions, and used similitudes by the ministry of the prophets' Hosea 12: 10 KJ21.

Visions mentioned in the Bible

Old Testament

To Abraham, concerning his descendants
Gen. 15: 1–17.

To Jacob
At Beersheba. Gen. 46: 2

To Moses
Of the burning bush.
"And the angel of the Lord appeared unto him in a flame of fire out of the midst of a bush; and he looked and, behold, the bush burned with fire, and the bush was not consumed.

3 And Moses said, 'I will now turn aside and see this great sight, why the bush is not burnt.'" Exodus 3: 2,3 KJ21

"And when forty years had expired, there appeared to him in the wilderness of Mount Sinai an angel of the Lord, in a flame of fire in a bush.

31 When Moses saw it, he wondered at the sight; and as he drew near to behold it, the voice of the Lord came unto him, saying,

32 'I am the God of thy fathers, the God of Abraham and the God of Isaac and the God of Jacob.' Then Moses trembled and dared not behold."

Acts 7: 30–32 KJ21

Of the glory of God
Ex. 24: 9–11; Ex. 33: 18–23.

Of the Israelites, of the manifestation of the glory of God
Ex. 24: 10; Ex. 24: 17; Heb. 12: 18–21.

To Joshua, of the captain of the Lord's host
Josh. 5: 13–15.

To Balaam, in a trance
Num. 22: 22–35; 2 Pet. 2: 16.

To Samuel
1 Sam. 3: 2–15.

To Nathan
2 Sam. 7: 4,17.

To Elisha, at the translation of Elijah
2 Kgs. 2: 11.

To Elisha's servant, of the chariots of the Lord
2 Kgs. 6: 17.

To Micaiah
of the defeat of the Israelites; of the Lord on His throne; and of a lying spirit.
1 Kgs. 22: 17–23; 2 Chr. 18: 16–22

To David
Of the angel of the Lord by the threshing floor of Ornan.
1 Chr. 21: 15–18.

To Eliphaz
Job 4: 13–16.

To Isaiah
Of the Lord and His glory in the temple
Is. 6.
Of the valley of vision
Is. 22.

To Jeremiah
Of an almond rod.
Jer. 1: 11.
Of the seething pot.
Jer. 1: 13.

Visions (2)

Visions mentioned in the Bible, continued

Old Testament, continued

TO EZEKIEL
Of the glory of God.
Ezek. 1: 3; Ezek. 1: 12–14; Ezek. 23.
Of the roll.
Ezek. 2: 9.
Of the man of fire.
Ezek. 8–9.
Of the coals of fire.
Ezek. 10: 1–7.
Of the dry bones.
Ezek. 37: 1–14.
Of the city and temple.
Ezek. 40–48.
Of the waters.
Ezek. 47: 1–12.

TO NEBUCHADNEZZAR
Dan. 2: 28; Dan. 4: 5.

TO DANIEL
Of the four beasts.
Dan. 7.
Of the Ancient of days.
Dan. 7: 9–27.
Of the ram and the he goat.
Dan. 8.
Of the angel.
Dan. 10.

TO AMOS
Of grasshoppers.
Amos 7: 1–2.
Of fire.
Amos 7: 4.
Of a plumb line.
Amos 7: 7–8.

Of summer fruit.
Amos 8: 1–2.
Of the temple.
Amos 9: 1.

TO ZECHARIAH
Of horses.
Zech. 1: 8–11.
Of horns and carpenters.
Zech. 1: 18–21.
Of the high priest.
Zech. 3: 1–5.
Of the golden candlestick.
Zech. 4.
Of the flying roll.
Zech. 5: 1–4.
Of the mountains and chariots.
Zech. 6: 1–8.

New Testament

TO ZACHARIAS, IN THE TEMPLE
Luke 1: 13–22.

TO JOHN THE BAPTIST, AT THE
BAPTISM OF JESUS
Matt. 3: 16; Mark 1: 10; Luke 3: 22;
John 1: 32–34.

TO PETER, JAMES, AND JOHN, OF THE
TRANSFIGURATION OF JESUS AND THE
APPEARANCE OF MOSES AND ELIJAH
Matt. 17: 1–9; Luke 9: 28–36.

TO THE PEOPLE, OF THE TONGUES OF
FIRE AT PENTECOST
Acts 2: 2–3.

TO STEPHEN, OF CHRIST
Acts 7: 55–56.

TO PAUL
Of Christ, on the way to Damascus.

Acts 9: 3–6; 1 Cor. 9: 1.
Of Ananias.
Acts 9: 12.
Of a man of Macedonia, saying, "Come over into Macedonia, and help us".
Acts 16: 9.
In Corinth.
Acts 18: 9–10.
In a trance.
Acts 22: 17–21.
Of paradise.

"It is doubtless not expedient for me to glory. I will come to visions and revelations of the Lord:

2 I knew a man in Christ more than fourteen years ago (whether in the body I cannot tell, or whether out of the body I cannot tell – God knoweth). Such a one was caught up to the third Heaven.

3 And I knew such a man (whether in the body or out of the body I cannot tell – God knoweth),

4 and how he was caught up into Paradise, and heard unspeakable words which it is not lawful for a man to utter.

2 Corinthians 12: 1–4 KJ21

To Ananias, of Christ
Acts 9: 10–12.

To Cornelius, the centurion, of an angel
Acts 10: 3.

To Peter, of the sheet let down from heaven
Acts 10: 9–18.

To John, on the island of Patmos:
Of Christ and the golden candlesticks.
Rev. 1: 10–20.
The open door.

Rev. 4: 1.
A rainbow and throne.
Rev. 4: 2–3.
Twenty-four elders.
Rev. 4: 4.
Seven lamps.
Rev. 4: 5.
Sea of glass.
Rev. 4: 6; Rev. 15: 2.
Four living creatures.
Rev. 4: 6–8.
Book with seven seals.
Rev. 5: 1–5.
Golden vials.
Rev. 5: 8.
Of the six seals .
Rev. 6.
Four horses .
Rev. 6: 2–8.
Earthquake and celestial phenomena.
Rev. 6: 12–14.
Four angels .
Rev. 7: 1.
Sealing of the one hundred and forty-four thousand.
Rev. 7: 2–8.
Of the seventh seal and seven angels.
Rev. 8–11.
Of the censer .
Rev. 8: 5.
Hail and fire .
Rev. 8: 7.

Quote Unquote

"Many souls, to whom visions have never come, are incomparably more advanced in the way of perfection than others to whom many have been given."
John of the Cross

Visions (3)

Visions mentioned in the Bible, continued

New Testament, continued

TO JOHN, ON THE ISLAND OF PATMOS
The third part of sun and moon and stars darkened.
Rev. 8: 12.
Bottomless pit.
Rev. 9: 2.
Locusts.
Rev. 9: 3–11.
Four angels loosed from the Euphrates.
Rev. 9: 14.
Army of horsemen.
Rev. 9: 16–19.
Angel having a book.
Rev. 10: 1–10.
Seven thunders.
Rev. 10: 3–4.
Measurement of the temple.
Rev. 11: 1–2.
Two witnesses.
Rev. 11: 3–12.
Court of the Gentiles.
Rev. 11: 2.
Two olive trees and two candlesticks.
Rev. 11: 4.
The beast out of the bottomless pit.
Rev. 11: 7.
Fall of the city.
Rev. 11: 13.
Second and third woes.
Rev. 11: 14.
A woman clothed with the sun; birth of the man child.
Rev. 12.
A red dragon.
Rev. 12: 3–17.

War in heaven.
Rev. 12: 7–9.
The beast rising out of the sea.
Rev. 13: 1–10.
The beast coming out of the earth.
Rev. 13: 11–18.
The Lamb on Mount Zion.
Rev. 14: 1–5.
The angel having the everlasting gospel.
Rev. 14: 6–7.
The angel proclaiming the fall of Babylon.
Rev. 14: 8–13.
The Son of man with a sickle.
Rev. 14: 14–16.
Angel reaping the harvest.
Rev. 14: 14–20.
Angel coming out of the temple.
Rev. 14: 17–19.
An angel having power over fire.
Rev. 14: 18.
The vine and the winepress.
Rev. 14: 18–20.
Angels with the seven last plagues.
Rev. 15.
Temple opened.
Rev. 15: 5.
The plague upon the men who had the mark of the beast.
Rev. 16: 2.
Sea turned into blood.
Rev. 16: 3.
The seven angels with the seven vials of the wrath of God.
Rev. 16–17.
Destruction of Babylon.
Rev. 18.
Of the multitude praising.
Rev. 19: 1–9.
Of Him who is faithful and true riding

a white horse.

Rev. 19: 11–16.

Angel in the sun.

Rev. 19: 17–21.

Satan bound a thousand years.

Rev. 20: 1–3.

Thrones of judgment, the resurrection, and the loosing of Satan.

Rev. 20: 1–10.

Great white throne.

Rev. 20: 11.

Opening of the book of life.

Rev. 20: 12.

Death and hell.

Rev. 20: 14.

New Jerusalem.

"And I saw a new heaven and a new earth, for the first heaven and the first earth had passed away, and there was no more sea.

2 And I, John, saw the holy city, New Jerusalem, coming down from God out of Heaven, prepared as a bride adorned for her husband.

3 And I heard a great voice out of Heaven, saying, 'Behold, the tabernacle of God is with men, and He will dwell with them; and they shall be His people, and God Himself shall be with them and be their God.

4 And God shall wipe away all tears from their eyes, and there shall be no more death, neither sorrow, nor crying, neither shall there be any more pain; for the former things are passed away.'

5 And He that sat upon the throne said, 'Behold, I make all things new.' And He said unto me, 'Write, for these words are true and faithful.'

6 And He said unto me, 'It is done! I am Alpha and Omega, the beginning and the end. I will give unto him that is athirst of the fountain of the Water of Life freely.

7 He that overcometh shall inherit all things; and I will be his God, and he shall be my son.'"

Revelation 21: 1–7

River of life.

Rev. 22: 1.

Tree of life.

Rev. 22: 2.

Facts about visions

Sometimes withheld for a long time

1 Sam. 3: 1..

The withholding of a great calamity. Lack of visions could be a sign of spiritual aridity.

"Where there is no vision, the people perish; but he that keepeth the law, happy is he" Proverbs 29: 18 *KJ21*.

"Her gates are sunk into the ground; He hath destroyed and broken her bars. Her king and her princes are among the Gentiles; the law is no more; her prophets also find no vision from the Lord" Lamentations 2: 9 *KJ21*.

False prophets claimed to have seen visions. Jer. 14: 14; 23: 16.

God's prophets could interpret visions accurately.

Quote Unquote

"For years I have never seen sun, moon, flowers, snow, stars, no man except the interrogator who beat, but I can say I have seen heaven open, I have seen Jesus Christ, I have seen the angles and we were very happy there."

Richard Wurmbrand, before the Senate Judiciary Committee

Dreams

Introduction

God has frequently made use of dreams in communicating his will to men and women. They were often given at pivotal moments in a person's life, as in the case of Jacob and of Joseph, Mary's husband-to-be.

The Bible teaches that the influence of God's Spirit on the soul extends to its sleeping as well as its waking thoughts.

In the Christian dispensation, while we read of trances and visions in the New Testament, dreams are never referred to as a method of divine revelation.

Overview

God's will often revealed in dreams. Num. 12: 6; Job 33: 15.

"In a dream, in a vision of the night, when deep sleep falleth upon men, in slumberings upon the bed,

16 then He openeth the ears of men, and sealeth their instruction,

17 that He may withdraw man from his purpose, and hide pride from man."

Job 33: 15–17 KJ21

Examples of dreams in the Bible

OLD TESTAMENT
Abimelech, concerning Sarah.
Gen. 20: 3.
Jacob, about the ladder.

"And Jacob went out from Beersheba, and went toward Haran.

11 And he alighted upon a certain place, and tarried there all night, because the sun was set; and he took of the stones of that place and put them for his pillows, and lay down in that place to sleep.

12 And he dreamed, and behold, a ladder was set up on the earth, and the top of it reached to heaven; and behold, the angels of God were ascending and descending on it.

13 And behold, the Lord stood above it and said, 'I am the Lord God of Abraham thy father and the God of Isaac: The land whereon thou liest, to thee will I give it, and to thy seed.

14 And thy seed shall be as the dust of the earth, and thou shalt spread abroad to the west and to the east, and to the north and to the south; and in thee and in thy seed shall all the families of the earth be blessed.

15 And behold, I am with thee, and will keep thee in all places whither thou goest, and will bring thee again into this land; for I will not leave thee, until I have done that which I have spoken to thee of.'

16 And Jacob awaked out of his sleep, and he said, 'Surely the Lord is in this place, and I knew it not.'

17 And he was afraid and said, 'How fearsome is this place! This is none other than the house of God, and this is the gate of heaven.'"

Genesis 28: 10–17 KJ21

The ring-streaked cattle.
Gen. 31: 10–13.
About his going down into Egypt.
Gen. 46: 2.

Laban, concerning Jacob.
Gen. 31: 24.
Joseph and the sheaves.
Gen. 37: 5–10.
The dreams of the butler and baker.
Gen. 40: 8–23.
The dreams of Pharaoh.
Gen. 41: 1–36.
Interpreted by Joseph.
Gen. 40: 12–13; Gen. 40: 18–19;
Gen. 41: 25–32.
The Midianite, concerning the cake of barley.
Judg. 7: 13.
Solomon, concerning his choice of wisdom.
1 Kgs. 3: 3–15.
Nebuchadnezzar.
Dan. 2: 1,31; 4: 5,8.
Daniel, concerning the four beasts.
Dan. 7.

NEW TESTAMENT
Joseph, concerning Mary's innocence.
Matt. 1: 20,21.
Concerning fleeing to Egypt.
Matt. 2: 13.
Concerning the return to Palestine.
Matt. 2: 19–22.
Wise men. .
Matt. 2: 11,12..
Pilate's wife, concerning Jesus.
Matt. 27: 19.

False dreams

Dreams that deceive.
"It shall even be as when a hungry man dreameth, and behold, he eateth; but he awaketh, and his soul is empty. Or as when a thirsty man dreameth, and behold, he drinketh; but he awaketh, and behold, he is faint and his soul hath appetite. So shall the multitude of all the nations be that fight against Mount Zion" Isaiah 29: 8 KJ21.
Deut. 13: 1–5; Jer. 23: 25–32; Jer. 27: 9; Jer. 29: 8; Zech. 10: 2.

False prophets

False prophets pretended to receive revelations through.
Jer. 23: 25–28; 29: 8.
Such dreams should be disregarded.
Deut. 13: 1–3; Jer. 27: 9.
Prophets condemned for falsely claiming to have received dreams.
Jer. 23: 32.

Facts about dreams

It is wrong to trust in natural dreams.
Eccl. 5: 7.
People placed their faith in dreams.
Judg. 7: 15.
Dreams were often perplexing.
Gen. 40: 6; 41: 8; Job 7: 14; Dan. 2: 1; 4: 5.
Magicians were consulted about dreams.
Gen. 41: 8; Dan. 2: 2–4.
God the only interpreter of dreams.
Gen. 40: 8; 41: 16; Dan. 2: 27–30; 7: 16.

Dreams illustrate

Prosperity of sinners.
Job 20: 5–8, Ps. 73: 19,20.
Impure imaginations.
Jude 1: 8.
Enemies of the church.
Is. 29: 7,8.

Part Three
Facts From
The Old Testament

Part Three Contents in summary

Every Old Testament book: Overviews 698

Encouragement from Old Testament books................808

Old Testament people..846

Old Testament history and kings...............................868

Old Testament belief, worship and judges 892

Part Three Contents in detail

Every Old Testament book: Overviews

Genesis (1) 698

Genesis (2)..700

Exodus (1) 702

Exodus (2) 704

Leviticus..706

Numbers (1) 708

Numbers (2)..710

Deuteronomy (1) 712

Deuteronomy (2)...714

Joshua (1)..716

Joshua (2) 718

Judges (1) 720

Judges (2)..722

Ruth 724

1 Samuel (1)..726

1 Samuel (2) 728

2 Samuel 730

1 Kings (1)...732

1 Kings (2)...734

2 Kings..736

1 Chronicles (1) 738

1 Chronicles (2)...740

2 Chronicles 742

Ezra..744

Nehemiah 746

Esther 748

Job (1)...750

Job (2) 752

Psalms (1)..754

Psalms (2)..756

Psalms (3)..758

Proverbs (1)..760

Proverbs (2)..762

Ecclesiastes...764

Song of Solomon...766

Isaiah (1)..768

Isaiah (2)..770

Jeremiah (1)...772

Jeremiah (2)..774

Lamentations..776

Ezekiel (1)...778

Ezekiel (2)...780

Daniel...782

Hosea...784

Joel...786

Amos..788

Obadiah..790

Jonah..792

Micah...794

Nahum...796

Habakkuk...798

Zephaniah...800

Haggai..802

Zechariah..804

Malachi...806

Encouragement from Old Testament books

Encouragement from Old Testament books (1).........................808

Encouragement from Old Testament books (2).........................810

Genesis 812

Exodus 814

Leviticus and Numbers 816

Deuteronomy 818

Joshua, Judges, Ruth, 1 and 2 Samuel 820

1 and 2 Samuel, 1 Kings 822

2 Kings, 1 Chronicles, 2 Chronicles 824

Ezra, Nehemiah, Esther 826

Esther and Job 828

Psalms and Proverbs 830

Proverbs and Ecclesiastes 832

Ecclesiastes, Song of Solomon, Isaiah 834

Isaiah and Jeremiah 836

Lamentations, Ezekiel, Daniel, Hosea 838

Hosea, Joel, Amos, Obadiah, Jonah 840

Jonah, Micah, Nahum, Habakkuk, Zephaniah 842

Haggai, Zechariah, Malachi 844

Old Testament people

Noah 846

Abram, Abraham (1) 848

Abram, Abraham (2) 850

Abram, Abraham (3) 852

Esau and Jacob, and Joseph 854

Moses (1) 856

Moses (2) 858

Samuel 860

David, King of Israel (1) 862

David, King of Israel (2) 864

Solomon 866

Old Testament history and kings

Parallel passages in the historical books (1) 868

Parallel passages in the historical books (2)...............................870

Kings of Israel (1)..872

Kings of Israel (2) 874

Kings of Israel (3) 876

Kings of Israel (4)..878

Kings of Judah (1)..880

Kings of Judah (2) 882

Kings of Judah (3)..884

Kings of Judah (4) 886

Kings of Judah (5)..888

The Apocrypha...890

Old Testament belief, worship and judges

The Law (1) 892

The Law (2)...894

The Tabernacle (1)..896

The Tabernacle (2) 898

The priesthood (1)..900

The priesthood (2) 902

Tabernacle worship 904

The judges...906

The beginning of the Hebrew monarchy...............................908

Feasts, festivals, and fasts (1)...910

Feasts, festivals, and fasts (2) 912

Genesis (1)

An introduction

Names for Genesis

PENTATEUCH
The five books of Moses were collectively called the Pentateuch, a word of Greek origin meaning "the five-fold book."

TORAH
The Jews called them the Torah, i.e., "the law."

BERESHITH
The first book of the Pentateuch is called, by the Jews, Bereshith, i.e., "in the beginning," because this is the first word of the book.

GENESIS
It is generally known by the name of Genesis, i.e., "creation" or "generation," being the name given to it in the LXX as designating its character, because it gives an account of the origin of all things.

Divisions

Genesis is divided into two principal parts.

The first part (Gen. 1–11) gives a general history of mankind down to the time of the Dispersion.

The second part presents the early history of Israel down to the death and burial of Joseph (Gen. 12–50).

People

There are five main people in this book. Around these people the history of the successive periods is grouped:
Adam (Gen. 1–3),
Noah (Gen. 4–9),
Abraham (Gen. 10–25: 18),
Isaac (Gen. 25: 19–35: 29), and
Jacob (Gen. 36–50).

Prophecies

In this book we have several prophecies concerning Christ (Gen. 3: 15; 12: 3; 18: 18; 22: 18; 26: 4; 28: 14; 49: 10).

Authorship

The author of this book was Moses. Under divine guidance he may indeed have been led to make use of materials already existing, documents, or even of traditions in a trustworthy form that had come down to his time, purifying them from all that was unworthy; but the hand of Moses is clearly seen throughout in its composition.

Name, author, date

MEANING OF NAME OF BOOK
The book of beginnings.

AUTHOR
Moses.

APPROXIMATE DATE OF WRITING
1450–1410 B.C.

Statistics

PLACE OF BOOK IN BIBLE
1st Old Testament book.
1st Book of the Law.

NUMBER OF CHAPTERS
50

NUMBER OF VERSES
1,533

NUMBER OF WORDS
38,267

Main theme of book

God's choice of a nation, through whom he would bless all nations.

Keys to the understanding of book

KEY WORD/S
Beginnings; generations; account.

KEY PHRASE
In the beginning.

KEY PERSON/PEOPLE
Adam, Eve, Noah, Abraham, Sarah, Isaac, Rebekah, Esau, Jacob, Rachel, Joseph.

KEY CHAPTER/S
1; 12; 15; 17.

KEY VERSE/S
In the beginning God created the heaven and the earth.
Genesis 1: 1

And I will put enmity between thee and the woman, and between thy seed and her seed; it shall bruise thy head, and thou shalt bruise his heel.
Genesis 3: 15

And I will bless them that bless thee, and curse him that curseth thee: and in thee shall all families of the earth be blessed.
Genesis 12: 3

Jesus Christ in Genesis

WHO JESUS IS
The promised Seed.

JESUS FORESHADOWED AS A TYPE/ PORTRAITS OF CHRIST
Adam is a type of Christ, Romans 4: 15.
Abel's accepted blood sacrifice points to Jesus' sacrifice.
Melchizedek is a type of Christ, Hebrews 12: 3.
Joseph is also a type of Christ, as they were similar in numerous ways: both loved by their father, both hated, rejected and condemned though innocent.

Spiritual thought

Start with God.

Chapter by chapter breakdown

Chapter 1: The first account of creation

Chapter 2: A second account of creation

Chapter 3: The record of the fall of humankind

Chapter 4: Cain and Abel

Chapter 5: Potted histories: Adam to Noah

Chapter 6: The judgment of the Flood

Chapter 7: Entering the ark and the flooded earth

Chapter 8: The Flood recedes

Chapter 9: God's covenant; the rainbow

Genesis (2)

Chapter by chapter breakdown, continued

Chapter 10: Family lines after the Flood

Chapter 11: The tower of Babel

Chapter 12: God calls Abraham

Chapter 13: Abraham and Lot separate

Chapter 14: Abraham rescues Lot

Chapter 15: God's promise of children

Chapter 16: Hagar and Ishmael

Chapter 17: Circumcision

Chapter 18: Sarah and Abraham tested

Chapter 19: Destruction of Sodom and Gomorrah

Chapter 20: Abimelech is tested

Chapter 21: The birth of Isaac

Chapter 22: Abraham's severe test

Chapter 23: Abraham buries Sarah

Chapter 24: Finding a wife for Isaac

Chapter 25: Abraham dies

Chapter 26: Isaac in Philistine country

Chapter 27: Jacob gains Esau's blessing

Chapter 28: Jacob's dream

Chapter 29: Jacob's marriages

Chapter 30: Jacob's bargain with Laban

Chapter 31: Jacob flees from Laban

Chapter 32: Jacob fights with an angel

Chapter 33: Jacob makes peace with Esau

Chapter 34: Dinah is raped

Chapter 35: Jacob returns to Bethel

Chapter 36: The history of Esau

Chapter 37: Joseph's dreams

Chapter 38: Judah and Tamar

Chapter 39: Joseph and Potiphar's wife

Chapter 40: Joseph in prison

Chapter 41: Joseph interprets Pharaoh's dreams

Chapter 42: Joseph's brothers seek food in Egypt

Chapter 43: Joseph's brothers return to Egypt with Benjamin

Chapter 44: Joseph's cup goes missing

Chapter 45: Joseph reveals himself to his brothers

Chapter 46: Jacob and his family go to Egypt

Chapter 47: Jacob's family safe in Egypt

Chapter 48: Jacob blesses Ephraim and Manasseh

Chapter 49: Jacob's last words and death

Chapter 50: The death of Joseph

Insight from Matthew Henry

Genesis 1

VERSES 1–2

The first verse of the Bible gives us a satisfying and useful account of the origin of the earth and the heavens. The faith of humble Christians understands this better than the fancy of the most learned men. From what we see of heaven and earth, we learn the power of the great Creator. And let our make and place as men, remind us of our duty as Christians, always to keep heaven in our eye, and the earth under our feet. The Son of God, one with the Father, was with him when he made the world; nay, we are often told that the world was made by him, and nothing was made without him. Oh, what high thoughts should there be in our minds, of that great God whom we worship, and of that great Mediator in whose name we pray! And here, at the beginning of the sacred volume, we read of that Divine Spirit, whose work upon the heart of man is so often mentioned in other parts of the Bible. Observe, that at first there was nothing desirable to be seen, for the world was without form, and void; it was confusion, and emptiness. In like manner the work of grace in the soul is a new creation: and in a graceless soul, one that is not born again, there is disorder, confusion, and every evil work: it is empty of all good, for it is without God; it is dark, it is darkness itself: this is our condition by nature, till Almighty grace works a change in us.

VERSES 3–5

God said, Let there be light; he willed it, and at once there was light. Oh, the power of the word of God! And in the new creation, the first thing that is wrought in the soul is light: the blessed Spirit works upon the will and affections by enlightening the understanding. Those who by sin were darkness, by grace become light in the Lord. Darkness would have been always upon fallen man, if the Son of God had not come and given us an understanding. The light which God willed, he approved of. God divided the light from the darkness; for what fellowship has light with darkness? In heaven there is perfect light, and no darkness at all; in hell, utter darkness, and no gleam of light. The day and the night are the Lord's; let us use both to his honor, by working for him every day, and resting in him every night, meditating in his law both day and night.

VERSES 6–13

The earth was emptiness, but by a word spoken, it became full of God's riches, and his they are still. Though the use of them is allowed to man, they are from God, and to his service and honor they must be used. The earth, at his command, brings forth grass, herbs, and fruits. God must have the glory of all the benefit we receive from the produce of the earth. If we have, through grace, an interest in Him who is the Fountain, we may rejoice in him when the streams of temporal mercies are dried up.

VERSES 14–19

In the fourth day's work, the creation of the sun, moon, and stars is accounted for. All these are the works of God. The stars are spoken of as they appear to our eyes, without telling their number, nature, place, size, or motions; for the Scriptures were written, not to gratify curiosity, or make us astronomers, but to lead us to God, and make us saints. The lights of heaven are made to serve him; they do it faithfully, and shine in their season without fail. We are set as lights in this world to serve God; but do we in like manner answer the end of our creation? We do not: our light does not shine before God, as his lights shine before us. We burn our Master's candles, but do not mind our Master's work.

Exodus (1)

An introduction

Names for Exodus

Exodus
Exodus is the name given in the LXX to the second book of the Pentateuch. It means "departure" or "outgoing." This name was adopted in the Latin translation, and from there into other languages.

Ve-eleh shemoth
The Hebrews called it by the first words, according to their custom, Ve-eleh shemoth (i.e., "and these are the names").

Contents

It contains,
  (1) An account of the increase and growth of the Israelites in Egypt (Ex. 1).
  (2) Preparations for their exodus from Egypt (Ex. 2–12: 36).
  (3) Their journey from Egypt to Sinai (Ex. 12: 37–19: 2).
  (4) The giving of the law and the establishment of the institutions by which the organization of the people was completed, the theocracy, "a kingdom of priest and an holy nation" (Ex. 19: 3–40).

Period covered

The book covers the time from the death of Joseph to the erection of the tabernacle in the wilderness.

Authorship

The authorship of this book, as well as of that of the other books of the Pentateuch, is to be ascribed to Moses. The unanimous voice of tradition and all internal evidences abundantly support this opinion.

Name, author, date

Meaning of name of book
Exit, going out, departure.

Author
Moses.

Approximate date of writing
1450–1410 B.C.

Statistics

Place of book in Bible
2nd Old Testament book.
2nd Book of the Law.

Number of chapters
40

Number of verses
1,213

Number of words
32,692

Main theme of book

Redemption is portrayed in the Passover, and deliverance in the Exodus.

Keys to the understanding of book

Key word/s
Redemption. "Redeem" is used 9 times.

Key phrase
Pass over you, 12: 13.

Key person/people
Moses, Aaron, Miriam, Pharaoh.

Key chapter/s
12–14. As the cross is the central event in the New Testament, the Exodus is the central event in the Old Testament.

Key verse/s
Wherefore say unto the children of Israel, I am the Lord, and I will bring you out from under the burdens of the Egyptians, and I will rid you out of their bondage, and I will redeem you with a stretched out arm, and with great judgments.
Exodus 6: 6

Now therefore, if ye will obey my voice indeed, and keep my covenant, then ye shall be a peculiar treasure unto me above all people: for all the earth is mine: 6 And ye shall be unto me a kingdom of priests, and an holy nation. These are the words which thou shalt speak unto the children of Israel.
Exodus 19: 5–6

Jesus Christ in Exodus

Who Jesus is
The Passover Lamb.

Jesus foreshadowed as a type/ portraits of Christ
1 Moses
2 The Passover
3 The seven feasts
4 The Exodus
5 The manna and the water
6 The tabernacle
7 The high priest

Spiritual thought
Come out for God.

Chapter by chapter breakdown
Chapter 1: A new king in Egypt
Chapter 2: The birth of Moses
Chapter 3: Moses and the burning bush
Chapter 4: Moses returns to Egypt
Chapter 5: Moses in conflict with Pharaoh
Chapter 6: The family of Moses and Aaron
Chapter 7: The River Nile is turned to blood
Chapter 8: Frogs, gnats, and flies
Chapter 9: Death of animals, boils, and hail
Chapter 10: Locusts and darkness
Chapter 11: The death of the firstborn is announced
Chapter 12: The Passover and the Exodus
Chapter 13: The festival of unleavened bread
Chapter 14: Crossing the Red Sea
Chapter 15: The Song of Moses
Chapter 16: Food miraculously provided
Chapter 17: Water from a rock
Chapter 18: Jethro meets the Israelites
Chapter 19: The Israelites at Mount Sinai
Chapter 20: The Ten Commandments
Chapter 21: Laws about the rights of people
Chapter 22: Laws about repayment, and moral and religious laws

Exodus (2)

Chapter by chapter breakdown, continued

Chapter 23: The seventh day and the seventh year, and three national festivals

Chapter 24: The covenant is ratified

Chapter 25: The covenant box, the special table, and the lampstand

Chapter 26: The tent of the Lord's presence

Chapter 27: The altar and tabernacle enclosure

Chapter 28: The clothes for the priests and the breast-piece

Chapter 29: Instructions for Aaron's ordination and the daily offerings

Chapter 30: Instructions for using the tabernacle

Chapter 31: Instructions for building the tabernacle, and the sign of the covenant

Chapter 32: Moses prays for Israel's salvation

Chapter 33: God shows Moses his glory

Chapter 34: The second set of stone tablets, and the renewal of the covenant

Chapter 35: Rules for the Sabbath, and the craftsmen for the tabernacle

Chapter 36: Making the tabernacle

Chapter 37: Making the furniture for the tabernacle

Chapter 38: Making the altar and bronze basin, and the materials used

Chapter 39: Clothes for the priests

Chapter 40: The tent is put up and filled with God's glory

Insight from Matthew Henry

Exodus 12

1. The paschal lamb was typical.

Christ is our Passover, 1 Cor. 5: 7. Christ is the Lamb of God, John 1: 29; often in the Revelation he is called the Lamb. It was to be in its prime; Christ offered up himself in the midst of his days, not when a babe at Bethlehem. It was to be without blemish; the Lord Jesus was a Lamb without spot: the judge who condemned Christ declared him innocent. It was to be set apart four days before, denoting the marking out of the Lord Jesus to be a Savior, both in the purpose and in the promise. It was to be slain, and roasted with fire, denoting the painful sufferings of the Lord Jesus, even unto death, the death of the cross. The wrath of God is as fire, and Christ was made a curse for us. Not a bone of it must be broken, which was fulfilled in Christ, John 19: 33, denoting the unbroken strength of the Lord Jesus.

2. The sprinkling of the blood was typical.

The blood of the lamb must be sprinkled, denoting the applying of the merits of Christ's death to our souls; we must receive the atonement, Romans 5: 11. Faith is the bunch of hyssop, by which we apply the promises, and the benefits of the blood of Christ laid up in them, to ourselves. It was to be sprinkled on the door-posts, denoting the open profession we are to make of faith in Christ. It was not to be sprinkled upon the threshold; which cautions us to take heed of trampling under foot the blood of the covenant. It is precious blood, and must be precious to us. The blood, thus sprinkled, was a means of preserving the Israelites from the destroying angel, who had nothing to do where the blood was. The blood of Christ is the believer's protection from the wrath of God, the curse of the law, and the damnation of hell, Romans 8: 1.

3. The solemn eating of the lamb was typical of our gospel duty to Christ.

The paschal lamb was not to be looked upon only, but to be fed upon. So we must by faith make Christ our own; and we must receive spiritual strength and nourishment from him, as from our food, see John 6: 53,55 . It was all to be eaten; those who by faith feed upon Christ, must feed upon a whole Christ; they must take Christ and his yoke, Christ and his cross, as well as Christ and his crown. It was to be eaten at once, not put by till morning. To-day Christ is offered, and is to be accepted while it is called to-day, before we sleep the sleep of death. It was to be eaten with bitter herbs, in remembrance of the bitterness of their bondage in Egypt; we must feed upon Christ with sorrow and brokenness of heart, in remembrance of sin. Christ will be sweet to us, if sin be bitter. It was to be eaten standing, with their staves in their hands, as being ready to depart. When we feed upon Christ by faith, we must forsake the rule and the dominion of sin; sit loose to the world, and every

thing in it; forsake all for Christ, and reckon it no bad bargain, Hebrews 13: 13,14.

4. The feast of unleavened bread was Christ Jesus the Lord, we must continually delight ourselves in Christ Jesus.

No manner of work must be done, that is, no care admitted and indulged, which does not agree with, or would lessen this holy joy. The Jews were very strict as to the Passover, so that no leaven should be found in their houses. It must be a feast kept in charity, without the leaven of malice; and in sincerity, without the leaven of hypocrisy. It was by an ordinance for ever; so long as we live we must continue feeding upon Christ, rejoicing in him always, with thankful mention of the great things he has done for us.

Leviticus

An introduction

Leviticus, the third book of the Pentateuch, is given this name in the Vulgate, after the LXX, because it mainly deals with the work of the Levites.

Divisions

In the first section of the book (Lev. 1–17), which concentrates on the worship itself, there is,

(1) A series of laws (Lev. 1–7)

a) regarding sacrifices, burnt-offerings, meat-offerings, and thank-offerings (Lev. 1–3),

b) sin-offerings and trespass-offerings (Lev. 4; 5),

c) followed by the law of the priestly duties in connection with the offering of sacrifices (Lev. 6; 7).

(2) An historical section (Lev. 8–10),

a) giving an account of the consecration of Aaron and his sons (Lev. 8);

b) Aaron's first offering for himself and the people (Lev. 9);

c) Nadab and Abihu's presumption in offering "strange fire before Jehovah," and their punishment (Lev. 10).

(3) Laws concerning purity, and the sacrifices and ordinances for putting away impurity (Lev. 11–16).

(4) Laws marking the separation between Israel and the heathen (Lev. 17–20).

(5) Laws about the personal purity of the priests, and their eating of the holy things (Lev. 20; 21); about the offerings of Israel, that they were to be without blemish (Lev. 22: 17–33); and about the due celebration of the great festivals (Lev. 23; 25).

(6) Then follow promises and warnings to the people about obedience to these commandments, closing with a section on vows.

The various ordinances contained in this book were all delivered in the space of a month (Cf. Ex. 40: 17; Num. 1: 1), the first month of the second year after the Exodus. It is the third book of Moses.

No book contains more of the very words of God. He is almost throughout the whole of it the direct speaker. This book is a prophecy of things to come, a shadow whereof the substance is Christ and his kingdom. The principles on which this book is to be interpreted are laid down in the Epistle to the Hebrews. It contains in its complicated ceremonial the gospel of the grace of God.

Name, author, date

MEANING OF NAME OF BOOK
Levitical book.

Author

Moses.

Approximate date of writing

1450–1410 B.C.

Statistics

PLACE OF BOOK IN BIBLE
3rd Old Testament book.
3rd Book of the Law.

NUMBER OF CHAPTERS. 27

NUMBER OF VERSES. 859

NUMBER OF WORDS. 24,546

Main theme of book

God's chosen people must approach God in a holy way.

Keys to the understanding of book

KEY WORD/S
Holiness, 87 times; holy, 65 times.

KEY PHRASE
Be ye holy, for I am holy, 11: 44.

KEY PERSON/PEOPLE
Moses and Aaron.

KEY CHAPTER/S
16, the Day of Atonement.

KEY VERSE/S
For the life of the flesh is in the blood: and I have given it to you upon the altar to make an atonement for your souls: for it is the blood that maketh an atonement for the soul.
Leviticus 17: 11

Jesus Christ in Leviticus

WHO JESUS IS
The scapegoat.

JESUS FORESHADOWED AS A TYPE/
PORTRAITS OF CHRIST
1 The five offerings
2 The high priest
3 The seven feasts

Spiritual thought

Getting right with God.

Chapter by chapter breakdown

Chapter 1: Burnt offerings
Chapter 2: Cereal offerings
Chapter 3: Peace offerings
Chapter 4: Sin offerings
Chapter 5: Guilt offerings
Chapter 6: Laws for administering offerings
Chapter 7: Laws for administering guilt and peace offerings
Chapter 8: Consecration of priests
Chapter 9: Sacrifices are offered
Chapter 10: Rules for the priests
Chapter 11: Animals that may and may not be eaten
Chapter 12: Cleansing after childbirth
Chapter 13: Cases of skin disease
Chapter 14: Cleansing if skin disease is cured
Chapter 15: Uncleanliness from discharges
Chapter 16: The Day of Atonement
Chapter 17: Blood is sacred
Chapter 18: Forbidden relationships
Chapter 19: Rules for life: love your neighbor
Chapter 20: Laws of penalties
Chapter 21: Rules for godly living for priests
Chapter 22: Holiness of the offerings
Chapter 23: The religious calendar
Chapter 24: An example of sin and punishment
Chapter 25: The seventh year, and restorations
Chapter 26: Reward and punishment
Chapter 27: Rules about vows and tithes

Insight from Matthew Henry

Leviticus 11

VERSES 10–16
The blood is now allowed for the nourishment of our bodies; it is no longer appointed to make an atonement for the soul. Now the blood of Christ makes atonement.

Numbers (1)

An introduction

Names for Numbers

IN THE WILDERNESS
The fourth of the books of the Pentateuch, is called in Hebrew *bemidbar*, i.e., "in the wilderness."

NUMBERS
In the LXX version it is called "Numbers," and this name is now the usual title of the book. It is so called because it contains a record of the numbering of the people in the wilderness of Sinai (Num. 1–4), and of their numbering afterwards on the plain of Moab (Num. 26).

Historical interest

This book is of special historical interest as it furnishes us with details about the route the Israelites took in the wilderness and their principal encampments.

Divisions

It may be divided into three parts:
  1. The numbering of the people at Sinai, and preparations for their resuming their march (Num. 1–10: 10). The sixth chapter gives an account of the vow of a Nazarite.
  2. An account of the journey from Sinai to Moab, the sending out of the spies and the report they brought back, and the murmurings (eight times) of the people at the hardships they experienced (Num. 10: 11–21: 20).
  3. The events in the plain of

Moab before crossing the Jordan (Num. 21: 21–Num. 36).

Period covered

The period covered in the history extends from the second month of the second year after the Exodus to the beginning of the eleventh month of the fortieth year, in all about thirty-eight years and ten months; a dreary period of wanderings, during which that disobedient generation all died in the wilderness. They were fewer in number at the end of their wanderings than when they left the land of Egypt. We see in this history, on the one hand, the unceasing care of the Almighty over his chosen people during their wanderings; and, on the other hand, the murmurings and rebellions by which they offended their heavenly Protector, drew down repeated marks of his displeasure, and provoked him to say that they should "not enter into his rest" because of their unbelief (Heb. 3: 19).

Authorship

This, like the other books of the Pentateuch, bears evidence of having been written by Moses.

The book of the wars of the Lord

The expression "the book of the wars of the Lord," occurring in Num. 21: 14, has given rise to much discussion. But, after all, what this book was is uncertain, whether some writing of Israel not now extant, or some writing of the Amorites which contained songs and triumphs of their king Sihon's victories, out of which Moses may cite this testimony, as Paul sometimes does out of heathen poets (Acts 17: 28; Titus 1: 12).

Name, author, date

MEANING OF NAME OF BOOK
Numbering.

AUTHOR
Moses.

APPROXIMATE DATE OF WRITING
1450–1410 B.C.

Statistics

PLACE OF BOOK IN BIBLE
4th Old Testament book.
4th Book of the Law.

NUMBER OF CHAPTERS
36

NUMBER OF VERSES
1,288

NUMBER OF WORDS
32,902

Main theme of book

The journey to the Promised Land.

Keys to the understanding of book

KEY WORD/S
Wanderings.

KEY PHRASE
These are the journeys, 33: 1.

KEY PERSON/PEOPLE
Moses, Aaron, Miriam, Joshua, Caleb, Balak.

KEY CHAPTER/S
14, where Israel refuses to conquer the Promised Land.

KEY VERSE/S
Because all those men which have seen my glory, and my miracles, which I did in Egypt and in the wilderness, and have tempted me now these ten times, and have not hearkened to my voice; Surely they shall not see the land which I sware unto their fathers, neither shall any of them that provoked me see it.
Numbers 14: 22,23

And the Lord spake unto Moses and Aaron, Because ye believed me not, to sanctify me in the eyes of the children of Israel, therefore ye shall not bring this congregation into the land which I have given them.
Numbers 20: 12

Jesus Christ in Numbers

WHO JESUS IS
The bronze snake.

JESUS FORESHADOWED AS A TYPE/ PORTRAITS OF CHRIST
1   The snake which was lifted up
2   The rock which quenched thirst
3   The pillar of cloud and fire
4   The red heifer

Spiritual thought

Arriving by God's grace.

Numbers (2)

Chapter by chapter breakdown

Chapter 1: The first census

Chapter 2: The arrangement of the camp

Chapter 3: The census of the Levites

Chapter 4: The ministry of the Levites

Chapter 5: The law of jealousy

Chapter 6: The Nazirite vows

Chapter 7: The offerings of the leaders

Chapter 8: The consecration of the Levites

Chapter 9: The second Passover, and the fiery cloud

Chapter 10: Israel leaves Mount Sinai

Chapter 11: Moses complains, and the quails

Chapter 12: Miriam and Aaron complain

Chapter 13: The mission and report of the spies

Chapter 14: Rebellion and judgment in the camp

Chapter 15: Rules for the priests

Chapter 16: Rebellion against Moses and Aaron

Chapter 17: Aaron's blossoming rod

Chapter 18: Rules for the priests and Levites

Chapter 19: Purification of the red heifer

Chapter 20: The people complain, and the death of Aaron

Chapter 21: The bronze serpent

Chapter 22: Balak, Balaam and his talking donkey

Chapter 23: Balaam's first prophecies

Chapter 24: Balaam's third and fourth prophecies

Chapter 25: Moab seduces Israel

Chapter 26: The second census

Chapter 27: Joshua is to succeed Moses

Chapter 28: Seasonal offerings

Chapter 29: Offering for New Year, Day of Atonement, and Festival of Shelters

Chapter 30: Laws about vows

Chapter 31: Judgment on Midian

Chapter 32: Division of the land east of Jordan

Chapter 33: Summary of Israel's journeys

Chapter 34: The boundaries of the land

Chapter 35: Levitical cities and cities of refuge

Chapter 36: Inheritance of married women

Insight from Matthew Henry

Numbers 21

VERSES 1–3

Before the people began their march round the country of Edom, the king of Arad, a Canaanite, who inhabited the southern part of the country, attacked them in the wilderness, and took some prisoners. This was to lead the Israelites to look more thoroughly to the Lord.

VERSES 4–9

The children of Israel were wearied by a long march round the land of Edom. They speak discontentedly of what God had done for them, and distrustfully of what he would do. What will they be pleased with, whom manna will not please?

Let not the contempt which some cast on the word of God, make us value it less. It is the bread of life, substantial bread, and will nourish those who by faith feed upon it, to eternal life, whoever may call it light bread.

We see the righteous judgment God brought upon them for murmuring. He sent fiery serpents among them, which bit or stung many to death.

It is to be feared that they would not have owned the sin, if they had not felt the smart; but they relent under the rod. And God made a wonderful provision for their relief.

The Jews themselves say it was not the sight of the brazen serpent that cured; but in looking up to it, they looked up to God as the Lord that healed them.

There was much gospel in this. Our Savior declared, John 3: 14,15 , that as Moses lifted up the serpent in the wilderness, so the Son of man must be lifted up, that whatsoever believeth in him, should not perish. Compare their disease and ours.

Sin bites like a serpent, and stings like an adder. Compare the application of their remedy and ours.

They looked and lived, and we, if we believe, shall not perish.

It is by faith that we look unto Jesus, Hebrews 12: 2.

Whosoever looked, however desperate his case, or feeble his sight, or distant his place, was certainly and perfectly cured.

The Lord can relieve us from dangers and distresses, by means which human reason never would have devised.

Oh that the venom of the old serpent, inflaming men's passions, and causing them to commit sins which end in their eternal destruction, were as sensibly felt, and the danger as plainly seen, as the Israelites felt pain from the bite of the fiery serpents, and feared the death which followed!

Then none would shut their eyes to Christ, or turn from his gospel.

Then a crucified Savior would be so valued, that all things else would be accounted loss for him; then, without delay, and with earnestness and simplicity, all would apply to him in the appointed way, crying, Lord, save us; we perish! Nor would any abuse the freeness of Christ's salvation, while they reckoned the price which it cost him.

VERSES 10–20
We have here the removes of the children of Israel, till they came to the plains of Moab, from whence they passed over Jordan into Canaan. The end of their pilgrimage was near. "They set forward."

It were well if we did thus; and the nearer we come to heaven, were so much the more active and abundant in the work of the Lord.

The wonderful success God granted to his people, is here spoken of, and, among the rest, their actions on the river Arnon, at Vaheb in Suphah, and other places on that river.

Deuteronomy (1)

An introduction

Volumes

In all the Hebrew manuscripts the Pentateuch forms one roll or volume divided into larger and smaller sections called *parshioth* and *sedarim*. It is not easy to say when it was divided into five books. This was probably first done by the Greek translators of the book, whom the Vulgate follows.

Names for Deuteronomy

DEUTERONOMION
The fifth of these books was called by the Greeks Deuteronomion, i.e., the second law, hence our name Deuteronomy, or a second statement of the laws already promulgated.

THESE ARE THE WORDS
The Jews designated the book by the two first Hebrew words that occur, 'Elle haddabharim, i.e., "These are the words." They divided it into eleven *parshioth*. In the English Bible it contains thirty-four chapters.

Division

It consists chiefly of three discourses delivered by Moses a short time before his death. They were spoken to all Israel in the plains of Moab, in the eleventh month of the last year of their wanderings.

The first discourse (Deut. 1–4: 40) recapitulates the chief events of the last forty years in the wilderness, with earnest exhortations to obey the divine ordinances, and warnings against the danger of forsaking the God of their fathers.

The second discourse (Deut. 5–26: 19) is in effect the body of the whole book. The first address is introductory to it. It contains practically a recapitulation of the law already given by God at Mount Sinai, together with many admonitions and injunctions about how to live when they were settled in Canaan.

The concluding discourse (Deut. 27–30) relates almost wholly to the solemn sanctions of the law, the blessings to the obedient, and the curse that would fall on the rebellious. He solemnly warns them to adhere faithfully to the covenant God had made with them, and so secure for themselves and their posterity the promised blessings.

THREE APPENDICES
These addresses to the people are followed by what may be called three appendices, namely
(1) a song which God had commanded Moses to write (Deut. 32: 1–47);
(2) the blessings he pronounced on the separate tribes (Deut. 33); and
(3) the story of his death (Deut. 32: 48–52) and burial (Deut. 34), written by some other hand, probably that of Joshua.

These farewell addresses of Moses to the tribes of Israel he had so long led in the wilderness "glow in each line with the emotions of a great leader recounting to his contemporaries the marvelous story of their common experience. The enthusiasm they kindle, even to-day, though obscured by translation, reveals their matchless adaptation to the circumstances under which they were first spoken. Confidence for the future is evoked by remembrance of the past. The same God who had done mighty works for the tribes since the Exodus would cover their head in the day of battle with the nations of Palestine, soon to be invaded. Their great lawgiver stands before us, vigorous in his old age, stern in his abhorrence of evil, earnest in his zeal for God, but mellowed in all relations to earth by his nearness to heaven. The commanding wisdom of his enactments, the dignity of his position as the founder of the nation and the first of prophets, enforce his utterances. But he touches our deepest emotions by the human tenderness that breathes in all his words. Standing on the verge of life, he speaks as a father giving his parting counsels to those he loves; willing to depart and be with God he has served so well, but fondly lengthening out his last farewell to the dear ones of earth. No book can compare with Deuteronomy in its mingled sublimity and tenderness."

Geikie

Authorship

The whole style and method of this book, its tone and its peculiarities of conception and expression, show that it must have come from one hand. That the author was none other than Moses is established by the following considerations:

(1) The uniform tradition both of the Jewish and the Christian Church down to recent times.

(2) The book professes to have been written by Moses (Deut. 1: 1; 29: 1; 31: 1, 9–11, etc.), and was obviously intended to be accepted as his work.

(3) The incontrovertible testimony of our Lord and his apostles (Matt. 19: 7,8; Mark 10: 3,4; John 5: 46,47; Acts 3: 22; 7: 37; Rom. 10: 19) establishes the same conclusion.

(4) The frequent references to it in the later books of the canon (Josh. 8: 31; 1 Kings 2: 9; 2 Kings 14: 6; 2 Chr. 23: 18; 25: 4; 34: 14; Ezra 3: 2; 7: 6; Neh. 8: 1; Dan. 9: 11,13) prove its antiquity; and

(5) the archaisms found in it are in harmony with the age in which Moses lived.

(6) Its style and allusions are also strikingly consistent with the circumstances and position of Moses and of the people at that time.

This body of positive evidence cannot be set aside by the conjectures and reasoning of modern critics, who contended that the book was somewhat like a forgery, introduced among the Jews some seven or eight centuries after the Exodus.

Name, author, date

MEANING OF NAME OF BOOK
Second law.

AUTHOR
Moses.

Deuteronomy (2)

Approximate date of writing

1410 B.C.

Statistics

PLACE OF BOOK IN BIBLE
5th Old Testament book.
5th Book of the Law.

NUMBER OF CHAPTERS
34

NUMBER OF VERSES
959

NUMBER OF WORDS
28,461

Main theme of book

The danger of forgetting God.

Keys to the understanding of book

KEY WORD/S
Covenant, 27 times
Love, 17 times
Remember
Obedience

KEY PHRASE
Observe and do, 12: 1.

KEY PERSON/PEOPLE
Moses and Joshua.

KEY CHAPTER/S
27; 29.

KEY VERSE/S
Only take heed to thyself, and keep thy soul diligently, lest thou forget the things which thine eyes have seen, and lest they depart from thy heart all the days of thy life: but teach them thy sons, and thy sons' sons.
Deuteronomy 4: 9

Take heed unto yourselves, lest ye forget the covenant of the Lord your God, which he made with you, and make you a graven image, or the likeness of any thing, which the Lord thy God hath forbidden thee.
Deuteronomy 4: 23

(For the Lord thy God is a merciful God;) he will not forsake thee, neither destroy thee, nor forget the covenant of thy fathers which he sware unto them.
Deuteronomy 4: 31

And thou shalt love the Lord thy God with all thine heart, and with all thy soul, and with all thy might.
Deuteronomy 6: 5

And now, Israel, what doth the Lord thy God require of thee, but to fear the Lord thy God, to walk in all his ways, and to love him, and to serve the Lord thy God with all thy heart and with all thy soul, To keep the commandments of the Lord, and his statutes, which I command thee this day for thy good?
Deuteronomy 10: 12–13

I call heaven and earth to record this day against you, that I have set before you life and death, blessing and cursing: therefore choose life, that both thou and thy seed may live: That thou mayest love the Lord thy God, and that thou mayest obey his voice, and that thou mayest cleave unto him: for he is thy life, and the length of thy days: that

thou mayest dwell in the land which the Lord sware unto thy fathers, to Abraham, to Isaac, and to Jacob, to give them.
Deuteronomy 30: 19–20

Jesus Christ in Deuteronomy

WHO JESUS IS
The Lawgiver.

JESUS FORESHADOWED AS A TYPE/
PORTRAITS OF CHRIST
Moses as a type of Christ, 18: 15.
Moses as prophet, 34: 10–12; priest, 32: 31–35, and king, 33: 4–5.

Spiritual thought

Reflect on where you are spiritually.

Chapter by chapter breakdown

Chapter 1: Judges appointed, spies sent out

Chapter 2: Wandering in the desert for thirty-eight years

Chapter 3: Land east of Jordan conquered

Chapter 4: Summary of God's covenant

Chapter 5: The Ten Commandments

Chapter 6: Command to teach the law

Chapter 7: Command to conquer Canaan

Chapter 8: Command to remember the Lord

Chapter 9: Israel's disobedience to God

Chapter 10: The covenant is renewed

Chapter 11: Victory is dependent on obedience

Chapter 12: Detailed instructions for worship

Chapter 13: Warning against idolatry

Chapter 14: Laws about food and tithes

Chapter 15: Laws about debts, slaves, and the firstborn

Chapter 16: Laws about feasts

Chapter 17: Instructions for a king

Chapter 18: Laws about prophecy

Chapter 19: Cities of refuge, and laws of witnesses

Chapter 20: Laws about war

Chapter 21: Laws about unsolved murders, and other laws

Chapter 22: Laws about sexual purity

Chapter 23: Laws about exclusion from God's people

Chapter 24: Divorce and remarriage

Chapter 25: Duty to a dead brother

Chapter 26: Laws about tithes, and Israel's vows

Chapter 27: The curse of disobedience

Chapter 28: Warnings of the covenant

Chapter 29: The Lord's covenant in the land of Moab

Chapter 30: Promise of repentance and forgiveness

Chapter 31: Joshua to succeed Moses

Chapter 32: The Song of Moses

Chapter 33: Moses blesses Israel

Chapter 34: The death of Moses

Insight from Matthew Henry

Deuteronomy 6

VERSES 4–5
Here is a brief summary of religion, containing the first principles of faith and obedience.

Joshua (1)

An introduction

The book of Joshua contains a history of the Israelites from the death of Moses to that of Joshua.

Divisions

It consists of three parts:

(1) The history of the conquest of the land (Josh. 1–12).

(2) The allotment of the land to the different tribes, with the appointment of cities of refuge, the provision for the Levites (Josh. 13–22), and the dismissal of the eastern tribes to their homes. This section has been compared to the Doomsday Book of the Norman conquest of England.

(3) The farewell addresses of Joshua, with an account of his death (Josh. 23,24).

Place in Old Testament

This book stands first in the second of the three sections of the Old Testament,

(1) the Law,

(2) the Prophets,

(3) the "other writings" – *Hagiographa*, into which the Jewish Church divided the Old Testament.

Authorship

There is every reason for concluding that the uniform tradition of the Jews is correct when they assign the authorship of the book to Joshua, all except the concluding section; the last verses (Josh. 24: 29–33) were added by some other hand.

Two difficulties

There are two difficulties connected with this book which have given rise to much discussion,

(1) The miracle of the standing still of the sun and moon on Gibeon. This occurred in Joshua's impassioned prayer of faith, as quoted (Josh. 10: 12–15) from the "Book of Jasher." There are many explanations given of these words. They need, however, present no difficulty if we believe in the possibility of God's miraculous interposition on behalf of his people. Whether it was caused by the refraction of the light, or by some other means, we know not.

(2) Another difficulty arises out of the command given by God utterly to exterminate the Canaanites. "Shall not the Judge of all the earth do right?" It is enough that Joshua clearly knew that this was the will of God, who employs his terrible agencies, famine, pestilence, and war, in the righteous government of this world. The Canaanites had sunk into a state of immorality and corruption so foul and degrading that they had to be rooted out of the land with the edge of the sword. The Israelites' sword, in its bloodiest executions, wrought a work of mercy for all the countries of the earth to the very end of the world.

This book resembles the Acts of the Apostles in the number and variety of historical incidents it records, and in its many references to people and places; and as in the latter case the epistles of Paul confirm its historical accuracy by their incidental allusions and coincidences, so in the former modern discoveries confirm its historicity. The Amarna tablets are among the most remarkable discoveries of the age. Dating from about 1480 B.C. down to the time of Joshua, and consisting of official communications from Amorite, Phoenician, and Philistine chiefs to the king of Egypt, they afford a glimpse into the actual condition of Palestine prior to the Hebrew invasion, and illustrate and confirm the history of the conquest. A letter, also still extant, from a military officer, "master of the captains of Egypt," dating from near the end of the reign of Rameses II., gives a curious account of a journey, probably official, which he undertook through Palestine as far north as to Aleppo, and an insight into the social condition of the country at that time. Among the things brought to light by this letter and the Amarna tablets is the state of confusion and decay that had now fallen on Egypt. The Egyptian garrisons that had held possession of Palestine from the time of Thothmes III, some two hundred years before, had now been withdrawn. The way was thus opened for the Hebrews. In the history of the conquest there is no mention of Joshua having encountered any Egyptian force. The tablets contain many appeals to the king of Egypt for help against the inroads of the Hebrews, but no help seems ever to have been sent. Is not this just such a state of things as might have been anticipated as the result of the disaster of the Exodus? In many points the progress of the conquest is remarkably

illustrated by the tablets. The value of modern discoveries in their relation to Old Testament history has been thus well described:

"The difficulty of establishing the charge of lack of historical credibility, as against the testimony of the Old Testament, has of late years greatly increased. The outcome of recent excavations and explorations is altogether against it.

As long as these books contained, in the main, the only known accounts of the events they mention, there was some plausibility in the theory that perhaps these accounts were written rather to teach moral lessons than to preserve an exact knowledge of events. It was easy to say in those times men had not the historic sense. But the recent discoveries touch the events recorded in the Bible at very many different points in many different generations, mentioning the same persons, countries, peoples, events that are mentioned in the Bible, and showing beyond question that these were strictly historic. The point is not that the discoveries confirm the correctness of the biblical statements, though that is commonly the case, but that the discoveries show that the peoples of those ages had the historic sense, and, specifically, that the biblical narratives they touch are narratives of actual occurrences."

Joshua (2)

Name, author, date

Meaning of name of book
Named after its central figure, Joshua, meaning salvation

Author
Joshua.

Approximate date of writing
1370 B.C.

Statistics

Place of book in Bible
6th Old Testament book.
1st historical book.

Number of chapters
24

Number of verses
658

Number of words
18,858

Main theme of book
The conquest and portioning of the land of promise.

Keys to the understanding of book

Key word/s
Conquest, Possession, Victory.

Key phrase
Dividing the land.

Key person/people
Joshua, Rahab, Caleb.

Key chapter/s
1; 24; 27.

Key verse/s
This book of the law shall not depart out of thy mouth; but thou shalt meditate therein day and night, that thou mayest observe to do according to all that is written therein: for then thou shalt make thy way prosperous, and then thou shalt have good success. Have not I commanded thee? Be strong and of a good courage; be not afraid, neither be thou dismayed: for the LORD thy God is with thee whithersoever thou goest.
Joshua 1: 8,9

So Joshua took the whole land, according to all that the LORD said unto Moses; and Joshua gave it for an inheritance unto Israel according to their divisions by their tribes. And the land rested from war.
Joshua 11: 23

And the LORD gave them rest round about, according to all that he sware unto their fathers: and there stood not a man of all their enemies before them; the LORD delivered all their enemies into their hand. There failed not ought of any good thing which the LORD had spoken unto the house of Israel; all came to pass.
Joshua 21: 44,45

Jesus Christ in Joshua

Who Jesus is
Prophet, Priest, King.

JESUS FORESHADOWED AS A TYPE/
PORTRAITS OF CHRIST

1 Joshua, as a type of Christ
2 Rahab, as a type of Christ

Spiritual thought

Possess your possessions.

Chapter by chapter breakdown

Chapter 1: Joshua is commissioned to be Israel's leader

Chapter 2: The spies are sent out

Chapter 3: Crossing the River Jordan

Chapter 4: Erecting a memorial

Chapter 5: Joshua prepares Israel spiritually

Chapter 6: Victory at Jericho;

Chapter 7: Defeat at Ai

Chapter 8: Victory at Ai;

Chapter 9: Failure with the Gibeonites

Chapter 10: Victory over the Amorites

Chapter 11: Conquering northern Canaan, and summary of conquests

Chapter 12: Kings conquered by Moses and Joshua

Chapter 13: Tribal boundaries; Chapter 14: Land for Caleb

Chapter 15: Land for Judah

Chapter 16: Boundaries of Joseph and Ephraim

Chapter 17: Boundaries of the half tribe of Manasseh

Chapter 18: Boundaries of Benjamin

Chapter 19: Boundaries of seven tribes

Chapter 20: Six cities of refuge

Chapter 21: The levitical cities selected

Chapter 22: The altar of witness

Chapter 23: Reminders from history

Chapter 24: Renewing the covenant, and deaths of Joshua and Eleazar

Insight from Matthew Henry

Joshua 1

VERSES 5–9

Joshua is to make the law of God his rule. He is charged to meditate therein day and night, that he might understand it. Whatever affairs of this world we have to mind, we must not neglect the one thing needful. All his orders to the people, and his judgments, must be according to the law of God. Joshua must himself be under command; no man's dignity or dominion sets him above the law of God. He is to encourage himself with the promise and presence of God. Let not the sense of thine own infirmities dishearten thee; God is all-sufficient. I have commanded, called, and commissioned thee to do it, and will be sure to bear thee out in it.

Judges (1)

An introduction

Names for Judges

JUDGES
The book of Judges is so called because it contains the history of the deliverance and rule over Israel by the men who bore the title of the "judges." The book of Ruth originally formed part of this book, but about A.D. 450 it was separated from it and placed in the Hebrew scriptures immediately after the Song of Solomon.

Contents

The book contains,
(1) An introduction (Judg. 1–3: 6), connecting it with the previous narrative in Joshua, as a "link in the chain of books."
(2) The history of the thirteen judges (Judg. 3: 7–16: 31). See table.

Samson's exploits probably synchronize with the period immediately preceding the national repentance and reformation under Samuel (1 Sam. 7: 2–6).

After Samson came Eli, who was both high priest and judge. He directed the civil and religious affairs of the people for forty years, at the close of which the Philistines again invaded the land and oppressed it for twenty years. Samuel was raised up to deliver the people from this oppression, and he judged Israel for some twelve years, when the direction of affairs fell into the hands of Saul, who was anointed king. If Eli and Samuel are included, there were then

fifteen judges. But the chronology of this whole period is uncertain.
(3) The historic section of the book is followed by an appendix (Judg. 17–21), which has no formal connection with that which goes before. It records (a) the conquest (Judg. 17, 18) of Laish by a section of the tribe of Dan; and (b) the almost total extinction of the tribe of Benjamin by the other tribes, because they helped the men of Gibeah (Judg. 19–21). This section properly belongs to the period only a few years after the death of Joshua. It shows the religious and moral degeneracy of the people.

Authorship

The author of this book was most probably Samuel. The internal evidence both of the first sixteen chapters and of the appendix warrants this conclusion. It was probably composed during Saul's reign, or at the very beginning of David's. The words in Judg. 18: 30, 31, imply that it was written after the taking of the Ark by the Philistines, and after it was set up at Nob (1 Sam. 21). In David's reign the Ark was at Gibeon (1 Chr. 16: 39).

Name, author, date

MEANING OF NAME OF BOOK
The book is named after the judges were the leaders who ruled Israel.

AUTHOR
The book of Judges is anonymous. Traditionally Samuel has been thought of as its author.

Thirteen Judges	Years
FIRST PERIOD (Judg. 3: 7–5)	
Servitude under Chushan-rishathaim of Mesopotamia	8
OTHNIEL delivers Israel – rest	40
Servitude under Eglon of Moab: Ammon, Amalek	18
EHUD's deliverance – rest	80
SHAMGAR	Unknown
Servitude under Jabin of Hazor in Canaan	20
DEBORAH [BARAK]	40
First period total of years	206
SECOND PERIOD (Judg. 6–10: 5)	
Servitude under Midian, Amalek, and children of the east	7
GIDEON	40
ABIMELECH, Gideon's son, reigns as king over Israel	3
TOLA	23
JAIR	22
Second period total of years	95
THIRD PERIOD (Judg. 10: 6–12)	
Servitude under Ammonites with the Philistines	18
JEPHTHAH	6
IBZAN	7
ELON	10
ABDON	8
Third period total of years	49
FOURTH PERIOD (Judg. 13–16)	
Servitude under Philistines	40
SAMSON	20
Fourth period total of years	60
Total of four periods	410

APPROXIMATE DATE OF WRITING
1043–1004 B.C.

Statistics

PLACE OF BOOK IN BIBLE
7th Old Testament book.
2nd historical book.

NUMBER OF CHAPTERS: 21

NUMBER OF VERSES: 618

NUMBER OF WORDS: 18,976

Main theme of book

This book links Joshua and the arrival
of God's people in the Promised Land
to the kings Saul and David.

Keys to the understanding of book

KEY WORD/S
Delivered, 28 times
Cycles, 2: 20,21
Evil, 14 times
Judge, judged, judgment, 22 times

KEY PHRASE
Neither did, 1: 27.

KEY PERSON/PEOPLE
The judges: Othniel, Ehud, Shamgar,
Deborah and Barak, Gideon, Tola and
Jair, Jephthah, Ibzan, Elon, and Abdon,
and Samson.

Judges (2)

KEY CHAPTER/S
2, where Israel's backsliding is
described.

KEY VERSE/S
And the anger of the Lord was hot
against Israel; and he said, Because
that this people hath transgressed my
covenant which I commanded their
fathers, and have not hearkened unto
my voice; I also will not henceforth
drive out any from before them of the
nations which Joshua left when he died.
Joshua 2: 20,21

In those days there was no king in
Israel: every man did that which was
right in his own eyes.
Joshua 21: 25

Jesus Christ in Judges

WHO JESUS IS
Judge of the whole earth.

JESUS FORESHADOWED AS A TYPE/
PORTRAITS OF CHRIST
Deliverer, 3: 9.
The angel of the Lord, 6: 12.

Spiritual thought

Take heed, in case you fall.

Chapter by chapter breakdown

Chapter 1: Israel fails to complete the
conquest
Chapter 2: God's judgment for not
completing the conquest
Chapter 3: The southern campaign
Chapter 4: The northern campaign
Chapter 5: Song of Deborah and Barak
Chapter 6: Gideon is called

Chapter 7: Defeat of the Midianites
Chapter 8: Gideon as judge, and his
death
Chapter 9: Abimelech
Chapter 10: Israel sins
Chapter 11: Jephthah and his daughter
Chapter 12: Ibzan, Elon, and Abdon
Chapter 13: Samson's miraculous birth
Chapter 14: Samson's sinful marriage
Chapter 15: Samson as judge
Chapter 16: Samson's decline and fall
Chapter 17: An example of personal
idolatry
Chapter 18: An example of tribal
idolatry
Chapter 19: Personal and tribal
immorality
Chapter 20: War between Israel and
Dan
Chapter 21: The need for a king

Insight from Matthew Henry

Judges 16

VERSES 4–17
Samson had been more than once
brought into mischief and danger by
the love of women, yet he would not
take warning, but is again taken in the
same snare, and this third time is fatal.

VERSES 18–21
See the fatal effects of false security.
Satan ruins men by flattering them into
a good opinion of their own safety, and
so bringing them to mind nothing, and
fear nothing; and then he robs them
of their strength and honor, and leads

them captive at his will. When we sleep our spiritual enemies do not. Samson's eyes were the inlets of his sin, (ver. 1,) and now his punishment began there. Now the Philistines blinded him, he had time to remember how his own lust had before blinded him. The best way to preserve the eyes, is, to turn them away from beholding vanity. Take warning by his fall, carefully to watch against all fleshly lusts; for all our glory is gone, and our defense departed from us, when our separation to God, as spiritual Nazarites, is profaned.

VERSES 22–24
Samson's afflictions were the means of bringing him to deep repentance. By the loss of his bodily sight the eyes of his understanding were opened; and by depriving him of bodily strength, the Lord was pleased to renew his spiritual strength. The Lord permits some few to wander wide and sink deep, yet he recovers them at last, and marking his displeasure at sin in their severe temporal sufferings, preserves them from sinking into the pit of destruction. Hypocrites may abuse these examples, but true Christians will be more humble, and dependent on the Lord, more fervent in prayer to be kept from falling, and in praise for being preserved; and, if they fall, they will be kept from sinking into despair.

VERSES 25–31
Nothing fills up the sins of any person or people faster than mocking and misusing the servants of God, even thought it is by their own folly that they are brought low. God put it into Samson's heart, as a public person,

thus to avenge on them God's quarrel, Israel's, and his own. That strength which he had lost by sin, he recovers by prayer. That it was not from passion or personal revenge, but from holy zeal for the glory of God and Israel, appears from God's accepting and answering the prayer. The house was pulled down, not by the natural strength of Samson, but by the almighty power of God. In his case it was right he should avenge the cause of God and Israel. Nor is he to be accused of self-murder. He sought not his own death, but Israel's deliverance, and the destruction of their enemies. Thus Samson died in bonds, and among the Philistines, as an awful rebuke for his sins; but he died repentant. The effects of his death typified those of the death of Christ, who, of his own will, laid down his life among transgressors, and thus overturned the foundation of Satan's kingdom, and provided for the deliverance of his people. Great as was the sin of Samson, and justly as he deserved the judgments he brought upon himself, he found mercy of the Lord at last; and every penitent shall obtain mercy, who flees for refuge to that Savior whose blood cleanses from all sin. But here is nothing to encourage any to indulge sin, from a hope they shall at last repent and be saved.

Ruth

An introduction

The book of Ruth was originally a part of the Book of Judges, but it now forms one of the twenty-four separate books of the Hebrew Bible.

The history it contains refers to a period perhaps about one hundred and twenty-six years before the birth of David. It gives

(1) an account of Naomi's going to Moab with her husband, Elimelech, and of her subsequent return to Bethlehem with her daughter-in-law;

(2) the marriage of Boaz and Ruth; and

(3) the birth of Obed, from whom David sprang.

The author of this book was probably Samuel, according to Jewish tradition.

"Brief as this book is, and simple as is its story, it is remarkably rich in examples of faith, patience, industry, and kindness, nor less so in indications of the care which God takes of those who put their trust in him."

Name, author, date

MEANING OF NAME OF BOOK
The book is named after Ruth.

AUTHOR
The book of Ruth is anonymous.

APPROXIMATE DATE OF WRITING
1000 B.C.

Statistics

PLACE OF BOOK IN BIBLE
8th Old Testament book.
3rd historical book.

NUMBER OF CHAPTERS: 4

NUMBER OF VERSES: 85

NUMBER OF WORDS: 2,587

Main theme of book

From the time of the judges this book illustrates loyalty and faith.

Keys to the understanding of book

KEY WORD/S
Kinsman, 14 times
Redeem, 9 times

KEY PHRASE
Near of kin.

KEY PERSON/PEOPLE
Ruth, Naomi, Boaz.

KEY CHAPTER/S
4.

KEY VERSE/S
And Ruth said, Entreat me not to leave thee, or to return from following after thee: for whither thou goest, I will go; and where thou lodgest, I will lodge: thy people shall be my people, and thy God my God.
Ruth 1: 16

And now, my daughter, fear not; I will do to thee all that thou requirest: for all the city of my people doth know that thou art a virtuous woman.
Ruth 3: 11

And the women said unto Naomi, Blessed be the Lord, which hath not left thee this day without a kinsman, that his name may be famous in Israel. Ruth 4:14

JESUS CHRIST IN RUTH

WHO JESUS IS
Our Kinsman-Redeemer.

JESUS FORESHADOWED AS A TYPE/ PORTRAITS OF CHRIST
The Kinsman-Redeemer portrays the work of Christ.

Spiritual thought
God's providential care.

Chapter by chapter breakdown
Chapter 1: Ruth comes to Bethlehem
Chapter 2: Ruth meets Boaz
Chapter 3: Ruth claims the protection
   of the kinsmen
Chapter 4: Boaz marries Ruth

Insight from Matthew Henry

Ruth 1
VERSES 6–14
Naomi began to think of returning, after the death of her two sons. When death comes into a family, it ought to reform what is amiss there. Earth is made bitter to us, that heaven may be made dear. Naomi seems to have been a person of faith and piety. She dismissed her daughters-in-law with prayer. It is very proper for friends, when they part, to part with them thus in love.

VERSES 15–18
See Ruth's resolution, and her good affection to Naomi. Orpah was loth to part from her; yet she did not love her well enough to leave Moab for her sake. Thus, many have a value and affection for Christ, yet come short of salvation by him, because they will not forsake other things for him. They love him, yet leave him, because they do not love him enough, but love other things better. Ruth is an example of the grace of God, inclining the soul to choose the better part. Naomi could desire no more than the solemn declaration Ruth made. See the power of resolution; it silences temptation. Those that go in religious ways without a stedfast mind, stand like a door half open, which invites a thief; but resolution shuts and bolts the door, resists the devil and forces him to flee.

VERSES 19–22
Naomi and Ruth came to Bethlehem. Afflictions will make great and surprising changes in a little time. May God, by his grace, fit us for all such changes, especially the great change! Naomi signifies "pleasant," or "amiable"; Mara, "bitter," or "bitterness." She was now a woman of a sorrowful spirit. She had come home empty, poor, a widow and childless. But there is a fullness for believers of which they never can be emptied; a good part which shall not be taken from those who have it. The cup of affliction is a "bitter" cup, but she owns that the affliction came from God. It well becomes us to have our hearts humbled under humbling providences. It is not affliction itself, but affliction rightly borne, that does us good.

1 Samuel (1)

An introduction

Names for 1 and 2 Samuel

BOOKS OF THE KINGDOM
The LXX translators regarded the books of Samuel and of Kings as forming one continuous history, which they divided into four books, which they called "Books of the Kingdom."

BOOKS OF THE KINGS
The Vulgate version followed this division, but styled them "Books of the Kings."

FIRST BOOK OF KINGS
These books of Samuel they accordingly called the "First" and "Second" Books of Kings, and not, as in the modern Protestant versions, the "First" and "Second" Books of Samuel.

Authorship

The authors of the books of Samuel were probably Samuel, Gad, and Nathan.

SAMUEL
Samuel penned the first twenty-four chapters of the first book.

GAD
Gad, the companion of David (1 Sam. 22: 5), continued the history.

NATHAN
Nathan completed it, probably arranging the whole in the form in which we now have it (1 Chr. 29: 29).

Contents

The contents of the books.

1 SAMUEL
The first book comprises a period of about a hundred years, and nearly coincides with the life of Samuel. It contains:
  (1) the history of Eli (1 Sam. 1–4);
  (2) the history of Samuel (1 Sam. 5–12);
  (3) the history of Saul, and of David in exile (1 Sam. 13–31).

2 SAMUEL
The second book, comprising a period of perhaps fifty years, contains a history of the reign of David:
  (1) over Judah (2 Sam. 1–4), and
  (2) over all Israel (2 Sam. 5–24), mainly in its political aspects. The last four chapters of Second Samuel may be regarded as a sort of appendix recording various events, but not chronologically.

Gaps

These books do not contain complete histories. Frequent gaps are met with in the record, because their object is to present a history of the kingdom of God in its gradual development, and not of the events of the reigns of the successive rulers.

It is noticeable that the section (2 Sam. 11: 2–12: 29) containing an account of David's sin in the matter of Bathsheba is omitted in the corresponding passage in 1 Chr. 20.

Name, author, date

MEANING OF NAME OF BOOK
Originally one book with 2 Samuel,
1 Samuel is named after the last judge
and first prophet, Samuel.

AUTHOR
The book of 1 Samuel is anonymous.

APPROXIMATE DATE OF WRITING
930 B.C.

Statistics

PLACE OF BOOK IN BIBLE
9th Old Testament book.
4th historical book.

NUMBER OF CHAPTERS
31

NUMBER OF VERSES
810

NUMBER OF WORDS
25,061

Main theme of book

An account of the early kings of Israel.

Keys to the understanding of book

KEY WORD/S
King and kingdom
Transition
Anoint, 7 times
Rejected, 7 times

KEY PHRASE
Thy servant heareth, 3: 9.

KEY PERSON/PEOPLE
Samuel
Saul
David

KEY CHAPTER/S
8, where Israel demands a king
15, where kingship passes to David
from Saul.

KEY VERSE/S
But now thy kingdom shall not
continue: the Lord hath sought him a
man after his own heart, and the Lord
hath commanded him to be captain
over his people, because thou hast not
kept that which the Lord commanded
thee.
1 Samuel 13: 14

And Samuel said, Hath the Lord as
great delight in burnt offerings and
sacrifices, as in obeying the voice of
the Lord? Behold, to obey is better than
sacrifice, and to hearken than the fat of
rams.
1 Samuel 15: 22

Jesus Christ in 1 Samuel

WHO JESUS IS
The descendant of David, Romans 1: 3.

JESUS FORESHADOWED AS A TYPE/
PORTRAITS OF CHRIST
1   Samuel, as a type of Christ
2   David, as a type of Christ

Spiritual thought

Keeping God's lamp shining.

1 Samuel (2)

Chapter by chapter breakdown

Chapter 1: Hannah's prayer and the birth of Samuel

Chapter 2: Eli and his family

Chapter 3: The call of Samuel

Chapter 4: The Philistines capture the covenant box (the Ark)

Chapter 5: The covenant box in the land of the Philistines

Chapter 6: The return of the covenant box

Chapter 7: Samuel judges Israel

Chapter 8: The people demand a king

Chapter 9: Saul is chosen and anointed king

Chapter 10: Saul is acclaimed as king

Chapter 11: Saul defeats the Ammonites

Chapter 12: Samuel speaks to the people

Chapter 13: War against the Philistines

Chapter 14: Jonathan and the Philistine defeat

Chapter 15: War against Amalek, and rejection of Saul as king

Chapter 16: God anoints David as king

Chapter 17: God confirms David over Saul

Chapter 18: Saul attempts to kill David

Chapter 19: Saul continues to try to kill David

Chapter 20: David flees, but Jonathan remains his friend

Chapter 21: David is protected by Achish at Gath

Chapter 22: Saul kills God's priests

Chapter 23: Saul chases David

Chapter 24: David spares Saul's life

Chapter 25: David marries Abigail

Chapter 26: Saul admits his guilt

Chapter 27: David joins the Philistines

Chapter 28: Saul visits a medium

Chapter 29: David is spared from fighting Saul

Chapter 30: David fights against the Amalekites

Chapter 31: Saul and Jonathan are killed

Insight from Matthew Henry

1 Samuel 3

VERSES 1–10
The call which Divine grace designs shall be made effectual; will be repeated till it is so, till we come to the call. Eli, perceiving that it was the voice of God that Samuel heard, instructed him what to say. Though it was a disgrace to Eli, for God's call to be directed to Samuel, yet he told him how to meet it. Let us never fail to teach those who are coming after us, even such as will soon be preferred before us.

VERSES 11–18
What a great deal of guilt and corruption is there in us, concerning which we may say, It is the iniquity which our own heart knoweth; we are conscious to ourselves of it! Those who do not restrain the sins of others, when it is in their power to do it, make themselves partakers of the guilt, and will be charged as joining in it. In his remarkable answer to this awful sentence, Eli acknowledged that the Lord had a right to do as he saw good, being assured that he would do nothing

wrong. The meekness, patience, and humility contained in those words, show that he was truly repentant; he accepted the punishment of his sin.

1 Samuel 20

VERSES 1–10
The trials David met with, prepared him for future advancement. Thus the Lord deals with those whom he prepares unto glory. He does not put them into immediate possession of the kingdom, but leads them to it through much tribulation, which he makes the means of fitting them for it. Let them not murmur at his gracious appointment, nor distrust his care; but let them look forward with joyful expectation to the crown which is laid up for them. Sometimes it appears to us that there is but a step between us and death; at all times it may be so, and we should prepare for the event. But though dangers appear most threatening, we cannot die till the purpose of God concerning us is accomplished; nor till we have served our generation according to his will, if we are believers. Jonathan generously offers David his services. This is true friendship. Thus Christ testifies his love to us, Ask, and it shall be done for you; and we must testify our love to him, by keeping his commandments.

VERSES 11–23
Jonathan faithfully promises that he would let David know how he found his father affected toward him. It will be kindness to ourselves and to ours, to secure an interest in those whom God favors, and to make his friends

ours. True friendship rests on a firm basis, and is able to silence ambition, self-love, and undue regard for others. But who can fully understand the love of Jesus, who gave himself as a sacrifice for rebellious, polluted sinners! how great then ought to be the force and effects of our love to him, to his cause, and his people!

VERSES 24–34
None were more constant than David in attending holy duties; nor had he been absent, but self-preservation obliged him to withdraw. In great peril present opportunities for Divine ordinances may be waved. But it is bad for us, except in case of necessity, to omit any opportunity of attending on them. Jonathan did wisely and well for himself and family, to secure an interest in David, yet for this he is blamed. It is good to take God's people for our people. It will prove to our advantage at last, however it may now be thought against our interest.

VERSES 35–42
The separation of two such faithful friends was grievous to both, but David's case was the more deplorable, for David was leaving all his comforts, even those of God's sanctuary. Christians need not sorrow, as men without hope; but being one with Christ, they are one with each other, and will meet in his presence ere long, to part no more; to meet where all tears shall be wiped from their eyes.

2 Samuel

An introduction

See this section under 1 Samuel.

Name, author, date

MEANING OF NAME OF BOOK
Originally one book with 1 Samuel,
2 Samuel is named after the last judge
and first prophet, Samuel.

AUTHOR
The book of 2 Samuel is anonymous.

APPROXIMATE DATE OF WRITING
930 B.C.

Statistics

PLACE OF BOOK IN BIBLE
10th Old Testament book.
5th historical book.

NUMBER OF CHAPTERS
24

NUMBER OF VERSES
695

NUMBER OF WORDS
20,612

Main theme of book

David's reign.

KEYS TO THE UNDERSTANDING OF
BOOK

KEY WORD/S
David, 267 times

KEY PHRASE
Before the Lord, 6: 17.

KEY PERSON/PEOPLE
David, Bathsheba, Nathan, Absolom,
Joab, Amnon, and Ahithophel.

KEY CHAPTER/S
5, David is king over all Israel.
11, David's sin.

KEY VERSE/S
And when thy days be fulfilled, and
thou shalt sleep with thy fathers, I will
set up thy seed after thee, which shall
proceed out of thy bowels, and I will
establish his kingdom. He shall build an
house for my name, and I will stablish
the throne of his kingdom for ever.
2 Samuel 7: 12,13

The Lord rewarded me according
to my righteousness: according to
the cleanness of my hands hath he
recompensed me.
2 Samuel 22: 21

Jesus Christ in 2 Samuel

WHO JESUS IS
The Anointed One.

JESUS FORESHADOWED AS A TYPE/
PORTRAITS OF CHRIST
David, as a type of Christ
Jesus is David's Lord, 7: 4–17

Spiritual thought

God calls and anoints.

Chapter by chapter breakdown

Chapter 1: The death of King Saul
Chapter 2: War between Israel and
   Judah

Chapter 3: Abner's murder

Chapter 4: Ish-Bosheth's murder

Chapter 5: David's reign in Jerusalem

Chapter 6: The covenant box comes to Jerusalem

Chapter 7: David's covenant

Chapter 8: David's military triumphs

Chapter 9: David's kindness to Mephibosheth

Chapter 10: David triumphs over Ammon and Syria

Chapter 11: David, Bathsheba, and Uriah

Chapter 12: Nathan rebukes David

Chapter 13: Tamar is raped: Absalom's revenge on Amnon

Chapter 14: Joab arranges for Absalom's restoration

Chapter 15: Absalom rebels, and David flees Jerusalem

Chapter 16: David, Ziba, and Shimei

Chapter 17: Absalom's reign

Chapter 18: Absalom's murder

Chapter 19: David returns to Jerusalem

Chapter 20: Sheba's rebellion

Chapter 21: Famine, and war with Philistia

Chapter 22: Psalms of thanksgiving

Chapter 23: Deeds of David's mighty men

Chapter 24: The census and the plague

Insight from Matthew Henry

2 Samuel 11

VERSES 1–5

Observe the occasions of David's sin; what led to it.

1. Neglect of his business. He tarried at Jerusalem. When we are out of the way of our duty, we are in temptation.

2. Love of ease: idleness gives great advantage to the tempter.

3. A wandering eye. He had not, like Job, made a covenant with his eyes, or, at this time, he had forgotten it. And observe the steps of the sin. See how the way of sin is down-hill; when men begin to do evil, they cannot soon stop.

VERSES 14–27

Adulteries often occasion murders, and one wickedness is sought to be covered by another. The beginnings of sin are much to be dreaded; for who knows where they will end? Can such a person be indeed a child of God? Though grace be not lost in such an awful case, the assurance and consolation of it must be suspended. All David's life, spirituality, and comfort in religion, we may be sure were lost. No man in such a case can have evidence to be satisfied that he is a believer. The higher a man's confidence is, who has sunk in wickedness, the greater his presumption and hypocrisy. Let not any one who resembles David in nothing but his transgressions, bolster up his confidence with this example. Let him follow David in his humiliation, repentance, and his other eminent graces, before he thinks himself only a backslider, and not a hypocrite. Let no one who opposes the truth say, These are the fruits of faith! No; they are the effects of corrupt nature. Let us all watch against the beginnings of self-indulgence, and keep at the utmost distance from all evil.

1 Kings (1)

An introduction

Names for 1 and 2 Kings

THIRD AND FOURTH BOOKS OF KINGS
The two books of Kings formed
originally but one book in the Hebrew
Scriptures. The present division into
two books was first made by the LXX,
which now, with the Vulgate, numbers
them as the third and fourth books of
Kings, the two books of Samuel being
the first and second books of Kings.

Contents

ANNALS
They contain the annals of the Jewish
nation from the accession of Solomon
to the subjugation of the kingdom by
Nebuchadnezzar and the Babylonians
(apparently a period of about four
hundred and fifty-three years).

Comparison with Chronicles

The books of Chronicles are more
comprehensive in their contents than
those of Kings. The latter synchronize
with 1 Chr. 28–2 Chr. 36: 21. While in
the Chronicles greater prominence is
given to the priestly or Levitical office,
in the Kings greater prominence is
given to the kingly.

Authorship

UNCERTAIN
The authorship of these books is
uncertain.

LINKS WITH THE BOOK OF JEREMIAH
There are some portions of them and of

Jeremiah that are almost identical, e.g.,
2 Kings 24: 18–25 and Jer. 52; 39: 1–10;
40: 7–41: 10.

2 KINGS AND JEREMIAH
There are also many coincidences
between Jeremiah and Kings (2 Kings
21–23 and Jer. 7: 15; 15: 4; 19: 3, etc.),
and events recorded in Kings of which
Jeremiah had personal knowledge.Was
Jeremiah or Ezra the author?

These facts countenance in some
degree the tradition that Jeremiah was
the author of the books of Kings.

But the more probable supposition is
that Ezra, after the Captivity, compiled
them from documents written perhaps
by David, Solomon, Nathan, Gad, and
Iddo, and that he arranged them in the
order in which they now exist.

In the threefold Jewish division of the
Scriptures, these books are reckoned to
be among the "Prophets."

Frequently quoted

They are frequently quoted or alluded
to by our Lord and his apostles
(Matt. 6: 29; 12: 42; Luke 4: 25,26; 10: 4;
cf. 2 Kings 4: 29; Mark 1: 6; cf. 2 Kings
1: 8; Matt. 3: 4, etc.).

Sources

A number of the sources of the
narrative are referred to:
(1) "the book of the acts of Solomon"
(1 Kings 11: 41);
(2) the "book of the chronicles of the
kings of Judah" (1 Kings 14: 29; 15: 7,23,
etc.);

(3) the "book of the chronicles of the kings of Israel" (1 Kings 14: 19; 15: 31; 16: 14,20,27, etc.).

Date

The date of its composition was some time between 561 B.C., the date of the last chapter (2 Kings 25), when Jehoiachin was released from captivity by Evil-merodach, and 538 B.C., the date of the decree of deliverance by Cyrus.

Name, author, date

MEANING OF NAME OF BOOK
1 and 2 Kings were originally one book. The original title of the book is taken from the opening word of 1 Kings, "king."

AUTHOR
The book of 1 Kings is anonymous.

APPROXIMATE DATE OF WRITING
550 B.C.

Statistics

PLACE OF BOOK IN BIBLE
11th Old Testament book.
6th historical book.

NUMBER OF CHAPTERS
22

NUMBER OF VERSES
816

NUMBER OF WORDS
24,524

Main theme of book

With 2 Kings, 1 Kings is the history of the kings of Israel and Judah from Solomon to the Babylonian captivity.

Keys to the understanding of book

KEY WORD/S
Kingdom, 357 times
Division

KEY PHRASE
David his father

KEY PERSON/PEOPLE
Solomon
Jeroboam
Rehoboam,
Elijah and Elisha
Ahab and Jezebel.

KEY CHAPTER/S
12 and the division of the kingdom.

KEY VERSE/S
And if thou wilt walk before me, as David thy father walked, in integrity of heart, and in uprightness, to do according to all that I have commanded thee, and wilt keep my statutes and my judgments: Then I will establish the throne of thy kingdom upon Israel for ever, as I promised to David thy father, saying, There shall not fail thee a man upon the throne of Israel.
1 Kings 9: 4,5

Wherefore the Lord said unto Solomon, Forasmuch as this is done of thee, and thou hast not kept my covenant and my statutes, which I have commanded thee, I will surely rend the kingdom from thee, and will give it to thy servant.
1 Kings 11: 11

1 Kings (2)

KEY VERSE/S, CONTINUED
Howbeit I will not rend away all the kingdom; but will give one tribe to thy son for David my servant's sake, and for Jerusalem's sake which I have chosen.
1 Kings 11: 13

Jesus Christ in 1 Kings

WHO JESUS IS
King of kings.

Spiritual thought

A king reigns from his throne.

Chapter by chapter breakdown

Chapter 1: Solomon is appointed king
Chapter 2: Solomon is established as king
Chapter 3: Solomon asks for wisdom
Chapter 4: Solomon's rule over Israel
Chapter 5: The materials and laborers used to build the temple
Chapter 6: The completion of the temple
Chapter 7: Solomon's house and the temple's furniture
Chapter 8: Dedication of the temple
Chapter 9: The Lord appears to Solomon again
Chapter 10: Visit from the Queen of Sheba
Chapter 11: Solomon's unfaithfulness and his death
Chapter 12: The cause of the kingdom's division
Chapter 13: Jeroboam's evil ways
Chapter 14: Judgment on Jeroboam

Chapter 15: Reigns of Abijam and Asa in Judah
Chapter 16: Five kings of Israel: Baasha, Elah, Zimri, Omri, and Ahab
Chapter 17: Elijah's ministry in the drought
Chapter 18: Miracle of fire on Mount Carmel
Chapter 19: God's help for the depressed Elijah
Chapter 20: War with Syria
Chapter 21: Ahab murders Naboth for his vineyard
Chapter 22: Defeat by Syria, and death of Ahab

Insight from Matthew Henry

1 Kings 10

VERSES 1–13
The queen of Sheba came to Solomon to hear his wisdom, thereby to improve her own. Our Savior mentions her inquiries after God, by Solomon, as showing the stupidity of those who inquire not after God, by our Lord Jesus Christ. By waiting and prayer, by diligently searching the Scriptures, by consulting wise and experienced Christians, and by practicing what we have learned, we shall be delivered from difficulties. Solomon's wisdom made more impression upon the queen of Sheba than all his prosperity and grandeur. There is a spiritual excellence in heavenly things, and in consistent Christians, to which no reports can do justice. Here the truth exceeded; and

all who, through grace, are brought to commune with God, will say the one half was not told them of the pleasures and the advantages of wisdom's ways. Glorified saints, much more, will say of heaven, pronounced them happy that constantly attended Solomon. With much more reason may we say of Christ's servants, Blessed are they that dwell in his house; they will be still praising him. She made a noble present to Solomon. What we present to Christ, he needs not, but will have us do so to express our gratitude. The believer who has been with Jesus, will return to his station, discharge his duties with readiness, and from better motives; looking forward to the day when, being absent from the body, he shall be present with the Lord.

VERSES 14–29
Solomon increased his wealth. Silver was nothing accounted of. Such is the nature of worldly wealth, plenty of it makes it the less valuable; much more should the enjoyment of spiritual riches lessen our esteem of all earthly possessions. If gold in abundance makes silver to be despised, shall not wisdom, and grace, and the foretastes of heaven, which are far better than gold, make gold to be lightly esteemed? See in Solomon's greatness the performance of God's promise, and let it encourage us to seek first the righteousness of God's kingdom. This was he, who, having tasted all earthly enjoyments, wrote a book, to show the vanity of all worldly things, the vexation of spirit that attends them, and the folly of setting our

hearts upon them: and to recommend serious godliness, as that which will do unspeakably more to make us happy, that all the wealth and power he was master of; and, through the grace of God, it is within our reach.

Chapter 17
VERSES 1–7
God wonderfully suits men to the work he designs them for. The times were fit for an Elijah; an Elijah was fit for them. The Spirit of the Lord knows how to fit men for the occasions. Elijah let Ahab know that God was displeased with the idolaters, and would chastise them by the want of rain, which it was not in the power of the gods they served to bestow. Elijah was commanded to hide himself. If Providence calls us to solitude and retirement, it becomes us to go: when we cannot be useful, we must be patient; and when we cannot work for God, we must sit still quietly for him. The ravens were appointed to bring him meat, and did so. Let those who have but from hand to mouth, learn to live upon Providence, and trust it for the bread of the day, in the day. God could have sent angels to minister to him; but he chose to show that he can serve his own purposes by the meanest creatures, as effectually as by the mightiest. Elijah seems to have continued thus above a year.

2 Kings

An introduction

See this section under 1 Kings.

Name, author, date

MEANING OF NAME OF BOOK
1 and 2 Kings were originally one book. The original title of the book is taken from the opening word of 1 Kings, "king."

AUTHOR
The book of 2 Kings is anonymous.

APPROXIMATE DATE OF WRITING
550 B.C.

Statistics

PLACE OF BOOK IN BIBLE
12th Old Testament book.
7th historical book.

NUMBER OF CHAPTERS: 25

NUMBER OF VERSES: 719

NUMBER OF WORDS: 23,532

Main theme of book

With 1 Kings, 2 Kings is the history of the kings of Israel and Judah from Solomon to the Babylonian captivity.

Keys to the understanding of book

KEY WORD/S
King, more than 400 times
Prophet, 34 times
Evil; Captivity

KEY PHRASE
According to the word of the Lord, 1: 17.

KEY PERSON/PEOPLE
Elijah, Elisha, Josiah, Naaman, Hezekiah.

KEY CHAPTER/S
25

KEY VERSE/S
Know now that there shall fall unto the earth nothing of the word of the Lord, which the Lord spake concerning the house of Ahab: for the Lord hath done that which he spake by his servant Elijah.
2 Kings 10: 10

And the Lord said, I will remove Judah also out of my sight, as I have removed Israel, and will cast off this city Jerusalem which I have chosen, and the house of which I said, My name shall be there.
2 Kings 23: 27

Jesus Christ in 2 Kings

WHO JESUS IS
King of kings.

JESUS FORESHADOWED AS A TYPE/ PORTRAITS OF CHRIST
Elijah as a type of John the Baptist, who was the forerunner of Christ.
Elisha as a type of Christ.

Spiritual thought

Praying for a double portion of the Spirit, 2: 9.

Chapter by chapter breakdown

Chapter 1: King Ahaziah of Israel
Chapter 2: Elijah hands over to Elisha

Chapter 3: Rebellion of Moab

Chapter 4: Elisha's miraculous ministry

Chapter 5: Healing of Naaman

Chapter 6: More of Elisha's miracles

Chapter 7: Elisha's prophecies

Chapter 8: Kings of Syria, Israel, and Judah

Chapter 9: Jehu is anointed king: Ahab's family is killed

Chapter 10: Baal worshipers killed; death of Jehu

Chapter 11: Queen Athaliah of Judah

Chapter 12: King Joash of Judah

Chapter 13: King Jehoahaz and King Jehoash of Israel

Chapter 14: King Amaziah of Judah

Chapter 15: Azariah of Judah, and five evil kings of Israel

Chapter 16: King Ahaz of Judah

Chapter 17: King Hoshea of Israel

Chapter 18: Hezekiah's early reign, and Jerusalem besieged

Chapter 19: Assyria's letter and Hezekiah's faith in God

Chapter 20: Hezekiah's illness, recovery, and death

Chapter 21: The evil reigns of Manasseh and Amon

Chapter 22: Josiah repairs the temple and the finding of the book of the law

Chapter 23: Josiah removes pagan worship and celebrates the Passover

Chapter 24: Nebuchadnezzar captures Jerusalem

Chapter 25: The destruction of the temple and exile

Insight from Matthew Henry

2 Kings 20

VERSES 1–11

Hezekiah was sick unto death, in the same year in which the king of Assyria besieged Jerusalem. A warning to prepare for death was brought to Hezekiah by Isaiah. Prayer is one of the best preparations for death, because by it we fetch in strength and grace from God, to enable us to finish well. He wept sorely: some gather from hence that he was unwilling to die; it is in the nature of man to dread the separation of soul and body. There was also something peculiar in Hezekiah's case; he was now in the midst of his usefulness. Let Hezekiah's prayer, see Is. 38, interpret his tears; in that is nothing which is like his having been under that fear of death, which has bondage or torment. Hezekiah's piety made his sick-bed easy. "O Lord, remember now"; he does not speak as if God needed to be put in mind of any thing by us; nor, as if the reward might be demanded as due; it is Christ's righteousness only that is the purchase of mercy and grace. Hezekiah does not pray, Lord, spare me; but, Lord, remember me; whether I live or die, let me be thine. God always hears the prayers of the broken in heart, and will give health, length of days, and temporal deliverances, as much and as long as is truly good for them. Means were to be used for Hezekiah's recovery; yet, considering to what a height the disease was come, and how suddenly it was checked, the cure was miraculous.

1 Chronicles (1)

An introduction

Names for Chronicles

ACTS OF THE DAYS
1 and 2 Chronicles were originally one. They bore the title in the Masoretic Hebrew Dibre hayyamim, i.e., "Acts of the Days."

CHRONICLES
This title was rendered by Jerome in his Latin version Chronicon, and hence "Chronicles."

PARALEIPOMENA
In the Septuagint version the book is divided into two, and bears the title Paraleipomena, i.e., "things omitted," or "supplements," because it contains many things omitted in the Books of Kings.

Contents

The contents of these books fall under four heads.

(1)The first nine chapters of Book I contain little more than a list of genealogies in the line of Israel down to the time of David.

(2) The remainder of the first book contains a history of the reign of David.

(3) The first nine chapters of Book II contain the history of the reign of Solomon.

(4) The remaining chapters of the second book contain the history of the separate kingdom of Judah to the time of the return from Babylonian Exile.

Date

The time of the composition of the Chronicles was, there is every ground to conclude, subsequent to the Babylonian exile, probably between 450 and 435 B.C. The contents of this twofold book, both as to matter and form, correspond closely with this idea. The close of the book records the proclamation of Cyrus permitting the Jews to return to their own land, and this forms the opening passage of the Book of Ezra, which must be viewed as a continuation of the Chronicles.

Language

The peculiar form of the language, being Aramaean in its general character, harmonizes also with that of the books which were written after the exile.

Authorship

The author was certainly contemporary with Zerubbabel, details of whose family history are given (1 Chr. 3: 19).

The time of the composition being determined, the question of the authorship may be more easily decided.

WAS EZRA THE AUTHOR?
According to Jewish tradition, which was universally received down to the middle of the seventeenth century, Ezra was regarded as the author of the Chronicles. There are many points of resemblance and of contact between the Chronicles and the Book

of Ezra which seem to confirm this opinion. The conclusion of the one and the beginning of the other are almost identical. In their spirit and characteristics they are the same, showing thus also an identity of authorship.

In their general scope and design these books are not so much historical as didactic. The principal aim of the writer appears to be to present moral and religious truth. He does not give prominence to political events, as is done in Samuel and Kings, but to ecclesiastical institutions.

"The genealogies, so uninteresting to most modern readers, were really an important part of the public records of the Hebrew state. They were the basis on which not only the land was distributed and held, but the public services of the temple were arranged and conducted, the Levites and their descendants alone, as is well known, being entitled and first fruits set apart for that purpose."

The "Chronicles" are an epitome of the sacred history from the days of Adam down to the return from Babylonian exile, a period of about 3,500 years. The writer gathers up "the threads of the old national life broken by the Captivity."

Sources

The sources from which the chronicler compiled his work were public records, registers, and genealogical tables belonging to the Jews. These are referred to in the course of the book (1 Chr. 27: 24; 29: 29; 2 Chr. 9: 29; 12: 15; 13: 22; 20: 34; 24: 27; 26: 22; 32: 32;

33: 18,19; 27: 7; 35: 25). There are in Chronicles, and the books of Samuel and Kings, forty parallels, often verbal, proving that the writer both knew and used these records (1 Chr. 17: 18; cf. 2 Sam. 7: 18–20; 1 Chr. 19; cf. 2 Sam. 10, etc.).

Comparison with Samuel and Kings

As compared with Samuel and Kings, the Book of Chronicles omits many particulars there recorded (2 Sam. 6: 20–23; 9; 11; 14–19, etc.), and includes many things peculiar to itself (1 Chr. 12; 22; 23–26; 27; 28; 29, etc.). Twenty whole chapters, and twenty-four parts of chapters, are occupied with matter not found elsewhere. It also records many things in fuller detail, as the list of David's heroes (1 Chr. 12: 1–37), the removal of the Ark from Kirjath-jearim to Mount Zion (1 Chr. 13; 15: 2–24; 16: 4–43; cf. 2 Sam. 6), Uzziah's leprosy and its cause (2 Chr. 26: 16–21; cf. 2 Kings 15: 5), etc.

It has also been observed that another peculiarity of the book is that it substitutes modern and more common expressions for those that had then become unusual or obsolete. This is seen particularly in the substitution of modern names of places, such as were in use in the writer's day, for the old names; thus Gezer (1 Chr. 20: 4) is used instead of Gob (2 Sam. 21: 18), etc.

1 Chronicles (2)

An introduction, continued

HAGIOGRAPHA
The Books of Chronicles are ranked among the khethubim or hagiographa.

Allusions to

They are alluded to, though not directly quoted, in the New Testament (Heb. 5: 4; Matt. 12: 42; 23: 35; Luke 1: 5; 11: 31,51).

Name, author, date

MEANING OF NAME OF BOOK
1 and 2 Chronicles were originally one book.
    They are called "Chronicles" in the sense that they record the events and times of the part of Israel's history.

AUTHOR
The book of 1 Chronicles is anonymous.

APPROXIMATE DATE OF WRITING
450–425 B.C.

Statistics

PLACE OF BOOK IN BIBLE
13th Old Testament book.
8th historical book.

NUMBER OF CHAPTERS
29

NUMBER OF VERSES
942

NUMBER OF WORDS
20,369

Main theme of book

History of David's reign.

Keys to the understanding of book

KEY WORD/S
Reigned

KEY PHRASE
Build thee an house, 29: 16.

KEY PERSON/PEOPLE
David, Nathan, Bathsheba, and Uriah.

KEY CHAPTER/S
17, God's promise to establish his throne forever.

KEY VERSE/S
Then all Israel gathered themselves to David unto Hebron, saying, Behold, we are thy bone and thy flesh. And moreover in time past, even when Saul was king, thou wast he that leddest out and broughtest in Israel: and the Lord thy God said unto thee, Thou shalt feed my people Israel, and thou shalt be ruler over my people Israel. Therefore came all the elders of Israel to the king to Hebron; and David made a covenant with them in Hebron before the Lord; and they anointed David king over Israel, according to the word of the Lord by Samuel.
1 Chronicles 11: 1–3

And it shall come to pass, when thy days be expired that thou must go to be with thy fathers, that I will raise up thy seed after thee, which shall be of thy sons; and I will establish his kingdom. He shall build me an house, and I will stablish his throne for ever. I will be his father, and he shall be my son: and I will not take my mercy away from him, as I took it from him that was before thee: But I will settle him in mine house and in my kingdom for ever: and his throne shall be established for evermore.

1 Chronicles 17: 11–14

Thine, O Lord, is the greatness, and the power, and the glory, and the victory, and the majesty: for all that is in the heaven and in the earth is thine; thine is the kingdom, O Lord, and thou art exalted as head above all.

1 Chronicles 29: 11

Jesus Christ in 1 Chronicles

WHO JESUS IS
King of kings, and Lord of lords.

JESUS FORESHADOWED AS A TYPE/
PORTRAITS OF CHRIST
David is a type of Christ.

Spiritual thought

Learning from the history of God's people.

Chapter by chapter breakdown

Chapter 1: Genealogy from Adam to Abraham, and from Abraham to Jacob

Chapter 2: Genealogy from Jacob to David

Chapter 3: Genealogy from David to the captivity

Chapter 4: Genealogy of Judah and Simeon

Chapter 5: Genealogy of Reuben, Gad, and Manasseh

Chapter 6: Genealogy of Levi

Chapter 7: Genealogy of Issachar, Benjamin, Naphtali, Manasseh, Ephraim, and Asher

Chapter 8: Genealogy of Benjamin

Chapter 9: Genealogy of the remnant

Chapter 10: Death of Saul

Chapter 11: David becomes king, takes Jerusalem, and his mighty men

Chapter 12: Those who came to David at Ziklag and who came to Hebron to proclaim him king

Chapter 13: The failed attempt to take the Ark to Jerusalem

Chapter 14: David's prosperous reign

Chapter 15: Preparations for the removal of the Ark and its removal

Chapter 16: Celebrating the Ark's arrival in Jerusalem

Chapter 17: David is not allowed to build the temple

Chapter 18: David's victories and his officials

Chapter 19: Battle against the Ammonites

Chapter 20: Rabbah is captured

Chapter 21: David's sinful census

Chapter 22: David's preparations for the temple

Chapter 23: The work of the Levites

Chapter 24: Work given to the priests

Chapter 25: The temple musicians

Chapter 26: The temple guards

Chapter 27: Government officials

Chapter 28: David's last words to his officials and to Solomon

Chapter 29: David praises God, and summary of his reign

2 Chronicles

An introduction

See this section under 1 Chronicles.

Name, author, date

MEANING OF NAME OF BOOK
1 and 2 Chronicles were originally one book. They are called "Chronicles" in the sense that they record the events and times of the part of Israel's history.

AUTHOR
The book of 1 Chronicles is anonymous.

APPROXIMATE DATE OF WRITING
450–425 B.C.

Statistics

PLACE OF BOOK IN BIBLE
14th Old Testament book
9th historical book

NUMBER OF CHAPTER:S 36

NUMBER OF VERSES: 822

NUMBER OF WORDS: 26,074

Main theme of book

History of reign of Solomon and kings of Judah.

Keys to the understanding of book

KEY WORD/S
Established

KEY PHRASE
Prepareth his heart to seek God, 30–18,19.

Key person/people

Josiah, Rehoboam, Solomon.

KEY CHAPTER/S
34 and the finding of the book of the Law.

KEY VERSE/S
If my people, which are called by my name, shall humble themselves, and pray, and seek my face, and turn from their wicked ways; then will I hear from heaven, and will forgive their sin, and will heal their land.
2 Chronicles 7: 14

And he went out to meet Asa, and said unto him, Hear ye me, Asa, and all Judah and Benjamin; The Lord is with you, while ye be with him; and if ye seek him, he will be found of you; but if ye forsake him, he will forsake you.
2 Chronicles 15: 2

For the eyes of the Lord run to and fro throughout the whole earth, to show himself strong in the behalf of them whose heart is perfect toward him. Herein thou hast done foolishly: therefore from henceforth thou shalt have wars.
2 Chronicles 16: 9

Jesus Christ in 2 Chronicles

WHO JESUS IS
The God of history.

JESUS FORESHADOWED AS A TYPE/
PORTRAITS OF CHRIST
The temple foreshadows Christ.

Spiritual thought

Give the King his due honor.

Chapter by chapter breakdown

Chapter 1: Solomon's request for wisdom

Chapter 2: Preparations for building the temple

Chapter 3: Building the temple

Chapter 4: The temple's furnishings

Chapter 5: The Ark taken into the temple

Chapter 6: Solomon's sermon and prayer

Chapter 7: The temple's dedication, and the Lord's reply to Solomon

Chapter 8: Solomon's other building

Chapter 9: The Queen of Sheba visits Solomon and Solomon's death

Chapter 10: Division of the kingdom

Chapter 11: Rehoboam strengthens Judah and Rehoboam's family

Chapter 12: Egyptians invade Judah

Chapter 13: Abijah of Judah

Chapter 14: Asa's reforms and victory against the Cushites

Chapter 15: King Asa's reforms

Chapter 16: Hanani the prophet, and the end of Asa's reign

Chapter 17: Jehoshaphat king of Judah

Chapter 18: Micaiah prophecies against Ahab; Ahab killed

Chapter 19: Jehoshaphat is reprimanded and Jehoshaphat's reforms

Chapter 20: Jehoshaphat defeats Moab and Ammon

Chapter 21: King Jehoram of Judah

Chapter 22: King Ahaziah of Judah

Chapter 23: Rebellion against Athaliah, Jehoiada's reforms

Chapter 24: Joash repairs the temple but then falls into idolatry

Chapter 25: King Amaziah of Judah

Chapter 26: King Uzziah of Judah

Chapter 27: King Jotham of Judah

Chapter 28: King Ahaz of Judah

Chapter 29: Hezekiah's good reign in Judah and his sacrifice of atonement

Chapter 30: Preparations for and two celebrations of the Passover

Chapter 31: Hezekiah's religious reforms

Chapter 32: Assyrians threaten Jerusalem; Hezekiah's wealth, illness, and death

Chapter 33: King Manasseh of Judah

Chapter 34: Josiah's positive religious reforms

Chapter 35: Passover is kept by Josiah; Josiah killed in battle

Chapter 36: Last four kings of Judah; fall of Jerusalem and exile

Insight from Matthew Henry

2 Chronicles 6

The order of Solomon's prayer is to be observed. First and chiefly, he prays for repentance and forgiveness, which is the chief blessing, and the only solid foundation of other mercies: he then prays for temporal mercies; thereby teaching us what things to mind and desire most in our prayers. This also Christ hath taught us in his perfect pattern and form of prayer, where there is but one prayer for outward, and all the rest are for spiritual blessings. The temple typified the human nature of Christ, in whom dwelleth all the fullness of the Godhead bodily. The ark typified his obedience and sufferings, by which repenting sinners have access to a reconciled God, and communion with him.

Ezra

An introduction

The book of Ezra is the record of events occurring at the close of the Babylonian exile.

It was at one time included in Nehemiah, as the Jews regarded them as one volume. The two are still listed in the Vulgate version as I and II Esdras.

Divisions

It consists of two principal divisions:

(1) The history of the first return of exiles, in the first year of Cyrus (536 B.C.), till the completion and dedication of the new temple, in the sixth year of Darius Hystapes (515 B.C.), Ezra 1–6. From the close of the sixth to the opening of the seventh chapter there is a blank in the history of about sixty years.

(2) The history of the second return under Ezra, in the seventh year of Artaxerxes Longimanus, and of the events that took place at Jerusalem after Ezra's arrival there (Ezra 7–10).

The book thus contains memorabilia connected with the Jews, from the decree of Cyrus (536 B.C.) to the reformation by Ezra (456 B.C.), extending over a period of about eighty years.

No quotations

There is no quotation from this book in the New Testament, but there never has been any doubt about its being canonical.

Authorship

Ezra was probably the author of this book, at least of the greater part of it (cf. Ezra 7: 27,28; 8: 1, etc.), as he was also of the Books of Chronicles, the close of which forms the opening passage of Ezra.

Name, author, date

MEANING OF NAME OF BOOK
The book is named after Ezra, whose name means "help."

AUTHOR
The book of Ezra is anonymous, but Ezra is the most likely person to have written it.

APPROXIMATE DATE OF WRITING
455–440 B.C.

Statistics

PLACE OF BOOK IN BIBLE
15th Old Testament book.
10th historical book.

NUMBER OF CHAPTERS: 10

NUMBER OF VERSES: 280

NUMBER OF WORDS: 7,441

Main theme of book

Ezra records two returns of God's people from Babylon to Jerusalem and the rebuilding of the temple.

Keys to the understanding of book

KEY WORD/S
Build

Temple, 25 times.
Jerusalem, 48 times.

KEY PHRASE
The word of the Lord, 1: 1.

KEY PERSON/PEOPLE
Cyrus, Ezra, Jeshua, and Zerubbabel.

KEY CHAPTER/S
6 and the temple's dedication.

KEY VERSE/S
Now these are the children of the
province that went up out of the
captivity, of those which had been
carried away, whom Nebuchadnezzar
the king of Babylon had carried away
unto Babylon, and came again unto
Jerusalem and Judah, every one unto
his city.
Ezra 2: 1

And the children of Israel, which were
come again out of captivity, and all
such as had separated themselves unto
them from the filthiness of the heathen
of the land, to seek the Lord God of
Israel, did eat, And kept the feast of
unleavened bread seven days with
joy: for the Lord had made them joyful,
and turned the heart of the king of
Assyria unto them, to strengthen their
hands in the work of the house of God,
the God of Israel.
Ezra 6: 21,22

For Ezra had prepared his heart to seek
the law of the Lord, and to do it, and to
teach in Israel statutes and judgments.
Ezra 7: 10

Jesus Christ in Ezra
WHO JESUS IS
Lord of heaven and earth.

JESUS FORESHADOWED AS A TYPE/
PORTRAITS OF CHRIST
The restoration and forgiveness of
Christ is portrayed in the whole book.

Spiritual thought
Repairing God's spiritual temple.

Chapter by chapter breakdown
Chapter 1: Cyrus allows the exiles to
return
Chapter 2: List of exiles who returned
Chapter 3: Worship restarted, and the
temple foundation laid
Chapter 4: The Jews encounter
opposition
Chapter 5: Searching the records
Chapter 6: Rebuilding the temple is
finished
Chapter 7: Ezra arrives in Jerusalem
Chapter 8: List of exiles who returned
under Ezra
Chapter 9: Ezra's prayer after learning
about inter-marriage with non-Jews
Chapter 10: Ezra's plans to end
marriages with non-Jews

Insight from Matthew Henry

Ezra 1
VERSES 1–4
The Lord stirred up the spirit of Cyrus.
The hearts of kings are in the hand of
the Lord. God governs the world by
his influence on the spirits of men;
whatever good they do, God stirs up
their spirits to do it.

Nehemiah

An introduction

Authorship

The author of this book was no doubt Nehemiah himself. There are parts of the book written in the first person (Neh. 1–7; 12: 27–47; 13). But there are also parts of it in which Nehemiah is spoken of in the third person (Neh. 8; 9; 10). It is supposed that these parts may have been written by Ezra; of this, however, there is no distinct evidence. These parts had their place assigned them in the book, there can be no doubt, by Nehemiah. He was the responsible author of the whole book, with the exception of Neh. 12: 11,22,23.

Date

The date at which the book was written was probably about 431–430 B.C., when Nehemiah had returned the second time to Jerusalem after his visit to Persia.

Divisions

The book, which may historically be regarded as a continuation of the book of Ezra, consists of four parts.

(1) An account of the rebuilding of the wall of Jerusalem, and of the register Nehemiah had found of those who had returned from Babylon (Neh. 1–7).

(2) An account of the state of religion among the Jews during this time (Neh. 8–10).

(3) Increase of the inhabitants of Jerusalem; the census of the adult male population, and names of the chiefs, together with lists of priests and Levites (Neh. 11: 1–12: 26).

(4) Dedication of the wall of Jerusalem, the arrangement of the temple officers, and the reforms carried out by Nehemiah (Neh. 12: 27–Neh. 13).

Closes the Old Testament

This book closes the history of the Old Testament. Malachi the prophet was contemporary with Nehemiah.

Name, author, date

MEANING OF NAME OF BOOK
The book is named after Nehemiah, whose name means "Comfort of the Lord."

AUTHOR
The book of Nehemiah is attributed to Nehemiah, 1: 1, and parts of it are clearly Nehemiah's memoirs.

APPROXIMATE DATE OF WRITING
445–425 B.C.

Statistics

PLACE OF BOOK IN BIBLE
16th Old Testament book.
11th historical book.

NUMBER OF CHAPTERS: 13

NUMBER OF VERSES: 406

NUMBER OF WORDS: 10,438

Main theme of book

Nehemiah leading the third return of God's people from Babylon to Jerusalem.

Keys to the understanding of book

KEY WORD/S
Prayer
Work
Wall, walls, 33 times
Jerusalem
Build, rebuilding

KEY PHRASE
Arise and build, 2: 20.

KEY PERSON/PEOPLE
Nehemiah, Artaxerxes, Sanballet, Ezra.

KEY CHAPTER/S
9 and the completion of the temple and reaffirmation of loyalty to God's covenant.

KEY VERSE/S
Remember, I beseech thee, the word that thou commandedst thy servant Moses, saying, If ye transgress, I will scatter you abroad among the nations: But if ye turn unto me, and keep my commandments, and do them; though there were of you cast out unto the uttermost part of the heaven, yet will I gather them from thence, and will bring them unto the place that I have chosen to set my name there.
Nehemiah 1: 8,9

So they read in the book in the law of God distinctly, and gave the sense, and caused them to understand the reading.
Nehemiah 8: 8

Jesus Christ in Nehemiah

WHO JESUS IS
Lord of heaven and earth.

JESUS FORESHADOWED AS A TYPE/ PORTRAITS OF CHRIST
Nehemiah portrays Christ through his restoration of the walls of Jerusalem.

Spiritual thought

Having a mind to do God's work.

Chapter by chapter breakdown

Chapter 1: Nehemiah learns of Jerusalem's plight
Chapter 2: Nehemiah goes to Jerusalem
Chapter 3: Nehemiah organizes the work in Jerusalem
Chapter 4: Nehemiah encounters opposition
Chapter 5: The poor are oppressed; Nehemiah's generosity
Chapter 6: The rebuilding of the walls of Jerusalem is completed
Chapter 7: List of those who returned from exile with Zerubbabel
Chapter 8: Ezra reads the Law
Chapter 9: The Jews confess their sins in prayer
Chapter 10: The covenant is renewed
Chapter 11: The residents of Jerusalem and the people in the villages
Chapter 12: Lists of priests and Levites and other lists of people
Chapter 13: Nehemiah's reforms

Insight from Matthew Henry

Nehemiah 1

When God has work to do, he will never want instruments to do it with. Nehemiah lived at ease, and in honor, but does not forget that he is an Israelite, and that his brethren are in distress.

Esther

An introduction

Authorship

The authorship of this book is unknown. It must obviously have been written after the death of Ahasuerus (the Xerxes of the Greeks), which took place in 465 B.C. The minute and particular account also given of many historical details makes it probable that the writer was contemporary with Mordecai and Esther. Hence we may conclude that the author was one of the Jews of the dispersion.

History book

This book is more purely historical than any other book of Scripture; and it has this remarkable peculiarity that the name of God does not occur in it from first to last in any form. It has, however, been well observed that "though the name of God be not in it, his finger is." The book wonderfully exhibits the providential government of God.

Name, author, date

MEANING OF NAME OF BOOK
The book is named after Esther whose name means "myrtle."

AUTHOR
The book of Esther is anonymous.

APPROXIMATE DATE OF WRITING
470–465 B.C.

Statistics

PLACE OF BOOK IN BIBLE
17th Old Testament book.

12th historical book.

NUMBER OF CHAPTERS: 10

NUMBER OF VERSES: 167

NUMBER OF WORDS: 5,637

Main theme of book

The Israelites escape from the threat of extermination.

Keys to the understanding of book

KEY WORD/S
Providence
Deliverance

KEY PHRASE
For such a time as this, 4: 14.

KEY PERSON/PEOPLE
Esther, Haman, Mordecai, Xerxes (Ahasuerus).

KEY CHAPTER/S
8, which states that many people became Jews.

KEY VERSE/S
For if thou altogether holdest thy peace at this time, then shall there enlargement and deliverance arise to the Jews from another place; but thou and thy father's house shall be destroyed: and who knoweth whether thou art come to the kingdom for such a time as this?
Esther 4: 14

And in every province, and in every city, whithersoever the king's commandment and his decree came,

the Jews had joy and gladness, a feast and a good day. And many of the people of the land became Jews; for the fear of the Jews fell upon them.
Esther 8:17

Jesus Christ in Esther

WHO JESUS IS
Savior of God's people.

JESUS FORESHADOWED AS A TYPE/
PORTRAITS OF CHRIST
Esther is seen as a type of Christ when she was prepared to die for her people in order to bring about their salvation.

Spiritual thought

God alone is to be trusted.

Chapter by chapter breakdown

Chapter 1: Queen Vashti is deposed

Chapter 2: Esther becomes the new queen

Chapter 3: Haman plots to kill the Jews

Chapter 4: Esther agrees to seek the king's help

Chapter 5: Esther goes before the king; Haman plots against Mordecai

Chapter 6: The king honors Mordecai, while Haman sulks

Chapter 7: Haman's fall from grace

Chapter 8: The king's new decree saves the Jews

Chapter 9: The Jews defeat their enemies and institute the Feast of Purim

Chapter 10: Mordecai is honored

Insight from Matthew Henry

Esther 4

VERSES 5–17

We are prone to shrink from services that are attended with peril or loss. But when the cause of Christ and his people demand it, we must take up our cross, and follow him. When Christians are disposed to consult their own ease or safety, rather than the public good, they should be blamed. The law was express, all knew it. It is not thus in the court of the King of kings: to the footstool of his throne of grace we may always come boldly, and may be sure of an answer of peace to the prayer of faith. We are welcome, even into the holiest, through the blood of Jesus. Providence so ordered it, that, just then, the king's affections had cooled toward Esther; her faith and courage thereby were the more tried; and God's goodness in the favor she now found with the king, thereby shone the brighter. Haman no doubt did what he could to set the king against her. Mordecai suggests, that it was a cause which, one way or other, would certainly be carried, and which therefore she might safely venture in. This was the language of strong faith, which staggered not at the promise when the danger was most threatening, but against hope believed in hope. He that by sinful devices will save his life, and will not trust God with it in the way of duty, shall lose it in the way of sin. Divine Providence had regard to this matter, in bringing Esther to be queen.

Job (1)

An introduction

Authorship

Many different opinions exist about the authorship of this book.

INTERNAL EVIDENCE
From internal evidence, such as the similarity of sentiment and language to those in the Psalms and Proverbs (see Ps. 88 and 89), the prevalence of the idea of "wisdom," and the style and character of the composition, it is supposed by some to have been written in the time of David and Solomon.

Others argue that it was written by Job himself, or by Elihu, or Isaiah, or perhaps more probably by Moses, who was "learned in all the wisdom of the Egyptians, and mighty in words and deeds" (Acts 7: 22). He had opportunities in Midian for obtaining the knowledge of the facts related. But the authorship is altogether uncertain.

Historical poem

As to the character of the book, it is a historical poem, one of the greatest and sublime poems in all literature. Job was a historical person, and the localities and names were real and not fictitious.

It is "one of the grandest portions of the inspired Scriptures, a heavenly-replenished storehouse of comfort and instruction, the patriarchal Bible, and a precious monument of primitive theology. It is to the Old Testament what the Epistle to the Romans is to the New."

It is a didactic narrative in a dramatic form.

Quoted in the New Testament

This book was apparently well known in the days of Ezekiel, 600 B.C. (Ezek. 14: 14). It formed a part of the sacred Scriptures used by our Lord and his apostles, and is referred to as a part of the inspired Word (Heb. 12: 5; 1 Cor. 3: 19).

Contents

The subject of the book is the trial of Job, its occasion, nature, endurance, and issue.

It exhibits the harmony of the truths of revelation and the dealings of Providence, which are seen to be at once inscrutable, just, and merciful. It shows the blessedness of the truly pious, even in the middle of acute afflictions, and thus ministers comfort and hope to tried believers of every age. Many important lessons are contained in this book which is profitable for doctrine, for reproof, for correction, and for instruction in righteousness (2 Tim. 3: 16).

It consists of,

(1) An historical introduction in prose (Job 1, 2).

(2) The controversy and its solution, in poetry (Job 3–42: 6).

Job's despondent lamentation (Job 3) is the occasion of the controversy which is carried on in three sets of dialogues between Job and his three friends.

The first set gives the commencement of the controversy (Job 4–14); the second the growth of the controversy (Job 15–21); and the third the height of the controversy (Job 22–27).

This is followed by the solution of the controversy in the speeches of Elihu and the address of Jehovah, followed by Job's humble confession (Job 42: 1–6) of his own fault and folly.

(3) The third division is the historical conclusion, in prose (Job 42: 7–15).

J. W. Dawson

Sir J. W. Dawson says: "It would now seem that the language and theology of the book of Job can be better explained by supposing it to be a portion of Minean [Southern Arabia] literature obtained by Moses in Midian than in any other way. This view also agrees better than any other with its references to natural objects, the art of mining, and other matters."

Name, author, date

MEANING OF NAME OF BOOK
The book is named after Job, whose name means both "persecuted one" and "repent."

AUTHOR
The book of Job is anonymous.

APPROXIMATE DATE OF WRITING
It is not known when this book was written, but it may have been the first book of the Old Testament to be written.

Statistics

PLACE OF BOOK IN BIBLE
18th Old Testament book.
2nd poetical book.

NUMBER OF CHAPTERS
42

NUMBER OF VERSES
1,070

NUMBER OF WORDS
10,102

Main theme of book

Why do the seemingly innocent suffer?

Keys to the understanding of book

KEY WORD/S
Sovereignty (key concept)
Tried
Affliction, hardship, misery, 9 times
Righteous, righteousness, 20 times

KEY PHRASE
Blessed be the name of the Lord, 21.

KEY PERSON/PEOPLE
Job, Satan, Eliphaz, Bildad, Zopher, and Elihu.

KEY CHAPTER/S
38, where Job becomes conscious of God.
42, where Job bows before God's majesty.

Job (2)

KEY VERSE/S
Though he slay me, yet will I trust in him: but I will maintain mine own ways before him.
Job 13:15

But he knoweth the way that I take: when he hath tried me, I shall come forth as gold.
Job 23:10

Touching the Almighty, we cannot find him out: he is excellent in power, and in judgment, and in plenty of justice: he will not afflict. Men do therefore fear him: he respecteth not any that are wise of heart.
Job 37: 23,24

I have heard of thee by the hearing of the ear: but now mine eye seeth thee. herefore I abhor myself, and repent in dust and ashes.
Job 42: 5,6

And the Lord turned the captivity of Job, when he prayed for his friends: also the Lord gave Job twice as much as he had before.
Job 42:10

Jesus Christ in Job

WHO JESUS IS
The Friend who sticks closer than a brother.

JESUS FORESHADOWED AS A TYPE/ PORTRAITS OF CHRIST
Job calls out for a Mediator and acknowledges a Redeemer.

Spiritual thought
Allow God to rule in our lives.

Chapter by chapter breakdown
Chapter 1: Job's circumstances
Chapter 2: Satan's second attack; Job's four friends arrive
Chapter 3: Job's first speech
Chapter 4: Eliphaz says that the innocent do not suffer
Chapter 5: Eliphaz continues his reply
Chapter 6: Job expresses his deep anguish
Chapter 8: Bildad's first speech
Chapter 9: Job argues his case
Chapter 10: Job questions his oppression
Chapter 11: Zophar's first speech
Chapter 12: Job says that only God knows everything
Chapter 13: Job reproves his friends and expresses his confidence in God
Chapter 14: Job mourns that man has only one life
Chapter 15: Eliphaz's second speech
Chapter 16: Job accuses his friends of being miserable
Chapter 17: Job says his hope is not in life, but in death
Chapter 18: Bildad's second speech
Chapter 19: Job replies to Bildad
Chapter 20: Zophar's second speech
Chapter 21: Job replies to Zophar
Chapter 22: Eliphaz's third speech
Chapter 23: Job will come out refined like pure gold
Chapter 24: Job says that God seems indifferent to wickedness

Chapter 25: Bildad's third speech
Chapter 26: Job replies to Bildad
Chapter 27: Job boasts of his
righteousness
Chapter 28: Job says that men cannot
achieve wisdom
Chapter 29: Job recalls his happy past
Chapter 30: Job outlines his present
humiliation
Chapter 31: Job maintains that he is
innocent
Chapter 32: Elihu intervenes in the
discussion
Chapter 33: Elihu's first proposition
Chapter 34: Elihu's second proposition
Chapter 35: Elihu's third proposition
Chapter 36: Elihu says that God is
disciplining Job
Chapter 37: Elihu observes God's power
Chapter 38: God questions Job
Chapter 39: God reminds Job of the
animal kingdom
Chapter 40: God shows Job how feeble
he is
Chapter 41: God compares Job's power
with that of the leviathan
Chapter 42: Job repents and is fully
restored

Insight from Matthew Henry

Job 42

VERSES 7–9

After the Lord had convinced and humbled Job, and brought him to repentance, he owned him, comforted him, and put honor upon him. The devil had undertaken to prove Job a hypocrite, and his three friends had condemned him as a wicked man; but if God say, Well done, thou good and faithful servant, it is of little consequence who says otherwise.

Job's friends had wronged God, by making prosperity a mark of the true church, and affliction a certain proof of God's wrath.

Job had referred things to the future judgment and the future state, more than his friends, therefore he spake of God that which was right, better than his friends had done.

And as Job prayed and offered sacrifice for those that had grieved and wounded his spirit, so Christ prayed for his persecutors, and ever lives, making intercession for the transgressors.

Job's friends were good men, and belonged to God, and He would not let them be in their mistake any more than Job; but having humbled him by a discourse out of the whirlwind, he takes another way to humble them. They are not to argue the matter again, but they must agree in a sacrifice and a prayer, and that must reconcile them.

Those who differ in judgment about lesser things, yet are one in Christ the great Sacrifice, and ought therefore to love and bear with one another. When God was angry with Job's friends, he put them in a way to make peace with him. Our quarrels with God always begin on our part, but the making peace begins on his.

Peace with God is to be had only in his own way, and upon his own terms.

Psalms (1)

An introduction

Authorship

MORE THAN ONE AUTHOR
The psalms were produced by various authors.

"Only a portion of the Book of Psalms claims David as its author. Other inspired poets in successive generations added now one now another contribution to the sacred collection, and thus in the wisdom of Providence it more completely reflects every phase of human emotion and circumstances than it otherwise could." But it is specially to David and his contemporaries that we owe this precious book.

DAVID
In the "titles" of the psalms, the genuineness of which there is no sufficient reason to doubt, 73 are ascribed to David.

Peter and John (Acts 4: 25) ascribe to him also the second psalm, which is one of the 48 that are anonymous. About two-thirds of the whole collection have been ascribed to David.

JUDUTHUN
Ps. 39, 62, and 77 are addressed to Jeduthun, to be sung after his manner or in his choir.

ASAPH
Ps. 50 and 73–83 are addressed to Asaph, as the master of his choir, to be sung in the worship of God.

SONS OF KORAH
The "sons of Korah," who formed a leading part of the Kohathite singers (2 Chr. 20: 19), were entrusted with the arranging and singing of Ps. 42,44–49, 84,85,87, and 88.

Hagiographa

In Luke 24: 44 the word "psalms" means the Hagiographa, i.e., the holy writings, one of the sections into which the Jews divided the Old Testament.

Date

None of the psalms can be proved to have been of a later date than the time of Ezra and Nehemiah, hence the whole collection extends over a period of about 1000 years. There are in the New Testament 116 direct quotations from the Psalter.

Divisions

The Psalter is divided, like the Pentateuch, into five books, each closing with a doxology or benediction:

(1) The first book comprises the first 41 psalms, all of which are ascribed to David except Ps. 1, 2, 10, and 33, which, though anonymous, may also be ascribed to him.

(2) The second book consists of the next 31 psalms (Ps. 42–72), 18 of which are ascribed to David and 1 to Solomon (Ps. 72). The rest are anonymous.

(3) The third book contains 17 psalms (Ps. 73–89), of which Ps. 86 is ascribed to David, Ps. 88 to Heman the Ezrahite, and Ps. 89 to Ethan the Ezrahite.

(4) The fourth book also contains 17 psalms (Ps. 90–106), of which Ps. 90 is ascribed to Moses, and Ps. 101 and 103 to David.

(5) The fifth book contains the remaining psalms, 44 in number. Of these, 15 are ascribed to David, and Ps. 127 to Solomon.

Great hallel

Ps. 136 is generally called "the great hallel." But the Talmud includes also Ps. 120–135. Ps. 113–118, inclusive, constitute the hallel recited at the three great feasts, at the new moon, and on the eight days of the feast of dedication. "It is presumed that these several collections were made at times of high religious life: the first, probably, near the close of David's life; the second in the days of Solomon; the third by the singers of Jehoshaphat (2 Chr. 20: 19); the fourth by the men of Hezekiah (2 Chr. 29, 30, 31); and the fifth in the days of Ezra."

Worship songs

The Mosaic ritual makes no provision for the service of song in the worship of God. David first taught the Church to sing the praises of the Lord. He first introduced into the ritual of the tabernacle music and song.

Diverse names are given to the psalms.

(1) Some bear the Hebrew designation *shir* (Gr. ode, a song). Thirteen have this title. It means the flow of speech, as it were, in a straight line or in a regular strain. This title includes secular as well as sacred song.

(2) Fifty-eight psalms bear the designation (Heb.) *mitsmor* (Gr. *psalmos*, a psalm), a lyric ode, or a song set to music; a sacred song accompanied with a musical instrument.

(3) Ps. 145, and many others, have the designation (Heb.) *tehillah* (Gr. *hymnos*, a hymn), meaning a song of praise; a song the prominent thought of which is the praise of God.

(4) Six psalms (Ps. 16, 56–60) have the title (Heb.) *michtam*.

(5) Ps. 7 and Hab. 3 bear the title (Heb.) *shiggaion*.

Name, author, date

MEANING OF NAME OF BOOK
This book was named "book of praises."

AUTHOR
The book itself says that it was written by several people, including King David.

APPROXIMATE DATE OF WRITING
The Psalms were written over many centuries, from 1410 to 430 B.C.

Psalms (2)

Statistics

PLACE OF BOOK IN BIBLE
19th Old Testament book.
3rd poetical book.

NUMBER OF CHAPTERS
150

NUMBER OF VERSES
2,461

NUMBER OF WORDS
43,743

Main theme of book

The psalms were Israel's hymnbook.

Keys to the understanding of book

KEY WORD/S
Praise, more than 150 times
Worship
Bless, blessing, bless, more than 100 times

KEY PHRASE
Praise the Lord, 7: 17.

KEY PERSON/PEOPLE
The focus of the psalms is God rather than people. David and Korah are mentioned.

KEY CHAPTER/S
23
100, where worship and praise are central.

KEY VERSE/S
Let the words of my mouth, and the meditation of my heart, be acceptable in thy sight, O Lord, my strength, and my redeemer.
Psalm 19: 14

Give unto the Lord the glory due unto his name; worship the Lord in the beauty of holiness.
Psalm 29: 2

O come, let us sing unto the Lord: let us make a joyful noise to the rock of our salvation.
Psalm 95: 1

My mouth shall speak the praise of the Lord: and let all flesh bless his holy name for ever and ever.
Psalm 145: 21

Jesus Christ in Psalms

WHO JESUS IS
Jesus is Lord, 110: 1.

JESUS FORESHADOWED AS A TYPE/ PORTRAITS OF CHRIST
In the psalms Christ is seen as prophet, priest, king, the Son of Man, and the Son of God.

Spiritual thought

Be like the psalmist and come to know the Lord in a deeper way.

Chapter by chapter breakdown

Psalm 1: Contrasting two ways of life
Psalm 2: The Lord's Anointed
Psalm 3: Victory in the face of defeat
Psalm 4: Evening prayer for deliverance
Psalm 5: Morning prayer for guidance
Psalm 6: Prayer for God's mercy

Psalm 7: A prayer for justice

Psalm 8: God's glory and humankind's dominion

Psalm 9: Praise for victory over enemies

Psalm 10: The psalmist complains of the wickedness of the wicked

Psalm 11: God tests the sons of men

Psalm 12: The pure words of God

Psalm 13: A prayer asking for God's immediate answer

Psalm 14: The characteristics of the godless

Psalm 15: The characteristics of the godly

Psalm 16: A confident prayer about God's goodness

Psalm 17: Hidden under God's wings

Psalm 18: Thanksgiving for God's deliverance

Psalm 19: God's deeds and God's word

Psalm 20: Trust in God, not in chariots and horses

Psalm 21: Triumph of the King

Psalm 22: The psalm of the cross

Psalm 23: The psalm of the divine Shepherd

Psalm 24: The psalm of the King of Glory

Psalm 25: Acrostic prayer for instruction

Psalm 26: A plea to be examined by the Lord

Psalm 27: Trust in the Lord and do not be afraid

Psalm 28: A prayer for help

Psalm 29: God's powerful voice

Psalm 30: Thanksgiving for dramatic deliverance

Psalm 31: Be of good courage

Psalm 32: The fruit of forgiveness

Psalm 33: God considers all humankind's deeds

Psalm 34: Seek the Lord

Psalm 35: Request for God's intervention

Psalm 36: God's loving-kindness

Psalm 37: Rest in the Lord

Psalm 38: Sin's heavy burden

Psalm 39: Recall your lifespan

Psalm 40: Delight to do God's will

Psalm 41: Joy in helping the poor

Psalm 42: Why are you depressed?

Psalm 43: Prayer for God's deliverance

Psalm 44: Prayer for God's deliverance

Psalm 45: The psalm of the great King

Psalm 46: God is our refuge and strength

Psalm 47: The Lord will subdue all nations

Psalm 48: The praise of Mount Zion

Psalm 49: Riches cannot redeem

Psalm 50: Everyone will be judged by the Lord

Psalm 51: Confession and forgiveness of sin

Psalm 52: The Lord will judge the deceitful

Psalm 53: A picture of the godless

Psalm 54: Assurance of the divine favor and protection

Psalm 55: Cast your burden on the Lord

Psalm 56: Fear in the middle of trials

Psalm 57: Prayer in the middle of trouble

Psalm 58: Wicked judges will be judged

Psalm 59: Prayer for deliverance from violent people

Psalm 60: Prayer for the deliverance of the nation

Psalms (3)

Chapter by chapter breakdown, continued

Psalm 61: A prayer when overwhelmed

Psalm 62: Wait for God

Psalm 63: Thirst for God

Psalm 64: A prayer for God's protection

Psalm 65: God's care of nature

Psalm 66: Remember what God has done

Psalm 67: God will rule the earth

Psalm 68: God is the Father of the fatherless

Psalm 69: Prayer for God to come close

Psalm 70: Prayer for the poor and needy

Psalm 71: Prayers that God would deliver and save

Psalm 72: The Messiah's rule

Psalm 73: The perspective of eternity

Psalm 74: A prayer asking God to remember his covenant

Psalm 75: God is the Judge

Psalm 76: God's wonderful power

Psalm 77: When overwhelmed, recall God's greatness

Psalm 78: God continues to guide, despite unbelief

Psalm 79: Jerusalem's defilement will be avenged

Psalm 80: Israel pleads for God's mercy

Psalm 81: God's longing for Israel's obedience

Psalm 82: Israel's judges rebuked

Psalm 83: Plea for God to destroy Israel's enemies

Psalm 84: The joy of living with God

Psalm 85: A prayer for revival

Psalm 86: Teach my your way, O Lord

Psalm 87: Glorious Zion, city of God

Psalm 88: Crying from the depths of affliction

Psalm 89: Claiming God's promises in affliction

Psalm 90: Teach us to number our days

Psalm 91: Living under the shadow of the Almighty

Psalm 92: It is good to praise the Lord

Psalm 93: God's majesty

Psalm 94: Revenge belongs only to God

Psalm 95: A call to worship the Lord

Psalm 96: Make known God's glory

Psalm 97: The Lord reigns in power that cannot be resisted

Psalm 98: Sing a new song to the Lord

Psalm 99: Exult in the Lord our God

Psalm 100: Serve the Lord with gladness

Psalm 101: Commitment to a holy life

Psalm 102: The prayer of an overwhelmed believer

Psalm 103: Bless the Lord, all you people!

Psalm 104: A psalm remembering God's creation

Psalm 105: Remember, God keeps his promises

Psalm 106: We have sinned

Psalm 107: God satisfies the longing soul

Psalm 108: A cry for help from God's right hand

Psalm 109: A song of those who have been slandered

Psalm 110: The coming of the Priest-King-Judge

Psalm 111: Praise for God's tender care

Psalm 112: The blessings of those who fear God

Psalm 113: God's wonderful grace

Psalm 114: Praise God for the Exodus

Psalm 115: To God alone be the glory

Psalm 116: Remember all that God has done

Psalm 117: The praise of God's people

Psalm 118: It is better to trust God than any human being

Psalm 119: An acrostic psalm in praise of the Scriptures

Psalm 120: A cry from the depths of distress

Psalm 121: God is our Protector

Psalm 122: Pray for the peace of Jerusalem

Psalm 123: A plea for God's mercy

Psalm 124: God is on our side

Psalm 125: Trust in the Lord

Psalm 126: Sow in tears, reap in joy

Psalm 127: Children are God's gift

Psalm 128: May God's blessing rest on the God-fearing

Psalm 129: A cry of the persecuted

Psalm 130: My soul waits for the Lord

Psalm 131: A childlike faith

Psalm 132: Trust in the God of David

Psalm 133: The beauty of unity among God's people

Psalm 134: Praise the Lord in the evening

Psalm 135: God has done great things

Psalm 136: God's mercy endures forever

Psalm 137: Tears in exile

Psalm 138: God answered my prayer

Psalm 139: Search me, O God

Psalm 140: Protect me from violent people

Psalm 141: Set a guard, O Lord, over my mouth

Psalm 142: A prayer for help

Psalm 143: Teach me to do your will

Psalm 144: What is man?

Psalm 145: Speak of God's great deeds

Psalm 146: Do not place your trust in princes

Psalm 147: God heals the broken-hearted

Psalm 148: All creation praises the Lord

Psalm 149: The Lord takes pleasure in his people

Psalm 150: Praise the Lord

Insight from Matthew Henry

Psalm 23

The believer is taught to express his satisfaction in the care of the great Pastor of the universe, the Redeemer and Preserver of men. With joy he reflects that he has a shepherd, and that shepherd is Jehovah. A flock of sheep, gentle and harmless, feeding in verdant pastures, under the care of a skilful, watchful, and tender shepherd, forms an emblem of believers brought back to the Shepherd of their souls. The greatest abundance is but a dry pasture to a wicked man, who relishes in it only what pleases the senses; but to a godly man, who by faith tastes the goodness of God in all his enjoyments, though he has but little of the world, it is a green pasture. The Lord gives quiet and contentment in the mind, whatever the lot is.

Proverbs (1)

An introduction

The book of Proverbs is a collection of moral and philosophical maxims on a wide range of subjects presented in a poetic form.

This book sets out the "philosophy of practical life. It is the sign to us that the Bible does not despise common sense and discretion. It impresses upon us in the most forcible manner the value of intelligence and prudence and of a good education. The whole strength of the Hebrew language and of the sacred authority of the book is thrown upon these homely truths. It deals, too, in that refined, discriminating, careful view of the finer shades of human character so often overlooked by theologians, but so necessary to any true estimate of human life" (*Stanley's Jewish Church*).

Authorship

As to the origin of this book, "it is probable that Solomon gathered and recast many proverbs which sprang from human experience in preceding ages and were floating past him on the tide of time, and that he also elaborated many new ones from the material of his own experience. Towards the close of the book, indeed, are preserved some of Solomon's own sayings that seem to have fallen from his lips in later life and been gathered by other hands" (*Arnot's Laws from Heaven*).

Divisions

This book is usually divided into three parts:

(1) Consisting of Prov. 1–9, which contain an exhibition of wisdom as the highest good.

(2) Consisting of Prov. 10–24.

(3) Containing proverbs of Solomon "which the men of Hezekiah, the king of Judah, collected" (Prov. 25–29).

Two supplements

These are followed by two supplements,

(1) "The words of Agur" (Prov. 30); and

(2) "The words of king Lemuel" (Prov. 31).

Solomon

Solomon is said to have written three thousand proverbs, and those contained in this book may be a selection from these (1 Kings 4: 32).

New Testament quotations

In the New Testament there are thirty-five direct quotations from this book or allusions to it.

Name, author, date

MEANING OF NAME OF BOOK
The Hebrew word for "proverbs" means to rule or to govern.

AUTHOR
The book of Proverbs was written mainly by Solomon.

APPROXIMATE DATE OF WRITING
The proverbs written by Solomon were written by the time of his death in 931 B.C.

Statistics

PLACE OF BOOK IN BIBLE
20th Old Testament book.
3rd poetical book.

NUMBER OF CHAPTERS
31

NUMBER OF VERSES
915

NUMBER OF WORDS
15,043

Main theme of book

Moral discernment.

Keys to the understanding of book

KEY WORD/S
Wisdom, wise, 110 times
Instruction, teaching, taught, 23 times

KEY PHRASE
The fear of the Lord, 9: 10.

KEY PERSON/PEOPLE
The book of Proverbs is several collections of proverbs and does not focus on people.

KEY CHAPTER/S
8 and the value of wisdom
31 and its high view of women

KEY VERSE/S
A wise man will hear, and will increase learning; and a man of understanding shall attain unto wise counsels: To understand a proverb, and the interpretation; the words of the wise, and their dark sayings. The fear of the Lord is the beginning of knowledge: but fools despise wisdom and instruction.
Proverbs 1: 5–7

Trust in the Lord with all thine heart; and lean not unto thine own understanding. In all thy ways acknowledge him, and he shall direct thy paths.
Proverbs 3: 5,6

Keep thy heart with all diligence; for out of it are the issues of life.
Proverbs 4: 23

The fear of the Lord is the beginning of wisdom: and the knowledge of the holy is understanding.
Proverbs 9: 10

Jesus Christ in Proverbs

WHO JESUS IS
The Truth.

JESUS FORESHADOWED AS A TYPE/
PORTRAITS OF CHRIST
Chapter 8 personifies wisdom.
Jesus is our wisdom, 1 Corinthians 1: 30.

Spiritual thought

Learning wisdom in God's school.

Proverbs (2)

Chapter by chapter breakdown

Chapter 1: The purpose of proverbs

Chapter 2: Seek wisdom

Chapter 3: The benefits of wisdom

Chapter 4: Avoid the wicked and guard your heart

Chapter 5: Adultery is out, faithfulness is in

Chapter 6: Do not be lazy

Chapter 7: Do not commit adultery

Chapter 8: In praise of wisdom

Chapter 9: Wisdom and folly are contrasted

Chapter 10: The godly and the wicked are contrasted

Chapter 11: The godly and the wicked are contrasted

Chapter 12: The godly and the wicked are contrasted

Chapter 13: The godly and the wicked are contrasted

Chapter 14: The godly and the wicked are contrasted

Chapter 15: The godly and the wicked are contrasted

Chapter 16: Encouraging godly lives

Chapter 17: Encouraging godly lives

Chapter 18: Encouraging godly lives

Chapter 19: Encouraging godly lives

Chapter 20: Encouraging godly lives

Chapter 21: Encouraging godly lives

Chapter 22: Encouraging godly lives

Chapter 23: Proverbs concerning a variety of situations

Chapter 24: Proverbs concerning a variety of situations

Chapter 25: Relationships with kings, neighbors, enemies, and yourself

Chapter 26: Relationships with fools, the lazy, and gossips

Chapter 27: Proverbs concerning various activities

Chapter 28: Proverbs concerning various activities

Chapter 29: Proverbs concerning various activities

Chapter 30: The proverbs of Agur

Chapter 31: The wise woman

Insight from Matthew Henry

Proverbs 8

VERSES 1–11

The will of God is made known by the works of creation, and by the consciences of men, but more clearly by Moses and the prophets. The chief difficulty is to get men to attend to instruction. Yet attention to the words of Christ, will guide the most ignorant into saving knowledge of the truth. Where there is an understanding heart, and willingness to receive the truth in love, wisdom is valued above silver and gold.

VERSES 12–21

Wisdom, here is Christ, in whom are all the treasures of wisdom and knowledge; it is Christ in the word, and Christ in the heart; not only Christ revealed to us, but Christ revealed in us. All prudence and skill are from the Lord. Through the redemption of Christ's precious blood, the riches of his grace abound in all wisdom and prudence. Man found out many inventions for ruin; God found one for our recovery. He hates pride and arrogance, evil ways and froward conversation; these render men unwilling to hear his humbling, awakening, holy instructions. True religion gives men the best counsel in all difficult cases, and helps to make their way plain. His wisdom makes all truly happy who receive it in the love of Christ Jesus. Seek him early, seek him earnestly, seek him before any thing else. Christ never said, Seek in vain. Those who love Christ, are such as have seen his loveliness, and have had his love shed abroad in their hearts; therefore they are happy. They shall be happy in this world, or in that which is beyond compare better. Wealth gotten by vanity will soon be diminished, but that which is well got, will wear well; and that which is well spent upon works of piety and charity, will be lasting. If they have not riches and honor in this world, they shall have that which is infinitely better. They shall be happy in the grace of God. Christ, by his Spirit, guides believers into all truth, and so leads them in the way of righteousness; and they walk after the Spirit. Also, they shall be happy in the glory of God hereafter. In Wisdom's promises, believers have goods laid up, not for days and years, but for eternity; her fruit therefore is better than gold.

VERSES 22–31

The Son of God declares himself to have been engaged in the creation of the world. How able, how fit is the Son of God to be the Savior of the world, who was the Creator of it! The Son of

God was ordained, before the world, to that great work. Does he delight in saving wretched sinners, and shall not we delight in his salvation?

VERSES 32–36

Surely we should hearken to Christ's voice with the readiness of children. Let us all be wise, and not refuse such mercy. Blessed are those who hear the Savior's voice, and wait on him with daily reading, meditation, and prayer. The children of the world find time for vain amusements, without neglecting what they deem the one thing needful. Does it not show contempt of Wisdom's instructions, when people professing godliness, seek excuses for neglecting the means of grace? Christ is Wisdom, and he is Life to all believers; nor can we obtain God's favor, unless we find Christ, and are found in him. Those who offend Christ deceive themselves; sin is a wrong to the soul. Sinners die because they will die, which justifies God when he judges.

Proverbs 31

VERSES 1–9

When children are under the mother's eye, she has an opportunity of fashioning their minds aright. Those who are grown up, should often call to mind the good teaching they received when children. The many awful instances of promising characters who have been ruined by vile women, and love of wine, should warn every one to avoid these evils.

Ecclesiastes

An introduction

Names for Ecclesiastes

KOHELETH

The name of this book, Ecclesiastes, comes from the Greek rendering of the Hebrew Koheleth, which means "Preacher."

Authorship

The old and traditional view of the authorship of this book attributes it to Solomon. This view can be satisfactorily maintained, though others date it from the Captivity. The writer represents himself implicitly as Solomon (1: 12).

THE CONFESSION OF KING SOLOMON

It has been appropriately styled "The Confession of King Solomon." "The writer is a man who has sinned in giving way to selfishness and sensuality, who has paid the penalty of that sin in satiety and weariness of life, but who has through all this been under the discipline of a divine education, and has learned from it the lesson which God meant to teach him."

"The writer concludes by pointing out that the secret of a true life is that a man should consecrate the vigor of his youth of God." The key-note of the book is sounded in Eccl. 1: 2,

"Vanity of vanities! saith the Preacher, Vanity of vanities! all is vanity!" i.e., all man's efforts to find happiness apart from God are without result.

Name, author, date

MEANING OF NAME OF BOOK

The word "Ecclesiastes" means preacher.

AUTHOR

Solomon is the traditional author of Ecclesiastes.

APPROXIMATE DATE OF WRITING

935 B.C.

Statistics

PLACE OF BOOK IN BIBLE

21st Old Testament book.
4th historical book.

NUMBER OF CHAPTERS: 12

NUMBER OF VERSES: 222

NUMBER OF WORDS: 5,584

Main theme of book

Nothing in the world, apart from God, satisfies the human heart.

Keys to the understanding of book

KEY WORD/S

Vanity, 37 times

KEY PHRASE

Under the sun, 29 times

KEY PERSON/PEOPLE

Ecclesiastes does not focus on named people.

KEY CHAPTER/S

12 and its answer to the meaning of life.

KEY VERSE/S

Vanity of vanities, saith the Preacher, vanity of vanities; all is vanity. What

profit hath a man of all his labor which he taketh under the sun?
Ecclesiastes 1: 2,3

There is nothing better for a man, than that he should eat and drink, and that he should make his soul enjoy good in his labor. This also I saw, that it was from the hand of God.
Ecclesiastes 2: 24

Then shall the dust return to the earth as it was: and the spirit shall return unto God who gave it.
Ecclesiastes 12: 7

For God shall bring every work into judgment, with every secret thing, whether it be good, or whether it be evil.
Ecclesiastes 12: 14

Jesus Christ in Ecclesiastes

WHO JESUS IS
The great Preacher.

JESUS FORESHADOWED AS A TYPE/
PORTRAITS OF CHRIST
Ultimate satisfaction in life can only be found in Christ.

Spiritual thought

Happiness is not possible without God.

Chapter by chapter breakdown

Chapter 1: Illustrations of vanity
Chapter 2: Proof from experience that "All is vanity"
Chapter 3: God's plans cannot be changed
Chapter 4: Inequalities of life
Chapter 5: Insufficiencies of wealth
Chapter 6: Vanity of life is inescapable
Chapter 7: Wisdom and folly contrasted
Chapter 8: Inability to understand all of God's actions
Chapter 9: Judgment, enjoyment of life, and the value of wisdom
Chapter 10: Wisdom's characteristics
Chapter 11: Wisdom and business; wisdom and youth
Chapter 12: Remember God in your youth

Insight from Matthew Henry

Ecclesiastes 12

VERSES 1–7
We should remember our sins against our Creator, repent, and seek forgiveness. We should remember our duties, and set about them, looking to him for grace and strength. This should be done early, while the body is strong, and the spirits active. When a man has the pain of reviewing a misspent life, his not having given up sin and worldly vanities till he is forced to say, I have no pleasure in them, renders his sincerity very questionable. Then follows a figurative description of old age and its infirmities, which has some difficulties; but the meaning is plain, to show how uncomfortable, generally, the days of old age are. As the four verses, 2–5, are a figurative description of the infirmities that usually accompany old age, ver. 6 notices the circumstances which take place in the hour of death. If sin had not entered into the world, these infirmities would not have been known. Surely then the aged should reflect on the evil of sin.

Song of Solomon

An introduction

Names for Song of Solomon

CANTICLES
This book is called, after the Vulgate, the "Canticles."

SONG OF SONGS
It is the "song of songs" (Cant. 1: 1), as being the finest and most precious of its kind; the noblest song, "das Hohelied," as Luther calls it.

Authorship

The Solomonic authorship of this book has been called in question, but evidences, both internal and external, fairly establish the traditional view that it is the product of Solomon's pen.

Theme

It is an allegorical poem setting forth the mutual love of Christ and the Church, under the emblem of the bridegroom and the bride. (cf. Matt. 9: 15; John 3: 29; Eph. 5: 23,27,29; Rev. 19: 7–9; 21: 2,9; 22: 17. Cf. also Ps. 45; Is. 54: 4–6; 62: 4,5; Jer. 2: 2; 3: 1,20; Ezek. 16; Hos. 2: 16,19,20.)

Name, author, date

MEANING OF NAME OF BOOK
The Hebrew title comes from the opening verse. "The Song of Songs" is a superlative referring to Solomon's best song.

AUTHOR
Traditionally Solomon.

APPROXIMATE DATE OF WRITING
965 B.C.

Statistics

PLACE OF BOOK IN BIBLE
22nd Old Testament book.
5th historical book.

NUMBER OF CHAPTERS: 8

NUMBER OF VERSES: 117

NUMBER OF WORDS: 2,661

Main theme of book

The glory of married love.

Keys to the understanding of book

KEY WORD/S
Love
Beloved, 23 times

KEY PHRASE
My beloved is mine, and I am his, 2: 16.

KEY PERSON/PEOPLE
The bride, the king, and the daughters of Jerusalem.

KEY CHAPTER/S
1 and the love between the bride and bridegroom.

KEY VERSE/S
I am my beloved's, and his desire is toward me. 7: 10

Jesus Christ in Song of Solomon

WHO JESUS IS
The supreme lover.

JESUS FORESHADOWED AS A TYPE/ PORTRAITS OF CHRIST
In the New Testament the church is depicted as the bride of the Christ, and the Song of Solomon illustrates Christ's love for his people.

Spiritual thought

Love Christ wholeheartedly.

Chapter by chapter breakdown

Chapter 1: First song
Chapter 2: Second song
Chapter 3: Third song
Chapter 4: The groom praises the bride
Chapter 5: Fourth song
Chapter 6: Fifth song
Chapter 7: Fifth song
Chapter 8: Sixth song

Insight from Matthew Henry

Song of Solomon 1

VERSES 7–8
Observe the title given to Christ, O Thou whom my soul loveth. Those whose souls love Jesus Christ, earnestly desire to share in the privileges of his flock.

VERSES 9–17
The Bridegroom gives high praises of his spouse. In the sight of Christ believers are the excellent of the earth, fitted to be instruments for promoting his glory. The spiritual gifts and graces which Christ bestows on every true believer, are of the saints are many, but there is dependence upon each other. He who is the Author, will be the Finisher of the good work. The grace received from Christ's fullness, springs forth into lively exercises of faith, affection, and gratitude. Yet Christ, not his gifts, is most precious to them. The word translated "camphire," signifies "atonement or propitiation."

Christ is dear to all believers, because he is the propitiation for their sins. No pretender must have his place in the soul. They resolved to lodge him in their hearts all the night; during the continuance of the troubles of life. Christ takes delight in the good work which his grace has wrought on the souls of believers. This should engage all who are made holy, to be very thankful for that grace which has made those fair, who by nature were deformed. The spouse (the believer) has a humble, modest eye, discovering simplicity and godly sincerity; eyes enlightened and guided by the Holy Spirit, that blessed Dove. The church expresses her value for Christ. Thou art the great Original, but I am but a faint and imperfect copy. Many are fair to look at, yet their temper renders them unpleasant: but Christ is fair, yet pleasant.

The believer, ver. 16, speaks with praise of those holy ordinances in which true believers have fellowship with Christ. Whether the believer is in the courts of the Lord, or in retirement; whether following his daily labors, or confined on the bed of sickness, or even in a dungeon, a sense of the Divine presence will turn the place into a paradise.

Thus the soul, daily having fellowship with the Father, the Son, and the Holy Spirit, enjoys a lively hope of an incorruptible, undefiled, and unfading inheritance above.

Isaiah (1)

An introduction

Consists of prophecies delivered (Is. 1)

(1) in the reign of Uzziah (Is. 1–5),

(2) of Jotham (Is. 6),

(3) Ahaz (Is. 7–14: 28),

(4) the first half of Hezekiah's reign (Is. 14: 28–35),

(5) the second half of Hezekiah's reign (Is. 36–66).

Sixty-four years

Thus, counting from the fourth year before Uzziah's death (762 B.C.) to the last year of Hezekiah (698 B.C.), Isaiah's ministry extended over a period of sixty-four years.

Divisions

The book, as a whole, has been divided into three main parts:

(1) The first thirty-five chapters, almost wholly prophetic, Israel's enemy Assyria, present the Messiah as a mighty Ruler and King.

(2) Four chapters are historical (Is. 36–39), relating to the times of Hezekiah.

(3) Prophetical (Is. 40–66), Israel's enemy Babylon, describing the Messiah as a suffering victim, meek and lowly.

40–66

The genuineness of the section Is. 40–66 has been keenly opposed by able critics. They assert that it must be the production of a deutero-Isaiah,

who lived toward the close of the Babylonian captivity.

This theory was originated by Koppe, a German writer at the close of the last century. There are other portions of the book also (e.g., Is. 13; 24–27; and certain verses in Is. 14 and Is. 21) which they attribute to some other prophet than Isaiah. Thus they say that some five or seven, or even more, unknown prophets had a hand in the production of this book. The considerations which have led to such a result are various:

(1) They cannot, as some say, conceive it possible that Isaiah, living in 700 B.C., could foretell the appearance and the exploits of a prince called Cyrus, who would set the Jews free from captivity one hundred and seventy years after.

(2) It is alleged that the prophet takes the time of the Captivity as his standpoint, and speaks of it as then present; and

(3) that there is such a difference between the style and language of the closing section (Is. 40–66) and those of the preceding chapters as to necessitate a different authorship, and lead to the conclusion that there were at least two Isaiahs. But even granting the fact of a great diversity of style and language, this will not necessitate the conclusion attempted to be drawn from it. The diversity of subjects treated of and the peculiarities of the prophet's position at the time the prophecies were uttered will sufficiently account for this.

The unity of Isaiah

The arguments in favor of the unity of the book are quite conclusive. When the LXX version was made (about 250 B.C.) the entire contents of the book were ascribed to Isaiah, the son of Amoz. It is not called in question, moreover, that in the time of our Lord the book existed in the form in which we now have it. Many prophecies in the disputed portions are quoted in the New Testament as the words of Isaiah (Matt. 3: 3; Luke 3: 4–6; 4: 16–41; John 12: 38; Acts 8: 28; Rom. 10: 16–21). Universal and persistent tradition has ascribed the whole book to one author.

Besides this, the internal evidence, the similarity in the language and style, in the thoughts and images and rhetorical ornaments, all point to the same conclusion; and its local coloring and allusions show that it is obviously of Palestinian origin. The theory therefore of a double authorship of the book, much less of a manifold authorship, cannot be maintained. The book, with all the diversity of its contents, is one, and is, we believe, the production of the great prophet whose name it bears.

Name, author, date

MEANING OF NAME OF BOOK
Named after the prophet Isaiah whose name means "the salvation of Jehovah."

AUTHOR
Isaiah.

APPROXIMATE DATE OF WRITING
740–680 B.C.

Statistics

PLACE OF BOOK IN BIBLE
23rd Old Testament book.
1st major prophet.

NUMBER OF CHAPTERS
66

NUMBER OF VERSES
1,292

NUMBER OF WORDS
37,044

Main theme of book

God's salvation.

Keys to the understanding of book

KEY WORD/S
Salvation, 28 times

KEY PHRASE
The Holy One of Israel, 1: 4.

KEY PERSON/PEOPLE
Isaiah, Cyrus, Hezekiah, Sennacerib.

KEY CHAPTER/S
53 and its prophecy of the Messiah's atonement.

KEY VERSE/S
For unto us a child is born, unto us a son is given: and the government shall be upon his shoulder: and his name shall be called Wonderful, Counselor, The mighty God, The everlasting Father, The Prince of Peace.
Isaiah 9: 6,7

Isaiah (2)

KEY VERSE/S, CONTINUED
All we like sheep have gone astray;
we have turned every one to his own
way; and the Lord hath laid on him the
iniquity of us all.
Isaiah53: 6

Jesus Christ in Isaiah

WHO JESUS IS
Wonderful, Counselor, Everlasting
Father, Prince of Peace.

JESUS FORESHADOWED AS A TYPE/
PORTRAITS OF CHRIST
Isaiah describes and prophecies many
aspects of the life and ministry of
Christ, especially his death.

Spiritual thought

The Messiah is coming.

Chapter by chapter breakdown

Chapter 1: Judah's sickness
Chapter 2: The day of judgment
Chapter 3: Society's breakdown
Chapter 4: The Day of the Lord: the
    branch
Chapter 5: The Song of the Vineyard
Chapter 6: Isaiah's vision and calling
Chapter 7: The sign of Immanuel
Chapter 8: Comfort and warning
Chapter 9: The sign of the Prince of
    Peace
Chapter 10: A remnant will survive
Chapter 11: God's future king
Chapter 12: A song of salvation
Chapter 13: Prophecies against Babylon
Chapter 14: Prophecies against Assyria
    and Philistia

Chapter 15: Prophecies against Moab
Chapter 16: Moab's hopeless situation
Chapter 17: Prophecies against
    Damascus and Israel
Chapter 18: Prophecies against Egypt
Chapter 19: Prophecies against Egypt
Chapter 20: Prophecies against Egypt
Chapter 21: Prophecies against Babylon,
    Edom, and Arabia
Chapter 22: Prophecies against
    Jerusalem
Chapter 23: Prophecies against Tyre
Chapter 24: Warning about coming
    judgment
Chapter 25: Praise for kingdom
    blessings
Chapter 26: Israel's song of salvation
Chapter 27: Future restoration
Chapter 28: Israel and Judah are warned
Chapter 29: Jerusalem is warned
Chapter 30: The obstinate are warned
Chapter 31: Warning against an
    Egyptian alliance
Chapter 32: The King is coming
Chapter 33: A hymn of thanksgiving
Chapter 34: A warning to the nations
Chapter 35: The promise of restoration
    and transformation
Chapter 36: Sennacherib threatens
    Jerusalem
Chapter 37: Jerusalem's deliverance
    foretold
Chapter 38: Hezekiah's illness
Chapter 39: Envoys come from Babylon
Chapter 40: Comfort because of Israel's
    deliverance
Chapter 41: Comfort because of God's
    greatness
Chapter 42: Comfort because of God's
    Servant

Chapter 43: God is Israel's Redeemer
Chapter 44: The absurdity of idolatry
Chapter 45: Comfort through God using Cyrus
Chapter 46: Destruction of Babylon's idols
Chapter 47: Destruction of Babylon
Chapter 48: Israel is stubborn
Chapter 49: The Messiah's mission
Chapter 50: The Messiah's obedience
Chapter 51: The Messiah's encouragement to Israel
Chapter 52: The Messiah's atonement
Chapter 53: The Messiah's atonement
Chapter 54: The Messiah's promise of Israel's restoration
Chapter 55: The Messiah's global invitation
Chapter 56: The basis of worship
Chapter 57: The Messiah rebukes the wicked
Chapter 58: The blessings of true worship
Chapter 59: Israel's sins
Chapter 60: A vision of the new Jerusalem
Chapter 61: The year of the Lord's favor
Chapter 62: Jerusalem's future
Chapter 63: Salvation and judgment
Chapter 64: A prayer for deliverance
Chapter 65: The Lord's answer to the remnant
Chapter 66: A new heaven and a new earth

Insight from Matthew Henry

Isaiah 53

VERSES 1–3

Nowhere in all the Old Testament is it so plainly and fully prophesied, that Christ ought to suffer, and then to enter into his glory, as in this chapter. But to this day few discern, or will acknowledge, that Divine power which goes with the word. The authentic and most important report of salvation for sinners, through the Son of God, is disregarded. The low condition he submitted to, and his appearance in the world, were not agreeable to the ideas the Jews had formed of the Messiah. It was expected that he should come in pomp; instead of that, he grew up as a plant, silently, and insensibly. He had nothing of the glory which one might have thought to meet with him. His whole life was not only humble as to outward condition, but also sorrowful. Being made sin for us, he underwent the sentence sin had exposed us to. Carnal hearts see nothing in the Lord Jesus to desire an interest in him. Alas! by how many is he still despised in his people, and rejected as to his doctrine and authority!

VERSES 4–9

In these verses is an account of the sufferings of Christ; also of the design of his sufferings. It was for our sins, and in our stead, that our Lord Jesus suffered. We have all sinned, and have come short of the glory of God. Sinners have their beloved sin, their own evil way, of which they are fond. Our sins deserve all griefs and sorrows, even the most severe.

Jeremiah (1)

An introduction

Contents

The book of Jeremiah consists of twenty-three separate and independent sections, arranged in five books.

I. The introduction, chapter 1.

II. Reproofs of the sins of the Jews, consisting of seven sections:
(1) Jer. 2
(2) Jer. 3–6
(3) Jer. 7–10
(4) Jer. 11–13
(5) Jer. 14–17: 18
(6) Jer. 17: 19–20
(7) Jer. 21–24

III. A general review of all nations, in two sections:
(1) Jer. 46–49
(2) Jer. 25; with an historical appendix of three sections:
(a) Jer. 26
(b) Jer. 27
(c) Jer. 28, 29

IV. Two sections picturing the hopes of better times:
(1) Jer. 30, 31
(2) Jer. 32, 33; to which is added an historical appendix in three sections:
(a) Jer. 34: 1–7
(b) Jer. 34: 8–22
(c) Jer. 35

V. The conclusion, in two sections:
(1) Jer. 36
(2) Jer. 45
In Egypt, after an interval, Jeremiah is supposed to have added three sections, viz., Jer. 37–39; 40–43; and 44.

Messianic prophecies

The principal Messianic prophecies are found in Jer. 23: 1–8; 31: 31–40; and 33: 14–26. Jeremiah's prophecies are noted for the frequent repetitions found in them of the same words and phrases and imagery. They cover the period of about thirty years.

Not chronological

They are not recorded in the order of time. When and under what circumstances this book assumed its present form we know not.

Name, author, date

MEANING OF NAME OF BOOK
The book is named after Jeremiah the prophet whose name means "the one whom Jehovah appoints."

AUTHOR
Jeremiah.

APPROXIMATE DATE OF WRITING
627–580 B.C.

Statistics

PLACE OF BOOK IN BIBLE
24th Old Testament book.
2nd major prophet.

NUMBER OF CHAPTERS: 52

NUMBER OF VERSES: 1,364

NUMBER OF WORDS: 42,659

Main theme of book

Jeremiah's warnings about God's judgment on the people of Jerusalem.

Keys to the understanding of book

KEY WORD/S
Backsliding, 13 times
Return, 47 times

KEY PHRASE GO AND CRY, 2: 2

KEY PERSON/PEOPLE
Jeremiah.

KEY CHAPTER/S
31 with its wonderful promises in the middle of warnings about judgment.

KEY VERSE/S
But this thing commanded I them, saying, Obey my voice, and I will be your God, and ye shall be my people: and walk ye in all the ways that I have commanded you, that it may be well unto you. But they hearkened not, nor inclined their ear, but walked in the counsels and in the imagination of their evil heart, and went backward, and not forward.
Jeremiah 7: 23,24

For they have healed the hurt of the daughter of my people slightly, saying, Peace, peace; when there is no peace. Were they ashamed when they had committed abomination? nay, they were not at all ashamed, neither could they blush: therefore shall they fall among them that fall: in the time of their visitation they shall be cast down, saith the Lord.
Jeremiah 8: 11,12

Jesus Christ in Jeremiah

WHO JESUS IS
The weeping Prophet.

JESUS FORESHADOWED AS A TYPE/PORTRAITS OF CHRIST
The work of the Messiah is often depicted in Jeremiah: 23: 1–8
Jesus is the Righteous Branch.

Spiritual thought

Take heed lest you fall.

Chapter by chapter breakdown

Chapter 1: Jeremiah's call
Chapter 2: Judah's deliberate sins
Chapter 3: Judah ignores Israel's example
Chapter 4: Judah's destruction from the north
Chapter 5: Judah's sins
Chapter 6: Jerusalem will be destroyed
Chapter 7: The externals of religion
Chapter 8: Judgment on Judah is imminent
Chapter 9: Description of Judah's judgment
Chapter 10: The Lord is sovereign
Chapter 11: Judah and the broken covenant
Chapter 12: Jeremiah's complaint, and God's reply
Chapter 13: Enacted warnings
Chapter 14: Judah's drought is described
Chapter 15: Jeremiah complains again to the Lord
Chapter 16: When God departs

Jeremiah (2)

Chapter by chapter breakdown, continued

Chapter 17: The results of sin

Chapter 18: Learning from the potter

Chapter 19: The sign of the broken flask

Chapter 20: Jeremiah put in the stocks

Chapter 21: Jerusalem's defeat is predicted

Chapter 22: Kings condemned

Chapter 23: The Righteous Branch

Chapter 24: Two baskets of figs

Chapter 25: The seventy-year captivity

Chapter 26: Jeremiah on trial

Chapter 27: Jeremiah wears an ox yoke

Chapter 28: Jeremiah's conflict with the prophet Hananiah

Chapter 29: Jeremiah's letter to the Jews in Babylonia

Chapter 30: Restoration of the land

Chapter 31: Israel will return home

Chapter 32: Rebuilding Jerusalem

Chapter 33: Reconfirming the covenant

Chapter 34: Prophecies in Zedekiah's reign

Chapter 35: Message to the Recabites

Chapter 36: Scroll burning

Chapter 37: Jeremiah imprisoned

Chapter 38: Jeremiah dumped in a cistern

Chapter 39: Ebed-Melech rewarded; Jerusalem captured

Chapter 40: Jeremiah freed

Chapter 41: Murder and massacre

Chapter 42: "Don't flee to Egypt"

Chapter 43: Jeremiah taken to Egypt

Chapter 44: The Lord's message to the Jews in Egypt

Chapter 45: A message for Baruch

Chapter 46: Prophecies against Egypt

Chapter 47: Prophecies against Philistia

Chapter 48: Prophecies against Moab

Chapter 49: Prophecies against Ammon, Edom, Damascus, Kedar, and Hazor

Chapter 50: Babylon's defeat and desolation

Chapter 51: Babylon's destiny

Chapter 52: Jerusalem captured, the exile, and signs of hope

Insight from Matthew Henry

Jeremiah 1

VERSES 1–10

Jeremiah's early call to the work and office of a prophet is stated. He was to be a prophet, not to the Jews only, but to the neighboring nations. He is still a prophet to the whole world, and it would be well if they would attend to these warnings. The Lord who formed us, knows for what particular services and purposes he intended us. But unless he sanctify us by his new-creating Spirit, we shall neither be fit for his holy service on earth, nor his holy happiness in heaven. It becomes us to have low thoughts of ourselves. Those who are young, should consider that they are so, and not venture beyond their powers. But though a sense of our own weakness and insufficiency should make us go humbly about our work, it should not make us draw back when God calls us. Those who have messages to deliver from God, must not fear the face of man. The Lord, by a sign, gave

Jeremiah such a gift as was necessary. God's message should be delivered in his own words. Whatever wordly wise men or politicians may think, the safety of kingdoms is decided according to the purpose and word of God.

VERSES 11–19
God gave Jeremiah a view of the destruction of Judah and Jerusalem by the Chaldeans. The almond-tree, which is more forward in the spring than any other, represented the speedy approach of judgments. God also showed whence the intended ruin should arise. Jeremiah saw a seething-pot boiling, representing Jerusalem and Judah in great commotion. The mouth or face of the furnace or hearth, was toward the north; from whence the fire and fuel were to come. The northern powers shall unite. The cause of these judgments was the sin of Judah. The whole counsel of God must be declared. The fear of God is the best remedy against the fear of man. Better to have all men our enemies than God our enemy; those who are sure they have God with them, need not, ought not to fear, whoever is against them. Let us pray that we may be willing to give up personal interests, and that nothing may move us from our duty.

Jeremiah 40

VERSES 1–6
The captain of the guard seems to glory that he had been God's instrument to fulfill, what Jeremiah had been God's messenger to foretell. Many can see God's justice and truth with regard to others, who are heedless and blind as to themselves and their own sins. But, sooner or later, all men shall be made sensible that their sin is the cause of all their miseries. Jeremiah has leave to dispose of himself; but is advised to go to Gedaliah, governor of the land under the king of Babylon. It is doubtful whether Jeremiah acted right in this decision. But those who desire the salvation of sinners, and the good of the church, are apt to expect better times from slight appearances, and they will prefer the hope of being useful, to the most secure situations without it.

VERSES 7–16
Jeremiah had never in his prophecies spoken of any good days for the Jews, to come immediately after the captivity; yet Providence seemed to encourage such an expectation. But how soon is this hopeful prospect blighted! When God begins a judgment, he will complete it. While pride, ambition, or revenge, bears rule in the heart, men will form new projects, and be restless in mischief, which commonly ends in their own ruin. Who would have thought, that after the destruction of Jerusalem, rebellion would so soon have sprung up? There can be no thorough change but what grace makes. And if the miserable, who are kept in everlasting chains for the judgment of the great day, were again permitted to come on earth, the sin and evil of their nature would be unchanged.

Lamentations

An introduction

Names for Lamentations

How

The book of Lamentations is called in the Hebrew canon 'Ekhah, meaning "How," being the formula for the commencement of a song of wailing. It is the first word of the book (see 2 Sam. 1: 19–27).

LAMENTATIONS

The LXX adopted the name rendered "Lamentations" (Gr. *threnoi* = Heb. *qinoth*) now in common use, to denote the character of the book, in which the prophet mourns over the desolations brought on the city and the holy land by the Babylonians. In the Hebrew Bible it is placed among the Khethubim.

Authorship

As to its authorship, there is no room for hesitancy in following the LXX and the Targum in ascribing it to Jeremiah. The spirit, tone, language, and subject-matter are in accord with the testimony of tradition in assigning it to him. According to tradition, he retired after the destruction of Jerusalem by Nebuchadnezzar to a cavern outside the Damascus gate, where he wrote this book. That cavern is still pointed out. "In the face of a rocky hill, on the western side of the city, the local belief has placed 'the grotto of Jeremiah.' There, in that fixed attitude of grief which Michael Angelo has immortalized, the prophet may well be supposed to have mourned the fall of his country" (*Stanley, Jewish Church*).

Contents

The book consists of five separate poems.

In Lam. 1 the prophet dwells on the manifold miseries oppressed by which the city sits as a solitary widow weeping sorely.

In Lam. 2 these miseries are described in connection with the national sins that had caused them.

Lam. 3 speaks of hope for the people of God. The chastisement would only be for their good; a better day would dawn for them.

Lam. 4 laments the ruin and desolation that had come upon the city and temple, but traces it only to the people's sins.

Lam. 5 is a prayer that Zion's reproach may be taken away in the repentance and recovery of the people.

Acrostic poems

The first four poems (chapters) are acrostics, like some of the Psalms (Ps. 25,34,37,119), i.e., each verse begins with a letter of the Hebrew alphabet taken in order. The first, second, and fourth each have twenty-two verses, the number of the letters in the Hebrew alphabet. The third has sixty-six verses, in which each three successive verses begin with the same letter. The fifth is not acrostic.

Wailing Wall

Speaking of the "Wailing-place of the Jews" at Jerusalem, a portion of the old wall of the temple of Solomon, Schaff says: "There the Jews assemble every Friday afternoon to bewail the downfall of the holy city, kissing the stone wall and watering it with their tears. They repeat from their well-worn Hebrew Bibles and prayer-books the Lamentations of Jeremiah and suitable Psalms."

Name, author, date

MEANING OF NAME OF BOOK
Lamentations means "dirge" or "laments."

AUTHOR
The book of Lamentations is anonymous, but there are significant pointers in its pages which point to it being written by Jeremiah.

APPROXIMATE DATE OF WRITING
586 B.C.

Statistics

PLACE OF BOOK IN BIBLE
25th Old Testament book.
3rd major prophet

NUMBER OF CHAPTERS: 5

NUMBER OF VERSES: 154

NUMBER OF WORDS: 3,415

Main theme of book

God's great love for his people in the middle of their disaster.

Keys to the understanding of book

KEY WORD/S
Tears.

KEY PHRASE
Mourning and lamentations, 2: 5.

KEY PERSON/PEOPLE
The people of Jerusalem.

KEY CHAPTER/S
3 and its example of hope in God in a hopeless situation.

KEY VERSE/S
The Lord was as an enemy: he hath swallowed up Israel, he hath swallowed up all her palaces: he hath destroyed his strong holds, and hath increased in the daughter of Judah mourning and lamentation. And he hath violently taken away his tabernacle, as if it were of a garden: he hath destroyed his places of the assembly: the Lord hath caused the solemn feasts and sabbaths to be forgotten in Zion, and hath despised in the indignation of his anger the king and the priest.
Lamentations 2: 5,6

Jesus Christ in Lamentations

WHO JESUS IS
The Preacher of comfort

JESUS FORESHADOWED AS A TYPE/ PORTRAITS OF CHRIST
The prophet who told people to weep foreshadows Jesus' prophecies. Jesus was a Man of Sorrows.

Spiritual thought

The Lord is merciful.

Chapter by chapter breakdown

Chapter 1: Jerusalem's destruction
Chapter 2: God's anger
Chapter 3: A prayer for mercy
Chapter 4: Jerusalem, after its fall
Chapter 5: A prayer for restoration

Ezekiel (1)

An introduction

Contents

The book of Ezekiel consists mainly of three groups of prophecies. After an account of his call to the prophetical office (Ezek. 1–3: 21), Ezekiel

(1) utters words of denunciation against the Jews (Ezek. 3: 22–24), warning them of the certain destruction of Jerusalem, in opposition to the words of the false prophets (Ezek. 4: 1–3). The symbolical acts, by which the extremities to which Jerusalem would be reduced are described in Ezek. 4–5, show his intimate acquaintance with the Levitical legislation. (See Ex. 22: 30; Deut. 14: 21; Lev. 5: 2; 7: 18,24; 17: 15; 19: 7; 22: 8, etc.)

(2) Prophecies against various surrounding nations: against the Ammonites (Ezek. 25: 1–7), the Moabites (Ezek. 25: 8–11), the Edomites (Ezek. 25: 12–14), the Philistines (Ezek. 25: 15–17), Tyre and Sidon (Ezek. 26–28), and against Egypt (Ezek. 29–32).

(3) Prophecies delivered after the destruction of Jerusalem by Nebuchadnezzar: the triumphs of Israel and of the kingdom of God on earth (Ezek. 33–39); Messianic times, and the establishment and prosperity of the kingdom of God (Ezek. 40; Ezek. 48).

Quotations in New Testament

The closing visions of this book are referred to in the book of Revelation (Ezek. 38 = Rev. 20: 8; Ezek. 47: 1–8

= Rev. 22: 1,2). Other references to this book are also found in the New Testament. (Compare Rom. 2: 24 with Ezek. 36: 2; Rom. 10: 5, Gal. 3: 12 with Ezek. 20: 11; 2 Pet. 3: 4 with Ezek. 12: 22.)

Daniel, Noah, and Job

It may be noted that Daniel, fourteen years after his deportation from Jerusalem, is mentioned by Ezekiel (Ezek. 14: 14) along with Noah and Job, noted for his righteousness, and some five years later he is spoken of as pre-eminent for his wisdom (Ezek. 28: 3).

Symbolical and allegorical

Ezekiel's prophecies are characterized by symbolical and allegorical representations, "unfolding a rich series of majestic visions and of colossal symbols." There are a great many also of "symbolical actions embodying vivid conceptions on the part of the prophet" (Ezek. 4: 1–4; 5: 1–4; 12: 3–6; 24: 3–5; 37: 16, etc.) "The mode of representation, in which symbols and allegories occupy a prominent place, gives a dark, mysterious character to the prophecies of Ezekiel. They are obscure and enigmatical. A cloudy mystery overhangs them which it is almost impossible to penetrate. Jerome calls the book 'a labyrinth of the mysteries of God.' It was because of this obscurity that the Jews forbade any one to read it till he had attained the age of thirty."

Ezekiel and other Old Testament books

Ezekiel is singular in the frequency with which he refers to the Pentateuch (e.g., Ezek. 27; 28: 13; 31: 8; 36: 11,34; 47: 13, etc.). He shows also an acquaintance with the writings of Hosea (Ezek. 37: 22), Isaiah (Ezek. 8: 12; 29: 6), and especially with those of Jeremiah, his older contemporary (Jer. 24: 7,9; 48: 37).

Name, author, date

MEANING OF NAME OF BOOK
Named after the prophet Ezekiel, whose name means "God strengthens me."

AUTHOR
Ezekiel.

APPROXIMATE DATE OF WRITING
593–571 B.C.

Statistics

PLACE OF BOOK IN BIBLE
26th Old Testament book.
4th major prophet.

NUMBER OF CHAPTERS
48

NUMBER OF VERSES
1,273

NUMBER OF WORDS
39,407

Main theme of book

Ezekiel's messages to God's people in exile in Babylon.

Keys to the understanding of book

KEY WORD/S
Restoration
Vision

KEY PHRASE
Shall know that I am the Lord, 63 times.

KEY PERSON/PEOPLE
Ezekiel.

KEY CHAPTER/S
37 and its message of restoration.

KEY VERSE/S
1: 1

For I will take you from among the heathen, and gather you out of all countries, and will bring you into your own land. Then will I sprinkle clean water upon you, and ye shall be clean: from all your filthiness, and from all your idols, will I cleanse you. A new heart also will I give you, and a new spirit will I put within you: and I will take away the stony heart out of your flesh, and I will give you an heart of flesh.
Ezekiel 36: 24–26

Thus saith the Lord GOD; In the day that I shall have cleansed you from all your iniquities I will also cause you to dwell in the cities, and the wastes shall be builded. And the desolate land shall be tilled, whereas it lay desolate in the sight of all that passed by.

And they shall say, This land that was desolate is become like the garden of Eden.
Ezekiel 36: 33–35

Ezekiel (2)

Jesus Christ in Ezekiel

WHO JESUS IS

Jesus (spiritually) rebuilt God's temple.

JESUS FORESHADOWED AS A TYPE/
PORTRAITS OF CHRIST
The Messiah is depicted as the King
who rules, 21: 26,27, and as the true
Shepherd, 34: 11–31.

Spiritual thought

God is the great Restorer.

Chapter by chapter breakdown

Chapter 1: Ezekiel sees the glory of God

Chapter 2: Ezekiel is sent to Israel

Chapter 3: Ezekiel is instructed about
his ministry

Chapter 4: Three symbolic actions

Chapter 5: A fourth symbolic action,
and symbolic actions explained

Chapter 6: Destruction because of
idolatry

Chapter 7: The day of destruction
described

Chapter 8: Four abominations

Chapter 9: Vision of killing in
Jerusalem

Chapter 10: God's glory leaves the
temple

Chapter 11: The promise of restoration

Chapter 12: Pictures of the exile

Chapter 13: False prophets are
condemned

Chapter 14: Idolatry is condemned

Chapter 15: The parable of the vine

Chapter 16: Parable of Israel's marriage

Chapter 17: Parable of the two eagles

Chapter 18: Personal judgment on
personal sin

Chapter 19: Lament for Israel's princes

Chapter 20: Looking back on Israel's
past rebellion

Chapter 21: Jerusalem's great sins

Chapter 22: God's judgment on
Jerusalem

Chapter 23: Parable of two adulterous
sisters

Chapter 24: Jerusalem is besieged

Chapter 25: Judgment against Ammon,
Moab, Edom, and Philistia

Chapter 26: Destruction of Tyre

Chapter 27: Lament over Tyre

Chapter 28: The fall of the ruler of Tyre

Chapter 29: Prophecies against Egypt

Chapter 30: Egypt will be destroyed

Chapter 31: Egypt will fall like a cedar

Chapter 32: Further prophecies against
Egypt

Chapter 33: Ezekiel the watchman

Chapter 34: Message to the shepherds

Chapter 35: Judgment on Edom

Chapter 36: A new heart and a new
spirit

Chapter 37: New life for dry bones

Chapter 38: Prophecy against Gog

Chapter 39: God's plans for Israel

Chapter 40: The new temple

Chapter 41: The holy place, holy of
holies, and interior furniture

Chapter 42: The priests' rooms and
overall dimensions of the temple

Chapter 43: God's glory returns to the
temple

Chapter 44: Laws for the priesthood

Chapter 45: Rules for the prince; and
the festivals

Chapter 46: Additional princely duties

Chapter 47: The river flowing from the temple

Chapter 48: Division of the land among the tribes

Insight from Matthew Henry

Ezekiel 1

VERSES 26–28

The eternal Son, the second Person in the Trinity, who afterwards took the human nature, is here denoted. The first thing observed was a throne. It is a throne of glory, a throne of grace, a throne of triumph, a throne of government, a throne of judgment. It is good news to men, that the throne above the firmament is filled with One who appears, even there, in the likeness of a man. The throne is surrounded with a rainbow, the well-known emblem of the covenant, representing God's mercy and covenanted love to his people. The fire of God's wrath was breaking out against Jerusalem, but bounds should be set to it; he would look upon the bow, and remember the covenant.

Ezekiel 37

VERSES 1–14

No created power could restore human bones to life. God alone could cause them to live. Skin and flesh covered them, and the wind was then told to blow upon these bodies; and they were restored to life. The wind was an emblem of the Spirit of God, and represented his quickening powers. The vision was to encourage the

desponding Jews; to predict both their restoration after the captivity, and also their recovery from their present and long-continued dispersion. It was also a clear intimation of the resurrection of the dead; and it represents the power and grace of God, in the conversion of the most hopeless sinners to himself. Let us look to Him who will at last open our graves, and bring us forth to judgment, that He may now deliver us from sin, and put his Spirit within us, and keep us by his power, through faith, unto salvation.

VERSES 15–28

This emblem was to show the people, that the Lord would unite Judah and Israel. Christ is the true David, Israel's King of old; and those whom he makes willing in the day of his power, he makes to walk in his judgments, and to keep his statutes. Events yet to come will further explain this prophecy. Nothing has more hindered the success of the gospel than divisions. Let us study to keep the unity of the Spirit in the bond of peace; let us seek for Divine grace to keep us from detestable things; and let us pray that all nations may be obedient and happy subjects of the Son of David, that the Lord may be our God, and we may be his people for evermore.

Daniel

An introduction

The book of Daniel is placed by the Jews in that division of their Bible called the Hagiographa (Heb. Khethubim).

Divisions

It consists of two distinct parts. The first part, consisting of the first six chapters, is chiefly historical; and the second part, consisting of the remaining six chapters, is chiefly prophetical.

HISTORICAL
The historical part of the book treats of the period of the Captivity. Daniel is "the historian of the Captivity, the writer who alone furnishes any series of events for that dark and dismal period during which the harp of Israel hung on the trees that grew by the Euphrates. His narrative may be said in general to intervene between Kings and Chronicles on the one hand and Ezra on the other, or (more strictly) to fill out the sketch which the author of the Chronicles gives in a single verse in his last chapter: 'And them that had escaped from the sword carried he [i.e., Nebuchadnezzar] away to Babylon; where they were servants to him and his sons until the reign of the kingdom of Persia'" (2 Chr. 36: 20).

PROPHETIC
The prophetic part consists of three visions and one lengthy prophetical communication.

Genuineness disputed

The genuineness of this book has been much disputed, but the arguments in its favor fully establish its claims.

(1) We have the testimony of Christ (Matt. 24: 15; 25: 31; 26: 64) and his apostles (1 Cor. 6: 2; 2 Thess. 2: 3) for its authority; and

(2) the important testimony of Ezekiel (Ezek. 14: 14,20; 28: 3).

(3) The character and records of the book are also entirely in harmony with the times and circumstances in which the author lived.

(4) The linguistic character of the book is, moreover, just such as might be expected. Certain portions (Dan. 2: 4; 7) are written in the Babylonian language; and the portions written in Hebrew are in a style and form having a close affinity with the later books of the Old Testament, especially with that of Ezra. The writer is familiar both with the Hebrew and the Babylonian, passing from the one to the other just as his subject required. This is in strict accordance with the position of the author and of the people for whom his book was written. That Daniel is the writer of this book is also testified to in the book itself (Dan. 7: 1,28; 8: 2; 9: 2; 10: 1,2; 12: 4,5).

Name, author, date

MEANING OF NAME OF BOOK
The book is named after Daniel, whose name means "God is my judge."

AUTHOR
Daniel.

APPROXIMATE DATE OF WRITING
605–535 B.C.

Statistics

PLACE OF BOOK IN BIBLE
27th Old Testament book.
5th major prophet.

NUMBER OF CHAPTERS: 12

NUMBER OF VERSES: 357

NUMBER OF WORDS: 11,606

Main theme of book

God's messages to his people during their captivity in Babylon.

Keys to the understanding of book

KEY WORD/S
Kingdom, 57 times

KEY PHRASE
In the latter days, 2: 28.

KEY PERSON/PEOPLE
Daniel, Shadrach, Meshach, and Abed-nego, (Hananiah, Mishael, and Azariah). Nebuchadnezzar, Darius, Belshazzar, Cyrus, and Michael the archangel.

KEY CHAPTER/S
2, 9.

KEY VERSE/S
And in the days of these kings shall the God of heaven set up a kingdom, which shall never be destroyed: and the kingdom shall not be left to other people, but it shall break in pieces and consume all these kingdoms, and it shall stand for ever.   Daniel 2: 44

Jesus Christ in Daniel

WHO JESUS IS
Jesus is the stone cut without hands.

JESUS FORESHADOWED AS A TYPE/
PORTRAITS OF CHRIST
Christ is portrayed as the Son of Man, the Great Stone and the coming Messiah.

Spiritual thought

God will usher in his kingdom.

Chapter by chapter breakdown

Chapter 1: The personal history of Daniel

Chapter 2: Nebuchadnezzar's dream of the great image

Chapter 3: Nebuchadnezzar's image of gold

Chapter 4: Nebuchadnezzar's vision of a great tree

Chapter 5: Belshazzar and handwriting on the wall

Chapter 6: Darius' foolish decree

Chapter 7: Daniel's vision of four beasts

Chapter 8: Daniel's vision of a ram and a goat

Chapter 9: Daniel's vision of seventy weeks

Chapter 10: The appearance of the messenger

Chapter 11: A vision of kings

Chapter 12: The end time

Insight from Matthew Henry

Daniel 3

VERSES 1–7
Pride and bigotry cause men to require their subjects to follow their religion, whether right or wrong.

Hosea

An introduction

Background

The book of Hosea is the first of the "Minor Prophets." "The probable cause of the location of Hosea may be the thoroughly national character of his oracles, their length, their earnest tone, and vivid representations." This was the longest of the prophetic books written before the Captivity. Hosea prophesied in a dark and melancholy period of Israel's history, the period of Israel's decline and fall. Their sins had brought upon them great national disasters. "Their homicides and fornication, their perjury and theft, their idolatry and impiety, are censured and satirized with a faithful severity." Hosea was a contemporary of Isaiah.

Divisions

The book may be divided into two parts, the first containing Hos. 1–3, and symbolically representing the idolatry of Israel using imagery borrowed from the marriage relationship. The figures of marriage and adultery are common in the Old Testament writings and represent the spiritual relations between Jehovah and the people of Israel. Here we see the apostasy of Israel and their punishment, with their future repentance, forgiveness, and restoration.

The second part, containing Hos. 4–14, is a summary of Hosea's discourses, filled with denunciations, threats, exhortations, promises, and revelations of mercy.

Quotations

Quotations from Hosea are found in Matt. 2: 15; 9: 15; 12: 7; Rom. 9: 25,26. There are, in addition, various allusions to it in other places (Luke 23: 30; Rev. 6: 16, cf. Hos. 10: 8; Rom. 9: 25,26; 1 Pet. 2: 10, cf. Hos. 1: 10, etc.).

Writing style

As regards the style of this writer, it has been said that "each verse forms a whole for itself, like one heavy toll in a funeral knell." "Inversions (Hos. 7: 8; 9: 11,13; 12: 8), anacolutha (Hos. 9: 6; 12: 8, etc.), ellipses (Hos. 9: 4; 13: 9, etc.), paranomasias, and plays upon words, are very characteristic of Hosea (Hos. 8: 7; 9: 15; 10: 5; 11: 5; 12: 11)."

Name, author, date

MEANING OF NAME OF BOOK
This book is named after the prophet Hosea, whose name means "salvation."

AUTHOR
Hosea.

APPROXIMATE DATE OF WRITING
755–715 B.C.

Statistics

PLACE OF BOOK IN BIBLE
28th Old Testament book.
1st minor prophet.

NUMBER OF CHAPTERS: 14

NUMBER OF VERSES: 197

NUMBER OF WORDS: 5,175

Main theme of book

Israel's spiritual adultery is depicted in Hosea's wife's adultery.

Keys to the understanding of book

KEY WORD/S
Faithful love
Harlot, harlotry, 19 times

KEY PHRASE
Latter days, 3: 5.

KEY PERSON/PEOPLE
Hosea, Gomer.

KEY CHAPTER/S
4 and Israel's unfaithfulness.

KEY VERSE/S
Then said the Lord unto me, Go yet, love a woman beloved of her friend, yet an adulteress, according to the love of the Lord toward the children of Israel, who look to other gods, and love flagons of wine.
Hosea 3: 1

Hear the word of the Lord, ye children of Israel: for the Lord hath a controversy with the inhabitants of the land, because there is no truth, nor mercy, nor knowledge of God in the land.
Hosea 4: 1

And my people are bent to backsliding from me: though they called them to the most High, none at all would exalt him.
Hosea 11: 7

Jesus Christ in Hosea

WHO JESUS IS
The One who forgives and loves, even after being rejected.

JESUS FORESHADOWED AS A TYPE/ PORTRAITS OF CHRIST
Hosea's redemption of Gomer mirrors Christ's work of our redemption.

Spiritual thought

God's erring people must return to the Lord.

Chapter by chapter breakdown

Chapter 1: Hosea's marriage
Chapter 2: Israel's unfaithfulness, God's faithfulness
Chapter 3: Hosea buys his wife back
Chapter 4: Israel's sins
Chapter 5: Eventual restoration of Israel
Chapter 6: The covenant is deliberately broken
Chapter 7: Deliberate refusal to return to the Lord
Chapter 8: Deliberate idolatry
Chapter 9: God will reject Israel
Chapter 10: God's judgment on Israel
Chapter 11: God's love for Israel
Chapter 12: Israel and Judah are condemned
Chapter 13: Only God's love can save Israel
Chapter 14: God's promise to restore Israel

Insight from Matthew Henry

Hosea 11

VERSES 8–12
God is slow to anger, and is loth to abandon a people to utter ruin, who have been called by his name. When God was to give a sacrifice for sin he spared not his own Son.

Joel

An introduction

The prophet Joel

Joel was probably a resident in Judah, as his commission was directed to those people. He often mentions Judah and Jerusalem (Joel 1: 14; 2: 1,15,32; 3: 1,12,17,20,21).

Contents

The contents of this book are,

(1) A prophecy of a great public calamity then impending over the land, consisting of a want of water and an extraordinary plague of locusts (Joel 1: 1–2: 11).

(2) The prophet then calls on his countrymen to repent and to turn to God, assuring them of his readiness to forgive (Joel 2: 12–17), and foretelling the restoration of the land to its accustomed fruitfulness (Joel 2: 18–26).

(3) Then follows a Messianic prophecy, quoted by Peter (Acts 2: 39).

(4) Finally, the prophet foretells portents and judgments as destined to fall on the enemies of God (Joel 3).

Name, author, date

MEANING OF NAME OF BOOK
This book is named after the prophet Joel, whose name means "Jehovah is my God."

AUTHOR
Joel.

APPROXIMATE DATE OF WRITING
835 B.C.

Statistics

PLACE OF BOOK IN BIBLE
29th Old Testament book.
2nd minor prophet.

NUMBER OF CHAPTERS
3

NUMBER OF VERSES
73

NUMBER OF WORDS
2,034

Main theme of book

The Day of the Lord will come as God's judgment.

Keys to the understanding of book

KEY WORD/S
Repent

KEY PHRASE
The day of the Lord.

KEY CHAPTER/S
2

KEY VERSE/S
And the Lord shall utter his voice before his army: for his camp is very great: for he is strong that executeth his word: for the day of the Lord is great and very terrible; and who can abide it?
Joel 2: 11

And it shall come to pass, that whosoever shall call on the name of the Lord shall be delivered: for in mount Zion and in Jerusalem shall be

deliverance, as the Lord hath said, and in the remnant whom the Lord shall call.
Joel 2: 32

Jesus Christ in Joel

WHO JESUS IS
The hope of his people, 3: 16.

JESUS FORESHADOWED AS A TYPE/ PORTRAITS OF CHRIST
The promised Holy Spirit, also promised by Jesus, is fulfilled on the Day of Pentecost.

Spiritual thought

An alarm needs to be sounded.

Chapter by chapter breakdown

Chapter 1: The devastating plague of locusts
Chapter 2: The Day of the Lord will bring destruction
Chapter 3: Judgment on the nations

Insight from Matthew Henry

Joel 1

VERSES 1–7
The most aged could not remember such calamities as were about to take place. Armies of insects were coming upon the land to eat the fruits of it. It is expressed so as to apply also to the destruction of the country by a foreign enemy, and seems to refer to the devastations of the Chaldeans. God is Lord of hosts, has every creature at his command, and, when he pleases, can humble and mortify a proud, rebellious people, by the weakest and most contemptible creatures. It is just with God to take away the comforts which are abused to luxury and excess; and the more men place their happiness in the gratifications of sense, the more severe temporal afflictions are upon them. The more earthly delights we make needful to satisfy us, the more we expose ourselves to trouble.

VERSES 8–13
All who labor only for the meat that perishes, will, sooner or later, be ashamed of their labor. Those that place their happiness in the delights of sense, when deprived of them, or disturbed in the enjoyment, lose their joy; whereas spiritual joy then flourishes more than ever. See what perishing, uncertain things our creature-comforts are. See how we need to live in continual dependence upon God and his providence. See what ruinous work sin makes. As far as poverty occasions the decay of piety, and starves the cause of religion among a people, it is a very sore judgment. But how blessed are the awakening judgments of God, in rousing his people and calling home the heart to Christ, and his salvation!

VERSES 14–20
The sorrow of the people is turned into repentance and humiliation before God. With all the marks of sorrow and shame, sin must be confessed and bewailed.

Amos

An introduction

The prophet Amos

Amos was born in Tekoa, a town about 12 miles south-east of Bethlehem. He was a man of humble birth, neither a "prophet nor a prophet's son," but "an herdman and a dresser of sycomore trees," *RV*. He prophesied in the days of Uzziah, king of Judah, and was contemporary with Isaiah and Hosea (Amos 1: 1; 7: 14,15; Zech. 14: 5), who survived him a few years. Under Jeroboam II the kingdom of Israel rose to the zenith of its prosperity; but that was followed by the prevalence of luxury and vice and idolatry. At this period Amos was called from his obscurity to remind the people of the law of God's retributive justice, and to call them to repentance.

Divisions

The Book of Amos consists of three parts:

(1) The nations around are summoned to judgment because of their sins (Amos 1: 1–2: 3). He quotes Joel 3: 16.

(2) The spiritual condition of Judah, and especially of Israel, is described (Amos 2: 4–6: 14).

(3) In Amos 7: 1–9: 10 are recorded five prophetic visions.

(a) The first two (Amos 7: 1–6) refer to judgments against the guilty people.

(b) The next two (Amos 7: 7–9; 8: 1–3) point out the ripeness of the people for the threatened judgments. Amos 7: 10–

17 consists of a conversation between the prophet and the priest of Bethel.

(c) The fifth describes the overthrow and ruin of Israel (Amos 9: 1–10); to which is added the promise of the restoration of the kingdom and its final glory in the Messiah's kingdom.

Allusions

The style is peculiar in the number of the allusions made to natural objects and to agricultural occupations. Other allusions show also that Amos was a student of the law as well as a "child of nature." These phrases are peculiar to him: "Cleanness of teeth" [i.e., lack of bread] (Amos 4: 6); "The excellency of Jacob" (Amos 6: 8; 8: 7); "The high places of Isaac" (Amos 7: 9); "The house of Isaac" (Amos 7: 16); "He that createth the wind" (Amos 4: 13). Quoted, Acts 7: 42.

Name, author, date

MEANING OF NAME OF BOOK
This book is named after the prophet Amos, whose name means "burdened."

AUTHOR
Amos.

APPROXIMATE DATE OF WRITING
760–753 B.C.

Statistics

PLACE OF BOOK IN BIBLE
30th Old Testament book.
3rd minor prophet.

NUMBER OF CHAPTERS
9

NUMBER OF VERSES
146

NUMBER OF WORDS
4,217

Main theme of book

Judgment on Israel.

Keys to the understanding of book

KEY WORD/S
Judgment
Plumbline

KEY PHRASE
For three transgressions ... and for four, 1: 3.

KEY PERSON/PEOPLE
Amos.

KEY CHAPTER/S
9 and future restoration promised.

KEY VERSE/S
Behold, the days come, saith the Lord GOD, that I will send a famine in the land, not a famine of bread, nor a thirst for water, but of hearing the words of the Lord: And they shall wander from sea to sea, and from the north even to the east, they shall run to and fro to seek the word of the Lord, and shall not find it.
Amos 8: 11,12

Jesus Christ in Amos

WHO JESUS IS
The God of hosts, 4: 13.

JESUS FORESHADOWED AS A TYPE/
PORTRAITS OF CHRIST

Jesus is Judge.
Jesus is the Restorer.

Spiritual thought

Made use of the plumbline.

Chapter by chapter breakdown

Chapter 1: The sins of Damascus, Philistia, Phoenicia, Edom, and Ammon
Chapter 2: Moab, Judah, and Israel condemned
Chapter 3: God's judgment
Chapter 4: The willfulness of Israel
Chapter 5: Judgment on Israel is deserved
Chapter 6: Israel's end is near
Chapter 7: Visions of doom: locusts, fire, and plumbline
Chapter 8: Vision of the summer fruit
Chapter 9: God's destruction, but hope for the future

Insight from Matthew Henry

Amos 4

VERSES 1–5
What is got by extortion is commonly used to provide for the flesh. What is got by oppression cannot be enjoyed with satisfaction. How miserable are those whose confidence in unscriptural observances only prove that they believe a lie! Let us see to it that our faith, hope, and worship, are warranted by the Divine word.

Obadiah

An introduction

Divisions

The book of Obadiah consists of one chapter, "concerning Edom," its impending doom (Obad. 1–16), and the restoration of Israel (Obad. 17–21). This is the shortest book of the Old Testament.

Edom

Edom is the type of Israel's and of God's last foe (Is. 63: 1–4). These will finally all be vanquished, and the kingdom will be the Lord's (Cf. Ps. 22: 28).

Name, author, date

MEANING OF NAME OF BOOK
This book is named after the prophet Obadiah, whose name means "a servant."

AUTHOR
Obadiah.

APPROXIMATE DATE OF WRITING
848–841 B.C.

Statistics

PLACE OF BOOK IN BIBLE
31st Old Testament book.
4th minor prophet.

NUMBER OF CHAPTERS
1

NUMBER OF VERSES
21

NUMBER OF WORDS
670

Main theme of book
Edom's doom is foretold.

Keys to the understanding of book

KEY WORD/S
Judgment

KEY PHRASE
The house of Jacob shall possess their possessions, verse 17.

KEY PERSON/PEOPLE
Obadiah.

KEY VERSE/S
For the day of the Lord is near upon all the heathen: as thou hast done, it shall be done unto thee: thy reward shall return upon thine own head.
Obadiah 15

Jesus Christ in Obadiah

WHO JESUS IS
Your reward.

JESUS FORESHADOWED AS A TYPE/ PORTRAITS OF CHRIST
In Obadiah, Christ is the judge of the nations, the Savior of Israel and the Possessor of the kingdom.

Spiritual thought
Possess your possessions.

Chapter by chapter breakdown
Chapter 1: The judgment of Edom

Insight from Matthew Henry

Obadiah 17

After the destruction of the church's enemies is threatened, which will be completely accomplished in the great day of recompense, and that judgment for which Christ came once, and will come again, into this world, here follow precious promises of the salvation of the church, with which this prophecy concludes, and those of Joel and Amos did, which, however they might be in part fulfilled in the return of the Jews out of Babylon notwithstanding the triumphs of Edom in their captivity, as if it were perpetual, are yet, doubtless, to have their full accomplishment in that great salvation wrought out by Jesus Christ, to which all the prophets bore witness. It is promised here,

I. That there shall be salvation upon Mount Zion, that holy hill where God sets his anointed King (Ps. 2: 6): Upon Mount Zion shall be deliverance, v. 17. There shall be those that escape; so the margin. A remnant of Israel, upon the holy mountain shall be saved, v. 16. Christ said, Salvation is of the Jews, John 4: 22. God wrought deliverances for the Jews, typical of our redemption by Christ. But Mount Zion is the gospel church, from which the New-Testament law went forth, Is. 2: 3. There salvation shall be preached and prayed for; to the gospel church those are added who shall be saved; and for those who come in faith and hope to this Mount Zion deliverance shall be wrought from wrath and the curse, from sin, and death, and hell, while those who continue afar off shall be left to perish.

II. That, where there is salvation, there shall be sanctification in order to it: And there shall be holiness, to prepare and qualify the children of Zion for this deliverance; for wherever God designs glory he gives grace. Temporal deliverances are indeed wrought for us in mercy when with them there is holiness, when there is wrought in us a disposition to receive them with love and gratitude to God; when we are sanctified, they are sanctified to us. Holiness is itself a great deliverance, and an earnest of that eternal salvation which we look for. There, upon Mount Zion, in the gospel church, shall be holiness; for that is it which becomes God's house for ever, and the great design of the gospel, and its grace, is to plant and promote holiness. There shall be the Holy Spirit, the holy ordinances, the holy Jesus, and a select remnant of holy souls, in whom, and among whom, the holy God will delight to dwell. Note, Where there is holiness there shall be deliverance.

III. That this salvation and sanctification shall spread, and prevail, and get ground in the world: The house of Jacob, even this Mount Zion, with the deliverance and their holiness there wrought, shall possess their possessions; that is, the gospel church shall be set up among the heathen, and shall replenish the earth; the apostles of Christ by their preaching shall gain possession of the hearts of men.

Jonah

An introduction

Is the book a parable?

This book professes to give an account of what actually took place in the experience of the prophet. Some critics have sought to interpret the book as a parable or allegory, and not as a history. They have done so for various reasons. Thus

(1) some reject it on the ground that the miraculous element enters so largely into it, and that it is not prophetical but narrative in its form;

(2) others, denying the possibility of miracles altogether, hold that therefore it cannot be true history.

Jonah and Jesus

Jonah and his story are referred to by our Lord (Matt. 12: 39,40; Luke 11: 29), a fact to which the greatest weight must be attached. It is impossible to interpret this reference on any other theory. This one argument is of sufficient importance to settle the whole question. No theories devised for the purpose of getting rid of difficulties can stand against such a proof that the book is a veritable history.

Authorship

There is every reason to believe that this book was written by Jonah himself. It gives an account of

(1) his divine commission to go to Nineveh, his disobedience, and the punishment following (Jonah 1: 1–17);

(2) his prayer and miraculous

deliverance (Jonah 1: 17–2: 10);

(3) the second commission given to him, and his prompt obedience in delivering the message from God, and its results in the repentance of the Ninevites, and God's long-sparing mercy toward them (Jonah 3);

(4) Jonah's displeasure at God's merciful decision, and the rebuke tendered to the impatient prophet (Jonah 4). Nineveh was spared after Jonah's mission for more than a century. The history of Jonah may well be regarded "as a part of that great onward movement which was before the Law and under the Law; which gained strength and volume as the fullness of the times drew near" (Perowne's Jonah).

Name, author, date

MEANING OF NAME OF BOOK
This book is named after the prophet Jonah, whose name means "a dove."

AUTHOR
Jonah.

APPROXIMATE DATE OF WRITING
782–753 B.C.

Statistics

PLACE OF BOOK IN BIBLE
32nd Old Testament book.
5th minor prophet.

NUMBER OF CHAPTERS
4

NUMBER OF VERSES
48

NUMBER OF WORDS

1,321

Main theme of book

Salvation is proclaimed to the Gentiles.

Keys to the understanding of book

KEY WORD/S

Preach

KEY PHRASE

Arise and go.

KEY PERSON/PEOPLE

Jonah, the people of Nineveh.

KEY CHAPTER/S

3 and Nineveh's repentance.

KEY VERSE/S

They that observe lying vanities forsake their own mercy. But I will sacrifice unto thee with the voice of thanksgiving; I will pay that that I have vowed. Salvation is of the Lord.
Jonah 2 : 8,9

Jesus Christ in Jonah

WHO JESUS IS

The giver of salvation.

JESUS FORESHADOWED AS A TYPE/
PORTRAITS OF CHRIST

Jesus likened himself to Jonah, but to no other prophet.
The resurrection of Jesus is pictured by Jonah being in the big fish and being delivered.

Spiritual thought

I am lost if I do not preach the gospel.
See 1 Corinthians 9: 16.

Chapter by chapter breakdown

Chapter 1: Jonah is thrown overboard
Chapter 2: Jonah prays from inside the great fish
Chapter 3: Jonah goes to Nineveh
Chapter 4: The people of Nineveh repent

Insight from Matthew Henry

Jonah 2

VERSES 1–9

Observe when Jonah prayed. When he was in trouble, under the tokens of God's displeasure against him for sin: when we are in affliction we must pray. Being kept alive by miracle, he prayed. A sense of God's good-will to us, notwithstanding our offences, opens the lips in prayer, which were closed with the dread of wrath. Also, where he prayed; in the belly of the fish. No place is amiss for prayer. Men may shut us from communion with one another, but not from communion with God. To whom he prayed; to the Lord his God. This encourages even backsliders to return. What his prayer was. This seems to relate his experience and reflections, then and afterwards, rather than to be the form or substance of his prayer. Jonah reflects on the earnestness of his prayer, and God's readiness to hear and answer.

Micah

An introduction

Superscription

The superscription to this book states that the prophet exercised his office in the reigns of Jotham, Ahaz, and Hezekiah. It has been noted as remarkable that this book commences with the last words of another prophet, "Micaiah the son of Imlah" (1 Kings 22: 28): "Hearken, O people, every one of you."

Divisions

The book consists of three sections, each commencing with a rebuke, "Hear ye," etc., and closing with a promise,
(1) Micah 1; 2;
(2) Micah 3–5, especially addressed to the princes and leaders of the people;
(3) Micah 6–7, in which Jehovah is represented holding a controversy with his people: the whole book concludes with a song of triumph at the great deliverance which the Lord will achieve for his people. The closing verse is quoted in the song of Zacharias (Luke 1: 72,73).

Bethlehem

The prediction regarding the place "where Christ should be born," one of the most remarkable Messianic prophecies (Micah 5: 2), is quoted in Matt. 2: 6.

There are the following references to this book in the New Testament: Micah 5: 2 (cf. Matt. 2: 6; John 7: 42), Micah 7: 6 (cf. Matt. 10: 21,35,36), Micah 7: 20 (cf. Luke 1: 72,73).

Name, author, date

MEANING OF NAME OF BOOK
This book is named after the prophet Micah, whose name means "Who is like Jehovah?"

AUTHOR
Micah.

APPROXIMATE DATE OF WRITING
735–700 B.C.

Statistics

PLACE OF BOOK IN BIBLE
33rd Old Testament book.
6th minor prophet.

NUMBER OF CHAPTERS
7

NUMBER OF VERSES
105

NUMBER OF WORDS
3,153

Main theme of book

Judah's injustice is contrasted with God's justice.

Keys to the understanding of book

KEY WORD/S
Judgment
Restoration

KEY PHRASE
The Lord hath a controversy with his people, 6: 2.

Key person/people
Micah.

Key chapter/s
6 and 7 and the courtroom scene.

Key verse/s
Hear, all ye people; hearken, O earth, and all that therein is: and let the Lord GOD be witness against you, the Lord from his holy temple.
Micah 1: 2

Jesus Christ in Micah

Who Jesus is
The One who will be born in Bethlehem.

Jesus foreshadowed as a type/portraits of Christ
The predicted birthplace of Jesus is one of the clearest prophecies in the Old Testament.

Spiritual thought
Look to God if you want to live.

Chapter by chapter breakdown
Chapter 1: Samaria will be destroyed; the enemy approaches Jerusalem
Chapter 2: People who exploit the poor will be punished
Chapter 3: The leaders are judged
Chapter 4: The Lord's future reign, and the return from exile
Chapter 5: The promise about the coming King
Chapter 6: The Lord pleads for repentance
Chapter 7: The promise of final salvation

Insight from Matthew Henry

Micah 5

Verses 1–6
Having showed how low the house of David would be brought, a prediction of the Messiah and his kingdom is added to encourage the faith of God's people. His existence from eternity as God, and his office as Mediator, are noticed. Here is foretold that Bethlehem should be his birthplace. Hence it was universally known among the Jews, Matthew 2: 5. Christ's government shall be very happy for his subjects; they shall be safe and easy. Under the shadow of protection from the Assyrians, is a promise of protection to the gospel church and all believers, from the designs and attempts of the powers of darkness. Christ is our Peace as a Priest, making atonement for sin, and reconciling us to God; and he is our Peace as a King, conquering our enemies: hence our souls may dwell at ease in him. Christ will find instruments to protect and deliver. Those that threaten ruin to the church of God, soon bring ruin on themselves. This may include the past powerful effects of the preached gospel, its future spread, and the ruin of all antichristian powers. This is, perhaps, the most important single prophecy in the Old Testament: it respects the personal character of the Messiah, and the discoveries of himself to the world. It distinguishes his human birth from his existing from eternity.

Nahum

An introduction

Nineveh

The subject of this prophecy is the approaching complete and final destruction of Nineveh, the capital of the great and at that time flourishing Assyrian empire. Nineveh was a vast city and was then the center of the civilization and commerce of the world, a "bloody city all full of lies and robbery" (Nah. 3: 1), for it had robbed and plundered all the neighboring nations. It was strongly fortified on every side, defying every enemy; yet it was to be utterly destroyed as a punishment for the great wickedness of its inhabitants.

Jonah and Zephaniah

Jonah had already uttered his message of warning, and Nahum was followed by Zephaniah, who also predicted (Zeph. 2: 4–15) the destruction of the city, predictions which were remarkably fulfilled (625 B.C.) when Nineveh was destroyed apparently by fire, and the Assyrian Empire came to an end, an event which changed the face of Asia.

Name, author, date

MEANING OF NAME OF BOOK
This book is named after the prophet Nahum, whose name means "Consoler" or "Comforter."

AUTHOR
Nahum.

APPROXIMATE DATE OF WRITING
664–654 B.C.

Statistics

PLACE OF BOOK IN BIBLE
34th Old Testament book.
7th minor prophet.

NUMBER OF CHAPTERS
3

NUMBER OF VERSES
47

NUMBER OF WORDS
1,285

Main theme of book

Nineveh's destruction is foretold.

Keys to the understanding of book

KEY WORD/S
Justice

KEY PHRASE
An utter end, 1: 8,9.

KEY PERSON/PEOPLE
Nahum

KEY CHAPTER/S
1 and divine judgment and deliverance.

KEY VERSE/S
God is jealous, and the Lord revengeth; the Lord revengeth, and is furious; the Lord will take vengeance on his adversaries, and he reserveth wrath for

his enemies. The Lord is slow to anger, and great in power, and will not at all acquit the wicked: the Lord hath his way in the whirlwind and in the storm, and the clouds are the dust of his feet.
Nahum 1: 2,3

Behold, I am against thee, saith the Lord of hosts; and I will discover thy skirts upon thy face, and I will show the nations thy nakedness, and the kingdoms thy shame. And I will cast abominable filth upon thee, and make thee vile, and will set thee as a gazingstock. And it shall come to pass, that all they that look upon thee shall flee from thee, and say, Nineveh is laid waste: who will bemoan her? whence shall I seek comforters for thee?
Nahum 3: 5–7

Jesus Christ in Nahum

WHO JESUS IS
The Lord is good.

JESUS FORESHADOWED AS A TYPE/
PORTRAITS OF CHRIST
There are no direct Messianic prophecies in Nahum.

Spiritual thought
God's judgment is a reality.

Chapter by chapter breakdown

Chapter 1: A portrait of God
Chapter 2: Nineveh's destruction described
Chapter 3: Nineveh's destruction is deserved

Insight from Matthew Henry

Nahum 2

VERSES 1–10
Nineveh shall not put aside this judgment; there is no counsel or strength against the Lord. God looks upon proud cities, and brings them down. Particular account is given of the terrors wherein the invading enemy shall appear against Nineveh. The empire of Assyria is represented as a queen, about to be led captive to Babylon. Guilt in the conscience fills men with terror in an evil day; and what will treasures or glory do for us in times of distress, or in the day of wrath? Yet for such things how many lose their souls!

VERSES 11–13
The kings of Assyria had long been terrible and cruel to their neighbors, but the Lord would destroy their power. Many plead as an excuse for rapine and fraud, that they have families to provide for; but what is thus obtained will never do them any good. Those that fear the Lord, and get honestly what they have, shall not want for themselves and theirs. It is just with God to deprive those of children, or of comfort in them, who take sinful courses to enrich them. Those are not worthy to be heard again, that have spoken reproachfully of God. Let us then come to God upon his mercy-seat, that having peace with him through our Lord Jesus Christ, we may know that he is for us, and that all things shall work together for our everlasting good.

Habakkuk

An introduction

Contents

The prophecies of Habakkuk consist of three chapters, the contents of which are thus comprehensively described: "When the prophet in spirit saw the formidable power of the Babylonians approaching and menacing his land, and saw the great evils they would cause in Judea, he bore his complaints and doubts before Jehovah, the just and the pure (Hab. 1: 2–17). And on this occasion the future punishment of the Babylonians was revealed to him (Hab. 2). In Hab. 3 a presentiment of the destruction of his country, in the inspired heart of the prophet, contends with his hope that the enemy would be chastised."

The third chapter is a sublime song dedicated "to the chief musician," and therefore intended apparently to be used in the worship of God. It is "unequaled in majesty and splendor of language and imagery."

Quotations

The passage in Hab. 2: 4, "The just shall live by his faith," is quoted by the apostle in Rom. 1: 17. (Cf. Gal. 3: 12; Heb. 10: 37,38.)

Name, author, date

MEANING OF NAME OF BOOK
This book is named after the prophet Habakkuk, whose name means "embrace."

AUTHOR
Habakkuk.

APPROXIMATE DATE OF WRITING
609–605 B.C.

Statistics

PLACE OF BOOK IN BIBLE
35th Old Testament book.
8th minor prophet.

NUMBER OF CHAPTERS
3

NUMBER OF VERSES
56

NUMBER OF WORDS
1,476

Main theme of book

The just will live by faith.

Keys to the understanding of book

KEY WORD/S
Faith

KEY PHRASE
Why dost thou? 1: 3.

KEY PERSON/PEOPLE
Habakkuk.

KEY CHAPTER/S
3 and Habakkuk's faith.

KEY VERSE/S
Behold, his soul which is lifted up is not upright in him: but the just shall live by his faith.
Habakkuk 2: 4

Jesus Christ in Habakkuk

WHO JESUS IS
The holy One.

JESUS FORESHADOWED AS A TYPE/
PORTRAITS OF CHRIST
The word "salvation" which comes
three times in Habakkuk is the root
meaning of the word "Jesus."

Spiritual thought

God brings light, 3: 4.

Chapter by chapter breakdown

Chapter 1: Habakkuk's complaints
Chapter 2: God's hatred of injustice
Chapter 3: Habakkuk's prayer

Insight from Matthew Henry

Habakkuk 2

VERSES 1–4
When tossed and perplexed with
doubts about the methods of
Providence, we must watch against
temptations to be impatient. When
we have poured out complaints and
requests before God, we must observe
the answers God gives by his word,
his Spirit, and providences; what the
Lord will say to our case. God will not
disappoint the believing expectations
of those who wait to hear what he
will say unto them. All are concerned
in the truths of God's word. Though
the promised favor be deferred long,
it will come at last, and abundantly
recompense us for waiting. The
humble, broken-hearted, repenting
sinner, alone seeks to obtain an interest
in this salvation. He will rest his soul
on the promise, and on Christ, in
and through whom it is given. Thus
he walks and works, as well as lives

by faith, perseveres to the end, and
is exalted to glory; while those who
distrust or despise God's all-sufficiency
will not walk uprightly with him. The
just shall live by faith in these precious
promises, while the performance of
them is deferred. Only those made just
by faith, shall live, shall be happy here
and for ever.

VERSES 5–14
The prophet reads the doom of all
proud and oppressive powers that bear
hard upon God's people. The lusts of
the flesh, the lust of the eye, and the
pride of life, are the entangling snares
of men; and we find him that led Israel
captive, himself led captive by each of
these. No more of what we have is to
be reckoned ours, than what we come
honestly by. Riches are but clay, thick
clay; what are gold and silver but white
and yellow earth? Those who travel
through thick clay, are hindered and
dirtied in their journey; so are those
who go through the world in the midst
of abundance of wealth. And what
fools are those that burden themselves
with continual care about it; with a
great deal of guilt in getting, saving,
and spending it, and with a heavy
account which they must give another
day! They overload themselves with
this thick clay, and so sink themselves
down into destruction and perdition.
See what will be the end hereof; what
is gotten by violence from others,
others shall take away by violence.
Covetousness brings disquiet and
uneasiness into a family; he that is
greedy of gain troubles his own house.

Zephaniah

An introduction

Zephaniah the prophet

Zephaniah means "Jehovah has concealed," or "Jehovah of darkness."

The son of Cushi, and great-grandson of Hezekiah, Zephaniah prophesied in the days of Josiah, king of Judah (641–610 B.C.), and was contemporary with Jeremiah, with whom he had much in common.

Contents

The book of his prophecies consists of:

(1) An introduction (Zeph. 1:1–6), announcing the judgment of the world, and the judgment upon Israel, because of their transgressions.

(2) The description of the judgment (Zeph. 1:7–18).

(3) An exhortation to seek God while there is still time (Zeph. 2:1–3).

(4) The announcement of judgment on the heathen (Zeph. 2:4–15).

(5) The hopeless misery of Jerusalem (Zeph. 3:1–7).

(6) The promise of salvation (Zeph. 3:8–20).

Name, author, date

MEANING OF NAME OF BOOK
This book is named after the prophet Zephaniah, whose name means "hidden of Jehovah."

AUTHOR
Zephaniah.

APPROXIMATE DATE OF WRITING
640–612 B.C.

Statistics

PLACE OF BOOK IN BIBLE
366h Old Testament book.
9th minor prophet.

NUMBER OF CHAPTERS
3

NUMBER OF VERSES
53

NUMBER OF WORDS
1,617

Main theme of book

The day of the Lord will bring judgment and blessing.

Keys to the understanding of book

KEY WORD/S
Search

KEY PHRASE
The day of the Lord.

KEY PERSON/PEOPLE
Zephaniah.

KEY CHAPTER/S
3 and judgment and restoration.

KEY VERSE/S
Seek ye the Lord, all ye meek of the earth, which have wrought his judgment; seek righteousness, seek meekness: it may be ye shall be hid in the day of the Lord's anger.
Zephaniah 2:3

Jesus Christ in Zephaniah

WHO JESUS IS
The Lord who is with his people.

JESUS FORESHADOWED AS A TYPE/
PORTRAITS OF CHRIST
Jesus fulfils the promises mentioned in
Zephaniah, 3: 9–20.

Spiritual thought

As you make your spiritual journey,
sing, 3: 14.

Chapter by chapter breakdown

Chapter 1: Judah is judged
Chapter 2: Oracles against the nations
Chapter 3: Salvation on the Day of the
     Lord

Insight from Matthew Henry

Zephaniah 3

VERSES 8–13
The purifying doctrines of the gospel,
or the pure language of the grace of
the Lord, would teach men to use the
language of humility, repentance, and
faith. Purity and piety in common
conversation is good. The pure and
happy state of the church in the latter
days seems intended. The Lord will
shut out boasting, and leave men
nothing to glory in, save the Lord
Jesus, as made of God to them wisdom,
righteousness, sanctification, and
redemption. Humiliation for sin, and
obligations to the Redeemer, will make
true believers upright and sincere,
whatever may be the case among mere
professors.

VERSES 14–20
After the promises of taking away
sin, follow promises of taking away
trouble. When the cause is removed,
the effect will cease. What makes a
people holy, will make them happy.
The precious promises made to the
purified people, were to have full
accomplishment in the gospel. These
verses appear chiefly to relate to the
future conversion and restoration of
Israel, and the glorious times which
are to follow. They show the abundant
peace, comfort, and prosperity of
the church, in the happy times yet to
come. He will save; he will be Jesus;
he will answer the name, for he will
save his people from their sins. Before
the glorious times foretold, believers
would be sorrowful, and objects
of reproach. But the Lord will save
the weakest believer, and cause true
Christians to be greatly honored where
they had been treated with contempt.
One act of mercy and grace shall
serve, both to gather Israel out of their
dispersions and to lead them to their
own land. Then will God's Israel be
made a name and a praise to eternity.
The events alone can fully answer the
language of this prophecy. Many are
the troubles of the righteous, but they
may rejoice in God's love. Surely our
hearts should honor the Lord, and
rejoice in him, when we hear such
words of condescension and grace. If
now kept from his ordinances, it is our
trial and grief; but in due time we shall
be gathered into his temple above. The
glory and happiness of the believer will
be perfect.

Haggai

An introduction

Contents

The book of Haggai consists of two brief, comprehensive chapters. The object of the prophet was generally to urge the people to proceed with the rebuilding of the temple.

Chapter one consists of the first address (Hag. 1: 2–11) and its effects (Hag. 1: 12–15).

Chapter two contains,
  (1) The second prophecy (Hag. 2: 1–9), which was delivered a month after the first.
  (2) The third prophecy (Hag. 2: 10–19), delivered two months and three days after the second; and
  (3) The fourth prophecy (Hag. 2: 20–23), delivered on the same day as the third.
These discourses are referred to in Ezra 5: 1; 6: 14; Heb. 12: 26. (Cf. Hag. 2: 7,8,22.)

Name, author, date

MEANING OF NAME OF BOOK
This book is named after the prophet Haggai, whose name means "festival" or "my feast."

AUTHOR
Haggai.

APPROXIMATE DATE OF WRITING
520 B.C.

Statistics

PLACE OF BOOK IN BIBLE
37th Old Testament book.
10th minor prophet.

NUMBER OF CHAPTERS
2

NUMBER OF VERSES
38

NUMBER OF WORDS
1,131

Main theme of book

The rebuilding of the temple in Jerusalem.

Keys to the understanding of book

KEY WORD/S
Build

KEY PHRASE
Be strong and work, 2: 4.

KEY PERSON/PEOPLE
Haggai, Zerubbabel, and Joshua (the high priest).

KEY CHAPTER/S
2 and the amazing Messianic prophecy.

KEY VERSE/S
Thus saith the Lord of hosts; Consider your ways. Go up to the mountain, and bring wood, and build the house; and I will take pleasure in it, and I will be glorified, saith the Lord.
Haggai 1: 7,8

And I will shake all nations, and the desire of all nations shall come: and I will fill this house with glory, saith the Lord of hosts. The silver is mine, and the gold is mine, saith the Lord of hosts. The glory of this latter house shall be greater than of the former, saith the Lord of hosts: and in this place will I give peace, saith the Lord of hosts. Haggai 2: 7–9

Jesus Christ in Haggai

WHO JESUS IS
The Word of the Lord.

JESUS FORESHADOWED AS A TYPE/ PORTRAITS OF CHRIST
Zerubbabel foreshadows Christ.

Spiritual thought

First things should be put first.

Chapter by chapter breakdown

Chapter 1 :A call to build the house of the Lord
Chapter 2: Looking to the future

Insight from Matthew Henry

Haggai 1

VERSES 1–11
Observe the sin of the Jews, after their return from captivity in Babylon. Those employed for God may be driven from their work by a storm, yet they must go back to it. They did not say that they would not build a temple, but, Not yet. Thus men do not say they will never repent and reform, and be religious, but, Not yet. And so the great business we were sent into the world to do, is not done. There is a proneness in us to think wrongly of discouragements in our duty, as if they were a discharge from our duty, when they are only for the trial of our courage and faith. They neglected the building of God's house, that they might have more time and money for worldly affairs. That the punishment might answer to the sin, the poverty they thought to prevent by not building the temple, God brought upon them for not building it. Many good works have been intended, but not done, because men supposed the proper time was not come. Thus believers let slip opportunities of usefulness, and sinners delay the concerns of their souls, till too late. If we labor only for the meat that perishes, as the Jews here, we are in danger of losing our labor; but we are sure it shall not be in vain in the Lord, if we labor for the meat which lasts to eternal life. If we would have the comfort and continuance of temporal enjoyments, we must have God as our Friend. See also Luke 12: 33. When God crosses our temporal affairs, and we meet with trouble and disappointment, we shall find the cause is, that the work we have to do for God and our own souls is left undone, and we seek our own things more than the things of Christ. How many, who plead that they cannot afford to give to pious or charitable designs, often lavish ten times as much in needless expenses on their houses and themselves! But those are strangers to their own interests, who are full of care to adorn and enrich their own houses, while God's temple in their hearts lies waste.

Zechariah

An introduction

Zechariah the prophet

Zechariah was a prophet of Judah, and like Ezekiel belonged to a priestly family. He describes himself (Zech. 1: 1) as "the son of Berechiah." In Ezra 5: 1 and 6: 14 he is called "the son of Iddo," who was properly his grandfather. His prophetical career began in the second year of Darius (520 B.C.), about sixteen years after the return of the first company from exile. He was contemporary with Haggai (Ezra 5: 1).

Contents

His book consists of two distinct parts, chapters 1 to 8, inclusive, and 9 to the end. It begins with a preface (Zech. 1: 1–6), which recalls the nation's past history, for the purpose of presenting a solemn warning to the present generation. Then follows a series of eight visions (Zech. 1: 7–6: 8), succeeding one another in one night, which may be regarded as a symbolical history of Israel, intended to bring consolation to the returned exiles and to bring them hope. The symbolical action, the crowning of Joshua (Zech. 6: 9–15), describes how the kingdoms of the world become the kingdom of God's Christ. Zech. 7 and 8, delivered two years later, are an answer to the question whether the days of mourning for the destruction of the city should be any longer kept, and an encouraging address to the people, assuring them of God's presence and blessing.

The second part of the book (Zech. 9–14) bears no date. It is probable that a considerable interval separates it from the first part. It consists of two burdens. The first burden (Zech. 9–11) gives an outline of the course of God's providential dealings with his people down to the time of the Advent. The second burden (Zech. 12–14) points out the glories that await Israel in "the latter day," the final conflict and triumph of God's kingdom.

Name, author, date

MEANING OF NAME OF BOOK
This book is named after the prophet Zechariah, whose name means "one whom Jehovah remembers."

AUTHOR
Zechariah.

APPROXIMATE DATE OF WRITING
520–480 B.C.

Statistics

PLACE OF BOOK IN BIBLE
38th Old Testament book.
11th minor prophet.

NUMBER OF CHAPTERS
14

NUMBER OF VERSES
211

NUMBER OF WORDS
6,444

Main theme of book
Israel's future blessings are foretold.

Keys to the understanding of book

KEY WORD/S
Turn

KEY PHRASE
The Word of the Lord, 13 times.
The Lord of hosts, 53 times.

KEY PERSON/PEOPLE
Zechariah.

KEY CHAPTER/S
14 and the siege of Jerusalem.

KEY VERSE/S
Thus saith the Lord; I am returned unto Zion, and will dwell in the midst of Jerusalem: and Jerusalem shall be called a city of truth; and the mountain of the Lord of hosts the holy mountain. Zechariah 8: 3

Jesus Christ in Zechariah

WHO JESUS IS
The Branch.

JESUS FORESHADOWED AS A TYPE/ PORTRAITS OF CHRIST
The angel of the Lord, 3: 1,2.
The righteous Branch, 3: 8.
The stone with seven eyes, 3: 9.
The King-Priest, 6: 13
The King who revealed his humility, 9: 9,10
The good Shepherd who is rejected, 11: 4–13.
The righteous King, chapter 14.

Spiritual thought
The Lord will yet comfort Zion, 1: 17.

Chapter by chapter breakdown
Chapter 1: Two visions: the man on the red horse; the four horns
Chapter 2: The man with the measuring line
Chapter 3: Joshua the priest is accused and acquitted
Chapter 4: The golden lampstand and the olive trees
Chapter 5: The flying scroll, and the woman in the basket
Chapter 6: The vision of the four chariots
Chapter 7: A call to repentance
Chapter 8: Jerusalem's wonderful future
Chapter 9: Judgment on the surrounding nations, and the Messiah-King
Chapter 10: The Lord promises deliverance
Chapter 11: The good shepherd and the bad shepherds
Chapter 12: Jerusalem is saved, and the way of salvation
Chapter 13: Impurity abolished, and the remnant refined
Chapter 14: The Messiah's reign

Insight from Matthew Henry

Zechariah 7
VERSES 8–14
God's judgments upon Israel of old for their sins, were written to warn Christians. The law of God lays restraint upon the heart.

Malachi

An introduction

Divisions

The contents of the book consists of three sections, preceded by an introduction (Mal. 1: 1–5), in which the prophet reminds Israel of Jehovah's love of them.

The first section (Mal. 1: 6–2: 9) contains a stern rebuke addressed to the priests who had despised the name of Jehovah, and been leaders in a departure from his worship and from the covenant, and for their partiality in administering the law.

In the second (Mal. 2: 9–16) the people are rebuked for their intermarriages with idolatrous heathen.

In the third (Mal. 2: 17–4: 6) he addresses the people as a whole, and warns them of the coming of the God of judgment, preceded by the advent of the Messiah.

Quotations

This book is frequently referred to in the New Testament (Matt. 11: 10; 17: 12; Mark 1: 2; 9: 11,12; Luke 1: 17; Rom. 9: 13).

Name, author, date

MEANING OF NAME OF BOOK
This book is named after the prophet Malachi, whose name means "Jehovah's messenger."

AUTHOR
Malachi.

APPROXIMATE DATE OF WRITING
432–424 B.C.

Statistics

PLACE OF BOOK IN BIBLE
39th Old Testament book.
12th minor prophet.

NUMBER OF CHAPTERS
4

NUMBER OF VERSES
55

NUMBER OF WORDS
1.783

Main theme of book

Appeal to backsliders.

Keys to the understanding of book

KEY WORD/S
Messenger

KEY PHRASE
Yet ye say, 2: 17.

KEY PERSON/PEOPLE
Malachi.

KEY CHAPTER/S
3 and its foretelling of the coming of the Lord.

KEY VERSE/S
Ye have wearied the Lord with your words. Yet ye say, Wherein have we wearied him? When ye say, Every one that doeth evil is good in the sight of the Lord, and he delighteth in them; or, Where is the God of judgment?
Malachi 2: 17

Behold, I will send my messenger,
and he shall prepare the way before
me: and the Lord, whom ye seek, shall
suddenly come to his temple, even the
messenger of the covenant, whom ye
delight in: behold, he shall come, saith
the Lord of hosts.
Malachi 3: 1

But unto you that fear my name shall
the Sun of righteousness arise with
healing in his wings; and ye shall go
forth, and grow up as calves of the stall.
Malachi 4: 2

Behold, I will send you Elijah the
prophet before the coming of the great
and dreadful day of the Lord: And he
shall turn the heart of the fathers to the
children, and the heart of the children
to their fathers, lest I come and smite
the earth with a curse.
Malachi 4: 5,6

Jesus Christ in Malachi

WHO JESUS IS
The Sun of Righteousness.

JESUS FORESHADOWED AS A TYPE/
PORTRAITS OF CHRIST
The prediction of the messenger who
will prepare the way for the Lord.

Spiritual thought

Listen to God's messengers.

Chapter by chapter breakdown

Chapter 1: God loves Israel, but indicts
the priests
Chapter 2: Israel's faithlessness in
worship and marriage
Chapter 3: Robbing God, tithing and
God's blessing

Chapter 4: The Day of the Lord, and the
coming of Elijah

Insight from Matthew Henry

Malachi 4

VERSES 1–3
Here is a reference to the first and to
the second coming of Christ: God has
fixed the day of both. Those who do
wickedly, who do not fear God's anger,
shall feel it. It is certainly to be applied
to the day of judgment, when Christ
shall be revealed in flaming fire; to
execute judgment on the proud, and
all that do wickedly. In both, Christ is a
rejoicing Light to those who serve him
faithfully. By the Sun of Righteousness
we understand Jesus Christ. Through
him believers are justified and
sanctified, and so are brought to see
light. His influences render the sinner
holy, joyful, and fruitful. It is applicable
to the graces and comforts of the Holy
Spirit, brought into the souls of men.
Christ gave the Spirit to those who are
his, to shine in their hearts, and to be a
Comforter to them, a Sun and a Shield.
That day which to the wicked will burn
as an oven, will to the righteous be
bright as the morning; it is what they
wait for, more than those that wait for
the morning. Christ came as the Sun,
to bring, not only light to a dark world,
but health to a distempered world.
Souls shall increase in knowledge and
spiritual strength. Their growth is as
that of calves of the stall, not as the
flower of the field, which is slender and
weak, and soon withers.

Encouragement from Old Testament books (1)

Classification of Old Testament books

The Old Testament has thirty-nine books, which fall into four categories:

- the books of law
- the books of history
- the books of poetry
- the books of prophecy.

Literary genre

A wide variety of literary genres are found among the books of the Old Testament:

- Historical narrative
- Song
- Romance
- Didactic treatise
- Personal correspondence
- Memoirs
- Satire
- Biography
- Autobiography
- Law
- Prophecy
- Parable
- Allegory

Old Testament authors

The writers of the Old Testament came from different backgrounds.

Kings – David, Solomon

Political leader – Moses

Governor – Daniel

Priest – Ezra

General – Joshua

Shepherd – Amos

Cupbearer – Nehemiah

AUTHORS OF INDIVIDUAL BOOKS
Some of the books of the Old Testament have easily identifiable authors but others are still unknown. The authorship of some books is still uncertain. The list below gives the traditionally authors of the Old Testament books.

Genesis: Moses

Exodus: Moses

Leviticus: Moses

Numbers: Moses

Deuteronomy: Moses

Joshua: Authors unknown

Judges: Authors unknown

Ruth: Authors unknown

1 and 2 Samuel: Authors unknown

1 and 2 Kings: Authors unknown

1 and 2 Chronicles: Authors unknown

Ezra: Ezra

Nehemiah: Nehemiah

Esther: Author unknown

Job: Author unknown

Psalms: The Psalms were written by a number of people: King David, Moses, Solomon, the sons of Korah, the sons of Asaph, and Ethan the Ezrahite. Some Psalms remain anonymous.

Proverbs: King Solomon, with Proverbs 30 written by Agur and Proverbs 31 written by Lemuel.

Ecclesiastes: Author unknown

Song of Solomon: King Solomon

Isaiah: Isaiah

Jeremiah: Jeremiah

Lamentations: Jeremiah

Ezekiel: Ezekiel

Daniel: Daniel

Hosea: Hosea

Joel: Joel

Amos: Amos

Obadiah: Obadiah

Jonah: Jonah

Micah: Micah

Nahum: Nahum

Habakkuk : Habakkuk

Zephaniah: Zephaniah

Haggai: Haggai

Zechariah: Zechariah

Malachi: Malachi

Word of God

God's Word is called by a wide variety of names in the Bible.

Book

Ps. 40: 7; Rev. 22: 19

Book of the Lord

Is. 34: 16

Book of the Law

Neh. 8: 3; Gal. 3: 10

Good Word of God

Heb. 6: 5

Holy Scriptures

Rom. 1: 2; 2 Tim. 3: 15

Law of the Lord

Ps. 1: 2; Is. 30: 9

Oracles of God

Rom. 3: 2; 1 Pet. 4: 11

Scriptures

1 Cor. 15: 3

Scriptures of Truth

Dan. 10: 21

Sword of the Spirit

Eph. 6: 17

Encouragement from Old Testament books (2)

Word of God, continued

The Word
James 1: 21–23; 1 Pet. 2: 2

Word of God
Luke 11: 28; Heb. 4: 12

Word of Christ
Col. 3: 16

Word of Life
Phil. 2: 16

Word of Truth
2 Tim. 2: 15; James 1: 18

Likened to:

Seed
Matt. 13: 3–8; Matt. 13: 18–23;
Matt. 13: 37,38; Mark 4: 3–20;
Mark 4: 26–32; Luke 8: 5–15

A two-edged sword
Heb. 4: 12

To be read publicly:

General references
Deut. 31: 11–13; Josh. 8: 33–35;
2 Kgs. 23: 2; 2 Chr. 17: 7–9; Neh. 8: 1–8;
Neh. 8: 13; Neh. 8: 18; Jer. 36: 6;
Acts 13: 15; Acts 13: 27; Col. 4: 16;
1 Thess. 5: 27

The people stood and responded by saying, "Amen"
Neh. 8: 5–6; Ex. 24: 7; Deut. 27: 12–26

Expounded
Neh. 8: 8

Expounded by Jesus
Luke 4: 16–27; Luke 24: 27; Luke 24: 45

Searched
Acts 17: 11
Searching of, enjoined
John 5: 39; John 7: 52

Texts of, to be written on doorposts
Deut. 6: 9; Deut. 11: 20

Not to be added to, or taken from
Deut. 4: 2; Deut. 12: 32; Rev. 22: 18,19

Conviction of sin from reading
2 Kgs. 22: 9–13; 2 Chr. 17: 7–10; 2 Chr. 34

Fulfilled by Jesus
Matt. 5: 17; Luke 24: 27; John 19: 24

Testify of Jesus
GENERAL REFERENCES
John 5: 39; Acts 10: 43; Acts 18: 28;
1 Cor. 15: 3

Introductions
The following pages give introductions to each Old Testament book as well as some verses from most of the books.
   Most of the introductions are

taken from one of the all-time classic translations of the Bible, the Geneva Bible, first published in 1599. This was the first study Bible to be published and the introductions are taken from its introductions to each Old Testament book. A few of the introductions are by Adam Clarke, and a few by the great Non-Conformist Bible commentator, Matthew Henry.

There are many individual verses in the Old Testament which, even if we do not know their context, warm the heart. A selection of these verses come with the above introductions.

Alphabetical list of Bible books

Acts

Amos

1 and 2 Chronicles
Colossians
1 Corinthians
2 Corinthians

Daniel
Deuteronomy

Ecclesiastes
Ephesians
Esther
Exodus
Ezekiel
Ezra

Galatians
Genesis

Habakkuk
Haggai
Hebrews
Hosea

Isaiah

James
Jeremiah
Job
Joel
John
1,2,3 John
Jonah
Joshua
Jude
Judges

1 and 2 Kings

Lamentations
Leviticus
Luke

Malachi
Mark
Matthew
Micah

Nahum
Nehemiah
Numbers

Obadiah

1 and 2 Peter
Philemon
Philippians
Proverbs
Psalms

Revelation
Romans
Ruth

1 and 2 Samuel
Song of Solomon
1 and 2 Thessalonians
1 and 2 Timothy

Titus

Zechariah
Zephaniah

Genesis

Introduction

Moses in effect declares three things, which are in this book chiefly to be considered:

First, that the world and all things in it were created by God, and to praise his Name for the infinite graces, with which he had endued him, fell willingly from God through disobedience, who yet for his own mercies sake restored him to life, and confirmed him in the same by his promise of Christ to come, by whom he should overcome Satan, death and hell.

Secondly, that the wicked, unmindful of God's most excellent benefits, remained still in their wickedness, and so falling most horribly from sin to sin, provoked God (who by his preachers called them continually to repentance) at length to destroy the whole world.

Thirdly, he assures us by the examples of Abraham, Isaac, Jaco,b and the other the patriarchs, that his mercies never fail those whom he chooses to be his Church, and to profess his Name in earth, but in all their afflictions and persecutions he assists them, sends comfort, and delivers them, so that the beginning, increase, preservation, and success of it might be attributed to God only.

Moses shows by the examples of Cain, Ishmael, Esau, and others, who were noble in man's judgment, that this Church depends not on the estimation and nobility of the world: and also by the fewness of those, who have at all times worshiped him purely according to his word that it stands not in the multitude, but in the poor and despised, in the small flock and little number, that man in his wisdom might be confounded, and the name of God praised forever.

1599 Geneva Study Bible

Verses of encouragement

Gen. 1: 26

"And God said, Let Us make man in Our image, after Our likeness: and let them have dominion over the fish of the sea, and over the fowl of the air, and over the cattle, and over all the earth, and over every creeping thing that creepeth upon the earth."

Gen. 12: 2–3

"And I will make of thee a great nation, and I will bless thee, and make thy name great; and thou shalt be a blessing. And I will bless them that bless thee, and curse him that curseth thee: and in thee shall all families of the earth be blessed."

Gen. 15: 1

"After these things the Word of the LORD came unto Abram in a vision, saying, Fear not, Abram: I am thy Shield, and thy Exceeding Great Reward."

Gen. 15: 6

"And he believed in the LORD; and He counted it to him for righteousness."

Gen. 17: 6–7

"And I will make thee exceeding fruitful, and I will make nations of thee, and kings shall come out of thee. And I will establish My Covenant between Me and thee and thy seed after thee in their generations for an Everlasting Covenant, to be a God unto thee, and to thy seed after thee."

Gen. 18: 14

"Is any thing too hard for the LORD?"

Gen. 18: 17

"And the LORD said, Shall I hide from Abraham that thing which I do."

Gen. 18: 25

"That be far from Thee to do after this manner, to slay the righteous with the wicked: and that the righteous should be as the wicked, that be far from Thee: Shall not the Judge of all the earth do right?"

Gen. 21: 22

"And it came to pass at that time, that Abimelech and Phichol the chief captain of his host spake unto Abraham, saying, God is with thee in all that thou doest."

Gen. 24: 40

"And he said unto me, The LORD, before Whom I walk, will send His Angel with thee, and prosper thy way."

Gen. 26: 3

"Sojourn in this land, and I will be with thee, and will bless thee; for unto thee, and unto thy seed, I will give all these countries, and I will perform the oath which I sware unto Abraham thy father."

Exodus

Introduction

After Jacob by God's commandment in Gen. 46: 3 had brought his family into Egypt, where they remained for four hundred years, and from seventy people grew to an infinite number so that the king and the country endeavored both by tyranny and cruel slavery to suppress them: the Lord according to his promise in Gen. 15: 14 had compassion on his Church, and delivered them, but plagued their enemies in most strange and varied ways.

The more the tyranny of the wicked raged against his Church, the more his heavy judgments increased against them, till Pharaoh and his army were drowned in the sea, which gave an entry and passage to the children of God. As the ingratitude of man is great, so they immediately forgot God's wonderful benefits and although he had given them the Passover as a sign and memorial of the same, yet they fell to distrust, and tempted God with various complaining and grudging against him and his ministers: sometimes out of ambition, sometimes lack of drink or meat to satisfy their lusts, sometimes idolatry, or such like.

For this reason, God punished them with severe rods and plagues, that by his correction they might turn to him for help against his scourges, and earnestly repent for their rebellion and wickedness. Because God loves them to the end, whom he has once begun to love, he punished them not as they deserved, but dealt with them mercifully, and with new benefits labored to overcome their malice: for he still governed them and gave them his word and Law, both concerning the way to serve him, and also the form of judgments and civil policy: with the intent that they would not serve God after as they pleased, but according to the order, that his heavenly wisdom had appointed.

Ex. 14: 13,14 "And Moses said unto the people, Fear ye not, stand still, and see the salvation of the LORD, which He will shew to you to day: for the Egyptians whom ye have seen to day, ye shall see them again no more for ever. The LORD shall fight for you, and ye shall hold your peace."

1599 Geneva Study Bible

Verses of encouragement

Ex. 15: 11

"Who is like unto Thee, O LORD, among the gods? who is like Thee, glorious in holiness, fearful in praises, doing wonders?"

Ex. 15: 17

"Thou shalt bring them in, and plant them in the mountain of Thine inheritance, in the place, O LORD, which Thou hast made for Thee to dwell in, in the Sanctuary, O LORD, which Thy hands have established."

Ex. 19: 5

"Now therefore, if ye will obey My voice indeed, and keep My Covenant, then ye shall be a peculiar treasure unto Me above all people: for all the earth is Mine."

Ex. 33: 13–14

"Now therefore, I pray Thee, if I have found grace in Thy sight, shew me now Thy way, that I may know Thee, that I may find grace in Thy sight: and consider that this nation is Thy people. And He said, My presence shall go with thee, and I will give thee rest."

The Ten Commandments and the teaching of Jesus

The New Testament records some teaching of Jesus which can be linked to each of the Ten Commandments.

1st commandment and Matt. 22: 37. Jesus said to him, "'You shall love the LORD your God with all your heart, with all your soul, and with all your mind.'" Matthew 22: 37 NKJV

2nd commandment and John 4: 24. "God is Spirit, and those who worship Him must worship in spirit and truth." John 4: 24 NKJV

3rd commandment and Matt. 5: 34. "But I say to you, do not swear at all: neither by heaven, for it is God's throne." Matthew 5: 34 NKJV

4th commandment and Mark 2: 27; Luke 13: 14–16.
"The Sabbath was made for man, and not man for the Sabbath." Mark 2: 27 NKJV

5th commandment and Matt. 15: 4–6, 19: 19; Mark 7: 10.
"For Moses said, 'Honor your father and your mother'; and, 'He who curses father or mother, let him be put to death.'" Mark 7: 10 NKJV

6th commandment and Matt. 5: 21. "You have heard that it was said to those of old, 'You shall not murder.'" Matthew 5: 21 NKJV

7th commandment and Matt. 5: 28; 19: 9,18.

8th commandment and Matt. 15: 19.

9th commandment and Matt. 12: 34–37.

10th commandment and Matt. 5: 28. "But I say to you that whoever looks at a woman to lust for her has already committed adultery with her in his heart." Matthew 5: 28 NKJV

Leviticus and Numbers

Leviticus

Introduction

As God daily by most singular benefits declared himself mindful of his Church: he did not want them to have opportunity to trust either in themselves, or to depend on others, either for lack of physical things, or anything that belonged to his divine service and religion. Therefore he ordained various kinds of duties and sacrifices, to assure them of forgiveness for their offenses (if they offered them in true faith and obedience.)

Also he appointed the priests and Levites, their apparel, offices, conversation, and portion; he showed what feasts they should observe, and when. Moreover, he declares by these sacrifices and ceremonies that the reward of sin is death, and that without the blood of Christ the innocent Lamb, there can be no forgiveness of sins. Because they should not give priority to their own inventions (which God detested, as appears by the terrible example of Nadab and Abihu) he prescribed even to the least things, what they should do, what beasts they should offer and eat, what diseases were contagious and to be avoided, how they should purge all types of filthiness and pollution, whose company they should flee, what marriages were lawful, and what customs were profitable.

After declaring these things, he promised favor and blessing to those who keep his laws, and threatened his curse to those who transgressed them.

1599 Geneva Study Bible

Verses of encouragement

Lev. 23: 10–11

"Speak unto the children of Israel, and say unto them, When ye be come into the land which I give unto you, and shall reap the harvest thereof…"

Lev. 25: 23

"The land shall not be sold for ever: for the land is Mine; for ye are strangers and sojourners with Me."

Lev. 26: 9

"For I will have respect unto you, and make you fruitful, and multiply you, and establish My Covenant with you."

Lev. 26: 12

"And I will walk among you, and will be your God, and ye shall be My people."

Numbers

Introduction

In that as God has appointed that his Church in this world shall be under the cross, both so they could learn not to put their trust in worldly things, and also feel his comfort, when all other help fails: he did not immediately bring his people, after their departure out of Egypt, into the land which he had promised them: but led them to and fro for the space of forty years, and kept them in continual exercises before they enjoyed it, to try their faith, teach them to forget the world, and to depend on him. Which trial greatly profited, to discern the wicked and the hypocrites from the faithful and true servants of God, who served him with pure heart, while the other, preferring their earthly lusts to God's glory, and making religion to serve their purpose, complained when they lacked enough to satisfy their lusts, and despised those who God had appointed as rulers over them. By reason of which they provoked God's terrible judgments against them, and are set forth as a notable example for all ages, to beware how they abuse God's word, prefer their own lusts to his will, or despise his ministers. Nonetheless, God is always true to his promise, and governs his people by his Holy Spirit, that either they fall not to such inconveniences, or else return to him quickly in true repentance: and therefore he continues his graces toward them, he gives them ordinances and instructions, as well for religion, as outward policy: he preserves them against all deceit and conspiracy, and gives them many victories against their enemies. To avoid all controversies that might arise, he takes away the occasions, by dividing among all the tribes, both the land which they had won, and that also which he had promised, as seemed best to his godly wisdom.

1599 Geneva Study Bible

Verses of encouragement

Num. 6: 24–26

"The LORD bless thee, and keep thee: The LORD make His face shine upon thee, and be gracious unto thee: The LORD lift up His countenance upon thee, and give thee peace."

Num. 14: 8

"If the LORD delight in us, then He will bring us into this land, and give it us; a land which floweth with milk and honey."

Num. 14: 21

"But as truly as I live, all the earth shall be filled with the glory of the LORD."

Deuteronomy

Introduction

The wonderful love of God toward his Church is actively set forth in this book. Even through their ingratitude and many rebellions against God, for the space of forty years. (Deut. 9: 7) they deserved to have been cut off from the number of his people, and forever to have been deprived of the use of his holy word and ordinances: yet he ever preserved his Church even for his own mercy's sake, and would still have his name called upon among them. Wherefore he brings them into the land of Canaan, destroys their enemies, gives them their country, towns, and goods, and exhorts them by the example of their fathers (whose infidelity, idolatry, adulteries, complaining, and rebellions, he had most severely punished) to fear and obey the Lord, to embrace and keep his law without adding to it or diminishing from it.

For by his word he would be known to be their God, and they his people, by his word he would govern his Church, and by the same they would learn to obey him: by his word he would discern the false prophet from the true, light from darkness, ignorance from knowledge, and his own people from all the other nations and infidels: teaching them by it to refuse and detest, destroy and abolish whatever is not agreeable to his holy will, seem it otherwise never so good or precious in the eyes of man. For this cause God promised to raise up kings and governors, for the setting forth of his word and preservation of his Church: giving to them a special charge for the executing of it: whom therefore he wills to exercise themselves diligently in the continual study and meditation of the same: that they might learn to fear the Lord, love their subjects, abhor covetousness and vices, and whatever offends the majesty of God. As he had before instructed their fathers in all things belonging both to his spiritual service and also for the maintenance of that society which is between men: so he prescribes here anew all such laws and ordinances, which either concern his divine service, or else are necessary for a common good: appointing to every estate and degree their charge and duty: as well, how to rule and live in the fear of God, as to nourish friendship toward their neighbors, and to preserve the order which God has established among men: threatening most horrible plagues to them that transgress his commandments, and promising blessings and happiness to those who observe and obey them.

1599 Geneva Study Bible

Verses of encouragement

Deut. 4: 40

"Thou shalt keep therefore His statutes, and His Commandments, which I command thee this day, that it may go well with thee, and with thy children after thee, and that thou mayest prolong thy days upon the earth, which the LORD thy God giveth thee, for ever."

Deut. 6: 6–7

"And these Words, which I command thee this day, shall be in thine heart: And thou shalt teach Them diligently unto thy children, and shalt talk of Them when thou sittest in thine house, and when thou walkest by the way, and when thou liest down, and when thou risest up."

Deut. 7: 6

"For thou art an holy people unto the LORD thy God: the LORD thy God hath chosen thee to be a special people unto Himself, above all people that are upon the face of the earth."

Deut. 7: 9

"Know therefore that the LORD thy God, He is God, the faithful God, which keepeth Covenant and mercy with them that love Him and keep His Commandments to a thousand generations."

Deut. 8: 3

"And He humbled thee, and suffered thee to hunger, and fed thee with manna, which thou knewest not, neither did thy fathers know; that He might make thee know that man doth not live by bread only, but by every Word that proceedeth out of the mouth of the LORD doth man live."

Deut. 14: 2

"For thou art an holy people unto the LORD thy God, and the LORD hath chosen thee to be a peculiar people unto Himself, above all the nations that are upon the earth."

Deut. 29: 9

"Keep therefore the Words of this Covenant, and do Them, that ye may prosper in all that ye do."

Deut. 29: 29

"The secret things belong unto the LORD our God: but those things which are revealed belong unto us and to our children for ever, that we may do all the Words of this Law."

Joshua, Judges, Ruth, 1 and 2 Samuel

Joshua

Introduction

In this book the Holy Spirit sets most lively before us the accomplishment of God's promise, who as he promised by the mouth of Moses, that a prophet would be raised up to the people like him, whom he wills to obey, (Deut. 18: 15): so he shows himself true to his promise, as at all other times, and after the death of Moses his faithful servant, he raises up Joshua to be ruler and governor over his people, that they should neither be discouraged for lack of a captain, nor have reason to distrust God's promises later. So that Joshua might be confirmed in his calling, and the people also might have no opportunity to grudge, as though he were not approved by God: he is adorned with most excellent gifts and graces from God, both to govern the people with counsel, and to defend them with strength, that he lacks nothing which either belongs to a valiant captain, or a faithful minister. So he overcomes all difficulties, and brings them into the land of Canaan: which according to God's ordinance he divides among the people and appoints their borders: he established laws and ordinances, and put them in remembrance of God's revealed benefits, assuring them of his grace and favor if they obey God, and of his plagues and vengeance if they disobey him. This history represents Jesus Christ the true Joshua, who leads us into eternal happiness, signified to us by this land of Canaan.

1599 Geneva Study Bible

Verses of encouragement

Josh. 1: 7–9 "Only be thou strong and very courageous, that thou mayest observe to do according to all the Law, which Moses My servant commanded thee: turn not from it to the right hand or to the left, that thou mayest prosper whithersoever thou goest. This Book Of The Law shall not depart out of thy mouth; but thou shalt meditate therein day and night, that thou mayest observe to do according to all that is written therein: for then thou shalt make thy way prosperous, and then thou shalt have good success. Have not I commanded thee? Be strong and of a good courage; be not afraid, neither be thou dismayed: for the Lord thy God is with thee whithersoever thou goest."

Josh. 1: 13 "Remember the Word which Moses the servant of the Lord commanded you, saying, The Lord your God hath given you rest, and hath given you this land."

Judges

Introduction

After the death of Joshua the Israelites purpose to attack the remaining Canaanites; and the tribe of Judah is directed to go up first, 1, 2.

Judah and Simeon unite, attack the Canaanites and Perrizites, kill ten thousand of them, take Adoni-bezek prisoner, cut off his thumbs and great toes, and bring him to Jerusalem, where he dies, 3–7.

Jerusalem conquered, 8.

A new war with the Canaanites under the direction of Caleb, 9–11.

Kirjath-sepher taken by Othniel, on which he receives, as a reward, Achsah, the daughter of Caleb and with her a south land with springs of water, 12–15.

The Kenites dwell among the people, 16.

Judah and Simeon destroy the Canaanites in Zephath, Gaza, etc., 17–19.

Hebron is given to Caleb, 20.

Of the Benjamites, house of Joseph, tribe of Manasseh, 21–27.

The Israelites put the Canaanites to tribute, 28.

Of the tribes of Ephraim, Zebulun, Asher, and Naphtali, 29–33.

The Amorites force the children of Dan into the mountains, 34–36.

Adam Clarke

Ruth

Introduction

This book is called Ruth, who is the main person spoken of in this writing. In which also the state of the Church is set forth figuratively, being subject to many afflictions and yet eventually God gives good and joyful offspring, teaching us to abide with patience till God delivers us out of troubles. In this also it is described how Jesus Christ, who according to the flesh came from

David, proceeded by Ruth, of whom the Lord Jesus promised to come, nonetheless she was a Moabite of base condition, and a stranger to the people of God; declaring to us by it that the Gentiles would be sanctified by him, and joined with his people, and that there would be one sheepfold, and one shepherd. It would appear that this account belongs to the time of the judges.

1599 Geneva Study Bible

Verse of encouragement

Ruth 1: 10 "But Ruth said:
'Entreat me not to leave you,
Or to turn back from following after you;
For wherever you go, I will go;
And wherever you lodge, I will lodge;
Your people shall be my people,
And your God, my God.'"

1 and 2 Samuel

1 Samuel

INTRODUCTION

As God had ordained in (Deut. 17: 14), that when the Israelites entered the land of Canaan, he would appoint a king for them: so here in the first book of Samuel the state of the people under their first king Saul is declared. Not content with the order that God had temporarily appointed for the government of his Church, they demanded a king, so that they might be as other nations.

1 and 2 Samuel, 1 Kings

1 and 2 Samuel, continued

1 Samuel, continued

INTRODUCTION, CONTINUED

As well they thought they would be better off, not because they could serve God better by it, but because they would be under the safeguard of him who represented Jesus Christ the true deliverer. Therefore God gave them a tyrant and a hypocrite to rule over them, so that they might learn that a king is not sufficient to defend them, unless God by his power preserves and keeps them. Therefore he punishes the ingratitude of his people, and sends them continual wars both at home and abroad. Also, because Saul, whom God had given to the honor of a king out of nothing, did not acknowledge God's mercy to him, but rather disobeyed the word of God and was not zealous of his glory, he was removed from his estate by God, and David the true figure of Messiah was placed in his stead. His patience, modesty, constancy, persecution by open enemies, feigned friends, and deceitful flatterers, is left to the Church and to every member of it, as a pattern and example of their state and calling.

1599 Geneva Study Bible

Verse of encouragement

1 Sam. 25: 6
"And thus shall ye say to him that liveth in prosperity, Peace be both to thee, and peace be to thine house, and peace be unto all that thou hast."

2 Samuel

INTRODUCTION

This book and the former are called Samuel, because they contain the conception, birth and the whole course of his life, and also the lives and acts of two kings, that is, of Saul and David, whom he anointed and consecrated kings by the ordinance of God. The first book contains those things which God brought to pass among this people under the government of Samuel and Saul. This second book declares the noble acts of David, after the death of Saul when he began to reign, to the end of his kingdom, and how it was expanded by him. It also contains the great troubles and dangers he sustained both within his house and without, the horrible and dangerous insurrections, uproars, and treasons wrought against him, partly by false counselors, feigned friends and flatterers and partly by his own children and people. By God's assistance he overcame all difficulties, and enjoyed his kingdom in rest and peace. In the person of David the Scripture sets forth Christ Jesus the chief king, who came from David according to the flesh, and was persecuted on every side with outward and inward enemies, as well in his own person, as in his members, but at length he overcomes all his enemies, and gives his Church victory against all power both spiritual and temporal; and so reigns with them, king for ever.

1599 Geneva Study Bible

Verses of encouragement

2 Sam. 22: 2–3
"The Lord is my Rock, and my Fortress, and my Deliverer; The God Of My Rock; in Him will I trust: He is my Shield, and the Horn Of My Salvation, my High Tower, and my Refuge, my Savior; Thou savest me from violence."

2 Sam. 22: 20–21
"He brought me forth also into a large place: He delivered me, because He delighted in me. The Lord rewarded me according to my righteousness according to the cleanness of my hands hath He recompensed me."

2 Sam. 22: 29–34
"For Thou art my Lamp, O Lord: and the Lord will lighten my darkness. For by Thee I have run through a troop: by my God have I leaped over a wall. As for God, His way is perfect; the Word of the Lord is tried: He is a Buckler to all them that trust in Him. For who is God, save the Lord? and who is a Rock, save our God? God is my Strength and Power: and He maketh my way perfect. He maketh my feet like hinds' feet: and setteth me upon my high places."

2 Sam. 22: 47
"The Lord liveth; and blessed be my Rock; and exalted be the God of the Rock Of My Salvation."

1 Kings

Introduction

Because the children of God should expect no continual rest and quietness in this world, the Holy Spirit sets before our eyes in this book the variety and change of things, which came to the people of Israel from the death of David, Solomon, and the rest of the kings, to the death of Ahab. Declaring that flourishing kingdoms, unless they are preserved by God's protection, (who then favors them when his word is truly set forth, virtue esteemed, vice punished, and concord maintained) fall to decay and come to nothing as appears by the dividing of the kingdom under Rehoboam and Jeroboam, who were one people before and now by the just punishment of God were made two. Judah and Benjamin were under Rehoboam, and this was called the kingdom of Judah. The other ten tribes held with Jeroboam, and this was called the kingdom of Israel. The king of Judah had his throne in Jerusalem, and the king of Israel in Samaria, after it was built by Omri Ahab's father. Because our Savior Christ according to the flesh, comes from the stock of David, the genealogy of the kings of Judah is here described, from Solomon to Joram the son of Jehoshaphat, who reigned over Judah in Jerusalem as Ahab did over Israel in Samaria.

1599 Geneva Study Bible

Verse of encouragement

1 Kgs. 5: 4
"But now the Lord my God hath given me rest on every side, so that there is neither adversary nor evil occurrent."

2 Kings, 1 Chronicles, 2 Chronicles

2 Kings

Introduction

This second book contains the acts of the kings of Judah and Israel: that is, of Israel, from the death of Ahab to the last king Hoshea, who was imprisoned by the king of Assyria, and his city Samaria taken, and the ten tribes led into captivity by the just plague of God for their idolatry and disobedience to God. Also of Judah, from the reign of Jehoram son of Jehoshaphat to Zedekiah, who for contemning the Lord's commandment by his prophets, and neglecting his many admonitions by famine and other means was taken by his enemies, saw his sons most cruelly slain before his face, and his own eyes put out, as the Lord had declared to him before by his prophet Jeremiah. By the just vengeance of God for contempt of his word Jerusalem was destroyed, the temple burnt, and he and all his people were led away captives into Babylon. In this book are notable examples of God's favor toward those rulers and people who obey his prophets, and embrace his word: and contrariwise of his plagues on those who neglect his ministers, and do not obey his commandments.

1599 Geneva Study Bible

1 Chronicles

Introduction

The laws comprehend both these books in one, which the Grecians because of the length, divide into two: and they are called Chronicles, because they note briefly the history from Adam to the return from their captivity in Babylon. But these are not the books of Chronicles which are mentioned in the books of the kings of Judah and Israel, which set forth the story of both kingdoms, and later perished in the captivity, but an abridgement of the same, and were gathered by Ezra, as the Jews write after their return from Babylon. This first book contains a brief rehearsal of the children of Adam to Abraham, Isaac, Jacob, and the twelve patriarchs, chiefly of Judah, and the reign of David, because Christ came from him according to the flesh. Therefore it shows his acts both concerning civil government, and also the administration concerning religion, for the good success of which he rejoices and gives thanks to the Lord.

1599 Geneva Study Bible

Verses of encouragement

1 Chr. 4: 10 "And Jabez called on the God of Israel, saying, Oh that Thou wouldest bless me indeed, and enlarge my coast, and that Thine hand might be with me, and that Thou wouldest keep me from evil, that it may not grieve me!

And God granted him that which he requested."

1 Chr. 16: 27 "Glory and honor are in His presence; strength and gladness are in His place."

1 Chr. 29: 11 "Thine, O Lord, is the greatness, and the power, and the glory, and the victory, and the majesty: for all that is in the heaven and in the earth is Thine; Thine is the Kingdom, O Lord, and Thou art exalted as Head Above All."

2 Chronicles

Introduction

This second book contains in brief the contents of the two books of the kings: that is, from the reign of Solomon to the destruction of Jerusalem and the Babylonian captivity. In this story some things are told in more detail than in the books of the kings and therefore help greatly in the understanding of the prophets. Three things are chiefly to be considered here: First, that when the godly kings saw the plagues of God prepared against their country for sin, they turned to the Lord and by earnest prayer were heard, and the plagues removed. Secondly, while the good rulers always loved the prophets of God and were zealous to set forth his religion throughout their dominions, it offended God greatly that the wicked hated his ministers, deposed them and set up idolatry and attempted to serve God according to the fantasy of men. Thus we have the chief acts from the beginning of the world to the

rebuilding of Jerusalem in the 32nd year of Darius, in total 3568 years and six months.

1599 Geneva Study Bible

Verses of encouragement

2 Chr. 9: 8 "Blessed be the Lord thy God, which delighted in thee to set thee on His Throne, to be king for the Lord thy God."

2 Chr. 16: 8 "Were not the Ethiopians and the Lubims a huge host, with very many chariots and horsemen? yet, because thou didst rely on the Lord, He delivered them into thine hand. For the eyes of the Lord run to and fro throughout the whole earth, to shew Himself strong in the behalf of them whose heart is perfect toward Him."

2 Chr. 20: 15 "Thus saith the Lord unto you, Be not afraid nor dismayed by reason of this great multitude; for the battle is not yours, but God's."

2 Chr. 20: 17 "Ye shall not need to fight in this battle: set yourselves, stand ye still, and see the salvation of the Lord with you, O Judah and Jerusalem: fear not, nor be dismayed; to morrow go out against them: for the Lord will be with you."

2 Chr. 20: 20 "Jehoshaphat stood and said, Hear me, O Judah, and ye inhabitants of Jerusalem; Believe in the Lord your God, so shall ye be established; believe His prophets, so shall ye prosper."

2 Chr. 26: 5 "And he sought God in the days of Zechariah, who had understanding in the visions of God: and as long as he sought the Lord, God made him to prosper."

Ezra, Nehemiah, Esther

Ezra

Introduction

As the Lord is always merciful to his Church, and does not punish them, but so that they should see their own miseries, and be exercised under the cross, that they might contemn the world, and aspire to the heavens: so after he had visited the Jews, and kept them in bondage seventy years in a strange country among infidels and idolaters, he remembered his tender mercies and their infirmities, and therefore for his own sake raised up a deliverer, and moved both the heart of the chief ruler to pity them, and also by him punished those who had kept them in slavery. Nonetheless, lest they should grow into a contempt of God's great benefits, he keeps them still in exercise, and raises domestic enemies, who try as much as they can to hinder their worthy enterprises: yet by the exhortation of the prophet they went forward little by little till their work was finished. The author of this book was Ezra, who was a priest and scribe of the Law, as in Ezra 7: 6. He returned to Jerusalem the sixth year of Darius, who succeeded Cyrus, that is, about fifty years after the first return under Zerubbabel, when the temple was built. He brought with him a great company and much treasure, with letters to the king's officers for all things needed for the temple: and at his coming he fixed that which was amiss, and set things in order.

1599 Geneva Study Bible

Verses of encouragement

Ezra 6: 14 "And the elders of the Jews builded, and they prospered through the prophesying of Haggai the prophet and Zechariah the son of Iddo. And they builded, and finished it, according to the Commandment of the God of Israel."

Ezra 7: 10 "For Ezra had prepared his heart to seek the law of the Lord, and to do it, and to teach in Israel statutes and judgments."

Nehemiah

Introduction

God, in all ages and at all times, sets up worthy persons for the convenience and profit of his Church, as now within the compass of seventy years he raised up various excellent men for the preservation of his people after their return from Babylon. Zerubbabel, Ezra, and Nehemiah, of which the first was their captain to bring them home, and provided that the temple was built: the second reformed their manners and planted religion: and the third built up the walls, delivered the people from oppression and provided that the law of God was carried out among them. He was a godly man, and in great authority with the king, so that the king favored him greatly and gave him letters to accomplish all the things he desired. This book is also called the second of Ezra by the Latins because he was the author of it.

1599 Geneva Study Bible

Verses of encouragement

Neh. 1: 8–11 "Remember, I beseech thee, the word that thou commandedst thy servant Moses, saying, If ye transgress, I will scatter you abroad among the nations: But if ye turn unto me, and keep my commandments, and do them; though there were of you cast out unto the uttermost part of the heaven, yet will I gather them from thence, and will bring them unto the place that I have chosen to set my name there. Now these are thy servants and thy people, whom thou hast redeemed by thy great power, and by thy strong hand. O Lord, I beseech thee, let now thine ear be attentive to the prayer of thy servant, and to the prayer of thy servants, who desire to fear thy name: and prosper, I pray thee, thy servant this day, and grant him mercy in the sight of this man. For I was the king's cupbearer."

Neh. 2: 20 "Then answered I them, and said unto them, The God of Heaven, He will prosper us; therefore we His servants will arise and build."

Neh. 5: 9 "Also I said, It is not good that ye do: ought ye not to walk in the fear of our God because of the reproach of the heathen our enemies?"

Neh. 6: 3 "And I sent messengers unto them, saying, I am doing a great work, so that I cannot come down: why should the work cease, whilst I leave it, and come down to you?"

Neh. 6: 15,16 "So the wall was finished in the twenty and fifth day of the month Elul, in fifty and two days. And it came to pass, that when all our enemies heard thereof, and all the heathen that were about us saw these things, they were much cast down in their own eyes: for they perceived that this work was wrought of our God."

Neh. 8: 8 "So they read in the book in the law of God distinctly, and gave the sense, and caused them to understand the reading."

Neh. 8: 10 "Then He said unto them, Go your way, eat the fat, and drink the sweet, and send portions unto them for whom nothing is prepared: for this day is holy unto our Lord: neither be ye sorry; for the joy of the Lord is your strength."

Esther

Introduction

Because of the variety of names, by which they used to call their kings, and the number of years in which the Hebrews and the Greeks vary, various authors write concerning that Ahasuerus but it seems in Dan. 9: 1 that he was Darius king of the Medes and son of Astyages also called Ahasuerus which was a name of honor and signified great and chief as chief head. In this is declared the great mercies of God toward his church: who never fails them in their greatest dangers.

Esther and Job

Esther, continued

Introduction, continued

But when all hope of worldly help fades, he stirs up some, by whom he sends comfort and deliverance.

In this also is described the ambition, pride and cruelty of the wicked when they come to honor and their sudden fall when they are at their highest and how God preserves and prefers them who are zealous of his glory and have a care and love for their brethren.

1599 Geneva Study Bible

Verse of encouragement

Esther 4: 14
"For if you remain completely silent at this time, relief and deliverance will arise for the Jews from another place, but you and your father's house will perish. Yet who knows whether you have come to the kingdom for such a time as this?"

Job

Introduction

In this history the example of patience is set before our eyes.

This holy man Job was not only extremely afflicted in outward things and in his body, but also in his mind and conscience, by the sharp temptation of his wife and friends: who by their vehement words and subtle disputations brought him almost to despair.

They set forth God as a sincere judge, and mortal enemy to him who had cast him off, therefore in vain he should seek him for help.

These friends came to him under pretence of consolation, and yet they tormented him more than all his afflictions did. Even so, he constantly resisted them, and eventually succeeded.

In this story we must note that Job maintains a good cause, but handles it badly. His adversaries have an evil matter, but they defend it craftily. Job held that God did not always punish men according to their sins, but that he had secret judgments, of which man knew not the cause, and therefore man could not reason against God in it, but he should be convicted.

Moreover, he was assured that God had not rejected him, yet through his great torments and afflictions he speaks many inconveniences and shows himself as a desperate man in many things, and as one that would resist God, and this is his good cause which he handles well.

Again the adversaries maintain with many good arguments that God punishes continually according to the trespass, grounding on God's providence, his justice, and man's sins, yet their intention is evil; for they labor to bring Job into despair, and so they maintain an evil cause.

Ezekiel commends Job as a just man, (Ezek. 14: 14) and James sets out his patience for an example, (James 5: 11).

1599 Geneva Study Bible

Verses of encouragement

Job 5: 19–22,25
"He shall deliver thee in six troubles: yea, in seven there shall no evil touch thee. In famine He shall redeem thee from death: and in war from the power of the sword. Thou shalt be hid from the scourge of the tongue: neither shalt thou be afraid of destruction when it cometh. At destruction and famine thou shalt laugh: neither shalt thou be afraid of the beasts of the earth... Thou shalt know also that thy seed shall be great, and thine offspring as the grass of the earth."

Job 8: 7
"Though thy beginning was small, yet thy latter end should greatly increase."

Job 17: 9
"The righteous also shall hold on his way, and he that hath clean hands shall be stronger and stronger."

Job 22: 21–26
"Acquaint now thyself with Him, and be at peace: thereby good shall come unto thee. Receive, I pray thee, the Law from His mouth, and lay up His words in thine heart. If thou return to the Almighty, thou shalt be built up, thou shalt put away iniquity far from thy tabernacles. Then shalt thou lay up gold as dust, and the gold of Ophir as the stones of the brooks. Yea, the Almighty shall be thy defense, and thou shalt have plenty of silver. For then shalt thou have thy delight in the Almighty, and shalt lift up thy face unto God."

Job 28: 28
"Behold, the fear of the Lord, that is wisdom; and to depart from evil is understanding."

Job 29: 12–13
"Because I delivered the poor that cried, and the fatherless, and him that had none to help him. The blessing of him that was ready to perish came upon me: and I caused the widow's heart to sing for joy."

Job 36: 7
"He withdraweth not His eyes from the righteous: but with kings are they on the throne; yea, He doth establish them for ever, and they are exalted."

Job 36: 11
"If they obey and serve Him, they shall spend their days in prosperity, and their years in pleasures."

Job 42: 10,12,15–17
"And the Lord turned the captivity of Job, when he prayed for his friends: also the Lord gave Job twice as much as he had before... So the Lord blessed the latter end of Job more than his beginning: for he had fourteen thousand sheep, and six thousand camels, and a thousand yoke of oxen, and a thousand she asses... And in all the land were no women found so fair as the daughters of Job: and their father gave them inheritance among their brethren. After this lived Job an hundred and forty years, and saw his sons, and his sons' sons, even four generations. So Job died, being old and full of days."

Psalms and Proverbs

Psalms

Introduction

This book of psalms is given to us by the Holy Spirit, to be esteemed as a precious treasure in which all things are contained that bring to true happiness in this present life as well as in the life to come. For the riches of true knowledge and heavenly wisdom, are here set open for us, to take of it most abundantly. If we would know the great and high majesty of God, here we may see the brightness of it shine clearly. If we would seek his incomprehensible wisdom, here is the school of the same profession. If we would comprehend his inestimable bounty, and approach near to it, and fill our hands with that treasure, here we may have a most lively and comfortable taste of it.

If we would know where our salvation lies and how to attain to everlasting life, here is Christ our Redeemer, and Mediator most evidently described. The rich man may learn the true use of his riches. The poor man may find full contentment. He who will rejoice will know true joy, and how to keep measure in it. They who are afflicted and oppressed will see what their comfort exists in, and how they should praise God when he sends them deliverance. The wicked and the persecutors of the children of God will see how the hand of God is always against them: and though he permits them to prosper for a while,

yet he bridles them, so much so that they cannot touch a hair of one's head unless he permits them, and how in the end their destruction is most miserable. Briefly here we have most present remedies against all temptations and troubles of mind and conscience, so that being well practiced in this, we may be assured against all dangers in this life, live in the true fear and love of God, and at length attain the incorruptible crown of glory, which is laid up for all who love the coming of our Lord Jesus Christ.

1599 Geneva Study Bible

Verses of encouragement

Ps. 4: 3 "But know that the Lord hath set apart him that is godly for Himself: the Lord will hear when I call unto Him."

Ps. 4: 8 "I will both lay me down in peace, and sleep: for Thou, Lord, only makest me dwell in safety."

Ps. 7: 1 "O Lord my God, in Thee do I put my trust: save me from all them that persecute me, and deliver me."

Ps. 12: 6 "The Words of the Lord are pure words: as silver tried in a furnace of earth, purified seven times."

Ps. 13: 6 "I will sing unto the Lord, because He hath dealt bountifully with me."

Ps. 16: 1 "Preserve me, O God: for in Thee do I put my trust."

Ps. 16: 6–8 "The lines are fallen unto me in pleasant places; yea, I have a goodly heritage. I will bless the Lord, Who hath given me Counsel: my reins also instruct me in the night seasons. I have set the Lord always before me: because He is at my right hand, I shall not be moved."

Ps. 16: 11 "Thou wilt shew me the path of life: in Thy presence is fullness of joy; at Thy right hand there are pleasures for evermore."

Ps. 18: 1,2 "I will love Thee, O Lord, my Strength. The Lord is my Rock, and my Fortress, and my Deliverer; my God, my Strength, in Whom I will trust; my Buckler, and the Horn Of My Salvation, and my High Tower."

Ps. 19: 14 "Let the words of my mouth, and the meditation of my heart, be acceptable in Thy sight, O Lord, my Strength, and my Redeemer."

Ps. 24: 1 "The earth is the Lord's, and the fullness thereof; the world, and they that dwell therein."

Ps. 27: 1 "The Lord is my Light and my Salvation; whom shall I fear? the Lord is The Strength Of My Life; of whom shall I be afraid?"

Ps. 27: 4 "One thing have I desired of the Lord, that will I seek after; that I may dwell in the House of the Lord all the days of my life, to behold the beauty of the Lord, and to enquire in His Temple."

Ps. 27: 14 "Wait on the Lord: be of good courage, and He shall strengthen thine heart: wait, I say, on the Lord."

Proverbs

Introduction

The wonderful love of God toward his Church is declared in this book: for as much as the sum and effect of the whole Scriptures is here set forth in these brief sentences, which partly contain doctrine, and partly manners, and also exhortations to both: of which the first nine Chapters are as a preface full of grave sentences and deep mysteries, to assure the hearts of men to the diligent reading of the parables that follow: which are left as a precious jewel to the Church, of those three thousand parables mentioned in 1 Kgs. 4: 32 and were gathered and committed to writing by Solomon's servants and incited by him.

1599 Geneva Study Bible

Verses of encouragement

Prov. 1: 33 "But whoso hearkeneth unto Me shall dwell safely, and shall be quiet from fear of evil."

Prov. 2: 8 "He keepeth the paths of judgment, and preserveth the way of His saints."

Prov. 2: 10–11 "When Wisdom entereth into thine heart, and Knowledge is pleasant unto thy soul; Discretion shall preserve thee, Understanding shall keep thee."

Proverbs and Ecclesiastes

Proverbs, continued

Verses of encouragement, continued

Prov. 3: 1–2 "My son, forget not My Law; but let thine heart keep My Commandments: For length of days, and long life, and peace, shall They add to thee."

Prov. 3: 5,6,8–10 "Trust in the Lord with all thine heart; and lean not unto thine own understanding. In all thy ways acknowledge Him, and He shall direct thy paths... It shall be health to thy navel, and marrow to thy bones. Honor the Lord with thy substance, and with the firstfruits of all thine increase: So shall thy barns be filled with plenty, and thy presses shall burst out with new wine."

Prov. 3: 13 "Happy is the man that findeth Wisdom, and the man that getteth Understanding."

Prov. 3: 16–18 "Length of days is in her right hand; and in her left hand riches and honor. Her ways are ways of pleasantness, and all her paths are peace. She is a Tree Of Life to them that lay hold upon her: and happy is every one that retaineth her."

Prov. 4: 7–10 "Wisdom is the principal thing; therefore get Wisdom: and with all thy getting get Understanding. Exalt Her, and She shall promote thee: She shall bring thee to honor, when thou dost embrace Her. She shall give to thine head an Ornament of Grace: a Crown of Glory shall she deliver to thee. Hear, O My son, and receive My Sayings; and the years of thy life shall be many."

Prov. 8: 11 "For Wisdom is better than rubies; and all the things that may be desired are not to be compared to it."

Prov. 8: 18 "Riches and honor are with Me; yea, durable riches and righteousness."

Prov. 8: 34,35 "Blessed is the man that heareth Me, watching daily at My Gates, waiting at the posts of My Doors. For whoso findeth Me findeth Life, and shall obtain favor of the Lord."

Prov. 9: 11 "For by Me thy days shall be multiplied, and the years of thy life shall be increased."

Prov. 10: 11 "The mouth of a righteous man is a well of life: but violence covereth the mouth of the wicked."

Prov. 11: 28 "He that trusteth in his riches shall fall: but the righteous shall flourish as a branch."

Prov. 12: 28 "In the way of Righteousness is life; and in the pathway thereof there is no death."

Prov. 14: 26,27 "In the fear of the Lord is strong confidence: and His children shall have a place of Refuge. The fear of the Lord is a Fountain Of Life, to depart from the snares of death."

Prov. 15: 1 "A soft answer turneth away wrath: but grievous words stir up anger."

Prov. 15: 20 "A wise son maketh a glad father: but a foolish man despiseth his mother."

Prov. 16: 3 "Commit thy works unto the Lord, and thy thoughts shall be established."

Prov. 17: 22 "A merry heart doeth good like a medicine: but a broken spirit drieth the bones."

Prov. 22: 4 "By humility and the fear of the Lord are riches, and Honor, and Life."

Prov. 22: 6 "Train up a child in The Way he should go: and when he is old, he will not depart from it."

Prov. 25: 11 "A word fitly spoken is like apples of gold in pictures of silver."

Prov. 28: 10 "Whoso causeth the righteous to go astray in an evil way, he shall fall himself into his own pit: but the upright shall have good things in possession."

Ecclesiastes

Introduction

Solomon as a preacher and one that desired to instruct all in the way of salvation, describes the deceivable vanities of this world: that man should not be addicted to anything under the sun, but rather inflamed with the desire of the heavenly life: therefore he confutes their opinions, which set their happiness either in knowledge or in pleasures, or in dignity and riches, wishing that man's true happiness

consists in that he is united with God and will enjoy his presence: so that all other things must be rejected, save in as much as they further us to attain to this heavenly treasure, which is sure and permanent, and cannot be found in any other save in God alone.

1599 Geneva Study Bible

Verses of encouragement

Eccl. 1: 2,3 "Vanity of vanities, saith the Preacher, vanity of vanities; all is vanity. What profit hath a man of all his labor which he taketh under the sun?"

Eccl. 2: 24 "There is nothing better for a man, than that he should eat and drink, and that he should make his soul enjoy good in his labor. This also I saw, that it was from the hand of God."

Eccl. 5: 18 "Behold that which I have seen: it is good and comely for one to eat and to drink, and to enjoy the good of all his labor that he taketh under the sun all the days of his life, which God giveth him: for it is his portion."

Eccl. 5: 19 "Every man also to whom God hath given riches and wealth, and hath given him power to eat thereof, and to take his portion, and to rejoice in his labor; this is the gift of God."

Ecclesiastes, Song of Solomon, Isaiah

Ecclesiastes, continued

Verses of encouragement, continued

Eccl. 11: 1 "Cast thy bread upon the waters: for thou shalt find it after many days."

Eccl. 12: 7 "Then shall the dust return to the earth as it was: and the spirit shall return unto God who gave it."

Eccl. 12: 13,14 "Let us hear the conclusion of the whole matter: Fear God, and keep his commandments: for this is the whole duty of man. For God shall bring every work into judgment, with every secret thing, whether it be good, or whether it be evil."

Song of Solomon

Introduction

This book is a Divine allegory, which represents the love between Christ and his church of true believers, under figures taken from the relation and affection that subsist between a bridegroom and his espoused bride; an emblem often employed in Scripture, as describing the nearest, firmest, and most sure relation. There is no character in the church of Christ, and no situation in which the believer is placed, but what may be traced in this book, as humble inquirers will find, on comparing it with other Scriptures, by the assistance of God the Holy Spirit, in answer to their

supplications. Much, however, of the language has been misunderstood by expositors and translators. The difference between the customs and manners of Europe, and those of the East, must especially be kept in view. The little acquaintance with eastern customs possessed by most of our early expositors and translators, has in many cases prevented a correct rendering. Also, the changes in our own language, during the last two or three centuries, affect the manner in which some expressions are viewed, and they must not be judged by modern notions. But the great outlines, rightly interpreted, fully accord with the affections and experience of the sincere Christian.

Matthew Henry

Verses of encouragement

Song of Songs 2: 16 "My beloved is mine, and I am his: he feedeth among the lilies."

Song of Songs 5: 10–12 "My beloved is white and ruddy, the chiefest among ten thousand. His head is as the most fine gold, his locks are bushy, and black as a raven. His eyes are as the eyes of doves by the rivers of waters, washed with milk, and fitly set."

"Song of Songs 6: 3 "I am my beloved's, and my beloved is mine: he feedeth among the lilies."

Song of Songs 7: 10 "I am my beloved's, and his desire is toward me."

Song of Songs 8: 7 "Many waters cannot quench love, neither can the floods drown it: if a man would give all the substance of his house for love, it would utterly be contemned."

Isaiah

Introduction

God, according to his promise in Deut. 18: 15 that he would never leave his Church destitute of a prophet, has from time to time accomplished the same: whose office was not only to declare to the people the things to come, of which they had a special revelation, but also to interpret and declare the law, and to apply particularly the doctrine contained briefly in it, for the use and profit of those to whom they thought it chiefly to belong, and as the time and state of things required.

Principally in the declaration of the law, they had respect to three things which were the ground of their doctrine: first, to the doctrine contained briefly in the two tables: secondly to the promises and threatenings of the law: and thirdly to the covenant of grace and reconciliation grounded on our Savior Jesus Christ, who is the end of the law. To which they neither added nor diminished, but faithfully expounded the sense and meaning of it.

As God gave them understanding of things, they applied the promises particularly for the comfort of the Church and the members of it, and also denounced the menaces against the enemies of the same: not for any care or regard to the enemies, but to assure the Church of their safeguard by the destruction of their enemies. Concerning the doctrine of reconciliation, they have more clearly entreated it than Moses, and set forth more lively Jesus Christ, in whom this covenant of reconciliation was made. In all these things Isaiah surpassed all the prophets, and was diligent to set out the same, with vehement admonitions, reprehensions, and consolations: ever applying the doctrine as he saw that the disease of the people required.

He declares also many notable prophecies which he had received from God, concerning the promise of the Messiah, his office and kingdom, the favor of God toward his Church, the calling of the Gentiles and their union with the Jews. Which are principal points contained in this book, and a gathering of his sermons that he preached. Which after certain days that they had stood upon the temple door (for the manner of the prophets was to post the sum of their doctrine for certain days, that the people might the better mark it as in (Is. 8: 1, Hab. 2: 2)) the priests took it down and reserved it among their registers. By God's providence these books were preserved as a monument to the Church forever. Concerning his person and time he was of the king's stock and prophesied more than sixty-four years, from the time of Uzziah to the reign of Manasseh who was his son-in-law and by whom he was put to death.

Isaiah and Jeremiah

Isaiah, continued

Introduction, continued

In reading of the prophets, this one thing among others is to be observed, that they speak of things to come as though they were now past because of the certainty of it, and that they could not but come to pass, because God had ordained them in his secret counsel and so revealed them to his prophets.

1599 Geneva Study Bible

Verses of encouragement

Is. 1: 18,19 "Come now, and let us reason together, saith the Lord: though your sins be as scarlet, they shall be as white as snow; though they be red like crimson, they shall be as wool. If ye be willing and obedient, ye shall eat the good of the land."

Is. 7: 14,15 "Therefore the Lord Himself shall give you a sign; Behold, a virgin shall conceive, and bear a Son, and shall call His name Immanuel. Butter and honey shall He eat, that He may know to refuse the evil, and choose the good."

Is. 9: 6 "For unto us a Child is born, unto us a Son is given: and the government shall be upon His shoulder: and His name shall be called Wonderful, Counselor, The Mighty God, The Everlasting Father, The Prince of Peace."

Is. 10: 27 "And it shall come to pass in that day, that his burden shall be taken away from off thy shoulder, and his yoke from off thy neck, and the yoke shall be destroyed because of the Anointing."

Is. 12: 2,3 "Behold, God is my Salvation; I will trust, and not be afraid: for the Lord JEHOVAH is my strength and my song; he also is become my salvation. therefore with joy shall ye draw water out of the wells of salvation."

Jeremiah

Introduction

The prophet Jeremiah born in the city of Anathoth in the country of Benjamin, was the son of Hilkiah, whom some think to be he that found the book of the law and gave it to Josiah. This prophet had excellent gifts from God, and most evident revelations of prophecy, so that by the commandment of the Lord he began very young to prophecy, that is, in the thirteenth year of Josiah, and continued eighteen years under the king, three months under Jehoahaz and under Jehoiakim eleven years, three months under Jehoiachin, and under Zedekiah eleven years to the time that they were carried away into Babylon. So that this time amounts to above forty years, besides the time that he prophesied after the captivity. In this book he declares with tears and lamentations, the destruction of Jerusalem and the captivity of the people, for their idolatry, covetousness, deceit, cruelty, excess, rebellion, and contempt of God's word, and for the consolation of the Church reveals the just time of their deliverance. Here chiefly are to be considered three things. First the rebellion of the wicked, who wax more stubborn and obstinate, when the prophets admonish them most plainly of their destruction. Next how the prophets and ministers of God should not be discouraged in their vocation, though they are persecuted and rigorously handled by the wicked, for God's cause. Thirdly though God shows his just judgment against the wicked, yet will he ever show himself a preserver of his Church, and when all means seem to men's judgment to be abolished, then will he declare himself victorious in preserving his.

1599 Geneva Study Bible

Verses of encouragement

Jer. 7: 23 "But this thing commanded I them, saying, Obey My Voice, and I will be your God, and ye shall be My people: and walk ye in all the ways that I have commanded you, that it may be well unto you."

Jer. 15: 21 "And I will deliver thee out of the hand of the wicked, and I will redeem thee out of the hand of the terrible."

Jer. 17: 7,8 "Blessed is the man that trusteth in the Lord, and whose hope the Lord is. For he shall be as a Tree Planted By The Waters, and that spreadeth out her roots by The River, and shall not see when heat cometh,

but her leaf shall be green; and shall not be careful in the year of drought, neither shall cease from yielding fruit."

Jer. 29: 11–13 "For I know the thoughts that I think toward you, saith the Lord, thoughts of peace, and not of evil, to give you an expected end. then shall ye call upon Me, and ye shall go and pray unto Me, and I will hearken unto you. And ye shall seek Me, and find Me, when ye shall search for Me with all your heart."

Jer. 30: 17 "For I will restore health unto thee, and I will heal thee of thy wounds, saith the Lord; because they called thee an Outcast, saying, This is Zion, whom no man seeketh after."

Jer. 32: 27 "Behold, I am the Lord, the God of all flesh: is there any thing too hard for Me?"

Jer. 33: 3 "Call unto Me, and I will answer thee, and shew thee great and mighty things, which thou knowest not."

Jer. 33: 11 "The voice of joy, and the voice of gladness, the voice of the bridegroom, and the voice of the bride, the voice of them that shall say, Praise the Lord of hosts: for the Lord is Good; for His mercy endureth for ever: and of them that shall bring the sacrifice of praise into the House of the Lord."

Lamentations, Ezekiel, Daniel, Hosea

Lamentations

Introduction

It is evident that Jeremiah was the author of the Lamentations which bear his name. The book was not written till after the destruction of Jerusalem by the Chaldeans. May we be led to consider sin as the cause of all our calamities, and under trials exercise submission, repentance, faith, and prayer, with the hope of promised deliverance through God's mercy.

Matthew Henry

Verses of encouragement

Lam. 3: 22,23 "It is of the Lord's Mercies that we are not consumed, because His compassions fail not. They are new every morning: GREAT is thy Faithfulness."

Lam. 3: 24 "The Lord is my Portion, saith my soul; therefore will I hope in Him."

Lam. 3: 25 "The Lord is Good unto them that wait for Him, to the soul that seeketh Him."

Ezekiel

Introduction

After Jehoiachin by the counsel of Jeremiah and Ezekiel had yielded himself to Nebuchadnezzar, and so went into captivity with his mother and various of his princes and of the people, some began to repent and murmur that they had obeyed the prophet's counsel, as though the things which they had prophesied would not come to pass, and therefore their estate would still be miserable under the Chaldeans. By reason of which he confirms his former prophecies, declaring by new visions and revelations shown to him, that the city would most certainly be destroyed, and the people grievously tormented by God's plagues, in so much that they who remained would be brought into cruel bondage. Lest the godly despair in these great troubles, he assures them that God will deliver his church at his appointed time and also destroy their enemies, who either afflicted them, or rejoiced in their miseries. The effect of the one and the other would be chiefly performed under Christ, of whom in this book are many notable promises, and in whom the glory of the new temple would perfectly be restored. He prophesied these things in Chaldea, at the same time that Jeremiah prophesied in Judah, and there began in the fifth year of Jehoiachin's captivity.

1599 Geneva Study Bible

Verses of encouragement

Ezek. 36: 11 "And I will multiply upon you man and beast; and they shall increase and bring fruit: and I will settle you after your old estates, and will do better unto you than at your beginnings: and ye shall know that I am the Lord."

Daniel

Introduction

The great providence of God, and his singular mercy toward his Church are set forth here most vividly, who never leaves his own destitute, but now in their greatest miseries and afflictions gives them Prophets, such as Ezekiel and Daniel, whom he adorned with special graces of his Holy Spirit. And Daniel above all others had most special revelations of such things as would come to the Church, even from the time that they were in captivity, to the last end of the world, and to the general resurrection, as of the four Monarchies and empires of all the world, that is, of the Babylonians, Persians, Grecians, and Romans. Also of the certain number of the times even until Christ, when all ceremonies and sacrifices would cease, because he would be the accomplishment of them: moreover he shows Christ's office and the reason of his death, which was by his sacrifice to take away sins, and to bring everlasting life. And as from the beginning God always exercised his people under the cross, so he teaches here, that after Christ is offered, he will still leave this exercise to his Church, until the dead rise again, and Christ gathers his own into his kingdom in the heavens.

1599 Geneva Study Bible

Verses of encouragement

Dan. 2: 44 "And in the days of these kings shall the God of heaven set up a kingdom, which shall never be destroyed: and the kingdom shall not be left to other people, but it shall break in pieces and consume all these kingdoms, and it shall stand for ever."

Dan. 7: 14 "And there was given him dominion, and glory, and a kingdom, that all people, nations, and languages, should serve him: his dominion is an everlasting dominion, which shall not pass away, and his kingdom that which shall not be destroyed."

Dan. 11: 32 "And such as do wickedly against the covenant shall he corrupt by flatteries: but the people that do know their God shall be strong, and do exploits."

Dan. 12: 3 "And they that be wise shall shine as the brightness of the firmament; and they that turn many to righteousness as the stars for ever and ever."

Hosea

Introduction

After the ten tribes had fallen away from God by the wicked and subtle counsel of Jeroboam, the son of Neba, and instead of his true service commanded by his word, worshiped him according to their own imaginings and traditions of men, giving themselves to most vile idolatry and superstition, the Lord from time to time sent them Prophets to call them to repentance. But they grew even worse and worse, and still abused God's benefits.

Hosea, Joel, Amos, Obadiah, Jonah

Hosea, continued

Introduction, continued

Therefore now when their prosperity was at the highest under Jeroboam, the son of Joash, God sent Hosea and Amos to the Israelites (as he did at the same time send Isaiah and Micah to those of Judah) to condemn them for their ingratitude. And whereas they thought themselves to be greatly in the favor of God, and to be his people, the Prophet calls them bastards and children born in adultery: and therefore shows them that God would take away their kingdom, and give them to the Assyrians to be led away captives.

Thus Hosea faithfully executed his office for the space of seventy years, though they remained still in their vices and wickedness and derided the Prophets, and condemned God's judgments. And because they would neither be discouraged with threatening only, nor should they flatter themselves by the sweetness of God's promises, he sets before them the two principal parts of the Law, which are the promise of salvation, and the doctrine of life. For the first part he directs the faithful to the Messiah, by whom alone they would have true deliverance: and for the second, he uses threatenings and menaces to bring them from their wicked manners and vices: and this is the chief scope of all the Prophets, either by God's promises to allure them to be godly, or else by threatenings of his judgments to scare

them from vice. And even though the whole Law contains these two points, yet the Prophets moreover note distinctly both the time of God's judgments and the manner.

1599 Geneva Study Bible

Verses of encouragement

Hosea 6: 1–3 "Come, and let us return to the Lord;
For He has torn, but He will heal us;
He has stricken, but He will bind us up.
After two days He will revive us;
On the third day He will raise us up,
That we may live in His sight.
Let us know,
Let us pursue the knowledge of the Lord.
His going forth is established as the morning;
He will come to us like the rain,
Like the latter and former rain to the earth."

Joel

Introduction

The Prophet Joel first rebukes those of Judah, that being now punished with a great plague of famine, still remain obstinate. Secondly, he threatens greater plagues, because they grow daily to a more hardness of heart and rebellion against God in spite of his punishments. Thirdly, he exhorts them to repentance, showing that it must be earnest, and proceed from the heart, because they had grievously offended

God. And in doing this, Joel promises that God will be merciful, and not forget his covenant that he made with their fathers, but will send his Christ, who will gather the scattered sheep, and restore them to life and liberty, even though they seem to be dead.

1599 Geneva Study Bible

Verses of encouragement

Joel 2: 26 "And ye shall eat in plenty, and be satisfied, and praise the Name of the Lord your God, that hath dealt wondrously with you: and My people shall never be ashamed."

Amos

Introduction

Among many other Prophets that God raised up to admonish the Israelites of his plagues for their wickedness and idolatry, he stirred up Amos, who was a herdman or shepherd of a poor town, and gave him both knowledge and constancy to reprove all estates and degrees, and to make known God's horrible judgments against them, unless they repented in time. And he showed them, that if God did not spare the other nations around them, who had lived as it were in ignorance of God compared to them, but for their sins punished them, then they could look for nothing, but a horrible destruction, unless they turned to the Lord in true repentance. And finally, he comforts the godly with hope of the coming of the Messiah, by whom they would have perfect deliverance and salvation.

1599 Geneva Study Bible

Verse of encouragement

Amos 3: 7 "Surely the Lord GOD will do nothing, but He revealeth His secret unto His servants the prophets."

Obadiah

Introduction

The Idumeans, who came from Esau, were mortal enemies always to the Israelites, who came from Jacob, and therefore did not only vex them continually with various types of cruelty, but also stirred up others to fight against them. Therefore when they were now in their greatest prosperity, and did most triumph against Israel, which was in great affliction and misery, God raised up his Prophet to comfort the Israelites. For God had now determined to destroy their adversaries, who did so severely vex them, and to send them those who would deliver them, and set up the kingdom of the Messiah which he had promised.

1599 Geneva Study Bible

Jonah

Introduction

When Jonah had long prophesied in Israel and had little profited, God gave him specific charge to go and denounce his judgments against Nineveh, the chief city of the Assyrians, because he had appointed that those who were of the heathen, should convert by the mighty power of his word.

Jonah, Micah, Nahum, Habakkuk, Zephaniah

Jonah, continued

Introduction, continued

And this was so that within three day's preaching, Israel might see how horribly they had provoked God's wrath, who for the space of so many years, had not converted to the Lord, for so many prophets and such diligent preaching. He prophesied under Jonah, and Jeroboam; (2 Kgs. 14: 25).

1599 Geneva Study Bible

Micah

Introduction

Micah the prophet of the tribe of Judah served in the work of the Lord concerning Judah and Israel at least thirty years: during which time Isaiah prophesied. He declares the destruction first of the one kingdom, and then of the other, because of their manifold wickedness, but chiefly because of their idolatry. And to this end he notes the wickedness of the people, the cruelty of the princes and governors, and the allowing of the false prophets, and the delighting in them. Then he sets forth the coming of Christ, his kingdom, and the felicity of it. This Prophet was not that Micah who resisted Ahab and all his false prophets, (1 Kgs. 22: 8) but another with the same name.

1599 Geneva Study Bible

Verses of encouragement

Mic. 6: 8 "He hath shewed thee, O man, what is Good; and what doth the Lord require of thee, but to do justly, and to love Mercy, and to walk humbly with thy God?"

Nahum

Introduction

The people of Nineveh provoked God's just judgment against them, in afflicting his people. Therefore their city Nineveh was destroyed, and Meroch-baladan, king of Babel (or as some think, Nebuchadnezzar) enjoyed the empire of the Assyrians. But because God has a continual care for his Church, he stirs up his Prophet to comfort the godly, showing that the destruction of their enemies would be for their consolation: and as it seems, he prophesies around the time of Hezekiah, and not in the time of Manasseh his son, as the Jews write.

1599 Geneva Study Bible

Verses of encouragement

Nah. 1: 7 "The Lord is Good, a strong hold in the day of trouble; and He knoweth them that trust in Him."

Habakkuk

Introduction

The Prophet complains to God, considering the great felicity of the wicked, and the miserable oppression of the godly, who endure all types of affliction and cruelty, and yet can see no end. Therefore he had this revelation shown to him by God, that the Chaldeans would come and take them away as captives, so that they could look for no end of their troubles as yet, because of their stubbornness and rebellion against the Lord. And lest the godly should despair, seeing this horrible confusion, he comforts them by this, that God will punish the Chaldeans their enemies, when their pride and cruelty will be at height. And for this reason he exhorts the faithful to patience by his own example, and shows them a form of prayer, with which they should comfort themselves.

1599 Geneva Study Bible

Verses of encouragement

Hab. 2: 14 "For the earth shall be filled with the Knowledge of the glory of the Lord, as the waters cover the sea."

Hab. 3: 18 "Yet I will rejoice in the Lord, I will joy in the God of my salvation."

Hab. 3: 19 "The Lord God is my strength, and He will make my feet like hinds' feet, and He will make me to walk upon mine high places."

Zephaniah

Introduction

Seeing the great rebellion of the people, and that there was now no hope of amendment, he gives notice of the great judgment of God, which was at hand, showing that their country would be utterly destroyed, and they would be carried away captives by the Babylonians. Yet for the comfort of the faithful he prophesied of God's vengeance against their enemies, such as the Philistines, Moabites, Assyrians, and others, to assure them that God had a continual care over them. And as the wicked would be punished for their sins and transgressions, so he exhorts the godly to patience, and to trust to find mercy by reason of the free promise of God made to Abraham: and therefore quietly to wait until God shows them the effect of that grace, by which in the end they should be gathered to him, and counted as his people and children.

1599 Geneva Study Bible

Verses of encouragement

Zeph. 2: 3 "Seek ye the Lord, all ye meek of the earth, which have wrought his judgment; seek righteousness, seek meekness: it may be ye shall be hid in the day of the Lord's anger."

Zeph. 3: 12,13 "I will also leave in the midst of thee an afflicted and poor people, and they shall trust in the name of the Lord. The remnant of Israel shall not do iniquity, nor speak lies; neither shall a deceitful tongue be found in their mouth: for they shall feed and lie down, and none shall make them afraid."

Zeph. 3: 20 "At that time will I bring you again, even in the time that I gather you: for I will make you a name and a praise among all people of the earth, when I turn back your captivity before your eyes, saith the Lord."

Haggai, Zechariah, Malachi

Haggai

Introduction

When the time of the seventy years captivity prophesied by Jeremiah was expired, God raised up Haggai, Zechariah, and Malachi, to comfort the Jews, and to exhort them to the building of the temple, which was a figure of the spiritual Temple and Church of God, whose perfection and excellency depended on Christ. And because all were given to their own pleasures and benefits, he declares that that plague of famine, which God then sent among them, was a just reward for their ingratitude, in that they condemned God's honor, who had delivered them. Yet he comforts them, if they will return to the Lord, with the promise of great felicity, since the Lord will finish the work that he has begun, and send Christ whom he had promised, and by whom they would attain to perfect joy and glory.

1599 Geneva Study Bible

Verses of encouragement

Hag. 1: 8 "Go up to the mountain, and bring wood, and build the house; and I will take pleasure in it, and I will be glorified, saith the Lord."

Hag. 2: 7–9 "And I will shake all nations, and the desire of all nations shall come: and I will fill this House with Glory, saith the Lord of hosts. The silver is Mine, and the gold is Mine, saith the Lord of hosts. The Glory of

this latter House shall be greater than of the former, saith the Lord of hosts: and in this place will I give Peace, saith the Lord of hosts."

Zechariah

Introduction

Two months after Haggai had begun to prophesy, Zechariah was also sent of the Lord to help him in the labor, and to confirm the same doctrine. First therefore, he puts them in remembrance for what reason God had so severely punished their fathers: and yet comforts them if they will truly repent, and not abuse this great benefit of God in their deliverance which was a figure of that true deliverance, that all the faithful should have from death and sin, by Christ. But because they remained still in their wickedness, and lack of desire to set forth God's glory, and were not yet made better by their long banishment, he rebukes them most sharply: yet for the comfort of the repentant, he ever mixes the promise of grace, that they might by this means be prepared to receive Christ, in whom all should be sanctified to the Lord.

1599 Geneva Study Bible

Verses of encouragement

Zech. 2: 5 "For I, saith the Lord, will be unto her a wall of fire round about, and will be the glory in the midst of her."

Zech. 9: 16–17 "And the Lord their God shall save them in that day as the flock of His people: for they shall be as the stones of a crown, lifted up as an ensign upon His land. For how great is His goodness, and how great is His beauty! corn shall make the young men cheerful, and new wine the maids."

Zech. 13: 9 "And I will bring the third part through the fire, and will refine them as silver is refined, and will try them as gold is tried: they shall call on My Name, and I will hear them: I will say, It is My people: and they shall say, The Lord is my God."

Malachi

Introduction

This Prophet was one of the three who God raised up for the comfort of the Church after the captivity, and after him there was no one else until John the Baptist was sent, which was either a token of God's wrath, or an admonition that they should with more fervent desires look for the coming of the Messiah. He confirms the same doctrine, that the two former do: chiefly he reproves the priests for their covetousness, and because they served God after their own fantasies, and not according to the direction of his word. He also notes certain distinct sins, which were then among them, such as the marrying of idolatrous and many wives, murmurings against God, impatience, and things such as these. Nonetheless, for the comfort of the godly he declares that God would not forget his promise made to their fathers, but would send Christ his messenger, in whom the covenant would be accomplished, whose coming would be terrible to the wicked, and bring all consolation and joy to the godly.

1599 Geneva Study Bible

Verses of encouragement

Mal. 3: 6 "For I am the Lord, I change not; therefore ye sons of Jacob are not consumed."

Mal. 3: 10–12 "Bring ye all the tithes into the storehouse, that there may be meat in Mine house, and prove Me now herewith, saith the Lord of hosts, if I will not open you the windows of Heaven, and pour you out a blessing, that there shall not be room enough to receive it. And I will rebuke the devourer for your sakes, and he shall not destroy the fruits of your ground; neither shall your vine cast her fruit before the time in the field, saith the Lord of hosts. And all nations shall call you blessed: for ye shall be a Delightsome Land, saith the Lord of hosts."

Mal. 3: 16,17 "Then they that feared the Lord spake often one to another: and the Lord hearkened, and heard it, and a book of remembrance was written before Him for them that feared the Lord, and that thought upon His Name. And they shall be Mine, saith the Lord of hosts, in that day when I make up My jewels; and I will spare them, as a man spareth his own son that serveth him."

Noah

Overview of Noah

General references

Gen. 5: 28,29

Builds an ark and saves his family from the flood

Gen. 6: 14–22; Gen. 7–8; Matt. 24: 38; Luke 17: 27; Heb. 11: 7; 1 Pet. 3: 20

Builds an altar and offers sacrifices

Gen. 8: 20,21

Covenant and rainbow

Receives God's covenant. No more flood. Rainbow given as a token of the covenant

Gen. 8: 20; Gen. 8: 22; Gen. 9: 9–17

Noah becomes drunk and curses Canaan

Gen. 9: 20–27

His blessing upon Shem and Japheth

Gen. 9: 26,27

Dies at the age of nine hundred and fifty years

Gen. 9: 28,29

Life of Noah

NOAH WAS THE GRANDSON OF METHUSELAH
For two hundred and fifty years he was a contemporary with Adam, and the son of Lamech, who was about fifty years old when Adam died. (Gen. 5: 25–29).

PATRIARCH
As a patriarch Adam is the link between the old and the new world.

SECOND PROGENITOR
He is the second great progenitor of the human family.

TYPE OF JESUS
The words of his father Lamech at his birth ("And he called his name Noah, saying, This *same* shall comfort us concerning our work and toil of our hands, because of the ground which the Lord hath cursed" Gen. 5: 29) were prophetic and designated Noah as a type of Jesus, Him who is the true "rest and comfort" of men under the burden of life (Matt. 11: 28).

THREE SONS
After he had lived for five hundred years he had three sons, Shem, Ham, and Japheth (Gen. 5: 32).

CHARACTER OF
Noah was a "just man and perfect in his generation," and "walked with God" (Compare Ezek. 14: 14,20).

Worldwide corruption

Because people became more and more corrupt, and God decided to rid the earth of them (Gen. 6: 7).

Promised deliverance

But God made a covenant with Noah. He promised to deliver him from the threatened flood (Gen. 6: 18).

Ark

So Noah was ordered to build an ark (Gen. 6: 14–16) to save himself and his family.

MASSIVE BUILDING PROJECT
It took one hundred and twenty years to build the ark (Gen. 6: 3), during which time Noah was constantly made fun of by wicked people (1 Pet. 3: 18–20; 2 Pet. 2: 5).

BUILT OF GOPHER-WOOD
When the ark of "gopher-wood" (mentioned only here) was completed the living creatures that had been selected entered into it; and then Noah and his wife and sons and daughters-in-law entered it, and the "Lord shut him in" (Gen. 7: 16).

Judgment

The judgment which had been threatened now fell on the guilty world, "the world that then was, being overflowed with water, perished" (2 Pet. 3: 6).

The ark floated on the waters for one hundred and fifty days, and then rested on the mountains of Ararat (Gen. 8: 3,4). But some many weeks passed before God's permission was given him to leave the ark (Gen. 8: 6–14).

First altar

On leaving the ark the first thing Noah did was to erect an altar, which is the first one ever mentioned.

He offered sacrifices of thanks and praise to God, who entered into a covenant with him, the first covenant between God and humankind, granting him possession of the earth by a new and special charter, which remains in force to the present time (Gen. 8: 21–9: 17). As a sign and witness of this covenant, the rainbow was set apart by God, as a sure pledge that never again would the earth be destroyed by a flood.

The rainbow promise

"And God spake unto Noah, and to his sons with him, saying,

And I, behold, I establish my covenant with you, and with your seed after you; . . . This is the token of the covenant which I make between me and you and every living creature that is with you, for perpetual generations:

I do set my bow in the cloud, and it shall be for a token of a covenant between me and the earth.

And it shall come to pass, when I bring a cloud over the earth, that the bow shall be seen in the cloud:

And I will remember my covenant, which is between me and you and every living creature of all flesh; and the waters shall no more become a flood to destroy all flesh.

And the bow shall be in the cloud; and I will look upon it, that I may remember the everlasting covenant between God and every living creature of all flesh that is upon the earth" Genesis 9: 8,9, 12–16.

Noah after the flood

Noah "lived after the flood three hundred and fifty years, and he died" (Gen. 9: 28,29).

Abram, Abraham (1)

Summary

Birth

He was born in Ur of the Chaldees, and was a direct descendant of Shem (Genesis 11: 10–32).

His call

The Lord first spoke to him in Ur of Chaldees (Genesis 12: 1; Acts 7: 1–5).

The promises

God gave Abraham two great promises:
- that he would make from him a great nation, bless him, make his name great, make him a blessing, bless those who blessed him, and curse those who cursed him;
- that in him should all families of the earth be blessed (Genesis 12: 1–3).

These promises were subsequently renewed on Mount Moriah (Genesis 22: 1–18).

FULFILMENT OF PROMISES
These promises were subsequently fulfilled in:
- the covenant dedicated at Mount Sinai (Exodus 24: 1–8),
- the new covenant (Galatians 4: 22–31).

Overview

Son of Terah
  Gen. 11: 26–27
Marries Sarah
  Gen. 11: 29
Lives in Ur, but moves to Haran
  Gen. 11: 31; Neh. 9: 7; Acts 7: 4
Lives in Canaan
  Gen. 12: 4–6; Acts 7: 4
Called by God
  Gen. 12: 1–3; Josh. 24: 3; Neh. 9: 7;
  Is. 51: 2; Acts 7: 2,3; Heb. 11: 8
Canaan given to
  Gen. 12: 1; Gen. 12: 7; Gen. 15: 7–21;
  Ezek. 33: 24
Lives in Bethel
  Gen. 12: 8
Travels in Egypt
  Gen. 12: 10–20; Gen. 26: 1
Gives Lot the first choice of land
  Gen. 13; Gen. 14: 13; Gen. 35: 27
Lives in Gerar
  Gen. 20; Gen. 21: 22–34
Defeats Chedorlaomer
  Gen. 14: 5–24; Heb. 7: 1
Is blessed by Melchizedek
  Gen. 14: 18–20; Heb. 7: 1–10
God's covenant with
  Gen. 15; Gen. 17: 1–22; Mic. 7: 20;
  Luke 1: 73; Rom. 4: 13; Rom. 15: 8;
  Heb. 6: 13,14; Gal. 3: 6–18; Gal. 3: 29;
  Gal. 4: 22–31
Name changed to Abraham
  Gen. 17: 5; Neh. 9: 7
Circumcision of
  Gen. 17: 10–14; Gen. 17: 23–27

Angels appear to
Gen. 18: 1–16; Gen. 22: 11; Gen. 22: 15;
Gen. 24: 7

His questions about the destruction of
the righteous and wicked in Sodom
Gen. 18: 23–32

Witnesses the destruction of Sodom
Gen. 19: 27,28

Ishmael born to
Gen. 16: 3; Gen. 16: 15

Lives in Gerar; deceives Abimelech
concerning Sarah, his wife
Gen. 20

Isaac born to
Gen. 21: 2,3; Gal. 4: 22–30

Sends Hagar and Ishmael away
Gen. 21: 10–14; Gal. 4: 22–30

Trial of his faith in the offering of Isaac
Gen. 22: 1–19; Heb. 11: 17; James 2: 21

Sarah, his wife, dies
Gen. 23: 1,2

He purchases a place for her burial, and
buries her in a cave
Gen. 23: 3–20

Marries Keturah
Gen. 25: 1

Provides a wife for Isaac
Gen. 24

Children of
Gen. 16: 15; Gen. 21: 2,3; Gen. 25: 1–4;
1 Chr. 1: 32–34

Testament of
Gen. 25: 5,6

Wealth of
Gen. 13: 2; Gen. 24: 35; Is. 51: 2

Age of, at different periods
Gen. 12: 4; Gen. 16: 16; Gen. 21: 5;
Gen. 25: 7

Death of
Gen. 15: 15; Gen. 25: 8–10

Friend of God
Is. 41: 8; 2 Chr. 20: 7; James 2: 23

Piety of
Gen. 12: 7,8; Gen. 13: 4; Gen. 13: 18;
Gen. 18: 19; Gen. 20: 7; Gen. 21: 33;
Gen. 22: 3–13; Gen. 26: 5; Neh. 9: 7,8;
Rom. 4: 16–18; 2 Chr. 20: 7; Is. 41: 8;
James 2: 23

A prophet
Gen. 20: 7

Faith of
Gen. 15: 6; Rom. 4: 1–22; Gal. 3: 6–9;
Heb. 11: 8–10; Heb. 11: 17–19;
James 2: 21–24

Unselfishness of
Gen. 13: 9; Gen. 21: 25–30

Held in high esteem
Matt. 3: 9; Luke 13: 16; Luke 13: 28;
Luke 19: 9; John 8: 33–40; John 8: 52–
59

Abram, Abraham (2)

Life of Abraham

Named

Abraham, father of a multitude, son of Terah, named (Gen. 11: 27) before his older brothers Nahor and Haran, because he was the heir of the promises. Until he was seventy years old, Abram stayed in the country of his birth. Then, with his father and his family and household, he left the city of Ur, and went 300 miles north to Haran, where he lived for fifteen years.

He left because of God's call (Acts 7: 2–4). There is no mention of this first call in the Old Testament; it is implied, however, in Gen. 12.

Second call

While they stayed in Haran, Terah died aged 205 years. Abram now received a second and more definite call, accompanied by a promise from God (Gen. 12: 1,2). He then left Haran, taking his nephew Lot with him, "not knowing whither he went" (Heb. 11: 8). He trusted implicitly in the guidance of God who had called him.

Nomadic life

Abram now started his migratory life, and lived in tents. Passing along the valley of the Jabbok, in Canaan, he set up his first encampment at Sichem (Gen. 12: 6), in the vale or oak-grove of Moreh, between Ebal on the north and Gerizim on the south. Here he received the great promise, "I will make of thee a great nation," etc. (Gen. 12: 2,3,7).

Spiritual blessings

This promise included not only temporal but also spiritual blessings. It implied that he was the chosen ancestor of the great Deliverer whose coming had been long ago predicted (Gen. 3: 15). Soon after this he moved to the mountain district between Bethel, then called Luz, and Ai, towns about two miles apart, where he built an altar to "Jehovah." He moved again into the southern part of Palestine, called by the Hebrews the Negeb; but was forced to go down into Egypt on account of a famine. This took place when the Hyksos, a Semitic race, held the Egyptians in their grip. Here Abram tried to deceive the Pharaoh and was rebuked by him for this (Gen. 12: 18). Sarai was given back to Abram and Pharaoh showered him with presents, advising him to leave the country. He returned to Canaan richer than when he left it, "in cattle, in silver, and in gold" (Gen. 12: 8; 13: 2. Cf. Ps. 105: 13,14).

Abram's generosity

Abram then moved northward, and returned to a place near Bethel. Here disputes arose between Lot's shepherds and Abram's about watering and pasturing their livestock. Abram generously gave Lot his choice of the pasture-ground. (Cf. 1 Cor. 6: 7.) He chose the well-watered plain which included the city of Sodom and moved there. In this way the uncle and nephew were separated. Immediately after this Abram was encouraged as the promises already made to him were repeated. He then moved to the plain of Mamre, in Hebron. He finally settled here, pitching his tent under a famous oak or terebinth tree, called "the oak of Mamre" (Gen. 13: 18). This was his third resting-place in the land.

Rescues nephew

Some fourteen years before this, while Abram was still in Chaldea, Palestine had been invaded by Chedorlaomer, King of Elam, who forced the five cities in the plain to which Lot had moved, to pay tribute to him. This tribute became a heavy burden, and after twelve years the people in these cities rebelled. As a result of this, Chedorlaomer, who had a treaty with four other kings, decimated the whole country, plundering the towns, and carrying the inhabitants away as slaves. Among those treated in this way was Lot.

On hearing of the disaster that had fallen on his nephew, Abram immediately gathered together a group of 318 armed men, and was joined by the Amorite chiefs Mamre, Aner, and Eshcol. They pursued Chedorlaomer, and caught up with him near the springs of the Jordan. They attacked and routed his army, and brought back all the spoils that had been carried away. Returning by way of Salem, i.e., Jerusalem, the king of that place, Melchizedek, came out to meet them with refreshments. Abram presented him with a tenth of the spoils, in

recognition of his character as a priest of the most high God (Gen. 14: 18–20).

Hagar

Having returned to his home at Mamre, the promises already made to him by God were repeated and enlarged (Gen. 13: 14). "The word of the Lord" (an expression occurring here for the first time) "came to him" (Gen. 15: 1). He now understood about the future of the nation that would stem from him. Sarai, now seventy-five years old, in her impatience, persuaded Abram to take Hagar, her Egyptian maid, as a concubine, intending that the resulting child should be reckoned as her own. Ishmael was therefore brought up in this way, and was thought of as the heir of these promises (Gen. 16). When Ishmael was thirteen years old, God again revealed yet more explicitly his purpose.

Abram, Abraham (3)

Abram to Abraham

As a further sign of the certain fulfillment of this purpose the patriarch's name was now changed from Abram to Abraham (Gen. 17: 4,5), and the rite of circumcision was instituted as a sign of the covenant. It was then announced that the heir to these covenant promises would be the son of Sarai, even though she was now ninety years old. It was also said that his name would be Isaac. At the same time, Sarai's name was changed to Sarah. On that day when God revealed his purposes in this way, Abraham and his son Ishmael and all the males of his household were circumcised (Gen. 17).

Angelic visitors

Three months after this, as Abraham sat at the entrance of his tent, he saw three men approaching. They accepted his hospitality, and, sat down under an oak-tree.

One of the three visitors was none other than the Lord, and the other two were angels in the form of men. The Lord renewed his promise of a son by Sarah, who was rebuked for her unbelief. Abraham accompanied the three as they set out on their journey. The two angels went on toward Sodom; while the Lord stayed behind and talked with Abraham, telling him about the destruction that was about to fall on that guilty city. The patriarch prayed earnestly on behalf of the doomed city. But as not even ten righteous people were found in it, for whose sake the city would have been spared, the threatened destruction fell on it; and early next morning Abraham saw the smoke of the fire that consumed it as the "smoke of a furnace" (Gen. 19: 1–28).

Abimelech

After staying for fifteen years in Mamre, Abraham moved southward, and pitched his tent among the Philistines, near Gerar. There Abraham's sad instance of prevarication with Abimelech the King occurred (Gen. 20). Soon after this event, the patriarch left the vicinity of Gerar, and moved down the fertile valley about 25 miles to Beer-sheba. It was probably here that Isaac was born when Abraham was a hundred years old.

Jealousy

Sarah and Hagar became jealous of each other, for Hagar's son, Ishmael, was no longer Abraham's heir. Sarah insisted that both Hagar and her son should be sent away. This was done, but not with Abraham's approval (Gen. 21: 12).

Gap

At this point there is a gap in the patriarch's biography of about twenty-five years. These years of peace and happiness were spent at Beer-sheba. The next time we see him his faith is severely tested.

Severe trial

He is suddenly commanded to offer up Isaac, the heir of all the promises, as a sacrifice on one of the mountains of Moriah. His faith stood the test (Heb. 11: 17–19). He obeyed in a spirit of unhesitating obedience; and when about to kill his son, whom he had laid on the altar, a ram, which was caught in bushes, was seized and offered in his stead.

The Lord will provide

As a result of this that place was called Jehovah-jireh, i.e., "The Lord will provide." The promises made to Abraham were again confirmed (and this was the last recorded word of God to the patriarch); and he descended the mount with his son, and returned to his home at Beer-sheba (Gen. 22: 19), where he stayed for some years, and then moved northward to Hebron.

Death of Sarah

Some years after this Sarah died at Hebron, aged 127 years. Abraham now needed to acquire a burying-place.

Cave of Machpelah

So he bought the cave of Machpelah, from Ephron the Hittite (Gen. 23); and buried Sarah there.

Then he had to provide a wife for Isaac, and so he sent his steward, Eliezer, to Haran (or Charran, Acts 7: 2), where his brother Nahor and his family lived (Gen. 11: 31).

The result was that Rebekah, the daughter of Nahor's son Bethuel, became Isaac's wife (Gen. 24). At the age of 175 years, 100 years after he had first entered the land of Canaan, he died, and was buried in the old family burying-place at Machpelah (Gen. 25: 7–10).

Names of Abraham

Abraham is called

"the friend of God" (James 2: 23),

"faithful Abraham" (Gal. 3: 9),

"the father of us all" (Rom. 4: 16).

Esau and Jacob, and Joseph

Esau and Jacob

Isaac's wife, Rebekah, was barren, and so Isaac prayed to the Lord and as a result Rebekah conceived (Genesis 25: 21). Rebekah had twin boys, Esau and Jacob.

Before they were born, the Lord selected Jacob, as Isaac, to succeed to all the promises made to Abraham (Genesis 25: 21–23; Romans 9: 9–12).

Jacob subsequently:

Bought Esau's birthright (Genesis 25: 24–34) cheated him out of the patriarchal blessing (Genesis 27: 1–40).
Jacob was sent away to Haran (Genesis 27: 41–28: 7).
During this journey the two great promises were renewed (Genesis 13: 1–3; Genesis 28: 10–15).
Esau settled in Mount Seir (Genesis 36: 8; Deuteronomy 2: 1–5).
Jacob remained in Padanaram twenty years (Genesis 29: 1–15; Genesis 31: 36–41), and then returned to Canaan (Genesis 31: 1–55; Genesis 35: 27).
Jacob was the father of the twelve patriarchs (Gen. 35: 21–26; Acts 7: 8).

Joseph

His father's favorite child, Gen. 33: 2; Gen. 37: 3,4; Gen. 37: 35; Gen. 48: 22; 1 Chr. 5: 2; John 4: 5
His prophetic dreams, Gen. 37: 5–11
Sold into Egypt, Gen. 37: 27,28
His father is told that he was killed by wild animals, Gen. 37: 29–35
Is bought by Potiphar, one of Pharaoh's officers , Gen. 37: 36
Prospers because of God's help, Gen. 39: 2–5; Gen. 39: 21; Gen. 39: 23
Is falsely accused, and thrown into prison, Gen. 39–40; Ps. 105: 18
Interprets dreams of Pharaoh, Gen. 41: 1–37
Is promoted to the second most important person in the land, at the age of at thirty, Gen. 41: 37–46; Ps. 105: 19–22
Provides for the coming years of famine, Gen. 41: 46–57

Joseph's character

His kindness, Gen. 40: 7,8
His integrity, Gen. 39: 7–12
His humility, Gen. 41: 16; Gen. 45: 7–9
His wisdom, Gen. 41: 33–57
His piety, Gen. 41: 51,52
His faith, Gen. 45: 5–8

Son of Jacob and Rachel

The elder of the two sons of Jacob by Rachel (Gen. 30: 23,24), who, at his birth, said, "God hath taken away my reproach."

"The Lord shall add to me another son" (Gen. 30: 24).

The coat of "many colors" "Now Israel loved Joseph more than all his children, because he was the son of his old age," and he "made him a long garment with sleeves" (Gen. 37: 3, RV marg.), i.e., a garment worn by the children of nobles. The phrase may also be rendered, "a coat of many pieces," i.e., a patchwork of many small pieces of various colors.

Jealous hatred

When he was about seventeen years old Joseph found that his brothers were full of jealous hatred toward him (Gen. 37: 4). They "hated him, and could not speak peaceably unto him." Their anger increased when he told them his dreams (Gen. 37: 11).

Sold as slave

Jacob wanting to hear news about his sons, who had gone to Shechem with their flocks, some 60 miles from Hebron, sent Joseph to them. As soon as the brothers saw Joseph coming they hatched a plot, and would have killed him had not Reuben intervened.

They eventually sold him to Ishmaelite traders for twenty pieces (shekels) of silver, ten pieces less than the price of a slave, for "they cared little what they had for him, if so be they were rid of him." These merchants took Joseph to Egypt where they sold him as a slave to Potiphar, an "officer of Pharaoh's, and captain of the guard" (Gen. 37: 36).

Joseph's promotion

Pharaoh was pleased with Joseph's wisdom in interpreting his dreams, and with his wise counsel. He promoted him to be governor of Egypt (Gen. 41: 46), and gave him the name of Zaphnath-paaneah. He was married to Asenath, the daughter of the priest of On, and thus became a member of the priestly class. Joseph was now about thirty years old.

Joseph's family go to Egypt

During this famine Joseph's brethren also came down to Egypt to buy corn. Eventually, (Gen. 42–45), Joseph told his brothers to bring Jacob and his family to the land of Egypt, saying, "I will give you the good of the land of Egypt, and ye shall eat the fat of the land. Regard not your stuff; for the good of all the land is yours." So Jacob and his family, numbering seventy people, together with "all that they had," went down to Egypt. They were allowed to settle in Goshen, where Joseph met his father, and "fell on his neck, and wept on his neck a good while" (Gen. 46: 29).

Joseph's death

Joseph and Asenath had two sons, Manasseh and Ephraim (Gen. 41: 50). Joseph told his brothers that when the time came that God would "bring them unto the land which he swore to Abraham, to Isaac, and to Jacob," they would carry his bones out of Egypt. Joseph died, aged one hundred and ten years old, and "they embalmed him, and he was put in a coffin" (Gen. 50: 26). At the time of the Exodus Joseph's descendants carried his remains with them during their forty years' wanderings, and eventually buried him in Shechem, in the piece of land which Jacob bought from the sons of Hamor (Josh. 24: 32; cf. Gen. 33: 19).

With the death of Joseph the patriarchal age of the history of Israel came to a close.

Moses (1)

First forty years of his life

The important incidents of this period of his life were:

he was concealed by his mother (Ex. 2: 1,2);

he was placed in an ark of bulrushes (Ex. 2: 3);

he was discovered by Pharaoh's daughter and named Moses because he was drawn out of the water (Ex. 2: 3–10);

he was adopted by Pharaoh's daughter and educated (Ex. 2: 9,10; Acts 7: 20–22);

he refused to be called the son of Pharaoh's daughter (Hebrews 11: 24);

he visited his brethren (Acts 7: 23);

he killed an Egyptian (Ex. 2: 11,12; Acts 7: 24,25);

his brethren failed to understand him (Ex. 2: 14; Acts 7: 22–28);

he fled to Midian (Acts ex; Ex. 2: 15; Acts 7: 29).

Second forty years of his life

The important incidents of this period of his life were:

he met the daughters of Jethro, the priest of Midian, at the well and watered their flocks (Ex. 2: 16,17);

he was invited into Jethro's house (Ex. 2: 17–20);

he married Zipporah (Ex. 2: 21);

the birth of his son Gershom (Ex. 2: 22);

the death of the king of Egypt (Ex. 2: 23–25);

an angel appearing to him in the burning bush at Mount Horeb (Ex. 3: 1–16; Acts 7: 30).

Third forty years of his life

The important incidents of this period of his life were:

he was commissioned as the deliverer of his brethren (Ex. 2: 7–22; Ex. 3: 1–6; Acts 7: 31–35);

he returned to Egypt with his family, and with Jethro's blessing (Ex. 4: 18–20);

the Lord appeared to him and confirmed his commission (Ex. 4: 21–23);

he met his brother Aaron (Ex. 4: 27);

they told their brethren about their mission (Ex. 4: 29–31);

Pharaoh refused to release the Hebrews (Ex. 5: 1–4);

the Passover was instituted (Ex. 12: 1–29);

Pharaoh gave his consent for the Hebrews to leave Egypt (Ex. 12: 31–36);

the miracle at the Red Sea (Ex. 14: 9–22);

the destruction of the Egyptians (Ex. 14: 23–31);

the song of triumph (Ex. 15: 1–19);

the miracle at Marah (Ex. 15: 23–26);

the provision of manna (Ex. 16: 1–15);

the keeping of a Sabbath (Ex. 16: 16–35);

the visit of Jethro and the return of his family (Ex. 18: 1–6);

he accepted Jethro's counsel (Ex. 18: 13–26);

the arrival at Sinai (Ex. 19: 1);

the Lord's covenant with the people (Ex. 19: 3–8);

the giving of the ten commandments (Ex. 20: 1–17);

he received instructions about the tabernacle (Ex. 25: 1–40);

he destroyed the idolatrous worship inaugurated by Aaron (Ex. 32: 1–33);

he set up his tabernacle or tent apart from the people (Ex. 33: 1–11);

he saw the passing glory of the Lord (Ex. 33: 12–23);

the second visit into the mount and the renewal of the tablets of stone (Ex. 34: 1–28);

his shining face (Ex. 34: 29–35);

request for material to build the tabernacle (Ex. 35: 1–35);

setting up of the tabernacle (Ex. 40: 1–38);

he acted as priest at the consecration of Aaron and his sons (Leviticus 8: 1–36);

he numbered the people (Numbers 1: 1–46);

the consecration of the Levites (Numbers 8: 1–26);

the second Passover (Numbers 9: 1–15);

leaving Sinai (Numbers 10: 11–13);

seventy elders appointed to assist him (Numbers 11: 16–30);

Miriam and Aaron's negative actions (Numbers 12: 1–13);

he sent twelve spies into Canaan (Numbers 13: 1–16);

Moses (2)

Third forty years of his life, continued

The important incidents of this period of his life were: continued

the rebellion in the camp (Numbers 14: 1–35);

the rebellion of Korah (Numbers 16: 1–40);

the plague in the camp (Numbers 16: 41–50);

the budding of Aaron's rod (Numbers 17: 1–13);

he sinned at Meribah (Numbers 20: 1–13);

the death of Aaron (Numbers 20: 22–29);

his brethren were bitten by snakes (Numbers 21: 1–9);

the defeat of the Amorites (Numbers 21: 21–35);

Balak and Balaam resisted him (Numbers 22: 1–41; Numbers 23: 1–30; Numbers 24: 1–25);

idolatry in the camp of Israel (Numbers 25: 1–15);

the second numbering (Numbers 26: 1–65);

The appointment of the successor (Numbers 27: 15–23);

war with the Midianites (Numbers 31: 1–54);

he gave the Reubenites, the Gadites and the half-tribe of Manasseh the privilege of living on the east side of the Jordan (Numbers 32: 1–42);

he wrote the travels of the children of Israel (Numbers 33: 1–49);

he described the borders of the land of promise (Numbers 34: 1–29);

he went over the law in the plains of Moab (Deut. 1: 1–5);

he emphasized the law about vows (Deut. 23: 21–23);

he begged the Lord to allow him to enter into the land of promise, but his request was refused (Deut. 3: 21–28);

he finished recording the law and put the book in the Ark of the covenant (Deut. 31: 24–26);

he composed his last song (Deut. 32: 1–44);

he gave his parting blessing to the tribes (Deut. 33: 1–29);

he climbed to the summit of Pisgah, and viewed the land promised to Abraham, Isaac and Jacob (Deut. 34: 1–4).

Moses as a leader

He led the Hebrew nation as its leader for forty years (Ex. 7: 7; Deut. 29: 1–5; Deut. 34: 1–7; Acts 7: 30–36).

Moses as a priest

He acted as priest during the temporary worship at Mount Sinai (Ex. 24: 1–8), and at the consecration of Aaron and his sons (Leviticus 8: 1–30).

Moses' character

Good aspects to his character include:

His refusal to be called the son of Pharaoh's daughter and his choice to suffer affliction with God's people shows how much he loved his brethren (Ex. 2: 11,12; Hebrews 11: 23–27);

his attempt to be excused from the leadership of his people reveals his humility (Ex. 3: 7–22; Ex. 4: 1–13);

his address to the people at the Red Sea, while the Egyptians were sweeping down on them, demonstrates his extraordinary faith (Ex. 14: 13–18);

listening to all the complaints of Israel and passing judgment on them from morning until night shows his great perseverance (Ex. 18: 13);

his acceptance of advice from his father-in-law shows that he was open to change (Ex. 18: 17–27);

his destruction of the golden calf reveals his desire for God alone to be honored (Ex. 32: 19–28);

his refusal to rebuke Eldad and Medad for prophesying shows that he was not a jealous person (Numbers 11: 27–29);

his prayer to the Lord to forgive his sister Miriam reveals his meek and forgiving spirit (Numbers 12: 1–13);

his suppression of the insurrection inaugurated by Korah reveals his courage (Numbers 16: 1–40).

Moses' disobedience

God did not allow him to enter into the Promised Land because of one sin (Numbers 20: 1–13).

But Moses did stand on the mountain in the beloved country in the company of Elijah, Peter, James, John, and the Lord Jesus (Matthew 17: 1–13).

Moses' death

He died on Mount Pisgah, and was buried by the Lord in a valley in the land of Moab, but the exact site of his grave was never known (Deut. 34: 1–7).

Samuel

Overview

Miraculous birth of
1 Sam. 1: 7–20

Consecrated to God before his birth
1 Sam. 1: 11; 1 Sam. 1: 22; 1 Sam. 1: 24–28

His mother's song of thanksgiving
1 Sam. 2: 1–10
"Hannah prayed and said,
'My heart exults in the Lord;
my strength is exalted in my God.
My mouth derides my enemies,
because I rejoice in my victory.
  2 There is no Holy One like the Lord,
no one besides you;
there is no Rock like our God.
  3 Talk no more so very proudly,
let not arrogance come from your mouth;
for the Lord is a God of knowledge,
and by him actions are weighed.
  4 The bows of the mighty are broken,
but the feeble gird on strength.
  5 Those who were full have hired themselves out for bread,
but those who were hungry are fat with spoil.
The barren has borne seven,
but she who has many children is forlorn.
  6 The Lord kills and brings to life;
he brings down to Sheol and raises up.
  7 The Lord makes poor and makes rich;
he brings low, he also exalts.
  8 He raises up the poor from the dust;
he lifts the needy from the ash heap,
to make them sit with princes
and inherit a seat of honor.
For the pillars of the earth are the Lord's,
and on them he has set the world.
  9 "He will guard the feet of his faithful ones,
but the wicked shall be cut off in darkness;
for not by might does one prevail.
  10 The Lord! His adversaries shall be shattered;
the Most High will thunder in heaven.
The Lord will judge the ends of the earth;
he will give strength to his king,
and exalt the power of his anointed.'"
1 Samuel 1: 1–10 NRSV

Served in God's house
1 Sam. 2: 11; 1 Sam. 2: 18,19

Blessed by God
"And the boy Samuel grew up in the presence of the Lord" 1 Sam. 2: 21 NRSV.
  "As Samuel grew up, the Lord was with him and let none of his words fall to the ground.
  20 And all Israel from Dan to Beer-sheba knew that Samuel was a trustworthy prophet of the Lord" 1 Sam. 3: 19,20 NRSV.

His vision about the house of Eli
1 Sam. 3: 1–18

A prophet of the Israelites
1 Sam. 3: 20,21; 1 Sam. 4: 1

A judge of Israel, his judgment seat at Bethel, Gilgal, Mizpeh, and Ramah
1 Sam. 7: 15–17

Organizes the tabernacle service
1 Chr. 9: 22; 1 Chr. 26: 28; 2 Chr. 35: 18

Israelites repent because of his reproofs
1 Sam. 7: 4–6

The Philistines defeated as a result of his prayers and sacrifices
1 Sam. 7: 7–14

Makes his corrupt sons judges in Israel
1 Sam. 8: 1–3

He objects to the people asking for a king
1 Sam. 8: 4–22

Anoints Saul king of Israel
1 Sam. 9–10
"Samuel took a vial of oil and poured it on his head, and kissed him; he said, 'The Lord has anointed you ruler over his people Israel. You shall reign over the people of the Lord and you will save them from the hand of their enemies all around'" 1 Samuel 10: 1 NRSV.

Reproves Saul
1 Sam. 13: 11–15; 1 Sam. 15

Anoints David to be king
1 Sam. 16

Shelters David when escaping from Saul
1 Sam. 19: 18

Death of; the lament for him
"Now Samuel died; and all Israel assembled and mourned for him. They buried him at his home in Ramah" 1 Sam. 25: 1 NRSV.

His integrity as judge and ruler
1 Sam. 12: 1–5; Ps. 99: 6; Jer. 15: 1; Heb. 11: 32
"Samuel said to all Israel, 'I have listened to you in all that you have said to me, and have set a king over you.

2 See, it is the king who leads you now; I am old and gray, but my sons are with you. I have led you from my youth until this day.

3 Here I am; testify against me before the Lord and before his anointed. Whose ox have I taken? Or whose donkey have I taken? Or whom have I defrauded? Whom have I oppressed? Or from whose hand have I taken a bribe to blind my eyes with it? Testify against me and I will restore it to you.'

4 They said, 'You have not defrauded us or oppressed us or taken anything from the hand of anyone.'

5 He said to them, 'The Lord is witness against you, and his anointed is witness this day, that you have not found anything in my hand." And they said, 'He is witness.'"
1 Samuel 12: 1–5 NRSV

David, King of Israel (1)

Overview

Genealogy of
Ruth 4: 18–22; 1 Sam. 16: 11;
1 Sam. 17: 12; 1 Chr. 2: 3–15; Matt. 1: 1–6;
Luke 3: 31–38

A shepherd
1 Sam. 16: 11

Kills a lion and a bear
1 Sam. 17: 34–36

Anointed king, while a youth, by
Samuel
1 Sam. 16: 1; 1 Sam. 16: 13; Ps. 89: 19–37

Chosen by God
Ps. 78: 70

Armor bearer and musician at Saul's
court
1 Sam. 16: 21–23

Kills Goliath
1 Sam. 17

Love for Jonathan
1 Sam. 18: 1–4

A popular and discreet person
1 Sam. 18

Saul's jealousy of
1 Sam. 18: 8–30

Is deceived by Merab, and given Michal
as his wife
1 Sam. 18: 17–27

Jonathan prays for
1 Sam. 19: 1–7

Defeats the Philistines
1 Sam. 19: 8

Saul tries to kill him; he escapes to
Ramah, and lives at Naioth
1 Sam. 19: 9–24

Jonathan makes covenant with him
1 Sam. 20

Escapes to Nob, and receives
shewbread and Goliath's sword from
Abimelech
1 Sam. 21: 1–6; Matt. 12: 3,4

Escapes to Gath
1 Sam. 21: 10–15

Saves Keilah
1 Sam. 23: 1–13

Makes second covenant with Jonathan
1 Sam. 23: 16–18

Goes to the desert of Ziph and is
betrayed to Saul
1 Sam. 23: 13–26

Writes a psalm on the betrayal,
Psalm 54

Goes to Engedi
1 Sam. 23: 29

Does not take his opportunity to kill
Saul
1 Sam. 24

Marries Nabal's widow, Abigail, and
Ahinoam
1 Sam. 25

Lives in the desert of Ziph, has
opportunity to kill Saul, but only takes
his spear
1 Sam. 26

Flees to Achish and lives in Ziklag
1 Sam. 27

List of men who join him
1 Chr. 12: 1–22

Is refused permission to accompany the Philistines to battle against the Israelites
1 Sam. 28: 1,2; 1 Sam. 29

Rescues the people of Ziklag, who had been captured by the Amalekites
1 Sam. 30

Death and burial of Saul and his sons
1 Sam. 31; 2 Sam. 21: 1; 2 Sam. 21: 14

Kills the person who killed Saul
2 Sam. 1: 1–16

Lamentation over Saul
2 Sam. 1: 17–27

Lives for one year and four months at Ziklag
1 Sam. 27: 7

Goes to Hebron, and is anointed king by Judah
2 Sam. 2: 1–4; 2 Sam. 2: 11; 2 Sam. 5: 5; 1 Kgs. 2: 11; 1 Chr. 3: 4; 1 Chr. 11: 1–3

List of those who join him at Hebron
1 Chr. 12: 23–40

Ishbosheth, son of Saul, crowned
2 Sam. 2–4

David defeats Ishbosheth
2 Sam. 2: 13–32; 2 Sam. 3: 4

Demands the restoration of Michal
2 Sam. 3: 14–16

Abner joins David, but is killed by Joab
2 Sam. 3

Punishes Ishbosheth's murderers
2 Sam. 4

Anointed king over all Israel, after reigning over Judah at Hebron seven and a half years, and reigns thirty-three years
2 Sam. 2: 11; 2 Sam. 5: 5; 1 Chr. 3: 4; 1 Chr. 11: 1–3; 1 Chr. 12: 23–40; 1 Chr. 29: 27

Captures Jerusalem
2 Sam. 5: 6; 1 Chr. 11: 4–8; Is. 29: 1

Builds a palace
2 Sam. 5: 11; 2 Chr. 2: 3

Friendship of, with Hiram, king of Tyre
2 Sam. 5: 11; 1 Kgs. 5: 1

David, King of Israel (2)

Overview continued

Fame of
1 Chr. 14: 17

Philistines defeated by him
2 Sam. 5: 17–25

Ark brought to Jerusalem
2 Sam. 6: 1–16; 1 Chr. 13

Organized the tabernacle service
1 Chr. 9: 22; 1 Chr. 15: 16–24;
1 Chr. 16: 4–6; 1 Chr. 16: 37–43

Offers sacrifice, distributes gifts, and
blesses the people
2 Sam. 6: 17–19

Wishes to build a temple, is forbidden,
but receives promise that his seed
should reign forever
2 Sam. 7: 12–16; 2 Sam. 23: 5;
1 Chr. 17: 11–14; 2 Chr. 6: 16; Ps. 89: 3,4;
Ps. 132: 11,12; Acts 15: 16; Rom. 15: 12

Conquers the Philistines, Moabites, and
Syria
2 Sam. 8

Treats Mephibosheth with great
kindness
2 Sam. 9: 6; 2 Sam. 19: 24–30

Defeats the combined armies of the
Ammonites and Syrians
2 Sam. 10; 1 Chr. 19

Commits adultery with Bathsheba
2 Sam. 11: 2–5

Causes the death of Uriah
2 Sam. 11: 6–25

Takes Bathsheba as his wife
2 Sam. 11: 26,27

Is rebuked by the prophet Nathan
2 Sam. 12: 1–14

Repents and confesses his guilt
Ps. 6; Ps. 32; Ps. 38–40; Ps. 51

Death of his infant son
2 Sam. 12: 15–23

Solomon is born
2 Sam. 12: 24,25

Ammonites defeated
2 Sam. 12: 26–31

Amnon's crime, his murder by
Absalom, and Absalom's flight
2 Sam. 13

Absalom's return
2 Sam. 14: 1–24

David flees from Jerusalem
2 Sam. 15: 13–37

Shimei curses him
2 Sam. 16

Crosses the Jordan
2 Sam. 17: 21–29

Absalom's defeat and death
2 Sam. 18

Laments the death of Absalom
2 Sam. 18: 33; 2 Sam. 19: 1–4

Returns to Jerusalem
2 Sam. 20: 1–3

Buries Saul's bones, and his sons'
2 Sam. 21: 12–14

Defeats the Philistines
2 Sam. 21: 15–22; 1 Chr. 20: 4–8

Marries Abishag
1 Kgs. 1: 1–4

Reorganizes the tabernacle service
1 Chr. 22–26; 2 Chr. 7: 6; 2 Chr. 8: 14

Solomon appointed to the throne
1 Kgs. 1; 1 Chr. 23: 1

Delivers his charge to Solomon
1 Kgs. 2: 1–11; 1 Chr. 22: 6–19; 1 Chr. 28–
29

Last words of
2 Sam. 23: 1–7

Death of
1 Kgs. 2: 10; 1 Chr. 29: 28; Acts 2: 29,30

Sepulcher of
Acts 2: 29

Characteristics of David

DEVOUTNESS OF
1 Sam. 13: 14; 2 Sam. 6: 5; 2 Sam. 6: 14–
18; 2 Sam. 7: 18–29; 2 Sam. 8: 11;
2 Sam. 24: 25; 1 Kgs. 3: 14; 1 Chr. 17: 16–
27

JUSTICE IN ADMINISTRATION
2 Sam. 8: 15; 1 Chr. 18: 14

DISCREETNESS OF
1 Sam. 18: 14; 1 Sam. 18: 30

MEEKNESS OF
1 Sam. 24: 7; 1 Sam. 26: 11; 2 Sam. 16: 11;
2 Sam. 19: 22,23

MERCIFUL
2 Sam. 19: 23

David as:

MUSICIAN
1 Sam. 16: 21–23; 1 Chr. 15: 16;
1 Chr. 23: 5; 2 Chr. 7: 6; 2 Chr. 29: 26;
Neh. 12: 36; Amos 6: 5

PROPHET
2 Sam. 23: 2–7; 1 Chr. 28: 19;
Matt. 22: 41–46; Acts 2: 25–38;
Acts 4: 25

Type of Christ

Ps. 2; Ps. 16; Ps. 18: 43; Ps. 69: 7–9;
Ps. 69: 20,21; Ps. 69: 26; Ps. 69: 29;
Ps. 89: 19–37

JESUS CALLED SON OF DAVID
Matt. 9: 27; Matt. 12: 23; Matt. 15: 22;
Matt. 20: 30,31; Matt. 21: 9; Matt. 22: 42;
Mark 10: 47,48; Luke 18: 37; Luke 18: 39

PROPHECIES CONCERNING HIM AND
HIS KINGDOM
Num. 24: 17; Num. 24: 19; 2 Sam. 7: 11–
16; 1 Chr. 17: 9–14; 1 Chr. 22; 2 Chr. 6: 5–
17; 2 Chr. 13: 5; 2 Chr. 21: 7; Ps. 89: 19–37;
Is. 9: 7; Is. 16: 5; Is. 22: 20–25; Jer. 23: 5;
Jer. 33: 15–26; Luke 1: 32,33

Solomon

Overview

Son of David by Bathsheba
2 Sam. 12: 24; 1 Kgs. 1: 13; 1 Kgs. 1: 17;
1 Kgs. 1: 21

Named Jedidiah, by Nathan the
prophet
2 Sam. 12: 24,25

Ancestor of Joseph
Matt. 1: 6

Succeeds David to the throne of Israel
1 Kgs. 1: 11–48; 1 Kgs. 2: 12; 1 Chr. 23: 1;
1 Chr. 28; Eccl. 1: 12

Anointed king a second time
1 Chr. 29: 22

His prayer for wisdom, and his vision
1 Kgs. 3: 5–14; 2 Chr. 1: 7–12

Covenant renewed in a vision after the
dedication of the temple
1 Kgs. 9: 1–9; 2 Chr. 7: 12–22

His rigorous reign
1 Kgs. 2

Builds the temple
1 Kgs. 5–6; 1 Kgs. 9: 10; 1 Chr. 6: 10;
2 Chr. 2–4; 2 Chr. 7: 11; Jer. 52: 20;
Acts 7: 45–47

Dedicates the temple
1 Kgs. 8; 2 Chr. 6

Renews the ministry of the priests and
Levites, and the forms of service in line
with Moses' commandment and the
regulations of David
2 Chr. 8: 12–16; 2 Chr. 35: 4; Neh. 12: 45

Builds his palace
1 Kgs. 3: 1; 1 Kgs. 7: 1; 1 Kgs. 7: 8;
1 Kgs. 9: 10; 2 Chr. 7: 11; 2 Chr. 8: 1;
Eccl. 2: 4

Builds his house of the forest of
Lebanon
1 Kgs. 7: 2–7

Builds for Pharaoh's daughter
1 Kgs. 7: 8–12; 1 Kgs. 9: 24; 2 Chr. 8: 11;
Eccl. 2: 4

Ivory throne of
1 Kgs. 7: 7; 1 Kgs. 10: 18–20

Halls for judgment
1 Kgs. 7: 7

Builds Millo, the wall of Jerusalem,
the cities of Hazor, Megiddo, Gezer,
Bethhoron, Baalath, Tadmor, store
cities, and cities for chariots, and for
cavalry
1 Kgs. 9: 15–19; 2 Chr. 9: 25

Provides an armory
1 Kgs. 10: 16,17

Plants vineyards and orchards
Eccl. 2: 4–6

Imports apes and peacocks
1 Kgs. 10: 22

Musicians and musical instruments of
his court
1 Kgs. 10: 12; 2 Chr. 9: 11; Eccl. 2: 8

The splendor of his court
1 Kgs. 10: 5–9; 1 Kgs. 10: 12; 2 Chr. 9: 3–8;
Eccl. 2: 9; Matt. 6: 29; Luke 12: 27

Commerce of
1 Kgs. 9: 28; 1 Kgs. 10: 11,12; 1 Kgs. 10: 22;
1 Kgs. 10: 28,29; 2 Chr. 1: 16,17;
2 Chr. 8: 17,18; 2 Chr. 9: 13–22;
2 Chr. 9: 28

Is visited by the queen of Sheba
1 Kgs. 10: 1–13; 2 Chr. 9: 1–12

Wealth of
1 Kgs. 9; 1 Kgs. 10: 10; 1 Kgs. 10: 14,15;
1 Kgs. 10: 23; 1 Kgs. 10: 27; 2 Chr. 1: 15;
2 Chr. 9: 1; 2 Chr. 9: 9; 2 Chr. 9: 13;
2 Chr. 9: 24; 2 Chr. 9: 27; Eccl. 1: 16

Has seven hundred wives and three
hundred concubines
1 Kgs. 11: 3; Deut. 17: 17

Their influence over him
1 Kgs. 11: 4

Marries one of Pharaoh's daughters
1 Kgs. 3: 1

Builds idolatrous temples
1 Kgs. 11: 1–8; 2 Kgs. 23: 13

Extent of his conquests
1 Kgs. 4: 21; 1 Kgs. 4: 24; 1 Kgs. 8: 65;
2 Chr. 7: 8; 2 Chr. 9: 26

Receives tribute
1 Kgs. 4: 21; 1 Kgs. 9: 21; 2 Chr. 8: 8

Officers of
1 Kgs. 2: 35; 1 Kgs. 4: 1–19; 2 Chr. 8: 9,10

Military equipment of
1 Kgs. 4: 26; 1 Kgs. 4: 28; 1 Kgs. 10: 16,17;
1 Kgs. 10: 26; 1 Kgs. 10: 28; 2 Chr. 1: 14;
2 Chr. 9: 25; Deut. 17: 15,16

Wisdom and fame of
1 Kgs. 4: 29–34; 1 Kgs. 10: 3,4;
1 Kgs. 10: 8; 1 Kgs. 10: 23,24;

1 Chr. 29: 24,25; 2 Chr. 9: 2–7;
2 Chr. 9: 22,23; Eccl. 1: 16; Matt. 12: 42

Piety of
1 Kgs. 3: 5–15; 1 Kgs. 4: 29; 1 Kgs. 8

Beloved of God
2 Sam. 12: 24

Justice of, illustrated in his judgment of
the two harlots
1 Kgs. 3: 16–28

Oppressions of
1 Kgs. 12: 4; 2 Chr. 10: 4

Reigns forty years
2 Chr. 9: 30

Death of
2 Chr. 9: 29–31

Prophecies concerning
2 Sam. 7: 12–16; 1 Kgs. 11: 9–13;
1 Chr. 17: 11–14; 1 Chr. 28: 6,7; Ps. 132: 11

A type of Christ
Ps. 45: 2–17; Ps. 72 765

Parallel passages in the historical books (1)

Overlap

Even a cursory read through the historical books of the Old Testament, 1 and 2 Samuel, 1 and 2 Kings, and 1 and 2 Chronicles reveals much overlap of material between the books.

Parallel passages

The following lists of references show the parallel passages between the books of Samuel and Kings on the one hand, and the books of Chronicles on the other.

List of references emphasize different viewpoints

1 From this list of references it is easy to identify the similar sections in the different books.

2 The lists underline the different viewpoints of these books.

Different viewpoints

1 and 2 Samuel and 1 and 2 Kings have a similar viewpoint of the historical events they record, and this is different from that found in 1 and 2 Chronicles.

HUMAN STANDPOINT
1 and 2 Samuel and 1 and 2 Kings view history from a human standpoint, as they would be seen by the natural eye.

DIVINE STANDPOINT
1 and 2 Chronicles view the same events but from a divine standpoint. They view them with a spiritual perspective.

1 and 2 Samuel and 1 and 2 Kings view events in their historical context, while 1 and 2 Chronicles often add

the moral aspect seen in the recorded event. In the former we have the historic record; in the latter we have the divine reason for it, which often comes in the form of divine "words" and judgment on the event.

SAUL'S DEATH
An example of these two different approaches is seen in how Saul's death is recorded.

"So Saul died, and his three sons, and his armor bearer, and all his men, that same day together" 1 Samuel 31: 6.

"So Saul died for his transgression which he committed against the Lord, even against the word of the Lord, which he kept not, and also for asking counsel of one that had a familiar spirit, to inquire of it; And inquired not of the Lord: therefore he slew him, and turned the kingdom unto David the son of Jesse" 1 Chronicles 10: 13,14.

Different amount of space given to the same events

The different viewpoints of 1 and 2 Samuel and 1 and 2 Kings, and that of 1 and 2 Chronicles accounts for the amount of space they devote to the same historic event.

For example, in the former books there are three chapters (that is 88 verses) given to the secular events of Hezekiah's reign (recorded in 2 Kings 8, 19, and 20), but only three verses (in 2 Kings 18: 4–6) given to his great religious reformation.

"He removed the high places, and brake the images, and cut down the groves, and brake in pieces the brazen serpent that Moses had made: for unto those days the children of Israel did burn incense to it: and he called it Nehushtan.

5 He trusted in the Lord God of Israel; so that after him was none like him among all the kings of Judah, nor any that were before him.

6 For he clave to the Lord, and departed not from following him, but kept his commandments, which the Lord commanded Moses."

2 Kings 18: 4–6

In Chronicles this is exactly reversed. Three chapters (which amount to 84 verses) are devoted to his reformation (2 Chr. 29–31), while one chapter (or 32 verses) suffices for the secular events of his reign.

In the same way Jehoshaphat's three alliances with Ahab can be spiritually and morally understood only from 2 Chr. 17, of which there is not a word in 1 and 2 Kings.

ORDER OF EVENTS

The two different viewpoints of 1 and 2 Samuel, 1 and 2 Kings, and 1 and 2 Chronicles also determine the order in which the events which they record are treated.

In the books of Kings the events are recorded in chronological order; while in Chronicles this order is sometimes ignored, in order to bring the moral causes or consequences of the two events together, so a comparison or contrast can be made. Examples of this are the list of David's mighty men; David's numbering the people, and the account of the plague.

1 and 2 Samuel and 1 and 2 Kings give the whole history of Israel's kingdom.

1 and 2 Chronicles only record the events which relate to the house of David and the tribe of Judah.

Table of parallel passages in 1 and 2 Samuel, 1 and 2 Kings, and 1 and 2 Chronicles

1 Samuel	1 Chronicles
1 Sam. 27	1 Chron. 12: 1–7
29: 1–3	12: 19–22
31	10
2 Samuel	**1 Chronicles**
2 Sam. 5: 1–5	1 Chr. 11: 1–3
5: 6–10	11: 4–9
5: 11–16	14: 1–7
5: 17–25	14: 8–17
6: 1–11	13
6: 12–23	15 and 16
7	17
8	18
10	19
11: 1–27	20: 1
12: 29–31	20: 1–3
23: 8–39	11: 10–47
24: 1–9	21: 1–6
24: 1–9	27: 23,24
24: 10–17	21: 7–17
24: 18–24	21: 18–22: 1
1 Kings	**1 Chronicles**
1 Kings 2: 1	23: 1
2: 1–4	28: 20,21
2: 10–12	29: 23–30

Parallel passages in the historical books (2)

Parallel passages in 1 and 2 Samuel, 1 and 2 Kings, and 1 and 2 Chronicles

1 Kings	2 Chronicles
2: 46	1: 1
3: 4–15	1: 2–13
5	2
6	3: 1–14; 4: 9
7: 15–21	3: 15–17
7: 23–26	4: 2–5
7: 38–46	4: 6,10,17
7: 47–50	4: 18–22
7: 51	5: 1
8	5: 2–7: 10
9: 1–9	7: 11–22
9: 10–28	8
10: 1–13	9: 1–12

1 Kings and 2 Chronicles

1 Kings 10: 1–13 and 2 Chronicles 9: 1–12 are a good example of the similarity between passages in 1 Kings and 2 Chronicles

"Now when the queen of Sheba heard of the fame of Solomon concerning the name of the Lord, she came to test him with hard questions. She came to Jerusalem with a very great retinue, with camels that bore spices, very much gold, and precious stones; and when she came to Solomon, she spoke with him about all that was in her heart. So Solomon answered all her questions; there was nothing so difficult for the king that he could not explain it to her. And when the queen of Sheba had seen all the wisdom of Solomon, the house

that he had built, the food on his table, the seating of his servants, the service of his waiters and their apparel, his cupbearers, and his entryway by which he went up to the house of the Lord, there was no more spirit in her. Then she said to the king: 'It was a true report which I heard in my own land about your words and your wisdom. However I did not believe the words until I came and saw with my own eyes; and indeed the half was not told me. Your wisdom and prosperity exceed the fame of which I heard.'"   *1 Kings 10: 1–8*

"Now when the queen of Sheba heard of the fame of Solomon, she came to Jerusalem to test Solomon with hard questions, having a very great retinue, camels that bore spices, gold in abundance, and precious stones; and when she came to Solomon, she spoke with him about all that was in her heart. So Solomon answered all her questions; there was nothing so difficult for Solomon that he could not explain it to her. And when the queen of Sheba had seen the wisdom of Solomon, the house that he had built, the food on his table, the seating of his servants, the service of his waiters and their apparel, his cupbearers and their apparel, and his entryway by which he went up to the house of the Lord, there was no more spirit in her.

Then she said to the king: "It was a true report which I heard in my own land about your words and your wisdom. However I did not believe their words until I came and saw with my own eyes; and indeed the half of the greatness of your wisdom was not told me. You exceed the fame of which I heard.'"   *2 Chronicles 9: 1–6*

1 Kings	2 Chronicles
10: 14–25	9: 13–24
10: 26–29	9: 25–28; 1: 14–17
11: 41–43	9: 29,31
12: 1–19	10
12: 21–24	11: 1–4
12: 25	11: 5–12
12: 26–31	11: 13–17
14: 22–24	12: 1
14: 25–28	12: 2–12
14: 21,29–31	12: 13–16
15: 1	13: 1,2
15: 6	13: 2–21
15: 7,8	13: 22; 14: 1
15: 11,12	14: 1–5
15: 13–15	15: 16–18
15: 16–22	16: 1–6
15: 23,24	16: 11–14
22: 1–20,44	18
22: 41–43	17: 1; 20: 31–33
22: 45	20: 34
22: 47–49	20: 35–37
22: 50	21: 1

2 Kings	2 Chronicles
1: 1; 3: 4,5	20: 1–3
8: 16–19	21: 2–7
8: 20–22	21: 8–15
8: 23,24	21: 18–20
8: 25–27	22: 1–4
8: 28,29; 9: 1–28	22: 5–7,9
10: 11–14	22: 8
11: 1–3	22: 10–12
11: 4–20	23
11: 21; 12: 1–3	24: 1–3
12: 6–16	24: 4–14
12: 17,18	24: 23,24
12: 19–21	24: 25–27

14: 1–6	25: 1–4
14: 7	25: 11–16
14: 8–14	25: 17–24
14: 17–20	25: 25–28
14: 21,22;	15: 1–42; 6: 1–15
15: 6,7,27,28	26: 22,23
15: 32–35	27: 1–8
15: 38	27: 9
16: 1,2	28: 1,2
16: 3,4,6	28: 2–8
16: 7	28: 16–19
15: 29	28: 20
16: 8–18	28: 21–25
16: 19,20	28: 26,27
18: 1–3	29: 1,2
18: 13	Isaiah 36: 1
18: 14–16	2 Chronicles 32: 2–8
20: 1–11	32: 24; Isaiah 38
20: 12–19	Isaiah 39: 1–8
18: 17–37	2 Chr 32: 9–19; Is 36: 2–22
19: 1–5	2 Chr 32: 20; Is 37: 1–4
19: 6,7	Is 37: 6,7
19: 8–19	2 Chron 32: 17; Is 37: 8–20
19: 20–37	2 Ch 32: 21; Is 37: 21–38
20: 20,21	2 Chron 32: 32,33
21: 1–16	33: 1–9
21: 17,18	33: 18–20
21: 19–26	33: 21–25
22: 1,2	34: 1–7
22: 3–20	34: 8–28
23: 1–3	34: 29–32
23: 21–23	35: 1–19
23: 24–26	34: 33
23: 28–30	35: 20–27
23: 30–33	36: 1–3
23: 34–37	36: 4,5
24: 8,9	36: 9
24: 15–17	36: 10
24: 18,19	36: 11,12
24: 20	36: 13–16
25: 8–21	36: 18–21

Kings of Israel (1)

Kings of Israel and Judah

Kings of Israel

This chronological list of the kings of Israel shows how long they each reigned for.

1. Jeroboam, twenty-two years
2. Nadab, about two years
3. Baasha, twenty-four years
4. Elah, two years
5. Zimri, seven days
6. Omri, twelve years
7. Ahab, twenty-two years
8. Ahaziah, two years
9. Jehoram, twelve years
10. Jehu, twenty-eight years
11. Jehoahaz, seventeen years
12. Jehoash, sixteen years
13. Jeroboam II, forty-one years
14. Zachariah, six months
15. Shallum, one month
16. Menahem, ten years
17. Pekahiah, two years
18. Pekah, twenty years
19. Hoshea, nine years

Kings of Judah

This chronological list of the kings of Judah shows how long they each reigned for.

1. Rehoboam, seventeen years
2. Abijah, or Abijam, three years
3. Asa, forty-one years
4. Jehoshaphat, twenty-five years
5. Jehoram, eight years
6. Ahaziah, one year
7. Athaliah's usurpation, six years
8. Joash, or Jehoash, forty years
9. Amaziah, twenty-nine years
10. Uzziah, or Azariah, fifty-two years
11. Jotham, sixteen years
12. Ahaz, sixteen years
13. Hezekiah, twenty-nine years
14. Manasseh, fifty-five years
15. Amon, two years
16. Josiah, thirty-one years
17. Jehoahaz, Josiah's son, three months
18. Jehoiakim, Josiah's son, eleven years
19. Jehoiachin, or Jeconiah, Jehoiakim's son, three months
20. Zedekiah, or Mattaniah, Josiah's son, eleven years

Kingdom of Israel

JEROBOAM, THE FIRST KING OF ISRAEL

SUMMARY

1 Kings 11: 26–40, 1 Kings 12–14, 2 Chronicles 10

- Fled to Egypt to escape Solomon
- Returned when Rehoboam became king
- Became first king of Israel
- Set up golden calves in Dan and Bethel
- Set up priesthood and worship for calves
- Reigned 22 years
- A bad king

Details of reign
During Solomon's building projects he met a young man called Jeroboam, the son of Nebat an Ephrathite, who

was industrious, and he put him in charge of the house of Joseph (1 Kings 11: 26–29).

Later, as Jeroboam was going out of Jerusalem, he was met by the prophet Ahijah who assured him that he should reign over ten of the tribes of Israel (1 Kings 11: 29–39).

Solomon, on hearing of this, attempted to kill Jeroboam. So Jeroboam fled to Egypt (1 Kings 11: 40).

After the accession of Rehoboam to the throne the people sent for Jeroboam. Jeroboam joined his countrymen in requesting the new king to lighten their burdens which he refused to do. So Jeroboam led the revolt against him (1 Kings 11: 1–24; 1 Chronicles 10: 1–19).

Jeroboam established himself at Shechem. To prevent the people from going to Jerusalem to worship, Jeroboam set up two golden calves, one at Bethel and the other at Dan, assuring the people that these were the gods that had brought them out of the land of Egypt (1 Kings 12: 25–30).

Jeroboam reigned twenty-two years (1 Kings 14: 19,20). He reigned contemporaneously with Rehoboam seventeen years (1 Kings 12: 1–20; 1 Kings 14: 20; 2 Chronicles 14: 20), Abijah three years (1 Kings 14: 31–15: 2), and with Asa two years (1 Kings 14: 20,31; 1 Kings 15: 1,2,8–10; 2 Chronicles 12: 13).

AHIJAH THE PROPHET

The prophet Ahijah ministered during the reign of Jeroboam (1 Kings 14: 1–18).

NADAB, THE SECOND KING OF ISRAEL

Summary

1 Kings 15: 25–32
• Son of Jereboam
• Killed by Baasha
• Reigned 2 years
• A bad king

Details

Jeroboam was succeeded by his son Nadab. His uneventful reign lasted for only two years (1 Kings 15: 25).

BAASHA, THE THIRD KING OF ISRAEL

Summary

1 Kings 15: 33–16: 7
• Killed Nadab and the whole household of Jereboam
• Fought with Asa, king of Judah
• Reigned 24 years
• A bad king

Details

Second dynasty.

Nadab was overthrown and succeeded by Baasha, who, as soon as he became king exterminated the house of Jeroboam (1 Kings 15: 2–30).

He reigned contemporaneously with Asa (1 Kings 15: 9,10,33).

JEHU THE PROPHET

The prophet Jehu lived during the reign of Baasha (1 Kings 16: 1–4).

Kings of Israel (2)

Kingdom of Israel, continued

ELAH, THE FOURTH KING OF ISRAEL

Summary
1 Kings 16: 8–14
• Son of Baasha
• Reigned 2 years
• Killed by Zimri
• A bad king

Details
King. Baasha was succeeded by his son Elah, who reigned for two years contemporaneously with Asa, king of Judah (1 Kings 15: 9,10; 1 Kings 16: 6–8).

ZIMRI, THE FIFTH KING OF ISRAEL

Summary
1 Kings 16: 8–20
• Killed Elah and the whole household of Baasha
• Reigned 7 days
• Killed himself
• A bad king

Details
Third dynasty.
Elah was assassinated by His servant Zimri who, as soon as he ascended the throne, destroyed all the house of Baasha.
Zimri reigned Contemporaneously with Asa for seven days (1 Kings 15: 9,10; 1 Kings 16: 8–30).

OMRI, THE SIXTH KING OF ISRAEL

Summary
1 Kings 16: 15–28
• Commander of army
• Built Samaria
• Reigned 12 years (6 in Tirzah)
• A bad king

Details
Fourth dynasty.
Zimri was succeeded by Omri. He reigned six years in undisputed authority. He was contemporary with Asa (1 Kings 15: 9,10; 1 Kings 16: 21–23). The main achievement of Omri's reign was the founding of the city of Samaria (1 Kings 16: 23,24). His reign was characterized by evil (1 Kings 16: 25–27).

AHAB, THE SEVENTH KING OF ISRAEL.

Summary
1 Kings 16–22, 2 Chronicles 18
• Married Jezebel the Sidonian
• Served Baal and did more evil than any other king
• Coveted Naboth's vineyard
• Killed in battle against Aram
• Reigned 22 years
• A bad king

Details
Omri was succeeded by his son Ahab (1 Kings 16: 28). He introduced idolatry into the court of Israel, and his reign was marked by its great disregard for God's law (1 Kings 16: 9–17: 24).
He reigned contemporaneously with Asa four years (1 Kings 15: 9,10; 1 Kings 16: 29) and Jehoshaphat eighteen years (1 Kings 22;41,42).

MICAIAH AND ELIJAH THE PROPHETS
During Ahab's reign two notable prophets ministered.

MICAIAH

Ahab formed a military alliance with Jehoshaphat, and they went to war against the king of Syria. Before they went into the battle, Ahab called Micaiah whose predictions about the battle were fulfilled (2 Chronicles 18: 1–34).

ELIJAH

Elijah was a faithful prophet to God at a time when idolatry held sway in Ahab's court, and when Israel seemed to have forsaken the Lord (1 Kings 16: 29–17: 1).

The main events in Elijah's life were:

His prediction, in front of King Ahab, that there would be no more rain until he said so (1 Kings 17: 1; James 5: 17);

he was fed by ravens on the banks of the River Cherith (1 Kings 17: 2–7);

he stayed at Zarephath (1 Kings 17: 8–16);

he restored the widow's son (1 Kings 17: 17–24);

he rebuilt the Lord's altar and destroyed the prophets of Baal (1 Kings 18: 20–40);

at the end of the drought he raced from Carmel to Jezreel (1 Kings 18: 41–46);

he fled from Jezebel's anger (1 Kings 19: 1–3);

he sat down under a juniper tree and prayed that he might die (1 Kings 19: 4);

the angel of the Lord appeared to him, fed him, and strengthened him (1 Kings 19: 5–8);

the Lord spoke to him at Mount Sinai and assured him that there were seven thousand in Israel who had not bowed their knees to Baal (1 Kings 19: 9–18);

by the Lord's authority he anointed Elisha of Abelmeholah as his successor (1 Kings 19: 15–21);

he predicted the terrible end of Ahab and his wife (1 Kings 21: 17–29);

he called fire down from heaven (2 Kings 1: 1–12; Luke 9: 54);

he predicted the death of Ahaziah (2 Kings 1: 13–18);

he was carried to heaven in a chariot of fire (2 Kings 2: 1–18).

AHAZIAH, THE EIGHTH KING OF ISRAEL

Summary

1 Kings 22: 51–53; 2 Kings 1
- Did evil, worshiping the Baal
- Fell through lattice and became ill
- Sent to Baal about sickness, but heard from Elijah
- Reigned 2 years
- A bad king

Details

Ahab was succeeded by his son Ahaziah. He followed in the footsteps of his wicked ancestors (1 Kings 22: 51–53). As a result of an accident he became dangerously sick ill. He sent messengers to ask Baalzebub, the god of Ekron, if he would recover. The angel of the Lord commanded Elijah to go and tell the messengers to tell the king that he would die.

Kings of Israel (3)

Kingdom of Israel, continued

AHAZIAH, THE EIGHTH KING OF
ISRAEL, CONTINUED

Details
When Ahaziah recognized the
identity of the prophet Elijah he sent a
deputation of soldiers requesting him
to come to him at once. Eventually the
prophet went to the king and predicted
his imminent death (2 Kings 1: 1–16).
Ahaziah reigned contemporaneously
with Jehoshaphat two years (1 Kings
22: 42–51; 2 Kings 3: 1).

JEHORAM, THE NINTH KING OF ISRAEL

Summary
2 Kings 3,9
• Joined with Judah and Edom to fight
  Moab
• Killed in Jezreel by Jehu
• Reigned 12 years
• A bad king

Details
Ahaziah was succeeded by his brother
Jehoram (2 Kings 1: 17; 2 Kings 3: 1). His
reign was characterized by evil (2 Kings
3: 1,2).

He fought unsuccessfully against the
king of Moab (2 Kings 3: 1–27). He
reigned contemporaneously with
Jehoshaphat (2 Kings 3: 1), Jehoram
(1 Kings 22: 42; 2 Kings 3: 1; 2 Kings
9: 29; 2 Chronicles 21: 1,5), and Ahaziah
(2 Kings 9: 29;

ELISHA THE PROPHET
The main events in his life were:
he was anointed by Elijah as his

successor (1 Kings 19: 19–21);

he received a double portion of the
spirit of Elijah (2 Kings 2: 9–15);

he told king Jehoram how to obtain
water during his campaign against the
Moabites (2 Kings 3: 10–20);

he increased the widow's oil (2 Kings
4: 1–7);

he raised the Shunammite's son from
the dead (2 Kings 4: 8–38);

he performed a great miracle at Gilgal
(2 Kings 4: 39–41);

he miraculously fed a large group of
people (2 Kings 4: 42–44);

he healed Naaman's leprosy (2 Kings
5: 1–19);

he brought leprosy on the house of
Gehazi (2 Kings 5: 20–27);

he was captured by the Syrians (2 Kings
6: 13–18);

he led the Syrians to Samaria, sent
them away, and so won a great victory
over them (2 Kings 6: 19–24);

he predicted the sudden provision of
a great amount of food, during the
famine of Samaria (2 Kings 7: 1,2);

his prediction was fulfilled (2 Kings
7: 3–20);

he carried out the commission
originally given to Elijah (1 Kings 19: 15–
18; 2 Kings 8: 1–15; 2 Kings 9: 1–13).

JEHU, THE TENTH KING OF ISRAEL

Summary
2 Kings 9–10
• Anointed by Elisha
• Killed Jehoram and shot Ahaziah

king of Judah
- Had Jezebel killed
- Killed 70 sons of Ahab
- Killed Ahaziah king of Judah's relatives
- Destroyed temple of Baal and killed worshipers
- Reigned 28 years
- A bad king

Details

Fifth dynasty.

Jehoram was killed and succeeded by Jehu, the son of Jehoshaphat, the son of Nimshi.

He inaugurated a reform by killing Jezebel, the sons of Ahab, and the prophets of Baal (2 Kings 9: 1–10: 28). Because of his success in the destruction of evil, the Lord promised him that his children would succeed him for the next four generations (2 Kings 10: 29–34).

Jehu was contemporary with Athaliah seven years (2 Kings 10: 36; 2 Kings 11: 1–4) and Jehoash twenty-one years (2 Kings 12: 1).

JEHOAHAZ, THE ELEVENTH KING OF ISRAEL

Summary

2 Kings 13: 1–9
- God gave Israel to Aram because of his evil
- Reigned 17 years
- A bad king

Details

Jehu was succeeded by his son Jehoahaz, who reigned in Samaria seventeen years (2 Kings 18: 1). His reign was characterized by continuing idolatrous practices inaugurated by Jeroboam. The Lord delivered Isreal into the hands of the Syrians. Jehoahaz seemed to be penitent but did not reform (2 Kings 12: 2–8).

He was contemporary with Jehoash seventeen years (2 Kings 12: 1; 2 Kings 13: 1).

JOASH, THE TWELFTH KING OF ISRAEL

Summary

2 Kings 13: 10–25
- Conferred with Elisha about Aram
- Struck ground 3 times with arrows
- Defeated Aram 3 times
- A bad king

Details

Jehoahaz was succeeded by his son Joash, who followed in the footsteps of his wicked predecessors.

During Elisha's last illness he was visited by Joash. Elisha told Joash that he would defeat the Syrians three times (2 Kings 13: 14–19).

Joash reigned sixteen years, and was contemporary with Jehoash two years (2 Kings 13: 9,10; 2 Kings 12: 1; 2 Kings 14: 1) and Amaziah fourteen years (2 Kings 14: 1,2).

JEROBOAM II, THE THIRTEENTH KING OF ISRAEL

Summary

2 Kings 14: 23–29
- Restored Israel's border as Jonah had said
- Reigned 41 years
- A bad king

Kings of Israel (4)

Kingdom of Israel, continued

JEROBOAM II, THE THIRTEENTH KING OF ISRAEL, CONTINUED

Details

Joash was succeeded by his son Jeroboam, who we know as Jeroboam II.

He regained Israel's coast from the "entering of Hamath unto the sea of the plain," in line with Jonah the son of Amittai's prophecy (2 Kings 14: 23–25).

He was contemporary with Amaziah fifteen years (2 Kings 14: 1,2,23) and Uzziah fourteen years (2 Kings 15: 1).

JONAH THE PROPHET

Jonah the prophet ministered during the reign of Jeroboam II (2 Kings 14: 23–25).

The main events in his life were:

he received a commission from the Lord to go unto the great city of Nineveh and preach there (Jonah 1: 1,2);

he was thrown into the sea and swallowed by a great fish (Jonah 1: 3–17);

he prayed to the Lord and was delivered (Jonah 2: 1–10);

the people of Nineveh repented as a result of his preaching (Jonah 4: 1–11).

INTERREGNUM

About twenty-four years elapsed between the death of Jeroboam II, and the accession of Zachariah (2 Kings 14: 23; 2 Kings 15: 1,8).

ZACHARIAH, THE FOURTEENTH KING OF ISRAEL

Summary

2 Kings 15: 8–12
- Fulfilled prophecy concerning his sons
- Killed by Shallum
- A bad king

Details

Jeroboam II was succeeded by his son Zachariah. In him was fulfilled the Lord's promise to Jehu (2 Kings 14: 29; 2 Kings 15: 8–12).

He reigned six months contemporaneously with Uzziah (2 Kings 15: 1,2,8).

SHALLUM, THE FIFTEENTH KING OF ISRAEL

Summary

2 Kings 15: 10–16
- Reigned one month
- Killed by Menahem
- A bad king

Details

Sixth dynasty.

Zachariah was killed and succeeded by Shallum who reigned contemporaneously with Uzziah (2 Kings 15: 1,2,10,13).

MENAHEM, THE SIXTEENTH KING OF ISRAEL

Summary

2 Kings 15: 14–22
- Paid 1000 talent tribute to Assyria
- Reigned 10 years
- A bad king

Details

Seventh dynasty.

Shallum was killed and succeeded by Menahem.

His reign was characterized by great wickedness, war and excessive taxation (2 Kings 15: 14–22).

He reigned contemporaneously with Uzziah (2 Kings 15: 1,2,17).

PEKAHIAH, THE SEVENTEENTH KING OF ISRAEL

Summary

2 Kings 15: 22–26
- Reigned 2 years
- Killed by Pekah
- A bad king

Details

Menahem was succeeded by his son Pekahiah. His reign was also characterized by wickedness.

He reigned contemporaneously with Uzziah (2 Kings 15: 1,2,22–24).

PEKAH, THE EIGHTEENTH KING OF ISRAEL

Summary

2 Kings 15: 25–37
- Pekahiah's officer
- Killed Pekahiah
- Part of land captured by Assyria during his reign
- Reigned 20 years
- Killed by Hoshea
- A bad king

Details

Eighth dynasty.

Pekahiah was killed and succeeded by Pekah (2 Kings 15: 25–27).

He followed in the footsteps of his predecessors (2 Kings 15: 28).

He was contemporary with Uzziah for about one year (2 Kings 15: 1,2), and with Jotham for sixteen years (2 Kings 15: 32,33; (2 Kings 16: 1).

INTERREGNUM

There was an interregnum of about eight years between the death of Pekah and the accession of Hoshea (2 Kings 15: 27; 2 Kings 16: 1,2; 2 Kings 17: 1).

HOSHEA, THE NINETEENTH KING OF ISRAEL

Summary

2 Kings 15: 29–30; 2 Kings 17: 1–6
- Paid tribute to Assyria
- Turned to Egypt to conspire against Assyria
- Taken captive
- Reigned 9 years, then Israel was destroyed.
- A bad king

Details

Ninth dynasty.

Pekah was killed and succeeded by Hoshea (2 Kings 15: 30).

During Hoshea's reign, Israel was taken into captivity by the Assyrians into captivity, and their country was occupied by their enemies (2 Kings 17: 1–41).

Kings of Judah (1)

Kingdom of Judah

REHOBOAM, FIRST KING OF JUDAH

Summary

1 Kings 12: 1–24; 1 Kings14: 21–31;
2 Chronicles 10–12
• Split kingdom
• Attempted to fight Israel
• Forsook God's law
• Served Shishak
• Built high places, Ashrerim
• Reigned 17 years
• A bad king

Details

Solomon was succeeded by his son,
Rehoboam (1 Kings 12: 43).

He ignored the counsel of the old
men and followed the counsel of the
young men, and refused to reduce
taxation (1 Kings 12: 1–15; 2 Chronicles
10: 1–15).

This caused ten of the tribes to
rebel against his authority. He decided
to suppress the rebellion, but was
warned by God not to make war
against his brethren (1 Kings 12: 16–24;
2 Chronicles 10: 16–19).

Rehoboam moved to Jerusalem,
built cities and fortified strongholds
(2 Chronicles 11: 5–12).

Rehoboam had many wives
(Deuteronomy 14: 14–18; 2 Chronicles
11: 18–23).

After he established his throne, he
ignored the law of the Lord and was
punished by Shishak, king of Egypt
(2 Chronicles 12: 1–12).

There was constant war between
Jeroboam and Rehoboam (1 Kings 15: 6).

He was contemporary with
Jeroboam (1 Kings 12: 1–20; 1 Kings
14: 20).

SHEMAIAH THE PROPHET

Shemaiah, the prophet, ministered
during Rehoboam's reign. He told
Rehoboam the Lord's command not to
go to war against the ten tribes when
they rebelled against his authority
(1 Kings 12: 22–24).

ABJIAM, SECOND KING OF JUDAH

Summary

1 Kings 15: 1–8; 2 Chronicles 13
• Fought Jereboam with God's help
• Had many wives and children
• Did evil like father
• Reigned 3 years
• A bad king

Details

Rehoboam was succeeded by his
son Abijam. He walked in the ways
of his father and sinned against God
(1 Kings 15: 1–5). The war that had
begun between the two kingdoms was
continued during the reign of Abijam,
and finally resulted in the defeat of
Jeroboam (2 Chronicles 13: 1–20).

During the latter part of Abijam's
reign he married fourteen wives
(2 Chronicles 13: 21,22).

He reigned contemporaneously with
Jeroboam (1 Kings 14: 20 1 Kings 15: 1,2).

ASA, THIRD KING OF JUDAH

Summary

1 Kings 15: 9–24; 2 Chronicles 14–16
• Removed idols and turned to God

- Fought Ethiopia with God's power
- Had rest in the land for many years
- Entered a covenant with people to follow God
- Became ill but sought help from doctors, not God
- Reigned 41 years
- A good king

Details

Abijam was succeeded by his son Asa (1 Kings 15: 8). He inaugurated a reformation and removed all the idols his father had made; he stopped his mother from being queen, and destroyed her idol.

He followed the Lord, (1 Kings 15: 9–15).

Asa enlarged his army (2 Chronicles 14: 1–8).

He defeated the powerful troops of Zerah the Ethiopian (2 Chronicles 14: 9–15).

He was greatly encouraged by Oded, the prophet, and made a covenant to seek and serve the Lord (2 Chronicles 15: 8–19).

Asa was rebuked by Hanani because he had relied on the Syrians to assist him in war. The king was so angry that he imprisoned him, and also oppressed some of the people (2 Chronicles 16: 7–10).

Asa's closing years were clouded by disease and sorrow; he went for help from doctors and not the Lord.

Asa was contemporary with seven of the kings of Israel:

Jeroboam, two years (1 Kings 14: 20,31; 1 Kings 15: 1,2; 2 Chronicles 12: 13);

Nadab, two years (1 Kings 14: 20;

1 Kings 15: 25);

Baasha, twenty-four years (1 Kings 15: 33);

Elah, two years (1 Kings 16: 8);

Zimri, seven days (1 Kings 16: 8–10,15);

Omri, six years (1 Kings 16: 23,28,29);

Ahab, three years (1 Kings 16: 29).

Tibni and Omri vie for throne 1 Kings 16: 21–22.

AZARIAH, ODED, AND HANANI THE PROPHETS

The prophets Azariah (2 Chronicles 15: 1,2), Oded (2 Chronicles 15: 8), and Hanani ministered during the reign of Asa (2 Chronicles 15: 1–8; 2 Chronicles 16: 7–10).

JEHOSHAPHAT, FOURTH KING OF JUDAH

Summary

1 Kings 22; 2 Chronicles 17–20
- Took pride in God's ways
- Received tribute from Philistines and Arabians
- Allied with Ahab by marriage
- Reigned 25 years
- A good king

Details

Asa was succeeded by his son Jehoshaphat (1 Kings 15: 24).

He continued his father's work by fortifying the land and destroying the remains of idolatrous worship.

Kings of Judah (2)

Kingdom of Judah, continued

JEHOSHAPHAT, FOURTH KING OF JUDAH

Details
He also appointed Levites to go to the cities to teach the people the law of the Lord (2 Chronicles 17: 1–9).

Jehoshaphat's reign was a peaceful one (2 Chronicles 17: 10).

He assisted Ahab in a campaign against Ramothgilead, which resulted in the death of the king of Israel (2 Chronicles 18: 1–34).

Jehoshaphat was contemporary with Ahab seventeen years (1 Kings 16: 29; 1 Kings 22: 41,50,51), Ahaziah two years (1 Kings 22: 51), Jehoram six years (2 Kings 3: 1).

JEHU AND JAHAZIEL THE PROPHETS
The prophets Jehu, the son of Hanani (2 Chronicles 19: 1–3), and Jahaziel ministered during the reign of Jehoshaphat (2 Chronicles 20: 14–17).

JEHORAM, FIFTH KING OF JUDAH

Summary
2 Kings 8: 16–24, 2 Chronicles 21
• Married Ahab's daughter
• Made high places in Judah
• Reigned 8 years
• A bad king

Details
Jehoshaphat was succeeded by his son Jehoram (2 Chronicles 21: 1). His reign was characterized by murder, war, devastation, and great trouble (2 Chronicles 21: 1–20).

He was contemporary with Jehoram, king of Israel (1 Kings 22: 42; 2 Kings 3: 1; 2 Kings 9: 29).

AHAZIAH, SIXTH KING OF JUDAH

Summary
2 Kings 8: 25–29; 2 Chronicles 22: 1–9
• Did evil as counseled by house of Ahab
• Went with Jehoram to fight Aram
• Reigned 1 year
• Killed by Jehu while visiting Jehoram
• A bad king
• Details
Jehoram was succeeded by Ahaziah. His reign was characterized by his wickedness (2 Chronicles 22: 1–4).

He went to Jezreel to visit Joram, king of Israel, who had been wounded in war with the Syrians, where he was killed by Jehu, the son of Nimshi (2 Chronicles 22: 5–9).

Ahaziah reigned contemporaneously with Jehoram (2 Kings 3: 1; 2 Kings 8: 24–26).

ATHALIAH, SEVENTH KING OF JUDAH

Summary
2 Kings 11, 2 Chronicles 22: 10–23: 21
• Killed royal offspring
• Killed by Jehoiadah
• Reigned 6 years
• A bad queen

Details
Athaliah, the usurper, attempted to kill off the whole royal household as soon as Ahaziah died (2 Kings 11: 1–3; 2 Chronicles 22: 10–12).

She reigned contemporaneously with Jehu about six years (2 Kings 9: 1–12; 2 Kings 10: 36; 2 Kings 11: 1–4).

JOASH, EIGHTH KING OF JUDAH

Summary

2 Kings 12; 2 Chronicles 24
- Son of Ahaziah by Zibiah of Beersheba
- 7 years old when he became king
- Hidden from Athaliah by Jehoiadah the priest
- Commissioned temple repairs
- Turned form God after the death of Jehoiadah
- Was killed by his servants
- Reigned 40 years
- A good king

Details

Athaliah was succeeded Joash, the son of Ahaziah. He was saved from being killed by Athaliah by Jehoiadah and was hidden for six years (2 Kings 11: 1–3).

In his seventh year, led by Jehoiadah, the priest, the people made him king and killed Athaliah (2 Kings 11: 4–16).

At his coronation the people destroyed and broke down the house of Baal, destroyed idols, and killed the idolatrous priest (2 Kings 11: 17–21).

The young king, under the instruction of Jehoiadah the priest, honored the Lord (2 Kings 12: 1,2).

The most important event in the reign of Jehoash was the repairing of the house of the Lord (2 Kings 12: 4–18 2 Chronicles 24: 1–4).

After the death of Jehoiadah, the people and king were unfaithful to the Lord. The Lord sent prophets to them,

but they would not listen to them.

Zechariah, the son of Jehoiadah, was stoned to death (2 Chronicles 24: 15–22).

Joash was assassinated by his own servants (2 Kings 12: 20,21; 2 Chronicles 24: 23–26).

Joash was contemporary with Jehu about twenty-one years (2 Kings 10: 36; 2 Kings 12: 1), Jehoahaz seventeen years (2 Kings 13: 1), Jehoash about two years (2 Kings 13: 10).

AMAZIAH, NINTH KING OF JUDAH

Summary

2 Kings 14: 1–22; 2 Chronicles 25
- Killed men who murdered his father
- Did right, but not wholeheartedly
- Killed Edomites in battle with God's help
- Brought back Edom's idols and worshiped them
- Was killed by conspirators
- Reigned 29 years
- A good king

Details

Jehoash was succeeded by his son Amaziah (2 Chronicles 24: 27). Amaziah's reign was a mixture of good and evil. He defeated the Edomites in battle. Subsequently he challenged the king of Israel but was defeated (2 Chronicles 25: 1–28).

Kings of Judah (3)

Kingdom of Judah, continued

AMAZIAH, NINTH KING OF JUDAH

Details

Amaziah was contemporary with
Joash fourteen years (2 Kings 13: 10;
2 Kings 14: 1,2) and Jeroboam II fifteen
years (2 Kings 14: 23).

INTERREGNUM

There was an interregnum of twelve
years between the death of Amaziah
and the succession of Uzziah (2 Kings
14: 1,2,23; 2 Kings 15: 1,2).

AZARIAH, OR UZZIAH, TENTH KING OF JUDAH

Summary

2 Kings 15: 1–7; 2 Chronicles 26
• Sought God and did right
• Conquered Philistines and Arabians
• Received tribute from Ammonites
• After becoming strong, acted
  corruptly
• Struck down with leprosy for
  burning incense in temple
• Reigned 52 years and died a leper
• A good king

Details

Amaziah was succeeded by his
Son Uzziah. His reign was similar
to his predecessors. He had a large
standing army, and was successful
in war because the Lord helped him
(2 Chronicles 26: 1–15).

On account of his great success he
became disobedient to the law of God,
and attempted to perform the duties of
priest, and the Lord made him a leper
(2 Chronicles 26: 16–21).

AMOS AND JOEL THE PROPHETS

The prophet Amos ministered during
the reigns of Uzziah king of Judah
and Jeroboam II, king of Israel (Amos
1: 1). Joel also probably ministered
about this time (Joel 1: 1). Joel's most
important prophecy relates to the
beginning of the gospel (Joel 2: 28–32;
Acts 2: 1–41).

JOTHAM, ELEVENTH KING OF JUDAH

Summary

2 Kings 15: 32–38; 2 Chronicles 27
• Did right
• Fought and subdued Ammonites
• Reigned 16 yrs
• A good king

Details

Uzziah was succeeded by his son
Jotham, whose reign was characterized
by a successful conflict against the
Ammonites. His success is attributed
to his faithfulness to the Lord his God
(2 Chronicles 27: 1–7).

Jotham reigned sixteen years
contemporaneously with Pekah
(2 Kings 15: 27,32,33).

AHAZ, TWELFTH KING OF JUDAH

Summary

2 Kings 16; 2 Chronicles 28
• Did evil, even committing child
  sacrifice
• God delivered his kingdom to Aram
  and Israel
• Israel took 200,000 captives but
  returned them
• Sent to Assyria for help, but they
  attacked instead

- Turned to gods of Damascus
- Reigned 16 yrs
- A bad king

Details

Jotham was succeeded by his son Ahaz, whose reign was characterized by the most appalling acts of wickedness performed by any of the kings of Judah (2 Chronicles 28: 1–27).

HEZEKIAH

Summary

2 Kings 18–20; 2 Chronicles 29–32; Isaiah 36–39

- Son of Ahaz
- Cleansed temple and consecrated Levitical priests
- Offered burnt offerings to God
- Celebrated the Passover
- Tore down idols and their altars
- Relied on God to save him from Assyria's threats
- Grew ill and prayed, God granted him 15 years life
- Reigned 29 years

Details

Ahaz was succeeded by his son Hezekiah (2 Kings 18: 1). He followed in the steps of his forefather David (2 Kings 18: 1–3).

His reign was notable for:

the destruction of high places, and images (2 Kings 18: 4);

the opening of the house of the Lord (2 Chronicles 29: 1–18);

the subjugation of the Philistines (2 Kings 18: 8);

the captivity of Israel (2 Kings 18: 9–12);

the comfort brought him by Isaiah

the son of Amoz when he was greatly troubled by the threats of Rabshakeh the servant of the king of Assyria, and the final throwing off of the Assyrian yoke by the destruction of the army by the angel of the Lord (2 Kings 18: 13–37; 2 Kings 19: 1–37);

his miraculous restoration to health and the backward movement of the shadow on the dial (2 Kings 20: 1–11);

his mistake in showing his treasures to the ambassadors of the king of Babylon (2 Kings 20: 12–19);

the keeping of the Passover of the Lord (2 Chronicles 30: 1–27);

he fortified and improved Jerusalem (2 Chronicles 32: 1–31).

CAPTIVITY

2 Kings 17; Israelites taken into captivity by the Assyrians.

ISAIAH, HOSEA, MICAH AND NAHUM
THE PROPHETS

The prophets Isaiah, Hosea, Micah and Nahum ministered during the reigns of the last three or four kings of Judah, (Isaiah 1: 1; Hosea 1: 1; Micah 1: 1; Nahum 1: 1).

Isaiah

The main events in Isaiah's life were:

the beginning of his public ministry in the days of Uzziah, king of Judah, when he denounced the wickedness of Judah and Israel (Isaiah 1: 1–31);

Kings of Judah (4)

Kingdom of Judah, continued

ISAIAH, HOSEA, MICAH AND NAHUM
THE PROPHETS

Isaiah

he predicted that the word of the Lord would go out from Jerusalem, and that eventually the nations would beat their implements of war into implements of peace and learn war no more (Isaiah 2: 1–4);

his vision of the glory of God (Isaiah 6: 1–12);

he comforted Ahaz, the king of Judah, and assured him that a virgin should conceive and bear a son whose name should be Immanuel (Isaiah 7: 1–16);

he predicted the birth of Jesus Christ and the triumphs of his kingdom (Isaiah 9: 1–7);

he predicted the gathering again of Israel (Isaiah 10: 20–27; Isaiah 11: 11–16; Isaiah 14: 1–3);

he predicted the downfall of Babylon (Isaiah 13: 1–22);

he predicted the destruction of Moab (Isaiah 15: 1–9; Isaiah 16: 1–14);

he predicted the downfall of Damascus (Isaiah 17: 1–3);

he predicted the downfall of Egypt (Isaiah 19: 1–25);

he comforted Hezekiah, and predicted the overthrow of the Assyrians (2 Kings 19: 6–37; Isaiah 37: 6–38);

his prediction about the sickness and restoration of Hezekiah and the sign given him (2 Kings 20: 1–11; Isaiah 38: 1–8);

he condemned Hezekiah for showing his treasures to the ambassadors of the king of Babylon and predicted the captivity of the people of Judah (2 Kings 20: 12–19; Isaiah 39: 1–8);

he predicted the restoration of the captives and the rebuilding of the temple under Cyrus (Isaiah 44: 28; Isaiah 45: 1–13);

he predicted the humiliation and sufferings of the Messiah (Isaiah 53: 1–12);

he predicted the call of the Gentiles (Isaiah 54: 1–4; Isaiah 60: 1–11);

he heard with prophetic ear the invitation of the gospel (Isaiah 55: 1–5; Matthew 11: 28–30);

he predicted the giving of the new name (Isaiah 62: 1–4; Acts 11: 1–26);

he described the conquering march of the Messiah (Isaiah 63: 1–9).

Hosea

The most important feature of Hosea's prophecy is his denunciation of the sins of his countrymen and telling them the reason for all their troubles – their lack of knowledge (Hosea 4: 1–6).

Micah

Micah predicted the proclamation of the word of the Lord from Jerusalem and the destruction of the implements of war (Micah 4: 1–5) and also predicted the birth of Messiah at Bethlehem (Micah 5: 2).

Nahum

Nahum predicted the destruction of Nineveh (Nahum 1: 1–3: 19).

MANASSEH, FOURTEENTH KING OF JUDAH

Summary
2 Kings 21: 1–18; 2 Chronicles 33: 10–20
- Rebuilt high places
- Put idols in the temple
- Taken by Assyrians to Babylon
- Returned to Jerusalem and tore down idols
- Ordered people to serve God
- Reigned 55 years
- A bad king

Details
Hezekiah was succeeded by his son Manasseh (2 Kings 20: 21). In the early part of this reign he restored the idolatrous practice that had been destroyed by Hezekiah (2 Chronicles 33: 1–10). As a punishment the Lord allowed the king of Assyria to carry off Manasseh a prisoner in chains to Babylon.

During his stay there he became humble before God.

He was restored to his throne and during the latter part of his reign he honored the Lord (2 Chr. 33: 11–20).

AMON, FIFTEENTH KING OF JUDAH

Summary
2 Kings 21: 19–36; 2 Chronicles 33: 21–25
- Did evil
- Killed by his servants
- Reigned 2 years
- A bad king

Details
Manasseh was succeeded by his son Amon, who reigned wickedly for two years (2 Kings 21: 18–22; 2 Chronicles 33: 20–24).

JOSIAH, SIXTEENTH KING OF JUDAH

Summary
2 Kings 22: 1 – 23: 30, 2 Chronicles 34–35
- 8 years old when he became king
- Did right and purged idolatry
- Repaired the temple
- Read book of Law
- Celebrated Passover
- Attacked Pharaoh Necho of Egypt and was killed
- Death lamented by Jeremiah
- Reigned 31 years
- A good king

Details
Amon was succeeded by his son Josiah (2 Kings 21: 26).

Many years before his birth, the prophet of the Lord had predicted that he would be a reformer (2 Kings 13: 1,2).

Josiah lived and worked in strict obedience to God's law.

In the eighteenth year of his reign, he began to repair the house of the Lord. During the work Hilkiah, the priest, discovered the book of the law and Shaphan, the scribe, read it before the king. When the king heard it he expressed his great concern about the condition of Israel.

Kings of Judah (5)

Kingdom of Judah, continued

JOSIAH, SIXTEENTH KING OF JUDAH

Details

The Lord however assured him that he would live and die in peace (2 Kings 22: 3–20).

After this Josiah pushed ahead with the work of reformation with great zeal.

He eventually destroyed the altar at Bethel and burned the bones of the priests according to the predictions of the Prophet (2 Kings 23: 1–20).

After the land had been purged of idolatry, Josiah kept the feast of the Passover (2 Chronicles 35: 1–19).

Josiah was killed in a battle with Pharaoh Necho, the king of Egypt, and he was buried in Jerusalem (2 Kings 23: 29,30 2 Chronicles 35: 20–27).

ZEPHANIAH AND HABAKKUK THE PROPHETS

The prophet Zephaniah ministered during Josiah's reign (Zephaniah 1: 1); as did, most probably, Habakkuk, (Habakkuk 1: 1).

JEHOAHAZ, SEVENTEENTH KING OF JUDAH

Summary

2 Kings 23: 31–35; 2 Chronicles 26: 1–4
- Did evil
- Imprisoned by king of Egypt
- Reigned 3 months, died in Egypt
- An evil king

Details

The people of the land made Jehoahaz king in his father's place. He reigned for three months and was then dethroned by the king of Egypt (2 Chronicles 36: 1–3).

JEHOIAKIM, EIGHTEENTH KING OF JUDAH

Summary

2 Kings 23: 36–24: 7; 2 Chronicles 36: 5–8
- Son of Josiah, brother of Jehoahaz
- Also called "Eliakim"
- Did evil
- Babylon besieged Jerusalem
- Reigned 11 years
- A bad king

Details

Jehoahaz was succeeded by Jehoiakim, whose wicked reign lasted eleven years. He was taken into captivity by Nebuchadnezzar the king of Babylon (2 Chronicles 36: 5–8).

JEHOIACHIN, NINETEENTH KING OF JUDAH

Summary

2 Kings 24: 8–12; 2 Kings 25: 27–30; 2 Chronicles 36: 9–10
- Taken captive by Nebuchadnezzar of Babylon
- In 37th year of exile, released to eat at king's table
- Reigned 3 months and 10 days
- A bad king

Details

Jehoiakim was succeeded by Jehoiachin, whose wicked reign lasted three months and ten days, after which he was taken into captivity by the king of Babylon (2 Chronicles 36: 9,10).

ZEDEKIAH, TWENTIETH KING OF JUDAH

Summary

2 Kings 24: 18–25: 7; 2 Chronicles 36: 11–14

- Also called "Mattaniah"
- Rebelled against Babylon after vowing allegiance
- Captured by Babylon
- Sons killed before his eyes
- Blinded, bound, and brought to Babylon
- Reigned 11 years, then Jerusalem fell to Babylon
- A bad king

Details

Jehoiachin was succeeded by Zedekiah, who reigned wickedly for eleven years. He made a unsuccessful attempt to throw off the Babylonian rule. The evil that had existed for centuries culminated in the destruction of the house of the Lord and the captivity of his people (2 Chronicles 36: 11–21).

JEREMIAH AND OBADIAH THE PROPHETS

The prophets Jeremiah and probably Obadiah ministered during the closing years of the kingdom of Judah (Jeremiah 1: 1–3; Obadiah 1: 1).

Jeremiah

He was called to the prophetic office in the days of Josiah (Jeremiah 1: 1,2);

he denounced Jerusalem and Judah because of their sins (Jeremiah 2: 1–37; Jeremiah 3: 1–10);

he told the people of the Lord's willingness to accept them if they would repent (Jeremiah 3: 11–25);

he was thrown into prison by Pashur (Jeremiah 20: 1,2);

he foretold the seventy years' captivity (Jeremiah 25: 11,12);

he fled from Jehoiakim to Egypt (Jeremiah 26: 12–21);

he condemned the false prophet Hananiah (Jeremiah 28: 1–16);

he predicted the restoration of Judah and Israel (Jeremiah 30: 1–3);

he predicted the establishment of a new covenant (Jeremiah 31: 31–34);

he predicted the downfall of Jerusalem (2 Chronicles 36: 11–21; Jeremiah 39: 1–10);

he was treated well by Nebuzaradan (Jeremiah 39: 11–14; Jeremiah 40: 1–5);

he went into Egypt with a few of his countrymen (Jeremiah 43: 5–7);

he predicted the overthrow of Egypt by the king of Babylon, and the destruction of all the Jews who went into Egypt except a small remnant (Jeremiah 43: 8–13; Jeremiah 44: 1–28);

he predicted the downfall of Babylon (Jeremiah 50: 1–46; Jeremiah 51: 1–64).

Obadiah

Obadiah prophesied against Edom (Obadiah 1: 1–21).

CAPTIVITY

2 Kings 25, 2 Chronicles 36: 15–23, Jeremiah 39–43; Judah taken captive by the Babylonians.

The Apocrypha

Old Testament Apocrypha

The Old Testament Apocrypha consists of the following books
- The First Book of Esdras
- The Second Book of Esdras
- Tobit
- Judith
- Additions to the Book of Esther
- The Wisdom of Solomon
- Ecclesiasticus or the Wisdom of Jesus, son of Sirach
- Baruch
- A Letter of Jeremiah
- Additions to the Book of Daniel: The Prayer of Azariah; and the Song of the Three Jews; Susanna; Bell and the Dragon
- 1 Maccabees
- 2 Maccabees
- 3 Maccabees
- 4 Maccabees
- 1 Esdras
- 2 Esdras
- Prayer of Manasseh
- Psalm 151

What is the Apocrypha?

Aocrypha means "hidden things," in Greek or "spurious," and is the name given to the non-canonical books which are found in the LXX and Latin Vulgate versions of the Old Testament, and were included in all the English translations made in the 16th century, but which have no claim to be part of the inspired Word of God.

They are not accepted by Protestants as inspired writings. The Roman Catholic church accepts 12 of these books as "deuterocanonical," that is, inspired, but not on the same level as the other books of the Old and New Testament.

They were written between 200 B.C. and A.D. 200.

Protestants have sometimes referred to these books as the "pseudepigrapha," which means "false writings."

Reasons for rejecting the Apocrypha

Protestants have advanced the following reasons for rejecting these additional books to the Bible.

Although it is possible to find just a few possible allusions to the apocryphal books by New Testament writers (Hebrews 11: 35 compares with 2 Maccabees 7, 12) there is not one direct quotation from them.

No New Testament writer ever refers to any of these fourteen or fifteen books as authoritative.

Christ never quoted from them.

The apostles never quoted from them.

The apocrypha is not once quoted by any of the New Testament writers, even though they frequently quote from the LXX.

Our Lord and his apostles confirmed by their authority the Jewish canon of the Old Testament, which was the same in all respects as we now have it.

The Apocrypha was never part of the Old Testament Hebrew canon.

The apocryphal books do not claim

to be the Word of God or the work of prophets.

These books were not written in Hebrew but in Greek during the "period of silence," from the time of Malachi, after which oracles and direct revelations from God ceased until the Christian era.

The contents of the books themselves show that they were no part of Scripture.

The Belgic Confession

ARTICLE 6: THE DIFFERENCE BETWEEN THE CANONICAL AND APOCRYPHAL BOOKS

We distinguish these holy books from the apocryphal, namely,

The Church may read and take instruction from these so far as they agree with the canonical books. They are, however, far from having such power and authority that we may confirm from their testimony any point of faith or of the Christian religion; much less may they be used to detract from the authority of the holy books.

Even early Catholic Church leaders who were familiar with the Hebrew texts clearly distinguish canonical and Apocrypha writings. The writings of Cyril of Jerusalem, St. Jerome, and Bishop Melito of Sardis (A.D. 170) indicate a recognition of the difference between inspired Holy text and the Apocrypha. Church leaders such as Origen, Tertullian, and Hilary of Poitiers, exclude the Apocrypha from Sacred canon in their own lists of canonical books.

Official Roman Catholic teaching

Official Roman Catholic teaching states that "Jerome distinguished between canonical books and ecclesiastical books. The latter he judged were circulated by the Church as good spiritual reading but were not recognized as authoritative Scripture. The situation remained unclear in the ensuing centuries...For example, John of Damascus, Gregory the Great, Walafrid, Nicolas of Lyra, and Tostado continued to doubt the canonicity of the deuterocanonical books. According to Catholic doctrine, the proximate criterion of the biblical canon is the infallible decision of the Church. This decision was not given until rather late in the history of the Church at the Council of Trent. The Council of Trent definitively settled the matter of the Old Testament canon. That this had not been done previously is apparent from the uncertainty that persisted up to the time of Trent."

New Catholic Encyclopedia, The Canon

The Law (1)

Covenant of circumcision

After Abram had been in the land of promise twenty-four years, the Lord made a covenant with him and changed his name to Abraham (Genesis 12: 4,5; Genesis 17: 1–5).

The Lord decided to make him into a great nation (Genesis 17: 6,7).

Circumcision

(A) It was a visible mark on the body.
(B) It was restricted to males from Abraham's family.
(C) The children were circumcised on the eighth day.
(D) The uncircumcised were to be excluded from the covenant (Genesis 17: 6–14).

"This is my covenant, which you shall keep, between me and you and your offspring after you: Every male among you shall be circumcised. You shall circumcise the flesh of your foreskins, and it shall be a sign of the covenant between me and you. Throughout your generations every male among you shall be circumcised when he is eight days old, including the slave born in your house and the one bought with your money from any foreigner who is not of your offspring. Both the slave born in your house and the one bought with your money must be circumcised. So shall my covenant be in your flesh an everlasting covenant. Any uncircumcised male who is not circumcised in the flesh of his foreskin shall be cut off from his people; he has broken my covenant."

Genesis 17: 10–14 NRSV

Receiving the law at Mount Sinai

The important events at Mount Sinai were:

The people entered into a covenant with the Lord (Exodus 19: 1–8).

The people and priests were sanctified (Exodus 19: 9–25).

The Ten Commandments were given (Exodus 19: 1–25; Exodus 20: 1–17; Deuteronomy 5: 1–22).

The people were frightened by the Lord's voice and asked Moses to speak to them (Exodus 20: 18–21).

Moses spent forty days and nights with the Lord on Mount Sinai (Exodus 24: 1,2,9–18).

Moses received instructions concerning the tabernacle (Exodus 25: 1–40).

Moses was told to set Aaron and his sons apart for priestly work (Exodus 28: 1).

Bezaleel and Aholiab were instructed to head up the building of the house of the Lord (Exodus 31: 1–6).

The Lord gave Moses two tablets of stone with the Ten Commandments written on them (Exodus 31: 18).

The people, led by Aaron, lapsed into idolatry (Exodus 32: 1–6).

Moses pleaded on their behalf but broke the tablets of stone after he came down from the mountain (Exodus 32: 7–24).

The Levites showed their devotion to the Lord's cause (Exodus 32: 25–35).

Moses had a glimpse of the glory of God (Exodus 33: 12–23).

The tablets of stone were renewed (Exodus 34: 1–28).

Moses returned from the mountain, built an altar and made sacrifices on it (Exodus 24: 3–5; Exodus 35: 29–35).

The people entered into a covenant with the Lord again (Exodus 24: 7,8; Hebrews 9: 18–21).

Moses called on the people for a freewill offering of material for the building of the tabernacle (Exodus 35: 1–29).

The people gave so generously that they had to be restrained Ex. 36: 1–7).

The tabernacle was set up (Exodus 40: 1–38).

Aaron and his sons were consecrated and fire descended on the bronze altar (Leviticus 8: 1–36; Leviticus 9: 1–24).

Nadab and Abihu were killed for dishonoring God (Leviticus 10: 1,2).

The Levites were consecrated (Numbers 8: 1–26).

The second Passover was observed (Numbers 9: 1–15).

Regulations for the whole camp were given (Numbers 2: 1–34).

The leaders made their offerings (Numbers 7: 1–9).

The people were numbered (Numbers 1: 1–46).

The giving of the Law

The Ten Commandments

These commandments were proclaimed by the Lord, in person, from Mount Sinai (Exodus 19: 1–25; Exodus 20: 1–17; Heb. 12: 18–20). They:

- required strict submission to the one true and living God;
- prohibited idolatry in all forms;
- prohibited the taking of the name of the Lord in vain;
- required the keeping of the Sabbath;
- required the people to honor their parents;
- prohibited murder;
- prohibited adultery;
- prohibited stealing;
- prohibited the bearing of false witness;
- and prohibited covetousness (Exodus 20: 1–17).

These commandments were given to Moses on stone tablets so he could teach them to the people (Exodus 24: 12), and preserve them (Exodus 31: 18). These tables were placed in the Ark of the Lord for safekeeping (Deuteronomy 10: 1–5; Hebrews 9: 4).

Names given to these commandments

These commandments were called:

- "the words of the covenant," because they constituted the basis of the covenant between the Lord and his people (Exodus 20: 1–17; Exodus 34: 28);
- "the testimony," because they constantly testified to the fact that the Lord had spoken to them (Exodus 20: 1–17; Exodus 25: 16);
- "the tables of the covenant," because the words of the covenant were written by God (Exodus 31: 18; Exodus 32: 15,16; Deuteronomy 9: 7–11)

The Law (2)

Laws previously given

The law proclaimed by Jehovah from Mount Sinai was the first law that was given to the whole nation. Laws had previously been given to individuals only:

the law forbidding the eating
of the fruit of the tree of life
(Genesis 2: 16,17);
the law of marriage (Genesis 2: 24);
the law of sacrifice (Genesis 4: 1–7;
Hebrews 11: 4);
the law against eating blood, and
murder (Genesis 9: 4–6);
and the law of circumcision
(Genesis 17: 1–14).

Two reasons are given for the keeping of the sabbath day:

the resting of the Lord on the seventh
day;
the deliverance of the Hebrews
from bondage (Exodus 20: 8–11;
Deuteronomy 5: 12–15).

Unique aspects of the Law of Moses

ITS NATIONAL ASPECTS

The law of Moses was given to, and for, just one nation (Exodus 19: 1–25; Exodus 20: 1–17; Deuteronomy 5: 1–33; Malachi 4: 4). It developed national worship. Before this law for the whole nation, worship was confined to the family (Genesis 12: 6,7; Genesis 46: 1–3).

In the Law of Moses God recorded his name on the altar (Exodus 20: 24–26), and required all Israel to meet there and worship through the divinely ordained priesthood (Numbers 18: 1–7;

Deuteronomy 12: 12–16). The law of Moses was given orally (Exodus 20: 1–23), and perpetuated,

by being written on tables of stone
(Exodus 24: 12; Exodus 31: 18),
by being written in a book
(Exodus 24: 4,7,8; Deuteronomy 31: 24–26; Hebrews 9: 18,19),

and it was made a part of the national life by being taught to each new generation, spoken about in their homes, tied to their forearms, written on the doorposts of their houses, on their gates (Deuteronomy 27: 1–8), and publicly proclaimed to the nation (Deuteronomy 11: 26–32; Deuteronomy 31: 9–13).

ITS SIMPLICITY

The law of Moses was given to a nation that had recently been in slavery, and was appropriate for that situation. God intended that they should understand and obey it, for:

most people were ignorant about
it, and inclined to be unfaithful to
him (Exodus 20: 1–5; Deuteronomy
27: 1–8);
through it they received knowledge
about sin (Exodus 20: 1–7;
Numbers 25: 1–15; Romans 3: 19–21);
it united them to God and to each other
(Deuteronomy 7: 12–16);
it carried with it a blessing and a curse
(Deuteronomy 11: 26–32);
it foreshadowed the gospel of Christ
(Colossians 2: 17; Hebrews 10: 1).

ITS GREAT BLESSINGS

The blessings of the law were:

- possession of the land promised to their fathers (Deuteronomy 7: 1–13; Deuteronomy 30: 16),
- long life (Deuteronomy 30: 20),
- prosperity in this world (Deuteronomy 28: 1–14),
- protection from their enemies (Deut. 20: 10–18; 23: 14),
- authority over other nations (Deuteronomy 15: 5,6; Deuteronomy 26: 19; Deuteronomy 28: 12,13).

ITS TERRIBLE CURSES

The curses of the law were many and terrible (Deuteronomy 27: 11–26; Deuteronomy 28: 15–68). In addition to this, many crimes were punishable with death or expulsion from the congregation of Israel:

Murder (Exodus 21: 12–14; Numbers 35: 30),

unlawfully injuring a servant (Exodus 21: 20,21),

death by uncontrolled animals (Exodus 21: 28–30),

robbery at night (Exodus 22: 2–4),

idolatry (Exodus 22: 20; Lev. 20: 1–5),

witchcraft (Exodus 22: 18; Leviticus 20: 27),

oppressing the widow or fatherless (Exodus 22: 22–24),

disobedience to priests or judges (Exodus 22: 28; Deuteronomy 17: 12),

neglect of certain rituals (Exodus 30: 18–21),

breaking the Sabbath (Exodus 31: 15,16; Numbers 15: 32–36),

adultery (Leviticus 20: 10),

incest (Leviticus 20: 11,12),

sodomy (Leviticus 20: 13),

bestiality (Leviticus 20: 15,16),

disrespect to parents (Leviticus 20: 9),

blasphemy (Leviticus 24: 16),

approaching the tabernacle in the wrong way (Numbers 1: 51),

false prophecy (Deuteronomy 13: 1–5),

enticing people into idolatry (Deuteronomy 13: 6–11),

gluttony and drunkenness (Deuteronomy 21: 18–21),

rape (Deuteronomy 22: 13–27),

kidnapping (Deuteronomy 24: 7),

eating leavened bread at the feast of unleavened bread (Exodus 12: 15–17),

making or using the sacred oil for anointing (Exodus 30: 23–33),

making or using the holy perfume (Exodus 30: 34–38),

eating the sacrifices of peace offerings, being unclean (Leviticus 17: 10–14),

exposing the nakedness of close relatives (Leviticus 18: 6–18,29),

eating the sacrifices of peace offerings on the third day (Leviticus 19: 5–8),

doing work on the day of atonement (Leviticus 23: 27–30),

neglecting to keep the Passover (Numbers 9: 13).

Election

Abraham (Genesis 12: 1–3), Isaac (Genesis 26: 1–5), Jacob (Genesis 28: 10–14), and the nation of Israel were elected so that God's purposes could be seen by all.

The law, however, provided for strangers (Exodus 20: 10; Leviticus 19: 33,34). It provided a home for the Edomites (Deuteronomy 2: 1–5), and, for example, allowed the Edomites and the Egyptians into their congregation (Deuteronomy 23: 7,8).

The Tabernacle (1)

A revelation and a type

The tabernacle with all that was linked to it was a revelation from God , and was typical of the new and living way (Hebrews 8: 4,5; Hebrews 9: 1–10). This building was not the product of human thought but was both a revelation and a prophecy. The Lord said: "Look that thou make them after their pattern, which was showed thee in the mount" (Exodus 25: 40).

The Lord gave Moses the plan and made him responsible for carrying it out (Exodus 25: 9).

The tabernacle workers

The Lord specifically called Bezaleel the son of Uri of the tribe of Judah, and Aholiab the son of Ahisamach of the tribe of Dan, and inspired them for the work (Exodus 31: 1–7). They were also empowered to teach others (Exodus 35: 30–35). They were assisted by the men and women of Israel (Exodus 35: 25,26; Exodus 36: 1,2).

The materials of the tabernacle

metals: gold, silver, brass;
fabrics: purple, scarlet and white linen, and cloth made of goats' hair;
wood: shittim wood.

All these things were provided by the people through their free will offerings. They also made the clothes for the priests (Exodus 25: 1–40; Exodus 35: 1–35).

The liberality of the people was so great that Moses had to restrain them (Exodus 36: 5–7).

The court of the tabernacle

The court was a kind of fence or protection for the tabernacle; it surrounded it (Exodus 27: 9–18). Materials used in its construction were:
• brass,
• silver,
• and linen (Exodus 27: 9–19).

COURT'S FOUNDATION
The court's foundation was made up of sixty sockets of brass which were placed as follows:
• twenty on the north side,
• ten on the west end,
• twenty on the south side,
• and ten on the east end.
Into these slotted sixty pillars of brass, on which silver hooks were attached, onto which were hung linen curtains.

The curtains for the doors had ornamental needle-work on them while the other curtains were plain (Exodus 38: 8–20).

MEASUREMENTS OF THE COURT
Assuming eighteen inches to the cubit, the court, when completed, was one hundred and fifty feet long, seventy-five feet wide, and seven and a half feet high (Exodus 27: 18).

FURNITURE OF THE COURT
The only furniture in the court consisted of:
• the altar for burnt sacrifices, and
• the bronze basin (Exodus 40: 28–30).

Entering the tabernacle

The court was entered through a door, the holy place was entered through a door, and the holy of holies was entered through a door.

The people were allowed to enter the court (Exodus 40: 28,29; Leviticus 1: 1–3 Psalms 5: 7; Psalms 84: 2,10; Psalms 100: 4), but they were excluded from the tabernacle on pain of death (Numbers 1: 51).

The priests, Aaron's sons, were allowed to enter the holy place (Leviticus 1: 1–17; Hebrews 9: 6), but only the high priest was allowed to enter the holy of holies, and he only once a year (Leviticus 16: 1–34; Hebrews 9: 7).

The tabernacle as a type

The court was a type of the world, the holy place was a type of the church, and the holy of holies, a type of heaven.

The rooms of the tabernacle

The tabernacle was divided into two separate rooms by a richly embroidered curtain called the vail or curtain (Exodus 26: 31–33).

"You shall make a curtain of blue, purple, and crimson yarns, and of fine twisted linen; it shall be made with cherubim skillfully worked into it … You shall hang the curtain under the clasps, and bring the ark of the covenant in there, within the curtain; and the curtain shall separate for you the holy place from the most holy" Exodus 26: 31,33 NRSV.

THE FIRST ROOM WAS CALLED
- the holy place (Exodus 26: 34),
- the tent of the congregation (Exodus 40: 26), and
- the first tabernacle (Hebrews 9: 6).

THE FURNITURE IN THE HOLY PLACE
- table of showbread,
- candlestick, and
- altar of incense (Exodus 40: 24–27).

THE SECOND ROOM WAS CALLED
- the most holy place (Exodus 26: 33),
- the holy place within the vail (Leviticus 16: 2), and
- holy sanctuary.

THE COVERINGS OF THE TABERNACLE
The tabernacle had four separate coverings:
- the first or inner covering,
- the goats' hair covering,
- the covering of rams' skins dyed red,
- the covering of badgers' skins (Exodus 26: 1–14).

Significance of the tabernacle as a type

It is clear that the New Testament writers viewed the tabernacle and its contents as a spiritual type.

Viewed in the light of Jesus' teaching, and death, it is easy to see how the law and tabernacle prefigured or foreshadowed good things to come (Hebrews 8: 1–5 Hebrews 9: 1–10; Hebrews 10: 1).

The Tabernacle (2)

Significance of the tabernacle as a type, continued

"Now the main point in what we are saying is this: we have such a high priest, one who is seated at the right hand of the throne of the Majesty in the heavens, a minister in the sanctuary and the true tent that the Lord, and not any mortal, has set up. For every high priest is appointed to offer gifts and sacrifices; hence it is necessary for this priest also to have something to offer. Now if he were on earth, he would not be a priest at all, since there are priests who offer gifts according to the law. They offer worship in a sanctuary that is a sketch and shadow of the heavenly one; for Moses, when he was about to erect the tent, was warned, 'See that you make everything according to the pattern that was shown you on the mountain.'"

Hebrews 8: 1–5 NRSV

"Now even the first covenant had regulations for worship and an earthly sanctuary. For a tent was constructed, the first one, in which were the lampstand, the table, and the bread of the Presence; this is called the Holy Place. Behind the second curtain was a tent called the Holy of Holies. In it stood the golden altar of incense and the ark of the covenant overlaid on all sides with gold, in which there were a golden urn holding the manna, and Aaron's rod that budded, and the tablets of the covenant; above it were the cherubim of glory overshadowing the mercy seat. Of these things we

cannot speak now in detail.

Such preparations having been made, the priests go continually into the first tent to carry out their ritual duties; but only the high priest goes into the second, and he but once a year, and not without taking the blood that he offers for himself and for the sins committed unintentionally by the people. By this the Holy Spirit indicates that the way into the sanctuary has not yet been disclosed as long as the first tent is still standing. This is a symbol of the present time, during which gifts and sacrifices are offered that cannot perfect the conscience of the worshiper, but deal only with food and drink and various baptisms, regulations for the body imposed until the time comes to set things right."

Hebrews 9: 1–10 NRSV

Various types

THE COURT
The court was a type of the world (Exodus 27: 9–18; Revelation 11: 1,2).

THE ALTAR OF BURNT SACRIFICES
The altar of burnt sacrifices was a type of the Cross of Christ (Exodus 40: 29; John 12: 32,33).

THE BASIN
the basin was a type of Christ (Exodus 30: 18–21; 1 John 1: 7; 1 Peter 1: 22).

FIRST CURTAIN
The first curtain or door was a type of the dividing line between the world and

the Church (Exodus 26: 36,27; John 3: 5; Acts 2: 38; 1 Corinthians 12: 13).

HOLY PLACE

The holy place was a type of the Church (Exodus 26: 33; Hebrews 8: 2).

SHOWBREAD

The showbread was a type of Christ (Exodus 40: 4; Leviticus 24: 5–9; Matthew 28: 20; John 6: 48–63).

CANDLESTICK

The candlestick was a type of Christ and the light of the gospel in the Church (Exodus 40: 7; Leviticus 24: 1,2; John 1: 4–9; John 3: 20,21; 2 Corinthians 4: 4–6).

ALTAR OF INCENSE

The altar of incense was a type of our worship (Exodus 30: 1–10; Malachi 1: 11; Revelation 8: 3).

SECOND CURTAIN

The second curtain was a type of the dividing line between the Church and heaven (Exodus 26: 39; Hebrews 10: 19–21).

THE HOLY OF HOLIES

The holy of holies was a type of heaven (Exodus 26: 33; Hebrews 9: 24);

"Therefore, my friends, since we have confidence to enter the sanctuary by the blood of Jesus, by the new and living way that he opened for us through the curtain (that is, through his flesh)..."

Hebrews 10: 19,20 NRSV

MERCY SEAT

The mercy seat was a type of our mercy seat which is in heaven (Exodus 25: 10–22; 1 Timothy 2: 5,6; Hebrews 4: 14–16); and

"Since, then, we have a great high priest who has passed through the heavens, Jesus, the Son of God, let us hold fast to our confession. For we do not have a high priest who is unable to sympathize with our weaknesses, but we have one who in every respect has been tested as we are, yet without sin. Let us therefore approach the throne of grace with boldness, so that we may receive mercy and find grace to help in time of need."

Hebrews 4: 14–16 NRSV

LIGHT

The light that filled the tabernacle was a type of the Holy Spirit who fills the Church (Exodus 40: 33–38; 1 Corinthians 3: 16,17).

The priesthood (1)

Overview

From the time that the smoke of Abel's sacrifice ascended to God to the death of Jesus Christ on the cross, the history of the human race is closely linked with altars, priests, and sacrifices. To start with every man was his own priest. Cain and Abel "brought" their sacrifices and presented them to Jehovah (Genesis 4: 1–5). After the flood, Noah, acknowledging God's goodness, erected an altar on the purified earth and offered sacrifices to his great Deliverer (Genesis 8: 20). Later on, the head of the family officiated at the altar and led the family worship.

Examples of altars and sacrifices

Abram built altars at Sichem, between Bethel and Hai (Genesis 12: 6–8; Genesis 13: 1–3) and on Mount Moriah (Genesis 22: 1–9;

Isaac built an altar at Beersheba (Genesis 26: 18,23–25);

Jacob offered sacrifices at Beersheba on his way to Egypt (Genesis 46: 1).

Before the Exodus there was no priesthood. No special law regulated the offering of sacrifices; but the sacrifices were undoubtedly offered in obedience to God's command (Genesis 4: 1–5; Genesis 22: 1–9; Genesis 35: 1–3; Romans 10: 17; Hebrews 11: 4).

God was gradually preparing the people he had chosen. He was separating them from other nations.

During their time in Egypt the chosen people absorbed the evil ways from the people who surrounded them.

The Passover

During their last night in Egypt the angel of the Lord passed through the land of Egypt, killing all the firstborn, of both humans and animals from among the Egyptians (Exodus 12: 1–29). To commemorate that God preserved all the firstborn of the children of Israel, he ordered that the firstborn of humans and animals should be dedicated to him (Exodus 13: 2,11–16). Later, God chose the entire tribe of Levi in place of the firstborn of the children of Israel, and the cattle of the Levites in the place of their cattle (Numbers 3: 40–43).

The Levites

The first sign of the selection of the Levites is seen in the choice of Moses and Aaron (Exodus 3: 1–10 Exodus 4: 14–16). The Levites first showed their devotion to God when Moses returned from the mountain and found all Israel engaged in idol worship. In response to Moses' invitation they went to him, and, at his command, killed many of the idolaters (Exodus 32: 1–28).

THE LEVITE TRIBE WAS DIVIDED AS FOLLOWS:
Aaron and his sons were to be priests (Exodus 28: 1; Numbers 18: 1–7);

the Kohathites were given the responsibility of transporting the holy vessels of the tabernacle and court (Numbers 4: 1–15);

the Gershonites were put in charge of the coverings, curtains, cords, or fabrics of the tabernacle (Numbers 4: 21–28);

the Merarites were put in charge of the boards, bars, pillars, sockets, pins, and cords of the tabernacle and court, and the tools needed in setting them up (Numbers 4: 29–33).

CONSECRATION OF THE LEVITES
The rites in which the Levites were consecrated to the Lord's service were: first, they had purifying water sprinkled on them; they then shaved themselves and washed their clothes. Then they offered a young bullock as a burnt offering, and a second bullock for a sin offering; the Israelites laid their hands on the heads of the Levites as an offering from the Israelites; the Levites then placed their hands on their burnt offering and sin offering which were killed, and atonement was made for them (Numbers 8: 5–15).

The priests' clothes

The clothes of the ordinary priest were made from fine linen and consisted of tunic, sashes and headdresses (Exodus 28: 40–42; Exodus 39: 27–29).

The high priest's clothes

"Then Moses brought Aaron and his sons forward, and washed them with water. He put the tunic on him, fastened the sash around him, clothed him with the robe, and put the ephod on him. He then put the decorated band of the ephod around him, tying the ephod to him with it. He placed the breast piece on him, and in the breast piece he put the Urim and the Thummim. And he set the turban on his head, and on the turban, in front, he set the golden ornament, the holy crown, as the LORD commanded Moses."
Leviticus 8: 6–9.

EPHOD
"He made the ephod of gold, of blue, purple, and crimson yarns, and of fine twisted linen. Gold leaf was hammered out and cut into threads to work into the blue, purple, and crimson yarns and into the fine twisted linen, in skilled design. They made for the ephod shoulder-pieces, joined to it at its two edges.

The decorated band on it was of the same materials and workmanship, of gold, of blue, purple, and crimson yarns, and of fine twisted linen; as the Lord had commanded Moses.

"The onyx stones were prepared, enclosed in settings of gold filigree and engraved like the engravings of a signet, according to the names of the sons of Israel. He set them on the shoulder-pieces of the ephod, to be stones of remembrance for the sons of Israel; as the Lord had commanded Moses.

The priesthood (2)

The clothes of the high priest, continued

EPHOD, CONTINUED

He made the breast piece, in skilled work, like the work of the ephod, of gold, of blue, purple, and crimson yarns, and of fine twisted linen. It was square; the breast piece was made double, a span in length and a span in width when doubled. They set in it four rows of stones. A row of carnelian, chrysolite, and emerald was the first row; and the second row, a turquoise, a sapphire, and a moonstone; and the third row, a jacinth, an agate, and an amethyst; and the fourth row, a beryl, an onyx, and a jasper; they were enclosed in settings of gold filigree. There were twelve stones with names corresponding to the names of the sons of Israel; they were like signets, each engraved with its name, for the twelve tribes. They made on the breast piece chains of pure gold, twisted like cords; and they made two settings of gold filigree and two gold rings, and put the two rings on the two edges of the breast piece; and they put the two cords of gold in the two rings at the edges of the breast piece. Two ends of the two cords they had attached to the two settings of filigree; in this way they attached it in front to the shoulder-pieces of the ephod. Then they made two rings of gold, and put them at the two ends of the breast piece, on its inside edge next to the ephod. They made two rings of gold, and attached them in front to the lower part of the two shoulder-pieces of the ephod, at its joining above the decorated band of the ephod. They bound the breast piece by its rings to the rings of the ephod with a blue cord, so that it should lie on the decorated band of the ephod, and that the breast piece should not come loose from the ephod; as the Lord had commanded Moses."

Exodus 39: 2–21

EPHOD

An ephod was one of the sacred garments worn by the high priest.

Described
Ex. 28: 6–14; Ex. 28: 31–35; Ex. 25: 7

Making of
Ex. 39: 2–26

Breastplate attached to
Ex. 28: 22–29

Worn by Aaron
Ex. 39: 5

Used as an oracle
1 Sam. 23: 9; 1 Sam. 23: 12; 1 Sam. 30: 7,8

AN INFERIOR, WAS WORN:
By ordinary priests
1 Sam. 22: 18

By Samuel
1 Sam. 2: 18

By David
2 Sam. 6: 14

It was called "coat"
Ex. 28: 40; Ex. 29: 8; Ex. 39: 27; Ex. 40: 14; Lev. 8: 13; Lev. 10: 5

the Ephod from Israel

Hos. 3: 4

Length of office

All the priests remained in their office from the time of their consecration until their death (Hebrews 7: 23,28).

The firstborn of Aaron's family became the high priest.

"The sacred vestments of Aaron shall be passed on to his sons after him; they shall be anointed in them and ordained in them" Exodus 29: 29. See also Numbers 20: 20–29.

Name given to the high priest

The high priest was known as the Anointed priest (Leviticus 4: 3–16; Psalms 133: 1–3).

At the consecration of Aaron and his sons the anointing oil was poured profusely upon Aaron's head (Leviticus 8: 12).

He was also anointed with blood and oil combined, while the other priests were only anointed with the blood and oil (Leviticus 8: 30).

Duties of the priests

The priests, Aaron's sons, officiated at the bronze altar and in the holy place every day (Leviticus 1: 1–17; Hebrews 9: 6).

PUBLIC DUTIES OF THE HIGH PRIEST
The high priest was required to:

Look after the golden candlestick,

burn incense morning and evening (Exodus 30: 1–10), and

stand in front of the ark of the covenant and make atonement for the children of Israel once every year (Leviticus 16: 1–34 Hebrews 10: 9).

He was also required to teach the people the law of God (Leviticus 10: 8–11; Deuteronomy 17: 8–13).

Priests as types

TYPES OF CHRISTIANS
The priests were types of Christians (Exodus 29: 38–42; Romans 12: 1; Hebrews 10: 5–7).

TYPE OF JESUS
The high priest was a type of Jesus Christ (Leviticus 16: 1–34; Hebrews 10: 7–14).

Tabernacle worship

Constant worship

At the inauguration of the tabernacle service by the consecration of Aaron and his sons (Exodus 40: 1–38; Leviticus 8: 1–36), fire fell from heaven upon the altar of burnt sacrifices.

"On the eighth day Moses summoned Aaron and his sons and the elders of Israel. He said to Aaron, 'Take a bull calf for a sin offering and a ram for a burnt offering, without blemish, and offer them before the Lord. And say to the people of Israel, "Take a male goat for a sin offering; a calf and a lamb, yearlings without blemish, for a burnt offering; and an ox and a ram for an offering of well-being to sacrifice before the Lord; and a grain offering mixed with oil. For today the Lord will appear to you."' … Then Moses said to Aaron, 'Draw near to the altar and sacrifice your sin offering and your burnt offering, and make atonement for yourself and for the people; and sacrifice the offering of the people, and make atonement for them; as the Lord has commanded.'"

Leviticus 9: 1–4,7 NRSV

They had to keep it burning continually (Leviticus 6: 12,13).

They also had to keep the golden lamps in the holy place burning continually (Leviticus 24: 1–3).

The showbread was "set in order before the Lord continually" (Leviticus 24: 5–9).

The constant worship was made up of sacrifices, and bread offerings.

Daily sacrifices

Every day the priests offered on the bronze altar two lambs, one in the morning, and the other in the evening. With each lamb, they offered flour, oil and wine (Exodus 29: 38–43; Numbers 28: 1–8). Twice as many offerings were made on the Sabbath (Numbers 28: 9,10).

Type of offerings

The burnt offering

The burnt offering was an animal sacrifice and was totally consumed on the bronze altar (Leviticus 1: 1–17).

The meat offering

Only part of the meat offering was burnt, and the rest of it was eaten by Aaron and his sons (Leviticus 2: 1–16).

The peace offering

Part of the peace offering was burnt on the altar, and the rest of it was eaten by the priests and the worshiper (Leviticus 3: 1–17; Leviticus 7: 11–38).

The sin offering

Part of the sin offering was burned on the altar of burnt offerings and the rest was burnt outside the camp (Leviticus 4: 1–35).

The trespass offering

The trespass offering was offered in a similar way to the sin offering

(Leviticus 7: 1–7). It differed from all the other offerings because restitution had to be made by the worshiper (Leviticus 5: 1–19; Leviticus 6: 1–7; Leviticus 7: 1–7).

"The Lord spoke to Moses, saying: When any of you sin and commit a trespass against the Lord by deceiving a neighbor in a matter of a deposit or a pledge, or by robbery, or if you have defrauded a neighbor, or have found something lost and lied about it – if you swear falsely regarding any of the various things that one may do and sin thereby – when you have sinned and realize your guilt, and would restore what you took by robbery or by fraud or the deposit that was committed to you, or the lost thing that you found, or anything else about which you have sworn falsely, you shall repay the principal amount and shall add one-fifth to it. You shall pay it to its owner when you realize your guilt."

Leviticus 6: 1–5 NRSV

Three times a year

All male Hebrews had to come before the Lord three times a year,
• at the Passover,
• at the feast of Weeks and
• at the feast of tabernacles
(Exodus 23: 14–19; Leviticus 23: 1–44). At these feasts many sacrifices were offered (Numbers 28: 16–31; Numbers 29: 1–40).

Day of Atonement

This was by far the most important day in the Hebrew calendar. It was the day on which reconciliation with God was made for the entire nation. After

the ordinary morning sacrifice was presented (Exodus 28: 38–42), a special offering was made, consisting of one young bullock, seven lambs, one ram, one kid of the goats, accompanied by meat offerings of flour mingled with oil (Numbers 29: 7–11).

The bullock

The high priest took the blood from the bullock of the sin offering and sprinkled it on the mercy seat and seven times upon the ground before the mercy seat. This was the sin offering for himself and his family.

The first lamb

After making this atonement for himself and his household, he killed the goat for a sin offering for the people. He took its blood and sprinkled it on the mercy seat and seven times upon the ground before the mercy seat. After he came out of the most holy place he placed some of the goat's blood on the horns of the altar of incense and on the horns of the bronze altar. He also sprinkled blood with his finger on the bronze altar seven times. This atonement was for the priests, tabernacle, and people.

The second lamb

The second sacrificial lamb was the sin offering for the people and was called the scapegoat. The high priest confessed the sins of the people over it by laying his hands on its head. Then the goat was led into the desert by a man selected for the task.

The judges

Tribal leaders

After the death of Joshua the children of Israel asked the Lord for a leader, and he gave them Judah.

"After the death of Joshua, the Israelites inquired of the Lord, "Who shall go up first for us against the Canaanites, to fight against them?" The Lord said, "Judah shall go up. I hereby give the land into his hand" Judges 1: 1,2 NRSV.

Judah subsequently formed an alliance with Simeon, and won a number of battles (Judges 1: 3–20).

The other tribes, however, did not expel the inhabitants of the land, but made them pay tribute to them (Judges 1: 21–36).

Destruction of Canaanites

The Lord destroyed the Canaanites because of their sin and to fulfill his promise made to Abraham, Isaac, and Jacob (Deuteronomy 7: 1–5; Deuteronomy 9: 5).

The angel's visit

After the people had failed to drive out the inhabitants of Canaan, the Lord sent an angel to them at Bochim.

The angel told them that their enemies would be thorns in their sides and that their gods should be snares to them.

"Now the angel of the Lord went up from Gilgal to Bochim, and said, 'I brought you up from Egypt, and brought you into the land that I had promised to your ancestors. I said, "I will never break my covenant with you. For your part, do not make a covenant with the inhabitants of this land; tear down their altars." But you have not obeyed my command. See what you have done! So now I say, I will not drive them out before you; but they shall become adversaries to you, and their gods shall be a snare to you.' When the angel of the Lord spoke these words to all the Israelites, the people lifted up their voices and wept. So they named that place Bochim, and there they sacrificed to the Lord."

Judges 2: 1–5 NRSV

Idolatry

The people served the Lord in the days of Joshua and during the time of the next generation.

But after that generation died, they turned away from the Lord and served Baal and Ashtaroth. So the Lord handed them over to their enemies. Then the Israelites cried to the Lord and he sent them judges (Judges 2: 6–23).

Surrounded by strangers

From this time on the children of Israel were surrounded by the
• Canaanites,
• Hittites,
• Amorites,
• Perizzites,
• Hivites and
• Jebusites (Judges 3: 1–5).

Contrary to God's command, they intermarried with these nations, (Deuteronomy 7: 1–6), and forgot the Lord their God, and served Baalim and the groves.

"... they took their daughters as wives for themselves, and their own daughters they gave to their sons; and they worshiped their gods" Judges 3: 6,7 NRSV.

List of the judges of Israel

GENERAL REFERENCES

Judg. 2: 16–19

"For about forty years he put up with them in the wilderness. After he had destroyed seven nations in the land of Canaan, he gave them their land as an inheritance for about four hundred fifty years. After that he gave them judges until the time of the prophet Samuel."

Acts 13: 19,20 NRSV

JUDGES
Othniel
   Judg. 3: 9–11
Ehud
   Judg. 3: 15–30
Shamgar
   Judg. 3: 31
Deborah
   Judg. 4–5
Gideon
   Judg. 6: 11–40; Judg. 7–8
Abimelech
   Judg. 9: 1–54
Tola
   Judg. 10: 1–2
Jair
   Judg. 10: 3–5
Jephthah
   Judg. 11; Judg. 12: 1–7

Ibzan
   Judg. 12: 8–10
Elon
   Judg. 12: 11–12
Abdon
   Judg. 12: 13–14
Samson
   Judg. 13–16
Eli judged Israel
   1 Sam. 4: 18
Samuel as judge
   1 Sam. 7: 6; 1 Sam. 7: 15–17
The sons of Samuel
   1 Sam. 8: 1–5

Ruth

During the times of the judges Elimelech of Bethlehem, with his wife Naomi and their two sons, Mahlon and Chilion, went to live in the land of Moab. The two sons married women from Moab. Then the father and two sons died, and Naomi decided to return to her own country, suggesting to her daughters-in-law that it would be best for them to stay in the country where they had been born. Orpah, the wife of Chilion, agreed to this, but Ruth stayed with Naomi (Ruth 1: 1–18).

They returned to Bethlehem, and Ruth looked after Naomi by gleaning the fields (Ruth 1: 19–2: 23).

She married Boaz and had a son Obed. Obed was the father of Jesse, who, in turn, was the father of David, and also an ancestor of Christ (Ruth 3: 1–4: 22; Matthew 1: 1–17).

The beginning of the Hebrew monarchy

Reasons leading to a monarchy

Disregard for God's law

In Samuel's old age, his sons Joel and Abiah were made judges in Beersheba, but they disregarded the Lord's law (Deuteronomy 16: 18,19), and refused to walk in the footsteps of their illustrious father (1 Samuel 8: 1–3). The elders met at Ramah, expressed their dissatisfaction to Samuel, and asked him to make them a king to judge them like other nations (1 Samuel 8: 4,5).

"You are old and your sons do not follow in your ways; appoint for us, then, a king to govern us, like other nations" 1 Samuel 8: 5 NRSV.

Request granted

The Lord had previously intimated through Moses that the time would come when they would want a king, (Deuteronomy 17: 14–20; 26: 19). The request from the elders greatly displeased Samuel, and he prayed for the Lord's guidance. The Lord told him to grant their request, but to warn the people that this would only bring trouble on them.

Saul made king

Samuel anointed Saul to be king. (1 Samuel 10: 1). As soon as Saul left from Samuel, God gave him a new heart.

OVERVIEW OF SAUL'S LIFE
A Benjamite, son of Kish
1 Sam. 9: 1–2

Sons of
1 Chr. 8: 33

His personal appearance
1 Sam. 9: 2; 1 Sam. 10: 23

Made king of Israel
1 Sam. 9–10; 1 Sam. 11: 12–15; Hos. 13: 11

Lives at Gibeah
1 Sam. 14: 2; 1 Sam. 15: 34; Is. 10: 29

Defeats the Philistines
1 Sam. 13; 1 Sam. 14: 46; 1 Sam. 14: 52

Defeats the Amalekites
1 Sam. 15

Is reproved by Samuel for usurping the priestly functions
1 Sam. 13: 11–14

Is reproved for disobedience in not killing the Amalekites; the loss of his kingdom foretold
1 Sam. 15

Dedicates the spoils of war
1 Sam. 15: 21–25; 1 Chr. 26: 28

Sends messengers to Jesse, asking that David be sent to him as musician and armor-bearer
1 Sam. 16: 17–23

Defeats the Philistines after Goliath is killed by David
1 Sam. 17

His jealousy of David; gives his daughter, Michal, to be David's wife; becomes David's enemy
1 Sam. 18

"The next day an evil spirit from God rushed upon Saul, and he raved within his house, while David was playing the lyre, as he did day by day. Saul had his spear in his hand;

11 and Saul threw the spear, for he thought, "I will pin David to the wall." But David eluded him twice.

12 Saul was afraid of David, because the Lord was with him but had departed from Saul.

13 So Saul removed him from his presence, and made him a commander of a thousand; and David marched out and came in, leading the army.

14 David had success in all his undertakings; for the Lord was with him.

15 When Saul saw that he had great success, he stood in awe of him.

16 But all Israel and Judah loved David; for it was he who marched out and came in leading them"

1 Samuel 18: 10–16 NRSV

Tries to kill David; Jonathan speaks up for David but incurs Saul's displeasure; David's loyalty to him; Saul's repentance; prophesies
1 Sam. 19

Listens to Doeg speaking against Ahimelech, and kills the priest and his family. Chases after David into the desert of Ziph
1 Sam. 23

Pursues David to Engedi
1 Sam. 24: 1–6

His life saved by David
1 Sam. 24: 5–8

David is again betrayed to Saul, by the Ziphites; Saul pursues him to the hill of Hachilah; his life spared again by David; his confession, and his blessing upon David
1 Sam. 26

His kingdom invaded by Philistines; seeks counsel from the witch of Endor, who foretells his death
1 Sam. 28: 3–25; 1 Sam. 29: 1

Is defeated, and with his sons is killed
1 Sam. 31

Their bodies exposed in Bethshan; rescued by the people of Jabesh and burned; bones of, buried under a tree at Jabesh
1 Sam. 31; 2 Sam. 1–2; 1 Chr. 10

His death a judgment on account of his sins

"So Saul died for his unfaithfulness; he was unfaithful to the Lord in that he did not keep the command of the Lord; moreover, he had consulted a medium, seeking guidance,

14 and did not seek guidance from the Lord. Therefore the Lord put him to death and turned the kingdom over to David son of Jesse"

1 Chr. 10: 13,14 NRSV

Feasts, festivals, and fasts (1)

Overview

Annual festivals instituted by Moses:

Called solemn feasts
Num. 15: 3; 2 Chr. 8: 13; Lam. 2: 6;
Ezek. 46: 9
Set feasts
Num. 29: 39; Ezra 3: 5
Appointed feasts
Is. 1: 14
To be kept with rejoicing
Lev. 23: 40; Deut. 16: 11–14;
2 Chr. 30: 21–26; Ezra 6: 22;
Neh. 8: 9–12; Neh. 8: 17; Ps. 42: 4;
Ps. 122: 4; Is. 30: 29; Zech. 8: 19
Divine protection given during
Ex. 34: 24

Three major feasts

The three main festivals were Passover,
Pentecost, Tabernacles:
All males were required to attend
Ex. 23: 17; Ex. 34: 23; Deut. 16: 16;
Ps. 42: 4; Ps. 122: 4; Ezek. 36: 38; Luke
2: 44; John 4: 45; John 7
Strangers were allowed to attend
John 12: 20; Acts 2: 1–11
Attended by women
1 Sam. 1: 3; 1 Sam. 1: 9; Luke 2: 41

OBSERVED
In the book of Leviticus, God
commanded the Israelites to observe
the following feasts and festivals.

By Jesus
Matt. 26: 17–20; Luke 2: 41,42; Luke
22: 15; John 2: 13; John 2: 23; John 5: 1;
John 7: 10; John 10: 22

By Paul
Acts 18: 21; Acts 19: 21; Acts 20: 6;
Acts 20: 16; Acts 24: 11; Acts 24: 17

Sabbath

This fell on the seventh day of the week
and no work was allowed to be done on
the Sabbath. It was a day of rest and a
sign of God's covenant (Exodus 20: 8–
11).

The Israelites were not allowed to
leave their homes (Exodus 16: 29), or
light fires throughout their habitations
on the Sabbath day (Exodus 35: 1–3).
Breaking the Sabbath was punished by
the death penalty (Numbers 15: 32–36).

THE SABBATICAL YEAR
The land, as well as the people were to
rest every seventh year (Leviticus 25: 1–
7,18–22).

The jubilee

This came round every fifty years.
Slaves were released and everyone
received back his property. All debts
were cancelled. The land had to lie
fallow. The price of everything in Israel
was regulated by its distance from the
jubilee (Leviticus 25: 14–17).

"You shall count off seven weeks
of years, seven times seven years, so
that the period of seven weeks of years
gives forty-nine years. Then you shall
have the trumpet sounded loud; on the
tenth day of the seventh month – on
the day of atonement – you shall have
the trumpet sounded throughout all
your land. And you shall hallow the
fiftieth year and you shall proclaim

liberty throughout the land to all its inhabitants. It shall be a jubilee for you: you shall return, every one of you, to your property and every one of you to your family. That fiftieth year shall be a jubilee for you: you shall not sow, or reap the aftergrowth, or harvest the unpruned vines. For it is a jubilee; it shall be holy to you: you shall eat only what the field itself produces.

In this year of jubilee you shall return, every one of you, to your property." Leviticus 25: 8–13 NRSV

The Passover

This feast originated in Egypt was given this name because the angel of death passed over of the houses of the Hebrews.

To commemorate this event, the symbol of their salvation, and how God led them out of Egypt, they kept the feast of unleavened bread (Exodus 12: 1–29).

The law of Moses laid down regulations about how the feast should be observed.

It was eaten on the night of the fifteenth of month of Abib, as the Hebrew day ended at sunset (Leviticus 23: 32).

They killed the paschal lamb at sunset on the fourteenth Abib (Exodus 12: 1–6; Deuteronomy 16: 1–8).

The feast of unleavened bread began with the Passover and ended on the twenty-first day of the month at sunset (Exodus 12: 14–19; Leviticus 23: 1–8).

No uncircumcised person was allowed to take part in the paschal feast (Exodus 12: 43–51).

Special offerings were made at the feast consisting of,
- two young bullocks,
- one ram,
- seven lambs, and
- one goat,

The above eleven animals were offered each day for seven days, amounting to a total of seventy-seven animals (Numbers 28: 16–25).

They also ate unleavened bread for 7 days.

The first day of each month

On the first day of each month, throughout the year, the Israelites were commanded to offer:
- two young bullocks,
- one ram,
- seven lambs, and
- one kid of the goats (Numbers 28: 11–15).

Feast of Weeks

This feast was known as,
- feast of harvest (Exodus 23: 16).
- feast of weeks (Exodus 34: 22),
- day of first fruits (Numbers 28: 26), and
- Pentecost (Acts 2: 1).

FIFTY DAYS
This feast was observed fifty days after the Passover (Leviticus 23: 15,16; Deuteronomy 16: 9–12).

They began to count the fifty days from the day after the first sabbath of the feast of unleavened bread, that is on the sixteenth day of Abib (Exodus 12: 11–20; Leviticus 23: 4–16).

Feasts, festivals, and fasts (2)

Feast of Weeks, continued

During this feast they offered:
- two loaves made of the first fruits of the land,
- seven lambs,
- one young bullock,
- two rams,
- one male goat, and
- two one-year-old male lambs

This made a total of thirteen animals (Leviticus 23: 15–21; Numbers 28: 26–31).

The feast of Weeks was a celebration of the firstfruits of the harvest.

Feast of Trumpets

This feast was held on the first day of the seventh month of each year. It was a day of rest marked by the blowing of trumpets (Numbers 29: 1).

During this feast they offered:
- one young bullock,
- one ram,
- seven lambs of the first year, and
- one kid of the goats (Numbers 29: 1–6).

Feast of Tabernacles

This feast was also known as the feast of ingathering, and the feast of booths and celebrated the harvest.

It was the third of the annual feasts that had to be kept and attended by all Jewish men (Exodus 23: 16).

It was commemorated fifty days after the feast of firstfruits, from the fifteenth of Tishri, and lasted seven days (Leviticus 23: 33–44).

It was kept as follows:

The people lived in booths (huts) made out of branches from trees. This commemorated their temporary homes during their travels through the desert.

"The LORD spoke to Moses, saying:

34 Speak to the people of Israel, saying: On the fifteenth day of this seventh month, and lasting seven days, there shall be the festival of booths to the LORD.

35 The first day shall be a holy convocation; you shall not work at your occupations.

36 Seven days you shall present the LORD'S offerings by fire; on the eighth day you shall observe a holy convocation and present the LORD'S offerings by fire; it is a solemn assembly; you shall not work at your occupations. . . .

39 Now, the fifteenth day of the seventh month, when you have gathered in the produce of the land, you shall keep the festival of the LORD, lasting seven days; a complete rest on the first day, and a complete rest on the eighth day.

40 On the first day you shall take the fruit of majestic trees, branches of palm trees, boughs of leafy trees, and willows of the brook; and you shall rejoice before the LORD your God for seven days.

41 You shall keep it as a festival to the LORD seven days in the year; you shall keep it in the seventh month as a statute forever throughout your generations.

42 You shall live in booths for seven days; all that are citizens in Israel shall live in booths,

43 so that your generations may know that I made the people of Israel live in booths when I brought them out of the land of Egypt: I am the LORD your God"

Leviticus 23: 24–43 NRSV

Fasts

The only fast laid down by the law of Moses occurred on the Day of Atonement Lev. 23: 26–32. It is called "the fast" (Acts 27: 9).

The only other periodical fast mentioned in the Old Testament is in Zech. 7: 1–7; 8: 19, from which it appears that during their captivity the Jews observed four annual fasts, see Ex. 32: 19; Jer. 52: 12, 13; Jer. 41: 1,2; Jer. 52: 4; Ezek. 33: 21; 2 Kings25: 1,

Additionally there is the fast mentioned in Esther 4: 16.

NATIONAL FASTS
Public national fasts were held because of sin or to ask the Lord for some divine favor: 1 Sam. 7: 6; 2 Chr. 20: 3; Jer. 36: 6–10; Neh. 9: 1.

LOCAL FASTS
There were also local fasts: Judg. 20: 26; 2 Sam. 1: 12; 1 Sam. 31: 13; 1 Kings 21: 9–12; Ezra 8: 21–23; Jonah 3: 5–9.

PRIVATE FASTS
There are many examples of private occasional fasting (1 Sam. 1: 7; 20: 34; 2 Sam. 3: 35; 12: 16; 1 Kings 21: 27; Ezra 10: 6; Neh. 1: 4; Dan. 10: 2, 3).

Moses fasted forty days (Ex. 24: 18; 34: 28), and so also did Elijah (1 Kings 19: 8).

Our Lord fasted forty days in the wilderness (Matt. 4: 2).

FASTS MISUSUED
On some occasions the practice of fasting was abused (Is. 58: 4; Jer. 14: 12; Zech. 7: 5).

Our Lord rebuked the Pharisees for their hypocritical way of fasting (Matt. 6: 16). Jesus himself appointed no fast.

The early Christians, however, observed the ordinary fasts of the law (Acts 13: 3; 14: 23; 2 Cor. 6: 5).

Part Four
Facts From
The New Testament

Part Four Contents in summary

Every New Testament book: Overviews........................922

Studies in the New Testament.......................................990

Encouragement from every New Testament book.....1004

Messianic prophecies...1062

Parables and miracles..1086

The resurrection of Jesus..1090

Conversions in Acts...1094

The early church..1100

Part Four Contents in detail

Every New Testament book: Overviews

Matthew (1) 922

Matthew (2) 924

Mark (1) 926

Mark (2) 928

Luke (1) 930

Luke (2) 932

John 934

Acts (1) 936

Acts (2) 938

Romans (1) 940

Romans (2) 942

1 Corinthians (1) 944

1 Corinthians (2) 946

2 Corinthians 948

Galatians (1) 950

Galatians (2) 952

Ephesians (1) 954

Ephesians (2) 956

Philippians 958

Colossians 960

1 Thessalonians 962

2 Thessalonians 964

1 Timothy 966

2 Timothy 968

Titus 970

Philemon 972

Hebrews 974

James 976

1 Peter 978

2 Peter 980

1 John 982

2 John and 3 John 984

Jude 986

Revelation 988

Studies in the New Testament

Analysis of New Testament books (1) 990

Analysis of New Testament books (2) 992

Authors of the New Testament 994

The synoptic Gospels 996

New Testament letters and Aramaic words 998

Harmony of the accounts of the resurrection, the resurrection
appearances, and the ascension (1) 1000

Harmony of the accounts of the resurrection, the resurrection
appearances, and the ascension (2) 1002

Encouragement from every New Testament book

Matthew, Mark 1004

Mark, Luke 1006

Luke, John 1008

John 1010

Acts, Romans 1012

Romans, 1 Corinthians 1014

1 Corinthians 1016

1 Corinthians, 2 Corinthians 1018

2 Corinthians, Galatians 1020

Galatians, Ephesians 1022

Ephesians 1024

Ephesians, Philippians 1026

Philippians, Colossians...1028

1 Thessalonians 1030

2 Thessalonians, 1 Timothy..1032

1 Timothy, 2 Timothy...1034

2 Timothy, Titus..1036

Philemon, Hebrews 1038

Hebrews...1040

Hebrews, James...1042

James, 1 Peter 1044

1 Peter...1046

2 Peter, 1 John...1048

1 John, 2 John, 3 John...1050

Jude, Revelation (1)..1052

Revelation (2)...1054

Revelation (3)...1056

Symbols found in Revelation (1)..1058

Symbols found in Revelation (2)..1060

Messianic prophecies

Messianic prophecies in the Old Testament (1)........................1062

Messianic prophecies in the Old Testament (2) 1064

Messianic prophecies in the Old Testament (3).........................1066

Messianic prophecies in the Old Testament (4) 1068

Messianic prophecies in the Old Testament (5).........................1070

Messianic prophecies in the Old Testament (6) 1072

Prophecies about the Messiah's birth and life...........................1074

Prophecies about the Messiah's ministry.................................1076

Prophecies about the Messiah's death (1) 1078

Prophecies about the Messiah's death (2)................................1080

Prophecies about the Messiah's resurrection and ascension 1082

The Messiah's return 1084

Parables and miracles

All the miracles of Jesus...1086

All the parables of Jesus...1088

The resurrection of Jesus

The resurrection of Jesus (1)...1090

The resurrection of Jesus (2)...1092

Conversions in Acts

Conversions in Acts (1)..1094

Conversions in Acts (2)..1096

Conversions in Acts (3)..1098

The early church

Church (1)..1100

Church (2)..1102

The church of Christ (1)..1104

The church of Christ (2)..1106

Worship...1108

Praise..1110

Baptism...1112

Lord's Supper...1114

Paul (1)..1116

Paul (2)..1118

The persecuted Paul...1120

The teachings of Paul...1122

Matthew (1)

An introduction

Authorship

The author of this book was beyond a doubt the Matthew, an apostle of our Lord, whose name it bears. He wrote the Gospel of Christ according to his own plans and aims, and from his own point of view, as did also the other "evangelists."

Date of writing

As to the time of its composition, there is little in the Gospel itself to indicate. It was evidently written before the destruction of Jerusalem (Matt. 24), and some time after the events it records. The probability is that it was written between the years A.D. 60 and 65.

Readership

The thought forms and expression used by the writer show that this Gospel was written for Jewish Christians of Palestine.

Purpose of Gospel

His great object is to prove that Jesus of Nazareth was the promised Messiah, and that in him the ancient prophecies had their fulfillment. The Gospel is full of allusions to those passages of the Old Testament in which Christ is predicted and foreshadowed. The one aim pervading the whole book is to show that Jesus is he "of whom Moses in the law and the prophets did write." This Gospel contains no fewer than sixty-five references to the Old Testament, forty-three of these being direct verbal citations, thus greatly outnumbering those found in the other Gospels. The main feature of this Gospel may be expressed in the motto, "I am not come to destroy, but to fulfill."

Characteristics of Gospel

The leading characteristic of this Gospel is that it presents the kingly glory of Christ, and shows him to be the true heir to David's throne. It is the Gospel of the kingdom. Matthew uses the expression "kingdom of heaven" (thirty-two times), while Luke uses the expression "kingdom of God" (thirty-three times).

Use of Latin

Some Latinized forms occur in this Gospel, as kodrantes (Matt. 5: 26), for the Latin *quadrans*, and phragello (Matt. 27: 26), for the Latin *flagello*. It must be remembered that Matthew was a tax-gatherer for the Roman government, and hence in contact with those using the Latin language.

Written independently

As for the relationship between the Gospels, we must maintain that each writer of the synoptics (the first three Gospels) wrote independently of the other two, Matthew being probably first in point of time.

Matthew, Mark, and Luke

Out of a total of 1071 verses, Matthew has 387 in common with Mark and Luke, 130 with Mark, 184 with Luke; only 387 being unique to itself.

Divisions

The book is rightly divided into these four parts:

(1) Containing the genealogy, the birth, and the infancy of Jesus (Matt. 1; 2).

(2) The discourses and actions of John the Baptist preparatory to Christ's public ministry (Matt. 3; 4: 11).

(3) The discourses and actions of Christ in Galilee (Matt. 4: 12–20: 16).

(4) The sufferings, death, and resurrection of our Lord (Matt. 20: 17–28).

Name, author, date

AUTHOR
Matthew, one of Jesus' 12 apostles.

APPROXIMATE DATE OF WRITING
A.D. 58–68

Statistics

PLACE OF BOOK IN BIBLE
1st New Testament book
1st Gospel

NUMBER OF CHAPTERS
28

NUMBER OF VERSES
1,071

NUMBER OF WORDS
23,684

Main theme of book

To explain to Jews that Jesus was their Messiah.

Keys to the understanding of book

KEY WORD/S
King, Kingdom, 50 times, Messiah

KEY PHRASE
King of the Jews
That it might be fulfilled

KEY CHAPTER/S
12 with the Pharisees rejecting Jesus.
16 and Peter's confession of Christ.

KEY VERSE/S
The book of the generation of Jesus Christ, the son of David, the son of Abraham.
Matthew 1: 1

Behold, a virgin shall be with child, and shall bring forth a son, and they shall call his name Emmanuel, which being interpreted is, God with us.
Matthew 1: 23

And Simon Peter answered and said, Thou art the Christ, the Son of the living God.
Matthew 16: 16–19

Matthew (2)

KEY VERSE/S, CONTINUED
And Jesus came and spake unto them, saying, All power is given unto me in heaven and in earth. Go ye therefore, and teach all nations, baptizing them in the name of the Father, and of the Son, and of the Holy Ghost: Teaching them to observe all things whatsoever I have commanded you: and, lo, I am with you alway, even unto the end of the world. Amen.
Matthew 28:18–20

Christ is seen as
King.

Spiritual thought
The need for repentance.

Chapter by chapter breakdown
Chapter 1: Jesus' family tree and birth
Chapter 2: Jesus' infancy
Chapter 3: John the Baptist and the baptism of Jesus
Chapter 4: The temptation of Jesus
Chapter 5: The Beatitudes, salt and light, and the Law
Chapter 6: Jesus rejects pharisaical practices
Chapter 7: Jesus encourages true religion
Chapter 8: Healing miracles and the demands of discipleship
Chapter 9: More miracles
Chapter 10: The mission of the Twelve
Chapter 11: Jesus' answer about John the Baptist
Chapter 12: The opposition of the Pharisees

Chapter 13: The parables of the kingdom
Chapter 14: Execution of John the Baptist
Chapter 15: Rejection by scribes and Pharisees
Chapter 16: Warnings about religious leaders, and Peter's confession
Chapter 17: Jesus' transfiguration and teaching the Twelve
Chapter 18: The Church's lifestyle
Chapter 19: Divorce, children, and a rich young man
Chapter 20: Parable of the workers in the vineyard, and Jesus in Judea
Chapter 21: Jesus enters Jerusalem and his public ministry there
Chapter 22: Parables and questions
Chapter 23: Jesus denounces the Pharisees and teachers of the law, and weeps over Jerusalem
Chapter 24: Jesus teaches about the end of the age
Chapter 25: Jesus predicts judgment at his coming
Chapter 26: The Last Supper and Jesus on trial
Chapter 27: Jesus before Pilate, and his death and burial
Chapter 28: The resurrection of Jesus

Insight from Matthew Henry

Matthew 28

VERSES 11–15
Those men promise more than they can perform, who undertake to save a man harmless in doing a willful sin.

But this falsehood disproved itself. Had the soldiers been all asleep, they could not have known what passed. If any had been awake, they would have roused the others and prevented the removal; and certainly if they had been asleep, they never would have dared to confess it; while the Jewish rulers would have been the first to call for their punishment. Again, had there been any truth in the report, the rulers would have prosecuted the apostles with severity for it. The whole shows that the story was entirely false. And we must not charge such things to the weakness of the understanding, but to the wickedness of the heart. God left them to expose their own course. The great argument to prove Christ to be the Son of God, is his resurrection; and none could have more convincing proofs of the truth of that than these soldiers; yet they took bribes to hinder others from believing. The plainest evidence will not affect men, without the work of the Holy Spirit.

VERSES 16–20
This evangelist passes over other appearances of Christ, recorded by Luke and John, and hastens to the most solemn; one appointed before his death, and after his resurrection. All that see the Lord Jesus with an eye of faith, will worship him. Yet the faith of the sincere may be very weak and wavering. But Christ gave such convincing proofs of his resurrection, as made their faith to triumph over doubts. He now solemnly commissioned the apostles and his ministers to go forth among all nations.

The salvation they were to preach, is a common salvation; whoever will, let him come, and take the benefit; all are welcome to Christ Jesus. Christianity is the religion of a sinner who applies for salvation from deserved wrath and from sin; he applies to the mercy of the Father, through the atonement of the incarnate Son, and by the sanctification of the Holy Spirit, and gives up himself to be the worshiper and servant of God, as the Father, Son, and Holy Ghost, three Persons but one God, in all his ordinances and commandments. Baptism is an outward sign of that inward washing, or sanctification of the Spirit, which seals and evidences the believer's justification. Let us examine ourselves, whether we really possess the inward and spiritual grace of a death unto sin, and a new birth unto righteousness, by which those who were the children of wrath become the children of God. Believers shall have the constant presence of their Lord always; all days, every day. There is no day, no hour of the day, in which our Lord Jesus is not present with his churches and with his ministers; if there were, in that day, that hour, they would be undone. The God of Israel, the Savior, is sometimes a God that hideth himself, but never a God at a distance. To these precious words Amen is added. Even so, Lord Jesus, be thou with us and all thy people; cause thy face to shine upon us, that thy way may be known upon earth, thy saving health among all nations.

Mark (1)

An introduction

Mark and Peter

It is the current and apparently well-founded tradition that Mark derived his information mainly from the discourses of Peter. In his mother's house he would have abundant opportunities of obtaining information from the other apostles and their coadjutors, yet he was "the disciple and interpreter of Peter" specially.

Date of writing

As to the time when it was written, the Gospel furnishes us with no definite information. Mark makes no mention of the destruction of Jerusalem, hence it must have been written before that event, and probably about A.D. 63.

Readersip

It was intended primarily for Romans. This appears probable when it is considered that it makes no reference to the Jewish law, and that the writer takes care to interpret words which a Gentile would be likely to misunderstand, such as, "Boanerges" (Mark 3: 17); "Talitha cumi" (Mark 5: 41); "Corban" (Mark 7: 11); "Bartimaeus" (Mark 10: 46); "Abba" (Mark 14: 36); "Eloi," etc. (Mark 15: 34). Jewish usages are also explained (Mark 7: 3; 14: 3; 14: 12; 15: 42). Mark also uses certain Latin words not found in any of the other Gospels, as "speculator" (Mark 6: 27, rendered, AV, "executioner;" RV, "soldier of his guard"), "xestes" (a corruption of sextarius, rendered "pots," Mark 7: 4,8), "quadrans" (Mark 12: 42, rendered "a farthing"), "centurion" (Mark 15: 39,44,45). He only twice quotes from the Old Testament (Mark 1: 2; 15: 28).

Characteristics of Gospel

The characteristics of this Gospel are,

(1) the absence of the genealogy of our Lord,

(2) whom he represents as clothed with power, the "lion of the tribe of Judah."

(3) Mark also records with wonderful minuteness the very words (Mark 3: 17; 5: 41; 7: 11,34; 14: 36) as well as the position (Mark 9: 35) and gestures (Mark 3: 5,34; 5: 32; 9: 36; 10: 16) of our Lord.

(4) He is also careful to record particulars of people (Mark 1: 29,36; 3: 6,22, etc.), number (Mark 5: 13; 6: 7, etc.), place (Mark 2: 13; 4: 1; 7: 31, etc.), and time (Mark 1: 35; 2: 1; 4: 35, etc.), which the other evangelists omit.

(5) The phrase "and straightway" occurs nearly forty times in this Gospel; while in Luke's Gospel, which is much longer, it is used only seven times, and in John only four times.

"The Gospel of Mark," says Westcott, "is essentially a transcript from life. The course and issue of facts are imaged in it with the clearest outline." "In Mark we have no attempt to draw up a continuous narrative. His Gospel is a rapid succession of vivid pictures loosely strung together without much attempt to bind them into a whole or give the events in their natural sequence. This pictorial power is that which specially characterizes this evangelist, so that 'if any one desires to know an evangelical fact, not only in its main features and grand results, but also in its most minute and so to speak more graphic delineation, he must betake himself to Mark.'"

Motto

The leading principle running through this Gospel may be expressed in the motto: "Jesus came... preaching the gospel of the kingdom" (Mark 1: 14).

Matthew, Mark, and Luke

Out of a total of 662 verses, Mark has 406 in common with Matthew and Luke, 145 with Matthew, 60 with Luke, and at most 51 unique to itself.

Name, author, date

AUTHOR
Mark.

APPROXIMATE DATE OF WRITING
A.D. 55–65

Statistics

PLACE OF BOOK IN BIBLE
2nd New Testament book.
2nd Gospel.

NUMBER OF CHAPTERS
16

NUMBER OF VERSES
678

NUMBER OF WORDS
15,171

Main theme of book

Jesus is God's Servant and Redeemer.

Keys to the understanding of book

KEY WORD/S
Servant, Straightway (immediately), 42 times

KEY PHRASE
Servant of the Lord

KEY CHAPTER/S
8 and the change of emphasis in Jesus' ministry.
10 and Christ's purpose of his work.

KEY VERSE/S
And when he had called the people unto him with his disciples also, he said unto them, Whosoever will come after me, let him deny himself, and take up his cross, and follow me. For whosoever will save his life shall lose it; but whosoever shall lose his life for my sake and the gospel's, the same shall save it. For what shall it profit a man, if he shall gain the whole world, and lose his own soul? Or what shall a man give in exchange for his soul?
Mark 8: 34–37

Mark (2)

KEY VERSE/S, CONTINUED
For even the Son of man came not to be ministered unto, but to minister, and to give his life a ransom for many.
Mark 10: 45

Christ is seen as
God's righteous servant.

Spiritual thought
Jesus' deeds show who he is.

Chapter by chapter breakdown
Chapter 1: Jesus' baptism, temptation, and first followers

Chapter 2: Jesus heals a paralyzed man, calls Levi, and answers questions

Chapter 3: Jesus appoints the Twelve

Chapter 4: Four parables and the calming of the lake

Chapter 5: Four miracles

Chapter 6: The Twelve; John the Baptist beheaded, and 5,000 fed

Chapter 7: Inner purity and two healing miracles

Chapter 8: Jesus feeds four thousand, and Peter's confession

Chapter 9: Transfiguration, demon-possession, and prediction of death

Chapter 10: Jesus teaches his disciples and heals Bartimaeus

Chapter 11: Jesus enters Jerusalem and the barren fig tree

Chapter 12: Opposition from the leaders in Jerusalem

Chapter 13: The destruction of the temple prophesied and other of Jesus' prophecies

Chapter 14: The Last Supper and Gethsemane

Chapter 15: Pilate, and Jesus' crucifixion and burial

Chapter 16: Jesus' resurrection

Insight from Matthew Henry

Mark 14

VERSES 32–42

He now tasted death, in all the bitterness of it. This was that fear of which the apostle speaks, the natural fear of pain and death, at which human nature startles. Can we ever entertain favorable, or even slight thoughts of sin, when we see the painful sufferings which sin, though but reckoned to him, brought on the Lord Jesus? Shall that sit light upon our souls, which sat so heavy upon his? Was Christ in such agony for our sins, and shall we never be in agony about them? How should we look upon him whom we have pierced, and mourn! It becomes us to be exceedingly sorrowful for sin, because he was so, and never to mock at it. Christ, as Man, pleaded, that, if it were possible, his sufferings might pass from him. As Mediator, he submitted to the will of God, saying, Nevertheless, not what I will, but what thou wilt; I bid it welcome. See how the sinful weakness of Christ's disciples returns, and overpowers them. What heavy clogs these bodies of ours are to our souls! But when we see trouble at the door, we should get ready for it. Alas, even believers often look at the Redeemer's sufferings in a drowsy manner, and instead of being ready to die with Christ, they are not even prepared to watch with him one hour.

VERSES 43–52
Because Christ appeared not as a temporal prince, but preached repentance, reformation, and a holy life, and directed men's thoughts, and affections, and aims to another world, therefore the Jewish rulers sought to destroy him. Peter wounded one of the band. It is easier to fight for Christ than to die for him. But there is a great difference between faulty disciples and hypocrites. The latter rashly and without thought call Christ Master, and express great affection for him, yet betray him to his enemies. Thus they hasten their own destruction.

VERSES 53–65
We have here Christ's condemnation before the great council of the Jews. Peter followed; but the high priest's fire-side was no proper place, nor his servants proper company, for Peter: it was an entrance into temptation. Great diligence was used to procure false witnesses against Jesus, yet their testimony was not equal to the charge of a capital crime, by the utmost stretch of their law. He was asked, Art thou the Son of the Blessed? that is, the Son of God. For the proof of his being the Son of God, he refers to his second coming. In these outrages we have proofs of man's enmity to God, and of God's free and unspeakable love to man.

VERSES 66–72
Peter's denying Christ began by keeping at a distance from him. Those that are shy of godliness, are far in the way to deny Christ. Those who think it dangerous to be in company with Christ's disciples, because thence they may be drawn in to suffer for him, will find it much more dangerous to be in company with his enemies, because there they may be drawn in to sin against him. When Christ was admired and flocked after, Peter readily owned him; but will own no relation to him now he is deserted and despised. Yet observe, Peter's repentance was very speedy. Let him that thinketh he standeth take heed lest he fall; and let him that has fallen think of these things, and return to the Lord with weeping.

Luke (1)

An introduction

Authorship

This Gospel was written by Luke. He does not claim to have been an eye-witness of our Lord's ministry, but to have gone to the best sources of information within his reach, and to have written an orderly narrative of the facts (Luke 1: 1–4). The authors of the first three Gospels wrote under the guidance of the Holy Spirit.

Style of writing

Each writer has some things, both in matter and style, peculiar to himself, yet all the three have much in common.

Names of Luke's Gospel

Luke's Gospel has been called
• the Gospel of the nations, full of mercy and hope, assured to the world by the love of a suffering Savior;
• the Gospel of the saintly life;
• the Gospel for the Greeks;
• the Gospel of the future;
• the Gospel of progressive Christianity, of the universality and gratuitousness of the gospel;
• the historic Gospel;
• the Gospel of Jesus as the good Physician and the Savior of mankind;
• the Gospel of the Fatherhood of God and the brotherhood of man;
• the Gospel of womanhood;
• the Gospel of the outcast, of the Samaritan, the publican, the harlot, and the prodigal;
• the Gospel of tolerance.

Characteristic of Gospel

The main characteristic of this Gospel, as Farrar remarks, is expressed in the motto, "Who went about doing good, and healing all that were oppressed of the devil" (Acts 10: 38; cf. Luke 4: 18). Luke wrote for the "Hellenic world." This Gospel is indeed "rich and precious."

Matthew, Mark, and Luke

Out of a total of 1151 verses,
Luke has 389 in common with Matthew and Mark,
176 in common with Matthew alone,
41 in common with Mark alone,
leaving 544 unique to himself.
In many instances all three use identical language.

Unique parables

There are seventeen of our Lord's parables peculiar to this Gospel.

Miracles

Luke also records seven of our Lord's miracles which are omitted by Matthew and Mark.

Synoptics

The synoptic Gospels are related to each other after the following scheme. If the contents of each Gospel be represented by 100, then when compared this result is obtained in the following table.

That is, thirteen-fourteenths of Mark, four-sevenths of Matthew, and two-fifths of Luke are taken up in describing

Synoptic Gospels	Peculiarities	Coincidences	Total
Mark	7	93	100
Matthew	42	58	100
Luke	59	41	100

the same things in very similar language.

Polished writer

Luke's style is more finished and classical than that of Matthew and Mark. There is less in it of the Hebrew idiom. He uses a few Latin words (Luke 12: 6; 7: 41; 8: 30; 11: 33; 19: 20), but no Syriac or Hebrew words except *sikera*, an exciting drink of the nature of wine, but not made of grapes (from Heb. *shakar*, "he is intoxicated," Lev. 10: 9), probably palm wine.

Old Testament references

This Gospel contains twenty-eight distinct references to the Old Testament.

Date of writing

The date of its composition is uncertain. It must have been written before the Acts, the date of the composition of which is generally fixed at about A.D. 63 or 64. This Gospel was written, therefore, probably about A.D. 60 or 63, when Luke may have been at Caesarea in attendance on Paul, who was then a prisoner. Others have conjectured that it was written at Rome during Paul's imprisonment there. But on this point no positive certainty can be attained.

Luke and Paul

It is commonly supposed that Luke wrote under the direction, if not at the dictation of Paul. Many words and phrases are common to both; see table:

Compare	With
Luke 4: 22	Col. 4: 6
Luke 4: 32	1 Cor. 2: 4
Luke 6: 36	2 Cor. 1: 3
Luke 6: 39	Rom. 2: 19
Luke 9: 56	2 Cor. 10: 8
Luke 10: 8	1 Cor. 10: 27
Luke 11: 41	Titus 1: 15
Luke 18: 1	2 Thess. 1: 11
Luke 21: 36	Eph. 6: 18
Luke 22: 19,20	1 Cor. 11: 23–29
Luke 24: 46	Acts 17: 3
Luke 24: 34	1 Cor. 15: 5

Name, author, date

AUTHOR
Luke.

APPROXIMATE DATE OF WRITING
Early 60s A.D.

Luke (2)

Statistics

PLACE OF BOOK IN BIBLE
3rd New Testament book.
3rd Gospel.

NUMBER OF CHAPTERS
24

NUMBER OF VERSES
1,151

NUMBER OF WORDS
25,944

Main theme of book

To present an accurate account of the
life, death, and resurrection of Jesus.

Keys to the understanding of book

KEY WORD/S
Seek, save

KEY PHRASE
Son of Man

KEY CHAPTER/S
15 and its three parables.

KEY VERSE/S
For the Son of man is come to seek and
to save that which was lost.
Luke 19:10

Christ is seen as

The Son of Man.

Spiritual thought

Jesus is the Friend of sinners.

Chapter by chapter breakdown

Chapter 1: Events before Jesus' birth and
birth of John the Baptist

Chapter 2: The birth of Jesus and events
during his childhood

Chapter 3: John the Baptist's ministry
and Jesus' baptism

Chapter 4: Jesus' temptation, rejection
at Nazareth, and early miracles

Chapter 5: Miracles of Jesus and the
calling of Levi

Chapter 6: Jesus chooses the Twelve
and teaches them

Chapter 7: Two miracles, John the
Baptist, and in the home of a Pharisee

Chapter 8: The parable of the sower and
three miracles

Chapter 9: Feeding of the five thousand,
Jesus' transfiguration, and Peter's
confession

Chapter 10: The mission of the seventy-
two disciples and the parable of the
good Samaritan

Chapter 11: The Lord's Prayer and
further teaching

Chapter 12: Jesus teaches a large crowd

Chapter 13: A healing, three kingdom
parables, and weeping over Jerusalem

Chapter 14: Jesus teaches the Pharisees,
and teaches about discipleship

Chapter 15: The lost sheep, lost coin,
and lost son

Chapter 16: Jesus teaches about money

Chapter 17: Ten lepers cured, and
teaching on the Second Coming

Chapter 18: Jesus and prayer, children,
sacrifice, and his own death and
resurrection

Chapter 19: Zacchaeus, entering
Jerusalem, and cleansing the temple
Chapter 20: Jesus' public teaching in
Jerusalem
Chapter 21: Jesus commends a
widow, prophecies and commands
watchfulness
Chapter 22: The Last Supper,
Gethsemane, and Peter's denial
Chapter 23: Jesus' trials, crucifixion, and
burial
Chapter 24: Jesus' resurrection and
ascension

Insight from Matthew Henry

Luke 15

VERSES 1–10
The parable of the lost sheep is very
applicable to the great work of man's
redemption. The lost sheep represents
the sinner as departed from God, and
exposed to certain ruin if not brought
back to him, yet not desirous to return.
Christ is earnest in bringing sinners
home. In the parable of the lost piece
of silver, that which is lost, is one piece,
of small value compared with the rest.
Yet the woman seeks diligently till she
finds it. This represents the various
means and methods God makes use of
to bring lost souls home to himself, and
the Savior's joy on their return to him.
How careful then should we be that our
repentance is unto salvation!

VERSES 11–16
The parable of the prodigal son shows
the nature of repentance, and the Lord's
readiness to welcome and bless all who
return to him. It fully sets forth the
riches of gospel grace; and it has been,

and will be, while the world stands,
of unspeakable use to poor sinners,
to direct and to encourage them in
repenting and returning to God. It is
bad, and the beginning of worse, when
men look upon God's gifts as debts due
to them. The great folly of sinners, and
that which ruins them, is, being content
in their life-time to receive their good
things. Our first parents ruined themselves and all their race, by a foolish
ambition to be independent, and this
is at the bottom of sinners' persisting
in their sin. We may all discern some
features of our own characters in that
of the prodigal son. A sinful state is of
departure and distance from God. A
sinful state is a spending state: willful
sinners misemploy their thoughts and
the powers of their souls, misspend
their time and all their opportunities.
A sinful state is a wanting state. Sinners want necessaries for their souls;
they have neither food nor raiment for
them, nor any provision for hereafter.
A sinful state is a vile, slavish state. The
business of the devil's servants is to
make provision for the flesh, to fulfill
the lusts thereof, and that is no better
than feeding swine. A sinful state is a
state of constant discontent. The wealth
of the world and the pleasures of the
senses will not even satisfy our bodies;
but what are they to precious souls! A
sinful state is a state which cannot look
for relief from any creature. In vain do
we cry to the world and to the flesh;
they have that which will poison a soul,
but have nothing to give which will feed
and nourish it. A sinful state is a state of
death. A sinner is dead in trespasses and
sins, destitute of spiritual life.

John

An introduction

Authorship

The genuineness of this Gospel, i.e., the fact that the apostle John was its author, is beyond all reasonable doubt. In recent times, from about 1820, many attempts have been made to impugn its genuineness, but without success.

Purpose of Gospel

The design of John in writing this Gospel is stated by himself (John 20: 31). It was at one time supposed that he wrote for the purpose of supplying the omissions of the synoptic Gospels, but there is no evidence for this.

"There is here no history of Jesus and his teaching after the manner of the other evangelists. But there is in historical form a representation of the Christian faith in relation to the person of Christ as its central point; and in this representation there is a picture on the one hand of the antagonism of the world to the truth revealed in him, and on the other of the spiritual blessedness of the few who yield themselves to him as the Light of life" (Reuss).

Contents

After the prologue (John 1: 1–5), the historical part of the book begins with John 1: 6, and consists of two parts. The first part (John 1: 6–12) contains the history of our Lord's public ministry from the time of his introduction to it by John the Baptist to its close. The second part (John 13–21) presents our Lord in the retirement of private life and in his intercourse with his immediate followers (John 13–17), and gives an account of his sufferings and of his appearances to the disciples after his resurrection (John 18–21).

Special features

The peculiarities of this Gospel are the place it gives

(1) to the mystical relation of the Son to the Father, and

(2) of the Redeemer to believers;

(3) the announcement of the Holy Ghost as the Comforter;

(4) the prominence given to love as an element in the Christian character. It was obviously addressed primarily to Christians.

Name, author, date

AUTHOR
John, one of Jesus' 12 apostles.

APPROXIMATE DATE OF WRITING
A.D. 69–90

Statistics

PLACE OF BOOK IN BIBLE
4th New Testament book.
4th Gospel.

NUMBER OF CHAPTERS
21

NUMBER OF VERSES
879

NUMBER OF WORDS
25,944

Main theme of book

The spiritual meaning of Jesus' life and teaching.

Keys to the understanding of book

KEY WORD/S
Believe, 98 times
Witness, 21 times
Love 20 times

KEY PHRASE
Eternal life, 35 times

KEY CHAPTER/S
3 and Jesus' conversation with Nicodemus.
17 and Jesus' prayer to his Father.

KEY VERSE/S
For God so loved the world, that he gave his only begotten Son, that whosoever believeth in him should not perish, but have everlasting life. John 3: 16

Christ is seen as

Son of God.

Spiritual thought

God showed his great love by sending Jesus.

Chapter by chapter breakdown

Chapter 1: Special introduction, John the Baptist, and first disciples
Chapter 2: Water into wine and cleansing the temple
Chapter 3: Jesus and Nicodemus
Chapter 4: Jesus and the woman of Samaria
Chapter 5: Opposition at the feast in Jerusalem
Chapter 6: Jesus is the bread of life
Chapter 7: Jesus is the water of life
Chapter 8: The woman caught in adultery, and Jesus the Light of the world
Chapter 9: Jesus heals a blind man
Chapter 10: Jesus is the good shepherd
Chapter 11: Jesus brings Lazarus back to life
Chapter 12: Jesus enters Jerusalem and teaches
Chapter 13: Jesus washes his disciples' feet
Chapter 14: Jesus teaches about the promised Holy Spirit
Chapter 15: Jesus is the true vine
Chapter 16: Jesus gives the Holy Spirit and predicts his own death and resurrection
Chapter 17: Jesus prays to his Father
Chapter 18: Jesus' arrest and trials
Chapter 19: Jesus' death and burial
Chapter 20: Jesus' resurrection and first resurrection appearances
Chapter 21: Further resurrection appearances of Jesus

Insight from Matthew Henry

John 3

VERSE 16
Here is God's love in giving his Son for the world. God so loved the world; so really, so richly. Behold and wonder, that the great God should love such a worthless world!

Acts (1)

An introduction

Names for Acts

TREATISE
The author styles his Gospel as a "treatise" (Acts 1: 1).

THE ACTS
It was early called "The Acts,"

THE GOSPEL OF THE HOLY GHOST
"The Gospel of the Holy Ghost," and

THE GOSPEL OF THE RESURRECTION
"The Gospel of the Resurrection."

SOME ACTS OF CERTAIN APOSTLES
It contains no account of any of the apostles except Peter and Paul. John is noticed only three times; and all that is recorded of James, the son of Zebedee, is his execution by Herod. It is rightly therefore not the history of the "Acts of the Apostles," a title which was given to the book at a later date, but of "Acts of Apostles," or more correctly, of "Some Acts of Certain Apostles."

Authorship

As regards its authorship, it was certainly the work of Luke, the "beloved physician" (cf. Luke 1: 1–4; Acts 1: 1). This is the uniform tradition of antiquity, although the writer nowhere makes mention of himself by name. The style and idiom of the Gospel of Luke and of the Acts, and the usage of words and phrases common to both, strengthen this opinion. The writer first appears in the narrative in Acts 16: 11, and then disappears till Paul's return to Philippi two years afterwards, when he and Paul left that place together (Acts 20: 6), and the two seem henceforth to have been constant companions to the end. He was certainly with Paul at Rome (Acts 28; Col. 4: 14). Thus he wrote a great portion of that history from personal observation. For what lay beyond his own experience he had the instruction of Paul. If, as is very probable, 2 Timothy was written during Paul's second imprisonment at Rome, Luke was with him then as his faithful companion to the last (2 Tim. 4: 11). Of his subsequent history we have no certain information.

Purpose of Gospel

The design of Luke's Gospel was to give an exhibition of the character and work of Christ as seen in his history till he was taken up from his disciples into heaven; and of the Acts, as its sequel, to give an illustration of the power and working of the gospel when preached among all nations, "beginning at Jerusalem."

The opening sentences of the Acts are just an expansion and an explanation of the closing words of the Gospel. In this book we have just a continuation of the history of the church after Christ's ascension. Luke here carries on the history in the same spirit in which he had commenced it. It is only a book of beginnings, a history of the founding of churches, the initial steps in the formation of the Christian society in the different places visited by the apostles. It records a cycle of "representative events."

Power of Jesus

All through the narrative we see the ever-present, all-controlling power of the ever-living Savior. He works all and in all in spreading abroad his truth among men and women by his Spirit and through the work of his apostles.

Date of writing

The time of the writing of this history may be gathered from the fact that the narrative extends down to the close of the second year of Paul's first imprisonment at Rome. It could not therefore have been written earlier than A.D. 61 or 62, nor later than about the end of A.D. 63. Paul was probably put to death during his second imprisonment, about A.D. 64, or, as some think, 66.

Place of writing

The place where the book was written was probably Rome, to which Luke accompanied Paul.

Key to contents

The key to the contents of the book is in Acts 1: 8, "Ye shall be witnesses unto me both in Jerusalem, and in all Judea, and in Samaria, and unto the uttermost part of the earth." After referring to what had been recorded in a "former treatise" of the sayings and doings of Jesus Christ before his ascension, the author proceeds to give an account of the circumstances connected with that event, and then records the leading facts with reference to the spread and triumphs of Christianity over the world during a period of about thirty years. The record begins with Pentecost (A.D. 33) and ends with Paul's first imprisonment (A.D. 63 or 64). The whole contents of the book may be divided into these three parts:

Divisions

(1) Chaps. 1–12, describing the first twelve years of the Christian church. This section has been entitled "From Jerusalem to Antioch." It contains the history of the planting and extension of the church among the Jews by the ministry of Peter.

(2) Chaps. 13–21, Paul's missionary journeys, giving the history of the extension and planting of the church among the Gentiles.

(3) Chaps. 21–28, Paul at Rome, and the events which led to this. Chaps. 13–28 have been entitled "From Antioch to Rome."

No mention of Paul's writings

In this book it is worthy of note that no mention is made of the writing by Paul of any of his epistles. This may be accounted for by the fact that the writer confined himself to a history of the planting of the church, and not to that of its training or edification.

Acts (2)

An introduction, continued

No mention of Paul's writings, continued

The relation, however, between this history and the epistles of Paul is of such a kind, i.e., brings to light so many coincidences, as to prove the genuineness and authenticity of both, as is so ably shown by Paley in his *Horce Paulince.*

"No ancient work affords so many tests of veracity; for no other has such numerous points of contact in all directions with contemporary history, politics, and topography, whether Jewish, or Greek, or Roman."

Lightfoot

Name, author, date

AUTHOR
Luke.

APPROXIMATE DATE OF WRITING
62 A.D.

Statistics

PLACE OF BOOK IN BIBLE
5th New Testament book.
1st historical book.

NUMBER OF CHAPTERS
28

NUMBER OF VERSES
1,007

NUMBER OF WORDS
24,250

Main theme of book

To trace the growth of Christianity from Jerusalem throughout the Roman Empire.

Keys to the understanding of book

KEY WORD/S
Witness, witnesses, Holy Spirit

KEY PHRASE
Promise of the Father

KEY CHAPTER/S
2 and the outpouring of the Holy Spirit on the day of Pentecost.

KEY VERSE/S
But ye shall receive power, after that the Holy Ghost is come upon you: and ye shall be witnesses unto me both in Jerusalem, and in all Judea, and in Samaria, and unto the uttermost part of the earth.
Acts 1: 8

And they continued steadfastly in the apostles' doctrine and fellowship, and in breaking of bread, and in prayers.
Acts 2: 42

Christ is seen as

The ascended Lord.

Spiritual thought

God's spiritual power is now fully available.

Chapter by chapter breakdown

Chapter 1: The ascension of Jesus, and waiting for the Spirit

Chapter 2: The coming of the Holy
Spirit and Peter's sermon

Chapter 3: Peter heals and preaches

Chapter 4: Peter and John arrested, and
Peter before the Sanhedrin

Chapter 5: Ananias and Sapphira,
miracles and persecution

Chapter 6: Deacons appointed, and
Stephen before the council

Chapter 7: Stephen's sermon and
martyrdom

Chapter 8: The expansion of the Church

Chapter 9: Saul's conversion

Chapter 10: Peter and Cornelius

Chapter 11: Peter defends his ministry,
and the Antioch church

Chapter 12: Herod's persecution

Chapter 13: First part of Paul's first
missionary journey

Chapter 14: Second part of Paul's first
missionary journey

Chapter 15: The Jerusalem Council

Chapter 16: First part of Paul's second
missionary journey

Chapter 17: Second part of Paul's
second missionary journey

Chapter 18: Paul's ministry in Corinth

Chapter 19: Paul's ministry in Ephesus

Chapter 20: Second part of Paul's third
missionary journey

Chapter 21: Paul is arrested

Chapter 22: Paul's defense before the
mob

Chapter 23: Plot to kill Paul

Chapter 24: Paul before Felix

Chapter 25: Paul appeals to the
Emperor

Chapter 26: Paul is tried before Agrippa

Chapter 27: Paul sails for Rome and is
shipwrecked

Chapter 28: Paul arrives in Rome to a
two-year house arrest

Insight from Matthew Henry

Acts 1

VERSES 6–11

They were earnest in asking about
that which their Master never had
directed or encouraged them to seek.
Our Lord knew that his ascension and
the teaching of the Holy Spirit would
soon end these expectations, and
therefore only gave them a rebuke; but
it is a caution to his church in all ages,
to take heed of a desire of forbidden
knowledge. He had given his disciples
instructions for the discharge of their
duty, both before his death and since
his resurrection, and this knowledge
is enough for a Christian. It is enough
that he has engaged to give believers
strength equal to their trials and
services; that under the influence of
the Holy Spirit they may, in one way
or other, be witnesses for Christ on
earth, while in heaven he manages their
concerns with perfect wisdom, truth,
and love. When we stand gazing and
trifling, the thoughts of our Master's
second coming should quicken and
awaken us: when we stand gazing and
trembling, they should comfort and
encourage us. May our expectation of it
be stedfast and joyful, giving diligence
to be found of him blameless.

Romans (1)

An introduction

Place of writing

This epistle was probably written at Corinth. Phoebe (Rom. 16: 1) of Cenchrea brought it to Rome, and Gaius of Corinth entertained the apostle at the time of his writing it (Rom. 16: 23; 1 Cor. 1: 14), and Erastus was treasurer of the city of Corinth (2 Tim. 4: 20).

Date of writing

The precise time at which it was written is not mentioned in the epistle, but it was obviously written when the apostle was about to "go unto Jerusalem to minister unto the saints," i.e., at the close of his second visit to Greece, during the winter preceding his last visit to that city (Rom. 15: 25; cf. Acts 19: 21; 20: 2,3,16; 1 Cor. 16: 1–4), early in A.D. 58.

Background to letter

It is highly probable that Christianity was planted in Rome by some of those who had been at Jerusalem on the day of Pentecost (Acts 2: 10). At this time the Jews were very numerous in Rome, and their synagogues were probably resorted to by Romans also, who in this way became acquainted with the great facts regarding Jesus as these were reported among the Jews. Thus a church composed of both Jews and Gentiles was formed at Rome. Many of the brethren went out to meet Paul

on his approach to Rome. There are evidences that Christians were then in Rome in considerable numbers, and had probably more than one place of meeting (Rom. 16: 14,15).

Purpose of letter

The object of the apostle in writing to this church was to explain to them the great doctrines of the gospel. His epistle was a "word in season." Himself deeply impressed with a sense of the value of the doctrines of salvation, he opens up in a clear and connected form the whole system of the gospel in its relation both to Jew and Gentile. This epistle is peculiar in this, that it is a systematic exposition of the gospel of universal application. The subject is here treated argumentatively, and is a plea for Gentiles addressed to Jews. In the Epistle to the Galatians, the same subject is discussed, but there the apostle pleads his own authority, because the church in Galatia had been founded by him.

Contents

After the introduction (Rom. 1: 1–15), the apostle presents in it various aspects of the doctrine of justification by faith (Rom. 1: 16–11: 36) on the ground of the imputed righteousness of Christ. He shows that salvation is all of grace, and only of grace. This main section of his letter is followed by various practical exhortations (Rom. 12: 1–15: 13), which are followed by a conclusion containing personal explanations and salutations, which contain the names of twenty-four Christians at Rome, a benediction, and a doxology (Rom. 15: 14–16).

Author, date

AUTHOR
Paul.

APPROXIMATE DATE OF WRITING
A.D. 57

Statistics

PLACE OF BOOK IN BIBLE
6th New Testament book.
1st letter written by Paul.

NUMBER OF CHAPTERS
16

NUMBER OF VERSES
433

NUMBER OF WORDS
9,447

Main theme of book

A systematic explanation of the Christian gospel.

Keys to the understanding of book

KEY WORD/S
Law, 78 times
Righteousness and righteous, 66 times
Faith, 62 times
Sin, 60 times
Death, 42 times
Justification and justify, 17 times

KEY PHRASE
In Christ, 33 times
The righteousness of God, 1: 17

KEY CHAPTER/S
3 and its statement about universal sin.

KEY VERSE/S
For I am not ashamed of the gospel of Christ: for it is the power of God unto salvation to every one that believeth; to the Jew first, and also to the Greek. For therein is the righteousness of God revealed from faith to faith: as it is written, The just shall live by faith.
Romans 1: 16,17

But now the righteousness of God without the law is manifested, being witnessed by the law and the prophets; Even the righteousness of God *which is* by faith of Jesus Christ unto all and upon all them that believe: for there is no difference: For all have sinned, and come short of the glory of God.
Romans 3: 21–23

Therefore being justified by faith, we have peace with God through our Lord Jesus Christ.
Romans 5: 1

Christ is seen as

The Lord our righteousness.

Spiritual thought

We can approach God clothed in his righteousness.

Romans (2)

Chapter by chapter breakdown

Chapter 1: Greetings, prayer, and theme

Chapter 2: God will be our judge

Chapter 3: Why the Jews did not believe, and righteousness described

Chapter 4: Righteousness illustrated

Chapter 5: Peace with God, and salvation from God's wrath

Chapter 6: Sanctification and sin

Chapter 7: Sanctification and the Law

Chapter 8: Sanctification and the Holy Spirit

Chapter 9: What about the Jews?

Chapter 10: Israel rejected Jesus and the prophets

Chapter 11: Israel's future and her restoration

Chapter 12: Christian behavior in the Church and in the world

Chapter 13: Christians, and the authorities, and their neighbors

Chapter 14: The principles of Christian freedom

Chapter 15: Paul's missionary plans

Chapter 16: Paul greets his many friends in Rome

Insight from Matthew Henry

Romans 5

VERSES 1–5

A blessed change takes place in the sinner's state, when he becomes a true believer, whatever he has been. Being justified by faith he has peace with God.

The holy, righteous God, cannot be at peace with a sinner, while under the guilt of sin. Justification takes away the guilt, and so makes way for peace.

This is through our Lord Jesus Christ; through him as the great Peace-maker, the Mediator between God and man. The saints' happy state is a state of grace. Into this grace we are brought, which teaches that we were not born in this state.

We could not have got into it of ourselves, but we are led into it, as pardoned offenders. Therein we stand, a posture that denotes perseverance; we stand firm and safe, upheld by the power of the enemy. And those who have hope for the glory of God hereafter, have enough to rejoice in now.

Tribulation worketh patience, not in and of itself, but the powerful grace of God working in and with the tribulation. Patient sufferers have most of the Divine consolations, which abound as afflictions abound. It works needful experience of ourselves.

This hope will not disappoint, because it is sealed with the Holy Spirit as a Spirit of love.

It is the gracious work of the blessed Spirit to shed abroad the love of God in the hearts of all the saints. A right sense of God's love to us, will make us not ashamed, either of our hope, or of our sufferings for him.

VERSES 6–11

Christ died for sinners; not only such as were useless, but such as were guilty and hateful; such that their everlasting destruction would be to the glory of God's justice.

Christ died to save us, not in our sins, but from our sins; and we were yet sinners when he died for us. Nay, the carnal mind is not only an enemy to God, but enmity itself.

But God designed to deliver from sin, and to work a great change. While the sinful state continues, God loathes the sinner, and the sinner loathes God, Zechariah 11: 8. And that for such as these Christ should die, is a mystery; no other such an instance of love is known, so that it may well be the employment of eternity to adore and wonder at it.

Again; what idea had the apostle when he supposed the case of some one dying for a righteous man?

And yet he only put it as a thing that might be. Was it not the undergoing this suffering, that the person intended to be benefited might be released therefrom?

But from what are believers in Christ released by his death?

Not from bodily death; for that they all do and must endure. The evil, from which the deliverance could be effected only in this astonishing manner, must be more dreadful than natural death. There is no evil, to which the argument can be applied, except that which the apostle actually affirms, sin, and wrath, the punishment of sin, determined by the unerring justice of God. And if, by Divine grace, they were thus brought to repent, and to believe in Christ, and thus were justified by the price of his blood shedding, and by faith in

that atonement, much more through him who died for them and rose again, would they be kept from falling under the power of sin and Satan, or departing finally from him.

The living Lord of all, will complete the purpose of his dying love, by saving all true believers to the uttermost. Having such a pledge of salvation in the love of God through Christ, the apostle declared that believers not only rejoiced in the hope of heaven, and even in their tribulations for Christ's sake, but they gloried in God also, as their unchangeable Friend and all-sufficient Portion, through Christ only.

1 Corinthians (1)

An introduction

Place and date of writing

This letter was written from Ephesus (1 Cor. 16: 8) about the time of the Passover in the third year of the apostle's stay there (Acts 19: 10; 20: 31), and when he had formed the purpose to visit Macedonia, and then return to Corinth (probably A.D. 57).

Unwelcome news

The news which had reached him, however, from Corinth frustrated his plan. He had heard of the abuses and contentions that had arisen among them, first from Apollos (Acts 19: 1), and then from a letter they had written him on the subject, and also from some of the "household of Chloe," and from Stephanas and his two friends who had visited him (1 Cor. 1: 11; 16: 17). Paul thereupon wrote this letter, for the purpose of checking the factious spirit and correcting the erroneous opinions that had sprung up among them, and remedying the many abuses and disorderly practices that prevailed. Titus and a brother whose name is not given were probably the bearers of the letter (2 Cor. 2: 13; 8: 6,16–18).

Divisions

The epistle may be divided into four parts:

(1) The apostle deals with the subject of the lamentable divisions and party strifes that had arisen among them (1 Cor. 1–4).

(2) He next treats of certain cases of immorality that had become notorious among them. They had apparently totally disregarded the very first principles of morality (1 Cor. 5; 6).

(3) In the third part he discusses various questions of doctrine and of Christian ethics in reply to certain communications they had made to him. He especially rectifies certain flagrant abuses regarding the celebration of the Lord's supper (1 Cor. 7–14).

(4) The concluding part (1 Cor. 15; 16) contains an elaborate defense of the doctrine of the resurrection of the dead, which had been called in question by some among them, followed by some general instructions, intimations, and greetings.

Characteristics of letter

This epistle "shows the powerful self-control of the apostle in spite of his physical weakness, his distressed circumstances, his incessant troubles, and his emotional nature. It was written, he tells us, in bitter anguish, 'out of much affliction and pressure of heart... and with streaming eyes' (2 Cor. 2: 4); yet he restrained the expression of his feelings, and wrote with a dignity and holy calm which he thought most calculated to win back his erring children."

Author, date

AUTHOR
Paul.

APPROXIMATE DATE OF WRITING
A.D. 55,56

Statistics

PLACE OF BOOK IN BIBLE
7th New Testament book.
2nd letter written by Paul.

NUMBER OF CHAPTERS
16

NUMBER OF VERSES
437

NUMBER OF WORDS
9,489

Main theme of book

Correction given to the Corinthians for their unchristian behavior.

Keys to the understanding of book

KEY WORD/S
Wisdom, 29 times

KEY PHRASE
Wisdom, and righteousness, 1: 30

KEY CHAPTER/S
13 and love being the Christian way to live.
15 and Jesus' resurrection.

KEY VERSE/S
But of him are ye in Christ Jesus, who of God is made unto us wisdom, and righteousness, and sanctification, and redemption.
1 Corinthians 1: 30

There hath no temptation taken you but such as is common to man: but God is faithful, who will not suffer you to be tempted above that ye are able; but will with the temptation also make a way to escape, that ye may be able to bear it.
1 Corinthians 10: 13

1 Corinthians (2)

Christ is seen as

The firstfruits of the dead, 15: 20.

Spiritual thought

God is the source of all spiritual gifts.

Chapter by chapter breakdown

Chapter 1: Introduction and divisions

Chapter 2: True wisdom and the Spirit

Chapter 3: The nature of ministers

Chapter 4: Paul's ministry is misunderstood

Chapter 5: Sexual immorality among Christians

Chapter 6: Taking a fellow-Christian to court, and sexual immorality

Chapter 7: Counsel about marriage

Chapter 8: Christian freedom, and the weaker Christian

Chapter 9: Paul's Christian freedom

Chapter 10: The correct use of Christian freedom

Chapter 11: Public prayer and disorder at the Lord's Supper

Chapter 12: The importance and correct use of spiritual gifts

Chapter 13: Paul's hymn on love

Chapter 14: Prophecy, tongues, and public worship

Chapter 15: Teaching about the resurrection

Insight from Matthew Henry

1 Corinthians 13

VERSES 1–3
Without this love, the most glorious gifts are of no account to us, of no esteem in the sight of God. A clear head and a deep understanding, are of no value without a benevolent and charitable heart. There may be an open and lavish hand, where there is not a liberal and charitable heart. Doing good to others will do none to us, if it be not done from love to God, and good-will to men. If we give away all we have, while we withhold the heart from God, it will not profit. Nor even the most painful sufferings. How are those deluded who look for acceptance and reward for their good works, which are as scanty and defective as they are corrupt and selfish!

VERSES 4–7
Some of the effects of charity are stated, that we may know whether we have this grace; and that if we have not, we may not rest till we have it. This love is a clear proof of regeneration, and is a touchstone of our professed faith in Christ. In this beautiful description of the nature and effects of love, it is meant to show the Corinthians that their conduct had, in many respects, been a contrast to it. Charity is an utter enemy to selfishness; it does not desire or seek its own praise, or honor, or profit, or pleasure. Not that charity destroys all regard to ourselves,

or that the charitable man should neglect himself and all his interests. But charity never seeks its own to the hurt of others, or to neglect others. It ever prefers the welfare of others to its private advantage. How good-natured and amiable is Christian charity! How excellent would Christianity appear to the world, if those who profess it were more under this Divine principle, and paid due regard to the command on which its blessed Author laid the chief stress! Let us ask whether this Divine love dwells in our hearts. Has this principle guided us into becoming behavior to all men? Are we willing to lay aside selfish objects and aims? Here is a call to watchfulness, diligence, and prayer.

VERSES 8–13
Charity is much to be preferred to the gifts on which the Corinthians prided themselves. From its longer continuance, it is a grace, lasting as eternity. The present state is a state of childhood, the future that of manhood. Such is the difference between earth and heaven. What narrow views, what confused notions of things, have children when compared with grown men! Thus shall we think of our most valued gifts of this world, when we come to heaven. All things are dark and confused now, compared with what they will be hereafter. They can only be seen as by the reflection in a mirror, or in the description of a riddle; but hereafter our knowledge will be free from all obscurity and error. It is the light of heaven only, that will remove all clouds and darkness that hide the

face of God from us. To sum up the excellences of charity, it is preferred not only to gifts, but to other graces, to faith and hope. Faith fixes on the Divine revelation, and assents thereto, relying on the Divine Redeemer. Hope fastens on future happiness, and waits for that; but in heaven, faith will be swallowed up in actual sight, and hope in enjoyment. There is no room to believe and hope, when we see and enjoy. But there, love will be made perfect. There we shall perfectly love God. And there we shall perfectly love one another.

2 Corinthians

An introduction

Shortly after writing his first letter to the Corinthians, Paul left Ephesus, where intense excitement had been aroused against him, the evidence of his great success, and proceeded to Macedonia. Pursuing the usual route, he reached Troas, the port of departure for Europe. Here he expected to meet with Titus, whom he had sent from Ephesus to Corinth, with tidings of the effects produced on the church there by the first epistle; but was disappointed (1 Cor. 16: 9; 2 Cor. 1: 8; 2: 12,13). He then left Troas and proceeded to Macedonia; and at Philippi, where he tarried, he was soon joined by Titus (2 Cor. 7: 6,7), who brought him good news from Corinth, and also by Timothy. Under the influence of the feelings awakened in his mind by the favorable report which Titus brought back from Corinth, this second epistle was written. It was probably written at Philippi, or, as some think, Thessalonica, early in the year A.D. 58, and was sent to Corinth by Titus. This letter he addresses not only to the church in Corinth, but also to the saints in all Achaia, i.e., in Athens, Cenchrea, and other cities in Greece.

Contents

The contents of this epistle may be thus arranged:

(1) Paul speaks of his spiritual labors and course of life, and expresses his warm affection toward the Corinthians (2 Cor. 1–7).

(2) He gives specific directions regarding the collection that was to be made for their poor brethren in Judea (2 Cor. 8; 9).

(3) He defends his own apostolic claim (2 Cor. 10–13), and justifies himself from the charges and insinuations of the false teacher and his adherents.

Insight into Paul

This epistle, it has been well said, shows the individuality of the apostle more than any other. "Human weakness, spiritual strength, the deepest tenderness of affection, wounded feeling, sternness, irony, rebuke, impassioned self-vindication, humility, a just self-respect, zeal for the welfare of the weak and suffering, as well as for the progress of the church of Christ and for the spiritual advancement of its members, are all displayed in turn in the course of his appeal." (Lias, *Second Corinthians*)

Result of letter?

Of the effects produced on the Corinthian church by this epistle we have no definite information. We know that Paul visited Corinth after he had written it (Acts 20: 2,3), and that on that occasion he stayed there for three months. In his letter to Rome, written at this time, he sent greetings from some of the principal members of the church to the Romans.

Author, date

AUTHOR
Paul.

APPROXIMATE DATE OF WRITING
56 A.D.

Statistics

PLACE OF BOOK IN BIBLE
8th New Testament book.
3rd letter written by Paul.

NUMBER OF CHAPTERS
13

NUMBER OF VERSES
257

NUMBER OF WORDS
6,092

Main theme of book

Paul's defense against attacks of false
apostles.

Keys to the understanding of book

KEY WORD/S
Boast/glory

KEY PHRASE
Renewed day by day, 4:16.

KEY CHAPTER/S
5 and the promise of being with Christ
eternally.

KEY VERSE/S
For which cause we faint not; but
though our outward man perish, yet
the inward man is renewed day by day.
2 Corinthians 4:16

Therefore if any man be in Christ, he is
a new creature: old things are passed
away; behold, all things are become
new.
2 Corinthians 5:17

Christ is seen as

Our sufficiency.

Spiritual thought

God's grace is all we need.

Chapter by chapter breakdown

Chapter 1: Giving thanks for God's
   comfort
Chapter 2: Punishment and forgiveness
Chapter 3: All ability is from God, and
   the superiority of the new covenant
Chapter 4: Paul's ministry, a most
   unlikely apostle, and Christian hope
Chapter 5: Death and future glory
Chapter 6: Reconciliation among
   Christians, and separation from
   unbelievers
Chapter 7: Meeting Titus, and response
   to Paul's letter
Chapter 8: Will you follow Macedonia's
   example in giving money?
Chapter 9: Giving money is a spiritual
   act
Chapter 10: Discipline
Chapter 11: The apostle and his
   sufferings
Chapter 12: Boast about your weakness,
   and Paul's proposed third visit
Chapter 13: Examine yourselves, and
   greetings

Galatians (1)

An introduction

Authorship

The genuineness of this epistle is not called in question. Its Pauline origin is universally acknowledged.

Occasion of writing

The churches of Galatia were founded by Paul himself (Acts 16: 6; Gal. 1: 8; 4: 13,19). They seem to have been composed mainly of converts from heathenism (Gal. 4: 8), but partly also of Jewish converts, who probably, under the influence of Judaizing teachers, sought to incorporate the rites of Judaism with Christianity, and by their active zeal had succeeded in inducing the majority of the churches to adopt their views (Gal. 1: 6; 3: 1). This epistle was written for the purpose of counteracting this Judaizing tendency, and of recalling the Galatians to the simplicity of the gospel, and at the same time also of vindicating Paul's claim to be a divinely-commissioned apostle.

Time and place of writing

The epistle was probably written very soon after Paul's second visit to Galatia (Acts 18: 23). The references of the epistle appear to agree with this conclusion. The visit to Jerusalem, mentioned in Gal. 2: 1–10, was identical with that of Acts 15, and it is spoken of as a thing of the past, and consequently the epistle was written subsequently to the council of Jerusalem. The similarity between this epistle and that to the Romans has led to the conclusion that they were both written at the same time, namely, in the winter of A.D. 57–8, during Paul's stay in Corinth (Acts 20: 2,3). This to the Galatians is written on the urgency of the occasion, tidings having reached him of the state of matters; and that to the Romans in a more deliberate and systematic way, in exposition of the same great doctrines of the gospel.

Contents of

The great question discussed is, Was the Jewish law binding on Christians? The epistle is designed to prove against the Jews that men are justified by faith without the works of the law of Moses. After an introductory address (Gal. 1: 1–10) the apostle discusses the subjects which had occasioned the epistle.

(1) He defends his apostolic authority (Gal. 1: 11–19; 2: 1–14);

(2) shows the evil influence of the Judaizers in destroying the very essence of the gospel (Gal. 3 and 4);

(3) exhorts the Galatian believers to stand fast in the faith as it is in Jesus, and to abound in the fruits of the Spirit, and in a right use of their Christian freedom (Gal. 5: 1–6: 10);

(4) and then concludes with a summary of the topics discussed, and with the benediction.

Galatians and Romans

The Epistle to the Galatians and that to the Romans taken together "form a complete proof that justification is not to be obtained meritoriously either by works of morality or by rites and ceremonies, though of divine appointment; but that it is a free gift, proceeding entirely from the mercy of God, to those who receive it by faith in Jesus our Lord."

Conclusion

In the conclusion of the epistle (Gal. 6: 11) Paul says, "Ye see how large a letter I have written with mine own hand." It is implied that this was different from his normal custom, which was simply to write the concluding salutation with his own hand, indicating that the rest of the epistle was written by another hand. Regarding this conclusion, Lightfoot, in his Commentary on the epistle, says: "At this point the apostle takes the pen from his amanuensis, and the concluding paragraph is written with his own hand. From the time when letters began to be forged in his name (2 Thess. 2: 2; 3: 17) it seems to have been his practice to close with a few words in his own handwriting, as a precaution against such forgeries... In the present case he writes a whole paragraph, summing up the main lessons of the epistle in terse, eager, disjointed sentences. He writes it, too, in large, bold characters (Gr. *pelikois grammasin*), that his hand-writing may reflect the energy and determination of his soul."

Author, date

AUTHOR
Paul

APPROXIMATE DATE OF WRITING
A.D. 49

Statistics

PLACE OF BOOK IN BIBLE
9th New Testament book.
4th letter written by Paul.

NUMBER OF CHAPTERS
6

NUMBER OF VERSES
149

NUMBER OF WORDS
3,098

Galatians (2)

Main theme of book

Paul's attack on Christians reverting to legalism.

Keys to the understanding of book

KEY WORD/S
Freedom

KEY PHRASE
Justification by faith

KEY CHAPTER/S
3 and justification by faith.

KEY VERSE/S
Knowing that a man is not justified by the works of the law, but by the faith of Jesus Christ, even we have believed in Jesus Christ, that we might be justified by the faith of Christ, and not by the works of the law: for by the works of the law shall no flesh be justified.
Galatians 2: 16

Stand fast therefore in the liberty wherewith Christ hath made us free, and be not entangled again with the yoke of bondage.
Galatians 5: 1

Christ is seen as

The One who frees us from the grip and consequences of sin.

Spiritual thought

We have been redeemed from the curse of the law.

Chapter by chapter breakdown

Chapter 1: Paul explains why he had authority to preach the gospel.
Chapter 2: Paul's authority and his gospel
Chapter 3: Paul gives the content of the gospel
Chapter 4: Salvation is through faith, not through obeying the Jewish Law
Chapter 5: Paul's description of Christian freedom
Chapter 6: The gospel and service and separation from the world

Insight from Matthew Henry

Galations 6

VERSES 1–5
We are to bear one another's burdens. So we shall fulfill the law of Christ. This obliges to mutual forbearance and compassion toward each other, agreeably to his example. It becomes us to bear one another's burdens, as fellow-travelers. It is very common for a man to look upon himself as wiser and better than other men, and as fit to dictate to them. Such a one deceives himself; by pretending to what he has not, he puts a cheat upon himself, and sooner or later will find the sad effects. This will never gain esteem, either with God or men. Every one is advised to prove his own work. The better we know our own hearts and ways, the less shall we despise others, and the

more be disposed to help them under infirmities and afflictions. How light soever men's sins seem to them when committed, yet they will be found a heavy burden, when they come to reckon with God about them. No man can pay a ransom for his brother; and sin is a burden to the soul. It is a spiritual burden; and the less a man feels it to be such, the more cause has he to suspect himself. Most men are dead in their sins, and therefore have no sight or sense of the spiritual burden of sin. Feeling the weight and burden of our sins, we must seek to be eased thereof by the Savior, and be warned against every sin.

VERSES 6–11

Many excuse themselves from the work of religion, though they may make a show, and profess it. They may impose upon others, yet they deceive themselves if they think to impose upon God, who knows their hearts as well as actions; and as he cannot be deceived, so he will not be mocked. Our present time is seed time; in the other world we shall reap as we sow now. As there are two sorts of sowing, one to the flesh, and the other to the Spirit, so will the reckoning be hereafter. Those who live a carnal, sensual life, must expect no other fruit from such a course than misery and ruin. But those who, under the guidance and influences of the Holy Spirit, live a life of faith in Christ, and abound in Christian graces, shall of the Spirit reap life everlasting. We are all very apt to tire in duty, particularly in doing good. This we should

carefully watch and guard against. Only to perseverance in well-doing is the reward promised. Here is an exhortation to all to do good in their places. We should take care to do good in our life-time, and make this the business of our lives. Especially when fresh occasions offer, and as far as our power reaches.

Ephesians (1)

An introduction

Overview

This letter was written by Paul from Rome about the same time as that to the Colossians, which in many points it resembles.

Contents of letter.

The Epistle to the Colossians is mainly polemical, designed to refute certain theosophic errors that had crept into the church there. Paul's letter to the Ephesians does not seem to have originated in any special circumstances, but is simply a letter springing from Paul's love to the church there, and indicative of his earnest desire that they should be fully instructed in the profound doctrines of the gospel.

Contents

It contains:

(1) the greeting (Eph. 1: 1,2);

(2) a general description of the blessings the gospel reveals, as to their source, means by which they are attained, purpose for which they are bestowed, and their final result, with a fervent prayer for the further spiritual enrichment of the Ephesians (Eph. 1: 3–2: 10);

(3) "a record of that marked change in spiritual position which the Gentile believers now possessed, ending with an account of the writer's selection to and qualification for the apostolate of heathendom, a fact so considered as

to keep them from being dispirited, and to lead him to pray for enlarged spiritual benefactions on his absent sympathizers" (Eph. 2: 12–3: 21);

(4) a chapter on unity as undisturbed by diversity of gifts (Eph. 4: 1–16);

(5) special injunctions bearing on ordinary life (Eph. 4: 17–6: 10);

(6) the imagery of a spiritual warfare, mission of Tychicus, and valedictory blessing (Eph. 6: 11–24).

Planting of the church at Ephesus. Paul's first and hurried visit for three months to Ephesus is recorded in Acts 18: 19–21. The work he began on this occasion was continued by Apollos (Acts 18: 24–26) and Aquila and Priscilla. On his second visit, early in the following year, he stayed at Ephesus "three years," for he found it was the key to the western provinces of Asia Minor. Here "a great door and effectual" was opened to him (1 Cor. 16: 9), and the church was established and strengthened by his assiduous labors there (Acts 20: 20,31). From Ephesus as a center the gospel spread abroad "almost throughout all Asia" (Acts 19: 26). The word "mightily grew and prevailed" despite all the opposition and persecution he encountered.

The church at Ephesus

On his last journey to Jerusalem the apostle landed at Miletus, and summoning together the elders of the church from Ephesus, delivered to them his remarkable farewell charge

(Acts 20: 18–35), expecting to see them no more.

Parallels

The following parallels between this epistle and the Milesian charge may be traced:

(1) Acts 20: 19 = Eph. 4: 2. The phrase "lowliness of mind" occurs nowhere else.

(2) Acts 20: 27 = Eph. 1: 11. The word "counsel," as denoting the divine plan, occurs only here and Heb. 6: 17.

(3) Acts 20: 32 = Eph. 3: 20. The divine ability.

(4) Acts 20: 32 = Eph. 2: 20. The building upon the foundation.

(5) Acts 20: 32 = Eph. 1: 14,18. "The inheritance of the saints."

Place and date of the writing of the letter. It was evidently written from Rome during Paul's first imprisonment (Eph. 3: 1; 4: 1; 6: 20), and probably soon after his arrival there, about the year 62, four years after he had parted with the Ephesian elders at Miletus.

Occasion of letter

There seems to have been no special occasion for the writing of this letter, as already noted. Paul's object was plainly not polemical. No errors had sprung up in the church which he sought to point out and refute. The object of the apostle is "to set forth the ground, the cause, and the aim and end of the church of the faithful in Christ. He speaks to the Ephesians as a type or sample of the church universal." The church's foundations, its course, and its end, are his theme. "Everywhere the foundation of the church is the will of the Father; the course of the church is by the satisfaction of the Son; the end of the church is the life in the Holy Spirit." In the Epistle to the Romans, Paul writes from the point of view of justification by the imputed righteousness of Christ; here he writes from the point of view specially of union to the Redeemer, and hence of the oneness of the true church of Christ. "This is perhaps the profoundest book in existence." It is a book "which sounds the lowest depths of Christian doctrine, and scales the loftiest heights of Christian experience."

The fact that the apostle evidently expected the Ephesians to understand it is an evidence of the "proficiency which Paul's converts had attained under his preaching at Ephesus."

Ephesians and Colossians

Relation between this epistle and that to the Colossians. "The letters of the apostle are the fervent outburst of pastoral zeal and attachment, written without reserve and in unaffected simplicity; sentiments come warm from the heart, without the shaping out, pruning, and punctilious arrangement of a formal discourse. There is such a fresh and familiar transcription of feeling, so frequent an introduction of colloquial idiom, and so much of conversational frankness and vivacity, that the reader associates the image of the writer with every paragraph, and the ear seems to catch and recognize the very tones of living address."

Ephesians (2)

An introduction, continued

Ephesians and Colossians, continued

"Is it then any matter of amazement that one letter should resemble another, or that two written about the same time should have so much in common and so much that is peculiar? The close relation as to style and subject between the epistles to Colosse and Ephesus must strike every reader. Their precise relation to each other has given rise to much discussion. The great probability is that the epistle to Colosse was first written; the parallel passages in Ephesians, which amount to about forty-two in number, having the appearance of being expansions from the epistle to Colosse. See table comparison:

Compare	with
Ephesians 1: 7	Colossians 1: 14
Ephesians 1: 10	Colossians 1: 20
Ephesians 3: 2	Colossians 1: 25
Ephesians 5: 19	Colossians 3: 16
Ephesians 6: 22	Colossians 4: 8
Ephesians 1: 19–2: 5	Colossians 2: 12,13
Ephesians 4: 2–4	Colossians 3: 12–15
Ephesians 4: 16	Colossians 2: 19
Ephesians 4: 32	Colossians 3: 13
Ephesians 4: 22–24	Colossians 3: 9,10
Ephesians 5: 6–8	Colossians 3: 6–8
Ephesians 5: 15,16	Colossians 4: 5
Ephesians 6: 19,20	Colossians 4: 3,4
Ephesians 5: 22–6: 9	Colossians 3: 18–4: 1

"The style of this epistle is exceedingly animated, and corresponds with the state of the apostle's mind at the account which their messenger had brought him of their faith and holiness (Eph. 1: 15), and transported with the consideration of the unsearchable wisdom of God displayed in the work of man's redemption, and of his astonishing love toward the Gentiles in making them partakers through faith of all the benefits of Christ's death, he soars high in his sentiments on those grand subjects, and gives his thoughts utterance in sublime and copious expression."

Author, date

AUTHOR
Paul.

APPROXIMATE DATE OF WRITING
A.D. 61,62

Statistics

PLACE OF BOOK IN BIBLE
10th New Testament book.
5th letter written by Paul.

NUMBER OF CHAPTERS
6

NUMBER OF VERSES
155

NUMBER OF WORDS
3,098

Main theme of book

The believer's spiritual position living in Christ.

Keys to the understanding of book

KEY WORD/S
Fullness
Walk
Warfare
Wealth

KEY PHRASE
In the heavenlies, 2: 6

KEY CHAPTER/S
6 and spiritual warfare.

KEY VERSE/S
Blessed be the God and Father of our Lord Jesus Christ, who hath blessed us with all spiritual blessings in heavenly places in Christ.
Ephesians 1: 3

For by grace are ye saved through faith; and that not of yourselves: it is the gift of God: Not of works, lest any man should boast. For we are his workmanship, created in Christ Jesus unto good works, which God hath before ordained that we should walk in them.
Ephesians 2: 8–10

Finally, my brethren, be strong in the Lord, and in the power of his might. Put on the whole armor of God, that ye may be able to stand against the wiles of the devil.
Ephesians 6: 10,11

Christ is seen as

The Head of the church.

Spiritual thought

Fullness of life is in Christ.

Chapter by chapter breakdown

Chapter 1: Greetings and prayer
Chapter 2: The resurrection life and unity
Chapter 3: A revealed mystery
Chapter 4: The nature of the Christian Church
Chapter 5: Challenging evil; wives and husbands
Chapter 6: Fighting the spiritual battle

Insight from Matthew Henry

Ephesians 6

VERSES 19–24
The gospel was a mystery till made known by Divine revelation; and it is the work of Christ's ministers to declare it. The best and most eminent ministers need the prayers of believers. Those particularly should be prayed for, who are exposed to great hardships and perils in their work. Peace be to the brethren, and love with faith. By peace, understand all manner of peace; peace with God, peace of conscience, peace among themselves. And the grace of the Spirit, producing faith and love, and every grace. These he desires for those in whom they were already begun.

Philippians

An introduction

Overview

This letter was written by Paul during the two years when he was "in bonds" in Rome (Phil. 1: 7–13), probably early in the year A.D. 62 or in the end of 61. The Philippians had sent Epaphroditus, their messenger, with contributions to meet the necessities of the apostle; and on his return Paul sent back with him this letter. With this precious communication Epaphroditus sets out on his homeward journey. "The joy caused by his return, and the effect of this wonderful letter when first read in the church of Philippi, are hidden from us. And we may almost say that with this letter the church itself passes from our view. To-day, in silent meadows, quiet cattle browse among the ruins which mark the site of what was once the flourishing Roman colony of Philippi, the home of the most attractive church of the apostolic age. But the name and fame and spiritual influence of that church will never pass. To myriads of men and women in every age and nation the letter written in a dungeon at Rome, and carried along the Egnatian Way by an obscure Christian messenger, has been a light divine and a cheerful guide along the most rugged paths of life" (*Professor Beet*).

The church at Philippi was the first-fruits of European Christianity. Their attachment to the apostle was very fervent, and so also was his affection for them. They alone of all the churches helped him by their contributions, which he gratefully acknowledges (Acts 20: 33–35; 2 Cor. 11: 7–12; 2 Thess. 3: 8). The pecuniary liberality of the Philippians comes out very conspicuously (Phil. 4: 15). "This was a characteristic of the Macedonian missions, as 2 Cor. 8 and 9 amply and beautifully prove. It is remarkable that the Macedonian converts were, as a class, very poor (2 Cor. 8: 2); and the parallel facts, their poverty and their open-handed support of the great missionary and his work, are deeply harmonious. At the present day the missionary liberality of poor Christians is, in proportion, really greater than that of the rich" (Moule's *Philippians*).

Contents

The contents of this epistle give an interesting insight into the condition of the church at Rome at the time it was written. Paul's imprisonment, we are informed, was no hindrance to his preaching the gospel, but rather "turned out to the furtherance of the gospel." The gospel spread very extensively among the Roman soldiers, with whom he was in constant contact, and the Christians grew into a "vast multitude." It is plain that Christianity was at this time making rapid advancement in Rome.

Philippians and Romans

The doctrinal statements of this epistle bear a close relation to those of the

Epistle to the Romans. Compare also Phil. 3: 20 with Eph. 2: 12,19, where the church is presented under the idea of a city or commonwealth for the first time in Paul's writings. The personal glory of Christ is also set forth in almost parallel forms of expression in Phil. 2: 5–11, compared with Eph. 1: 17–23; 2: 8; and Col. 1: 15–20. "This exposition of the grace and wonder of His personal majesty, personal self-abasement, and personal exaltation after it," found in these epistles, "is, in a great measure, a new development in the revelations given through St. Paul" (Moule). Other minute analogies in forms of expression and of thought are also found in these epistles of the captivity.

Author, date

AUTHOR
Paul.

APPROXIMATE DATE OF WRITING
62,63 A.D.

Statistics

PLACE OF BOOK IN BIBLE
11th New Testament book.
6th letter written by Paul.

NUMBER OF CHAPTERS
4

NUMBER OF VERSES
104

NUMBER OF WORDS
2,002

Main theme of book

In the joyful letter Paul urges the Philippians to be united and humble.

Keys to the understanding of book

KEY WORD/S
Joy, rejoice, 16 times

KEY PHRASE
Rejoice in the Lord

KEY CHAPTER/S
2 and the humility of Jesus.

KEY VERSE/S
For to me to live is Christ, and to die is gain.
Philippians 1: 21

I know both how to be abased, and I know how to abound: every where and in all things I am instructed both to be full and to be hungry, both to abound and to suffer need.
Philippians 4: 12

I can do all things through Christ which strengtheneth me.
Philippians 4: 13

Christ is seen as

Our strength.

Spiritual thought

We can have the mind of Christ.

Chapter by chapter breakdown

Chapter 1: Paul's present circumstances
Chapter 2: Having Christ's mind
Chapter 3: Knowing Christ
Chapter 4: Joy in contentment

Colossians

An introduction

Overview

This letter was written by Paul at Rome during his first imprisonment there (Acts 28:16,30), probably in the spring of A.D. 57, or, as some think, 62, and soon after he had written his Epistle to the Ephesians. Like some of his other epistles (e.g., those to Corinth), this seems to have been written in consequence of information which had somehow been conveyed to him of the internal state of the church there (Col. 1:4–8). Its object was to counteract false teaching. A large part of it is directed against certain speculatists who attempted to combine the doctrines of Oriental mysticism and asceticism with Christianity, thereby promising the disciples the enjoyment of a higher spiritual life and a deeper insight into the world of spirits. Paul argues against such teaching, showing that in Christ Jesus they had all things. He sets out the majesty of his redemption. The mention of the "new moon" and "sabbath days" (Col. 2:16) shows also that there were here Judaizing teachers who sought to draw away the disciples from the simplicity of the gospel.

Divisions

Like most of Paul's epistles, this consists of two parts, a doctrinal and a practical.

(1) The doctrinal part comprises the first two chapters. His main theme is developed in chapter 2. He warns them against being drawn away from him in whom dwelt all the fullness of the Godhead, and who was the head of all spiritual powers. Christ was the head of the body of which they were members; and if they were truly united to him, what needed they more?

(2) The practical part of the epistle (Col. 3–4) enforces various duties naturally flowing from the doctrines expounded. They were exhorted to mind things that are above (Col. 3:1–4), to mortify every evil principle of their nature, and to put on the new man (Col. 3:5–14). Many special duties of the Christian life are also insisted upon as the fitting evidence of the Christian character. Tychicus was the bearer of the letter, as he was also of that to the Ephesians and to Philemon, and he would tell them of the state of the apostle (Col. 4:7–9). After friendly greetings (Col. 4:10–14), he bids them interchange this letter with that he had sent to the neighboring church of Laodicea. He then closes this brief but striking epistle with his usual autograph salutation.

Colossians and Ephesians

There is a remarkable resemblance between this epistle and that to the Ephesians.

Author, date

AUTHOR
Paul.

APPROXIMATE DATE OF WRITING
A.D. 60,61

Statistics

PLACE OF BOOK IN BIBLE
12th New Testament book.
7th letter written by Paul.

NUMBER OF CHAPTERS
4

NUMBER OF VERSES
95

NUMBER OF WORDS
1,998

Main theme of book

Christ is central creation, redemption
and the Christian life.

Keys to the understanding of book

KEY WORD/S
Supremacy
Sufficiency
Fullness

KEY PHRASE
With Christ

KEY CHAPTER/S
1 and Christ living in Christians.

KEY VERSE/S
For in him dwelleth all the fullness
of the Godhead bodily. And ye are
complete in him, which is the head of
all principality and power.
Colossians 2: 9,10

If ye then be risen with Christ, seek
those things which are above, where
Christ sitteth on the right hand of God.
Set your affection on things above, not
on things on the earth.
Colossians 3: 1,2

Christ is seen as

Being pre-eminent.

Spiritual thought

Jesus is to be crowned lord of all.

Chapter by chapter breakdown

Chapter 1: Greetings, prayer, and the
    pre-eminence of Christ
Chapter 2: Freedom in Jesus
Chapter 3: Living the risen life with
    Christ
Chapter 4: Prayer and wisdom, and
    personal greetings

Insight from Matthew Henry

Colossians 4

VERSES 2–6
No duties can be done aright, unless
we persevere in fervent prayer, and
watch therein with thanksgiving. The
people are to pray particularly for
their ministers. Believers are exhorted
to right conduct toward unbelievers.
Be careful in all converse with them,
to do them good, and recommend
religion by all fit means. Diligence in
redeeming time, commends religion to
the good opinion of others. Even what
is only carelessness may cause a lasting
prejudice against the truth. Let all
discourse be discreet and seasonable,
as becomes Christians. Though it be
not always of grace, it must always be
with grace. Though our discourse be of
that which is common, yet it must be
in a Christian manner. Grace is the salt
which seasons our discourse, and keeps
it from corrupting.

1 Thessalonians

An introduction

First letter

The first epistle to the Thessalonians was the first of all Paul's epistles. It was in all probability written from Corinth, where he abode a "long time" (Acts 18: 11,18), early in the period of his residence there, about the end of A.D. 52.

Reason for writing

It was occasioned by the return of Timothy from Macedonia, bearing tidings from Thessalonica regarding the state of the church there (Acts 18: 1–5; 1 Thess. 3: 6). While, on the whole, the report of Timothy was encouraging, it also showed that various errors and misunderstandings regarding the tenor of Paul's teaching had crept in among them. He addresses them in this letter with the view of correcting these errors, and especially to exhort them to purity of life, reminding them that their sanctification was the great end desired by God for them.

2 Thessalonians

The second epistle to the Thessalonians was probably also written from Corinth, and not many months after the first.

The occasion of the writing of this epistle was the arrival of tidings that the tenor of the first epistle had been misunderstood, especially with reference to the second advent of Christ. The Thessalonians had embraced the idea that Paul had taught that "the day of Christ was at hand," that Christ's coming was just about to happen. This error is corrected (2 Thess. 2: 1–12), and the apostle prophetically announces what first must take place. "The apostasy" was first to arise. Various explanations of this expression have been given, but that which is most satisfactory refers it to the Church of Rome.

Author, date

AUTHOR
Paul.

APPROXIMATE DATE OF WRITING
A.D. 51

Statistics

PLACE OF BOOK IN BIBLE
13th New Testament book.
8th letter written by Paul.

NUMBER OF CHAPTERS
5

NUMBER OF VERSES
89

NUMBER OF WORDS
1,857

Main theme of book

In the light of Christ's coming, live a pure life.

Keys to the understanding of book

KEY WORD/S
Sanctification

KEY PHRASE
The coming of the Lord

KEY CHAPTER/S
4 and Jesus' second coming.

KEY VERSE/S
For they themselves show of us what manner of entering in we had unto you, and how ye turned to God from idols to serve the living and true God; And to wait for his Son from heaven, whom he raised from the dead, *even* Jesus, which delivered us from the wrath to come.
1 Thessalonians 1: 9,10

For this cause also thank we God without ceasing, because, when ye received the word of God which ye heard of us, ye received it not *as* the word of men, but as it is in truth, the word of God, which effectually worketh also in you that believe.
1 Thessalonians 2: 13

Wherefore when we could no longer forbear, we thought it good to be left at Athens alone; And sent Timotheus, our brother, and minister of God, and our fellowlaborer in the gospel of Christ, to establish you, and to comfort you concerning your faith: That no man should be moved by these afflictions: for yourselves know that we are appointed thereunto.
1 Thessalonians 3: 1–3

Christ is seen as
The Lord who will return.

Spiritual thought
We must walk in the light.

Chapter by chapter breakdown
Chapter 1: Paul commends their spiritual growth
Chapter 2: Paul's foundation of the Church, and Satan's attack
Chapter 3: Paul's great concern
Chapter 4: Sexual morality, earning a living, and the dead
Chapter 5: The Day of the Lord, and holy living

Insight from Matthew Henry

1 Thessalonians 5

VERSES 23–28
The apostle prays that they might be sanctified more perfectly, for the best are sanctified but in part while in this world; therefore we should pray for, and press toward, complete holiness. And as we must fall, if God did not carry on his good work in the soul, we should pray to God to perfect his work, till we are presented faultless before the throne of his glory. We should pray for one another; and brethren should thus express brotherly love. This epistle was to be read to all the brethren. Not only are the common people allowed to read the Scriptures, but it is their duty, and what they should be persuaded to do. The word of God should not be kept in an unknown tongue, but transplanted, that as all men are concerned to know the Scriptures, so they all may be able to read them. The Scriptures should be read in all public congregations, for the benefit of the unlearned especially.

2 Thessalonians

An introduction

See this section under 1 Thessalonians.

Author, date

AUTHOR
Paul.

APPROXIMATE DATE OF WRITING
A.D. 51

Statistics

PLACE OF BOOK IN BIBLE
14th New Testament book.
9th letter written by Paul.

NUMBER OF CHAPTERS
3

NUMBER OF VERSES
47

NUMBER OF WORDS
1,042

Main theme of book

Paul corrects misunderstandings about
Jesus' second coming.

Keys to the understanding of book

KEY WORD/S
Destruction
Judgment
Retribution
Waiting

KEY PHRASE
In Christ

KEY CHAPTER/S
2 and its corrective teaching about
Jesus' return.

KEY VERSE/S
Let no man deceive you by any
means: for *that day shall not come*, except
there come a falling away first, and
that man of sin be revealed, the son of
perdition.
2 Thessalonians 2: 2

But we are bound to give thanks alway
to God for you, brethren beloved of
the Lord, because God hath from the
beginning chosen you to salvation
through sanctification of the Spirit and
belief of the truth: Whereunto he called
you by our gospel, to the obtaining of
the glory of our Lord Jesus Christ.
2 Thessalonians 2: 13,14

And we have confidence in the Lord
touching you, that ye both do and will
do the things which we command you.
And the Lord direct your hearts into
the love of God, and into the patient
waiting for Christ.
2 Thessalonians 3: 4,5

Christ is seen as

Returning Lord.

Spiritual thought

Live in the light of Jesus' return.

Chapter by chapter breakdown

Chapter 1: Encouragement in
persecution
Chapter 2: Explanation about the Day
of the Lord
Chapter 3: Pray for us, God is faithful,
don't be idle

Insight from Matthew Henry

2 Thessalonians 3

VERSES 1–5

Those who are far apart still may meet together at the throne of grace; and those not able to do or receive any other kindness, may in this way do and receive real and very great kindness. Enemies to the preaching of the gospel, and persecutors of its faithful preachers, are unreasonable and wicked men. Many do not believe the gospel; and no wonder if such are restless and show malice in their endeavors to oppose it.

The evil of sin is the greatest evil, but there are other evils we need to be preserved from, and we have encouragement to depend upon the grace of God. When once the promise is made, the performance is sure and certain.

The apostle had confidence in them, but that was founded upon his confidence in God; for there is otherwise no confidence in man. He prays for them for spiritual blessings. It is our sin and our misery, that we place our affections upon wrong objects. There is not true love of God, without faith in Jesus Christ. If, by the special grace of God, we have that faith which multitudes have not, we should earnestly pray that we may be enabled, without reserve, to obey his commands, and that we may be enabled, without reserve, to the love of God, and the patience of Christ.

VERSES 6–15

Those who have received the gospel, are to live according to the gospel. Such as could work, and would not, were not to be maintained in idleness. Christianity is not to countenance slothfulness, which would consume what is meant to encourage the industrious, and to support the sick and afflicted. Industry in our callings as men, is a duty required by our calling as Christians. But some expected to be maintained in idleness, and indulged a curious and conceited temper. They meddled with the concerns of others, and did much harm.

It is a great error and abuse of religion, to make it a cloak for idleness or any other sin. The servant who waits for the coming of his Lord aright, must be working as his Lord has commanded. If we are idle, the devil and a corrupt heart will soon find us somewhat to do.

The mind of man is a busy thing; if it is not employed in doing good, it will be doing evil. It is an excellent, but rare union, to be active in our own business, yet quiet as to other people's. If any refused to labor with quietness, they were to note him with censure, and to separate from his company, yet they were to seek his good by loving admonitions.

The Lord is with you while you are with him. Hold on your way, and hold on to the end.

1 Timothy

An introduction

Overview

Paul in this epistle speaks of himself as having left Ephesus for Macedonia (1 Tim. 1: 3), and hence not Laodicea, as mentioned in the subscription; but probably Philippi, or some other city in that region, was the place where this epistle was written. During the interval between his first and second imprisonments he probably visited the scenes of his former labors in Greece and Asia, and then found his way into Macedonia, whence he wrote this letter to Timothy, whom he had left behind in Ephesus.

Date of writing

It was probably written about A.D. 66 or 67.

Contents

The epistle consists mainly,
(1) of counsels to Timothy regarding the worship and organization of the Church, and the responsibilities resting on its several members; and
(2) of exhortation to faithfulness in maintaining the truth amid surrounding errors.

Author, date

AUTHOR
Paul.

APPROXIMATE DATE OF WRITING
A.D. 62–66

Statistics

PLACE OF BOOK IN BIBLE
15th New Testament book.
10th letter written by Paul.

NUMBER OF CHAPTERS
6

NUMBER OF VERSES
113

NUMBER OF WORDS
2,269

Main theme of book

A leadership manual for Christian workers.

Keys to the understanding of book

KEY WORD/S
Godliness

KEY PHRASE
In Christ

KEY CHAPTER/S
3 and qualifications for God's leaders.

KEY VERSE/S
These things write I unto thee, hoping to come unto thee shortly: But if I tarry long, that thou mayest know how thou oughtest to behave thyself in the house of God, which is the church of the living God, the pillar and ground of the truth.
1 Timothy 3: 14,15

But thou, O man of God, flee these things; and follow after righteousness, godliness, faith, love, patience, meekness. Fight the good fight of faith, lay hold on eternal life, whereunto thou art also called, and hast professed a good profession before many witnesses.

1 Timothy 6: 11,12

Christ is seen as

The One who now lives in glory.

Spiritual thought

Guard the gospel.

Chapter by chapter breakdown

Chapter 1: False teachers and correct Christian doctrine

Chapter 2: Praying in public, and women in public worship

Chapter 3: Qualifications for Christian leadership

Chapter 4: False teachers

Chapter 5: Church discipline

Chapter 6: Having the correct attitude

Insight from Matthew Henry

1 Timothy 6

VERSES 11–16

It ill becomes any men, but especially men of God, to set their hearts upon the things of this world; men of God should be taken up with the things of God. There must be a conflict with corruption, and temptations, and the powers of darkness. Eternal life is the crown proposed for our encouragement. We are called to lay hold thereon. To the rich must especially be pointed out their dangers and duties, as to the proper use of wealth. But who can give such a charge, that is not himself above the love of things that wealth can buy? The appearing of Christ is certain, but it is not for us to know the time. Mortal eyes cannot bear the brightness of the Divine glory. None can approach him except as he is made known unto sinners in and by Christ. The Godhead is here adored without distinction of Persons, as all these things are properly spoken, whether of the Father, the Son, or the Holy Ghost. God is revealed to us, only in and through the human nature of Christ, as the only begotten Son of the Father.

VERSES 17–21

Being rich in this world is wholly different from being rich toward God. Nothing is more uncertain than worldly wealth. Those who are rich, must see that God gives them their riches; and he only can give to enjoy them richly; for many have riches, but enjoy them poorly, not having a heart to use them. What is the best estate worth, more than as it gives opportunity of doing the more good? Showing faith in Christ by fruits of love, let us lay hold on eternal life, when the self-indulgent, covetous, and ungodly around, lift up their eyes in torment. That learning which opposes the truth of the gospel, is not true science, or real knowledge, or it would approve the gospel, and consent to it. Those who advance reason above faith, are in danger of leaving faith. Grace includes all that is good, and grace is an earnest, a beginning of glory; wherever God gives grace, he will give glory.

2 Timothy

An introduction

Overview

This letter was probably written a year or so after 1 Timothy, and from Rome, where Paul was for a second time a prisoner, and was sent to Timothy by the hands of Tychicus. In it he entreats Timothy to come to him before winter, and to bring Mark with him (compare Phil. 2: 22). He was anticipating that "the time of his departure was at hand" (2 Tim. 4: 6), and he exhorts his "son Timothy" to all diligence and steadfastness, and to patience under persecution (2 Tim. 1: 6–15), and to a faithful discharge of all the duties of his office (2 Tim. 4: 1–5), with all the solemnity of one who was about to appear before the Judge of quick and dead.

Author, date

AUTHOR
Paul

APPROXIMATE DATE OF WRITING
A.D. 67

Statistics

PLACE OF BOOK IN BIBLE
16th New Testament book.
11th letter written by Paul.

NUMBER OF CHAPTERS
4

NUMBER OF VERSES
83

NUMBER OF WORDS
1,703

Main theme of book

How to successfully engage in the spiritual battle.

Keys to the understanding of book

KEY WORD/S
Charge

KEY PHRASE
Afflictions of the gospel, 1: 8.

KEY CHAPTER/S
2 and the Christian ministry.

KEY VERSE/S
For God hath not given us the spirit of fear; but of power, and of love, and of a sound mind.
2 Timothy 1: 7

Study to show thyself approved unto God, a workman that needeth not to be ashamed, rightly dividing the word of truth.
2 Timothy 2: 15

Christ is seen as

The One who judges with justice.

Spiritual thought

We have responsibility in the Christian fellowship.

Chapter by chapter breakdown

Chapter 1: Speaking as a spiritual father
Chapter 2: Characteristics of a faithful
   minister
Chapter 3: A snapshot of the last days
Chapter 4: Paul's impending
   martyrdom

Insight from Matthew Henry

2 Timothy 4

VERSES 6–8
The blood of the martyrs, though
not a sacrifice of atonement, yet was
a sacrifice of acknowledgment to the
grace of God and his truth. Death
to a good man, is his release from
the imprisonment of this world, and
his departure to the enjoyments of
another world. As a Christian, and a
minister, Paul had kept the faith, kept
the doctrines of the gospel. What
comfort will it afford, to be able to
speak in this manner toward the end
of our days! The crown of believers is a
crown of righteousness, purchased by
the righteousness of Christ. Believers
have it not at present, yet it is sure, for it
is laid up for them. The believer, amidst
poverty, pain, sickness, and the agonies
of death, may rejoice.

VERSES 9–13
The love of this world, is often the
cause of turning back from the truths
and ways of Jesus Christ. Paul was
guided by Divine inspiration, yet he
would have his books. As long as we
live, we must still learn. The apostles

did not neglect human means, in
seeking the necessaries of life, or their
own instruction. Let us thank the
Divine goodness in having given us
so many writings of wise and pious
men in all ages; and let us seek that by
reading them our profiting may appear
to all.

VERSES 14–18
There is as much danger from false
brethren, as from open enemies. It is
dangerous having to do with those
who would be enemies to such a man
as Paul.
   The Christians at Rome were forward
to meet him, but when there seemed to
be a danger of suffering with him, then
all forsook him. God might justly be
angry with them, but he prays God to
forgive them.
   The apostle was delivered out of
the mouth of the lion, that is, of Nero,
or some of his judges. If the Lord
stands by us, he will strengthen us
in difficulties and dangers, and his
presence will more than supply every
one's absence.

VERSES 19–22
We need no more to make us happy,
than to have the Lord Jesus Christ
with our spirits; for in him all spiritual
blessings are summed up.
   It is the best prayer we can offer for
our friends, that the Lord Jesus Christ
may be with their spirits, to sanctify
and save them, and at last to receive
them to himself. Many who believed
as Paul, are now before the throne,
giving glory to their Lord: may we be
followers of them.

Titus

An introduction

This letter was probably written about the same time as the first epistle to Timothy, with which it has many affinities.

Paley's *Horœ Paulinœ*

"Both letters were addressed to people left by the writer to preside in their respective churches during his absence. Both letters are principally occupied in describing the qualifications to be sought for in those whom they should appoint to offices in the church; and the ingredients of this description are in both letters nearly the same. Timothy and Titus are likewise cautioned against the same prevailing corruptions, and in particular against the same misdirection of their cares and studies. This affinity obtains not only in the subject of the letters, which from the similarity of situation in the persons to whom they were addressed might be expected to be somewhat alike, but extends in a great variety of instances to the phrases and expressions. The writer accosts his two friends with the same salutation, and passes on to the business of his letter by the same transition (compare 1 Tim. 1: 2,3 with Titus 1: 4,5; 1 Tim. 1: 4 with Titus 1: 13,14; 3: 9; 1 Tim. 4: 12 with Titus 2: 7,15)."

Date of writing

The date of its composition may be concluded from the circumstance that it was written after Paul's visit to Crete (Titus 1: 5). That visit could not be the one referred to in Acts 27: 7, when Paul was on his voyage to Rome as a prisoner, and where he continued a prisoner for two year. We may suppose that after his release Paul sailed from Rome into Asia and took Crete by the way, and that there he left Titus "to set in order the things that were wanting." From there he went to Ephesus, where he left Timothy, and from Ephesus to Macedonia, where he wrote First Timothy, and thence to Nicopolis in Epirus, from which place he wrote to Titus, about A.D. 66 or 67.

Author, date

AUTHOR
Paul.

APPROXIMATE DATE OF WRITING
A.D. 63

Statistics

PLACE OF BOOK IN BIBLE
17th New Testament book.
12th letter written by Paul.

NUMBER OF CHAPTERS
3

NUMBER OF VERSES
46

NUMBER OF WORDS
921

Main theme of book

How an elder should minister to his Christian fellowship.

Keys to the understanding of book

KEY WORD/S
Faith
Grace
Profitable

KEY PHRASE
Good deeds

KEY CHAPTER/S
2 and instructions for Christian belief and behavior.

KEY VERSE/S
For this cause left I thee in Crete, that thou shouldest set in order the things that are wanting, and ordain elders in every city, as I had appointed thee.
Titus 1: 5

Not by works of righteousness which we have done, but according to his mercy he saved us, by the washing of regeneration, and renewing of the Holy Ghost.
Titus 3: 5

Christ is seen as

The Savior.

Spiritual thought

Live in line with your Christian beliefs.

Chapter by chapter breakdown

Chapter 1: Appoint elders
Chapter 2: Sound teaching
Chapter 3: Keep up the good deeds

Insight from Matthew Henry

Titus 3

VERSES 1–7
Spiritual privileges do not make void or weaken, but confirm civil duties. Mere good words and good meanings are not enough without good works.

They were not to be quarrelsome, but to show meekness on all occasions, not toward friends only, but to all men, though with wisdom, James 3: 13.

And let this text teach us how wrong it is for a Christian to be churlish to the worst, weakest, and most abject.

The servants of sin have many masters, their lusts hurry them different ways; pride commands one thing, covetousness another.

Thus they are hateful, deserving to be hated. It is the misery of sinners, that they hate one another; and it is the duty and happiness of saints to love one another.

And we are delivered out of our miserable condition, only by the mercy and free grace of God, the merit and sufferings of Christ, and the working of his Spirit. God the Father is God our Savior.

He is the fountain from which the Holy Spirit flows, to teach, regenerate, and save his fallen creatures; and this blessing comes to mankind through Christ.

The spring and rise of it, is the kindness and love of God to man. Love and grace have, through the Spirit, great power to change and turn the heart to God. Works must be in the saved, but are not among the causes of their salvation.

Philemon

An introduction

Overview

This letter was written from Rome at the same time as the epistles to the Colossians and Ephesians, and was sent also by Onesimus. It was addressed to Philemon and the members of his family.

Purpose of letter

It was written for the purpose of interceding for Onesimus, who had deserted his master Philemon and been "unprofitable" to him. Paul had found Onesimus at Rome, and had there been instrumental in his conversion, and now he sends him back to his master with this letter.

Private letter

This epistle has the character of a strictly private letter, and is the only one of such epistles preserved to us. "It exhibits the apostle in a new light. He throws off as far as possible his apostolic dignity and his fatherly authority over his converts. He speaks simply as Christian to Christian. He speaks, therefore, with that peculiar grace of humility and courtesy which has, under the reign of Christianity, developed the spirit of chivalry and what is called 'the character of a gentleman,' certainly very little known in the old Greek and Roman civilization" (*Dr. Barry*).

Author, date

AUTHOR
Paul.

APPROXIMATE DATE OF WRITING
A.D. 60,61

Statistics

PLACE OF BOOK IN BIBLE
18th New Testament book.
13th letter written by Paul.

NUMBER OF CHAPTERS
1

NUMBER OF VERSES
25

NUMBER OF WORDS
445

Main theme of book

Paul's personal plea to Philemon to take back his runaway slave.

Keys to the understanding of book

KEY WORD/S
Receive
Forgiveness

KEY PHRASE
In Christ

KEY VERSE/S
Not now as a servant, but above a servant, a brother beloved, specially to me, but how much more unto thee, both in the flesh, and in the Lord?
Philemon, verse 16

Christ is seen as

The One who pays our debt.

Spiritual thought

Christian principles override society's standards.

Chapter by chapter breakdown

Chapter 1: Take back your runaway slave

Insight from Matthew Henry

VERSES 1–7

Faith in Christ, and love to him, should unite saints more closely than any outward relation can unite the people of the world. Paul in his private prayers was particular in remembering his friends. We must remember Christian friends much and often, as their cases may need, bearing them in our thoughts, and upon our hearts, before our God. Different sentiments and ways in what is not essential, must not make difference of affection, as to the truth. He inquired concerning his friends, as to the truth, growth, and fruitfulness of their graces, their faith in Christ, and love to him, and to all the saints. The good which Philemon did, was matter of joy and comfort to him and others, who therefore desired that he would continue and abound in good fruits, more and more, to God's honor.

VERSES 8–14

It does not lower any one to condescend, and sometimes even to beseech, where, in strictness of right, we might command: the apostle argues from love, rather than authority, in behalf of one converted through his means; and this was Onesimus. In allusion to that name, which signifies "profitable," the apostle allows that in time past he had been unprofitable to Philemon, but hastens to mention the change by which he had become profitable. Unholy persons are unprofitable; they answer not the great end of their being. But what happy changes conversion makes! of evil, good; of unprofitable, useful. No prospect of usefulness should lead any to neglect their obligations, or to fail in obedience to superiors. One great evidence of true repentance consists in returning to practice the duties which have been neglected. In his unconverted state, Onesimus had withdrawn, to his master's injury; but now he had seen his sin and repented, he was willing and desirous to return to his duty. Little do men know for what purposes the Lord leaves some to change their situations, or engage in undertakings, perhaps from evil motives. Had not the Lord overruled some of our ungodly projects, we may reflect upon cases, in which our destruction must have been sure.

VERSES 15–22

When we speak of the nature of any sin or offense against God, the evil of it is not to be lessened; but in a penitent sinner, as God covers it, so must we. Such changed characters often become a blessing to all among whom they reside.

Hebrews

An introduction

Its canonicity

All the results of critical and historical research to which this epistle has been specially subjected abundantly vindicate its right to a place in the New Testament canon among the other inspired books.

Its authorship

A considerable variety of opinions on this subject has at different times been advanced. Some have maintained that its author was Silas, Paul's companion. Others have attributed it to Clement of Rome, or Luke, or Barnabas, or some unknown Alexandrian Christian, or Apollos.

Date and place of writing

It was certainly written before the destruction of Jerusalem (Heb. 13:10).

To whom addressed.

Plainly it was intended for Jewish converts to the faith of the gospel, probably for the church at Jerusalem.

Purpose

Its design was to show the true end and meaning of the Mosaic system, and its symbolical and transient character. It proves that the Levitical priesthood was a "shadow" of that of Christ, and that the legal sacrifices prefigured the great and all-perfect sacrifice he offered for us. It explains that the gospel was designed, not to modify the law of Moses, but to supersede and abolish it. Its teaching was fitted, as it was designed, to check that tendency to apostatize from Christianity and to return to Judaism which now showed itself among certain Jewish Christians. The supreme authority and the transcendent glory of the gospel are clearly set forth, and in such a way as to strengthen and confirm their allegiance to Christ.

Divisions

It has two parts: (a) doctrinal (Heb. 1–10:18), and (b) practical (Heb. 10:19–13:25). There are found in it many references to portions of the Old Testament. It may be regarded as a treatise supplementary to the Epistles to the Romans and Galatians, and as an inspired commentary on the book of Leviticus.

Author, date

AUTHOR
This letter is anonymous.

APPROXIMATE DATE OF WRITING
A.D. 64–68

Statistics

PLACE OF BOOK IN BIBLE
19th New Testament book.
1st letter not written by Paul.

NUMBER OF CHAPTERS
13

NUMBER OF VERSES
303

NUMBER OF WORDS
6,913

Main theme of book

How Christ is superior to all of Judaism.

Keys to the understanding of book

KEY WORD/S
Better, 13 times
Heaven, heavenly, 15 times
Perfect

KEY PHRASE
The word of God is . . . powerful, 4: 12.

KEY CHAPTER/S
11 and its hall of fame of Old Testament followers of God.

KEY VERSE/S
Now faith is the substance of things hoped for, the evidence of things not seen.
Hebrews 11: 1

Wherefore seeing we also are compassed about with so great a cloud of witnesses, let us lay aside every weight, and the sin which doth so easily beset *us*, and let us run with patience the race that is set before us, Looking unto Jesus the author and finisher of *our* faith; who for the joy that was set before him endured the cross, despising the shame, and is set down at the right hand of the throne of God.
Hebrews 12: 1,2

Christ is seen as

Our eternal High Priest.

Spiritual thought

Christians are those who look unto Jesus.

Chapter by chapter breakdown

Chapter 1: The pre-eminence of Jesus Christ
Chapter 2: God's program of salvation
Chapter 3: Christ is superior to Moses
Chapter 4: The Christian's rest and Jesus the High Priest
Chapter 5: Jesus the great High Priest
Chapter 6: Christian maturity
Chapter 7: Melchizedek
Chapter 8: The new covenant
Chapter 9: A superior sacrifice
Chapter 10: The finality of Jesus' sacrifice
Chapter 11: Examples of faith
Chapter 12: How to live by faith
Chapter 13: An exhortation to love

Insight from Matthew Henry

Hebrews 11

VERSES 1–3
Faith always has been the mark of God's servants, from the beginning of the world. Where the principle is planted by the regenerating Spirit of God, it will cause the truth to be received, concerning justification by the sufferings and merits of Christ. And the same things that are the object of our hope, are the object of our faith. It is a firm persuasion and expectation, that God will perform all he has promised to us in Christ.

James

An introduction

Authorship

The author was James the Less, the Lord's brother, one of the twelve apostles. He was one of the three pillars of the Church (Gal. 2: 9).

Readers

It was addressed to the Jews of the dispersion, "the twelve tribes scattered abroad."

Purpose

The object of the writer was to enforce the practical duties of the Christian life. "The Jewish vices against which he warns them are, formalism, which made the service of God consist in washings and outward ceremonies, whereas he reminds them (James 1: 27) that it consists rather in active love and purity; fanaticism, which, under the cloak of religious zeal, was tearing Jerusalem in pieces (James 1: 20); fatalism, which threw its sins on God (James 1: 13); meanness, which crouched before the rich (James 2: 2); falsehood, which had made words and oaths playthings (James 3: 2–12); partisanship (James 3: 14); evil speaking (James 4: 11); boasting (James 4: 16); oppression (James 5: 4). The great lesson which he teaches them as Christians is patience, patience in trial (James 1: 2), patience in good works (James 1: 22–25), patience under provocation (James 3: 17), patience under oppression (James 5: 7), patience

under persecution (James 5: 10); and the ground of their patience is that the coming of the Lord draweth nigh, which is to right all wrong (James 5: 8)."

Faith and works

"Justification by works," which James contends for, is justification before man, the justification of our profession of faith by a consistent life. Paul contends for the doctrine of "justification by faith"; but that is justification before God, a being regarded and accepted as just by virtue of the righteousness of Christ, which is received by faith.

Author, date

AUTHOR
James.

APPROXIMATE DATE OF WRITING
A.D. 45–49

Statistics

PLACE OF BOOK IN BIBLE
20th New Testament book.
2nd letter not written by Paul.

NUMBER OF CHAPTERS
5

NUMBER OF VERSES
108

NUMBER OF WORDS
2,309

Main theme of book

Practical ways in which to live the Christian life.

Keys to the understanding of book

KEY WORD/S
Faith, 16 times
Works, working

KEY PHRASE
Be ye doers of the Word

KEY CHAPTER/S
1 and being tested and tempted.

KEY VERSE/S
But wilt thou know, O vain man, that faith without works is dead?
James 2: 20

Christ is seen as

The One who draws close to us.

Spiritual thought

God draws close to us as soon as we seek to draw close to him.

Chapter by chapter breakdown

Chapter 1: The test of faith
Chapter 2: Faith and discrimination and good deeds
Chapter 3: Controlling the tongue and producing wisdom
Chapter 4: Humility and depending on God
Chapter 5: The triumph of faith

Insight from Matthew Henry

James 3

VERSES 1–12
We are taught to dread an unruly tongue, as one of the greatest evils. The affairs of mankind are thrown into confusion by the tongues of men. Every age of the world, and every condition of life, private or public, affords examples of this. Hell has more to do in promoting the fire of the tongue than men generally think; and whenever men's tongues are employed in sinful ways, they are set on fire of hell. No man can tame the tongue without Divine grace and assistance. The apostle does not represent it as impossible, but as extremely difficult. Other sins decay with age, this many times gets worse; we grow more froward and fretful, as natural strength decays, and the days come on in which we have no pleasure. When other sins are tamed and subdued by the infirmities of age, the spirit often grows more tart, nature being drawn down to the dregs, and the words used become more passionate. That man's tongue confutes itself, which at one time pretends to adore the perfections of God, and to refer all things to him; and at another time condemns even good men, if they do not use the same words and expressions. True religion will not admit of contradictions: how many sins would be prevented, if men would always be consistent! Pious and edifying language is the genuine produce of a sanctified heart; and none who understand Christianity, expect to hear curses, lies, boastings, and revilings from a true believer's mouth, any more than they look for the fruit of one tree from another. But facts prove that more professors succeed in bridling their senses and appetites, than in duly restraining their tongues.

1 Peter

An introduction

Overview

This epistle is addressed to "the strangers scattered abroad," i.e., to the Jews of the Dispersion (the Diaspora).

Its object is to confirm its readers in the doctrines they had been already taught. Peter has been called "the apostle of hope," because this epistle abounds with words of comfort and encouragement fitted to sustain a "lively hope."

It contains about thirty-five references to the Old Testament.

Contents

He counsels

(1) to steadfastness and perseverance under persecution (1 Pet. 1–2: 10);

(2) to the practical duties of a holy life (1 Pet. 2: 11–3: 13);

(3) he adduces the example of Christ and other motives to patience and holiness (1 Pet. 3: 14–4: 19); and

(4) concludes with counsels to pastors and people (1 Pet. 5).

Author, date

AUTHOR
Peter

APPROXIMATE DATE OF WRITING
A.D. 63,64

Statistics

PLACE OF BOOK IN BIBLE
21st New Testament book.
3rd letter not written by Paul.

NUMBER OF CHAPTERS
5

NUMBER OF VERSES
105 .

NUMBER OF WORDS
2,482

Main theme of book

Face underserved suffering and persecution with Christian hope.

Keys to the understanding of book

KEY WORD/S
Suffer, suffering, 16 times

KEY PHRASE
Suffering for Christ

KEY CHAPTER/S
4 and coping under persecution.

KEY VERSE/S
Wherein ye greatly rejoice, though now for a season, if need be, ye are in heaviness through manifold temptations: That the trial of your faith, being much more precious than of gold that perisheth, though it be tried with fire, might be found unto praise and honor and glory at the appearing of Jesus Christ.
1 Peter 1: 6,7

Beloved, think it not strange concerning the fiery trial which is to try you, as though some strange thing happened unto you: But rejoice,

inasmuch as ye are partakers of Christ's sufferings; that, when his glory shall be revealed, ye may be glad also with exceeding joy.
1 Peter 4: 12,13

Christ is seen as

The perfect sacrificial Lamb, 1: 19.

Spiritual thought

Christian hope is founded on God's promises.

Chapter by chapter breakdown

Chapter 1: Hope and holiness
Chapter 2: Living stones, slaves of God, and the example of Jesus' suffering
Chapter 3: How to suffer
Chapter 4: Suffering as a Christian
Chapter 5: Submit to God

Insight from Matthew Henry

1 Peter 5

VERSES 1–4
The apostle Peter does not command, but exhorts. He does not claim power to rule over all pastors and churches. It was the peculiar honor of Peter and a few more, to be witnesses of Christ's sufferings; but it is the privilege of all true Christians to partake of the glory that shall be revealed. These poor, dispersed, suffering Christians, were the flock of God, redeemed to God by the great Shepherd, living in holy love and communion, according to the will

of God. They are also dignified with the title of God's heritage or clergy; his peculiar lot, chosen for his own people, to enjoy his special favor, and to do him special service. Christ is the chief Shepherd of the whole flock and heritage of God. And all faithful ministers will receive a crown of unfading glory, infinitely better and more honorable than all the authority, wealth, and pleasure of the world.

VERSES 5–9
Humility preserves peace and order in all Christian churches and societies; pride disturbs them. Where God gives grace to be humble, he will give wisdom, faith, and holiness. To be humble, and subject to our reconciled God, will bring greater comfort to the soul than the gratification of pride and ambition. But it is to be in due time; not in thy fancied time, but God's own wisely appointed time. Does he wait, and wilt not thou? What difficulties will not the firm belief of his wisdom, power, and goodness get over! Then be humble under his hand. Cast "all your care"; personal cares, family cares, cares for the present, and cares for the future, for yourselves, for others, for the church, on God. These are burdensome, and often very sinful, when they arise from unbelief and distrust, when they torture and distract the mind, unfit us for duties, and hinder our delight in the service of God.

2 Peter

An introduction

Authenticity

The question of the authenticity of this epistle has been much discussed, but the weight of evidence is wholly in favor of its claim to be the production of the apostle whose name it bears. It appears to have been written shortly before the apostle's death (2 Pet. 1: 14). This epistle contains eleven references to the Old Testament. It also contains (2 Pet. 3: 15,16) a remarkable reference to Paul's epistles. Some think this reference is to 1 Thess. 4: 13–5: 11. A few years ago, among other documents, a parchment fragment, called the "Gospel of Peter," was discovered in a Christian tomb at Akhmim in Upper Egypt. Origen, Eusebius, and Jerome refer to such a work, and hence it has been concluded that it was probably written about the middle of the second century. It professes to give a history of our Lord's resurrection and ascension. While differing in not a few particulars from the canonical Gospels, the writer shows plainly that he was acquainted both with the synoptics and with the Gospel of John. Though apocryphal, it is of considerable value as showing that the main facts of the history of our Lord were then widely known.

Author, date

AUTHOR
Peter

APPROXIMATE DATE OF WRITING
A.D. 65,66

Statistics

PLACE OF BOOK IN BIBLE
22nd New Testament book.
4th letter not written by Paul.

NUMBER OF CHAPTERS
3

NUMBER OF VERSES
61

NUMBER OF WORDS
1,559

Main theme of book

How to defeat dangerous false teachers.

Keys to the understanding of book

KEY WORD/S
Knowledge
False teachers

KEY PHRASE
Knowledge of God, 1: 2

KEY CHAPTER/S
1 and the divine inspiration of Scripture.

KEY VERSE/S
Knowing this first, that no prophecy of the Scripture is of any private interpretation.
2 Peter 1: 20,21

That ye may be mindful of the words which were spoken before by the holy prophets, and of the commandment of us the apostles of the Lord and Savior.
2 Peter 3: 2

Christ is seen as

The Lord of glory.

Spiritual thought

Christians are never to cease growing.

Chapter by chapter breakdown

Chapter 1: Cultivating a Christian
character
Chapter 2: False teachers condemned
Chapter 3: Confidence in Jesus' return

Insight from Matthew Henry

2 Peter 1

VERSES 1–11
Faith unites the weak believer to Christ,
as really as it does the strong one, and
purifies the heart of one as truly as of
another; and every sincere believer
is by his faith justified in the sight of
God. Faith worketh godliness, and
produces effects which no other grace
in the soul can do. In Christ all fullness
dwells, and pardon, peace, grace, and
knowledge, and new principles, are
thus given through the Holy Spirit. The
promises to those who are partakers
of a Divine nature, will cause us to
inquire whether we are really renewed
in the spirit of our minds; let us turn
all these promises into prayers for the
transforming and purifying grace of
the Holy Spirit. The believer must add
knowledge to his virtue, increasing
acquaintance with the whole truth and
will of God. We must add temperance

to knowledge; moderation about
worldly things; and add to temperance,
patience, or cheerful submission to
the will of God. Tribulation worketh
patience, whereby we bear all
calamities and crosses with silence and
submission.

To patience we must add
godliness: this includes the holy
affections and dispositions found
in the true worshiper of God; with
tender affection to all fellow Christians,
who are children of the same Father,
servants of the same Master, members
of the same family, travelers to the
same country, heirs of the same
inheritance.

Wherefore let Christians labor to
attain assurance of their calling, and of
their election, by believing and well-
doing; and thus carefully to endeavor,
is a firm argument of the grace and
mercy of God, upholding them so that
they shall not utterly fall.

Those who are diligent in the work
of religion, shall have a triumphant
entrance into that everlasting kingdom
where Christ reigns, and they shall
reign with him for ever and ever;
and it is in the practice of every good
work that we are to expect entrance to
heaven.

VERSES 12–15
We must be established in the belief of
the truth, that we may not be shaken by
every wind of doctrine; and especially
in the truth necessary for us to know in
our day, what belongs to our peace, and
what is opposed in our time.

1 John

An introduction

Authorship

This letter was evidently written by John the evangelist, and probably also at Ephesus, and when the writer was in advanced age.

Purpose

The purpose of the apostle (1 John 1: 1–4) is to declare the Word of Life to those to whom he writes, in order that they might be united in fellowship with the Father and his Son Jesus Christ.

UNION WITH GOD
He shows that the means of union with God are, on the part of Christ, his atoning work (1 John 1: 7; 2: 2; 3: 5; 4: 10,14; 5: 11,12) and his advocacy (1 John 2: 1); and on the part of man,
• holiness (1 John 1: 6),
• obedience (1 John 2: 3),
• purity (1 John 3: 3),
• faith (1 John 3: 23; 4: 3; 5: 5), and
• love (1 John 2: 7,8; 3: 14; 4: 7; 5: 1).

Author, date

AUTHOR
John

APPROXIMATE DATE OF WRITING
A.D. 86–90

Statistics

PLACE OF BOOK IN BIBLE
23rd New Testament book.
5th letter not written by Paul.

NUMBER OF CHAPTERS
5

NUMBER OF VERSES
105

NUMBER OF WORDS
2,523

Main theme of book

How to know for certain that you are Christ's follower.

Keys to the understanding of book

KEY WORD/S
Know
Love
Fellowship
Abiding
Righteousness

KEY PHRASE
If we say

KEY CHAPTER/S
1 and restoration of fellowship with God.

KEY VERSE/S
That which we have seen and heard declare we unto you, that ye also may have fellowship with us: and truly our fellowship is with the Father, and with his Son Jesus Christ. And these things write we unto you, that your joy may be full.
1 John 1: 3,4

If we confess our sins, he is faithful and just to forgive us our sins, and to cleanse us from all unrighteousness.
1 John 1: 9

These things have I written unto you that believe on the name of the Son of God; that ye may know that ye have eternal life, and that ye may believe on the name of the Son of God.
1 John 5:13

Christ is seen as

The Son of God.

Spiritual thought

We are meant to be quietly confident about being Christians.

Chapter by chapter breakdown

Chapter 1: Eyewitness and fellowship
Chapter 2: Obeying and loving God, and dealing with heretics
Chapter 3: Being God's children and showing Christian love
Chapter 4: Testing the spirits, and the proof of love
Chapter 5: Grounds for assurance

Insight from Matthew Henry

1 John 5

VERSES 9–12
Nothing can be more absurd than the conduct of those who doubt as to the truth of Christianity, while in the common affairs of life they do not hesitate to proceed on human testimony, and would deem any one out of his senses who declined to do so. The real Christian has seen his guilt and

misery, and his need of such a Savior. He has seen the suitableness of such a Savior to all his spiritual wants and circumstances. He has found and felt the power of the word and doctrine of Christ, humbling, healing, quickening, and comforting his soul. He has a new disposition, and new delights, and is not the man that he formerly was. Yet he finds still a conflict with himself, with sin, with the flesh, the world, and wicked powers. But he finds such strength from faith in Christ, that he can overcome the world, and travel on toward a better. Such assurance has the gospel believer: he has a witness in himself, which puts the matter out of doubt with him, except in hours of darkness or conflict; but he cannot be argued out of his belief in the leading truths of the gospel. Here is what makes the unbeliever's sin so awful; the sin of unbelief. He gives God the lie; because he believes not the record that God gave of his Son. It is in vain for a man to plead that he believes the testimony of God in other things, while he rejects it in this. He that refuses to trust and honor Christ as the Son of God, who disdains to submit to his teaching as Prophet, to rely on his atonement and intercession as High Priest, or to obey him as King, is dead in sin, under condemnation; nor will any outward morality, learning, forms, notions, or confidences avail him.

VERSES 13–17
Upon all this evidence, it is but right that we believe on the name of the Son of God. Believers have eternal life in the covenant of the gospel.

2 John and 3 John

2 John

An introduction

This letter is addressed to "the elect lady," and closes with the words, "The children of thy elect sister greet thee"; but some would read instead of "lady" the proper name Kyria. Of the thirteen verses composing this epistle seven are in the First Epistle. The person addressed is commended for her piety, and is warned against false teachers.

Author, date

AUTHOR
John.

APPROXIMATE DATE OF WRITING
A.D. 86–90

Statistics

PLACE OF BOOK IN BIBLE
24th New Testament book.
6th letter not written by Paul.

NUMBER OF CHAPTERS: 1

NUMBER OF VERSES: 13

NUMBER OF WORDS: 303

Main theme of book

Truth is of utmost importance.

Keys to the understanding of book

KEY WORD/S
Love

KEY PHRASE
The doctrine of Christ, verse 9.

KEY VERSE/S
And this is love, that we walk after his commandments. This is the command-

ment, That, as ye have heard from the beginning, ye should walk in it.
2 John, verse 6

Christ is seen as

The Truth.

Spiritual thought

Christians are to walk in the truth.

Chapter by chapter breakdown

Chapter 1: Abiding in God's commands

Insight from Matthew Henry

VERSES 1–3
Religion turns compliments into real expressions of respect and love. An old disciple is honorable; an old apostle and leader of disciples is more so. The letter is to a noble Christian matron, and her children; it is well that the gospel should get among such: some noble persons are called. Families are to be encouraged and directed in their love and duties at home. Those who love truth and piety in themselves, should love it in others; and the Christians loved this lady, not for her rank, but for her holiness. And where religion truly dwells, it will abide for ever. From the Divine Persons of the Godhead, the apostle craves grace, Divine favor, and good-will, the spring of all good things. It is grace indeed that any spiritual blessing should be given to sinful mortals. Mercy, free pardon, and forgiveness; for those already rich in grace, need continual forgiveness.

3 John

An introduction

This letter is addressed to Caius, or Gaius, but whether to the Christian of that name in Macedonia (Acts 19: 29) or in Corinth (Rom. 16: 23) or in Derbe (Acts 20: 4) is uncertain. It was written for the purpose of commending to Gaius some Christians who were strangers in the place where he lived, and who had gone thither for the purpose of preaching the gospel (3 John 7).

Author, date

AUTHOR
John.

APPROXIMATE DATE OF WRITING
A.D. 86–90

Statistics

PLACE OF BOOK IN BIBLE
25th New Testament book.
7th letter not written by Paul.

NUMBER OF CHAPTERS: 1

NUMBER OF VERSES: 13

NUMBER OF WORDS: 299

Main theme of book

Who should be welcomed and who should be rejected.

Keys to the understanding of book

KEY WORD/S
Truth

KEY PHRASE
Walk in truth, verse 4

KEY VERSE/S
Beloved, follow not that which is evil, but that which is good. He that doeth good is of God: but he that doeth evil

hath not seen God.
3 John, verse 11

Christ is seen as

Christ, although not mentioned by name in this letter, is nevertheless the source of truth.

Spiritual thought

The truth is to be spread.

Chapter by chapter breakdown

Chapter 1: Christian fellowship

Insight from Matthew Henry

VERSES 13–14
Here is the character of Demetrius. A name in the gospel, or a good report in the churches, is better than worldly honor. Few are well spoken of by all; and sometimes it is ill to be so. Happy those whose spirit and conduct commend them before God and men. We must be ready to bear our testimony to them; and it is well when those who commend, can appeal to the consciences of such as know most of those who are commended. A personal conversation together often spares time and trouble, and mistakes which rise from letters; and good Christians may well be glad to see one another. The blessing is, Peace be to you; all happiness attend you. Those may well salute and greet one another on earth, who hope to live together in heaven. By associating with and copying the example of such Christians, we shall have peace within, and live at peace with the brethren.

Jude

An introduction

Authorship

The author of this letter was "Judas, the brother of James" the Less (Jude 1), called also Lebbaeus (Matt. 10: 3) and Thaddaeus (Mark 3: 18).

Genuineness of letter

The genuineness of this epistle was early questioned, and doubts regarding it were revived at the time of the Reformation; but the evidences in support of its claims are complete. It has all the marks of having proceeded from the writer whose name it bears.

Time and place of writing

There is nothing very definite to determine the time and place at which it was written. It was apparently written in the later period of the apostolic age, for when it was written there were persons still alive who had heard the apostles preach (Jude 17). It may thus have been written about A.D. 66 or 70, and apparently in Palestine.

Readership

The epistle is addressed to Christians in general (Jude 1), and its purpose is to put them on their guard against some false teachers to whom they were exposed. The style of the epistle is that of an "impassioned invective, in the impetuous whirlwind of which the writer is hurried along, collecting example after example of divine vengeance on the ungodly; heaping epithet upon epithet, and piling image upon image, and, as it were, laboring for words and images strong enough to depict the polluted character of the licentious apostates against whom he is warning the Church; returning again and again to the subject, as though all language was insufficient to give an adequate idea of their profligacy, and to express his burning hatred of their perversion of the doctrines of the gospel."

Jude and 2 Peter

The striking resemblance this epistle bears to 2 Peter suggests the idea that the author of the one had seen the epistle of the other.

Doxology

The doxology with which the epistle concludes is regarded as the finest in the New Testament.

Author, date

AUTHOR
Jude.

APPROXIMATE DATE OF WRITING
A.D. 67–80

Statistics

PLACE OF BOOK IN BIBLE
26th New Testament book.
8th letter not written by Paul.

NUMBER OF CHAPTERS
1

NUMBER OF VERSES
25

NUMBER OF WORDS
613

Main theme of book

False teachers are exposed.

Keys to the understanding of book

KEY WORD/S
Kept

KEY PHRASE
Keep yourselves in the love of God, verse 21.

KEY VERSE/S
Now unto him that is able to keep you from falling, and to present *you* faultless before the presence of his glory with exceeding joy, To the only wise God our Savior, *be* glory and majesty, dominion and power, both now and for ever. Amen.
Jude, verses 24,25

Christ is seen as

The only wise God, verse 25.

Spiritual thought

False teachers are to be opposed.

Chapter by chapter breakdown

Chapter 1: Defeating false teachers

Insight from Matthew Henry

VERSES 1–4
Christians are called out of the world, from the evil spirit and temper of it; called above the world, to higher

and better things, to heaven, things unseen and eternal; called from sin to Christ, from vanity to seriousness, from uncleanness to holiness; and this according to the Divine purpose and grace.

If sanctified and glorified, all the honor and glory must be ascribed to God, and to him alone. As it is God who begins the work of grace in the souls of men, so it is he who carries it on, and perfects it.

Let us not trust in ourselves, nor in our stock of grace already received, but in him, and in him alone. The mercy of God is the spring and fountain of all the good we have or hope for; mercy, not only to the miserable, but to the guilty. Next to mercy is peace, which we have from the sense of having obtained mercy. From peace springs love; Christ's love to us, our love to him, and our brotherly love to one another.

The apostle prays, not that Christians may be content with a little; but that their souls and societies may be full of these things. None are shut out from gospel offers and invitations, but those who obstinately and wickedly shut themselves out. But the application is to all believers, and only to such.

It is to the weak as well as to the strong. Those who have received the doctrine of this common salvation, must contend for it, earnestly, not furiously. Lying for the truth is bad; scolding for it is not better. Those who have received the truth must contend for it.

Revelation

An introduction

Overview

The Apocalypse is the closing book and the only prophetical book of the New Testament canon.

Authorship

The author of this book was undoubtedly John the apostle. His name occurs four times in the book itself (Rev. 1: 1,4,9; 22: 8), and there is every reason to conclude that the "John" here mentioned was the apostle. In a manuscript of about the twelfth century he is called "John the divine," but no reason can be assigned for this appellation.

Date of writing

The date of the writing of this book has generally been fixed at A.D. 96, in the reign of Domitian. There are some, however, who contend for an earlier date, A.D. 68 or 69, in the reign of Nero. Those who are in favor of the later date appeal to the testimony of the Christian father Irenaeus, who received information relative to this book from those who had seen John face to face. He says that the Apocalypse "was seen no long time ago."

Revelation and Gospel of John

As for the relationship between this book and the Gospel of John, it has been well observed that "the leading ideas of both are the same. The one gives us in a magnificent vision, the other in a great historic drama, the supreme conflict between good and evil and its issue. In both Jesus Christ is the central figure, whose victory through defeat is the issue of the conflict. In both the Jewish dispensation is the preparation for the gospel, and the warfare and triumph of the Christ is described in language saturated with the Old Testament The difference of date will go a long way toward explaining the difference of style." (Plummer's *Gospel of St. John*).

Author, date

AUTHOR
John.

APPROXIMATE DATE OF WRITING
A.D. 90–96

Statistics

PLACE OF BOOK IN BIBLE
27th New Testament book
1st apocalyptic book

NUMBER OF CHAPTERS
22

NUMBER OF VERSES
404

NUMBER OF WORDS
12,000

Main theme of book

Prophecies about God's redemption and judgment.

Keys to the understanding of book

KEY WORD/S
Overcometh

KEY PHRASE
He that hath an ear let him hear.

KEY CHAPTER/S
19 and Christ's coming in glory.

KEY VERSE/S
Behold, he cometh with clouds; and every eye shall see him, and they *also* which pierced him: and all kindreds of the earth shall wail because of him. Even so, Amen.
Revelation 1: 7

I am Alpha and Omega, the beginning and the ending, saith the Lord, which is, and which was, and which is to come, the Almighty.
Revelation 1: 8

Write the things which thou hast seen, and the things which are, and the things which shall be hereafter.
Revelation 1: 19

Behold, I stand at the door, and knock: if any man hear my voice, and open the door, I will come in to him, and will sup with him, and he with me.
Revelation 3: 20

Christ is seen as
The First and the Last.

Spiritual thought
Jesus Christ has revealed to us everything we need to know.

Chapter by chapter breakdown
Chapter 1: The revelation of Jesus
Chapter 2: Letters to the first four of the seven churches
Chapter 3: The last three of the seven letters to the churches
Chapter 4: God's throne
Chapter 5: The sealed scroll
Chapter 6: Six seals opened
Chapter 7: Sealing and martyrs
Chapter 8: The seventh seal, the censer and the first four trumpets
Chapter 9: The fifth and sixth trumpet
Chapter 10: The little scroll
Chapter 11: The two witnesses and the seventh trumpet
Chapter 12: The woman, war in heaven and on earth
Chapter 13: The beast from the sea, and from the land
Chapter 14: The vision of the Lamb and of the harvest
Chapter 15: The victory song of the redeemed
Chapter 16: The bowls of God's anger
Chapter 17: Overthrow of the great prostitute
Chapter 18: Babylon's fall
Chapter 19: The marriage of the Lamb, and the rider on the white horse
Chapter 20: Binding Satan and the reign of the martyrs, Gog and Magog, and the final judgment
Chapter 21: The new Jerusalem
Chapter 22: The river of life

Insight from Matthew Henry

Revelation 3

VERSES 14–22
Laodicea was the last and worst of the seven churches of Asia. Here our Lord Jesus styles himself, "The Amen"; one steady and unchangeable in all his purposes and promises. If religion is worth anything, it is worth every thing. Christ expects men should be in earnest. How many professors of gospel doctrine are neither hot nor cold.

Analysis of New Testament books (1)

This table shows:
- The number of chapters in each New Testament book
- The number of verses in each chapter
- The total number of verses in each book
- The total number of words in each book

Book Name	Total Chapters	1	2	3	4	5	6	7	8	9	10	11	12	13	14
Matt.	28	25	23	17	25	48	34	29	34	38	42	30	50	58	36
Mark	16	45	28	35	41	43	56	37	38	50	52	33	44	37	72
Luke	24	80	52	38	44	39	49	50	56	62	42	54	59	35	35
John	21	51	25	36	54	47	71	53*	59	41	42	57	50	38	31
Acts	28	26	47	26	37	42	15	60	40	43	48	30	25	52	28
Rom.	16	32	29	31	25	21	23	25	39	33	21	36	21	14	23
1 Cor.	16	31	16	23	21	13	20	40	13	27	33	34	31	13	40
2 Cor.	13	24	17	18	18	21	18	16	24	15	18	33	21	13	.
Gal.	6	24	21	29	31	26	18	.	.	.	.	.	.	.	.
Eph.	6	23	22	21	32	33	24	.	.	.	.	.	.	.	.
Phil.	4	30	30	21	23	.	.	.	.	.	.	.	.	.	.
Col.	4	29	23	25	18	.	.	.	.	.	.	.	.	.	.
1 Thess.	5	10	20	13	18	28	.	.	.	.	.	.	.	.	.
2 Thess.	3	12	17	18	.	.	.	.	.	.	.	.	.	.	.
1 Tim.	6	20	15	16	16	25	21	.	.	.	.	.	.	.	.
2 Tim.	4	18	26	17	22	.	.	.	.	.	.	.	.	.	.
Titus	3	16	15	15	.	.	.	.	.	.	.	.	.	.	.
Phile.	1	25	.	.	.	.	.	.	.	.	.	.	.	.	.
Heb.	13	14	18	19	16	14	20	28	13	28	39	40	29	25	.
James	5	27	26	18	17	20	.	.	.	.	.	.	.	.	.
1 Peter	5	25	25	22	19	14	.	.	.	.	.	.	.	.	.
2 Peter	3	21	22	18	.	.	.	.	.	.	.	.	.	.	.
1 John	5	10	29	24	21	21	.	.	.	.	.	.	.	.	.
2 John	1	13	.	.	.	.	.	.	.	.	.	.	.	.	.
3 John	1	15	.	.	.	.	.	.	.	.	.	.	.	.	.
Jude	1	25	.	.	.	.	.	.	.	.	.	.	.	.	.
Rev.	22	20	29	22	11	14	17	17	13	21	11	19	17	18	20
TOTAL	260	.	.	.	.	.	.	.	.	.	.	.	.	.	.

- And the total number of chapters, verses and words in the whole New Testament.
- These figures are based on the Greek words of the New Testament, as found in the *Analytical Greek New Testament* and they are not based on the English translation of the New Testament.

15	16	17	18	19	20	21	22	23	24	25	26	27	28	Total Verses	Total Words
39	28	27	35	30	34	46	46	39	51	46	75	66	20	1071	18345
47	20*	.	.	.	.	.	.	.	.	.	.	.	.	678	11304
32	31	37	43	48	47	38	71	56	53	.	.	.	.	1151	19482
27	33	26	40	42	31	25	.	.	.	.	.	.	.	879	15635
40	40	34	28	40*	38	40	30	35	27	27	32	44	31	1005	18451
33	27	.	.	.	.	.	.	.	.	.	.	.	.	433	7111
58	24	.	.	.	.	.	.	.	.	.	.	.	.	437	6829
.	.	.	.	.	.	.	.	.	.	.	.	.	.	256	4477
.	.	.	.	.	.	.	.	.	.	.	.	.	.	149	2230
.	.	.	.	.	.	.	.	.	.	.	.	.	.	155	2422
.	.	.	.	.	.	.	.	.	.	.	.	.	.	104	1629
.	.	.	.	.	.	.	.	.	.	.	.	.	.	95	1582
.	.	.	.	.	.	.	.	.	.	.	.	.	.	89	1481
.	.	.	.	.	.	.	.	.	.	.	.	.	.	47	823
.	.	.	.	.	.	.	.	.	.	.	.	.	.	113	1591
.	.	.	.	.	.	.	.	.	.	.	.	.	.	83	1238
.	.	.	.	.	.	.	.	.	.	.	.	.	.	46	659
.	.	.	.	.	.	.	.	.	.	.	.	.	.	25	335
.	.	.	.	.	.	.	.	.	.	.	.	.	.	303	4953
.	.	.	.	.	.	.	.	.	.	.	.	.	.	108	1742
.	.	.	.	.	.	.	.	.	.	.	.	.	.	105	1684
.	.	.	.	.	.	.	.	.	.	.	.	.	.	61	1099
.	.	.	.	.	.	.	.	.	.	.	.	.	.	105	2141
.	.	.	.	.	.	.	.	.	.	.	.	.	.	13	245
.	.	.	.	.	.	.	.	.	.	.	.	.	.	15	219
.	.	.	.	.	.	.	.	.	.	.	.	.	.	25	461
8	21	18	24	21	15	27	21	.	.	.	.	.	.	404	9852
.	.	.	.	.	.	.	.	.	.	.	.	.	.	7955	138,020

Analysis of New Testament books (2)

The four Gospels

Name	No. of chs	Author
Matthew	28	Matthew
Mark	16	Mark
Luke	24	Luke
John	21	John
Acts	28	Luke

The 21 letters

Name	No. of chs	Author
Romans	16	Paul
1 Corinthians	16	Paul
2 Corinthians	13	Paul
Galatians	6	Paul
Ephesians	6	Paul
Philippians	4	Paul
Colossians	4	Paul
1 Thessalonians	5	Paul
2 Thessalonians	3	Paul
1 Timothy	6	Paul
2 Timothy	4	Paul
Titus	3	Paul
Philemon	1	Paul
Hebrews	13	unknown
James	5	James
1 Peter	5	Peter
2 Peter	3	Peter
1 John	5	John
2 John	1	John
3 John	1	John
Jude	1	Jude

The book of Revelation

Name	No. of chs	Author
Revelation	2	John

The order of the New Testament books

It can be confusing to open the New Testament for the first time.

The following facts about the canonical arrangement of the New Testament are helpful to keep in mind.

New Testament books by category

BIOGRAPHY

Matthew	Luke
Mark	John

HISTORY

Acts

PAUL'S LETTERS

Romans	1 Thessalonians
1 Corinthians	2 Thessalonians
2 Corinthians	1 Timothy
Galatians	2 Timothy
Ephesians	Titus
Philippians	Philemon
Colossians	

NON-PAULINE LETTERS

Hebrews	1 John
James	2 John
1 Peter	3 John
2 Peter	Jude

PROPHECY

Revelation

1 The order is not chronological

The 27 books of the New Testament are not in chronological order. The books, as set out in the New Testament, are not in the order in which they were written.

2 An overview of the New Testament books

The New Testament opens with four accounts of the life of Jesus recorded in the Gospels, Matthew, Mark, Luke, and John.

Then the growth of the Christian Church as it is recorded in Acts, and the New Testament letters follow.

The last book of the New Testament, the book of Revelation symbolically describes the end of time.

3 Luke and Acts

Luke

The Gospel of Luke and the book of Acts, also known as the Acts of the Apostles were both written by Luke. Acts is the second volume of Luke's two-volume work, but now John's Gospel separates them.

Acts

The Acts of the Apostles contains no account of any of the apostles except Peter and Paul. John is noticed only three times; and all that is recorded of James, the son of Zebedee, is his execution by Herod. It is properly therefore not the history of the "Acts of the Apostles," a title which was given to the book at a later date, but of "Acts of Apostles," or more correctly, of "Some Acts of Certain Apostles."

4 Paul's letters

Paul's letters can be divided into two groups. There are the letters he wrote to Christian communities and those he wrote to individuals.

Christian fellowships

Paul's letters to Christian fellowships are Romans, 1 Corinthians, 2 Corinthians, Galatians, Ephesians, Philippians, Colossians, 1 Thessalonians, 2 Thessalonians.

Individual letters

Paul's letters to individuals are 1 Timothy, 2 Timothy, Titus, Philemon. Paul's letters as they are arranged in the New Testament are not in chronological order. They are (nearly) arranged in decreasing order of length.

5 The letter to the Hebrews

This letter is anonymous and is the first letter to follow Paul's thirteen New Testament letters.

6 The other New Testament letters

The letters by James, Peter, John, and Jude are sometimes called the Catholic or General Epistles. They are listed in decreasing order of length, although letters written by the same apostle are grouped together.

7 The book of Revelation

The New Testament does not end with a letter but with a book from a totally different category, apocalyptic, with its descriptions of new heavens, new earth and new Jerusalem.

Authors of the New Testament

The traditional authors of the books of the New Testament with the books attributed to them are as follows:

Writer	Book
Matthew	Gospel of Matthew
Mark	Gospel of Mark
Luke	Gospel of Luke
	Acts
John	Gospel of John
	1 John
	2 John
	3 John
	Revelation
Peter	1 Peter
	2 Peter
James	James
Jude	Jude
Paul	Romans
	1 Corinthians
	2 Corinthians
	Galatians
	Ephesians
	Philippians
	Colossians
	1 Thessalonians
	2 Thessalonians
	1 Timothy
	2 Timothy
	Titus
	Philemon
Anonymous	Hebrews

Sketches of the New Testament authors

Next to nothing is known about some New Testament authors, while a great deal is known about others.

1 MATTHEW

Mathew, who is the same person known as Levi, was tax collector by trade.

As a tax collector Matthew would have been literate and quite capable of writing a Gospel.

He was chosen by Jesus to be one of the twelve Apostles.

2 MARK

Mark is the same person known as "John Mark." Mark was his Latin surname, John was his Jewish name.

John Mark worked for the spread of the gospel with his cousin Barnabas, a prominent figure in the early church, as well as with Peter and Paul. His close links with the apostles qualified him to write his Gospel.

3 LUKE

Luke is not mentioned by name in either his Gospel or his other writing, the book of Acts. However, he receives a passing mention in Colossians 4:14; Philemon 24; 2 Timothy 4:11 where we learn that Luke was a doctor and a fellow worker of Paul who accompanied Paul on some of his missionary journeys.

Luke's writings reveal him to be a careful historian as well as a spiritually motivated disciple of Jesus.

4 JOHN

John, along with his brother James, was one of the twelve apostles. John is the only New Testament writer to have written surviving New Testament letters as well as a Gospel. He is also the traditional author of the book of Revelation. John was called the "... disciple whom Jesus loved" and is believed to have been especially close to Jesus.

5 PETER

Peter became the leader and spokesman for the twelve Apostles. With brother Andrew, another of the twelve, he was also a fisherman. Along with James and John Peter was a member of the inner three disciples of Jesus.

6 PAUL

The apostle Paul is not mentioned in the Gospels and he was not one of the original twelve apostles. After his conversion the risen Jesus appointed Paul to preach the gospel to non-Jewish people.

Paul used his many gifts and talents in his tireless ministry of founding churches and building up churches through his missionary tours, lectures and sermons ,and letters.

7 JAMES

James, the traditional author of the letter of James was also a half-brother of Jesus. While not one of the twelve apostles James was a leader in the early church in Jerusalem and chaired the important council held in Jerusalem at which it was confirmed that ceremonial aspects of the law of Moses no longer need to be observed, Acts 12: 17; 15: 13,19; Gal. 2: 9.

8 JUDE

Jude was also a half-brother of Jesus, younger brother of James, and the author of the letter bearing his name.

The feel of a letter

New Testament letters often read well in a modern paraphrase. Here is part of 3 John.

"The Pastor, to my good friend Gaius: How truly I love you! We're the best of friends, and I pray for good fortune in everything you do, and for your good health – that your everyday affairs prosper, as well as your soul! I was most happy when some friends arrived and brought the news that you persist in following the way of Truth. Nothing could make me happier than getting reports that my children continue diligently in the way of Truth!

... Friend, don't go along with evil. Model the good. The person who does good does God's work. The person who does evil falsifies God, doesn't know the first thing about God.

Everyone has a good word for Demetrius – the Truth itself stands up for Demetrius! We concur, and you know we don't hand out endorsements lightly.

I have a lot more things to tell you, but I'd rather not use pen and ink. I hope to be there soon in person and have a heart-to-heart talk.

Peace to you. The friends here say hello. Greet our friends there by name."

The Message

The synoptic Gospels

The first three gospels, Matthew, Mark, and Luke are often called the synoptic Gospels meaning "see the same" (Syn = same, Optic = see).

The synoptic Gospels see with one eye. The synoptic Gospels, in contrast with John's Gospel, tend to view Jesus' ministry from the same perspective.

Forty-two common passages

There are forty-two passages in the Synoptics which are found in more than one Gospel.

1. John the Baptist, Mark 1: 2–8; Luke 3: 1–18; Matthew 3: 1–12.

2. Baptism of Jesus, Mark 1: 9–11; Luke 3: 21,22; Matt. 3: 13–17.

3. Temptation of Jesus, Mark 1: 12,13; Luke 4: 1–13; Matt. 4: 1–11.

4. Jesus' return to Galilee, and arrival at Capernaum, Mark 1: 14; Luke 4: 14; Matthew 4: 12,13.

5. Peter's mother-in-law healed, Mark 1: 29–34; Luke 4: 38–41; Matthew 8: 14–17.

6. A leper healed, Mark 1: 40–45; Luke 5: 12–16; Matthew 8: 2–4.

7. Paralytic healed, Mark 2: 1–12; Luke 5: 17–26; Matthew 9: 1–8.

8. Call of Matthew, Mark 2: 13–22; Luke 5: 27–39; Matthew 9: 9–17.

9. Jesus goes with his disciples through the corn-fields, Mark 2: 23–28; Luke 6: 1–5; Matthew 12: 1–8.

10. Man with shriveled hand healed, Mark 3: 1–6; Luke 6: 6–11; Matthew 12: 9–15.

11. Preparation for the Sermon on the Mount, Mark 3: 7–19; Luke 6: 12–16; Matthew 4: 23–25.

12. Jesus accused of casting out devils with the assistance of Beelzebub, Mark 3: 20–30; Matthew 12: 22–45

13. Arrival of the mother and family of Jesus, Mark 3: 31–35; Luke 8: 19–21; Matthew 12: 46–50.

14. Parable of the sower, Mark 4: 1–34; Luke 8: 4–18; Matthew 13: 1–34.

15. Jesus crosses the sea, and the storm, Mark 4: 35–41; Luke 8: 22–25; Matthew 8: 18–27.

16. Events in the country of the Gadarenes, Mark 5: 1–20; Luke 8: 26–39; Matthew 8: 28–34.

17. The daughter of Jairus restored to life, Mark 5: 21–43; Luke 8: 40–56; Matthew 9: 18–26.

18. Jesus sends out the twelve apostles, Mark 6: 7–13; Luke 9: 1–6; Matthew 10: 1–42.

19. Jesus' fame reaches the court of Herod, Matthew 14: 1–12; Mark 6: 14–29; Luke 9: 7–9.

20. Five thousand men fed, Matthew 14: 13–21; Mark 6: 30–44; Luke 9: 10–17.

21. Jesus is acknowledged to be the

Messiah by the apostles, Matthew 16: 13–28; Mark 8: 27; 9: 1; Luke 9: 18–27.

22. Transfiguration of Jesus, Matthew 17: 1–10; Mark 9: 2–9; Luke 9: 28–36.

23. Jesus heals a demoniac whom his apostles were unable to heal, Matthew 17: 14–21; Mark 9: 14–29; Luke 9: 37–43.

24. Jesus foretells his death, Matthew 17: 22,23; Mark 9: 30–32; Luke 9: 43–45.

25. Argument among the disciples about precedence, Matthew 18: 1–5; Mark 9: 33–37; Luke 9: 46–48.

26. Jesus blesses children who are brought to him, Matthew 19: 13–30; Mark 10: 13–31; Luke 18: 15–30.

27. Jesus again foretells his death, Matthew 20: 17–19; Mark 10: 32–34; Luke 18: 31–34.

28. Blind men at Jericho healed, Matthew 20: 29–34; Mark 10: 46–52; Luke 18: 35–43.

29. Jesus' public entry into Jerusalem, Matthew 21: 1–11; Mark 11: 1–10; Luke 19: 29–44.

30. Jesus ejects the traders from the temple, Matt. 21: 12–14; Mark 11: 15–17; Luke 19: 45, 46.

31. Jesus called to account by the chief priests and elders for teaching publicly in the temple, Matt. 21: 23–27,33–46; Mark 11: 27; 12: 12; Luke 20: 1–19.

32. Paying tax to Caesar, and marriage with a brother's widow, Matthew 22: 15–33; Mark 12: 13–34; Luke 20: 20–40.

33. Jesus' discussion with the Pharisees about the Messiah being called Lord, by David, Matthew 22: 41–46; Mark 12: 35–37; Luke 20: 41–44.

34. The Pharisees censured by Jesus, Matthew 23: 1, etc.; Mark 12: 38–40; Luke 20: 45–47.

35. Jesus foretells the destruction of Jerusalem, Matthew 24: 1–36; Mark 13: 1–36; Luke 21: 5–36.

36. Prelude to Jesus' passion, Matthew 26: 1–5; Mark 14: 1,2; Luke 22: 1,2.

37. Bribery of Judas, and the celebration of the Passover, Matthew 26: 14–29; Mark 14: 10–25; Luke 22: 3–23.

38. Jesus goes to the Mount of Olives, Matthew 26: 30–46; Mark 14: 26–42; Luke 22: 39–46.

39. Jesus is arrested, Matthew 26: 47–58; Mark 14: 43–54; Luke 22: 47–55.

40. Peter's denial of Jesus, Matthew 26: 69; 27: 19; Mark 14: 66; 15: 10; Luke 22: 56; 23: 17.

41. The crucifixion and death of Jesus, Matt. 27: 20–66; Mark 15: 11–47; Luke 23: 18–56.

42. The resurrection of Jesus, Matthew 28: 1, etc.; Mark 16: 1, etc.; Luke 24: 1, etc.

New Testament letters and Aramaic words

New Testament letters

The Epistles differ in their nature from any other portion of the Scriptures. They are a series of letters to the newly planted churches of the first century, or to individual church members. Most of them were written by apostles. There are twenty-one letters in the New Testament.

Table of New Testament letters

Name of letter	Number of chapters
Romans	16
1 Corinthians	16
2 Corinthians	13
Galatians	6
Ephesians	6
Philippians	4
Colossians	4
1 Thessalonians	5
2 Thessalonians	3
1 Timothy	6
2 Timothy	4
Titus	3
Philemon	1
Hebrews	13
James	5
1 Peter	5
2 Peter	3
1 John	5
2 John	1
3 John	1
Jude	1

The authors

The writers of these letters were Peter, James, John, Jude, and Paul. Some of the other apostles may have written letters, but if so, they no longer exist.

The purpose

These letters were written, some to particular congregations of believers; some to the church at large, and others to individuals; to encourage, reprove, correct false teaching, and give special instruction in doctrine and in how to live as a Christian.

The source

The authors of the New Testament letters were all apostles, or were closely linked to the apostolic circle, and were under the guidance of the Holy Spirit as they wrote.

Classification

The New Testament letters have been classified as follows:

1. The group of letters known as "the Pauline Epistles" obviously refer to those written by the Apostle Paul. These may be subdivided into:

(1) The Doctrinal, addressed to special churches – Romans, Corinthians, Galatians, Philippians, Colossians, Thessalonians.

(2) Pastoral, addressed to the evangelists, Timothy and Titus.

(3) Special, addressed to an individual – Philemon.

2. General Epistles, addressed to the church at large. These are,

(1) One of James;

(2) Two of Peter;

(3) Three of John;

(4) One of Jude.

3. The letter to the Hebrews.

Aramaic words in the New Testament

1. Abba; Mark 14: 36; Rom; 8: 15; Gal. 4: 6.

2. Ainias; Acts 9: 33,34.

3. Akeldama; Acts 1: 19.

4. Alphaios; Matt. 10: 3; Mark 2: 14; 3: 18; Luke 6: 15; Acts 1: 13.

5. Annas; Luke 3: 2; John 18: 13,24; Acts 4: 6.

6. Bar-abbas; Matt. 27: 16,17,20,21,26; Mark 15: 7,11,15; Luke 23: 18; John 18: 40.

7. Bartholomaios; Matt. 10: 3; Mark 3: 18; Luke 6: 14; Acts 1: 13.

8. Bar-iesous; Acts 13: 6.

9. Bar-iona; Matt. 16: 17; See No; 27,below.

10. Bar-nabas; Acts 4: 36,c; 1 Cor. 9: 6; Gal. 2: 1,9,13; Col. 4: 10.

11. Bar-sabas; Acts 1: 23; 15: 22.

12. Bar-timaios; Mark 10: 46.

13. Beel-zeboul; Matt. 10: 25; 12: 24,27; Mark 3: 22; Luke 11: 15,18,19.

14. Bethesda; John 5: 2.

15. Bethsaida; Matt. 11: 21; Mark 6: 45; 8: 22; Luke 9: 10; 10: 13; John 1: 44; 12: 21.

16. Bethphage; Matt. 21: 1; Mark 11: 1; Luke 19: 29.

17. Boanerges; Mark 3: 17.

18. Gethsemanei; Matt. 26: 36; Mark 14: 32.

19. Golgotha; Matt. 27: 33; Mark 15: 22; John 19: 17.

20. Eloi; Mark 15: 34.

21. Ephphatha; Mark 7: 34.

22. Zakchaios; Luke 19: 2,5,8.

23. Zebedaios; Matt. 4: 21,21; 10: 2; 20: 20; 26: 37; 27: 56; Mark 1: 19,10; 3: 17; 10: 35; Luke 5: 10; John 21: 2.

24. Eli; Matt. 27: 46.

25. Thaddaios; Matt. 10: 3; Mark 3: 18.

26. Thomas; Matt. 10: 3; Mark 3: 18; Luke 6: 15; John 11: 16; 14: 5; 20: 24,26,27,28,29; 21: 2; Acts 1: 13.

27. Ioannes; John 1: 42; 21: 15,16,17.

28. Kephas; John 1: 42; 1 Cor. 1: 12; 3: 22; 9: 5; 15: 5; Gal. 2: 9.

29. Kleopas; Luke 24: 18.

30. Klopas; John 19: 25.

31. Lama; Matt. 27: 46; Mark 15: 34.

32. Mammonas; Matt. 6: 24; Luke 16: 9,11,13.

33. Maran-atha; 1 Cor. 16: 22 (= Our Lord,come!).

34. Martha; Luke 10: 38,40,41; John 11: 1.

35. Mattaios; Matt. 9: 9; 10: 3; Mark 3: 18; Luke 6: 15; Acts 1: 13,26.

36. Nazareth; Matt. 2: 23; 4: 13; 21: 11; Mark 1: 9; Luke 1: 26; 2: 4,39,51; 4: 16; John 1: 45,46; Acs 10: 38.

37. Pascha; Matt. 26: 2,17,18,19; Mark 14: 1,12,12,14,16; Luke 2: 41; 22: 1,7,8,11,13,15; John 2: 13,23; 6: 4; 11: 55,55; 12: 1; 13: 1; 18: 28,39; 19: 14; Acts 12: 4; 1 Cor. 5: 7; Heb. 11: 28.

38. Rabboni,Rabbouni; Mark 10: 51; John 20: 16.

39. Raka; Matt. 5: 22.

40. Sabachthani; Matt. 27: 46; Mark 15: 34.

41. Sabbata; Matt. 12: 1,5,10,11,12.

42. Tabitha; Acts 9: 36,40.

43. Talitha kumi; Mark 5: 41.

44. Hosanna (in Aram; = Save us; in Heb. = Help us); Matt. 21: 9,9,15; Mark 11: 9,10; John 12: 13.

Harmony of the accounts of the resurrection, the resurrection appearances, and the ascension (1)

General points

Variations in content

One thing should always be borne in mind by everyone who reads the Gospels. The record of each event is what it is stated by all the evangelists.

Just because one detail in a story is omitted by one Gospel writer does not prove that either of the Gospels are false. Each Gospel is an independent witness to the great facts of the life and death of Jesus.

The order of events in the Gospels

The Gospels are not contradicting each other just because they record certain events in a different order from each other. In fact, none of the four Gospel writers ever claim that the events they have presented in their Gospels are in chronological order.

1. The Resurrection

1. Jesus was laid in the tomb on Friday evening, having been hurriedly wrapped in linen with myrrh and aloes, John 19: 39,40.

The women also prepared spices on the same evening to embalm him, Luke 23: 56. As it was too late that night to complete the preparation, they deferred it until the first day of the week, resting on the Sabbath, Luke 23: 56.

2. Early on the first day of the week, the women completed their preparation of the spices. "When the Sabbath was over, Mary Magdalene, Mary the mother of James, and Salome bought spices so they could embalm him" Mark 16: 1, *The Message.*

3. They went to the grave just the day was about to dawn, just as the light appeared in the east, but too dark to see everything clearly. It was "in the end of the Sabbath, as it began to dawn toward the first day of the week," Matt. 28: 1. "Very early in the morning, at the rising of the sun," or as the sun was about to rise, Mark 16: 2. "Very early in the morning," Luke 24: 1. "Early, while it was yet dark," John 20: 1.

4. The people who came to the tomb were:
- Mary Magdalene, Matt. 28: 1; John 20: 1;
- Mary the mother of James and Joses, Matt. 28: 1; Luke 24: 10; Mark 15: 40;
- Salome, the wife of Zebedee, and mother of James and John, cf. Matt. 27: 56; Mark 15: 40;
- Joanna, the wife of Chuza, Herod's steward, cf. Luke 24: 10; 8: 3; and
- Some others who are not specified, Luke 24: 1,10.

5. The reasons for going to the tomb:
(1) To see the grave, Matt. 28: 1.
(2) To embalm Jesus, or to finish embalming him, Mark 16: 1; Luke 24: 1.

6. While they were on the way to the tomb they discussed who should roll away the stone for them, so that they might gain access to the body of Jesus, Mark 16: 3.

7. When they arrived they found that there had been an earthquake, so that the stone was rolled away, Matt. 28: 2; Mark 16: 4.

8. The angel who rolled the stone away had sat on it, and had been seen by the guards and had frightened them. He did not, however, appear here to the women, but only to the guards, Matt. 28: 2–4.

9. When they arrived at the tomb, Mary Magdalene, greatly upset by what she saw, and probably thinking that the body had been stolen, left the other women, and ran to the city, to inform the disciples, John 20: 2.

10. While Mary Magdalene was away, the others women probably looked in the garden as they searched for the body.

The tomb was large enough for them to enter. There "the angel spake unto them," Matt. 28: 5.

"They saw a young man" – that is, an angel who looked like a young man – "sitting on the right side," Mark 16: 5. When they entered he was sitting; as they entered he rose and stood, Luke 24: 4. Luke adds that there was another angel with him, Luke 24: 4; this other angel was not seen when they entered the tomb as mentioned by Mark, but was seen when they had gone into the tomb, as mentioned by Luke.

11. The angel told them to go and tell the disciples and Peter, Matt. 28: 7; Mark 16: 7; and to assure them that Jesus would see them in Galilee. He also reminded them about what Jesus had said when they were in Galilee, Luke 24: 6,7.

12. They went at once toward the city, but took a different route from the one that Mary had taken, so that they did not meet her when she was returning from the city with Peter and John, Matt. 28: 8, Mark 16: 8. "They said nothing to any man," Luke 24: 9,10.

Harmony of the accounts of the resurrection, the resurrection appearances, and the ascension (2)

1. The Resurrection, continued

13. After they were gone Mary Magdalene returned to the tomb, following Peter and John, who came running, John 20: 2–9. They examined the tomb, and found that the body was really gone, but they did not know the reason for this. They had not seen the other women who had been told the reason for this by the angel. Mary Magdalene had left the women before the angel had spoken to them. So, at this point, she did not know why Jesus' body was not there.

14. Peter and John then left the tomb, returned to the city, and left Mary alone, John 20: 10.

15. While Mary was there alone she looked into the tomb, and saw two angels, probably the same that had appeared to the other women, John 20: 11–13.

16. Jesus appeared to Mary while she sat alone, John 20: 14–18.

"Now when she had said this, she turned around and saw Jesus standing there, and did not know that it was Jesus. Jesus said to her, 'Woman, why are you weeping? Whom are you seeking?'

She, supposing Him to be the gardener, said to Him, 'Sir, if You have carried Him away, tell me where You have laid Him, and I will take Him away.' Jesus said to her, 'Mary!' She turned and said to Him, 'Rabboni!' (which is to say, Teacher). Jesus said to her, 'Do not cling to Me, for I have not yet ascended to My Father; but go to My brethren and say to them, 'I am ascending to My Father and your Father, and to My God and your God.'" Mary Magdalene came and told the disciples that she had seen the Lord, and that He had spoken these things to her." *John 20: 14–18.*

Thus, according to Mark 16: 9, he appeared to Mary Magdalene "first."

17. Mary then went to tell the disciples that she had seen him, but they did not completely believe her, John 20: 18; Mark 16: 10,11.

18. Later Jesus appeared to the other women, Matt. 28: 9: "As they went to tell his disciples, behold, Jesus met them, saying, All hail." Probably this was not long after he had appeared to Mary Magdalene. They would naturally return to the disciples, and find out if he had been seen by anyone. In Luke 24: 10 it is said that it was Mary Magdalene, and Joanna, and Mary the mother of James, that told these things to the disciples.

2. Appearances of Jesus after the Resurrection

1. To Mary Magdalene, John 20: 14; Mark 16: 9.
2. To the other women, Matt. 28: 9.
3. To Peter, 1 Cor. 15: 5; Luke 24: 34.

4. To two disciples as they were going to Emmaus, Mark 16: 12–13; Luke 24: 13–32.

5. The same day, in the evening, to the apostles, but without Thomas, 1 Cor. 15: 5; Mark 16: 14; Luke 24: 36; John 20: 19,24.

6. To the apostles when Thomas was present, John 20: 24–29.

7. In Galilee, at the Sea of Tiberias, to Peter, Thomas, Nathaniel, James, and John, and two others, John 21: 1–14. This is said to be the third time that he showed himself to the disciples – that is, to the apostles when they were together, John 21: 14.

8. To the disciples on a mountain in Galilee, Matt. 28: 16.

9. To more than 500 brethren at once, 1 Cor. 15: 6.

10. To James, one of the apostles, 1 Cor. 15: 7.

11. To all the apostles together, 1 Cor. 15: 7. He was seen by them forty days after he rose.

12. To the apostles at his ascension, Luke 24: 50,51; Acts 1: 9,10.

13. To Paul, 1 Cor. 15: 8; Acts 9: 3–5; 22: 6–10.

3. The ascension

1. It was forty days after his resurrection, Acts 1: 3.

2. He ascended from the Mount of Olives, near Bethany, Luke 24: 50; Acts 1: 12.

3. It was in the presence of all the apostles, Luke 24: 50; Acts 1: 9,10.

4. He was received into a cloud, and ascended to heaven, Acts 1: 9,11; Luke 24: 51; Eph. 1: 20–22.

Matthew, Mark

Matthew

Introduction

The first of the Gospels has been assigned by the Church, from the earliest times, to Matthew, one of the Twelve Apostles, and in all ages has been given the first place in the New Testament. He was the son of Alphæus, as we learn from Luke, who also calls him Levi (Luke 5: 27–29). He calls himself "Matthew the publican," refusing to conceal in his own history the despised calling that had engaged him before he entered the service of Christ. He was a Jew, but had so far lost the national feeling that he was a collector of the hateful Roman tribute at Capernaum, and was sitting at the receipt of custom when called by our Lord to leave all and to follow him. His history of the Savior shows, however, that he was more dominated by Jewish ideas than the writers of the other three gospels. Of the life of Matthew, after the death of the Savior, we have no information, for no reliance can be placed upon the traditions concerning his later history.

The Gospel of Matthew shows the methodical habits of a business man, for of all the writers he is most systematic in his arrangement. He gives by far the fullest accounts of the Sermon on the Mount, the charge to the Apostles (Matt. ch. 10), the Discourse on Blasphemy against the Holy Spirit, the Arraignment of the Scribes and Pharisees, of the Parables, and of the Prophecies concerning the Overthrow of the Jewish State. It has always been held that Matthew wrote before the other New Testament writers, and wrote especially for Jewish Christians. It is therefore supposed that he wrote first either in the common language of Judea at that time, the Aramaic, which was spoken by the Savior and his Apostles, or else in the pure Hebrew, which was then generally understood. This, however, is an unsettled question, and the Greek which we now possess, was, it is almost certain, written in Matthew's lifetime. There are no data for determining the exact time and place where it was written, but it was probably composed about the middle of the first century, within twenty years of the crucifixion.

Whether written originally in Hebrew or not, it can hardly be doubted that Matthew wrote for Jewish readers. He takes for granted a familiarity with Jewish customs, laws, and localities, to a far greater extent than the other writers. Dean Alford says: "The whole narrative proceeds more upon a Jewish view of matters, and is concerned more to establish that point, which to a Jewish convert would be most important, namely, that Jesus is the Messiah prophesied in the Old Testament. Hence the commencement of his genealogy from Abraham and David; hence the frequent notice of the necessity of this or that event happening, because it was foretold by the prophets; hence the constant opposition of our Lord's spiritually ethical teaching to the carnal formalistic ethics of the Scribes and Pharisees."

B.W. Johnson, *The People's New Testament*

Verses of encouragement

Matt. 4: 4 "But he answered and said, It is written, Man shall not live by bread alone, but by every Word that proceedeth out of the mouth of God."

Matt. 5: 16 "Let your Light so shine before men, that they may see your good works, and glorify your Father which is in Heaven."

Matt. 6: 20,21 "But lay up for yourselves treasures in Heaven, where neither moth nor rust doth corrupt, and where thieves do not break through nor steal: For where your treasure is, there will your heart be also."

Matt. 6: 33 "But seek ye first the Kingdom of God, and His Righteousness; and all these things shall be added unto you."

Matt. 7: 7,8 "Ask, and it shall be given you; seek, and ye shall find; knock, and it shall be opened unto you: For every one that asketh receiveth; and he that seeketh findeth; and to him that knocketh it shall be opened."

Matt. 28: 18–20 "And Jesus came and spake unto them, saying, All power is given unto Me in Heaven and in earth. Go ye therefore, and teach all nations, baptizing them in the Name of the Father, and of the Son, and of the Holy Ghost: Teaching them to observe all things whatsoever I have commanded you: and, lo, I am with you alway, even unto the end of the world. Amen."

Mark

Introduction

I. CONCERNING THIS WITNESS. HIS NAME IS MARK

Marcus was a Roman name, and a very common one, and yet we have no reason to think, but that he was by birth a Jew; but as Saul, when he went among the nations, took the Roman name of Paul, so he of Mark, his Jewish name perhaps being Mardocai; so Grotius. We read of John whose surname was Mark, sister's son to Barnabas, whom Paul was displeased with (Acts 15: 37,38), but afterward had a great kindness for, and not only ordered the churches to receive him (Col. 4: 10), but sent for him to be his assistant, with this recommendation, He is profitable to me for the ministry (2 Tim. 4: 11); and he reckons him among his fellow-laborers, Philemon 24.

We read of Marcus whom Peter calls his son, he having been an instrument of his conversion (1 Pet. 5: 13); whether that was the same with the other, and, if not, which of them was the penman of this gospel, is altogether uncertain.

Mark, Luke

Mark, continued

Introduction, continued

I. CONCERNING THIS WITNESS. HIS
NAME IS MARK, CONTINUED
It is a tradition very current among
the ancients, that St. Mark wrote
this gospel under the direction of St.
Peter, and that it was confirmed by
his authority; so Hieron, "Mark, the
disciple and interpreter of Peter, being
sent from Rome by the brethren, wrote
a concise gospel." And Tertullian
says, "Mark, the interpreter of Peter,
delivered in writing the things which
had been preached by Peter." But
as Dr. Whitby very well suggests,
Why should we have recourse to the
authority of Peter for the support of
this gospel, or say with St. Jerome that
Peter approved of it and recommended
it by his authority to the church to be
read, when, though it is true Mark was
no apostle, yet we have all the reason
in the world to think that both he and
Luke were of the number of the seventy
disciples, who companied with the
apostles all along (Acts 1: 21), who had
a commission like that of the apostles
(Luke 10: 19, compared with Mark
16: 18), and who, it is highly probable,
received the Holy Ghost when they
did (Acts 1: 15; 2: 1–4), so that it is no
diminution at all to the validity or value
of this gospel, that Mark was not one of
the twelve, as Matthew and John were?
St. Jerome saith that, after the writing
of this gospel, he went into Egypt, and
was the first that preached the gospel
at Alexandria, where he founded
a church, to which he was a great
example of holy living. He so adorned,
by his doctrine and his life, the church
which he founded, that his example
influenced all the followers of Christ.

II. CONCERNING THIS TESTIMONY
Mark's gospel repeats much of
Matthew's but many remarkable
circumstances being added to the
stories there related, but not many
new matters. When many witnesses
are called to prove the same fact, upon
which a judgment is to be given, it
is not thought tedious, but highly
necessary, that they should each of
them relate it in their own words, again
and again, that by the agreement of the
testimony the thing may be established;
and therefore we must not think this
book of Scripture needless, for it is
written not only to confirm our belief
that Jesus is the Christ the Son of God,
but to put us in mind of things which
we have read in the foregoing gospel,
that we may give the more earnest
heed to them, lest at any time we let
them slip; and even pure minds have
need to be thus stirred up by way of
remembrance. It was fit that such great
things as these should be spoken and
written, once, yea twice, because man
is so unapt to perceive them, and so
apt to forget them. There is no ground
for the tradition, that this gospel was
written first in Latin, though it was
written at Rome; it was written in
Greek, as was St. Paul's epistle to the

Romans, the Greek being the more universal language

Matthew Henry

Verses of encouragement

Mark 4: 24 "And He said unto them, Take heed what ye hear: with what measure ye mete, it shall be measured to you: and unto you that hear shall more be given."

Mark 11: 24 " Therefore I say unto you, What things soever ye desire, when ye pray, believe that ye receive them, and ye shall have them."

Luke

Introduction

The third Gospel is assigned by the common voice of the primitive Church to Luke, "the beloved physician" and companion of Paul. Of his earlier history nothing is recorded. There is no proof that he ever saw the Lord or that he became a believer until some time after his death. He was not a Jew, his name is Greek, his style and modes of thought point to Greek training, and it has been generally believed that he was one of "the Grecians who turned to the Lord" in the great commercial city of Antioch where the first Gentile church beyond Palestine was founded. From the incidental references to himself in the Acts we learn that he was the constant companion of the later ministry of the great apostle to the Gentiles, and this is confirmed by the allusions to him in the Epistles. From Col. 4: 14; Philem. 24; 2 Tim. 4: 11, we learn that he was a Gentile, a physician, that he remained with Paul in his imprisonment at Cæsarea and attended him to Rome, where he was his companion during his long sufferings

The Gospel of Luke differs from the other three in its sources of information. Matthew wrote as an eye witness; Mark probably recalled the recollections of Peter; John recalled his own personal memories of the life and words of the Lord, but Luke draws from the authentic sources of information then accessible, and he carefully presents the results in an orderly narrative. There are reasons for believing that during the period when Paul was a prisoner at Cæsarea, Luke, under his direction, set in order the facts of the Life of Christ in order to furnish an account fitted for the use of Gentile converts, and Gentiles who desired to learn of the Lord. "As Paul was the apostle, so in a faint degree Gentile Luke was the evangelist, of the Gentiles. He traces the genealogy up, not merely to Abraham, but Adam, the son of God. He makes Christ's first teachings at Nazareth commemorate the extension of God's mercy beyond the limits of Israel. Luke 4: 16–30. He shows how the sinner is forgiven upon condition of obedient faith. Luke 7: 36–50. The publican is, in Paul's favorite term, justified. Evidently their narrative of the Lord's supper is the same tradition. Luke 24: 34; 1 Cor. 15: 5.

Luke, John

Luke, continued

Introduction

Luke's two books, his Gospels and the Acts, are properly two successive parts of one Christian history; and as the latter terminates at the point where Paul has lived two years at Rome, in the year 64, so the Gospel must have been written before that period, namely during the 27 years after Christ's death. For as Luke terminates his Acts abruptly with the close of Paul's two years' imprisonment, without adding a syllable of that apostle's later history, it is very certain that the Acts was published at that time. Yet, we know from the preface to Acts that the Gospel had been already written. Thus, it is evident, that it was written 27 years after the crucifixion."

B.W. Johnson, *The People's New Testament*

Verses of encouragement

Luke 1: 37 "For with God nothing shall be impossible."

Luke 6: 38 "Give, and it shall be given unto you; good measure, pressed down, and shaken together, and running over, shall men give into your bosom. For with the same measure that ye mete withal it shall be measured to you again."

Luke 11: 36 "If thy whole body therefore be full of Light, having no part dark, the whole shall be full of Light, as when the bright shining of a candle doth give thee light."

Luke 15: 4–7 "What man of you, having a hundred sheep, if he loses one of them, does not leave the ninety-nine in the wilderness, and go after the one which is lost until he finds it? And when he has found it, he lays it on his shoulders, rejoicing. And when he comes home, he calls together his friends and neighbors, saying to them, 'Rejoice with me, for I have found my sheep which was lost!' I say to you that likewise there will be more joy in heaven over one sinner who repents than over ninety-nine just persons who need no repentance."

Luke 18: 27 "And He said, The things which are impossible with men are possible with God."

John

Introduction

The author of the Fourth Gospel was John, the son of Zebedee and Salome, the brother of James, in early life a Galilean fisherman, but afterwards an apostle of Jesus Christ. In less than a hundred years after his death Christian writers living in different quarters of the world, whose writings are still extant, show us that this was the universal belief of the church. Indeed, the testimony to the authorship is stronger than can be furnished that Josephus wrote his Jewish history, that Cæsar wrote his Commentaries, or in behalf of any uninspired writing of antiquity, and would never have been questioned had not a class of rationalistic critics arisen who wished to set aside the lofty views of the personality and mission of the Savior which are so prominent a feature of the Fourth Gospel. We know from John 21: 24, that it was written by an eye-witness and by a beloved disciple. There were only three disciples who were admitted to the most intimate relations with Jesus – Peter, James, and John. As it was not written by either of the first two, John must be the author. So the early church unanimously testifies. Irenæus, who learned of one who had been intimate with John and who wrote near the middle of the second century, affirms that he was the author. It is credited to John in the canon of Muratori, the first catalogue of the New Testament writings, written A.D. 175. It is also spoken of by Theophilus of Antioch A.D. 175, and by Clement of Alexandria, near the same time, and in the latter part of the second century it was translated into the Syriac and Latin versions of the New Testament. Besides these direct recognitions there are evident allusions to it and quotations from it in a number of epistles and treatises of Ignatius, Hermas, Polycarp, Papias, and others, which belong to the first half of the second century. Indeed, it is quoted within twenty years of John's death.

PLACE AND TIME
We do not know certainly when or where the Fourth Gospel was written. Irenæus, who lived in the second century, and who was the religious pupil of Polycarp, the martyr who was educated at the feet of John, declares that it was written at Ephesus, after the other three had been written. Its internal character indicates that it was written outside of Judea, after the fall of the temple, and after certain heresies began to be developed. John was still at Jerusalem A.D. 50 (Gal. chapter 2); it is almost certain that he did not go to Ephesus until after the death of Paul, about A.D. 67, and it is probable that he did not leave the city of Jerusalem, permanently, until the storm of destruction began to gather, which broke in A.D. 70. As the testimony of the early church is unanimous that his later years were passed at Ephesus and in that region, he probably went there about this date. After this, and before his death, which took place near the close of the century, the Gospel was written.

JOHN
John, the author, was brought up to his father's calling, and even followed it after he was first pointed to Christ. While he was an "unlearned man" (Acts 4: 13), in the sense that he never attended the rabbinical schools, he had such an education in Hebrew and in the Scriptures as all respectable Jewish families were wont to give their children. In connection with every synagogue was a school in which children were taught reading, writing, and the rudiments of science.

John

John, continued

Introduction

JOHN, CONTINUED

The children of Jewish common people were better educated than those of any other country in the world. Jesus found John among the disciples of John the Baptist, who at once pointed him and his companions to Christ. We next meet him at the sea of Galilee, fishing, and there Jesus gave him a permanent call. From this time onward he steadfastly followed the Master, and with James and Peter, formed an inner circle nearer the Lord. These three, only, witness the resurrection of Jairus' daughter, see the glory of the transfiguration, and the agony of the garden. John and Peter follow Christ, after his arrest, and the first goes openly into the house of Caiaphas, to the trial before Pilate, and to the cross, till all was over. When the news of the resurrection came he and Peter were the first to reach the sepulcher.

To him Jesus committed the care of his own mother, while dying on the cross, and it is probable that he remained in Judea to attend to this sacred charge while she lived. From about the time of the overthrow of Jerusalem he changed his residence to Ephesus, where he probably lived until he died, near the close of the first century. The testimony of the early church would place his death after A.D. 98. It was during this later period that he wrote his Gospel, his Epistles, was exiled to Patmos, and there wrote his Revelation.

CHARACTER OF GOSPEL

The character of John's Gospel, written after his fellow apostles had gone to rest, differs in some respects from the others. It alone follows the chronological order of events, gives an account of the Judæan ministry of our Lord, shows that his ministry lasted for over three years, gives the account of the resurrection of Lazarus and of the wonderful discourse to the disciples the night that he was betrayed. It omits much with which the church was already familiar through the other Gospels, presents much that they had not recorded, and recognizes certain false doctrines which had begun to be taught. It is the gospel of the Incarnation, of Love, and the most Spiritual of the Gospels. It alone unfolds fully the great doctrine of the Comforter. The great end, however, that the writer had before him in all he wrote is given in his own words: These are written that ye might believe that Jesus is the Christ, the Son of God; and that believing ye might have life through his name.

B.W. Johnson, The People's New Testament

Verses of encouragement

John 1: 12 "But as many as received Him, to them gave He Power to become the sons of God, even to them that believe on His Name."

John 1: 17 "For the Law was given by Moses, but Grace and Truth came by Jesus Christ."

John 3: 3 "Jesus answered and said unto him, Verily, verily, I say unto thee, Except a man be born again, he cannot see the Kingdom of God."

John 3: 16 "For God so loved the world, that He gave His Only Begotten Son, that whosoever believeth in Him should not perish, but have Everlasting Life."

John 3: 36 "He that believeth on the Son hath Everlasting Life: and he that believeth not the Son shall not see life; but the wrath of God abideth on him."

John 5: 24 "Verily, verily, I say unto you, He that heareth My Word, and believeth on Him that sent Me, hath Everlasting Life, and shall not come into condemnation; but is passed from death unto Life."

John 6: 63 "It is the Spirit that quickeneth; the flesh profiteth nothing: the WORDS that I speak unto you, They are Spirit, and They are Life."

John 7: 38 "He that believeth on Me, as the Scripture hath said, out of his belly shall flow rivers of living water."

John 8: 12 "Then spake Jesus again unto them, saying, I am the Light of the world: he that followeth Me shall not walk in darkness, but shall have The Light of Life."

John 8: 32 "And ye shall know the Truth, and the Truth shall make you free."

John 10: 14 "I am the Good Shepherd, and know My sheep, and am known of Mine."

John 11: 25,26 "Jesus said unto her, I am The Resurrection, and The Life: he that believeth in Me, though he were dead, yet shall he Live: And whosoever Liveth and believeth in Me shall never die. Believest thou this?"

John 14: 1–3 "Let not your heart be troubled: ye believe in God, believe also in Me. In My Father's House are many mansions: if it were not so, I would have told you. I go to prepare a place for you. And if I go and prepare a place for you, I will come again, and receive you unto Myself; that where I am, there ye may be also."

John 14: 26,27 "But the Comforter, Which is the Holy Ghost, Whom the Father will send in My Name, He shall teach you all things, and bring all things to your remembrance, whatsoever I have said unto you. Peace I leave with you, My Peace I give unto you: not as the world giveth, give I unto you. Let not your heart be troubled, neither let it be afraid."

John 17: 15 "I pray not that Thou shouldest take them out of the world, but that Thou shouldest keep them from the evil."

Acts, Romans

Acts

Introduction

This book unites the Gospels to the Epistles. It contains many particulars concerning the apostles Peter and Paul, and of the Christian church from the ascension of our Savior to the arrival of St. Paul at Rome, a space of about thirty years. St. Luke was the writer of this book; he was present at many of the events he relates, and attended Paul to Rome. But the narrative does not afford a complete history of the church during the time to which it refers, nor even of St. Paul's life.

PURPOSE OF ACTS

The object of the book has been considered to be,

1. To relate in what manner the gifts of the Holy Spirit were communicated on the day of Pentecost, and the miracles performed by the apostles, to confirm the truth of Christianity, as showing that Christ's declarations were really fulfilled.

2. To prove the claim of the Gentiles to be admitted into the church of Christ. This is shown by much of the contents of the book. A large portion of the Acts is occupied by the discourses or sermons of various persons, the language and manner of which differ, and all of which will be found according to the persons by whom they were delivered, and the occasions on which they were spoken. It seems that most of these discourses are only the substance of what was actually delivered. They relate nevertheless fully to Jesus as the Christ, the anointed Messiah.

Matthew Henry

Verses of encouragement

Acts 1: 8 "But ye shall receive Power, after that the Holy Ghost is come upon you: and ye shall be witnesses unto Me both in Jerusalem, and in all Judaea, and in Samaria, and unto the uttermost part of the earth."

Acts 2: 25,26 "For David speaketh concerning Him, I foresaw the Lord always before my face, for He is on my right hand, that I should not be moved: Therefore did my heart Rejoice, and my tongue was Glad; moreover also my flesh shall rest in Hope."

Acts 2: 28 "Thou hast made known to me The Ways Of Life; Thou shalt make me full of Joy with Thy Countenance."

Acts 10: 34,35 "Then Peter opened his mouth, and said, Of a Truth I perceive that God is no respecter of persons: But in every nation He that feareth Him, and worketh Righteousness, is accepted with Him."

Acts 10: 38 "How God anointed Jesus of Nazareth with the Holy Ghost and with Power: Who went about doing good, and healing all that were oppressed of the devil; for God was with Him."

Acts 16: 31 "And they said, Believe on the Lord Jesus Christ, and thou shalt be saved, and thy house."

Acts 17: 28 "For in Him we live, and move, and have our being; as certain also of your own poets have said, For we are also His offspring."

Acts 20: 35 "I have shewed you all things, how that so laboring ye ought to support the weak, and to remember the Words of the Lord Jesus, how He said, It is more blessed to give than to receive."

Romans

Introduction

The depth of thought, logical reasoning, and profound comprehension of the divine government shown in this Epistle have always been recognized.

Luther says, "It is the chief part of the New Testament."

Meyer, that it is "the grandest, boldest, most complete composition of Paul."

Godet terms it "the cathedral of the Christian faith."

That it should be what Coleridge says, "the most profound work in existence," is not wonderful when we bear in mind that it was written by the greatest of the apostles, in the full vigor of his manhood, at the height of his activity, and addressed to the church of the great imperial city which was the center of influence and power for the whole world.

In this mighty capital, under the shadow of the palace of the Cæsars, in some unknown way, a congregation of believers had been gathered. It is certain that long before any apostle had set foot in Italy, churches had been formed in Puteoli and in Rome (Acts 28: 14,15). Possibly the "strangers of Rome," who listened to Peter on the day of Pentecost, had carried back the Gospel, and had formed the nucleus; but it is probable that the constant influx of strangers from all portions of the empire had carried many of the converts made around the Eastern Mediterranean to the great political center of the world.

The greetings of the last chapter of this Epistle show that Paul had many acquaintances among the number, and the names seem to imply that most of them were Greeks. Indeed, while there was a Jewish element in the church, it can hardly be doubted that the majority of the believers were of Gentile origin. Various passages in the Epistles, such as 1: 5–7; 11: 13,25,28; 14: 1; 15: 15,16, give indications of a Gentile preponderance.

OCCASION OF WRITING
The occasion of writing was the desire of the apostle to labor in the great city, a desire which had thus far been hindered, and the opportunity was furnished by the departure of Phoebe from Corinth to Rome. Still firm in his purpose to see and preach in Rome, a letter to the church would tend to prepare the way.

Romans, 1 Corinthians

Romans, continued

Introduction

OCCASION OF WRITING

As they had never been visited by an apostle, and as at that time there was no New Testament in existence to which they could go for instruction, it is not strange that there should be an imperfect comprehension, on the part of many, of great principles of Christian doctrine, and there was doubtless need that the relations of Jew and Gentile, and of the Law and the Gospel, should be set forth with all possible clearness. The great theme of the Epistle is set forth in chap. 1: 16,17: "The Gospel is the Power of God unto Salvation to every one that believeth; to the Jew first, and also to the Greek." The great doctrine is that salvation is not through the Law by works of the Law, but through the Gospel accepted by Faith. The righteousness of God, the righteousness which brings justification in the sight of God, does not come from legal works, but comes from God who gives this righteousness to those who believe upon and accept his Son. This great doctrinal theme is discussed with many illustrations and in various phases through chapters 1–11, and in chapters 12–14 the apostle passes to exhortations and practical applications, while the sixteenth and last chapter is devoted to salutations of various saints in Rome known to the apostle.

B.W. Johnson, *The People's New Testament*

Verses of encouragement

Rom. 1: 17 "For therein is the Righteousness of God revealed from faith to faith: as it is written, The just shall live by Faith."

Rom. 4: 20,21 "He staggered not at The Promise Of God through unbelief; but was strong in faith, giving Glory to God; And being fully persuaded that, what He had Promised, He was able also to perform."

Rom. 5: 1 "Therefore being justified by Faith, we have Peace with God through our Lord Jesus Christ."

Rom. 5: 5 "And Hope maketh not ashamed; because the Love of God is shed abroad in our hearts by the Holy Ghost Which is given unto us."

Rom. 5: 17 "For if by one man's offense death reigned by one; much more they which receive Abundance Of Grace and of The Gift Of Righteousness shall reign in life by One, Jesus Christ."

Rom. 6: 14 "For sin shall not have dominion over you: for ye are not under the Law, but under Grace."

Rom. 6: 23 "For the wages of sin is death; but the Gift Of God is Eternal Life Through Jesus Christ Our Lord."

Rom. 8: 1,2 "There is therefore now no condemnation to them which are in Christ Jesus, who walk not after the flesh, but after the Spirit. For The Law Of The Spirit Of Life In Christ Jesus hath made me free from the law of sin and death."

Rom. 8: 11 "But if the Spirit of Him that raised up Jesus from the dead dwell IN you, He that raised up Christ from the dead shall also quicken your mortal bodies by His Spirit that dwelleth IN you."

Rom. 8: 28 "And we know that all things work together for good to them that love God, to them who are The Called according to His purpose."

Rom. 8: 31,32 "What shall we then say to these things? If God be for us, who can be against us? He that spared not His Own Son, but delivered Him up for us all, how shall He not with Him also freely give us all things?"

Rom. 10: 17 "So then Faith cometh by hearing, and hearing by the Word Of God."

Rom. 12: 21 "Be not overcome of evil, but overcome evil with Good."

1 Corinthians

Introduction

The Epistles of Paul, like the prophecies of Jeremiah or Amos, were often called out by the mistakes, errors, and sins of the churches which he had planted, and were intended to correct them. The newly planted churches were in the midst of heathens and were composed in great part of those who had early heathen training. It is not wonderful that converts from such populations, unused to Christian morality, knowing little of the Old Testament Scriptures,

and without the New Testament, should sometimes go astray, or become the victims of false teachers. Yet the church of all ages has reason to be thankful for the circumstances which called out the collection of Inspired Letters on practical Christian life so essential to its instructions as we find in the Epistles of Paul. In order to gain the greatest profit from these it is necessary that the reader be informed concerning the conditions which called out each letter, what were the circumstances of each church, what were the wants the Apostle sought to supply and the sins he sought to correct.

CONDITIONS AT CORINTH

I will endeavor to explain in the case of the church at Corinth, what were these conditions. Though letters were written to other churches planted by Paul earlier than the one we are now considering, the First Epistle to the church of Corinth is the first of the letters of this class that we reach in the present arrangement of the New Testament. In the eighteenth chapter of Acts the account is found of the planting of this church.

1 Corinthians

1 Corinthians, continued

Introduction, continued

CONDITIONS AT CORINTH, CONTINUED

At that time, about A.D. 54, the Apostle sojourned in that great city for the space of a year and six months, preaching at first in the synagogue and afterwards in the house of Justus. A large congregation was gathered as the result of his labors, composed in part of Jews, but with a much larger number of Gentiles. After Paul departed to other fields of labor Apollos, an eloquent and learned Alexandrian Jew who has been instructed in the gospel by Priscilla and Aquila, the companions of Paul, visited Corinth and continued the work. Paul "planted, Apollos watered" (1 Cor. 3: 6).

The congregation which had begun its career so auspiciously was in a great commercial center, with a mixed and dissolute population, and could not but meet with many temptations. The city, situated on the Isthmus which connected southern Greece with the mainland of Europe, with the advantage of two harbors on either sea, and of a citadel as impregnable as Gibraltar on the lofty Acrocorinthus, had for centuries been influential in Grecian history but had in 146 B.C. been taken by the Romans and reduced to ruins. One hundred years later Julius Cæsar had founded it a second time, planting a Roman military colony on the old site, and the commanding situation soon restored its ancient

prosperity and splendor. It was about a century after its second founding that it was visited by Paul. It was then the great commercial city in Europe with the exception of Rome, and no cities of the East surpassed it save Antioch and Alexandria. It is estimated to have had a population of about four hundred thousand people, as cosmopolitan as is usually found in a great commercial center; Romans, Greeks, Jews, Syrians, Egyptians, sailors, traders, and slaves.

It would be strange if there was a high standard of morals in the mixed population of a commercial metropolis, nor were morals held in high regard anywhere in the heathen world. One fact will illustrate the shameless condition of the city. At the date of this Epistle there was standing there a vast and renowned temple of Venus, called the temple of Aphrodite Pandemos, "the Venus of all the people," which had a thousand consecrated priestesses, every priestess dedicated to the service of Aphrodite, or in other words to harlotry. The temple of worship, consecrated to religion, was a gigantic brothel! Indeed, even in that dissolute age when immorality was the rule in all the heathen world, Corinth had so bad an eminence that the word "to Corinthianize" had become a synonym for an impure life. It is not wonderful that amid such influences some of the Gentiles who had become members of the Corinthian Church showed the influence of their old habits, nor that the apostle found it necessary to rebuke licentiousness again and again.

But what especially called out this Epistle were the tidings of divisions in the church which had been brought to him at Ephesus by members of the household of Chloe, one of the principal members. Paul had confined himself while at Corinth to the simple principles of the gospel and scrupulously abstained from the philosophical discussions so dear to the Greek mind (1 Cor. 1: 17–22; 2: 1–5). Apollos, schooled in the philosophy of Alexandria, and not yet so thoroughly grounded in the gospel as Paul, evidently engaged in some philosophical speculations. It is also manifest that some of the Judaizing teachers who constantly followed in the footsteps of the great Apostle and sought to Judaize the churches, had come to Corinth, and by exalting Peter, in order to depreciate Paul, had formed another party. Hence there were various factions whose discords rent the body of Christ; one party claiming to be Pauline; another making Apollos its leader; still another claiming to be of Cephas, and still a fourth, whatever it may have been, claiming to be of Christ. The four chapters of the Epistle, the first in order, are a vigorous indignant and arraignment of these schisms.

Other questions discussed were suggested to him by a letter brought to him at Ephesus by Corinthian brethren begging a solution of various difficulties; on marriage, the veiling of women in assemblies, on sacrificial feasts, and perhaps on the nature of the resurrection from the dead.

This Epistle was written at Ephesus while Paul was engaged in his ministry of three years in that city (Acts 19: 1–41; Acts 20: 31; 1 Cor. 16: 8). The time when it was written can be determined with no little certainty to have been the spring of A.D. 57. That this Epistle is genuine has been conceded by all respectable critics, both ancient and modern.

B.W. Johnson, *The People's New Testament*

Verses of encouragement

1 Cor. 1: 30 "But of Him are ye in Christ Jesus, Who of God is made unto us Wisdom, and Righteousness, and Sanctification, and Redemption."

1 Cor. 2: 7 "But we speak the Wisdom Of God in a mystery, even the Hidden Wisdom, which God ordained before the world unto our Glory."

1 Cor. 2: 9 "But as it is written, Eye hath not seen, nor ear heard, neither have entered into the heart of man, The Things which God hath prepared for them that love Him."

1 Cor. 2: 14 "But the natural man receiveth not The Things of the Spirit of God: for they are foolishness unto him: neither can he know them, because they are Spiritually discerned."

1 Cor. 2: 16 "For who hath known the mind of the Lord, that he may instruct Him? But we have The Mind Of Christ."

1 Corinthians, 2 Corinthians

1 Corinthians, continued

Verses of encouragement, continued

1 Cor. 3: 21–23 "Therefore let no man glory in men. For all things are yours; Whether Paul, or Apollos, or Cephas, or the world, or life, or death, or things present, or things to come; all are yours; And ye are Christ's; and Christ is God's."

1 Cor. 4: 20 "For the Kingdom of God is not in word, but in Power."

1 Cor. 6: 14 "And God hath both raised up the Lord, and will also raise up us by His Own Power."

1 Cor. 10: 16 "The Cup Of Blessing which we bless, is it not The Communion Of The Blood Of Christ? The Bread which we break, is it not The Communion Of The Body Of Christ?"

1 Cor. 13: 1–7 "Though I speak with the tongues of men and of angels, and have not Charity, I am become as sounding brass, or a tinkling cymbal. And though I have the gift of prophecy, and understand all mysteries, and all knowledge; and though I have all faith, so that I could remove mountains, and have not Charity, I am nothing. And though I bestow all my goods to feed the poor, and though I give my body to be burned, and have not Charity, it profiteth me nothing. Charity suffereth long, and is kind; Charity envieth not; Charity vaunteth not Itself, is not puffed up, Doth not behave Itself unseemly, seeketh not Her own, is not easily provoked, thinketh no evil; Rejoiceth not in iniquity, but rejoiceth in the Truth; Beareth all things, believeth all things, hopeth all things, endureth all things."

1 Cor. 15: 57,58 "But thanks be to God, Which giveth us the VICTORY through our Lord Jesus Christ. Therefore, my beloved brethren, be ye stedfast, unmoveable, always abounding in the work of the Lord, forasmuch as ye know that your labor is not in vain in the Lord."

2 Corinthians

Introduction

The second Letter to the Church at Corinth is the supplement of the first. It is due to the same circumstances which called out the first, and to the effects that were produced in the church at Corinth by the receipt of the first letter. We can almost be thankful for the disorders which occasioned these two letters, not only on account of the rich fund of practical instruction which they contain, but on account of the picture which they present of a Gentile Church, composed of those who had so recently been heathen, in the first century of Christianity. They recall us to the immorality which had to be overcome, the obstacles in the way of a Christian life, and the mighty triumph which the gospel achieved over human nature itself in establishing the spiritual reign of Christ where the sensuality of heathen worship had before prevailed.

The first letter was written at Ephesus in the spring of A.D. 57; the second was written a few months later at some point in Macedonia where Paul had journeyed to visit the churches of that province before extending his tour to Corinth. We learn from the nineteenth and twentieth chapters of Acts that not long after the first letter was written, Demetrius and his fellow-craftsman aroused the terrible riot at Ephesus in which Paul so nearly lost his life (2 Cor. 1: 8–10), and that immediately after, at the urgency of the brethren, he started on his long contemplated journey to visit the churches of Europe. He had expected to meet Titus at Troas with word from Corinth concerning the effect of his first letter and was greatly disappointed when he did not find him there (2 Cor. 2: 13). Hence, although a fine opening for planting the gospel was presented, he pressed on to Macedonia. Here he met Titus, who was on his way to him, and was greatly rejoiced when he learned that his letter had been well received and his commands obeyed (2 Cor. 7: 5–7). Still the circumstances required another letter before his coming and the second letter was written, not only to express his joy over the better state of things in the church, but in order to convey further counsels.

DIVISIONS

This Epistle naturally divides itself into three parts. In the first part, embracing chapters 1–7, the Apostle portrays his feelings over the condition of matters in Corinth, his anxiety, and his relief after the coming of Titus; in chapters 8, 9, the second part, he takes up the great collection of the Gentile churches for the poor at Jerusalem on which he had so deeply set his heart; in the third part, chapters 10–13, he repels the insinuations of Judaizing teachers who were seeking, not only in Corinth but everywhere, to destroy Paul's influence so as to bring the churches under the bondage of the Jewish law. In this section he presents those wonderful details concerning what his service of Christ had cost him in earthly sufferings.

The whole letter is written in the expectation of soon being at Corinth, an expectation which we know from Acts, chapter 20 was realized.

B.W. Johnson, The People's New Testament

Verses of encouragement

2 Cor. 2: 14 "Now thanks be unto God, which always causeth us to TRIUMPH in Christ, and maketh manifest the savor of His Knowledge by us in every place."

2 Cor. 3: 6 "Who also hath made us able ministers of the New Testament; not of the letter, but of the Spirit: for the letter killeth, but the Spirit giveth Life."

2 Cor. 3: 17,18 "Now the Lord is that Spirit: and where the Spirit of the Lord is, there is Liberty. . . .

2 Corinthians, Galatians

2 Corinthians, continued

Verses of encouragement, continued

...But we all, with open face beholding as in a glass the Glory Of The Lord, are changed into the Same Image from glory to glory, even as by the Spirit of the Lord."

2 Cor. 4: 18 "While we look not at the things which are seen, but at the things which are not seen: for the things which are seen are temporal; but the things which are not seen are Eternal."

2 Cor. 5: 7 "(For we walk by Faith, not by sight:)."

2 Cor. 5: 17 "Therefore if any man be in Christ, he is a New Creature: old things are passed away; behold, all things are become new."

2 Cor. 5: 21 "For He hath made Him to be sin for us, Who knew no sin; that we might be made The Righteousness Of God in Him."

Galatians

Introduction

This Epistle differs from most of those written by Paul, in that it is not addressed specially to the church in some great city, but to the churches throughout a district of the Roman Empire. Galatia will be seen on any map of the empire in the apostolic period in the interior of the great peninsula called Asia Minor, which was the theater of so large a part of the labors of Paul. The people were of the Gallic stock, had marched from the Rhine to Greece, and thence into Asia about 280 B.C., and had conquered a home in the interior of Asia Minor, which henceforth took a new name from the people (Galli, or Gauls) who made it their seat. They learned the Greek language, but retained in part their old tongue and the traits of their race. Cæsar describes the Gauls as restless and changeable, characteristics still of the French, and this epistle shows that the Galatians were not unlike their European kinsmen.

It was on Paul's second great missionary tour, about A.D. 51, that he in company with Silas and Timothy passed through from Lycaonia in Phrygia and Galatia, and planted the seeds of the Christian faith (Acts 16: 6). On his third missionary journey, about A.D. 54 or 55, he "went over all the country of Galatia and Phrygia in order, strengthening all the disciples" (Acts 18: 23). The gospel was received with great readiness; and the apostle himself welcomed as "an angel of God" (Gal. 4: 14). A part of the converts were no doubt Jews of whom, according to Josephus, there were many in Galatia, but the greater part were Gentiles.

The Epistles of Paul were mostly called out by evils in the churches which he had planted which called for correction. That to the Galatians is not an exception. At a period not long after his second visit tidings came to him that excited his alarm and indignation. That restless wing of the church which clung to Judaism as well as Christianity, which had troubled the church at Antioch (Acts 15: 1), which had made necessary the council at Jerusalem (Acts 15: 5–30), whose evil work at Corinth we note in both Epistles, but especially in the second, whose continual warfare made one of Paul's sorest afflictions "perils among false brethren," had sent its emissaries into Galatia and had taught that it was needful that the Gentile Christians be circumcised and submit to the law of Moses in order to be saved. In order to carry their end they also insisted that Paul was not a true apostle, or was at least inferior to the original Twelve who had seen Christ and been instructed by him in person. It is true that in the Council at Jerusalem they had been defeated, but they kept up their work, and it required a life long struggle on the part of Paul to emancipate the church from Judaism. These men seemed to follow him everywhere, and a considerable part of his epistles is devoted to correcting the errors due to their influence.

The Galatian letter is an indignant protest against and refutation of the Judaizing teachers. In the first two chapters he shows that his apostleship was not derived from the other apostles, but from Christ; that the gospel that he taught was not revealed to him by them, but by his Lord; that he had never met them as an inferior, but on an equal footing; that it was agreed between them that Peter, James, and John would devote their labors to the Circumcision, while he and Barnabas should go to the Uncircumcision, and that on one occasion it was needful for him to rebuke and correct Peter on the very question of the proper attitude toward Gentile Christians.

In the Second Part of the Letter, chapters 3 and 4, he contrasts the free gospel salvation by a living faith in Christ with the slavish legalism of the false teachers who would virtually place Moses in the stead of Christ. The Third Part, the 5th and 6th chapters, is devoted mainly to practical duties which grow out of the gospel.

The Place where written and the Date of the Epistle can be determined only approximately. It must have been written after Paul's two visits to Galatia, the last of which was in A.D. 54 or 55. It must have been written not very long after the second visit.

There are many points of resemblance between Epistle and that to the Romans which indicate that they were written nearly at the same time; since this epistle is the less elaborate, it was probably written first. There are also points of resemblance to Second Corinthians which indicate that they belong to the same period. All these facts point to the last year of the Third Missionary Journey, or about A.D. 57. As we learn from Acts that this period was spent in Ephesus, Macedonia, and Corinth, it must have been written at one of these places.

Galatians, Ephesians

Galatians, continued

Introduction

It only remains to say concerning its Genuineness, "that the internal evidences of the authorship of Paul is so strong that no sane divine has ever denied or even doubted it" (*Schaff*). There is no other writer of the early church who could have written it. It bears the Pauline stamp in every line.

B.W. Johnson, The People's New Testament

St. Paul wrote this epistle because, after his departure from the Galatian churches, Jewish-Christian fanatics moved in, who perverted Paul's Gospel of man's free justification by faith in Christ Jesus.

The world bears the Gospel a grudge because the Gospel condemns the religious wisdom of the world. Jealous for its own religious views, the world in turn charges the Gospel with being a subversive and licentious doctrine, offensive to God and man, a doctrine to be persecuted as the worst plague on earth.

As a result we have this paradoxical situation: The Gospel supplies the world with the salvation of Jesus Christ, peace of conscience, and every blessing. Just for that the world abhors the Gospel.

These Jewish-Christian fanatics who pushed themselves into the Galatian churches after Paul's departure, boasted that they were the descendants of Abraham, true ministers of Christ, having been trained by the apostles themselves, that they were able to perform miracles.

Against these boasting, false apostles, Paul boldly defends his apostolic authority and ministry. Humble man that he was, he will not now take a back seat. He reminds them of the time when he opposed Peter to his face and reproved the chief of the apostles.

Martin Luther

Verses of encouragement

Gal. 2: 20 "I am crucified with Christ: nevertheless I live; yet not I, but Christ liveth in me: and The Life which I now live in the flesh I live by The Faith of the Son of God, Who loved me, and gave Himself for me."

Gal. 3: 7,9 "Know ye therefore that they which are of Faith, the same are the children of Abraham... So then they which be of Faith are blessed with faithful Abraham."

Gal. 3: 11 "But that no man is justified by the Law in the sight of God, it is evident: for, The Just shall live by Faith."

Gal. 3: 13,14 "Christ hath redeemed us from the curse of the Law, being made A Curse for us: for it is written, Cursed is every one that hangeth on a tree: That The Blessing Of Abraham might come on the Gentiles through Jesus Christ; that we might receive The Promise Of The Spirit through faith."

Gal. 3: 29 "And if ye be Christ's, then are ye Abraham's seed, and heirs according to The Promise."

Gal. 4: 7 "Wherefore thou art no more a servant, but a son; and if a son, then an heir of God through Christ."

Gal. 5: 13,14 "For, brethren, ye have been called unto Liberty; only use not Liberty for an occasion to the flesh, but by Love serve one another. For all the Law is fulfilled in one Word, even in this; Thou shalt love thy neighbor as thyself."

Gal. 5: 16 "This I say then, Walk in the Spirit, and ye shall not fulfill the lust of the flesh."

Gal. 5: 22,23 "But The Fruit Of The Spirit is Love, Joy, Peace, Longsuffering, Gentleness, Goodness, Faith, Meekness, Temperance: against such there is no Law."

Gal. 6: 7–10 "Be not deceived; God is not mocked: for whatsoever a man soweth, that shall he also reap. For he that soweth to his flesh shall of the flesh reap corruption; but he that soweth to the Spirit shall of the Spirit reap Life Everlasting. And let us not be weary in well doing: for in Due Season we shall reap, if we faint not. As we have therefore opportunity, let us do good unto all men, especially unto them who are of The Household Of Faith."

Ephesians

Introduction

Critical students of the New Testament are not in agreement concerning the Epistle upon the study of which we now enter. Their difference is not concerning its right to a place in the sacred Scriptures, nor concerning its authorship, but whether it was addressed by Paul to the church at Ephesus, or to some other church. The reasons which have suggested a doubt are briefly as follows: One of the three most ancient and trusted manuscripts, the Vatican, omits at Ephesus in the first verse; the heretic Marcion, in the third century, ascribes it to the Laodiceans; Basil, in the fourth century, speaks of the absence of the words at Ephesus in the manuscript; in chapter 1: 15, Paul speaks as if his knowledge of the Ephesians had been gained by report rather than by personal acquaintance; and in Col. 4: 16, Paul speaks of an Epistle to the Laodiceans, which has been lost unless this be the Epistle of which he speaks. These facts had such weight with the authors of Conybeare and Howson's *Life of Paul* that they affirm the "one thing certain to be that the Epistle was not directed to the Ephesians."

But, in the Vatican, as well as in all other most valued manuscripts, the heading is The Epistle of Paul to the Ephesians; in the Vatican the words "at Ephesus," are not in in verse 1, and are only supplied in the margin.

Ephesians

Ephesians, continued

Introduction

No manuscript is in existence which supplies these words by any other name; in the second century, at a time when there could have been no doubt about the facts, it is spoken of by the Fathers as "The Epistle to the Ephesians," as though the matter was not under discussion; the remark of Paul in 1:15, about hearing of their faith, has an exact parallel in Philemon 5, and yet Philemon was his own convert (verse 19), and is entirely natural when we remember that several years had passed since he had last seen them; the absence of at Ephesus in a few manuscripts of the fourth century, and in the Vatican, as well as all other difficulties, can be explained without the necessity of denying that the Epistle was addressed to the Ephesians. Hence the great majority of critics have agreed in following the authority of existing manuscripts and of the ancient church in the statement that the Epistle was addressed to the great congregation founded by its writer in the capital of proconsular Asia, which had enjoyed his apostolic labors for a longer period than any other of which a record has come down to us.

The city of Ephesus, a Grecian city on the Asiatic coast almost exactly east of Athens, was a great commercial metropolis in the first century, and the capital of the Roman province which was called by the name of Asia. Its greatest distinction hitherto had been, not its commercial pre-eminence, but the splendid temple of Diana, which was counted one of the Seven Wonders of the world. The city lay upon the edge of a plain, which extended to the sea, and in its artificial harbor were seen the ships from all the ports of the eastern Mediterranean. In our times, half-buried ruins are the only relics of its former greatness. We can still see the proofs of its former magnificence in the outlines of the great theater (Acts 19: 29), and in the ruins of the temple of Diana (Acts 19: 27). The modern Turkish village of Agasalouk, a wretched hamlet, is nearly two miles distant from the site of the Ephesus of the times of Paul.

The Ephesian church was virtually founded by Paul. About the close of his second missionary journey (Acts 18: 19–21) he paused at Ephesus on his way to Jerusalem and preached in the Jewish synagogue. Leaving Priscilla and Aquila to follow up the impression which he had made, he went on, but returned on his third missionary journey (Acts 19: 1), at which time he spent about three years (Acts 20: 31), preaching the gospel with a success which threatened to effect an entire revolution in the city and province (Acts 19: 17–20), and finally stirred up the avaricious fears of certain trades which profited by the old superstitions to such an extent that a commotion was aroused which caused him to leave the city. Since that date he had not seen Ephesus, though he had met the elders of the church at Miletus when on his way to Jerusalem (Acts 20: 17).

It is not possible to determine the date of this Epistle with exactness. It was written at a time when Paul was a prisoner (6: 20), and hence must have been written either at Cæsarea or at Rome. Meyer inclines to the first place, but the general consensus of opinion is that it belongs to the group of the Epistles which were sent forth from his Roman prison. Tychicus was the messenger to whom, on the same journey, were entrusted both this (6: 21) and the Epistle to Colosse (Col. 4: 7).

It was probably written to meet certain difficulties which were arising in the church. It was asked why the imperfections of Judaism and the errors of the Gentile religions existed so many ages before the gospel was revealed? Was the gospel an afterthought of God? Probably the leading thought is that, "The church of Jesus Christ, in which Jew and Gentile are made one, is a creation of the Father, through the Son, in the Holy Spirit, decreed from eternity, and destined for eternity." In chapters 1–3, he shows the church was foreordained of God, that it had been redeemed, and that Jew and Gentile have been made one in Christ. In chapters 4–6, the Apostle enters upon a practical application, enforcing unity, love, newness of life, walking in the strength of the Lord, and the armor of God.

B.W. Johnson, *The People's New Testament*

Verses of encouragement

Eph. 1: 3 "Blessed be the God and Father of our Lord Jesus Christ, Who hath blessed us with All Spiritual Blessings in Heavenly Places in Christ."

Eph. 1: 17–28 "That the God of our Lord Jesus Christ, the Father Of Glory, may give unto you The Spirit Of Wisdom And Revelation in the Knowledge Of Him: The eyes of your understanding being Enlightened; that ye may know what is The Hope Of His Calling, and what The Riches Of The Glory Of His Inheritance in the saints."

Eph. 2: 6–8 "And hath raised us up together, and made us sit together in Heavenly Places in Christ Jesus: That in the ages to come He might shew The Exceeding Riches Of His Grace In His Kindness Toward Us through Christ Jesus. For by Grace are ye saved through Faith; and that not of yourselves: it is The Gift of God."

Eph. 2: 10 "For we are His Workmanship, created in Christ Jesus unto Good Works, which God hath before ordained that we should walk in Them."

Eph. 3: 8 "Unto me, who am less than the least of all saints, is this Grace given, that I should preach among the Gentiles The Unsearchable Riches Of Christ."

Ephesians, Philippians

Ephesians, continued

Verses of encouragement, continued

Eph. 3: 16–20 "That He would grant you, according to The Riches Of His Glory, to be strengthened with Might by His Spirit in the inner man; That Christ may dwell in your hearts by Faith; that ye, being rooted and grounded in Love, May be able to comprehend with all saints what is the breadth, and length, and depth, and height; And to know the Love Of Christ, which passeth knowledge, that ye might be filled with all The Fullness Of God. Now unto Him that is able to do Exceeding Abundantly Above All That We Ask Or Think, according to The Power That Worketh In Us."

Eph. 4: 15 "But speaking the Truth in Love, may grow up into Him in all things, which is The Head, even Christ."

Eph. 4: 27 "Neither give place to the devil."

Eph. 4: 29,30 "Let no corrupt communication proceed out of your mouth, but that which is Good to the use of Edifying, that it may minister Grace unto the hearers. And grieve not The Holy Spirit Of God, whereby ye are sealed unto the Day Of Redemption."

Eph. 4: 32 "And be ye Kind one to another, Tenderhearted, forgiving one another, even as God for Christ's sake hath forgiven you."

Eph. 5: 20 "Giving thanks always for all things unto God and the Father in the Name of our Lord Jesus Christ."

Eph. 6: 12,13 "For we wrestle not against flesh and blood, but against principalities, against powers, against the rulers of the darkness of this world, against spiritual wickedness in high places. Wherefore take unto you The Whole Armor Of God, that ye may be able to withstand in the evil day, and having done all, to stand."

Eph. 6: 16 "Above all, taking The Shield Of Faith, wherewith ye shall be able to quench ALL the fiery darts of the wicked."

Philippians

Introduction

This letter is the outpouring of the love of the founder of the Philippian Church toward one of the most affectionate, faithful, and self-forgetful of all congregations which he had planted. It has been remarked that there is no breath of censure for the Philippian saints, except in so far as it is implied in the tender exhortation to Euodias and Syntyche found in chap. 4: 2. The history of the origin of the church and the memory of the loving remembrances of the Philippians help to explain the affectionate tenderness of the letter.

The account of the founding of the church at Philippi, which occurred in

A.D. 50 or 51, is given in the sixteenth chapter of Acts. Led by a vision at Troas the apostle, on his second great missionary journey, crossed into Europe, landing at Neapolis, and proceeding from thence at once to Philippi, which was "the chief city of that part of Macedonia." This city had already some claims to a place in history. It received its name from Philip of Macedon, the father of Alexander the Great, who added to his dominions the little Thracian town which existed there before, rebuilt and fortified it, and gave it its new name in the year 358 B.C.. In 42 B.C., about ninety-two years before Paul visited it, it was the field of the decisive battle between Brutus and Cassius, the leaders of the Republicans, and the Triumvirate of Imperialists, one of whom was subsequently Augustus Cæsar. But the place has a higher interest to the Christian world from the fact that here was planted the first congregation of Christians that ever existed on the soil of Europe.

It was not only the scene of gospel triumphs but of suffering for the cross of Christ. Here it was that Paul and Silas were beaten, cast into the stocks in the inner prison, by the grace of God converted and baptized their jailer and his household before the dawn, and were honorably released by the magistrates in the morning, as Roman citizens, unjustly beaten and imprisoned. When Paul continued his journey westward, the recently founded Philippian church followed him with support, contributing more than once to his necessities (4: 15,16), and when the tidings came that he was

a prisoner in Rome their old affection showed itself still again by sending one of their members, Epaphroditus, with the offerings of the church as a provision for his wants (2: 25; 4: 10–18). It seems to have been the return of Epaphroditus from this ministration of their love, to which we are indebted for this letter.

It was written from the city of Rome, during the first imprisonment of Paul, and probably toward its close, perhaps in the year A.D. 63. The mention of his bonds (1: 12), of the Prætorian camp of Cæsar's household (4: 22), as well as other allusions (1: 25; 2: 24) all show that Paul was in the Roman capital at the time of writing.

This epistle has always been accepted by the church. It is Pauline in doctrine, and in diction, abounds probably to a greater extent than other epistles in personal details, and is in full agreement with all the historical facts which can be gathered from the history of the times, and from the allusions in Acts and the other epistles. It bears every mark of having been written by Paul from the scene of his imprisonment to the beloved church which he had planted and for which he had suffered.

B.W. Johnson, *The People's New Testament*

Philippians, Colossians

Philippians, continued

Verses of encouragement

Php 1: 6 "Being confident of this very thing, that He Which Hath Begun A Good Work In You will perform it until the day of Jesus Christ."

Php 3: 1 "Finally, my brethren, Rejoice in the Lord. To write the same things to you, to me indeed is not grievous, but for you it is safe."

Php 3: 14–15 "I press toward the mark for The Prize Of The High Calling of God in Christ Jesus. Let us therefore, as many as be Perfect, be thus minded: and if in any thing ye be otherwise minded, God shall reveal even this unto you."

Php 4: 1 "Therefore, my brethren dearly beloved and longed for, my Joy and Crown, so stand fast in the Lord, my dearly beloved."

Php 4: 4 "Rejoice in the Lord alway: and again I say, Rejoice."

Colossians

Introduction

Colosse was a city of considerable size more than four hundred years before the date of this letter, when visited by Xenophon as the Ten Thousand marched up into Central Asia, and is mentioned by Herodotus still earlier. At this time, however, it was overshadowed in importance by

Laodicea, and at the present the ruins are less imposing than those of either Laodicea or Hierapolis.

We learn in the Sixteenth Chapter of Acts that Paul, on his second missionary journey, passed from Cilicia through the pass in the great Taurus chain of mountains, which has always been the highway from the coast to the interior; paused a little while in Lydia; took Timothy in his train of attendants, and then passed through Phrygia and Galatia. And, a second time, after his European tour, he returned and "went over all the country of Phrygia and Galatia, strengthening the disciples" (Acts 18: 23). Yet it is probable that he did not personally plant the gospel in Colosse, and possibly did not even pass through the valley of the Lycus. The words of Chapter 2: 1, are understood to mean that he had never met with the church in person, and indeed there is a marked difference between the tone of this letter and the familiar personal appeals of letters addressed to churches that he had certainly planted, like those of Philippi and Galatia.

Besides, Epaphras seems to be named (1: 7) as the founder, or at least the evangelist, of the church. Yet, since Epaphras must have been one of his own converts, and was working under his general supervision, Paul held himself responsible for its condition, and looked after its welfare, as after all the churches planted within the sphere of his labors.

It is easy to discover from certain portions of the letter why it was written. Phrygia was a sort of border land between religions. The light, joyous polytheism of the Greeks here met the deep, solemn mysticism of the East. In addition, large colonies of Jews had been transplanted from Babylon to this region by one of the Macedonian monarchs of Syria, and brought with them a Judaism which had been greatly modified by the doctrines of Zoroaster. The Epistle gives us ample ground for concluding that there was danger of these mongrel philosophies corrupting the simplicity of the gospel of Christ, and that Paul's object was to fortify the church against doctrine which would result in evil.

Concerning the genuineness of this Epistle, it has always had a place in the New Testament canon, and has never been questioned except by Baur, and some other critics of the Tubingen school who have thought that it gave too high an exaltation to Christ. This might be answered by replying that it exalts Christ no more than Philippians and other Epistles which are conceded to be of Pauline origin. Their theories have been overthrown not only by historical arguments, but by the internal evidence of the Epistle itself. Indeed, as Meyer remarks, "the forging of such an Epistle as this would be far more wonderful than its genuineness."

It was written at Rome, during Paul's imprisonment, probably in A.D. 62, the same date as Ephesians and Philemon, and was sent to the church by the hands of Tychicus (4: 7) and Onesimus (4: 9).

B.W. Johnson, *The People's New Testament*

Verses of encouragement

Col. 1: 13–14 "Who hath delivered us from the power of darkness, and hath translated us into the Kingdom of His dear Son: In Whom we have Redemption through His Blood, even the Forgiveness of sins."

Col. 1: 20 "And, having made Peace through The Blood Of His Cross, by Him to reconcile all things unto Himself; by Him, I say, whether they be things in earth, or things in Heaven."

Col. 2: 3 "In Whom are hid all The Treasures of Wisdom and Knowledge."

Col. 2: 6,7 "As ye have therefore received Christ Jesus the Lord, so walk ye in Him: Rooted and built up in Him, and established in the Faith, as ye have been taught, abounding therein with Thanksgiving."

Col. 2: 15 "And having spoiled principalities and powers, He made a shew of them openly, triumphing over them in it."

1 Thessalonians

Introduction

This epistle bears the distinction of being the first in the order of time of the letters written by the Apostle Paul which have been preserved. Indeed it is the earliest of any of the epistolary Books of the New Testament, the beginning of that body of writing to which the churches are so much indebted. It was written at least five or six years before the great doctrinal and ecclesiastical treatises known as the Roman, Galatian, and the Corinthian Letters, and with the Second Letter to the Thessalonians which followed it by only a few months, it shares the distinction of being the only epistles that came into existence before the beginning of Paul's third great missionary journey. These epistles, so long antedating the others, differ also from them in character.

Written only a short time after the church at Thessalonica was founded, and called forth by the trials and needs of a young congregation which he felt it in his heart to visit again, but was prevented, they illustrate the apostolic instruction given to a newly organized church, composed of Gentiles, suffering under the persecution of both Jewish and heathen adversaries. They are fresh in allusion to the experiences of Paul while among them, and reveal his deep solicitude when forced away.

When the apostle, on his third missionary journey, passed into Europe, he first planted a church at Philippi, but after a little season was driven from there by heathen persecution. Then, attended by Silas and Timothy, he went westward along the great Egnatian Way, the Roman road which led through Greece to Macedonia.

He did not pause until he reached Thessalonica, nearly a hundred miles westward, the chief city of Macedonia, situated around a noble harbor at the head of the Aegean Sea. Its situation on the great Roman thoroughfare, its position on the extremity of the sea, and the rich country in its rear, had contributed to make it a great commercial city, with a mixed population of Greeks, Romans, and Jews, the first being the most numerous.

Here, where there was a synagogue, the apostle paused, found employment to meet his frugal wants, and began to preach among his own countrymen. "And some of them believed, and consorted with Paul and Silas; and of the devout Greeks a great multitude, and of the chief women not a few."

But soon after the unbelieving Jews stirred up an uproar which made it necessary for Paul and Silas to leave, and the brethren sent them away by night. Going from thence to Berea to the southwest, they first labored there, and later the apostolic labors were extended to Athens and to Corinth. Shortly after Paul's departure from Thessalonica, the persecutions which had driven him away turned upon the church (2: 14; 3: 3), a circumstance that made him yearn to return (3: 5). Twice he resolved to do so but was prevented (2:18). Finally he sent back Timothy from Athens (3:1, 2), and when Timothy returned to him at Corinth, to which he had proceeded, the message which he brought was the occasion of this epistle, an epistle full of comfort, instruction and encouragement, but withal, containing also the instruction in righteousness so much needed by a congregation of those so recently heathen and addicted to heathen vices.

It is interesting to know that this church, honored with the first of the apostolic epistles, long continued to enjoy a glorious history. It was afterwards visited by the apostle more than once; and is often mentioned in the history of the church.

Though for more than four hundred years under the sway of the Turk, the majority of its population has always continued to profess the religion of Christ. The city is still great and flourishing, in point of commerce the third in the Turkish empire, possessing a population estimated all the way from 75,000 to 100,000. Of these about one-half are Greek Christians, and the remainder nearly equally divided between Mohammedans and Jews. The excellence of the harbor makes it a constant object of eastern diplomacy, and at this time one of the obstacles in the way of settling the "Eastern Question" is to determine what power shall be awarded Thessalonica.

As to the date of the epistle, it can be nearly determined. About A.D. 52, the church here was planted. From thence the apostle went to Berea and Athens. From the latter, probably several months after leaving Thessalonica, he sent Timothy back.

Several months more would intervene before Timothy could return at Corinth. It is therefore probable that the letter was written in A.D. 53, perhaps at least a year after the planting of the church.

B.W. Johnson, *The People's New Testament*

Verses of encouragement

1 Thess. 4: 16,17 "For the Lord Himself shall descend from Heaven with a shout, with the voice of the Archangel, and with The Trump of God: and the dead in Christ shall rise first: Then we which are alive and remain shall be caught up together with them in the clouds, to meet the Lord in the air: and so shall we ever be with the Lord."

1 Thess. 5: 9,10 "For God hath not appointed us to wrath, but to obtain Salvation by our Lord Jesus Christ, Who died for us, that, whether we wake or sleep, we should live together with Him."

1 Thess. 5: 15–18 "See that none render evil for evil unto any man; but ever follow that which is Good, both among yourselves, and to all men. Rejoice evermore. Pray without ceasing. In every thing give thanks: for this is The Will Of God In Christ Jesus concerning you."

2 Thessalonians, 1 Timothy

2 Thessalonians

Introduction

The circumstances connected with the planting of the Church at Thessalonica, the character of the surroundings, and the trials of the young Christian brotherhood have all been explained in the introduction to the preceding epistle, to which I refer the reader. Those circumstances called for a second letter, which must have followed the first after an interval of only a few months, the only instance save that of the Corinthian letters in which the apostle directed two successive epistles to the same congregation.

That the Second Epistle is followed soon after the First is indicated (1) by the fact that almost the same state of affairs is described in each: There was persecution and trial, there was an eager expectation of the speedy Advent of the Lord, excepting that in the Second Epistle the excitement had led to greater extremes, and in each certain ones are described who were neglecting their ordinary employments as unnecessary in view of the Lord's coming. Compare 2 Thess. 3: 6–14 with 1 Thess. 4: 10–12, and 1 Thess. 2: 9. In the second place both Silas and Timothy were present with Paul at the writing of each epistle. Compare the opening salutations.

The reasons for writing the letter are apparent. The conditions that called out the preceding letter still existed,

and the information brought by the messenger who had carried the letter showed the need of further instruction. The principal object is to correct the erroneous belief that the day of the Lord's coming was very close at hand. This belief had received the more currency because some reported that Paul had so declared, and had even so stated in a letter. Hence he now shows that certain great events must precede that day, and that these events are yet future. He again enforces the teaching of the Lord that the time is unknown, and charges that all follow their usual employments.

This epistle, like the First, was evidently written during Paul's long stay at Corinth, and both may be assigned to the same year.

B.W. Johnson, The People's New Testament

Verses of encouragement

2 Thess. 1: 11,12 "Wherefore also we pray always for you, that our God would count you worthy of this calling, and fulfill all the good pleasure of his goodness, and the work of faith with power: That the name of our Lord Jesus Christ may be glorified in you, and ye in him, according to the grace of our God and the Lord Jesus Christ."

2 Thess. 2: 13–17 "But we are bound to give thanks alway to God for you, brethren beloved of the Lord, because God hath from the beginning chosen you to salvation through sanctification of the Spirit and belief

of the truth: Whereunto he called you by our gospel, to the obtaining of the glory of our Lord Jesus Christ. Therefore, brethren, stand fast, and hold the traditions which ye have been taught, whether by word, or our epistle. Now our Lord Jesus Christ himself, and God, even our Father, which hath loved us, and hath given us everlasting consolation and good hope through grace, Comfort your hearts, and stablish you in every good word and work."

2 Thess. 3: 3 "But the Lord is faithful, Who shall stablish you, and keep you from evil."

1 Timothy

Introduction

Four of the epistles of Paul are addressed to persons; one, that of Philemon, on personal matters; the other three to evangelists who had long labored under his directions, and who were charged at the time they were written with responsible trusts in which they needed his instructions. From the circumstance that Timothy and Titus were each exercising the care of the churches of a district these have been called the Pastoral epistles. Yet the words Shepherd or Pastor, flock, and feed do not occur in them, as they do in John 21: 16; Acts 20: 28; Eph. 4: 11; 1 Pet. 5: 2, but at the same time the duties implied in those relations are strongly urged. They deal more intimately with church organization and church culture, than any of the other epistles.

If the generally accepted view of the date of these three epistles is received they have the common feature of belonging to the closing years of the apostle's life. The epistles of Ephesians, Philippians, Colossians, and Philemon, are the epistles of the captivity. On the hypothesis of Paul's release from the first imprisonment at Rome, in accordance with the universal statement of the early church, these epistles are held to have been written after his release, and after he had once more made a tour of the churches which he planted in Asia and Europe. Certain allusions in these epistles can only be explained by assigning them a date as late as this. The apostle had, after a circuit of the churches of Asia Minor, come into Macedonia, and from thence sent back to Timothy, who had been left in charge of the work in the city and district of Ephesus, instructions and admonitions which would be of service to him in his duties. Well aware of the difficulties he would meet at Ephesus, of the factious spirit of certain false teachers, the epistle is written not only to show him how he ought to act, but in order to support him by its authority. It was probably writen a little more than a year before the apostle's martyrdom at Rome.

Timothy, to whom it is directed, was his own "son in the gospel." From the Acts and the Epistles the outlines of his history are easily gathered. He was born in the Asiatic district of Lycaonia. His father was a Greek but his mother a Jewess.

1 Timothy, 2 Timothy

1 Timothy, continued

Introduction, continued

From his infancy he was instructed by his mother and grandmother, who names have been preserved, in the Hebrew scriptures, but had remained, probably at the demand of his father, uncircumcised. Converted by Paul, showing good gifts among the Lycaonian churches, Paul determined to make him a traveling assistant, and as it would aid much in enabling him to reach Jews, he had him circumcised. Indeed a Mamzer, a "bastard," as a child of a Jewish mother and heathen father was called by the Jews, would have had no access to the synagogue without circumcision.

From this time the allusions to Timothy in connection with Paul's work are so frequent that, did space permit, we could easily trace his course. Finally, we find him attending Paul to Jerusalem on the occasion when Paul was made a captive. During the imprisonment at Cæsarea he was probably absent, sent to the churches by Paul, but after the arrival at Rome, as we learn from "the Epistles of the Captivity," he again joined him. He had probably attended him on his last tour of the churches of Asia, was left behind at Ephesus, was there the recipient of two letters, which are the last allusions to him in the New Testament, unless he be "the angel of the church of Ephesus" named in Rev. 2: 1, as some have supposed.

The genuineness of the Pastoral epistles was never questioned in the primitive church. It only remains to be added that nothing has ever been written which contains, in the same space, so much that is indispensable to the preacher, the pastor, and to every church official.

B.W. Johnson, *The People's New Testament*

Verses of encouragement

1 Tim. 1: 15 "This is a Faithful Saying, and worthy of all acceptation, that Christ Jesus came into the world to save sinners; of whom I am chief."

1 Tim. 1: 17 "Now unto The King Eternal, Immortal, Invisible, The Only Wise God, be honor and glory for ever and ever. Amen."

1 Tim. 2: 5 "For there is One God, and One Mediator between God and men, the man Christ Jesus."

1 Tim. 4: 8 "For bodily exercise profiteth little: but Godliness is profitable unto all things, having Promise of the life that now is, and of that which is to come."

1 Tim. 6: 6 "But Godliness with contentment is great gain."

1 Tim. 6: 11 "But thou, O man of God, flee these things; and follow after Righteousness, Godliness, Faith, Love, Patience, Meekness."

1 Tim. 6: 17,18 "Charge them that are rich in this world, that they be not high-minded, nor trust in uncertain riches, but in The Living God, Who giveth

us richly all things to enjoy; That they do Good, that they be rich in Good Works, ready to distribute, willing to communicate."

2 Timothy

Introduction

The Second Epistle to Timothy has a melancholy interest as the last letter which Paul ever wrote, written from his second imprisonment in Rome, only a short time before his martyrdom. In the Introduction to First Timothy the uniform first testimony of the early church that Paul was released, shortly after the close of Acts, and engaged for several years in missionary work, was stated. On this point the testimony is clear, and goes back even to Clement of Rome, a companion of Paul named in one of his epistles, who states in his Epistle to the Corinthians that Paul was enabled to carry out his purpose of preaching the gospel in the extreme West. This verdict of antiquity is supported by criticism, and the allusions in the three Pastoral epistles can only be explained by conceding that there was a release, a period of missionary activity, and finally a second arrest, and imprisonment in Rome.

Shortly after the first was written Paul is supposed to have again visited Ephesus, to have gone from thence, in company with Titus, to Crete. The latter was left in charge of the work there when Paul left for Europe (Titus 1: 5). Where the Epistle to Titus was written cannot be certainly known, but it was at some point on the route from Crete to Nicopolis, a city situated on the Grecian shore of the Adriatic Sea (Titus 3: 12). If Paul reached there for the winter, as he proposed, it is probable that here he was again arrested, and from thence borne to Rome to trial. The only writing extant that came from this second period of imprisonment is this letter.

Timothy, his "beloved son" in the gospel, was still laboring in distant Ephesus, but the aged apostle, about to go to rest from his weary labors, desired to see him once more in the flesh. Hence, he bids him come, as speedily as possible; but, lest he might arrive too late to receive his parting words, he impresses upon him in this letter, with the earnestness of a last charge, the various duties of his office, and especially of opposing the dangerous heresies which threatened to destroy the vitality Christianity.

B.W. Johnson, *The People's New Testament*

Verses of encouragement

2 Tim. 1: 7 "For God hath not given us the spirit of fear; but of Power, and of Love, and of a Sound Mind."

2 Tim. 2: 15 "Study to shew thyself approved unto God, a workman that needeth not to be ashamed, rightly dividing The Word Of Truth."

2 Timothy, Titus

2 Timothy, continued

Verses of encouragement

2 Tim. 2: 19 "Nevertheless the Foundation Of God standeth sure, having this seal, The Lord knoweth them that are His. And, Let every one that nameth The Name Of Christ depart from iniquity."

2 Tim. 2: 22 "Flee also youthful lusts: but follow Righteousness, Faith, Charity, Peace, with them that call on the Lord out of a pure heart."

2 Tim. 3: 16,17 "All Scripture is given by Inspiration Of God, and is profitable for Doctrine, for Reproof, for Correction, for Instruction In Righteousness: That the man of God may be Perfect, throughly furnished unto all Good Works."

2 Tim. 4: 2 "Preach the Word; be instant in season, out of season; Reprove, Rebuke, Exhort with all Longsuffering and Doctrine."

2 Tim. 4: 7,8 "I have fought a Good Fight, I have finished my Course, I have kept The Faith: Henceforth there is laid up for me a Crown Of Righteousness, which the Lord, The Righteous Judge, shall give me at that day: and not to me only, but unto all them also that Love His Appearing."

2 Tim. 4: 18 "And the Lord shall deliver me from every evil work, and will preserve me unto His Heavenly Kingdom: to Whom be Glory for ever and ever. Amen."

Titus

Introduction

The Epistle to Titus was written before the Second, and there is good reason to believe, after the First Epistle to Timothy. It belongs to a period when Paul was not a prisoner, and can hardly be assigned to that portion of his life which is covered by the historian of Acts. There is not in Acts any allusion whatever to a visit to Crete, or to churches in that great island, a fact that cannot be accounted for except by placing his Cretan missionary tour after his first imprisonment. It is probable that churches had been planted before his visit, as in Rome and many other places; that after his first letter to Timothy he returned to Ephesus, and from thence passed into the island. When he left, as the work of organization was left incomplete, Titus remained in order to "set in order the things that are wanting" (1: 5), and afterwards Paul wrote to him to give further instructions concerning the work. Hence the date of the letter will be somewhere from A.D. 65 to 68.

Crete is a great island, stretching one hundred and fifty miles from east to west, but only about thirty-five miles in width, mountainous but fertile, and had in 1867 a population of 210,000, mostly Greeks. It is closely connected with early Greek legend and history, and although under Turkish rule, is in full sympathy with the Kingdom of Greece. Its modern history is mainly a record of resistance to the Turkish power.

Titus, to whom the letter is addressed, was a Greek. He attended Paul to Jerusalem at the time the question of Gentile Christians was considered (Acts 15). Paul refused to allow him to be circumcised (Gal. 2: 1–5; 2 Cor. 2: 12; 7: 5–16). He bore Paul's first letter to Corinth, and is often referred to in the epistles, although his name is not mentioned in Acts. From 2 Tim. 4: 10, we learn that he was in Dalmatia, at the time Paul wrote from his prison, and we find (Titus 3: 15) that Paul bade him come from Crete to Nicopolis, which is on the same coast as Dalmatia. It is still claimed in Dalmatia that he was the missionary of that region.

The genuineness of the letter, like that to Timothy, was never questioned until a recent period, but every objection made by the rationalistic critics of the German school has been satisfactorily answered, and there is no reasonable ground for doubt that all three of the Pastoral Letters belong to the last years of the great apostle's life.

B.W. Johnson, The People's New Testament

Verses of encouragement

Titus 1: 15,16 "Unto the pure all things are pure: but unto them that are defiled and unbelieving is nothing pure; but even their mind and conscience is defiled. They profess that they know God; but in works they deny him, being abominable, and disobedient, and unto every good work reprobate."

Titus 2: 7,8 "In all things shewing thyself a pattern of Good Works: in Doctrine shewing uncorruptness, gravity, sincerity, Sound Speech, that cannot be condemned; that he that is of the contrary part may be ashamed, having no evil thing to say of you."

Titus 2: 11–14 "For The Grace Of God That Bringeth Salvation hath appeared to all men, Teaching us that, denying ungodliness and worldly lusts, we should live soberly, righteously, and Godly, in this present world; Looking for that Blessed Hope, and The Glorious Appearing Of The Great God And Our Savior Jesus Christ; Who gave Himself for us, that He might Redeem us from all iniquity, and Purify unto Himself a peculiar people, zealous of Good Works."

Titus 3: 1,2 "Put them in mind to be subject to principalities and powers, to obey magistrates, to be ready to every Good Work, To speak evil of no man, to be no brawlers, but Gentle, shewing all Meekness unto all men."

Titus 3: 5 "Not by works of righteousness which we have done, but according to His Mercy He saved us, by the washing of Regeneration, and renewing of the Holy Ghost."

Titus 3: 14 "And let ours also learn to maintain Good Works for necessary uses, that they be not unfruitful."

Philemon, Hebrews

Philemon

Introduction

This, the fourth of the personal letters of Paul, differs from the other three, as well as from all other epistles of Paul, in that it is neither doctrinal, nor intended for general church instruction. It has its interest in that it shows by a particular example the application of the great principles of Christian brotherhood to social life. It is written to Philemon, an active Christian of Colosse, a convert of Paul, in behalf of Onesimus, a runaway slave of Philemon, who had found refuge in Rome, had in some way been brought under Paul's instruction during his first Roman imprisonment, and had been brought to Christ. In Col. 4: 9 he is mentioned as belonging to Colosse, commended as a faithful and beloved brother who had been of great service, and it is there stated that he would return from Rome to his old home along with Tychicus, while this epistle explains the occasion of his return, and throws a practical light on the new relations of master and slave, which could not be done by precept alone.

A few words concerning ancient slavery will assist in an understanding of the lesson of the epistle. Slavery was universal. Aristotle, one of the most enlightened of the Greeks, held that the Creator had made the majority of the human race for slavery. Even the Mosaic law permitted the relation, but mitigated the condition of the slave by protective regulations which made Jewish slavery far the mildest in the world. Under the Roman law the slave was not considered a man, but a chattel without any civil rights whatever, completely at the mercy of his master. The master could sell him, give him away, torture him, crucify him, put him to death, even feed him to the fishes, and there was no law to interfere in his behalf. But when Christ came he introduced new relations between man and man. All in the church were a brotherhood. In Christ Jesus there was neither bond nor free, male nor female. All stood on a footing of equality before the Lord; all were brethren; all God's children, and to be bound to each other by the ties of brotherly love.

Such revolutionary ideas were sure in the course of time to destroy the condition of slavery, but in the meanwhile, Christianity sought to prepare men for the revolution before it was declared, and hence the relation was continued under new regulations. The servant was to continue to render faithful service to a master who was a brother beloved, and the master was to love and trust his servant as a brother, and to do unto him as he would be done by in such a relation. Hence in the early church thousands of masters and slaves met on an equal footing and often the slaves were the bishops who ruled the church and watched over the spiritual welfare of their masters.

Onesimus, an unconverted slave of Philemon, had fled, whether after or before his master's conversion, is unknown. When he was converted the principles of Christian teaching would require him to return, but the conditions of his return are explained in the affectionate letter which he carries back to Philemon. He returns a servant, but as a more than servant, "a brother beloved, both in the flesh, and in the Lord," and Philemon is desired to so receive him in a tender appeal to his consciousness of how much he owes to him who asks. He is reminded that Onesimus is Paul's own son in the gospel, as well as himself. A sense of the fault is exhibited, and forgiveness for the offender is required, not by the authority of apostolic power, but of love.

This epistle must have been written about the same time as that to the Colossians, and was carried by the same messengers. Its genuineness is accepted by almost all critical authorities, the rationalist Baur being the only notable exception.

B.W. Johnson, The People's New Testament

Verses of encouragement

Philemon verses 10–13 "I beseech thee for my son Onesimus, whom I have begotten in my bonds: Which in time past was to thee unprofitable, but now profitable to thee and to me: Whom I have sent again: thou therefore receive him, that is, mine own bowels: Whom I would have retained with me, that in thy stead he might have ministered unto me in the bonds of the gospel."

Hebrews

Introduction

That this Epistle is entitled to a place in the New Testament Scriptures has been discussed but little in comparison with the question of its authorship. It is quoted at large by Clement of Rome before the close of the first century, by Ignatius, Polycarp, Justin Martyr, Irenaeus, and others in the second century, is found in the Versions of the second century, is named in the Ancient Canons, and is affirmed to be a part of the Holy Scriptures by the Council of Antioch (A.D. 269) and of Nicea (A.D. 325); as well as by the later councils.

On the other hand, both the ancient and modern church have been divided concerning the writer to whom it is to be ascribed. Contrary to the usual custom the writer's name is not given in the opening verses, nor in the closing salutations. It differs somewhat in style from any other portion of the New Testament. Some have thought it improbable that Paul, the Apostle to the Gentiles, should have addressed an Epistle to the Hebrews; for these, and perhaps other reasons, many devout critics have held that it was written by Barnabas, or by Apollos, or by Luke, and even Clement of Rome has been named as the author. In the ancient church the East with one consent declared in favor of Paul, while the West asserted that it belonged to some other writer, though in modern times the Latin Church has decided the question by the weight of infallibility in favor of the apostle to the Gentiles.

Hebrews

Introduction, continued

Luther and Calvin both held that it was not Pauline, and have been followed by many moderns.

It is addressed to HEBREWS; evidently Hebrew Christians; probably not so much those of Jerusalem as the "Dispersion," the multitudes of Jewish Christians in Gentile lands. It shows that those addressed were persecuted, were in danger of being tempted to fall away, that they had not yet shed their blood for Christ, and, in order to strengthen them, the superiority of Christianity to Judaism is demonstrated by showing the superlative excellence of Christ. He is (1) superior to the prophets; (2) superior to the angels; (3) superior to Moses. (4) His priesthood is superior to that of Aaron, being a priest after the order of Melchizedek. (5) Then the superiority of the New Covenant to the Old is shown, being a better covenant, based upon better promises. This is shown in Chs. 8, 9, 10, and then follows in the remaining chapters an exhortation to steadfastness, based upon faith and strengthened by examples of the heroes of the faith.

It is evident from the closing words, whatever may have been the writer's reasons for not incorporating his name in the Epistle, that he was well known to those addressed. He asks their prayers, prays for them, speaks of visiting them with Timothy, and closes with the usual Pauline farewell benediction.

B.W. Johnson, *The People's New Testament*

Verses of encouragement

Heb. 1: 2–3 "Hath in these Last Days spoken unto us by His Son, Whom He hath appointed Heir Of All Things, by Whom also He made the worlds; Who being The Brightness Of His Glory, and The Express Image Of His Person, and upholding all things by The Word Of His Power, when He had by Himself purged our sins, sat down on the right hand of The Majesty On High."

Heb. 1: 14 "Are they not all Ministering Spirits, sent forth to minister for them who shall be heirs of Salvation?"

Heb. 2: 10,11 "For it became Him, for Whom are all things, and by Whom are all things, in bringing many sons unto glory, to make The Captain of their Salvation perfect through sufferings. For both He That Sanctifieth and they who are sanctified are all of One: for which cause He is not ashamed to call them brethren."

Heb. 2: 13 "And again, I will put my trust in Him. And again, Behold I and the children which God hath given me."

Heb. 4: 9 "There remaineth therefore a Rest to the people of God."

Heb. 4: 11 "Let us labor therefore to enter into that Rest, lest any man fall after the same example of unbelief."

Heb. 4: 12 "For the Word of God is quick, and powerful, and sharper than any two-edged sword, piercing even to the dividing asunder of soul and spirit, and of the joints and marrow, and is a Discerner of the thoughts and intents of the heart."

Heb. 4: 16 "Let us therefore come boldly unto the Throne Of Grace, that we may obtain Mercy, and find Grace to help in time of need."

Heb. 6: 17–18 "Wherein God, willing more abu,dantly to shew unto the heirs of Promise the Immutability Of His Counsel, confirmed it by an oath: That by two immutable things, in which it was impossible for God to lie, we might have a Strong Consolation, who have fled for refuge to lay hold upon the hope set before us."

Heb. 8: 12 "For I will be Merciful to their unrighteousness, and their sins and their iniquities will I remember no more."

Heb. 9: 27 "And as it is appointed unto men once to die, but after this The Judgment."

Heb. 10: 14 "For by one offering He hath perfected for ever them that are Sanctified."

Heb. 10: 19 "Having therefore, brethren, boldness to enter into the Holiest by the Blood of Jesus."

Heb. 10: 22,23 "Let us draw near with a true heart in full assurance of Faith, having our hearts sprinkled from an evil conscience, and our bodies washed with Pure Water. Let us hold fast the profession of our Faith without wavering; (for He is Faithful that Promised)."

Heb. 10: 38 "Now the Just shall live by Faith: but if any man draw back, My soul shall have NO pleasure in him."

Heb. 11: 1 "Now Faith is the substance of things hoped for, the evidence of things not seen."

Heb. 11: 3 "Through Faith we understand that the worlds were framed by the Word of God, so that things which are seen were not made of things which do appear."

Heb. 11: 6 "But without Faith it is impossible to please Him: for he that cometh to God must believe that He is, and that He is a Rewarder of them that diligently seek Him."

Heb. 12: 1,2 "Wherefore seeing we also are compassed about with So Great A Cloud Of Witnesses, let us lay aside every weight, and the sin which doth so easily beset us, and let us run with patience the race that is set before us, Looking unto Jesus The Author And Finisher Of Our Faith."

Hebrews, James

Verses of encouragement

Heb. 13: 1 "Let brotherly Love continue."

Heb. 13: 5,6 "Let your conversation be without covetousness; and be content with such things as ye have: for He hath said, I will never leave thee, nor forsake thee. So that we may boldly say, The Lord is my Helper, and I will not fear what man shall do unto me."

Heb. 13: 8 "Jesus Christ the same yesterday, and to day, and for ever."

Heb. 13: 20,21 "Now the God Of Peace, that brought again from the dead our Lord Jesus, that Great Shepherd Of The Sheep, through The Blood Of The Everlasting Covenant, Make you perfect in every Good Work to do His will, working in you that which is well pleasing in His sight, through Jesus Christ; to Whom be Glory for ever and ever. Amen."

James

Introduction

This epistle stands first in order of seven which have been called "General," from a very early period, because of the fact that they were not addressed, like those of Paul, to particular churches or individuals, in most cases, but to the churches generally. This is directed to "the Twelve Tribes of the Dispersion," a dedication which shows that it was designed for the instruction of Jewish Christians scattered abroad among the Gentile countries.

Yet there has been some dispute about the personality of the James who wrote this letter. There are three distinguished disciples which bear that name: James, the brother of John, one of the sons of Zebedee, one of the Twelve; James, the son of Alphæus, also an apostle, called James the Less (Mark 15: 40); and James, called by Paul in Galatians "the brother of our Lord," the man who appears in Acts, chapter 15, as wielding a pre-eminent influence in the church at Jerusalem. The epistle could not have been written by James, the brother of John, as he was slain by Herod (Acts 12: 2) before its date. The authorship must be ascribed either to James, the son of Alphæus, or to James, "the Lord's brother."

From the earliest ages the latter has been agreed upon as the writer. To this conclusion all the known facts point. He was a permanent resident of Jerusalem, and pre-eminent in the church; he seems to be the chief figure in "the Council of Jerusalem" described in Acts, chapter 15; he was one of the pillars of the church (Gal. 2: 9); hence he could speak authoritatively to Jewish Christians scattered abroad. It has, however, been held by many that he is the same as James, the son of Alphæus, and a cousin of Christ, instead of a brother. The argument in favor of this hypothesis is ingenious.

ARGUMENTS IN FAVOR OF COUSIN
THEORY

(1) It is held that Mary never bore any children but Jesus, and hence that "the brethren of the Lord" were her nephews.

(2) That Mary, the wife of Clopas (John 19: 25) was sister of Mary, the mother of Jesus.

(3) That Alphæus and Clopas are different forms of the same name.

(4) That the brethren of Jesus, "James and Joses and Simon and Judas," were the cousins of Jesus, and that at least two, James and Judas, were apostles

(5) This is supported by the fact that Jesus on the cross commits the care of his mother to John, which is held to prove that she could have no other sons.

ARGUMENTS IN FAVOR OF BEING JESUS'
BROTHER

In answer to this theory it may be said that

(1) it is improbable that the wife of Clopas was sister to Mary, a fact which would require two sisters to be of the same name. John names two pairs, Mary and her sister, and Mary, the wife of Clopas and Mary Magdalene. The sister was no doubt Salome, the mother of John, named as one of the four women in the other gospels, and whom John omits to name from the same motives which prevented him from ever naming himself. Hence John was the nephew of Mary, and this in connection with the fact that the brethren of Jesus were not then believers is sufficient explanation of John being assigned the duty of caring for the mother of Jesus.

(2) We are told positively that the brethren of Jesus were not believers, and this, too, in the closing portion of the last year of our Lord's ministry, a fact that clearly shows that none of these could have been of the number of the apostles.

(3) They are never called cousins of Jesus nor is there any proof that the Greek word which designates them as "brethren" is ever used in the sense of cousins in the New Testament.

(4) When these brethren had become believers, after the resurrection, they are distinguished from the Twelve (Acts 1: 14; 1 Cor. 9: 5), a fact which cannot be explained if at least two of the four were of the Twelve. It is true that in Gal. 1: 19 James is spoken of as an apostle, yet neither he nor Paul, the greatest of the apostles, was of the Twelve. These facts seem to me to clearly indicate that "James, the brother of the Lord," the author of this epistle, was not of the Twelve, and was a brother to the Lord Jesus in the sense that he was a child of Mary.

His prominence, however, in the early church may be gathered from the following references: Acts 12: 17; Acts 15: 19; Acts 21: 18; Gal. 1: 19; Gal. 2: 9; Gal. 2: 12. The New Testament is silent concerning his later history, but Josephus, the Jewish historian, has the following information about him.

James, 1 Peter

James, continued

Introduction, continued

Josephus says that shortly before the war that ended in the destruction of Jerusalem, about A.D. 63, "Ananias, the high priest, assembled the Sanhedrim, and brought before them the brother of Jesus, who is called the Christ, whose name was James, and some of his companions and delivered them to be stoned" (Antiq. xx. 9: 1). He was allowed to remain until not long before the overthrow of the Jewish state, and was then removed. Though not requiring the Gentile Christians to obey the law, he continued to teach its observance to the Jewish Christians, and to regard Christianity not so much the overthrow of the old covenant as its fulfillment and perfection. In this respect he did not have a clear vision like Paul but was on this account perhaps the better fitted to lead his own nation to Christ.

The epistle was almost certainly written at Jerusalem, and probably during the last decade of the life of the writer, was addressed to Jewish Christians, is not doctrinal but full of practical instruction in the duties of life
B.W. Johnson, *The People's New Testament*

Verses of encouragement

James 1: 2–4 "My brethren, count it all Joy when ye fall into divers temptations; Knowing this, that the trying of your Faith worketh Patience.

But let Patience have her perfect work, that ye may be Perfect and Entire, wanting nothing."

James 1: 5,6 "If any of you lack Wisdom, let him ask of God, that giveth to all men liberally, and upbraideth not; and It shall be given him. But let him ask in Faith, nothing wavering. For he that wavereth is like a wave of the sea driven with the wind and tossed."

James 1: 13 "Let no man say when he is tempted, I am tempted of God: for God cannot be tempted with evil, neither tempteth He any man."

James 1: 17 "Every Good Gift and every Perfect Gift is from Above, and cometh down from The Father Of Lights, with Whom is no variableness, neither shadow of turning."

James 1: 19 "Wherefore, my beloved brethren, let every man be swift to hear, slow to speak, slow to wrath."

James 1: 22 "But be ye Doers Of The Word, and not hearers only, deceiving your own selves."

James 1: 25 "But whoso looketh into the Perfect Law Of Liberty, and continueth therein, he being not a forgetful hearer, but a Doer of the work, this man shall be blessed in his deed."

James 1: 27 "Pure religion and undefiled before God and the Father is this, To visit the fatherless and widows in their affliction, and to keep himself unspotted from the world."

James 2: 26 "For as the body without

the spirit is dead, so Faith without works is dead also."

James 3: 2 "For in many things we offend all. If any man offend not in Word, the same is a perfect man, and able also to bridle the whole body."

James 3: 13 "Who is a wise man and endued with Knowledge among you? let him shew out of a Good Conversation his works with meekness of Wisdom."

James 3: 17 "But the Wisdom that is from Above is first Pure, then Peaceable, Gentle, and Easy To Be Intreated, full of Mercy and Good Fruits, without partiality, and without hypocrisy."

James 3: 18 "And the Fruit Of Righteousness is sown in Peace of them that make Peace."

James 4: 2 "Ye lust, and have not: ye kill, and desire to have, and cannot obtain: ye fight and war, yet ye have not, because ye ask not."

James 4: 6 "But He giveth more Grace. Wherefore He saith, God resisteth the proud, but giveth Grace unto the humble."

James 4: 7 "Submit yourselves therefore to God. Resist the devil, and he will flee from you."

James 4: 8 Draw nigh to God, and He will draw nigh to you. Cleanse your hands, ye sinners; and purify your hearts, ye double minded."

James 4: 10 "Humble yourselves in the sight of the Lord, and He shall lift you up."

James 5: 16 "Confess your faults one to another, and pray one for another, that ye may be healed. The effectual fervent prayer of a righteous man availeth much."

1 Peter

Introduction

Simon Peter, the author of this epistle, was by profession a Galilean fisherman, the son of Jonah, the brother of Andrew, who first brought him to Christ, and associated in business with the sons of Zebedee. He was in Jerusalem when Paul came there from Damascus (Gal. 1: 18; Acts 9: 26); and also fourteen years later at the council of Jerusalem (Acts, chapter 15; Gal. 2: 9), and Paul met him again at Antioch (Gal. 2: 11), the first time he appears elsewhere than in Judea. After this it is only his epistles which give us hints of his further life and labors, but it is evident from these and the traditions of the early church that as an "apostle of the circumcision" he finally turned from Judea to evangelize his own race in other lands.

1 Peter

Introduction, continued

Readership and place of writing

This brings us to the questions of the Persons addressed in this epistle, the Object in writing to them, and the Place from whence he wrote. Our limits allow only the briefest answers.

(1) It was directed to "the Sojourners of the Dispersion," who lived in five provinces of the Roman Empire, all of which had been evangelized by the apostle Paul. See 1 Peter, chapter 1. The Dispersion was a term applied to the Jewish race in lands outside of Judea. Hence, not forgetful of his apostleship to the circumcision (Gal. 2: 8) he addressed himself to Jews, but Jewish Christians, "the elect."

(2) His object was apparently to encourage them to press on courageously under trial and persecution. This encouragement and exhortation is set forth in an impetuous torrent which is thoroughly characteristic of the impetuous Peter. His style is lively, energetic, and pleasing, if somewhat wanting in the logical connection and precision of the great apostle to the Gentiles. An indirect object of Peter in writing was, doubtless, to give his support to the authority of Paul. The churches addressed were founded by Paul, but in them had subsequently appeared Judaizers (see introduction to Galatians) who had sought to undermine his authority. Peter recognizes the work, and his teaching is an indirect endorsement of Paul. It served to show the Jewish Christians that the two great apostles were in harmony.

(3) One question remains, where was the epistle written? Chapter 5: 13 shows that Peter was at Babylon at the time. It seems strange that there should be any question in view of the fact that in all the ancient world, the word Babylon without any other explanations always mean the great city on the Euphrates, or the territory adjacent, which took its name from the city. True, its former greatness was gone, and it was a Roman province, but it had been the home of tens of thousands of the Circumcision, the class to whom Peter directed his labors, ever since the Captivity. We know that in the latter part of the first century and in the second the Rabbinical schools of Babylon vied in importance with that at Tiberias, and that "the Prince of the Captivity" was a formidable potentate for a subject. It is opposed to all the facts of history to contend that there was not, at the date of this epistle, a great Jewish population on the banks of the Euphrates, and an indefinite passage of Josephus belonging to a period a generation earlier, would never have been used for this purpose had it not been that it is essential to the argument of the Papacy to give Peter a long residence at Rome. It is equally out of the question to assert that Peter in a plain, matter of fact letter, speaks of Rome by a name that was only applied to it later in a book of symbols,

with the statement that it is used as a symbol. Babylon had carried Israel into captivity; when pagan Rome did the same thing she became a mystical Babylon; and spiritual Rome also merited the designation by carrying into captivity the church of God. There is no reasonable ground for doubt that Peter extended his labors for his own race to Mesopotamia and from thence wrote this epistle. It was probably written toward the close of Paul's first imprisonment in Rome. There are reasons for thinking that Peter had seen the Ephesian letter, one of the epistles of Paul's imprisonment, and hence this Epistle was probably written as late, at least, as A.D. 63.

B.W. Johnson, *The People's New Testament*

Verses of encouragement

1 Pet. 1: 3–5 "Blessed be the God and Father of our Lord Jesus Christ, which according to His abundant Mercy hath begotten us again unto a lively Hope by the resurrection of Jesus Christ from the dead, To an Inheritance incorruptible, and undefiled, and that fadeth not away, reserved in Heaven for you, who are kept by the Power of God through Faith unto Salvation ready to be revealed in the Last Time."

1 Pet. 1: 16 "Because it is written, Be ye holy; for I Am Holy."

1 Pet. 1: 22,23 "Seeing ye have purified your souls in obeying the Truth through the Spirit unto unfeigned Love of the brethren, see that ye Love one another with a Pure Heart fervently: Being born again, not of corruptible seed, but of Incorruptible, by the Word of God, which Liveth And Abideth for ever."

1 Pet. 1: 25 "But the Word of the Lord endureth for ever. And this is the Word which by the Gospel is preached unto you."

1 Pet. 2: 5 "Ye also, as Lively Stones, are built up A Spiritual House, an holy priesthood, to offer up Spiritual sacrifices, acceptable to God by Jesus Christ."

1 Pet. 2: 9 "But ye are a Chosen Generation, a Royal Priesthood, an Holy Nation, a Peculiar People; that ye should shew forth the praises of Him Who hath called you out of darkness into His Marvelous Light."

1 Pet. 3: 12 "For the eyes of the Lord are over the righteous, and His ears are open unto their prayers: but the face of the Lord is against them that do evil."

1 Pet. 5: 5–7 "Likewise, ye younger, submit yourselves unto the elder. Yea, all of you be subject one to another, and be clothed with humility: for God resisteth the proud, and giveth Grace to the humble. Humble yourselves therefore under The Mighty Hand Of God, that He may exalt you in due time: Casting all your care upon Him; for He careth for you."

2 Peter, 1 John

2 Peter

Introduction

The Second Epistle of Peter is placed by Eusebius among the writings whose genuineness had been called in question by many, and it is not to be denied that there were differences in the early church concerning its right to a place in the canon. Yet it seems to have been quoted by several of the Fathers in the second century, and in the third the great Origen went so far as to write a commentary upon it. It was finally received by all the churches except the Syrian, in whose translation of the New Testament it was not embraced. It seems probable that it was written by him whose name appears in the salutation, but written some time later than the first, near the close of his life, and specially directed against certain heresies which were beginning to appear.

B.W. Johnson, *The People's New Testament*

Verses of encouragement

2 Pet. 1: 2–7 "Grace and Peace be multiplied unto you through the Knowledge of God, and of Jesus our Lord, According as His Divine Power hath given unto us all things that pertain unto Life and Godliness, through the Knowledge of Him that hath called us to Glory and Virtue: Whereby are given unto us Exceeding Great And Precious Promises: that by These ye might be partakers of the Divine Nature, having escaped the corruption that is in the world through lust. And beside this, giving all diligence, add to your Faith Virtue; and to Virtue Knowledge; And to Knowledge Temperance; and to Temperance Patience; and to Patience Godliness; And to Godliness Brotherly Kindness; and to Brotherly Kindness Charity."

2 Pet. 3: 8,9 "But, beloved, be not ignorant of this one thing, that one day is with the Lord as a thousand years, and a thousand years as one day. The Lord is not slack concerning His Promise, as some men count slackness; but is Longsuffering To Us-ward, not willing that any should perish, but that all should come to repentance."

2 Pet. 3: 18 "But grow in Grace, and in the Knowledge of our Lord and Savior Jesus Christ. To Him be Glory both now and for ever. Amen."

1 John

Introduction

This Epistle was written by John, the son of Zebedee, the beloved Disciple, an Apostle of Jesus Christ. The outlines of his history and character have been fully given in the Introduction to the Gospel of John (*People's New Testament*, Vol. I.) to which I refer the reader. Prominent in the Savior's earthly ministry, the active companion of Peter in the founding of the church in Judea, he was soon overshadowed in the Acts of the Apostles by the towering personalities of Peter and Paul. He is only named four times in the Acts, and his name only occurs once in the Epistles of Paul (Gal. 2: 9) in a passage which probably names the only occasion when he and Paul ever met face to face. The opinion of the early church was that his residence was in Palestine until the time approached for the overthrow of the Jewish state, and probably until he had been released from the sacred charge of the mother of Jesus by her death; that he then removed to Asia Minor to make his home at Ephesus among the great body of Gentile churches which had been robbed of the care of their founder, the great apostle to the Gentiles, by his martyrdom, and that in Ephesus he wrote the Epistles which are ascribed to him in the New Testament.

Like the Gospel by the same writer, the Epistle does not mention the name of its author, and we are indebted for the knowledge of the authorship to the uniform testimony of the early church, as well as to the similarity of thought and expression of the Gospel and the Epistle. I do not think the hypothesis of those destructive German critics who have such a mania for novelties, that the writer of Ephesus was not the Apostle John, but a Presbyter John of the second century, is worthy of serious consideration. Such a figment is incredible in view of the fact that the second century testifies that John the Apostle long lived at Ephesus, and died there, leaving the legacy of his life and writings to the churches. We have still extant the writings of those who affirm that they had been trained by men of God who had been trained under the direction of the aged apostle during his Ephesian residence. It may be added that this epistle is repeatedly quoted in the writings of the Fathers belonging to the second century, and is named, as well as the other two Epistles of John, in the first canon of the New Testament writings, the Canon Muratori, which belongs to the last half of the second century.

Its date is only a matter of conjecture. It is evident from the various false doctrines which the writer evidently had in view that it belongs to a later period than any other writings of the New Testament save those of John himself. It was probably written when John remained as the only survivor of the apostolic band, after his Gospel, and when certain heresies began to assume form. Why it should appear without either the names of the author or of the churches to which it was addressed is uncertain, but it does demonstrate that it is a genuine Epistle. A forged Epistle would be ascribed to an apostolic writer in order to gain its acceptance. The examples afforded by certain forged epistles of the early centuries, the so called Epistle to the Laodiceans for instance, settle this point. The peculiarities of the Epistle, which cannot be discussed in our limited space, will be best seen in the notes on the text.

B.W. *Johnson, The People's New Testament*

1 John, 2 John, 3 John

1 John, continued

Verses of encouragement

1 John 1: 7 "But IF we walk in the Light, as He is in the Light, we have fellowship one with another, and the Blood of Jesus Christ His Son cleanseth us from all sin."

1 John 1: 9 "IF we confess our sins, He is Faithful and Just to forgive us our sins, and to cleanse us from all unrighteousness."

1 John 2: 5 "But whoso keepeth His Word, in him verily is the Love of God perfected: hereby know we that we are in Him."

1 John 2: 10 "He that loveth his brother abideth in the Light, and there is none occasion of stumbling in him."

1 John 2: 14 "I have written unto you, fathers, because ye have known Him that is from The Beginning. I have written unto you, young men, because ye are strong, and The Word Of God abideth in you, and ye have overcome the wicked one."

1 John 2: 16 "For all that is in the world, the lust of the flesh, and the lust of the eyes, and the pride of life, is not of the Father, but is of the world."

1 John 3: 8 "He that committeth SIN is of the devil; for the devil sinneth from the beginning. For this purpose the Son of God was manifested, that He might destroy the works of the devil."

1 John 3: 22 "And whatsoever we ask, we receive of Him, because we keep His Commandments, and do those things that are pleasing in His sight."

1 John 4: 4 "Ye are of God, little children, and have overcome them: because Greater Is He that is in you, than he that is in the world."

1 John 4: 18,19 "There is no fear in Love; but Perfect Love casteth out fear: because fear hath torment. He that feareth is not made perfect in Love. We Love Him, because He first Loved us."

1 John 5: 4,5 "For whatsoever is born of God overcometh the world: and this is the VICTORY that overcometh the world, even our Faith. Who is he that overcometh the world, but he that believeth that Jesus is the Son of God?"

1 John 5: 14,15 "And this is the Confidence that we have in Him, that, if we ask any thing according to His Will, He heareth us: And if we know that He hear us, whatsoever we ask, we know that we have the petitions that we desired of Him."

1 John 5: 18 "We know that whosoever is born of God sinneth not; but he that is begotten of God keepeth himself, and that wicked one toucheth him not."

2 John

Introduction

There has always been a difference of opinion and discussion concerning the Second and Third Epistles ascribed to John, the apostle. Neither the ancient church nor the modern critics have been entirely agreed concerning the writer, the persons addressed, or even concerning their title to a place in the Canon. The limited space to which I am confined will not allow me to enter at length into these controversies, further than to say that every hypothesis which refers to the authorship to any one else than John, the apostle, rests upon filmy foundations. The conjecture that they were written by a "Presbyter John," who was a contemporary of the apostle, and also lived at Ephesus, is based upon a fragment preserved from Papias, a Father in the second century, who mentions what he had learned from "the elders," or ancients, and among them names "the Elder John," who was a personal disciple of Christ. Since in the very same sentence he names seven apostles and calls them not apostles, but "elders," or "ancients," those are hard pressed who assume that he meant by the "Elder John," some other personal disciple of Christ than the son of Zebedee. There is no evidence that any "John the elder" lived in the apostolic age, a separate life from John the apostle. In addition, the language, doctrine, and style of the two epistles point to the author of the fourth Gospel, and especially to the writer of the First Epistle of John.

B.W. Johnson, The People's New Testament

Verses of encouragement

2 John verse 4 "I rejoiced greatly that I found of thy children walking in truth, as we have received a commandment from the Father."

3 John

Introduction

That this third epistle was written by the author of the second, is agreed. The writer is "The Elder." All that has been said concerning the authorship of the second, therefore, applies to the third. The only hypothesis which is more than baseless conjecture is that which ascribes it to John the apostle, in his extreme old age, during his residence at Ephesus. Like the second this is addressed to an individual of whose personality we are uncertain, as the name Gaius, or Caius, occurs several times in the New Testament.

B.W. Johnson, The People's New Testament

Verses of encouragement

3 John 1: 2 "Beloved, I wish above all things that thou mayest prosper and be in health, even as thy soul prospereth."

3 John 1: 4 "I have no greater Joy than to hear that my children walk in Truth."

Jude, Revelation (1)

Jude

Introduction

The author of this epistle introduces himself as "Jude the brother of James." Among the apostles there was a "Judas (Jude) James," the word son or brother being unexpressed, and some have concluded that the "Judas, not Iscariot," of the twelve is the writer of this letter. It is more likely, however, that he was the brother of the James of Jerusalem, who became so prominent in the history of the Palestine church, and whom Paul speaks of as a "pillar." In the last fifteen years before the overthrow of Jerusalem he became the most influential personage among the Jewish Christians, and it was only natural that Jude, if his brother, should refer to that relationship in order to secure a more favorable hearing. That James was "the Lord's brother" (Gal. 1: 19), but among the brethren of the Lord there was a Jude also, whom we have every reason to believe to be the writer of this epistle. For a fuller discussion of the question, see the Introduction to the Epistle of James. There reasons will be found for the conclusion that James was not an apostle, and it would follow also that Jude was not of the twelve. Since the authors of the second and third gospels and of Acts were not apostles, it need not be thought strange that two of the epistles were by other holy men.

Another question of some interest arises from a comparison of Jude with Second Peter. The reader will find that Jude 3–18 is almost identical with 2 Peter 1: 5 and 2: 1–18. One or the other writer certainly had before him the work of the other. Critics are divided concerning which was the earlier writer, and reasons can be given for assigning the priority to each. It seems to me probable that the "Speaker's Commentary" is right in deciding in favor of Peter, and that Jude was written at a date not much later. It is probable that he found a part of Peter's epistle expressed his ideas so well that he modified it somewhat and inserted it in his letter. It is more likely that he would thus honor an apostolic letter of the renowned Peter than that Peter would borrow from him. On this hypothesis this epistle was written between A.D. 65 and 70, or shortly before the siege of Jerusalem.

We have no data for determining where it is written, but there seems to be no doubt that, like the epistles of Peter and of James, it was primarily addressed to Jewish Christians. It contains a salutation with reasons for writing (verse 4); then three examples of the punitive justice of God; following this is a particular account of the wicked ways of certain false teachers against which he would warn them; after this comes a concluding portion in which disciples are warned and exhorted, and the whole closes with one of the sublimest doxologies of the Bible.

B.W. Johnson, The People's New Testament

Verses of encouragement

Jude 1: 20–21 "But ye, beloved, building up yourselves on your Most Holy Faith, praying in the Holy Ghost, Keep yourselves in the Love of God, looking for the Mercy of our Lord Jesus Christ unto Eternal Life."

Jude 1: 24,25 "Now unto Him that is able to keep you from falling, and to present you faultless before the presence of His Glory with Exceeding Joy, To The Only Wise God our Savior, be Glory and Majesty, Dominion and Power, both now and for ever. Amen."

Revelation (1)

Introduction

When we open the Book of Revelation we discover, at once, a marked difference between it and any other portion of the New Testament. It is not history like the Gospels and Acts, nor practical discussions and instructions like the epistles, but we at once seem to breathe the atmosphere of prophets like Ezekiel and Daniel. As Ezekiel and Daniel were permitted to behold visions which revealed certain great events of the future, in a series of symbolic images, so there passes before the eyes of John a series of wonderful visions of which he makes record, and has left that record to the church for interpretation. The book is a book of prophecy. "God gave to him to show unto his servants the things which should shortly come to pass." In order to any clear understanding of the book

we must never lose sight of its object, as stated in the opening sentence. Its object is to reveal the future. Nor is its aim to reveal some limited events of the future, but to show the things which must come to pass. In other words, its aim is to unfold the outlines of coming history as far as that history affects the fortunes of the church.

The author

There is no book of the New Testament to whose authorship the testimony of history is more definite than that of the book of Revelation. Only a few years passed after the death of John, the apostle, until it was quoted and ascribed to him by writers who either knew him in person or who derived their information from those who sat at his feet. Among those early witnesses is Papias, born about A.D. 70, a disciple of John himself ("a hearer" of John, according to Irenæus) of whose writings only fragments have been preserved, but who is known to have quoted Revelation as the work of John. To him may be added Irenæus, born between A.D. 115 and A.D. 125, who tells us that he was long a pupil of Polycarp, of whom he states that Polycarp had learned many things of the aged apostle at whose feet he had long sat. Of course, with such opportunities he could not be ignorant of what John had written, yet he declares explicitly that he is the author of the Apocalypse.

Revelation (2)

Introduction, continued

Several more fathers of the second century are quoted as giving the same testimony, but it will suffice to add that it is named in the Canon Muratori, the first canon of the New Testament Scriptures, dated about A.D. 170, and all doubts concerning its genuineness seem to belong to later times. Nor is any fact of history better established than that John's last years were spent in that part of Asia with which the Book of Revelation is locally associated.

Date of writing

I believe that all the facts point to "near the end of the reign of Domitian, or about the year A.D. 96." It might be of service to add that the persecution of Nero, as far as known, was local and confined to Rome; that death, instead of banishment, was the favorite method of punishment with him; that it is not probable that he would have put to death Paul and Peter and banished John; and that there is no evidence that John, as early as A.D. 68, had ever visited the region of the seven churches. On the other hand, the persecution of Domitian was not local; we know also that he sent other Christians into exile; we know also that the later years of John's life were passed at Ephesus, and in the region of which it was the center.

The place of writing

That the visions of Revelation were seen upon the island of Patmos is a fact that rests upon the testimony of the writer himself. It is the universal testimony of the early church, that John survived the destruction of Jerusalem, that when the storm of war was gathering around that devoted city he, in obedience to the Lord's warning (Matt. 24: 16), fled from the coming desolation, and finally took up his abode in Ephesus, in the midst of the churches of Asia, founded by the apostle Paul. During his long sojourn in this region, which extended until the close of his life, he was banished in the persecution of the latter part of the reign of Domitian. Patmos, the place of exile, is simply a rocky prison house in the sea.

Methods of interpretation

There is probably no other portion of the Scriptures concerning the meaning of which the interpreters so widely differ. This has caused some readers to conclude that the work is a tissue of confused and perhaps incoherent utterances, thrown out in prophetic ecstasy, the interpretation of which is a hopeless attempt; and they have supposed that the attempted explanations only illustrated the vagaries and the failures of the commentators. The differences are due to the different systems of interpretation employed. Of these there are three principal ones, all containing some truth, but all also in danger of being pushed to extreme erroneous conclusions, and it is probable that every interpreter, who is not rationalistic, accepts some of the results of all three of these systems.

THE PRETERIST

According to this system the successive visions apply to events chiefly in the history of the Jewish nation and of pagan Rome. These events have occurred long since in the past. Many rationalistic writers insist that all events described must have taken place before the visions were written, and that there is no such thing as prediction. Hence these critics are called Preterists, but this view is not confined to them.

THE FUTURISTS

These insist that the predictions apply mainly to events yet in the future, and will be fulfilled in the future history of the literal Israel. They assert that Israel will again occupy Palestine, that the temple will be literally rebuilt; that the holy city shall be literally trodden down for 1,260 days by the Gentiles, etc. The Preterist system is right in asserting that much of Revelation applies to what is now past, and the Futurist is right this far, namely, that a portion applies to what is still future.

THE HISTORICAL

In my opinion this system is more nearly correct, and yet it needs to be modified by the others, and carefully guarded. It holds that a succession of historical events, future when John wrote but now in part in the past, are portrayed by a series of visions. The error must be avoided of supposing that the book is continuously historical from the beginning to the end. If it is borne in mind that there is more than one series of visions; that when one series ends another follows which is synchronous, at least in part; that a part of the events portrayed by symbols is not in the past, while another portion is in the future, I think the result of the Historical system will be found to be clear, harmonious, and surprisingly in correspondence with the visions of the prophet. It perhaps cannot be expected that even those who adopt this system will agree in every detail, but we do find that the great expositors of the historical school, embracing the majority of English commentators, are in substantial agreement.

A book of prophecy

It must always be kept in mind, however, that this book is a book of prophecy, intended to "shew the things which must shortly come to pass." John was a Seer. He recorded what he saw. The future was portrayed to him in a series of visions. The pictures which passed before his eyes represented future events. Hence, each is a symbolical representation of what was then future, and may now be past history. Thus, when the first seal is opened in chap. 6: 1,2, and a warrior is seen with a bow in his hand riding on a white horse in conquest, this must be interpreted as a sense-image which appropriately represents an event or epoch of history which was future when John was an exile on Patmos.

Revelation (3)

A book of prophecy, continued

Symbolical pictures follow each other in rapid succession as the seals are opened and the trumpets blown, a correct interpretation of which is to be sought not in literal fulfillment, but in events of which the sense-visions might be appropriate symbols.

The theme of Revelation

John states that the book is a record of things "which should shortly come to pass." He saw outlined in his vision events which were at that time in the future, but which were "shortly" to become history. No one would suppose that it was the divine purpose to reveal all the changing history of nations, races, and kingdoms for the last eighteen hundred years, and hence, a question necessary to interpretation is: To what countries and series of events do the predictions apply? If we turn to the Old Testament prophets we will be guided to a correct answer. The central thought in all their predictions is the future history of the people of God. All that they utter is related, either directly or indirectly, to the fortunes of Israel, temporal and spiritual, the typical nation, and the spiritual nation, or in other words, to the fortunes of the Jews and of the Church. With this great object before them they predict the fate of the great Gentile nations with whom the Jews came in contact, who influenced their fortunes, or became their oppressors. Hence we have Assyria, Babylon, Tyre, Egypt, etc., made burdens of prophecy.

Exactly the same is true of New Testament prophecy. The prophets speak of the future of Israel and of the Church, and necessarily reveal much concerning the opposing and persecuting nations. It was not in the mind of Christ to give in Revelation the outline of all history, but to outline the fortunes, tribulations and triumphs of the Church.

The Church was, in the earlier centuries, almost wholly within the bounds of the vast, persecuting empire of pagan Rome. Hence this opposing power would come before the prophetic vision, and we will find that the symbolism often refers to the Roman power. Let it be ever present to the mind of the reader that John was the victim of Roman persecution, and an exile on Patmos when he wrote; that he had never been beyond the boundaries of the Roman Empire, and that there is no historical authority for supposing that any apostle ever stepped upon soil that a Roman citizen would call foreign. Since this mighty empire affects so closely the interests of the Church, it is in harmony with all we know of prophecy to expect it to be the subject of prophetic vision. The general scope of the Book of Revelation is similar to that of the Old Testament prophets; that its primary object is to outline the history of the Church; that, in subordination to this primary object, it portrays the fortunes of the two great persecuting powers, pagan and

Papal Rome. The changing fortunes of the Church are portrayed, running like a golden thread through the dark panorama of history, until at last, in God's good time, the battle is fought to the end, the victory won, and the triumphant Church enjoys the fruition of all its sufferings and labors and the glories of the New Jerusalem.

B.W. Johnson, *The People's New Testament*

Verses of encouragement

Rev. 1: 18 "I am He that liveth, and was dead; and, behold, I am Alive For Evermore, Amen; and have the Keys Of Hell And Of Death."

Rev. 3: 20 "Behold, I stand at the door, and knock: if any man hear My Voice, and open the door, I will come in to him, and will sup with him, and he with Me."

Rev. 5: 10 "And hast made us unto our God kings and priests: and we shall reign on the earth."

Rev. 7: 12 "Saying, Amen: Blessing, and Glory, and Wisdom, and Thanksgiving, and Honor, and Power, and Might, be unto our God for ever and ever. Amen."

Rev. 12: 10,11 "And I heard a loud voice saying in Heaven, Now is come Salvation, and Strength, and The Kingdom of our God, and the Power of His Christ: for the accuser of our brethren is cast down, which accused them before our God day and night. And they overcame him by The blood of the Lamb, and by the Word of their Testimony; and they loved not their lives unto the death."

Rev. 15: 3 "And they sing the song of Moses the servant of God, and the song of the Lamb, saying, Great and Marvelous are Thy Works, Lord God Almighty; Just and True are Thy Ways, Thou King Of Saints."

Rev. 15: 4 "Who shall not fear Thee, O Lord, and glorify Thy Name? for Thou only art Holy: for all nations shall come and worship before Thee; for Thy Judgments are made manifest."

Rev. 19: 7 "Let us be Glad and Rejoice, and give Honor to Him: for The Marriage Of The Lamb is come, and His wife hath made herself ready."

Rev. 21: 6,7 "And He said unto me, It is done. I am Alpha and Omega, the Beginning and the End. I will give unto him that is athirst of The Fountain Of The Water Of Life freely. He that overcometh shall Inherit all things; and I will be his God, and he shall be My son."

Rev. 22: 16,17 "I Jesus have sent Mine angel to testify unto you these things in the churches. I am the Root And The Offspring Of David, and the Bright And Morning Star. And the Spirit and the Bride say, Come. And let him that heareth say, Come. And let him that is athirst come. And whosoever will, let him take the Water Of Life freely."

Symbols found in Revelation (1)

Overview

This list gives the most important symbols used by John, with their meanings.

Adultery – Idolatry or apostasy; especially the latter. As Christ is represented as a bridegroom and the church as a bride, apostasy, or unfaithfulness to him, would be spiritual adultery, and a false church properly represented as a harlot.

Angel – Any agent or messenger of the divine will. The term may be a symbol of any movement of nations, or in history which carries out the divine purposes.

Ascension to Heaven – Exaltation in power and glory. Prosperity.

Babylon – The city which carried Israel into captivity. Hence, a symbol of any power that renders them captive, whether it be pagan or Papal Rome.

Balances – A symbol of justice, but when used to denote the weighing out of food, a symbol of scarcity.

Black – The color of mourning; hence a symbol of calamity and sorrow.

Black Horse – The horse was not used as a beast of burden by the ancients, but for purposes of war. Hence it is a symbol of war, and a black horse is a symbol of calamitous war.

Blood – A symbol of war.

Beast – The term rendered beast in the Revision means a savage wild beast. Hence it is a symbol of a cruel, tyrannical persecuting power. The term used in chap. 4, rendered beasts in the Common Version, is not the same. Instead of "Four Beasts" that should be rendered "Four Living Creatures."

Binding – This symbol means to restrain, to hold; also to deprive of power and render helpless.

Book – The record of the divine will. To seal a book is to conceal its meaning, since ancient books were rolls and could not be read when sealed. To open seals is to disclose the meaning. To devour a book is to become master of its contents. The book with seven seals is the book of human destiny, an outline of the great events which connect themselves with the church until its final triumph. The opening of its seals is the revelation of future history.

Bow – The bow, a warlike weapon, when held in the hand is a symbol of war.

Bride – The spouse of Christ, the Church, the New Jerusalem.

Bridegroom – Jesus Christ.

Candlestick – A symbol of a church, which should be a light in the world. The seven golden candlesticks are the seven churches. A symbol of any light-giving agency.

Chain – A symbol of bondage or affliction. To chain is to render powerless. To bind Satan with a chain is to destroy his power.

Cloud – An emblem of power and majesty. To ride upon the clouds is to appear in glory and exaltation.

Crown – The symbol of royal majesty. To enjoy exaltation and honor. To receive the crown of life is to receive the honors of eternal life.

Darkness – The well known symbol of calamity and affliction.

Day – "I have given you a day for a year." One revolution of the earth on its axis is a symbol of its annual revolution in its orbit. "Twelve hundred and sixty days" means as many years.

Death – A symbol of destruction.

Dragon – The old pagan Roman Empire.

Earth – The ancient civilized world, which corresponded in John's time with the Roman Empire. Political powers.

Earthquake – Political and moral revolutions and convulsions of society. The shaking of the established order of things. The subversion of states and fortunes.

Eclipse – Or the darkening of heavenly bodies, means the obscuration of the glory of kings and potentates of which sun, moon, and stars are symbols.

Egypt – The place of spiritual bondage. A condition of sinfulness. Opposition to Christ.

Elders – Probably princes of righteousness.

False Prophets – A false spiritual power which falsely claims divine authority for its teaching.

Fire – Fierce destruction. Never the symbol of a blessing, but of a curse.

Fire from Heaven – Divine destruction; but fire brought down from heaven by the two-horned dragon means excommunication and anathemas of a false spiritual power.

Flood – Symbol of overpowering distress from persecution or any cause.

Forehead – A mark in the forehead means a public profession.

Grave – To put in the grave, signifies to consign to oblivion. "Not to suffer dead bodies to be put into the grave," means that they shall be remembered.

Symbols found in Revelation (2)

Hail – Ravages and destruction.

Hand – A mark in the hand means the manner of life, or practice.

Harlot – An idolatrous community. The great Harlot is the apostate church.

Heavens and the Earth – The world. The political and religious universe. A new heavens and new earth imply a passing away of the old order of things and the establishment of a new order.

Horse – Used only for warlike purposes by the ancients and hence a symbol of war. The color of the horse indicates the condition of his rider and the state of the war.

Horns – "The great horn of the first king"; Daniel. A symbol of kings, kingdoms, or power. Seven horns indicate enormous power.

Incense – The prayers of the saints.

Islands – European states. In the prophets the "isles of the sea" meant the countries in and beyond the Mediterranean; hence, Europe.

Jerusalem – The capital of Judea and the seat of the temple becomes a symbol of the church of Christ. The "holy city" is contrasted with the "great city," Jerusalem with Babylon, or the true with the false church.

Jezebel – An unholy woman is a symbol of an unholy influence in the church.

Key – A symbol of power to deliver or imprison, to open heaven or hell, or to shut them; of power to save or destroy.

King – Supreme power of any kind. A government; a kingdom.

Lamb – The symbol of a sinless, sacrificial offering. The Lamb of God is Christ slain as a lamb from the foundation of the world.

Lion – A symbol of kingly power.

Locusts – The locusts, a devouring pest bred in the deserts of Arabia, are a symbol of devouring Arabian armies. The Arabians under Mohammed.

Manna – The bread of life. The truth of Christ.

Measuring Rod – The standard by which the church is measured. The Word.

Mountain – Some person or power conspicuous among men. Highly elevated. A great prince or government. A burning mountain is a baleful, destructive power.

Moon – A symbol of powers, rulers, and great men which are not supreme. A light which shines by reflecting another light.

Merchants – A symbol of those who make a gain of godliness and traffic in religious privileges.

Palm – A symbol of joy or victory.

Pale Horse – An image of desolating war, and a reign of death.

Red Horse – An image of cruel, bloody war, distinguished by awful carnage.

River of Life – Christ is the fountain of life. The abundant, ever flowing life that Christ bestows, is fitly symbolized by a river. The river, and tree, of life mean essentially the same.

Rod – The symbol of rule. The rod of iron is a symbol of resistless sway.

Scarlet – This color, the color of blood, symbolizes bloody cruelty. A scarlet woman is a persecuting church.

Seven – The perfect number. Completeness.

Stars – Shining lights in the world. Conspicuous men, whether in the church or the state.

Sun – As the great light giver, in one sense a symbol of Christ. Also a supreme ruler. The moon and stars indicate great lights of society, but inferior to the sun.

Sword – A symbol of slaughter. Also of conquest. A sword in the hand indicates by carnal weapons. A sword proceeding from the mouth indicates conquests by the word of God.

Temple of God – The church of which the tabernacle and temple were types. The temple of God in heaven, open, is the abode of God, heaven itself, the church above.

Throne – A symbol of authority.

Trumpet – The blast of a trumpet signifies the forward march of armies, carnal or spiritual. Also the proclamation of war or peace.

Time – Time, times and half a time is an annual revolution of the earth, a year, two years, a half year, or three and a half years. "Seven times" passed over Nebuchadnezzar, or seven years.

Wine Press – A symbol of an effusion of blood and of distress.

White – To be clothed in white is to be innocent, pure, and to be triumphant.

White Horse – Triumphant and glorious war.

Whore – Apostate church.

Winds – Symbol of commotion; of mighty movements. The "Four Winds" are four invasions of the Roman Empire.

Witness – The two witnesses are the two Testaments, for such is the meaning of the latter word.

Messianic prophecies in the Old Testament (1)

Key Bible verse

"For unto us a Child is born, unto us a
Son is given:
and the government shall be upon his
shoulder:
and his name shall be called
Wonderful, Counselor,
The mighty God,
The everlasting Father,
The Prince of Peace."
Isaiah 9: 6

Have you ever noticed?

In the Bible prophecy covers a wide
area of topics. But it does not exclude
predictive prophecy.

One facet of biblical prophecy may
be defined as: "A prophecy is the future
told in advance by God through a
prophet."

Messianic prophecies

The word "Messiah" means "anointed
one." In Greek it is Christ, and for
Christians it refers to Jesus as God's
Son and chosen one. For Jews of Jesus'
time, it referred to the hope for a new
prophet or king.

There are hundreds of prophecies
about Jesus in the Old Testament. Every
detail of Jesus' life is spelled out in
advance, from his birth in Bethlehem
to his death on the cross.

OVER 300 MESSIANIC PROPHECIES
In the Old Testament there are at
least 300 prophecies which foretell
something about the expected and
long-awaited Messiah.

Locating the Messianic prophecies

It sometimes surprises us to see how
the New Testament writers interpret
certain verses in the Old Testament as
prophecies about the Messiah.

GENESIS
Gen. 3: 15 ... He will bruise Satan's head
   ... Heb. 2: 14; 1 John 3: 18
Gen. 9: 26,27 ... The God of Shem will
   be the Son of Shem ... Luke 3: 36
Gen. 12: 3 ... As Abraham's seed, will
   bless all nations ... Acts. 3: 25,26
Gen. 12: 7 ... The promise made to
   Abraham's descendants ... Gal. 3: 16
Gen. 14: 18 ... A priest after
   Melchizedek ... Heb. 6: 20
Gen. 14: 18 A king ... Heb. 7: 2
Gen. 14: 18 ... The Last Supper
   foreshadowed ... Matt. 26: 26–29
Gen. 17: 19 ... The descendant of Isaac
   ... Rom. 9: 7
Gen. 22: 8 ... The Lamb of God
   promised ... John 1: 29
Gen. 22:18 ... As Isaac's descendant
   will bless all nations ... Gal. 3: 16
Gen.26: 2–5 ... The descendant of
   Isaac promised as the Redeemer ...
   Heb.11: 18
Gen. 49: 10 ... The time of his coming
   ... Luke 2: 1–7; Gal. 4: 4
Gen. 49: 10 ... The descendant of Judah
   ... Luke 3: 33
Gen. 49: 10 ... Called Shiloh or One
   sent ... John 17: 3

EXODUS
Ex. 3: 13,14 ... The great "I Am" ...
John 4: 26

Ex. 12: 5 ... A Lamb without blemish ...
1 Pet. 1: 19

Ex. 12: 13 ... The blood of the Lamb
saves from wrath ... Rom. 5: 8

Ex. 12: 21–27 ... Christ is our Passover
... 1 Cor. 5;7

Ex. 12: 46 ... Not a bone of the Lamb to
be broken ... John 19: 31–36

Ex. 15: 11 ... His holy nature ... Luke
1: 35; Acts 4: 27

Ex. 17: 6 ... The spiritual rock of Israel
... 1 Cor. 10: 4

Ex. 33: 19 ... His merciful nature ...
Luke 1: 72

LEVITICUS

Lev. 16: 15–17 ... Christ's once-for-all
death foreshadowed ... Heb. 9: 7–14

Lev. 16: 27 ... Suffering outside the
camp ... Matt. 27: 33; Heb. 13: 11,12

Lev. 17: 11 ... Blood and the life of the
flesh ... Matt. 26: 28; Mark 10: 45

Lev. 17: 11 ... Blood that makes
atonement ... 1 John 3: 14–18

Lev. 23: 36,37 ... The drink-offering and
"If any man thirst." ... John 19: 31–36

NUMBERS

Num. 9: 12 ... Not a bone of his is
broken ... John 19: 31–36

Num. 21: 9 ... The snake on a pole and
Christ lifted up ... John 3: 14–18

Num. 24: 17 ... Time: "I shall see him,
but not now." ... Gal. 4: 4

DEUTERONOMY

Deut. 18: 15 ... "This is of a truth that
prophet." ... John 6: 14

Deut. 18: 15–16 ... "Had ye believed
Moses, ye would believe me." ...
John 5: 45–47

Deut. 18: 18 ... Sent by the Father to
speak his word ... John 8: 28,29

Deut. 18: 19 ... Whoever will not hear
must bear his sin ... John 12: 15

Deut. 21: 23 ... Cursed is anyone who
hangs on a tree ... Gal. 3: 10–13

"His body shall not remain all
night upon the tree, but thou shalt in
any wise bury him that day; (for he
that is hanged is accursed of God;)
that thy land be not defiled, which
the Lord thy God giveth thee for an
inheritance" Deuteronomy 21: 23

"Christ hath redeemed us from
the curse of the law, being made a
curse for us: for it is written, Cursed
is every one that hangeth on a tree"
Galatians 3: 13.

RUTH

Ruth 4: 4–9 ... Christ, our kinsman,
has redeemed us ... Eph. 1: 3–7

1 AND 2 SAMUEL

1 Sam. 2: 10 ... Shall be an anointed
king ... Matt. 28: 18; John 12: 15

2 Sam. 7: 12 ... David's descendant ...
Matt. 1: 1

2 Sam. 7: 14a ... The Son of God ...
Luke 1: 32

2 Sam. 7: 16 ... David's house
established forever ... Luke 3: 31;
Rev. 22: 16

Quote Unquote

"God gave the prophecies, not
to gratify men's curiosity by
enabling them to foreknow
things, but that after they were
fulfilled they might be interpreted
by the event, and his own
providence, not the interpreter's,
be thereby manifested to the
world."   *Isaac Newton*

Messianic prophecies in the Old Testament (2)

Key Bible verse

"Yea, mine own familiar friend, in whom I trusted, which did eat of my bread, hath lifted up his heel against me." Psalm 41: 9

2 KINGS

2 Kgs. 2: 11 ... The bodily ascension to heaven illustrated ... Luke 24: 51

1 CHRONICLES

1 Chr. 17: 11 ... David's descendant ... Matt. 1: 1; 9: 27

1 Chr. 17: 12,13a ... To reign on David's throne forever ... Luke 1: 32,33

1 Chr. 17: 13a ... "I will be his Father, He ... my Son." ... Heb. 1: 5

JOB

Job 19: 23–27 ... The resurrection predicted ... John 5: 24–29

PSALMS

Ps. 2: 1–3 ... The enmity of kings foreordained ... Acts 4: 25–28

Ps. 2: 2 ... To have the title, Anointed (Christ) ... Acts 2: 36

Ps. 2: 6 ... His holy nature ... John 8: 46; Rev. 3: 7

Ps. 2: 6 ... To have the title King ... Matt. 2: 2

Ps. 2: 7 ... Declared the Beloved Son ... Matt. 3;17

Ps. 2: 7,8 ... The crucifixion and resurrection intimated ... Acts 13: 29–33

Ps. 2: 12 ... Life comes through faith in him ... John 20: 31

Ps. 8: 2 ... The mouths of babes praise him ... Matt. 21: 16

Ps. 8: 5,6 ... His humiliation and exaltation ... Luke 24: 50–53; 1 Cor. 15: 27

Ps. 16: 10 ... Was not to see corruption ... Acts 2: 31

Ps. 16: 9–11 ... Was to rise from the dead ... John 20: 9

Ps. 17: 15 ... The resurrection predicted ... Luke 24: 6

Ps. 22: 1 ... Forsaken because of sins of others ... 2 Cor. 5: 21

Ps. 22: 1 ... Words spoken from Calvary, "My God ... " Mk. 15: 34

Ps. 22: 2 ... Darkness over Calvary ... Matt. 27: 45

Ps. 22: 7 ... They shoot out the lip and shake the head ... Matt. 27: 39

Ps. 22: 8 ... "He trusted in God, let him deliver him" ... Matt. 27: 43

Ps. 22: 9 ... Born the Savior ... Luke 2: 7

Ps. 22: 14 ... Died of a broken (ruptured) heart ... John 19: 34

Ps. 22: 14,15 ... Suffered agony on Calvary ... Mark 15: 34–37

Ps. 22: 15 He thirsted John 19: 28

Ps. 22: 16 ... They pierced his hands and his feet ... John 19: 34,37; 20: 27

Ps. 22: 17,18 ... Stripped him as people watched ... Luke 23: 34,35

Ps. 22: 18 ... They parted his garments ... John 19: 23,24

Ps. 22: 20,21 ... He committed himself to God ... Luke 23: 46

Ps. 22: 20,21 ... Satanic power bruising the Redeemer's heel ... Heb. 2: 14

Ps. 22: 22 ... His resurrection declared ... John 20: 17

Ps. 22: 27 ... He shall be the governor of the nations ... Col. 1: 16

Ps. 22: 31 ... "It is finished" ... John 19: 30

Ps. 23: 1 ... "I am the good shepherd" ... John 10: 11

Ps. 24: 3 ... His exaltation predicted ... Acts 1: 11; Phil. 2: 9

Ps. 30: 3 ... His resurrection predicted ... Acts 2: 32

Ps. 31: 5 ... "Into thy hands I commit my spirit" ... Luke 23: 46

Ps. 31: 11 ... His acquaintances fled from him ... Mk. 14: 50

Ps. 31: 13 ... They took counsel to put him to death ... John 11: 53

Ps. 31: 14,15 ... " He trusted in God, let him deliver him" ... Matt. 27: 43

Ps. 34: 20 ... Not a bone of him broken ... John 19: 31–36

Ps. 35: 11 ... False witnesses rose up against him ... Matt. 26: 59

Ps. 35: 19 ... He was hated without a cause ... John 15: 25

Ps. 38: 11 ... His friends stood afar off ... Luke 23: 49

Ps. 40: 2–5 ... The joy of his resurrection predicted ... John 20: 20

Ps. 40: 6–8 ... His delight-the will of the Father ... John 4: 34

Ps. 40: 9 ... He was to preach the righteousness in Israel ... Matt. 4: 17

Ps. 40: 14 ... Confronted by adversaries in the Garden ... John 18: 4–6

Ps. 41: 9 ... Betrayed by a close friend ... John 13: 18

Ps. 45: 2 ... Words of grace come from his lips ... Luke 4: 22

Ps. 45: 6 ... To bear the title, God or Elohim ... Heb. 1: 8

Ps. 45: 7 ... A special anointing by the Holy Spirit ... Matt. 3: 16; Heb. 1: 9

Ps. 45: 7,8 ... Called the Christ (Messiah or Anointed) ... Luke 2: 11

Ps. 55: 12–14 ... Betrayed by a friend, not an enemy ... John 13: 18

Ps. 55: 15 ... Unrepentant death of the betrayer ... Matt. 27: 3–5; Acts 1: 16–19

Ps. 68: 18 ... To give gifts to men ... Eph. 4: 7–16

Ps. 68: 18 ... Ascended into heaven ... Luke 24: 51

Ps. 69: 4 ... Hated without a cause ... John 15: 25

Ps. 69: 8 ... A stranger to own brethren ... Luke 8: 0,21

Ps. 69: 9 ... Zealous for the Lord's house ... John 2: 17

Ps. 69: 14–20 ... Messiah's anguish of soul before crucifixion ... Matt. 26: 36–45

Ps. 69: 20 ... "My soul is exceeding sorrowful." ... Matt. 26: 38

Ps. 69: 21 ... Given vinegar in thirst ... Matt. 27: 34

Ps. 69: 26 ... The Savior given and smitten by God ... John 17: 4; 18: 11

Ps. 72: 10,11 ... Important people would visit him ... Matt. 2: 1–11

Ps. 72: 16 ... The corn of wheat to fall into the ground ... John 12: 24

Ps. 72: 17 ... All nations shall be blessed by him ... Acts 2: 11,12,41

Ps. 78: 1,2 ... He would teach in parables ... Matt. 13: 34,35

Ps. 78: 2b ... To speak the wisdom of God with authority...Matt. 7: 29

Quote Unquote

"What is needed desperately today is prophetic insight. Scholars can interpret the past; it takes prophets to interpret the present."

A.W. Tozer

Messianic prophecies in the Old Testament (3)

Key Bible verse

"For the prophecy came not in old time by the will of man: but holy men of God spake as they were moved by the Holy Ghost." 2 Peter 1: 21

God's test about prophecy

God used prophets to speak and to write down his prophecies. To show that they were true God gave this test. "And if thou say in thine heart, How shall we know the word which the Lord hath not spoken? When a prophet speaketh in the name of the Lord, if the thing follow not, nor come to pass, that is the thing which the Lord hath not spoken, but the prophet hath spoken it presumptuously: thou shalt not be afraid of him." Deuteronomy 18: 21,22

Fulfilled prophecy authenticated the message and the messenger.

PSALMS, CONTINUED

Ps. 88: 8 ... They stood afar off and watched ... Luke 23: 49

Ps. 89: 27 ... Emmanuel to be above earthly kings ... Luke 1: 32,33

Ps. 89: 35–37 ... David's descendant, throne, kingdom endure forever ... Luke 1: 32,33

Ps. 89: 36,37 ... His faithful nature ... Rev. 1: 5

Ps. 90: 2 ... He is from everlasting ... John 1: 1

Ps. 91: 11,12 ... Identified as messianic; used to tempt Christ ... Luke 4;10,11

Ps. 97: 9 ... His exaltation predicted ... Acts 1: 11; Eph. 1: 20

Ps. 100: 5 ... His good nature ... Matt. 19: 16,17

Ps. 102: 1–11 ... The suffering and reproach of Calvary ... John 21: 16–30

Ps. 102: 25–27 ... Messiah is the pre-existent Son ... Heb. 1: 10–12

Ps. 109: 25 ... Ridiculed ... Matt. 27: 39

Ps. 110: 1 ... Son of David ... Matt. 22: 43

Ps. 110: 1 ... To ascend to the right hand of the Father ... Mark. 16: 19

Ps. 110: 1 ... David's son called Lord ... Matt. 22: 44,45

Ps. 110: 4 ... A priest after Melchizedek's order ... Heb. 6: 20

Ps. 112: 4 ... His compassionate and gracious nature ... Matt. 9;36

Ps. 118: 17,18 ... Messiah's resurrection assured ... Luke 24: 5–7; 1 Cor. 15: 20

Ps. 118: 22,23 ... The rejected stone is head of the corner ... Matt. 21: 42,43

Ps. 118: 26a ... The blessed One presented to Israel ... Matt. 21: 9

Ps. 118: 26b ... To come while temple standing ... Matt. 21: 12–15

Ps. 132: 11 ... The descendant of David ... Luke 1: 32

Ps. 138: 1–6 ... The supremacy of David's descendant amazes kings ... Matt. 2: 2–6

Ps. 147: 3,6 ... The earthly ministry of Christ described ... Luke 4: 18

Ps. 1: 23 ... He will send the Spirit of God ... John 16: 7

SONG OF SONGS

Song. 5: 16 ... The altogether lovely One ... John 1: 17

ISAIAH

Is. 6: 1 ... When Isaiah saw his glory ... John 12: 40,41

Is. 6: 9,10 ... Parables fall on deaf ears ... Matt. 13: 13–15

Is. 6: 9–12 ... Blinded to Christ and deaf to his words ... Acts. 28: 23–29

Is. 7: 14 ... To be born of a virgin ... Luke 1: 35

Is. 7: 14 ... To be Emmanuel – God with us ... Matt. 1: 18–23

Is. 8: 8 ... Called Emmanuel ... Matt. 28: 20

Is. 8: 14 ... A stone of stumbling, a Rock of offense ... 1 Pet. 2: 8

Is. 9: 1,2 ... His ministry to begin in Galilee ... Matt. 4: 12–17

Is. 9: 6 ... A child born: his humanity ... Luke 1: 31

Is. 9: 6 ... A Son given: his deity ... Luke 1: 32; John 1: 14; 1 Tim. 3: 16

Is. 9: 6 ... Declared to be the Son of God with power ... Rom. 1: 3,4

Is. 9: 6 ... The Wonderful One ... Luke 4: 22

Is. 9: 6 ... The Counselor ... Matt. 13: 54

Is. 9: 6 ... The Mighty God ... Matt. 11: 20

Is. 9: 6 ... The Everlasting Father ... John 8: 58

Is. 9: 6 ... The Prince of Peace ... John 16: 33

Is. 9: 7 ... To establish an everlasting kingdom ... Luke 1: 32,33

Is. 9: 7 ... His just nature ... John 5: 30

Is. 9: 7 ... No end to his government, throne, and peace ... Luke 1: 32,33

Is. 11: 1 ... Called a Nazarene: the Branch, ... Matt. 2: 23

Is. 11: 1 ... A rod out of Jesse: son of Jesse ... Luke 3: 23,32

Is. 11: 2 ... The anointed One by the Spirit ... Matt. 3: 16,17

Is. 11: 2 ... His wise and understanding nature ... John 4: 4–26

Is. 11: 4 ... His truthful nature ... John 14: 6

Is. 11: 10 ... The Gentiles seek him ... John 12: 18–21

Is. 12: 2 ... Called "God is my salvation" ... Matt. 1: 21

Is. 25: 8 ... The resurrection predicted ... 1 Cor. 15: 54

Is. 26: 19 ... His power of resurrection predicted ... John 11: 43,44

Is. 28: 16 ... The Messiah is the precious corner stone ... Acts 4: 11,12

Is. 29: 13 ... He indicated hypocritical obedience to his Word ... Matt. 15: 7–9

Is. 29: 14 ... The wise are confounded by the Word ... 1 Cor. 1: 18–31

Is. 32: 2 ... A refuge: a man shall be a hiding place ... Matt. 23: 37

Is. 35: 4 ... He will come and save you ... Matt. 1: 21

Is. 35: 5 ... To have a ministry of miracles ... Matt. 11: 4–6

Is. 40: 3,4 ... Preceded by forerunner ... John 1: 23

Is. 40: 9 ... "Behold your God." ... John 1: 36; 19: 14

Is. 40: 11 ... A shepherd – compassionate life-giver ... John 10: 10–18

Is. 42: 1–4 ... The Servant, as a faithful, patient redeemer ... Matt. 12: 18–21

Is. 42: 2 ... Meek and lowly ... Matt. 11: 28–30

Quote Unquote

The expectation of the Messiah is so strong in Isaiah, that Jerome calls his book not a prophecy, but the gospel: "He is not so much a prophet as an evangelist."

Messianic prophecies in the Old Testament (4)

Key Bible verse

"All we like sheep have gone astray; we have turned every one to his own way; and the Lord hath laid on him the iniquity of us all." Isaiah 53: 6

Bird's eye view of Messianic prophecies in Isaiah

The Prophet Isaiah predicted that the future Messiah would:
- Be rejected like the rejected stone in the building of the temple.
- Have his way prepared by a wilderness prophet.
- Spend time in Galilee teaching the people of Galilee.
- Warn others to avoid hypocrisy.
- Restore eyesight to the blind and hearing to the deaf.
- Make the lame walk.
- Be a gentle spirit filled servant.
- Teach both Jews and Gentiles.
- Teach people to take care of the hungry and the needs of others.
- Preach to the poor and would do a work of healing to comfort those in sorrow and to bring discomfort to the careless.
- Be taken a prisoner and unjustly given the death penalty.
- Be silent in his own defense when others would seek to kill him.
- Go through suffering that would change his appearance.
- Allow others to whip his back.
- Allow others to spit in his face.
- Die, not from the mistreatment of the people but from the weight of the sins of the world.
- Die with criminals.
- Have a burial site provided for by a rich person.

ISAIAH, CONTINUED

Is. 42: 3 ... He brings hope for the hopeless ... John 4

Is. 42: 4 ... The nations shall wait on his teachings ... John 12: 20–26

Is. 42: 6 ... The light of the Gentiles ... Luke 2: 32

Is. 42: 1,6 ... His is a worldwide compassion ... Matt. 28: 19,20

Is. 42: 7 ... Blind eyes opened ... John 9: 25–38

Is. 43: 11 ... He is the only Savior ... Acts 4: 12

Is. 44: 3 ... He will send the Spirit of God ... John 16: 7,13

Is. 45: 23 ... He will be the judge ... John 5: 22; Rom. 14: 11

Is. 48: 12 ... The First and the Last ... John 1: 30; Rev. 1: 8,17

Is. 48: 17 ... He came as a teacher ... John 3: 2

Is. 49: 1 ... Called from the womb: his humanity ... Matt. 1: 18

Is. 49: 5 ... A servant from the womb ... Luke 1: 31; Phil. 2: 7

Is. 49: 6 ... He is salvation for Israel ... Luke 2: 29–32

Is. 49: 6 ... He is the light of the Gentiles ... Acts 13: 47

Is. 49: 6 ... He is salvation unto the ends of the earth ... Acts 15: 7–18

Is. 49: 7 ... He is despised by the nation ... John 8: 48,49

Is. 50: 3 ... Heaven is clothed in darkness at his humiliation ... Luke 23: 44,45

Is. 50: 4 ... He is a learned counselor for the weary ... Matt. 11: 28,29

Is. 50: 5 ... The servant bound willingly to obedience ... Matt. 26: 39

Is. 50: 6a ... "I gave my back to the smiters." ... Matt. 27: 26

"I gave my back to the smiters, and my cheeks to them that plucked off the hair: I hid not my face from shame and spitting" Isaiah 50: 6.

"Then released he Barabbas unto them: and when he had scourged Jesus, he delivered him to be crucified" Matthew 27: 26.

Is. 50: 6b ... He was smitten on the cheeks ... Matt. 26: 67

Is. 50: 6c ... He was spat upon ... Matt. 27: 30

Is. 52: 7 ... To publish good tidings of peace ... Luke 4: 14,15

Is. 52: 13 ... The servant exalted ... Acts 1: 8–11; Eph. 1: 19–22

Is. 52: 13 ... Behold, my servant ... Matt. 17: 5; Phil. 2: 5–8

Is. 52: 14 ... The servant abused ... Luke 18: 31–34; Matt. 26: 67,68

Is. 52: 15 ... Nations startled by the servant's message ... Rom. 15: 18–21

Is. 52: 15 ... His blood shed to make atonement ... Rev. 1: 5

Is. 53: 1 ... His people would not believe him ... John 12: 37–38

Is. 53: 2a ... He would grow up in a poor family ... Luke 2: 7

Is. 53: 2b ... Appearance of an ordinary man ... Phil. 2: 7,8

Is. 53: 3a ... Despised ... Luke 4: 28,29

Is. 53: 3b ... Rejected ... Matt. 27: 21–23

Is. 53: 3c ... Great sorrow and grief ... Luke 19: 41,42

Is. 53: 3d ... Men hide from being associated with him ... Mark

14: 50–52

Is. 53: 4a ... He would have a healing ministry ... Luke 6: 17–19

Is. 53: 4b ... He would bear the sins of the world ... 1 Pet. 2: 24

Is. 53: 4c ... Thought to be cursed by God ... Matt. 27: 41–43

Is. 53: 5a ... Bears penalty for humankind's transgressions ... Luke 23: 33

Is. 53: 5b ... His sacrifice would bring peace between man and God ... Col. 1: 20

Is. 53: 5c ... His back would be whipped ... Matt. 27: 26

Is. 53: 6a ... He would be the sin-bearer for all humankind ... Gal. 1: 4

Is. 53: 6b ... God's will that he bear sin for all humankind ... 1 John 4: 10

Is. 53: 7a ... Oppressed and afflicted ... Matt. 27: 27–31

Is. 53: 7b ... Silent before his accusers ... Matt. 27: 12–14

Is. 53: 7c ... Sacrificial lamb ... John 1: 29

Is. 53: 8a ... Confined and persecuted ... Matt. 26: 47–27: 31

Is. 53: 8b ... He would be judged ... John 18: 13–22

> ## Quote Unquote
>
> Prophecy or prediction, was one of the functions of the prophet. It has been defined as a "miracle of knowledge, a declaration or description or representation of something future, beyond the power of human sagacity to foresee, discern, or conjecture."
>
> *M.G. Easton*

Messianic prophecies in the Old Testament (5)

Key Bible verse

"Behold, the days come, saith the Lord, that I will make a new covenant with the house of Israel, and with the house of Judah." Jeremiah 31: 31

Isaiah, continued

Is. 53: 8c ... Killed ... Matt. 27: 35

Is. 53: 8d ... Dies for the sins of the world ... 1 John 2: 2

Is. 53: 9a ... Buried in a rich man's grave ... Matt. 27: 57

Is. 53: 9b ... Innocent and had done no violence ... Mark 15: 3

Is. 53: 9c ... No deceit in his mouth ... John 18: 38

Is. 53: 10a ... God's will that he die for humankind ... John 18: 11

Is. 53: 10b ... An offering for sin ... Matt. 20: 28

Is. 53: 10c ... Resurrected and live forever ... Mark 16: 16

Is. 53: 10d ... He would prosper ... John 17: 1–5

Is. 53: 11a ... God fully satisfied with his suffering ... John 12: 27

Is. 53: 11b ... God's servant ... Rom. 5: 18,19

Is. 53: 11c ... He would justify man before God ... Rom. 5: 8,9

Is. 53: 11d ... The sin-bearer for all mankind ... Heb. 9: 28

Is. 53: 12a ... Exalted by God because of his sacrifice ... Matt. 28: 18

Is. 53: 12b ... He would give up his life to save humankind ... Luke 23: 46

Is. 53: 12c ... Grouped with criminals ... Luke 23: 32

Is. 53: 12d ... Sin-bearer for all humankind ... 2 Cor. 5: 21

Is. 53: 12e ... Intercede to God in behalf of humankind ... Luke 23: 34

Is. 55: 3 ... Resurrected by God ... Acts 13: 34

Is. 55: 4 ... A witness ... John 18: 37

Is. 59: 15–16a ... He would come to provide salvation ... John 6: 40

Is. 59: 15,16b ... Intercessor between man and God ... Matt. 10: 32

Is. 59: 20 ... He would come to Zion as their redeemer ... Luke 2: 38

Is. 61: 1,2a ... The Spirit of God upon him ... Matt. 3: 16–17

Is. 61: 1–2b ... The Messiah would preach the good news ... Luke 4: 17–21

Is. 61: 1–2c ... Provide freedom from the bondage of sin and death ... John 8: 31,32

Is. 61: 1,2 ... Proclaim a period of grace ... John 5: 24

JEREMIAH

Jer. 23: 5,6a ... Descendant of David ... Luke 3: 23–31

Jer. 23: 5–6b ... The Messiah would be God ... John 13: 13

Jer. 23: 5–6c ... The Messiah would be both God and Man ... 1 Tim. 3: 16

Jer. 31: 22 ... Born of a virgin ... Matt. 1: 18–20

Jer. 31: 31 ... The Messiah would be the new covenant ... Matt. 26: 28

Jer. 33: 14,15 ... Descendant of David ... Luke 3: 23–31

EZEKIEL

Ezek. 17: 22–24 ... Descendant of David ... Luke 3: 23–31

Ezek. 34: 23–24 ... Descendant of David ... Matt. 1: 1

DANIEL

Dan. 7: 13,14a ... He would ascend into heaven ... Acts 1: 9–11

Dan. 7: 13–14b ... Highly exalted ... Eph. 1: 20–22

Dan. 7: 13–14c ... His dominion would be everlasting ... Luke 1: 31–33

Dan. 9: 24a ... To make an end to sins ... Gal. 1: 3–5

Dan. 9: 24b ... He would be holy ... Luke 1: 35

Dan. 9: 25 ... Announced to his people after the decree to rebuild the city of Jerusalem ... John 12: 12,13

Dan. 9: 26a ... Killed ... Matt. 27: 35

Dan. 9: 26b ... Die for the sins of the world ... Heb. 2: 9

Dan. 9: 26c ... Killed before the destruction of the temple ... Matt. 27: 50,51

Dan. 10: 5–6 ... Messiah in a glorified state ... Rev. 1: 13–16

HOSEA

Hos. 13: 14 ... He would defeat death ... 1 Cor. 15: 55–57

JOEL

Joel 2: 32 ... Offer salvation to all humankind ... Rom. 10: 12,13

MICAH

Mic. 5: 2a ... Born in Bethlehem ... Matt. 2: 1,2

Mic. 5: 2b ... God's servant ... John 15: 10

Mic. 5: 2c ... From everlasting ... John 8: 58

HAGGAI

Hag. 2: 6–9 ... He would visit the second Temple ... Luke 2: 27–32

Hag. 2: 23 ... Descendant of Zerubbabel ... Luke 3: 23–27

ZECHARIAH

Zech. 3: 8 ... God's servant ... John 17: 4

Zech. 6: 12,13 ... Priest and king ... Heb. 8: 1

Zech. 9: 9a ... Greeted with rejoicing in Jerusalem ... Matt. 21: 8–10

Zech. 9: 9b ... Beheld as king ... John 12: 12,13

Zech. 9: 9c ... The Messiah would be just ... John 5: 30

Zech. 9: 9d ... The Messiah would bring salvation ... Luke 19: 10

Zech. 9: 9e ... The Messiah would be humble ... Matt. 11: 29

Zech. 9: 9f ... Presented to Jerusalem riding on a donkey ... Matt. 21: 6–9

Zech. 10: 4 ... The cornerstone ... Eph. 2: 20

Zech. 11: 4–6a ... At his coming, Israel to have unfit leaders ... Matt. 23: 1–4

Zech. 11: 4–6b ... Rejection causes God to remove his protection ... Luke 19: 41–44

Zech. 11: 4–6c ... Rejected in favor of another king ... John 19: 13–15

Zech. 11: 7 ... Ministry to the poor ... Matt. 9: 35,36

Zech. 11: 8a ... Unbelief forces Messiah to reject them ... Matt. 23: 33

Quote Unquote

"I have always said, I always say, that the studious perusal of the sacred volume will make better citizens, better fathers, and better husbands."

Thomas Jefferson, 1743–1826, third President of the United States

Messianic prophecies in the Old Testament (6)

The "impossibility" of Messianic prophecies

"In an attempt to determine the scientific significance of these prophetic fulfillments, a California mathematician, Peter Stoner, made an interesting experiment with one of his classes. Each member of the class was assigned a particular Messianic prophecy for study, with the purpose of determining the statistical chance that the particular event could have been predicted without supernatural inspiration.

THE LAWS OF MATHEMATICAL PROBABILITY

The laws of mathematical probability show that the probability of several chance occurrences, independent of each other, being accomplished simultaneously is the product of the probabilities of all the individual occurrences. Thus the probability of all these forty-eight prophecies being fulfilled simultaneously in one individual, the promised Messiah and Savior, was calculated as the product of all the separate probabilities.

FORTY-EIGHT PROPHECIES

Stoner considers forty-eight prophecies and says, 'we find the chance that any one man fulfilled all forty-eight prophecies to be 1 in 10^{157} [one in ten to the power 157] (a number that would be written as one, followed by 181 zeros). 1 in 10, 000, 000, 000, 000, 000, 000, 000, 000, 000,

000, 000, 000, 000, 000, 000, 000, 000, 000, 000, 000, 000, 000, 000, 000, 000, 000, 000, 000, 000, 000, 000, 000, 000, 000, 000, 000, 000, 000, 000, 000, 000, 000, 000, 000, 000, 000, 000, 000, 000, 000, 000, 000.
All of which amounts to clear mathematical proof that the Scriptures must have been divinely inspired."

Henry M. Morris

ZECHARIAH

Zech. 11: 8b … Despised … Mt. 27: 20

Zech. 11: 9 … Stops ministering to the those who rejected him … Matt. 13: 10-11

Zech. 11: 10-11a … Rejection causes God to remove protection … Luke. 19: 41–44

Zech. 11: 10-11b … The Messiah would be God … John 14: 7

Zech. 11: 12-13a … Betrayed for thirty pieces of silver … Matt. 26: 14,15

ZECHARIAH FORESHADOWED THE BETRAYAL OF JESUS FOR THIRTY PIECES OF SILVER

Zechariah, in Zechariah 11: 12,13, writing about 520 and 518 b.c., spoke about a person who would receive thirty pieces of silver for betraying someone.

"And I said unto them, If ye think good, give me my price; and if not, forbear. So they weighed for my price thirty pieces of silver. And the Lord said unto me, Cast it unto the potter: a goodly price that I was prised at of them."

This foreshadowed an event that took place about 500 years later. Matthew 26:15 explains that Judas was paid thirty silver coins for his betrayal of Jesus. Judas made it possible for Jesus to be arrested without being surrounded by a large crowd of his own followers.

"And said unto them, What will ye give me, and I will deliver him unto you? And they covenanted with him for thirty pieces of silver. And from that time he sought opportunity to betray him" Matthew 26: 15,16.

Zechariah also prophesied that thirty pieces of silver would be thrown into the house of the Lord: "And I took the thirty pieces of silver, and cast them to the potter in the house of the Lord" Zechariah 11: 13.

Matthew, in Matthew 27: 5-7, records how this five hundred year old prophecy was precisely fulfilled when Judas tossed the money into the Temple (the house of the Lord) and the money was used to buy a potter's field as a burial place for foreigners.

"And he cast down the pieces of silver in the temple, and departed, and went and hanged himself. And the chief priests took the silver pieces, and said, It is not lawful for to put them into the treasury, because it is the price of blood. And they took counsel, and bought with them the potter's field, to bury strangers in."
Matthew 27: 5-7

Quote Unquote

"I see many contradictory religions, and consequently all false save one. Each wants to be believed on its own authority, and threatens unbelievers. I do not therefore believe them. Every one can say this; every one can call himself a prophet. But I see that Christian religion wherein prophecies are fulfilled; and that is what every one cannot do."

Blaise Pascal

Prophecies about the Messiah's birth and life

Key Bible verse

"This is he concerning whom it is written, Behold, I send my messenger before Your face, who shall make ready Your way before You." Luke 7: 27

Have you ever noticed?

Matthew used the following phrase, or a similar one, sixteen times in relation to the events surrounding Jesus' life: "This was done that it might be fulfilled what was spoken of the prophet…"

Just for the record

1. The Messiah would be the "Seed of a Woman."
Prophecy, Genesis 3: 15
Fulfillment, Galatians 4: 4; Revelation 12: 5

2. The Messiah would be in the line of Shem.
Prophecy, Genesis 9: 26,27
Fulfillment, Luke 3: 36

3. The Messiah would be in the line of Abraham.
Prophecy, Genesis 18: 18
Fulfillment, Galatians 3: 16; Matthew 1: 1

4. The Messiah would be in the line of Isaac.
Prophecy, Genesis 17: 19; Genesis 21: 11 NIV
Fulfillment, Matthew 1: 2

5. The Messiah would be in the line of Jacob.

Prophecy, Numbers 24: 17
Fulfillment, Matthew 1: 2

6. The Messiah would descend from the tribe of Judah.
Prophecy, Genesis 49: 10
Fulfillment, Luke 3: 33; Hebrews 7: 14; Revelation 5: 5

7. The Messiah would descend from David and rule on his throne.
Prophecies
"And there shall come forth a rod out of the stem of Jesse, and a Branch shall grow out of his roots; and the spirit of the Lord shall rest upon him." Isaiah 11: 1,2

"Once for all I have sworn by My Holiness that cannot be violated, I will not lie to David: his offspring shall endure forever, and his throne shall continue as the sun before Me." Psalm 89: 35,36 *Amplified Bible*

"Of the increase of his government and of peace, there shall be no end, upon the throne of David and over his kingdom, to establish it and to uphold it with justice and with righteousness from that latter time forth, even for evermore. The zeal of the Lord of Hosts will perform this." Isaiah 9: 7 *Amplified Bible*
Fulfillment
"A record of the genealogy of Jesus Christ the Son of David." Matthew 1: 1 *Amplified Bible.*
"The Lord God shall give unto to him the throne of his father, David." Luke 1: 32
"I am the root and the offspring of David." Revelation 22: 16 *Amplified Bible*

8. The Messiah would be born by a virgin.
Prophecy, Isaiah 7: 14
Fulfillment, Matthew 1: 18

9. The Messiah would be born in Bethlehem.
Prophecy
"But you, Bethlehem Ephratah, you are little to be among the clans of Judah, yet out of you shall One come forth for Me Who is to be Ruler in Israel; whose goings forth have been from of old, from ancient days." Micah 5: 2
Fulfillment
"Now when Jesus was born in Bethlehem of Judea in the days of Herod the king." Matthew 2: 1.

PROPHECIES ABOUT SPECIFIC EVENTS IN THE MESSIAH'S LIFE

10. The Messiah would be born during a time of massacre.
Prophecy, Jeremiah 31: 15
Fulfillment, Matthew 2: 16.

11. The Messiah would come from Egypt as a child.
Prophecy
"When Israel was a child, then I loved him, and called my son out of Egypt." Hosea 11: 1
Fulfillment
"And having risen, he took the Child and his mother by night and withdrew to Egypt, and remained there until Herod's death. This was to fulfill what the Lord had spoken by the prophet, Out of Egypt have I called My Son." Matthew 2: 14,15

12. The Messiah would be called a "Nazarene."
Prophecy, Isaiah 11: 1
Fulfillment, Matthew 2: 23

13. The Messiah would be preceded by a forerunner.
Prophecies, Isaiah 40: 3; Malachi 3: 1; Malachi 4: 5
Fulfillment, Matthew 3: 1–3; John 1: 23; Luke 7: 27
"The voice of him that crieth in the wilderness, Prepare ye the way of the Lord, make straight in the desert a highway for our God" Isaiah 40: 3.
"He said, I am the voice of one crying in the wilderness, Make straight the way of the Lord, as said the prophet Esaias" John 1: 23

14. The Messiah would begin his ministry in Galilee.
Prophecy, Isaiah 9: 1,2
Fulfillment, Matthew 4: 12–14

Quote Unquote
"The Old Testament contains over 300 references to the Messiah that were fulfilled in Jesus."
Josh. McDowell

Prophecies about the Messiah's ministry

Key Bible verse

"And beginning at Moses and all the prophets, he expounded unto them in all the scriptures the things concerning himself." Luke 24: 27

Have you ever noticed?

The whole of the New Testament clearly shows that Jesus fulfilled the Old Testament prophecies about the predicted Messiah.

A New Testament perspective

Messianic prophecies can be studied by looking at the verses in the Gospels which are fulfillments of Old Testament prophecies.

Matt. 4: 12–16 with Is. 9: 1,2 speak of humankind being enlightened.

Luke 4: 16–21 with Is. 61: 1–3 where sight is given to the blind.

Matt. 12: 17–21 with Is. 42: 1–4. Justice is proclaimed.

Luke 2: 32 with Is. 42: 6; Is. 49: 6. Light is given to the Gentiles.

John 6: 45 with Is. 54: 13. Everyone will be taught by God.

Matt. 8: 16,17 with Is. 53: 4. The sick will be healed.

Matt. 13: 34,35 with Ps. 78: 2. Teaching will be in parables.

Just for the record

1. The Messiah would bring salvation for both Jews and Gentiles.
Prophecies, Jeremiah 50: 6; Isaiah 42: 1

Fulfillment, Matthew 15: 24; Matthew 12: 21

"Behold my servant, whom I uphold; mine elect, in whom my soul delighteth; I have put my spirit upon him: he shall bring forth judgment to the Gentiles." Isaiah 42: 1

"And in his name shall the Gentiles trust." Matthew 12: 21.

2. The Holy Spirit would rest upon the Messiah.
Prophecies
"And the Spirit of the Lord shall rest upon him, the spirit of wisdom and understanding, the spirit of counsel and might, the spirit of knowledge and of the reverential and obedient fear of the Lord." Isaiah 11: 2 *Amplified Bible*
"The Spirit of the Lord God is upon me." Isaiah 61: 1
Fulfillment
"And when Jesus was baptized..the heavens were opened and he John saw the Spirit of God descending like a dove and alighting on him." Matthew 3: 16 *Amplified Bible*.
"The Spirit of the Lord is upon me." Luke 4: 18 *Amplified Bible*

3. The Messiah would proclaim God's messages.
Prophecies, Psalm 40: 7,9; Isaiah 61: 1
Fulfillment, Luke 4: 17–21; Luke 8: 1

4. The Messiah would be a teacher.
Prophecies, Isaiah 50: 4; Job 36: 22
Fulfillment, Luke 4: 22; John 3: 2; John 8: 2.

5. The Messiah would teach in parables
Prophecy, Psalm 78: 2

Fulfillment, Matthew 13: 3

6. The Messiah would perform miracles.
Prophecy, Isaiah 35: 5,6
Fulfillment, Matthew 11: 3–5

7. The Messiah would bear our sorrows.
Prophecy, Isaiah 53: 4,5
Fulfillment, Matthew 8: 16,17

"Surely he hath borne our griefs, and carried our sorrows: yet we did esteem him stricken, smitten of God, and afflicted. But he was wounded for our transgressions, he was bruised for our iniquities: the chastisement of our peace was upon him; and with his stripes we are healed." Isaiah 53: 4,5.

"When the even was come, they brought unto him many that were possessed with devils: and he cast out the spirits with his word, and healed all that were sick: That it might be fulfilled which was spoken by Esaias the prophet, saying, Himself took our infirmities, and bare our sicknesses". Matthew 8: 16,17

8. The Messiah would be rejected by his people.
Prophecy, Isaiah 53: 3
Fulfillment, John 1: 11

9. The Messiah would suffer greatly.
Prophecy
"A man of sorrows and pains, and acquainted with grief...oppressed and afflicted." Isaiah 53: 3,7
Fulfillment
"He began to show grief and distress of mind and was deeply depressed. Then He said to them, My soul is very sad and deeply grieved, so that I am almost dying of sorrow." Matthew

26: 37,38 Amplified Bible
"He must ... suffer many things." Matthew 16: 21 Amplified Bible
"And He said to them, Thus it is written, that the Christ, the Messiah, should suffer..." Luke 24: 46 Amplified Bible
"Although He was a Son, He learned active, special obedience through what He suffered." Hebrews 5: 8 Amplified Bible

10. The Messiah would pray.
Prophecy, Isaiah 53: 12
Fulfillment, Luke 6: 12; Hebrews 5: 7;
    Hebrews 7: 25

11. The Messiah would be praised while riding the colt of a donkey.
Prophecy, Zechariah 9: 9
Fulfillment, John 12: 12–15

Quote Unquote

"Jesus is the central figure of the Bible. His birth as the Jewish Messiah and Savior of the world was prophesied by Old Testament authors. Christ fulfilled 100 percent of all the Old Testament predictions of the birth, life, death, and resurrection of the Messiah. The New Testament makes an even more revolutionary claim: that Jesus Christ is the center of all biblical prophecy."

Campus Crusade for Christ

Prophecies about the Messiah's death (1)

Key Bible verse

"Then He said to them, This is what I told you while I was still with you, that everything which is written concerning Me in the Law of Moses and the prophets and the Psalms must be fulfilled. Then He thoroughly opened up their minds to understand the Scriptures." Luke 24: 44,45 *Amplified Bible*

Have you ever noticed?

There are more prophecies about Jesus' death in the Old Testament than any other topic.

An overview

One way of viewing the Bible is to link its books with the theme of the Messiah.
The Messiah, Hebrew for Anointed One, or Christ in Greek, can be seen:

IN THE OLD TESTAMENT:
The books of the Law give the FOUNDATION for Christ.
The history books display the PREPARATION for Christ.
The poetry expresses the ASPIRATION for Christ.
The books of prophecy declare the EXPECTATION for Christ.

IN THE NEW TESTAMENT:
The Gospels describe the MANIFESTATION of Christ.
The Acts detail the PROPAGATION of Christ.

The Letters proclaim the INTERPRETATION of Christ.
The book of Revelation is the CONSUMMATION of all things in Christ.

Just for the record

FROM THE PSALMS, OTHER THAN PSALM 22
1. The Messiah would be betrayed by a friend.
Prophecies, Psalm 41: 9; Psalm 55: 12–14
Fulfillment, Matthew 26: 21;
    John 13: 18,21

2. The Messiah would be accused by false witnesses.
Prophecies, Psalm 35: 11; Psalm 109: 2
Fulfillment, Matthew 26: 59

3. The Messiah would be silent before his accusers.
Prophecy, Psalm 38: 13,14
Fulfillment, 1 Peter 2: 23

4. The Messiah would be ridiculed.
Prophecies, Psalm 109: 25; Psalm 42: 10;
    Luke 4: 23
Fulfillment, Matthew 27: 39; Mark
    15: 29–31; Mark 15: 32; Luke 23: 35,36

5. The Messiah would be extremely thirsty.
Prophecies, Psalm 69: 21; Psalm 69: 3
Fulfillment, Matthew 27: 34; Matthew 27: 48

6. The Messiah would commit his Spirit to God.
Prophecy
    "Into Your hand I commit my spirit."
Psalm 31: 5 *Amplified Bible*

Fulfillment

"And Jesus, crying out with a loud voice, said, Father, into Your hands I commit My Spirit! And with these words, He expired." Luke 23: 46 *Amplified Bible*

7. The Messiah's friends would stand at a distance from him.
Prophecies, Psalm 38: 11; Psalm 87: 8
Fulfillment, Luke 23: 49

Have you ever noticed?

The exquisite details recorded in Psalm 22 highlight the amazing accuracy of David's prophetic picture of the Messiah's crucifixion.

Q and A

Where does the apostle Paul identify Jesus as "our Passover lamb" who "has been sacrificed"? In 1 Corinthians 5: 7.

Just for the record

PROPHECIES ABOUT THE MESSIAH'S DEATH FROM PSALM 22
1. The Messiah would have his hands and feet pierced.
Prophecy, Psalm 22: 16
Fulfillment, John 20: 27

2. The Messiah would be ridiculed.
Prophecy

All who see me laugh at me and mock me; they shoot out the lip, they shake the head saying, he trusted and rolled himself on the Lord, that He would deliver him. Let him deliver him, seeing He delights in him!" Psalm 22: 7,8

Fulfillment

"In the same way the chief priests with the scribes and elders made sport of him saying,...He trusts in God; let God deliver him now, if He cares for him and will have him, for He said, I am the son of God." Matthew 27: 41,43

3. The Messiah's clothes would be gambled for.
Prophecy, Psalm 22: 18
Fulfillment, John 19: 23,24

4. The Messiah would be stared at in public.
Prophecy, Psalm 22: 17
Fulfillment, Luke 23: 35

5. The Messiah would be deserted by God.
Prophecy

"My God, my God, why have you forsaken me?" Psalm 22: 1
Fulfillment

"Jesus cried with a loud voice, Eli, Eli, lama sabachthani? that is, My God, My God, why have You abandoned Me?" Matthew 27: 46

6. The Messiah would be extremely thirsty.
Prophecy, Psalm 22: 15
Fulfillment, John 19: 28

7. The state of the Messiah's heart.
Prophecy

"I am poured out like water...my heart is like wax, it is softened with anguish, and melted down within me." Psalm 22: 14
Fulfillment

John 19: 34 and "This is He who came by with water and blood." 1 John 5: 6

Prophecies about the Messiah's death (2)

Key Bible verse

"And Paul, as his manner was, went in unto them, and three sabbath days reasoned with them out of the scriptures, Opening and alleging, that Christ must needs have suffered, and risen again from the dead." Acts 17: 2,3

Overview

PROPHECIES ABOUT THE DEATH OF THE MESSIAH FROM OLD TESTAMENT BOOKS OTHER THAN THE PSALMS

Just for the record

1. The Messiah would be sold for thirty pieces of silver.
Prophecy
   "So they weighed out for my price thirty pieces of silver." Zechariah 11: 12
Fulfillment
   "And said, What are you willing to give me if I hand him over to you? And they weighed out and paid him thirty pieces of silver." Matthew 26: 15

2. The thirty pieces of silver would be returned for a potter's field.
Prophecy, Zechariah 11: 13
Fulfillment, Matthew 27: 5–7

3. The Messiah would be forsaken by his disciples.
Prophecy, Zechariah 13: 7
Fulfillment, Mark 14: 27

4. The Messiah would be silent before his accusers.
Prophecy, Isaiah 53: 7
Fulfillment, Matthew 27: 2,14

5. The Messiah would be hit across the face.

Prophecies, Zechariah 13: 7; Micah 5: 1
Fulfillment, Matthew 27: 30; Matthew 26: 67

6. The Messiah would be spat upon.
Prophecy, Isaiah 50: 6
Fulfillment, Matthew 26: 67,68; Matthew 27: 30

7. The Messiah would be whipped on the back.
Prophecy, Isaiah 50: 6
Fulfillment, Mark 15: 15

8. The Messiah's body would be disfigured.
Prophecy, Isaiah 52: 14
Fulfillment, Luke 22: 64

9. The Messiah's body would be pierced.
Prophecy, Zechariah 12: 10
Fulfillment, John 19: 34; John 19: 37

10. The Messiah would be killed alongside the guilty.
Prophecy, Isaiah 53: 9,12
Fulfillment, Mark 15: 27,28

11. The Messiah would pray for his persecutors.
Prophecy, Isaiah 53: 12
Fulfillment, Luke 23: 34

12. The Messiah would be stared at in public.
Prophecy, Isaiah 52: 14
Fulfillment, Matthew 27: 36

13. The Messiah's bones would not be broken.
Prophecies
   "Neither shall you break a bone of it." Exodus 12: 46
   "They shall leave none of it until the morning, nor break any bone of it. . . ."

Numbers 9: 12
Fulfillment

"But when they came to Jesus, and they saw that he was already dead, they did not break his legs...For these things took place that the Scripture might be fulfilled verified, carried out Not one of his bones shall be broken." John 19: 33,36

14. Darkness will cover the earth.
Prophecy, Amos 8: 9
Fulfillment, Matthew 27: 45

15. The Messiah would be buried with the rich.
Prophecy

"And they assigned him a grave with the wicked, and with a rich man in his death..." Isaiah 53: 9
Fulfillment

"When it was evening, there came a rich man from Arimathea, named Joseph, who was also a disciple of Jesus. He went to Pilate and asked for the body of Jesus, and Pilate ordered that it be given him. And Joseph took the body and rolled it up in a clean linen cloth used for swathing dead bodies, and laid it in his own fresh undefiled tomb, which he had hewn in the rock; and he rolled a big boulder over the door and went away." Matthew 27: 57–60

16. The Messiah's death would be a voluntary and substitutionary one.
Prophecy

"...He poured out his life unto death, and He let himself be regarded as a criminal and be numbered with the transgressors, yet he bore and took away the sin of many..." Isaiah 53: 12b

"But He was wounded for our transgressions, He was bruised for our guilt and iniquities; the chastisement needful to obtain peace and well being for us was upon him, and with the stripes that wounded him we are healed and made whole....All we like sheep have gone astray, we have turned every one to his own way; and the Lord has made to light on him the guilt and iniquity of us all...My Servant shall justify and make many righteous upright and in right standing with God; for He shall bear their iniquities and their guilt with the consequences, says the Lord." Isaiah 53: 5,6,11

"I gave My back to the smiters, and my cheeks to those who plucked off the hair; I hid not my face from shame and spitting." Isaiah 50: 6
Fulfillment

John 10: 11; Matthew 20: 28; and "He personally bore our sins in his own body to the tree as to an alter and offered himself on it, that we might die cease to exist to sin and live to righteousness. By his wounds you have been healed." 1 Peter 2: 24

Quote Unquote

"Jesus literally died of a broken heart. Not only was it punctured by the soldier's sword thrust, but the extreme mental and spiritual torture was so great that his heart was ruptured before the point of the sword pierced it. Appearance of the blood and water indicated that the lymphatic fluid apparently had separated from the red blood, producing 'blood and water.'"   *Herbert Lockyer*

Prophecies about the Messiah's resurrection and ascension

Key Bible verse

"Why should it be thought incredible by any of you that God raises the dead?"

Acts 26: 8

Have you ever noticed?

Psalm 110 can only refer, as the Jews fully acknowledged, to the royal dignity, priesthood, victories, and triumphs of the Messiah.

"The Lord said unto my Lord, Sit thou at my right hand, until I make thine enemies thy footstool.

2 The Lord shall send the rod of thy strength out of Zion: rule thou in the midst of thine enemies.

3 Thy people shall be willing in the day of thy power, in the beauties of holiness from the womb of the morning: thou hast the dew of thy youth.

4 The Lord hath sworn, and will not repent, Thou art a priest for ever after the order of Melchizedek.

5 The Lord at thy right hand shall strike through kings in the day of his wrath.

6 He shall judge among the heathen, he shall fill the places with the dead bodies; he shall wound the heads over many countries.

7 He shall drink of the brook in the way: therefore shall he lift up the head."

Psalm 110: 1–7

The Lord

See Ps. 8: 1; Matt. 22: 42–46; Mark 12: 35–37; Luke 22: 41.

Sit

See Mark 16: 19; Act 2: 34; Eph. 1: 20–22; Heb. 12: 2, 1; Pet. 3: 22.

Until

See Ps. 2: 6–9; Ps. 45: 6,7; 1 Cor. 15: 25; Heb. 1: 3,13; Heb. 10: 12,13

Just for the record

1. The Messiah would not be bound to the power of death.
Prophecies, Psalm 16: 10; Psalm 30: 3
Fulfillment, Mark 16: 5–6; Acts 13: 35

2. The Messiah would destroy the power of death for others.
Prophecies

"Your dead shall live, O Lord; the bodies of our dead saints shall rise. You who dwell in the dust, awake and sing for joy!" Isaiah 26: 19

"And many of those who sleep in the dust of the earth shall awake, some to everlasting life and some to shame and everlasting contempt and abhorrence." Daniel 12: 2

"O Death, where are your plagues? O Sheol, where are your destructions?" Hosea 13: 14

"He will swallow up death in victory– He will abolish death forever; and the Lord God will wipe away tears from off all faces; and the reproach of his people He will take away from off all the earth; for the Lord has spoken it." Isaiah 25: 8

Fulfillment

"Jesus said to her, I am Myself the Resurrection and the Life. Whoever believes in Me, although he may die, yet he shall live." John 11: 25

"It is that purpose and grace which He now has made known and has fully disclosed and made real to us through the appearing of our Savior Jesus Christ Who annulled death and made it of no effect, and brought life and immortality – that is, immunity from eternal death – to light through the Gospel." 2 Timothy 1: 10

"And when this perishable puts on the imperishable and this that was capable of dying puts on freedom from death, then shall be fulfilled the Scripture that says, Death is swallowed up utterly vanquished, forever in and unto victory. O death, where is your victory? O death, where is your sting?" 1 Corinthians 15: 54–55

"Jesus suffered death, in order that by the grace unmerited favor of God to us sinners He might experience death for every individual person...He himself in a similar manner partook of the same nature, that by going through death He might bring to nought and make of no effect him who had the power of death, that is, the devil; and also that He might deliver and completely set free all those who through the haunting fear of death were held in bondage throughout the whole course of their lives." Hebrews 2: 9,14,15

3. The Messiah would be raised on the third day.

Prophecies, Jonah 1: 17; John 2: 19; Matthew 12: 40; Mark 8: 31

Fulfillment, Luke 24: 1–3,6; Luke 24: 45,46

4. The Messiah would ascend to heaven.

Prophecy, Psalm 68: 18

Fulfillment, Mark 16: 19; Luke 24: 51; Acts 1: 9

Quote Unquote

"Psalm 110: 1 gives special insight concerning Christ's ascension after the resurrection.

'The Lord said unto my Lord, Sit thou at my right hand, until I make shine enemies thy footstool.'

Literally, this reads:

'Jehovah said unto Adonai,' using two names of God.

The Father is apparently speaking to the Son.

This particular verse is applied to Christ no less than five times in the New Testament."

Henry M. Morris

The Messiah's return

Key Bible verses

"When the Son of man comes in his glory his majesty and splendor and all the holy angels with him, then He will sit on the throne of his glory. All nations shall be gathered before him and He will separate them the people from one another as a shepherd separates his sheep from the goats." Matthew 25: 31,32

Have you ever noticed?

The Second Coming of Christ is mentioned some 318 times in the New Testament. This is more than any other basic doctrine.

Prophecies about the Messiah's second coming

Just for the record

1. Christ will return a second time. Prophecies

"And then they will see the Son of man coming in a cloud with great transcendent and overwhelming power and all his kingly glory majesty and splendor." Luke 21: 27

"Men of Galilee, why do you stand gazing into heaven? This same Jesus, Who was caught away and lifted up from among you into heaven will return in just the same way in which you saw him go into heaven." Acts 1: 11

"Lo, He is coming with the clouds, and every eye will see him, even those who pierced him; and all the tribes of the earth shall gaze upon him and beat their breasts and mourn and lament over him. Even so must it be. Amen." Revelation 1: 7

"For just as the lightening flashes from the east and shines and is seen as far as the west, so will the coming of the Son of man be...Then they will see the Son of man coming on the clouds of heaven with power and great glory – in brilliancy and splendor." Matthew 24: 27,30

"For the Lord himself will descend from heaven with a loud cry of summons, with the shout of an archangel, and with the blast of the trumpet of God." 1 Thessalonians 4: 16a

2. Christ will return to judge the nations.
Prophecies, Matthew 25: 31–32;
    1 Corinthians 4: 5; 2 Timothy 4: 1;
    2 Corinthians 5: 10; John 5: 22
""When the Son of man shall come in his glory, and all the holy angels with him, then shall he sit upon the throne of his glory: And before him shall be gathered all nations: and he shall separate them one from another, as a shepherd divideth his sheep from the goats." Matthew 25: 31,32.

3. The exact time of his return is unknown.
Prophecies, Matthew 24: 36,44;
    1 Thessalonians 5: 2; Revelation 16: 15,
    Matthew 25: 13

Prophecies about the signs accompanying the Messiah's return

Key Bible verse

"For false Christs and false prophets will arise, and they will show great signs and wonders, so as to deceive and lead astray, if possible, even the elect God's chosen ones." Matthew 24: 24

Have you ever noticed?

Some of the most bizarre and wildly inaccurate statements about the Christian faith are made concerning the end of the world. To be clear about what Jesus did and did not say on this subject read all of Matthew chapters 24 and 25.

Just for the record

1. It will be a time when people are deceived.
Prophecies
    "Be careful that no one misleads you – deceiving you and leading you into error. For many will come in on the strength of My name – appropriating the name which belongs to Me – saying, I am the Messiah, the Christ; and they will lead many astray. . . ."
Matthew 24: 4,5

2. False Christs will appear.
Prophecy, Matthew 24: 24

3. It will be a time when people ignore God.
Prophecy, Matthew 24: 37

4. The appearance of the "man of lawlessness."
Prophecy, 2 Thessalonians 2: 3,4

5. Demonic teaching will be rife.
Prophecy, 1 Timothy 4: 1

6. A time when true religion is rejected.
Prophecy, 2 Timothy 3: 1, 4,5

7. A time when God's followers must stay alert
Prophecy, 1 Thessalonians 5: 4

8. Signs will indicate the proximity of Jesus' return.
Prophecy
    "From the fig tree learn its lesson: as soon as its young shoots become soft and tender and it puts out its leaves, you know of a surety that summer is near. So also when you see these signs all taken together coming to pass, you may know of a surety that he is near, at the very doors." Matthew 24: 32,33

Quote Unquote

"I believe that as Jesus Christ has once come in grace, so also is he to come a second time in glory."
Benjamin B. Warfield

All the miracles of Jesus

Four Greek words

In the New Testament these four Greek words are used to describe miracles:

(1) *Semeion*, a "sign," i.e., an evidence of a divine commission; an attestation of a divine message (Matt. 12: 38,39; 16: 1, ; Mark 8: 11; Luke 11: 16; 23: 8; John 2: 11,18,23; Acts 6: 8, etc.); evidence of the presence of God.

(2) *Terata*, "wonders"; events that evoke astonishment in those who observe them (Acts 2: 19).

(3) *Dunameis*, "mighty works"; deeds performed by a superhuman power (Acts 2: 22; Rom. 15: 19; 2 Thess. 2: 9).

(4) *Erga*, "works"; the deeds of Jesus, (John 5: 20,36).

Miracles are seals of a divine mission.

Miracles Recorded in the Gospels		
Unique to Matthew		
1. Two blind men healed		Matt. 9: 27–31
2. Coin in the fish's mouth		Matt. 17: 24–27
Unique to Mark		
1. The deaf and dumb man		Mark 7: 31–37
2. The blind man of Bethsaida		Mark 8: 22–26
Unique to Luke		
1. Jesus passes unseen through the crowd		Luke 4: 28–30
2. The miraculous catch of fish		Luke 5: 4–11
3. The raising of the widow's son at Nain		Luke 7: 11–18
4. The woman in the synagogue healed		Luke 13: 11–17
5. Man with swollen arms and legs healed		Luke 14: 1–6
6. The ten lepers		Luke 17: 11–19
7. The healing of Malchus		Luke 22: 50,51
Unique to John		
1. Water made wine		John 2: 1–11
2. Nobleman's son healed at Capernaum		John 4: 46–54
3. Paralyzed man in Jerusalem healed		John 5: 1–9
4. Man born blind healed		John 9: 1–7
5. Lazarus raised from the dead		John 11: 38–44
6. Catch of fish		John 21: 1–14
Common to Matthew and Mark		
1. Daughter of Canaanite woman healed	Matt. 15: 28	Mark 7: 24
2. Four thousand fed	Matt. 15: 32	Mark 8: 1
3. Fig tree cursed	Matt. 21: 18	Mark 11: 12
Common to Matthew and Luke		
1. Centurion's servant healed	Matt. 8: 5	Luke 7: 1
2. Blind and dumb demoniac healed	Matt. 12: 22	Luke 11: 14

Common to Mark and Luke			
1. Demon-possessed man healed in synagogue at Capernaum		Mark 1: 23	Luke 4: 33
Common to Matthew, Mark, and Luke			
1. Peter's wife's mother healed	Matt. 8: 14	Mark 1: 30	Luke 4: 38
2. Storm stilled	Matt. 8: 23	Mark 4: 37	Luke 8: 22
3. Demoniacs of Gadara healed	Matt. 8: 28	Mark 5: 1	Luke 8: 26
4. Leper healed	Matt. 8: 2	Mark 1: 40	Luke 5: 12
5. Jairus's daughter brought back to life	Matt. 9: 23	Mark 5: 23	Luke 8: 41
6. Woman with severe bleeding healed	Matt. 9: 20	Mark 5: 25	Luke 8: 43
7. Paralyzed man healed	Matt. 9: 2	Mark 2: 3	Luke 5: 18
8. Man with paralyzed hand healed	Matt. 12: 10	Mark 3: 1	Luke 6: 6
9. Epileptic boy healed	Matt. 17: 14	Mark 9: 14	Luke 9: 37
10. Two blind men healed	Matt. 20: 29	Mark 10: 46	Luke 18: 35
Common to Matthew, Mark ,and John			
Jesus walks on the sea	Matt. 14: 25	Mark 6: 48	John 6: 15
Common to all the evangelists			
Jesus feeds 5000	Matt. 14: 15	Mark 6: 30	Luke 9: 10	John 6: 1–14
In addition to the above miracles, there are four miraculous events linked to Jesus' life –			
1. The conception by the Holy Spirit		Luke 1: 35	
2. The transfiguration		Matt. 17: 1–8	
3. The resurrection		John 21: 1–14	
4. The ascension		Luke 2: 42–51	

The feeding of the 5000

This is the only miracle recorded in all four Gospels.

"And the apostles, when they were returned, declared unto him what things they had done. And he took them, and withdrew apart to a city called Bethsaida.

11 But the multitudes perceiving it followed him: and he welcomed them, and spake to them of the kingdom of God, and them that had need of healing he cured.

12 And the day began to wear away; and the twelve came, and said unto him, Send the multitude away, that they may go into the villages and country round about, and lodge, and get provisions: for we are here in a desert place.

13 But he said unto them, Give ye them to eat. And they said, We have no more than five loaves and two fishes; except we should go and buy food for all this people.

14 For they were about five thousand men. And he said unto his disciples, Make them sit down in companies, about fifty each.

15 And they did so, and made them all sit down.

16 And he took the five loaves and the two fishes, and looking up to heaven, he blessed them, and brake; and gave to the disciples to set before the multitude.

17 And they ate, and were all filled: and there was taken up that which remained over to them of broken pieces, twelve baskets."

Luke 9: 10–17 ASV

All the parables of Jesus

Parables and allegories

The parables spoken by Jesus are all recorded in the synoptic (i.e., the first three) Gospels. The fourth Gospel contains no parables as such, although the illustration of the good shepherd (John 10: 1–16) has all the essential features of a parable.

John's allegory

"Jesus therefore said unto them again, Verily, verily, I say unto you, I am the door of the sheep.

8 All that came before me are thieves and robbers: but the sheep did not hear them.

9 I am the door; by me if any man enter in, he shall be saved, and shall go in and go out, and shall find pasture.

10 The thief cometh not, but that he may steal, and kill, and destroy: I came that they may have life, and may have it abundantly.

11 I am the good shepherd: the good shepherd layeth down his life for the sheep.

12 He that is a hireling, and not a shepherd, whose own the sheep are not, beholdeth the wolf coming, and leaveth the sheep, and fleeth, and the wolf snatcheth them, and scattereth them:

13 he fleeth because he is a hireling, and careth not for the sheep.

14 I am the good shepherd; and I know mine own, and mine own know me,

15 even as the Father knoweth me, and I know the Father; and I lay down my life for the sheep.

16 And other sheep I have, which are not of this fold: them also I must bring, and they shall hear my voice: and they shall become one flock, one shepherd."

John 10: 7–16 ASV

All the New Testament parables

Parables Recorded in the Gospels	
Unique to Matthew	
1. The tares	Matt. 13: 24–30
2. The hid treasure	Matt. 13: 44
3. The pearl of great price	Matt. 13: 45, 46
4. The drag net	Matt. 13: 47–50
5. The unmerciful servant	Matt. 18: 23–35
6. The laborers in the vineyard	Matt. 20: 1–16
7. The two sons	Matt. 21: 28–32
8. Marriage of the king's son	Matt. 22: 1–14
9. The ten virgins	Matt. 25: 1–13
10. The talents	Matt. 25: 14–30
11. Sheep and goats	Matt. 25: 31–46

Unique to Mark		
1. The seed growing secretly		Mark 4: 26–29
2. Watchfulness		Mark 13: 34–35
Unique to Luke		
1. The two debtors		Luke 7: 41–43
2. The good Samaritan		Luke 10: 25–37
3. The importunate friend at midnight		Luke 11: 5–8
4. The rich fool		Luke 12: 16–21
5. The servants watching		Luke 12: 35–40
6. The steward		Luke 12: 42–48
7. Barren fit tree		Luke 13: 6–9
8. The great supper		Luke 14: 16–24
9. Building a tower, and a king going to war		Luke 14: 28–33
10. The lost piece of silver		Luke 15: 8–10
11. The prodigal son		Luke 15: 11–32
12. The unjust steward		Luke 16: 1–13
13. The rich man and Lazarus		Luke 16: 19–31
14. The master and servant		Luke 17: 7–10
15. The unjust judge and the importunate widow		Luke 18: 1–8
16. The Pharisee and publican		Luke 18: 10–14
17. The pounds		Luke 19: 12–27

There are no parables, apart from a special form of allegory, found in John. The word translated "parable" in John 10: 6 is not the word so translated in the Synoptics. The word which John uses (*paroimia*) is better translated "allegory." It occurs elsewhere only in John 16: 25,29 and 2 Peter 2: 22, where it is translated "proverb."

Common to Matthew and Luke		
1. The house on the rock and on the sand	Matt. 7: 24–27	Luke 6: 46–49
2. Leaven	Matt. 13: 33,34	Luke 13: 18–21
3. The lost sheep	Matt. 18: 12–14	Luke 15: 1–10

Common to Matthew, Mark, and Luke			
1. Candle under a bushel	Matt. 5: 15	Mark 4: 21	Luke 8: 16
2. New cloth and an old garment	Matt. 9: 16	Mark 2: 21	Luke 5: 36
3. New wine in old bottles	Matt. 9: 17	Mark 2: 22	Luke 5: 37,38
4. The sower	Matt. 13: 1–23	Mark 4: 1–9	Luke 8: 4–15
5. The mustard seed	Matt. 13: 31,32	Mark 4: 30–34	Luke 13: 18–20
6. The vineyard	Matt. 21: 33–46	Mark 12: 1–12	Luke 20: 9–19
7. The fig tree	Matt. 24: 32–35	Mark 13: 28–31	Luke 21: 29–33

Interpreting parables

A parable is a true-to-life story told to illustrate one central truth. In general, the details do not have independent significance but are simply inserted to make the story realistic. It is a mistake to attach doctrinal meaning to every detail unless the Bible does so.

The resurrection of Jesus (1)

Overview

The whole of the New Testament revelation rests on the historical fact of the resurrection of Jesus.

Peter's first sermon

On the day of Pentecost Peter argues for the necessity of Christ's resurrection from the prediction in Ps. 16 (Acts 2: 24–28).

Jesus' teaching

In Jesus' own teaching he often spoke quite clearly about his resurrection (Matt. 20: 19; Mark 9: 9; 14: 28; Luke 18: 33; John 2: 19–22).

"Jesus answered and said unto them, Destroy this temple, and in three days I will raise it up. 20 Then said the Jews, Forty and six years was this temple in building, and wilt thou rear it up in three days?

21 But he spake of the temple of his body.

22 When therefore he was risen from the dead, his disciples remembered that he had said this unto them; and they believed the scripture, and the word which Jesus had said." John 2: 19–21

Ten appearances

Ten different appearances of the risen Lord Jesus Christ are recorded in the New Testament.

They may be arranged as follows:

(1) To Mary Magdalene at the sepulcher alone

This is recorded at some length only by John (John 20: 11–18), but is alluded to by Mark (Mark 16: 9–11).

(2) To some women

"The other Mary," Salome, Joanna, and others, as they returned from the tomb. Matthew (Matt. 28: 1–10) alone gives an account of this. (Compare Mark 16: 1–8, and Luke 24: 1–11.)

(3) To Peter

To Simon Peter alone on the day of the resurrection. (See Luke 24: 34; 1 Cor. 15: 5.)

(4) To two disciples

To the two disciples on the way to Emmaus on the day of the resurrection, recorded in full only by Luke (Luke 24: 13–35. cf. Mark 16: 12,13).

(5) To the ten disciples

Thomas was not present. This was in Jerusalem in the evening of Jesus' resurrection day. John records this (John 20: 19–24).

(6) To the eleven disciples

This time, Thomas was present with the other ten apostles. It happened in Jerusalem (Mark 16: 14–18; Luke 24: 33–40; John 20: 26–28. See also 1 Cor. 15: 5).

(7) To the disciples when fishing on the Sea of Galilee

Only John (John 21: 1–23) records this event.

(8) To more than five hundred

To the eleven, and to more than five hundred Christian brethren at the same time, in Galilee (1 Cor. 15: 6; cf. Matt. 28: 16–20).

(9) To James

We are not given any details about this resurrection appearance (1 Cor. 15: 7). ". . . he was buried, and that he rose again the third day according to the scriptures:

And that he was seen of Cephas, then of the twelve:

After that, he was seen of above five hundred brethren at once; of whom the greater part remain unto this present, but some are fallen asleep.

After that, he was seen of James; then of all the apostles.

And last of all he was seen of me also, as of one born out of due time."

1 Corinthians 15: 4–8

(10) To the apostles just before the ascension

They went with him from Jerusalem to Mount Olivet, and there they saw him ascend "till a cloud received him out of their sight" (Mark 16: 19; Luke 24: 50–52; Acts 1: 4–10).

No apparition

It is worth noting that on most of these resurrection appearances Jesus allows his disciples ample opportunity to check that his resurrection was real.

The resurrection of Jesus (2)

He spoke with them face to face

They touched him (Matt. 28: 9; Luke 24: 39; John 20: 27).

He ate bread with them (Luke 24: 42,43; John 21: 12, 13).

Appearing to Paul

Paul claimed to have had a personal resurrection appearance of Jesus at Damascus. Paul refers to it as an appearance of the risen Savior (Acts 9: 3–9,17; 1 Cor. 15: 8; 9: 1).

Additional evidence

It is implied by Luke (Acts 1: 3) that there may have been other appearances of Jesus about which we have no record.

Trinitarian act

The resurrection is spoken of as the work:

(1) of God the Father
(Ps. 16: 10; Acts 2: 24; 3: 15; Rom. 8: 11; Eph. 1: 20; Col. 2: 12)
    "Now the God of peace, that brought again from the dead our Lord Jesus, that great shepherd of the sheep, through the blood of the everlasting covenant" Hebrews 13: 20.

(2) of Christ himself
(John 2: 19)
"No man taketh it from me, but I lay it down of myself. I have power to lay it down, and I have power to take it again.

This commandment have I received of my Father" John 10: 18.

(3) of the Holy Spirit
"For Christ also hath once suffered for sins, the just for the unjust, that he might bring us to God, being put to death in the flesh, but quickened by the Spirit" 1 Peter 3: 18.

What the resurrection means

The resurrection of Jesus is a victory over death and the grave for all his followers.

    The importance of Christ's resurrection can be seen in the fact that if he did indeed rise from the dead the gospel is true, but if he did not rise the gospel is false.

    The resurrection of Jesus is evidence of the Father's acceptance of Jesus' work of redemption.

    His resurrection proves that he made atonement for our sins.

    Jesus' resurrection also assures us that the resurrection of all believers will take place (Rom. 8: 11; 1 Cor. 6: 14; 15: 47–49; Phil. 3: 21; 1 John 3: 2).

    As Jesus lives, so we will live also.

    Jesus' resurrection showed that he was indeed the Son of God. It authenticated all his claims (John 2: 19; 10: 17).

What if Jesus did not rise?

"If Christ did not rise, the whole scheme of redemption is a failure, and all the predictions and anticipations of its glorious results for time and for eternity, for men and for angels of every rank and order, are proved to be chimeras.

'But now is Christ risen from the dead, and become the first-fruits of them that slept.'

Therefore the Bible is true from Genesis to Revelation. The kingdom of darkness has been overthrown, Satan has fallen as lightning from heaven, and the triumph of truth over error, of good over evil, of happiness over misery is for ever secured."

Hodge

'fold up the linen.'"

Matthew Henry, commenting on John 20: 1–10

Maybe the disciples stole Jesus' body?

The Roman soldiers were bribed (Matt. 28: 12–14) to circulate a report about Jesus' resurrection in which they would say, "his disciples came by night and stole him away while we slept."

"The grave-clothes in which Christ had been buried were found in very good order, which serves for an evidence that his body was not 'stolen away while men slept.'

Robbers of tombs have been known to take away 'the clothes' and leave the body; but none ever took away 'the body' and left the clothes, especially when they were 'fine linen' and new (Mark 15: 46).

Any one would rather choose to carry a dead body in its clothes than naked.

Or if they that were supposed to have stolen it would have left the grave-clothes behind, yet it cannot be supposed they would find leisure to

Conversions in Acts (1)

Bible conversions consisted of:

Hearing: Rom. 10: 13–17
Believing: Acts 2: 44
Repenting: Acts 2: 38
Confessing the name of Jesus:
  Rom. 10: 10; Acts 8: 37
Being baptized: Acts 2: 38
Living faithfully to death: Rev. 2: 10

Conversions in the book of Acts

WHAT THEY DID:
  HEARD
  BELIEVED
  REPENTED
  CONFESSED
  WERE BAPTIZED

Who was converted:

JEWS AT PENTECOST
Acts 2: 37–41

THE ETHIOPIAN EUNUCH
Acts 8: 37,38

SAMARITANS
Acts 8: 6; Acts 8: 12

SAUL OF TARSUS
Gal. 2: 16; Acts 9: 18; Acts 22: 16

CORNELIUS
Acts 10: 34–48

LYDIA
Acts 16: 14,15

PHILIPPIAN JAILOR
Acts 16.31–33

CORINTHIANS
Acts 18: 8

Baptism and conversion

Every person whose conversion is
recorded in the New Testament was
baptized.

1. Day of Pentecost

Acts 2: 36–47
About 3000 people believed that day.

Summary
They heard, they believed, they
repented, they were baptized, and
continued steadfastly in the Christian
faith.

Bible record
"'Therefore let all the house of Israel
know assuredly that God has made this
Jesus, whom you crucified, both Lord
and Christ.'

37 Now when they heard this, they
were cut to the heart, and said to Peter
and the rest of the apostles, 'Men and
brethren, what shall we do?'

38 Then Peter said to them, 'Repent,
and let every one of you be baptized
in the name of Jesus Christ for the
remission of sins; and you shall receive
the gift of the Holy Spirit.

39 For the promise is to you and to
your children, and to all who are afar
off, as many as the Lord our God will
call."

A Vital Church Grows
"40 And with many other words he
testified and exhorted them, saying, 'Be
saved from this perverse generation.'

41 Then those who gladly received
his word were baptized; and that day

about three thousand souls were added to them.

42 And they continued steadfastly in the apostles' doctrine and fellowship, in the breaking of bread, and in prayers.

43 Then fear came upon every soul, and many wonders and signs were done through the apostles.

44 Now all who believed were together, and had all things in common,

45 and sold their possessions and goods, and divided them among all, as anyone had need.

46 So continuing daily with one accord in the temple, and breaking bread from house to house, they ate their food with gladness and simplicity of heart,

47 praising God and having favor with all the people. And the Lord added to the church daily those who were being saved."

Acts 2: 36–47 NKJV

2. Samaria

Acts 8: 4–13
Both men and women were saved.

Summary
They heard, they believed, and they were baptized.

Bible record
"Christ Is Preached in Samaria

4 Therefore those who were scattered went everywhere preaching the word.

5 Then Philip went down to the city of Samaria and preached Christ to them.

6 And the multitudes with one accord heeded the things spoken by Philip, hearing and seeing the miracles which he did.

7 For unclean spirits, crying with a loud voice, came out of many who were possessed; and many who were paralyzed and lame were healed.

8 And there was great joy in that city."

The Sorcerer's Profession of Faith

"9 But there was a certain man called Simon, who previously practiced sorcery in the city and astonished the people of Samaria, claiming that he was someone great,

10 to whom they all gave heed, from the least to the greatest, saying, 'This man is the great power of God.'

11 And they heeded him because he had astonished them with his sorceries for a long time."

12 But when they believed Philip as he preached the things concerning the kingdom of God and the name of Jesus Christ, both men and women were baptized.

13 Then Simon himself also believed; and when he was baptized he continued with Philip, and was amazed, seeing the miracles and signs which were done."

Acts 8: 4–13 NKJV

Quote Unquote

"Conversion is a great and glorious work of God's power, at once changing the heart, and infusing life into the dead soul, though the grace then implanted displays itself more gradually in some than in others."

Jonathan Edwards

Conversions in Acts (2)

3. Ethiopian eunuch

Acts 8: 26–39

Summary
He heard, he believed, he confessed, and he was baptized.

Bible record
"Christ Is Preached to an Ethiopian

26 Now an angel of the Lord spoke to Philip, saying, 'Arise and go toward the south along the road which goes down from Jerusalem to Gaza.' This is desert.

27 So he arose and went.
And behold, a man of Ethiopia, a eunuch of great authority under Candace the queen of the Ethiopians, who had charge of all her treasury, and had come to Jerusalem to worship,

28 was returning. And sitting in his chariot, he was reading Isaiah the prophet.

29 Then the Spirit said to Philip, 'Go near and overtake this chariot.'

30 So Philip ran to him, and heard him reading the prophet Isaiah, and said, 'Do you understand what you are reading?'

31 And he said, 'How can I, unless someone guides me?' And he asked Philip to come up and sit with him.

32 The place in the Scripture which he read was this: 'He was led as a sheep to the slaughter; And as a lamb before its shearer is silent, So He opened not His mouth.

33 In His humiliation His justice was taken away, And who will declare His generation? For His life is taken from the earth.'

34 So the eunuch answered Philip and said, 'I ask you, of whom does the prophet say this, of himself or of some other man?'

35 Then Philip opened his mouth, and beginning at this Scripture, preached Jesus to him.

36 Now as they went down the road, they came to some water. And the eunuch said, 'See, here is water. What hinders me from being baptized?'

37 Then Philip said, 'If you believe with all your heart, you may.' And he answered and said, 'I believe that Jesus Christ is the Son of God.'

38 So he commanded the chariot to stand still. And both Philip and the eunuch went down into the water, and he baptized him.

39 Now when they came up out of the water, the Spirit of the Lord caught Philip away, so that the eunuch saw him no more; and he went on his way rejoicing."

Acts .8: 26–39 NKJV

4. Paul (Saul)

Acts 9: 1–20; 22: 6–16

Summary
He heard, he believed and he was baptized.

Bible record
"'Now it happened, as I journeyed and came near Damascus at about noon, suddenly a great light from heaven shone around me.

7 And I fell to the ground and heard a voice saying to me, "Saul, Saul, why are

you persecuting Me?"

8 So I answered, "Who are You, Lord?' And He said to me, "I am Jesus of Nazareth, whom you are persecuting."

9 "And those who were with me indeed saw the light and were afraid, but they did not hear the voice of Him who spoke to me.

10 So I said, "What shall I do, Lord?" And the Lord said to me, "Arise and go into Damascus, and there you will be told all things which are appointed for you to do."

11 And since I could not see for the glory of that light, being led by the hand of those who were with me, I came into Damascus.

12 Then a certain Ananias, a devout man according to the law, having a good testimony with all the Jews who dwelt there,

13 came to me; and he stood and said to me, "Brother Saul, receive your sight." And at that same hour I looked up at him.

14 Then he said, "The God of our fathers has chosen you that you should know His will, and see the Just One, and hear the voice of His mouth.

15 For you will be His witness to all men of what you have seen and heard.

16 And now why are you waiting? Arise and be baptized, and wash away your sins, calling on the name of the Lord.""'

Acts 22: 6–16 NKJV

5. Cornelius

Acts 10: 1–48; 11: 1–18
Cornelius and his whole household.

Summary

They heard, they believed, and they were baptized.

Bible record

"Preaching to Cornelius' Household

34 Then Peter opened his mouth and said: 'In truth I perceive that God shows no partiality.

35 But in every nation whoever fears Him and works righteousness is accepted by Him.

Quote Unquote

"Conversion marks the conscious beginning, not only of the putting away of the old man, a fleeing from sin, but also of the putting on of the new man, a striving for holiness of life."

Louis Berkhof

Conversions in Acts (3)

5. Cornelius, continued

36 The word which God sent to the children of Israel, preaching peace through Jesus Christ – He is Lord of all –

37 that word you know, which was proclaimed throughout all Judea, and began from Galilee after the baptism which John preached:

38 how God anointed Jesus of Nazareth with the Holy Spirit and with power, who went about doing good and healing all who were oppressed by the devil, for God was with Him.

39 And we are witnesses of all things which He did both in the land of the Jews and in Jerusalem, whom they killed by hanging on a tree.

40 Him God raised up on the third day, and showed Him openly,

41 not to all the people, but to witnesses chosen before by God, even to us who ate and drank with Him after He arose from the dead.

42 And He commanded us to preach to the people, and to testify that it is He who was ordained by God to be Judge of the living and the dead.

43 To Him all the prophets witness that, through His name, whoever believes in Him will receive remission of sins.'

The Holy Spirit Falls on the Gentiles

44 While Peter was still speaking these words, the Holy Spirit fell upon all those who heard the word.

45 And those of the circumcision who believed were astonished, as many as came with Peter, because the gift of the Holy Spirit had been poured out on the Gentiles also.

46 For they heard them speak with tongues and magnify God.

Then Peter answered,

47 'Can anyone forbid water, that these should not be baptized who have received the Holy Spirit just as we have?'

48 And he commanded them to be baptized in the name of the Lord. Then they asked him to stay a few days."

Acts 10: 34–48 NKJV

6. Lydia

Acts 16: 13–15
Lydia and her whole household.

Summary

They heard, they believed, and they were baptized.

Bible record

"And on the Sabbath day we went out of the city to the riverside, where prayer was customarily made; and we sat down and spoke to the women who met there.

14 Now a certain woman named Lydia heard us. She was a seller of purple from the city of Thyatira, who worshiped God. The Lord opened her heart to heed the things spoken by Paul.

15 And when she and her household were baptized, she begged us, saying, 'If you have judged me to be faithful to the Lord, come to my house and stay.' So she persuaded us."

Acts 16: 13–15 NKJV

7. Philippian jailer

Acts 16: 23,34
And his whole household.

Summary
They heard, they believed, and they
were baptized.

Bible record
"And when they had laid many
stripes on them, they threw them into
prison, commanding the jailer to keep
them securely.

24 Having received such a charge,
he put them into the inner prison and
fastened their feet in the stocks.
The Philippian Jailer Saved

25 But at midnight Paul and Silas
were praying and singing hymns to
God, and the prisoners were listening
to them.

26 Suddenly there was a great
earthquake, so that the foundations
of the prison were shaken; and
immediately all the doors were opened
and everyone's chains were loosed.

27 And the keeper of the prison,
awaking from sleep and seeing the
prison doors open, supposing the
prisoners had fled, drew his sword and
was about to kill himself.

28 But Paul called with a loud voice,
saying, 'Do yourself no harm, for we
are all here.'

29 Then he called for a light, ran in,
and fell down trembling before Paul
and Silas. 30 And he brought them out
and said, 'Sirs, what must I do to be
saved?'

31 So they said, 'Believe on the Lord
Jesus Christ, and you will be saved, you
and your household.'

32 Then they spoke the word of the
Lord to him and to all who were in his
house.

33 And he took them the same hour
of the night and washed their stripes.
And immediately he and all his family
were baptized.

34 Now when he had brought them
into his house, he set food before them;
and he rejoiced, having believed in God
with all his household."

Acts 16: 23–34 NKJV

8. Corinthians

Acts 18: 8
This involved "many" people.

Summary
They heard, they believed, and they
were baptized.

Bible record
"When Silas and Timothy had come
from Macedonia, Paul was compelled
by the Spirit, and testified to the Jews
that Jesus is the Christ.

6 But when they opposed him and
blasphemed, he shook his garments
and said to them, 'Your blood be upon
your own heads; I am clean. From now
on I will go to the Gentiles.'

7 And he departed from there and
entered the house of a certain man
named Justus, one who worshiped
God, whose house was next door to the
synagogue.

8 Then Crispus, the ruler of the
synagogue, believed on the Lord with
all his household. And many of the
Corinthians, hearing, believed and were
baptized."

Acts 18: 5–8 NKJV

Church (1)

Overview

Old Testament

THE CONGREGATION

Ex. 12: 3; Ex. 12: 6; Ex. 12: 19; Ex. 12: 47;
Ex. 16: 1,2; Ex. 16: 9,10; Ex. 16: 22;
Lev. 4: 13; Lev. 4: 15; Lev. 10: 17;
Lev. 24: 14

New Testament

CHURCH

Matt. 16: 18; Matt. 18: 17; Acts 2: 47;
1 Cor. 11: 18; 1 Cor. 14: 19; 1 Cor. 14: 23;
1 Cor. 14: 28; 1 Cor. 14: 33,34; 1 Cor. 15: 9;
Gal. 1: 13

Variety of names

As a collective body of believers the
church is given a variety of names in
the Old Testament and in the New
Testament which describe its different
aspects.

Assembly of the saints
Ps. 89: 7

Assembly of the upright
Ps. 111: 1

Body of Christ
Eph. 1: 22,23; Col. 1: 24

Branch, planted by God
Is. 60: 21

Bride of Christ
Rev. 21: 9
"And there came unto me one of
the seven angels which had the seven
vials full of the seven last plagues,
and talked with me, saying, Come
hither, I will shew thee the bride, the
Lamb's wife" Revelation 21: 9.

Church of God
Acts 20: 28

Church of the living God
1 Tim. 3: 15

Church of the firstborn
Heb. 12: 23

City of the living God
Heb. 12: 22

Congregation of saints
Ps. 149: 1

Congregation of the Lord's poor
Ps. 74: 19

Family in heaven and earth
Eph. 3: 15

Flock, God's flock
Ezek. 34: 15; 1 Pet. 5: 2
"I will feed my flock, and I will
cause them to lie down, saith the
Lord GOD" Ezekiel 34: 15.
"Feed the flock of God which is
among you, taking the oversight
thereof, not by constraint, but
willingly; not for filthy lucre, but of a
ready mind" 1 Peter 5: 2.

Fold, Christ's fold
John 10: 16

General assembly of the firstborn
Heb. 12: 23
"To the general assembly and
church of the firstborn, which are
written in heaven, and to God the
Judge of all, and to the spirits of just
men made perfect" Hebrews 12: 23.

Golden candlestick
Rev. 1: 20

God's building
1 Cor. 3: 9

God's husbandry
1 Cor. 3: 9

God's heritage

Joel 3: 2; 1 Pet. 5: 3
Habitation of God
  Eph. 2: 22
Heavenly Jerusalem
  Gal. 4: 26; Heb. 12: 22
Holy city
  Rev. 21: 2
Holy mountain
  Zech. 8: 3
Holy hill
  Ps. 2: 6; Ps. 15: 1
House of God
  1 Tim. 3: 15; Heb. 10: 21
    "But if I tarry long, that thou
  mayest know how thou oughtest to
  behave thyself in the house of God,
  which is the church of the living God,
  the pillar and ground of the truth"
  1 Timothy 3: 15.
    "And having an high priest over the
  house of God" Hebrews 10: 21.
The God of Jacob
  Is. 2: 3
House of Christ
  Heb. 3: 6
Household of God
  Eph. 2: 19
Inheritance
  Ps. 28: 9; Is. 19: 25
Israel of God
  Gal. 6: 16
    "And as many as walk according
  to this rule, peace be on them, and
  mercy, and upon the Israel of God"
  Galatians 6: 16
Kingdom of God
  Matt. 6: 33; Matt. 12: 28; Matt. 19: 24;
  Matt. 21: 31
Kingdom of heaven
  Matt. 3: 2; Matt. 4: 17; Matt. 10: 7;
  Matt. 5: 3; Matt. 5: 10; Matt. 5: 19,20
His kingdom

Ps. 103: 19; Ps. 145: 12; Matt. 16: 28;
Luke 1: 33
My kingdom
  John 18: 36
Thy kingdom
  Ps. 45: 6; Ps. 145: 11; Ps. 145: 13;
  Matt. 6: 10; Luke 23: 42
Lamb's bride
  Rev. 22: 17
Lamb's wife
  Rev. 19: 7–9; Rev. 21: 9
Lot of God's inheritance
  Deut. 32: 9
Mount Zion
  Heb. 12: 22
Mountain of the Lord's house
  Is. 2: 2
New Jerusalem
  Rev. 21: 2
Pillar and ground of the truth
  1 Tim. 3: 15
    "But if I tarry long, that thou
  mayest know how thou oughtest to
  behave thyself in the house of God,
  which is the church of the living God,
  the pillar and ground of the truth"
  1 Timothy 3: 15.
Place of God's throne
  Ezek. 43: 7
Pleasant portion
  Jer. 12: 10
Sanctuary of God
  Ps. 114: 2
Spiritual house
  1 Pet. 2: 5
    "Ye also, as lively stones, are
  built up a spiritual house, an holy
  priesthood, to offer up spiritual
  sacrifices, acceptable to God by Jesus
  Christ" 1 Peter 2: 5.
Strength and glory of God
  Ps. 78: 61

Church (2)

Variety of names, continued

Sought out, a city not forsaken
Is. 62:12
The Lord's portion
Deut. 32:9
Temple of God
1 Cor. 3:16,17
"Know ye not that ye are the temple of God, and that the Spirit of God dwelleth in you?
17 If any man defile the temple of God, him shall God destroy; for the temple of God is holy, which temple ye are." 1 Corinthians 3:16,17
Temple of the living God
2 Cor. 6:16
Vineyard
Jer. 12:10; Matt. 21:41

Facts about the Christian church

Christ's love for
John 10:8; John 10:11,12; Eph. 5:25–32; Rev. 3:9
All that ever came before me are thieves and robbers: but the sheep did not hear them. . . .I am the good shepherd: the good shepherd giveth his life for the sheep. But he that is an hireling, and not the shepherd, whose own the sheep are not, seeth the wolf coming, and leaveth the sheep, and fleeth: and the wolf catcheth them, and scattereth the sheep." John 10:8,11,12
"Husbands, love your wives, even as Christ also loved the church, and gave himself for it;
26 That he might sanctify and cleanse it with the washing of water by the word,
27 That he might present it to himself a glorious church, not having spot, or wrinkle, or any such thing; but that it should be holy and without blemish.
28 So ought men to love their wives as their own bodies. He that loveth his wife loveth himself.
29 For no man ever yet hated his own flesh; but nourisheth and cherisheth it, even as the Lord the church:
30 For we are members of his body, of his flesh, and of his bones.
31 For this cause shall a man leave his father and mother, and shall be joined unto his wife, and they two shall be one flesh.
32 This is a great mystery: but I speak concerning Christ and the church." Ephesians 5:25–32
"Behold, I will make them of the synagogue of Satan, which say they are Jews, and are not, but do lie; behold, I will make them to come and worship before thy feet, and to know that I have loved thee." Revelation 3:9.
Loved by believers
Ps. 87:7; Ps. 137:5; 1 Cor. 12:25; 1 Thess. 4:9
Is prayed for
Ps. 122:6; Is. 62:6
Dear to God
Is. 43:4
Safe under his care
Ps. 46:1,2; Ps. 46:5
Salt and light of the world
Matt. 5:13

Militant
Song 6: 10; Phil. 2: 25; 2 Tim. 2: 3;
2 Tim. 4: 7; Phile. 1: 2
God defends
Ps. 89: 18; Is. 4: 5; Is. 49: 25;
Matt. 16: 18
God provides ministers for
Jer. 3: 15; Eph. 4: 11,12
Is glorious
Ps. 45: 13; Eph. 5: 27
Is clothed in righteousness
Rev. 19: 8
Believers continually added to, by the
Lord
Acts 2: 47; Acts 5: 14; Acts 11: 24
Unity of
Rom. 12: 5; 1 Cor. 10: 17; 1 Cor. 12: 12;
Gal. 3: 28; Eph. 4: 4
Privileges of
Ps. 36: 8; Ps. 87: 5
Worship of, to be attended
Heb. 10: 25
Harmonious fellowship of
Ps. 133; John 13: 34; Acts 4: 32;
Phil. 1: 4; Phil. 2: 1; 1 John 1: 3,4
"That which we have seen and
heard declare we unto you, that
ye also may have fellowship with
us: and truly our fellowship is with
the Father, and with his Son Jesus
Christ.
4 And these things write we unto
you, that your joy may be full."
1 John 1: 3,4
Divisions in, to be shunned
Rom. 16: 17; 1 Cor. 1: 10; 1 Cor. 3: 3
Baptized into by one Spirit
1 Cor. 12: 13
Ministers commanded to feed
Acts 20: 28
Is edified by the word
Rom. 12: 6; 1 Cor. 14: 4; 1 Cor. 14: 13;

Col. 3: 16
Is strengthened by Christ
"But speaking the truth in love,
may grow up into him in all things,
which is the head, even Christ:
16 From whom the whole body
fitly joined together and compacted
by that which every joint supplieth,
according to the effectual working
in the measure of every part, maketh
increase of the body unto the
edifying of itself in love." Ephesians
4: 15,16
The wicked persecute
Acts 8: 1–3; 1 Thess. 2: 14–15
"And Saul was consenting unto his
death. And at that time there was a
great persecution against the church
which was at Jerusalem; and they
were all scattered abroad throughout
the regions of Judaea and Samaria,
except the apostles.
2 And devout men carried Stephen
to his burial, and made great
lamentation over him.
3 As for Saul, he made havoc of
the church, entering into every
house, and haling men and women
committed them to prison."
Acts 8: 1–3
Not to be despised
1 Cor. 11: 22
Defiling of, will be punished
1 Cor. 3: 17
Extent of, predicted
Is. 2: 2; Ezek. 17: 22–24; Dan. 2: 34,35

The church of Christ (1)

Prophecies about it

Isaiah and Micah

Isaiah and Micah predicted that the law would go from Zion and the word of the Lord from Jerusalem (Isaiah 2: 1–3; Micah 4: 1–3).

Jeremiah

Jeremiah predicted that the Lord would establish a new covenant with the house of Israel and the house of Judah, which would be unlike the covenant that he made with their fathers when he brought them out of Egypt, that he would put his laws in their minds and write them in their hearts, that they would know the Lord and that their sins would no longer be remembered (Jeremiah 31: 31–34; Hebrews 8: 7–13).

Daniel

Daniel predicted that God would set up a kingdom that would never be destroyed and that would shatter all other kingdoms, and stand forever (Daniel 2: 44).

Foundation of the church

Isaiah

Isaiah predicted that a foundation stone would be laid in Zion (Isaiah 28: 16). That stone is Christ (Matthew 16: 13–20; Romans 9: 32,33; 1 Corinthians 3: 10,11; Ephesians 2: 19–22).

"Now therefore ye are no more strangers and foreigners, but fellow citizens with the saints, and of the household of God;

20 And are built upon the foundation of the apostles and prophets, Jesus Christ himself being the chief corner *stone.*" Ephesians 2: 19,20

Head of the Church

Jesus Christ

Jesus Christ is the head of the Church (Colossians 1: 18 Ephesians 5: 23).

"And he is the head of the body, the church: who is the beginning, the firstborn from the dead; that in all *things* he might have the preeminence" Colossians 1: 18.

In the future

The general drift of Bible teaching about God's kingdom or church prior to the death of Christ is in the future.

It was in the future when God made promises to Abraham (Genesis 12: 1–3), to Isaac (Genesis 26: 1–5; (Genesis 28: 10–14);

it was in the future when Jacob prophesied the coming of Shiloh (Genesis 49: 1,8–10; Hebrews 2: 14; Revelation 1: 1–5);

it was in the future when Moses predicted the coming of One whose authority would be supreme (Deuteronomy 18: 15–18);

it was in the future when Isaiah predicted the collecting together of the

Gentiles (Isaiah 54: 1–3; Isaiah 62: 1–4); it was in the future when John the Baptist preached in the Judean desert (Matthew 3: 1–13); it was in the future when Jesus announced to his disciples that some of them would live to see it come with power (Mark 9: 1); it was in the future when Jesus visited Caesarea Philippi (Matthew 16: 13–17); it was in the future, near the end of the earthly life of Jesus, for the disciples were expecting it to appear immediately (Luke 19: 11–27); it was in the future when Jesus was on the cross (Luke 23: 42,43); it was in the future after the death of Jesus on the cross (Mark 15: 43); it was in the future, just before the ascension (Acts 1: 6,7).

Pentecost and the birth of the church

Prior to Pentecost the church or kingdom is spoken of as being in the future, but after Pentecost that day it is spoken of as having arrived and actually existing (Acts 2: 41; Acts 5: 11; Acts 8: 1; Hebrews 12: 28).

It was necessary to abolish the first institution in order to establish the second (Hebrews 10: 9).

"Then said he, Lo, I come to do thy will, O God. He taketh away the first, that he may establish the second" Hebrews 10: 9.

But the first was not taken away during Jesus' life, for the curtain in the temple was not torn from top to bottom until he breathed his last breath (Matthew 27: 51; Ephesians 2: 13–16).

The new institution would be characterized by the complete blotting out of sins (Jeremiah 31: 31–34), and as the blood of animal sacrifices could never take away sin, it was imperative for Jesus to die before this work could be achieved (Matthew 26: 28; Romans 5: 9; Hebrews 9: 14–22; Hebrews 10: 4; 1 Peter 1: 18,19).

The church was bought by Jesus and was not his until he paid the price (Matthew 20: 28; 1 Corinthians 6: 19,20).

The body could not exist without the spirit (1 Corinthians 6: 19,20; James 2: 26) and the Spirit was not given until Jesus was glorified (John 7: 38,39; Acts 1: 5).

The prophets, Jesus Christ and his apostles all state that God's church or kingdom would begin at Jerusalem (Psalms 110: 1–4; Isaiah 2: 1–3; Isaiah 62: 1,2; Joel 2: 28–32; Micah 4: 1,2; Luke 24: 45–53; Acts 1: 5–8; Acts 2: 1–47; Acts 8: 1; Galatians 4: 21–31).

"When the day of Pentecost had come, they were all together in one place.

2 And suddenly there came from heaven a noise like a violent rushing wind, and it filled the whole house where they were sitting.

3 And there appeared to them tongues as of fire distributing themselves, and they rested on each one of them.

4 And they were all filled with the Holy Spirit and began to speak with other tongues, as the Spirit was giving them utterance."

Acts 2: 1–4, NASB

The church of Christ (2)

Pentecost and the birth of the church, continued

A unique day

The work was inaugurated on the first Pentecost after the ascension of Christ. This day is unique. There is no other day in history like the day of Pentecost.

The beginning

The Holy Spirit came into the world in a new and special way as the apostles started to evangelize the world (John 14: 16–18; John 16: 7–11; Acts 2: 1–4).

Fulfilled prophecies

The prophecies were fulfilled on the day of Pentecost (Isaiah 2: 1–3; Psalms 110: 1–4; Joel 2: 28–32; Micah 4: 1,2; Acts 2: 1–47).

Peter and the other apostles began to bind and free people in the name of Jesus (Matthew 16: 18; Matthew 18: 18; Acts 2: 37,38).

The apostles proclaimed a law of remission of sins in the name of Jesus (Matthew 28: 18–20; Acts 2: 37).

The apostles started preaching in the wake of the last and great commission (Mark 16: 15,16; Acts 2: 14–36).

Entering the church

In general terms, the way into the Church is the gospel.

Jesus and his inspired apostles laid down certain conditions about how to enter the church.

One condition is faith

Faith:

its importance (Hebrews 11: 6);

it is taking God at His word (Romans 4: 21);

its unity (Ephesians 4: 5–13);

its basis is Jesus Christ (John 8: 24; 1 Corinthians 3: 10,11);

it is produced by hearing the gospel (John 20: 30,31; Romans 10: 17);

"Brethren, my heart's desire and prayer to God for Israel is, that they might be saved" Romans 10: 17.

it purifies the heart (Acts 15: 9);

its effect on life (James 2: 17–26).

ANOTHER CONDITION IS REPENTANCE
REPENTANCE:
God is willing for men to repent (Ezekiel 18: 25–32; 2 Peter 3: 9);

people, with God's grace, are able to repent, for salvation depends on it (Luke 13: 1–5);

the motives that produce it are the goodness of God (Romans 2: 4), and the fear of judgment (Acts 17: 30,31; 2 Corinthians 7: 10);

it is a change of mind resulting in a change or reformation of life (Isaiah 55: 7; Isaiah 7: 5; Matthew 3: 7; James 3: 7–10).

Baptism

The New Testament teaches that members of the Christian church should be baptized (Matthew 3: 14–17; Matthew 28: 18–20; Mark 16: 15,16;

John 3: 5; Acts 2: 38; Romans 6: 1–3; 1 Corinthians 12: 13; Galatians 3: 26,27; Ephesians 4: 5; Ephesians 5: 26; Colossians 2: 12; Hebrews 10: 22; 1 Peter 3: 21).

The Christian life

Every member of the body of Christ is required to live a godly life in this world (Titus 2: 11–14; 2 Peter 1: 5–7).

Witnessing

Members of God's church are called to be witnesses to Jesus. This is sometimes referred to as "confessing the faith."

Church members are required to confess Christ (Matthew 10: 32,33).

This can be done in a great variety of ways, including by word of mouth (Romans 10: 9,10).

Witnessing to our faith in Jesus includes some kind of public witness in the presence of other people (John 12: 42; Acts 19: 18; 1 Timothy 6: 12–14).

Meeting together

The first Christians met together on the first day of the week to break bread (Acts 20: 7). Apart from baptism, the Lord's Supper is the only other sacrament Jesus instituted.

Giving money

The early Christians were told to contribute to the Lord's work in proportion to their God-given resources (1 Corinthians 16: 1,2).

Names for the church

In New Testament times the Church was called the Church of Christ (Romans 16: 16) or the Church of God (1 Corinthians 1: 1,2).

Names of church members

The members of the church of Christ were called, individually,

- saints (Romans 1: 7);
- children of God (Romans 8: 16);
- heirs of God (Romans 8: 16);
- brethren (Romans 12: 1);
- sons of God (1 John 3: 2);
- Christians (Acts 11: 26; 1 Peter 4: 16).

The spread of the church

The early church was absorbed with evangelism. The apostles began by preaching in Jerusalem and then in the surrounding country (Acts 2: 37–42 Acts 4: 1–4; Acts 5: 14; Acts 6: 7). Soon Philip, the evangelist, introduced the gospel in the city of Samaria with great success (Acts 8: 1–25), and Peter introduced it to the Gentiles when he visited Cornelius' home (Acts 10: 1–48; Acts 11: 1–26). By the end of the book of Acts it is apparent that the gospel had spread like wildfire throughout the known world and that Paul had achieved one of his dearly held ambitions and had arrived in Rome where he spent two years spreading the good news about Jesus.

Worship

Worship only God

True worship can only be given to God.

Homage given to any object is sinful because it is idolatry.

This must never be given to any created being (Ex. 34: 14; Is. 2: 8).

"For thou shalt worship no other god: for the Lord, whose name is Jealous, is a jealous God" Exodus 34: 14.

See also, Ex. 20: 3; Deut. 5: 7; Deut. 6: 13; Matt. 4: 10; Luke 4: 8; Acts 10: 26; Acts 14: 15; Col. 2: 18; Rev. 19: 10; Rev. 22: 8.

Peter refused to be worshiped (Acts 10: 25,26) as did an angel (Rev. 22: 8,9).

Worshiping Jesus

There is no question but that we should worship Jesus.

OLD TESTAMENT REFERENCES
Josh. 5: 14,15; Ps. 45: 11; Ps. 45: 17; Ps. 72: 15

NEW TESTAMENT REFERENCES
Matt. 2: 2; Matt. 2: 11; Matt. 9: 18; Matt. 14: 33; Matt. 15: 25; Matt. 20: 20; Matt. 28: 9; Matt. 28: 16,17; Mark 3: 11; Mark 5: 6,7; Mark 11: 9,10; Matt. 21: 9; John 12: 13; Luke 4: 41; Luke 5: 8; Luke 23: 42; Luke 24: 52; John 5: 23; John 9: 38; Acts 7: 59,60; Acts 1: 24; 1 Cor. 1: 2; 2 Cor. 12: 8–9; Phil. 2: 10,11; 1 Tim. 1: 12; Heb. 1: 6; 2 Pet. 3: 18; Rev. 5: 8,9; Rev. 5: 12–14; Rev. 7: 10

"Saying with a loud voice, Worthy is the Lamb that was slain to receive power, and riches, and wisdom, and strength, and honor, and glory, and blessing.

13 And every creature which is in heaven, and on the earth, and under the earth, and such as are in the sea, and all that are in them, heard I saying, Blessing, and honor, and glory, and power, be unto him that sitteth upon the throne, and unto the Lamb for ever and ever.

14 And the four beasts said, Amen. And the four and twenty elders fell down and worshiped him that liveth for ever and ever."

Revelation 5: 12–14

Worshiping God

It is not possible to measure a person's devotion to God by the length of time they spend in prayer or the number of church services they attend. However, it is instructive to note that worshiping God was a major event in the life of the Old Testament followers of God.

Time given over to God

The children of Israel were redeemed by the Lord (Exodus 15: 1–19), and so they belonged to Him. The law required them to give a large amount of their time to his service.

TIME GIVEN: TO THE PASSOVER
Counting one day for the Sabbath, the Israelites were required to give six days to the feast of the Passover and unleavened bread each year (Leviticus 23: 4–8).   6 days.

To the Feast of the Weeks

They were required to give one day to this feast each year (Leviticus 23: 15–21). 1 day.

To the Feast of Tabernacles

Counting one day for the Sabbath, they were required to give six days to this feast each year (Leviticus 23: 34–42). 6 days.

To the Sabbath

They were required to give fifty-one days to the Sabbath each year (Leviticus 23: 3). 51 days.

To the Day of Atonement

They were required to give one day to the atonement each year (Leviticus 23: 26–32). 1 day.

To the Feast of New Moons

Counting one day for the feast of trumpets, they were required to give eleven days to this feast each year (Numbers 28: 11–15; Numbers 29: 1–5 Amos 8: 5). 11 days.

Total

This gives a total of seventy-six days each year.

Psalmist

The psalmist frequently captures his heartfelt desire and love of worshiping the Lord.

"One *thing* have I desired of the Lord, that will I seek after; that I may dwell in the house of the Lord all the days of my life, to behold the beauty of the Lord, and to inquire in his temple" Psalm 27: 4.

"Honor and majesty *are* before him: strength and beauty *are* in his sanctuary.

7 Give unto the Lord, O ye kindreds of the people, give unto the Lord glory and strength.

8 Give unto the Lord the glory *due unto* his name: bring an offering, and come into his courts.

9 O worship the Lord in the beauty of holiness: fear before him, all the earth.

10 Say among the heathen *that* the Lord reigneth: the world also shall be established that it shall not be moved: he shall judge the people righteously.

11 Let the heavens rejoice, and let the earth be glad; let the sea roar, and the fullness thereof.

12 Let the field be joyful, and all that *is* therein: then shall all the trees of the wood rejoice

13 Before the Lord: for he cometh, for he cometh to judge the earth: he shall judge the world with righteousness, and the people with his truth."

Psalm 96: 6–13

Praise

Overview

One of the main components of
Christian worship should always be
praise.

Old Testament praise

SONG OF MOSES
After crossing through the Red Sea
Ex. 15: 1–19

SONG OF MIRIAM
Ex. 15: 21

SONG OF DEBORAH
After defeating the Canaanites
Judg. 5

SONG OF HANNAH
1 Sam. 2: 1–10

SONGS OF DAVID

*Celebrating his deliverance from the hand
of Saul*
2 Sam. 22

Bringing the Ark to Zion
1 Chr. 16: 8–36

At the end of David's reign
1 Chr. 29: 10–19

THE SONG WHEN SOLOMON BROUGHT
THE ARK INTO THE TEMPLE
2 Chr. 5: 13

Psalms of Israel

FOR GOD'S GOODNESS TO
Ps. 46; Ps. 48; Ps. 65–66; Ps. 68; Ps. 76;
Ps. 81; Ps. 85; Ps. 98; Ps. 105; Ps. 124;
Ps. 126; Ps. 129; Ps. 135–136

FOR GOD'S GOODNESS TO RIGHTEOUS
MEN
Ps. 23; Ps. 34; Ps. 36; Ps. 91; Ps. 100;
Ps. 103; Ps. 107; Ps. 117; Ps. 121

FOR GOD'S GOODNESS TO
INDIVIDUALS
Ps. 9; Ps. 18; Ps. 22; Ps. 30; Ps. 40; Ps. 75;
Ps. 103; Ps. 108; Ps. 116; Ps. 118; Ps. 138;
Ps. 144

FOR GOD'S ATTRIBUTES
Ps. 8; Ps. 19; Ps. 22; Ps. 24; Ps. 29; Ps. 33;
Ps. 47; Ps. 50; Ps. 65–66; Ps. 76–77;
Ps. 92–93; Ps. 95–99; Ps. 104; Ps. 111;
Ps. 113–115; Ps. 134; Ps. 139; Ps. 147–148;
Ps. 150

Additional scriptures relating to praise

It is hard to exaggerate how much the
Bible teaching about praising God.

OLD TESTAMENT
Gen. 14: 20; Ex. 15: 1,2; Deut. 10: 21;
Judg. 5: 3; 2 Sam. 22: 4; Ps. 18: 3;
1 Chr. 16: 31; 1 Chr. 16: 33,34; 1 Chr. 16: 36;
1 Chr. 23: 30; 2 Chr. 7: 3; Neh. 9: 5,6;
Job 36: 24

Psalms
The scores of hymns of praise in the
book of Psalms can be categorized in a
number of different ways.

1 *Individual thanksgiving psalms*
In these the psalmist publicly gives
thanks to God for his assistance for
something that God has done for him
or will do for him. Such thanksgiving
psalms include:

a. A proclamation of praise
b. A summary of his praise
c. Witness about his deliverance
d. A vow to continue praising God. See Psalms 18; 30; 32; 34; 40; 41; 66; 106; 116; and 138

2 Communal thanksgiving psalms
There are a number of psalms in which the nation, rather than an individual, is giving praise to God. See Psalms 124; 129.

3 General psalms of praise
These psalms major more on praise than on thanksgiving, praising God for his greatness. See Psalms 8; 19; 29; 103; 104; 139; 148; 150.

4 Psalms of descriptive praise
These psalms concentrate on God's attributes and actions and give him praise for these. See Psalms 33; 36; 105; 111; 113; 117; 135; 136; 146; 147.

Prophets
Is. 12: 1–6; Is. 24: 14–16; Is. 25: 1; Is. 35: 10; Is. 38: 18,19; Is. 42: 10–12; Is. 43: 21; Is. 49: 13; Is. 51: 3; Is. 52: 7–10; Is. 61: 3; Jer. 31: 7; Jer. 33: 11; Dan. 2: 20; Dan. 2: 23; Dan. 4: 37; Jonah 2: 9

NEW TESTAMENT

Gospels
Matt. 26: 30; Mark 14: 26; Luke 1: 46–55; Luke 1: 67–75; Luke 2: 20; Luke 17: 15,16; Luke 19: 37,38; Luke 24: 52,53.

Acts
Acts 2: 46,47; Acts 4: 24; Acts 16: 25

Letters
Rom. 11: 36; Rom. 16: 27; 1 Cor. 14: 15; 1 Cor. 15: 57; Eph. 1: 3; Eph. 3: 20,21; Eph. 5: 19; Phil. 4: 20; 1 Tim. 1: 17; Heb. 2: 12; Heb. 13: 15; James 5: 13;

1 Pet. 1: 3; 1 Pet. 2: 9; 1 Pet. 4: 11; 1 Pet. 5: 11; 2 Pet. 3: 18; Jude 1: 25

Book of Revelation
Rev. 1: 6; Rev. 14: 7

Praise in heaven
Neh. 9: 6; Job 38: 7; Ps. 103: 20,21; Ps. 148: 2; Ps. 148: 4; Is. 6: 3; Ezek. 3: 12; Luke 2: 13,14; Luke 15: 10; Luke 15: 7; Rev. 1: 6; Rev. 4: 8–11; Rev. 5: 9–14; Rev. 7: 9–12; Rev. 11: 16,17; Rev. 14: 2,3; Rev. 15: 3,4; Rev. 19: 1–7

"After these things I saw, and behold, a great multitude, which no man could number, out of every nation and of all tribes and peoples and tongues, standing before the throne and before the Lamb, arrayed in white robes, and palms in their hands;

10 and they cry with a great voice, saying, Salvation unto our God who sitteth on the throne, and unto the Lamb.

11 And all the angels were standing round about the throne, and about the elders and the four living creatures; and they fell before the throne on their faces, and worshiped God,

12 saying, Amen: Blessing, and glory, and wisdom, and thanksgiving, and honor, and power, and might, be unto our God for ever and ever. Amen."

Revelation 7: 9–12 ASV.

Baptism

The institution of baptism

Christian baptism was instituted by Jesus (Matt. 28: 19,20).

"Go out and train everyone you meet, far and near, in this way of life, marking them by baptism in the threefold name: Father, Son, and Holy Spirit. 20 Then instruct them in the practice of all I have commanded you. I'll be with you as you do this, day after day after day, right up to the end of the age."

Matthew 28: 19,20 The Message

Meaning of baptism and dipping

The words "baptize" and "baptism" are simply Greek words transferred into English.

It means to dip a thing into an element or liquid.

OLD TESTAMENT WASHINGS

In the LXX, the Greek version of the Old Testament, it is used of the ablutions and baptisms required by the Mosaic law. These were effected by immersion, and the same word, "washings" (Heb. 9: 10,13,19,21) or "baptisms," is used of them all.

BAPTISMS RECORDED IN ACTS

All of the instances of baptism recorded in the Acts of the Apostles (Acts 2: 38–41; 8: 26–39; 9: 17,18; 22: 12–16; 10: 44–48; 16: 32–34) suggests the idea that it was by dipping the person who is being baptized into water.

The purpose and result of baptism

OVERVIEW

Christian baptism is to be born of God, that is, born again.
John 1: 12,13; 3: 1–7.

JESUS AND NICODEMUS

"After dark one evening, a Jewish religious leader named Nicodemus, a Pharisee,

2 came to speak with Jesus. 'Teacher,' he said, 'we all know that God has sent you to teach us. Your miraculous signs are proof enough that God is with you.'

3 Jesus replied, 'I assure you, unless you are born again, you can never see the Kingdom of God.'

4 'What do you mean?' exclaimed Nicodemus. 'How can an old man go back into his mother's womb and be born again?'

5 Jesus replied, 'The truth is, no one can enter the Kingdom of God without being born of water and the Spirit.

6 Humans can reproduce only human life, but the Holy Spirit gives new life from heaven.

7 So don't be surprised at my statement that you must be born again."

John 3: 1–7 NLT

TO BECOME CHILDREN OF GOD BY FAITH

"So you are all children of God through faith in Christ Jesus. And all who have been united with Christ in baptism have been made like him." Galatians 3: 26,27 *NLT*

TO SET A PERSON FREE FROM SINS

"Peter replied, 'Each of you must turn from your sins and turn to God, and be baptized in the name of Jesus Christ for the forgiveness of your sins. Then you will receive the gift of the Holy Spirit.'"
Acts 2: 38, *NLT*

"And now, why delay? Get up and be baptized, and have your sins washed away, calling on the name of the Lord."
Acts 22: 16 *NLT*

TO BE SAVED
1 Peter 3: 21; Mark 16: 16; Titus 3: 5–7

TO BECOME A DISCIPLE
Matthew 28: 19,20

TO BE ABLE TO ENTER THE KINGDOM OF GOD
John 3: 3

TO BE UNITED TO JESUS
"Some of us are Jews, some are Gentiles, some are slaves, and some are free. But we have all been baptized into Christ's body by one Spirit, and we have all received the same Spirit."
1 Corinthians 12: 13 *NLT*

TO BE MADE ALIVE IN JESUS
"When you came to Christ, you were 'circumcised,' but not by a physical procedure. It was a spiritual procedure – the cutting away of your sinful nature.
12 For you were buried with Christ when you were baptized. And with him you were raised to a new life because you trusted the mighty power of God, who raised Christ from the dead.

13 You were dead because of your sins and because your sinful nature was not yet cut away. Then God made you alive with Christ. He forgave all our sins.
14 He canceled the record that contained the charges against us. He took it and destroyed it by nailing it to Christ's cross."
Colossians 2: 11–14

TO CALL ON THE NAME OF THE LORD SO THAT OUR SINS MIGHT BE WASHED AWAY
"And now, why delay? Get up and be baptized, and have your sins washed away, calling on the name of the Lord."
Acts 22: 16 *NLT*

TO HAVE A CLEAR CONSCIENCE
"let us go right into the presence of God, with true hearts fully trusting him. For our evil consciences have been sprinkled with Christ's blood to make us clean, and our bodies have been washed with pure water." Hebrews 10: 22 *NLT*.
See also, 1 Peter 3: 21

TO PUT TO DEATH A SINFUL WAY OF LIFE
Romans 6: 2–18

TO BE RAISED UP TO WALK A NEW LIFE
Romans 6: 4; Colossians 2: 12; 3: 1–17

Lord's Supper

Names for the Lord's Supper

Lord's Supper

It is referred to as the "Lord's Supper."

"When ye come together therefore into one place, this is not to eat the Lord's supper."
1 Corinthians 11: 20

Lord's table

It is referred to as "the Lord's table."

"You cannot drink from the cup of the Lord and from the cup of demons, too. You cannot eat at the Lord's Table and at the table of demons, too."
1 Corinthians 10: 21 NLT

Communion and cup of blessing

It is referred to as "communion," and as the "cup of blessing."

"The cup of blessing which we bless, is it not the communion of the blood of Christ? The bread which we break, is it not the communion of the body of Christ?"
1 Corinthians 10: 16, NLT

Breaking of bread

It is referred to as "breaking of bread."

"And they continued steadfastly in the apostles' doctrine and fellowship, and in breaking of bread, and in prayers." Acts 2: 42

Eucharist

In the early Church it was called also "Eucharist," or giving of thanks (Cf. Matt. 26: 27).

"And when He had taken a cup and given thanks, He gave it to them, saying, "Drink from it, all of you . . .""
Matthew 26: 27 NASB

Mass

Today the Roman Catholic Church uses the name "mass," a name derived from the words at the end of the service: Ite, *missa est*, i.e., "Go, it is [you are] discharged."

The institution

The account of the institution of the Lord's Supper is given by the three Synoptic writers, in:
• Matt. 26: 26–29,
• Mark 14: 22–25,
• Luke 22: 19,20.
The fullest account is given by Matthew.

Matthew's account

"During the meal Jesus took some bread in his hands. He blessed the bread and broke it. Then he gave it to his disciples and said, "Take this and eat it. This is my body."

27 Jesus picked up a cup of wine and gave thanks to God. He then gave it to his disciples and said, "Take this and drink it.

28 This is my blood, and with it God makes his agreement with you. It will be poured out, so that many people will have their sins forgiven.

29 From now on I am not going to drink any wine, until I drink new wine with you in my Father's kingdom."
Matthew 26: 26–29 CEV

Not found in John's Gospel

In John's Gospel the actual institution of the Lord's Supper is not mentioned. But John, uniquely, does include the important incident that took place during the Lord's Supper, him washing the disciples' feet.

Paul

But Paul also gives an account of the institution of the Lord's Supper.

"Then after he had given thanks, he broke it and said, 'This is my body, which is given for you. Eat this and remember me.'

25 After the meal, Jesus took a cup of wine in his hands and said, 'This is my blood, and with it God makes his new agreement with you. Drink this and remember me.'

26 The Lord meant that when you eat this bread and drink from this cup, you tell about his death until he comes."

1 Corinthians 11: 24–26 CEV

Purpose of the Lord's Supper

The Lord's Supper was given:

(1) To commemorate the death of Christ: "This do in remembrance of me."

(2) To signify, seal, and apply to believers all the benefits of the new covenant. In this ordinance Christ confirms his promises to his people, and they on their part solemnly consecrate themselves to him and to his service.

Bread and wine

Bread

The elements used to represent Christ's body and blood are bread and wine. The kind of bread, whether leavened or unleavened, is not specified. Christ would have used unleavened bread because it was at that time on the paschal table.

Wine

Wine was used (Matt. 26: 26–29).

Feeding on Jesus

Believers are said to "feed" on Christ's body and blood,

(1) not with the mouth in any kind of physical way, but

(2) in a spiritual way,

(3) by faith, which is the mouth or hand of the soul. This they do:

(4) by the power of the Holy Ghost. This "feeding" on Christ, however, takes place not in the Lord's Supper alone, but whenever we exercise faith in Jesus.

Till he come

The Lord's Supper is a permanent ordinance in the Christian Church and is to be observed "till he come" again.

Paul (1)

Paul's background

Called Saul
Acts 8: 1; Acts 9: 1; Acts 13: 9
A member of the tribe of Benjamin
Rom. 11: 1; Phil. 3: 5
Personal appearance of
2 Cor. 10: 1; 2 Cor. 10: 10; 2 Cor. 11: 6
Born in Tarsus
Acts 9: 11; Acts 21: 39; Acts 22: 3
Educated at Jerusalem in the school of
Gamaliel
Acts 22: 3; Acts 26: 4
A zealous Pharisee
Acts 22: 3; Acts 23: 6; Acts 26: 5;
2 Cor. 11: 22; Gal. 1: 14; Phil. 3: 5
A Roman
Acts 16: 37; Acts 22: 25–28
Persecutes the Christians; present at,
and gives consent to, the stoning of
Stephen
Acts 7: 58; Acts 8: 1; Acts 8: 3;
Acts 9: 1; Acts 22: 4
Sent to Damascus with letters for
the arrest and return to Jerusalem of
Christians
Acts 9: 1,2

Paul's conversion

His vision and conversion
Acts 9: 3–22; Acts 22: 4–19;
Acts 26: 9–15; 1 Cor. 9: 1; 1 Cor. 15: 8;
Gal. 1: 13; 1 Tim. 1: 12,13
Is baptized
Acts 9: 18; Acts 22: 16
Called to be an apostle
Acts 22: 14–21; Acts 26: 16–18;
Rom. 1: 1; 1 Cor. 1: 1; 1 Cor. 9: 1,2;
1 Cor. 15: 9; Gal. 1: 1; Gal. 1: 15,16;

Eph. 1: 1; Col. 1: 1; 1 Tim. 1: 1;
1 Tim. 2: 7; 2 Tim. 1: 1; 2 Tim. 1: 11;
Titus 1: 1; Titus 1: 3

Paul's ministry

Preaches in Damascus
Acts 9: 20; Acts 9: 22
Is persecuted by the Jews
Acts 9: 23,24
Escapes by being let down from the
wall in a basket; goes to Jerusalem
Acts 9: 25,26; Gal. 1: 18,19
Welcomed by the disciples in Jerusalem
Acts 9: 26–29
Goes to Caesarea
Acts 9: 30; Acts 18: 22
Sent to the Gentiles
Acts 13: 2,3; Acts 13: 47,48;
Acts 22: 17–21; Rom. 11: 13;
Rom. 15: 16; Gal. 1: 15–24
Has Barnabas as his companion
Acts 11: 25,26
Teaches at Antioch
Acts 11: 26
Brings the contributions of the
Christians in Antioch to the Christians
in Jerusalem
Acts 11: 27–30
Returns with John to Antioch
Acts 12: 25
Visits Seleucia
Acts 13: 4
Visits Cyprus
Acts 13: 4
Preaches at Salamis
Acts 13: 5
Preaches at Paphos
Acts 13: 6
Sergius Paulus, deputy of the country,

is a convert of

Acts 13: 7–12

Challenges Elymas the sorcerer

Acts 13: 6–12

Visits Perga in Pamphylia

Acts 13: 13

Visits Antioch in Pisidia, and preaches
in the synagogue

Acts 13: 14–41

His message received gladly by the
Gentiles

Acts 13: 42; Acts 13: 49

Persecuted and thrown out

Acts 13: 50,51

Visits Iconium, and preaches to the
Jews and Greeks; is persecuted; escapes
to Lystra; goes to Derbe

Acts 14: 1–6

Heals a crippled man

Acts 14: 8–10

The people attempt to worship him

Acts 14: 11–18

Is persecuted by Jews from Antioch
and Iconium, and is stoned

Acts 14: 19; 2 Cor. 11: 25; 2 Tim. 3: 11

Escapes to Derbe, where he preaches
the gospel, and returns to Lystra, and to
Iconium, and to Antioch, teaches the
Christians, and ordains elders

Acts 14: 19–23

Revisits Pisidia, Pamphylia, Perga,
Attalia, and Antioch, in Syria, where he
stayed

Acts 14: 24–28

Argues against the Jewish Christians
who sought to impose circumcision

Acts 15: 1,2

Refers the question about circumcision
to the apostles and elders at Jerusalem

Acts 15: 2; Acts 15: 4

He tells the apostles at Jerusalem about
the miracles God had performed

among the Gentiles through them

Acts 15: 12

Returns to Antioch, accompanied by
Barnabas, Judas, and Silas, with letters
to the Gentiles

Acts 15: 22; Acts 15: 25

Makes his second missionary tour of
the churches

Acts 15: 36

Chooses Silas as his companion, and
passes through Syria and Cilicia

Acts 15: 36–41

Visits Lystra; circumcises Timothy

Acts 16: 1–5

Goes through Phrygia and Galatia; is
forbidden by the Holy Spirit to preach
in Asia; visits Mysia; plans to go to
Bithynia, but is restrained by the Spirit;
goes to Troas, where he has a vision
of a man saying, "Come over into
Macedonia, and help us"; immediately
proceeds to Macedonia

Acts 16: 6–10

Visits Samothracia and Neopolis;
comes to Philippi, the leading city of
Macedonia; visits a place of prayer by a
river; preaches the word; the merchant,
Lydia, of Thyatira, is converted and
baptized

Acts 16: 11–15

Expels an evil spirit from a slave-girl
who practiced divination

Acts 16: 16–18

Persecuted, beaten, and thrown into
prison with Silas; sings songs of praise
in prison; an earthquake shakes the
prison; he preaches to the alarmed
jailer, who believes, and is baptized
with his household

Acts 16: 19–34

Paul (2)

Paul's ministry, continued

Is released by the civil authorities as he is a Roman citizen

Acts 16: 35–39; 2 Cor. 6: 5; 2 Cor. 11: 25; 1 Thess. 2: 2

Is welcomed at Lydia's home

Acts 16: 40

Visits Amphipolis, and Apollonia, and Thessalonica, preaches in the synagogue

Acts 17: 1–4

Is persecuted

Acts 17: 5–9; 2 Thess. 1: 1–4

Escapes to Berea by night; preaches in the synagogue; not a few believe

Acts 17: 10–12

Persecuted by the Jews who come from Thessalonica; is taken by the Christian brethren to Athens

Acts 17: 13–15

Debates Mars' Hill with Greeks

Acts 17: 16–34

Visits Corinth; stays with Aquila and his wife, Priscilla, who were tentmakers; joins in the work of tent making; reasons in the synagogue every Sabbath; is rejected of the Jews; turns to the Gentiles; stays with Justus; teaches the word of God there for eighteen months

Acts 18: 1–11

Persecuted by Jews, sails to Syria, accompanied by Aquila and Priscilla

Acts 18: 12–18

Visits Ephesus, where he leaves Aquila and Priscilla; enters into a synagogue, where he reasons with the Jews; starts on his return journey to Jerusalem; visits Caesarea; passes through

Galatia and Phrygia, strengthening the disciples

Acts 18: 18–23

Returns to Ephesus; baptizes in the name of the Lord Jesus, and lays his hands upon the disciples, who are baptized with the Holy Spirit; preaches in the synagogue; stays in Ephesus for two years; heals the sick

Acts 19: 1–12

Reproves the exorcists; expels an evil spirit out of a man, and many believe, bringing their books of sorcery to be burned

Acts 19: 13–20; 1 Cor. 16: 8,9

Sends Timothy and Erastus into Macedonia, but stays himself in Asia

Acts 19: 21,22

His preaching of the gospel interferes with idol making; he is persecuted

Acts 19: 23–41; 2 Cor. 1: 8; 2 Tim. 4: 14

Moves on to Macedonia; goes to Greece and stays there for three months; returns through Macedonia, accompanied by Sopater, Aristarchus, Secundus, Gaius, Timothy, Tychicus, and Trophimus

Acts 20: 1–6

Visits Troas; preaches until day-break; restores to life the young man who fell from the window

Acts 20: 6–12

Visits Assos, Mitylene, Chios, Samos, Trogyllium, and Miletus, aiming to arrive in Jerusalem in time for Pentecost

Acts 20: 13–16

Sends for the elders of the church of Ephesus; tells them to take care of themselves and the flock over whom the Holy Spirit had made them overseers; kneels down and prays and leaves

Acts 20: 17–38

Visits Coos, Rhodes, Patara; sails for Tyre; stays at Tyre seven days; sails to Ptolemais; greets the brethren, and stays for one day

Acts 21: 1–7

Leaves for Caesarea; goes to the house of Philip, the Evangelist; is warned by Agabus not to go to Jerusalem; but nevertheless continues to travel to Jerusalem

Acts 21: 8–15

Is welcomed by the Christian brethren; reports about the things done among the Gentiles through his ministry; goes into the temple; uproar is created by Jews from Asia; he is thrown out of the temple; the chief captain of the garrison interposes and arrests him

Acts 21: 17–33

His defense

Acts 21: 33–40; Acts 22: 1–21

Is held prisoner

Acts 22: 24–30

Is brought before the council; his defense

Acts 22: 30; Acts 23: 1–5

Is returned to prison

Acts 23: 10

In a vision he is told that he will bear witness in Rome

Acts 23: 11

Jews conspire to kill him

Acts 23: 12–15

Conspiracy thwarted by his nephew

Acts 23: 16–22

Is escorted to Caesarea under military guard

Acts 23: 23–33

Kept in Herod's Judgment Hall in Caesarea

Acts 23: 35

His trial before Felix

Acts 24

Remains in custody for two years

Acts 24: 27

His trial before Festus

Acts 25: 1–12

Appeals to Caesar

Acts 25: 10–12

Before Agrippa

Acts 25: 13–27; Acts 26

Is taken to Rome in custody of Julius, a centurion, sails via the coasts of Asia; stops at Sidon, and at Myra

Acts 27: 1–5

Transferred to a ship of Alexandria; sails by way of Cnidus, Crete, Salamis, and the Fair Havens

Acts 27: 6–8

Predicts misfortune to the ship; his counsel not heeded, and the voyage resumed

Acts 27: 9–13

The ship in storm; the soldiers advise putting the prisoners to death; the centurion intervenes, and all two hundred and seventy-six people on board are saved

Acts 27: 14–44

Shipwreck, but all on board reach the island of Melita safely

Acts 27: 14–44

Treated kindly by the islanders

Acts 28: 1–2

Is bitten by a snake but miraculously survives

Acts 28: 3–6

The persecuted Paul

Paul's ministry, continued

Heals the ruler's father and others
   Acts 28: 7–10
Is delayed in Melita three months;
continues with voyage; delays
at Syracuse; sails via Rhegium
and Puteoli; meets brethren who
accompany him to Rome from Appii
forum; arrives at Rome; is handed over
to the captain of the guard; is allowed
to live under house arrest by himself in
custody of a soldier
   Acts 28: 11–16
Invites the leading Jews; states his
situation; is kindly received; expounds
the gospel; witnesses about the
kingdom of heaven
   Acts 28: 17–29
Lives for two years in his own rented
house, preaching and teaching
   Acts 28: 30,31
Supports himself
   Acts 18: 3; Acts 20: 33–35
Sickness of, in Asia
   2 Cor. 1: 8–11
Caught up to the third heavens
   2 Cor. 12: 1–4
Has "a thorn in the flesh"
   2 Cor. 12: 7–9; Gal. 4: 13,14

Paul and persecution

Paul's teaching about persecution

EXPECT PERSECUTION
Paul told fellow-Christians to expect to
be persecuted.
   "Indeed, all who want to live a godly
life in Christ Jesus will be persecuted"
2 Timothy 3: 12 NRSV.

ATTITUDE TOWARD PERSECUTORS
He also told them the attitude they
should have toward their persecutors.
   "Bless those who persecute you; bless
and do not curse them" Romans 12: 14
NRSV.

Paul's experience of persecution

Paul experienced a great deal of
persecution himself.

PERSECUTIONS ENDURED BY PAUL
   "After some time had passed, the
Jews plotted to kill him, but their plot
became known to Saul. They were
watching the gates day and night
so that they might kill him; but his
disciples took him by night and let him
down through an opening in the wall,
lowering him in a basket." Acts 9: 23–25
NRSV

PAUL AND SILAS IN PRISON
   "One day, as we were going to the
place of prayer, we met a slave-girl who
had a spirit of divination and brought
her owners a great deal of money by
fortune-telling. While she followed Paul
and us, she would cry out, 'These men
are slaves of the Most High God, who
proclaim to you a way of salvation.' She
kept doing this for many days. But Paul,
very much annoyed, turned and said
to the spirit, 'I order you in the name of
Jesus Christ to come out of her.' And it
came out that very hour.
   "But when her owners saw that their
hope of making money was gone,

they seized Paul and Silas and dragged them into the marketplace before the authorities. When they had brought them before the magistrates, they said, 'These men are disturbing our city; they are Jews and are advocating customs that are not lawful for us as Romans to adopt or observe.' The crowd joined in attacking them, and the magistrates had them stripped of their clothing and ordered them to be beaten with rods. After they had given them a severe flogging, they threw them into prison and ordered the jailer to keep them securely. Following these instructions, he put them in the innermost cell and fastened their feet in the stocks."   *Acts 16: 19–24 NRSV*

See also, Acts 2: 24; Acts 20: 22–24; Acts 21: 13; Acts 21: 27–33; Acts 22: 22–24; Acts 23: 10; Acts 23: 12–15; Rom. 8: 35–37; 1 Cor. 4: 9; 1 Cor. 4: 11–13; 2 Cor. 1: 8–10; 2 Cor. 4: 8–12; 2 Cor. 6: 4–5.

PAUL'S SUFFERINGS AS AN APOSTLE

"Are they ministers of Christ? I am talking like a madman – I am a better one: with far greater labors, far more imprisonments, with countless floggings, and often near death. Five times I have received from the Jews the forty lashes minus one. Three times I was beaten with rods. Once I received a stoning. Three times I was shipwrecked; for a night and a day I was adrift at sea; on frequent journeys, in danger from rivers, danger from bandits, danger from my own people, danger from Gentiles, danger in the city, danger in the wilderness, danger at sea, danger from false brothers and sisters; in toil and hardship, through many a sleepless night, hungry and thirsty, often without food, cold and naked. And, besides other things, I am under daily pressure because of my anxiety for all the churches. Who is weak, and I am not weak? Who is made to stumble, and I am not indignant?"
          2 Cor. 11: 23–29 NRSV

"If I must boast, I will boast of the things that show my weakness. The God and Father of the Lord Jesus (blessed be he forever!) knows that I do not lie. In Damascus, the governor under King Aretas guarded the city of Damascus in order to seize me, but I was let down in a basket through a window in the wall, and escaped from his hands."   *2 Cor. 11: 30–33 NRSV*

See also 2 Cor. 12: 10, Gal. 5: 11, Gal. 6: 17; 1 Thess. 3: 4; Phil. 1: 30; Phil. 2: 17,18; Col. 1: 24; 1 Thess. 2: 2; 1 Thess. 2: 14,15; 2 Tim. 1: 12, 2 Tim. 2: 9,10; 2 Tim. 3: 11,12.

"At my first defense no one came to my support, but all deserted me. May it not be counted against them! But the Lord stood by me and gave me strength, so that through me the message might be fully proclaimed and all the Gentiles might hear it. So I was rescued from the lion's mouth"
          2 Tim. 4: 16,17 NRSV

The teachings of Paul

The Law of Moses

The phrase "law of Moses" refers to all that was revealed through Moses. This is a major topic in the New Testament. Paul gave more teaching about the law of Moses than all of the other New Testament writers put together.

Pointing forwards

The law of Moses was only the shadow of good things to come (Colossians 2: 17; Hebrews 10: 1).

Fulfillment

Jesus Christ declared his intention to fulfill every word of the law (Matthew 5: 17,18), and he did it (Luke 24: 44).

Its limitations

The law could not:
bring about justification (Acts 13: 39);
produce righteousness (Galatians 2: 21);
produce life (Galatians 3: 21);
bring about perfection (Hebrews 7: 19);
free the conscience from a knowledge
   of sin (Hebrews 10: 1–4).

Impossible for anyone to keep

The law was given to and for Israel only (Exodus 19: 1–20: 17; Malachi 4: 4; John 1: 1–17).

There are many examples of this: All Hebrew males had to come before the Lord at a designated place three times a year (Exodus 23: 14–17; Exodus 12: 4–16);

the law commanded, on penalty of death, that no fire could be made on the sabbath day (Exodus 35: 1–3).

The law is abolished

It is declared: that the law is abolished (2 Corinthians 3: 6–13; Ephesians 2: 15); that Christ is the end of the law (Romans 10: 4); that it was the ministration of death (Exodus 32: 1–28), and that it is "done away" (2 Corinthians 3: 7); that Jesus took away the first that he might establish the second (Hebrews 10: 5–9); that it was nailed to the cross (Colossians 2: 14–16); that those who had been under it had been delivered from it (Romans 7: 6); that they were dead to it (Romans 7: 4);

that they were not under the law, but under grace (Romans 6: 14); that they were no longer under the schoolmaster of the law (Galatians 3: 24,25);

that they were not required to serve the law (Acts 15: 1–24; Galatians 3: 19); that the Christian who looked for justification under the law had fallen from grace (Galatians 5: 4);

that now the righteousness of God is revealed without the help of the law (Romans 3: 21,22).

Contrasted with the Gospel

ONE NATION: EVERYONE
The law was intended for one nation–Israel (Exodus 20: 1–17 Malachi 4: 4); the gospel of Christ is intended for the whole creation (Matthew 28: 18–20; Mark 16: 15,16).

BLOOD OF ANIMALS: BLOOD OF JESUS
The first covenant was dedicated with the blood of animals (Exodus 24: 6–8),

the new covenant was dedicated with the blood of Jesus Christ (1 Peter 1: 18,19).

ADMINISTERED BY PEOPLE: BY JESUS

The first institution was administered by frail men – the Levites (Leviticus 16: 1–34; Hebrews 7: 11–23); the second is administered by Jesus Christ, who was made priest, not by any human command, but "after the power of an endless life" (Hebrews 7: 16).

CIRCUMCISION OF THE FLESH: OF THE HEART

Circumcision of the flesh was a sign of the first (Genesis 17: 1–14; Leviticus 12: 1–13); circumcision of the heart and spirit is the sign of the second (Romans 2: 25).

TEMPORAL BLESSINGS: SPIRITUAL BLESSINGS

The law of Moses guaranteed to the obedient Hebrews temporal blessings (Deuteronomy 28: 1–6); the gospel of Christ guarantees spiritual blessings (1 Peter 1: 4).

LAND ON EARTH: HEAVEN

The law of Moses promised the land of Canaan to the Hebrews (Deuteronomy 30: 5–10); the gospel guarantees eternal life beyond the grave to those who honor the Lord (1 John 5: 20).

TAKING GOD'S NAME IN VAIN

The law of Moses prohibited the people from taking the name of the Lord in vain (Exodus 20: 7); the gospel teaches that anything beyond saying "yea" and "nay" is evil (Matthew 5: 37).

THE SABBATH

The law of Moses required the Hebrews to remember the Sabbath day (Exodus 20: 8–11); in apostolic times, the people of God remembered the Savior in the feast that he ordained (Matthew 26: 26–30; 1 Corinthians 11: 23–29) on the first day of the week (Acts 20: 7).

MURDER

The law of Moses prohibited murder (Exodus 20: 13); the gospel prohibits hatred (1 John 3: 15).

ADULTERY

The law of Moses forbade adultery (Exodus 20: 14); the gospel prohibits even lust (Matthew 5: 28).

STEALING AND FALSE WITNESS

The law of Moses prohibits stealing (Exodus 20: 15); the gospel prohibits stealing and requires goodness (Ephesians 4: 28).

The law of Moses forbade the bearing of false witness (Exodus 20: 16); the gospel requires us to speak the truth in love (Ephesians 4: 15).

COVETOUSNESS

The law of Moses prohibited covetousness (Exodus 20: 17); the gospel requires us to do good to men as we have the opportunities (Galatians 6: 10), and to love our neighbors as ourselves (Romans 13: 10).

Part Five
Fascinating Bible Facts

Part Five Contents in summary

Bible symbols 1128

Dark Bible topics 1132

Bible contradictions 1140

Bible promises 1144

Part Five Contents in Detail

Bible symbols

Bible symbols (1)..1128

Bible symbols (2) 1130

Dark Bible topics

Dark Bible topics (1) 1132

Dark Bible topics (2)..1134

Dark Bible topics (3)..1136

Dark Bible topics (4)..1138

Bible contradictions

Bible contradictions (1) 1140

Bible contradictions (2)..1142

Bible promises

Blessings promised to believers (1)..1144

Blessings promised to believers (2) 1146

Blessings promised to believers (3) 1148

Blessings promised to believers (4) 1150

Bible promises in times of need 1152

New Testament promises (1)..1154

New Testament promises (2) 1156

New Testament promises (3) 1158

New Testament promises (4)..1160

New Testament promises (5) 1162

Bible symbols (1)

1. Meaning of the word "symbol"

"Symbol" comes from two Greek words "syn" meaning "together" and "ballein" meaning to "throw." "Symbol" then, means literally "thrown together." A symbol is a representation, one thing standing for another.

2. Use of symbols of Scripture

Symbols are used in the Bible to explain concepts. A familiar symbol can sometimes communicate more effectively than hundreds of words.

3. Categories of symbols used in the Bible

Type of symbol	Example of symbol	Bible references
a) Symbolic actions	Sitting	Ps. 110: 1; Heb. 10: 11–18
b) Symbolic colors	White	Rev. 3: 4,5; 19:8. Isa.1: 18
c) Symbolic creatures	Dragon	Rev. 12: 9
Fox	Luke 13: 32	
d) Symbolic names	Nabal	1 Sam. 25: 25
e) Symbolic numbers	Three	2 Cor. 13: 1; 1 John.5: 7
f) Symbolic objects	Cup	Matt. 26: 39

4. How symbols should be interpreted

Inadvertently, some Bible students has come to misleading or even totally wrong interpretations about parts of the Bible because they have incorrectly interpreted the meaning of some symbols.

A) TAKE NOTE OF THE CONTEXT

Every symbol should be assessed by the verses, chapters, and book in which it appears.

A number of symbols mean different things in different parts of the Bible, so carefully observing the context of each occurrence of the symbol helps to determine its meaning.

Lion

A lion, for example, stands for:
- the devil, see 1 Peter 5: 8, where the devil is likened to a roaring lion;
- Jesus, see Revelation 5: 5, where Jesus is described as the Lion of Judah;
- God's faithful followers, see Proverbs 28: 1, where the righteous are said to be as bold as a lion.

B) LOOK FOR A SINGLE CHARACTERISTIC

It is usually best to think of a symbol standing for just one characteristic which is common to it and the matter being described.

Examples of single characteristics in symbols:

Milk

Milk, see Hebrews 5: 12 and 1 Peter 2: 2. Milk here symbolizes the foundational truth of God's Word. It is obvious that milk is a food that helps babies to grow.

Sun

Sun, see Revelation 1: 16. In this verse the sun is a symbol for the glory of God, as everyone knows that the sun is the brightest source of light in the sky.

c) LOOK FOR THE BIBLE'S OWN INTERPRETATION OF A SYMBOL
The Bible itself gives us the meaning of some of symbols it uses.

The prophet Isaiah mentions a "vineyard" in Isaiah 5: 1. Reading this we may have no idea what this vineyard stands for. But we are given the answer in Isaiah 5: 7, "For the vineyard of the Lord of hosts is the house of Israel."

5. Types and symbols

It is possible to draw a distinction between types used in the Bible and symbols found in the Bible.

1
A symbol is one thing standing for another.
A type is one thing prefiguring another.

2
A symbol is a figure of something which may belong to the past, present, or future.
A type is a figure which only refers to something in the future.

3
A symbol represents certain characteristics or qualities in that which it represents.
A type represents something or

someone that God has pre-ordained will come.

Example of a symbol and a type

In Psalm 18: 2 the word "rock" is a symbol. In 1 Corinthians 10: 4 the "rock" is Christ. Israel's wanderings in the wilderness, 1 Corinthians 10: 11, was a type. It pre-figured the experience of the Christian church and acts as a warning not to be like unbelieving Israel.

Bible symbols (2)

Actions	Meaning of action
1. Anointing	God's enabling for service
2. Being awake	Watchfulness
3. Bathing	Purification
4. Circumcision	Entering into God's covenant
5. Dancing	Joy
6. Fornication	Idolatry
7. Sitting	Finished work
8. Sleeping	Rest, and spiritual indifference

Man-made objects	Meaning of man-made objects
1. Altar	Place of sacrifice, and meeting with God
2. Anchor	Security for God's followers
3. Ark	Salvation
4. Armor	God's spiritual weapons
5. Axe	Judgment
6. Balances	Scarcity, and judgment
7. Barns	Human way of providing for the future
8. Basket	God's provision for our needs
9. Beam	Sin
10. Breastplate	Protection, and righteousness
11. Chair	Throne, and judgment

12. Cymbal	Expression of joy
13. Furnace	Trial
14. Gates	Place of judgment and decision-making in a city
15. Hammer	Word of God
16. Harps	Instrument of praise
17. Helmet	Protection, spiritual and physical
18. Incense	Prayer ascending to God
19. Lamp	Word of God, and God's Spirit
20. Linen	Righteousness
21. Sackcloth and ashes	Mourning, bereavement, and repentance
22. Sickle	God's judgment
23. Staff	God's protection and guidance
24. Sword	War, and Word of God
25. Well	Salvation

Natural objects	Meaning of natural objects
1. Clouds	God's presence
2. Fig tree	Israel, God's people
3. Fire	Judgment, and God's presence
4. Running water	The Holy Spirit
5. Olive tree	Israel, God's people
6. Vine	Israel, God's people
7. Wind	God's Spirit

Hand expressions

A number of the movements of the
hands and arms are used in a symbolic
way in the Bible.

Hand movement	Meaning
To relax the hand	To fail in duty
To wash hands	To indicate innocence or cleansing
To bury the hand	Laziness
To put the hand on the mouth	To be silent
To strengthen the hand	To be resolute
To drop the hands	A sign of weakness
To stretch out a hand	To receive divine help or punishment
To offer the hand	To give help
To lay hands on	To injure, or kill, or set apart for God's service and bless
To lift up a hand against	To rebel or attack
To place in the hand of	To be subject to
To be at the right hand of	To be in a position of authority
At your hand	From you
To put your hand to	To start work
Hollow of the hand	A place of security
To kiss someone else's hand	This showed reverence
To kiss your own hand	Was an act of worship
The Lord's hand is heavy	Experiencing punishment
Hand would not reach	Restricted power
To fill the hand	Act of commitment
Hand of the Lord upon	To prophecy
To require at the hand of	To have liability for
To put hand under the thigh	To take a solemn oath
To have one's hand with	To take sides with
To lift hands	To bless, or pray, or ask for help
To put your hand on your head	To display grief

Dark Bible topics (1)

Sexual sin (1)

The Bible pulls no punches when it comes to the misuse of God's good gift of sex. It gives many examples of sex sin in both the Old Testament and the New Testament.

People involved	Sin involved	Consequences of the sin
Sodom and Gomorrah (Jude 6–7, Genesis 18: 16–33, Genesis 19: 1–29, Ezekiel 16: 48–50)	Homosexuality Pride Gluttony Idleness Neglect of poor and needy	Both cities and the surrounding territory were destroyed by God
Lot and his daughters (Genesis 19: 30–38)	Incest Doubt: Daughters did not have faith that God would provide for them	The descendants (Ammonites and Moabites) became hated enemies of God's people
Judah and Tamar (Genesis 38)	Incest Deception Prostitution Manipulation/Control Hypocrisy	Tamar was almost executed Judah's sin was exposed Since Judah repented (v. 26), some consequences may have been averted Twin sons born out of wedlock
Reuben and his father's concubine (Genesis 35: 22; Genesis 49: 3,4; 1 Chronicles 5: 1)	Incest Defiled his father's marriage bed	Reuben lost his birth right Reuben and his descendants were cursed by Jacob
Joseph and Potiphar's wife (Genesis 39: 6–13)	Lust Lying Slander False accusation	Joseph loses trusted position in his master's house and is imprisoned on account of the false accusations

Israelites with Moabite and Midianite women (Numbers 25: 1–10)	Seduction Harlotry/Prostitution Adultery Idolatry	Israel was joined to the demon "Baal of Peor" through sexual worship God's anger was aroused and a plague ensued, killing 24,000 The guilty were executed Israel retaliates against Midian for their seduction (Numbers 31)
Samson (Judges 14–16)	Lust Pride Broken vows Manipulation/Control Anger Taking revenge Lying	Samson involved in several skirmishes with the Philistines Deceived by both his wives and eventually captured God's Spirit left Samson Samson's eyes gouged out by his captors Samson repented in captivity and God granted Samson's death wish to strike the Philistines
The Levite, the harlot concubine, and the Benjamite mob (Judges 19)	Prostitution Adultery Homosexuality Lust Fornication Rape Murder	The concubine died after being raped Israel declared war on the Benjamites; thousands died
David and Bathsheba (2 Samuel 11–12)	Lust/Coveting Murder Manipulation Conspiracy Lying Covering sin	David's son dies David brought reproach on God's name God spared David's life because he repented

Dark Bible topics (2)

Sexual sin (2)

People involved	Sin involved	Consequences of the sin
Amnon and Tamar (2 Samuel 13)	Lust/Coveting Conspiracy Fornication Hatred Lying Rape Incest	Tamar's marriage prospects were destroyed for life and she lived desolate in her brother Absalom's house Absalom murders Amnon in revenge
Absalom and his father's wives (2 Samuel 16: 21,22, 2 Samuel 18: 6–15)	Adultery Rebellion Dishonoring parents Incest Pride	Spiritual confusion; Absalom followed evil counsel
Solomon and his wives (1 Kings 11)	Love of pleasure Sexual idolatry Idolatry	Spiritual confusion Strife: God raised up several adversaries against Solomon because of his disobedience
Oholah (Ezekiel 23: 1–10,36–49; metaphorical for the northern kingdom of Samaria)	Spiritual adultery Lust Idolatry Fornication Prostitution Rebellion Adultery Child sacrifice Defiled God's sanctuary Profaned the Sabbath	God delivered her into the hands of her enemies, the Assyrians; the Assyrians plundered Samaria, taking some people captive and killing others The Assyrians executed God's judgment on Samaria
Oholibah (Ezekiel 23: 1–4,11–49; metaphorical for the southern kingdom of Judah)	Fornication Lust Prostitution Pride Rebellion Adultery Child sacrifice Defiled God's sanctuary Profaned Sabbaths	Oholibah was defiled by her Chaldean lovers and she alienated herself from her lovers

The New Testament

Sexual sins did not end at the close of the Old Testament. There are a number of examples of this in the New Testament. While it is always condemned, the whole Bible teaches that it may be repented of, as in the case of King David.

People involved	Sin involved	Consequences of the sin
The Romans (Romans 1: 20–32)	Pride	Became futile in their thoughts
	Idolatry	Their hearts were darkened
	Lust	God gave them up to uncleanness in the lusts of their hearts, to dishonor their bodies among themselves
	Sexual immorality	
	Homosexuality	
	Covetousness	God gave them up to their vile passions (homosexuality)
	Maliciousness	
	Envy	They burned in lust for one another and committed shameful acts
	Murder	
	Strife	They received due penalty for their acts
	Deceit	
	Evil-mindedness	God gave them over to a depraved mind
	Unforgiveness	They were filled with evil
	Rebellion	
	Gossip/Slander	
The sexually immoral brother and the Corinthian church (1 Corinthians 5: 1–13)	Incest	Paul instructed the church to:
	Pride	Not keep company with the unrepentant brother
	Tolerating sinful practice in the church	Deliver the brother to Satan in hopes that he would repent
The Jezebel spirit and the church (Revelation 2: 19–25)	Sexual immorality	Jezebel and those who sin with her will suffer intensely on a "bed of suffering" if they do not repent of Jezebel's ways
	Idolatry	
	False teaching	
	Spiritual adultery	
	Unrepentance	
	Studying Satan's "deep secrets" cult	

Dark Bible topics (3)

Witchcraft (1)

The Bible's teaching in summary

"For rebellion is as the sin of divination, and insubordination is as iniquity and idolatry..." 1 Samuel 15: 23 NAS

"For rebellion is as the sin of witchcraft..." 1 Samuel 15: 23

Defining witchcraft

Witchcraft is wanting to have spiritual power without submitting to God.

Witchcraft is a desire to be a spiritual free agent without submission to God and without regard for the Bible's teaching.

The dynamics of witchcraft

"You belong to your father, the devil, and you want to carry out your father's desire... When he lies, he speaks his native language, for he is a liar and the father of lies. Yet because I tell the truth, you do not believe me!" John 8: 44,45 NIV.

All supernatural power comes, ultimately, from either God or Satan. Satan empowers those who believe a lie. Witchcraft supports Satan's lies.

So anyone who opens himself or herself to them and then:
• mixes certain ingredients in a drink
• eats special herbs
• arranges candles in a certain configuration
• stares into a crystal ball

• turns over Tarot cards
• "reads" the stars
• draws certain symbols
will encourage evil spiritual forces to come into play.

But according to James 3: 15 such so-called "wisdom" does not come down from heaven but is earthly, unspiritual, of the devil.

Rebellion against God ranks as the greatest sin we can commit. Divination and witchcraft are often linked to each other in the teaching of the Bible.

"For rebellion is like the sin of divination, and arrogance like the evil of idolatry. Because you have rejected the word of the Lord, he has rejected you" 1 Samuel 15:23 NIV.

Witchcraft and God's followers

Witchcraft should never be allowed any foothold within the Christian church.

"Let no one be found among you... who practices divination or sorcery, interprets omens, engages in witchcraft, or cast spells, or who is a medium or spiritist." Deuteronomy 18: 10,11 NIV.

"For those nations, which you will dispossess, listen to those who practice witchcraft and to diviners, but as for you, the Lord your God has not allowed you to do so." Deuteronomy 18: 14 NAS.

The lure of sorcery should never be underestimated.

"Now for some time a man named Simon had practiced sorcery in the city and amazed all the people of Samaria. He boasted that he was someone great, and all the people, both high and low, gave him their attention and exclaimed, 'This man is the divine power known as the Great Power.' They followed him because he had amazed them for a long time with his magic." Acts 8: 9–11 NIV.

Fighting the lies

God's followers, in Bible times, as today, have to expose, condemn and root out all kinds of witchcraft.
In addition to those slain in battle, the Israelites had put to the sword Balaam son of Beor, who practiced divination. Joshua 13: 22 NIV.

"He ... practiced sorcery, divination and witchcraft, and consulted mediums and spiritists. He did much evil in the eyes of the Lord, provoking him to anger" 2 Chronicles 33: 6 NIV.

"Then the Lord said to me, 'The prophets are prophesying lies in my name. I have not sent them or appointed them or spoken to them. They are prophesying to you false visions, divinations, idolatries, and the delusions of their own minds.'" Jeremiah 14: 14 NIV.

"So do not listen to your prophets, your diviners, your interpreters of dreams, your mediums, or your sorcerers... Do not let the prophets and diviners among you deceive you. Do not listen to the dreams you encourage them to have." Jeremiah 27: 9,10 NIV.

We must be repentant

Like any other sinful activity Christians should repent if they have ever dabbled in or been deeply involved in witchcraft. One example of this is recorded in Acts.

"Many of them also which used curious arts brought their books together, and burned them before all men: and they counted the price of them, and found it fifty thousand pieces of silver" Acts 19: 19.

Dark Bible topics (4)

Witchcraft (2)

Clear Bible teaching

Evil activities, which are often widespread and accepted in today's society, need to be seen in the light of Scripture.

Evil activity	Bible teaching
1. Spells	Ezekiel 13: 6; Lamentations 3: 37
2. False Prophecies	Jeremiah 23: 25–38; Isaiah 28: 7–22
3. Incantations, Mantras	Matthew 6: 7; Ecclesiastes 5: 7
4. Potions	1 Timothy 4: 1–5; Matthew 15: 8–17
5. Tarot Cards	2 Timothy 2: 15; Micah 3: 6
6. Horoscopes	James 3: 13–15; Isaiah 47: 14,15
7. Spirit guides and false teachers	2 Timothy 4: 2–4; Acts 13: 10,11

Sorcery

Sorcery may be defined as divination by the (alleged) assistance of evil spirits.

Bible study on sorcery

FORBIDDEN AND DENOUNCED
Sorcery is forbidden in Leviticus 19: 26–28,31; 20: 6; Deuteronomy 18: 9–14, and it is denounced in Isaiah 8: 19; Malachi 3: 5.

PRACTICED
But sorcery was practiced:

In Old Testament

- By the Egyptians, Isaiah 19: 3,11,12
- By the magicians, Exodus 7: 11,22; 8: 7,18
- By Balaam, Numbers 22: 6; 23: 23; 22: 23
- By Jezebel, 2 Kings 9: 22
- By the Ninevites, Nahum 3: 4,5
- By the Babylonians, Isaiah 47: 9–13; Ezekiel 21: 21,22; Daniel 2: 2,10,27
- By Belshazzar, Daniel 5: 7,15
- By astrologers, Jeremiah 10: 2; Micah 3: 6,7
- By false prophets, Jeremiah 14: 14; 27: 9; 29: 8,9; Ezekiel 13: 6–9; 22: 28

In the New Testament

- By false prophets, Matthew 24: 24
- By Simon the Sorcerer, Acts 8: 9; 11
- By Elymas (Bar-Jesus), Acts 13: 8
- By the girl at Philippi, Acts 16: 16
- By charlatan Jews, Acts 19: 13
- By sons of Sceva, Acts 19: 14,15

Other instances of and information about of sorcery

To cease. Ezekiel 12: 23,24; 13: 23; Micah 5: 12.

False messages of. Ezekiel 21: 29; Zechariah 10: 2; 2 Thessalonians 2: 9.

Diviners will be confounded. Micah 3: 7.

Belongs to the works of the flesh.
Galatians 5: 20.

Wickedness of. 1 Samuel 15: 23.

Vainness of. Isaiah 44: 25.

Punishment for. Exodus 22: 18;
Leviticus 20: 27; Deuteronomy 13: 5.

Divining by mediums or spiritists.
Leviticus 20: 27; 1 Chronicles 10: 13;
2 Chronicles 33: 6; Isaiah 8: 19; 19: 3;
29: 4.

Diving by entrails. Ezekiel 21: 21.

Diving by images. 2 Kings 23: 24;
Ezekiel 21: 21.

Diving by rods. Hosea 4: 12.

Saul consulted the "witch" of Endor.
1 Samuel 28: 7–25.

Books of, destroyed. Acts 19: 19.

Note on witchcraft

The key Scriptures on witchcraft
are: 1 Samuel 15: 23; 2 Kings 9: 22;
2 Chronicles 33: 6; Micah 5: 12; Nahum
3: 4; Galatians 5: 20.

In the popular sense of the word no
mention is made either of witches or
of witchcraft in Scripture. The "witch
of En-dor" (1 Samuel 28: 7–25) was a
necromancer, that is, one who feigned
to hold conversations with the dead.

The girl with "a spirit of divination"
(Acts 16: 16) was possessed by an evil
spirit.

Bible teaching about various forms of divination

1. Augury, interpretation of omens, is
condemned: Deuteronomy 18: 9–14.
In 2 Kings 21: 6, King Manasseh
of Israel practiced such and did evil

before God ("soothsaying" *NKJV*;
"augury" *ASV*).

2 Psychics and fortune-tellers are
condemned: see 1 Corinthians 2: 11;
1 Kings 8: 39.

3 Spiritism and necromancy is
condemned: see Deuteronomy 18: 11.

Child sacrifice

Sadly, child sacrifice is still practiced
today.

God told his people not to sacrifice
their children to Molech: see Leviticus
18: 21; Deuteronomy 12: 31; 18: 10.

Bible contradictions (1)

Statement	Apparent contradiction	Resolution
1 God is satisfied with his creation "God saw all that he made, and it was very good." [Gen. 1: 31].	*1 God is dissatisfied with his creation* "The Lord was grieved that he had made man on earth, and his heart was filled with pain." [Gen. 6: 6]	This is not really a contradiction at all. For both statements are true. The first happened before the Fall, the second is true after humankind had rebelled against God.
2 God lives in chosen temples "I have heard your prayer and have chosen this place for myself as a temple of sacrifices... I have chosen and consecrated this temple so that my Name may be there forever. My eyes and my heart will always be there." [2 Chr. 7: 12,16]	*2 God does not live in temples* "However, the Most High does not live in houses made by men." [Acts 7: 48]	Just because it says that the Lord's "eyes and heart will always be there" it does not mean that God's presence cannot be elsewhere. God is transcendent and so reveals himself wherever he chooses.
3 God lives in light "who alone is immortal and who lives in unapproachable light whom no one has seen or can see." [1 Tim. 6: 16]	*God lives in darkness* "Clouds and darkness are round about him." [Ps. 97: 2]	Both verses are using metaphors which should not be interpreted literally. Both verses are expressing the same idea: the unsearchableness of God.
4 God is tired and rests "In six days the Lord made heaven and earth, and on the seventh day he rested, and was refreshed." [Ex. 31: 17]	*God is never tired and never rests* "The everlasting God, the Lord, the Creator of the ends of the earth, fainteth not, neither is weary." [Is. 40: 28]	The term "rested and was refreshed" is simply a vivid Oriental way of saying that God ceased from the work of creation and took delight in surveying the work.

5 God is not omnipresent and omniscient. God is everywhere present, sees and knows all things. "The eyes of the Lord are everywhere, keeping watch on the wicked and the good." [Proverbs 15: 3]	5 God is not omnipresent and omniscient. God is not everywhere present, neither sees nor knows all things "But the Lord came down to see the city and the tower that men were building." [Gen. 11: 5]	The verse from Genesis does not mean that God was ignorant about what was going on in Babel, but that he was now, as it were, turning his attention to it.
6 God knows the hearts of men and women "Then they prayed, 'Lord, you know everyone's heart. Show us which of these two you have chosen.'" [Acts 1: 24]	6 God tries men and women to find out what is in their heart "Remember how the Lord your God led you all the way in the desert these forty years, to humble you and test you in order to know what was in your hearts." [Deut. 8: 2]	God does know all about everyone. When Deuteronomy says that the Lord was testing his people in order to know their hearts it does not mean that God was ignorant, but rather, that the people would know that God knew all about them!
7 Christ warned his followers not to fear being killed "I tell you, my friends, do not be afraid of those who kill the body and after that can do no more." [Luke 12: 4 NIV]	7 Christ himself avoided the Jews for fear of being killed "After this, Jesus went around in Galilee, purposely staying away from Judea because the Jews there were waiting to take his life." [John 7:1 NIV]	Luke 12 records Jesus' general teaching that we should fear God more than men. John 7 does not say that Jesus was afraid that the Jews would kill him. He avoided them because it was not yet his time to die.

Bible contradictions (2)

"The Bible must be the invention either of good men or angels, bad men or devils, or of God. However, it was not written by good men, because good men would not tell lies by saying 'Thus saith the Lord'; it was not written by bad men because they would not write about doing good duty, while condemning sin, and themselves to hell; thus, it must be written by divine inspiration."

Charles Wesley

Statement	Apparent contradiction	Resolution
8 *Jesus would be in the grave for three days and three nights* "For as Jonas was three days and three nights in the whale's belly; so shall the Son of man be three days and three nights in the heart of the earth." [Matt. 12: 40]	8 *Jesus was only in the grave for one night* "Now when Jesus was risen early the first day of the week." [Mark 16:9]	Orientals thought of any part of a day or a day as a whole day or a whole night. So one whole day and two parts of a day, together with two nights, would be referred to as "three days and three nights."
9 *Jesus' mission was to bring peace* "And suddenly there was with the angel a multitude of the heavenly host praising God, and saying, Glory to God in the highest, and on earth peace, good will toward men." [Luke 2: 13,14]	9 *Jesus' mission was not to bring peace* "I did not come to bring peace, but a sword." [Mathew 10: 34]	The verse from Luke is speaking about Jesus' mission to the world through which he brought peace and forgiveness. The verse from Matthew refers to the division that is often caused as a result of individuals following Jesus.
10 *Killing is forbidden* "Thou shalt not kill." [Exodus 20: 13]	10 *Killing is commanded* "Now go and smite Amalek." [1 Samuel 15:3]	The Bible distinguishes between murder, which is forbidden, and capital punishment.

The skeptics guide to misinterpreting the Bible

1. Assuming that the unexplained is not explainable
2. Presuming the Bible guilty until proven innocent
3. Confusing our fallible interpretations with God's infallible revelation
4. Failing to understand the context of the passage.
5. Neglecting to interpret difficult passages in the light of clear ones
6. Basing a teaching on an obscure passage
7. Forgetting that the Bible is a human book with human characteristics
8. Assuming that a partial report is a false report
9. Demanding that NT citations of the OT always be exact quotations
10. Assuming that divergent accounts are false ones
11. Presuming that the Bible approves of all its records
12. Forgetting that the Bible uses non-technical, everyday language
13. Assuming that round numbers are false
14. Neglecting to note that the Bible uses different literary devices
15. Forgetting that only the original text, not every copy of Scripture, is without error
16. Confusing general statements with universal ones
17. Forgetting that latter revelation supersedes previous revelation

Statement	Apparent contradiction	Resolution
11 We are saved by good deeds "Ye see then how that by works a man is justified, and not by faith only." [James 2: 24]	11 We are not saved by good deeds "For by grace are ye saved through faith . . . not of works." [Ephesians 2: 8,9]	We are saved by faith, and that faith does good deeds. Goods deeds can never win salvation for us. But every Christian should be glad to serve Jesus and people.
12 Nobody has ever seen God "No man hath seen God at any time." [John 1: 18]	12 Moses saw God face to face "And the Lord spake unto Moses face to face, as a man speaketh unto his friend." [Exodus 33: 11]	Nobody has indeed ever seen God. The phrase "face to face" it is not meant to be taken literally. Rather, it conveys the idea of deep friendship.

Blessings promised to believers (1)

Promises of temporal blessings (1)

Theme	Bible references	Key promise
General promises to believers in the Psalms	Psalm 3: 8 Psalm 5: 12 Psalm 16: 6 Psalm 58: 11 Psalm 84: 11	"Surely goodness and mercy shall follow me all the days of my life: and I will dwell in the house of the Lord for ever" (Psalm 23: 6).
General promises to believers in the rest of the Old Testament	Proverbs 3: 32 Proverbs 10: 6,24,28 Proverbs 12: 2 Proverbs 13: 9,21 Ecclesiastes 8: 12 Isaiah 3: 10	"He that followeth after righteousness and mercy findeth life, righteousness, and honour" (Proverbs 21: 21).
General promises to believers in the New Testament	1 Corinthians 3: 21,22 1 Timothy 4: 8	"He that spared not his own Son, but delivered him up for us all, how shall he not with him also freely give us all things?" (Romans 8: 32).
Temporal blessings in general	Psalm 23: 1,5 Philippians 4: 19 1 Timothy 6: 6,17	"There is no want to them that fear him. They that seek the Lord shall not want any good thing" (Psalms 34: 9,10).
Food	Psalm 37: 3 Psalm 132: 15 Psalm 147: 14 Proverbs 13: 25 Joel 2: 26	"Behold the fowls of the air: for they sow not, neither do they reap, nor gather into barns; yet your heavenly Father feedeth them. Are ye not much better than they?" (Matthew 6: 26).

Clothing		"I say unto you, Take no thought for your life, what ye shall eat, or what ye shall drink; nor yet for your body, what ye shall put on. Is not the life more than meat, and the body than raiment? Wherefore, if God so clothe the grass of the field, which to day is, and to morrow is cast into the oven, shall he not much more clothe you, O ye of little faith? Therefore take no thought, saying, What shall we eat? or, What shall we drink? or, Wherewithal shall we be clothed? For your heavenly Father knoweth that ye have need of all these things" (Matthew 6: 25,30,31,32).
Life	Deuteronomy 6: 2 Job 5: 26 Psalm 34: 12–14 Psalm 91: 16 Proverbs 3: 2,16 Proverbs 9: 11	"Ye shall walk in all the ways which the LORD your God hath commanded you, that ye may live, and that it may be well with you, and that ye may prolong your days in the land which ye shall possess" (Deuteronomy 5: 33).
Health	Psalm 103: 3–5 Proverbs 4: 2	"Be not wise in thine own eyes: fear the Lord, and depart from evil. It shall be health to thy navel, and marrow to thy bones" (Proverbs 3: 7,8).

Blessings promised to believers (2)

Promises of temporal blessings (2)

Theme	Bible references	Key promise
Safety under divine protection	Deuteronomy 33: 12 1 Samuel 2: 9 Job 4: 7 Psalm 4: 8 Psalm 16: 8 Psalm 27: 1 Psalm 34: 20 Psalm 91: 1,2,4,10 Psalm 112: 7 Psalm 121: 1–8 Proverbs 3: 24 Isaiah 33: 16 Zechariah 2: 5	"When thou passest through the waters, I will be with thee; and through the rivers, they shall not overflow thee: when thou walkest through the fire, thou shalt not be burned; neither shall the flame kindle upon thee. For I am the Lord thy God, the Holy One of Israel, thy Savior" (Isaiah 43: 2,3).
Promises of peace	Leviticus 26: 6 Psalm 29: 11 Psalm 119: 165 Psalm 125: 5 Psalm 147: 14 Isaiah 26: 12	"My people shall dwell in a peaceable habitation, and in sure dwellings, and in quiet resting places" (Isaiah 32: 18).
Guidance	Psalm 37: 23 Psalm 48: 14 Psalm 73: 24 Proverbs 11: 5 Proverbs 16: 9 Isaiah 28: 26 Isaiah 42: 16	"In all thy ways acknowledge him, and he shall direct thy paths" (Proverbs 3: 6).

Promises linked to the troubles of life (1)

Theme	Bible references	Key promise
1 Preservation from trouble	Job 5: 19 Psalm 31: 23 Psalm 91: 10 Proverbs 12: 21 Proverbs 15: 19	"For this shall every one that is godly pray unto thee in a time when thou mayest be found: surely in the floods of great waters they shall not come nigh unto him. Thou art my hiding place; thou shalt preserve me from trouble; thou shalt compass me about with songs of deliverance" (Psalm 32: 6,7).
2 Deliverance from trouble	Psalm 68: 13 Psalm 71: 20 Psalm 146: 18 Proverbs 11: 8 Proverbs 12: 13 Jeremiah 31: 12,13 Hosea 6: 1	"Many are the afflictions of the righteous: but the Lord delivereth him out of them all" (Psalm 34: 19).
3 Support in trouble	Psalm 9: 9 Psalm 22: 24 Psalm 27: 10,14 Psalm 46: 1–3 Isaiah 50: 10 Lamentations 3: 31–33 Nahum 1: 7 Matthew 11: 28 2 Corinthians 4: 8,9	"Cast thy burden upon the LORD, and he shall sustain thee: he shall never suffer the righteous to be moved" (Psalm 55: 22). "Thou hast been a strength to the poor, a strength to the needy in his distress, a refuge from the storm, a shadow from the heat, when the blast of the terrible ones is as a storm against the wall" (Isaiah 25: 4).

Blessings promised to believers (3)

Promises linked to the troubles of life (2)

Theme	Bible references	Key promise
Deliverance from sickness	Exodus 15: 26 Exodus 23: 25 Deuteronomy 7: 15	"Behold, I will bring it health and cure, and I will cure them, and will reveal unto them the abundance of peace and truth" (Jeremiah 33: 6).
Support in sickness	Deuteronomy 7: 13	"The Lord will strengthen him upon the bed of languishing: thou wilt make all his bed in his sickness" (Psalm 41: 3).
Old age	Psalm 71: 9 Proverbs 16: 31	"And even to your old age I am he; and even to hoar hairs will I carry you: I have made, and I will bear; even I will carry, and will deliver you" (Isaiah 46: 4).
Deliverance from enemies	Psalm 37: 32,33,40 Psalm 97: 10 Psalm 112: 8 Luke 1: 71,74,75 Acts 18: 10	"The LORD your God ye shall fear; and he shall deliver you out of the hand of all your enemies" (2 Kings 17: 39).
Deliverance from oppression	Psalm 72: 4,14 Psalm 109: 31 Psalm 146: 7 Isaiah 54: 14	"For the oppression of the poor, for the sighing of the needy, now will I arise, saith the Lord; I will set him in safety from him that puffeth at him" (Psalm 12: 5).
Promises related to deliverance for: the helpless	Psalm 9: 18 Psalm 69: 33 Psalm 72: 2,12,13 Psalm 107: 41	"He raiseth up the poor out of the dust, and lifteth the needy out of the dunghill" (Psalm 113: 7).

Promises related to deliverance for the fatherless and widow	Exodus 22: 22–24 Deuteronomy 10: 18 Psalm 10: 14,18 Psalm 146: 9 Hosea 14: 3	"A father of the fatherless, and a judge of the widows, is God in his holy habitation" (Psalm 68:5).
Promises for the childless	Psalm 68: 6 Isaiah 56: 4,5	"He maketh the barren woman to keep house, and to be a joyful mother of children" (Psalm 113: 9).
Promises about deliverance from death	1 Samuel 2: 6 Deuteronomy 32: 39 Psalm 9: 13 Psalm 68: 20	"He will deliver his soul from going into the pit, and his life shall see the light" (Job 33: 28).

Blessings promised to believers (4)

Promises of spiritual blessings in this life

Theme	Bible references	Key promise
Promises in general about spiritual blessings in this life	Romans 8: 30 Galatians 6:16 Ephesians 1: 3,4,7,8 2 Peter 1: 3,4	"All the paths of the Lord are mercy and truth unto such as keep his covenant and his testimonies. The secret of the Lord is with them that fear him; and he will shew them his covenant" (Psalm 25: 10,14).
Justification	Isaiah 53: 11 Romans 5: 1,9,18,19 Romans 8: 1,33,34 Titus 3: 7	"Being justified freely by his grace through the redemption that is in Christ Jesus" (Romans 3: 24).
Pardon	Exodus 34: 7 Isaiah 43: 25 Isaiah 44: 22 Jeremiah 31: 34 Hebrews 10: 17	"Who is a God like unto thee, that pardoneth iniquity, and passeth by the transgression of the remnant of his heritage? He retaineth not his anger for ever, because he delighteth in mercy. He will turn again, he will have compassion upon us; he will subdue our iniquities; and thou wilt cast all their sins into the depths of the sea" (Micah 7: 18,19).
Reconciliation	Isaiah 27: 5 2 Corinthians 5: 18,19 Ephesians 2: 13–17 Colossians 1: 21–23 Hebrews 2: 7	"Being now justified by his blood, we shall be saved from wrath through him. For if, when we were enemies, we were reconciled to God by the death of his Son, much more, being reconciled, we shall be saved by his life" (Romans 5: 9,10).

Grace to fight sin	John 8: 23 Romans 7: 24,25 Romans 8: 2–4	"Walk in the Spirit, and ye shall not fulfil the lust of the flesh" (Galatians 5:16).
Grace to fight sin	John 8: 23 Romans 7: 24,25 Romans 8: 2–4	"Walk in the Spirit, and ye shall not fulfil the lust of the flesh" (Galatians 5:16).
Grace to overcome temptation	Romans 8: 37 2 Corinthians 12: 9 Hebrews 2: 18 2 Peter 2: 9 1 John 4: 4	"God is faithful, who will not suffer you to be tempted above that ye are able; but will with the temptation also make a way to escape, that ye may be able to bear it" (1 Corinthians 10: 13).
To grow in grace	Job 17: 9 Psalm 92: 12 Proverbs 4: 18 Malachi 4: 2 Matthew 13: 12 James 4: 6	"They go from strength to strength, every one of them in Zion appeareth before God" (Psalm 84: 7).
Grace to persevere	John 17: 11 Romans 8: 38,39 1 Thessalonians 5: 23,24 2 Thessalonians 3: 3 2 Corinthians 1: 21 1Corinthians 1: 8 Philippians 1: 6	"And I give unto them eternal life; and they shall never perish, neither shall any man pluck them out of my hand. My Father, which gave them me, is greater than all; and no man is able to pluck them out of my Father's hand" (John 10: 28,29). "Unto him that is able to keep you from falling, and to present you faultless before the presence of his glory with exceeding joy" (Jude 24).

Bible promises in times of need

Bible promises are especially treasured
by Christians during times of testing
and difficulty.

Theme	Key Bible promise	Other Bible promises
Discouragement	Psalms 147: 3 "He healeth the broken in heart, and bindeth up their wounds."	2 Corinthians 12: 9 Isaiah 41: 10,131 Peter 5: 7 1 Corinthians 10: 13
Faith	Mark 9: 23,24 "Jesus said unto him, If thou canst believe, all things are possible to him that believeth."	Matthew 9: 29 Matthew 17: 20,21 Jeremiah 32: 12,27 Ephesians 3: 20
Fear	Psalms 91: 5 "Thou shalt not be afraid for the terror by night; nor for the arrow that flieth by day."	Psalm 56: 3 Mark 5: 36 1 John 4: 18
Forgiveness	1 John 1: 9 "If we confess our sins, he is faithful and just to forgive us our sins, and to cleanse us from all unrighteousness."	Psalm 51: 17 Psalm 103: 12 Isaiah 55: 6,7 Isaiah 1: 18 Micah 7: 19 Luke 5: 32

God's love	John 3: 16,17 "For God so loved the world, that he gave his only begotten Son, that whosoever believeth in him should not perish, but have everlasting life. For God sent not his Son into the world to condemn the world; but that the world through him might be saved."	Isaiah 49: 15,16 1 John 3: 1 Romans 8: 32 Psalms 103: 13
Guidance	Psalms 32: 8 "I will instruct thee and teach thee in the way which thou shalt go: I will guide thee with mine eye."	Isaiah 31: 21 Romans 8: 28
Happiness	Psalms 16: 11 "Thou wilt show me the path of life: in thy presence is fullness of joy; at thy right hand there are pleasures for evermore."	Isaiah 12: 3 Habakkuk 3: 17–19 John 13: 17 Proverbs 29: 18
Hope	Jeremiah 17: 7 "Blessed is the man that trusteth in the Lord, and whose hope the Lord is."	1 Samuel 7: 12 Psalm 16: 9 Psalm 33: 18 Proverbs 14: 32 1 Corinthians 2: 9
Sickness	Jeremiah 30: 17 "For I will restore health unto thee, and I will heal thee of thy wounds, saith the Lord."	Job 5: 19 Psalm 34: 19 Psalm 119: 67,71 Isaiah 40: 31 James 5: 14–16 Matthew 9: 22

> man's faith is strengthened as he keeps
> promises of God before him and considers, not
> difficulties in the way of the things promised,
> but the character and resources of God Who has
> made the promise."
>
> *Paul Little*

Promises from Matthew's Gospel

Promise	Condition	Bible reference
1 Kingdom of heaven	The poor in spirit	Matthew 5: 3
2 Filled with righteousness	Seeking righteousness	Matthew 5: 6
3 Shall see God	Pure in heart	Matthew 5: 8
4 Called children of God	The peacemakers	Matthew 5: 9
5 Acknowledged before God the Father	Acknowledge Jesus before men	Matthew 10: 32
6 Rest for your soul	Taking Jesus' yoke	Matthew 11: 29
7 Jesus' mother, brother, sister	Doing the Father's will	Matthew 12: 50
8 Entering the kingdom of heaven	Become like little children	Matthew 18: 3
9 Greatest in the kingdom of heaven	Become humble like a little child	Matthew 18: 4
10 Receiving Jesus	Accepting a little child	Matthew 18: 5
11 Asking the Father for requests	Two Christians agreeing in prayer	Matthew 18: 19
12 The presence of Jesus	When Christians are together in Jesus' name	Matthew 18: 20
13 You will be saved	If you endure to the end	Matthew 24: 13
14 You can serve Jesus	If you serve the least of his brethren	Matthew 25: 40
15 I am will you always	If you teach the Christian message	Matthew 28: 19